EXPLORING MICROSOFT® OFFICE PROFESSIONAL FOR WINDOWS® 95

Volume II

VERSION 7.0

Thomson/McDuffie Campus
Library Information Center
388 Tech Dr. N.W.
Thomson, GA 30824

EXPLORING MICROSOFT® OFFICE PROFESSIONAL FOR WINDOWS® 95

Volume II

VERSION 7.0

Robert T. Grauer / Maryann Barber

University of Miami

Prentice Hall, Upper Saddle River, New Jersey 07458

isitions editor: Carolyn Henderson
orial/production supervisor: Greg Hubit Bookworks
rior and cover design: Suzanne Behnke
ior manufacturing supervisor: Paul Smolenski
itorial assistant: Audrey Regan

©1996 by Prentice Hall, Inc.
A Simon & Schuster Company
Upper Saddle River, New Jersey 07458

All rights reserved. No part of this book may be reproduced, in any form or by any means, without permission in writing from the publisher.

Printed in the United States of America
10 9 8 7 6 5 4 3 2 1

ISBN 0-13-486895-1

Prentice Hall International (UK) Limited, *London*
Prentice Hall of Australia Pty. Limited, *Sydney*
Prentice Hall of Canada Inc., *Toronto*
Prentice Hall Hispanoamericano, S.A., *Mexico*
Prentice Hall of India Private Limited, *New Delhi*
Prentice Hall of Japan, Inc., *Tokyo*
Simon & Schuster Asia Pte. Ltd., *Singapore*
Editora Prentice Hall do Brasil, Ltda., *Rio de Janeiro*

Contents

EXPLORING MICROSOFT EXCEL FOR WINDOWS 95

EXPLORING MICROSOFT ACCESS FOR WINDOWS 95

2

Many-to-Many Relationships: A More Complex System 57

3

Building Applications: Introduction to Macros and Prototyping 121

EXPLORING MICROSOFT POWERPOINT FOR WINDOWS 95

PREFACE

Exploring Microsoft Office Professional Volume II was created in response to the increasingly popular second course in microcomputer applications. It consists of selected chapters and appendices that constitute the intermediate and advanced material from individual books in the *Exploring Windows* series. Its companion title, *Exploring Microsoft Office Professional Volume I,* contains selected chapters with introductory material. Instructors who teach courses that focus on a single application should consider the stand-alone texts: *Exploring Microsoft Word Version 7.0, Exploring Microsoft Excel Version 7.0, Exploring Microsoft Access Version 7.0, Exploring Microsoft PowerPoint Version 7.0,* and *Exploring the Internet.*

The *Exploring Windows* series is different from other books, both in its scope and in the way in which material is presented. Students learn by doing. Concepts are stressed and memorization is minimized. Shortcuts and other important information are consistently highlighted in the many tips that appear throughout the series. Every chapter contains an average of three guided exercises to be completed at the computer, which enable students to master the material.

Each book in the *Exploring Windows* series is accompanied by a comprehensive Instructor's Resource Manual with tests, transparency masters, PowerPoint lectures, and student/instructor resource disks. Instructors can also use the Prentice Hall Computerized Online Testing System to prepare customized tests for their courses and may obtain Interactive Multimedia courseware as a further supplement. The *Exploring Windows* series is part of the Prentice Hall custom binding program.

What's New

Exploring Microsoft Office Professional Volume II is a new addition to the *Exploring Windows* series and contains material on the four major applications in Microsoft Office for Windows 95. Our coverage of Microsoft Word includes tables, styles, desktop publishing, mail merge, and a thorough introduction to the Internet Assistant to create Web pages. The Excel portion includes list management, three-dimensional workbooks, macros, auditing, Solver, and data mapping. The Access chapters develop a variety of databases containing both one-to-many and many-to-many relationships, and include coverage of subforms, advanced queries, prototyping, and macros. The PowerPoint section utilizes object linking and embedding to incorporate a variety of objects into a presentation and includes coverage of multimedia.

We believe, however, that our most important feature is the expanded end-of-chapter material, which provides a wide variety of student assignments. Every chapter contains 15 *multiple-choice questions* (with answers) so that students can test themselves quickly and objectively. Every chapter has *four conceptual problems* that do not require participation at the computer. Every chapter also has *four computer-based practice exercises* to build student proficiency. And finally, every chapter ends with *four case studies* in which the student is given little guidance in the means of solution. This unique *15-by-four-by-four-by-four* format provides substantial opportunity for students to master the material while simultaneously giving instructors considerable flexibility in student assignments.

FEATURES AND BENEFITS

A 22-page appendix introduces the Internet Assistant to create HTML documents through Microsoft Word. Students learn how to create a home page and how to create links from their page to other Web documents.

Chapter 2 in Word presents the basics of desktop publishing and its implementation in Microsoft Word. Students learn how to merge text with graphics to create professional-looking documents without reliance on external sources.

D

APPENDIX D: THE INTERNET ASSISTANT: INTRODUCTION TO HTML

OVERVIEW

The ***Internet***[1] is a network of networks that connects computers across the country and around the world. It grew out of a government project that began in 1969 to test the feasibility of a network for scientists and military personnel to share messages and data, no matter where they were. Known originally as the ARPAnet (Advanced Research Projects Agency), the original network of four computers grew exponentially to include tens of thousands of computers at virtually every major university and government agency and an ever-increasing number of private corporations. To say that the Internet is large is a gross understatement, but by its very nature, it's impossible to say just how large the Internet really is. The Internet is not a single network, but a collection of networks. How many networks there are, and how many users are connected to those networks, is of no importance as long as you yourself have access.

The ***World Wide Web*** (WWW, or simply the Web) is a means of connecting the resources on the Internet to one another. The Web is based on the technology of ***hypertext*** and ***hypermedia,*** which link computer-based documents in nonlinear fashion. Unlike a traditional document, which is read sequentially from top to bottom, a hypertext document includes links to other documents, which can be viewed at the reader's discretion. Hypermedia is similar in concept except that it provides links to graphic and video files in addition to text files.

To explore the Web, you need a program called a ***browser,*** which requests files from other computers on the Internet, then displays the hypertext (or hypermedia) documents on your computer. A ***home page*** is the first document a user sees when he or she connects to a particular

[1]See Grauer and Barber, Appendix D: The Internet and World Wide Web in *Exploring Windows 95 and Essential Computer Concepts,* Prentice Hall, 1996, for a 20-page introduction to the Internet. Alternatively, see Grauer and Marks, *Exploring the Internet,* Prentice Hall, 1996, for more detailed information.

135

previously done by others who were skilled in their respective areas. Thus, in addition to learning the commands within Microsoft Word to implement desktop publishing, you need to learn the basics of graphic design.

The chapter focuses on desktop publishing as it is implemented in Microsoft Word, followed by a brief introduction to graphic design. We show you how to create a multicolumn document, how to import graphic images, and how to edit those images as embedded objects. We also present material on bullets and lists, borders and shading, and section formatting, all of which will be used to create a newsletter in this chapter. Finally, we discuss several guidelines of graphic design to help you create a more polished document.

THE NEWSLETTER

The chapter is organized around the newsletter in Figure 2.1, which illustrates basic capabilities in ***desktop publishing.*** The hands-on exercises help you create the newsletter(s) in the figure. We think you will be pleased at how easy the process is and hope that you go on to create more sophisticated designs.

Figure 2.1a shows the newsletter as it exists on the data disk. We supply the text, but the formatting will be up to you. Figure 2.1b shows the newsletter at the end of the first hands-on exercise. It contains balanced newspaper columns, a ***masthead*** (a heading for the newsletter) that is set between thick parallel lines, and a bulleted list.

Figure 2.1c displays a more interesting design that contains a graphic, columns of different widths, a vertical line to separate the columns, and a dropped capital letter to emphasize the lead article. The figure uses shading to emphasize a specific paragraph and a ***reverse*** (white text on a black background) to accentuate the masthead.

Figure 2.1d illustrates an alternate design using three columns rather than two. The figure incorporates a ***pull quote*** (a phrase or sentence taken from an article) to emphasize a point. It also uses a more dynamic masthead that was developed with Microsoft WordArt (an application that is included with Microsoft Office).

The choice among the various newsletters in the figure is one of personal taste. All of the newsletters contain the identical text, but vary in their presentation of the written material. The easy part of desktop publishing is to implement a specific design using commands within Microsoft Word. The more difficult aspect is to create the design in the first place. We urge you therefore to experiment freely and to realize that good design is often the result of trial and error.

ADDING INTEREST

Boxes, shading, and reverses (light text on a dark background) add interest to a document. Horizontal (vertical) lines are also effective in separating one topic from another, emphasizing a subhead, or calling attention to a pull quote (a phrase or sentence taken from the article to emphasize a key point).

Typography

Typography—the selection of typefaces, styles, and sizes—is a critical element in the design of any document. Accordingly, you need to be familiar with the basic terminology of typography as it is used in the context of desktop publishing. A

54 MICROSOFT WORD 7.0

(a) Text for the Newsletter

The Athlete's Hi

(b) At End of Exercise 1

The Athlete's Hi

(c) At End of Exercise 3

(d) An Alternate Design

FIGURE 2.1 The Newsletter

DESKTOP PUBLISHING 55

Copying Worksheets

Objective: Open multiple workbooks; use the Windows Arrange command to tile the open workbooks; copy a worksheet from one workbook to another. Use Figure 2.5 as a guide in the exercise.

STEP 1: Open a New Workbook

- Start Excel. If necessary, click the **New button** on the Standard toolbar to open a new workbook.
- Delete all worksheets except for Sheet1:
  - Click the tab for **Sheet2.** Press the **▶| key** to scroll to the last sheet in the workbook (Sheet16).
  - Press the **Shift key** as you click the tab for Sheet 16. (Sheets 2 through 16 should be selected and their worksheet tabs appear in white.)
  - Point to the tab for **Sheet16** and click the **right mouse button** to display a shortcut menu. Click **Delete.** Click **OK** in response to the warning that the selected sheets will be permanently deleted.
- The workbook should contain only Sheet1 as shown in Figure 2.5a. Save the workbook as **Corporate Sales** in the **Exploring Excel folder.**

THE DEFAULT WORKBOOK

A new workbook contains 16 worksheets, but you can change the default value to any number. Pull down the Tools menu, click Options, then click the General tab. Click the up (down) arrow in the Sheets in New Workbook text box to enter a new default value, then click OK to exit the Options dialog box and continue working. The next time you open a new workbook, it will contain the new number of worksheets.

STEP 2: Open the Individual Workbooks

- Pull down the **File menu.** Click **Open** to display the Open dialog box as shown in Figure 2.5a.
- Click the **Atlanta workbook,** then press and hold the **Ctrl key** as you click the **Boston** and **Chicago workbooks** to select all three workbooks at the same time.
- Click **Open** to open the selected workbooks. The workbooks will be opened one after another with a brief message appearing on the status bar as each workbook is opened.
- Pull down the **Window menu,** which should indicate the four open workbooks at the bottom of the menu. Only the Chicago workbook is visible at this time.
- Click **Arrange** to display the Arrange Windows dialog box. If necessary, select the Tile option, then click **OK.** You should see four open workbooks as shown in Figure 2.5b. (Do not be concerned if your workbooks are arranged differently from ours.)

60 EXPLORING MICROSOFT EXCEL 7.0

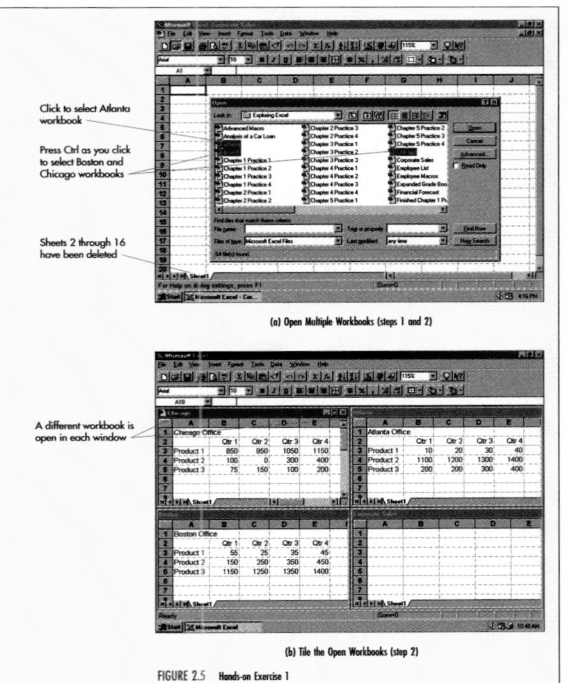

(a) Open Multiple Workbooks (steps 1 and 2)

(b) Tile the Open Workbooks (step 2)

FIGURE 2.5 Hands-on Exercise 1

CONSOLIDATING DATA 61

A total of 48 in-depth tutorials (hands-on exercises) guide the reader at the computer. Each tutorial is illustrated with large, full-color screen captures that are clear and easy to read. Each tutorial is accompanied by numerous tips that present different ways to accomplish a given task, but in a logical and relaxed fashion.

Object Linking and Embedding is stressed throughout the series. This exercise, for example, links a Word document to an Excel worksheet and chart. Appendix C in Access implements a mail merge using an Access database and a Word Form letter.

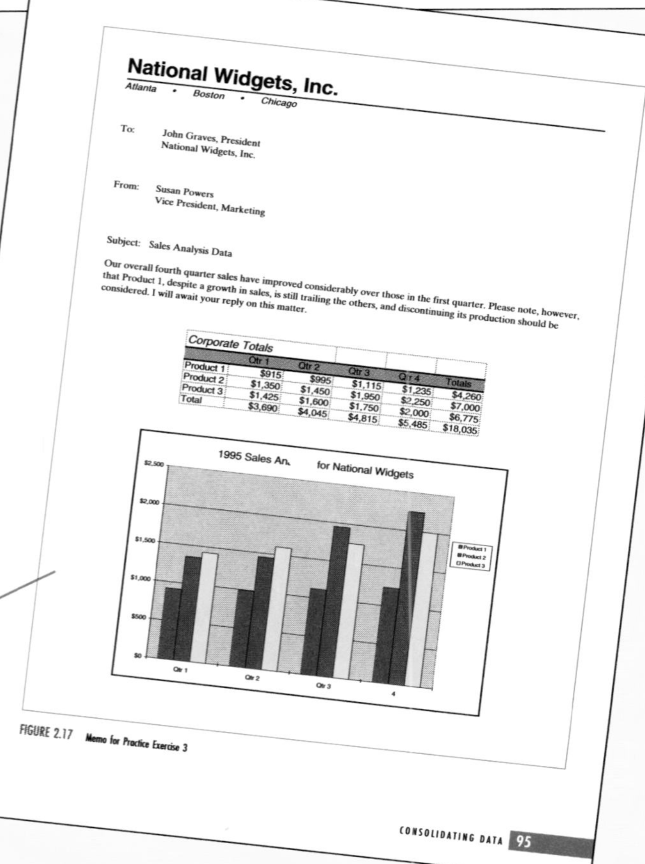

National Widgets, Inc.

Atlanta • Boston • Chicago

To: John Graves, President
National Widgets, Inc.

From: Susan Powers
Vice President, Marketing

Subject: Sales Analysis Data

Our overall fourth quarter sales have improved considerably over those in the first quarter. Please note, however, that Product 1, despite a growth in sales, is still trailing the others, and discontinuing its production should be considered. I will await your reply on this matter.

Corporate Totals

	Qtr 1	Qtr 2	Qtr 3	Qtr 4	Totals
Product 1	$915	$995	$1,115	$1,235	$4,260
Product 2	$1,350	$1,450	$1,950	$2,250	$7,000
Product 3	$1,425	$1,600	$1,750	$2,000	$6,775
Total	$3,690	$4,045	$4,815	$5,485	$18,035

FIGURE 2.17 Memo for Practice Exercise 3

CONSOLIDATING DATA 95

4. Answer the following with respect to the workbook(s) shown in Figure 2.14:
   a. How many workbooks are open in Figure 2.14?
   b. Which workbook is the source workbook? Which workbook is the dependent workbook?
   c. Which workbook contains an external reference?
   d. What is the active workbook? What is the active worksheet in this workbook? What is the active cell?
   e. What are the contents of the formula bar? Why are the drive and folder shown for the San Diego workbook, but not for the Miami workbook?

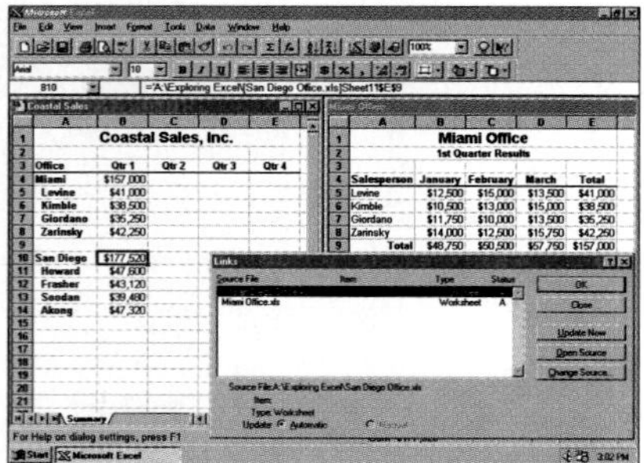

FIGURE 2.14 Screen for Problem 4

PRACTICE WITH MICROSOFT EXCEL 7.0

1. A partially completed version of the workbook in Figure 2.15 can be found on the data disk as *Volume II Chapter 2 Practice 1*. This workbook contains worksheets for the individual sections but does not contain the summary worksheet.
   a. Retrieve the *Volume II Chapter 2 Practice 1* workbook from the data disk, then open multiple windows so that the display on your monitor matches Figure 2.15.
   b. Complete the individual worksheets by adding the appropriate formulas (functions) to compute the class average on each test.
   c. Add a summary worksheet that includes the test averages from each of the sections as shown in the figure.

92 EXPLORING MICROSOFT EXCEL 7.0

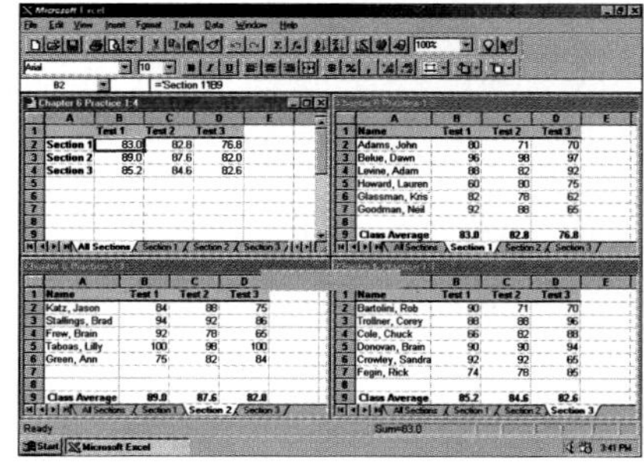

FIGURE 2.15 Screen for Practice Exercise 1

   d. Add a documentation worksheet that includes your name as the grading assistant, the date of modification, and lists all of the worksheets in the workbook.
   e. Print the entire workbook and submit it to your instructor.

2. A partially completed version of the workbook in Figure 2.16 can be found on the data disk as *Volume II Chapter 2 Practice 2*. The workbook contains a separate worksheet for each month of the year as well as a summary worksheet for the entire year. Thus far, only the months of January, February, and March are complete. Each monthly worksheet tallies the expenses for five departments in each of four categories to compute a monthly total for each department. The summary worksheet displays the total expense for each department.
   a. Retrieve the *Volume II Chapter 2 Practice 2* workbook from the data disk, then open multiple windows so that the display on your monitor matches Figure 2.16.
   b. Use the Group Editing feature to select the worksheets for January, February, and March simultaneously. Enter the formula to compute the monthly total for each department in each month.
   c. Use the Group Editing feature to format the worksheets.
   d. Enter the appropriate formulas in the summary worksheet to compute the year-to-date totals for each department.
   e. Add an additional worksheet for the month of April. Assume that department 1 spends $100 in each category, department 2 spends $200 in each category, and so on. Update the summary worksheet to include the expenses for April.
   f. Add a documentation worksheet that includes your name, the date of modification, plus a description of each worksheet within the workbook.
   g. Print the entire workbook (all five worksheets), then print the cell formulas for the summary worksheet only.

CONSOLIDATING DATA 93

Every chapter contains an abundant variety of thought-provoking exercises that review and extend the material. There are objective multiple-choice questions, conceptual problems that do not require interaction with the computer, guided computer exercises, and less-structured case studies.

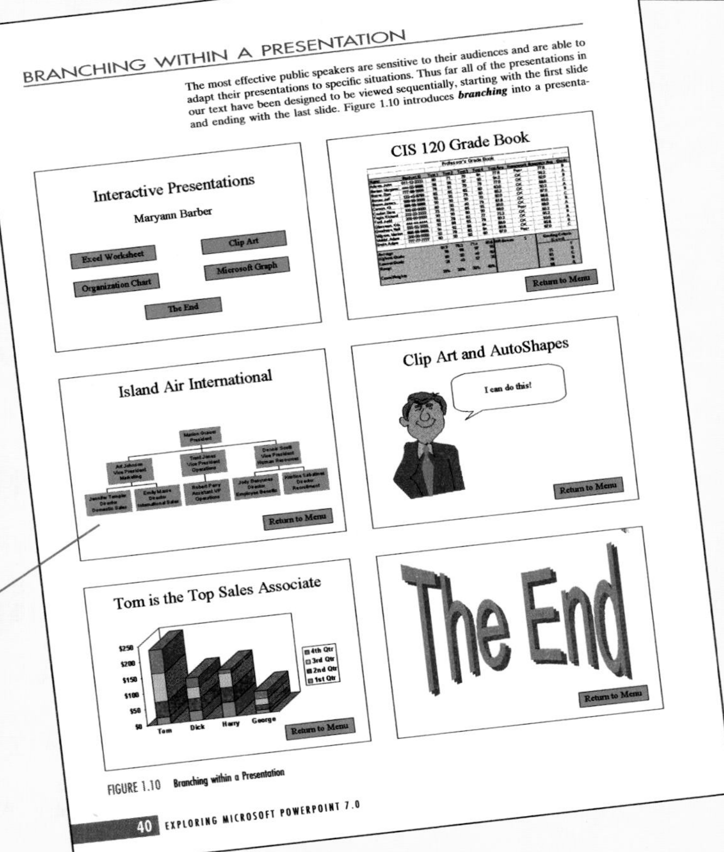

BRANCHING WITHIN A PRESENTATION

The most effective public speakers are sensitive to their audiences and are able to adapt their presentations to specific situations. Thus far all of the presentations in our text have been designed to be viewed sequentially, starting with the first slide and ending with the last slide. Figure 1.10 introduces ***branching*** into a presentation

FIGURE 1.10 Branching within a Presentation

40 EXPLORING MICROSOFT POWERPOINT 7.0

Students learn how to link or embed objects from various applications into a PowerPoint presentation. Nonsequential branching from one slide to another during the actual presentation is also covered.

Chapter 3 in Access shows students how to develop a complete application through macros and prototyping. This "capstone" chapter is the ideal basis for a semester-long project, as it enables students to develop realistic applications.

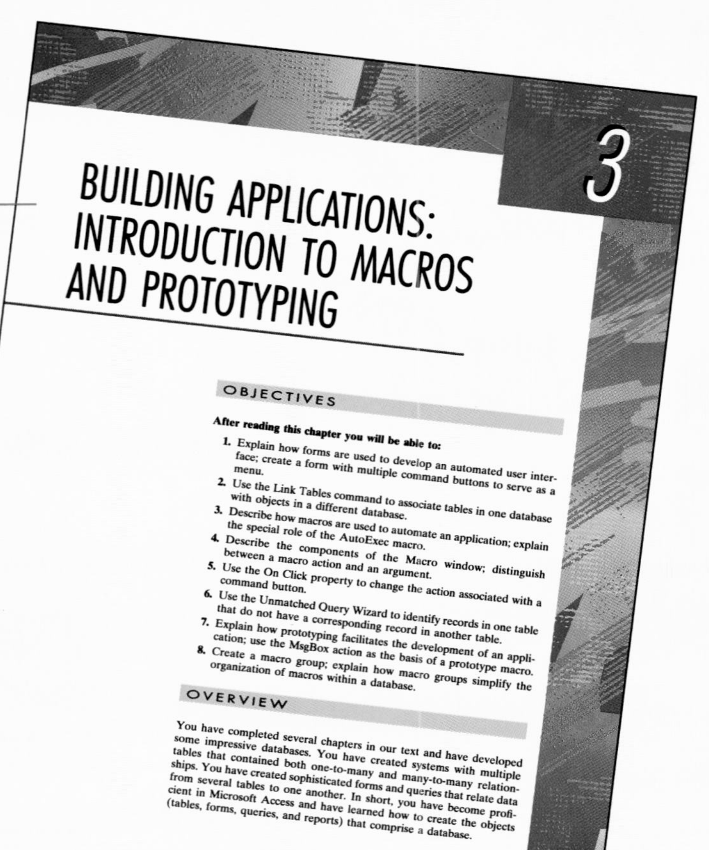

3

BUILDING APPLICATIONS: INTRODUCTION TO MACROS AND PROTOTYPING

OBJECTIVES

After reading this chapter you will be able to:

1. Explain how forms are used to develop an automated user interface; create a form with multiple command buttons to serve as a menu.
2. Use the Link Tables command to associate tables in one database with objects in a different database.
3. Describe how macros are used to automate an application; explain the special role of the AutoExec macro.
4. Describe the components of the Macro window; distinguish between a macro action and an argument.
5. Use the On Click property to change the action associated with a command button.
6. Use the Unmatched Query Wizard to identify records in one table that do not have a corresponding record in another table.
7. Explain how prototyping facilitates the development of an application; use the MsgBox action as the basis of a prototype macro.
8. Create a macro group; explain how macro groups simplify the organization of macros within a database.

OVERVIEW

You have completed several chapters in our text and have developed some impressive databases. You have created systems with multiple tables that contained both one-to-many and many-to-many relationships. You have created sophisticated forms and queries that relate data from several tables to one another. In short, you have become proficient in Microsoft Access and have learned how to create the objects (tables, forms, queries, and reports) that comprise a database.

121

Database design is stressed throughout the Access chapters through a variety of case studies. Full-color illustrations clarify the relationships among tables by highlighting the primary and foreign keys within a database.

forms created in this chapter are based on multiple table queries rather than tables. The queries themselves are of a more advanced nature. We show you how to create a parameter query, where you enter the criteria at the time you run the query. We also show you how to create queries that use the aggregate functions built into Access to perform calculations on groups of records.

The chapter contains four hands-on exercises to implement the case study. We think you will be pleased with what you have accomplished by the end of the chapter, working with a sophisticated system that is typical of real-world applications.

CASE STUDY: THE COMPUTER SUPER STORE

The case study in this chapter is set within the context of a computer store that requires a database for its customers, products, and orders. The store maintains the usual customer data (name, address, phone, etc.). It also keeps data about the products it sells, storing for each product a product ID, description, quantity on hand, quantity on order, and unit price. And finally, the store has to track its orders. It needs to know the date an order was received, the customer who placed it, the products that were ordered, and the quantity of each product.

Think, for a moment, about the tables that are necessary and the relationships between those tables, then compare your thoughts to our solution in Figure 2.1. You probably have no trouble recognizing the need for the Customers, Products, and Orders tables. Initially, you may be puzzled by the Order Details table, but you will soon appreciate why it is there and how powerful it is.

You can use the Customers, Products, and Orders tables individually to obtain information about a specific customer, product, or order, respectively. For example:

Query: What is Jeffrey Muddell's phone number?
Answer: Jeffrey Muddell's phone is (305) 253-3909.

Query: What is the price of a Pentium 133 system? How many are in stock?
Answer: A Pentium 133 sells for $2,599. Fifteen systems are in stock.

Query: When was Order O0003 placed?
Answer: Order O0003 was placed on April 18, 1996.

Other queries require you to relate the tables to one another. There is, for example, a ***one-to-many relationship*** between customers and orders. One customer can place many orders, but a specific order can be associated with only one customer. The tables are related through the CustomerID, which appears as the ***primary key*** in the Customers table and as a ***foreign key*** in the Orders table. Consider:

Query: What is the name of the customer who placed order number O0003?
Answer: Order O0003 was placed by Jeffrey Muddell.

Query: How many orders were placed by Jeffrey Muddell?
Answer: Jeffrey Muddell placed five orders: O0003, O0014, O0016, O0024, and O0025.

These queries require you to use two tables. To answer the first query, you would search the Orders table to find order O0003 and obtain the CustomerID (C0006 in this example). You would then search the Customers table for the

Customer ID	First Name	Last Name	Address	City	State	Zip Code	Phone Number
C0001	Benjamin	Lee	1000 Call Street	Tallahassee	FL	33340	(904) 327-4124
C0002	Eleanor	Milgrom	7245 NW 8 Street	Margate	FL	33065	(305) 974-1234
C0003	Neil	Goodman	4215 South 81 Street	Margate	FL	33065	(305) 444-5555
C0004	Nicholas	Colon	9020 N.W. 75 Street	Coral Springs	FL	33065	(305) 753-9887
C0005	Michael	Ware	276 Brickell Avenue	Miami	FL	33131	(305) 444-3980
C0006	Jeffrey	Muddell	9522 S.W. 142 Street	Miami	FL	33176	(305) 253-3909
C0007	Ashley	Geoghegan	7500 Center Lane	Coral Springs	FL	33070	(305) 753-7830
C0008	Serena	Sherard	5000 Jefferson Lane	Gainesville	FL	32601	(904) 375-6442
C0009	Luis	Couto	455 Bargello Avenue	Coral Gables	FL	33146	(305) 666-4801
C0010	Derek	Anderson	6000 Tigertail Avenue	Coconut Grove	FL	33120	(305) 446-8900
C0011	Lauren	Center	12380 S.W. 137 Avenue	Miami	FL	33186	(305) 385-4432
C0012	Robert	Slane	4508 N.W. 7 Street	Miami	FL	33131	(305) 635-3454

(a) Customers Table

Product ID	Product Name	Units In Stock	Units On Order	Unit Price
P0001	Pentium/75 System	50	0	$1,899.00
P0002	Pentium/90 System	25	5	$1,999.00
P0003	Pentium/100 System	125	15	$2,099.00
P0004	Pentium/120 System	25	50	$2,299.00
P0005	Pentium/133 System	15	25	$2,599.00
P0006	15" SVGA Monitor	50	0	$499.00
P0007	17" SVGA Monitor	25	10	$899.00
P0008	19" Multisync Monitor	50	20	$1,599.00
P0009	500 MB Hard Drive	15	20	$399.00
P0010	1 GB Hard Drive	25	15	$799.00
P0011	2 GB Hard Drive	10	0	$1,245.00
P0012	CD-ROM: 4X	40	0	$249.00
P0013	CD-ROM: 6X	50	15	$449.95
P0014	HD Floppy Disks	500	200	$9.99
P0015	HD Data Cartridges	100	50	$14.79
P0016	250 MB Tape Backup	15	3	$179.95
P0017	Serial Mouse	150	50	$69.95
P0018	Trackball	55	0	$59.95
P0019	Joystick	250	100	$39.95
P0020	Fax/Modem 28.8 Kbps	35	10	$189.95
P0021	Fax/Modem 14.4Kbps	20	0	$65.95
P0022	Laser Printer	100	15	$1,395.00
P0023	24Pin Dot Matrix	50	50	$249.95
P0024	Color Printer	125	25	$569.95
P0025	Windows 95	400	200	$95.95
P0026	Windows 95 Plus	150	50	$45.95
P0027	Norton Utilities 7.0	150	50	$115.95
P0028	Microsoft Scenes Screen Saver	75	25	$29.95
P0029	Microsoft Bookshelf	250	100	$129.95
P0030	Microsoft Cinemania	25	10	$59.95
P0031	Professional Photos on CD-ROM	15	0	$45.95

(b) Products Table

Order ID	Customer ID	Order Date
O0001	C0004	4/15/96
O0002	C0003	4/18/96
O0003	C0006	4/18/96
O0004	C0007	4/18/96
O0005	C0001	4/20/96
O0006	C0001	4/21/96
O0007	C0002	4/21/96
O0008	C0002	4/22/96
O0009	C0001	4/22/96
O0010	C0002	4/22/96
O0011	C0001	4/24/96
O0012	C0007	4/24/96
O0013	C0004	4/24/96
O0014	C0006	4/25/96
O0015	C0009	4/25/96
O0016	C0006	4/26/96
O0017	C0011	4/26/96
O0018	C0011	4/26/96
O0019	C0012	4/27/96
O0020	C0012	4/28/96
O0021	C0010	4/29/96
O0022	C0010	4/29/96
O0023	C0008	4/30/96
O0024	C0006	5/ 1/96
O0025	C0006	5/ 1/96

(c) Orders Table

Order ID	Product ID	Quantity
O0001	P0013	1
O0001	P0014	4
O0001	P0027	1
O0002	P0001	1
O0002	P0006	1
O0002	P0020	1
O0002	P0022	1
O0003	P0005	1
O0003	P0020	1
O0003	P0022	1
O0004	P0003	1
O0004	P0010	1
O0004	P0022	2
O0005	P0003	2
O0005	P0012	2
O0005	P0016	2
O0006	P0007	1
O0006	P0014	10
O0007	P0028	1
O0007	P0030	3
O0008	P0001	1
O0008	P0004	3
O0008	P0008	4
O0008	P0011	2
O0008	P0012	1
O0009	P0006	1
O0010	P0002	2
O0010	P0022	1
O0010	P0023	1
O0011	P0016	2
O0011	P0020	2
O0012	P0021	10
O0012	P0029	10
O0012	P0030	10
O0013	P0009	4
O0013	P0016	10
O0013	P0024	2
O0014	P0019	2
O0014	P0028	1
O0015	P0018	1
O0015	P0020	1
O0016	P0029	2
O0017	P0019	2
O0018	P0009	1
O0018	P0025	2
O0018	P0026	2
O0019	P0014	25
O0020	P0024	1
O0021	P0004	1
O0022	P0027	1
O0023	P0021	1
O0023	P0028	1
O0023	P0029	1
O0024	P0007	1
O0024	P0013	5
O0024	P0014	3
O0024	P0016	1
O0025	P0012	2
O0025	P0029	2

(d) Order Details Table

FIGURE 2.1 Super Store Database

Acknowledgments

We want to thank the many individuals who helped bring this project to fruition. We are especially grateful to our editors at Prentice Hall, Carolyn Henderson and P. J. Boardman, without whom the series would not have been possible. Cecil Yarbrough and Susan Hoffman did an outstanding job in checking the manuscript and proofs for technical accuracy. Suzanne Behnke developed the innovative and attractive design. Phyllis Bregman helped us to go online. Dave Moles produced the CD-ROM for the Instructor Manuals. Gretchen Marx of Saint Joseph College created the test bank. Carlotta Eaton of Radford University wrote the truly outstanding Instructor Manuals. Greg Hubit was in charge of production and kept the project on target from beginning to end. Paul Smolenski was senior manufacturing supervisor. Nancy Evans and Deborah Emry, our marketing managers at Prentice Hall, developed the innovative campaigns that made the series a success. We also want to acknowledge our reviewers who, through their comments and constructive criticism, greatly improved the *Exploring Windows* series.

Lynne Band, Middlesex Community College
Stuart P. Brian, Holy Family College
Carl M. Briggs, Indiana University School of Business
Kimberly Chambers, Scottsdale Community College
Alok Charturvedi, Purdue University
Jerry Chin, Southwest Missouri State University
Dean Combellick, Scottsdale Community College
Cody Copeland, Johnson County Community College
Larry S. Corman, Fort Lewis College
Janis Cox, Tri-County Technical College
Martin Crossland, Southwest Missouri State University
Paul E. Daurelle, Western Piedmont Community College
David Douglas, University of Arkansas
Carlotta Eaton, Radford University
Raymond Frost, Central Connecticut State University
James Gips, Boston College
Vernon Griffin, Austin Community College
Michael Hassett, Fort Hays State University
Wanda D. Heller, Seminole Community College
Bonnie Homan, San Francisco State University
Ernie Ivey, Polk Community College
Mike Kelly, Community College of Rhode Island
Jane King, Everett Community College
John Lesson, University of Central Florida
David B. Meinert, Southwest Missouri State University
Alan Moltz, Naugatuck Valley Technical Community College
Kim Montney, Kellogg Community College
Kevin Pauli, University of Nebraska
Mary McKenry Percival, University of Miami
Delores Pusins, Hillsborough Community College
Gale E. Rand, College Misericordia
Judith Rice, Santa Fe Community College
David Rinehard, Lansing Community College
Marilyn Salas, Scottsdale Community College
John Shepherd, Duquesne University
Helen Stoloff, Hudson Valley Community College
Mike Thomas, Indiana University School of Business
Suzanne Tomlinson, Iowa State University
Karen Tracey, Central Connecticut State University
Sally Visci, Lorain County Community College
David Weiner, University of San Francisco
Connie Wells, Georgia State University
Wallace John Whistance-Smith, Ryerson Polytechnic University
Jack Zeller, Kirkwood Community College

A final word of thanks to the unnamed students at the University of Miami who make it all worthwhile. And most of all, thanks to you, our readers, for choosing this book. Please feel free to contact us with any comments and suggestions.

Robert T. Grauer
RGRAUER@UMIAMI.MIAMI.EDU
http://www.bus.miami.edu/~rgrauer

Maryann Barber
MBARBER@UMIAMI.MIAMI.EDU
http://www.bus.miami.edu/~mbarber

MICROSOFT OFFICE FOR WINDOWS 95: FOUR APPLICATIONS IN ONE

OVERVIEW

Word processing, spreadsheets, and data management have always been significant microcomputer applications. The early days of the PC saw these applications emerge from different vendors with radically different user interfaces. WordPerfect, Lotus, and dBASE, for example, were dominant applications in their respective areas, and each was developed by a different company. The applications were totally dissimilar, and knowledge of one application did not help in learning another.

The widespread acceptance of Windows 3.1 promoted the concept of a common user interface, which required all applications to follow a consistent set of conventions. This meant that all applications worked essentially the same way, and it provided a sense of familiarity when you learned a new application, since every application presented the same user interface. The development of a suite of applications from a single vendor extended this concept by imposing additional similarities on all applications within the suite.

This introduction presents an overview of ***Microsoft Office for Windows 95*** and its four major applications—Word, Excel, PowerPoint, and Access. Our primary purpose is to emphasize the similarities between these applications and to help you extend your knowledge from one application to the next. You will find the same commands in the same menus. You will also recognize familiar toolbars and will be able to take advantage of similar keyboard shortcuts. Our goal is to show you how much you already know and to get you up and running as quickly as possible.

The introduction also discusses Schedule+ as well as shared applications and utilities such as the ClipArt Gallery and WordArt, which are included within Microsoft Office. We cover the Microsoft Binder, which enables you to keep related documents in one file. We discuss the Office Shortcut Bar and describe how to start an application and open a new or existing document. We introduce you to Object Linking and Embedding, which enables you to combine data from multiple applications into a single document. And finally, we include a hands-on exercise that lets you sit down at the computer and apply what you have learned.

> **TRY THE COLLEGE BOOKSTORE**
>
> Any machine you buy will come with Windows 95, but that is only the beginning since you must also obtain the application software you intend to run. Many first-time buyers are surprised that they have to pay extra for software, so you had better allow for software in your budget. Some hardware vendors will bundle (at no additional cost) Microsoft Office as an inducement to buy from them. If you have already purchased your system and you need software, the best place to buy Microsoft Office is the college bookstore, where it can be obtained at a substantial educational discount.

MICROSOFT OFFICE FOR WINDOWS 95

You have already studied the applications in Microsoft Office. This section reviews the common user interface with which you are familiar. Figure 1 displays a screen from each application in the Microsoft Office—Word, Excel, PowerPoint, and Access, in Figures 1a, 1b, 1c, and 1d, respectively. Look closely at Figure 1, and notice that each screen contains both an application window and a document window, and that each document window has been maximized within the application window. The title bars of the application and document windows have been merged into a single title bar that appears at the top of the application window. The title bar displays the application (e.g., Microsoft Word in Figure 1a) as well as the name of the document (Letter to My Instructor in Figure 1a) on which you are working.

All four screens in Figure 1 are similar in appearance even though the applications accomplish very different tasks. Each application window has an identifying icon, a menu bar, a title bar, and a minimize, maximize or restore, and a close button. Each document window has its own identifying icon, and its own minimize, maximize or restore, and close button. The Windows 95 taskbar appears at the bottom of each application window and shows the open applications. The status bar appears above the taskbar and displays information relevant to the window or selected object.

Each application in Microsoft Office uses a consistent command structure in which the same basic menus are found in all applications. The File, Edit, View, Insert, Tools, Window, and Help menus are present in all four applications. The same commands are found in the same menus. The Save, Open, Print, and Exit commands, for example, are contained in the File menu. The Cut, Copy, Paste, and Undo commands are found in the Edit menu.

The means for accessing the pull-down menus are consistent from one application to the next. Click the menu name on the menu bar, or press the Alt key plus the underlined letter of the menu name; for example, press Alt+F to pull down the File menu. If you already know some keyboard shortcuts in one application, there is a good chance that the shortcuts will work in another application. Ctrl+Home and Ctrl+End, for example, move to the beginning and end of a document, respectively. Ctrl+B, Ctrl+I, and Ctrl+U boldface, italicize, and underline text. Ctrl+X (the "X" is supposed to remind you of a pair of scissors), Ctrl+C, and Ctrl+V will cut, copy, and paste, respectively. You may not know what these

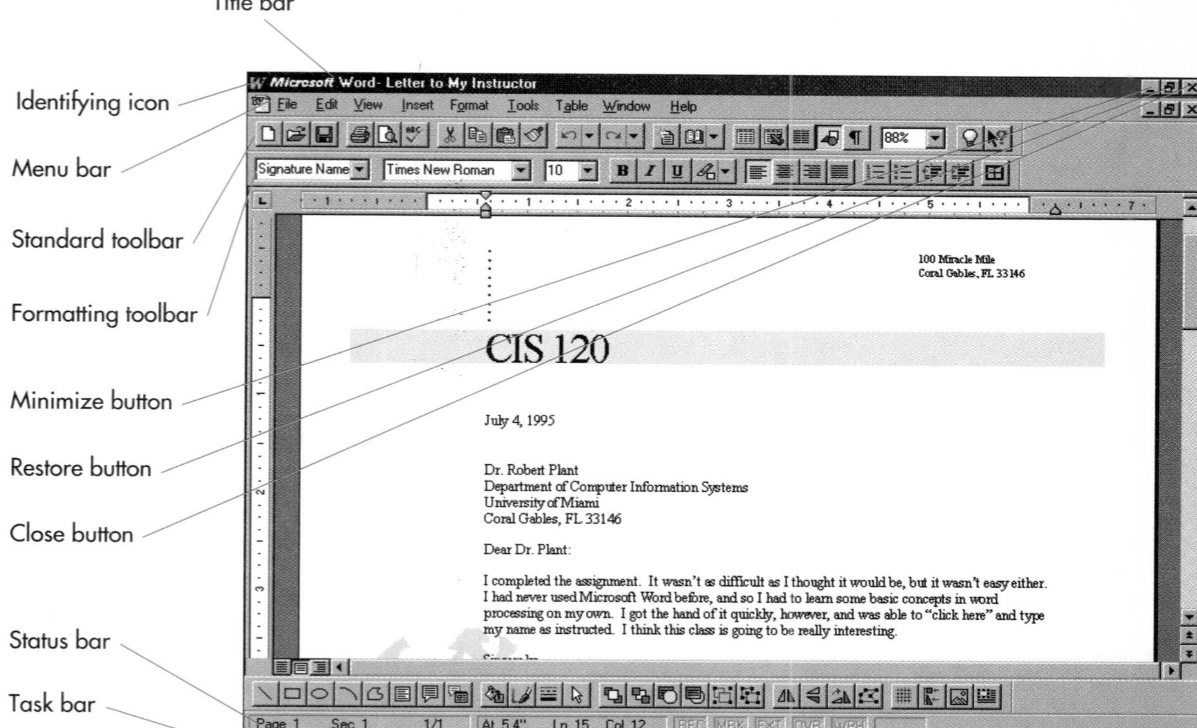

(a) Microsoft Word

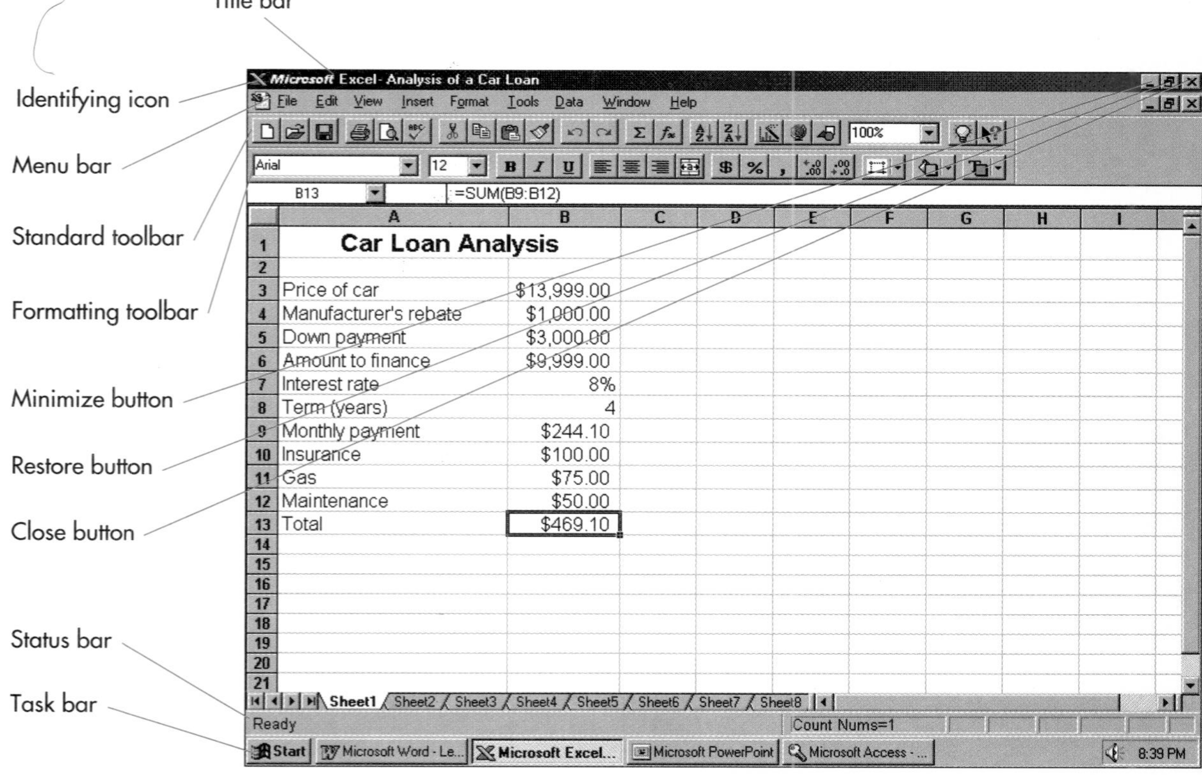

(b) Microsoft Excel

FIGURE 1 The Common User Interface

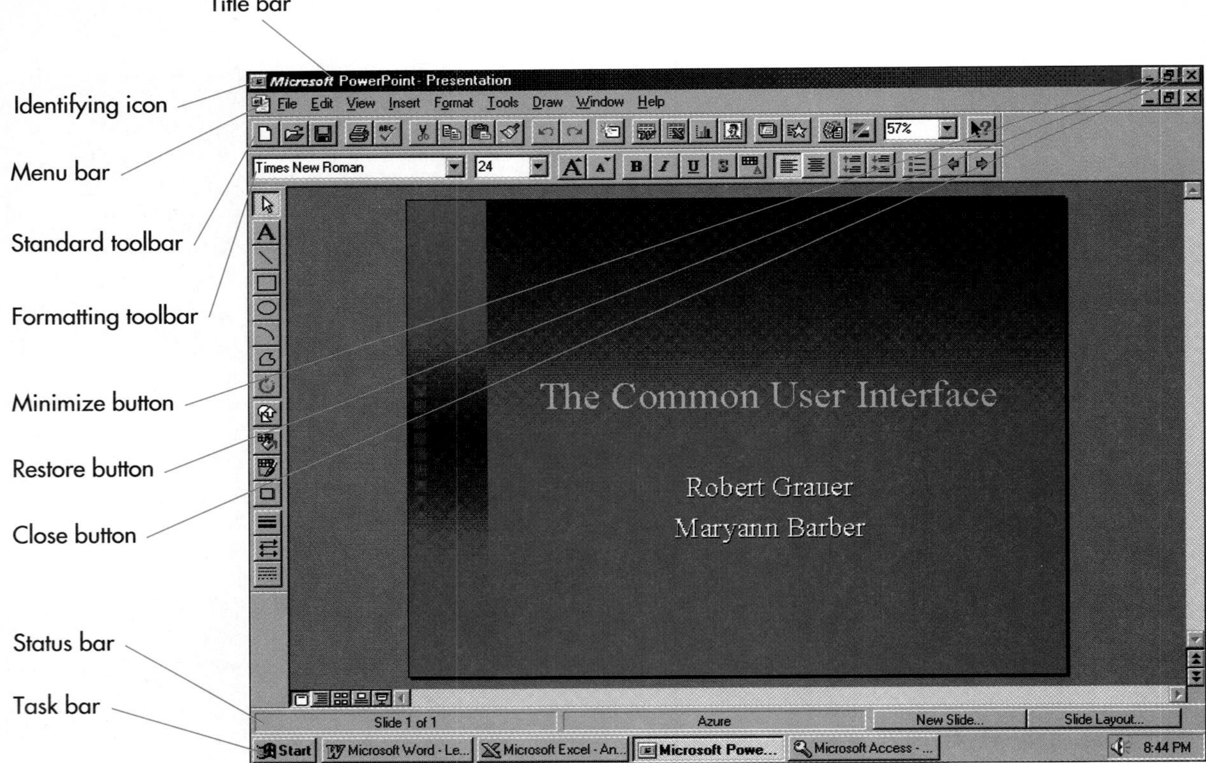

(c) Microsoft PowerPoint

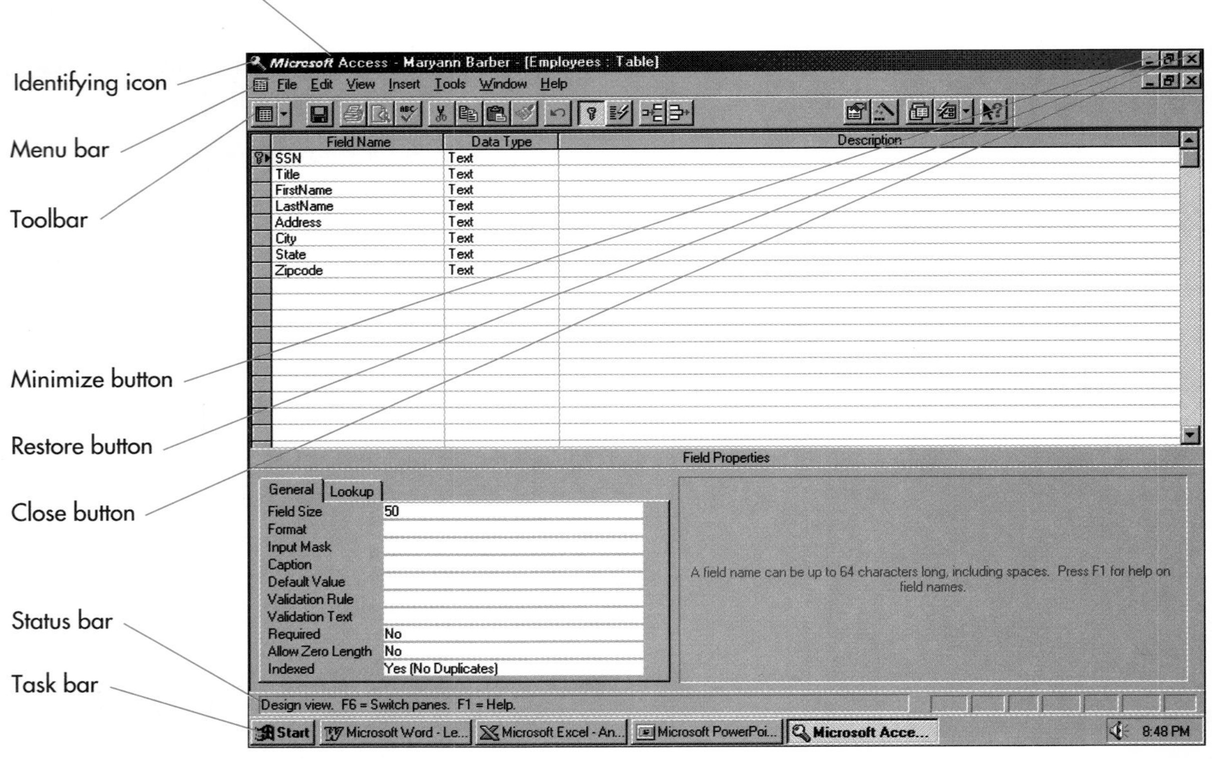

(d) Microsoft Access

FIGURE 1 The Common User Interface (continued)

commands do now, but once you learn how they work in one application, you will intuitively know how they work in the others.

All four applications use consistent (and often identical) dialog boxes. The dialog boxes to open and close a file, for example, are identical in every application. All four applications also share a common dictionary. The AutoCorrect feature (to correct common spelling mistakes) works identically in all four applications. The help feature also functions identically.

There are, of course, differences between the applications. Each application has its own unique menus and associated toolbars. Nevertheless, the Standard and Formatting toolbars in all applications contain many of the same tools (especially the first several tools on the left of each toolbar). The ***Standard toolbar*** contains buttons for basic commands such as Open, Save, or Print. It also contains buttons to cut, copy, and paste, and all of these buttons are identical in all four applications. The ***Formatting toolbar*** provides access to common formatting operations such as boldface, italics, or underlining, or changing the font or point size, and again, these buttons are identical in all four applications. ToolTips are present in all applications. Suffice it to say, therefore, that once you know one Office application, you have a tremendous head start in learning another.

MICROSOFT OFFICE VERSUS OFFICE PROFESSIONAL

Microsoft distributes two versions of the Office Suite: Standard Office and Office Professional. Both versions include Word, Excel, and PowerPoint. The Office Professional also has Microsoft Access. The difference is important when you are shopping and comparing prices from different sources. Be sure to purchase the version that is appropriate for your needs. Note, too, that Microsoft Access requires 12Mb of RAM. The other applications run adequately in 8Mb.

Online Help

Each application in the Microsoft Office has an extensive ***online help*** facility, as shown in Figure 2. Help is available at any time, and is accessed from the application's Help menu. (The Help screens in Figure 2 pertain to Microsoft Office, as opposed to a specific application, and were accessed through the Answer Wizard button on the Office Shortcut Bar.)

The ***Contents tab*** in Figure 2a is similar to the table of contents in an ordinary book. The major topics are represented by books, each of which can be opened to display additional topics. Each open book displays one or more topics, which may be viewed and/or printed to provide the indicated information.

The ***Index tab*** in Figure 2b is analogous to the index of an ordinary book. Type the first several letters of a topic, such as "he" in Figure 2b. Help then returns all of the topics beginning with the letters you entered. Select the topic you want, then display the topic for immediate viewing, or print it for later reference.

The ***Find tab*** (not shown in Figure 2) searches the text of the individual Help topics for a specific entry. It is similar in concept to an index except that it provides a more extensive list.

The ***Answer Wizard*** in Figure 2c lets you ask questions in your own words, then it returns the relevant help topics. The Help screen in Figure 2d was accessed from the selections provided by the Answer Wizard, and it, in turn, will lead you to new features in the individual applications.

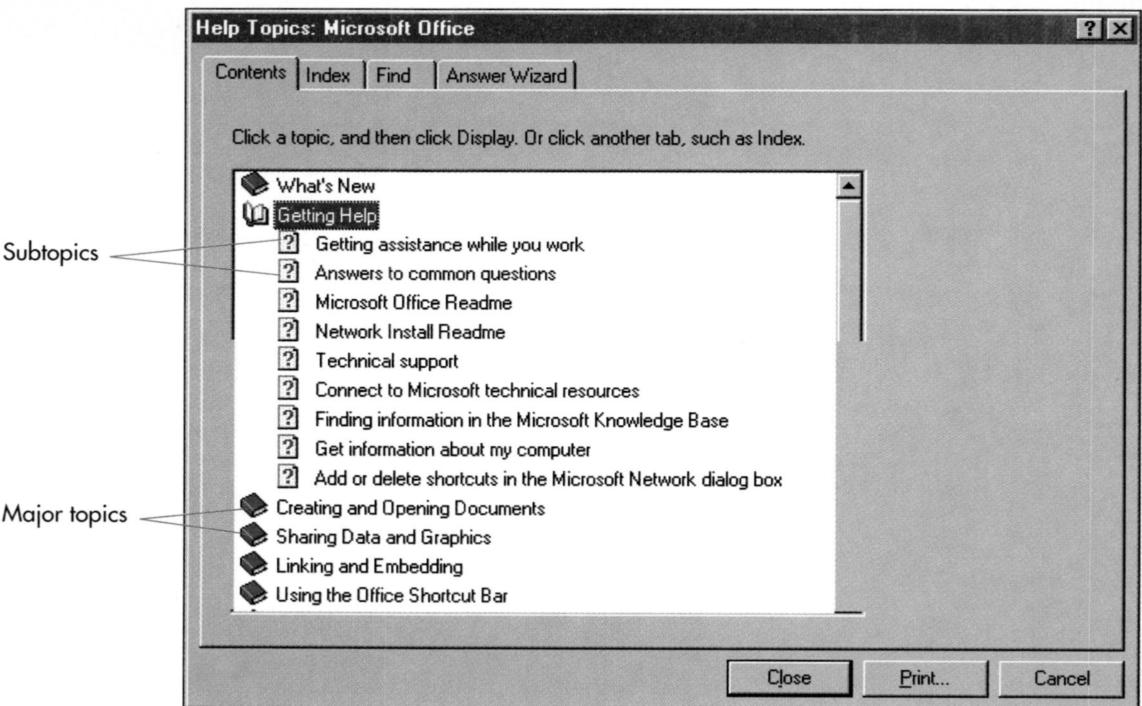

(a) Contents Tab

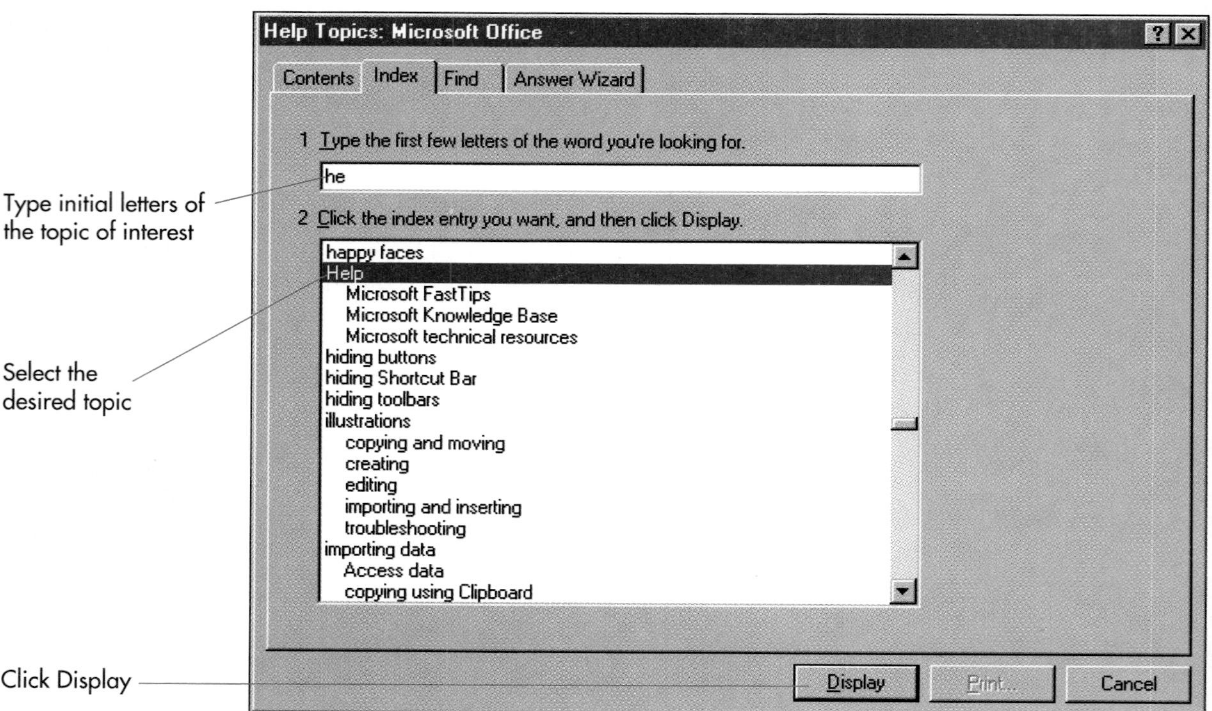

(b) Index Tab

FIGURE 2 Online Help

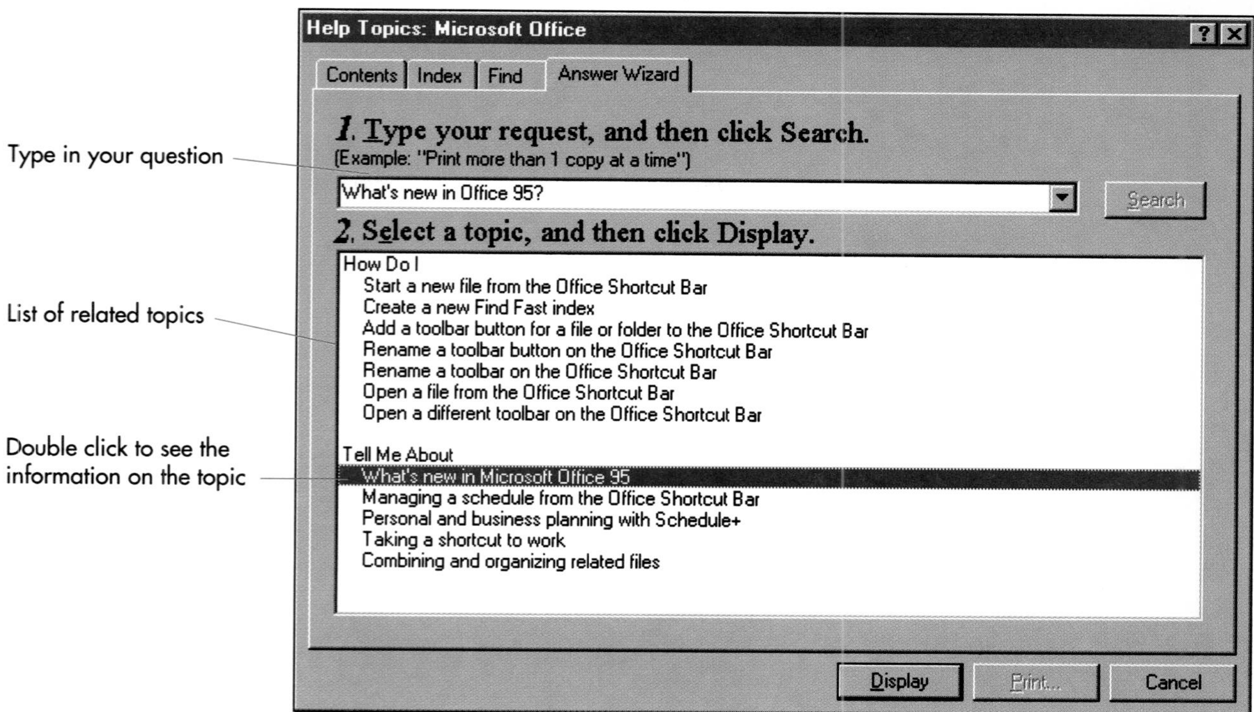

(c) Answer Wizard

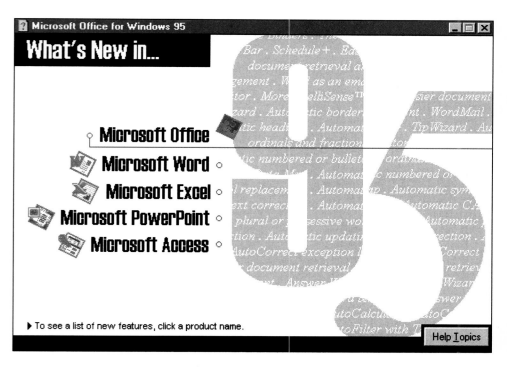

(d) What's New in Office 95?

FIGURE 2 **Online Help (continued)**

Office Shortcut Bar

The ***Microsoft Office Shortcut Bar*** provides immediate access to each application within Microsoft Office. It consists of a row of buttons and can be placed anywhere on the screen. The Shortcut Bar is anchored by default on the right side of the desktop, but you can position it along any edge, or have it "float" in the middle of the desktop. You can even hide it from view when it is not in use.

Figure 3a displays the Shortcut Bar as it appears on our desktop. The buttons that are displayed (and the order in which they appear) are established through the Customize dialog box in Figure 3b. (We show you how to customize the Shortcut Bar in the hands-on exercise that follows shortly.) Our Shortcut Bar contains a button for each Office application, a button for the Windows Explorer, and a button to access help.

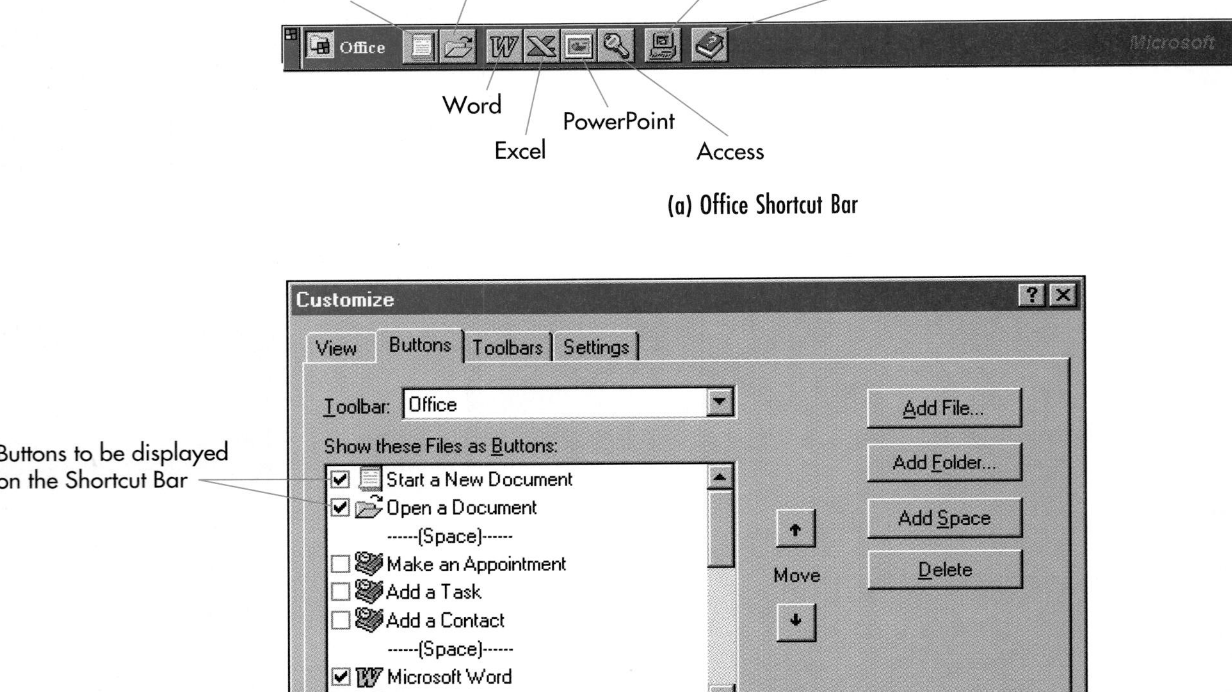

(a) Office Shortcut Bar

(b) Customize Dialog Box

FIGURE 3 Office Shortcut Bar

Docucentric Orientation

Our Shortcut Bar contains two additional buttons: to open an existing document and to start a new document. These buttons are very useful and take advantage of the "docucentric" orientation of Microsoft Office, which lets you think in terms of a document rather than the associated application. You can still open a document in traditional fashion, by starting the application (e.g., clicking its button on the Shortcut Bar), then using the File Open command to open the document. It's

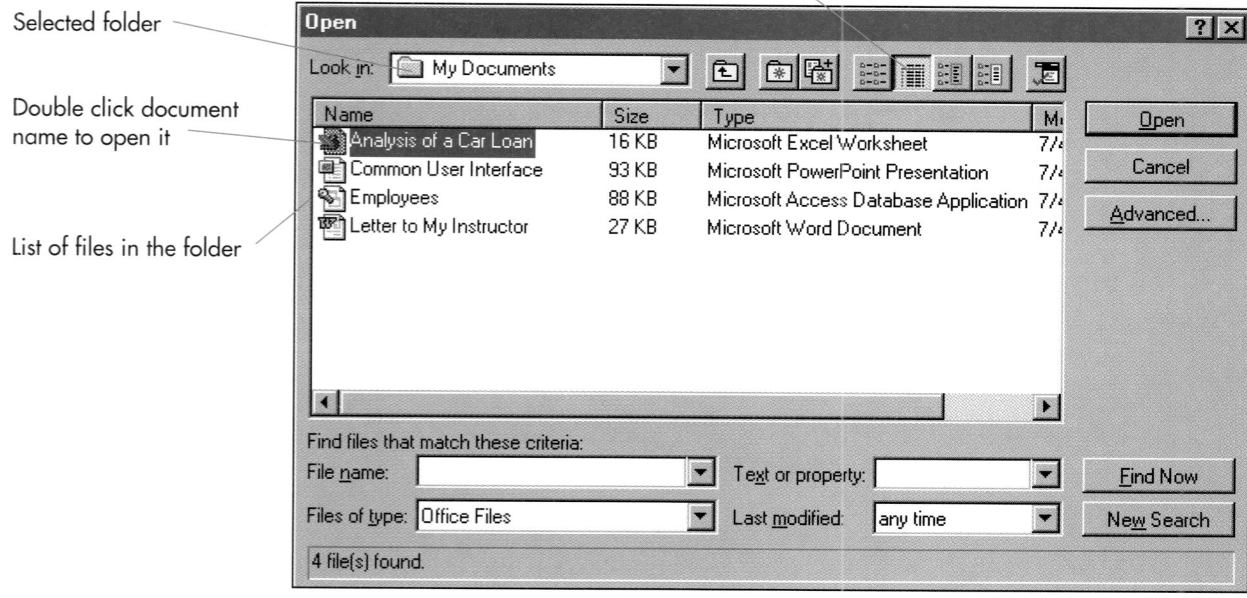

(a) Open an Existing Document

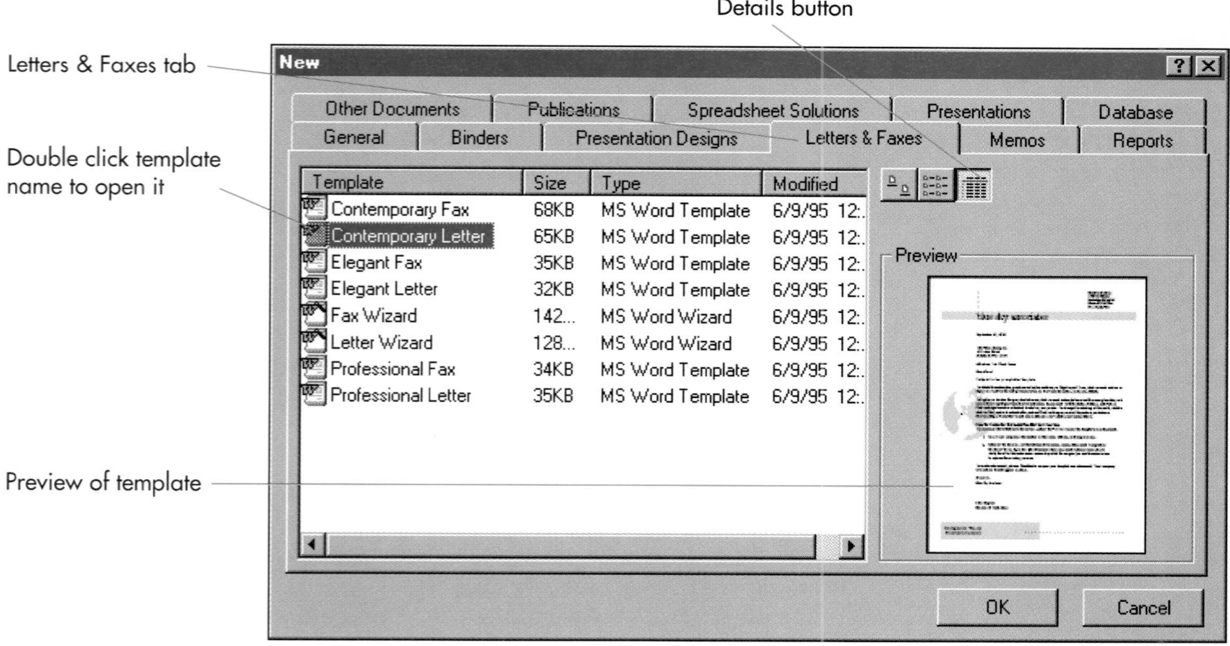

(b) Start a New Document

FIGURE 4 Document Orientation

easier, however, to locate the document, then double click its icon, which automatically loads the associated program.

Consider, for example, the Open dialog box in Figure 4a, which is displayed by clicking the Open a Document button on the Shortcut Bar. The Open dialog box is common to all Office applications, and it works identically in each application. The My Documents folder is selected in Figure 4a, and it contains four documents of various file types. The documents are displayed in the Details view, which shows the document name, size, file type, and date and time the document was last modified. To open any document—for example, "Analysis of a Car Loan"—just double click its name or icon. The associated application (Microsoft Excel in this example) will be started automatically; and it, in turn, will open the selected workbook.

The "docucentric" orientation also applies to new documents. Click the Start a New Document button on the Office Shortcut Bar, and you display the New dialog box in Figure 4b. Click the tab corresponding to the type of document you want to create, such as Letters & Faxes in Figure 4b, then click (select) various templates so that you can choose the one most appropriate for your purpose. Double click the desired template to start the application, which opens the template and enables you to create the document.

CHANGE THE VIEW

The toolbar in the Open dialog box displays the documents within the selected folder in one of several views. Click the Details button to switch to the Details view and see the date and time the file was last modified, as well as its size and type. Click the List button to display an icon representing the associated application, enabling you to see many more files than in the Details view. The Preview button lets you see a document before you open it. The Properties button displays information about the document, including the number of revisions.

BINDERS

The concept of a ***binder*** is new to Office 95. An Office binder, like a loose-leaf notebook or binder clip, keeps related documents together. Any number of Word, Excel, and/or PowerPoint documents can be placed into a binder and stored as a single file. (An Access database cannot be included.) The binder in Figure 5 contains six documents (three word documents, two spreadsheets, and a presentation). The left pane in the Microsoft Office Binder window shows the documents that make up the binder. The right pane displays the specific document on which you are working. To work on a different document (e.g., the Excel workbook named Forecast), just click its icon.

The documents within a binder are known as ***sections.*** The commands in the File menu apply to the binder as a whole, whereas the commands in the Section menu apply to the selected document (section). To print the entire binder, for example, you would execute the Print command from the File menu. To print a single document, however, you would execute the Print command from the Section menu. The Section menu is also used to add a new document to the binder and/or to delete or rename an existing document.

A CASE-SENSITIVE BINDER

The word *binder* is used in two different contexts in the discussion and is written with both an uppercase and a lowercase "b." Microsoft Office Binder (uppercase "B") is an application within Office 95. A binder (lowercase "b"), however, refers to a specific document created by the Binder application.

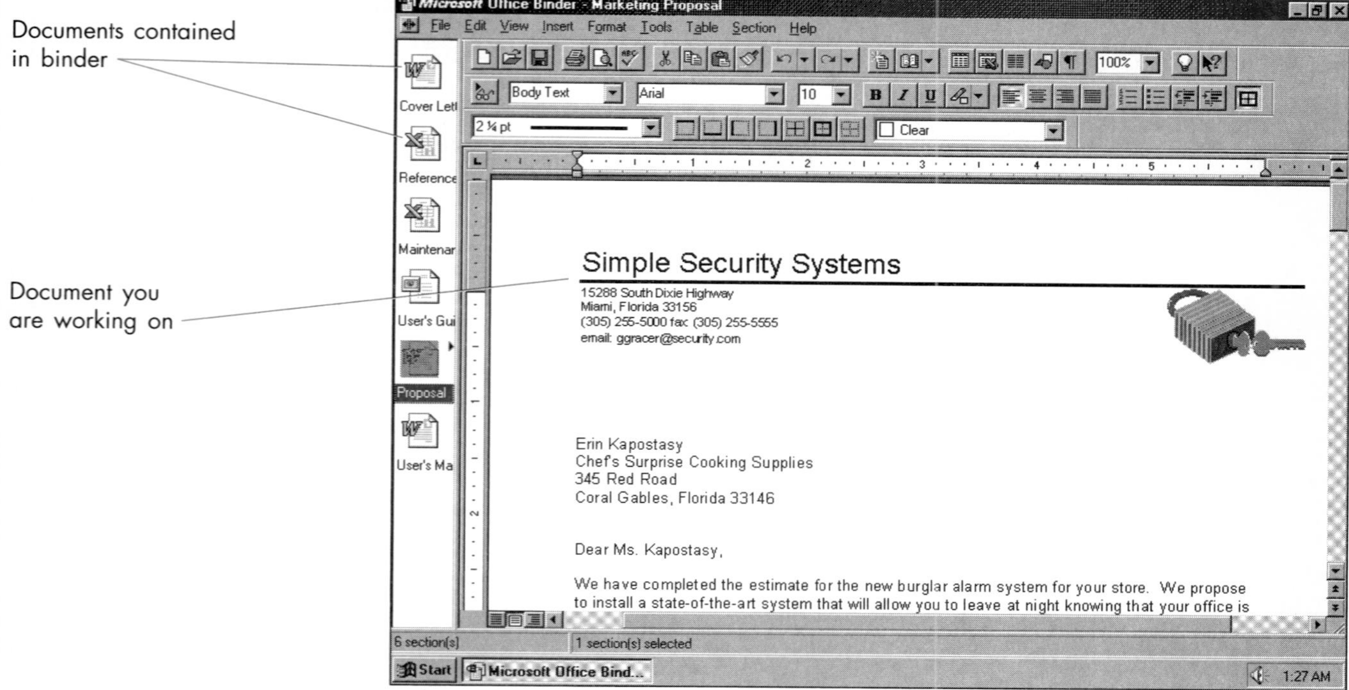

FIGURE 5 Binders

There is no requirement to use binders, and indeed, related documents can be stored in the same folder without creating a binder. Binders provide a convenience, however, in that a single Open command provides access to all of the documents in a binder without having to start the applications individually. A binder also ensures that the included documents are saved as a unit.

LEARNING BY DOING

Learning is best accomplished by doing, and so we come now to the first of many hands-on exercises that appear throughout the book. The exercises enable you to apply the concepts you have learned, then extend those concepts to further exploration on your own. This exercise focuses on the Office Shortcut Bar and assumes a basic knowledge of the Windows 95 desktop and associated mouse operations. It also guides you in creating a new binder based on an existing template that is accessed through the Start a New Document button.

DOWNLOAD THE DATA DISK

You can download the data disk for any book in the *Exploring Windows* series from Bob Grauer's home page (http://www.bus.miami.edu/~rgrauer). Use any Web browser to get to Bob's page, then click the link to the *Exploring Windows* series, where you choose the appropriate book and download the necessary file. (Be sure to read the associated "Read Me" file for additional instructions.) You can also click the link to CIS120, the microcomputer applications course at the University of Miami, to see Bob's syllabus and current assignment.

HANDS-ON EXERCISE 1

Introduction to Microsoft Office

Objective: To customize the Microsoft Office Shortcut Bar; to create an Office binder. Use Figure 6 as a guide in the exercise.

STEP 1: Welcome to Windows 95

- Turn on the computer and all of its peripherals. The floppy drive should be empty before you start your machine. This ensures that the system starts by reading files from the hard disk (which contains the Windows files), as opposed to a floppy disk (which does not).
- Your system will take a minute or so to get started, after which you should see the desktop in Figure 6a. Do not be concerned if the appearance of your desktop is different from ours.
- If you are new to Windows 95 and you want a quick introduction, click the **What's New** or **Windows Tour command buttons.** Follow the instructions in the boxed tip to display the dialog box if it does not appear on the system.
- Click the **Close button** to close the Welcome window and continue with the exercise.

TAKE THE WINDOWS 95 TOUR

Windows 95 greets you with a Welcome window that contains a command button to take you on a 10-minute tour of Windows 95. Click the command button and enjoy the show. You might also try the What's New command button for a quick overview of changes from Windows 3.1. If you do not see the Welcome window when you start Windows 95, click the Start button, click Run, type C:\WINDOWS\WELCOME in the Open text box, and press enter.

STEP 2: The Office Shortcut Bar

- We don't know why, but Microsoft does not make it easy to display the Office Shortcut bar. Click the **Start button,** click (or point to) the **Find command,** then click **Files or Folders** to display the Find Folders dialog box.
- Enter **Msoffice.exe** (the file you are searching for) in the Named Text box. Click the **down arrow** in the Look in list box, then enter **My Computer** to search all drives on your system.
- Click the **Find Now button** to initiate the search, which should display the program within the dialog box. Double click the icon for **Msoffice.exe** from within the Find dialog box to start the program and display the Office Shortcut Bar.
- You can position the Shortcut Bar anywhere on the desktop. Just point to an empty area on the bar, then click and drag to a new location.

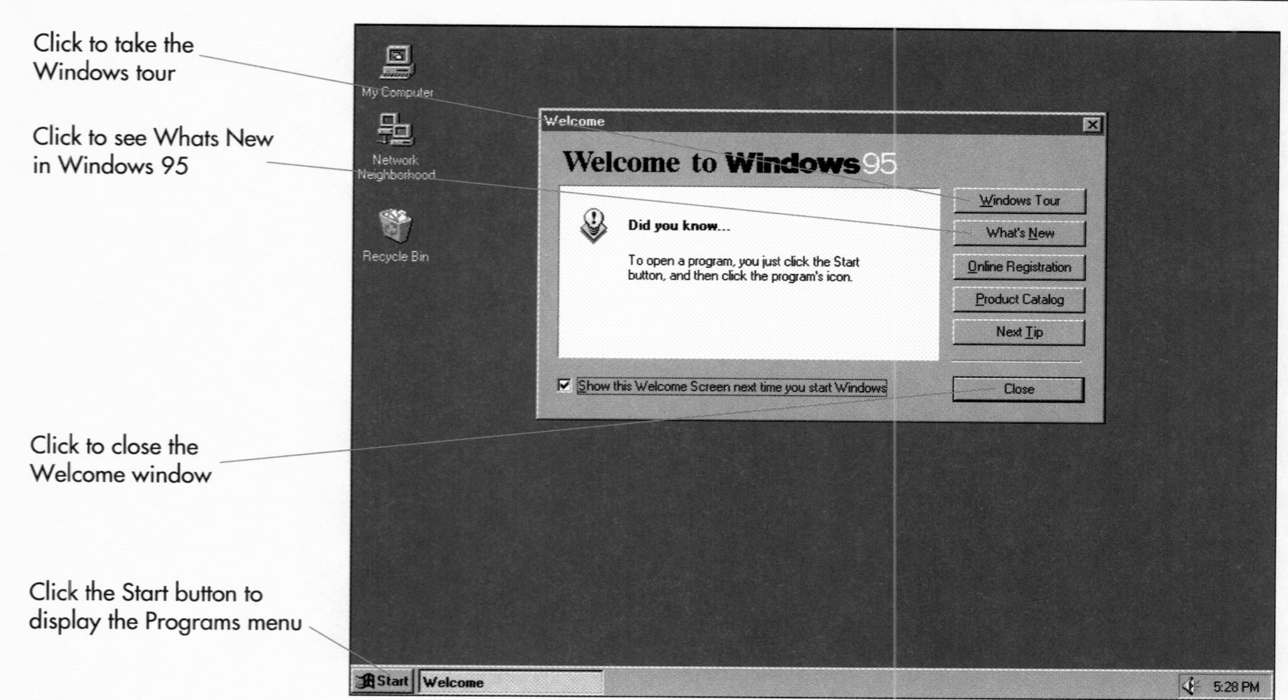

(a) Welcome to Windows 95 (step 1)

FIGURE 6 Hands-on Exercise 1

MODIFY THE START MENU

You can add your favorite programs to the Start menu so that you can execute it with a click of the button. Locate the program using Explorer or the Find command, then click and drag the icon for the program to the Start button on the taskbar. The next time you click the Start button you will see a (shortcut) icon corresponding to the program you dragged to the Start button.

STEP 3: Customize the Shortcut Bar

- Do not be concerned if your Shortcut Bar is different from Figure 6b since its appearance or content is easily changed.
- Point to an empty area of the Shortcut Bar, then click the **right mouse button** to display a Shortcut menu. Click **Customize** to display the Customize dialog box.
- If necessary, click the **View tab,** then check (or clear) the various option buttons according to the options you prefer. The settings do not take effect until you click the **OK command button** to close the dialog box.
- Clear the check box to Use the Standard Toolbar color, then click the **Change Color command button** to display the Color dialog box in Figure 6b.
- Click (select) a color, then click **OK** to accept the color change and close the Color dialog box. Click **OK** a second time to close the Customize dialog box and implement the changes.

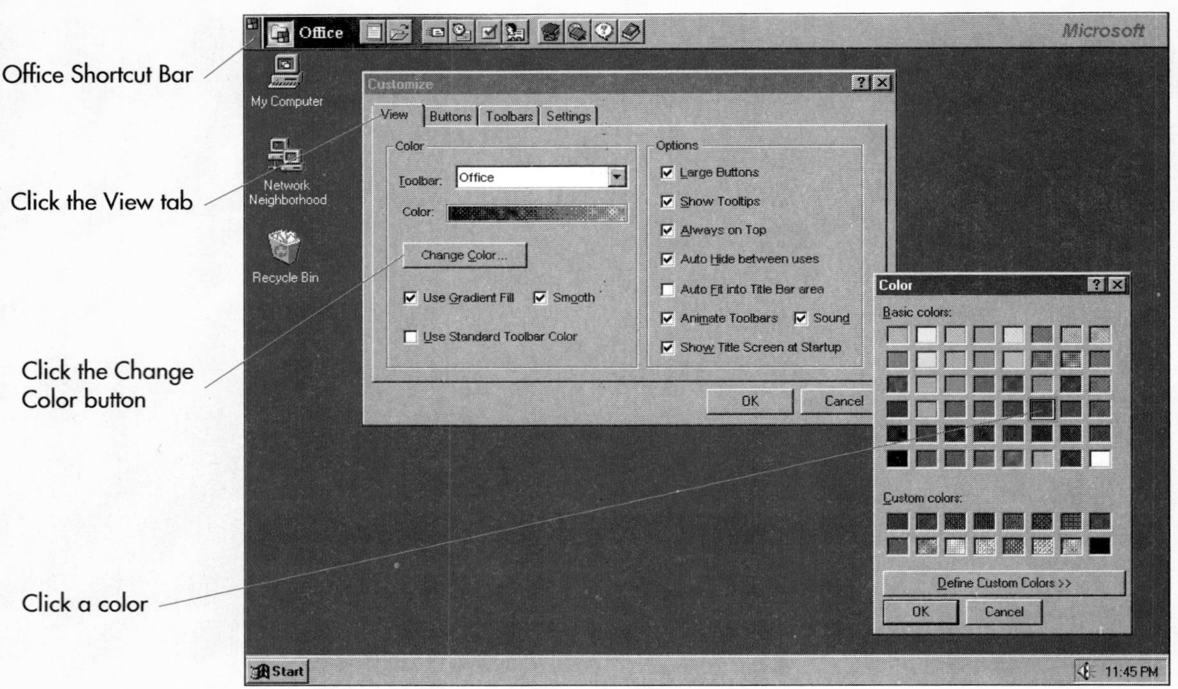

(b) Customize the Toolbar (step 3)

FIGURE 6 Hands-on Exercise 1 (continued)

AUTO HIDE THE SHORTCUT BAR

The Auto Hide option hides the Shortcut Bar between uses, giving you additional space on the desktop when you are in another application. Point to an empty space on the Shortcut Bar, click the right mouse button to display a menu, then check the Auto Hide command. (Clicking the command a second time removes the check and toggles the command off). To use the Shortcut Bar when it's hidden, point to the edge of the screen where the Shortcut Bar is docked, and the bar will appear. Click the appropriate button on the Shortcut Bar, then move the mouse back into the window containing your document to return to work.

STEP 4: Add/Remove Buttons

- Point to an empty area of the Shortcut Bar, then click the **right mouse button** to display a shortcut menu. Click **Customize** to display the Customize dialog box, then click the **Buttons tab** to display the dialog box in Figure 6c.
- Check (clear) the buttons you wish to display or hide. The effects of checking (or clearing) a button are visible immediately, without having to exit the dialog box; for example, checking the button for Microsoft Word displays the associated button immediately on the Shortcut Bar.
- Click **OK** to close the Customize dialog box.

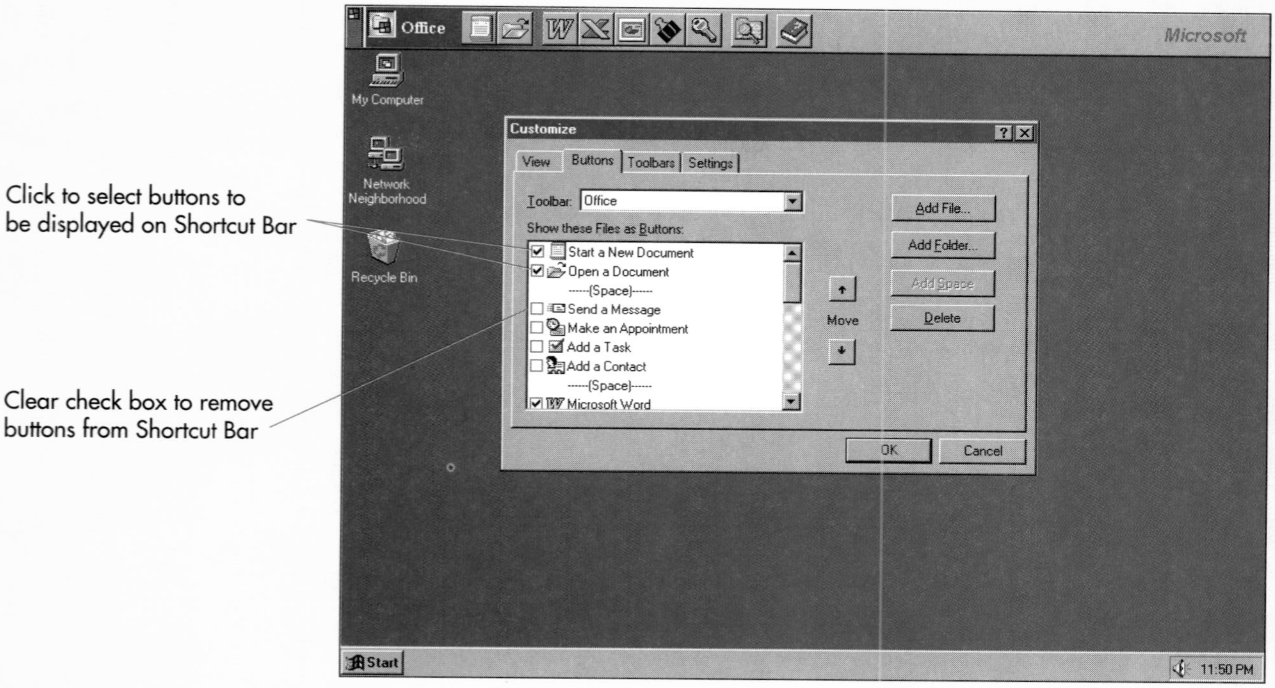

Click to select buttons to be displayed on Shortcut Bar

Clear check box to remove buttons from Shortcut Bar

(c) Add/Remove Buttons (step 4)

FIGURE 6 Hands-on Exercise 1 (continued)

ADD THE EXPLORER

The Windows Explorer is the primary means of file management within Windows 95, and thus, it is convenient to have it readily available. To add the Explorer to the Shortcut Bar, right click the Shortcut Bar, click the Customize command, click the Buttons tab, then scroll until you can check the box to add the Windows Explorer. Click OK to close the Customize dialog box. The Explorer has been added to the Shortcut Bar and is now a mouse click away.

STEP 5: Start a New Binder

➤ You can start a new binder in one of two ways:

- Click the **Start a New Document button** on the Microsoft Office toolbar to display the New dialog box, then click the **Binders tab** as shown in Figure 6d.
- Alternatively, you can click the **Start menu,** click **Programs,** then click **Microsoft Binder** to start the Microsoft Office Binder. Pull down the **File menu,** click **New Binder** to display the New Binder dialog box (similar to Figure 6d), then click the **Binders tab.**

➤ Click the **Details button** to change the view within the New (or New Binder) dialog box. Click and drag the border separating the Template and Size columns so that you can read the title of the template.

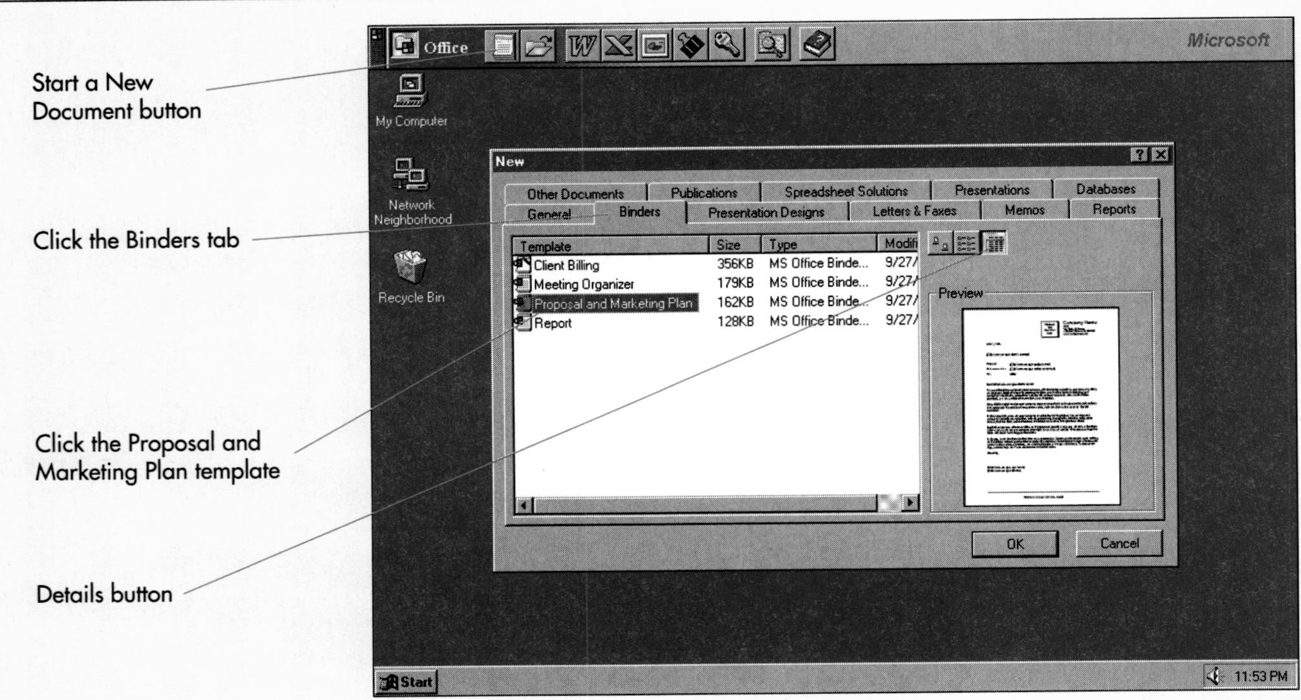

(d) Start a New Binder (step 5)

FIGURE 6 Hands-on Exercise 1 (continued)

➤ Select (click) the **Proposal and Marketing template** as shown in Figure 6d. (The preview for the selected document appears in the right of the dialog box.) Click **OK** to open the template for this binder.

ONLINE HELP

Online Help is available for Microsoft Office just as it is for any Windows application. Click the Answer Wizard button on the Office Shortcut Bar to display the dialog box containing Help Topics for Microsoft Office. The Help facility is intuitive and easy to use, and functions identically in every Windows application. The help displays are task-specific and fit in a single screen so that you don't have to scroll through large amounts of information.

STEP 6: Save the Binder

➤ If necessary, click the **maximize button** so that the Binder window takes the entire desktop, as shown in Figure 6e.

- The title bar indicates that you are running Microsoft Office Binder and that the name of the current binder is **Binder1.**

- The binder consists of six documents (four Word documents, one Excel workbook, and one PowerPoint presentation).
- The **Cover Letter document** is selected by default in the left pane and the document itself appears in the right pane. (To work on a different document just click its icon in the left pane.)
- Click the **Binder Contents button** to hide the left pane. Click the **Binder Contents button** a second time to redisplay the left pane.

➤ Pull down the **File menu** and click **Save Binder** (or click the **Save button** on the Standard toolbar) to display the Save Binder As dialog box in Figure 6e.

➤ Enter **Assignment 1** as the name of the binder. Click **Save.** The title bar changes to display Assignment 1 as the name of the binder.

THE FILE MENU VERSUS THE SECTION MENU

The commands in the File menu apply to the binder as a whole whereas the commands in the Section menu apply to a specific section (document). Thus to print the entire binder, you would pull down the File menu and select the Print Binder command. To print an individual document (section), however, you would select the Print command from the section menu. The Section menu is also used to add a new document to the binder and/or to delete or rename an existing document.

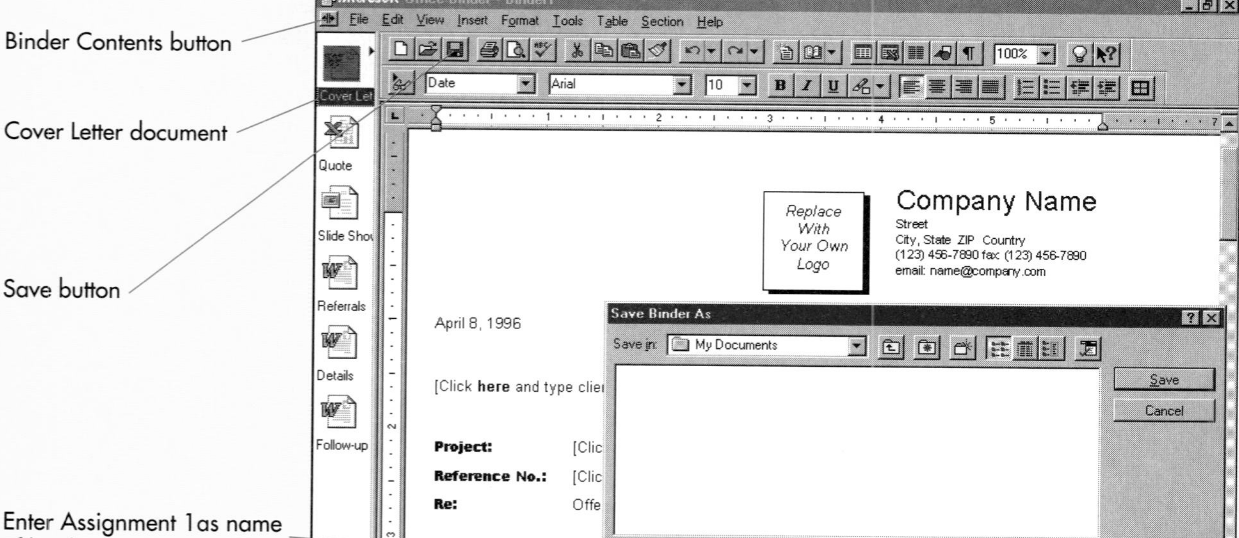

(e) Save the Binder (step 6)

FIGURE 6 Hands-on Exercise 1 (continued)

STEP 7: Insert a Graphic Logo

- ➤ If necessary, select the **Cover Letter document** in the left pane of the Binder window as shown in Figure 6f. Do not be concerned if the appearance of your screen is different from ours, as our Word view and zoom magnification may be different from yours.
- ➤ Select (click) the text box for the logo, which appears at the beginning of the letter. Press the **Del key** to delete the text box, which will be replaced by a graphic image.

> **FORMAT FRAME COMMAND**
>
> A graphic image should be placed into a frame (a special type of invisible container) immediately after it has been inserted into a document to facilitate positioning the object within the document. To do this, point to the graphic, click the right mouse button to display a shortcut menu, click the Frame Picture command, then click and drag the object (and its frame) to position it within the document. You can position a framed object more precisely by right clicking the object, selecting the Format Frame command from the shortcut menu, then entering the precise location of the frame within the Format Frame dialog box.

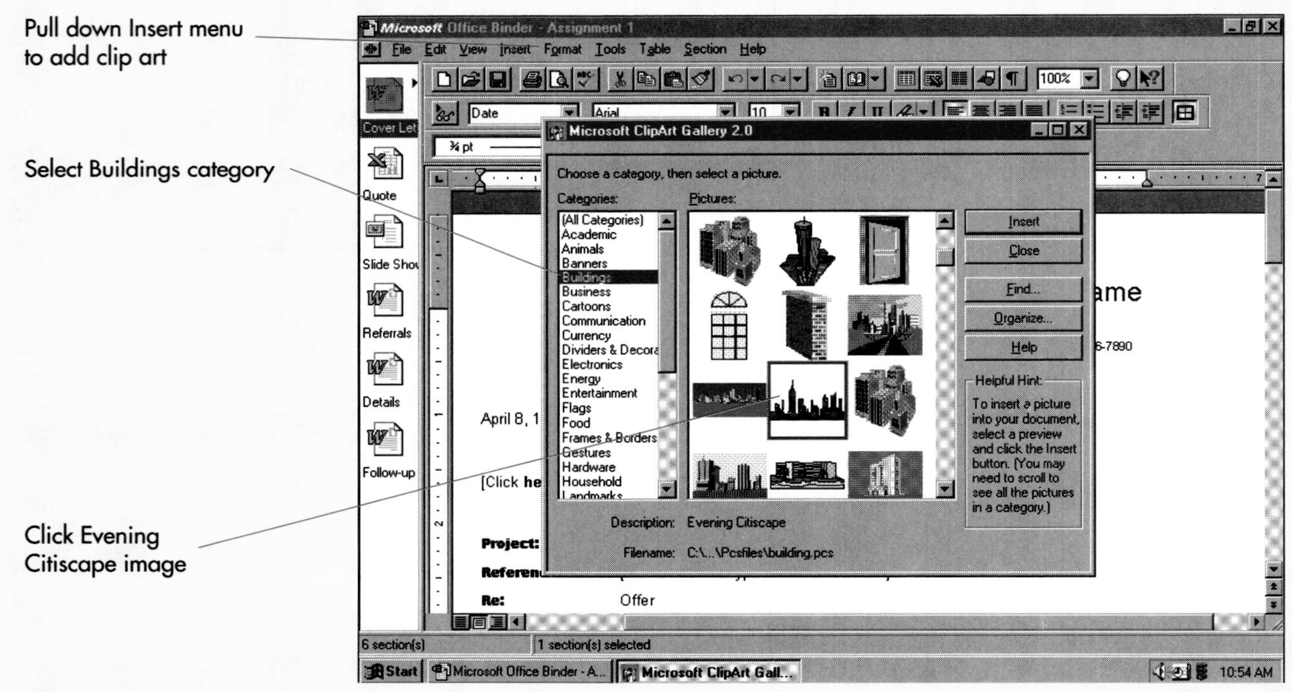

(f) Insert a Logo (step 7)

FIGURE 6 Hands-on Exercise 1 (continued)

➤ Pull down the **Insert menu,** click **Object** to display the Object dialog box, click the **Create New tab** (if necessary), then select **Microsoft ClipArt Gallery 2.0** from the list of displayed objects. You should see the Microsoft ClipArt Gallery 2.0 dialog box as shown in Figure 6f.

➤ Select (click) the **Buildings category,** select the **Evening Citiscape** clip art image, then click the **Insert button** to place the clip art into your document. Move and/or size the clip art image as described in the tip on the Format Frame command (page xxxiv).

STEP 8: Complete the Cover Letter

➤ The clip art image has been added to the letterhead as shown in Figure 6g. Follow the instructions within the template to complete the cover letter (use any text that is appropriate).

➤ Use the select-then-do methodology to replace the text in the template with your own words:

- The most basic way to select text is by dragging the mouse; that is, click at the beginning of the selection, press and hold the left mouse button as you move to the end of the selection, then release the mouse.
- To delete and replace text in one operation, select the text to be replaced, then just enter the new text.
- To boldface or italicize text, select the text, then click the Bold or Italics button on the Formatting toolbar. To left align, center, right align, or justify

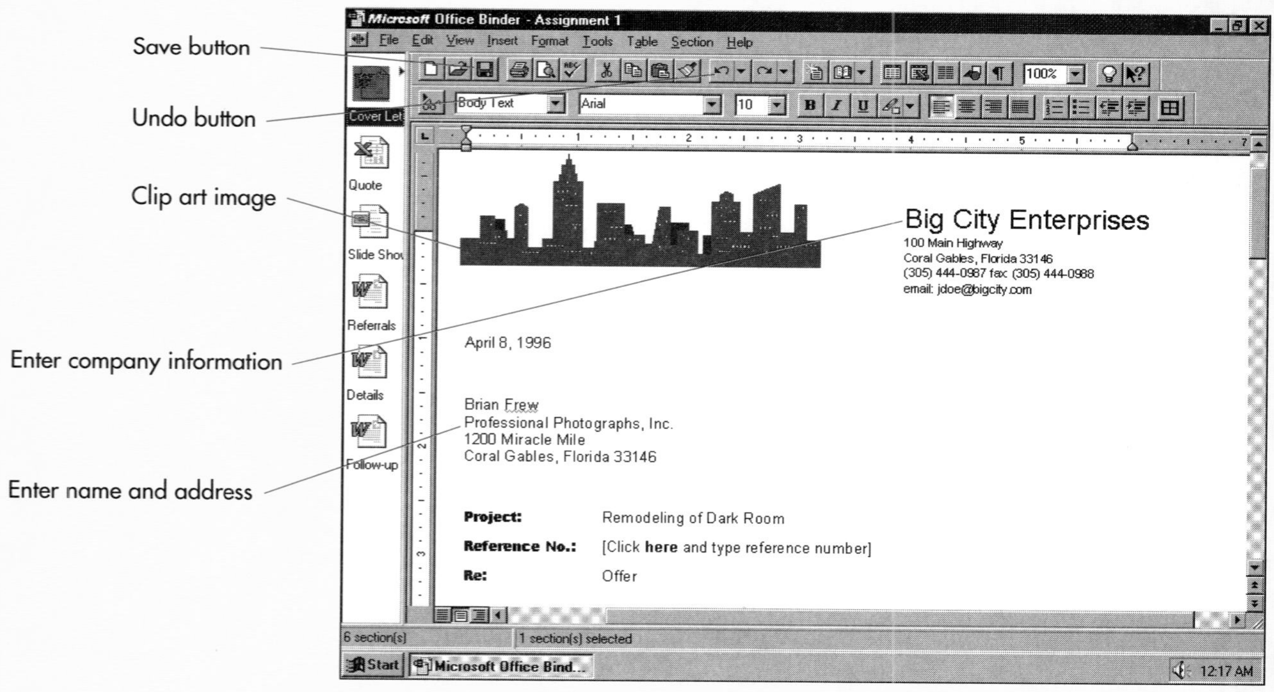

(g) Complete the Cover Letter (step 8)

FIGURE 6 Hands-on Exercise 1 (continued)

text, select the text, then click the appropriate button on the Formatting toolbar.

- Selected text is affected by any subsequent operation. The text remains selected until you click elsewhere in the document.

➤ Click the **Undo button** to reverse the last command or whenever something happens in your document that you didn't expect. (Word enables you to undo the last 100 changes to a document.)

➤ Click the **Save button** to save the changes to the document within the binder.

THE AUTOMATIC SPELL CHECK

A red wavy line under an entry indicates that the underlined word is either misspelled or not standard English, and hence not found in the Office dictionary. In either event, point to the underlined word, then click the right mouse button to display a shortcut menu. Select (click) the corrected spelling from the list of suggestions. You can also click the Add command to add the word to an auxiliary dictionary or the Ignore command to accept the word as it is.

STEP 9: Complete the Workbook

➤ Select the **Quote workbook** in the left pane of the Binder window to display the Excel worksheet in Figure 6h. The menu bar changes to reflect the Excel pull-down menus. The Standard and Formatting toolbars change as well.

➤ Point to any cell containing a tiny red dot to display a note containing information about the contents of that cell. The note in Figure 6h, for example, describes how to add a logo to the worksheet.

➤ Complete the client information at the top part of the worksheet by clicking in a cell and entering the appropriate information. Use the arrow keys to move from one cell to the next as you enter data.

➤ Enter the quantity, description, and unit price as shown in Figure 6h for Solid Wood Doors. Note that as soon as you press the enter key, the 395 is automatically formatted to $395.00 and the total ($790.00) is computed. Enter several additional items for your professor.

ADDING AND DELETING DOCUMENTS

A binder template provides a starting point from which you add, delete, or rename documents. To add (create) a new document, pull down the Section menu, click Add to display the Add Section dialog box, choose the type of document you want, then click OK. To add an existing document, pull down the Section menu, click the Add from File to display the Add from File dialog box, browse your system until you locate the document, then click OK to add the document to the binder. To delete (or rename) a document within the binder, point to the document in the left pane of the Binder window, click the right mouse button to display a shortcut menu, then click the appropriate command.

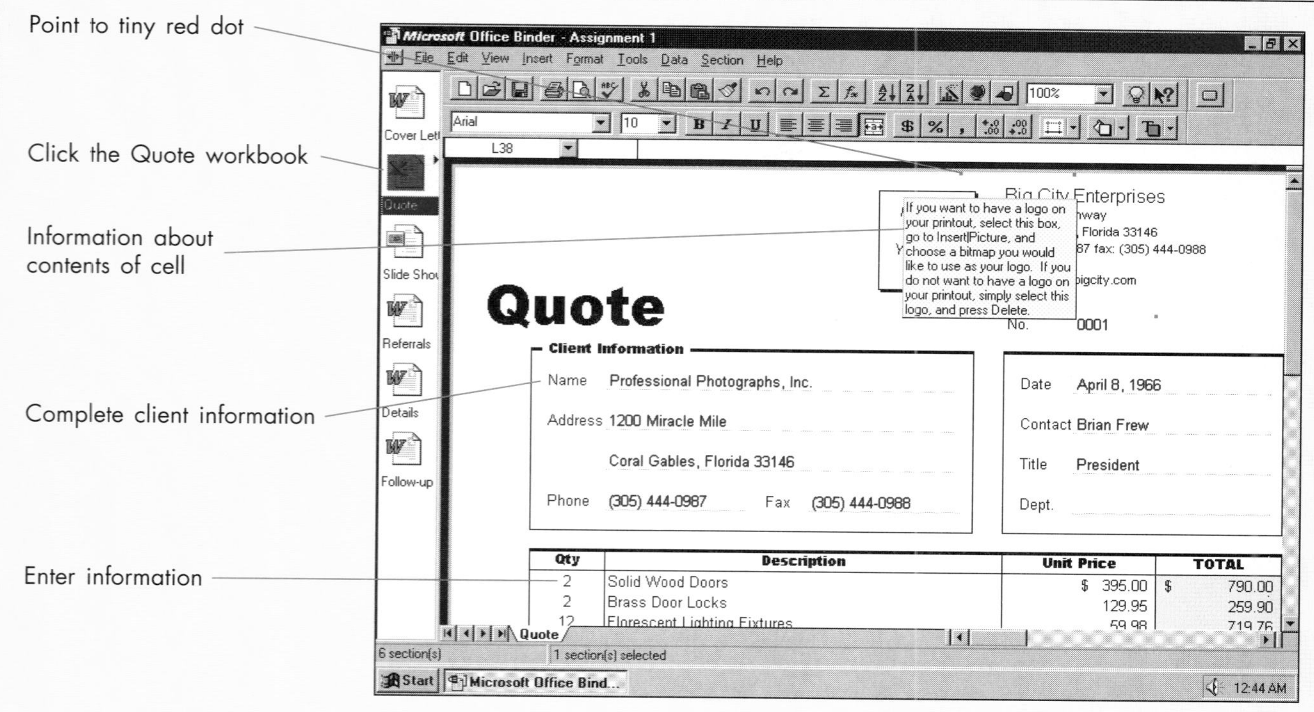

(h) The Spreadsheet (step 9)

FIGURE 6 Hands-on Exercise 1 (continued)

STEP 10: Print the Binder

- Click the **Cover Letter icon** in the left pane of the Binder window. When the Cover Letter is selected, the Quote workbook is automatically deselected.
- Now press and hold the **Ctrl key** as you click the **Quote icon.** Both documents (the Word Cover Letter and the Excel Quote) are selected, although only the Cover Letter is active.
- Experiment for a moment by pressing and holding the Ctrl key to select (deselect) additional documents within the Binder. End with only the Cover Letter and Quote selected, as shown in Figure 6i.

PAGE NUMBERS

The sections within a binder can be printed with consecutive page numbers provided page numbers have been added to the individual documents. To add page numbers to a Word document, pull down the Insert menu, click Page Numbers, then choose where you want the page numbers to appear. (Check the box to show numbers on the first page if you want a number on every page.) To add page numbers to an Excel worksheet, pull down the Section menu, select the Page Setup command, then choose (create) the appropriate header or footer. Note, too, that you can change the order of sections (and the associated page numbers) within a binder by dragging the icons within the left pane of the Binder window.

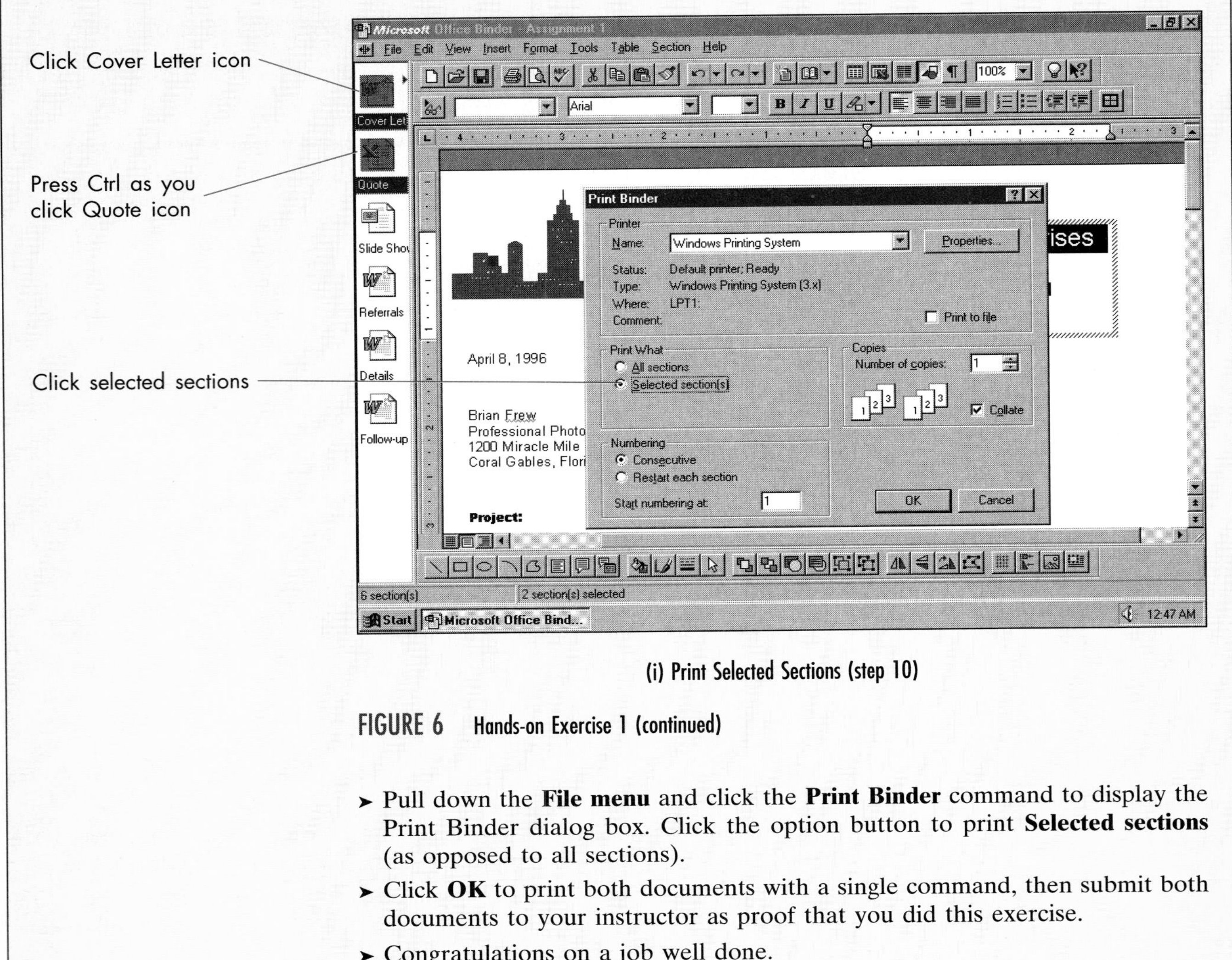

(i) Print Selected Sections (step 10)

FIGURE 6 Hands-on Exercise 1 (continued)

- Pull down the **File menu** and click the **Print Binder** command to display the Print Binder dialog box. Click the option button to print **Selected sections** (as opposed to all sections).
- Click **OK** to print both documents with a single command, then submit both documents to your instructor as proof that you did this exercise.
- Congratulations on a job well done.

SHARED APPLICATIONS AND UTILITIES

Microsoft Office includes a fifth application, Schedule+, as well as several smaller applications and shared utilities. ***Schedule+*** can be started from the Office Shortcut Bar or from the submenu for Microsoft Office, which is accessed through the Programs command on the Start button. Figure 7a displays one screen from Schedule+, to give you some idea of what the application can do.

In essence, Schedule+ is a personal information manager that helps you schedule (and keep) appointments. It will display your schedule on a daily, weekly, or monthly basis. It will beep to remind you of appointments. It will also maintain a list of important phone numbers and contacts. Schedule+ is beyond the scope of our text, but it is an easy application to learn since it follows the common user interface and has a detailed help facility.

The other applications (or applets as they are sometimes known) are easy to miss because they do not appear as buttons on the Shortcut Bar. Nor do they appear as options on any menu. Instead, these applications are loaded from within one of the major applications, typically through the Insert Object command. Two

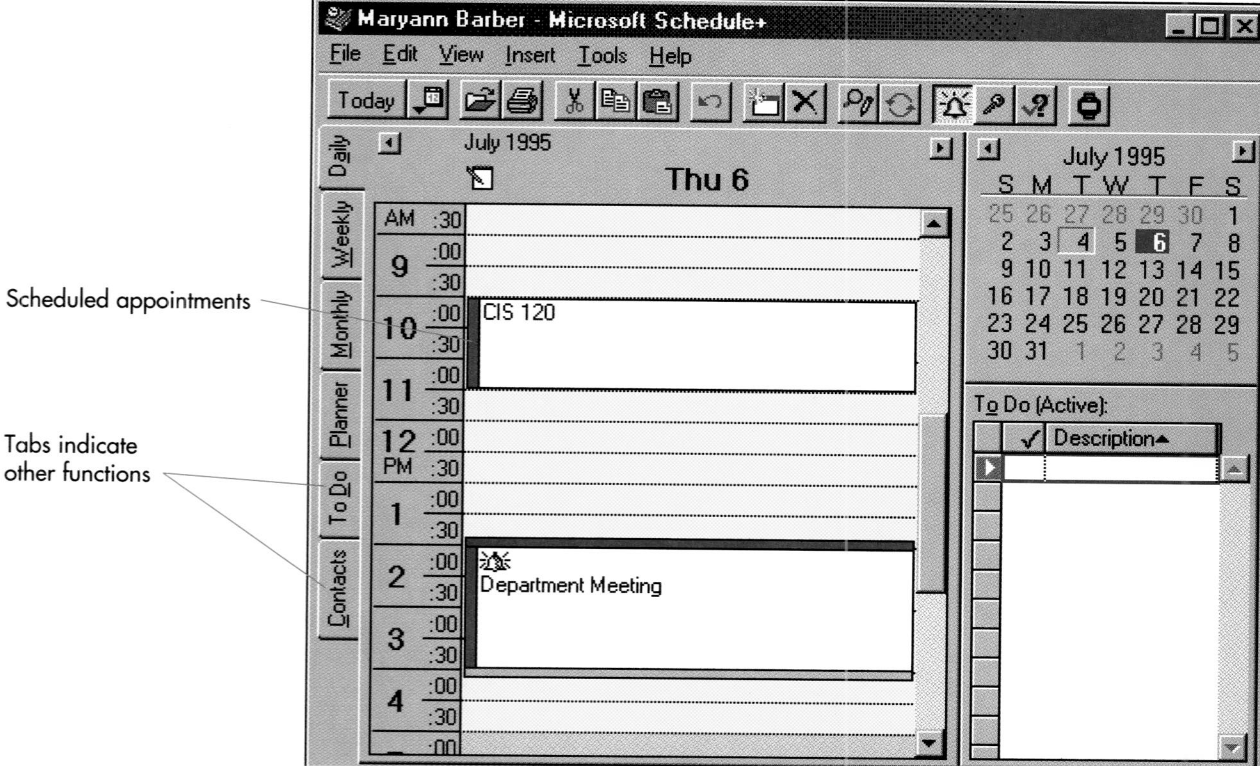

(a) Microsoft Schedule+

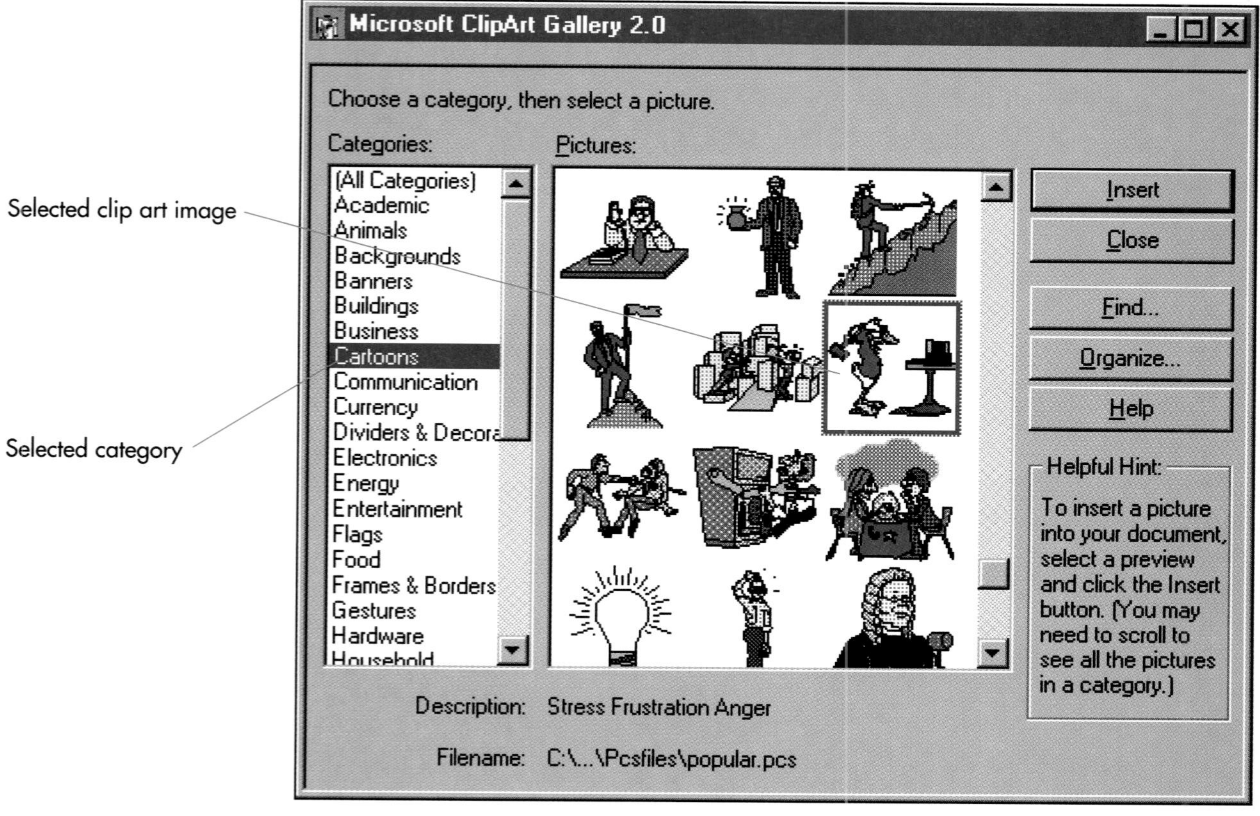

(b) ClipArt Gallery

FIGURE 7 Shared Applications

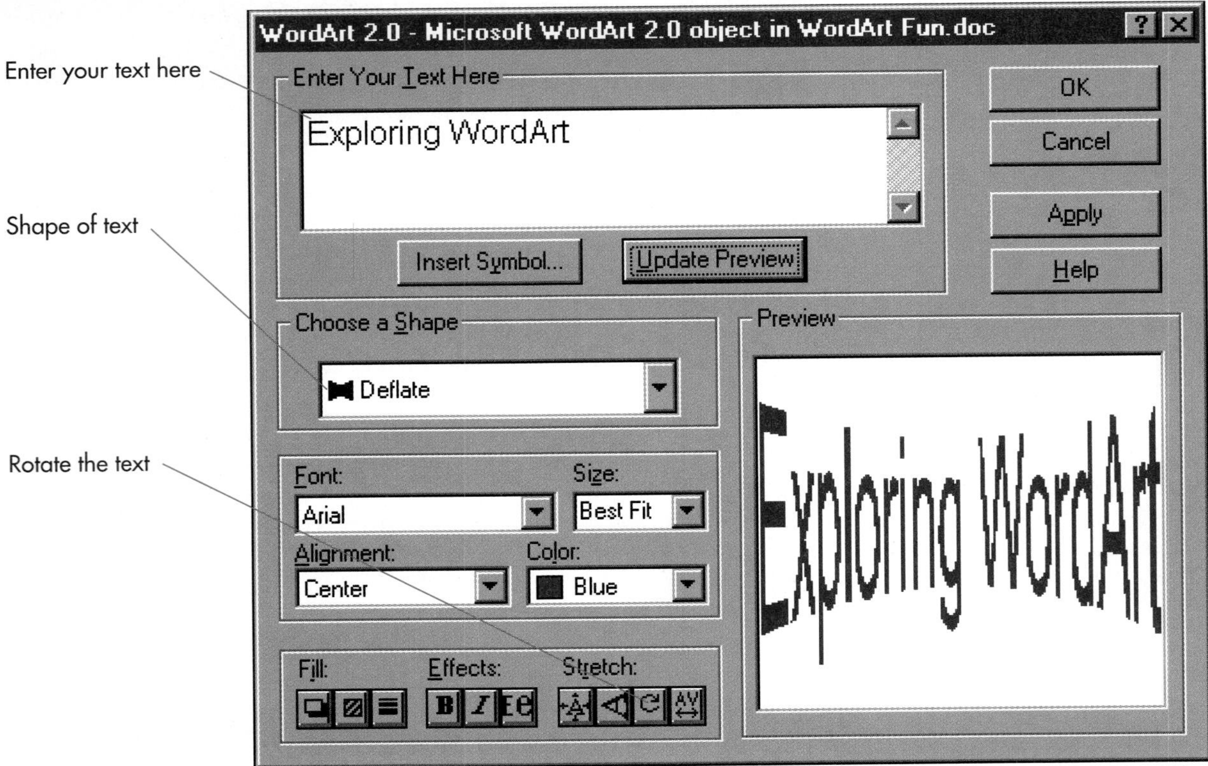

(c) WordArt

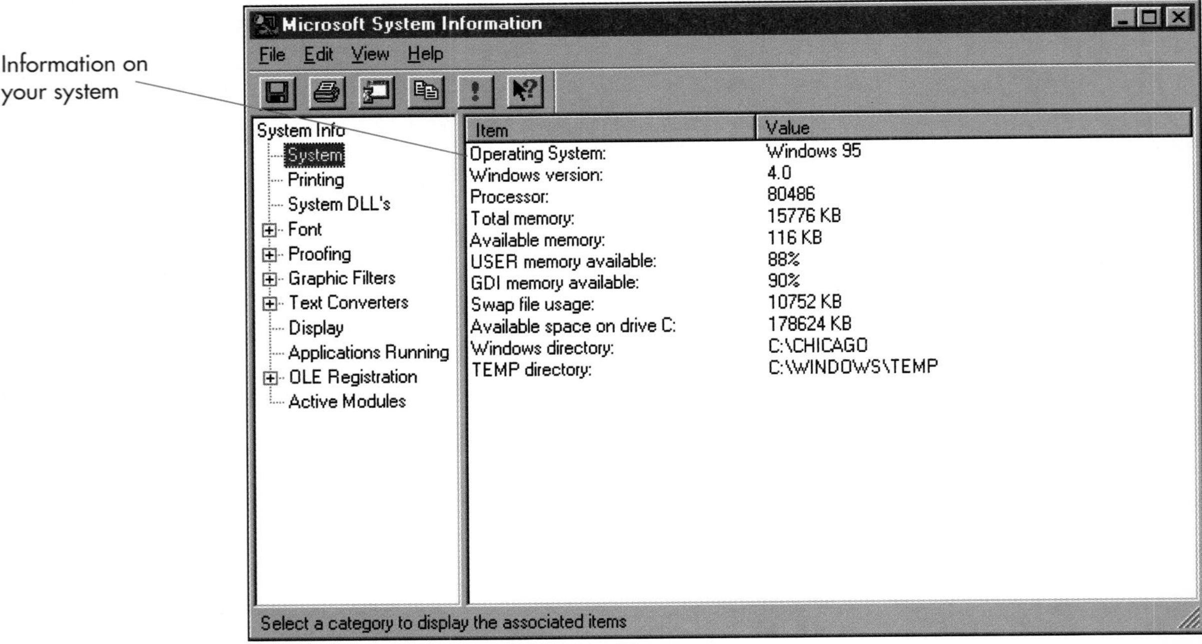

(d) Microsoft System Information

FIGURE 7 Shared Applications (continued)

of the more popular applications, the ***ClipArt Gallery*** and ***WordArt,*** are illustrated in Figures 7b and 7c, respectively.

The ClipArt Gallery contains more than 1,100 clip art images in 26 categories. Select a category such as Cartoons, select an image such as the duck smashing a computer, then click the Insert command button to insert the clip art into a document. Once an object is inserted into a document (regardless of whether it is a Word document, an Excel worksheet, a PowerPoint presentation, or an Access form or report), it can be moved and sized like any other Windows object.

WordArt enables you to create special effects with text. It lets you rotate and/or flip text, shade it, slant it, arch it, or even print it upside down. WordArt is intuitively easy to use. In essence, you enter the text in the dialog box of Figure 7c, choose a shape from the drop-down list box, then choose a font and point size. You can boldface or italicize the text or add special effects such as stretching or shadows.

The ***System Information Utility*** in Figure 7d is accessed from any major application by pulling down the Help menu, clicking the About button, then clicking the System Info command button. The utility provides detailed information about all aspects of your system. The information may prove to be invaluable should problems arise on your system and you need to supply technical details to support personnel.

THE OTHER SHARED APPLICATIONS

Microsoft Office includes several additional applications whose functions can be inferred from their names. The Equation Editor, Organization Chart, Data Map, and Graph utilities are accessed through the Insert Object command. All of these applications are straightforward and easy to use as they follow the common user interface and provide online help.

OBJECT LINKING AND EMBEDDING

The applications in Microsoft Office are thoroughly integrated with one another. They look alike and they work in consistent fashion. Equally important, they share information through a technology known as ***Object Linking and Embedding (OLE),*** which enables you to create a ***compound document*** containing data (objects) from multiple applications.

The compound document in Figure 8 was created in Word, and it contains objects (a worksheet and a chart) that were created in Excel. The letterhead uses a logo that was taken from the ClipArt Gallery, while the name and address of the recipient were drawn from an Access database. The various objects were inserted into the compound document through linking or embedding, which are actually two very different techniques. Both operations, however, are much more sophisticated than simply pasting an object, because with either linking or embedding you can edit the object by using the tools of the original application.

The difference between linking and embedding depends on whether the object is stored within the compound document (***embedding***) or in its own file (***linking***). An *embedded object* is stored in the compound document, which in turn becomes the only user (client) of that object. A *linked object* is stored in its own file, and the compound document is one of many potential clients of that object. The compound document does not contain the linked object per se, but only a representation of the object as well as a pointer (link) to the file containing the

Office of Residential Living

University of Miami • P.O. Box 243984 • Coral Gables, FL 33124

September 25, 1995

Mr. Jeffrey Redmond, President
Dynamic Dining Services
4329 Palmetto Lane
Miami, FL 33157

Dear Jeff,

As per our earlier conversation, occupancy is up in all of the dorms for the 1995 - 1996 school year. I have enclosed a spreadsheet and chart that show our occupancy rates for the 1992 - 1995 school years. Please realize, however, that the 1995 figures are projections, as the Fall 1995 numbers are still incomplete. The final 1995 numbers should be confirmed within the next two weeks. I hope that this helps with your planning. If you need further information, please contact me at the above address.

Dorm Occupancy

	1992	1993	1994	1995
Beatty	330	285	270	310
Broward	620	580	520	565
Graham	450	397	352	393
Rawlings	435	375	326	372
Tolbert	615	554	524	581

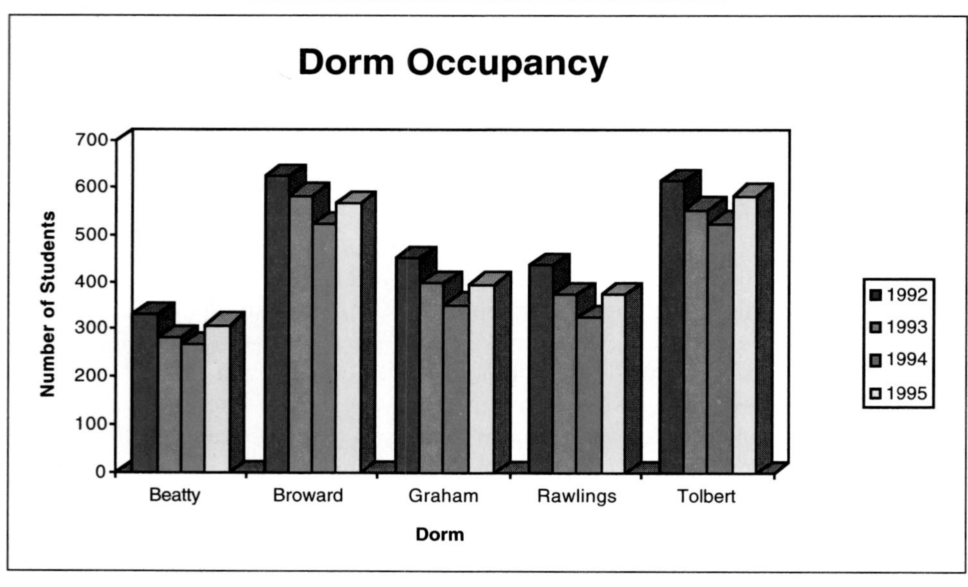

FIGURE 8 A Compound Document

object. The advantage of linking is that the document is updated automatically if the object changes.

The choice between linking and embedding depends on how the object will be used. Linking is preferable if the object is likely to change and the compound document requires the latest version. Linking should also be used when the same object is placed in many documents so that any change to the object has to be made in only one place. Embedding should be used if you need to take the object with you—for example, if you intend to edit the document on a different computer.

OBJECT LINKING AND EMBEDDING

Object Linking and Embedding (OLE) enables you to create a compound document containing objects (data) from multiple Windows applications. OLE is one of the major benefits of working in the Windows environment, but it would be impossible to illustrate all of the techniques in a single exercise. Accordingly, we have created the icon at the left to help you identify the many examples of object linking and embedding that appear throughout the *Exploring Windows* series.

SUMMARY

The common user interface requires every Windows application to follow a consistent set of conventions and ensures that all applications work basically the same way. The development of a suite of applications from a single vendor extends this concept by imposing additional similarities on all applications within the suite.

Microsoft distributes two versions of the Office Suite: Standard Office and Office Professional. Both versions include Word, Excel, and PowerPoint. The Office Professional also has Microsoft Access. Both versions also include a fifth application, Schedule+, as well as several smaller applications and shared utilities.

The Microsoft Office Shortcut Bar provides immediate access to each application in Microsoft Office. The Shortcut Bar is fully customizable with respect to the buttons it displays, its appearance, and its position on the desktop. The Open a Document and Start a New Document buttons enable you to think in terms of a document rather than the associated application.

An Office binder, like a loose-leaf notebook or binder clip, keeps related documents together. Any number of Office documents can be stored in a binder, which treats all of those documents as a single file.

Object Linking and Embedding (OLE) enables you to create a compound document containing data (objects) from multiple applications. Linking and embedding are different operations. The difference between the two depends on whether the object is stored within the compound document (embedding) or in its own file (linking).

KEY WORDS AND CONCEPTS

Answer Wizard	Common user interface	Formatting toolbar
ClipArt Gallery	Contents tab	Index tab
Compound document	Embedding	Linking

Microsoft Access
Microsoft Binder
Microsoft Excel
Microsoft Office Professional
Microsoft PowerPoint
Microsoft Standard Office
Microsoft Word
Object Linking and Embedding (OLE)
Microsoft Office Shortcut Bar
Online help
Schedule+
Standard toolbar
System Information Utility
WordArt

7

THE PROFESSIONAL DOCUMENT: FOOTNOTES, TABLES, AND STYLES

OBJECTIVES

After reading this chapter you will be able to:

1. Create a bulleted or numbered list; change the default character in either type of list.
2. Enter and/or edit footnotes and endnotes in a document.
3. Explain conceptually the use of the tables feature; create a table and insert it into a document.
4. Explain conceptually how styles automate the formatting process and provide a consistent appearance to common elements in a document.
5. Use the AutoFormat command to apply styles to an existing document; create, modify, and apply a style to selected elements of a document.
6. Define a section; explain how section formatting differs from character and paragraph formatting.
7. Create a header and/or a footer; establish different headers or footers for the first, odd, or even pages in the same document.
8. Insert page numbers into a document; use the Edit menu's Go To command to move directly to a specific page in a document.
9. Create and update a table of contents.

OVERVIEW

This chapter presents a series of features that give a document a professional look. It contains a wealth of information that will be especially useful the next time you have to write a term paper with specific formatting requirements. We show you how to insert footnotes and endnotes and how to convert one type of note to the other. We show you how to create a bulleted or numbered list to emphasize important items within a paper. We also introduce the tables feature, which is one of the most powerful features in Microsoft Word. Tables provide an easy way to arrange text, numbers, and/or graphics.

The second half of the chapter develops the use of styles, or sets of formatting instructions that provide a consistent appearance to similar elements in a document. We describe the AutoFormat command that assigns styles to an existing document and greatly simplifies the formatting process. We show you how to create a new style, how to modify an existing style, and how to apply those styles to text within a document. We also discuss several items associated with longer documents, such as page numbers, headers and footers, and a table of contents.

The chapter contains four hands-on exercises to apply the material at the computer. This is one more exercise than our earlier chapters, but we think you will appreciate the practical application of these very important capabilities within Microsoft Word.

BULLETS AND LISTS

A list helps to organize information by emphasizing important topics. A ***bulleted list*** emphasizes (and separates) the items. A ***numbered list*** sequences (and prioritizes) the items and is automatically updated to accommodate additions or deletions to the list. Either type of list could be created through normal formatting operations, but Microsoft Word facilitates the process through implementation of the ***Bullets and Numbering command*** within the Format menu. Execution of the command displays the Bullets and Numbering dialog box shown in Figure 1.1.

The tabs within the Bullets and Numbering dialog box enable you to specify the precise appearance of either type of list. Different bullets may be chosen as shown in Figure 1.1a, or different numbering schemes as in Figure 1.1b. A hanging indent may be specified for either type of list. Additional flexibility is provided by clicking the Modify command button in either dialog box to change the distance between the numbers or bullets and the associated text, and/or to modify the bullet or number style or appearance.

Bullets and numbering is implemented at the paragraph level and is illustrated in a hands-on exercise which follows shortly.

AUTOMATIC CREATION OF A NUMBERED LIST

Word will automatically create a numbered list any time you begin a line with a number or letter, followed by a period, tab, or right parenthesis, then continue with additional text on that line. Pressing the enter key at the end of the line or paragraph automatically generates the next sequential number or letter in the list. (Press the enter key twice to terminate the list.) To turn the autonumbering feature on or off, pull down the Tools menu, click Options, click the AutoFormat tab, then click the AutoFormat As You Type option button. Check (clear) the box for Automatic Numbered lists.

FOOTNOTES AND ENDNOTES

Every academic discipline has specific rules for incorporating footnotes or endnotes within a document. A ***footnote*** provides additional information about an item, such as its source, and appears at the bottom of the page where the reference occurs. An ***endnote*** is similar in concept but appears at the end of a document. A horizontal line separates the notes from the rest of the document.

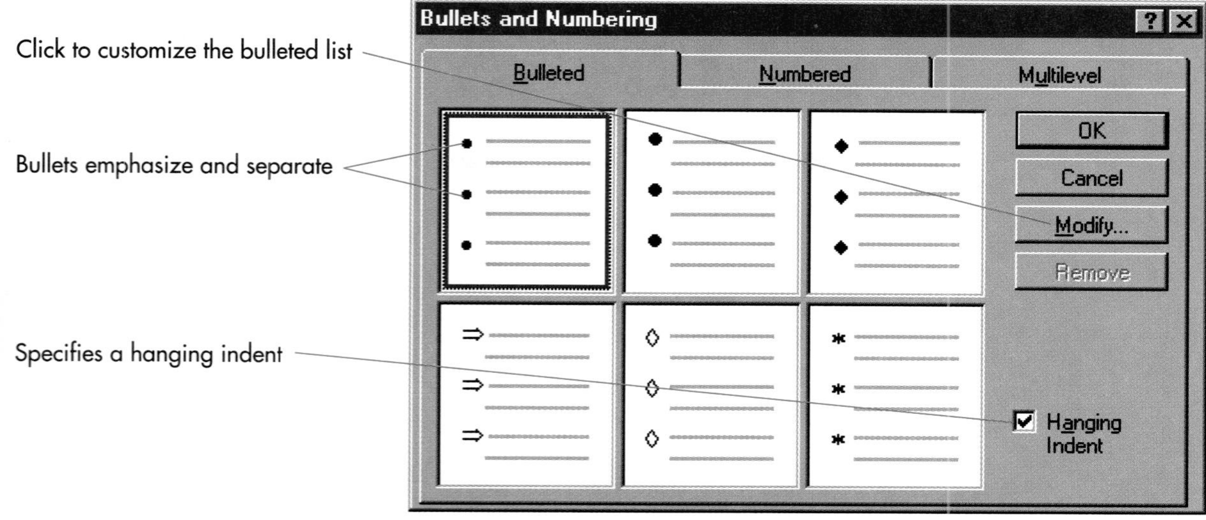

(a) Bulleted List

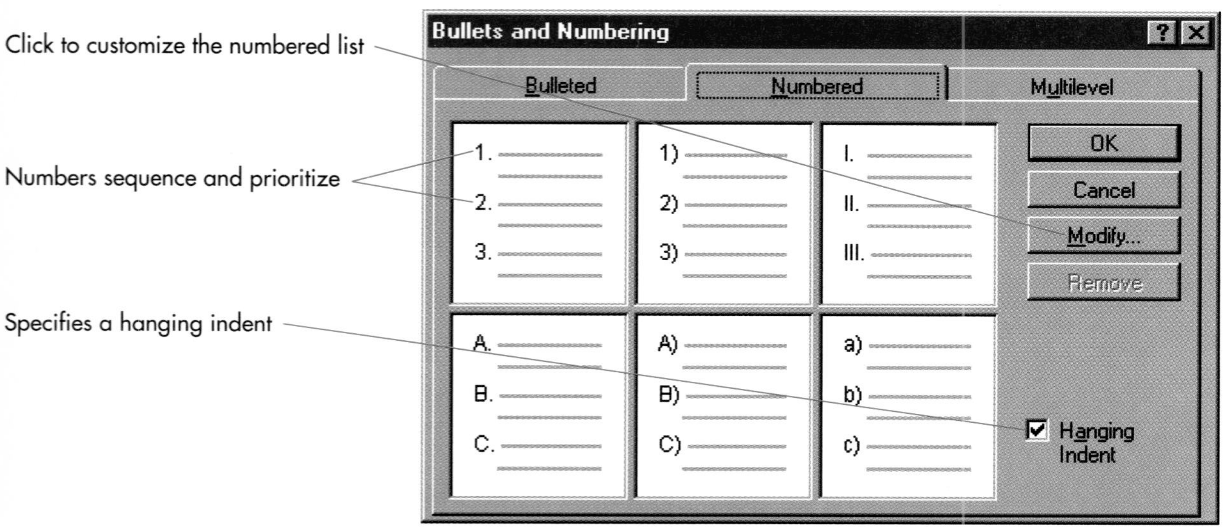

(b) Numbered List

FIGURE 1.1 Lists

The ***Insert Footnote command*** inserts a note into a document, and automatically assigns the next sequential number to that note. To create a note, position the insertion point where you want the reference, pull down the Insert menu, click Footnote to display the dialog box in Figure 1.2a, then choose either the Footnote or Endnote option button. A superscript reference is inserted into the document, and you will be positioned at the bottom of the page (a footnote) or at the end of the document (an endnote), where you enter the text of the note.

The Options command button in the Footnote and Endnote dialog box enables you to modify the formatting of either type of note as shown in Figure 1.2b. You can change the numbering format (e.g., to Roman numerals) and/or start numbering from a number other than one. You can also convert footnotes to endnotes or vice versa.

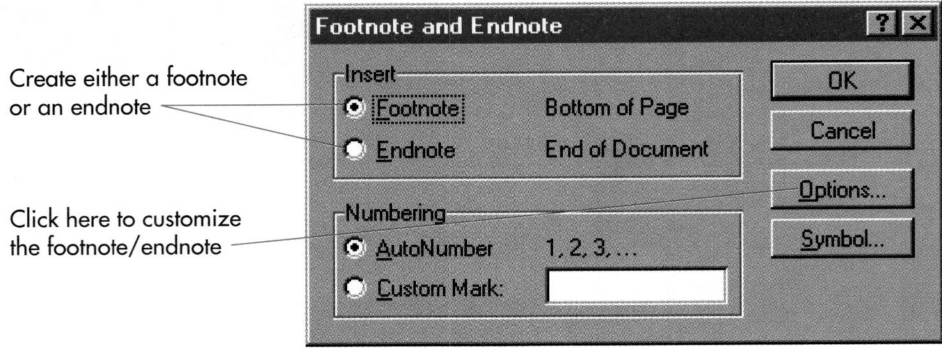

(a) Footnotes and Endnotes

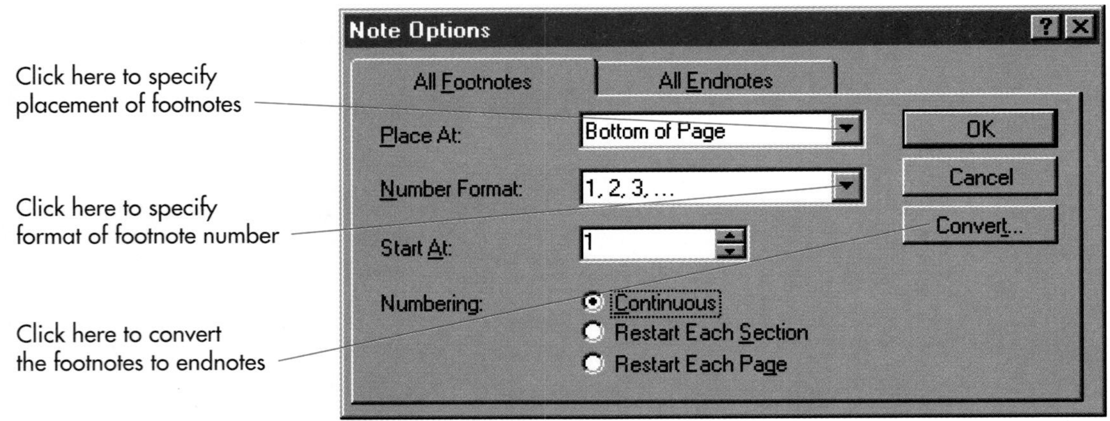

(b) Options

FIGURE 1.2 Footnotes and Endnotes

The Insert Footnote command is quite powerful and adjusts for last-minute changes, either in your writing or in your professor's requirements. It will, for example, renumber all existing notes to accommodate the addition or deletion of a footnote or endnote. [Existing notes are moved (or deleted) within a document by moving (deleting) the reference mark rather than the text of the footnote.]

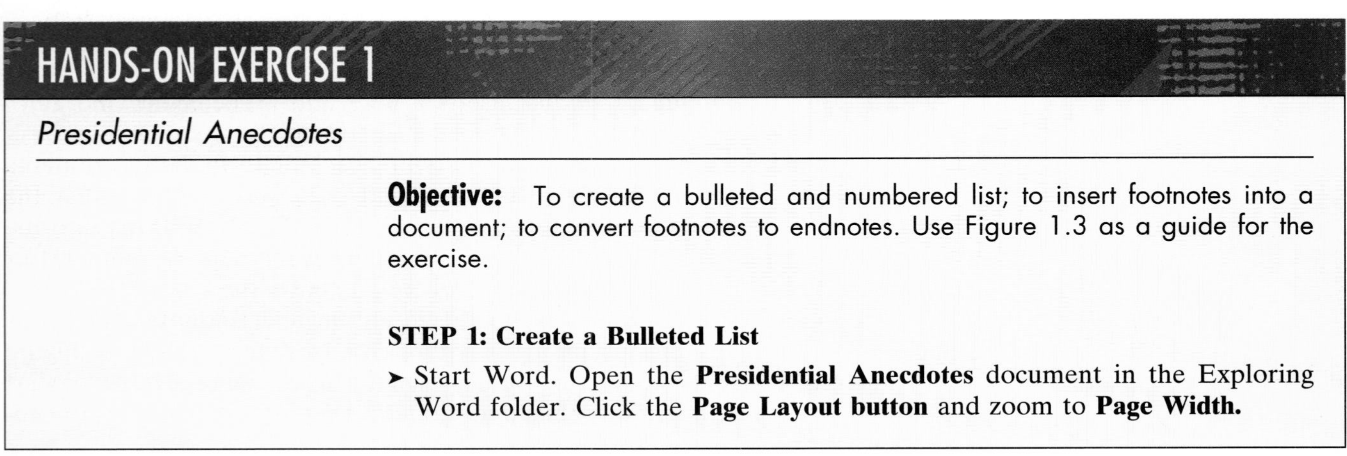

HANDS-ON EXERCISE 1

Presidential Anecdotes

Objective: To create a bulleted and numbered list; to insert footnotes into a document; to convert footnotes to endnotes. Use Figure 1.3 as a guide for the exercise.

STEP 1: Create a Bulleted List

➤ Start Word. Open the **Presidential Anecdotes** document in the Exploring Word folder. Click the **Page Layout button** and zoom to **Page Width.**

- Save the document as **Modified Presidential Anecdotes** so you can return to the original document if necessary.
- Click and drag to select the names of the presidents as shown in Figure 1.3a.
- Pull down the **Format menu.** Click **Bullets and Numbering.** If necessary, click the **Bulleted tab** to display the dialog box in the figure.
- Choose (click) a bullet style. Click **OK** to create the bulleted list and close the Bullets and Numbering dialog box.
- Check that the bulleted list is still selected. Click the **Bullets button** on the Standard toolbar to toggle the bullets off. Click the **Bullets button** a second time to restore the bullets.
- Click the **Increase Indent** button on the Formatting toolbar to indent the list to the next tab stop.

THE RIGHT MOUSE BUTTON

The right mouse button is the fastest way to access the Bullets and Numbering dialog box. Click and drag to select the items in a list, click the right mouse button to display a shortcut menu, then click the Bullets and Numbering command to display the dialog box. Click the appropriate tab (Bulleted or Numbered), click the style you want, then click the OK button to implement the list and close the dialog box.

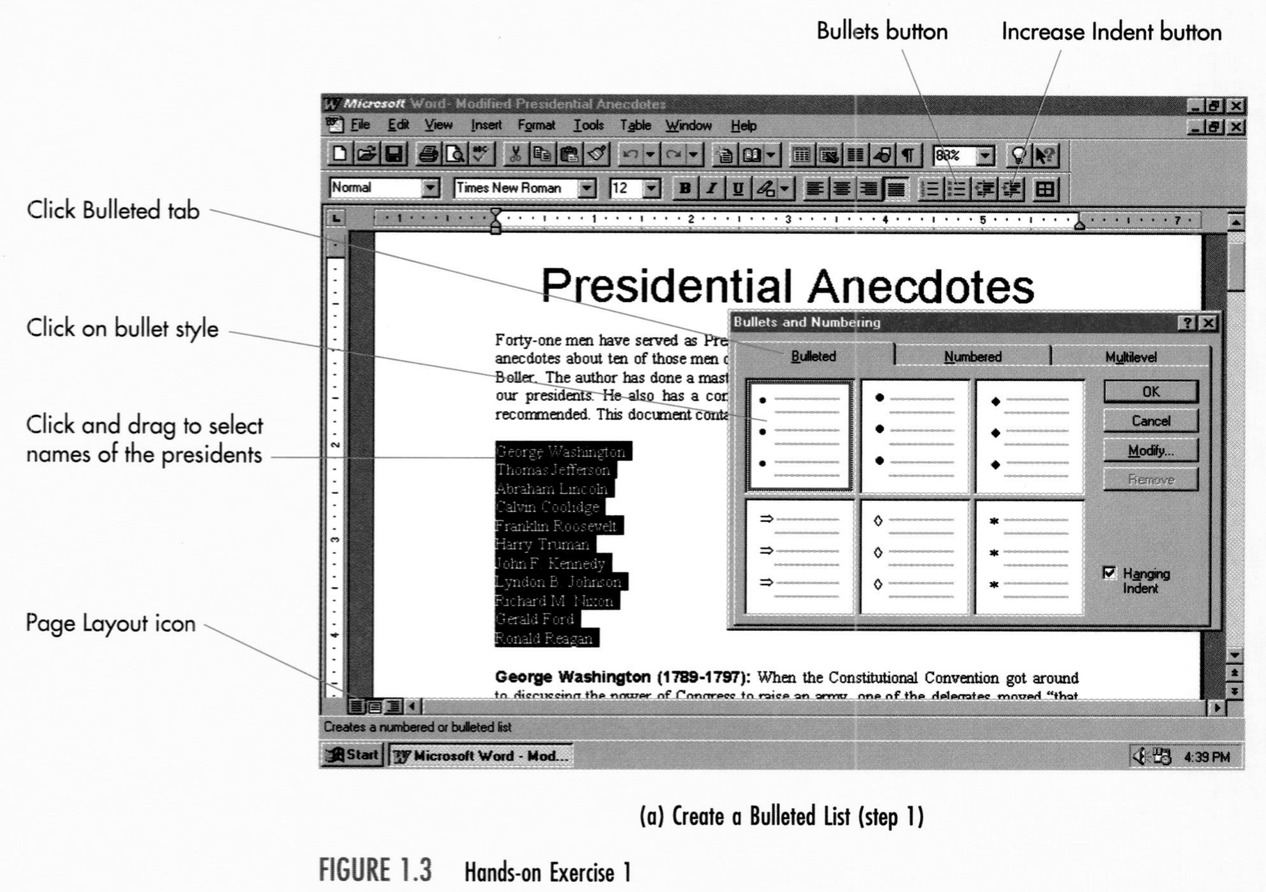

(a) Create a Bulleted List (step 1)

FIGURE 1.3 Hands-on Exercise 1

STEP 2: Create a Numbered List

- ➤ Check that the entire list is still selected. Click the **Numbering button** on the Formatting toolbar to convert the bulleted list to a numbered list.
- ➤ Click outside the list to deselect it. Click and drag to select **Franklin Roosevelt** as shown in Figure 1.3b. (You cannot select the number, only the text.)
- ➤ Press the **Del key** to erase the selected text, which automatically renumbers the rest of the list. (You may or may not have to press the **Del key** a second time to erase the number 5, depending on whether or not the paragraph mark was selected when you deleted Franklin Roosevelt.)

> **LISTS AND THE FORMATTING TOOLBAR**
>
> The Bullets and Numbering buttons on the Formatting toolbar facilitate the creation of either type of list. Click the Bullets button to create a bulleted list from selected items or to convert a numbered list to a bulleted list. Click the Numbering button to create a numbered list or to convert a bulleted list to numbers. The Bullets and Numbering buttons also function as toggle switches; for example, clicking the Bullets button when a bulleted list is already in effect will remove the bullets.

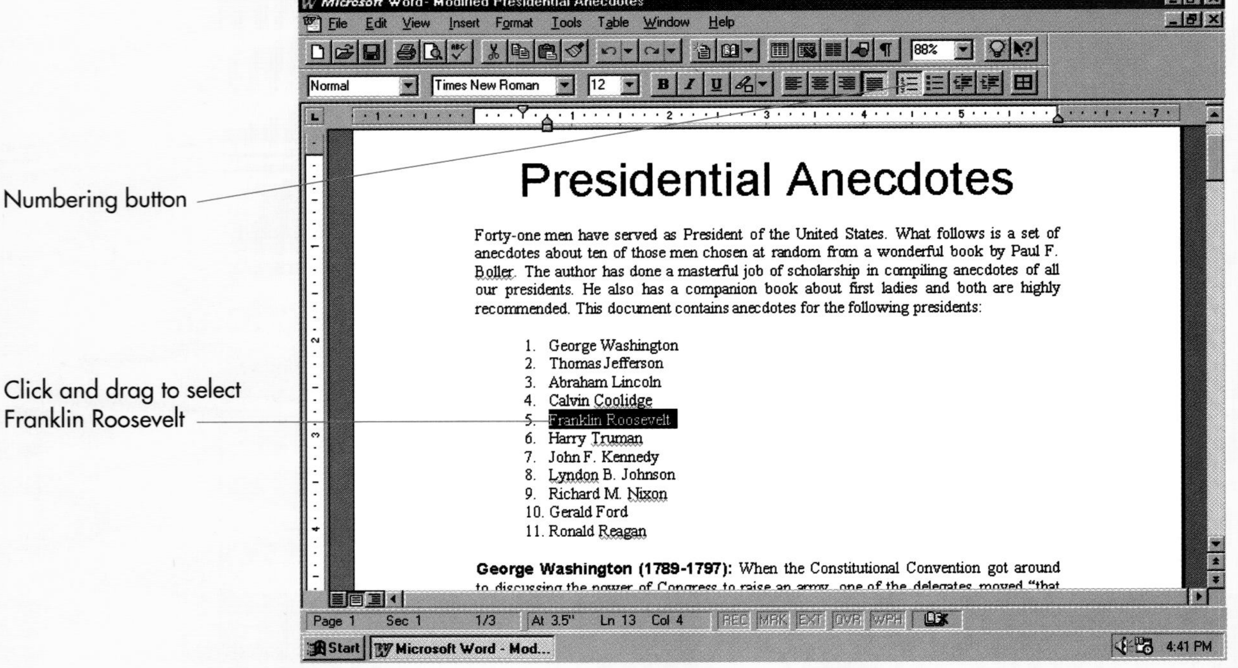

(b) Create a Numbered List (step 2)

FIGURE 1.3 Hands-on Exercise 1 (continued)

STEP 3: Create a Footnote

- Click the **drop-down arrow** on the **Zoom Control box** then click **Whole Page** to view the page before the footnotes are added. Click the **drop-down arrow** on the **Zoom Control box** a second time and click **Page Width** to facilitate the addition of the footnotes.
- Click immediately after the period following Paul Boller's name (the last word in the second sentence).
- Pull down the **Insert menu.** Click **Footnote** to display the Footnote and Endnote dialog box in Figure 1.3c.
- Click the **Footnote option button** as shown in the figure. Click **OK** to insert a footnote and close the dialog box.
- The insertion point moves automatically to the bottom of the page, where you will enter the text of the footnote. The existing footnotes are renumbered automatically to accommodate the new footnote.
- Type the text of the footnote, **Paul F. Boller, Jr., *Presidential Anecdotes,* Penguin Books (New York, NY, 1981).** Be sure to italicize the title of the book in your footnote.
- Save the document.

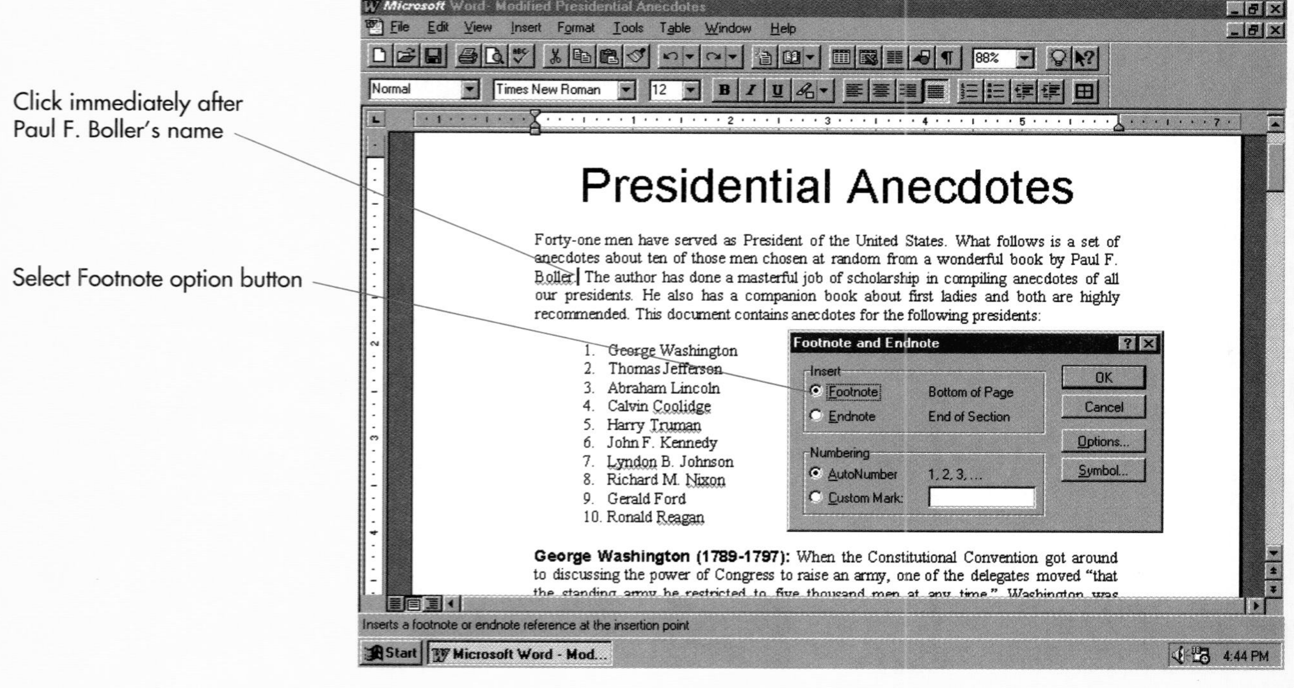

(c) Create a Footnote (step 3)

FIGURE 1.3 Hands-on Exercise 1 (continued)

FOOTNOTES AND STYLES

You can change the formatting (e.g., the font and point size) for individual footnotes just as you can change the formatting of any other element in a document. You can also change the formatting for all footnotes by changing the predefined style for the footnote text or reference. See the discussion on styles beginning on page 20 for additional information.

STEP 4: Renumber a Footnote

➤ The anecdotes in this document are out of chronological order in that Abraham Lincoln comes before Thomas Jefferson when it should be the other way around. The associated footnotes (Lincoln is currently number 3 and Jefferson is number 4) will be renumbered automatically when the associated text is moved. Thus:

- Select the paragraph containing the Lincoln anecdote (together with the blank line above the paragraph) as shown in Figure 1.3d.
- Drag the selected text below the anecdote for Thomas Jefferson. Release the mouse. The footnote for the Lincoln anecdote is renumbered to 4. The number of the Jefferson footnote changes to 3.

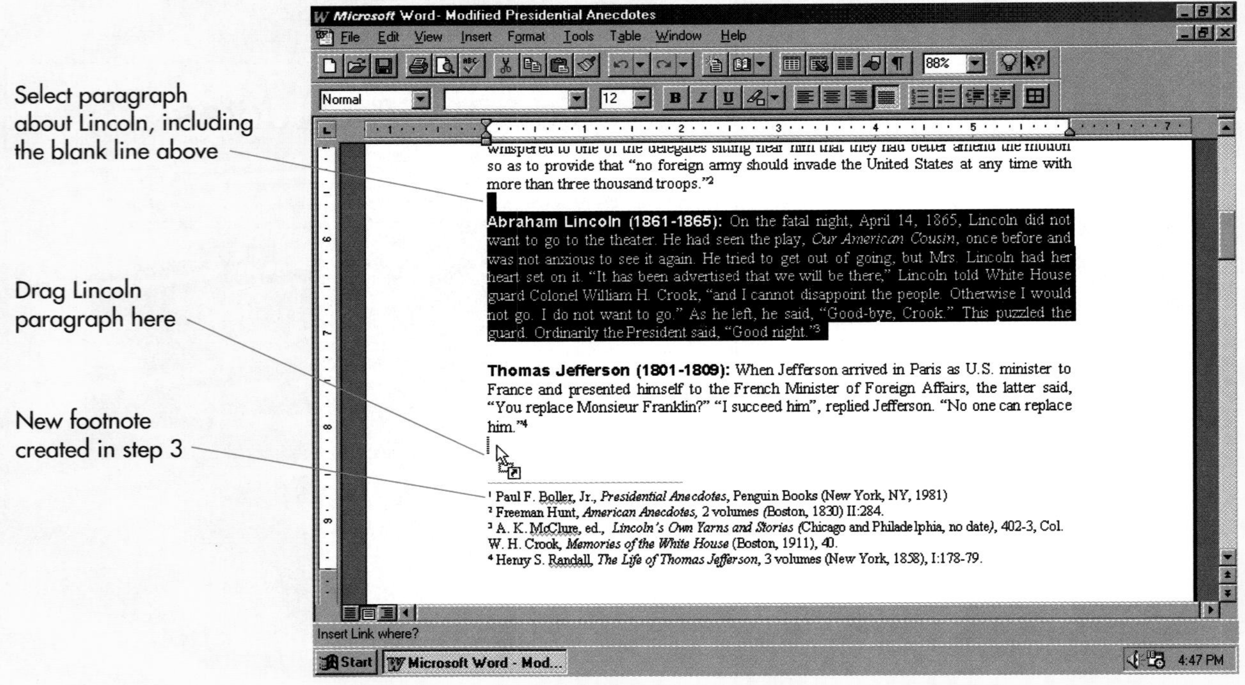

(d) Renumber a Footnote (step 4)

FIGURE 1.3 Hands-on Exercise 1 (continued)

➤ Click the **Undo button** to cancel the move. The Lincoln and Jefferson footnotes return to their original numbers, 3 and 4, respectively. Click the **Redo button** to restore the move and place the footnotes in their proper order.

➤ Save the document.

> **THE WRONG VIEW**
>
> Footnotes are visible only in the Page Layout view. Hence if you do not see a footnote, it is probably because you are in the wrong view, the Normal View, as opposed to the Page Layout view. Pull down the View menu and click the Page Layout command, or click the Page Layout button above the status bar. To edit (view) footnotes in the Normal view, double click the footnote reference mark, or pull down the View menu and click Footnote.

STEP 5: Delete a Footnote

➤ Click and drag to select the text of the second footnote as shown in Figure 1.3e. Press the **Del key** (in an attempt) to delete the footnote.

➤ The action is invalid and an error message appears. Click **OK** (or press **Esc**) to close the informational dialog box and continue working.

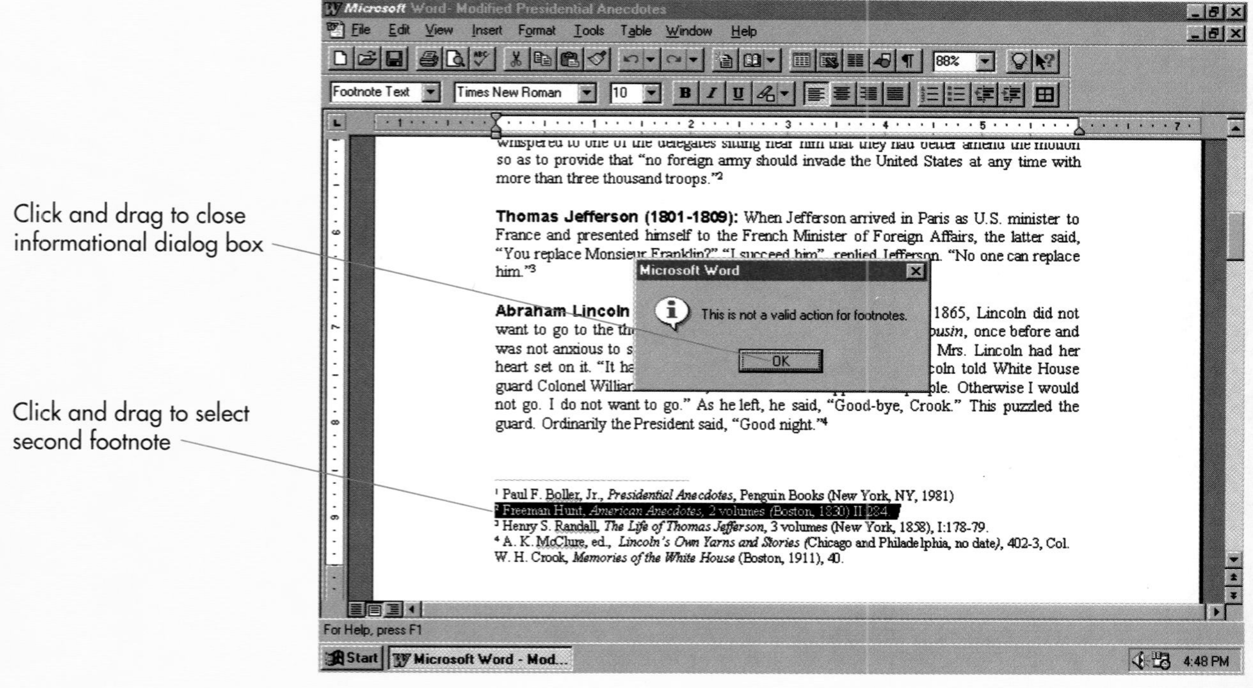

(e) Delete a Footnote (step 5)

FIGURE 1.3 Hands-on Exercise 1 (continued)

➤ Click and drag to select the reference mark for the second footnote. Press the **Del key.** The text for the second footnote is deleted, and the existing footnotes are renumbered.

➤ Click the **Undo button** to cancel the deletion as we want the footnote to remain. You now know that a footnote is deleted (or moved) by deleting (or moving) the reference mark rather than the text of the footnote.

STEP 6: Convert Footnotes to Endnotes

➤ Pull down **Insert menu.** Click **Footnote** to display the Footnote and Endnote dialog box. Click the **Options command button** to display the Note Options dialog box in Figure 1.3f.

➤ Click the **Convert command button** to display the Convert Notes dialog box. (Your dialog boxes may be positioned differently from those in the figure.)

➤ Click the option button to **Convert All Footnotes to Endnotes.** Click **OK** to implement the conversion and close the Convert Notes dialog box. Click **OK** to close the Note Options dialog box.

➤ Click **Close** to exit the Footnotes and Endnotes dialog box.

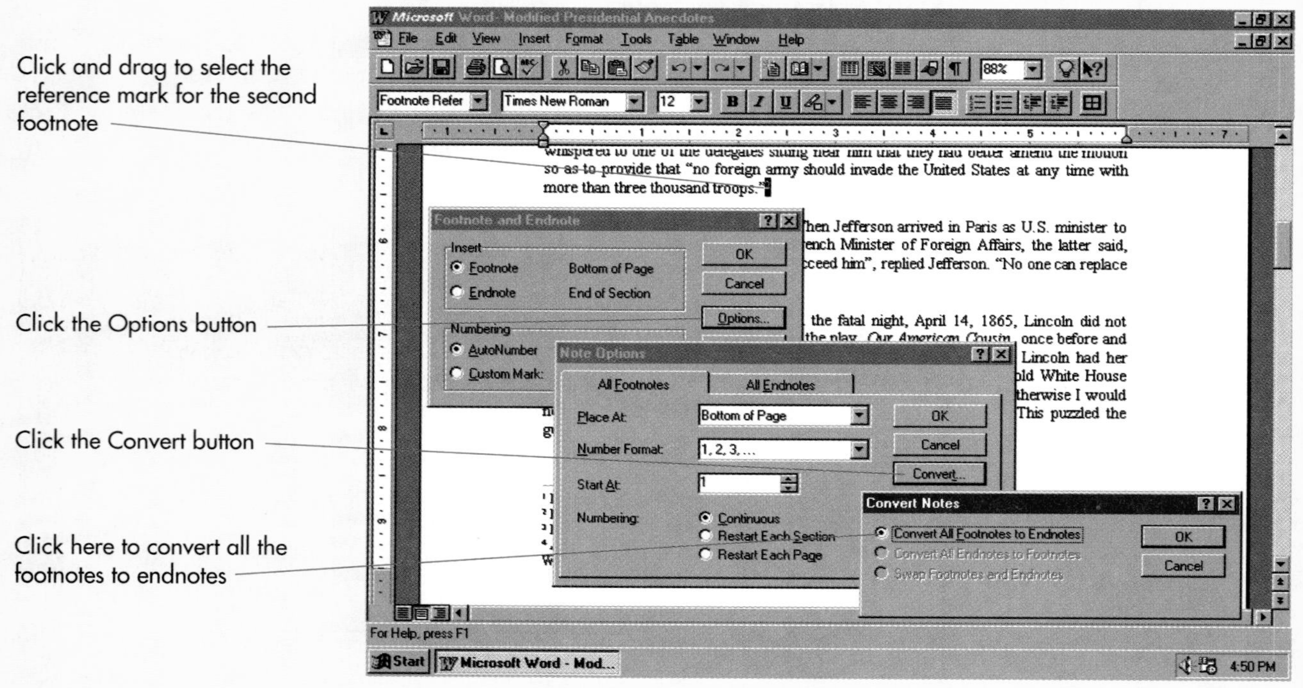

(f) Convert Footnotes to Endnotes (step 6)

FIGURE 1.3 Hands-on Exercise 1 (continued)

STEP 7: The Completed Document

➤ Press **Ctrl+end** to move to the end of the document, after the last anecdote but before the first endnote.

➤ Press **Ctrl+enter** to insert a page break. Type **References** in 24 point Arial. Click the **Center button** on the Formatting toolbar to center the heading. Add one or two blank lines as necessary.

➤ Pull down the **View menu.** Click **Zoom.** Click the **Many Pages option button,** then click the **monitor icon** to display a drop-down list, then click and drag to display three pages across. Release the mouse. Click **OK.**

➤ The completed document is shown in Figure 1.3g. Save the document a final time. Print the completed document and submit it to your instructor.

➤ Exit Word if you do not want to continue with the next exercise at this time.

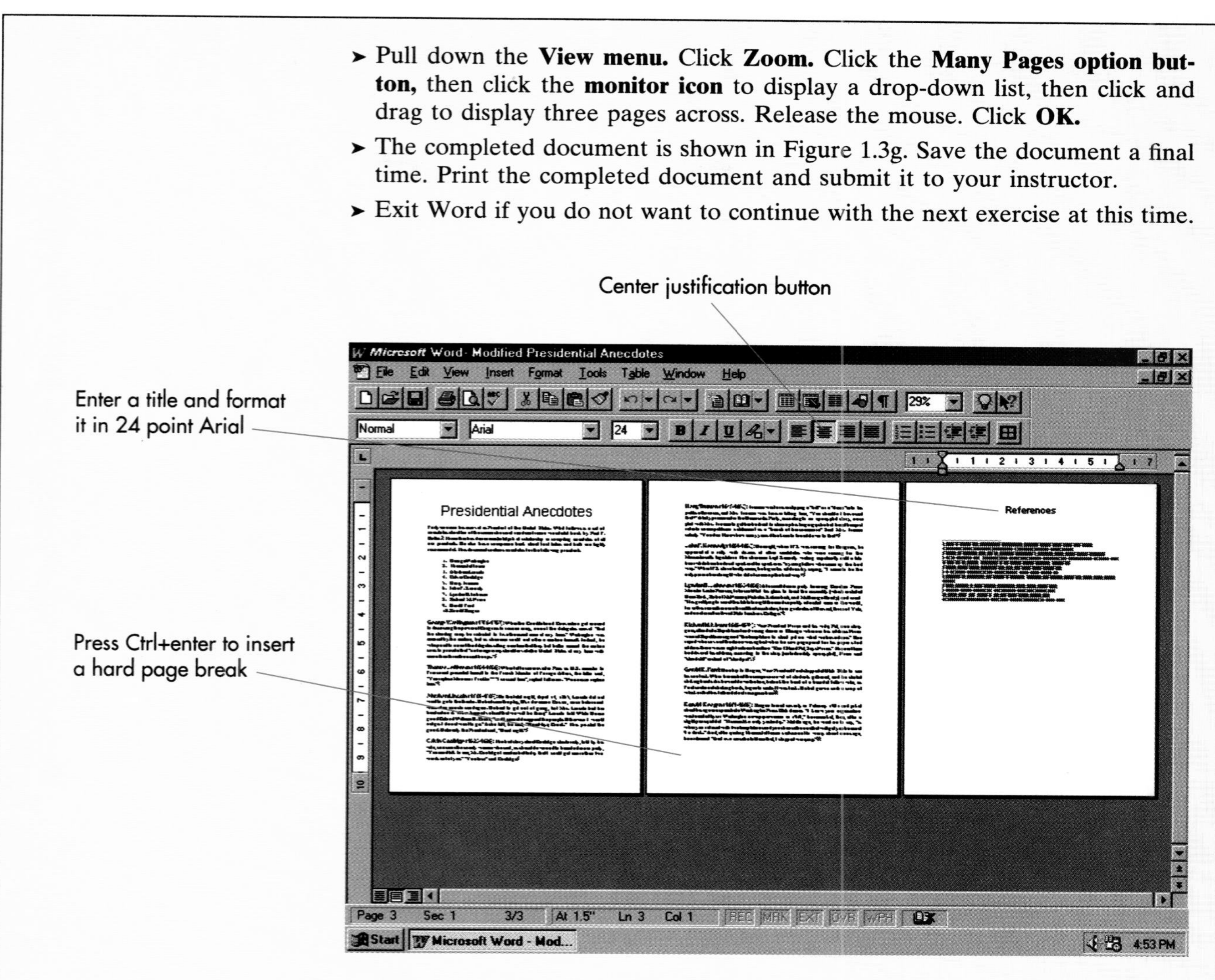

(g) The Completed Document (step 7)

FIGURE 1.3 Hands-on Exercise 1 (continued)

TABLES

The ***tables feature*** is one of the most powerful in Word and is the basis for an almost limitless variety of documents. The study schedule in Figure 1.4a, for example, is actually a 12 × 8 (12 rows and 8 columns) table as can be seen from the underlying structure in Figure 1.4b.

The rows and columns in a table intersect to form ***cells,*** which can contain text, numbers, and/or graphics. Commands operate on one or more cells. Individual cells can be joined together to form a larger cell as was done in the first and last rows of Figure 1.4. The rows within a table can be different heights, and each row may contain a different number of columns.

A table is created through the ***Insert Table command*** in the ***Table menu.*** The command produces a dialog box in which you enter the number of rows and columns. Once the table has been defined, you enter text in individual cells. Text wraps as it is entered within a cell, so that you can add or delete text in a cell

Weekly Class and Study Schedule							
	Monday	Tuesday	Wednesday	Thursday	Friday	Saturday	Sunday
8:00 AM							
9:00 AM							
10:00 AM							
11:00 AM							
12:00 PM							
1:00 PM							
2:00 PM							
3:00 PM							
4:00 PM							
Notes							

(a) Completed Table

(b) Underlying Structure

FIGURE 1.4 The Tables Feature

without affecting the text in other cells. You can format the contents of an individual cell the same way you format an ordinary paragraph; that is, you can change the font, use boldface or italics, change the alignment, or apply any other formatting command. You can also select multiple cells and apply the formatting to all selected cells at once.

The Insert and Delete commands in the Table menu enable you to add new rows or columns, or delete existing rows or columns. You can invoke other commands to shade and/or border selected cells or the entire table. It's easy, and as you may have guessed, it's time for another hands-on exercise.

LEFT ALIGNED **CENTERED** **RIGHT ALIGNED**

Many documents call for left, centered, and/or right aligned text on the same line, an effect that is achieved through setting tabs, or more easily through a table. To achieve the effect shown in the first line of this tip, create a 1 × 3 table (one row and three columns), type the text in the three cells, then use the buttons on the Formatting toolbar to left align, center, and right align the respective cells.

HANDS-ON EXERCISE 2

Tables

Objective: To create a table; to change row heights and column widths; to join cells together; to apply borders and shading to selected cells. Use Figure 1.5 as a guide in the exercise.

STEP 1: Page Setup

- Start Word. If necessary, open a new document. Pull down the **File menu.** Click **Page Setup.** If necessary, click the **Paper Size tab** to display the dialog box in Figure 1.5a. Click the **Landscape option button.**
- Click the **Margins tab.** Change the top and bottom margins to **.75** inch. Change the left and right margins to **.5** inch each. Click **OK** to accept the settings and close the dialog box.
- Change to the **Page Layout** view. Zoom to **Page Width.**
- Save the document as **My Study Schedule** in the Exploring Word folder.

THE INSERT TABLE BUTTON

The fastest way to create a table is to use the Insert Table button on the Standard toolbar. Click the Insert Table button to display a grid, then drag the mouse across and down the grid until you have the desired number of rows and columns. Release the mouse to create the table.

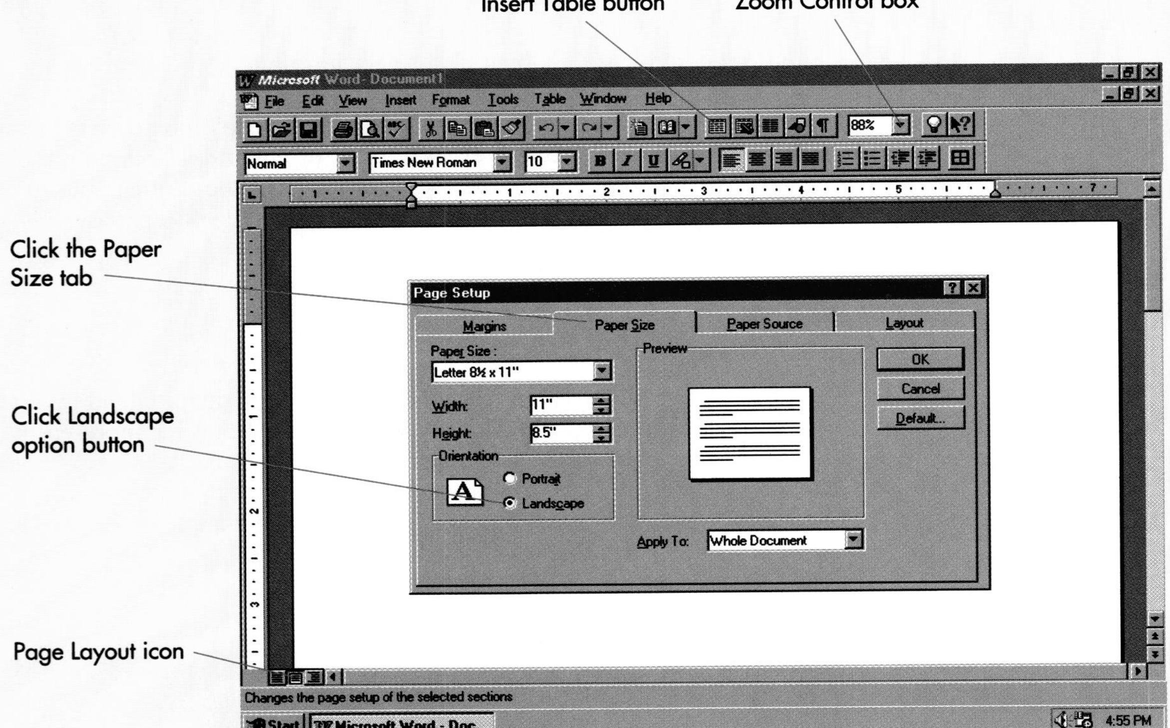

(a) Change the Orientation

FIGURE 1.5 Hands-on Exercise 2

STEP 2: Create the Table

- Pull down the **Table menu.** Click **Insert Table** to display the dialog box in Figure 1.5b. Enter **8** as the number of columns. Enter **12** as the number of rows.
- Click **OK** and the table will be inserted into the document. The cells in a table are separated by dotted lines known as gridlines, which appear on the monitor but not in the printed document.
- If you do not see the table, it is probably because the gridlines have been suppressed. Pull down the **Table menu** and click **Gridlines.**

TABLES AND THE SHOW/HIDE ¶ BUTTON

The Show/Hide ¶ button can be toggled on (off) to display (hide) the nonprinting characters associated with a table. The □ symbol indicates the end-of-cell (or end-of-row) marker and is analogous to the ¶ symbol at the end of a paragraph in a regular document.

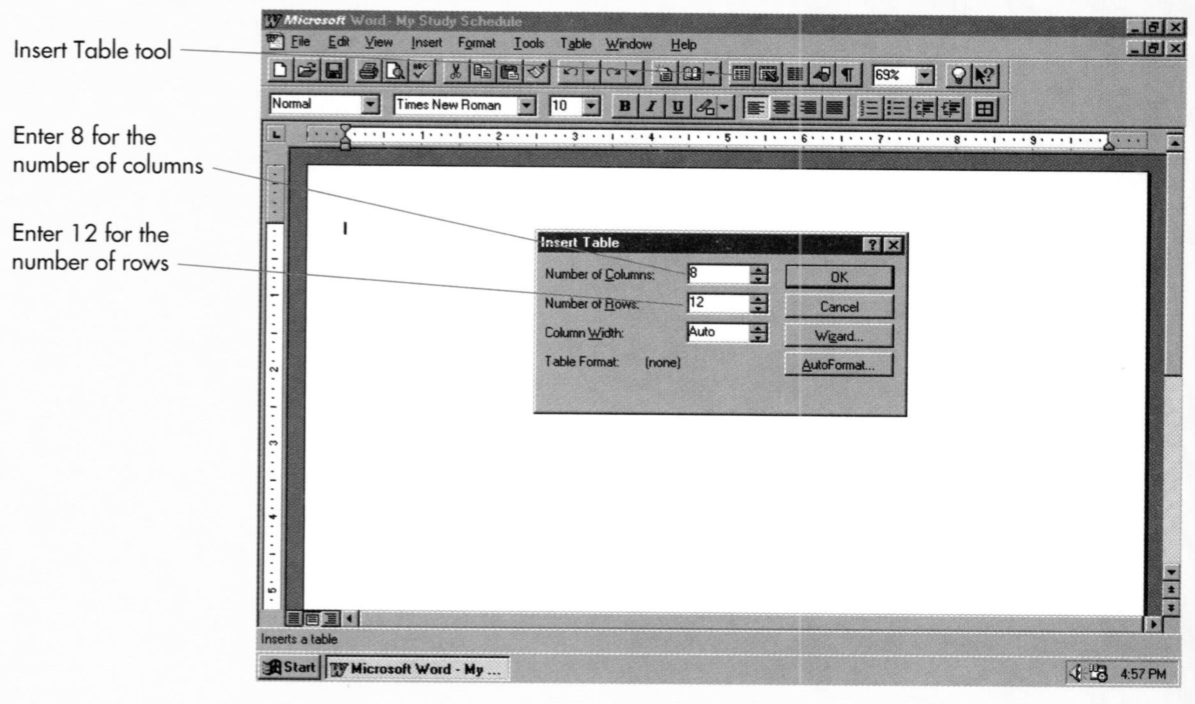

(b) Create the Table (step 2)

FIGURE 1.5 Hands-on Exercise 2 (continued)

STEP 3: Table Basics

➤ Practice moving within the table:
- If the cells in the table are empty (as they are now), press the **left** and **right arrow keys** to move from column to column. If the cells contain text (as they will later in the exercise), you must press **Tab** and **Shift+Tab** to move from column to column.
- Press the **up** and **down arrow keys** to move from row to row. This works for both empty cells and cells with text.

➤ Select a cell row, column, or block of contiguous cells:
- To select a single cell, click immediately to the right of the left gridline (the pointer changes to an arrow when you are in the proper position).

TABS AND TABLES

The Tab key functions differently in a table than in a regular document. Press the Tab key to move to the next cell in the current row (or to the first cell in the next row if you are at the end of a row). Press Tab when you are in the last cell of a table to add a new blank row to the bottom of the table. Press Shift+Tab to move to the previous cell in the current row (or to the last cell in the previous row). You must press Ctrl+Tab to insert a regular tab character within a cell.

- To select an entire row, click outside the table to the left of the first cell in that row.
- To select a column, click just above the top of the column (the pointer changes to a small black arrow).
- To select adjacent cells, drag the mouse over the cells.
- To select the entire table, drag the mouse over the table.

STEP 4: Merge the Cells

➤ Click outside the table to the left of the first cell in the first row to select the entire first row as shown in Figure 1.5c. Pull down the **Table menu.** Click **Merge Cells.**

➤ Type **Weekly Class and Study Schedule** and format the text in 24 point Arial bold. Center the text within the cell.

➤ Click outside the table to the left of the first cell in the last row to select the entire row. Pull down the **Table menu.** Click **Merge Cells** to join the cells into a single cell.

➤ Type **Notes:** and format the entry in 12 point Arial bold.

➤ Save the table.

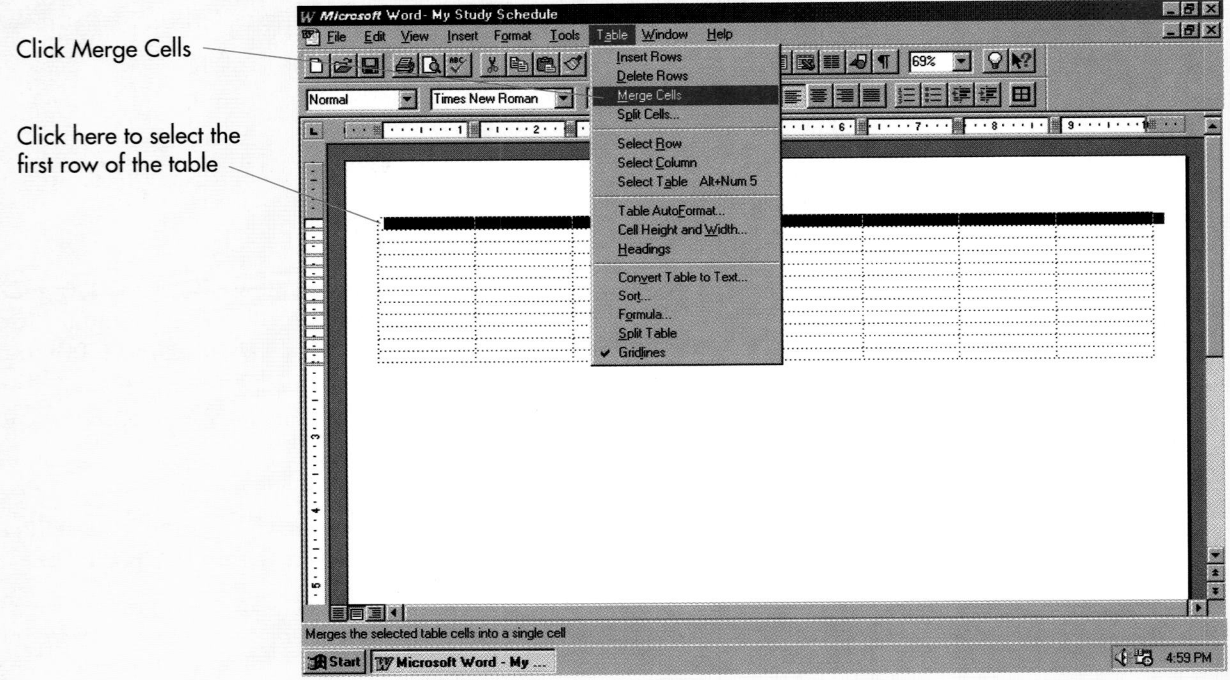

(c) Merge the Cells (step 4)

FIGURE 1.5 Hands-on Exercise 2 (continued)

STEP 5: Enter the Days and Hours

➤ Click the second cell in the second row. Type **Monday.**

➤ Press the **Tab** (or **right arrow) key** to move to the next cell. Type **Tuesday.** Continue until the days of the week have been entered.

➤ Use the Formatting Toolbar to change the font and alignment for the days of the week:

- Select the entire row. Click the **Bold button.**
- Click the **Font List box** to choose an appropriate font such as **Arial.**
- Click the **Font Size List box** to choose an appropriate size such as **10** point.
- Click the **Center button** on the Formatting toolbar.

➤ Click anywhere in the table to deselect the text and see the effect of the formatting change.

➤ Click the first cell in the third row. Type **8:00AM.** Press the **down arrow key** to move to the first cell in the fourth row. Type **9:00AM.**

➤ Continue in this fashion until you have entered the hourly periods up to **4:00PM.** Format as appropriate. (We right aligned the time periods and changed the font to Arial bold.) Your table should match Figure 1.5d. Save the table.

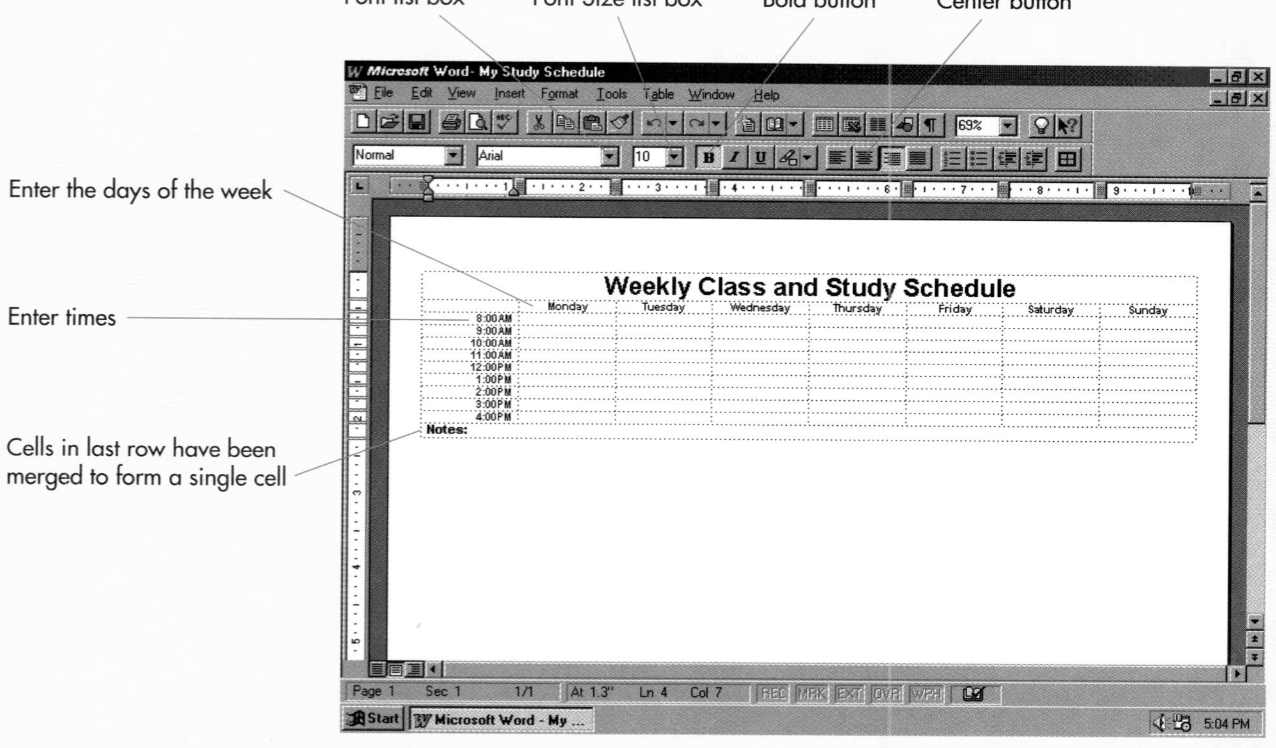

(d) Enter the Days and Hours (step 5)

FIGURE 1.5 Hands-on Exercise 2 (continued)

STEP 6: Change the Row Heights

➤ Click immediately after the word "notes." Press the **enter key** five times. The height of the cell increases automatically to accommodate the additional paragraphs.

➤ Select the cells containing the hours of the day. Pull down the **Table menu.** Click **Cell Height and Width** to display the dialog box in Figure 1.5e.

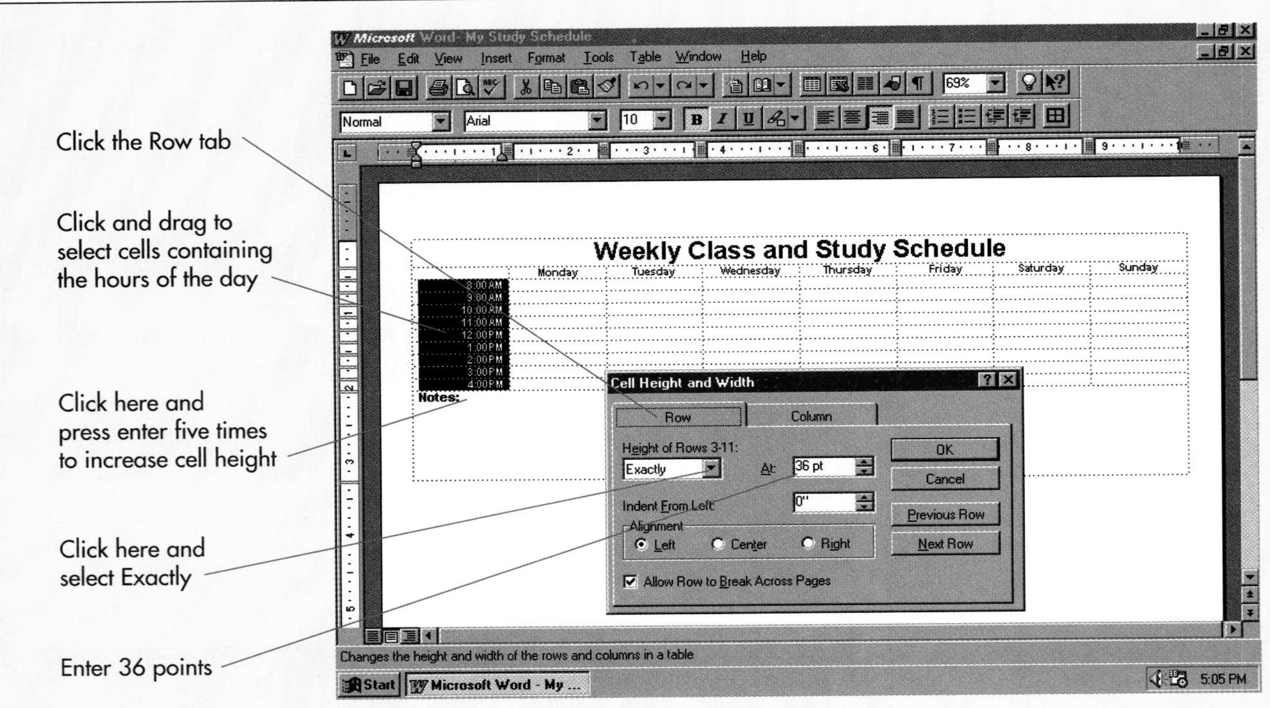
Click the Row tab
Click and drag to select cells containing the hours of the day
Click here and press enter five times to increase cell height
Click here and select Exactly
Enter 36 points
Weekly Class and Study Schedule
Cell Height and Width
Row
Column
Height of Rows 3-11:
Exactly
At:
36 pt
OK
Cancel
Previous Row
Next Row
Allow Row to Break Across Pages
Changes the height and width of the rows and columns in a table

(e) Change the Row Height (step 6)

FIGURE 1.5 Hands-on Exercise 2 (continued)

- If necessary, click the **Row tab.** Click the arrow for the Height of Rows list box. Click **Exactly,** then enter **36** (36 points is equal to ½ inch) in the At text box.
- Click **OK.** Click anywhere to deselect the text and see the new row heights.

STEP 7: Borders and Shading

- Pull down the **Table menu** and click **Select Table** (or drag the mouse over the entire table).
- Pull down the **Format menu.** Click **Borders and Shading** to display the dialog box in Figure 1.5f.
- If necessary, click the **Borders Tab.** Click **Grid** in the **Presets** area. Click **OK** to close the dialog box. Click anywhere in the table to deselect the table and see the effect of the Borders command.
- Select the first row in the table. Pull down the **Format menu** a second time. Click **Borders and Shading.**
- Click the **Shading Tab.** Click **10%** in the Shading list box. Experiment with different colors for borders or shading (if you have a color printer).
- Click **OK** to close the dialog box. Click outside the selected text to see the shading. Save the table.

STEP 8: The Completed Table

- Zoom to **Whole Page** to see the completed schedule as shown in Figure 1.5g.
- Print the table. Exit Word if you do not want to continue with the next exercise at this time.

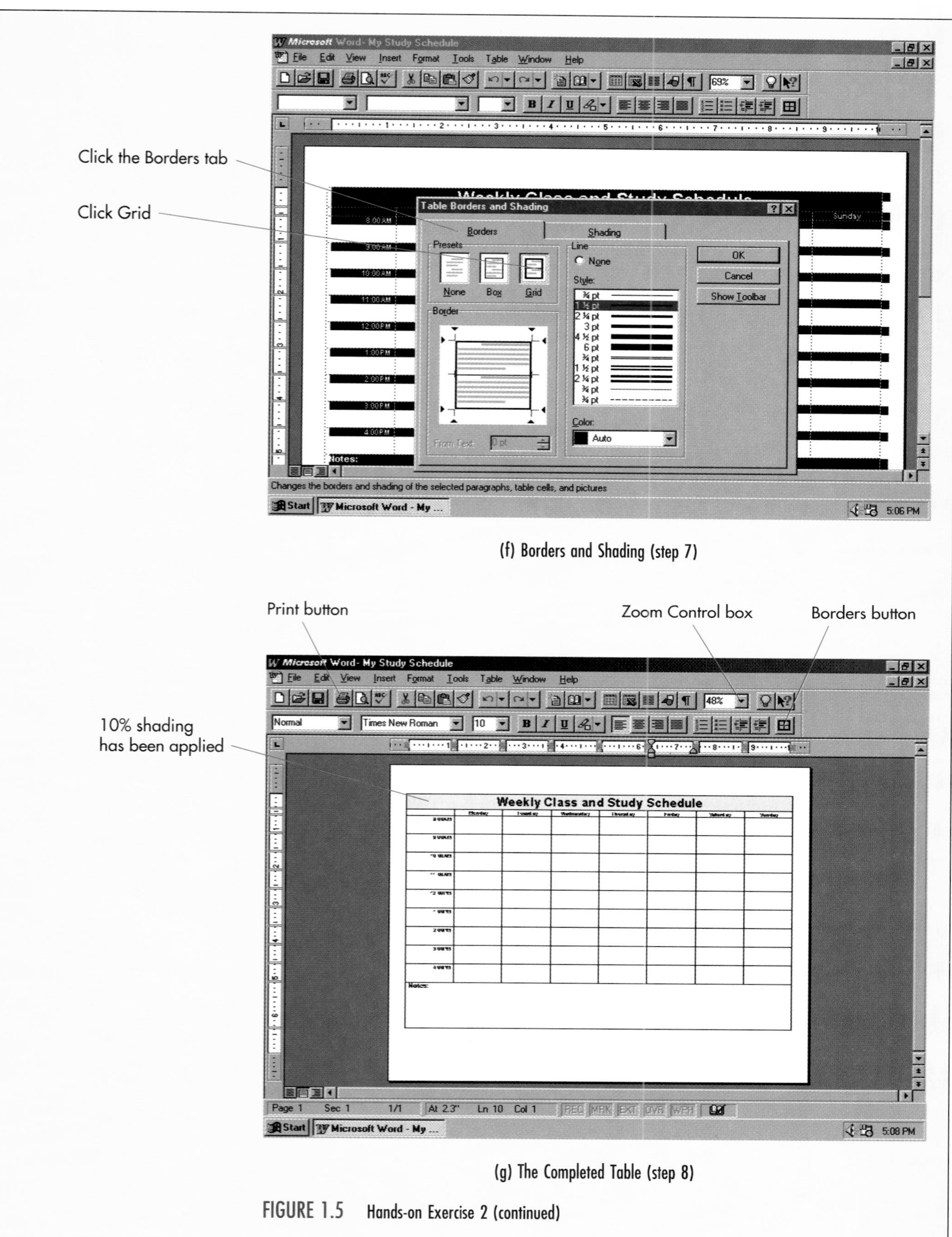

(f) Borders and Shading (step 7)

(g) The Completed Table (step 8)

FIGURE 1.5 Hands-on Exercise 2 (continued)

A characteristic of professional documents is the use of uniform formatting for each element. Different elements can have different formatting; for example, headings may be set in one font and the text under those headings in a different font. You may want the headings centered and the text justified.

If you are like most people, you will change your mind several times before arriving at a satisfactory design, after which you will want consistent formatting for each element in the document. You can use the Format Painter button (on the Standard toolbar) to copy the formatting from one occurrence of an element to another, but it still requires you to select the individual elements and paint each one whenever formatting changes.

A much easier way to achieve uniformity is to store the formatting information as a ***style,*** then apply that style to multiple occurrences of the same element within the document. Change the style and you automatically change all text defined by that style.

Styles are created on the character or paragraph level. A ***character style*** stores character formatting (font, size, and style) and affects only the selected text. A ***paragraph style*** stores paragraph formatting (alignment, line spacing, indents, tabs, text flow, and borders and shading, as well as the font, size, and style of the text in the paragraph). A paragraph style affects the current paragraph or multiple paragraphs if several paragraphs are selected. The ***Style command*** in the Format menu is used to create and/or modify either type of style, then enables you to apply that style within a document.

Execution of the Style command displays the dialog box shown in Figure 1.6, which lists the styles in use within a document. The ***Normal style*** contains the default paragraph settings (left aligned, single spacing, and a default font) and is automatically assigned to every paragraph unless a different style is specified. The ***Heading 1*** and ***Body Text*** styles are used in conjunction with the AutoFormat command, which applies these styles throughout a document. (The AutoFormat command is illustrated in the next hands-on exercise.) The ***Default Paragraph Font*** is a character style that specifies the (default) font for new text.

The Description box displays the style definition; for example, Times New Roman, 10 point, flush left, single spacing, and widow/orphan control. The Paragraph Preview box shows how paragraphs formatted in that style will appear. The Modify command button provides access to the Format Paragraph and Format Font commands to change the characteristics of the selected style. The Apply command button applies the style to all selected paragraphs or to the current paragraph. The New command button enables you to define a new style.

Styles automate the formatting process and provide a consistent appearance to a document. Any type of character or paragraph formatting can be stored within a style, and once a style has been defined, it can be applied to multiple occurrences of the same element within a document to produce identical formatting.

STYLES AND PARAGRAPHS

A paragraph style affects the entire paragraph; that is, you cannot apply a paragraph style to only part of a paragraph. To apply a style to an existing paragraph, place the insertion point anywhere within the paragraph, pull down the Style list box on the Formatting toolbar, then click the name of the style you want

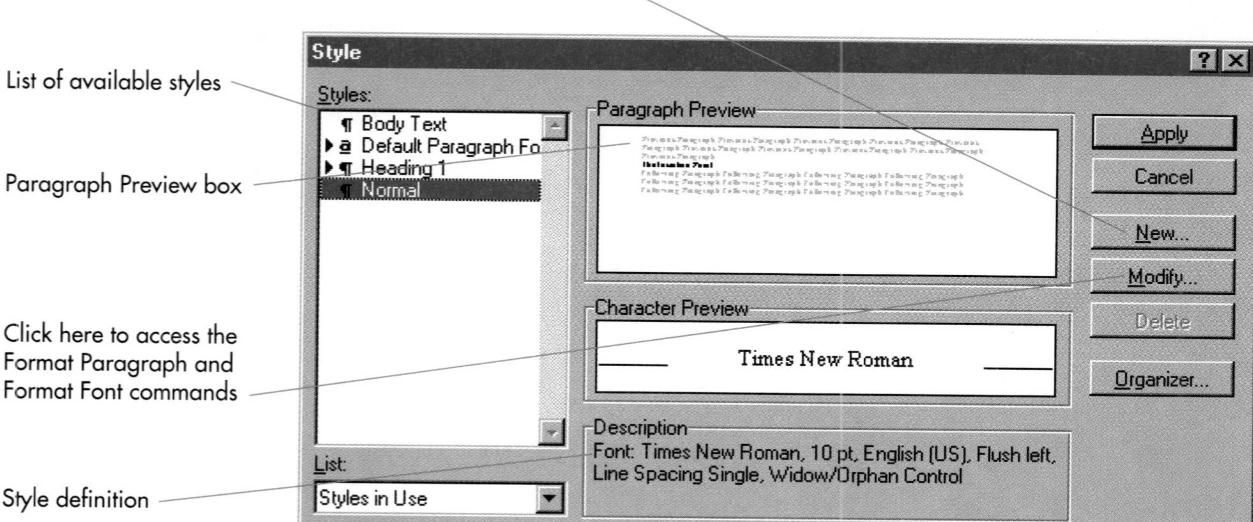

FIGURE 1.6 The Normal Style

The AutoFormat Command

The ***AutoFormat command*** enables you to format lengthy documents quickly, easily, and in a consistent fashion. In essence, the command analyzes a document and formats it for you. Its most important capability is the application of styles to individual paragraphs; that is, the command goes through an entire document, determines how each paragraph is used, then applies an appropriate style to each paragraph. The formatting process assumes that one-line paragraphs are headings and applies the predefined Heading 1 style to those paragraphs. It applies the Body Text style to ordinary paragraphs and can also detect lists and apply a numbered or bullet style to those lists.

The AutoFormat command will also add special touches to a document if you request those options. It can replace "ordinary quotation marks" with “smart quotation marks” that curl and face each other. It will also replace ordinal numbers (1st, 2nd, or 3rd) with the corresponding superscripts (1st, 2nd, or 3rd), or common fractions (1/2 or 1/4) with typographical symbols (½ or ¼).

AUTOMATIC BORDERS AND LISTS

The AutoFormat As You type option applies sophisticated formatting as text is entered. It creates a numbered list automatically any time a number is followed by a period, tab, or right parenthesis (press enter twice in a row to turn off the feature). It will also add a border to a paragraph any time you type three or more hyphens, equal signs, or underscores followed by the enter key. Pull down the Tools menu, click Options, click the AutoFormat tab, then click the AutoFormat As You Type option button to select the desired features.

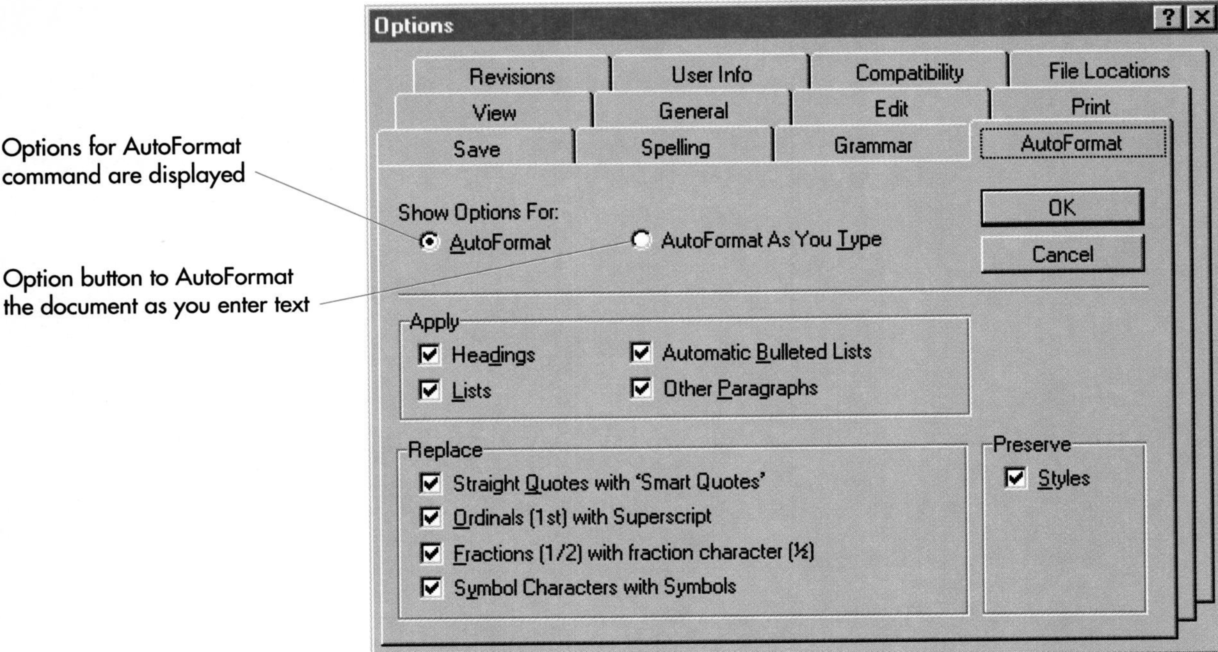

FIGURE 1.7 The AutoFormat Command

Options in the AutoFormat command are accessed from the dialog box shown in Figure 1.7. Once the options have been set, all formatting is done automatically by selecting the AutoFormat command from the Format menu. The changes are not final, however, as the command gives you the opportunity to review each formatting change individually, then accept the change or reject it as appropriate. (You can also format text automatically as it is entered according to the options specified under AutoFormat As You Type.)

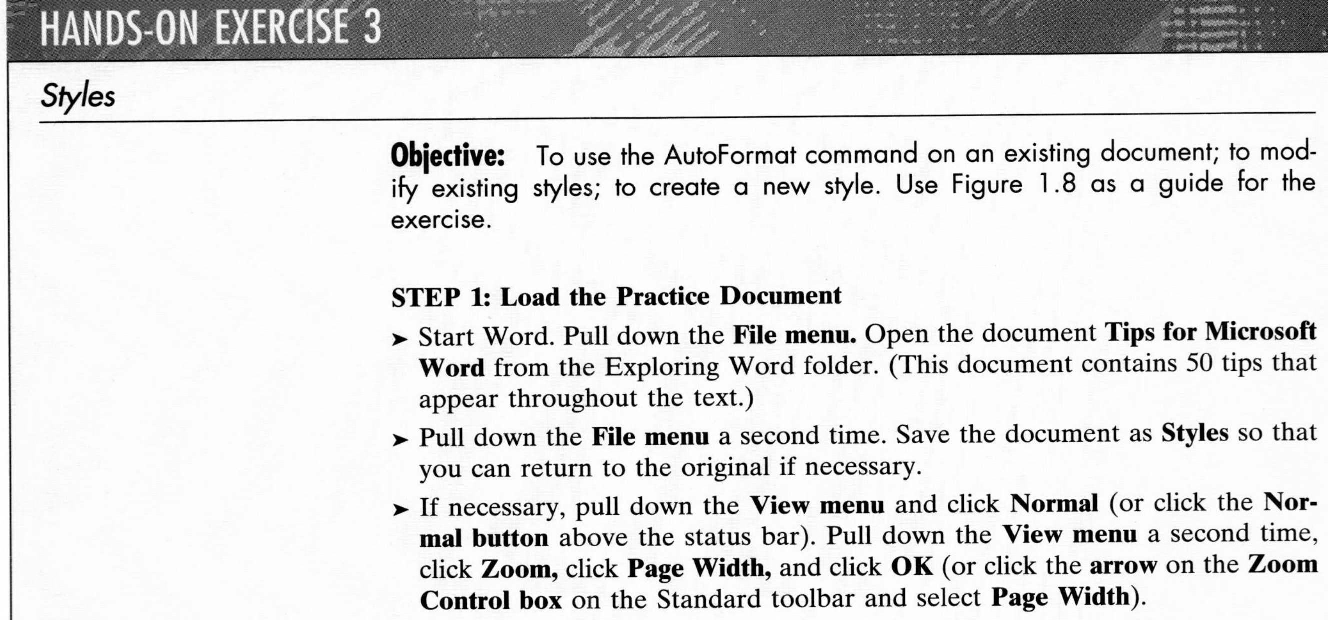

HANDS-ON EXERCISE 3

Styles

Objective: To use the AutoFormat command on an existing document; to modify existing styles; to create a new style. Use Figure 1.8 as a guide for the exercise.

STEP 1: Load the Practice Document

- Start Word. Pull down the **File menu.** Open the document **Tips for Microsoft Word** from the Exploring Word folder. (This document contains 50 tips that appear throughout the text.)
- Pull down the **File menu** a second time. Save the document as **Styles** so that you can return to the original if necessary.
- If necessary, pull down the **View menu** and click **Normal** (or click the **Normal button** above the status bar). Pull down the **View menu** a second time, click **Zoom,** click **Page Width,** and click **OK** (or click the **arrow** on the **Zoom Control box** on the Standard toolbar and select **Page Width**).

STEP 2: The AutoFormat Command

- Press **Ctrl+Home** to move to the beginning of the document. Pull down the **Format menu.** Click **AutoFormat** to display the dialog box in Figure 1.8a.
- Click the **Options command button.** Be sure that every check box is selected to implement the maximum amount of automatic formatting. Click the **OK button** to close the dialog box.
- Click the **OK command button** in the AutoFormat dialog box in Figure 1.8a to format the document. You will see a message at the left side of the status bar as the formatting is taking place, then you will see a newly formatted document behind a dialog box.
- Click the **Accept command button** to accept the formatting changes. Save the document.

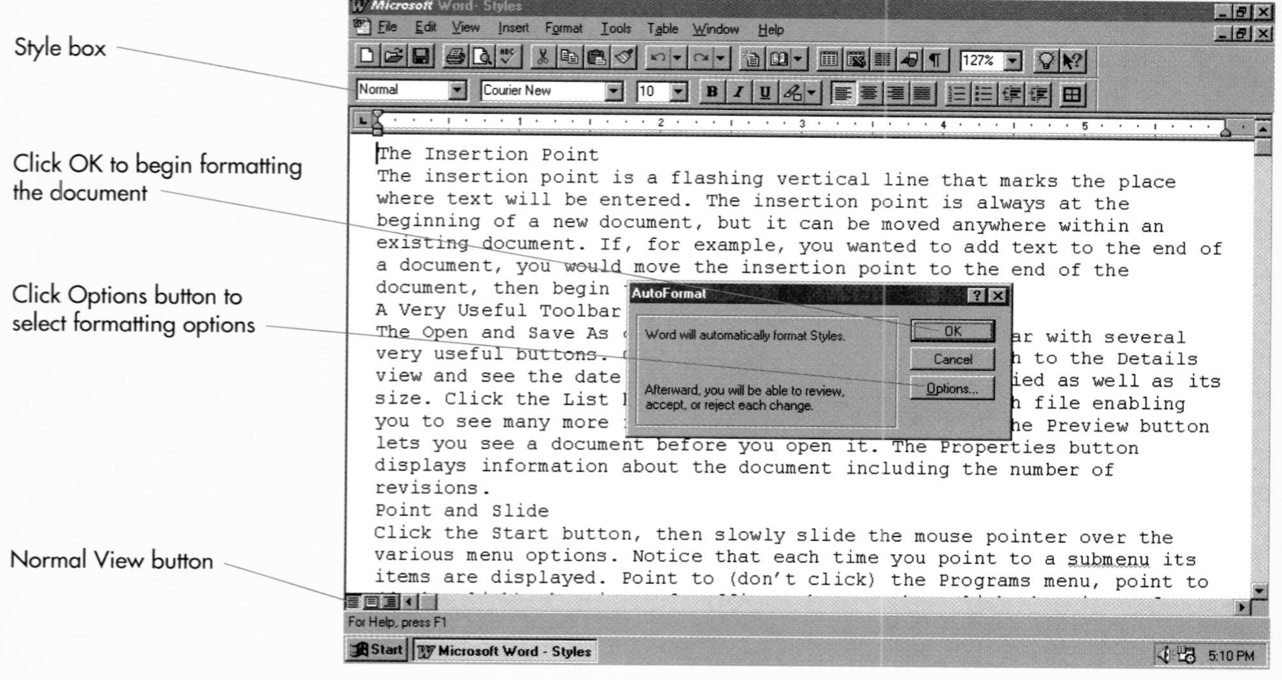

(a) AutoFormat Command (step 2)

FIGURE 1.8 Hands-on Exercise 3

STEP 3: Style Assignments

- Click anywhere in the heading of the first tip. The Style box on the Formatting toolbar displays Heading 1 to indicate that this style has been applied to the title of the tip.
- Click anywhere in the text of the first tip. The Style box on the Formatting toolbar displays Body Text to indicate that this style has been applied to the current paragraph.
- Click the title of any tip and you will see the Heading 1 style in the Style box. Click the text of any tip and you will see the Body Text style in the Style box.

STEP 4: Modify the Body Text Style

- ➤ Press **Ctrl+Home** to move to the beginning of the document. Click anywhere in the text of the first tip.
- ➤ Pull down the **Format menu.** Click **Style.** The Body Text style is automatically selected, and its characteristics are displayed within the description box.
- ➤ Click the **Modify command button** to produce the Modify Style dialog box in Figure 1.8b.
- ➤ Click the **Format command button.**
  - Click **Paragraph** to produce the Paragraph dialog box.
  - Click the **Indents and Spacing** tab.
  - Click the **arrow** on the **Alignment list box.** Click **Justified.**
  - Change the **Spacing After** to **12.**
  - Click the **Text Flow tab** on the Paragraph dialog box.
  - Click the **Keep Lines Together** check box so an individual tip will not be broken over two pages. Click **OK** to close the Paragraph dialog box.
- ➤ Click **OK** to close the Modify Style dialog box. Click the **Close command button** to return to the document. Save the document.

SPACE BEFORE AND AFTER

It's common practice to press the enter key twice at the end of a paragraph (once to end the paragraph, and a second time to insert a blank line before the next paragraph). The same effect can be achieved by setting the spacing before or after the paragraph using the Spacing Before or After list boxes in the Format Paragraph command. The latter technique gives you greater flexibility in that you can specify any amount of spacing (e.g., 6 points to leave only half a line) before or after a paragraph. It also enables you to change the spacing between paragraphs more easily because the spacing information can be stored within the paragraph style.

STEP 5: Review the Formatting

- ➤ All paragraphs in the document change automatically to reflect the new definition of the Body Text style.
- ➤ Click the **Help button** on the Standard toolbar; the mouse pointer changes to a large question mark. Click in any paragraph to display the formatting in effect for that paragraph as shown in Figure 1.8c.
- ➤ You will see formatting specifications for the Body Text style (Indent: Left 0″, Justified, Space After 12 pt, Keep Lines Together, Font Times New Roman, 10pt, and English (US)).
- ➤ Click in any other paragraph to see the formatting in effect for that paragraph.
- ➤ Click the **Help button** a second time (or press **Esc**) to return to normal editing.

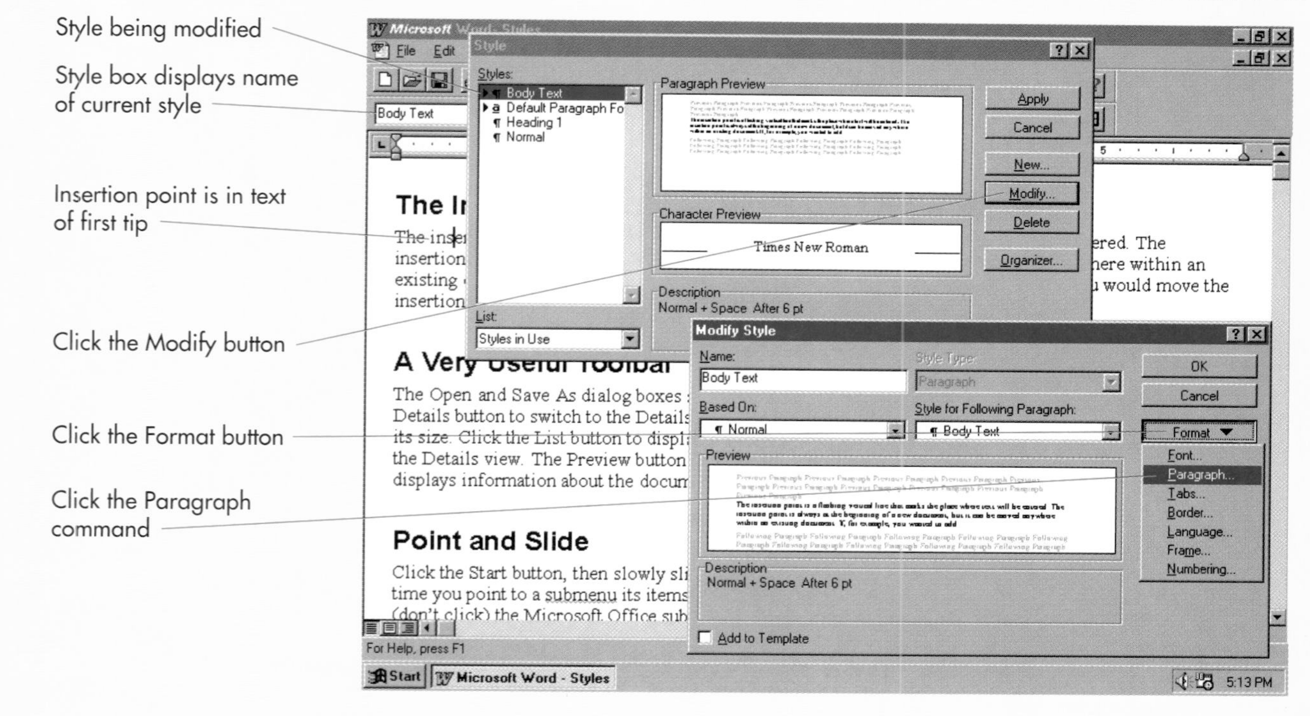

(b) Modify the Body Text Style (step 4)

Help button

Click in paragraph to display the formatting in effect

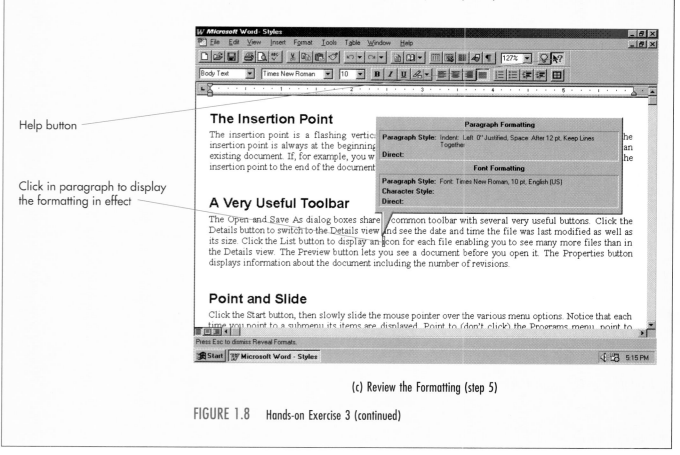

(c) Review the Formatting (step 5)

FIGURE 1.8 Hands-on Exercise 3 (continued)

HELP WITH FORMATTING

It's all too easy to lose sight of the formatting in effect, so Word provides a Help button on the Standard toolbar. Click the button, and the mouse pointer assumes the shape of a large question mark. Click anywhere in a document to display the formatting in effect at that point. Click the Help button a second time to exit Help.

STEP 6: Modify the Heading 1 Style

- Click anywhere in the title of the first tip. The Style box on the Formatting toolbar contains Heading 1 to indicate that this style has been applied to the current paragraph.
- Pull down the **Format menu.** Click **Style.** The Heading 1 style is automatically selected, and its characteristics are displayed within the description box.
- Click the **Modify command button** to produce the Modify Style dialog box.
- Click the **Format command button.**
  - Click **Paragraph** to produce the Paragraph dialog box. Click the **Indents and Spacing tab.**
  - Change the **Spacing After** to **0** (there should be no space separating the heading and the paragraph).
  - Change the **Spacing Before** to **0** (since there are already 12 points after the Body Text style as per the settings in step 6). Click **OK.**
  - Click the **Format command button** a second time.
  - Click **Font** to produce the Font dialog box.
  - Click **10** in the Font size box. Click **OK.**
- Click **OK** to close the Modify Style dialog box. Click the **Close command button** to return to the document and view the changes.
- Save the document.

MODIFY STYLES BY EXAMPLE

The Modify command button in the Format Style command is one way to change a style, but it prevents the use of the toolbar buttons; thus it's easier to modify an existing style by example. Select any text that is defined by the style you want to modify, then reformat that text using the Formatting toolbar, shortcut keys, or pull-down menus. Click the Style box on the Formatting toolbar, make sure the selected style is the correct one, press enter, then click OK when asked if you want to redefine the style.

STEP 7: Create a New Style

- Press **Ctrl+Home** to move to the beginning of the document. Press **Ctrl+enter** to create a page break for a title page.

- ➤ Move the insertion point above the page break. Press the **enter key** five to ten times to move to an appropriate position for the title.
- ➤ Click the **Show/Hide ¶ button** on the Standard toolbar to display the non-printing characters. Select the paragraph marks, pull down the **Style list** on the Formatting toolbar, and click **Normal.**
- ➤ Deselect the paragraph marks to continue editing.
- ➤ Place the insertion point to the left of the last hard return above the page break. Enter the title, **50 Tips in Microsoft Word,** and format it in 28 Point Arial Bold as shown in Figure 1.8d.
- ➤ Click the **Center button** on the Formatting toolbar.
- ➤ Check that the title is still selected, then click the **Styles List box** on the Formatting toolbar. The style name, Normal, is selected.
- ➤ Type **My Style** (the name of the new style). Press **enter.** You have just created a new style that we will use in the next exercise. Save the document.

MORE FONTS

We have restricted our design to the Arial and Times New Roman fonts because they are supplied with Windows and hence are always available. In all likelihood, you will have several additional fonts available, in which case you can modify the fonts in the Heading 1 and/or Body Text styles to create a completely different design.

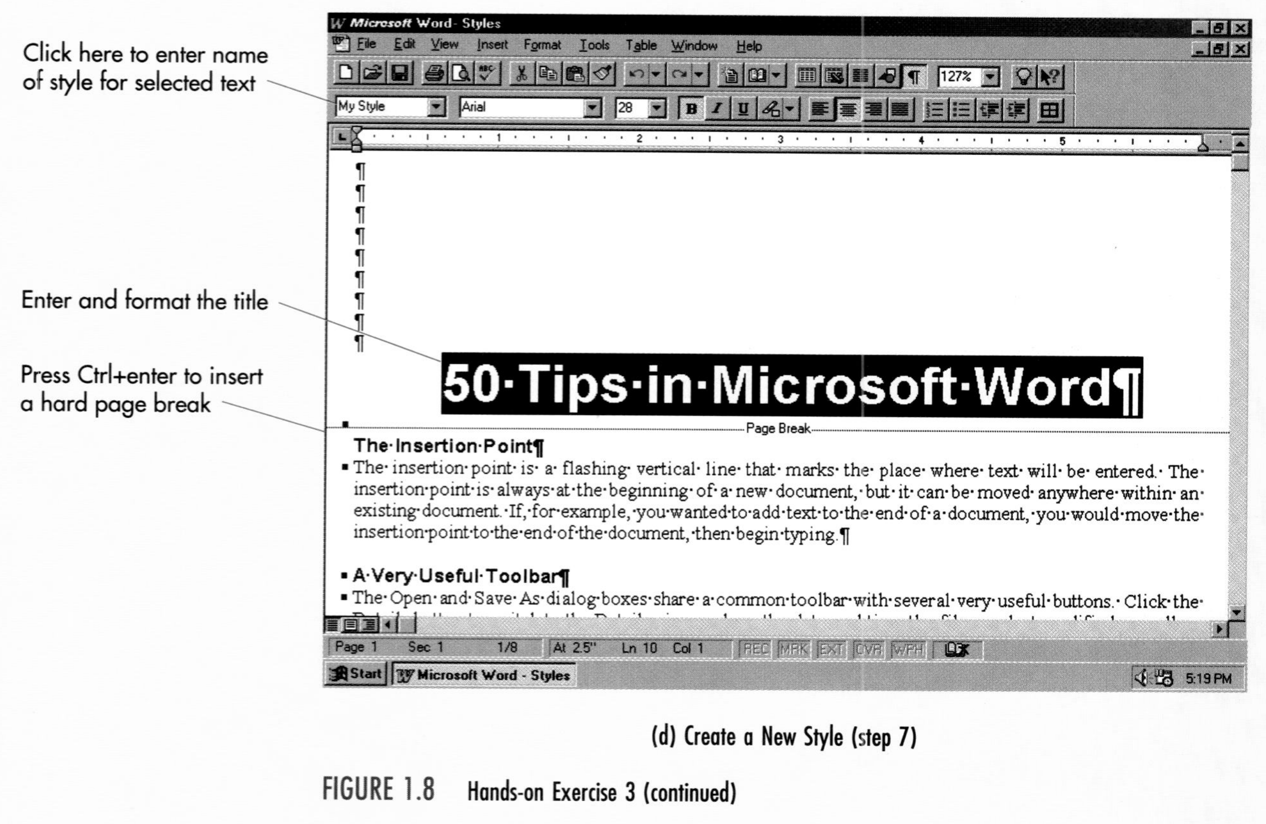

(d) Create a New Style (step 7)

FIGURE 1.8 Hands-on Exercise 3 (continued)

STEP 8: Complete the Title Page

- Click the **Page Layout button** on the status bar. Click the **arrow** on the **Zoom Control box** on the Standard toolbar. Click **Two Pages.**
- Scroll through the document to see the effects of your formatting.
- Press **Ctrl+Home** to return to the beginning of the document, then change to **Page Width** so that you can read what you are typing. Complete the title page as shown in Figure 1.8e.
- Click immediately to the left of the ¶ after the title to deselect the text. Press **enter** once or twice.
- Click the **arrow** on the **Font Size box** on the Formatting toolbar. Click **12.** Type **by Robert Grauer and Maryann Barber.** Press **enter.**
- Save the document. Print the document. Exit Word if you do not want to continue with the next exercise at this time.

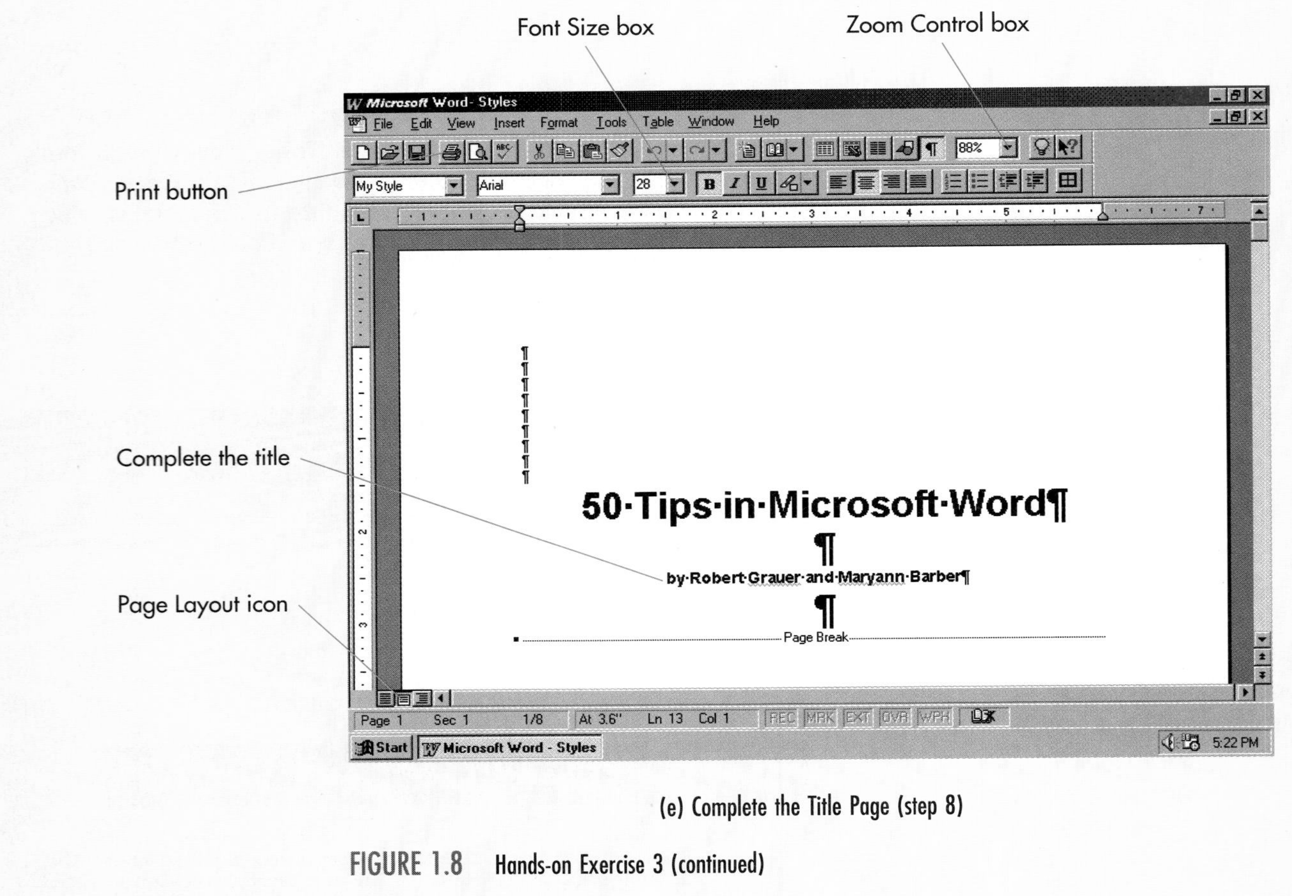

(e) Complete the Title Page (step 8)

FIGURE 1.8 Hands-on Exercise 3 (continued)

WORKING IN LONG DOCUMENTS

Long documents, such as term papers or reports, require additional formatting for better organization. These documents typically contain page numbers, headers and/or footers, and a table of contents. Each of these elements is discussed in turn and will be illustrated in a hands-on exercise.

Page Numbers

The ***Insert Page Numbers command*** is the easiest way to place ***page numbers*** into a document and is illustrated in Figure 1.9. The page numbers can appear at the top or bottom of a page, and can be left, centered, or right-aligned. Additional flexibility is provided as shown in Figure 1.9b; you can use Roman rather than Arabic numerals, and you need not start at page number one.

The Insert Page Number command is limited in two ways. It does not provide for additional text next to the page number, nor does it allow for different placements on the odd and even pages of a document as in a book or newsletter. Both restrictions are overcome by creating a header or footer which contains the page number.

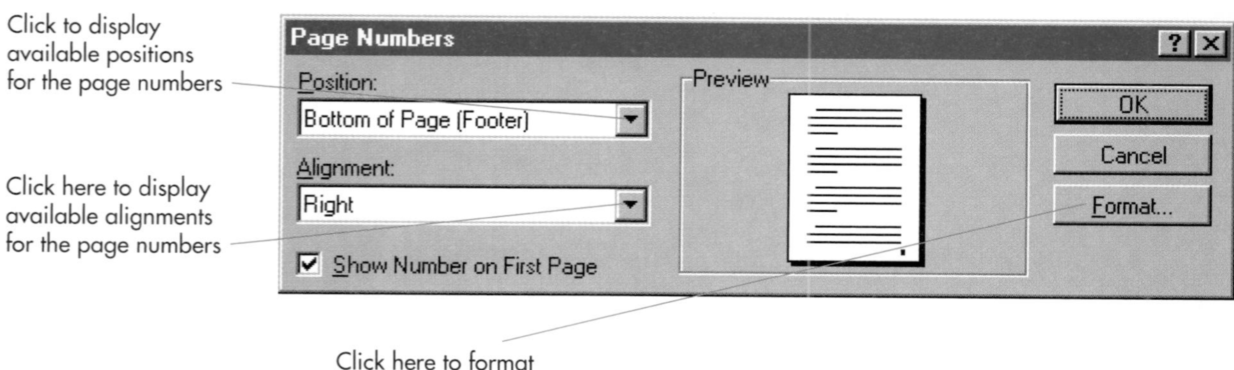

(a) Placement

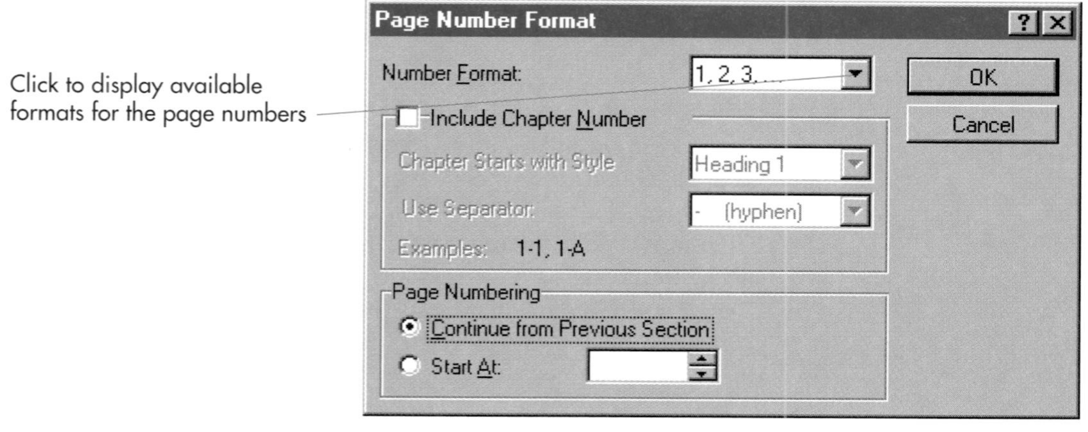

(b) Format

FIGURE 1.9 Page Numbers

Headers and Footers

Headers and footers give a professional appearance to a document. A ***header*** consists of one or more lines that are printed at the top of every page. A ***footer*** is printed at the bottom of the page. A document may contain headers but not footers, footers but not headers, or both headers and footers.

Headers and footers are created from the View menu. (A simple header or footer is also created automatically by the Insert Page Number command, depending on whether the page number is at the top or bottom of a page.) Headers and footers are formatted like any other paragraph and can be centered, left- or right-aligned. They can be formatted in any typeface or point size and can include special codes to automatically insert the page number, date and/or time a document is printed.

The advantage of using a header or footer (over typing the text yourself at the top or bottom of every page) is that you type the text only once, after which it appears automatically according to your specifications. The placement of the headers and footers is adjusted for changes in page breaks caused by the insertion or deletion of text in the body of the document.

Headers and footers can change continually throughout a document. The Page Setup dialog box (in the File menu) enables you to specify a different header or footer for the first page, and/or different headers and footers for the odd and even pages. If, however, you wanted to change the header (or footer) midway through a document, you would need to insert a section break at the point where the new header (or footer) is to begin.

Sections

Formatting in Word occurs on three levels. You are already familiar with formatting at the character and paragraph levels that have been used throughout the text. Formatting at the section level controls headers and footers, page numbering, page size and orientation, margins, and columns. All of the documents in the text so far have consisted of a single ***section,*** and thus any section formatting applied to the entire document. You can, however, divide a document into sections and format each section independently.

Formatting at the section level may appear complicated initially, but it gives you the ability to create more sophisticated documents. You can use section formatting to:

- ➤ Change the margins within a multipage letter where the first page (the letterhead) requires a larger top margin than the other pages in the letter.
- ➤ Change the orientation from portrait to landscape to accommodate a wide table at the end of the document.
- ➤ Change the page numbering, for example to use Roman numerals at the beginning of the document for a table of contents and Arabic numerals thereafter.
- ➤ Change the number of columns in a newsletter, which may contain a single column at the top of a page for the masthead, then two or three columns in the body of the newsletter.

In all instances, you determine where one section ends and another begins by using the ***Insert menu*** to create a ***section break.*** You also have the option of deciding how the section break will be implemented on the printed page; that is, you can specify that the new section continue on the same page, that it begin on a new page, or that it begin on the next odd or even page even if a blank page has to be inserted.

Word stores the formatting characteristics of each section in the section break at the end of a section. Thus, deleting a section break also deletes the section formatting, causing the text above the break to assume the formatting characteristics of the next section.

Figure 1.10 displays a multipage view of a ten-page document. The document has been divided into two sections, and the insertion point is currently on the

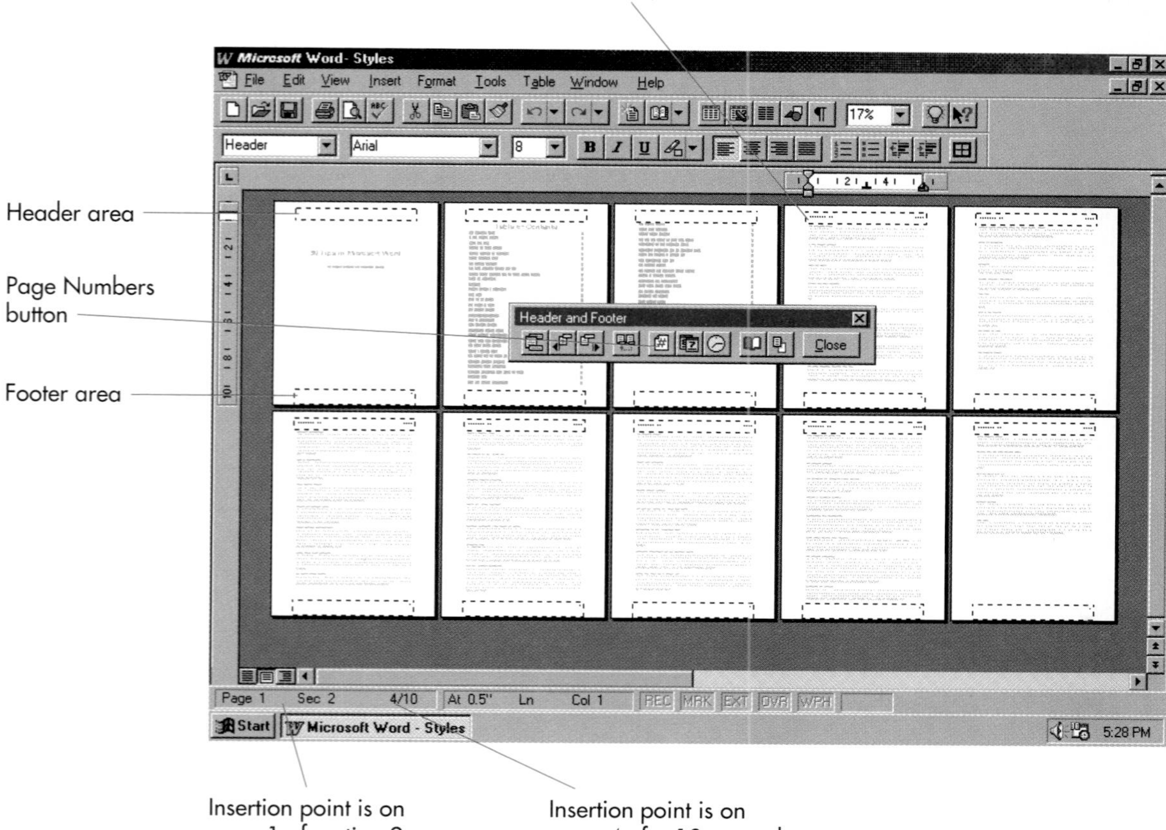

FIGURE 1.10 Headers and Footers

fourth page of the document (page four of ten), which is also the first page of the second section. Note the corresponding indications on the status bar and the position of the headers and footers throughout the document.

Figure 1.10 also displays the Headers and Footers toolbar, which contains various icons associated with these elements. As indicated, a header or footer may contain text and/or special codes—for example, the word "page" followed by a code for the page number. The latter is inserted into the header by clicking the appropriate button on the Headers and Footers toolbar.

THE SECTION VERSUS THE PARAGRAPH

Line spacing, alignment, tabs, and indents are implemented at the paragraph level. Change any of these parameters anywhere within the current (or selected) paragraph(s) and you change *only* those paragraph(s). Margins, headers and footers, page numbering, page size and orientation, and newspaper columns are implemented at the section level. Change these parameters anywhere within a section, and you change the characteristics of every page within that section.

Table of Contents

A ***table of contents*** lists headings in the order they appear in a document and the page numbers where the entries begin. Word will create the table of contents automatically, provided you have identified each heading in the document with a built-in heading style (Heading 1 through Heading 9). Word will also update the table automatically to accommodate the addition or deletion of headings and/or changes in page numbers brought about through changes in the document.

The table of contents is created through the ***Index and Tables command*** from the Insert menu as shown in Figure 1.11. You have your choice of several predefined formats and the number of levels within each format; the latter correspond to the heading styles used within the document. You can also choose the ***leader character*** and whether or not to right align the page numbers.

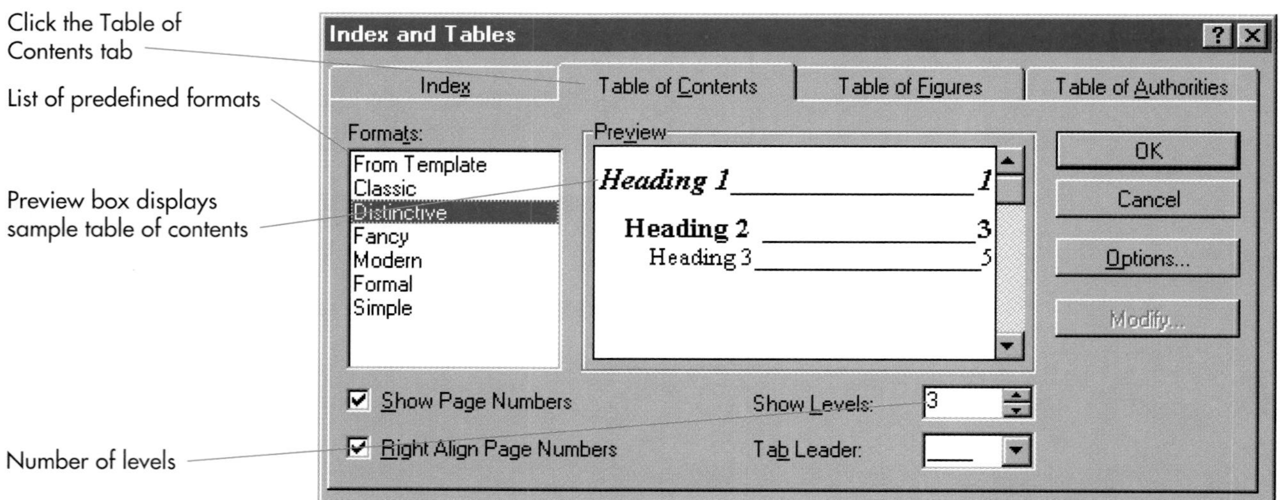

FIGURE 1.11 Index and Tables Command

The Go To Command

The ***Go To command*** moves the insertion point to the top of a designated page. The command is accessed from the Edit menu, or by pressing the F5 function key, or by double clicking the Page number on the status bar. After the command has been executed, you are presented with a dialog box in which you enter the desired page number. You can also specify a relative page number—for example, P+2 to move forward two pages, or P-1 to move back one page.

HANDS-ON EXERCISE 4

Working in Long Documents

Objective: To create a header (footer) that includes page numbers; to insert and update a table of contents; to insert a section break and demonstrate the Go To command; to view multiple pages of a document. Use Figure 1.12 as a guide for the exercise.

STEP 1: Applying a Style

- Open the **Styles document** from the first exercise. Scroll to the top of the second page. Click to the left of the first tip title. (If necessary, click the **Show/Hide ¶ button** on the Standard toolbar to hide the paragraph marks.)
- Type **Table of Contents.** Press the **enter key** two times.
- Click anywhere within the phrase "Table of Contents". Click the **arrow** on the **Styles list box** to pull down the styles for this document as shown in Figure 1.12a.
- Click **My Style** (the style you created at the end of the previous exercise). "Table of Contents" is centered in 28 point Arial bold according to the definition of My Style.

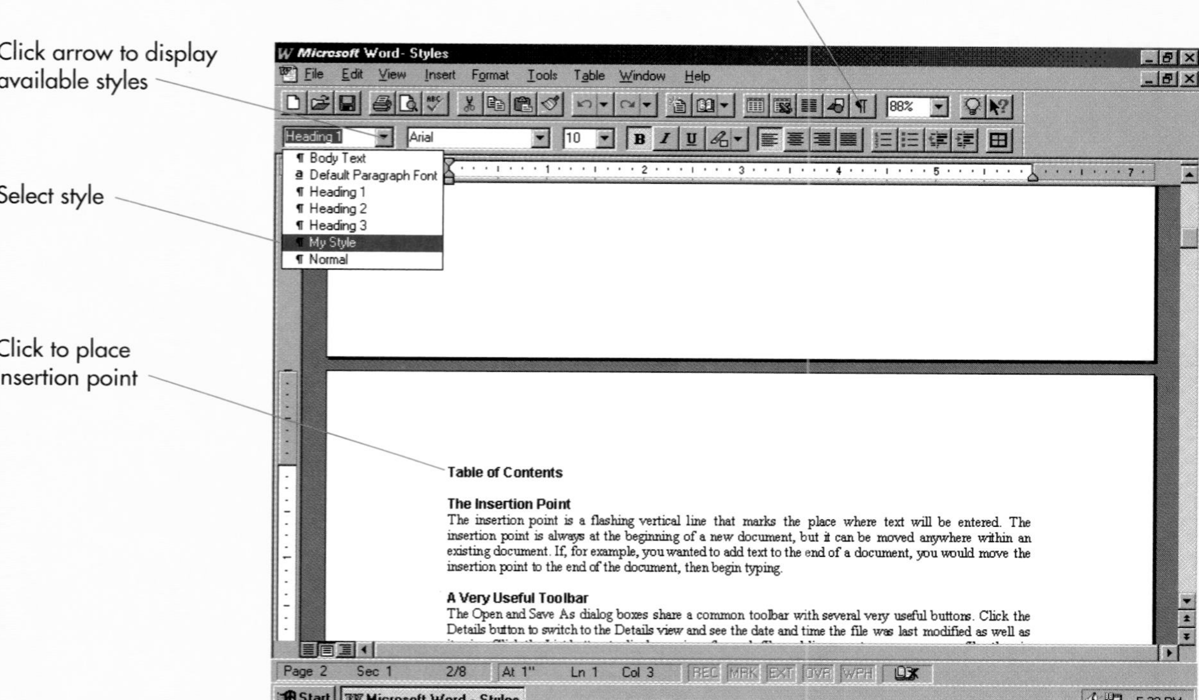

(a) Applying a Style (step 1)

FIGURE 1.12 Hands-on Exercise 4

STEP 2: View Many Pages

- Click the line immediately under the heading for the table of contents. Pull down the **View menu.** Click **Zoom** to display the dialog box in Figure 1.12b.
- Click the **monitor icon.** Click and drag the **page icon** within the monitor to display two pages down by five pages across as shown in the figure. Release the mouse.
- Click **OK.** The display changes to show all eight pages in the document.

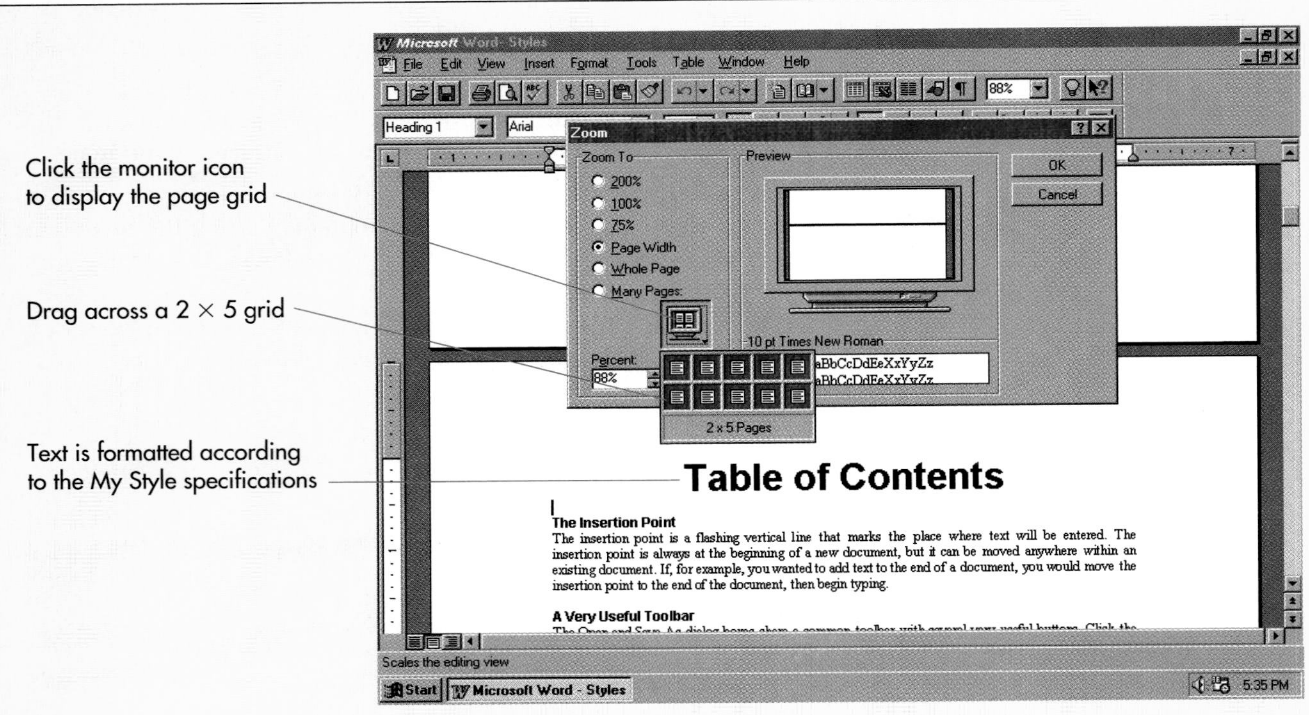

(b) View Zoom Command (step 2)

FIGURE 1.12 Hands-on Exercise 4 (continued)

STEP 3: Create the Table of Contents

- Pull down the **Insert menu.** Click **Index and Tables.** If necessary, click the **Table of Contents tab** to display the dialog box in Figure 1.12c.
- Check the boxes to **Show Page Numbers** and to **Right Align Page Numbers.**
- Click **Distinctive** in the **Formats list box.** Click the **arrow** in the **Tab Leader list box.** Choose a dot leader. Click **OK.** Word takes a moment to create the table of contents, which extends to two pages.

AUTOFORMAT AND THE TABLE OF CONTENTS

Word will create a table of contents automatically, provided you use the built-in heading styles to define the items for inclusion. If you have not applied the heading styles to the document, the AutoFormat command will do it for you. Once the heading styles are in the document, pull down the Insert command, click Index and Tables, then click the Table of Contents command.

STEP 4: Field Codes versus Field Text

- Click anywhere on the actual table of contents and it assumes a gray background. Click the **arrow** on the **Zoom Control box** on the Standard toolbar. Click **Page Width** in order to read the table of contents as in Figure 1.12d.

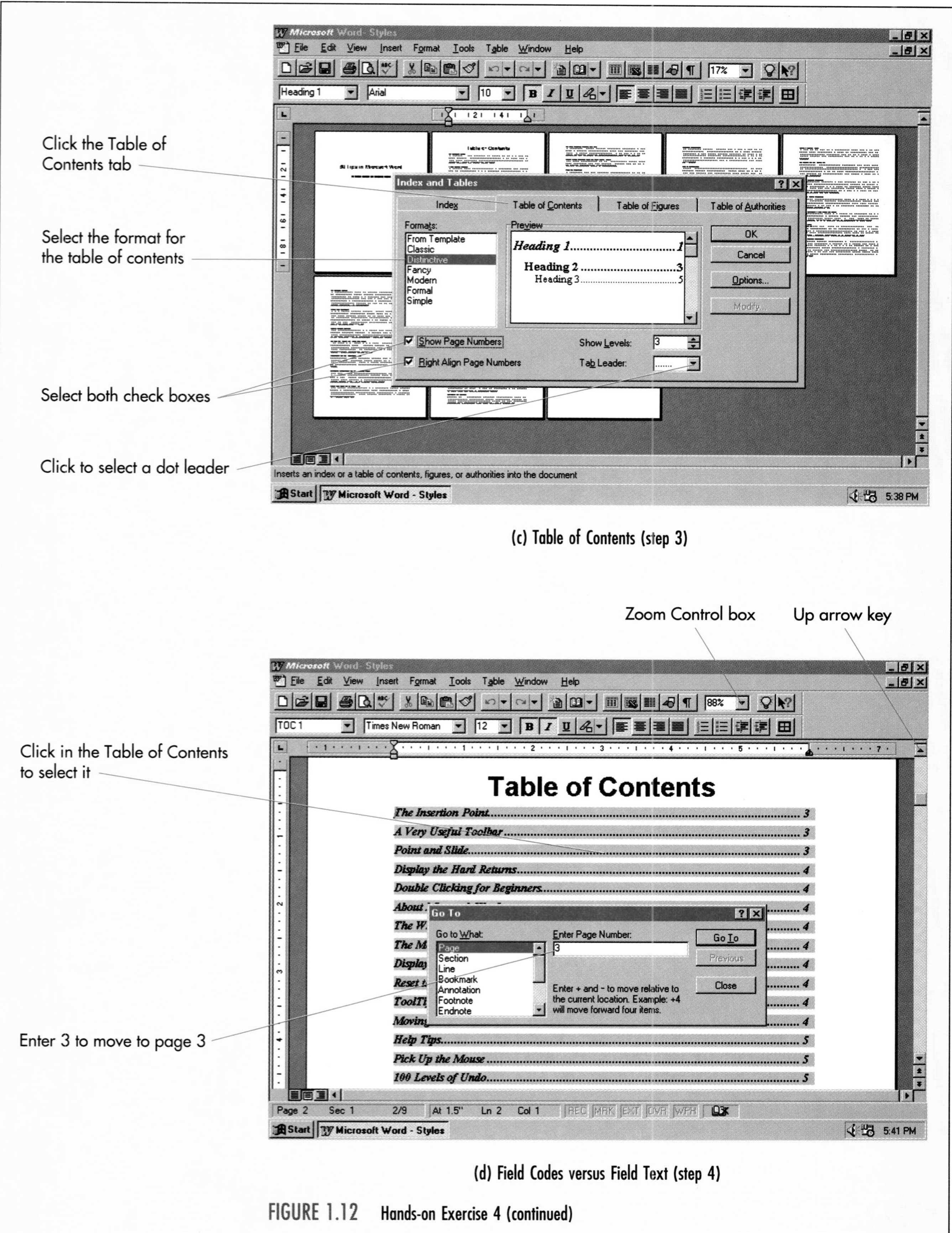

(c) Table of Contents (step 3)

(d) Field Codes versus Field Text (step 4)

FIGURE 1.12 Hands-on Exercise 4 (continued)

- Use the **up arrow key** to scroll to the beginning of the table of contents. Click in the first entry in the table of contents, then press **Shift+F9.** The entire table of contents is replaced by an entry similar to {TOC \o "1-3"} to indicate a field code; the exact code depends on your selections in step 4.
- Press **Shift+F9** a second time. The field code for the table of contents is replaced by text.
- Pull down the **Edit menu.** Click **Go To** to display the dialog box in Figure 1.12d.
- Type **3** and press the **enter key** to go to page 3. Click **Close.**

THE GO TO AND GO BACK COMMANDS

The F5 key is the shortcut equivalent of the Edit Go To command and produces a dialog box to move to a specific location (a page or section) within a document. The Shift+F5 combination executes the Go Back command and returns to a previous location of the insertion point; press Shift+F5 repeatedly to cycle through the last three locations of the insertion point.

STEP 5: Insert a Section Break

- Scroll down page three until you are at the end of the table of contents. Click to the left of the first tip heading as shown in Figure 1.12e.
- Pull down the **Insert menu.** Click **Break** to display the dialog box in Figure 1.12e.
- Click the **Next Page button** under Section Breaks. Click **OK** to create a section break, simultaneously forcing the first tip to begin on a new page.
- The status bar displays Page 1 Sec 2 to indicate you are on page one in the second section. (See the boxed tip on page numbering if the status bar indicates page 4.) The entry 4/10 indicates that you are physically on the fourth page of a ten-page document.

SECTIONS AND PAGE NUMBERING

Word gives you the option of numbering pages consecutively from one section to the next, or alternatively, of starting each section from page one. To view (change) the page numbering options in effect, pull down the Insert menu, click Page Numbers, click the Format command button, then click the option button for the page numbering you want. To start each section at page one, click the Start At option button, type 1 as the beginning page number, then click OK.

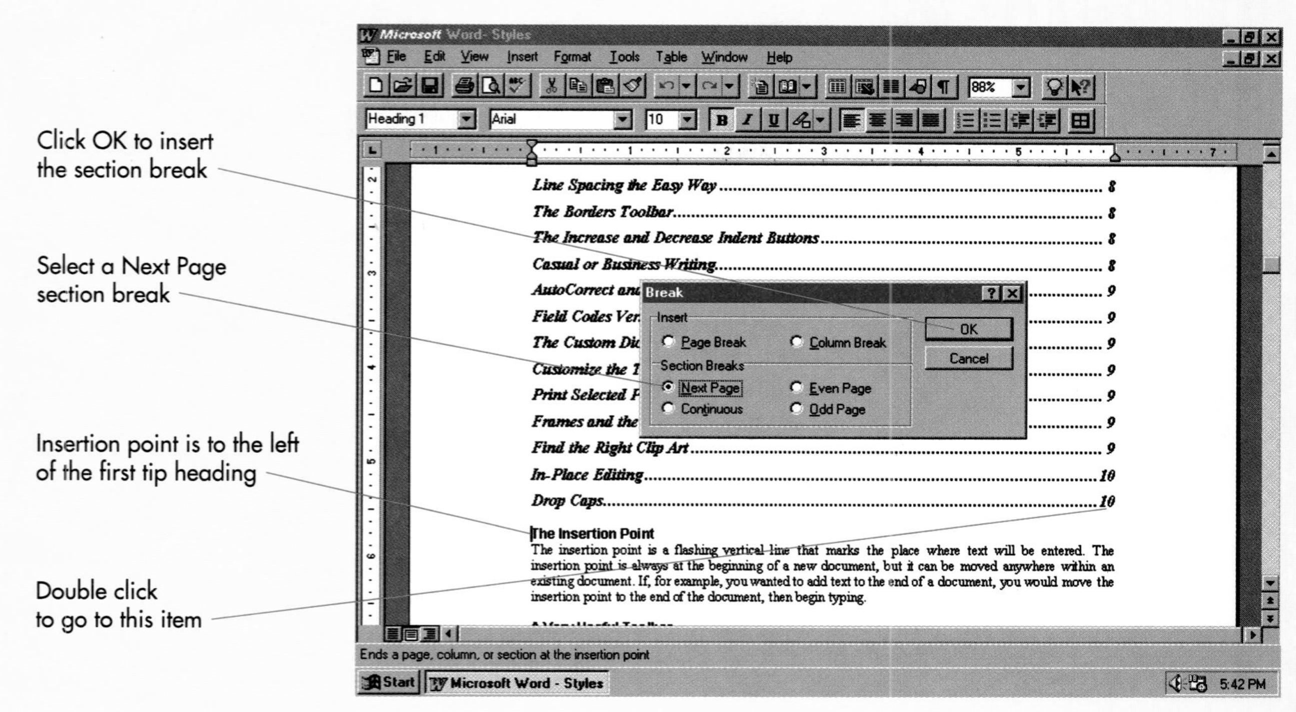
Click OK to insert the section break
Select a Next Page section break
Insertion point is to the left of the first tip heading
Double click to go to this item
Break
Insert
Page Break
Column Break
Section Breaks
Next Page
Even Page
Continuous
Odd Page
OK
Cancel
The Insertion Point
Ends a page, column, or section at the insertion point

(e) Inserting a Section Break (step 5)

FIGURE 1.12 Hands-on Exercise 4 (continued)

MOVING WITHIN LONG DOCUMENTS

Double click the page indicator on the status bar to display the dialog box for the ***Edit Go To command.*** You can also double click a page number in the table of contents (created through the Index and Tables command in the Insert menu) to go directly to the associated entry.

STEP 6: Create the Header

- Pull down the **File menu.** Click **Page Setup.** If necessary, click the **Layout tab** to display the dialog box in Figure 1.12f.
- If necessary, clear the box for Different Odd and Even Pages and for Different First Page, as all pages in this section (section two) are to have the same header. Click **OK.**

STEP 7: Create the Header (continued)

- Pull down the **View menu.** Click **Header and Footer** to produce the screen in Figure 1.12g. The text in the document is faded to indicate that you are editing the header, as opposed to the document.
- The "Same as Previous" indicator is on since Word automatically uses the header from the previous section. Click the **Same as Previous button** on the Header and Footer toolbar to toggle the indicator off in order to create a different header for this section. The indicator disappears from the header.

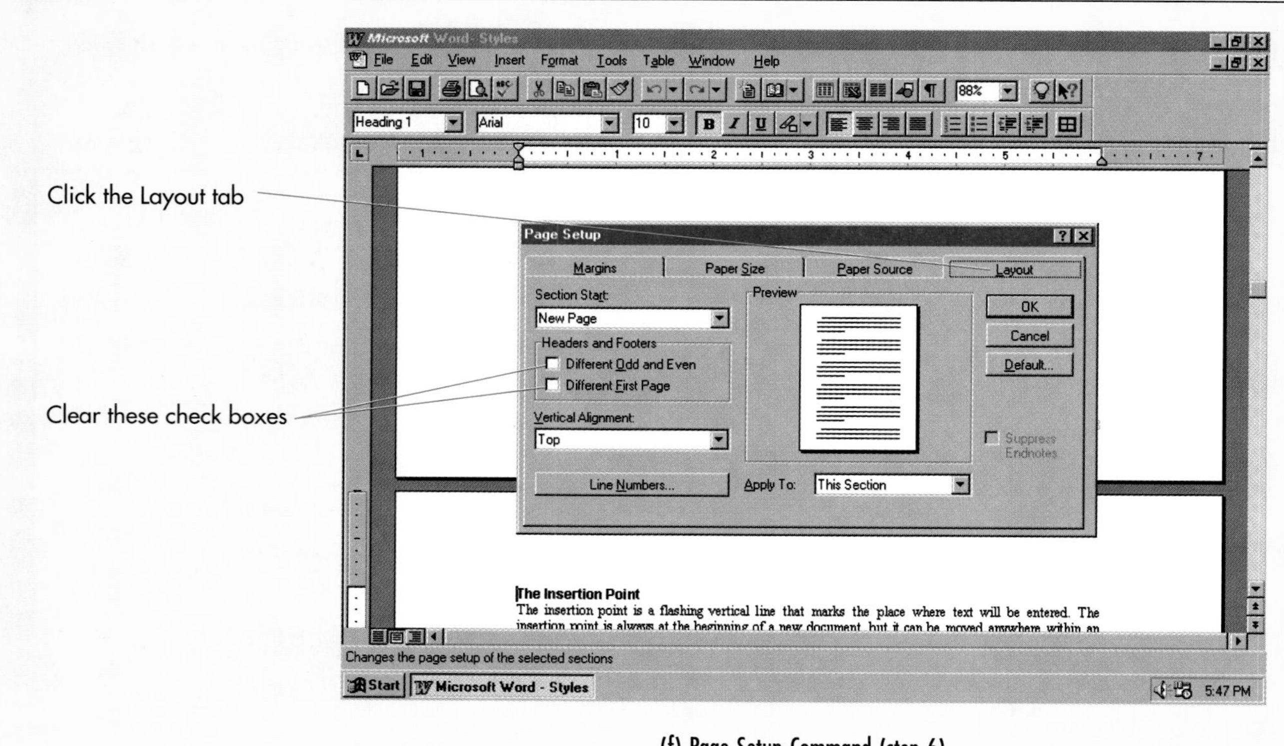

(f) Page Setup Command (step 6)

Click to display available fonts

Click here to enter text for header

Text is faded

Same as Previous button

Page Numbers button

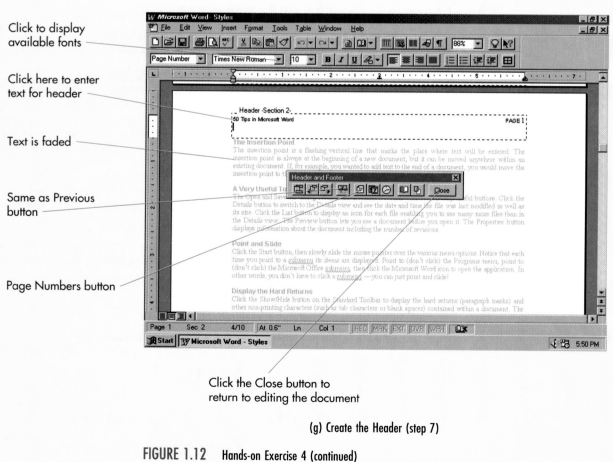

Click the Close button to return to editing the document

(g) Create the Header (step 7)

FIGURE 1.12 Hands-on Exercise 4 (continued)

- If necessary, click in the header. Click the **arrow** on the **Font list box** on the Formatting toolbar. Click **Arial.** Click the **arrow** on the Font size box. Click **8.** Type **50 Tips In Microsoft Word.**
- Press the **Tab key** twice. Type **PAGE.** Press the **space bar.** Click the **Page Numbers button** on the Header and Footer toolbar to insert a code for the page number. Press the **enter key** to insert a blank line in the header.
- Click the **Close button.** The header is faded, and the document text is available for editing.
- Save the document.

HEADERS AND FOOTERS

If you do not see a header or footer, it is most likely because you are in the wrong view. Headers and footers are displayed in the Page Layout view but not in the Normal view. (Click the Page Layout button on the status bar to change the view.) Even in the Page Layout view the header (footer) is faded, indicating that it cannot be edited unless it is selected (opened) by double clicking.

STEP 8: Update the Table of Contents

- Press **Ctrl+Home** to move to the beginning of the document. The status bar indicates Page 1, Sec 1.
- Click the **Next Page button** on the vertical scroll bar to move to the page containing the table of contents.
- Click anywhere in the table of contents and it assumes a gray background. The first tip, The Insertion Point, is shown to begin on page 3.
- Press the **F9 key** to update the table of contents. If necessary, click the **Update Entire Table** button as shown in Figure 1.12h, then click **OK.**
- The pages are renumbered to reflect the actual page numbers in the second section.

UPDATING THE TABLE OF CONTENTS

Use a shortcut menu to update the table of contents. Point anywhere in the table of contents, then press the right mouse button, to display a shortcut menu. Click Update Field, click the Update Entire Table command button, and click OK. The table of contents will be adjusted automatically to reflect page number changes as well as the addition or deletion of any items defined by any built-in heading style.

STEP 9: The Completed Document

- Pull down the **View menu.** Click **Zoom.** Click **Many Pages.** Click the **monitor icon.**

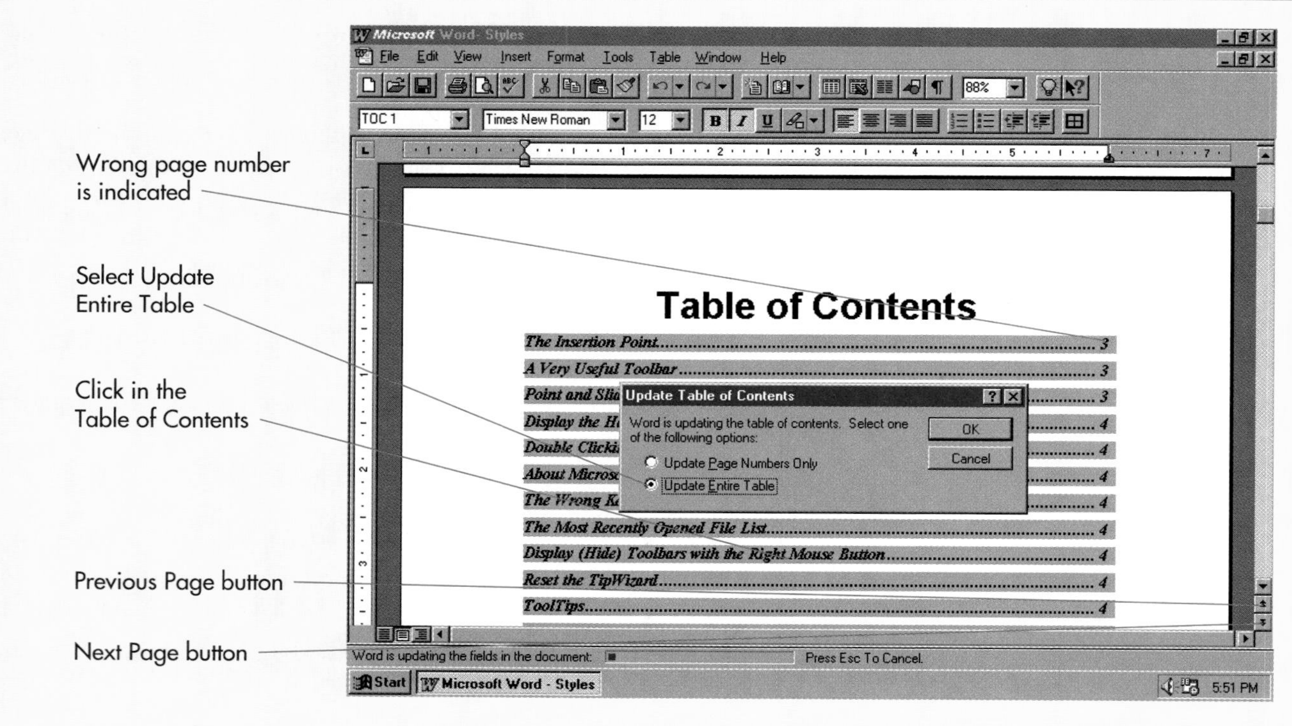

(h) Update the Table of Contents (step 8)

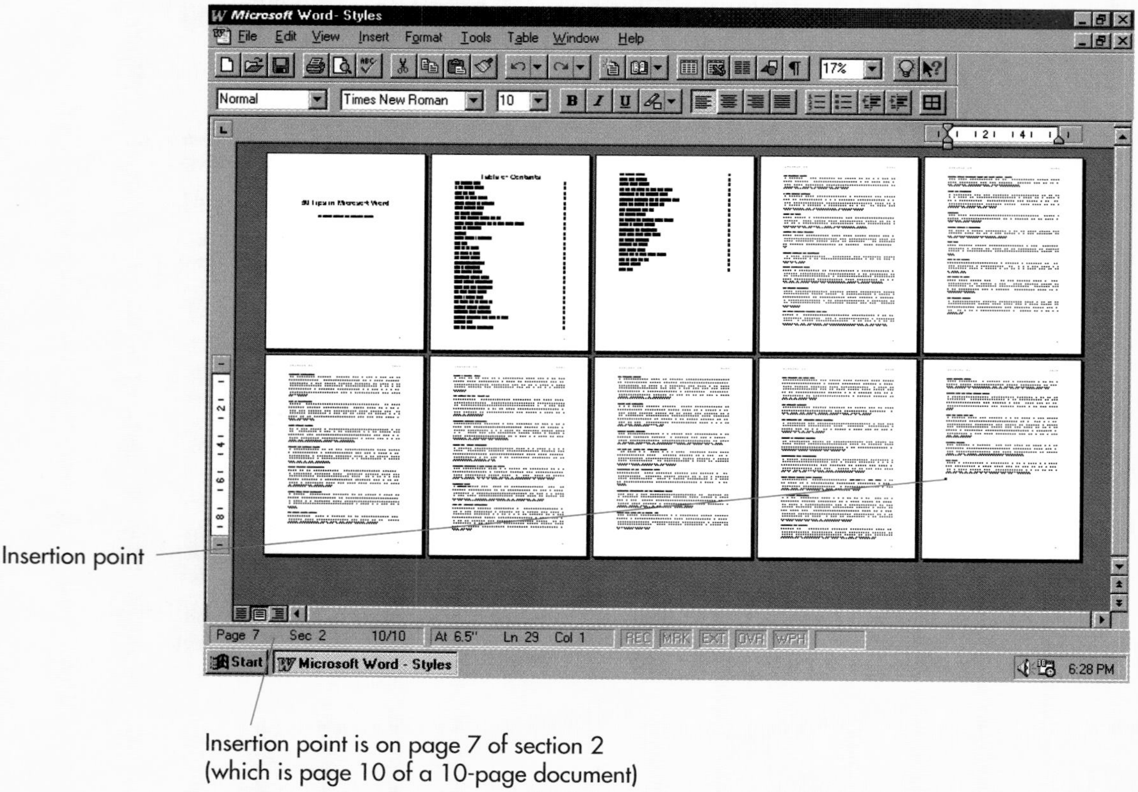

Insertion point

Insertion point is on page 7 of section 2
(which is page 10 of a 10-page document)

(i) The Completed Document (step 9)

FIGURE 1.12 Hands-on Exercise 4 (continued)

- Click and drag the **page icon** within the monitor to display two pages down by five pages. Release the mouse. Click **OK.**
- The completed document is shown in Figure 1.12i.
- Press **Ctrl+End** to move to the last page in the document.
- The status bar displays Page 7, Sec 2, 10/10 to indicate the seventh page in the second section, which is also the tenth page in the ten-page document.
- Save the document. Print the entire document. Exit Word.

BOOKMARKS

A ***bookmark*** is a predefined place in a document that is accessible through the Edit Go To command. Place the insertion point where you want the bookmark, pull down the Edit menu, click Bookmark, enter a name for the bookmark (40 or fewer characters consisting of letters, numbers, and/or the underscore), and click the Add command button. To return to the bookmark when subsequently editing the document, press the F5 key to display the dialog box for the Go To command, click Bookmark, choose the name of the bookmark from the displayed list, then click the Go To command button.

SUMMARY

A list helps to organize information by emphasizing important topics. A bulleted or numbered list can be created by clicking the appropriate button on the Formatting toolbar or by executing the Bullets and Numbering command in the Format menu.

Footnotes provide additional information about an item and appear at the bottom of the page where the reference occurs. Endnotes are similar in concept but appear collectively at the end of a document. The addition or deletion of a footnote or endnote automatically renumbers the notes that follow.

Tables represent a very powerful capability within Word and are created through the Insert Table command in the Table menu or by using the Insert Table button on the Standard toolbar. The cells in a table can contain text, numbers, and/or graphics. The cells in the table are separated by dotted lines known as gridlines, which appear on the monitor but not in the printed document.

A style is a set of formatting instructions that has been saved under a distinct name. Styles are created at the character or paragraph level and provide a consistent appearance to similar elements throughout a document. Existing styles can be modified to change the formatting of all text defined by that style.

The AutoFormat command analyzes a document and formats it for you. The command goes through an entire document, determines how each paragraph is used, then applies an appropriate style to each paragraph.

Formatting occurs at the character, paragraph, or section level. Section formatting controls margins, columns, page orientation and size, page numbering, and headers and footers. A header consists of one or more lines that are printed at the top of every (designated) page in a document. A footer is text that is printed at the bottom of designated pages. Page numbers may be added to either a header or footer.

A table of contents lists headings in the order they appear in a document with their respective page numbers. It can be created automatically, provided the built-in heading styles were previously applied to the items for inclusion. The Edit Go To command enables you to move directly to a specific page, section, or bookmark within a document.

KEY WORDS AND CONCEPTS

AutoFormat command
Body Text style
Bookmark
Bulleted list
Bullets and Numbering command
Cell
Character style
Default Paragraph Font style
Endnote
Footer
Footnote
Format Style command
Go To command
Header
Heading 1 style
Index and Tables command
Insert Footnote command
Insert menu
Insert Page Numbers command
Insert Table command
Leader character
Normal style
Numbered list
Page numbers
Paragraph style
Section
Section break
Style
Style command
Table menu
Table of contents
Tables feature

MULTIPLE CHOICE

1. Which of the following can be stored within a paragraph style?
   (a) Tabs and indents
   (b) Line spacing and alignment
   (c) Shading and borders
   (d) All of the above
2. What is the easiest way to change the alignment of five paragraphs scattered throughout a document, each of which has been formatted with the same style?
   (a) Select the paragraphs individually, then click the appropriate alignment button on the Formatting toolbar
   (b) Select the paragraphs at the same time, then click the appropriate alignment button on the Formatting toolbar
   (c) Change the format of the existing style, which changes the paragraphs
   (d) Retype the paragraphs according to the new specifications
3. The AutoFormat command will do all of the following except:
   (a) Apply styles to individual paragraphs
   (b) Apply boldface italics to terms that require additional emphasis
   (c) Replace ordinary quotes with smart quotes
   (d) Substitute typographic symbols for ordinary letters—such as © for (C)

4. Which of the following is true?
   (a) The addition or deletion of a footnote automatically renumbers the notes that follow
   (b) The addition or deletion of an endnote automatically renumbers the notes that follow
   (c) Both (a) and (b)
   (d) Neither (a) nor (b)

5. In which view do you see headers and/or footers?
   (a) Page Layout view
   (b) Normal view
   (c) Both (a) and (b)
   (d) Neither (a) nor (b)

6. Which of the following numbering schemes can be used with page numbers?
   (a) Roman numerals (I, II, III . . . or i, ii, iii)
   (b) Regular numbers (1, 2, 3, . . .)
   (c) Letters (A, B, C . . . or a, b, c)
   (d) All of the above

7. Which of the following is true regarding headers and footers?
   (a) Every document must have at least one header
   (b) Every document must have at least one footer
   (c) Both (a) and (b)
   (d) Neither (a) nor (b)

8. Which of the following is a *false* statement regarding lists?
   (a) A bulleted list can be changed to a numbered list and vice versa
   (b) The symbol for the bulleted list can be changed to a different character
   (c) The numbers in a numbered list can be changed to letters or roman numerals
   (d) The bullets or numbers cannot be removed

9. Page numbers can be specified in:
   (a) A header but not a footer
   (b) A footer but not a header
   (c) A header or a footer
   (d) Neither a header nor a footer

10. Which of the following is true regarding the formatting within a document?
    (a) Line spacing and alignment are implemented at the section level
    (b) Margins, headers, and footers are implemented at the paragraph level
    (c) Both (a) and (b)
    (d) Neither (a) nor (b)

11. What happens when you press the Tab key from within a table?
    (a) A Tab character is inserted just as it would be for ordinary text
    (b) The insertion point moves to the next column in the same row or the first column in the next row if you are at the end of the row
    (c) Both (a) and (b)
    (d) Neither (a) nor (b)

12. Which of the following is true, given that the status bar displays Page 1, Section 3, followed by 7/9?
    (a) The document has a maximum of three sections
    (b) The third section begins on page 7
    (c) The insertion point is on the very first page of the document
    (d) All of the above

13. The Edit Go To command enables you to move the insertion point to:
    (a) A specific page
    (b) A relative page forward or backward from the current page
    (c) A specific section
    (d) Any of the above

14. Once a table of contents has been created and inserted into a document:
    (a) Any subsequent page changes arising from the insertion or deletion of text to existing paragraphs must be entered manually
    (b) Any additions to the entries in the table arising due to the insertion of new paragraphs defined by a heading style must be entered manually
    (c) Both (a) and (b)
    (d) Neither (a) nor (b)

15. How do you print the lines separating the cells within a table in the printed document?
    (a) Select the gridlines option from the Table menu
    (b) Use the Format Border command
    (c) Either (a) or (b) but not both
    (d) Both (a) and (b) must be in effect at the same time

ANSWERS

1. d	**6.** d	**11.** b
2. c	**7.** d	**12.** b
3. b	**8.** d	**13.** d
4. c	**9.** c	**14.** d
5. a	**10.** d	**15.** b

EXPLORING MICROSOFT WORD 7.0

1. Use Figure 1.13 to match each action with its result; a given action may be used more than once or not at all.

Action		**Result**
a. Click at 1, click at 7	____	Change to landscape orientation
b. Click at 2	____	Insert page numbers into the document

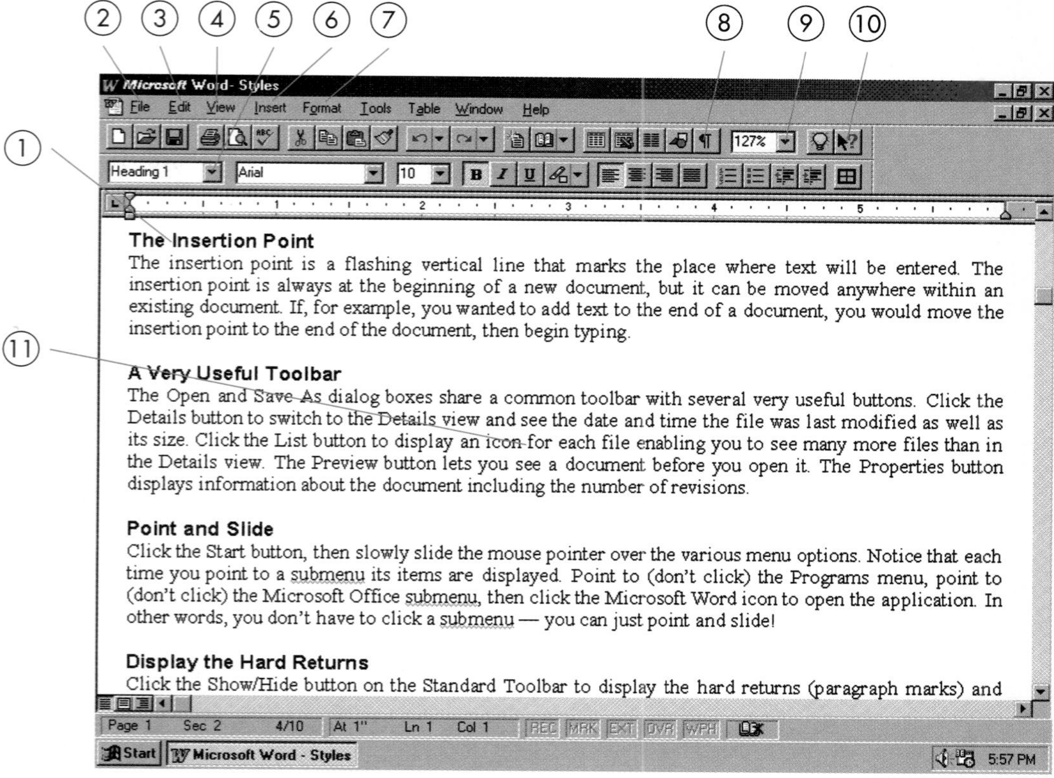

FIGURE 1.13 Screen for Problem 1

c. Click at 3	____	View the list of existing styles
d. Click at 4	____	Show the paragraph marks
e. Click at 5	____	Create a table of contents
f. Click at 6	____	Zoom to two pages
g. Click at 7	____	Go to page six
h. Click at 8	____	Edit the existing style
i. Click at 9	____	View the paragraph's formatting specifications
j. Click at 10, click at 11	____	Create a header

2. Adding emphasis: Figure 1.14 illustrates the use of a pull quote to add emphasis to a paragraph within a document. Figure 1.14a displays a paragraph set to the specifications of the style in Figure 1.14b.

a. What is the name of the style?

b. Which typeface, point size, and other font attributes are specified?

c. Which paragraph attributes are specified?

d. Which border attributes are specified?

e. What is the easiest way to create the style; that is, should the style be created before or after the commands in parts b through d are executed?

f. How would you modify the style to use a drop shadow rather than the parallel lines at the top and bottom?

g. How would you modify the style so that the text is shaded?

Horizontal rules are effective to separate one topic from another, emphasize a subhead, or call attention to a pull quote, a phrase or sentence taken from an article to emphasize a point.

(a) Printed Paragraph

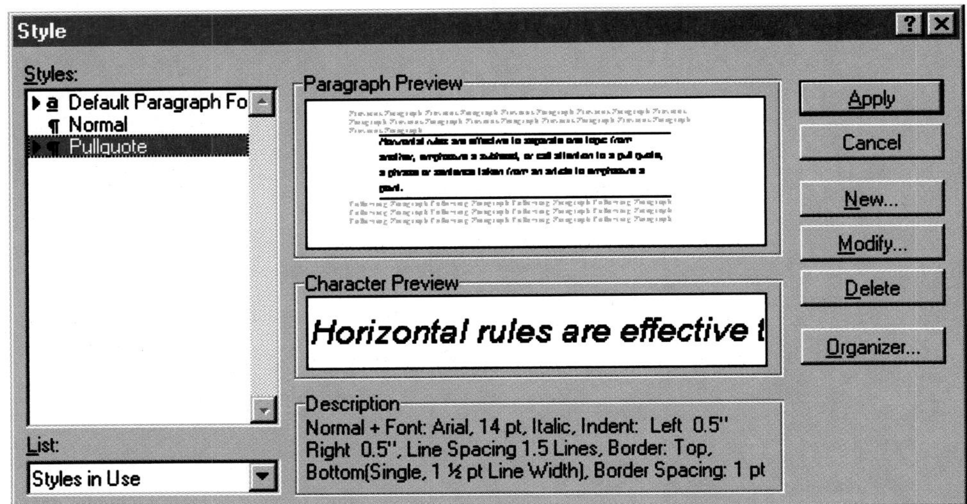

(b) Style Specifications

FIGURE 1.14 **Pull Quotes**

3. Answer the following with respect to the screen in Figure 1.15:
   a. How many sections are in the document? How many pages?
   b. What is the location of the insertion point? What does the indication "2/2" on the status bar mean?
   c. Which command was used to create the section break(s)?
   d. What is the orientation in the first section? In the second section?
   e. What are the margins in the first section? (Assume the default margins are in effect.) Are the margins the same in the second section?

4. Answer the following with respect to the screen displayed in Figure 1.16:
   a. What are the dimensions of the table? Which cells (if any) have been merged?
   b. What happens if you press the Tab key from within any cell in the table? If you press Ctrl+Tab?
   c. How does the appearance of the ruler change to reflect the fact that the insertion point is positioned within the table?
   d. Will the gridlines appear with the printed table? How do you place a border around the entire table so that the border prints with the table?
   e. Which command produced the dialog box in the figure?
   f. What is meant by automatic row height? What other way(s) will specify the height of a row?

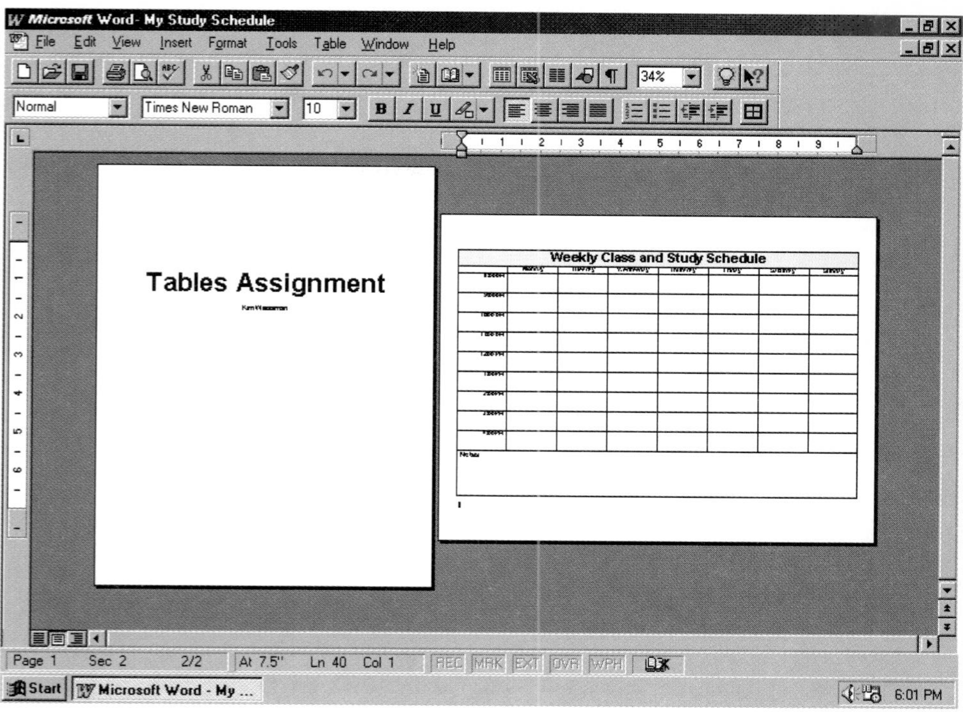

FIGURE 1.15 Screen for Problem 3

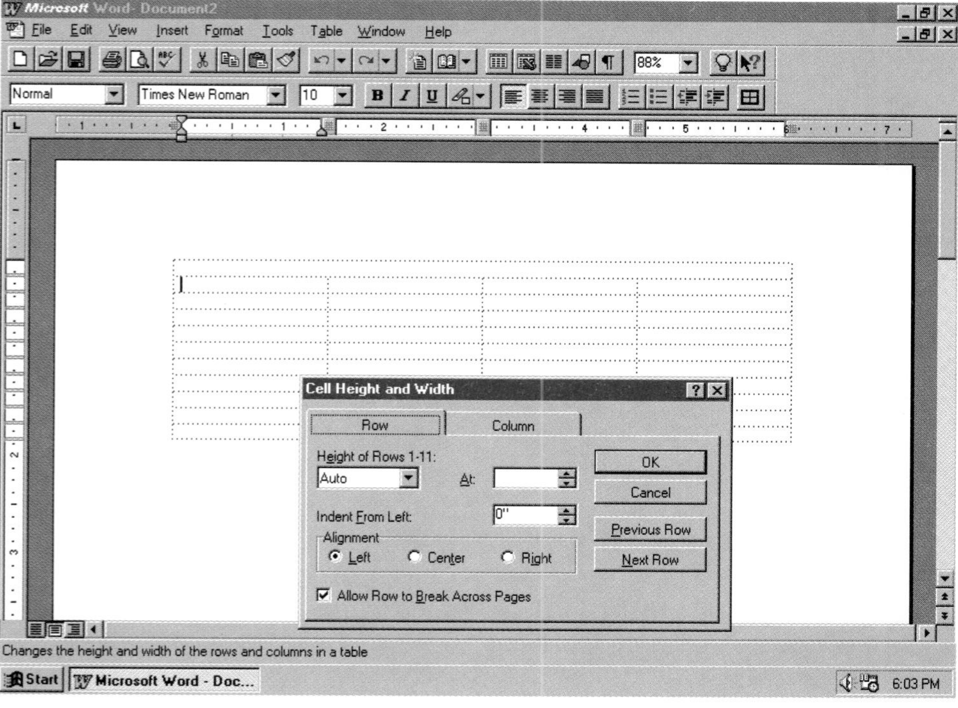

FIGURE 1.16 Screen for Problem 4

Practice with Microsoft Word 7.0

1. For the health conscious: Figure 1.17 displays the first five tips in a document describing tips for healthier living. Retrieve the document *Volume II Chapter 1 Practice 1* from the data disk, then modify it as follows:
   a. Use the AutoFormat command to apply the Heading 1 and Body Text styles throughout the document.
   b. Change the specifications for the Body Text and Heading 1 styles so that your document matches the document in the figure. The Heading 1 style calls for 12 point Arial bold with a blue top border (which requires a color printer). The Body Text style is 12 point Times New Roman, justified, with a ¼ inch left indent.
   c. Create a title page for the document consisting of the title, *Tips for Healthy Living,* the author, *Marion B. Grauer,* and an additional line, indicating that the document was prepared for you.
   d. Create a header for the document consisting of the title, *Tips for Healthy Living,* and a page number. The header is not to appear on the title page.

Start a Diet Journal

Keep a daily record of your weight and the foods you've eaten. Study your journal to become aware of your eating behavior. It will tell you when you're eating too much or if you're eating the wrong foods.

Why Do You Want to Lose Weight?

Write a list of reasons in your diet journal and refer to it often to sustain your motivation. Good health, good looks, more self-confidence, and new romantic possibilities are only the beginning.

Fighting Fatigue

Paradoxically, the more you do, the less tired you'll feel. Regular balanced exercise will speed up your metabolism, burn calories more efficiently, raise your energy level, and lift your spirits.

You Are What You Eat

Foods laden with fat, salt, and sugar leave you feeling lethargic and depressed. They set you up for more overeating. A nutritious low-fat diet has the opposite effect. You feel energized, revitalized, and happier.

"Water is the only drink for a wise man." Thoreau

Water is the perfect weight-loss beverage. It fills your stomach, curbs your appetite, and cleanses your entire system. Add a twist of lemon or lime to improve the taste, and drink eight glasses every day.

FIGURE 1.17 Document for Practice with Word Exercise 1

2. Sports fans: The tables feature is perfect to display the standings of any league, be it amateur or professional. Figure 1.18, for example, shows hypothetical standings in baseball and was a breeze. Pick any sport or league that you like and create a table with the standings as of today.

American League Standings as of June 4, 1995			
East	**Wins**	**Losses**	**Percent**
Boston Red Sox	22	11	.667
Baltimore Orioles	15	18	.455
Toronto Blue Jays	15	19	.441
Detroit Tigers	15	20	.429
New York Yankees	13	19	.406
Central	**Wins**	**Losses**	**Percent**
Cleveland Indians	23	10	.697
Kansas City Royals	18	15	.545
Milwaukee Brewers	15	19	.441
Chicago White Sox	13	20	.394
Minnesota Twins	11	25	.306
West	**Wins**	**Losses**	**Percent**
California Angels	22	13	.629
Seattle Mariners	19	15	.559
Texas Rangers	20	16	.556
Oakland A's	17	18	.486

FIGURE 1.18 Document for Practice with Word Exercise 2

3. Form design: The tables feature is ideal to create forms as shown by the document in Figure 1.19, which displays an employment application. Reproduce the document shown in the figure or design your own application. Submit the completed document to your instructor.

4. Graphics: A table may contain anything; text, graphics, or numbers as shown by the document in Figure 1.20, which displays a hypothetical computer advertisement. It's not complicated; in fact, it was really very easy; just follow the steps below:
   a. Create a 7 × 4 table.
   b. Merge all of the cells in row one and enter the heading. Merge all of the cells in row two and type the text describing the sale.
   c. Use the ClipArt Gallery to insert a picture into the table. (Various computer graphics are available in the Business and Technology categories.)
   d. Enter the sales data in rows three through seven of the table; all entries are centered within the respective cells.
   e. Use the Format Borders command to implement lines and shading, then print the completed document.

   Of course, it isn't quite as simple as it sounds, but we think you get the idea. Good luck and feel free to improve on our design.

Computer Consultants, Inc. Employee Application Form					
Last Name:		First Name:			Middle Name:
Address:					
City:		State:	Zip Code:		Telephone:
Date of Birth:	Place of Birth:			Citizenship:	
Highest Degree Attained: High School Diploma Bachelor's Degree Master's Degree Ph.D.	List Schools Attended (include years attended):				
List Specific Computer Skills:					
List Relevant Computer Experience:					
References (list name, title, and current mailing address): 1. 2. 3.					

FIGURE 1.19 Document for Practice with Word Exercise 3

Computers to Go

Our tremendous sales volume enables us to offer the fastest, most powerful series of Pentium computers at prices almost too good to be true. Each microprocessor is offered in a variety of configurations so that you get exactly what you need. All configurations include a local bus video, a 15-inch monitor, a mouse, and Windows 95.

Capacity	Configuration 1 8 Mb RAM 540 Mb Hard Drive	Configuration 2 16 Mb RAM 1 Gb Hard Drive	Configuration 3 24 Mb RAM 2 Gb Hard Drive
Pentium - 60 Mz	$1,999	$2,099	$2,599
Pentium - 75 Mz	$2,199	$2,399	$2,899
Pentium - 100 Mz	$2,399	$2,699	$3,199
Pentium - 120 Mz	$2,599	$2,999	$3,499

FIGURE 1.20 Document for Practice with Word Exercise 4

CASE STUDIES

Milestones in Communications

We take for granted immediate news of everything that is going on in the world, but it was not always that way. Did you know, for example, that it took five months for Queen Isabella to hear of Columbus' discovery, or that it took two weeks for Europe to learn of Lincoln's assassination? We've done some research on milestones in communications and left the file for you (Milestones in Communications). It runs for two, three, or four pages, depending on the formatting, which we leave to you. We would like you to include a header, and we think you should box the quotations that appear at the end of the document (it's your call as to whether to separate the quotations or group them together). Please be sure to number the completed document and don't forget a title page.

The Term Paper

Go to your most demanding professor and obtain the formatting requirements for the submission of a term paper. Be as precise as possible; for example, ask about margins, type size, and so on. What are the requirements for a title page? Is there a table of contents? Are there footnotes or endnotes, headers or footers? What is the format for the bibliography? Summarize the requirements, then indicate the precise means of implementation within Microsoft Word.

Forms, Forms, and More Forms

Every business uses a multitude of forms. Job applicants submit an employment application, sales personnel process order forms, and customers receive invoices. Even telephone messages have a form of their own. The office manager needs forms for everything, and she has come to you for help. You remember reading something about a tables feature and suggest that as a starting point. She needs more guidance so you sit down with her and quickly design two forms that meet with her approval. Bring the two forms to class and compare your work with that of your classmates.

Tips for Windows 95

The *Tips for Windows 95* document on the data disk contains 36 tips for using Windows 95. The tips are not formatted, however, and we would like you to use the AutoFormat command to create an attractive document. There are lots of tips so a table of contents is also appropriate. Add a cover page with your name and date, then submit the completed document to your instructor.

2

DESKTOP PUBLISHING: CREATING A NEWSLETTER

OBJECTIVES

After reading this chapter you will be able to:

1. Describe one advantage and one disadvantage of using the Newsletter Wizard, as opposed to creating a document from scratch.
2. Create a multicolumn newsletter; explain how sections are used to vary the number of columns in a document.
3. Use the Format Borders command to create boxes, shading, and reverses within a newsletter.
4. Use the Insert Picture command to insert clip art into a document; explain how frames are used to move and/or size the graphic.
5. Differentiate between clicking and double-clicking an object; modify a picture using the drawing tools within Microsoft Word.
6. Discuss the importance of a grid in the design of a document; describe the use of white space as a design element.

OVERVIEW

Desktop publishing evolved through a combination of technologies including faster computers, laser printers, and sophisticated page composition software to manipulate text and graphics. Today's generation of word processors has matured to such a degree that it is difficult to tell where word processing ends and desktop publishing begins. Microsoft Word is, for all practical purposes, a desktop publishing program that can be used to produce all types of documents.

The essence of desktop publishing is the merger of text with graphics to produce a professional-looking document without reliance on external services. Desktop publishing will save you time and money because you are doing work that used to be done by others. In practice it is not as easy as it sounds, because you are doing work that was previously done by others who were skilled in their respective areas. Thus, in addition to learning the commands within Microsoft Word to implement desktop publishing, you need to learn the basics of graphic design.

The chapter focuses on desktop publishing as it is implemented in Microsoft Word, followed by a brief introduction to graphic design. We show you how to create a multicolumn document, how to import graphic images, and how to edit those images as embedded objects. We also present material on bullets and lists, borders and shading, and section formatting, all of which will be used to create a newsletter in this chapter. Finally, we discuss several guidelines of graphic design to help you create a more polished document.

THE NEWSLETTER

The chapter is organized around the newsletter in Figure 2.1, which illustrates basic capabilities in ***desktop publishing.*** The hands-on exercises help you create the newsletter(s) in the figure. We think you will be pleased at how easy the process is and hope that you go on to create more sophisticated designs.

Figure 2.1a shows the newsletter as it exists on the data disk. We supply the text, but the formatting will be up to you. Figure 2.1b shows the newsletter at the end of the first hands-on exercise. It contains balanced newspaper columns, a ***masthead*** (a heading for the newsletter) that is set between thick parallel lines, and a bulleted list.

Figure 2.1c displays a more interesting design that contains a graphic, columns of different widths, a vertical line to separate the columns, and a dropped capital letter to emphasize the lead article. The figure uses shading to emphasize a specific paragraph and a ***reverse*** (white text on a black background) to accentuate the masthead.

Figure 2.1d illustrates an alternate design using three columns rather than two. The figure incorporates a ***pull quote*** (a phrase or sentence taken from an article) to emphasize a point. It also uses a more dynamic masthead that was developed with Microsoft WordArt (an application that is included with Microsoft Office).

The choice among the various newsletters in the figure is one of personal taste. All of the newsletters contain the identical text, but vary in their presentation of the written material. The easy part of desktop publishing is to implement a specific design using commands within Microsoft Word. The more difficult aspect is to create the design in the first place. We urge you therefore to experiment freely and to realize that good design is often the result of trial and error.

> **ADDING INTEREST**
>
> Boxes, shading, and reverses (light text on a dark background) add interest to a document. Horizontal (vertical) lines are also effective in separating one topic from another, emphasizing a subhead, or calling attention to a pull quote (a phrase or sentence taken from the article to emphasize a key point).

Typography

Typography—the selection of typefaces, styles, and sizes—is a critical element in the design of any document. Accordingly, you need to be familiar with the basic terminology of typography as it is used in the context of desktop publishing. A

Contest Winner
Congratulations to Carol Vazquez Villar who submitted the winning entry for our logo. Carol wins a pair of running shoes, which she promises to show off at the upcoming Jungle Jog.

Warming Up
Ever pull a muscle running your first mile or playing your first game of tennis? You should have stretched before you started -- right? Not according to a panel of sports medicine experts put together by the National Strength and Conditioning Association.

Warming up, not stretching, is the most important thing you can do to prevent injuries. Muscles that are cold are not very pliable and thus are susceptible to injury. Even stretching should be put off until you warm up with a few minutes of light jogging to increase your metabolic rate and raise your body's core temperature. When should you stretch? After your exercise -- when your muscles are warm.

Cold muscles injure easily
Begin with light jogging
Stretch after exercising
Be kind to your muscles

Better Fit Than Fat
There is nothing like finishing a meal with a delicate French pastry or a luscious chocolate mousse, but how much will that indulgence cost in calories? And what will you look like on the beach if you keep treating yourself to such delights?

Exercise is important to weight control, giving you more caloric leeway in your diet and suppressing your appetite. The number of calories burned during physical exercise depends on many factors -- how big you are (thinner, smaller people burn fewer calories at the same activity level than heavier, larger people), how hard or fast you work out (the harder the labor or faster the speed, the more calories you burn per minute), the air temperature (the colder the weather, the more calories you burn), the clothes you wear, the type of activity you choose, and the amount of time you spend doing it.

Some sports burn more fat than others. Start-stop activities, such as tennis or sprinting, are primarily carbohydrate-burning activities and use 60-70% carbohydrates and only 40-30% fat. Continuous sports on the other hand, such as walking or jogging, consume 50 - 60% fat and 50-40% carbohydrates.

Any strenuous workout, be it jogging, energetic walking, biking, or swimming, is fine. The important thing is to make a commitment to exercise regularly, at least three to five times a week, every week. If you haven't exercised in a while, start off slowly and gradually build up to the level that you desire.

Exercise and Income
According to a recent Gallup poll, the higher a person's income, the more likely he or she is to exercise; for example, in households with an income over $30,000, 68% of the men and 60% of the women exercise regularly. In addition, people with college degrees are more likely to exercise than those with only high school diplomas.

The Sun and Your Skin
If you have blond or red hair and your eyes are blue, green, or gray, you are more prone to skin cancer. The harmful rays of the sun are the ultraviolet (UV) ones. Unlike the infrared rays that are screened by the clouds, the UV rays go right through. So even on overcast days you need to protect your skin with a sunscreen with a high SPF factor. The best sunscreens are those that contain PABA esters and benzophenones that protect against both UVA and UVB rays.

As a precaution against skin cancer, examine brown spots, birth marks, moles, and sores that don't heal within two weeks. See your doctor immediately if you notice any change in shape or color.

Jungle Jog
Run the trails at the City Zoo on Saturday, March 15th at 7:00 AM, then meet at the Pavilion for breakfast among the beasts. Robert Plant will defend his title from last year. 35:55 is the time to beat.

(a) Text for the Newsletter

The Athlete's Hi

Contest Winner
Congratulations to Carol Vazquez Villar who submitted the winning entry for our logo. Carol wins a pair of running shoes, which she promises to show off at the upcoming Jungle Jog.

Warming Up
Ever pull a muscle running your first mile or playing your first game of tennis? You should have stretched before you started -- right? Not according to a panel of sports medicine experts put together by the National Strength and Conditioning Association.

Warming up, not stretching, is the most important thing you can do to prevent injuries. Muscles that are cold are not very pliable and thus are susceptible to injury. Even stretching should be put off until you warm up with a few minutes of light jogging to increase your metabolic rate and raise your body's core temperature. When should you stretch? After your exercise -- when your muscles are warm.

- Cold muscles injure easily
- Begin with light jogging
- Stretch after exercising
- Be kind to your muscles

Better Fit Than Fat
There is nothing like finishing a meal with a delicate French pastry or a luscious chocolate mousse, but how much will that indulgence cost in calories? And what will you look like on the beach if you keep treating yourself to such delights?

Exercise is important to weight control, giving you more caloric leeway in your diet and suppressing your appetite. The number of calories burned during physical exercise depends on many factors -- how big you are (thinner, smaller people burn fewer calories at the same activity level than heavier, larger people), how hard or fast you work out (the harder the labor or faster the speed, the more calories you burn per minute), the air temperature (the colder the weather, the more calories you burn), the clothes you wear, the type of activity you choose, and the amount of time you spend doing it.

Some sports burn more fat than others. Start-stop activities, such as tennis or sprinting, are primarily carbohydrate-burning activities and use 60–70% carbohydrates and only 40–30% fat. Continuous sports on the other hand, such as walking or jogging, consume 50–60% fat and 50–40% carbohydrates.

Any strenuous workout, be it jogging, energetic walking, biking, or swimming, is fine. The important thing is to make a commitment to exercise regularly, at least three to five times a week, every week. If you haven't exercised in a while, start off slowly and gradually build up to the level that you desire.

Exercise and Income
According to a recent Gallup poll, the higher a person's income, the more likely he or she is to exercise; for example, in households with an income over $30,000, 68% of the men and 60% of the women exercise regularly. In addition, people with college degrees are more likely to exercise than those with only high school diplomas.

The Sun and Your Skin
If you have blond or red hair and your eyes are blue, green, or gray, you are more prone to skin cancer. The harmful rays of the sun are the ultraviolet (UV) ones. Unlike the infrared rays that are screened by the clouds, the UV rays go right through. So even on overcast days you need to protect your skin with a sunscreen with a high SPF factor. The best sunscreens are those that contain PABA esters and benzophenones that protect against both UVA and UVB rays.

As a precaution against skin cancer, examine brown spots, birth marks, moles, and sores that don't heal within two weeks. See your doctor immediately if you notice any change in shape or color.

Jungle Jog
Run the trails at the City Zoo on Saturday, March 15th at 7:00 AM, then meet at the Pavilion for breakfast among the beasts. Robert Plant will defend his title from last year. 35:55 is the time to beat.

(b) At End of Exercise 1

The Athlete's Hi

Contest Winner
Congratulations to Carol Vazquez Villar who submitted the winning entry for our logo. Carol wins a pair of running shoes, which she promises to show off at the upcoming Jungle Jog.

Warming Up
Ever pull a muscle running your first mile or playing your first game of tennis? You should have stretched before you started -- right? Not according to a panel of sports medicine experts put together by the National Strength and Conditioning Association.

Warming up, not stretching, is the most important thing you can do to prevent injuries. Muscles that are cold are not very pliable and thus are susceptible to injury. Even stretching should be put off until you warm up with a few minutes of light jogging to increase your metabolic rate and raise your body's core temperature. When should you stretch? After your exercise -- when your muscles are warm.

- Cold muscles injure easily
- Begin with light jogging
- Stretch after exercising
- Be kind to your muscles

Better Fit Than Fat
There is nothing like finishing a meal with a delicate French pastry or a luscious chocolate mousse, but how much will that indulgence cost in calories? And what will you look like on the beach if you keep treating yourself to such delights?

Exercise is important to weight control, giving you more caloric leeway in your diet and suppressing your appetite. The number of calories burned during physical exercise depends on many factors -- how big you are (thinner, smaller people burn fewer calories at the same activity level than heavier, larger people), how hard or fast you work out (the harder the labor or faster the speed, the more calories you burn per minute), the air temperature (the colder the weather, the more calories you burn), the clothes you wear, the type of activity you choose, and the amount of time you spend doing it.

Some sports burn more fat than others. Start-stop activities, such as tennis or sprinting, are primarily carbohydrate-burning activities and use 60–70% carbohydrates and only 40–30% fat. Continuous sports on the other hand, such as walking or jogging, consume 50–60% fat and 50–40% carbohydrates.

Any strenuous workout, be it jogging, energetic walking, biking, or swimming, is fine. The important thing is to make a commitment to exercise regularly, at least three to five times a week, every week. If you haven't exercised in a while, start off slowly and gradually build up to the level that you desire.

Exercise and Income
According to a recent Gallup poll, the higher a person's income, the more likely he or she is to exercise; for example, in households with an income over $30,000, 68% of the men and 60% of the women exercise regularly. In addition, people with college degrees are more likely to exercise than those with only high school diplomas.

The Sun and Your Skin
If you have blond or red hair and your eyes are blue, green, or gray, you are more prone to skin cancer. The harmful rays of the sun are the ultraviolet (UV) ones. Unlike the infrared rays that are screened by the clouds, the UV rays go right through. So even on overcast days you need to protect your skin with a sunscreen with a high SPF factor. The best sunscreens are those that contain PABA esters and benzophenones that protect against both UVA and UVB rays.

As a precaution against skin cancer, examine brown spots, birth marks, moles, and sores that don't heal within two weeks. See your doctor immediately if you notice any change in shape or color.

Jungle Jog
Run the trails at the City Zoo on Saturday, March 15th at 7:00 AM, then meet at the Pavilion for breakfast among the beasts. Robert Plant will defend his title from last year. 35:55 is the time to beat.

(c) At End of Exercise 3

The Athlete's Hi

Volume 1, Number 1 **Winter 1996**

Contest Winner
Congratulations to Carol Vazquez Villar who submitted the winning entry for our logo. Carol wins a pair of running shoes, which she promises to show off at the upcoming Jungle Jog.

Warming Up
Ever pull a muscle running your first mile or playing your first game of tennis? You should have stretched before you started -- right? Not according to a panel of sports medicine experts put together by the National Strength and Conditioning Association.

Warming up, not stretching, is the most important thing you can do to prevent injuries. Muscles that are cold are not very pliable and thus are susceptible to injury. Even stretching should be put off until you warm up with a few minutes of light jogging to increase your metabolic rate and raise your body's core temperature. When should you stretch? After your exercise -- when your muscles are warm.

- Cold muscles injure easily
- Begin with light jogging
- Stretch after exercising
- Be kind to your muscles

Better Fit Than Fat
There is nothing like finishing a meal with a delicate French pastry or a luscious chocolate mousse, but how much will that indulgence cost in calories? And what will you look like on the beach if you keep treating yourself to such delights?

Exercise is important to weight control, giving you more caloric leeway in your diet and suppressing your appetite. The number of calories burned during physical exercise depends on many factors -- how big you are (thinner, smaller people burn fewer calories at the same activity level than heavier, larger people), how hard or fast you work out (the harder the labor or faster the speed, the more calories you burn per minute), the air temperature (the colder the weather, the more calories you burn), the clothes you wear, the type of activity you choose, and the amount of time you spend doing it.

Some sports burn more fat than others. Start-stop activities, such as tennis or sprinting, are primarily carbohydrate-burning activities and use 60–70% carbohydrates and only 40–30% fat. Continuous sports, on the other hand, such as walking or jogging, consume 50–60% fat and 50–40% carbohydrates.

Any strenuous workout, be it jogging, energetic walking, biking, or swimming, is fine. The important thing is to make a commitment to exercise regularly, at least three to five times a week, every week. If you haven't exercised in a while, start off slowly and gradually build up to the level that you desire.

Exercise and Income
According to a recent Gallup poll, the higher a person's income, the more likely he or she is to exercise; for example, in households with an income over $30,000, 68% of the men and 60% of the women exercise regularly. In addition, people with college degrees are more likely to exercise than those with only high school diplomas.

"The important thing is to make a commitment to exercise regularly, at least three to five times a week, every week"

The Sun and Your Skin
If you have blond or red hair and your eyes are blue, green, or gray, you are more prone to skin cancer. The harmful rays of the sun are the ultraviolet (UV) ones. Unlike the infrared rays that are screened by the clouds, the UV rays go right through. So even on overcast days you need to protect your skin with a sunscreen with a high SPF factor. The best sunscreens are those that contain PABA esters and benzophenones that protect against both UVA and UVB rays.

As a precaution against skin cancer, examine brown spots, birth marks, moles, and sores that don't heal within two weeks. See your doctor immediately if you notice any change in shape or color.

Jungle Jog
Run the trails at the City Zoo on Saturday, March 15th at 7:00 AM, then meet at the Pavilion for breakfast among the beasts. Robert Plant will defend his title from last year. 35:55 is the time to beat.

(d) An Alternate Design

FIGURE 2.1 The Newsletter

font (such as Times New Roman or Arial) is a complete set of characters consisting of letters, numbers, and special symbols. ***Type size*** is measured in points, with 72 points to the inch. Large amounts of text are typically set in 10 or 12 point type. This book, for example, is set in 10 point type.

Typography influences the appearance of a document more than any other element. Good typography goes almost unnoticed, whereas poor typography calls attention to itself and distracts from the document. There are no hard and fast rules, only guidelines and common sense, and what works in one instance may not work in another.

One generally accepted guideline is to limit the number of typefaces in a document to two, but to use multiple styles and sizes of those typefaces. Boldface and/or italics are recommended for emphasis, as opposed to underlining or all uppercase letters. Different point sizes can also be used to differentiate between headings, subheadings, and text, but a variation of at least two points is necessary to be noticeable.

The point size should also be consistent with the length of a line or the width of a column. Larger point sizes require longer lines or wider columns. Conversely, the shorter the line or narrower the column, the smaller the point size. Very narrow columns or very short lines should be avoided because they are choppy and difficult to read. Overly wide columns or very long lines are just as bad because the reader can easily get lost.

Columns

The ***Columns command*** in the Format menu enables you to define ***newspaper-style columns*** in which text flows continuously from the bottom of one column to the top of the next. You specify the number of columns and, optionally, the space between columns. Microsoft Word does the rest, calculating the width of each col-

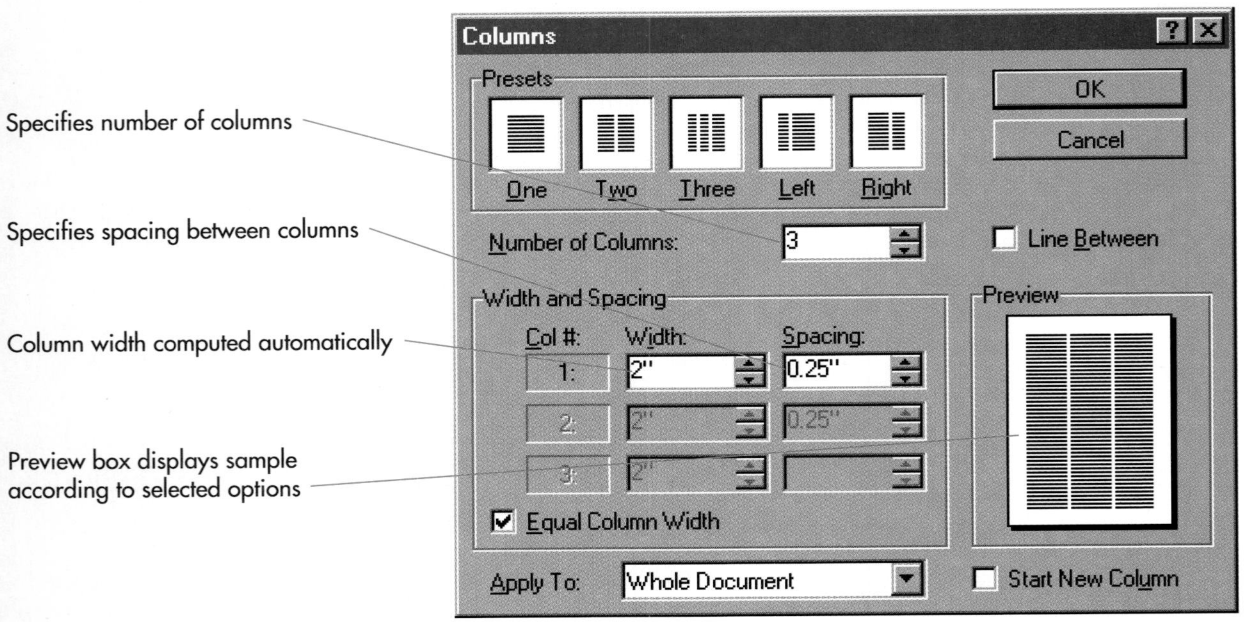

FIGURE 2.2 The Columns Command

umn according to the left and right margins on the page and the specified (default) space between columns.

The dialog box in Figure 2.2 specifies three equal columns with .25 inch between each column. The two-inch width of each column is computed automatically based on left and right page margins of one inch each and the ¼ inch spacing between columns. The space in the margins and between the columns, a total of 2½ inches in this example, is subtracted from the page width of 8½ inches. The remaining 6 inches is divided by three, resulting in a column width of two inches.

The number of columns can vary within a document. Each of the newsletters in Figure 2.1, for example, uses a single column at the top of the page for the masthead and multiple columns on the rest of the page. Columns are implemented at the section level, and thus a ***section break*** must be inserted whenever the column specification changes. (Section formatting was described in the previous chapter in conjunction with changing margins, headers and footers, page numbering, size, and orientation.)

UNEQUAL COLUMNS

Add interest to a document by creating columns of different widths. Pull down the Format menu, click Columns, then click the Left or Right icon in the Presets area. Change the number, width, and/or spacing between columns, and Microsoft Word automatically changes the other parameters to match your specifications. Add a line between columns by checking the Line Between box in the Columns dialog box.

THE NEWSLETTER WIZARD

At first glance the ***Newsletter Wizard*** appears to answer the prayers of the would-be desktop publisher. The Newsletter Wizard (one of several wizards in Microsoft Word) asks you a series of questions, then creates a template for you on which to base a document.

The Newsletter Wizard provides a considerable amount of flexibility as can be inferred from the screens in Figure 2.3a, b, c, and d, which let you specify the style, number of columns, title, and elements to include. The resulting template in Figure 2.3e is based on your answers, and further, incorporates good typography and other elements of graphic design.

What, then, is the drawback, and why would you not use the Newsletter Wizard for every newsletter you create? The problem is one of adaptability in that the wizard may not be suitable for the newsletter you wish to create. What if you wanted to include two graphics, rather than one, or you wanted the graphic(s) in a different position? What if you needed a newsletter with columns of varying width, or you wanted to include a pull quote or a reverse?

You could, of course, use the template created by the wizard as the starting point for the newsletter, then execute the necessary commands in Word to modify the document according to your specifications. You will find, however, that it is just as easy to create the newsletter from the beginning and bypass the wizard entirely. You will wind up with a superior document that is exactly what you need and not what the wizard thinks you need. Creating a newsletter is a lot easier than you might imagine, as you will see in the exercise that begins on page 59.

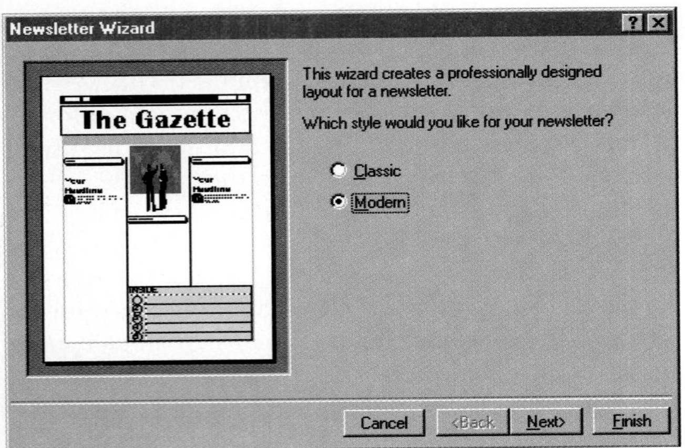

(a) The Newsletter Wizard

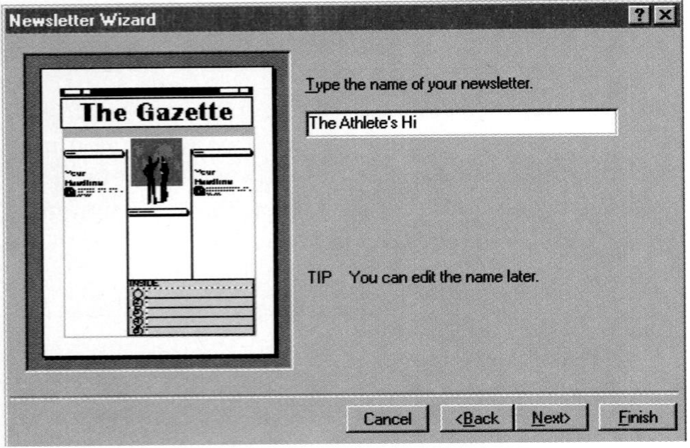

(b) Enter the Title

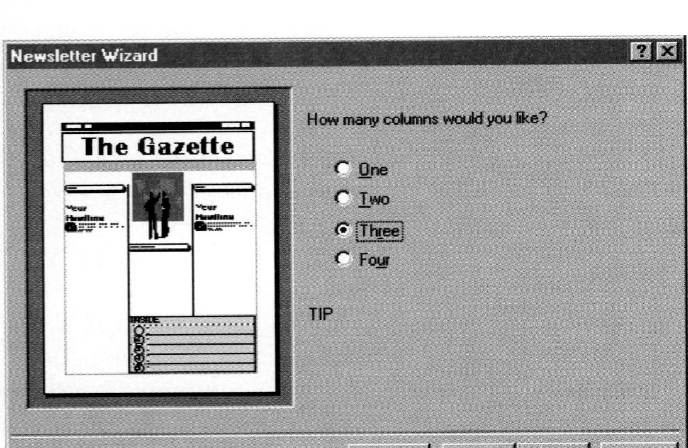

(c) Specify the Number of Columns

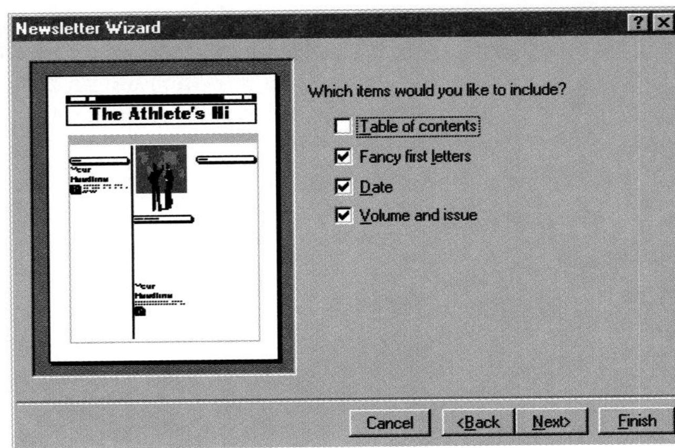

(d) Select the Items to Include

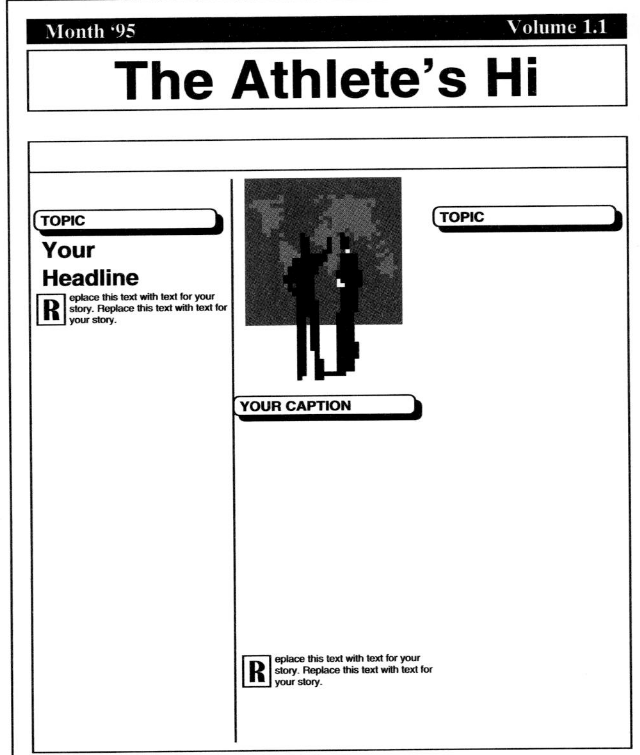

(e) The Completed Template

FIGURE 2.3 The Newsletter Wizard

HANDS-ON EXERCISE 1

Newspaper Columns

Objective: To create a multicolumn document with equal text in each column, to create a masthead, and to implement a bulleted or numbered list. Use Figure 2.4 as a guide for the exercise.

STEP 1: Load the Text of the Newsletter

- Start Word. Open the **Text for Newsletter** document in the Exploring Word folder.
- If necessary, click the **Page Layout button** on the status bar. Set the magnification (zoom) to **Page Width** to match the document in the figure.
- Save the document as **Modified Newsletter** so that you can return to the original document if necessary.

VIEWS AND COLUMNS

You must be in the Page Layout view, not the Normal view, in order to see columns displayed side-by-side within a document. Thus, if you do not see columns, it is probably because you are in the wrong view. Click the Page Layout button on the status bar to change the view, then click the arrow on the Zoom control box on the Standard toolbar to see as more or less of the page as necessary.

STEP 2: Newspaper Columns

- Pull down the **Format menu.** Click **Columns** to produce the dialog box in Figure 2.4a.
- Click the **Presets icon** for **Two.** The column width for each column and the spacing between columns will be determined automatically from the existing margins.
- If necessary, clear the **Line Between box.** Click **OK** to accept the settings and exit the dialog box. The text of the newsletter should be displayed in two columns.

THE COLUMNS BUTTON

The Columns button on the Standard toolbar is the fastest way to create columns in a document. Click the button, drag the mouse to choose the number of columns, then release the mouse to create the columns. The toolbar lets you change the number of columns, but not the spacing between columns. The toolbar is also limited in that you cannot create columns of different widths or select (deselect) a line between columns.

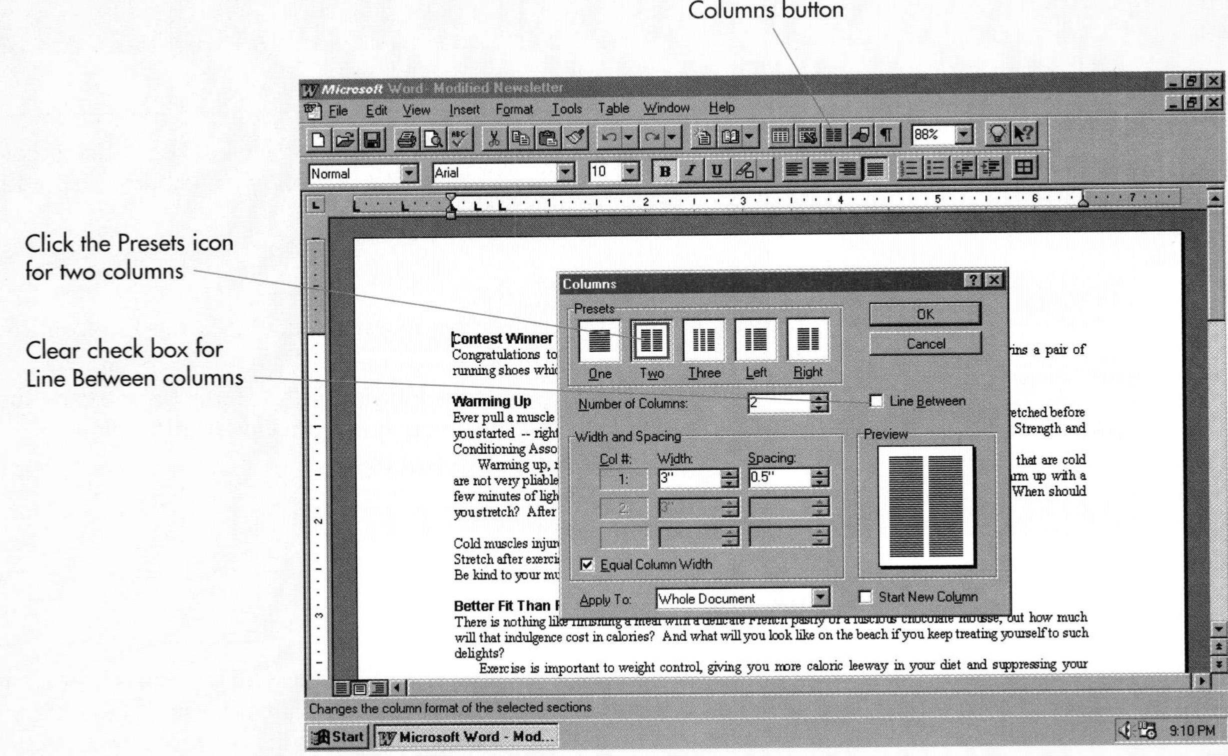

(a) Newspaper Columns (step 1)

FIGURE 2.4 Hands-on Exercise 1

STEP 3: Balance the Columns

- ➤ Use the **Zoom Control box** on the Standard toolbar to zoom to **Whole Page** to see the entire newsletter as in Figure 2.4b. Do not be concerned if the columns are of different lengths.
- ➤ Press **Ctrl+End** to move to the end of the document. Pull down the **Insert Menu.** Click **Break** to produce the dialog box of Figure 2.4b.
- ➤ Click the **Continuous button** under Section Breaks. Click **OK.** The columns should be balanced although one column may be one line longer (shorter) than the other.

USE THE RULER TO CHANGE COLUMN WIDTH

You can use the ruler to change column widths simply by dragging a column marker. Changing the width of one column in a document with equal-sized columns changes the width of all other columns so that they remain equal. Changing the width in a document with unequal columns changes only that column. You can also double click the top of the ruler to display the Page Setup dialog box, then click the Margins tab to change the left and right margins, which in turn will change the column width.

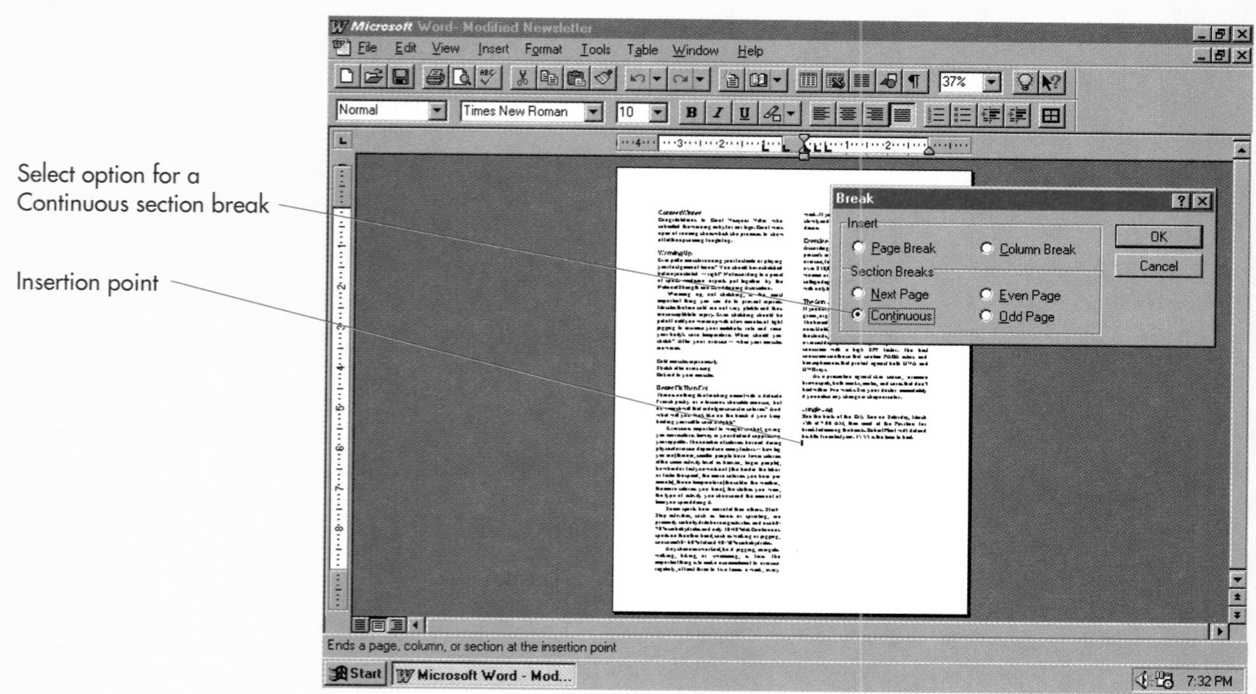

(b) Balance the Columns (step 3)

FIGURE 2.4 Hands-on Exercise 1 (continued)

STEP 4: Create the Masthead

- Use the **Zoom Control box** on the Standard toolbar to change to **Page Width.** Click the **Show/Hide ¶ button** to display the paragraph (and section) marks.
- Press **Ctrl+Home** to move to the beginning of the document.
- Pull down the **Insert menu.** Click **Break.** Click the **Continuous button.** Click **OK** to produce a double dotted line, indicating a section break as shown in Figure 2.4c.
- Click above the dotted line, which will place the insertion point to the left of the line. Check the status bar to be sure you are in section one, then format this section as a single column as follows:
  - Pull down the **Format menu,** click **Columns,** choose **One** from the Presets column formats, and click **OK,** or
  - Click the **Columns button** on the Standard toolbar and select one column.

COLUMNS AND SECTIONS

Columns are implemented at the section level, and thus a new section is required whenever the number of columns changes within a document. Select the text that is to be formatted in columns, click the Columns button on the Standard toolbar, then drag the mouse to set the desired number of columns. Microsoft Word will automatically insert the section breaks before and after the selected text.

- ➤ Type **The Athlete's Hi** and press **enter** twice. Select the newly entered text as shown in Figure 2.4c. Click the **Center button** on the Formatting toolbar. Change the font to **60 pt Arial Bold.**
- ➤ Save the newsletter.

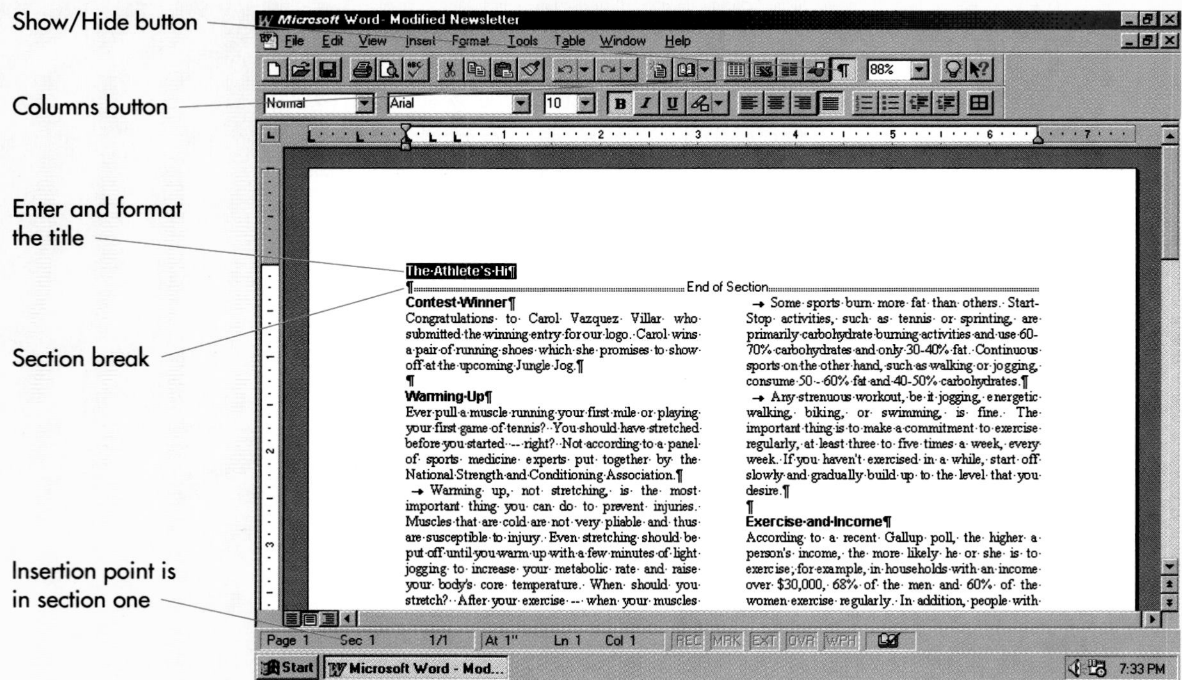

(c) Create the Masthead (step 4)

FIGURE 2.4 Hands-on Exercise 1 (continued)

STEP 5: Add Lines to the Masthead

- ➤ Press **Ctrl+Home** to move to the beginning of the newsletter. Click anywhere within the paragraph containing **The Athlete's Hi.**
- ➤ Pull down the **Format menu.** Click **Borders and Shading.** If necessary, click the **Borders tab** to produce the dialog box in Figure 2.4d.

BORDERS AND SHADING

The ***Borders and Shading command*** takes practice, but once you get used to it, you will love it. To place a border around multiple paragraphs (the paragraphs should have the same indents or else a different border will be placed around each paragraph), select the paragraphs prior to execution of the Borders and Shading command. Select (click) the line style you like, then click the Box or Shadow Preset button to place the border around the selected paragraphs. To change the border on one side, select (click) the side within the border model, then click the desired style. Click OK to exit the dialog box.

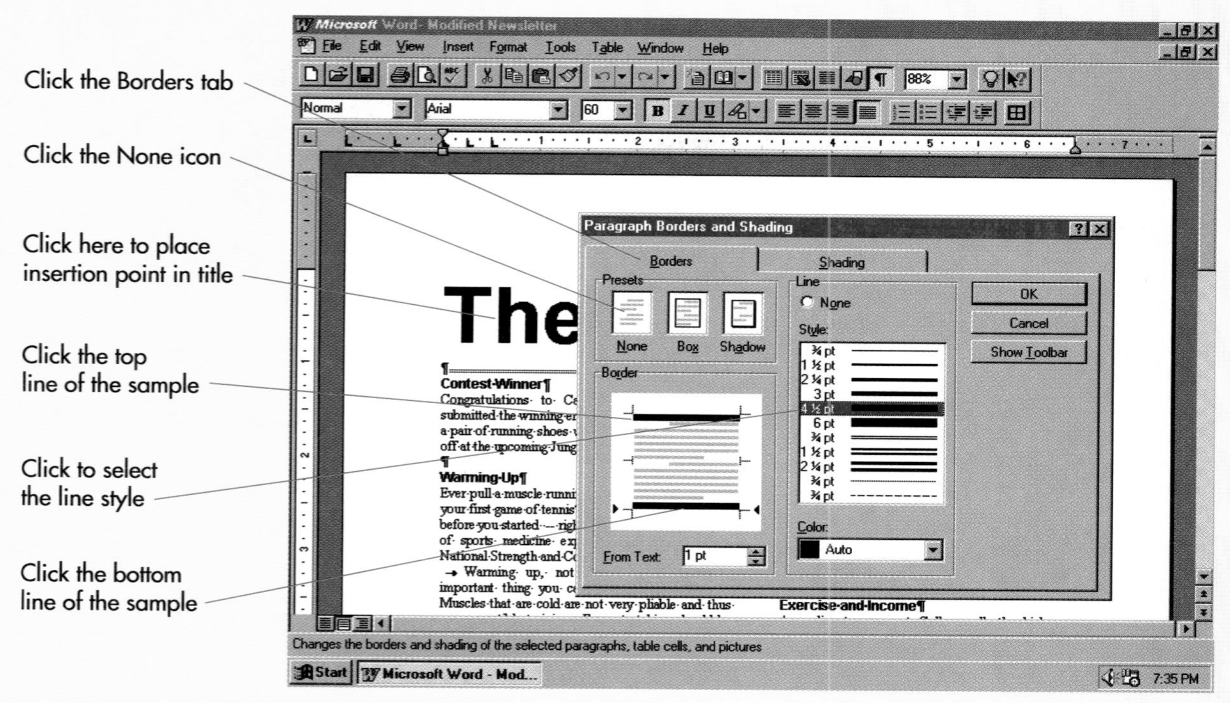
Click the Borders tab
Click the None icon
Click here to place insertion point in title
Click the top line of the sample
Click to select the line style
Click the bottom line of the sample
Paragraph Borders and Shading
Borders
Shading
Presets
None
Box
Shadow
Border
From Text
1 pt
Line
None
Style:
OK
Cancel
Show Toolbar
Color:
Auto
Changes the borders and shading of the selected paragraphs, table cells, and pictures

(d) Format the Masthead (step 5)

FIGURE 2.4 Hands-on Exercise 1 (continued)

- Click the **None icon** in the Presets area. Click the **top line** of the border model to apply a top border. Click the **4½** point line style. Click the **bottom line** of the model to apply the same line to the bottom border.
- Click **OK** to return to the document. The masthead should be enclosed in parallel horizontal lines.
- Save the newsletter.

STEP 6: Bulleted and Numbered Lists

- Scroll in the document until you come to the list at the end of the Warming Up paragraph. Select the entire list as shown in Figure 2.4e.
- Pull down the **Format menu.** Click **Bullets and Numbers.** If necessary, click the **Numbered tab** to produce the dialog box in the figure.
- Choose a number style. Click **OK** to return to the document, which now contains a numbered list.
- Click at the end of the first item on the list. Press the **enter key** to begin a new line and enter a new item, **Begin with light jogging.** Microsoft Word automatically renumbers the list to include the item you just typed.
- Drag the mouse to select all four items on the list (the numbers will not be highlighted). Click the **Bullets button** on the Formatting toolbar to change to a bulleted list.
- Click the **Increase Indent button** on the Formatting toolbar to indent the entire list to the next tab stop. Click the **Decrease Indent button** to move the list to the previous tab stop. Click the **Increase Indent button** a second time to end with the bulleted items indented one tab stop.
- Click anywhere in the document to deselect the text. Save the newsletter.

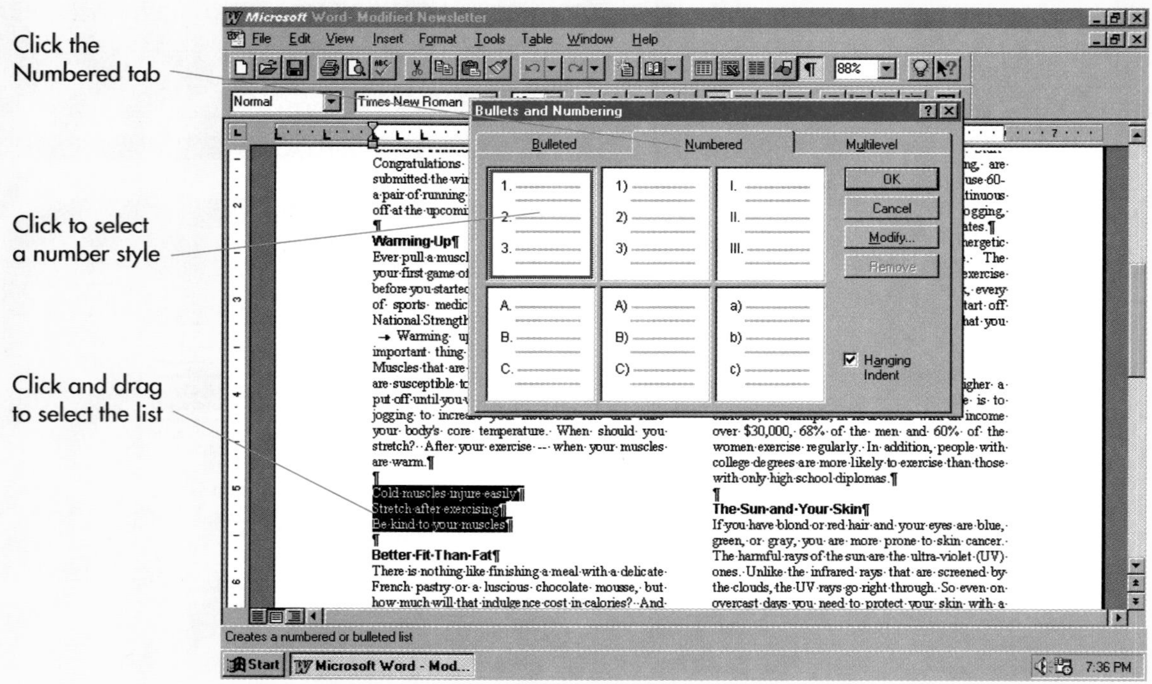

(e) Bullets and Numbering (step 6)

FIGURE 2.4 Hands-on Exercise 1 (continued)

LISTS AND THE FORMATTING TOOLBAR

The Formatting toolbar contains four buttons for use with bulleted and numbered lists. The Increase Indent and Decrease Indent buttons move the selected items one tab stop to the right and left, respectively. The Bullets button creates a bulleted list from unnumbered items or converts a numbered list to a bulleted list. The Numbering button creates a numbered list or converts a bulleted list to numbers. The Bullets and Numbering buttons also function as toggle switches; for example, clicking the Bullets button when a bulleted list is in effect will remove the bullets.

STEP 7: The Completed Newsletter

- Use the **Zoom Control box** on the Standard toolbar to zoom to **Whole Page** to see the entire newsletter as in Figure 2.4f.
- Click the **Show/Hide ¶ button** to suppress the paragraph markers.
- Pull down the **File menu.** Click **Exit** if you do not want to continue with the next exercise at this time. Click **Close** to close the document and remain in Word.

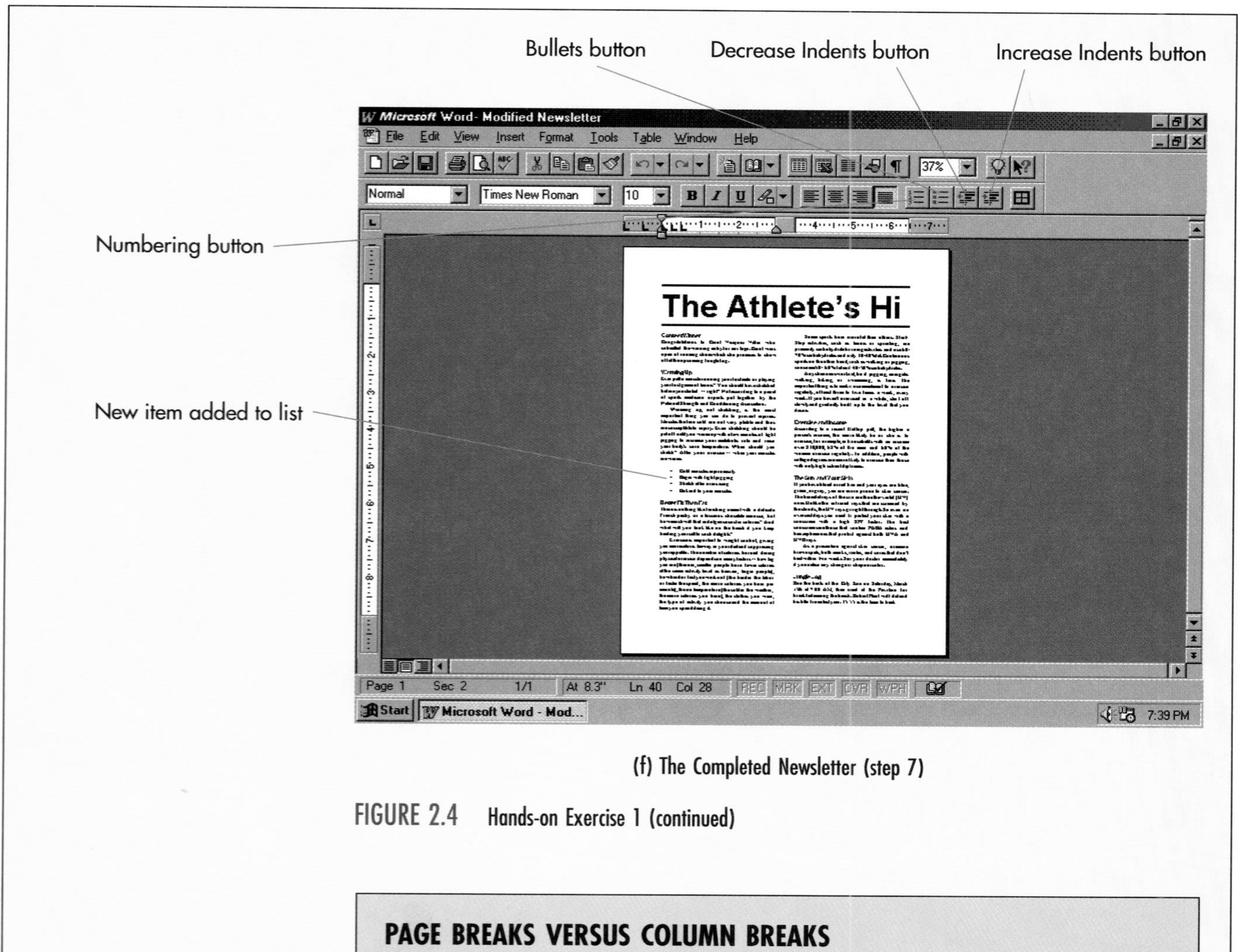

(f) The Completed Newsletter (step 7)

FIGURE 2.4 Hands-on Exercise 1 (continued)

PAGE BREAKS VERSUS COLUMN BREAKS

Press Ctrl+enter to create a hard page break in order to begin the next line on a new page. Press Ctrl+Shift+enter when columns are in effect to create a column break and begin the next line in a new column.

GRAPHICS

The right picture adds immeasurably to a document. ***Clip art*** (graphic images) is available from a variety of sources. You can use the Insert Object command to insert an image from the Microsoft ClipArt Gallery (an application included in Microsoft Office). You can also use the Insert Picture command to select from an entirely different set of clip art images.

The ***Insert Picture command*** enables you to select a clip art image from anywhere on your system. A set of sample images is installed automatically in a Clipart folder when you install Microsoft Word or Microsoft Office. Execution of the Insert Picture command displays the dialog box of Figure 2.5a, which lets you preview a picture prior to inserting it. The available pictures (e.g., the graphics in the Clipart folder) are shown in the Name list box. All you do is select (click) a graphic, then click the OK command button to insert the graphic into the document.

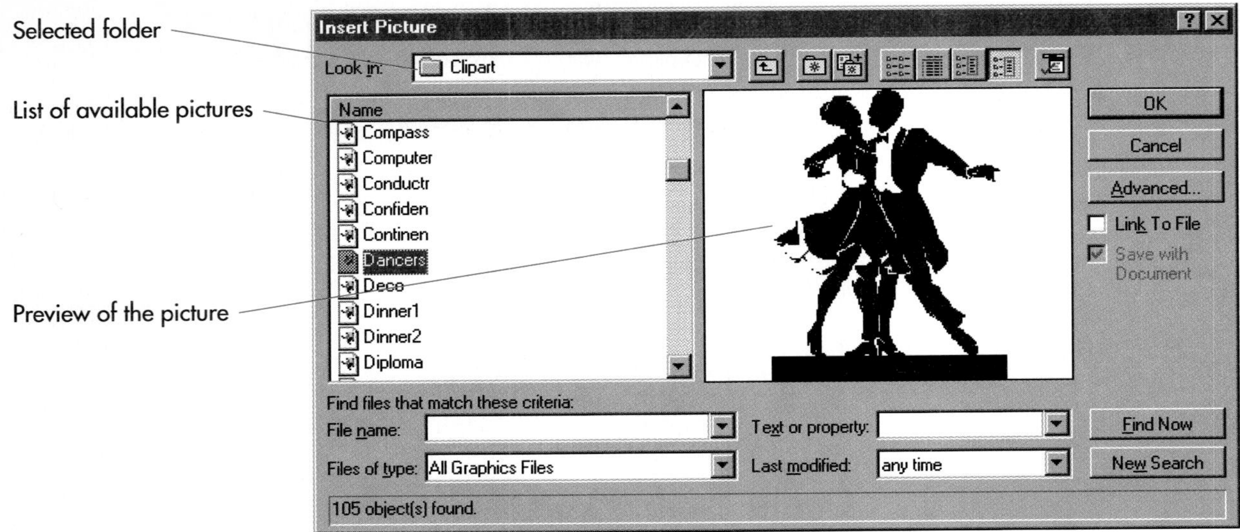

(a) Insert Picture Command

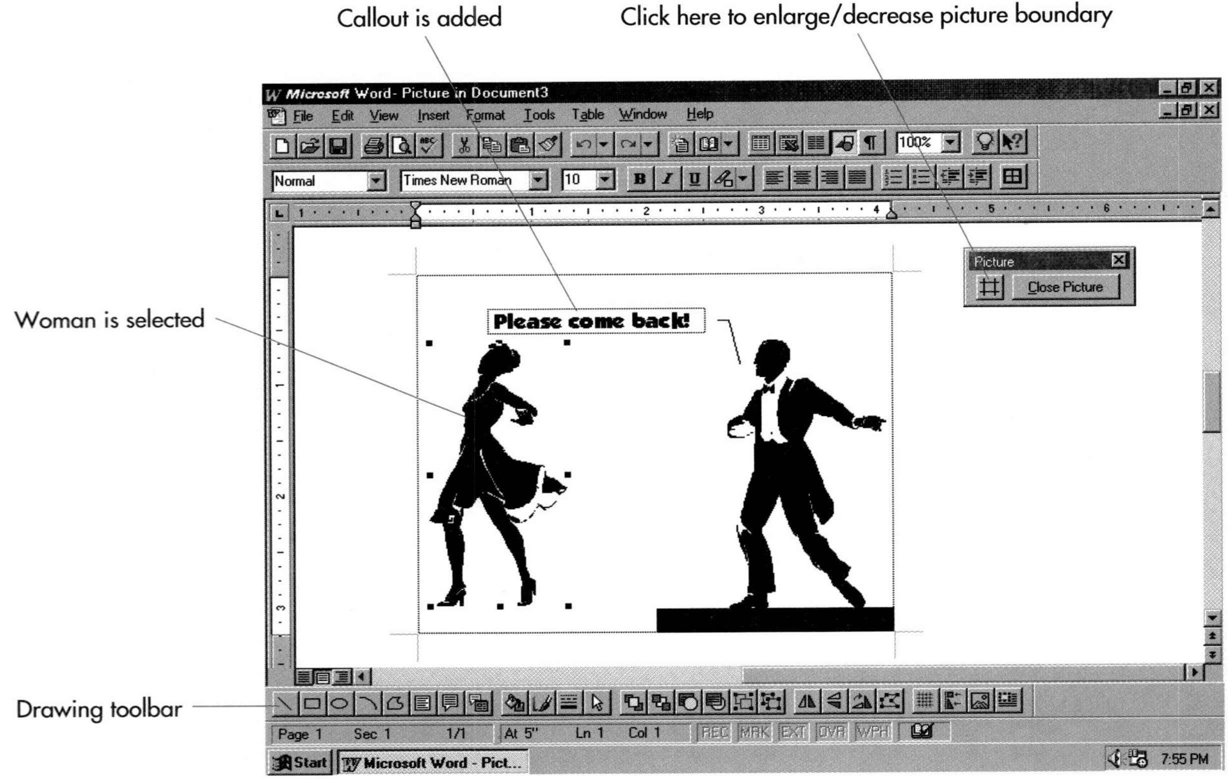

(b) Modifying a Picture

FIGURE 2.5 Graphics

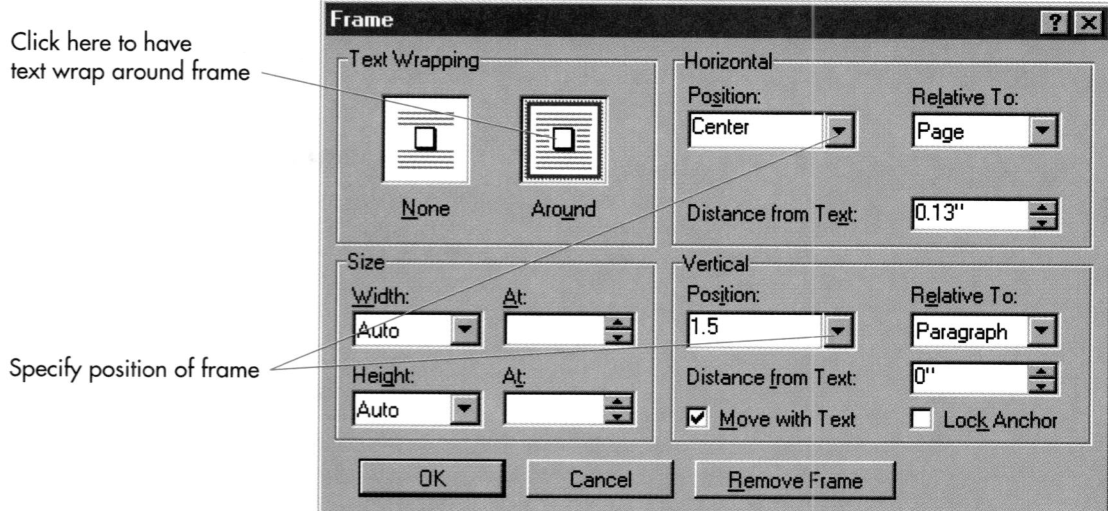

(c) Format Frame Command

Once a graphic has been inserted into a document, you can change its size, change its position, or even modify its content. Clicking the object selects it and lets you move or size the object within the document. Double clicking the object loads the drawing portion of Word in order to modify the picture. Once a graphic has been inserted into a document, you can change its size, change its position, or even modify its content. Clicking the object selects it and lets you move or size the object within the document. Double clicking the object loads the drawing portion of Word in order to modify the picture. Once a graphic has been inserted into a document, you can change its size, change its position, or even modify its content. Clicking the object selects it and lets you move or size the object within the document. Double clicking the object loads the drawing portion of Word in order to modify the picture. Once a

graphic has been inserted into a document, you can change its size, change its position, or even modify its content. Clicking the object selects it and lets you move or size the object within the document. Double clicking the object loads the drawing portion of Word in order to modify the picture. Once a graphic has been inserted into a document, you can change its size, change its position, or even modify its content. Clicking the object selects it and lets you move or size the object within the document. Double clicking the object loads the drawing portion of Word in order to modify the picture. Once a graphic has been inserted into a document, you can change its size, change its position, or even modify its content. Clicking the object selects it and lets you move or size the object within the document. Double clicking the object loads the drawing portion of Word in order to modify the picture.

(d) The Completed Document

FIGURE 2.5 Graphics (continued)

Once a graphic has been inserted into a document, you can change its size or position or even modify its content. Clicking the object selects it and lets you align or size the object within the document. Double clicking the object loads the program that created the graphic in order to modify the picture, as shown in Figure 2.5b.

Microsoft Word includes a complete set of drawing tools to create and/or modify the graphics supplied with Word. The picture is displayed in the window with the ***drawing toolbar*** displayed at the bottom of the window. You can add shapes, change colors, flip or rotate the image, or add callouts. (ToolTips are displayed when you point to a tool to indicate its function.) Online help is available just as it is for every other Windows application. So too is the Undo command, which we find invaluable.

The complete capabilities of the drawing program are beyond the present discussion, but you will be surprised at what you can do with a little bit of experimentation. We modified the Dancers graphic by selecting the woman, clicking the tool to rotate her about the vertical axis, then dragging her away from her partner. We also added a call out in which the man asks her to come back.

DROP CAPS

Drop caps add interest to a document and are created through the Drop Cap command in the Format menu. Click at the beginning of a paragraph (where the drop cap is to appear), pull down the Format Menu, and click Drop Cap. Choose the type of drop cap you want, its font, and the number of lines to drop, then click OK. The drop cap will be inserted into a frame in the document.

Frames

A ***frame*** is a special type of (invisible) container that holds an object such as a piece of clip art. It provides the easiest way to position an object within a document and/or to wrap text around the object. Anything at all can be placed into a frame—a picture, a table, a dropped capital letter, or an object created by another application, such as a spreadsheet created by Microsoft Excel.

Once an object has been placed in a frame, it can be dragged into position using the mouse or aligned more precisely using the dialog box within the ***Format Frame command*** shown in Figure 2.5c. The command enables you to specify the precise horizontal and vertical location of the frame. It also determines whether or not text is to wrap around the frame.

Figure 2.5d displays a document containing text and the Dancers graphic. (We decided to reunite our dancers and use the original picture). The text wraps around the graphic in accordance with the specifications in the Format Frame command of Figure 2.5c. The horizontal and vertical placement of the graphic are also consistent with the placement options within the Format Frame command. (Placing an object in a frame does not create a border for the object, which is done through the Borders and Shading command.)

TO FRAME OR NOT TO FRAME

Enclosing an object in a frame lets you position it freely on the page and/or wrap text around the object. Without a frame, the object is treated as an ordinary paragraph, and movement is restricted to one of three positions (left, center, or right). Text cannot be wrapped around an unframed object.

HANDS-ON EXERCISE 2

Graphics

Objective: Insert a picture into a document, then modify the picture to include your initials; frame the picture, then size and move the graphic within the document. Create a drop cap, boxed text, and reverse for emphasis. Use Figure 2.6 as a guide.

STEP 1: Load the Newsletter

- Open the **Modified Newsletter document** from the previous exercise. If necessary, change to the **Page Layout** view and zoom to **Page Width.**
- Pull down the **File menu,** click **Page Setup,** and if necessary, click the **Margins tab** to produce the dialog box in Figure 2.6a.

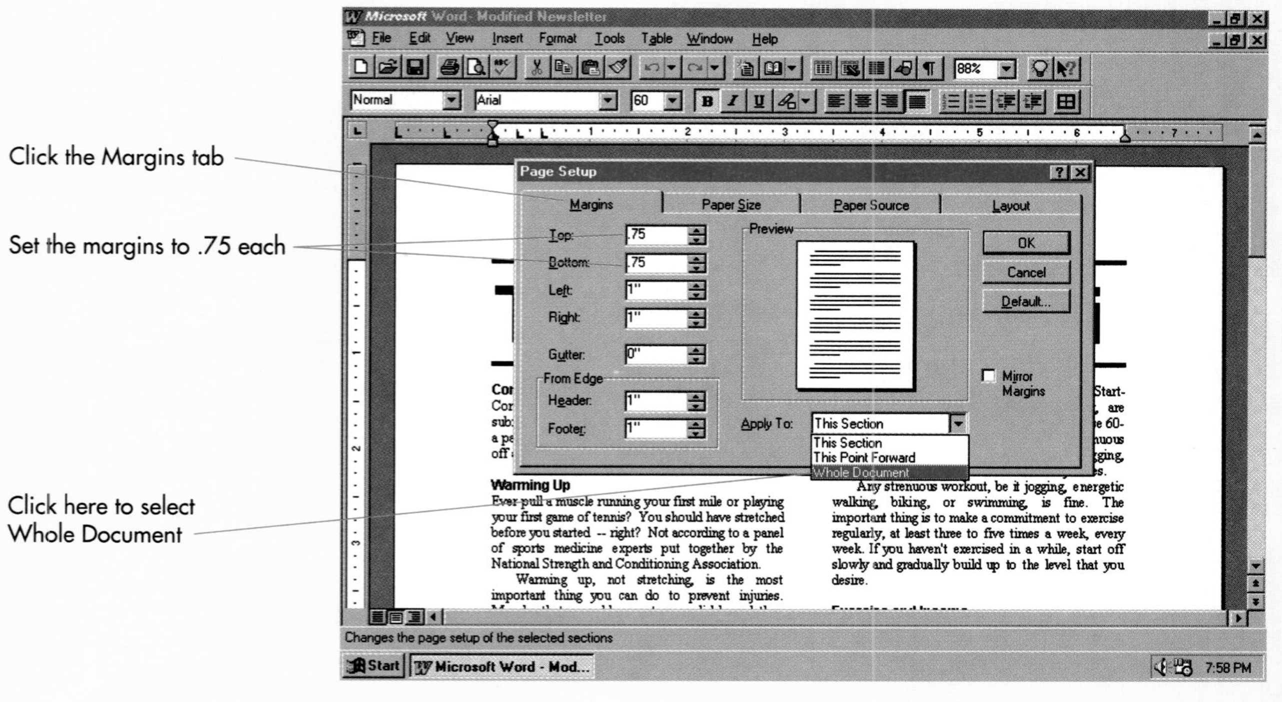

(a) Page Setup Command (step 1)

FIGURE 2.6 Hands-on Exercise 2

- Change the top and bottom margins to **.75** and **.75** as shown in the figure. Click the **arrow** in the **Apply To list box** and select **Whole Document.** Click **OK.**

STEP 2: Add the Graphic

- Click in the blank line at the end of the paragraph announcing the contest winner. Pull down the **Insert menu.** Click **Picture** to produce the dialog box of Figure 2.6b.
- The Clipart folder should already be selected, but if not, you must indicate where the clip art can be found.
    - Click the **down arrow** in the **Look in box.** Click drive C, the drive where Microsoft Word or Microsoft Office is typically installed.
    - Scroll until you can double click the **Winword** or **MSOffice folder** (depending on whether Word or Microsoft Office has been installed) to display its contents, which should include the Clipart folder. Double click the **Clipart folder.**
- The list of available figures should be visible as shown in Figure 2.6b. Click the **Preview button** if necessary, then scroll until you can select (click) the **Sports graphic.** Click **OK** to insert the figure into the document.
- Save the document.

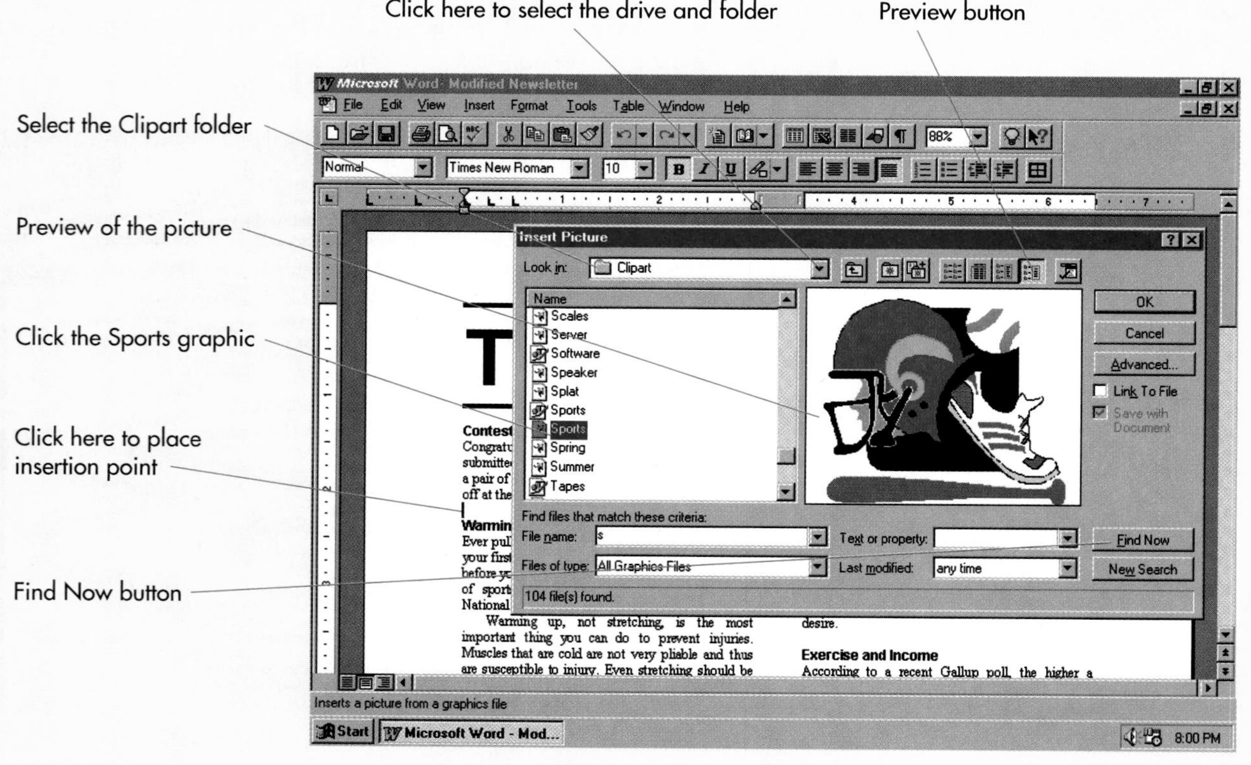

(b) Insert the Picture (step 2)

FIGURE 2.6 Hands-on Exercise 2 (continued)

THE FIND NOW COMMAND

The Find Now button, as its name implies, enables you to search for a specific graphic. Pull down the Insert menu, click Picture, then enter the (expected) title of the graphic you are searching for in the File name text box. Type "Sport", for example, if you are looking for a sports picture, then click the Find Now command button. Word will search for all graphic files that include "sport" in their title, then display only those files, making the selection of an appropriate picture much easier.

STEP 3: Insert a Frame

- Point to the graphic, then click the **left mouse button** to select the graphic and display the sizing handles. Pull down the **Insert menu.** Click **Frame.** The picture is now enclosed within a shaded border to indicate a frame.
- Check that the frame is still selected. Pull down the **Format menu.** Click **Frame** to produce the dialog box in Figure 2.6c.
  - Click the **arrow** on the **Horizontal Position box.** Click **Center.**
  - Click the **arrow** on the **Horizontal Relative To box.** Click **Column.**

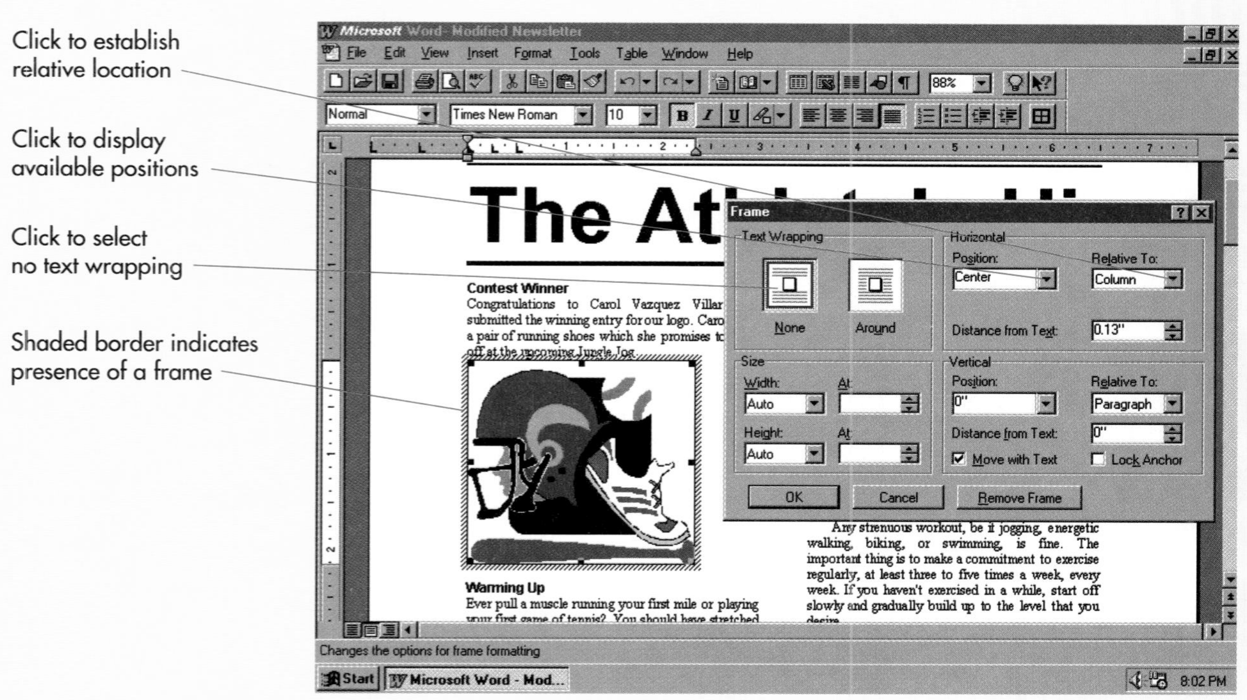

(c) Format the Frame (step 3)

FIGURE 2.6 Hands-on Exercise 2 (continued)

- The text may or may not wrap around the picture, depending on the size of the picture and the options in effect. (A minimum of one inch of text is required in order for the text to wrap.)
- If necessary, click the button to indicate **None** for Text Wrapping. Click **OK.** The sports picture should be centered within the left column.

➤ Save the newsletter.

PICTURES, FRAMES, AND SHORTCUT MENUS

Point to the border of a picture, then click the right mouse button to produce a shortcut menu. The commands in the menu will be appropriate for the selected object; that is, the menu will contain either the Frame Picture or the Format Frame command, depending on whether or not the graphic has already been framed.

STEP 4: Move and Size the Frame

➤ Use the **Zoom Control box** on the Standard toolbar to change to **Two Pages** as shown in Figure 2.6d; the newsletter may or may not spill to the second page, depending on the precise content of your document.

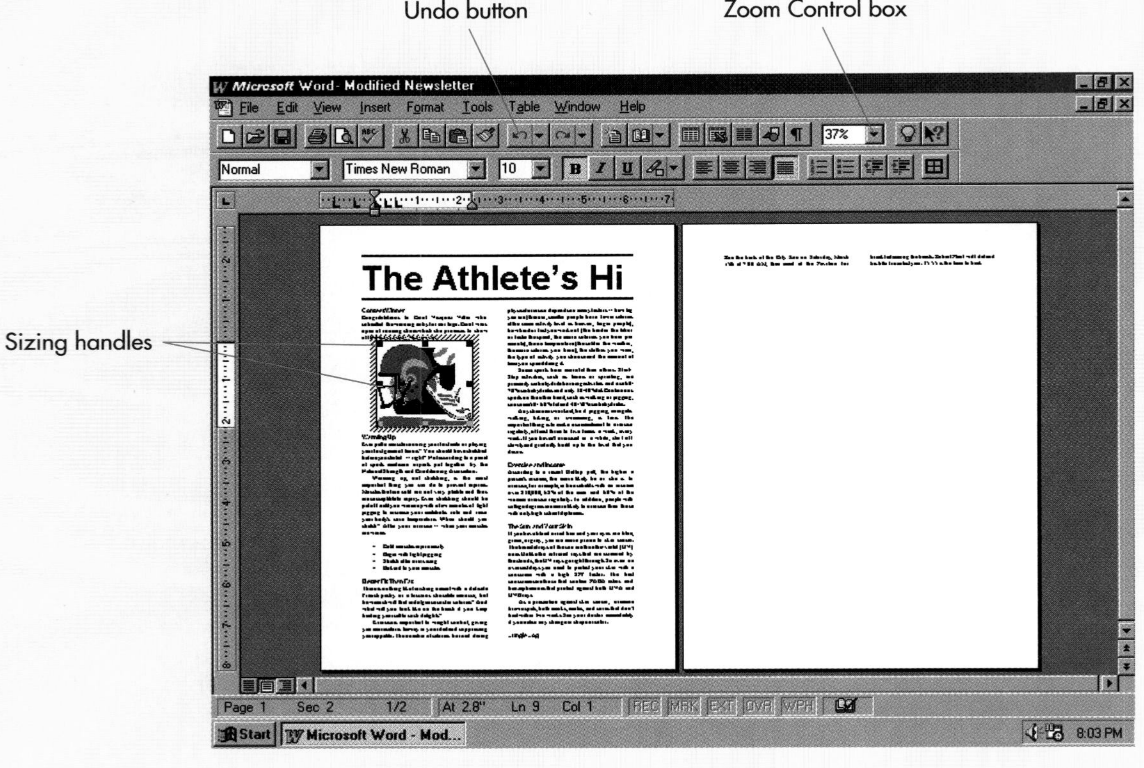

(d) Move and Size the Picture (step 4)

FIGURE 2.6 Hands-on Exercise 2 (continued)

➤ Point to the **graphic** (frame), then click the **left mouse button** to select the graphic and enclose it within the sizing handles. Experiment with moving and sizing the frame as follows:

- Drag a corner handle (the mouse pointer changes to a double arrow) to change the length and width simultaneously and keep the graphic in proportion.
- Drag a handle on the horizontal or vertical border to change one dimension only, which distorts the graphic.
- Drag any handle outward to increase the size of the picture or inward to shrink it.
- To move the frame, click the frame to select it, then drag the frame to its new position.
- To undo a move or sizing operation, click outside the frame to deselect it, then click the **Undo button** on the Standard toolbar.

➤ Move and/or size the frame so that the newsletter fits on a single page. Save the document.

STEP 5: Modify the Graphic

➤ Double click the **Sports graphic** in order to edit the picture in its own window as shown in Figure 2.6e. Click the **arrow** on the **Zoom Control box** on the toolbar and zoom to **200%.**

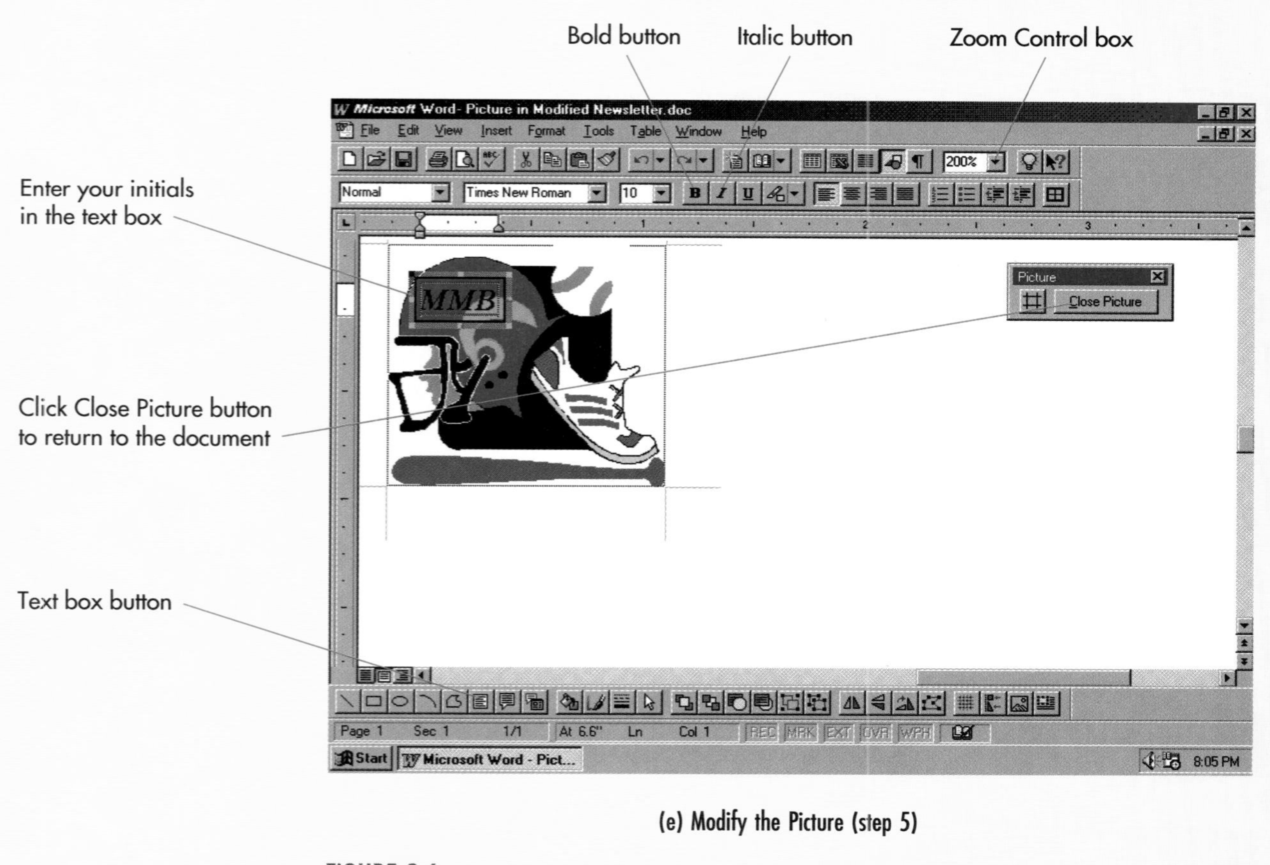

(e) Modify the Picture (step 5)

FIGURE 2.6 Hands-on Exercise 2 (continued)

- Click the **Text Box button** on the Drawing toolbar at the bottom of the window. Click the helmet in the drawing (the mouse pointer changes to a tiny cross) and drag the mouse to create a text box as shown in Figure 2.6e.
- Click the **Bold** and **Italics buttons** on the Formatting toolbar, then type your initials. (If you can't see all of your initials, click the border around the text box, then drag the sizing handles until you can see your initials.)
- Click the **Close Picture command button** to exit the drawing and return to the newsletter.

➤ Use the **Zoom Control box** to change to **Page Width.**

➤ Save the newsletter.

TO CLICK OR DOUBLE CLICK

Clicking an object selects the object and produces the sizing handles to move and/or size the object. Double clicking an object loads the application that created it and enables you to modify the object using the tools of that application.

STEP 6: The Masthead

➤ Press **Ctrl+Home** to move to the beginning of the document.

➤ Click the **Borders button** on the Formatting toolbar to display the Borders toolbar shown in Figure 2.6f.

➤ Click the **arrow** on the **Shading box** on the Borders toolbar. Choose **Solid (100%)** shading.

➤ Click outside the masthead to see the results. You should see white letters on a solid background (which is called a reverse).

➤ Save the newsletter.

STEP 7: Boxed and Shaded text

➤ Press **Ctrl+End** to move to the end of the newsletter. Select the paragraphs containing the Jungle Jog announcement along with its title.

➤ Click the **arrow** in the **Shading box** on the Borders toolbar. Choose **10%** shading.

➤ Click the **arrow** on the **Line style list box** to increase (decrease) the thickness of the line as you see fit. Click the **Outside border button** on the Borders toolbar to apply a border around the selected paragraphs.

➤ Click outside the selected text to see the results. Save the newsletter.

STEP 8: Add a Drop Cap

➤ Scroll to the beginning of the newsletter. Click immediately before the C in "Congratulations".

➤ Pull down the **Format menu.** Click **Drop Cap** to produce the dialog box in Figure 2.6g.

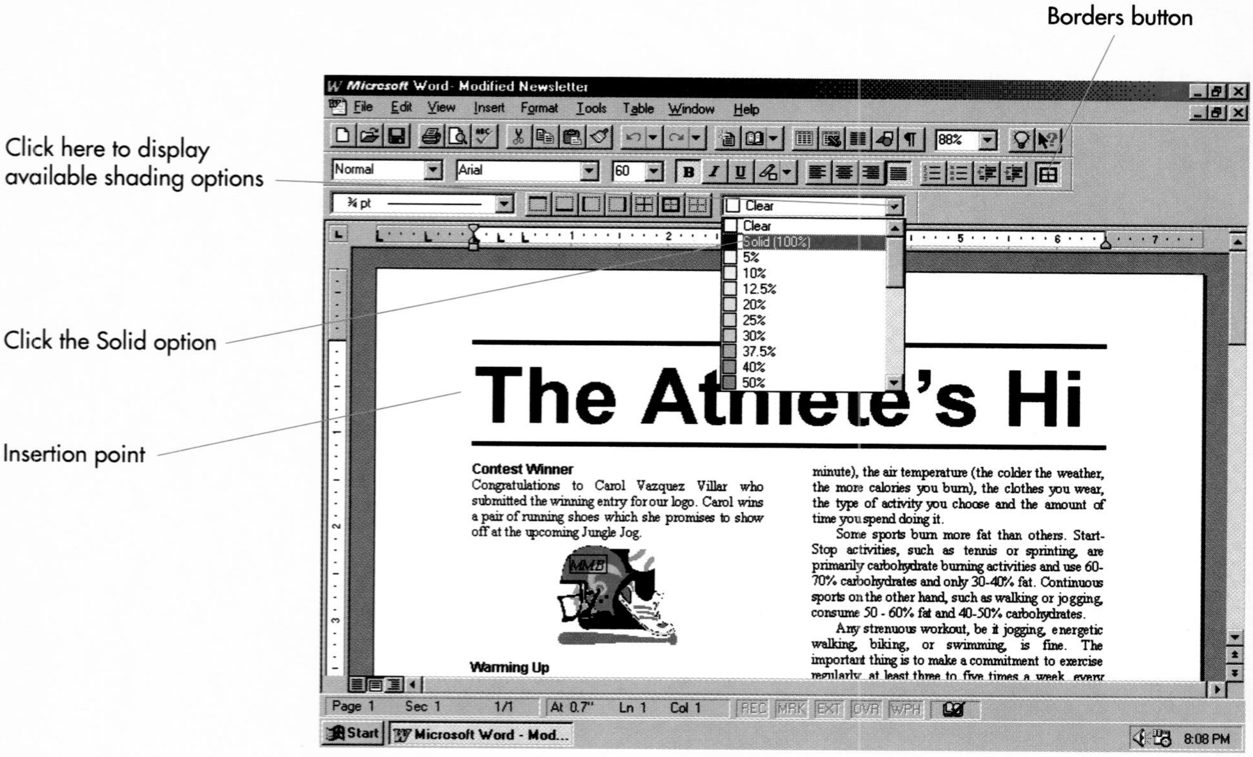

Borders button

Click here to display available shading options

Click the Solid option

Insertion point

(f) Borders and Shading (step 6)

Click here to select the Dropped cap

Click to the left of Congratulations

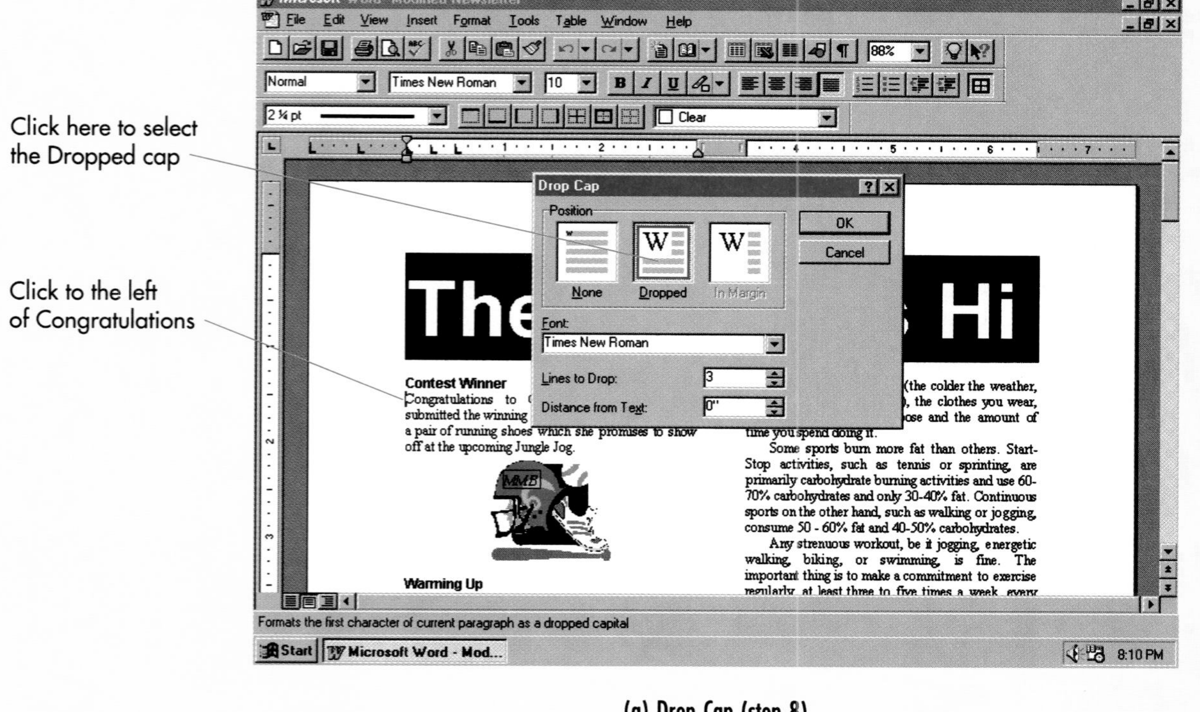

(g) Drop Cap (step 8)

FIGURE 2.6 Hands-on Exercise 2 (continued)

- Click the **Position icon** for **Dropped** as shown in the figure. You can also change the font, size (lines to drop), or distance from the text by clicking the arrow on the appropriate list box.
- Click **OK** to create the drop cap, exit the dialog box, and return to the document. Click outside the frame around the drop cap.
- Save the newsletter.

STEP 9: Change Column Formatting

- Click anywhere in the body of the newsletter, making sure you are in the second section.
- Pull down the **Format menu.** Click **Columns** to produce the dialog box in Figure 2.6h.
- Click the **Left Presets icon.** Change the width of the first column to **2″,** which automatically changes the width of the second column to 4″.
- Click the **Lines Between box.** Click **OK.**
- Use the **Zoom Control box** to zoom to **Whole Page** to display the completed newsletter as shown in Figure 2.6i. If necessary, size the graphic so that the newsletter fits on one page.
- Save the document a final time, then print the newsletter. Close the document. Exit Word.

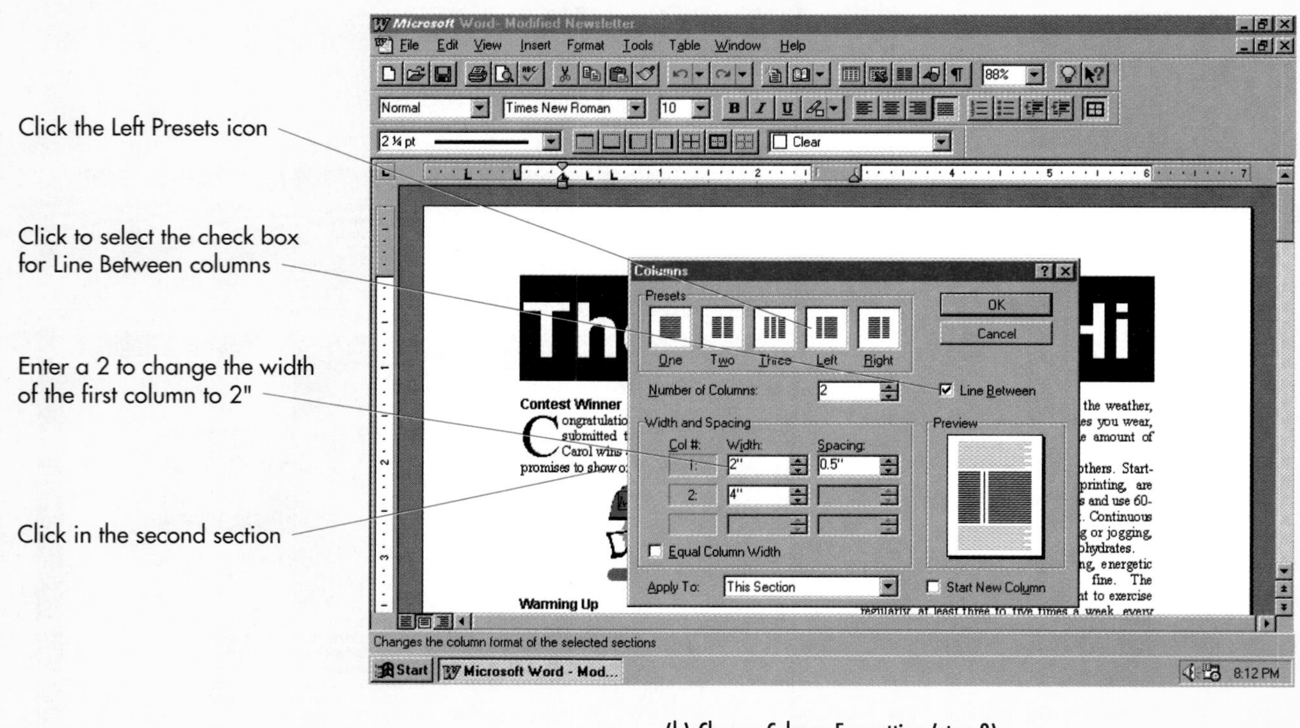

(h) Change Column Formatting (step 9)

FIGURE 2.6 Hands-on Exercise 2 (continued)

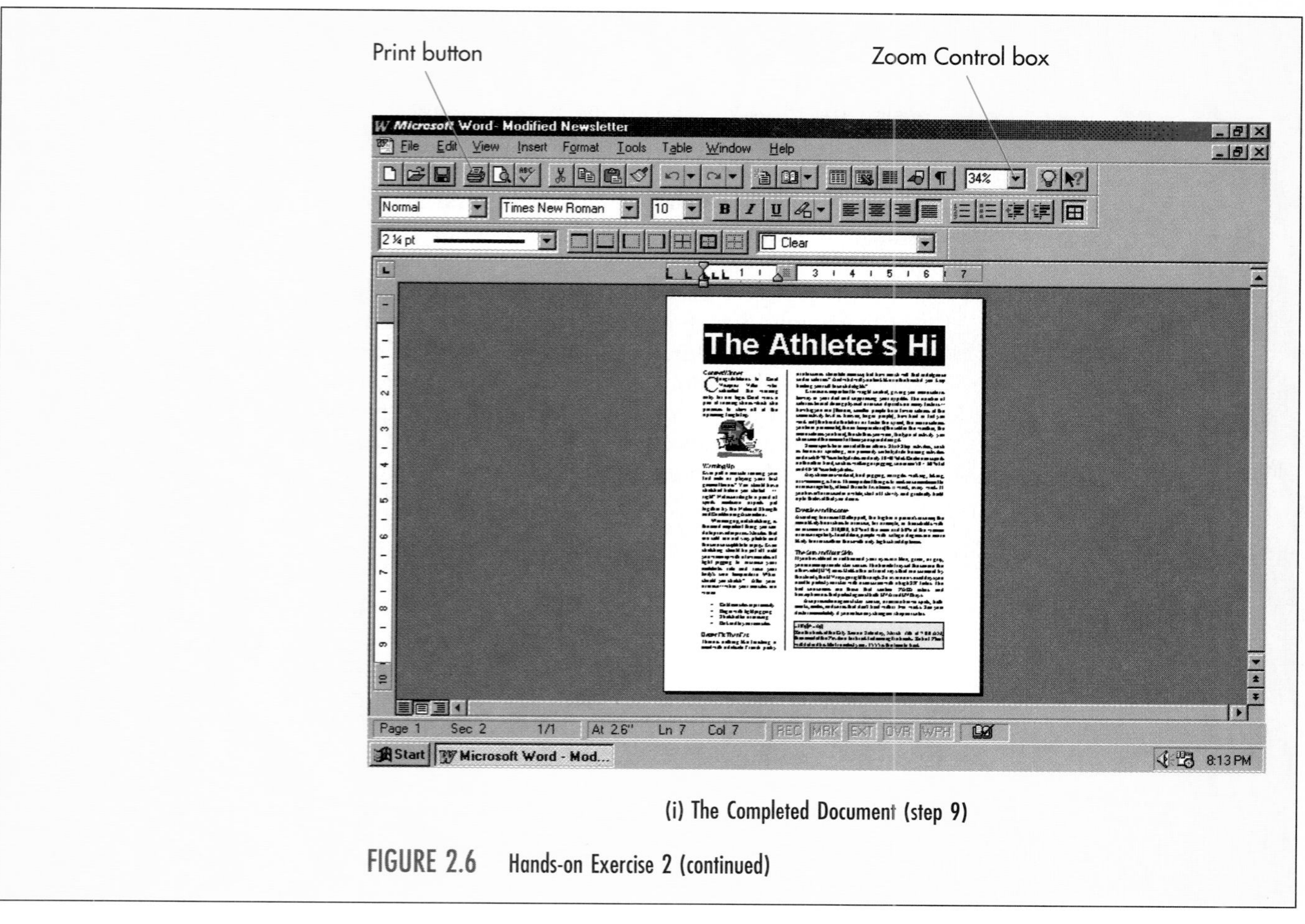

(i) The Completed Document (step 9)

FIGURE 2.6 Hands-on Exercise 2 (continued)

ELEMENTS OF GRAPHIC DESIGN

We trust you have completed the hands-on exercises without difficulty and that you were able to reproduce the newsletter. Realize, however, that the mere availability of Microsoft Word and a laser printer does not guarantee success in desktop publishing, any more than a word processor turns its author into a Shakespeare or a Hemingway. Other skills are necessary, and so we conclude with an introduction to basic principles of graphic design.

Much of what we say is subjective, and what works in one situation will not necessarily work in another. Your eye is the best judge of all, and you should stick to your own instincts. Experiment freely and realize that successful design is the result of trial and error. Seek inspiration from others by maintaining a file of publications, with examples of both good and bad design, and use the file as the basis for your own publications.

The Grid

The design of a document should be developed on a ***grid,*** an underlying, but *invisible,* set of horizontal and vertical lines that determine the placement of the major elements. A grid establishes the overall structure of a document by indicating the number of columns, the space between columns, the size of the margins, the placement of headlines, art, and so on. The grid does *not* appear in the printed document nor on the screen.

A grid may be simple or complex, but is always distinguished by the number of columns it contains. The three-column grid of Figures 2.7a and 2.7b is one of the most common and utilitarian designs. Figure 2.7c shows a four-column design for the same document, with unequal column widths to provide interest. Figure 2.7d illustrates a five-column grid that is often used with large amounts of text. Many other designs are possible as well. A one-column grid is used for term papers and letters. A two-column, wide and narrow format is appropriate for textbooks and manuals. Two- and three-column formats are used for newsletters and magazines.

The simple concept of a grid should make the underlying design of any document obvious, which in turn gives you an immediate understanding of page composition. Moreover, the conscious use of a grid will help you organize your material and result in a more polished and professional-looking publication. It will also help you to achieve consistency from page to page within a document (or from issue to issue of a newsletter). Indeed, much of what goes wrong in desktop publishing stems from failing to follow or use the underlying grid.

White Space

White space, or space that is free of text and art, is underutilized by most newcomers to graphic design. White space is essential, however, to provide contrast, and to give the eye a place to rest; conversely, the lack of white space makes a document crowded and difficult to read, as seen in Figure 2.8a.

White space is introduced into a document in several ways, but not every document will use every technique. White space will appear:

- Around a headline; surrounding a headline with white space gives it additional emphasis.
- In the page margins (left, right, top, and bottom); a minimum of one inch all around is a generally accepted guideline.
- Between columns in a multicolumn layout; the wider the columns, the more space is required between the columns.
- Between lines of text through adequate space between the lines.
- In paragraph indents and/or the ragged line endings of left-aligned type.
- Around a figure to emphasize the art.
- Between paragraphs through use of a paragraph spacing command; this subtlety increases the space after a hard carriage return and gives a more professional appearance than double spacing between paragraphs, which adds too much space.

White space can be used as a design element by leaving a column empty (or almost empty) as was done in Figures 2.8b and 2.8c. The use of vertical white space in this fashion is a very effective tool. White space is *not* attractive, however, when it is trapped in the middle of a page as in Figure 2.8d.

Emphasis

Good design makes it easy for the reader to determine what is important. ***Emphasis*** is achieved in several ways, the easiest being variations in type size and/or type style. Headings should be set in type sizes (at least two points) larger than the subheadings, which in turn should be larger than body copy. The use of **boldface** is effective as are *italics,* but both should be done in moderation. Shading, reverses (white letters on a black background), or boxes are also effective.

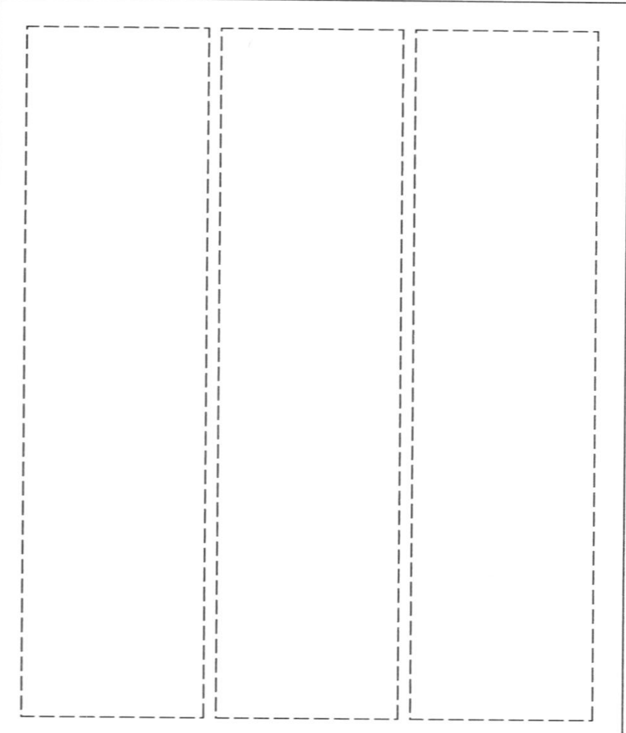

(a) Empty Three-column Grid

No can do

He felt more and more pressure to play the game of not playing. Maybe that's why he stepped in front of that truck.

People wonder why people do things like this, but all you have to do is look around and see all the stress and insanity each person in responsibility is required to put up with. There is no help or end in sight. It seems that managers are managing less and shoveling the workloads on to their underlings. This seems to be the overall response to the absence of raises or benefit packages they feel are their entitlement. Something must be done now!

People wonder why people do things like this, but all you have to do is look around and see all the stress and insanity each person in responsibility is required to put up with. There is no help or end in sight. It seems that managers are managing less and shoveling the workloads on to their underlings. This seems to be the overall response to the absence of raises or benefit packages they feel are their entitlement. Something must be done now!

People wonder why people do things like this, but all you have to do is look around and see all the stress and insanity each person in responsibility is required to put up with. There is no help or end in sight. It seems that managers are managing less and shoveling the workloads on to their underlings. This seems to be the overall response to the absence of raises or benefit packages they feel are their entitlement.

People wonder why people do things like this, but all you have to do is look around and see all the stress and insanity each person in responsibility is required to put up with. There is no help or end in sight. It seems that managers are managing less and shoveling the workloads on to their underlings. This seems to be the overall response to the absence of raises or benefit packages they feel are their entitlement. Something must be done now!

People wonder why people do things like this, but all you have to do is look around and see all the stress and insanity each person in responsibility is required to put up with. There is no help or end in sight. It seems that managers are managing less. Something must be done now!

People wonder why people do things like this, but all you have to do is look around and see all the stress and insanity each person in ▼

(b) Three-column Grid

No can do

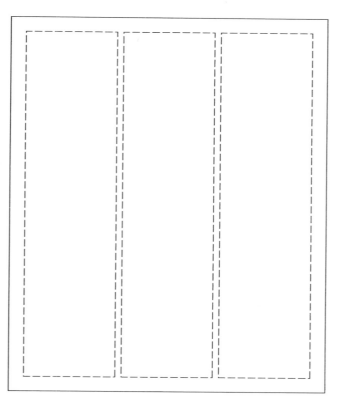

He felt more and more pressure to play the game of not playing. Maybe that's why he stepped in front of that truck.

People wonder why people do things like this, but all you have to do is look around and see all the stress and insanity each person in responsibility is required to put up with. There is no help or end in sight. It seems that managers are managing less and shoveling the workloads on to their underlings. This seems to be the overall response to the absence of raises or benefit packages they feel are their entitlement. Something must be done now!

People wonder why people do things like this, but all you have to do is look around and see all the stress and insanity each person in responsibility is required to put up with. There is no help or end in sight. It seems that managers are managing less and shoveling the workloads on to their underlings. This seems to be the overall response to the absence of raises or benefit packages they feel are their entitlement. Something must be done now!

People wonder why people do things like this, but all you have to do is look around and see all the stress and insanity each person in responsibility is required to put up with. There is no help or end in sight. It seems that managers are managing less and shoveling the workloads on to their underlings. This seems to be the overall response to the absence of raises or benefit packages they feel are their entitlement.

People wonder why people do things like this, but all you have to do is look around and see all the stress and insanity each person in responsibility is required to put up with. There is no help or end in sight. It seems that managers are managing less and shoveling the workloads on to their underlings. This seems to be the overall response to the absence of raises or benefit packages they feel are their entitlement. Something must be done now!

People wonder why people do things like this, but all you have to do is look around and see all the stress and insanity each person in responsibility is required to put up with. There is no help or end in sight. It seems that managers are managing less. Something must be done now!

People wonder why people do things like this, but all you have to do is look around and see all the stress and insanity each person in responsibility is required to put up with. There is no help or end in sight. It seems that managers are managing less and shoveling the workloads on to their underlings. This seems to be the overall response to the ▼

(c) Four-column Grid

People wonder why people do things like this, but all you have to do is look around and see all the stress and insanity each person in responsibility is required to put up with. There is no help or end in sight. It seems that managers are managing less and shoveling the workloads on to their underlings. This seems to be the overall response to the absence of raises or benefit packages they feel are their entitlement. Something must be done!

People wonder why people do things like this, but all you have to do is look around and see all the stress and insanity each person in responsibility is required to put up with. There is no help or end in sight. It seems that managers are managing less and shoveling the workloads on to their underlings. This seems to be the overall response to the absence of raises or benefit packages they feel are their entitlement. Something must be done now!

People wonder why people do things like this, but all you have to do is look around and see all the stress and insanity each person in responsibility is required to put up with. There is no help or end in sight. It seems that managers are managing less and shoveling the workloads on to their underlings. This seems to be the overall response to the absence of raises or benefit packages they feel are their entitlement. Something must be done now!

People wonder why people do things like this, but all you have to do is look around and see all the stress and insanity each person in responsibility is required to put up with. There is no help or end in sight. It seems that managers are managing less and shoveling the workloads on to their underlings. This seems to be the overall response to the absence of raises or benefit packages they feel are their entitlement. Something must be done now!

People wonder why people do things like this, but all you have to do is look around and see all the stress and insanity each person in responsibility is required to put up with. There is no help or end in sight. It seems that managers are managing less and shoveling the workloads on to their underlings. This seems to be the overall response to the absence of raises or benefit packages they feel are their entitlement. Something must be done!

He felt more and more pressure to play the game of not playing. Maybe that's why he stepped in front of that truck.

People wonder why people do things like this, but all you have to do is look around and see all the stress and insanity each person in responsibility is required to put up with. There is no help or end in sight. It seems that managers are managing less and shoveling the workloads on to their underlings. This seems to be the overall response to the absence of raises or benefit packages they feel are their entitlement. Something must be done!

People wonder why people do things like this, but all you have to do is look around and see all the stress and insanity each person in responsibility is required to put up with. There is no help or end in sight. It seems that managers are managing less and shoveling the workloads on to their underlings. Something must be done now!

People wonder why people do things like this, but all you have to do ▼

(d) Five-column Grid

FIGURE 2.7 The Grid System of Design

An Uninviting Morass of Text

I came to his garden alone, while the dew was still on the roses. Sweet fragrances and the song of birds filled the air. His voice I heard, soft and clear, saying that this is an organic garden. All the flowers, shrubs and trees were so beautiful not because of chemicals, but because of supplying the correct natural nutrients needed by each of them. There were no harmful insects because these plantings were strong and full of vitality. The birds, which also doubled as bug snatchers, were attracted by the various flowers and berries. Indeed Mrs. Crabtree was a lucky woman to have such a delightful garden and such an inspired man as Adam to tend it.

I came to his garden alone, while the dew was still on the roses. Sweet fragrances and the song of birds filled the air. His voice I heard, soft and clear, saying that this is an organic garden. All the flowers, shrubs and trees were so beautiful not because of chemicals, but because of supplying the correct natural nutrients needed by each of them. There were no harmful insects because these plantings were strong and full of vitality. The birds, which also doubled as bug snatchers, were attracted by the various flowers and berries. Indeed Mrs. Crabtree was a lucky woman to have such a delightful garden and such an inspired man as Adam to tend it.

I came to his garden alone, while the dew was still on the roses. Sweet fragrances and the song of birds filled the air. His voice I heard, soft and clear, saying that this is an organic garden. All the flowers, shrubs and trees were so beautiful not because of chemicals, but because of supplying the correct natural nutrients needed by each of them. There were no harmful insects because these plantings were strong and full of vitality. The birds, which also doubled as bug snatchers, were attracted by the various flowers and berries. Indeed Mrs. Crabtree was a lucky woman to have such a delightful garden and such an inspired man as Adam to tend it.

I came to his garden alone, while the dew was still on the roses. Sweet fragrances and the song of birds filled the air. His voice I heard, soft and clear, saying that this is an organic garden. All the flowers, shrubs and trees were so beautiful not because of chemicals, but because of supplying the correct natural nutrients needed by each of them. There were no harmful insects because these plantings were strong and full of vitality. The birds, which also doubled as bug snatchers, were attracted by the various flowers and berries. Indeed Mrs. Crabtree was a lucky woman to have such a delightful garden and such an inspired man as Adam to tend it.

I came to his garden alone, while the dew was still on the roses. Sweet fragrances and the song of birds filled the air. His voice I heard, soft and clear, saying that this is an organic garden. All the flowers, shrubs and trees were so beautiful not because of chemicals, but because of supplying the correct natural nutrients needed by each of them. There were no harmful insects because these plantings were strong and full of vitality. The birds, which also doubled as bug snatchers, were attracted by the various flowers and berries. Indeed Mrs. Crabtree was a lucky woman to have such a delightful garden and such an inspired man as Adam to tend it.

I came to his garden alone, while the dew was still on the roses. Sweet fragrances and the song of birds filled the air. His voice I heard, soft and clear, saying that this is an organic garden. All the flowers, shrubs and trees were so beautiful not because of chemicals, but because of supplying the correct ▼

(a) Crowded Page

A Page Should Leave a Place for the Bird to Fly

I came to his garden alone, while the dew was still on the roses. Sweet fragrances and the song of birds filled the air. His voice I heard, soft and clear, saying that this is an organic garden. All the flowers, shrubs and trees were so beautiful not because of chemicals, but because of supplying the correct natural nutrients needed by each of them. There were no harmful insects because these plantings were strong and full of vitality. The birds, which also doubled as bug snatchers, were attracted by the various flowers and berries. Indeed Mrs. Crabtree was a lucky woman and to have such a delightful garden and such an inspired man as Adam to tend it.

I came to his garden alone, while the dew was still on the roses. Sweet fragrances and the song of birds filled the air. His voice I heard, soft and clear, saying that this is an organic garden. All the flowers, shrubs and trees were so beautiful not because of chemicals, but because of supplying the correct natural nutrients needed by each of them. There were no harmful insects because these plantings were strong and full of vitality. The birds, which also doubled as bug snatchers, were attracted by the various flowers and berries. Indeed Mrs. Crabtree was a lucky woman and to have such a delightful garden and such an inspired man as Adam to tend it.

I came to his garden alone, while the dew was still on the roses. Sweet fragrances and the song of birds filled the air. His voice I heard, soft and clear, saying that this is an organic garden. All the flowers, shrubs and trees were so beautiful not because of chemicals, but because of supplying the correct natural nutrients needed by each of them. There were no harmful insects because these plantings were strong and full of vitality. The birds, which also doubled as bug snatchers, were attracted by the various flowers and berries. Indeed Mrs. Crabtree was a lucky woman and to have such a delightful garden and such an inspired man as Adam to tend it. ▼

(b) White Space

Picking Flowers from Mrs. Crabtree's Garden

I came to his garden alone, while the dew was still on the roses. Sweet fragrances and the song of birds filled the air. His voice I heard, soft and clear, saying that this is an organic garden. All the flowers, shrubs and trees were so beautiful not because of chemicals, but because of supplying the correct natural nutrients needed by each of them. There were no harmful insects because these plantings were strong and full of vitality. The birds, which also doubled as bug snatchers, were attracted by the various flowers and berries. Indeed Mrs. Crabtree was a lucky woman to have such a delightful garden and such an inspired man as Adam to tend it.

I came to his garden alone, while the dew was still on the roses. Sweet fragrances and the song of birds filled the air. His voice I heard, soft and clear, saying that this is an organic garden. All the flowers, shrubs and trees were so beautiful not because of chemicals, but because of supplying the correct natural nutrients needed by each of them. There were no harmful insects because these plantings were strong and full of vitality. The birds, which also doubled as bug snatchers, were attracted by the various flowers and berries. Indeed Mrs. Crabtree was a lucky woman to have such a delightful garden and such an inspired man as Adam to tend it.

I came to his garden alone, while the dew was still on the roses. Sweet fragrances and the song of birds filled the air. His voice I heard, soft and clear, saying that this is an organic garden. All the flowers, shrubs and trees were so beautiful not because of ▼

(c) Emphasis

Picking Flowers from Mrs. Crabtree's Garden

I came to his garden alone, while the dew was still on the roses. Sweet fragrances and the song of birds filled the air. His voice I heard, soft and clear, saying that this is an organic garden. All the flowers, shrubs and trees were so beautiful not because of chemicals, but because of supplying the correct natural nutrients needed by each of them. There were no harmful insects because these plantings were strong and full of vitality. The birds, which also doubled as bug snatchers, were attracted by the various flowers and berries. Indeed Mrs. Crabtree was a lucky woman to have such a delightful garden and such an inspired man as Adam to tend it.

I came to his garden alone, while the dew was still on the roses. Sweet fragrances and the song of birds filled the air. His voice I heard, soft and clear, saying that this is an organic garden. All the flowers, shrubs and trees were so beautiful not because of chemicals, but because of supplying the correct natural nutrients needed by each of them. There were no harmful insects because these plantings were strong and full of vitality. The birds, which also doubled as bug snatchers, were attracted by the various flowers and berries. Indeed Mrs. Crabtree was a lucky woman to have such a delightful garden and such an inspired man as Adam to tend it.

I came to his garden alone, while the dew was still on the roses. Sweet fragrances and the song of birds filled the air. His voice I heard, soft and clear, saying that this is an organic garden. All the flowers, shrubs and trees were so beautiful not because of chemicals, but because of supplying the correct natural nutrients needed by each of them. ▼

(d) Trapped White Space

FIGURE 2.8 White Space as a Design Element

Facing Pages

A multipage document such as a manual, newsletter, or brochure is typically viewed two pages at a time by the reader. If this is true for your publication, it makes sense to develop ***facing pages*** as a unit, as opposed to creating the pages individually. This is illustrated by Figure 2.9a, which shows individually balanced pages that do not look very good together. Figure 2.9b rearranges the same material in a more appealing fashion. Use the Page Layout view in Microsoft Word and zoom to two pages to work on your document.

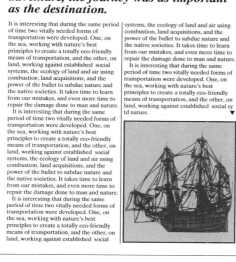

Tall Ships and Iron Horses: The Golden Age of Transportation?

It is interesting that during the same period of time two vitally needed forms of transportation were developed. One, on the sea, working with nature's best principles to create a totally eco-friendly means of transportation, and the other, on land, work-ing against established social systems, the ecology of land and air using combustion, land acquisitions, and the power of the bullet to subdue nature and the native societies. It takes time to learn from our mistakes, and even more time to repair the damage done to man and nature.

It is interesting that during the same period of time two vitally needed forms of transportation were developed. One, on the sea, working with nature's best principles to create a totally eco-friendly means of transportation, and the other, on land, work-ing against established social systems, the ecology of land and air using combustion, land acquisitions, and the power of the bullet to subdue nature and the native societies. It takes time to learn from our mistakes, and even more time to repair the damage done to man and nature.

It is interesting that during the same period of time two vitally needed forms of transportation were developed. One, on the sea, working with nature's best principles to create a totally eco-friendly means of transportation, and the other, on land, work-ing against established social systems, the ecology of land and air using combustion, land acquisitions, and the power of the bullet to subdue nature and the native ▼

In the days when travel was a real adventure, the journey was as important as the destination.

It is interesting that during the same period of time two vitally needed forms of transportation were developed. One, on the sea, working with nature's best principles to create a totally eco-friendly means of transportation, and the other, on land, working against established social systems, the ecology of land and air using combustion, land acquisitions, and the power of the bullet to subdue nature and the native societies. It takes time to learn from our mistakes, and even more time to repair the damage done to man and nature.

It is interesting that during the same period of time two vitally needed forms of transportation were developed. One, on the sea, working with nature's best principles to create a totally eco-friendly means of transportation, and the other, on land, working against established social systems, the ecology of land and air using combustion, land acquisitions, and the power of the bullet to subdue nature and the native societies. It takes time to learn from our mistakes, and even more time to repair the damage done to man and nature.

It is interesting that during the same period of time two vitally needed forms of transportation were developed. One, on the sea, working with nature's best principles to create a totally eco-friendly means of transportation, and the other, on land, working against established social systems, the ecology of land and air using combustion, land acquisitions, and the power of the bullet to subdue nature and the native societies. It takes time to learn from our mistakes, and even more time to repair the damage done to man and nature.

It is interesting that during the same period of time two vitally needed forms of transportation were developed. One, on the sea, working with nature's best principles to create a totally eco-friendly means of transportation, and the other, on land, working against established social sy td nature. ▼

(a) Pages Balanced Individually

Tall Ships and Iron Horses: The Golden Age of Transportation?

In the days when travel was a real adventure, the journey was as important as the destination.

It is interesting that during the same period of time two vitally needed forms of transportation were developed. One, on the sea, working with nature's best principles to create a totally eco-friendly means of transportation, and the other, on land, working against established social systems, the ecology of land and air using combustion, land acquisitions, and the power of the bullet to subdue nature and the native societies. It takes time to learn from our mistakes, and even more time to repair the damage done to man and nature.

It is interesting that during the same period of time two vitally needed forms of transportation were developed. One, on the sea, working with nature's best principles to create a totally eco-friendly means of transportation, and the other, on land, working against established social systems, the ecology of land and air using combustion, land acquisitions, and the power of the bullet to subdue nature and the native societies. It takes time to learn from our mistakes, and even more time to repair the damage done to man and nature. It takes time to learn from our mistakes, and even more time to repair the damage done to man and nature. It takes time to learn from our mistakes.

It is interesting that during the same period of time two vitally needed forms of transportation were developed. One, on the sea, working with nature's best principles to create a totally eco-friendly means of transportation, and the other, on land, working against established social systems, the ecology of land and air using combustion, land acquisitions, and the power of the bullet to subdue nature and the native societies. One, on the sea, working with nature's best principles to create a totally eco-friendly means of transportation, and the other, on land, working against established social systems, the ecology of land and air using combustion, land acquisitions, and the power of the bullet to subdue nature and the native societies. It takes time to learn from our mistakes, and even more time to repair the damage done to man and nature.

It takes time to learn from our mistakes, and even more time to repair the damage done to man and nature. ▼

(b) Pages Balanced as a Unit

FIGURE 2.9 Balancing Facing Pages

SUMMARY

The essence of desktop publishing is the merger of text with graphics to produce a professional-looking document. Proficiency in desktop publishing requires not only knowledge of Microsoft Word, but familiarity with the basics of graphic design.

The Newsletter Wizard can be used to create a template for a newsletter. It is preferable, however, to create the newsletter entirely in Microsoft Word so that it better suits your needs.

A document can be divided into any number of newspaper-style columns in which text flows from the bottom of one column to the top of the next. Columns are implemented by clicking the Columns button on the Standard toolbar or by selecting the Columns command from the Format menu. Sections are required if different column arrangements are present in the same document. The Page Layout view is required to see the columns displayed side-by-side.

The Insert Picture command places a picture into a document, which can subsequently be modified using the drawing tools within Microsoft Word. A frame facilitates moving and/or wrapping text around the graphic.

The successful use of desktop publishing requires knowledge of graphic design in addition to proficiency in Word. The use of a grid, white space, and appropriate emphasis are basic design techniques.

KEY WORDS AND CONCEPTS

Borders and Shading command
Clip art
Column break
Columns command
Desktop publishing
Drawing toolbar
Drop cap
Emphasis
Facing pages
Format Frame command
Frame
Grid
Insert Picture command
Masthead
Newsletter Wizard
Newspaper-style columns
Pull quote
Reverse
Section break
Typography
White space

MULTIPLE CHOICE

1. Which of the following *must* be specified by the user?
(a) The number of columns
(b) The width of each column
(c) Both (a) and (b)
(d) Neither (a) nor (b)

2. Which view enables you to see a multicolumn document as it will appear on the printed page?
(a) Normal view at any magnification
(b) Page Layout view at any magnification
(c) Normal or Page Layout view at 100% magnification
(d) Normal or Page Layout view at Full Page magnification

3. How is clip art inserted into a document?
   (a) Through the Insert Picture Command
   (b) Through the Microsoft ClipArt Gallery
   (c) Both (a) and (b)
   (d) Neither (a) nor (b)
4. What is the minimum number of sections in a three-column newsletter whose masthead extends across all three columns?
   (a) One
   (b) Two
   (c) Three
   (d) Four
5. What is the difference between clicking and double clicking an object such as the sports graphic in the newsletter?
   (a) Clicking selects the object; double clicking enables you to edit the object
   (b) Double clicking selects the object; clicking enables you to edit the object
   (c) Clicking changes to Normal view; double clicking changes to Page Layout view
   (d) Double clicking changes to Normal view; clicking changes to Page Layout view
6. Which of the following is correct with respect to page and column breaks?
   (a) Press Ctrl+enter to create a page break
   (b) Press Ctrl+Shift+enter to create a column break
   (c) Both (a) and (b)
   (d) Neither (a) nor (b)
7. Which of the following can be placed into a frame?
   (a) A picture or dropped capital letter
   (b) A table or object created by another application
   (c) Both (a) and (b)
   (d) Neither (a) nor (b)
8. Which of the following is controlled by the Format Frame command?
   (a) The horizontal and/or vertical placement of the frame
   (b) Wrapping (not wrapping) text around the framed object
   (c) Both (a) and (b)
   (d) Neither (a) nor (b)
9. What is the effect of dragging one of the four corner handles on a selected object?
   (a) The length of the object is changed but the width remains constant
   (b) The width of the object is changed but the length remains constant
   (c) The length and width of the object are changed in proportion to one another
   (d) Neither the length nor width of the object is changed
10. Which type size is the most reasonable for columns of text, such as those appearing in the newsletter created in the chapter?
   (a) 6 point
   (b) 10 point
   (c) 14 point
   (d) 18 point

11. A grid is applicable to the design of
    (a) Documents with one, two, or three columns and moderate clip art
    (b) Documents with four or more columns and no clip art
    (c) Both (a) and (b)
    (d) Neither (a) nor (b)

12. Which of the following is *not* an appropriate place to introduce white space in a document?
    (a) Between columns of a multicolumn document
    (b) Trapped in the middle of a page
    (c) In the page margins
    (d) Between paragraphs

13. Which of the following can be used to add emphasis to a document in the absence of clip art?
    (a) Boxes and shading
    (b) Pull quotes and reverses
    (c) Both (a) and (b)
    (d) Neither (a) nor (b)

14. Which of the following is a universally accepted guideline in the design of a document?
    (a) Use wider columns for larger type sizes
    (b) Use the same type size for the heading and text of an article
    (c) Both (a) and (b)
    (d) Neither (a) nor (b)

15. Which of the following are implemented at the section rather than the paragraph level?
    (a) Columns
    (b) Margins
    (c) Both (a) and (b)
    (d) Neither (a) nor (b)

ANSWERS

1. a	**6.** c	**11.** c
2. b	**7.** c	**12.** b
3. c	**8.** c	**13.** c
4. b	**9.** c	**14.** a
5. a	**10.** b	**15.** c

EXPLORING MICROSOFT WORD 7.0

1. Use Figure 2.10 to match each action with its result; a given action may be used more than once or not at all.

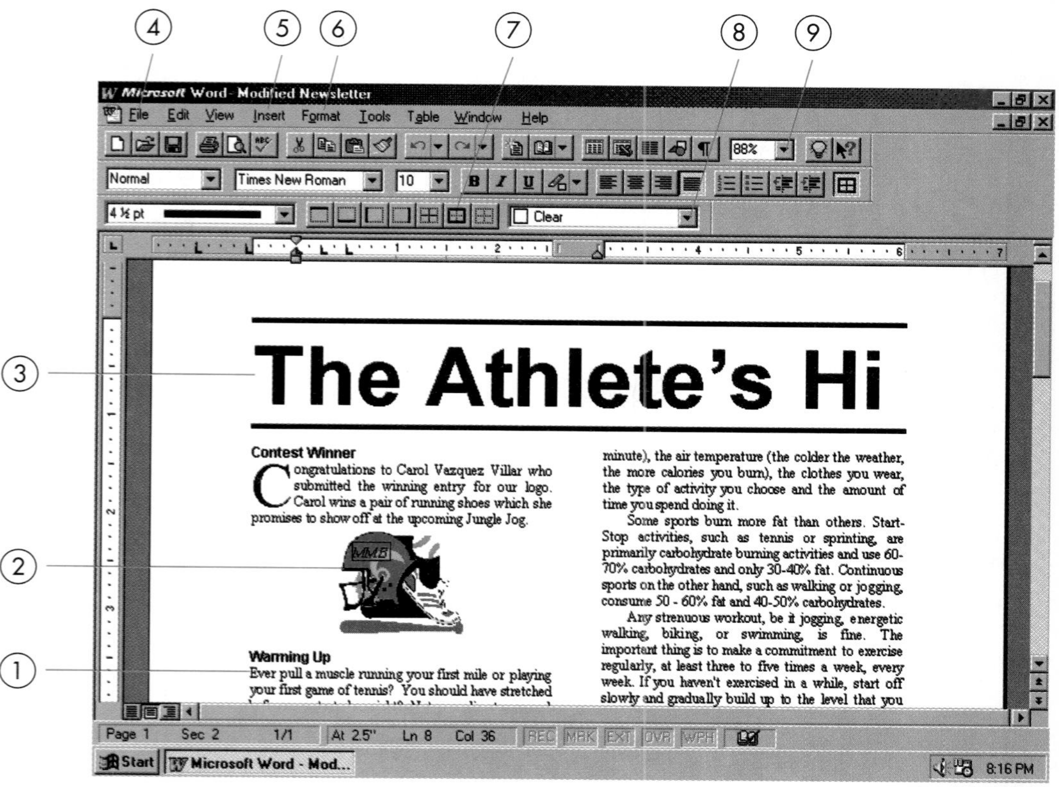

FIGURE 2.10 Screen for Problem 1

Action		Result
a. Click at 1, click at 6	____	Size the graphic
b. Double click at 2	____	Allow text to wrap around the graphic
c. Click at 2, drag a handle	____	Change the newsletter to three columns
d. Click at 2, click at 5	____	Modify the picture
e. Click at 2, click at 6	____	Insert the picture in a frame
f. Click at 2, click at 7	____	Put a border around the picture
g. Click at 3, click at 8	____	Shade the masthead
h. Click at 4	____	Add a drop cap for the second article
i. Click at 6	____	Change the zoom to Whole Page
j. Click at 9	____	Change the top and bottom margins

2. Answer the following with respect to the screen in Figure 2.11:

a. What is the name of the style that is in effect at the insertion point? What are the specifications for that style?

b. How would you change the typeface or point size for the style in part a?

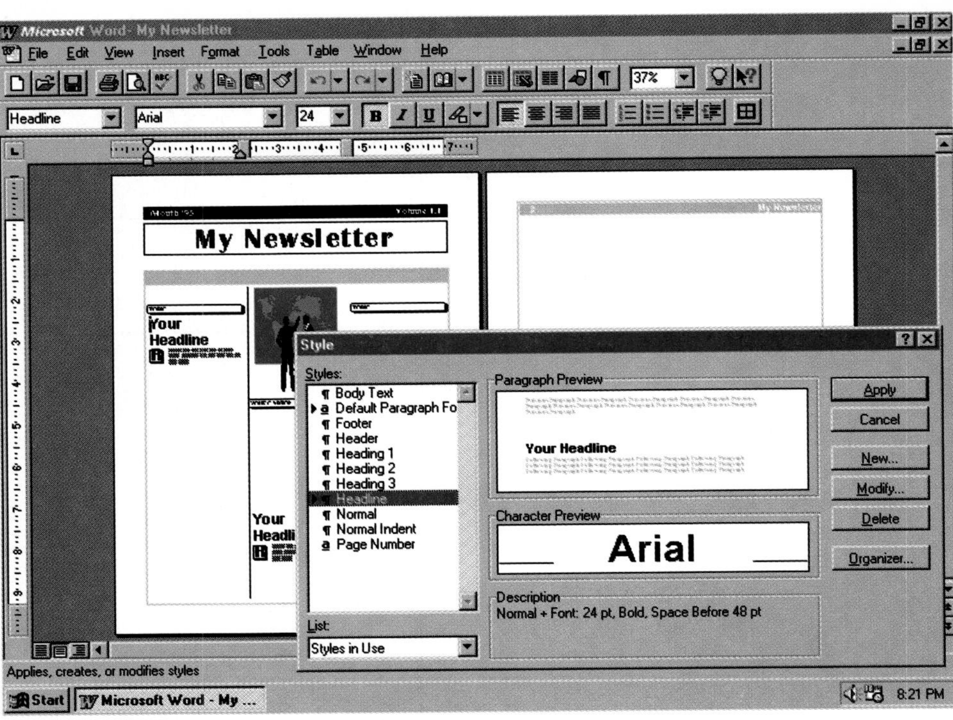

FIGURE 2.11 Screen for Problem 2

c. Which command displayed the dialog box in Figure 2.11? How can you use the dialog box to display the specifications for the Body Text style? How would you change the specifications for that style?
d. How was the newsletter in the figure created?

3. Answer the following with respect to the screen in Figure 2.12:
a. Which command produced the dialog box in the figure?
b. What are the left and right margins in effect? How wide is each column with the current margins?
c. How wide would each column be if you changed the left and right margins to .5 inch each and retained the current spacing between columns?
d. What would the width of each column be if you changed the margins and reduced the space between columns to .25 inch?
e. Which point size, 10 point or 12 point, would be preferable for the design in part d?
f. Explain why it is not possible to create a design of four unequal columns (2.5 inches for the first column and 1.5 inches for the other three columns) with left and right margins of .5 inch each?
g. Regardless of the parameters chosen, the document will not be displayed in columns after clicking the OK button and closing the dialog box. Why?

4. The examples in Figure 2.13 contain two versions of the same page, one that violates basic rules of design and one that follows them. Describe the problems in the poorly designed page, then indicate how they were corrected in the revised version.

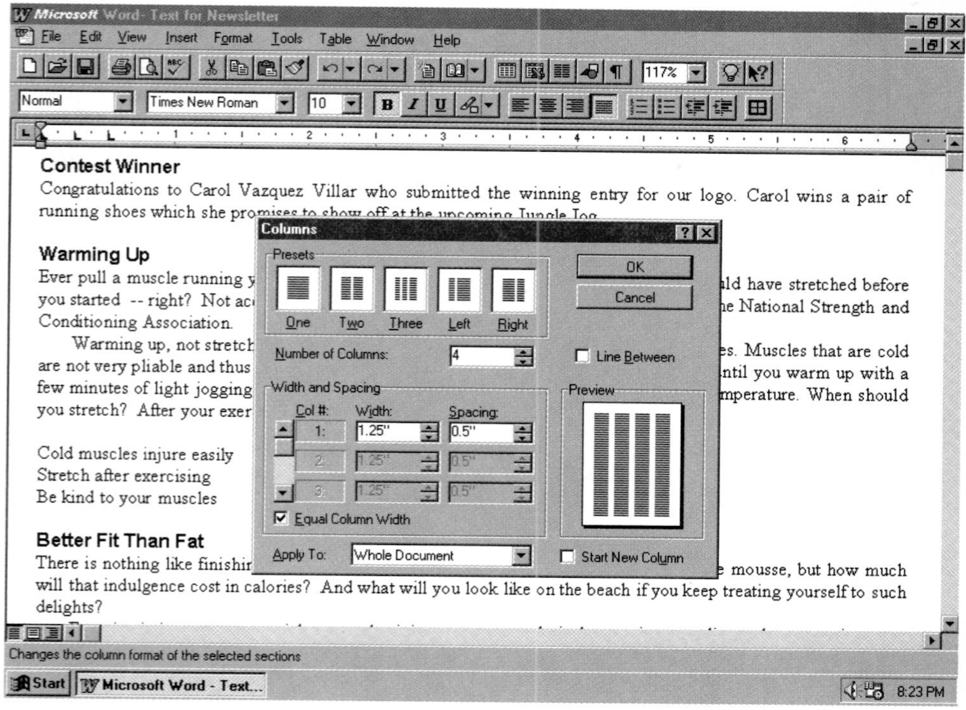

FIGURE 2.12 Screen for Problem 3

A Special Report: Living Latin

Something like eighty-five percent of the English language is derived from a mere ninety Latin root words.

Latin was one of the subjects which I really enjoyed in high school. Many people laugh at it because they say it is a useless, dead language. Churches do not even use it any more in their services, pity. Something like eighty-five percent of the English language is derived from a mere ninety latin root words. I cannot express how useful it was to have an understanding of latin when it came to memorizing the order, phylum and classification of organisms in zoology class, later on in college. My creative writing classes also got a shot in the arm because of it. It was also interesting to find out the toll that the dark ages took on the European civilization which the Romans had established for centuries. Latin is indeed living. But it is living quietly in the essence of western civilization.

Many people laugh at it because they say it is a useless, dead language. Churches do not even use it any more in their services, pity. Something like eighty-five percent of the English language is derived from a mere ninety latin root words.

I cannot express how useful it was to have an understanding of latin when it came to memorizing the order, phylum and classification of organisms in zoology class, later on in college. My creative writing classes also got a shot in the arm because of it. It was also interesting to find out the toll that the dark ages took on the European civilization which the Romans had established for centuries. Latin is indeed living. But it is living quietly in the essence of western civilization.

Latin was one of the subjects which I really enjoyed in high school. Many people laugh at it because they say it is a useless, dead language. Churches do not even use it any more in their services, pity. Something like eighty-five percent of the English language is derived from a mere ninety latin root words. I cannot express how useful it was to have an understanding of latin when it came to memorizing the order, phylum and classification of organisms in zoology class, later on in college. My creative writing classes also got a shot in the arm because of it. It was also interesting to find out the toll that the dark ages took on the European civilization which the Romans had established. My creative writing classes also got a shot in the arm because of it.

It was also interesting to find out the toll that the dark ages took on the European civilization which the Romans had established for centuries. Latin is indeed living. But it is living quietly in the essence of western civilization. I cannot express how useful it was to have an understanding of latin when it came to memorizing the order, phylum and classification ▼

Latin is indeed living. But it is living quietly in the essence of western civilization.

Poor Design

A Special Report: Living Latin

Latin was one of the subjects which I really enjoyed in high school. Many people laugh at it because they say it is a useless, dead language. Churches do not even use it any more in their services, pity. Something like eighty-five percent of the English language is derived from a mere ninety latin root words. I cannot express how useful it was to have an understanding of latin when it came to memorizing the order, phylum and classification of organisms in zoology class, later on in college. My creative writing classes also got a shot in the arm because of it. It was also interesting to find out the toll that the dark ages took on the European civilization which the Romans had established for centuries. Latin is indeed living. But it is living quietly in the essence of western civilization.

Many people laugh at it because they say it is a useless, dead language. Churches do not even use it any more in their services, pity. Something like eighty-five percent of the English language is derived from a mere ninety latin root words.

I cannot express how useful it was to have an understanding of latin when it came to memorizing the order, phylum and classification of organisms in zoology class, later on in college. My creative writing classes also got a shot in the arm because of it. It was also interesting to find out the toll that the dark ages took on the European civilization which the Romans had established for centuries. Latin is indeed living. But it is living quietly in the essence of western civilization.

Latin was one of the subjects which I really enjoyed in high school. Many people laugh at it because they say it is a useless, dead language. Churches do not even use it any more in their services, pity. Something like eighty-five percent of the English language is derived from a mere ninety latin root words. I cannot express how useful it was to have an understanding of latin when it came to memorizing the order, phylum and classification of organisms in zoology class, later on in college. My creative writing classes also got a shot in the arm because of it. It was also interesting to find out the toll that the dark ages took on the European civilization which the Romans had established. My creative writing classes also got a shot in the arm because of it.

It was also interesting to find out the toll that the dark ages took on the European civilization which the Romans had established. My creative writing classes also got a shot in the arm because of it. ▼

Latin is indeed living. But it is living quietly in the essence of western civilization.

Improved Design

(a) Example 1

FIGURE 2.13 Pages for Problem 4

(Adapted from Burns, Diane, and Venit, S., "What's Wrong with This Page?", *PC Magazine,* October 13, 1987.)

Living Latin Bulletin

Published by The Romulus and Remus Society of Southern California | Januarious MXMXCIV

Managers Required to Study Roman Classics

Latin was one of the subjects which I really enjoyed in high school. Many people laugh at it because they say it is a useless, dead language. Churches do not even use it any more in their services, pity. Something like eighty-five percent of the English language is derived from a mere ninety latin root words. I cannot express how useful it was to have an understanding of latin when it came to memorizing the order, phylum and classification of organisms in zoology class, later on in college. My creative writing classes also got a shot in the arm because of it. It was also interesting to find out the toll that the dark ages took on the European civilization which the Romans had established ▼

Group to Attend Archeological Dig

Latin was one of the subjects which I really enjoyed in high school. Many people laugh at it because they say it is a useless, dead language. Churches do not even use it

any more in their services, pity. Something like eighty-five percent of the English language is derived from a mere ninety latin root words. I cannot express how useful it was to have an understanding of latin when it came to memorizing the order, phylum and classification of organisms in zoology class, later on in college. My creative writing classes also got a shot in the ▼

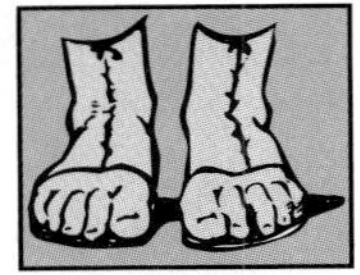

These Boots Were Made for Walkin'

Latin was one of the subjects which I really enjoyed in high school. Many people laugh at it because they say it is a useless, dead language. Churches do not even use it any more in their services, pity. Something like eighty-five percent of the English language is derived from a mere ninety latin root words. I cannot express how useful it was to have an understanding of latin when it came to memorizing the order, phylum . My creative writing classes also got a shot in wasalsoint ▼

Poor Design

Living Latin Bulletin

Published by The Romulus and Remus Society of Southern California | Januarious MXMXCIV

Managers Required to Study Roman Classics

Latin was one of the subjects which I really enjoyed in high school. Many people laugh at it because they say it is a useless, dead language. Churches do not even use it any more in their services, pity. Something like eighty-five percent of the English language is derived from a mere ninety latin root words. I cannot express how useful it was to have an understanding of latin when it came to memorizing the order, phylum and

classification of organisms in zoology class, later on in college. My creative writing classes also got a shot in the arm because of it. It was also interesting to find out the toll that the dark ages took on the European civilization which the Romans had established for centuries. Latin is indeed living. But it is living quietly in the essence of western civilization.

Archeological Dig

Latin was one of the subjects which I really enjoyed in high school. Many people laugh at it because they say it is a useless, dead language. Churches do not even use it any more in their services, pity. Something like eighty-five percent of the English language is derived from a mere ninety latin root words. I cannot express how useful it was to have an understanding of latin when it came to memorizing the order, phylum and classification of organisms in zoology class, later on in college. My creative writing classes also got a shot in the arm because of it. It was also interesting to find out the toll that the dark ages took on the European civilization which the Romans had established for centuries. Latin is indeed living. But it is living quietly in the essence of western civilization.

Latin was one of the subjects which I really enjoyed in high school. Many people laugh at it because they say it is a useless, dead language. Churches do not even use it any more in their services, pity. Something like eighty-five percent of the English language is derived from a mere ninety latin root words. I cannot express how useful it was to have an understanding of latin when it came to memorizing the order, phylum and classification of organisms in zoology class, later on in college. My creative writing classes also got a shot in the arm because of it. It was also interesting to find out the toll that the dark ages took on the European civilization which the Romans had established for centuries.

Walking Boots

Latin was one of the subjects which I really enjoyed in high school. Many people laugh at it because they say it is a useless, dead language. Churches do not even use it any more in their services, pity. Something like eighty-five percent of the English language is derived from a ▼

Improved Design

(b) Example 2

FIGURE 2.13 Pages for Problem 4 (continued)

Practice with Microsoft Word 7.0

1. The flyers in Figure 2.14 were created using the Insert Picture command to import the Jazz and Books graphics, respectively. Once the clip art was brought into the document, it was moved and sized as necessary to create the documents in the figure. It's easy, provided you remember to frame the picture as soon as you bring it into the document. Reproduce either or both of our flyers, or better yet, create your own.

2. Figure 2.15 displays three additional mastheads suitable for the newsletter that was developed in the chapter. Each masthead was created as follows:
   a. A two-by-two table was used in Figure 2.15a in order to right justify the date of the newsletter. The use of a table to right align text was suggested in the tip on page 13.
   b. A different font was used for the masthead in Figure 2.15b. The border around the masthead is a drop shadow.
   c. Microsoft WordArt was used to create the masthead in Figure 2.15c.

   Choose the masthead you like best, then modify the newsletter as it existed at the end of the second hands-on exercise to include the new masthead. Submit the modified newsletter to your instructor as proof that you did the hands-on exercises in this chapter as well as this problem.

UM Jazz Band

Plays Dixieland

Where: Gusman Hall

When: Friday,
November 10

Time: 8:00 PM

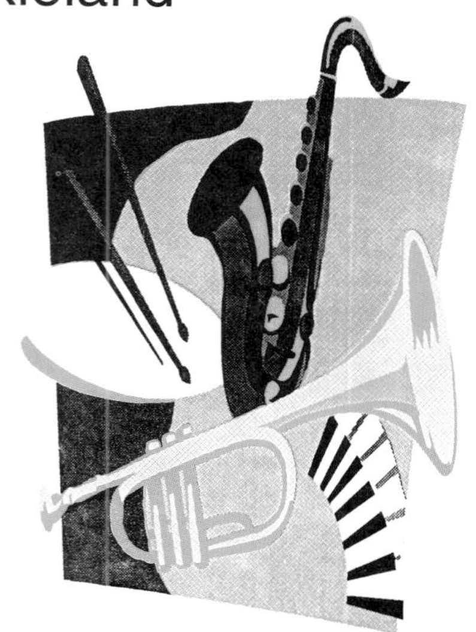

(a) UM Jazz Band

CIS 120 Study Sessions

For those who don't know a bit from a byte
Come to Stanford College this Tuesday night
We'll study the concepts that aren't always clear
And memorize terms that hackers hold dear

We'll hit the books from 7 to 10
And then on Thursday we'll do it again
It can't hurt to try us — so come on by
And give the CIS tutors that old college try!

(b) CIS 120 Study Sessions

FIGURE 2.14 Flyers for Practice with Word Exercise 1

The Athlete's Hi
Volume 1 November 1995

(a) With Volume Number and Date

The Athlete's Hi

(b) Alternate Font and Drop Shadow

The Athlete's Hi

(c) Microsoft WordArt

FIGURE 2.15 Mastheads for Practice with Word Exercise 2

3. Create a newsletter containing at least one graphic from the Clipart folder. The intent of this problem is simply to provide practice in graphic design. There is no requirement to write meaningful text, but the headings in the newsletter should follow the theme of the graphic.
   a. Select a graphic, then write one or two sentences in support of that graphic. If, for example, you choose the Books graphic, you could write a sentence describing how you intend to hit the books in an effort to boost your GPA and make the Dean's List.
   b. As indicated, there is no requirement to write meaningful text for the newsletter; just copy the sentences from part (a) once or twice to create a paragraph, then copy the paragraph several times to create the newsletter. You should, however, create meaningful headings to add interest to the document.
   c. Develop an overall design away from the computer—that is, with pencil and paper. Use a grid to indicate the placement of the articles, headings,

clip art, and masthead. You may be surprised to find that it is easier to master commands in Word than it is to design the newsletter; do not, however, underestimate the importance of graphic design in the ultimate success of your document.

   d. More is not better; that is, do not use too many fonts, styles, sizes, and clip art just because they are available. Don't crowd the page, and remember that white space is a very effective design element. There are no substitutes for simplicity and good taste.

4. A guide to smart shopping: This problem is more challenging than the previous exercises in that you are asked to consider content as well as design. The objective is to develop a one- (or two-) page document with helpful tips to the novice on buying a computer. We have, however, written the copy for you and put the file on the data disk.

   a. Open and print the *Volume II Chapter 2 Practice 4* document on the data disk, which takes approximately a page and a half as presently formatted. Read our text and determine the tips you want to retain and those you want to delete. Add other tips as you see fit.
   b. Examine the available clip art through the Insert Picture command or through the Microsoft ClipArt Gallery. There is no requirement, however, to include a graphic; that is, use clip art only if you think it will enhance the document.
   c. Consult a current computer magazine (or another source) to determine actual prices for one or more configurations, then include this information prominently in your document.
   d. Create the masthead for the document, then develop with pencil and paper a rough sketch of the completed document showing the masthead, the placement of the text, clip art, and special of the month (the configuration in part c).
   e. Return to the computer and implement the design of part d. Try to create a balanced publication that completely fills the space allotted; that is, your document should take exactly one or two pages (rather than the page and a half in the original document on the data disk).

Case Studies

Before and After

The best way to learn about the do's and don'ts of desktop publishing is to study the work of others. Choose a particular type of document—such as a newsletter, résumé, or advertising flyer—then collect samples of that document. Choose one sample that is particularly bad and redesign the document. You need not enter the actual text, but you should keep all of the major headings so that the document retains its identity. Add or delete clip art as appropriate. Bring the before and after samples to class and hold a contest to determine the most radical improvement.

Clip Art

Clip art—you see it all the time, but where do you get it, and how much does it cost? Some images are supplied with a word processor, but you grow tired of these and yearn for more. Scan the computer magazines and find at least two sources for additional clip art. Return to class with specific information on price and the nature of the clip art. Be sure to determine in advance how much disk space the clip art will require; the answer may surprise you.

The Flyer

It's rush week and you're the publicity chairperson for your fraternity or sorority. Needless to say, it's highly competitive and you need effective flyers to attract new members. This is an absolutely critical assignment, and people are counting on you. Don't blow it!

Intramurals

The ClipArt Gallery includes a Sports and Leisure category with graphics on many different sports. You have been appointed acting head of Campus Intramurals and need to create a flyer seeking participation in an upcoming league. Choose your sport, choose the graphic, and see how creative you can be.

A

APPENDIX A: OBJECT LINKING AND EMBEDDING

OVERVIEW

The ability to create a ***compound document*** is one of the primary advantages of the Windows environment. A compound document, such as the memo in Figure A.1, is a document that contains data (objects) from multiple applications. The memo was created in Microsoft Word, and it contains an object (a worksheet) that was created in Microsoft Excel. The ***container*** (the Word document) is created in the ***client application*** (Microsoft Word in this example). The object it contains (a worksheet) is created in the ***server application*** (Microsoft Excel in this example). ***Object Linking and Embedding*** (OLE—pronounced "OH-lay") is the means by which you develop compound documents.

The essential difference between linking and embedding is whether the object is stored within the compound document (embedding) or in its own file (linking). An ***embedded object*** is stored in the compound document, which in turn becomes the only user (client) of that object. A ***linked object*** is stored in its own file, and the compound document is one of many potential containers of that object. The compound document does not contain the linked object per se, but only a representation of the object as well as a pointer (link) to the file containing the object. The advantage of linking is that the object in the compound document is updated automatically if the object is changed in the source file in which it was created.

The choice between linking and embedding depends on how the object will be used. Linking is preferable if the object is likely to change, and the compound document requires the latest version. Linking should also be used when the same object is placed in many documents so that any change to the object has to be made in only one place. Embedding is preferable if you intend to edit the compound document on a computer other than the one on which it was created.

The exercise that follows shows you how to create the compound document in Figure A.1. The exercise uses the ***Insert Object command*** to embed a copy of the Excel worksheet into a Word document.

Lionel Douglas

402 Mahoney Hall • Coral Gables, Florida 33124

June 25, 1995

Dear Folks,

I heard from Mr. Black, the manager at University Commons, and the apartment is a definite for the Fall. Ken and I are very excited, and can't wait to get out of the dorm. The food is poison, not that either of us are cooks, but anything will be better than this! I have been checking into car prices (we are definitely too far away from campus to walk!), and have done some estimating on what it will cost. The figures below are for a Jeep Wrangler, the car of my dreams:

Price of car	$11,995			
Manufacturer's rebate	$1,000			
Down payment	$3,000		**My assumptions**	
Amount to be financed	$7,995		Interest rate	7.90%
Monthly payment	$195		Term (years)	4
Gas	$40			
Maintenance	$50			
Insurance	$100			
Total per month	$385			

My initial estimate was $471 based on a $2,000 down payment and a three year loan at 7.9%. I know this is too much so I plan on earning an additional $1,000 and extending the loan to four years. That will bring the total cost down to a more manageable level (see the above calculations). If that won't do it, I'll look at other cars.

Lionel

FIGURE A.1 A Compound Document

Once an object has been embedded into a document, it can be modified through ***in-place editing.*** In-place editing enables you to double click an embedded object (the worksheet) and change it, using the tools of the server application (Excel). In other words, you remain in the client application (Microsoft Word in this example), but you have access to the Excel toolbar and pull-down menus. In-place editing modifies the copy of the embedded object in the compound document. It does *not* change the original object because there is no connection (or link) between the object and the compound document.

HANDS-ON EXERCISE 1

Embedding

Objective: To embed an Excel worksheet into a Word document; to use in-place editing to modify the worksheet within Word. Use Figure A.2 as a guide in the exercise.

STEP 1: Open the Word Document

- Start Word. Open the **Car Request document** in the **Exploring Word folder.** Zoom to **Page Width** so that the display on your monitor matches ours.
- Save the document as **Modified Car Request** so that you can return to the original document if you edit the duplicated file beyond redemption.
- The date displayed on your monitor will be May 31, 1995, and needs to be updated. Point to the date field, click the **right mouse button** to display the shortcut menu in Figure A.2a, then click the **Update Field command.**

> **THE DATE FIELD**
>
> The Insert Date and Time command enables you to insert the date as a specific value (the date on which a document is created) or as a field. The latter will be updated automatically whenever the document is printed or when the document is opened in Page Layout view. Opening the document in the Normal view requires the date field to be updated manually.

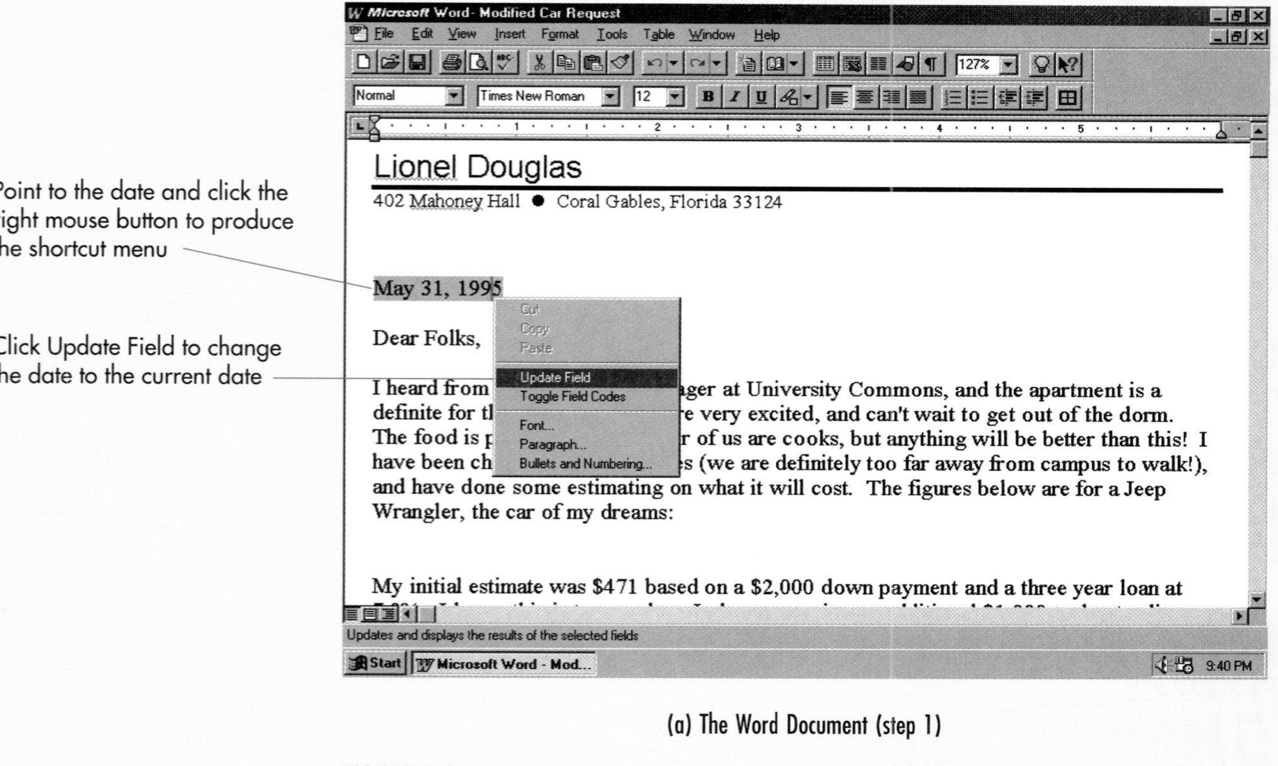

(a) The Word Document (step 1)

FIGURE A.2 Hands-on Exercise 1

STEP 2: Insert an Object

- Click the blank line above paragraph two as shown in Figure A.2b. This is the place in the document where the worksheet is to go.
- Pull down the **Insert menu**, and click the **Object command** to display the Object dialog box in Figure A.2b.
- Click the **Create from File tab,** then click the **Browse command button** in order to open the Browse dialog box and select the object.
- Click (select) the **Car Budget workbook** (note the Excel icon), which is in the Exploring Word folder.
- Click **OK** to select the workbook and close the Browse dialog box.

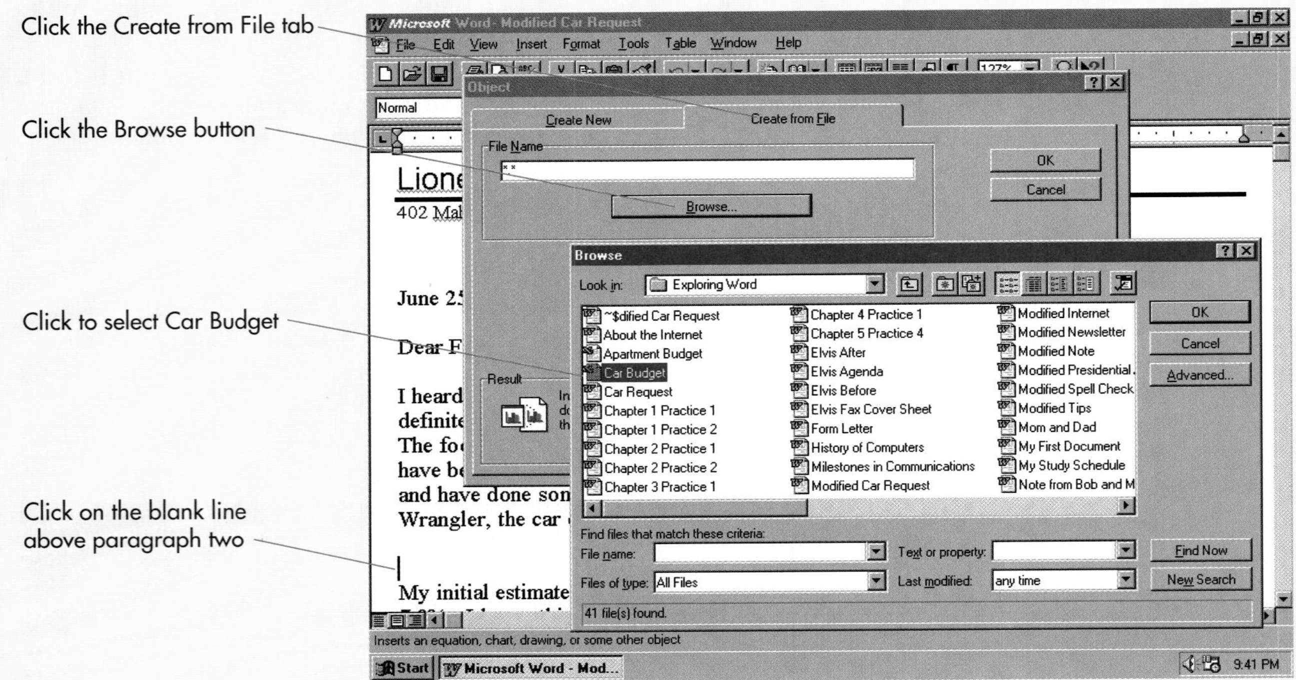

(b) Insert Object Command (step 2)

FIGURE A.2 Hands-on Exercise 1 (continued)

STEP 3: Insert an Object (continued)

- The file name of the object (Car Budget.xls) has been placed into the File Name text box, as shown in Figure A.2c.
- Verify that the Link to File and Display as Icon check boxes are clear, as shown in Figure A.2c. Note, too, the description at the bottom of the Object dialog box, which indicates that you will be able to edit the object using the application that created the file.
- Click **OK** to insert the Excel worksheet into the Word document. Save the document.

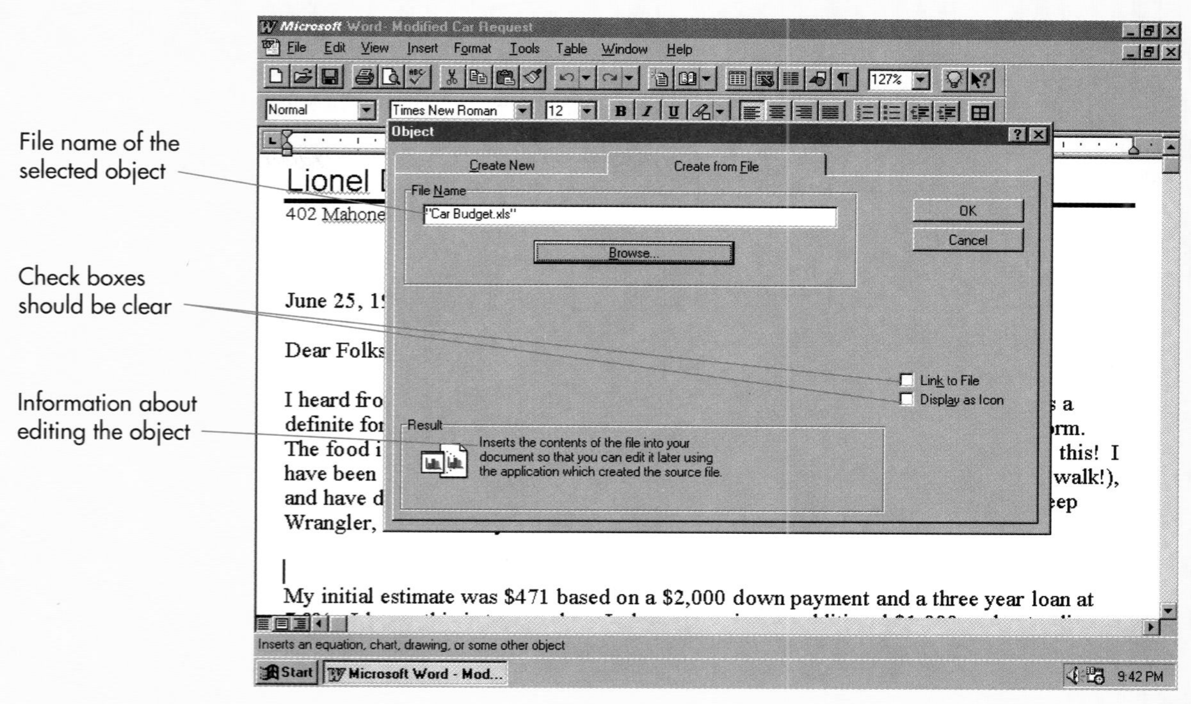

(c) Insert Object Command, continued (step 3)

FIGURE A.2 Hands-on Exercise 1 (continued)

STEP 4: Frame the Worksheet

- Point to the worksheet, then click the **right mouse button** to select the worksheet and display a shortcut menu. Click the **Frame Picture** command to frame the worksheet in order to position it more easily within the document.
- You will see the informational box in Figure A.2d, asking whether you want to switch to the Page Layout view. Click **Yes.** The worksheet is surrounded by a shaded (thatched) border to indicate a frame.

THE FORMAT FRAME COMMAND

All objects should be placed into a frame, a special type of (invisible) container in Microsoft Word that facilitates positioning an object within a Word document. An unframed object is treated as an ordinary paragraph, and movement is restricted to one of three alignments (left, center, or right). Additionally, text cannot be wrapped around an unframed object. A framed object, however, can be precisely positioned by right clicking the object, selecting the Format Frame command, then entering the information about the object's desired position.

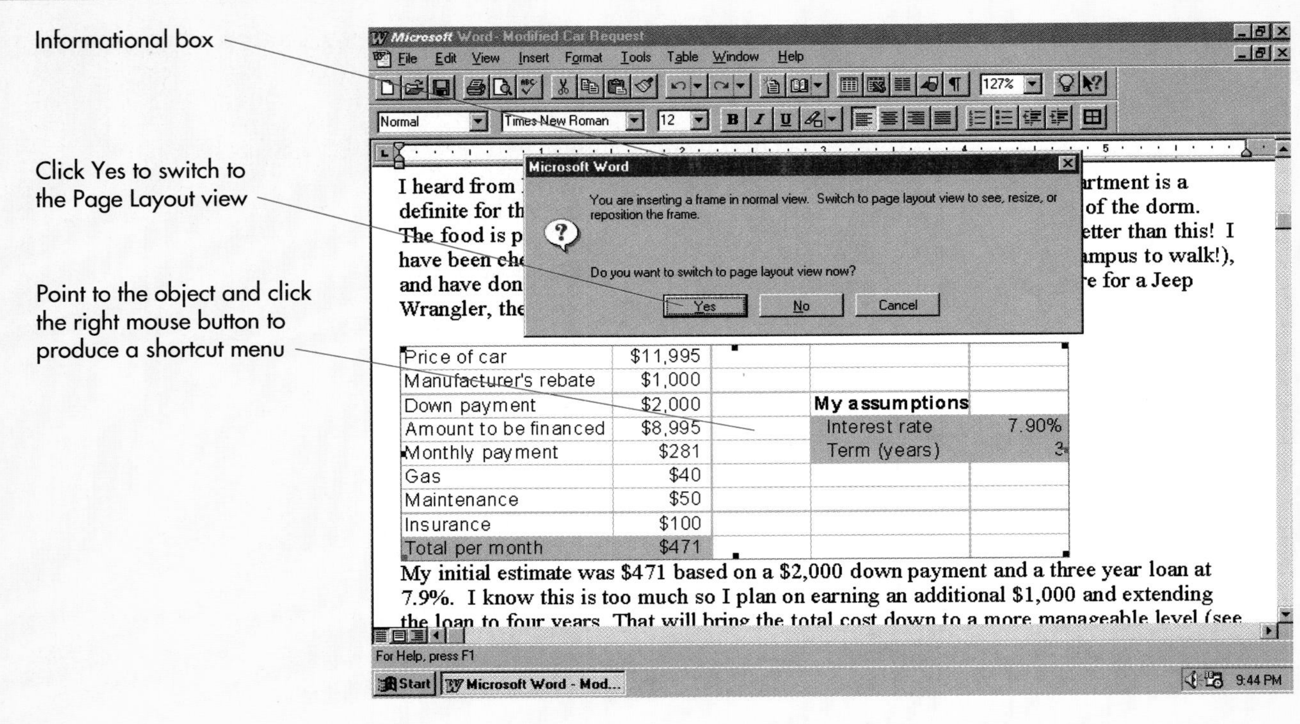

(d) Frame the Worksheet (step 4)

FIGURE A.2 Hands-on Exercise 1 (continued)

STEP 5: The Format Frame Command

- Pull down the **Format menu** and click **Frame** to display the Frame dialog box shown in Figure A.2e.
- Click the box for no text wrapping.
- Click the **drop-down arrow** on the list box for the Horizontal position and click **Center.** Click **OK** to accept the settings and close the Frame dialog box.
- The worksheet is centered within the memo, but you may want to insert a blank line(s) between the paragraphs to give the worksheet additional room.
- Save the document.

STEP 6: In-place Editing

- The worksheet should still be selected as indicated by the sizing handles. The monthly total of $471 needs to be changed to reflect Lionel's additional $1,000 for the down payment. Double click the worksheet object to edit the worksheet in place.
- Be patient as this step takes a while, even on a fast machine. The Excel grid, consisting of the row and column labels, will appear around the worksheet, as shown in Figure A.2f.
- You are still in Word, as indicated by the title bar (Microsoft Word - Modified Car Request), but the Excel toolbars are displayed.
- Click in cell **B3,** type the new down payment of **$3,000,** and press **enter.**
- Click in cell **E5,** type **4,** and press **enter.** The Monthly payment (cell B5) and Total per month (cell B9) drop to $195 and $385, respectively.

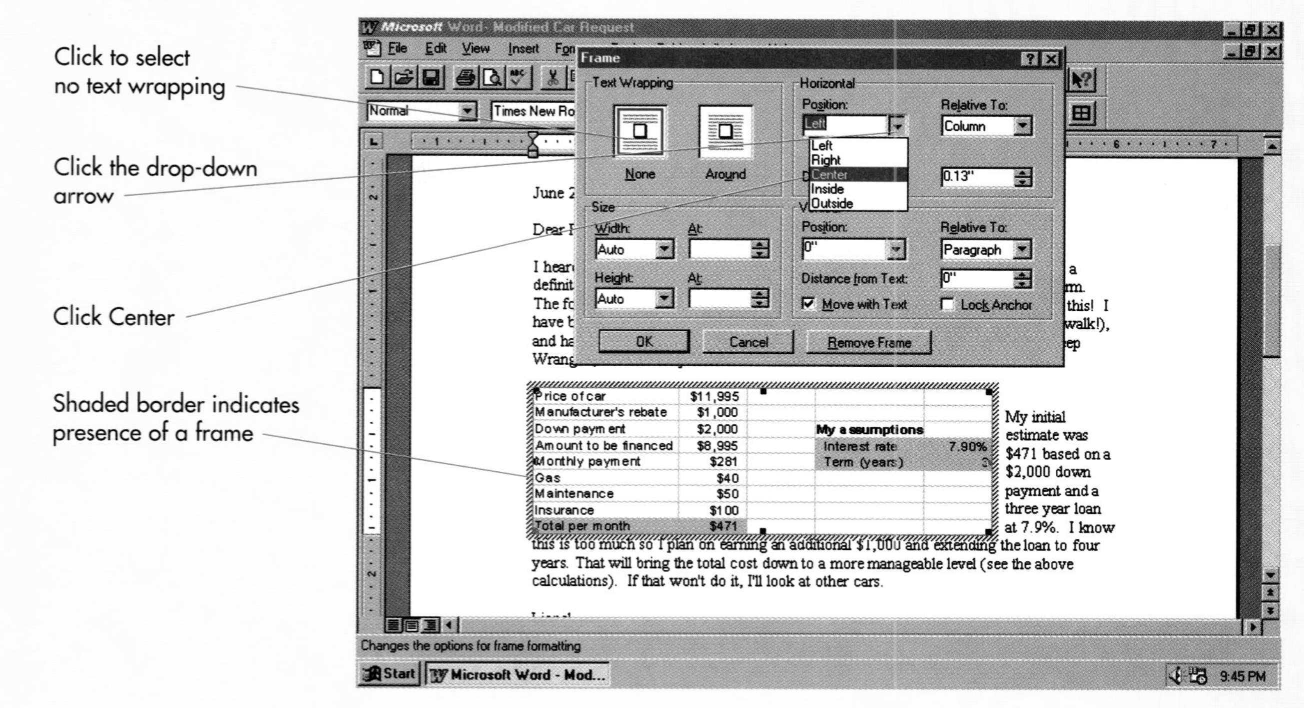

(e) Format Frame Command (step 5)

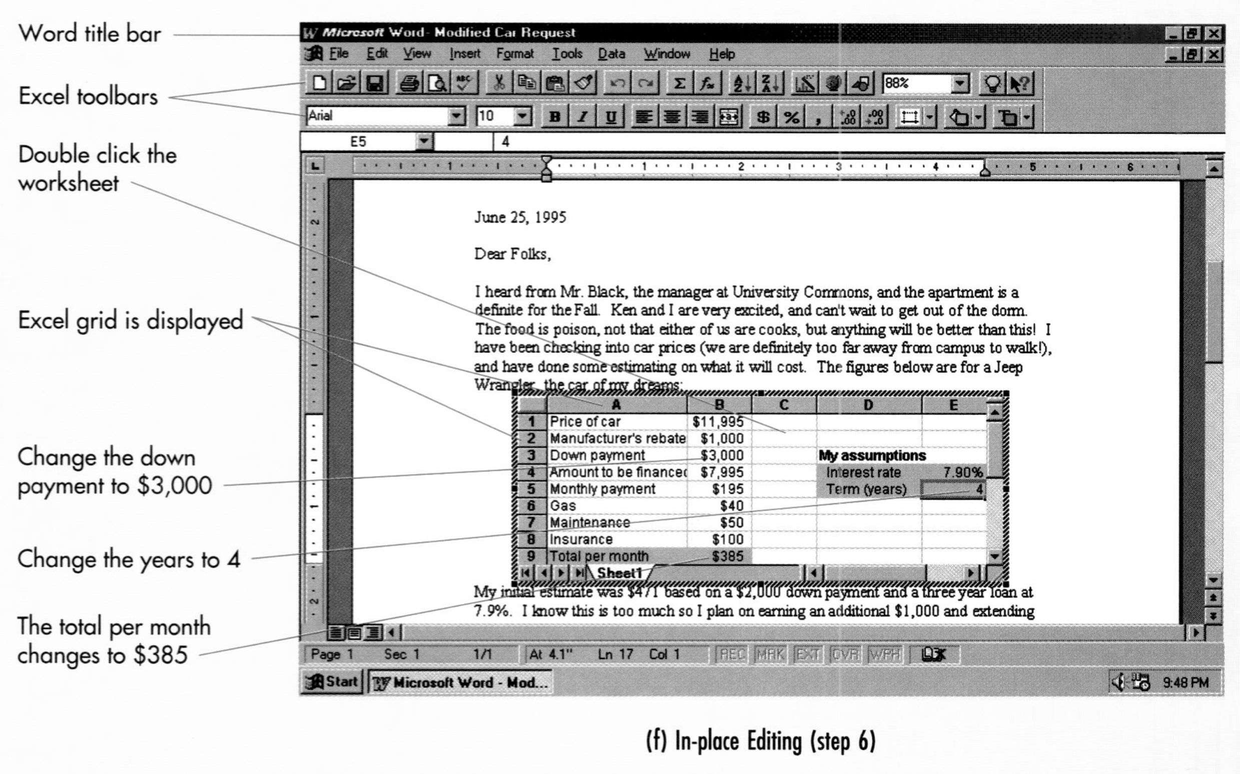

(f) In-place Editing (step 6)

FIGURE A.2 Hands-on Exercise 1 (continued)

IN-PLACE EDITING

In-place editing enables you to edit an embedded object using the toolbar and pull-down menus of the server application. Thus, when editing an Excel worksheet embedded into a Word document, the title bar is that of the client application (Microsoft Word), but the toolbars and pull-down menus reflect the server application (Excel). There are, however, two exceptions; the File and Window menus are those of the client application (Word) so that you can save the compound document and/or arrange multiple documents within the client application.

STEP 7: Save the Word Document

- ➤ Click anywhere outside the worksheet to deselect it and view the completed word document as shown in Figure A.2g.
- ➤ Pull down the **File menu** and click **Save** (or click the **Save button** on the Standard toolbar).
- ➤ Pull down the **File menu** a second time. Click **Exit** if you do not want to continue with the next hands-on exercise once this exercise is completed; otherwise click **Close** to remove the document from memory but leave Word open.

STEP 8: View the Original Object

- ➤ Click the **Start Button,** click (or point to) the **Programs menu,** then click **Microsoft Excel** to open the program.

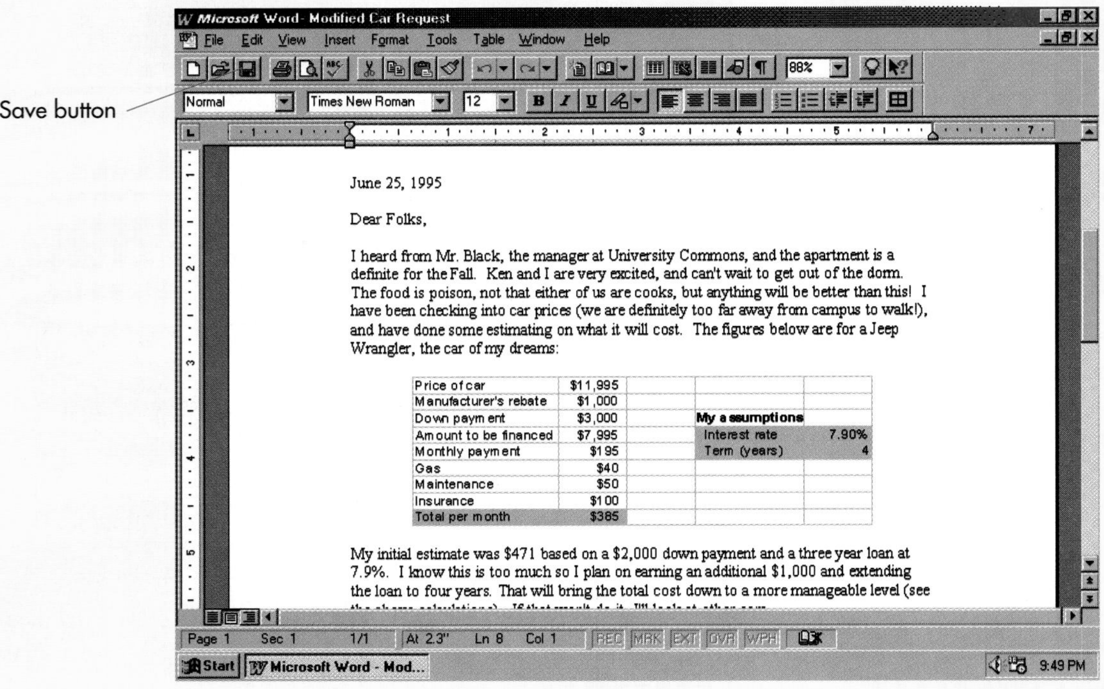

(g) The Completed Word Document (step 7)

FIGURE A.2 Hands-on Exercise 1 (continued)

- ➤ If necessary, click the **Maximize button** in the application window so that Excel takes the entire desktop, as shown in Figure A.2h.
- ➤ Pull down the **File menu** and click **Open** (or click the **Open button** on the Standard toolbar) to display the Open dialog box.
  - Click the **drop-down arrow** on the Look In list box. Click the appropriate drive, drive C or drive A, depending on the location of your data.
  - Double click the **Exploring Word folder** to make it the active folder.
  - Click (select) **Car Budget** to select the workbook that we have used throughout the exercise.
  - Click the **Open command button** to open the workbook, as shown in Figure A.2h.
  - Click the **Maximize button** in the document window (if necessary) so that the document window is as large as possible.
- ➤ You should see the original (unmodified) worksheet, with a down payment of $2,000, a three-year loan, a monthly car payment of $281, and total expenses per month of $471. The changes that were made in step 6 were made to the compound document and are *not* reflected in the source file.
- ➤ Pull down the **File menu.** Click **Exit** to exit Microsoft Excel.

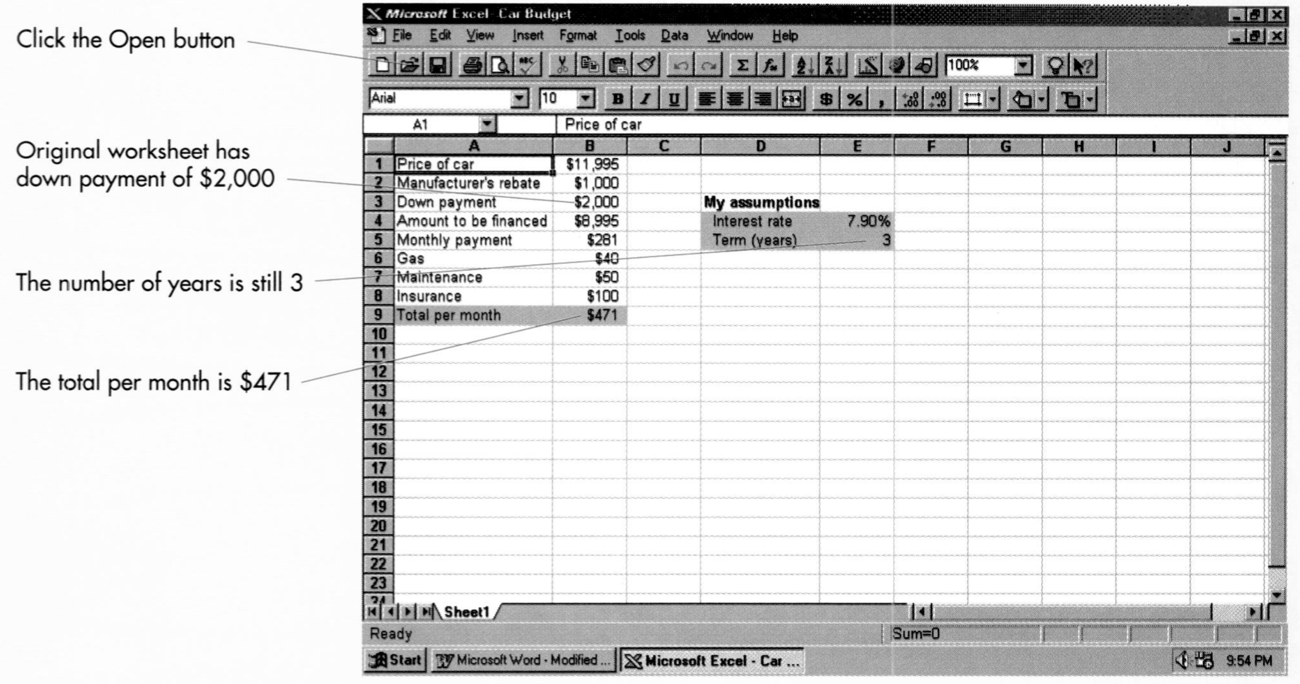

(h) The Original and Unmodified File (step 8)

FIGURE A.2 Hands-on Exercise 1 (continued)

The exercise just completed used embedding rather than linking to place a copy of the Excel worksheet into the Word document. The last step in the exercise demonstrated that the original worksheet was unaffected by changes made to the embedded copy within the compound document.

Linking is very different from embedding as you shall see in the next exercise. Linking maintains a dynamic connection between the server and client. Embedding does not. With linking, the object created by the server application

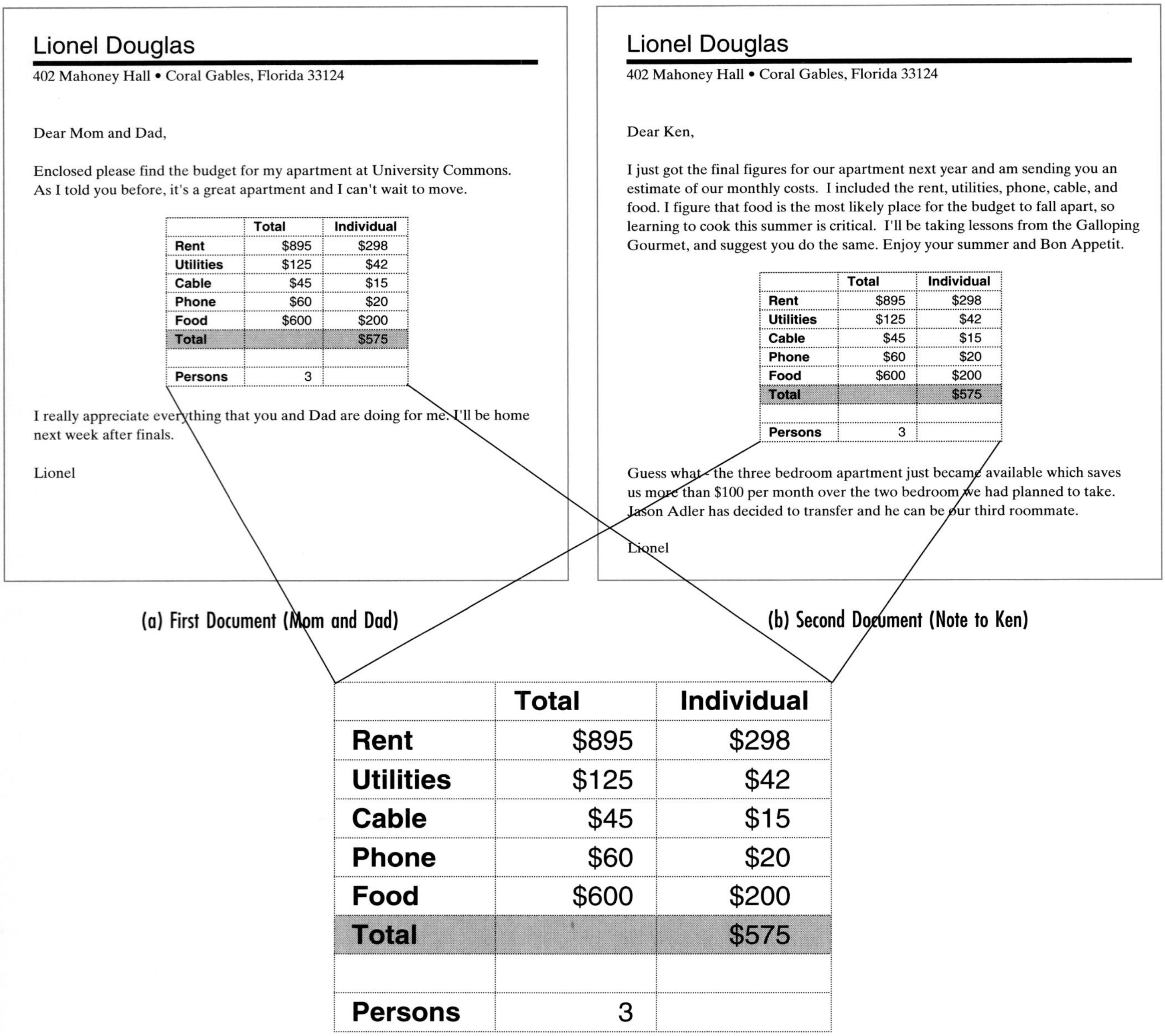

Lionel Douglas

402 Mahoney Hall • Coral Gables, Florida 33124

Dear Mom and Dad,

Enclosed please find the budget for my apartment at University Commons. As I told you before, it's a great apartment and I can't wait to move.

	Total	Individual
Rent	$895	$298
Utilities	$125	$42
Cable	$45	$15
Phone	$60	$20
Food	$600	$200
Total		$575
Persons	3	

I really appreciate everything that you and Dad are doing for me. I'll be home next week after finals.

Lionel

(a) First Document (Mom and Dad)

Lionel Douglas

402 Mahoney Hall • Coral Gables, Florida 33124

Dear Ken,

I just got the final figures for our apartment next year and am sending you an estimate of our monthly costs. I included the rent, utilities, phone, cable, and food. I figure that food is the most likely place for the budget to fall apart, so learning to cook this summer is critical. I'll be taking lessons from the Galloping Gourmet, and suggest you do the same. Enjoy your summer and Bon Appetit.

	Total	Individual
Rent	$895	$298
Utilities	$125	$42
Cable	$45	$15
Phone	$60	$20
Food	$600	$200
Total		$575
Persons	3	

Guess what - the three bedroom apartment just became available which saves us more than $100 per month over the two bedroom we had planned to take. Jason Adler has decided to transfer and he can be our third roommate.

Lionel

(b) Second Document (Note to Ken)

	Total	Individual
Rent	$895	$298
Utilities	$125	$42
Cable	$45	$15
Phone	$60	$20
Food	$600	$200
Total		$575
Persons	3	

(c) Worksheet (Apartment Budget)

FIGURE A.3 Linking

(e.g., an Excel worksheet) is tied to the compound document (e.g., a Word document) in such a way that any changes in the Excel worksheet are automatically reflected in the Word document. The Word document does not contain the worksheet per se, but only a representation of the worksheet, as well as a pointer (or link) to the Excel workbook.

Linking requires that an object be saved in its own file because the object does not actually exist within the compound document. Embedding, on the other hand, lets you place the object directly in a compound document without having to save it as a separate file. (The embedded object simply becomes part of the compound document.)

Consider now Figure A.3, in which the same worksheet is linked to two different documents. Both documents contain a pointer to the worksheet, which may be edited by double clicking the object in either compound document. Alternatively, you may open the server application and edit the object directly. In either case, changes to the Excel workbook are reflected in every compound document that is linked to the workbook.

The next exercise links a single Excel worksheet to two different Word documents. During the course of the exercise both applications (client and server) will be explicitly open, and it will be necessary to switch back and forth between the two. Thus, the exercise also demonstrates the multitasking capability within Windows 95 and the use of the taskbar to switch between the open applications.

HANDS-ON EXERCISE 2

Linking

Objective: To demonstrate multitasking and the ability to switch between applications; to link an Excel worksheet to multiple Word documents. Use Figure A.4 as a guide in the exercise.

STEP 1: Open the Word Document

- Check the taskbar to see whether there is a button for Microsoft Word indicating that the application is already active in memory. Start Word if you do not see its button on the taskbar.
- Open the **Mom and Dad document** in the **Exploring Word folder** as shown in Figure A.4a. The document opens in the Normal view (the view in which it was last saved). If necessary, zoom to **Page Width** so that the display on your monitor matches ours.
- Save the document as **Modified Mom and Dad.**

STEP 2: Open the Excel Worksheet

- Click the **Start button,** click (or point to) the **Programs menu,** then click **Microsoft Excel** to open the program.
- If necessary, click the **Maximize button** in the application window so that Excel takes the entire desktop. Click the **Maximize button** in the document window (if necessary) so that the document window is as large as possible.
- The taskbar should now contain buttons for both Microsoft Word and Microsoft Excel. Click either button to move back and forth between the open applications. End by clicking the Microsoft Excel button, since you want to work in that application.

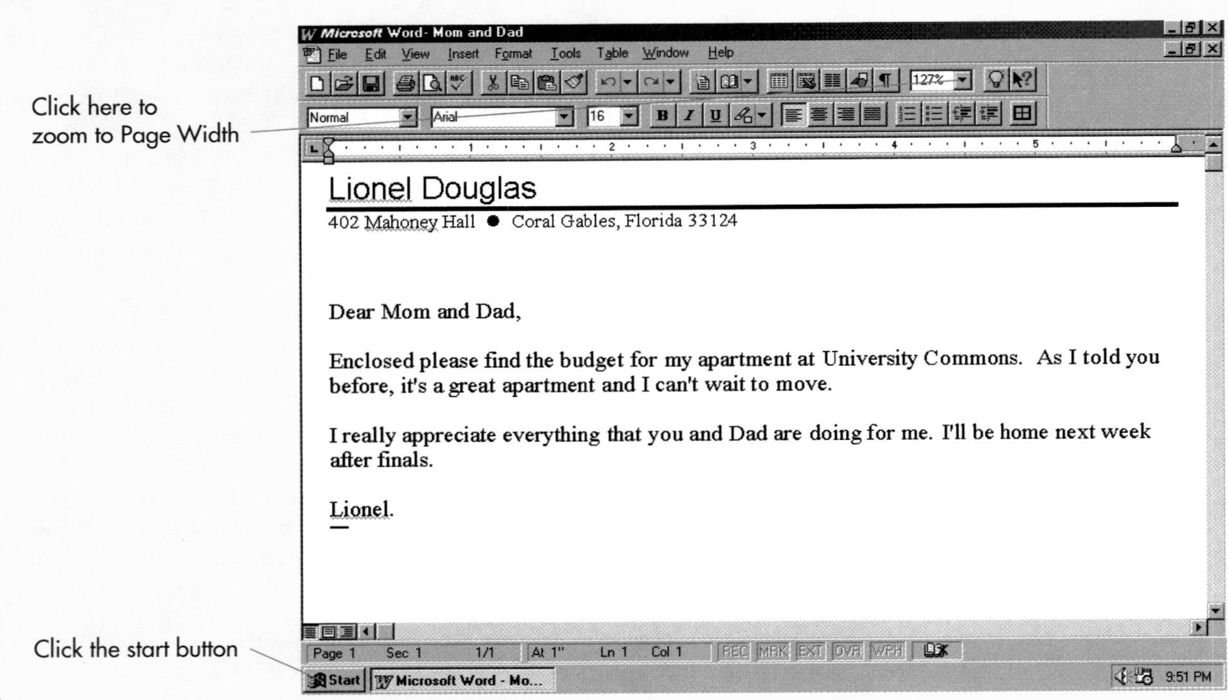

(a) Open the First Word Document (step 1)

FIGURE A.4 Hands-on Exercise 2

- Pull down the **File menu** and click **Open** (or click the **Open button** on the Standard toolbar) to display the Open dialog box in Figure A.4b.
- Click the **drop-down arrow** on the Look In list box. Click the appropriate drive, drive C or drive A, depending on the location of your data. Double click the **Exploring Word folder** to make it the active folder. Double click **Apartment Budget** to open the workbook.

THE COMMON USER INTERFACE

The ***common user interface*** provides a sense of familiarity from one Windows application to the next. Even if you have never used Excel, you will recognize many of the elements present in Word. Both applications share a common menu structure with consistent ways to execute commands from those menus. The Standard and Formatting toolbars are present in both applications. Many keyboard shortcuts are also common—for example Ctrl+Home and Ctrl+End to move to the beginning and end of a document.

STEP 3: Copy the Worksheet to the Clipboard

- Click in cell **A1.** Drag the mouse over cells **A1 through C9** so that the entire worksheet is selected as shown in Figure A.4c.

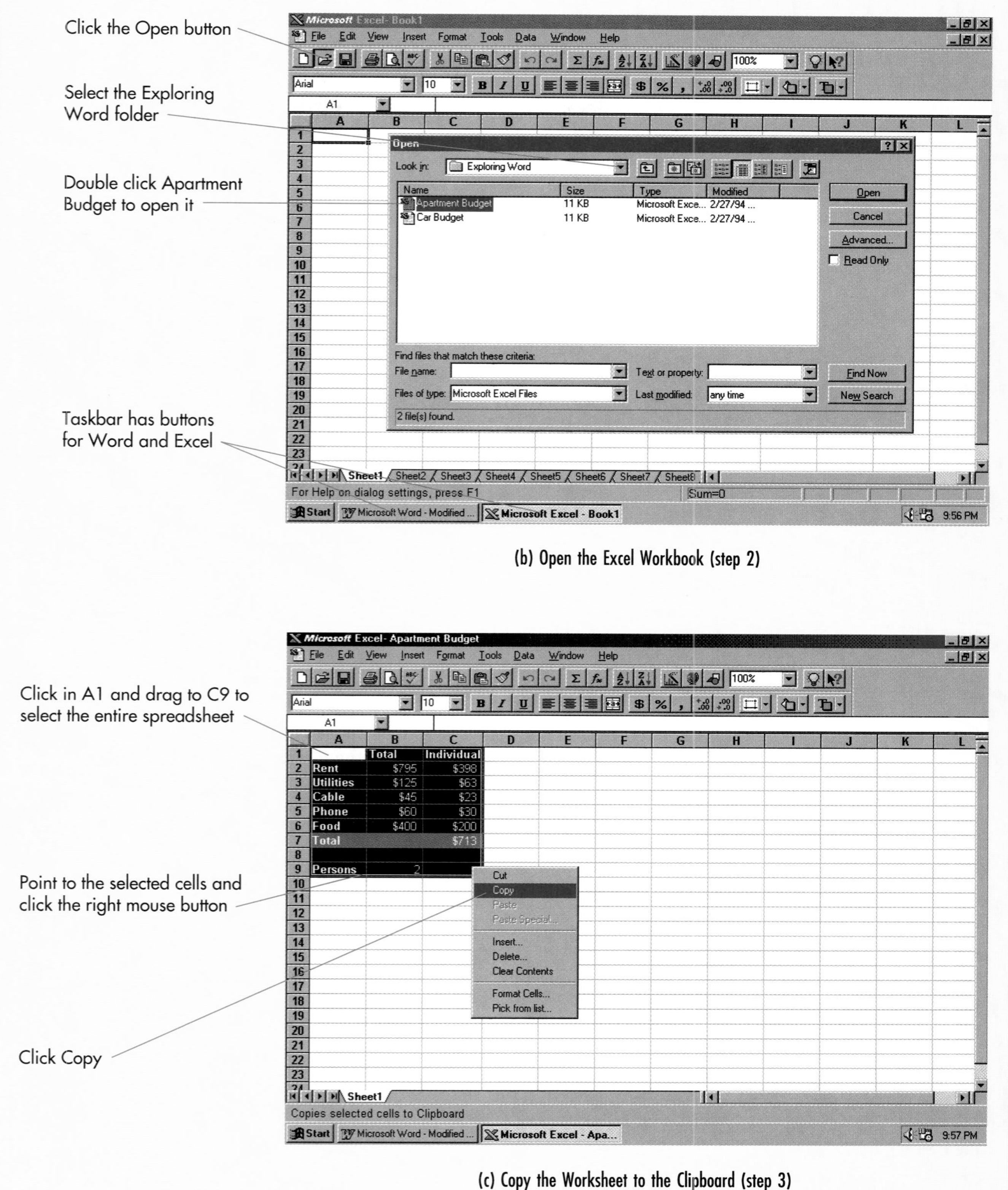

(b) Open the Excel Workbook (step 2)

(c) Copy the Worksheet to the Clipboard (step 3)

FIGURE A.4 Hands-on Exercise 2 (continued)

- ➤ Point to the selected cells, then click the **right mouse button** to display the shortcut menu shown in the figure. Click **Copy.** A moving border appears around the selected area in the worksheet, indicating that it has been copied to the clipboard.
- ➤ Click the **Microsoft Word button** on the taskbar to return to the Word document.

THE WINDOWS 95 TASKBAR

Multitasking, the ability to run multiple applications at the same time, is one of the primary advantages of the Windows environment. Each button on the taskbar appears automatically when its application or folder is opened and disappears upon closing. (The buttons on are resized automatically according to the number of open windows.) You can customize the taskbar by right clicking an empty area to display a shortcut menu, then clicking the Properties command. You can resize the taskbar by pointing to its inside edge, then dragging when you see a double-headed arrow. You can also move the taskbar to the left or right edge of the desktop, or to the top of the desktop, by dragging a blank area of the taskbar to the desired position.

STEP 4: Create the Link

- ➤ Click in the document between the two paragraphs. Press **enter** to enter an additional blank line.
- ➤ Pull down the **Edit menu.** Click **Paste Special** to produce the dialog box in Figure A.4d.
- ➤ Click the **Paste Link option button.** Click **Microsoft Excel Worksheet Object.** Click **OK** to insert the worksheet into the document. You may want to insert a blank line before and/or after the worksheet to make it easier to read.
- ➤ Save the document containing the letter to Mom and Dad.

LINKING VERSUS EMBEDDING

The ***Paste Special command*** will link or embed an object, depending on whether the Paste Link or Paste Option button is checked. Linking stores a pointer to the file containing the object together with a reference to the server application, and changes to the object are automatically reflected in all compound documents that are linked to the object. Embedding stores a copy of the object with a reference to the server application, but any changes to the copy of the object within the compound document are not reflected in the original object. With both linking and embedding, however, you can double click the object in the compound document to edit the object by using the tools of the server application.

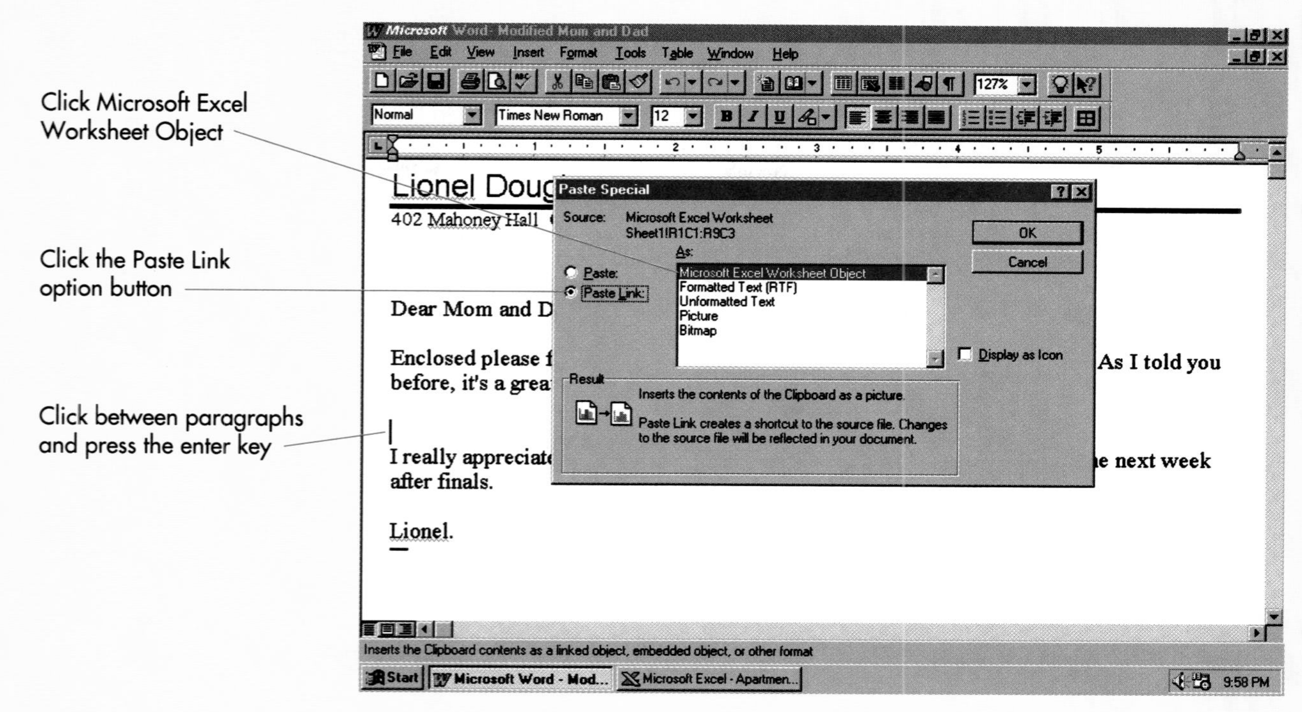

(d) Create the Link (step 4)

FIGURE A.4 Hands-on Exercise 2 (continued)

STEP 5: Open the Second Word Document

- Open the **Note to Ken document** in the **Exploring Word folder.** Save the document as **Modified Note to Ken** so that you can always return to the original document.
- The Apartment Budget worksheet is still in the clipboard since the contents of the clipboard have not been changed. Click at the end of the first paragraph (after the words Bon Appetit). Press the **enter key** to insert a blank line after the paragraph.
- Pull down the **Edit menu.** Click **Paste Special.** Click the **Paste Link option button.** Click **Microsoft Excel Worksheet Object.** Click **OK** to insert the worksheet into the document, as shown in Figure A.4e.
- If necessary, enter a blank line before or after the object to improve the appearance of the document. Save the document.
- Click anywhere on the worksheet to select the worksheet, as shown in Figure A.4e. The message on the status bar indicates you can double click the worksheet to edit the object.

STEP 6: Modify the Worksheet

- The existing spreadsheet indicates the cost of a two-bedroom apartment, but you want to show the cost of a three-bedroom apartment. Double click the worksheet in order to change it.
- The system pauses (the faster your computer, the better) as it switches back to Excel. Maximize the document window.
- Cells **A1 through C9** are still selected from step 3. Click outside the selected range to deselect the worksheet.

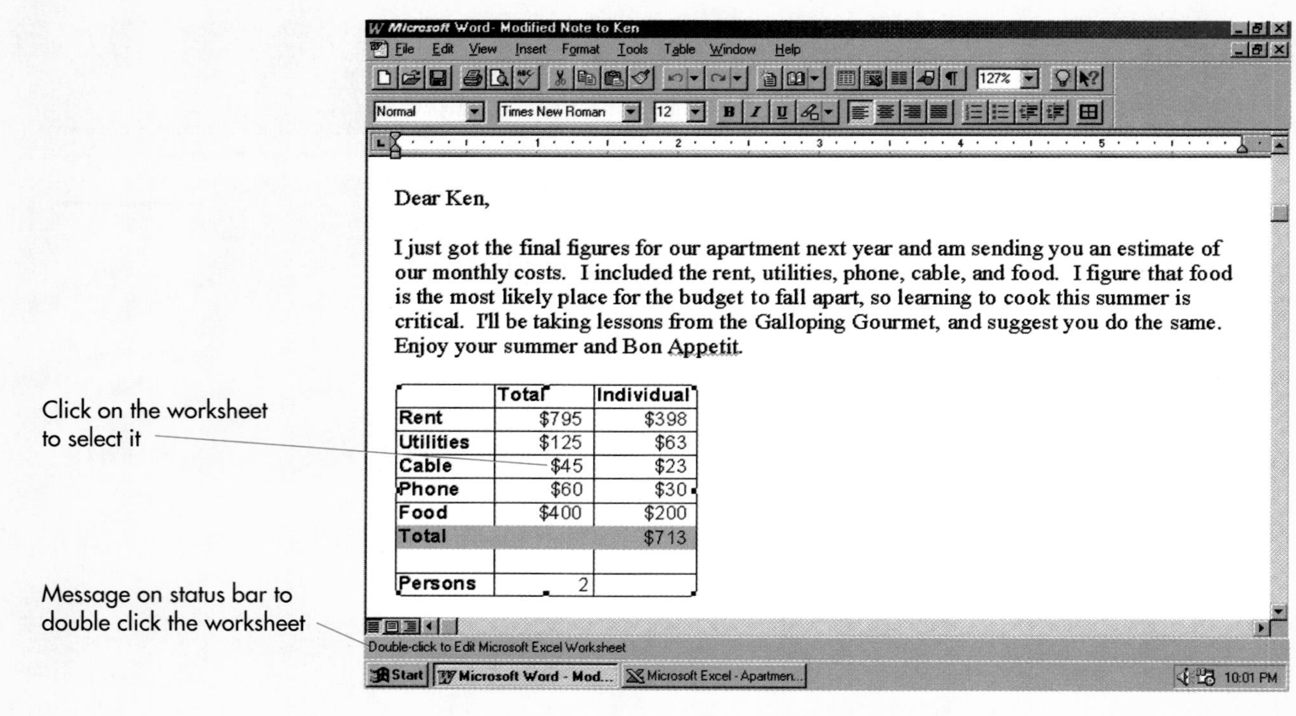
Microsoft Word - Modified Note to Ken
File Edit View Insert Format Tools Table Window Help
Normal
Times New Roman
12
127%
Dear Ken,
I just got the final figures for our apartment next year and am sending you an estimate of our monthly costs. I included the rent, utilities, phone, cable, and food. I figure that food is the most likely place for the budget to fall apart, so learning to cook this summer is critical. I'll be taking lessons from the Galloping Gourmet, and suggest you do the same. Enjoy your summer and Bon Appetit.
Click on the worksheet to select it
Message on status bar to double click the worksheet
Double-click to Edit Microsoft Excel Worksheet
Start
Microsoft Word - Mod...
Microsoft Excel - Apartmen...
10:01 PM

	Total	Individual
Rent	$795	$398
Utilities	$125	$63
Cable	$45	$23
Phone	$60	$30
Food	$400	$200
Total		$713
Persons	2	

(e) Open the Second Document (step 5)

FIGURE A.4 Hands-on Exercise 2 (continued)

- Click in cell **B2.** Type **$895** (the rent for a three-bedroom apartment).
- Click in cell **B6.** Type **$600** (the increased amount for food).
- Click in cell **B9.** Type **3** to change the number of people sharing the apartment. Press **enter.** The total expenses (in cell C9) change to $575, as shown in Figure A.4f.
- Save the worksheet.

STEP 7: View the Modified Document

- Click the **Microsoft Word button** on the taskbar to return to Microsoft Word and the note to Ken, as shown in Figure A.4g.
- The note to Ken displays the modified worksheet because of the link established earlier.
- Click at the end of the worksheet and to add the additional text shown in Figure A.4g to let Ken know about the new apartment.
- Save the document.

STEP 8: View the Completed Note to Mom and Dad

- Pull down the **Window menu.** Click **Modified Note to Mom and Dad** to switch to this document.
- The note to your parents also contains the updated worksheet (with three roommates) because of the link established earlier.
- Save the completed document.

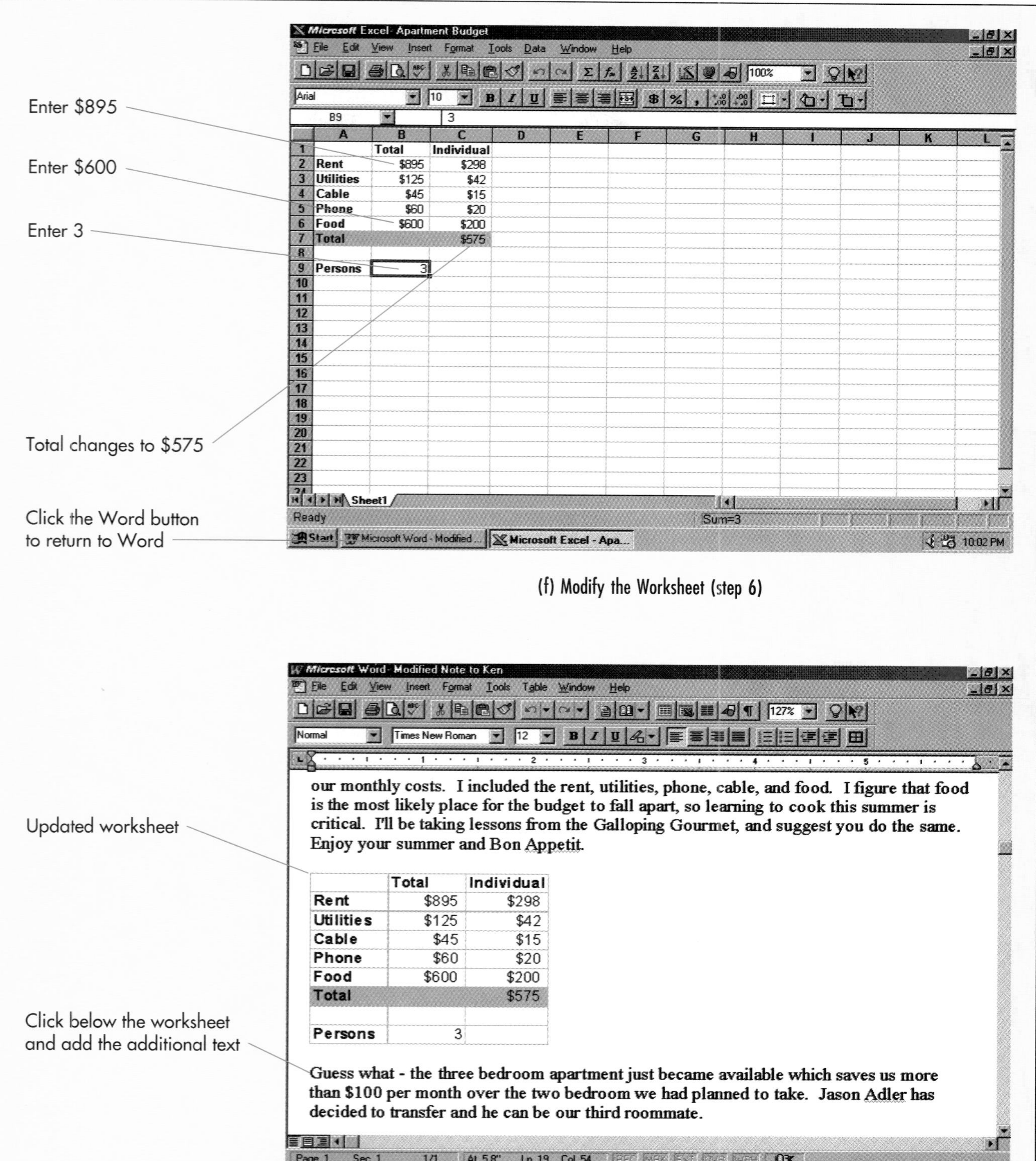

Enter $895
Enter $600
Enter 3
Total changes to $575
Click the Word button to return to Word
Microsoft Excel - Apartment Budget
Total
Individual
Rent $895 $298
Utilities $125 $42
Cable $45 $15
Phone $60 $20
Food $600 $200
Total $575
Persons 3
Sheet1
Ready
Sum=3
Updated worksheet
Click below the worksheet and add the additional text
Microsoft Word - Modified Note to Ken
our monthly costs. I included the rent, utilities, phone, cable, and food. I figure that food is the most likely place for the budget to fall apart, so learning to cook this summer is critical. I'll be taking lessons from the Galloping Gourmet, and suggest you do the same. Enjoy your summer and Bon Appetit.
Total
Individual
Rent $895 $298
Utilities $125 $42
Cable $45 $15
Phone $60 $20
Food $600 $200
Total $575
Persons 3
Guess what - the three bedroom apartment just became available which saves us more than $100 per month over the two bedroom we had planned to take. Jason Adler has decided to transfer and he can be our third roommate.

(f) Modify the Worksheet (step 6)

(g) View the Modified Document (step 7)

FIGURE A.4 Hands-on Exercise 2 (continued)

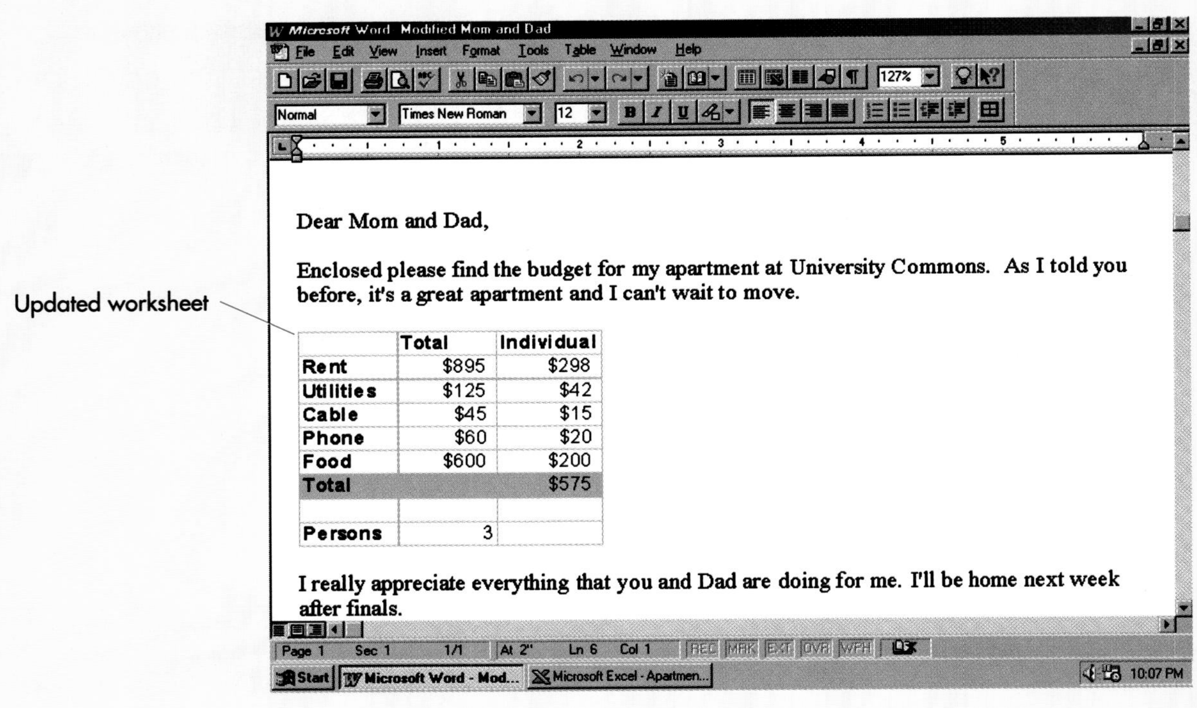

Updated worksheet
Microsoft Word Modified Mom and Dad
Dear Mom and Dad,
Enclosed please find the budget for my apartment at University Commons. As I told you before, it's a great apartment and I can't wait to move.
	Total	Individual
Rent	$895	$298
Utilities	$125	$42
Cable	$45	$15
Phone	$60	$20
Food	$600	$200
Total		$575
Persons	3	
I really appreciate everything that you and Dad are doing for me. I'll be home next week after finals.

(h) View the Modified Document (step 8)

FIGURE A.4 Hands-on Exercise 2 (continued)

> **ALT+TAB STILL WORKS**
>
> Alt+Tab was a treasured shortcut in Windows 3.1 that enabled users to switch back and forth between open applications. The shortcut also works in Windows 95. Press and hold the Alt key while you press and release the Tab key repeatedly to cycle through the open applications. Note that each time you release the Tab key the icon of a different application is selected in the small rectangular window that is displayed in the middle of the screen. Release the Alt key when you have selected the icon for the application you want.

STEP 9: Exit

- Exit Word. Save the files if you are requested to do so. The button for Microsoft Word disappears from the taskbar.
- Exit Excel. Save the files if you are requested to do so. The button for Microsoft Excel disappears from the taskbar.

SUMMARY

The essential difference between linking and embedding is that linking does not place the object into the compound document, but only a pointer (link) to the object. Embedding places (a copy of) the actual object into the compound document. Linking is dynamic in nature, whereas embedding is not.

Linking requires that the object be saved in its own file, and further that the link between the object and the compound (container) document be maintained. Linking is especially useful when the same object is present in multiple documents because any subsequent change to the object is made in only one place, but is automatically reflected in the multiple compound documents.

Embedding does not require the object to be saved in a separate file because the object is contained within the compound document. Embedding lets you give your colleague a copy of the compound document, without a copy of the object, and indeed, there need not be a separate file for the object. You would not, however, want to embed the same object into multiple documents because any subsequent change to the object would have to be made in every document.

KEY WORDS AND CONCEPTS

Client application
Clipboard
Common user interface
Compound document
Container
Dynamic connection
Embedded object
In-place editing
Insert Object command
Linked object
Multitasking
Object Linking and Embedding (OLE)
Paste Special command
Server application

B

APPENDIX B: MAIL MERGE

OVERVIEW

A ***mail merge*** takes the tedium out of sending ***form letters,*** as it creates the same letter many times, changing the name, address, and other information as appropriate from letter to letter. You might use a mail merge to look for a job upon graduation, when you send essentially the same letter to many different companies. The concept is illustrated in Figure B.1, in which John Smith drafts a letter describing his qualifications, then merges that letter with a set of names and addresses, to produce the individual letters.

The mail merge process uses two files as input, a main document and a data source. A set of form letters is created as output. The ***main document*** (e.g., the cover letter in Figure B.1a) contains standardized text together with one or more ***merge fields*** that indicate where variable information is to be inserted into the individual letters. The ***data source*** (the set of names and addresses in Figure B.1b) contains the information that varies from letter to letter.

The first row in the data source is called the header row and identifies the fields in the remaining rows. Each additional row contains the data to create one letter and is called a ***data record.*** Every data record contains the same fields in the same order—for example, Title, FirstName, LastName, and so on.

The main document and the data source work in conjunction with one another, with the merge fields in the main document referencing the corresponding fields in the data source. The first line in the address of Figure B.1a, for example, contains the entries in angled brackets, *<<Title>> <<FirstName>> <<LastName>>*. (These entries are not typed explicitly but are entered through special commands as described in the hands-on exercise that follows shortly.) The merge process examines each record in the data source and substitutes the appropriate field values for the corresponding merge fields as it creates the individual form letters. For example, the first three fields in the first record will

John H. Smith

426 Jenny Lake Drive • Coral Gables, FL 33146 • (305) 666-4801

June 25, 1995

« Title » «FirstName» «LastName»
«JobTitle»
«Company»
«Address1»
«City», «State» «PostalCode»

Dear «Title» «LastName»:

I am writing to inquire about a position with «Company» as an entry level computer programmer. I have just graduated from the University of Miami with a Bachelor's Degree in Computer Information Systems (May, 1995) and I am very interested in working for you. I have a background in both microcomputer applications (Windows 95, Word, Excel, PowerPoint, and Access) as well as extensive experience with programming languages (Visual Basic, C++ and COBOL). I feel that I am well qualified to join your staff as over the past two years I have had a great deal of experience designing and implementing computer programs, both as a part of my educational program and during my internship with Personalized Computer Designs, Inc.

I am eager to put my skills to work and would like to talk with you at your earliest convenience. I have enclosed a copy of my résumé and will be happy to furnish the names and addresses of my references, if you so desire. You may reach me at the above address and phone number. I look forward to hearing from you.

Sincerely,

John Smith

(a) The Main Document

FIGURE B.1 The Mail Merge

produce *Mr. Jason Frasher.* The same fields in the second record will produce *Ms. Elizabeth Schery,* and so on.

In similar fashion, the second line in the address of the main document contains the *<<JobTitle>>* field. The third line contains the *<<Company>>* field. The fourth line references the *<<Address1>>* field, and the last line contains the *<<City>>, <<State>,* and *<<PostalCode>>* fields. The salutation repeats the *<<Title>>* and *<<LastName>>* fields. The first sentence uses the *<<Company>>* field a second time. The mail merge prepares the letters one at a time, with one letter created for every record in the data source until the file of names and addresses is exhausted. The individual form letters are shown in Figure B.1c. Each letter begins automatically on a new page.

Title	FirstName	LastName	JobTitle	Company	Address1	City	State	PostalCode
Mr.	Jason	Frasher	President	Frasher Systems	100 S. Miami Avenue	Miami	FL	33103
Ms.	Elizabeth	Schery	Director of Personnel	Custom Computing	8180 Kendall Drive	Miami	FL	33156
Ms.	Lauren	Howard	President	Unique Systems	475 LeJeune Road	Coral Gables	FL	33146

(b) The Data Source

John H. Smith

426 Jenny Lake Drive • Coral Gables, FL 33146 • (305) 666-4801

June 25, 1995

Mr. Jason Frasher
President
Frasher Systems
100 S. Miami Avenue
Miami, FL 33103

Dear Mr. Frasher:

I am writing to inquire about a position with Frasher Systems as an entry level computer programmer.
I have just graduated from the University c
Systems (May, 1995) and I am very interes
microcomputer applications (Windows 95,
experience with programming languages (V
to join your staff as over the past two years
implementing computer programs, both as
with Personalized Computer Designs, Inc.

I am eager to put my skills to work and wo
enclosed a copy of my résumé and will be h
you so desire. You may reach me at the ab
from you.

Sincerely,

John Smith

John H. Smith

426 Jenny Lake Drive • Coral Gables, FL 33146 • (305) 666-4801

June 25, 1995

Ms. Elizabeth Schery
Director of Personnel
Custom Computing
8180 Kendall Drive
Miami, FL 33156

Dear Ms. Schery:

I am writing to inquire about a position with Custom Computing as an entry level computer programmer.
I have just graduated from the University of M
Systems (May, 1995) and I am very interested
microcomputer applications (Windows 95, W
experience with programming languages (Vis
to join your staff as over the past two years I h
implementing computer programs, both as a p
with Personalized Computer Designs, Inc.

I am eager to put my skills to work and would
enclosed a copy of my résumé and will be hap
you so desire. You may reach me at the abov
from you.

Sincerely,

John Smith

John H. Smith

426 Jenny Lake Drive • Coral Gables, FL 33146 • (305) 666-4801

June 25, 1995

Ms. Lauren Howard
President
Unique Systems
475 LeJeune Road
Coral Gables, FL 33146

Dear Ms. Howard:

I am writing to inquire about a position with Unique Systems as an entry level computer programmer. I have just graduated from the University of Miami with a Bachelor's Degree in Computer Information Systems (May, 1995) and I am very interested in working for you. I have a background in both microcomputer applications (Windows 95, Word, Excel, PowerPoint, and Access) as well as extensive experience with programming languages (Visual Basic, C++ and COBOL). I feel that I am well qualified to join your staff as over the past two years I have had a great deal of experience designing and implementing computer programs, both as a part of my educational program and during my internship with Personalized Computer Designs, Inc.

I am eager to put my skills to work and would like to talk with you at your earliest convenience. I have enclosed a copy of my résumé and will be happy to furnish the names and addresses of my references, if you so desire. You may reach me at the above address and phone number. I look forward to hearing from you.

Sincerely,

John Smith

(c) The Printed Letters

FIGURE B.1 The Mail Merge (continued)

> **FILE DESIGN**
>
> The zip code should be defined as a separate field in the data source in order to sort on zip code and take advantage of bulk mail. A person's first and last name should also be defined separately, so that you have access to either field, perhaps to create a friendly salutation such as Dear Joe or to sort on last name.

MAIL MERGE HELPER

The implementation of a mail merge in Microsoft Word is easy, provided you understand the basic concept. In essence, there are three things you must do:

1. Create and save the main document
2. Create and save the data source
3. Merge the main document and data source to create the individual letters

The Mail Merge command is located in the Tools menu. Execution of the command displays the ***Mail Merge Helper,*** which lists the steps in the mail merge process and guides you every step of the way.

The screen in Figure B.2 shows the Mail Merge Helper as it appears after steps 1 and 2 have been completed. The main document is the file *Finished Form Letter.doc.* The data source is the file *Names and Addresses.doc.* All that remains is to merge the files and create the individual form letters. The options in effect

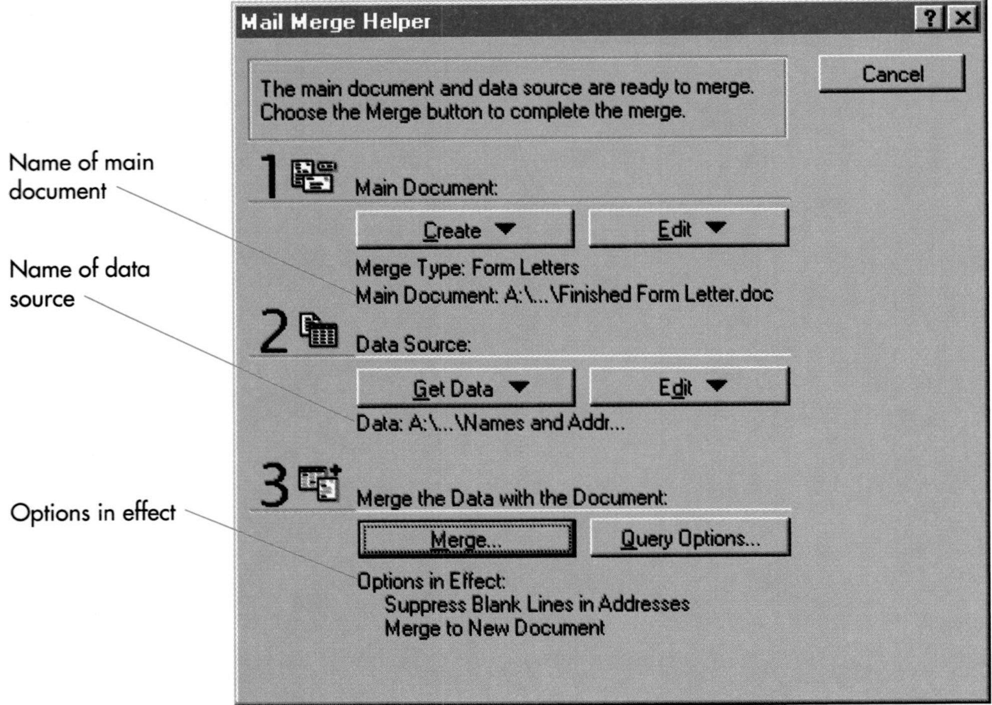

FIGURE B.2 Mail Merge Helper

indicate that the letters will be created in a new document and that blank lines, if any, in addresses (e.g., a missing company or title) will be suppressed. The Query Options command button lets you select and/or ***sort*** the records in the data source prior to the merge. These options are discussed after the hands-on exercise.

PAPER MAKES A DIFFERENCE

Most of us take paper for granted, but the right paper can make a significant difference in the effectiveness of the document. Reports and formal correspondence are usually printed on white paper, but you would be surprised how many different shades of white there are. Other types of documents lend themselves to colored paper for additional impact. In short, the choice of paper you use is far from an automatic decision. Our favorite source for paper is a company called PAPER DIRECT (1-800-APAPERS). Ask for a catalog, then consider the use of a specialty paper the next time you have an important project, such as the cover letter for your résumé.

HANDS-ON EXERCISE 1

Mail Merge

Objective: To create a main document and associated data source; to implement a mail merge and produce a set of form letters. Use Figure B.3 as a guide in the exercise.

STEP 1: Open the Cover Letter

- Open the **Form Letter document** in the **Exploring Word Folder** as shown in Figure B.3a. (The dialog box will not yet be displayed.)
  - If necessary, pull down the **View menu** and click **Page Layout** (or click the **Page Layout button** above the status bar).
  - If necessary, click the **Zoom Control arrow** to change to **Page Width.**
- Save the document as **Modified Form Letter** so that you can return to the original document if necessary.

THE LETTER WIZARD

It is the rare individual who has never been confronted by writer's block and the frustration of a blank screen and a flashing cursor. The Letter Wizard is Microsoft's attempt to get you started. Pull down the File menu, click New, click the Letters & Faxes tab in the New dialog box, then double click the Letter Wizard. The Wizard asks you a series of questions about the type of letter you want to write, then supplies a template for you to complete. It will even let you choose one of several prewritten letters, including a résumé cover letter. It's not perfect, but it is a starting point, and that may be all you need.

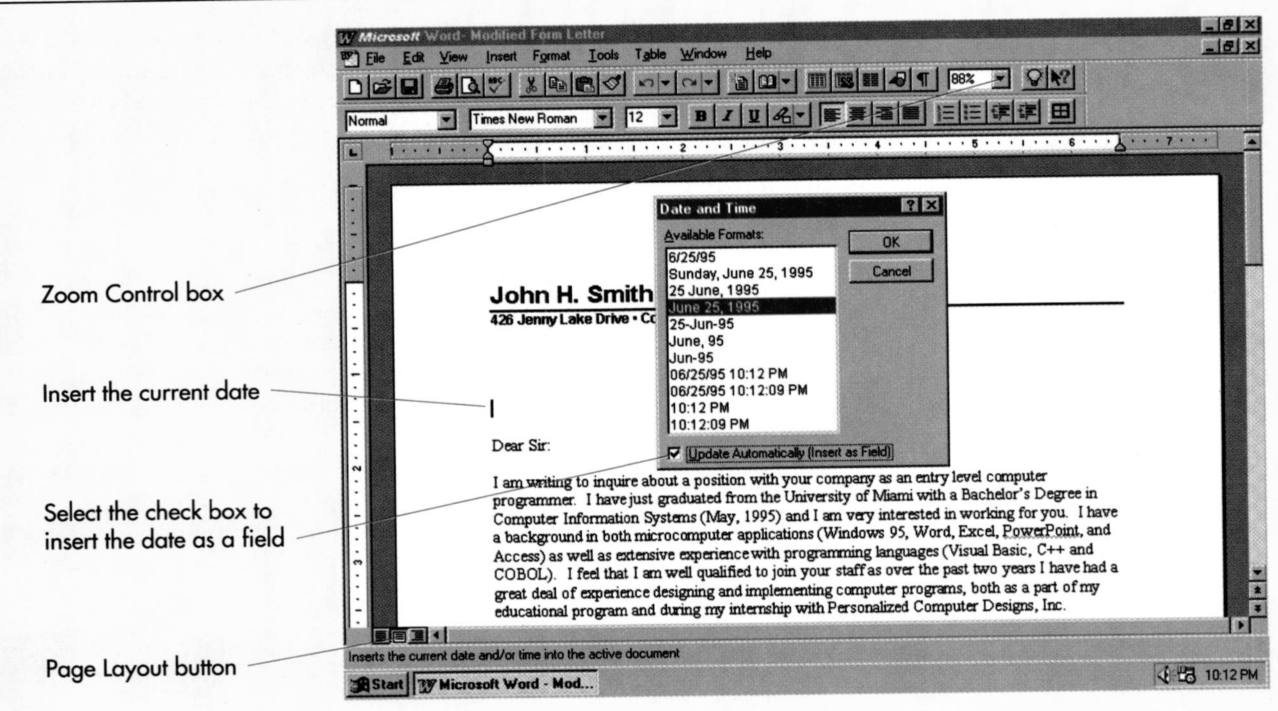

(a) Insert the Date (step 2)

FIGURE B.3 Hands-on Exercise 1

STEP 2: Insert Today's Date

- Click to the left of the "D" in Dear Sir, then press **enter** twice to insert two lines. Press the **up arrow** two times to return to the first line you inserted.
- Pull down the **Insert menu** and click the **Date and Time command** to display the dialog box in Figure B.3a.
- Select (click) the date format you prefer and, if necessary, check the box to insert the date as a field. Click **OK** to close the dialog box.

FIELD CODES VERSUS FIELD RESULTS

All fields are displayed in a document in one of two formats, as a ***field code*** or as a ***field result.*** A field code appears in braces and indicates instructions to insert variable data when the document is printed; a field result displays the information as it will appear in the printed document. You can toggle the display between the field code and field result by pressing Shift+F9 during editing.

STEP 3: Create the Main Document

- Pull down the **Tools menu.** Click **Mail Merge.** Click the **Create command button** under step 1 to create the main document as shown in Figure B.3b.
- Click **Form Letters,** then click **Active Window** to indicate that you will use the Form Letter document (in the active window) as the main document.

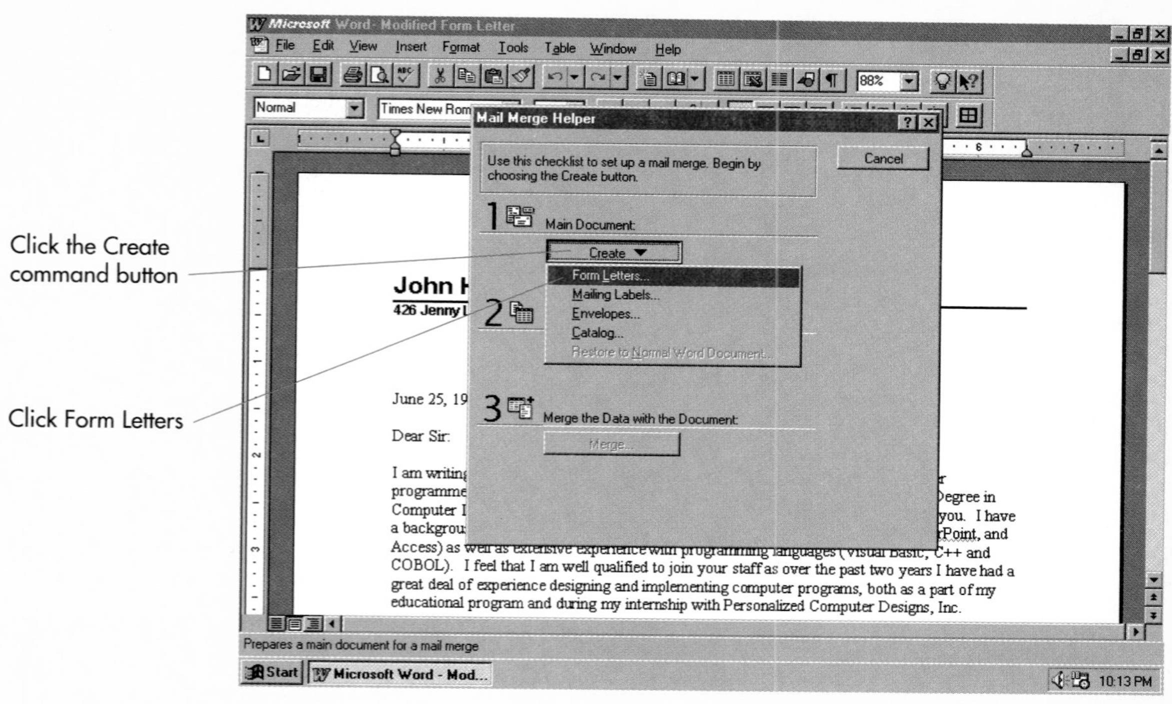

(b) Create the Main Document (step 3)

FIGURE B.3 Hands-on Exercise 1 (continued)

STEP 4: Create the Data Source

- Click **Get Data** under step 2, then click **Create Data Source** to display the dialog box in Figure B.3c.
- Word provides commonly used field names for the data source, but not all of the data fields are necessary. Click **Address2,** then click the **Remove Field Name command button.** Delete the Country, HomePhone, and WorkPhone fields in similar fashion.
- Click **OK** to complete the definition of the data source. You will then be presented with the Save As dialog box as you need to save the data source.
- Type **Names and Addresses** in the File Name text box as the name of the data source. Click **Save** to save the file.
- You will see a message indicating that the data source does not contain any data records. Click **Edit Data Source** in order to add records at this time.

STEP 5: Add the Data

- Enter data for the first record. Type **Mr.** in the Title field. Press **Tab** to move to the next (FirstName) field, and type **Jason.** Continue in this fashion until you have completed the first record as shown in Figure B.3d.
- Click **Add New** to enter the data for the next person to receive the letter:
  - Ms. Elizabeth Schery
  - Director of Personnel
  - Custom Computing
  - 8180 Kendall Drive
  - Miami, FL 33156

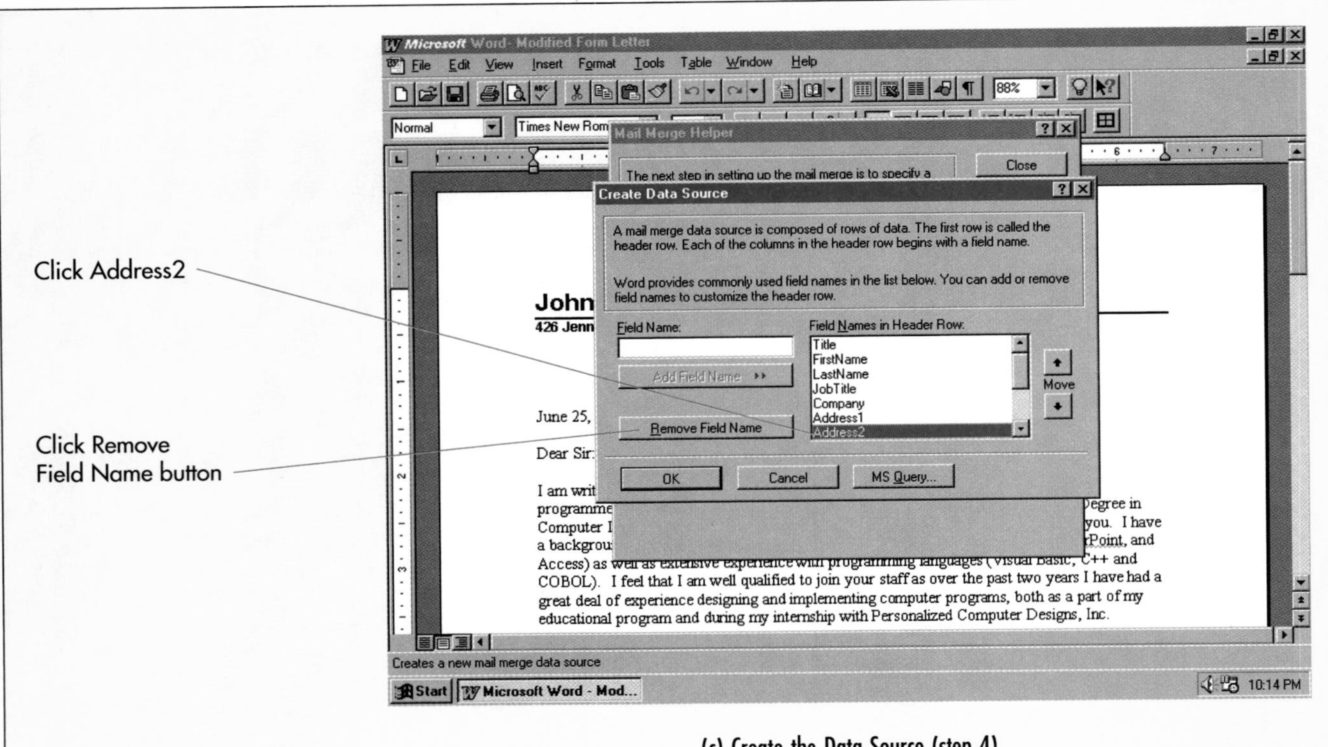
Click Address2
Click Remove Field Name button

(c) Create the Data Source (step 4)

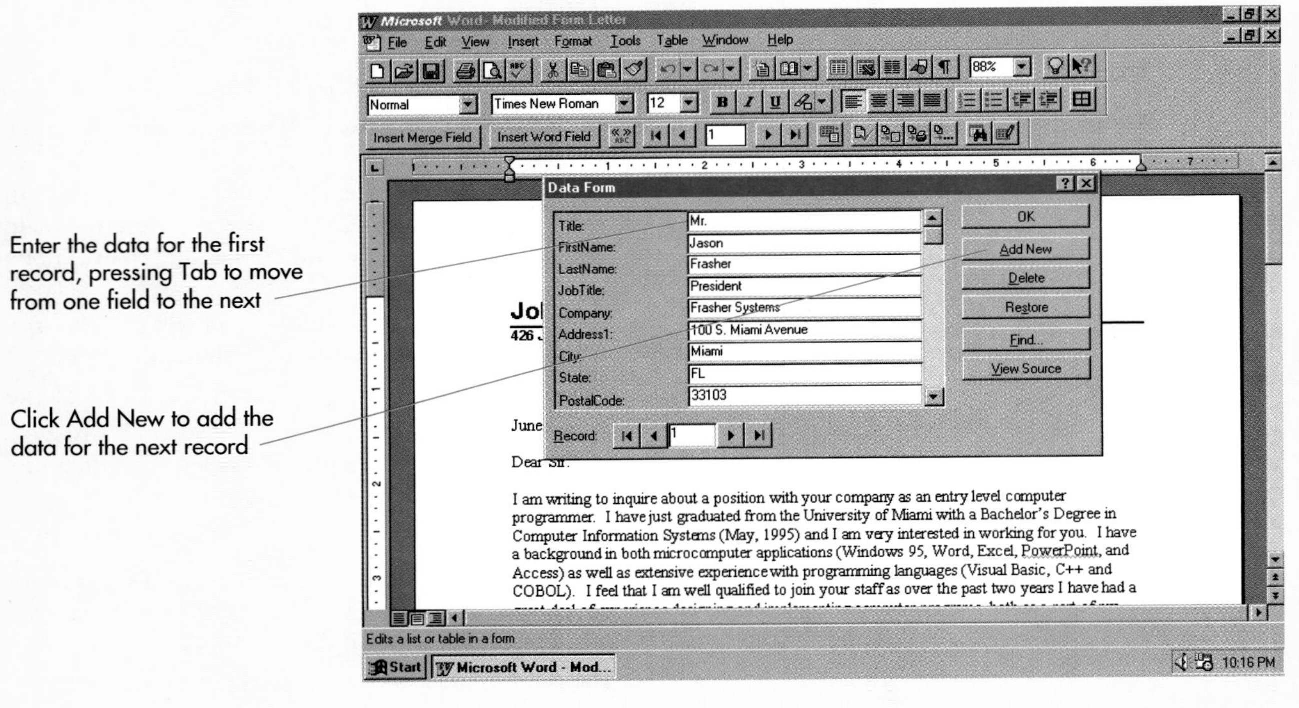
Enter the data for the first record, pressing Tab to move from one field to the next
Click Add New to add the data for the next record

(d) Adding Data (step 5)

FIGURE B.3 Hands-on Exercise 1 (continued)

➤ Click **Add New** to enter the data for the third and last recipient:

- Ms. Lauren Howard
- President
- Unique Systems
- 475 LeJeune Road
- Coral Gables, FL 33146

➤ Click **OK** to end the data entry and return to the main document. The Mail Merge toolbar is displayed immediately below the Formatting toolbar.

STEP 6: Add the Data Fields

➤ Click in the main document immediately below the date. Press **enter** to leave a blank line between the date and the first line of the address.

➤ Click the **Insert Merge Field button** on the Merge toolbar. Click **Title** from the list of fields within the data source. The title field is inserted into the main document and enclosed in angled brackets as shown in Figure B.3e.

➤ Press the **space bar** to add a space between the words. Click the **Insert Merge Field button** a second time. Click **FirstName.** Press the **space bar.**

➤ Click the **Insert Merge Field button** again. Click **LastName.**

➤ Press **enter** to move to the next line. Enter the remaining fields in the address as shown in Figure B.3e. Be sure to add a comma after the **City field** as well as a space.

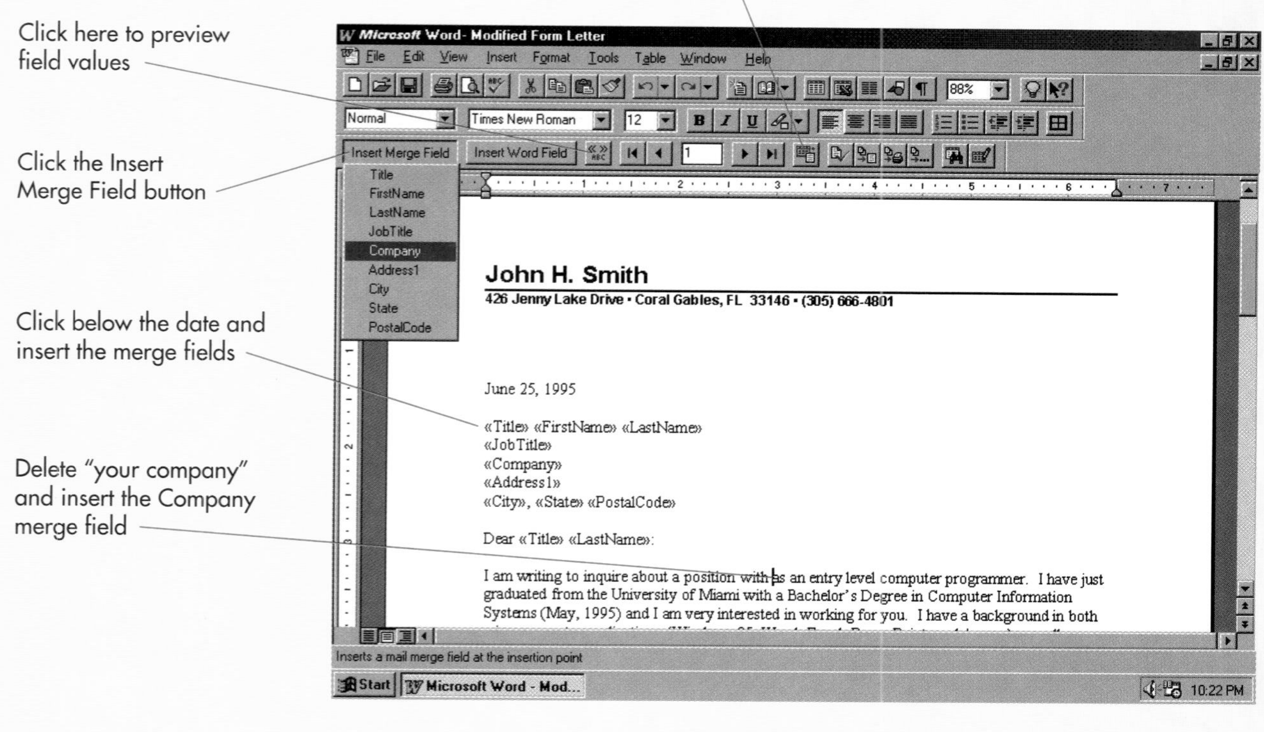

(e) Inserting Data Fields (step 6)

FIGURE B.3 Hands-on Exercise 1 (continued)

- Delete the word "Sir" in the salutation and replace it with the **Title** and **LastName fields.**
- Delete the words "your company" in the first sentence and replace them with the **Company field.**
- Save the main document.

STEP 7: The Mail Merge Toolbar

- The Mail Merge toolbar enables you to preview the form letters before they are created.
- Click the **<<abc>> button** on the Merge toolbar to display field values rather than field codes; you will see Mr. Jason Frasher instead of <<Title>> <<FirstName>> <<LastName>>, etc.
- The **<<abc>> button** functions as a toggle switch. Click it once and you switch from field codes to field values; click it a second time and you go from field values back to field codes. End with the field values displayed.
- Look at the text box on the Mail Merge toolbar, which displays the number 1 to indicate that the first record is displayed. Click the **▶ button** to display the form letter for the next record (Ms. Elizabeth Schery in our example).
- Click the **▶ button** again to display the form letter for the next record (Ms. Lauren Howard). The toolbar indicates you are on the third record. Click the **◀ button** to return to the previous (second) record.
- Click the **|◀ button** to move directly to the first record (Jason Frasher). Click the **▶| button** to display the form letter for the last record (Lauren Howard).
- Toggle the **<<abc>> button** to display the field codes.

STEP 8: The Mail Merge Helper

- Click the **Mail Merge Helper button** on the Merge toolbar to display the dialog box in Figure B.3f.
- The Mail Merge Helper shows your progress thus far:
  - The main document has been created and saved as Modified Form Letter.
  - The data source has been created and saved as Names and Addresses.
- Click the **Merge command button** to display the dialog box in Figure B.3g.

EDIT THE DATA SOURCE

Click the Mail Merge Helper button to display a dialog box with information about the mail merge, click the Edit command button under Data Source, then click the file containing the data source. Click the View Source command button to see multiple records in the data source displayed within a table; the first row contains the field names, and each succeeding row contains a data record. Edit the data source, then pull down the Window menu and click the name of the file containing the main document to continue working on the mail merge.

STEP 9: The Merge

- The selected options in Figure B.3g should already be set:
  - If necessary, click the **arrow** in the Merge To list box and select New document.

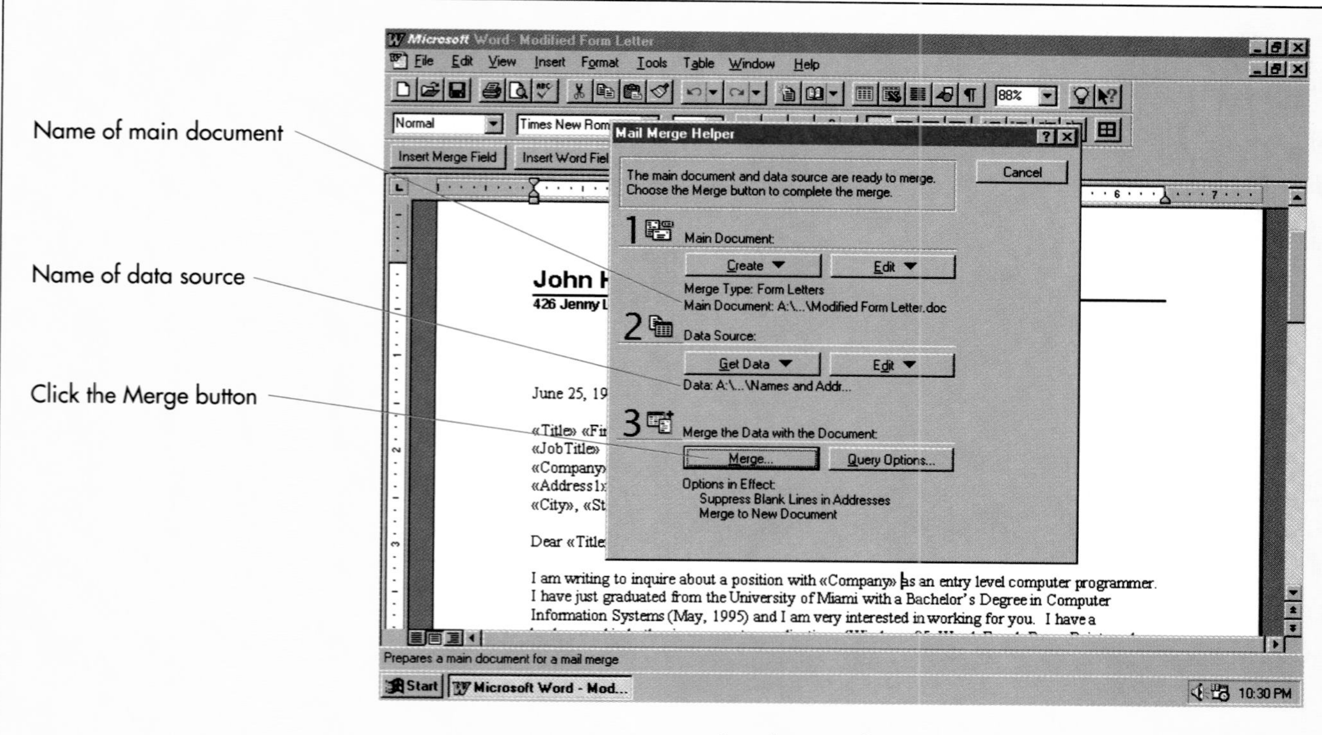

(f) Mail Merge Helper (step 8)

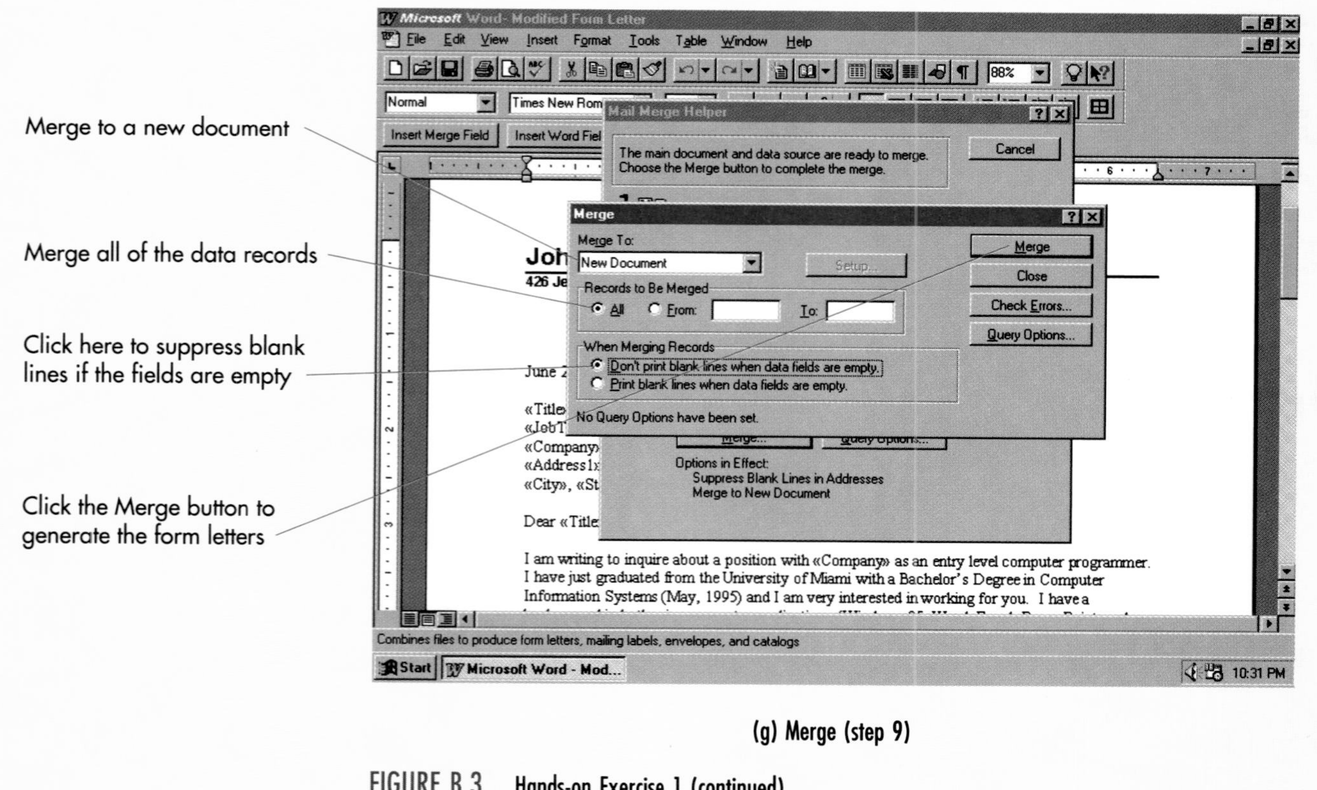

(g) Merge (step 9)

FIGURE B.3 Hands-on Exercise 1 (continued)

- If necessary, click the **All options button** to include all records in the data source.
- If necessary, click the **option button** to suppress blank lines if data fields are empty.

➤ Click the **Merge command button.** Word pauses momentarily, then generates the three form letters in a new document.

STEP 10: The Form Letters

➤ The title bar of the active window changes to Form Letters1. Scroll through the letters to review them individually.

➤ Pull down the **View menu.** Click **Zoom.** Click **Many Pages.** Click the **monitor icon,** then click and drag within the resulting dialog box to display three pages side by side. Click **OK.** You should see the three form letters as shown in Figure B.3h.

➤ Print the letters.

➤ Pull down the **File menu** and click **Exit** to exit Word. Pay close attention to the informational messages that ask whether to save the modified file(s):

- There is no need to save the merged document (Form Letters1) because you can always re-create the merged letters, provided you have saved the main document and data source.
- Save the Modified Form Letter and Names and Addresses documents if you are asked to do so.

➤ Congratulations on a job well done. Good luck in your job hunting!

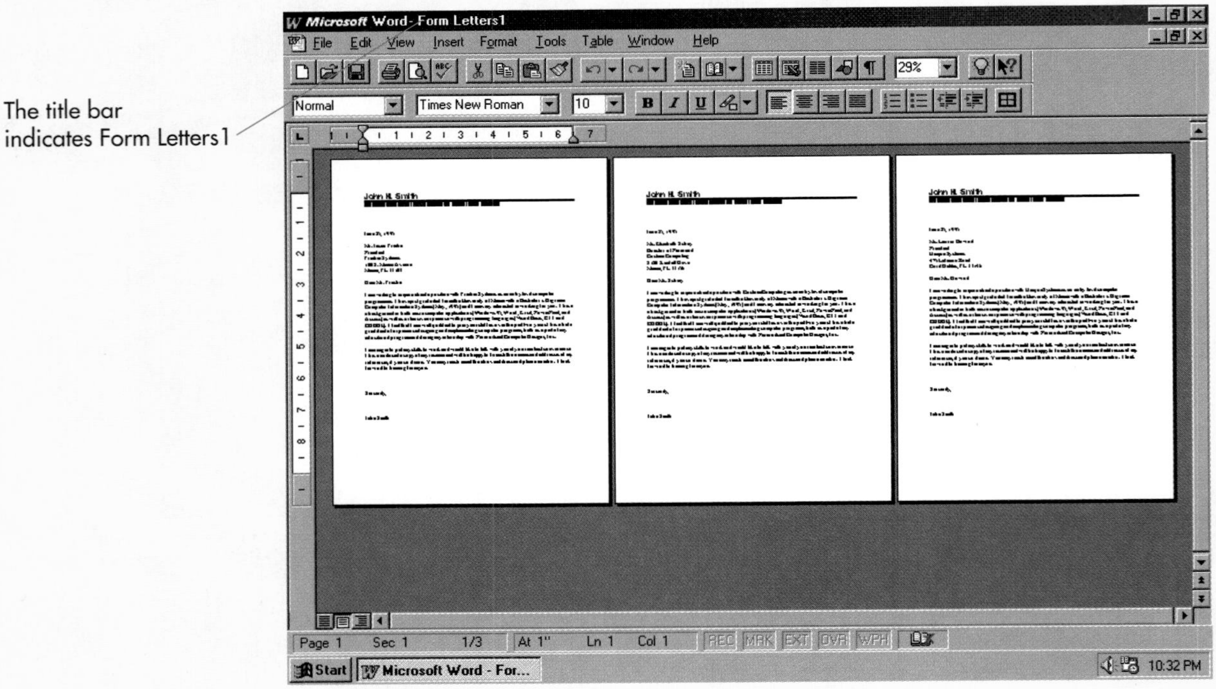

(h) The Individual Form Letters (step 10)

FIGURE B.3 Hands-on Exercise 1 (continued)

FINER POINTS OF MAIL MERGE

The hands-on exercise just completed acquaints you with the basics of a mail merge, but there is much more that you can do. You can, for example, sort the data source so that the form letters are printed in a different sequence—for example, by zip code to take advantage of bulk mail. You can also select (filter) the records that are to be included in the mail merge; that is, a letter need not be sent to every record in the data source.

Figure B.4 illustrates both options and is accessed through the Query Options command button in the Mail Merge Helper window. The records in the data source may be sorted on as many as three fields, as indicated in Figure B.4a, which sorts the records by postal code (zip code), and then by last name within the postal code. Both fields are in ascending (low to high) sequence.

The dialog box in Figure B.4b lets you establish selection criteria in order to specify which records from the data source are to be merged. The example in the figure will send letters only to those persons living in California. The implementation is straightforward, and you can impose additional rules or clear an existing rule by clicking the appropriate command button.

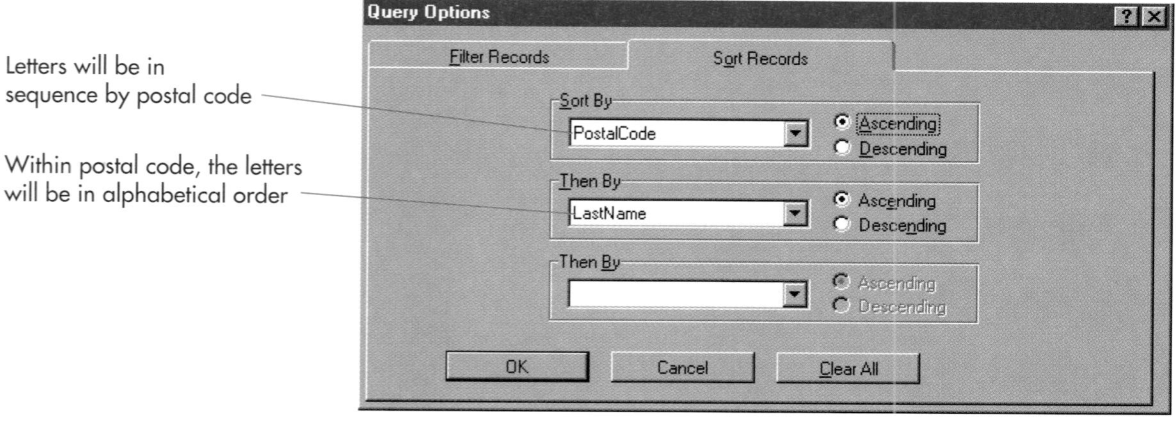

(a) Sorting Records

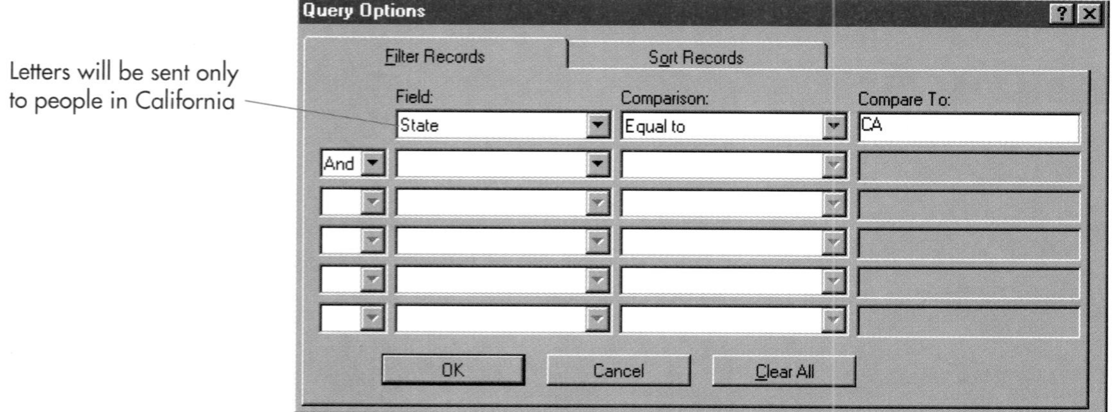

(b) Selecting Records

FIGURE B.4 Finer Points of Mail Merge

SUMMARY

A mail merge creates the same letter many times, changing only the variable data such as the addressee's name and address, from letter to letter. It is performed in conjunction with a main document and a data source, both of which exist as separate documents. The mail merge can be used to create a form letter for selected records, and/or print the form letters in a sequence different from the way the records are stored in the data source.

KEY WORDS AND CONCEPTS

Data source
Field
Field code
Field result
Filter
Form letter
Mail merge
Mail Merge Helper
Main document
Merge field
Record
Sort

C

APPENDIX C: TOOLBARS

OVERVIEW

Microsoft Word has nine predefined toolbars, which provide access to commonly used commands. The toolbars are displayed in Figure C.1 and are listed here for convenience. They are: the Borders, Database, Drawing, Formatting, Forms, Microsoft, Standard, TipWizard, and Word 2.0 toolbars. The Standard and Formatting toolbars are displayed by default and appear immediately below the menu bar.

In addition to the predefined toolbars, which are displayed continually, seven other toolbars appear only when their corresponding feature is in use. These toolbars appear (and disappear) automatically and are shown in Figure C.2. They are: the Equation Editor, Header/Footer, Macro, Mail Merge, Master Document, Outlining, and Picture toolbars.

The buttons on the toolbars are intended to be indicative of their function. Clicking the Printer button (the fourth button from the left on the Standard toolbar), for example, executes the Print command. If you are unsure of the purpose of any toolbar button, point to it, and a ToolTip will appear that displays its name.

You can display multiple toolbars at one time, move them to new locations on the screen, customize their appearance, or suppress their display.

- To display or hide a toolbar, pull down the View menu and click the Toolbars command. Select (deselect) the toolbar(s) that you want to display (hide). The selected toolbar(s) will be displayed in the same position as when last displayed. You may also point to any toolbar and click with the right mouse button to bring up a shortcut menu, after which you can select the toolbar to be displayed (hidden).
- To change the size of the buttons, display them in monochrome rather than color, suppress the display of the ToolTips or display the associated shortcut key (if available), pull down the View

menu, click Toolbars, and then select (deselect) the appropriate check box. Alternatively, you can click on any toolbar with the right mouse button, select Toolbars, and then select (deselect) the appropriate check box.

- Toolbars may be either docked (along the edge of the window) or left floating (in their own window). A toolbar moved to the edge of the window will dock along that edge. A toolbar moved anywhere else in the window will float in its own window. Docked toolbars are one tool wide (high), whereas floating toolbars can be resized by clicking and dragging a border or corner as you would with any other window.
  - To move a docked toolbar, click anywhere in the gray background area and drag the toolbar to its new location.
  - To move a floating toolbar, drag its title bar to its new location.
- To customize a toolbar, display the toolbar on the screen, pull down the View menu, click Toolbars, click the Customize command button, and select the Toolbars tab. Alternatively, you can click on any toolbar with the right mouse button, select Customize from the shortcut menu, and then click the Toolbars tab.
  - To move a button, drag the button to its new location on that toolbar or any other displayed toolbar.
  - To copy a button, press the Ctrl key as you drag the button to its new location on that toolbar or any other displayed toolbar.
  - To delete a button, drag the button off the toolbar and release the mouse button.
  - To add a button, select the category containing the button from the Categories list box and then drag the button to the desired location on the toolbar. (To see a description of a tool's function prior to adding it to a toolbar, click the tool in the Customize dialog box and read the displayed description.)
  - To restore a predefined toolbar to its default appearance, pull down the View menu, click Toolbars, select (highlight) the desired toolbar, and click the Reset command button.
- Buttons can also be moved, copied, or deleted without displaying the Customize dialog box.
  - To move a button, press the Alt key as you drag the button to the new location.
  - To copy a button, press the Alt and Ctrl keys as you drag the button to the new location.
  - To delete a button, press the Alt key and drag the button off the toolbar.
- To create your own toolbar, pull down the View menu, click Toolbars, and click the New command button. Alternatively, you can click on any toolbar with the right mouse button, select Toolbars from the shortcut menu, and then click the New command button.
  - Enter a name for the toolbar in the dialog box that follows. The name can be any length and can contain spaces.
  - The new toolbar will appear at the top left of the screen. Initially it will be big enough to hold only one button. Add, move, and delete buttons following the same procedures as outlined above. The toolbar will automatically size itself as new buttons are added and deleted.
  - To delete a custom toolbar, pull down the View menu, click Toolbars, and make sure that the custom toolbar to be deleted is the only one selected (highlighted). Click the Delete command button. Click Yes to confirm the deletion. (Note that a predefined toolbar cannot be deleted.)

Borders Toolbar

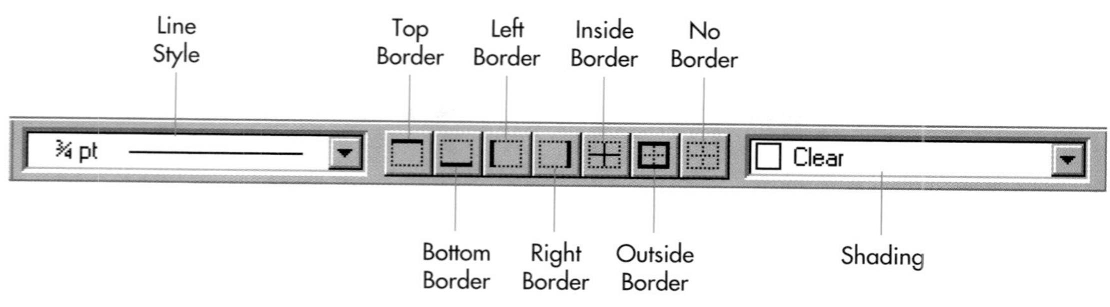

Database Toolbar

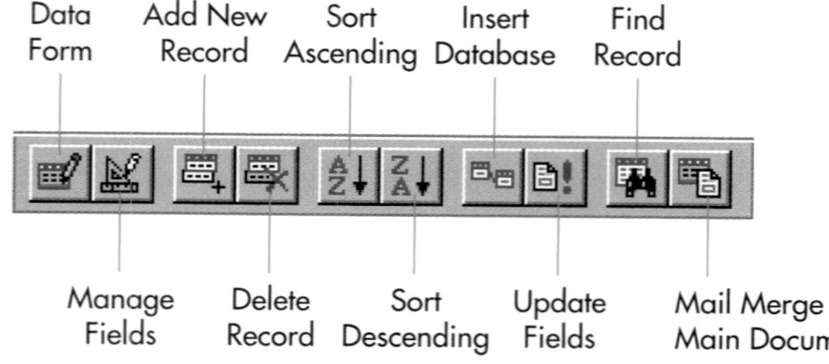

Drawing Toolbar

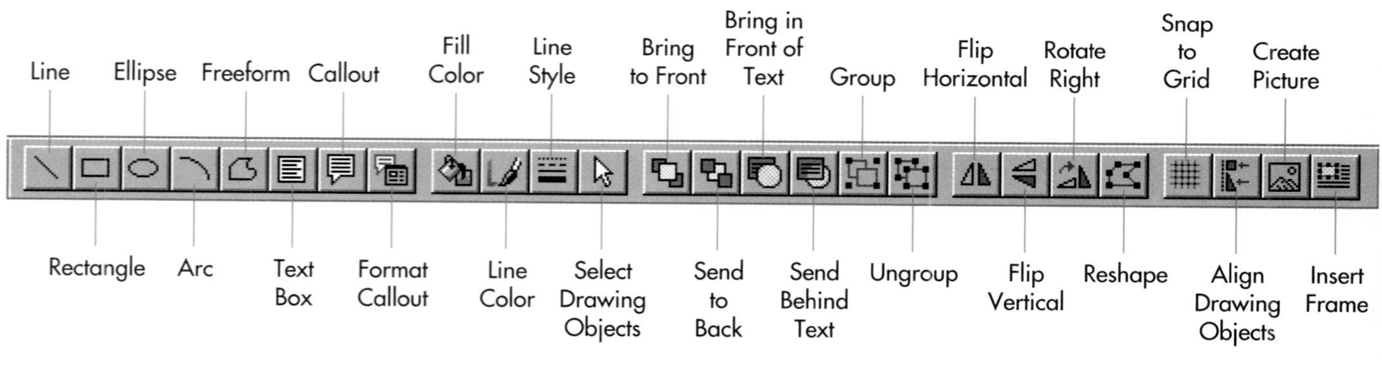

Formatting Toolbar

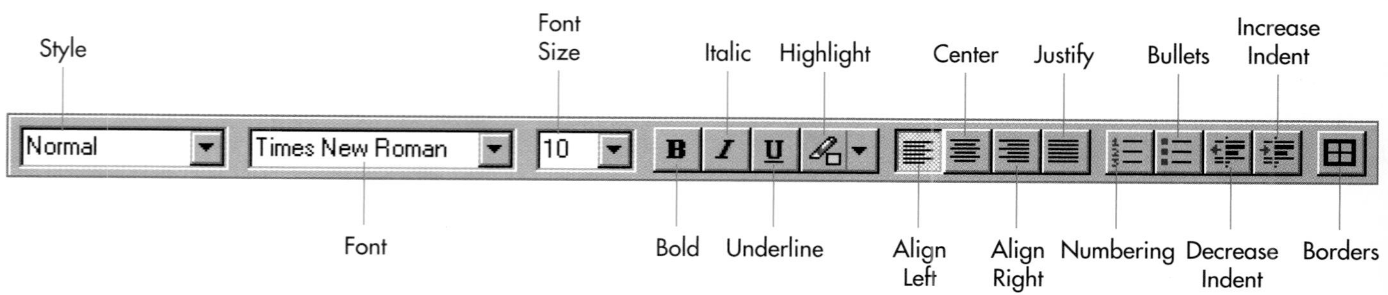

FIGURE C.1 Predefined Toolbars

Forms Toolbar

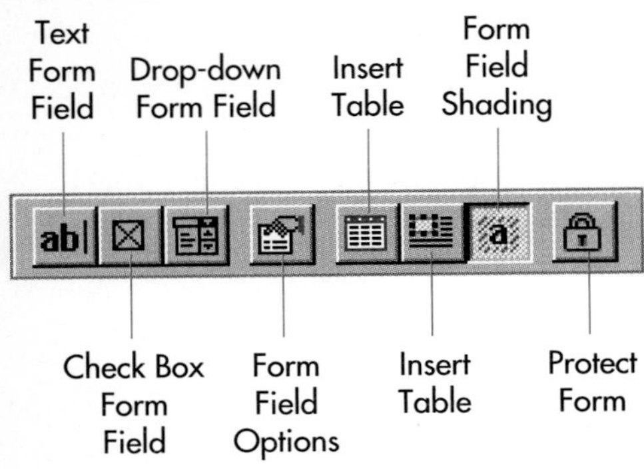

Microsoft Toolbar

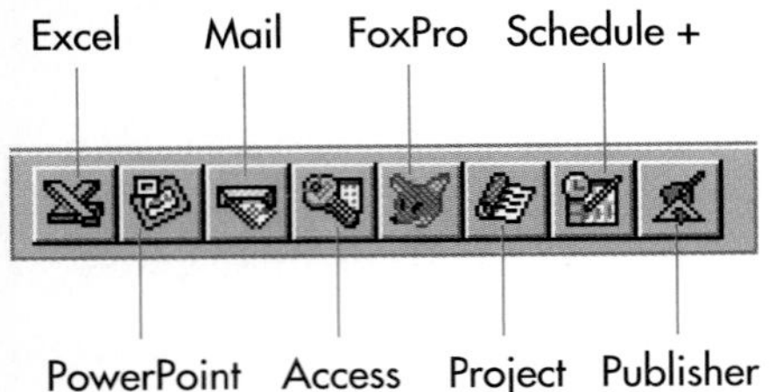

Standard Toolbar

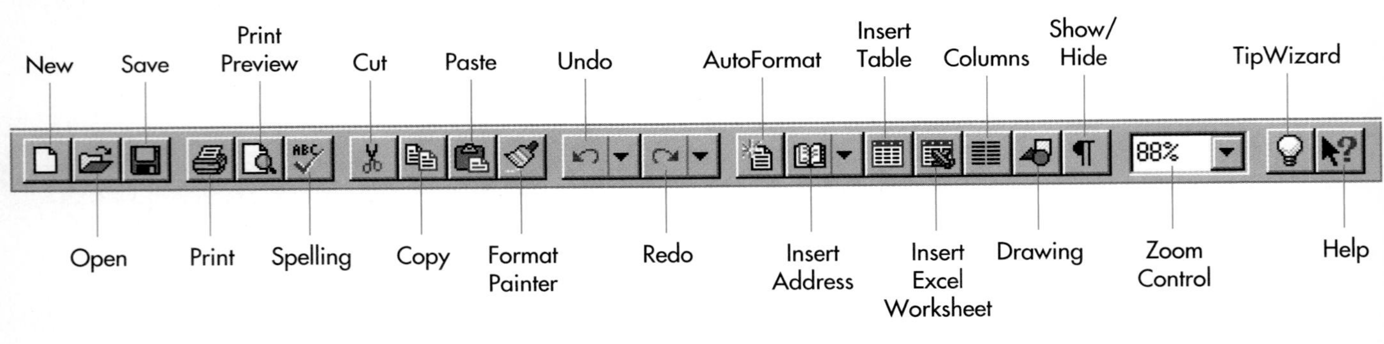

TipWizard Toolbar

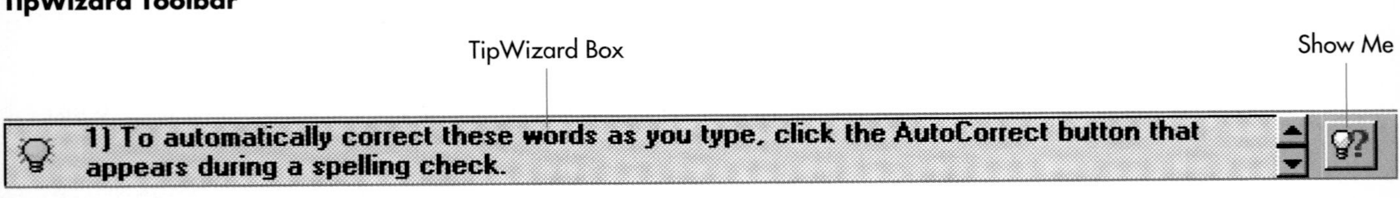

FIGURE C.1 Predefined Toolbars (continued)

Word 2.0 Toolbar

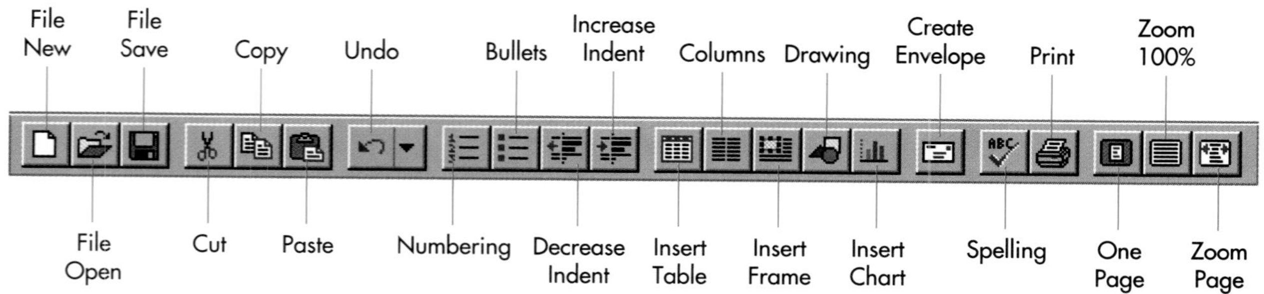

FIGURE C.1 Predefined Toolbars (continued)

Equation Editor Toolbar

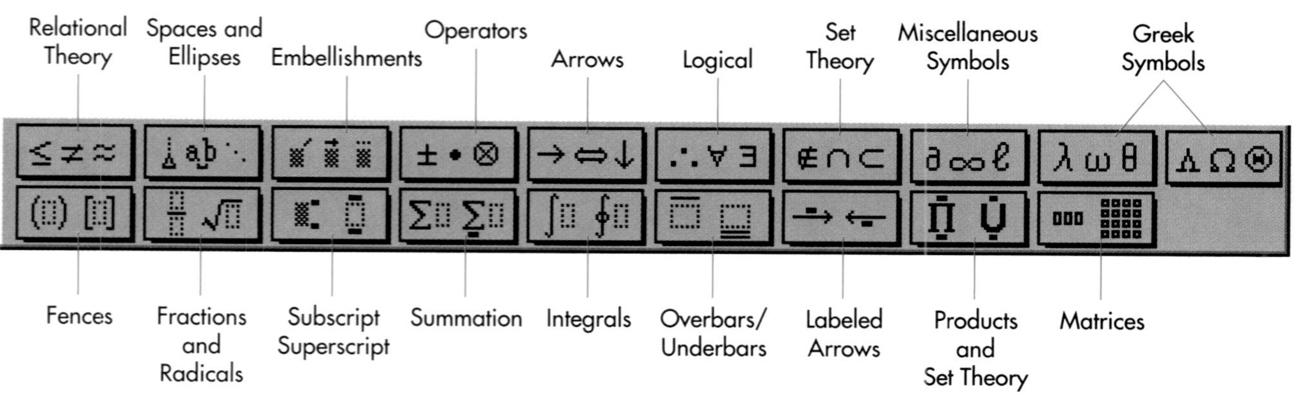

Header/Footer Toolbar

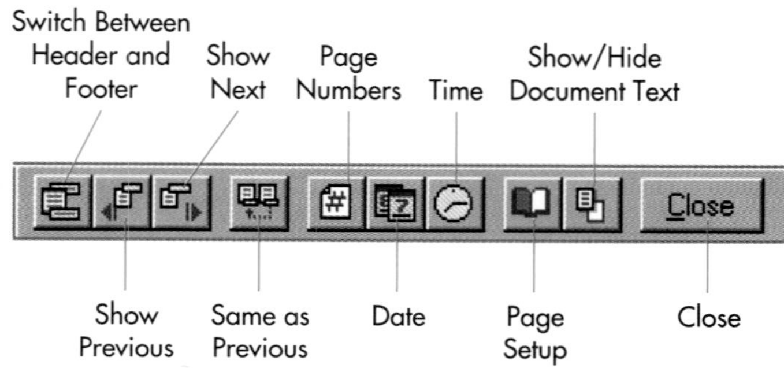

FIGURE C.2 Feature Toolbars

Macro Toolbar

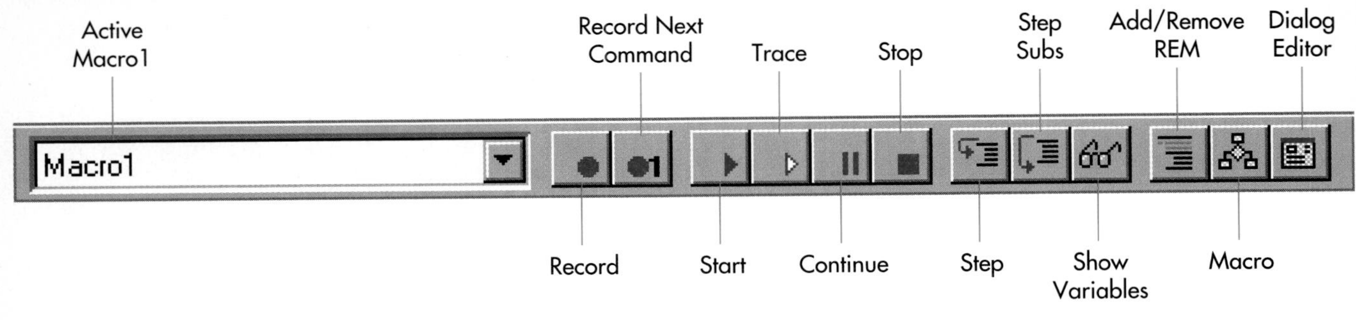

Mail Merge Toolbar

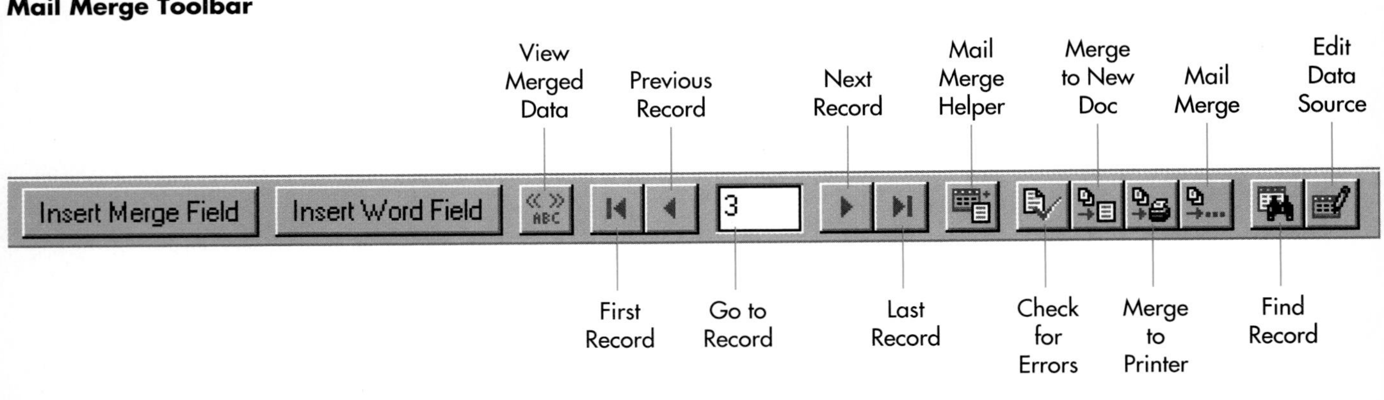

Master Document Toolbar

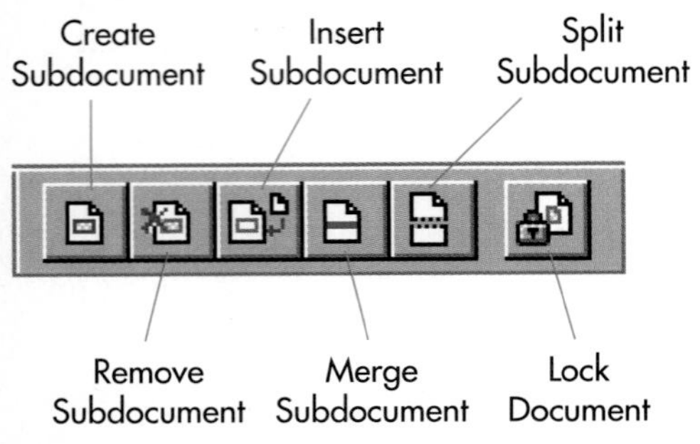

FIGURE C.2 Feature Toolbars (continued)

Outlining Toolbar

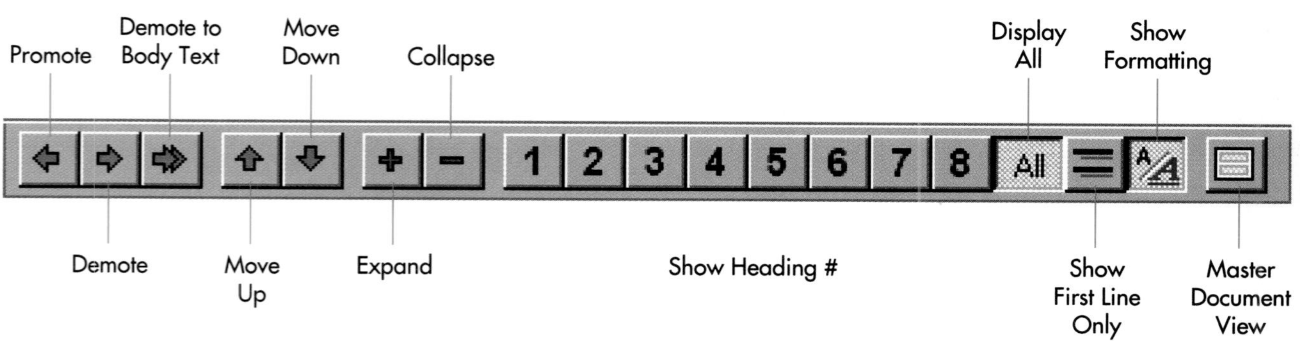

Picture Toolbar

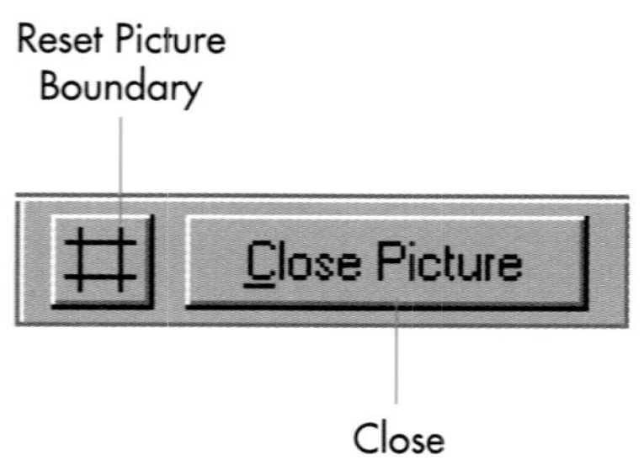

FIGURE C.2 Feature Toolbars (continued)

D

APPENDIX D: THE INTERNET ASSISTANT: INTRODUCTION TO HTML

OVERVIEW

The ***Internet***[1] is a network of networks that connects computers across the country and around the world. It grew out of a government project that began in 1969 to test the feasibility of a network for scientists and military personnel to share messages and data, no matter where they were. Known originally as the ARPAnet (Advanced Research Projects Agency), the original network of four computers grew exponentially to include tens of thousands of computers at virtually every major university and government agency and an ever-increasing number of private corporations. To say that the Internet is large is a gross understatement, but by its very nature, it's impossible to say just how large the Internet really is. The Internet is not a single network, but a collection of networks. How many networks there are, and how many users are connected to those networks, is of no importance as long as you yourself have access.

The ***World Wide Web*** (WWW, or simply the Web) is a means of connecting the resources on the Internet to one another. The Web is based on the technology of ***hypertext*** and ***hypermedia,*** which link computer-based documents in nonlinear fashion. Unlike a traditional document, which is read sequentially from top to bottom, a hypertext document includes links to other documents, which can be viewed at the reader's discretion. Hypermedia is similar in concept except that it provides links to graphic and video files in addition to text files.

To explore the Web, you need a program called a ***browser,*** which requests files from other computers on the Internet, then displays the hypertext (or hypermedia) documents on your computer. A ***home page*** is the first document a user sees when he or she connects to a particular

[1]See Grauer and Barber, Appendix D: The Internet and World Wide Web in *Exploring Windows 95 and Essential Computer Concepts,* Prentice Hall, 1996, for a 20-page introduction to the Internet. Alternatively, see Grauer and Marks, *Exploring the Internet,* Prentice Hall, 1996, for more detailed information.

Web address. All Web documents (pages) are created in ***Hypertext Markup Language*** (***HTML***), which consists of a set of codes that format a document for display in the World Wide Web.

This appendix shows you how to create a home page using the ***Internet Assistant,*** an add-on that is provided for use with Microsoft Word. You will learn how to display information and how to link your home page to other pages. The appendix is merely a beginning, however, as it covers only the most basic commands. You can learn more about HTML by conducting a search on the Web for the keywords, *HTML Guide* or *HTML Primer.* Several excellent references are available.

IT'S THE DOCUMENT, NOT THE BROWSER

It doesn't matter whether you use Netscape, Mosaic, the Internet Explorer, or one of several other commercially available browsers. All Web documents are written in HTML, and any browser can display any Web document. Some browsers are more sophisticated than others and support HTML extensions, which are beyond the commands discussed in this appendix.

INTRODUCTION TO HTML

Figure D.1 displays a home page similar to the one you will create in the hands-on exercises that follow shortly. Our page has the look and feel of Web pages you may have seen when you accessed the World Wide Web. It includes different types of formatting such as a bulleted list, underlined links, horizontal lines (rules) to separate elements on the page, and a heading displayed in a larger font. All of these elements are created by inserting codes, called ***HTML tags,*** into a document to identify the formatting that should be applied at that location. Figure D.1a displays the document as it would appear using Netscape (a popular Web browser). Figure D.1b shows the underlying HTML codes (tags) that are necessary to format the page.

HTML documents become less intimidating when you realize that the tags are enclosed in angle brackets and are used consistently from document to document. Most tags occur in pairs, at the beginning and end of the text to be formatted, with the ending code preceded by a slash. In Figure D.1b, for example, the text "John Doe's Home Page" is enclosed within the <TITLE> and </TITLE> tags. (The function of the Title tag is to indicate the text that will be displayed in the title bar of the browser's application window. Look at the title and other tags in Figure D.1b, then observe the effect of these tags as they are read and displayed by the browser in Figure D.1a.)

Tags can also be nested within one another. The welcome message that John has chosen to place at the top of his page is nested within codes that will center (<CENTER>) and boldface (<B>) the text as well as display it in a larger font size (<FONT SIZE=5>). Other tags are added as desired. Links to other pages (which are known as ***hyperlinks***) are enclosed within a pair of anchor tags <A> and </A> in which you specify the URL address of the document through the HREF parameter. Note, too, that a few tags appear individually, such as <P> or <HR> to indicate a new paragraph or horizontal rule, respectively.

Fortunately, however, it is not necessary to memorize HTML codes since you can usually determine their meaning from the codes themselves. Nor is it necessary for you to enter the tags explicitly into a document as you can take advantage of tools such as Microsoft's Internet Assistant to create the codes for you.

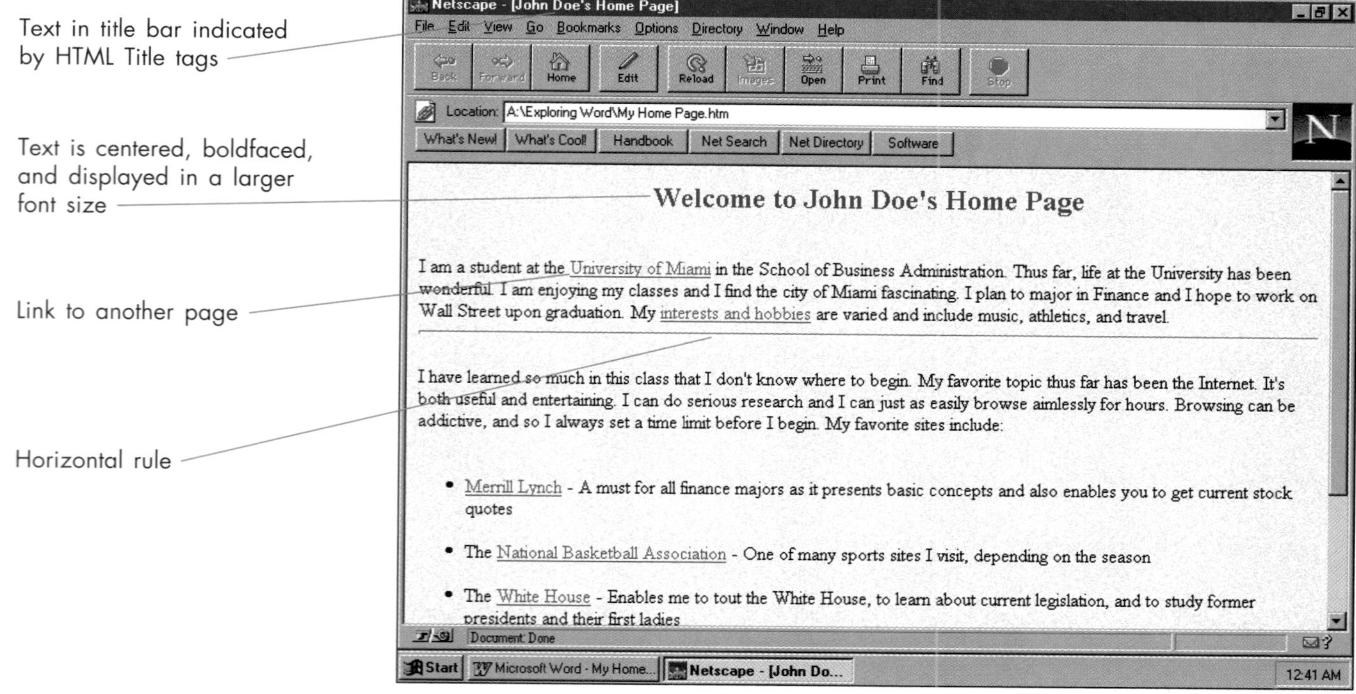

(a) A Web Browser

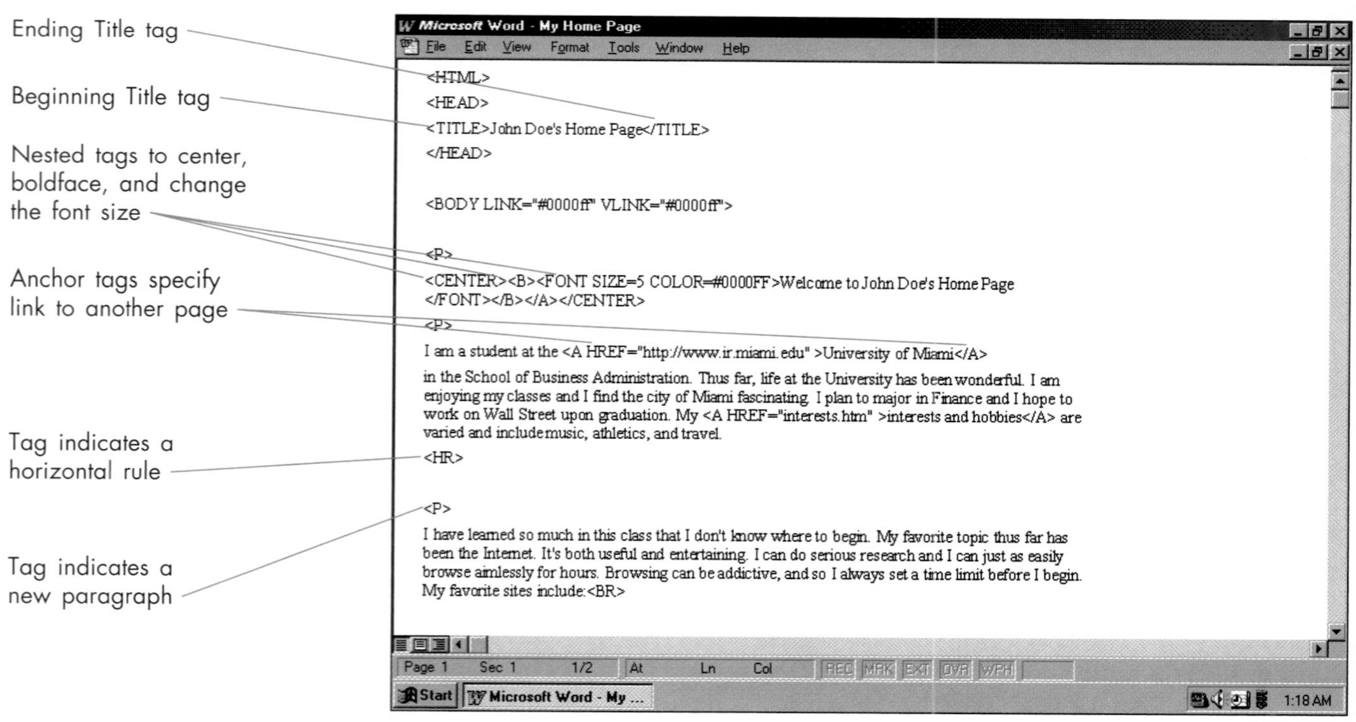

(b) HTML Codes

FIGURE D.1 A Home Page

THE HEAD AND THE BODY

An HTML document is composed of two parts—a head and a body. The head contains the text that will be displayed on the browser's title bar and is found between the <HEAD> and </HEAD> tags. The main portion (body) of the document is entered between the <BODY> and </BODY> tags, which contain the necessary codes to format the document for display on a Web browser.

The Internet Assistant

There are two ways to create a document containing HTML tags. The original (and more difficult) method is to explicitly enter the codes in a text editor such as Notepad (a Windows 95 accessory). The easier technique (and the only one you need to consider) is to use an HTML editor such as Microsoft's Internet Assistant, which creates the HTML tags for you. The Internet Assistant can be downloaded from Microsoft's home page, and when installed will automatically attach itself to Word, placing its own icon on the Formatting toolbar. To use the Internet Assistant, you create a document in Word as you normally would, then you save it as an HTML document. The Internet Assistant does the rest, generating the HTML tags needed to format the document. (The only items you need to enter explicitly are the URL addresses for the links to other documents.)

Figure D.2 shows how John Doe's home page appears in the Internet Assistant within Microsoft Word once it has been saved as an HTML document. Look carefully and you will see that the toolbars in Figure D.2 are subtly different from those you are used to seeing. Note, for example, the eyeglasses at the left of the

Standard and Formatting toolbars are subtly different

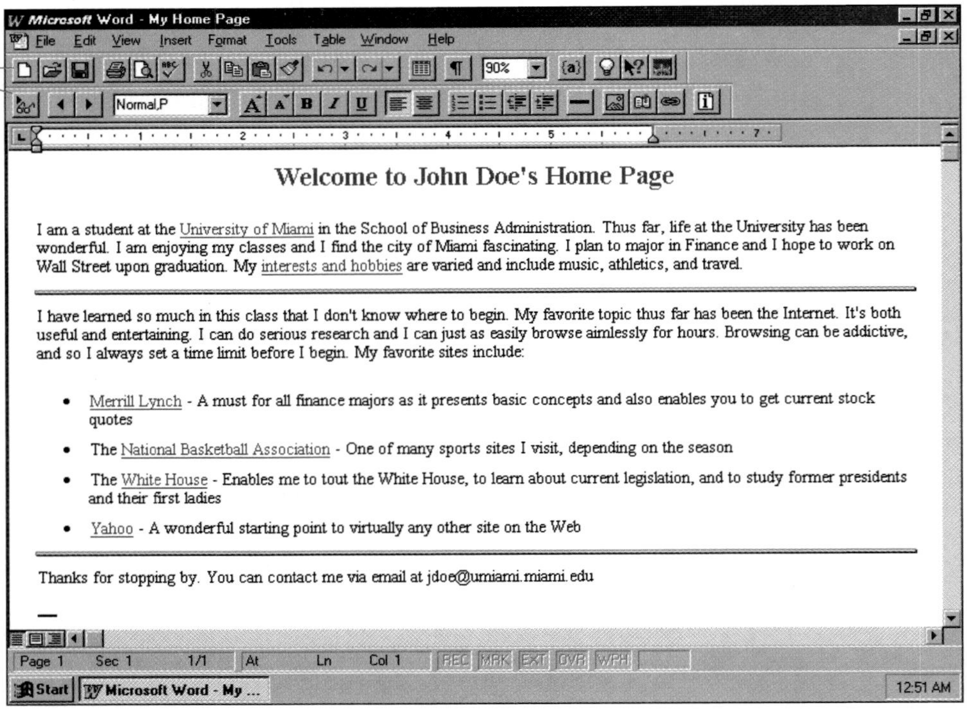

FIGURE D.2 The Internet Assistant

Formatting toolbar and the last several buttons on the right. Each of these buttons is associated with a specific command in the Internet Assistant, as explained in Figure D.3.

To create an HTML document using the Internet Assistant, you start Word in the usual fashion and enter the text of the document. Next, you pull down the File menu and save the document as an HTML file, at which point the Formatting and Standard toolbars change to display the buttons in Figure D.3. (The toolbars return to normal when you close the HTML document.) And finally, you complete the document by entering any additional HTML tags as appropriate; for example, click the Hyperlink button to insert a hyperlink into a document.

After you create a home page, you need to place it on a Web server so that other people will be able to access it. Thus, you need to check with your system administrator at school or work, or with your local Internet provider, to determine how to submit your page(s) when it is complete. Even if you do not actually place your page on the Web, you can still create and view it locally on your PC, as will be shown in the following exercise.

DOWNLOAD THE INTERNET ASSISTANT

The Internet Assistant is available at no charge from Microsoft. Use any Web browser to go to Microsoft's home page (http://www.microsoft.com), then click the link to Internet Resource Center. Select the appropriate version of the Internet Assistant (for Word 6.0 or Word 7.0 for Windows 95), then follow the instructions to download and install the Internet Assistant. The Internet Assistant will attach itself automatically to Microsoft Word.

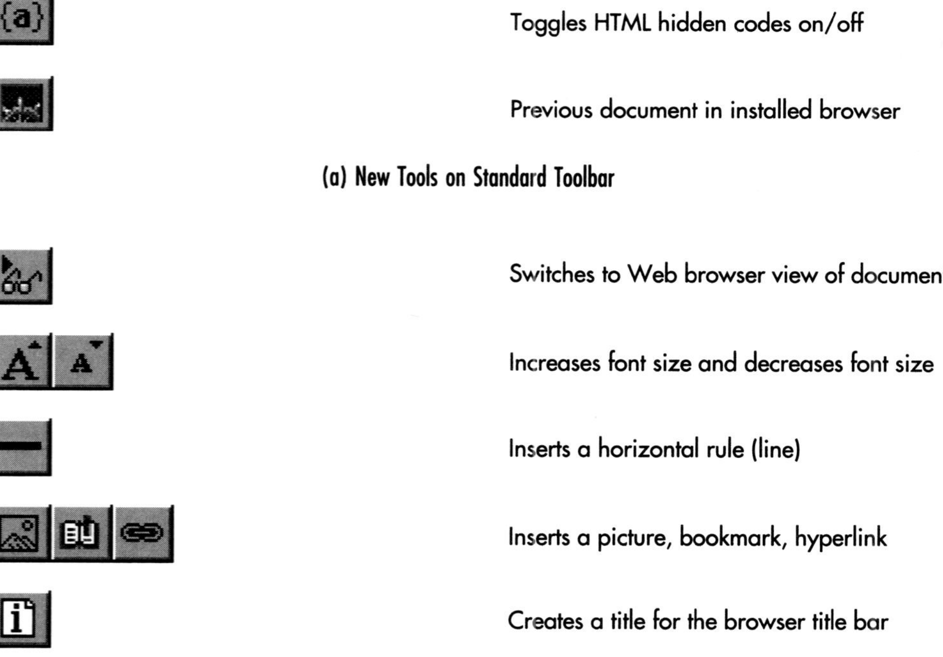

FIGURE D.3 Internet Assistant Buttons

HANDS-ON EXERCISE 1

Introduction to HTML

Objective: To convert a Word document to its HTML equivalent and to use the Internet Assistant to create a simple home page. Use Figure D.4 as a guide in the exercise.

STEP 1: Create the Document

- Start Word as you have done throughout the text. Change to the **Page Layout view,** then create a document similar to the one in Figure D.4a. Do not be concerned that you cannot see the entire page as you can add your own text as appropriate. (You can also refer to Figure D.2, which appeared previously in the appendix.)
- Use an appropriate font and type size. Boldface, center, and enlarge the title for your page.
- Enter the bullets for our links (Merrill Lynch, the National Basketball Association, and so on) or use your own. (See Table D.1 in the appendix for suggestions. You will need the addresses for those Web pages in the next hands-on exercise, although you do not enter the URL addresses at this time.)
- Pull down the **File menu** and click **Save** to display the Save As dialog box in Figure D.4a.
  - Select the appropriate drive and folder where you want to save your document, e.g., the Exploring Word folder or drive A or drive C.
  - Enter **My Home Page** as the name of the document.
  - Click the **drop-down arrow** next to the Save As type list box, then scroll until you can click **HTML Document** as shown in the figure.
  - Click the **Save button** to save the document.
- The display changes ever so slightly (the buttons change on the Formatting toolbar) to reflect that you are now working on an HTML document.

> **SOME FORMATTING IS LOST**
>
> The Save As command converts an existing Word document to its HTML equivalent. Some formatting (e.g., borders and shading) is lost in the process, but most is retained. To learn the limitations of the conversion process, pull down the Help menu, click Internet Assistant for Microsoft Word Help, open the book on HTML/Word Equivalents, then display the item that indicates what is lost when a Word document is converted to HTML

STEP 2: Complete the Formatting

- Click and drag to select the title of your document. Pull down the **Format menu,** then click **Font** to display the Font dialog box shown in Figure D.4b.
- Click the **drop-down arrow** on the Color list box, then click **Blue** to change the color of the selected text. Click **OK** to close the dialog box.

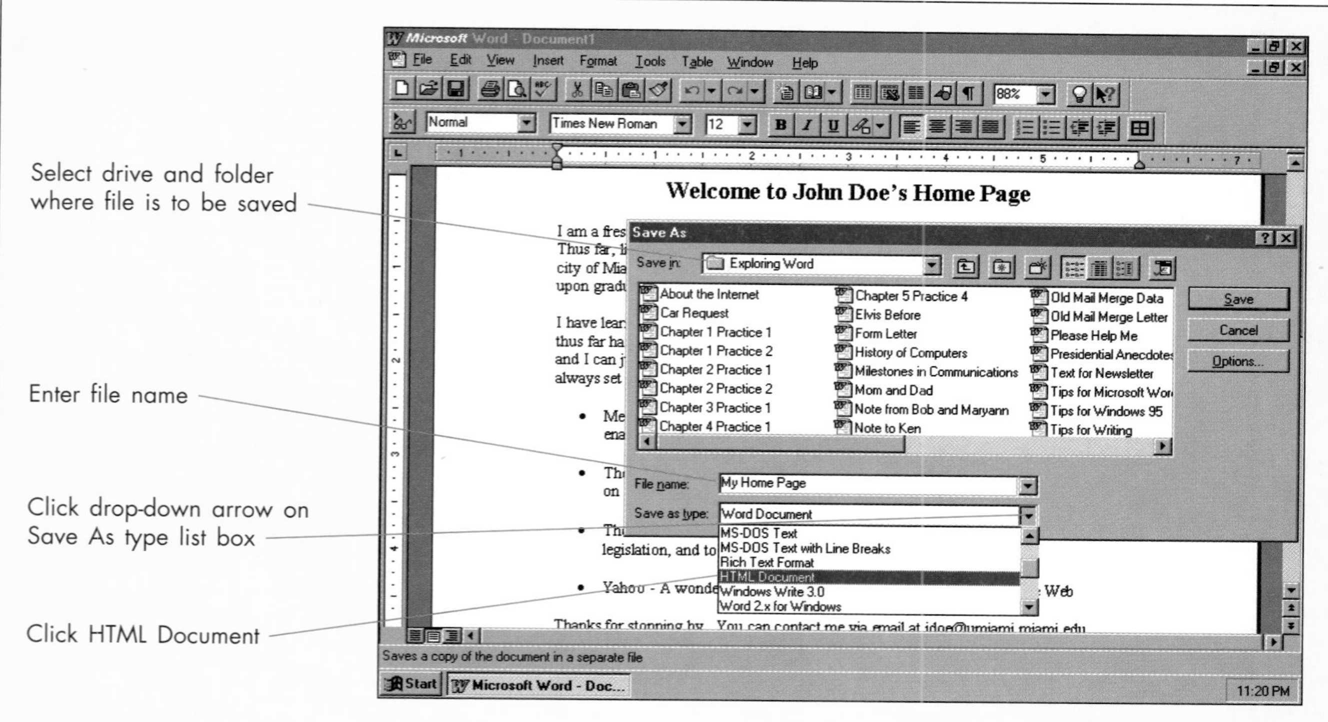

(a) Create a Document (step 1)

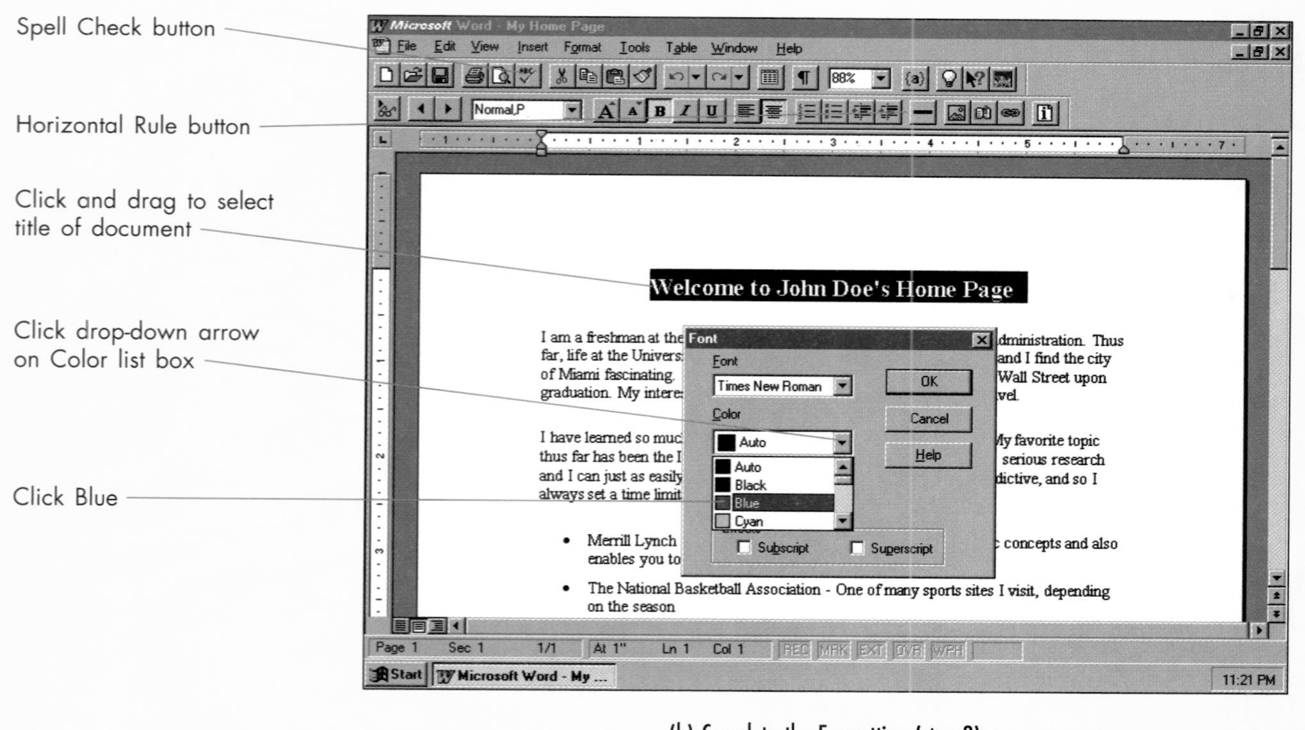

(b) Complete the Formatting (step 2)

FIGURE D.4 Hands-on Exercise 1

- Click at the end of the first paragraph, then click the **Horizontal Rule button** to insert a horizontal rule at the end of the paragraph. Click to the left of the paragraph that begins "Thanks for stopping by," then click the **Horizontal Rule button** a second time.
- Enter additional formatting as you see fit. Delete (or enter) blank lines before (after) the rules as necessary.
- Click the **Spelling button** to check your document for spelling. Save the document.

ABOUT THE INTERNET ASSISTANT

Pull down the Help menu and click About Internet Assistant for Microsoft Word to see the version of the Assistant you are using. Our exercise was done with version 2.0z, but it is quite possible that Microsoft will issue a new release by the time you do the exercise. A newer release may contain additional commands and/or display slightly different screens as you do the exercise.

STEP 3: Set the Background

- Pull down the **Format menu** and click **Background and Links** to display the dialog box in Figure D.4c. Click **Browse** to display the Insert Picture dialog box, which appears on top of the earlier box.

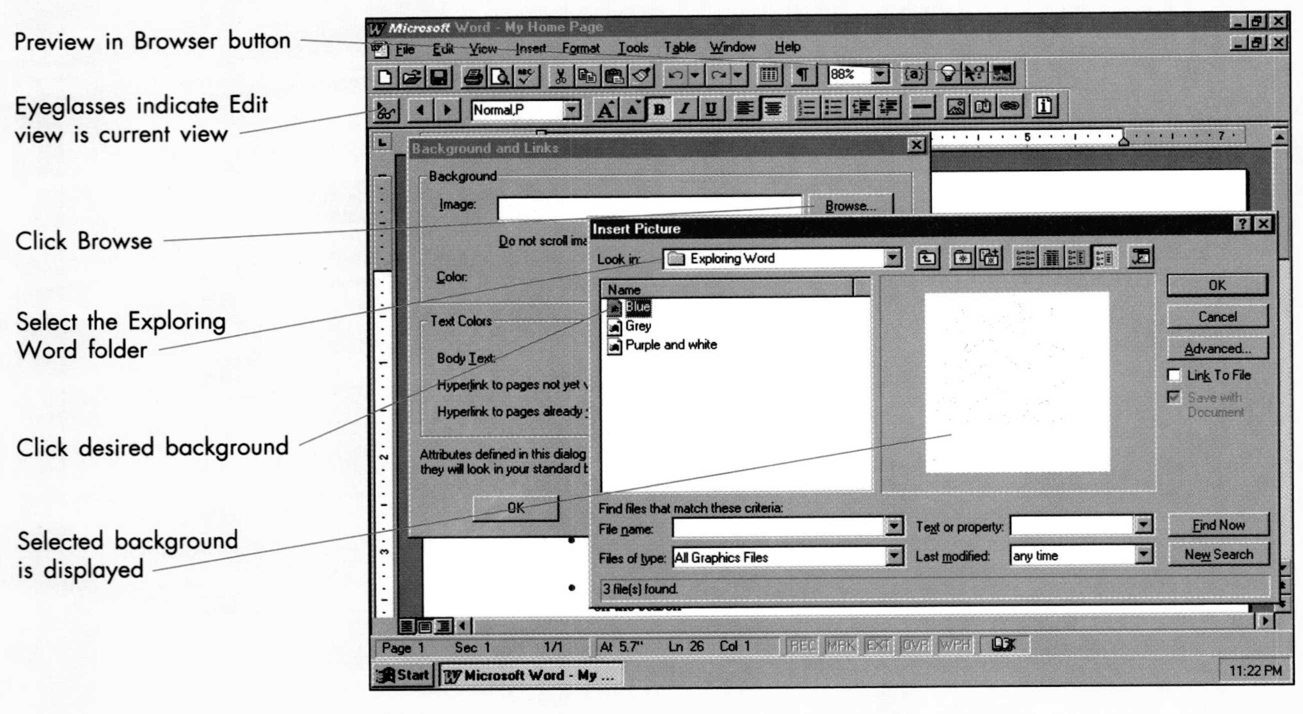

(c) Add a Background (step 3)

FIGURE D.4 Hands-on Exercise 1 (continued)

- ➤ Click the **drop-down arrow** on the Look in list box, then select the Exploring Word folder (on drive A or drive C), which contains three graphic files.
- ➤ Click each background in turn to see how it will appear. Click the background you prefer, click **OK** to select the background and close the Insert Picture dialog box, then click **OK** to close the Background and Links dialog box.
- ➤ A <BODY . . .> code appears in your document (to the left of the Welcome title), but the background itself is not yet visible. Save the document.

> **LEARN MORE ABOUT HTML**
>
> Use your favorite Web search engine to locate additional information about HTML. One excellent place to begin is the resource page on HTML that is maintained by the Library of Congress at http://lcweb.loc.gov/global/html.html. This site contains links to several HTML tutorials and also provides you with information about the latest HTML standard.

STEP 4: The Completed Page

- ➤ Click the **Preview in Browser button** on the Standard toolbar to see how your page will appear in the Internet Browser installed on your system. Click **Yes** if asked to save the document. (You can also preview the document by switching to the Web Browser view within the Internet Assistant, as described in the boxed tip below.)
- ➤ Netscape is the browser installed on our system, as can be seen in Figure D.4d. The URL address in Figure D.4d (A:\Exploring Word\My Home Page.htm) indicates that you are viewing the home page on a local drive (drive A) as opposed to an actual Web server.
- ➤ View your home page and write down any changes you want to make. Click the **Close button** to close the window and return to the Internet Assistant in order to modify the document.

> **TWO VIEWS**
>
> The Internet Assistant has two views, an Edit view and a Web Browser view, as indicated by the icon at the extreme left of the Formatting toolbar. The eyeglasses indicate that you are currently in the Edit view and are in the process of creating (modifying) a Web document. Click the eyeglasses and you switch to the Web Browser view (the icon changes to a pencil), which lets you preview the document using the Internet Assistant browser. Click the pencil and you return to the Edit view. You can use the Web Browser view to preview a Web document using the Assistant's browser, or alternatively you can click the Preview in Browser button to see the document in your regular browser (e.g., Netscape).

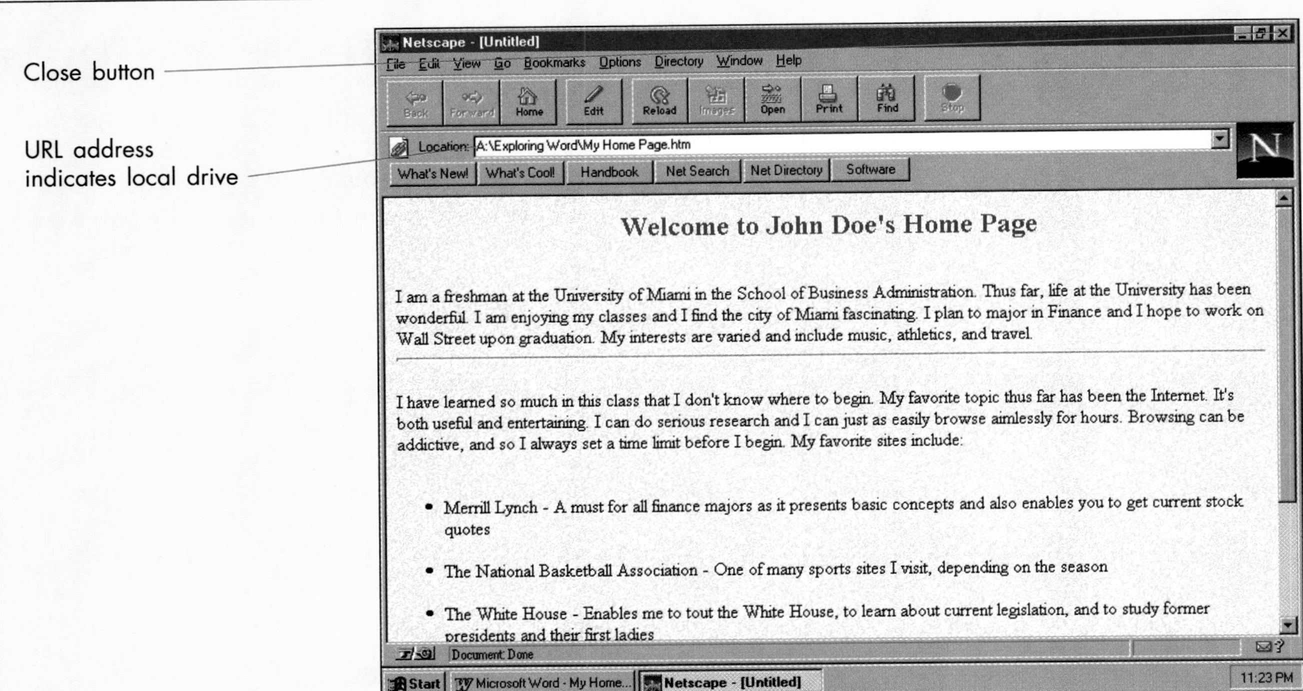
Close button
URL address indicates local drive
Netscape - [Untitled]
File Edit View Go Bookmarks Options Directory Window Help
Back Forward Home Edit Reload Images Open Print Find Stop
Location: A:\Exploring Word\My Home Page.htm
What's New! What's Cool! Handbook Net Search Net Directory Software
Welcome to John Doe's Home Page
I am a freshman at the University of Miami in the School of Business Administration. Thus far, life at the University has been wonderful. I am enjoying my classes and I find the city of Miami fascinating. I plan to major in Finance and I hope to work on Wall Street upon graduation. My interests are varied and include music, athletics, and travel.
I have learned so much in this class that I don't know where to begin. My favorite topic thus far has been the Internet. It's both useful and entertaining. I can do serious research and I can just as easily browse aimlessly for hours. Browsing can be addictive, and so I always set a time limit before I begin. My favorite sites include:
Merrill Lynch - A must for all finance majors as it presents basic concepts and also enables you to get current stock quotes
The National Basketball Association - One of many sports sites I visit, depending on the season
The White House - Enables me to tout the White House, to learn about current legislation, and to study former presidents and their first ladies
Document: Done
Start
Microsoft Word - My Home...
Netscape - [Untitled]
11:23 PM

(d) The Completed Page (step 4)

FIGURE D.4 Hands-on Exercise 1 (continued)

STEP 5: View the HTML Tags

- Pull down the **View menu** and click **HTML Source** to display the HTML source code as shown in Figure D.4e. The Internet Assistant has created all of the necessary HTML tags for you.
- Click and drag to select **Untitled** within the Title tags as shown in Figure D.4e. Enter **John Doe's Home Page,** which will be the text displayed in the title bar of the browser when the page is accessed.
- Change the word **freshman** to **student** within the body of the document. Make any other changes you want to the text of your page.
- Click the **Return to Edit Mode button** on the HTML toolbar (or pull down the **View menu** and click **Return to Edit Mode**), then click **Yes** when asked whether to save the changes. The HTML tags are no longer visible.
- Click the **Preview in Browser button** on the Standard toolbar to view your home page a second time. The entry in the title bar has changed, as has the text in the document, corresponding to the changes you just made. (The title in the document still reads "Welcome To" since the change you made affects only the title bar.)
- Close the Internet Browser. Exit Word if you do not want to continue with the next exercise at this time.

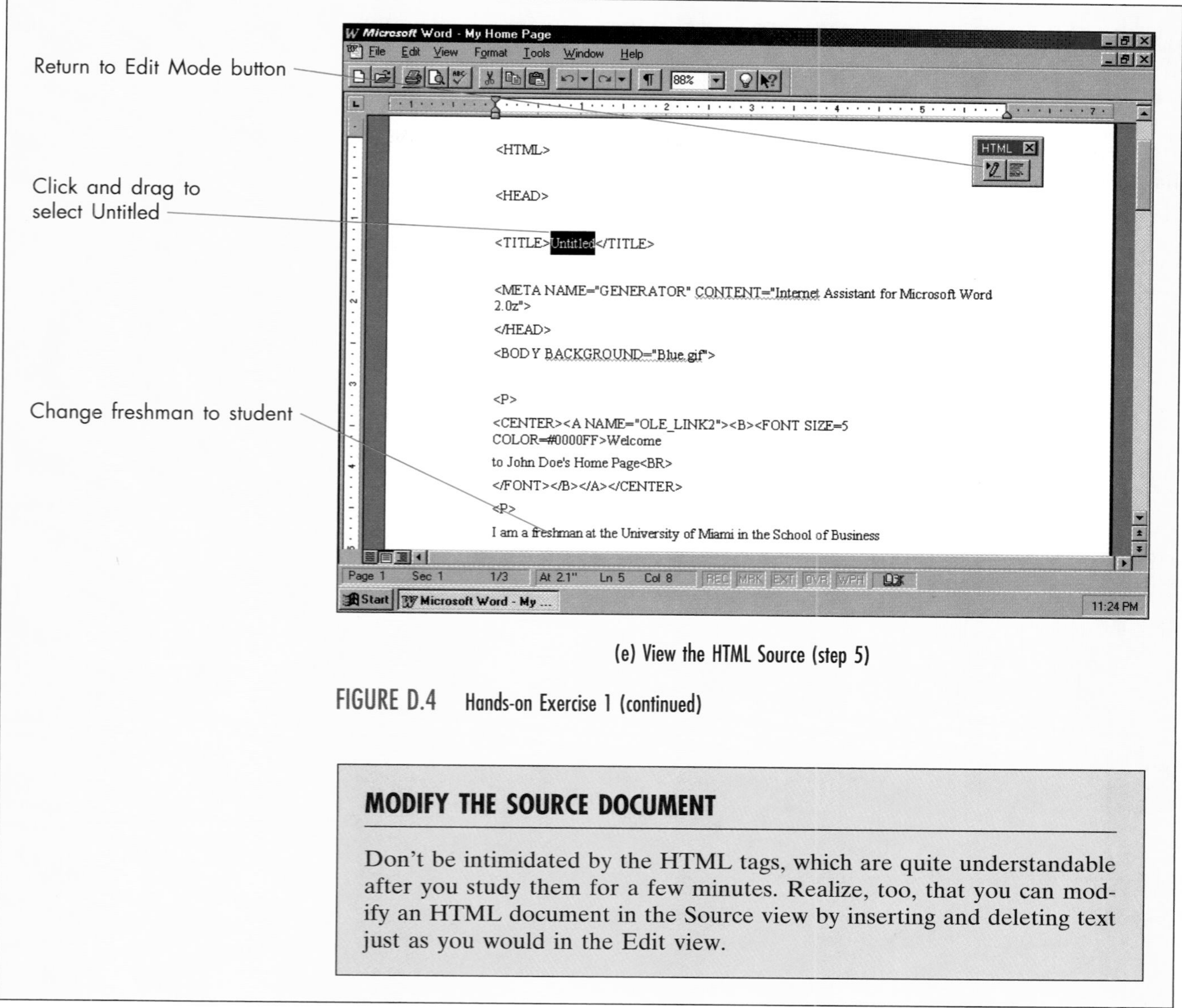

(e) View the HTML Source (step 5)

FIGURE D.4 Hands-on Exercise 1 (continued)

MODIFY THE SOURCE DOCUMENT

Don't be intimidated by the HTML tags, which are quite understandable after you study them for a few minutes. Realize, too, that you can modify an HTML document in the Source view by inserting and deleting text just as you would in the Edit view.

HYPERLINKS

The hands-on exercise just completed had you create a Web page without links of any kind. What makes the Web so fascinating, however, is the ability to link from one page to another. Assume, for example, that you are reading a Web document about the American Revolution and that you come to a reference to the Declaration of Independence. You can continue to read about the revolution or you can click the link to the Declaration of Independence. That document in turn may contain a link to Thomas Jefferson or Benjamin Franklin, and those documents may contain additional links to still other documents. The linked documents may be on the same server (computer) or they may be on an entirely different computer. Either way, you go from one document to another simply by clicking on the links of interest to you.

Figure D.5a displays your home page as it will appear at the end of the next hands-on exercise. It looks very similar to the page you just created except that it contains links to other Web documents. The links appear as underlined text, such as University of Miami or National Basketball Association. Click on a desired link and the browser (e.g., Netscape) displays the associated document. Note, too, that

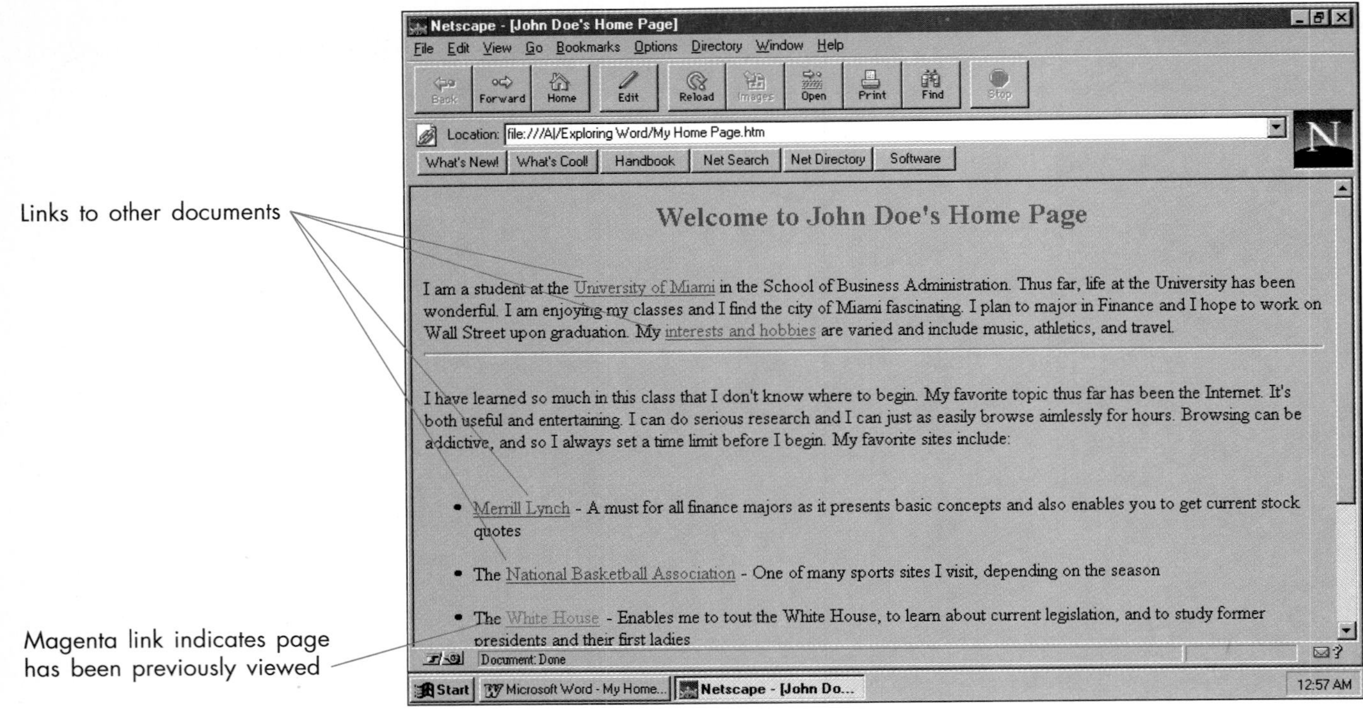
Netscape - [John Doe's Home Page]
File Edit View Go Bookmarks Options Directory Window Help
Back Forward Home Edit Reload Images Open Print Find Stop
Location: file:///A|/Exploring Word/My Home Page.htm
What's New! What's Cool! Handbook Net Search Net Directory Software
Links to other documents
Welcome to John Doe's Home Page
I am a student at the University of Miami in the School of Business Administration. Thus far, life at the University has been wonderful. I am enjoying my classes and I find the city of Miami fascinating. I plan to major in Finance and I hope to work on Wall Street upon graduation. My interests and hobbies are varied and include music, athletics, and travel.
I have learned so much in this class that I don't know where to begin. My favorite topic thus far has been the Internet. It's both useful and entertaining. I can do serious research and I can just as easily browse aimlessly for hours. Browsing can be addictive, and so I always set a time limit before I begin. My favorite sites include:
Merrill Lynch - A must for all finance majors as it presents basic concepts and also enables you to get current stock quotes
The National Basketball Association - One of many sports sites I visit, depending on the season
The White House - Enables me to tout the White House, to learn about current legislation, and to study former presidents and their first ladies
Magenta link indicates page has been previously viewed
Document: Done
Start Microsoft Word - My Home... Netscape - [John Do...
12:57 AM

(a) The Web Page

Text for link — URL address

Hyperlink: Text to Display: National Basketball Association; File or URL: http://www.nba.com; Bookmark Location in File: — OK, Cancel, Help, Unlink, Browse..., Link Path...

(b) External Link

Text for link — File name

Hyperlink: Text to Display: interests and hobbies; File or URL: interests.htm; Bookmark Location in File: — OK, Cancel, Help, Unlink, Browse..., Link Path...

(c) Local Link

FIGURE D.5 Hyperlinks

the links (underlined text) appear in one of two colors, blue or magenta. A blue link indicates that the associated page has not been previously displayed. Magenta, on the other hand, implies that the page has been viewed.

To create a link within your document, you need to know the URL address of the associated page, such as http://www.nba.com to display the home page for the National Basketball Association. You need not, however, concern yourself with the syntax of the HTML tags, as the Internet Assistant will prompt you for the necessary information via the Hyperlink dialog box in Figure D.5b. You enter the descriptive text that is to appear as an underlined link in your document followed by the URL address, then you click OK and the Internet Assistant does the rest.

Figure D.5c displays a second hyperlink dialog box through which you create a link to a local document (a document on your PC or on the LAN to which your PC is attached) rather than to an external Web page. The dialog box in Fig-

TABLE D.1 Interesting Web Sites

Site	URL
Bloomberg Personal	http://www.bloomberg.com
Bob Grauer's Home Page	http://www.bus.miami.edu/~rgrauer
Buena Vista Movie Plex	http://www.wdp.com
Business Week	http://www.businessweek.com
CIA	http://www.odci.gov/cia
CNN	http://www.cnn.com
CNN National Weather Information	http://www.cnn.com/WEATHER
Democratic National Committee	http://www.democrats.org
Entertainment Weekly	http://pathfinder.com/@@nvneUoJUtwMAQCSr/ew
ESPN	http://espnet.sportszone.com
Fidelity Investments	http://www.fid-inv.com
InfoSeek	http://guide.infoseek.com
Library of Congress	http://lcweb.loc.gov/homepage
Lycos	http://www.lycos.com
Merrill Lynch	http://www.ml.com
Microsoft	http://www.microsoft.com
Microsoft Cinemania	http://www.msn.com/cinemania
Music Television (MTV)	http://www.mtv.com
National Basketball Association	http://www.nba.com
National Football League	http://nflhome.com
National Science Foundation	http://stis.nsf.gov
New York Times	http://nytimesfax.com
PC magazine	http://www.zdnet.com/pcmag
Prentice Hall	http://www.prenhall.com
Republican Web Central	http://www.gop.org
Time magazine	http://pathfinder.com/@@nvneUoJUtwMAQCSr/time
U.S. Bureau of the Census	http://www.census.gov
U.S. News and World Report	http://www.usnews.com
Wall Street Journal	http://www.wsj.com
Webcrawler	http://www.webcrawler.com
White House	http://www.whitehouse.gov
Wire Services	http://www1.trib.com/NEWS
Yahoo	http://www.yahoo.com

ure D.5c contains a file name (interests.htm) rather than a URL address. This enables you to link one document, such as your home page, to a second document that describes your hobbies and interests in detail, which in turn can be linked to another document and so on. The documents can be stored locally, rather than on an Internet server, and can still be viewed through Netscape (or any other browser). Many organizations are taking advantage of this capability to create an ***intranet*** to disseminate information within an organization (which is available only to computers on a specific network) as opposed to placing the pages on the Internet itself.

VISIT OUR HOME PAGES

Visit Bob Grauer's home page (http://www.bus.miami.edu/~rgrauer) to view his current class assignments and/or download the data disk(s) for various texts in the *Exploring Windows* series. You can also click the link to the Internet supplement to access various search engines and/or to view a variety of interesting Web pages. Maryann Barber has her own page (http://www.bus.miami.edu/~mbarber) with a different set of assignments and links.

HANDS-ON EXERCISE 2

Hyperlinks

Objective: To use the Internet Assistant to add (internal and external) hyperlinks to another HTML document. Use Figure D.6 as a guide in the exercise.

STEP 1: Create a Second Web Document

➤ Start Word. Create a document describing your interests, such as the document in Figure D.6a. Your document does not have to be long, as its purpose is simply to demonstrate how you can link one Web document to another.

➤ Pull down the **File menu** and click **Save** to display the Save As dialog box in Figure D.6a. Save the document in the same drive and folder as you used in the previous exercise.

- Enter **Interests** as the name of the document.
- Click the **drop-down arrow** next to the Save As type list box, then scroll until you can click **HTML Document** as shown in the figure.
- Click the **Save button** to save the document.

➤ The display changes ever so slightly (the buttons change on the Formatting toolbar) to reflect that you are now working on an HTML document.

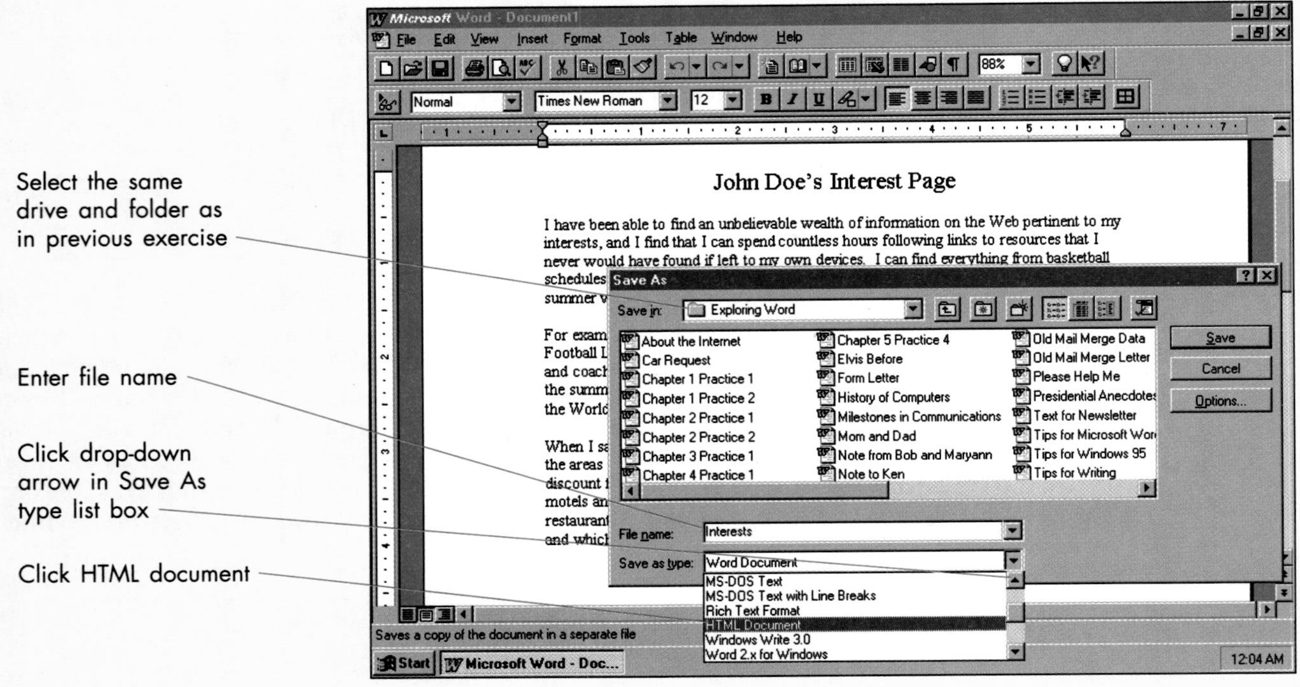

(a) Create the Second Document (step 1)

FIGURE D.6 Hands-on Exercise 2

ONLINE HELP

Online help is available for the Internet Assistant just as it is available for Microsoft Word. It contains detailed information about the Internet Assistant and should be used whenever you have a question about a specific command. Pull down the Help menu, then click Internet Assistant for Microsoft Word help. (You must have previously saved the document as an HTML document in order for this option to appear on the Help menu.)

STEP 2: Complete the Second Document

➤ Add the same background as in the previous exercise so that your pages have a consistent look. Thus:

- Pull down the **Format menu** and click **Background and Links.** Click **Browse** to display the Insert Picture dialog box, then select the same background as in the previous exercise.
- Click **OK** to select the background and close the Insert Picture dialog box, then click **OK** to close the Background and Links dialog box. A <BODY . . .> code appears in your document but the background itself is not yet visible.

➤ Complete the document, including additional formatting as necessary. Save the document, then click the **Preview in Browser button** on the Standard toolbar to preview the document. Close the browser.

➤ Pull down the **File menu** and click **Close** to close this document but remain in Word. Answer **Yes** if prompted to save your changes.

BE CONSISTENT

Your Web documents should have a consistent look from one page to another. If, for example, you use a special font or background in one document, you should use similarly formatted elements in related documents so that the user has a sense of continuity as he or she goes from one page to another.

STEP 3: Open Your Home Page

➤ Pull down the **File menu** and click **Open** (or click the **Open button** on the Standard toolbar). If necessary, change to the appropriate drive and folder.

➤ Your home page is not yet visible in the list of documents because only the Microsoft Word documents (as opposed to HTML documents) are displayed by default. Click the **drop-down arrow** on the Files of type list box, then select **All Files** as shown in Figure D.6b.

➤ Scroll (if necessary) until you can select **My Home Page** (the HTML document created in the first exercise), then click **Open** to open the document.

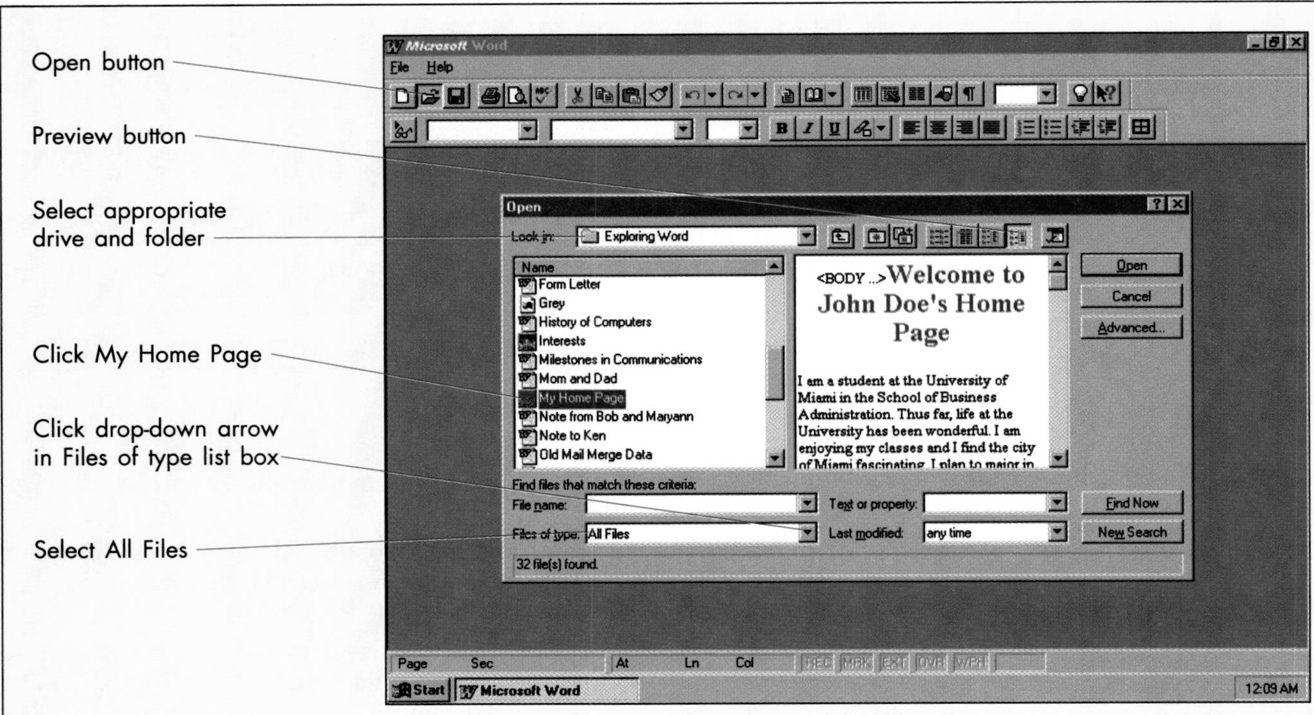

(b) Open Your Home Page (step 3)

FIGURE D.6 Hands-on Exercise 2 (continued)

A VERY USEFUL TOOLBAR

The Open and Save As dialog boxes share a common toolbar with several very useful buttons, three of which display different views. The Details view enables you to see the date and time the file was last modified as well as its size. The List button displays an icon for each file (omitting the details), which lets you see many more files at one time than in the Details view. Note, too, the different icons for the various file types (e.g., there are different icons for Word and HTML documents). The Preview button enables you to see the contents of a document before you open it.

STEP 4: Create the Link

- Read through your home page until you come to the phrase "My interests are varied and include," which appears at the end of the first paragraph. Click and drag to select the word **interests,** then press the **Del key** to delete the text (which you will replace with a hyperlink).
- Pull down the **Insert menu** and click **HyperLink** (or click the **Hyperlink button** on the Formatting toolbar) to display the Hyperlink dialog box in Figure D.6c.
- Check that you are positioned in the File or URL text box, then click the **Browse button** to display the Select File to Link dialog box shown in the fig-

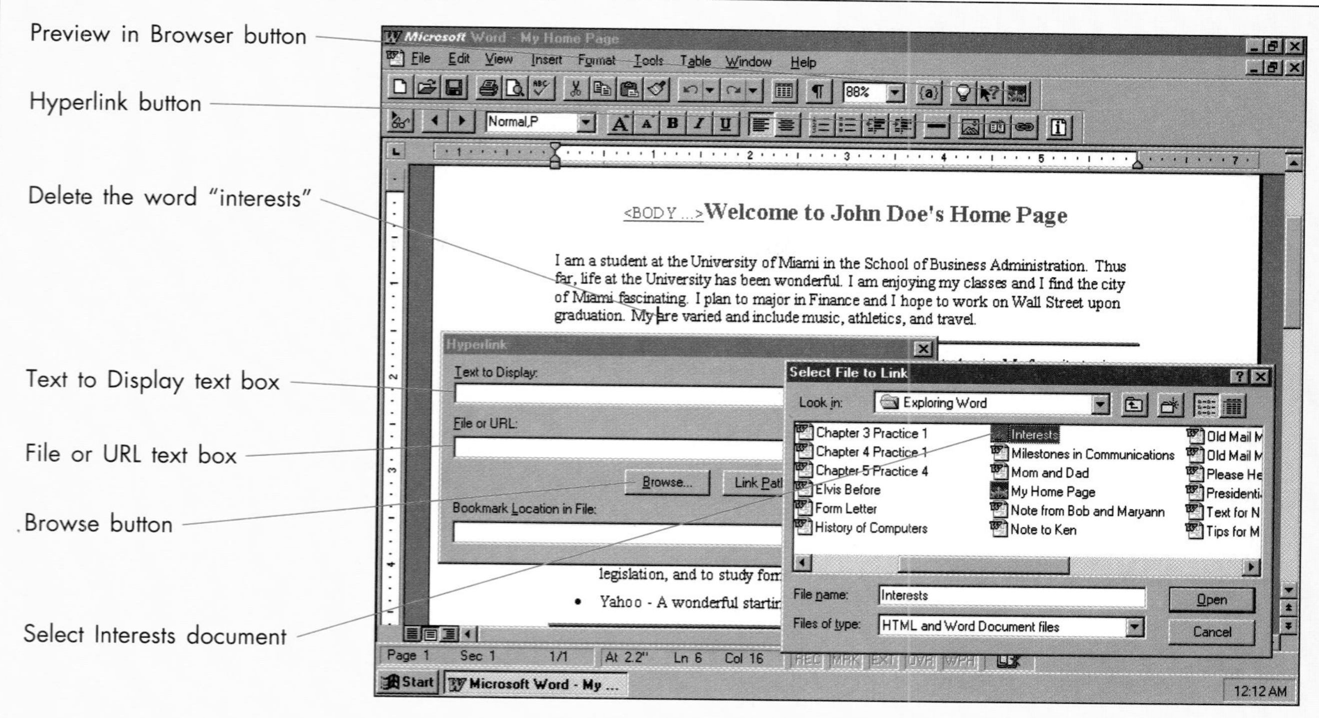

(c) Link to a Local Document (step 4)

FIGURE D.6 Hands-on Exercise 2 (continued)

ure. Select (click) the **Interests** document you created earlier, then click the **Open button** to select the file and close the Select File dialog box.

- Click in the **Text to Display** text box, then enter **interests and hobbies.** Click **OK** to close the Hyperlink dialog box. If necessary, add spaces between the link and the next word. Save the document.

CREATE A BOOKMARK

You can branch from one place to another within the same Web document through creation of one or more bookmarks. To do this, you need to create a bookmark, then create a link elsewhere in the document that takes you to the bookmark. Click where you want the bookmark to go (e.g., the top of your page), then click the Bookmark button on the Formatting toolbar to display the Bookmark dialog box. Enter the name of the bookmark such as TopOfPage (spaces are not allowed), then click Add to accept the name and close the dialog box. To create the link to the bookmark, press Ctrl+End to move to the end of your document, click the Hyperlink button to display the Hyperlink dialog box, then click the drop-down arrow on the Bookmark Location in File list box and select the bookmark you just created. Click in the Text to Display text box, enter an appropriate prompt (e.g., Return to the top of my page), then click OK. You now have a link from the bottom of your page to the top.

STEP 5: Test the Link

- Click the **hobbies and interests** link, which now appears on your home page. The text is selected but you haven't branched to the interests page because you are still in the Edit view of the Internet Assistant.
- Click the **Preview in Browser button** on the Standard toolbar to view the document using your default browser. (Alternatively, you can click the **eyeglass icon** to switch to the Web Browser view of the Internet Assistant.) Click **Yes** if prompted to save the document.
- Netscape is the browser installed on our system, as can be seen in Figure D.6d. The URL address (A:\Exploring Word\My Home Page.htm) that is displayed in the Location text box indicates that you are viewing the home page from a local drive (drive A) as opposed to an actual Web server.
- Point to the link (the mouse pointer changes to a hand with certain browsers to indicate a link), then click the **hobbies and interests** hyperlink you just created to view this page.

HYPERLINKS BEFORE AND AFTER

Hyperlinks are displayed in different colors, depending on whether the associated page has been displayed. Pull down the Format menu and click Background and Links to display the associated dialog box. Click the drop-down arrow next to the appropriate list box to change the color associated with hyperlinks before and after they are viewed. Click OK to accept your changes and close the dialog box.

Address indicates a local document

Click the interests and hobbies link

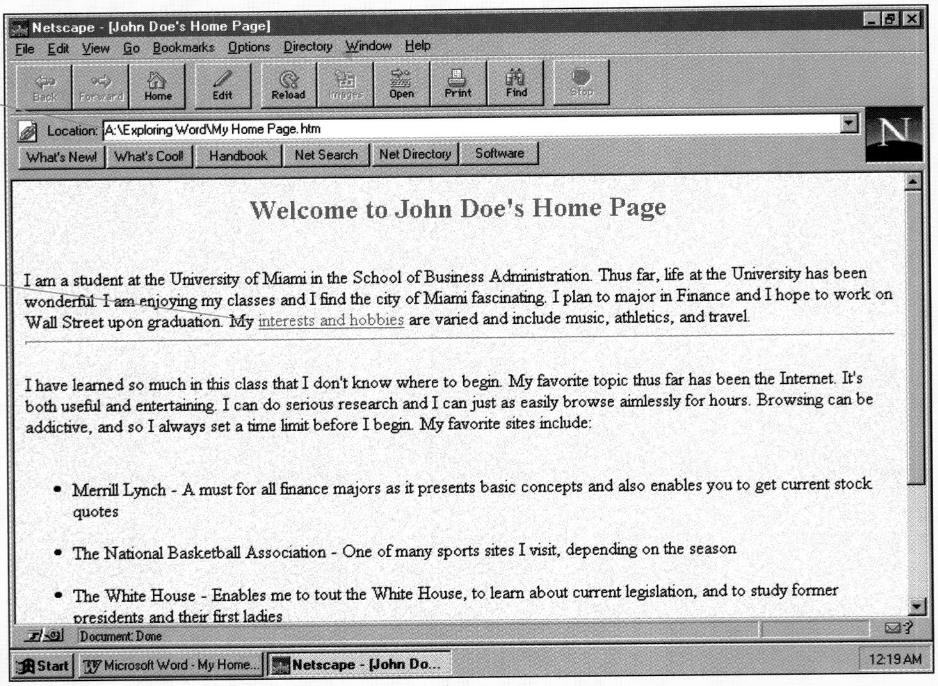

(d) Test the Link (step 5)

FIGURE D.6 Hands-on Exercise 2 (continued)

STEP 6: View Your Interests Page

- You should see your hobbies and interests as shown in Figure D.6e. The URL address in Figure D.6e (file://A:Exploring Word/Interests.htm) indicates that you are viewing this page from a local drive (drive A) as opposed to the actual server.
- Click the **back button** on the Netscape (or other browser) toolbar to return to your home page. The color of the hobbies and interests hyperlink has changed to indicate that you have viewed the associated page.
- Click the **Close button** to close the browser and return to your home page.

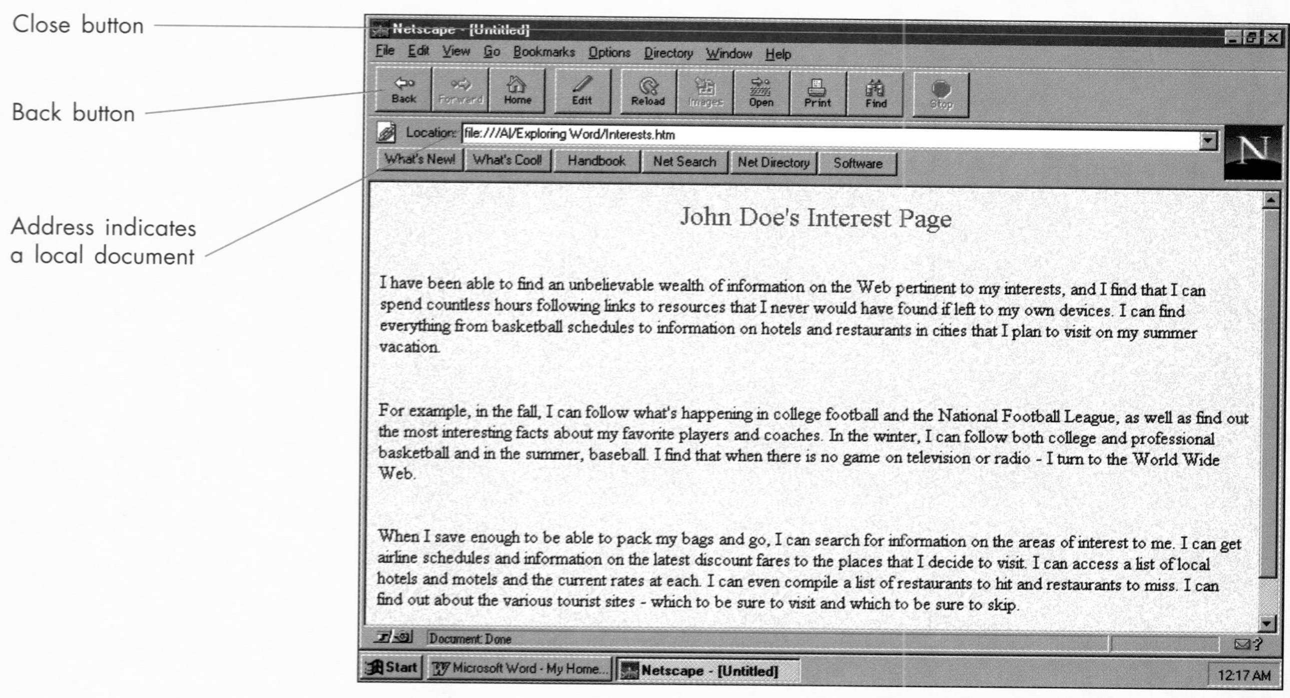

(e) View the Linked Page (step 6)

FIGURE D.6 Hands-on Exercise 2 (continued)

THE "INTRANET"

The ability to create links to local documents and to view those pages through a Web browser has given organizations an entirely new way to disseminate information. Tools such as the Internet Assistant facilitate the creation of attractive Web pages and enable you to link those pages to one another. The pages can be loaded onto a Web server and/or a local area network for use only within the organization. In this exercise, for example, you have created a home page (an HTML document) and linked it to another document stored on your hard drive. You could use the same technique to create a "help system" for an application in which the user clicks various key words to jump from one screen to the next. An organization simply extends that concept to deliver as much information as necessary, adding links as appropriate so that the user goes from one document to another as the need arises.

STEP 7: Create an External Link

- You should see your home page displayed within the Internet Assistant as shown in Figure D.6f. Click and drag to select the name of your school in the first line of the document, then press the **Del key** to delete the text, which you will replace with a hyperlink.
- Pull down the **Insert menu** and click **HyperLink** (or click the **Hyperlink button** on the Formatting toolbar) to display the Hyperlink dialog box in Figure D.6f.
- Check that you are positioned in the File or URL text box, then enter the URL of your college or university (e.g., **http://www.ir.miami.edu**) as shown in the figure.

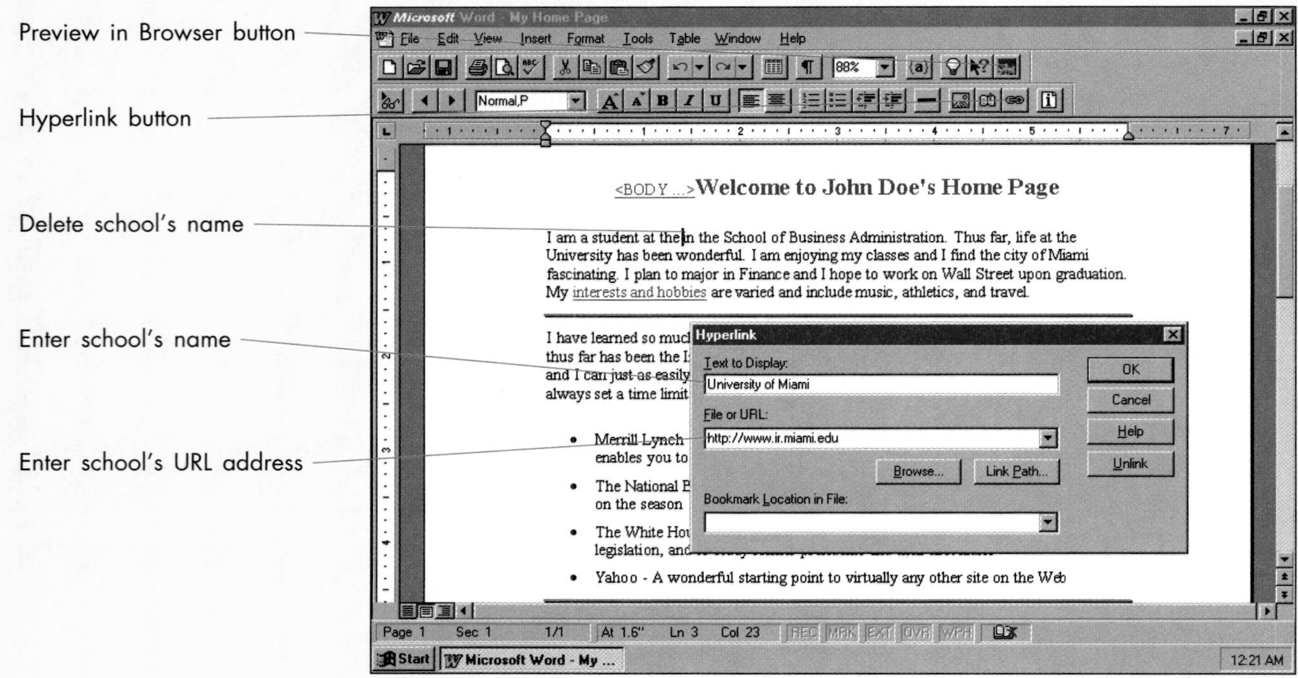

(f) Add the External Links (step 7)

FIGURE D.6 Hands-on Exercise 2 (continued)

LEARN FROM OTHERS

You can incorporate elements from existing Web pages into your own documents. Once you find a Web page of interest to you, pull down the View menu in your browser, then select the Source command to view the underlying HTML codes. Click and drag to select the codes you need, press Ctrl+C to copy the code into the Windows clipboard, then return to the Internet Assistant and the document on which you are working. Pull down the View menu from within the Internet Assistant, select HTML source to view the source code for your page, then press Ctrl+V to paste the codes into your document. *Do not, however, incorporate copyright material into your document.*

➤ Click in the **Text to Display** text box, then enter the name of your school (e.g., **the University of Miami**). Click **OK** to close the Hyperlink dialog box.

➤ Add the additional links for your other interests (see Table D.1), then save the document.

STEP 8: Test the External Link

➤ Click the **Preview in Browser button** on the Standard toolbar to view the document in your default browser. You should see your home page with the newly added links.

➤ Click the link to the **University of Miami.** Realize, however, that unlike the link to a local document in step 5, you need access to the Internet in order for this step to work.

➤ You should see the University of Miami (or your school's) home page as shown in Figure D.6g. The URL address displayed by Netscape corresponds to the address you entered in the Hyperlink dialog box in step 7.

➤ If you are unable to connect, it is most likely because you entered the URL incorrectly or because you are not connected to the Internet. To correct the problem, you need to close the browser and return to the Internet Assistant, where you should delete the invalid link, repeat step 7, then be sure you are connected to the Internet.

➤ If you link successfully, click the **back button** in your browser to return to your home page, then test the various other links to be sure that they are working.

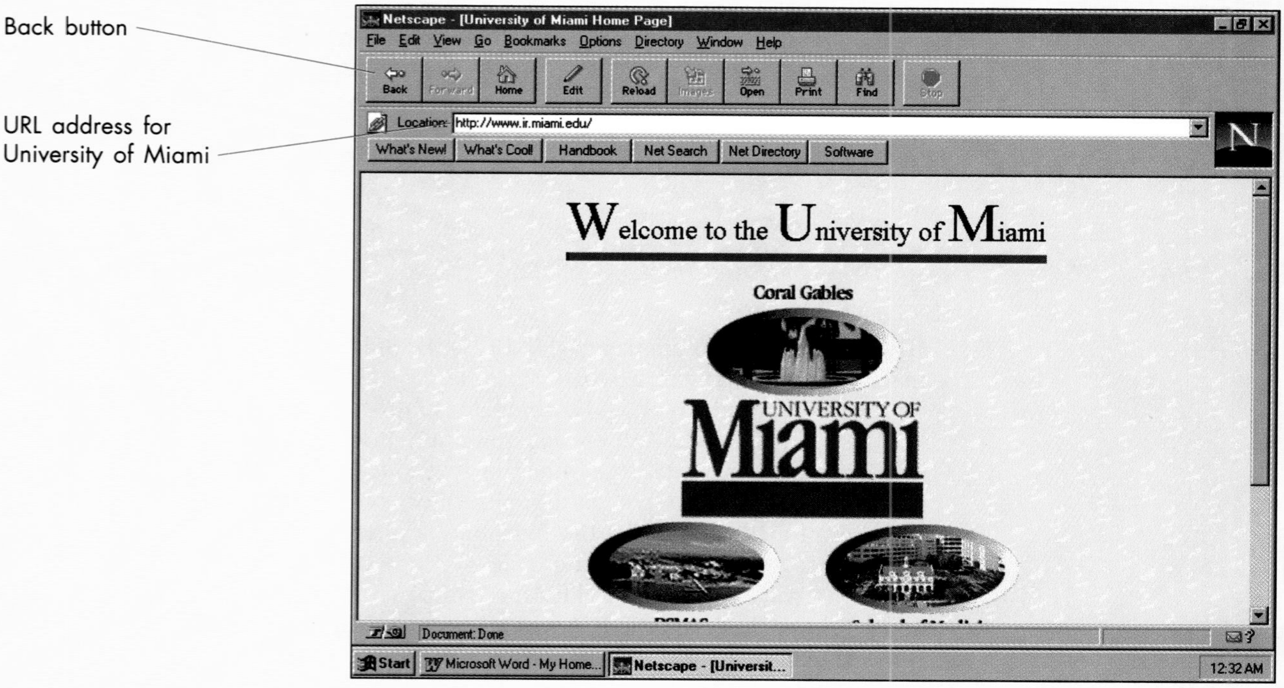

Back button

URL address for University of Miami

(g) Test the External Link (step 8)

FIGURE D.6 Hands-on Exercise 2 (continued)

ADD YOUR HOME PAGE TO THE LYCOS CATALOG

Now that you have created your page, you want others to know about it. You can add your page to various catalogs such as the Lycos Search Engine, which claims to index more than 90% of the Web. Go to the URL http://lycos.cs.cmu.edu/register.html#add and fill out the form. Wait a week or two, then try a search on your name. You should be cataloged on the Web!

STEP 9: Surf the Net

- Now that you are connected to the Internet, take a few minutes to relax and explore. You can go to specific pages or you can use various search engines to look for information on a specific topic.
- Exit your browser when you are finished surfing. Exit Word and the Internet Assistant. Congratulations on a job well done.

SET A TIME LIMIT

Your home page now contains hyperlinks to other Web pages. To test these links you need to connect to the Internet, which in turn enables you to "surf the Net." We warn you, however, that surfing can be addictive and time-consuming. Set a time limit before you begin, and stick to it when the time expires. Tomorrow is another day with new places to explore.

SUMMARY

Hypertext Markup Language (HTML) is the language used to create a Web page. In essence, HTML consists of a set of codes that format a document for display on the World Wide Web and also enables a document to link to other Web sites.

All HTML codes are enclosed in angle brackets and are in a consistent format from one document to another. A few codes appear individually, such as <P> or <HR> to indicate a new paragraph or horizontal rule, respectively. Most codes, however, appear in pairs at the beginning and end of the text to be formatted. A slash appears before the ending code.

One way to create an HTML document is to explicitly enter the codes in a text editor such as Notepad. Alternatively, you can use a tool such as Microsoft's Internet Assistant to create the codes for you. In essence, you create a document in Microsoft Word, then you save the document as an HTML file and let the Internet Assistant do the rest.

After a home page is created, it needs to be placed on a Web server so that other people will be able to access it. This, in turn, requires you to check with your system administrator if, in fact, your page is to become part of the World Wide Web. Even if your page is not placed on the Web, you can still view it locally on your PC through a Web browser.

HTML OR HTM

Hypertext documents are written in HTML (HyperText Markup Language) and display the extension HTML at the end of the URL address. Occasionally, however, you may see HTM (rather than HTML) when viewing the document in a browser (e.g., Netscape) if the document is stored on a server that does not support long file names. UNIX-based systems, which constitute the majority of Web servers, support long file names and so HTML is the more common extension.

KEYWORDS AND CONCEPTS

Browser
Home page
HTML
Hyperlink
Internet
Internet Assistant
Internet Explorer
Intranet
Netscape
Tag
World Wide Web

CASE STUDIES

Employment Opportunities

The Internet abounds with employment opportunities, help-wanted listings, and places to post your résumé. Your home page reflects your skills and experience to the entire world and represents an incredible opportunity never before available to college students. You can encourage prospective employers to visit your home page and make contact with hundreds more companies than would otherwise be possible. Update your home page to include a link to your résumé, and then surf the Net to find places to register it.

Personal Security

As in the real world, the virtual world of cyberspace harbors some strange people. For this reason, many experienced Internauts recommend against putting personal information on your home page. Write a short report indicating the pros and cons of placing personal information on your home page. Describe what you are willing to share on your home page, and indicate why you have made these choices.

Designer Home Pages

The earliest HTML standard, HTML I, was concerned with getting the pages, contents displayed regardless of what platform (Mac or PC, for example) the browser was installed on. With advancements in the standards, and with the exploding popularity of the Web, more emphasis is being placed on designing hot Web sites.

Develop some criteria you think make a Web site visually interesting. Search the Web for HTML design guidelines and incorporate them in your list. Write up a report on your findings.

Home Pages off the Web

Many companies are discovering HTML documents for internal use. Pick two companies, in two industries (hotel and toy manufacturing, for instance), and think of some uses they might have for hypertext documents. Write a two-page memo justifying to management why you should be given a summer internship to develop these documents.

7

LIST AND DATA MANAGEMENT: CONVERTING DATA TO INFORMATION

OBJECTIVES

After reading this chapter you will be able to:

1. Create a list within Excel; explain the importance of proper planning and design prior to creating the list.
2. Add, edit, and delete records in an existing list; explain the significance of data validation.
3. Distinguish between data and information; describe how one is converted to the other.
4. Describe the TODAY function and explain the use of date arithmetic.
5. Use the Sort command; distinguish between an ascending and a descending sort, and among primary, secondary, and tertiary keys.
6. Use the DSUM, DAVERAGE, DMAX, DMIN, and DCOUNT functions.
7. Use the AutoFilter and Advanced Filter commands to display a subset of a list.
8. Use the Subtotals command to summarize data in a list.
9. Create a pivot table and explain how it provides flexibility in data analysis.

OVERVIEW

All businesses maintain data in the form of lists. Companies have lists of their employees. Magazines and newspapers keep lists of their subscribers. Political candidates monitor voter lists, and so on. This chapter presents the fundamentals of list management as it is implemented in Excel. We begin with the definition of basic terms, such as field and record, then cover the commands to create a list, to add a new record, or to modify or delete an existing record.

The second half of the chapter distinguishes between data and information and describes how one is converted to the other. We introduce the AutoFilter and Advanced Filter commands that display selected records in a list. We use the Sort command to rearrange the list. We discuss database functions and the associated criteria range. We also introduce date functions and date arithmetic. The chapter ends with a discussion of subtotals and pivot tables, two powerful capabilities associated with lists.

All of this is accomplished using Excel, and although it may eventually be necessary for you to use a dedicated database program (e.g., Microsoft Access), you will be pleased with what you can do. The chapter contains three hands-on exercises, each of which focuses on a different aspect of data management.

LIST AND DATA MANAGEMENT

Imagine, if you will, that you are the personnel director of a medium-sized company with offices in several cities, and that you manually maintain employee data for the company. Accordingly, you have recorded the specifics of every individual's employment (name, salary, location, title, and so on) in a manila folder, and you have stored the entire set of folders in a file cabinet. You have written the name of each employee on the label of his or her folder and have arranged the folders alphabetically in the filing cabinet.

The manual system just described illustrates the basics of data management terminology. The set of manila folders corresponds to a ***file.*** Each individual folder is known as a ***record.*** Each data item (fact) within a folder is called a ***field.*** The folders are arranged alphabetically in the file cabinet (according to the employee name on the label) to simplify the retrieval of any given folder. Likewise, the records in a computer-based system are also in sequence according to a specific field known as a ***key.***

Excel maintains data in the form of a list. A ***list*** is an area in the worksheet that contains rows of similar data. A list can be used as a simple ***database,*** where the rows correspond to records and the columns correspond to fields. The first row contains the column labels or ***field names,*** which identify the data that will be entered in that column (field). Each additional row in the list contains a record. Each column represents a field. Each cell in the worksheet contains a value for a specific field in a specific record. Every record (row) contains the same fields (columns) in the same order as every other record.

Figure 1.1 contains an employee list with 13 records. There are four fields in every record—name, location, title, and salary. The field names should be meaningful and must be unique. (A field name may contain up to 255 characters, but you should keep them as short as possible so that a column does not become too wide and thus difficult to work with.) The arrangement of the fields within a record is consistent from record to record. The employee name was chosen as the key, and thus the records are in alphabetical order.

Normal business operations require that you make repeated trips to the filing cabinet to maintain the accuracy of the data. You will have to add a folder whenever a new employee is hired. In similar fashion, you will have to remove the folder of any employee who leaves the company, or modify the data in the folder of any employee who receives a raise, changes location, and so on.

Changes of this nature (additions, deletions, and modifications) are known as ***file maintenance*** and constitute a critical activity within any system. Indeed, without adequate file maintenance, the data in a system quickly becomes obsolete and the information useless. Imagine, if you will, the consequences of producing a payroll based on data that is six months old.

	A	B	C	D
1	Name	Location	Title	Salary
2	Adams	Atlanta	Trainee	$19,500
3	Adamson	Chicago	Manager	$52,000
4	Brown	Atlanta	Trainee	$18,500
5	Charles	Boston	Account Rep	$40,000
6	Coulter	Atlanta	Manager	$100,000
7	Frank	Miami	Manager	$75,000
8	James	Chicago	Account Rep	$42,500
9	Johnson	Chicag	Account Rep	$47,500
10	Manin	Boston	Accout Rep	$49,500
11	Marder	Chicago	Account Rep	$38,500
12	Milgrom	Boston	Manager	$57,500
13	Rubin	Boston	Account Rep	$45,000
14	Smith	Atlanta	Account Rep	$65,000

FIGURE 1.1 The Employee List

Nor is it sufficient simply to add (edit or delete) a record without adequate checks on the validity of the data. Look carefully at the entries in Figure 1.1 and ask yourself if a computer-generated report listing employees in the Chicago office will include Johnson. Will a report listing account reps include Manin? The answer to both questions is *no* because the data for these employees was entered incorrectly. Chicago is misspelled in Johnson's record (the "o" was omitted). Account rep is misspelled in Manin's title. *You* know that Johnson works in Chicago, but the computer does not, because it searches for the correct spelling. It also will omit Manin from a listing of account reps because of the misspelled title.

GARBAGE IN, GARBAGE OUT (GIGO)

A computer does exactly what you tell it to do, which is not necessarily what you want it to do. It is absolutely critical, therefore, that you validate the data that goes into a system, or else the associated information will not be correct. No system, no matter how sophisticated, can produce valid output from invalid input. In other words, garbage in—garbage out.

IMPLEMENTATION IN EXCEL

Creating a list is easy because there is little to do other than enter the data. You choose the area in the worksheet that will contain the list, then you enter the field names in the first row of the designated area. Each field name should be a unique text entry. The data for the individual records should be entered in the rows immediately below the row of field names.

Once a list has been created, you can edit any field, in any record, just as you would change the entries in an ordinary worksheet. The ***Insert Rows command*** lets you add new rows (records) to the list. The ***Insert Columns command*** lets you add additional columns (fields). The ***Delete command*** in the Edit menu enables you to delete a row or column. You can also use shortcut menus to execute commands more quickly. And finally, you can also format the entries within a list, just as you format the entries in any other worksheet.

LIST SIZE AND LOCATION

A list can appear anywhere within a worksheet and can theoretically be as large as an entire worksheet (16,384 rows by 256 columns). Practically, the list will be much smaller, giving rise to the following guideline for its placement: leave at least one blank column and one blank row between the list and the other entries in the worksheet. Excel will then be able to find the boundaries of the list automatically whenever a cell within the list is selected. It simply searches for the first blank row above and below the selected cell, and for the first blank column to the left and right of the selected cell.

Data Form Command

A ***data form*** provides an easy way to add, edit, and delete records in a list. The ***Form command*** in the Data menu displays a dialog box based on the fields in the list and contains the command buttons shown in Figure 1.2. Every record in the list contains the same fields in the same order (e.g., Name, Location, Title, and Salary in Figure 1.2), and the fields are displayed in this order within the dialog box. You do not have to enter a value for every field; that is, you may leave a field blank if the data is unknown.

Next to each field name is a text box into which data can be entered for a new record, or edited for an existing record. The scroll bar to the right of the data is used to scroll through the records in the list. The functions of the various command buttons are explained briefly:

New — Adds a record to the end of a list, then lets you enter data in that record. The formulas for computed fields, if any, are automatically copied to the new record.

Delete — Permanently removes the currently displayed record. The remaining records move up one row.

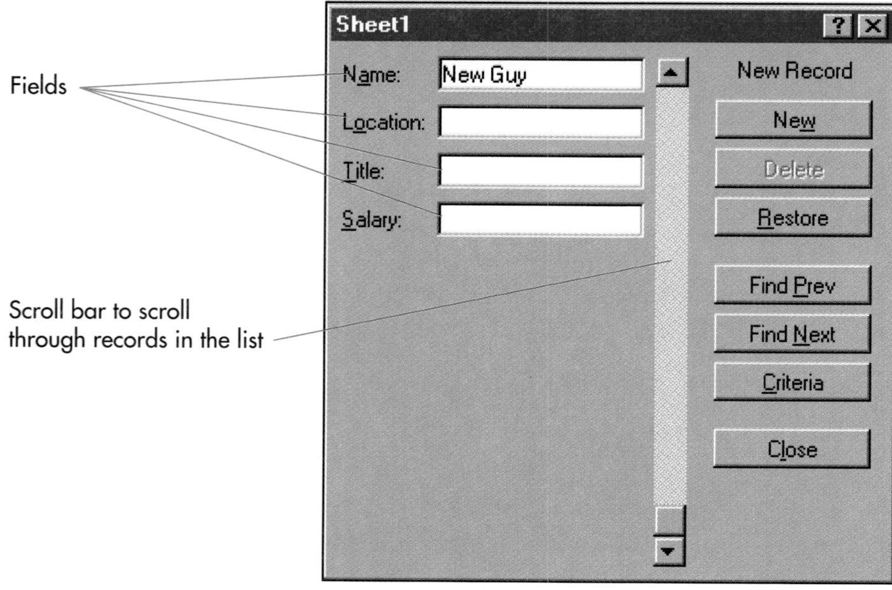

FIGURE 1.2 The Data Form Command

Restore — Cancels any changes made to the current record. (You must press the Restore button before pressing the enter key or scrolling to a new record.)
Find Prev — Displays the previous record (or the previous record that matches the existing criteria when criteria are defined).
Find Next — Displays the next record (or the next record that matches the existing criteria when criteria are defined).
Criteria — Displays a dialog box in which you specify the criteria for the Find Prev and/or Find Next command buttons to limit the displayed records to those that match the criteria.
Close — Closes the data form and returns to the worksheet.

Note, too, the What's This button (the question mark) on the title bar of the Data Form, which provides access to online help. Click the What's This button, then click any of the command buttons for an explanation. As indicated, the Data Form command provides an easy way to add, edit, and delete records in a list. It is not required, however, and you can use the Insert and Delete commands within the Edit menu as an alternate means of data entry.

Sort Command

The ***Sort command*** arranges the records in a list according to the value of one or more fields within that list. You can sort the list in ***ascending*** (low-to-high) or ***descending*** (high-to-low) ***sequence.*** (Putting a list in alphabetical order is considered an ascending sort.) You can also sort on more than one field at a time; for example, by location and then alphabetically by last name within each location. The field(s) on which you sort the list is (are) known as the key(s).

The records in Figure 1.3a are listed alphabetically (in ascending sequence according to employee name). Adams comes before Adamson, who comes before Brown, and so on. Figure 1.3b displays the identical records but in descending sequence by employee salary. The employee with the highest salary is listed first, and the employee with the lowest salary is last.

Figure 1.3c sorts the employees on two keys—by location, and by descending salary within location. Location is the more important, or ***primary key.*** Salary is the less important, or ***secondary key.*** The Sort command groups employees according to like values of the primary key (location), then within the like values of the primary key arranges them in descending sequence (ascending could have been chosen just as easily) according to the secondary key (salary). Excel provides a maximum of three keys—primary, secondary, and ***tertiary.***

CHOOSE A CUSTOM SORT SEQUENCE

Alphabetic fields are normally arranged in strict alphabetical order. You can, however, choose a custom sort sequence such as the days of the week or the months of the year. Pull down the Data menu, click Sort, click the Options command button, then click the arrow on the drop-down list box to choose a sequence other than the alphabetic. You can also create your own sequence. Pull down the Tools menu, click Options, click the Custom Lists tab, then enter the items in desired sequence in the List Entries Box. Click Add to create the sequence, then close the dialog box.

Records are listed in ascending sequence by employee name

	A	B	C	D
1	Name	Location	Title	Salary
2	Adams	Atlanta	Trainee	$19,500
3	Adamson	Chicago	Manager	$52,000
4	Brown	Atlanta	Trainee	$18,500
5	Charles	Boston	Account Rep	$40,000
6	Coulter	Atlanta	Manager	$100,000
7	Frank	Miami	Manager	$75,000
8	James	Chicago	Account Rep	$42,500
9	Johnson	Chicago	Account Rep	$47,500
10	Manin	Boston	Account Rep	$49,500
11	Marder	Chicago	Account Rep	$38,500
12	Milgrom	Boston	Manager	$57,500
13	Rubin	Boston	Account Rep	$45,000
14	Smith	Atlanta	Account Rep	$65,000

(a) Ascending Sequence (by name)

Records are listed in descending sequence by salary

	A	B	C	D
1	Name	Location	Title	Salary
2	Coulter	Atlanta	Manager	$100,000
3	Frank	Miami	Manager	$75,000
4	Smith	Atlanta	Account Rep	$65,000
5	Milgrom	Boston	Manager	$57,500
6	Adamson	Chicago	Manager	$52,000
7	Manin	Boston	Account Rep	$49,500
8	Johnson	Chicago	Account Rep	$47,500
9	Rubin	Boston	Account Rep	$45,000
10	James	Chicago	Account Rep	$42,500
11	Charles	Boston	Account Rep	$40,000
12	Marder	Chicago	Account Rep	$38,500
13	Adams	Atlanta	Trainee	$19,500
14	Brown	Atlanta	Trainee	$18,500

(b) Descending Sequence (by salary)

Location is the primary key (ascending sequence)

Salary is the secondary key (descending sequence)

	A	B	C	D
1	Name	Location	Title	Salary
2	Coulter	Atlanta	Manager	$100,000
3	Smith	Atlanta	Account Rep	$65,000
4	Adams	Atlanta	Trainee	$19,500
5	Brown	Atlanta	Trainee	$18,500
6	Milgrom	Boston	Manager	$57,500
7	Manin	Boston	Account Rep	$49,500
8	Rubin	Boston	Account Rep	$45,000
9	Charles	Boston	Account Rep	$40,000
10	Adamson	Chicago	Manager	$52,000
11	Johnson	Chicago	Account Rep	$47,500
12	James	Chicago	Account Rep	$42,500
13	Marder	Chicago	Account Rep	$38,500
14	Frank	Miami	Manager	$75,000

(c) Primary and Secondary Keys

FIGURE 1.3 The Sort Command

DATE ARITHMETIC

A date is stored internally as an integer number corresponding to the number of days in this century. January 1, 1900 is stored as the number 1; January 2, 1900 as the number 2; and so on. July 29, 1995 corresponds to the number 34909 as can

Displays the current date

Always displays same date

Age is calculated

	A	B	C	D
1		Cell Formulas	Date Format	Number Format
2	Today's Date	=TODAY()	7/29/95	34909
3	Birth Date	3/16/77	3/16/77	28200
4				
5	Elapsed Time (days)	=B2-B3		6709
6	Age (years)	=B5/365		18.4
7				
8		=IF(B6>=21,"Legal","Minor")		Minor

FIGURE 1.4 **Date Arithmetic**

be seen in Figure 1.4. The fact that dates are stored as integer numbers enables you to compute the number of elapsed days between two dates through simple subtraction. Age, for example, can be computed by subtracting a person's date of birth from today's date, and dividing the result by 365 (or more accurately by 365¼ to adjust for leap years).

The calculation of an individual's age requires the integer value of the current date, which is stored in the ***TODAY() function.*** Thus, whenever the worksheet is retrieved, the TODAY function will reflect the new date, and the calculated value of age will adjust automatically.

A specific date, such as March 16, 1977, is entered by typing the date in conventional fashion as 3/16/77. (Entering 00 for year, as in 1/21/00, signifies the year 2000.) Once entered, the date can be displayed in one of many formats. Note, too, the IF function in Figure 1.4, which examines the computed age, then displays an appropriate message indicating whether the individual is of legal age or still under the age of 21.

BIRTH DATE VERSUS AGE

An individual's age and birth date provide equivalent information, as one is calculated from the other. It might seem easier, therefore, to enter the age directly into the list and avoid the calculation, but this would be a mistake. A person's age changes continually, whereas the birth date remains constant. Thus, the date, and not the age, should be stored, so that the data in the list remains current. Similar reasoning applies to an employee's hire date and the length of service.

HANDS-ON EXERCISE 1

Creating and Maintaining a List

Objective: To add, edit, and delete records in an employee list; to introduce the Data Form and Data Sort commands; to use the spell check to validate data. Use Figure 1.5 as a guide in the exercise.

STEP 1: Open the Employee Workbook

➤ Start Excel. Open the **Employee List** workbook in the **Exploring Excel folder** as shown in Figure 1.5a.

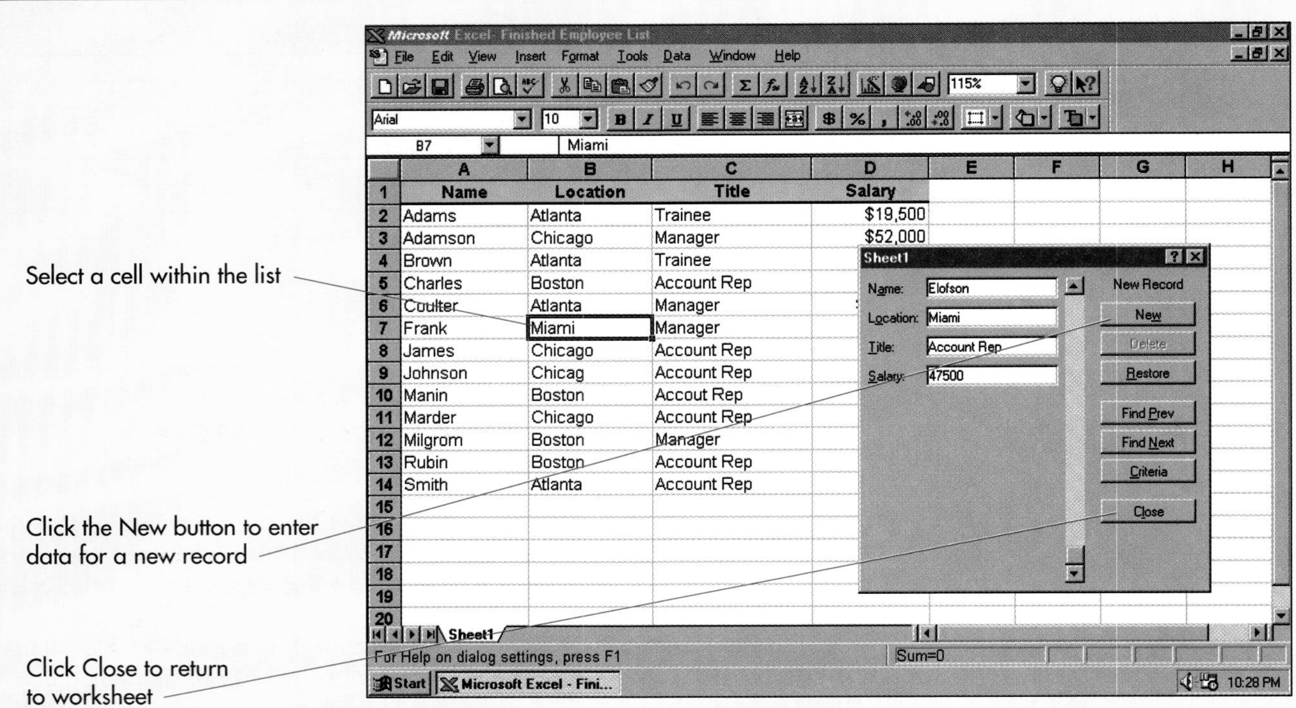

(a) The Data Form Command (step 2)

FIGURE 1.5 Hands-on Exercise 1

- Save the workbook as **Finished Employee List** so that you can always return to the original workbook.
- Reset the TipWizard.

EMPHASIZE THE COLUMN LABELS (FIELD NAMES)

Use a different font, alignment, style (boldface and/or italics), pattern, or border to distinguish the first row containing the field names from the remaining rows (records) in a list. This ensures that Excel will recognize the first row as a header row, enabling you to sort the list simply by selecting a cell in the list, then clicking the Ascending or Descending sort buttons on the Standard toolbar.

STEP 2: Add a Record (The Data Form Command)

- Click a single cell anywhere within the employee list (**cells A1** through **D14**). Pull down the **Data menu.** Click **Form** to display a dialog box with data for the first record in the list (Adams). Click the **New command button** to clear the text boxes and begin entering a new record.

- ➤ Enter the data for **Elofson** as shown in Figure 1.5a, using the Tab key to move from field to field within the data form. Click the **Close command button** after entering the salary. Elofson has been added to the list and appears in row 15.
- ➤ Save the workbook.

> **PRESS TAB, NOT ENTER**
>
> Press the Tab key to move to the next field within a data form. Press Shift+Tab to move to the previous field. Press the enter key only after the last field has been entered to move to the first field in the next record.

STEP 3: Add a Record (The Insert Rows Command)

- ➤ Click the **row heading** for **row 8.** Pull down the **Insert menu.** Click **Rows** as shown in Figure 1.5b.
- ➤ Add the data for **Gillenson,** who works in **Miami** as an **Account Rep** with a salary of **$55,000.**
- ➤ Save the workbook.

(b) The Insert Rows Command (step 3)

FIGURE 1.5 Hands-on Exercise 1 (continued)

THE FREEZE PANES COMMAND

The Freeze Panes command is useful with large lists as it prevents the column labels (field names) from scrolling off the screen. Click in the first column (field) of the first record. Pull down the Window menu, then click the Freeze Panes command. A horizontal line will appear under the field names to indicate that the command is in effect.

STEP 4: The Spell Check

- Select **cells B2:C16** as in Figure 1.5c. Pull down the **Tools menu** and click **Spelling** (or click the **Spelling button** on the Standard toolbar).
- Chicago is misspelled in cell B10 and flagged accordingly. Click the **Change command button** to accept the suggested correction and continue checking the document.
- Account is misspelled in cell C11 and flagged accordingly. Click **Account** in the Suggestions list box, then click the **Change command button** to correct the misspelling.
- Excel will indicate that it has finished checking the selected cells. Click **OK** to return to the worksheet.
- Save the workbook.

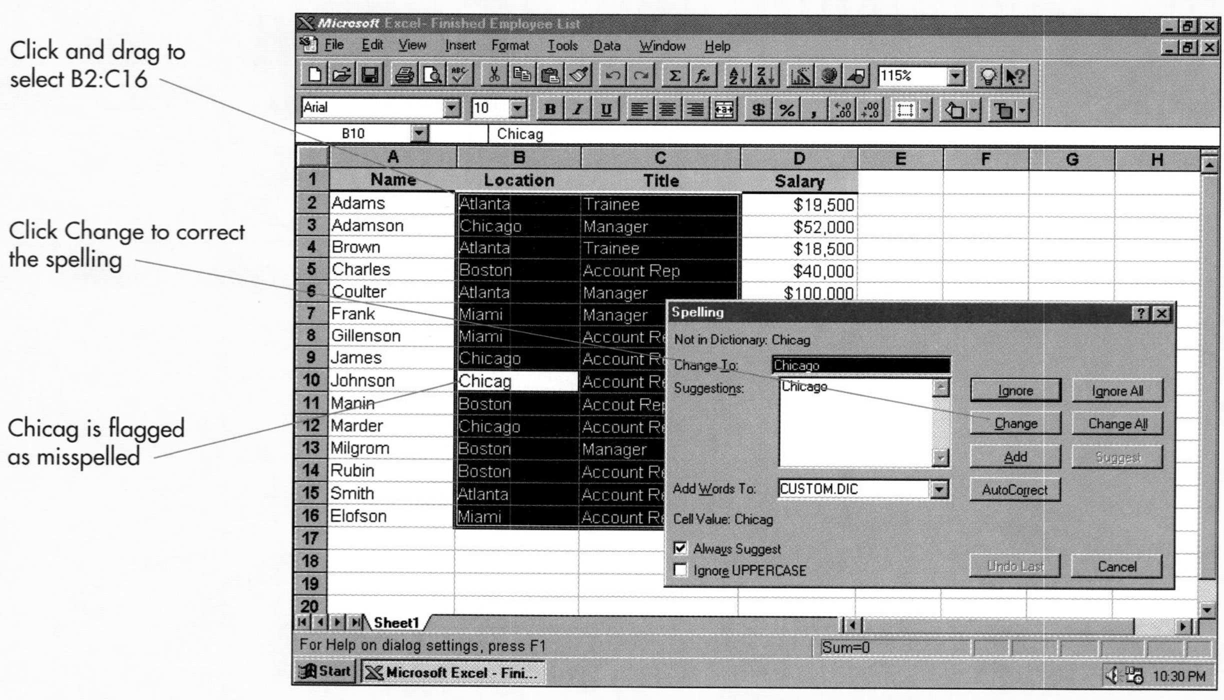

(c) The Spell Check (step 4)

FIGURE 1.5 Hands-on Exercise 1 (continued)

CREATE YOUR OWN SHORTHAND

The AutoCorrect feature is common to all Office applications and corrects mistakes as they are made according to entries in a predefined list. Type "teh", for example, and it is corrected automatically to "the" as soon as you press the space bar. You can use the feature to create your own shorthand by having it expand abbreviations such as "cis" for "Computer Informtion Systems". Pull down the Tools menu, click AutoCorrect, type the abbreviation in the Replace text box and the expanded entry in the With text box. Click the Add command button, then click OK to exit the dialog box and return to the document. The next time you type cis in a spreadsheet, it will automatically be expanded to Computer Information Systems.

STEP 5: Sort the List

➤ Click a single cell anywhere in the employee list (**cells A1** through **D16**). Pull down the **Data menu.** Click **Sort** to display the dialog box in Figure 1.5d.

- Click the **drop-down arrow** in the Sort By list box. Click **Location** as the primary key.

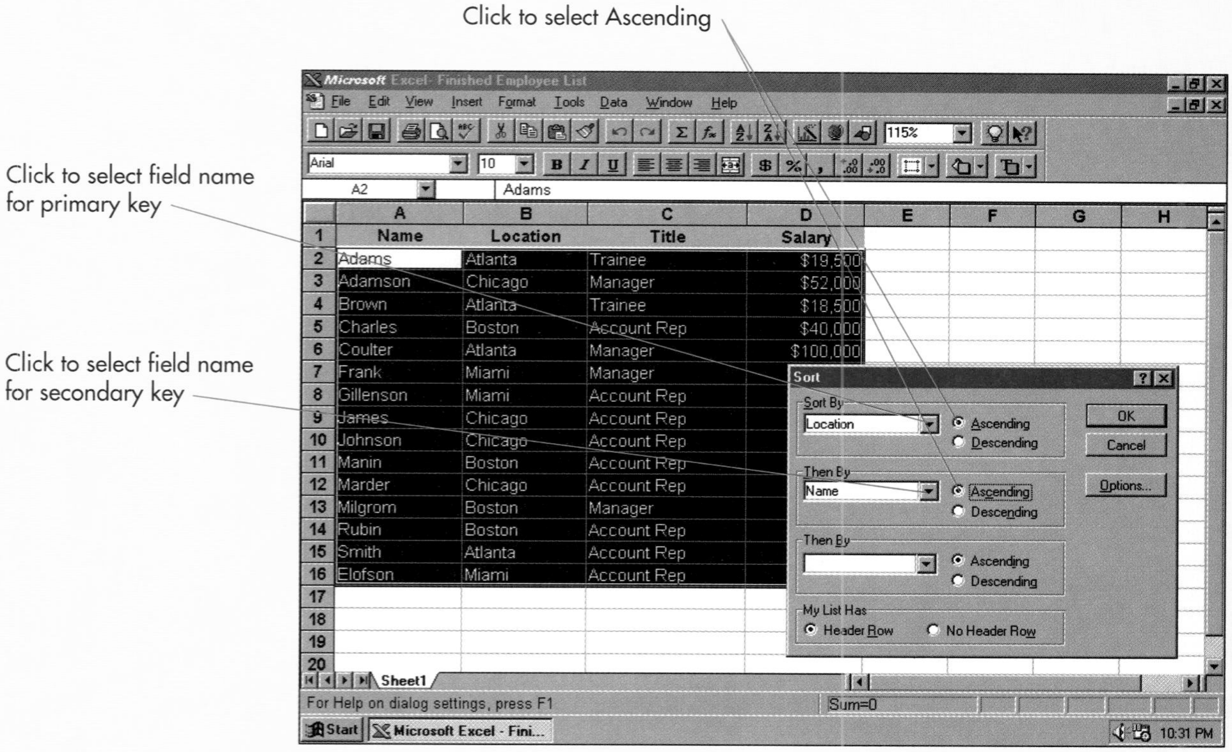

Click to select Ascending

Click to select field name for primary key

Click to select field name for secondary key

(d) Sort the Employee List (step 5)

FIGURE 1.5 Hands-on Exercise 1 (continued)

- Click the **drop-down arrow** in the first Then By list box. Click **Name** as the secondary key.
- Be Sure the **Header Row option button** is checked (so that the field names are not mixed in with the records in the list).
- Check that the **Ascending option button** is selected for both the primary and secondary keys.
- Click **OK** to sort the list and return to the worksheet.

➤ The employees are listed by location and alphabetically within location.

➤ Save the workbook.

USE THE SORT BUTTONS

Use the Sort Ascending or Sort Descending buttons on the Standard toolbar to sort on one or more keys. To sort on a single key, click any cell in the column containing the key, then click the appropriate button, depending on whether you want an ascending or a descending sort. You can also sort on multiple keys, by clicking either button multiple times, but the trick is to do it in the right order. Sort on the least significant field first, then work your way up to the most significant. For example, to sort a list by location, and name within location, sort by name first (the secondary key), then sort by location (the primary key).

STEP 6: Delete a Record

➤ A record may be deleted by using the Edit Delete command or the Data Form command; both methods will be illustrated to delete the record for Frank, which is currently in row 15.

➤ To delete a record by using the Edit Delete command:

- Click the **row heading** in **row 15** (containing the record for Frank, which is slated for deletion).
- Pull down the **Edit menu.** Click **Delete.** Frank has been deleted.

➤ Click the **Undo button** on the Standard toolbar. The record for Frank has been restored.

➤ To delete a record by using the Data Form command:

- Click a single cell within the employee list.
- Pull down the **Data menu.** Click **Form** to display the data form.
- Click the **down arrow** in the scroll bar until you come to the record for Frank.
- Click the **Delete command button.**
- Click **OK** in response to the warning message shown in Figure 1.5e. (The record cannot be undeleted as it could with the Edit Delete command.)
- Click **Close** to close the Data Form.

➤ Save the workbook.

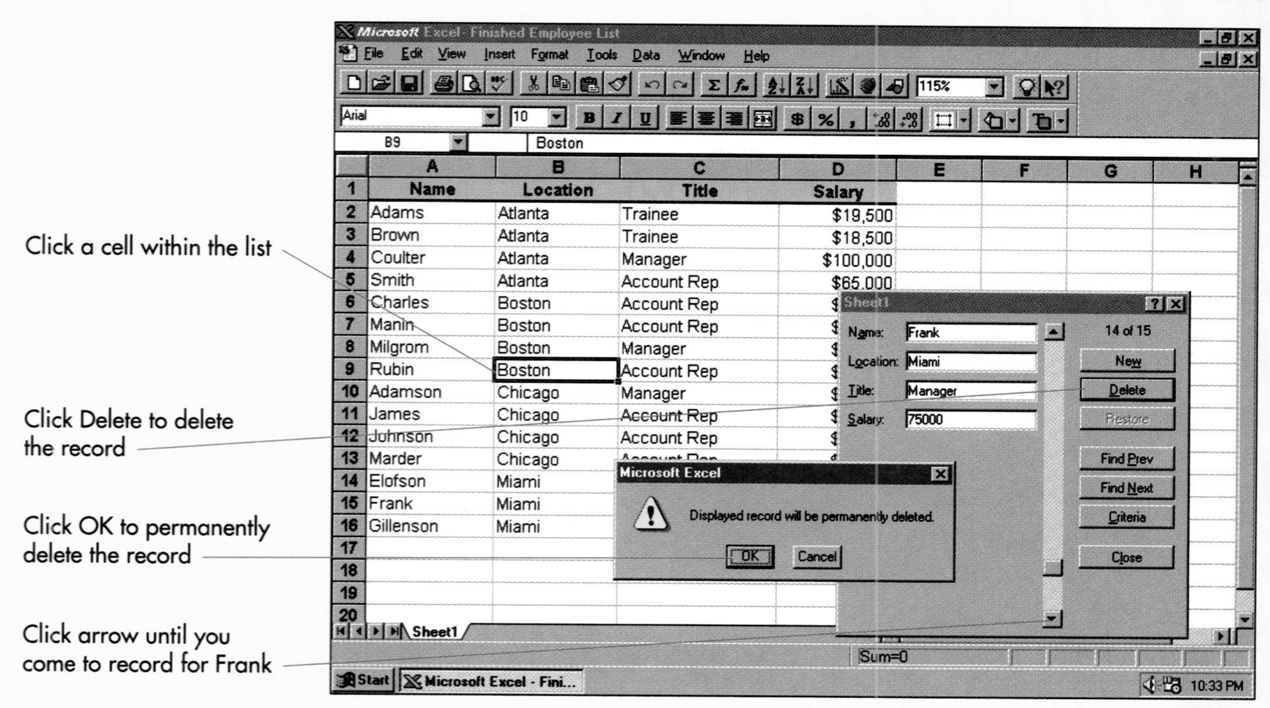

(e) Delete a Record (step 6)

FIGURE 1.5 Hands-on Exercise 1 (continued)

STEP 7: Insert a Field

- Click the **column heading** in **column D.** Click the **right mouse button** to display a shortcut menu. Click **Insert.** The employee salaries have been moved to column E.
- Click **cell D1.** Type **Hire Date** and press **enter.** Adjust the column width if necessary.

STEP 8: Enter the Hire Dates

- Dates may be entered in several different formats. Do not be concerned if Excel displays the date in a different format from the way you entered it.
  - Type **11/24/93** in cell D2. Press the **down arrow key.**
  - Type **Nov 24, 1993** in cell D3. Type a **comma** after the day, but do not type a period after the month. Press the **down arrow key** to move to cell D4.
  - Type **=Date(93,11,24)** in cell D4. Press the **down arrow key.**
  - Type **11-24-93** in cell D5.
- For ease of data entry, assume that the next several employees were hired on the same day, 3/16/92.
  - Click in **cell D6.** Type **3/16/92.** Press **enter.**
  - Click in **cell D6.** Click the **Copy button** on the Standard toolbar, which produces a moving border around cell D6. Drag the mouse over **cells D7** through **D10.** Click the **Paste button** on the Standard toolbar to complete the copy operation.
  - Press **Esc** to remove the moving border around cell D6.

- ➤ The last five employees were hired one year apart, beginning October 31, 1989.
  - Click in **cell D11** and type **10/31/89.**
  - Click in **cell D12** and type **10/31/90.**
  - Select **cells D11** and **D12.**
  - Drag the **fill handle** at the bottom of cell D12 over **cells D13, D14,** and **D15.** Release the mouse to complete the AutoFill operation.
- ➤ Save the workbook.

DATES AND THE FILL HANDLE

The AutoFill facility is the fastest way to create a series of dates. Enter the first two dates in the series, then select both cells and drag the fill handle over the remaining cells. Excel will create a series based on the increment between the first two cells; for example, if the first two dates are one month apart, the remaining dates will also be one month apart.

STEP 9: Format the Date

- ➤ Click in the **column heading** for **column D** to select the column of dates as in Figure 1.5f.
- ➤ Click the **right mouse button** to display a shortcut menu. Click **Format Cells.**
- ➤ Click the **Number tab** in the Format Cells dialog box. Click **Date** in the Category list box. Select (click) the date format shown in Figure 1.5f. Click **OK.**
- ➤ Click elsewhere in the workbook to deselect the dates. Reduce the width of column D as appropriate. Save the workbook.

DATES VERSUS FRACTIONS

A fraction is entered into a cell by preceding the fraction with an equal sign—for example, =1/4. The fraction is displayed as its decimal equivalent (.25) unless the cell is formatted to display fractions. Select the cell, pull down the Format menu, and click the Cells command. Click the Numbers tab, then choose Fraction from the Category list box. Omission of the equal sign, when entering a fraction, treats the entry as a date; that is, typing 1/4 (without the equal sign) will store the entry as a date and display it as January 4th (of the current year).

STEP 10: Exit Excel

- ➤ Click the **TipWizard button** to open the TipWizard box. Click the **up (down) arrow** to review the suggestions made by the TipWizard during the exercise.
- ➤ Close the workbook. Exit Excel if you do not want to continue with the next exercise at this time.

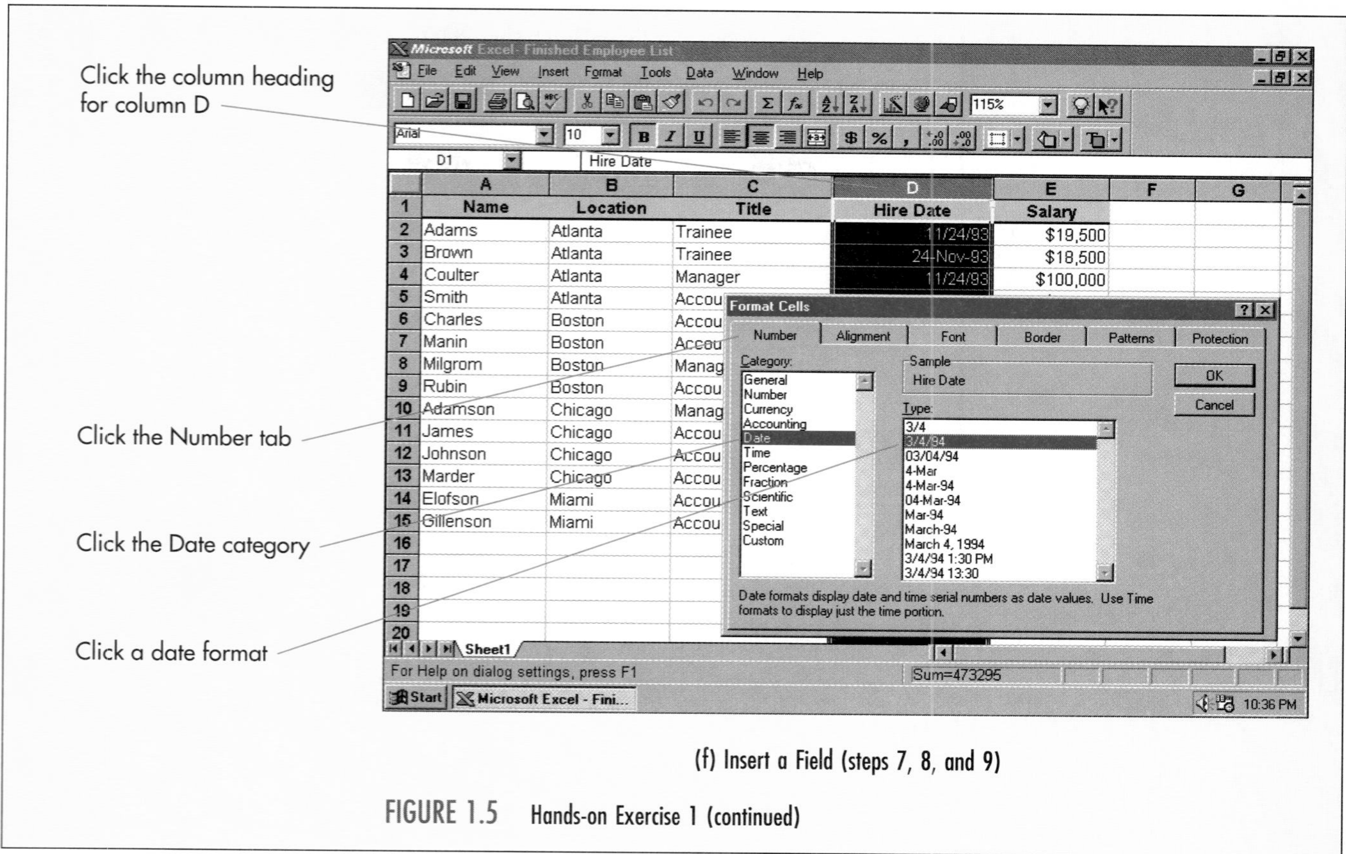

(f) Insert a Field (steps 7, 8, and 9)

FIGURE 1.5 Hands-on Exercise 1 (continued)

DATA VERSUS INFORMATION

Data and information are not synonymous. ***Data*** refers to a fact or facts about a specific record, such as an employee's name, title, or salary. ***Information,*** on the other hand, is data that has been rearranged into a form perceived as useful by the recipient. A list of employees earning more than $35,000 or a total of all employee salaries are examples of information produced from data about individual employees. Put another way, data is the raw material, and information is the finished product.

Decisions in an organization are based on information rather than raw data; for example, in assessing the effects of a proposed across-the-board salary increase, management needs to know the total payroll rather than individual salary amounts. In similar fashion, decisions about next year's hiring will be influenced, at least in part, by knowing how many individuals are currently employed in each job category.

Data is converted to information through a combination of database commands and functions whose capabilities are illustrated by the reports in Figure 1.6. The reports are based on the employee list as it existed at the end of the first hands-on exercise. Each report presents the data in a different way, according to the information requirements of the end-user. As you view each report, ask yourself how it was produced; that is, what was done to the data in order to produce the information?

Figure 1.6a contains a master list of all employees, listing employees by location, and alphabetically by last name within location. The report was created by sorting the list on two keys, location and name. Location is the more important or primary key. Name is the less important or secondary key. The sorted report

Location Report				
Name	Location	Title	Hire Date	Salary
Adams	Atlanta	Trainee	11/24/93	$19,500
Brown	Atlanta	Trainee	11/24/93	$18,500
Coulter	Atlanta	Manager	11/24/93	$100,000
Smith	Atlanta	Account Rep	11/24/93	$65,000
Charles	Boston	Account Rep	3/16/92	$40,000
Manin	Boston	Account Rep	3/16/92	$49,500
Milgrom	Boston	Manager	3/16/92	$57,500
Rubin	Boston	Account Rep	3/16/92	$45,000
Adamson	Chicago	Manager	3/16/92	$52,000
James	Chicago	Account Rep	10/31/89	$42,500
Johnson	Chicago	Account Rep	10/31/90	$47,500
Marder	Chicago	Account Rep	10/31/91	$38,500
Elofson	Miami	Account Rep	10/31/92	$47,500
Gillenson	Miami	Account Rep	10/31/93	$55,000

(a) Employees by Location and Name within Location

Employees Earning Between $40,000 and $60,000				
Name	Location	Title	Hire Date	Salary
Milgrom	Boston	Manager	3/16/92	$57,500
Gillenson	Miami	Account Rep	10/31/93	$55,000
Adamson	Chicago	Manager	3/16/92	$52,000
Manin	Boston	Account Rep	3/16/92	$49,500
Johnson	Chicago	Account Rep	10/31/90	$47,500
Elofson	Miami	Account Rep	10/31/92	$47,500
Rubin	Boston	Account Rep	3/16/92	$45,000
James	Chicago	Account Rep	10/31/89	$42,500
Charles	Boston	Account Rep	3/16/92	$40,000

(b) Employees Earning between $40,000 and $60,000

Summary Statistics	
Total Salary for Account Reps:	$430,500
Average Salary for Account Reps:	$47,833
Maximum Salary for Account Reps:	$65,000
Minimum Salary for Account Reps:	$38,500
Number of Account Reps:	9

(c) Account Rep Summary Data

FIGURE 1.6 Data versus Information

groups employees according to like values of the primary key (location), then within the primary key, groups the records according to the secondary key (name).

The report in Figure 1.6b displays a subset of the records in the list, which includes only those employees that meet specific criteria. The criteria can be based on any field, or combination of fields; in this case, employees whose salary is between $40,000 and $60,000 (inclusive). The employees are shown in descending order of salary so that the employee with the highest salary is listed first.

The report in Figure 1.6c displays summary statistics for the selected employees—in this example, the salaries for the account reps within the company. Reports of this nature omit the salaries of individual employees (known as detail lines), in order to present an aggregate view of the organization.

> **CITY, STATE, AND ZIP CODE—ONE FIELD OR THREE?**
>
> The answer depends on whether the fields are referenced as a unit or individually. However, given the almost universal need to sort or select on zip code, it is almost invariably defined as a separate field. An individual's last name, first name, and middle initial are defined as individual fields for the same reason.

AutoFilter Command

A ***filtered list*** displays a subset of records that meet a specific criterion or set of criteria. It is created by the ***AutoFilter command*** (or the Advanced Filter command discussed in the next section). Both commands temporarily hide those records (rows) that do not meet the criteria. The hidden records are *not* deleted; they are simply not displayed.

Figure 1.7a displays the employee list in alphabetical order. Figure 1.7b displays a filtered version of the list in which only the Atlanta employees (in rows 2, 4, 6, and 15) are visible. The remaining employees are still in the worksheet but are not shown as their rows are hidden.

Execution of the AutoFilter command places drop-down arrows next to each column label (field name). Clicking a drop-down arrow produces a list of the

Drop-down arrows appear next to each field name

Click here to display only the Atlanta employees

(All)
(Top 10...)
(Custom...)
Atlanta
Boston
Chicago
Miami
(Blanks)

	A	B	C	D	E
1	Name	Location	Title	Hire Date	Salary
2	Adams		Trainee	11/24/93	$19,500
3	Adamson		Manager	3/16/92	$52,000
4	Brown		Trainee	11/24/93	$18,500
5	Charles		Account Rep	3/16/92	$40,000
6	Coulter		Manager	11/24/93	$100,000
7	Elofson		Account Rep	10/31/92	$47,500
8	Gillenson	Miami	Account Rep	10/31/93	$55,000
9	James	Chicago	Account Rep	10/31/89	$42,500
10	Johnson	Chicago	Account Rep	10/31/90	$47,500
11	Manin	Boston	Account Rep	3/16/92	$49,500
12	Marder	Chicago	Account Rep	10/31/91	$38,500
13	Milgrom	Boston	Manager	3/16/92	$57,500
14	Rubin	Boston	Account Rep	3/16/92	$45,000
15	Smith	Atlanta	Account Rep	11/24/93	$65,000

(a) Unfiltered List

Only Atanta employees are displayed

	A	B	C	D	E
1	Name	Location	Title	Hire Date	Salary
2	Adams	Atlanta	Trainee	11/24/93	$19,500
4	Brown	Atlanta	Trainee	11/24/93	$18,500
6	Coulter	Atlanta	Manager	11/24/93	$100,000
15	Smith	Atlanta	Account Rep	11/24/93	$65,000

(b) Filtered List (Atlanta employees)

FIGURE 1.7 Filter Command

Click drop-down arrow to further filter the list to Atlanta Managers

	A	B	C	D	E
1	Name	Location	Title	Hire Date	Salary
2	Adams	Atlanta	(All)	11/24/93	$19,500
4	Brown	Atlanta	(Top 10...) (Custom...)	11/24/93	$18,500
6	Coulter	Atlanta	Account Rep	11/24/93	$100,000
15	Smith	Atlanta	Manager	11/24/93	$65,000
16			Trainee		
17			(Blanks) (NonBlanks)		

(c) Imposing a Second Condition

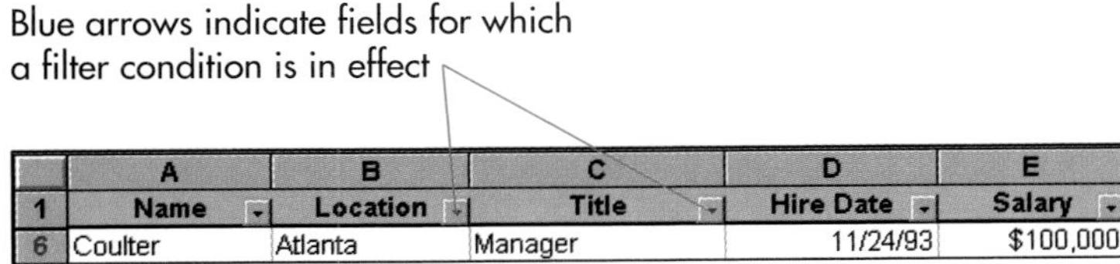

Blue arrows indicate fields for which a filter condition is in effect
A
B
C
D
E
1
Name
Location
Title
Hire Date
Salary
6
Coulter
Atlanta
Manager
11/24/93
$100,000

(d) Filtered List (Atlanta managers)

FIGURE 1.7 Filter Command (continued)

unique values for that field, enabling you to establish the criteria for the filtered list. Thus, to display the Atlanta employees, click the drop-down arrow for Location, then click Atlanta.

A filter condition can be imposed on multiple columns as shown in Figure 1.7c. The filtered list in Figure 1.7c contains just the Atlanta employees. Clicking the arrow next to Title, then clicking Manager, will filter the list further to display the employees who work in Atlanta *and* who have Manager as a title. Only one employee meets both conditions, as shown in Figure 1.7d. The drop-down arrows next to Location and Title are displayed in blue to indicate that a filter is in effect for these columns.

The AutoFilter command has additional options as can be seen from the drop-down list box in Figure 1.7c. (All) removes existing criteria in the column and effectively "unfilters" the list. (Custom. . .) enables you to use the relational operators (=, >, <, >=, <=, or <>) within a criterion. (NonBlanks) and (Blanks) select the records that contain, or do not contain, data in the specified field, and are useful in data validation.

Advanced Filter Command

The ***Advanced Filter command*** extends the capabilities of the AutoFilter command in two important ways. It enables you to develop more complex criteria than are possible with the AutoFilter Command. It also enables you to copy the selected records to a separate area in the worksheet. The Advanced Filter command is illustrated in detail in the hands-on exercise that follows shortly.

Criteria Range

The ***criteria range*** is used with both the Advanced Filter command and the database functions that are discussed in the next section. It is defined independently of the list on which it operates and exists as a separate area in the worksheet. A criteria range must be at least two rows deep and one column wide as illustrated in Figure 1.8.

First row is field names

Second row is value for filter condition

Name	Location	Title	Hire Date	Salary
	Atlanta			

(a) Employees Who Work in Atlanta

Multiple values in same row

Name	Location	Title	Hire Date	Salary
	Atlanta	Account Rep		

(b) Account Reps Who Work in Atlanta (AND condition)

Multiple values in different rows

Name	Location	Title	Hire Date	Salary
	Atlanta			
		Account Rep		

(c) Employees Who Work in Atlanta or Who Are Account Reps (OR condition)

Relational operators can be used with dates and numeric fields

Name	Location	Title	Hire Date	Salary
			<1/1/93	

(d) Employees Hired before January 1, 1993

Name	Location	Title	Hire Date	Salary
				>$40,000

(e) Employees Who Earn More Than $40,000

Upper boundary

Lower boundary

Name	Location	Title	Hire Date	Salary	Salary
				>$40,000	<$60,000

(f) Employees Who Earn More Than $40,000 but Less Than $60,000

Returns all records with no entry in this field

Name	Location	Title	Hire Date	Salary
	=			

(g) Employees without an Entry in Location

Empty row returns every record in the list

Name	Location	Title	Hire Date	Salary

(h) All Employees (a blank row)

FIGURE 1.8 The Criteria Range

The simplest criteria range consists of two rows and as many columns as there are fields in the list. The first row contains the field names as they appear in the list. The second row holds the value(s) you are looking for. The criteria range in Figure 1.8a selects the employees who work in Atlanta.

Multiple values in the same row are connected by an AND and require that the selected records meet *all* of the specified criteria. The criteria range in Figure 1.8b identifies the account reps in Atlanta; that is, it selects any record in which the Location field is Atlanta *and* the Title field is Account Rep.

Values entered in multiple rows are connected by an OR in which the selected records satisfy *any* of the indicated criteria. The criteria range in Figure 1.8c will identify employees who work in Atlanta *or* whose title is Account Rep.

Relational operators may be used with date or numeric fields to return records within a designated range. The criteria range in Figure 1.8d selects the employees hired before January 1, 1993. The criteria range in Figure 1.8e returns employees whose salary is greater than $40,000.

An upper and lower boundary may be established for the same field by repeating the field within the criteria range. This was done in Figure 1.8f, which returns all records in which the salary is greater than $40,000 but less than $60,000.

The equal and unequal signs select records with empty and nonempty fields, respectively. An equal sign with nothing after it will return all records without an entry in the designated field; for example, the criteria range in Figure 1.8g selects any record that is missing a value for the Location field. An unequal sign (<>) with nothing after it will select all records with an entry in the field.

An empty row in the criteria range returns *every* record in the list, as shown in Figure 1.8h. All criteria are *case insensitive* and return records with any combination of upper- and lowercase letters that match the entry.

THE IMPLIED WILD CARD

Any text entry within a criteria range is treated as though it were followed by the asterisk ***wild card;*** that is, *New* is the same as *New**. Both entries will return New York and New Jersey. To match a text entry exactly, begin with an equal sign, enter a quotation mark followed by another equal sign, the entry you are looking for, and the closing quotation mark—for example, ="=New" to return only the entries that say New.

Database Functions

The ***database functions*** DSUM, DAVERAGE, DMAX, DMIN, and DCOUNT operate on *selected* records in a list. These functions parallel the regular statistical functions (SUM, AVERAGE, MAX, MIN, and COUNT) except that they affect only records that satisfy the established criteria.

The summary statistics in Figure 1.9 are based on the salaries of the managers in the list, rather than all employees. Each database function includes the criteria range in cells A17:E18 as one of its arguments, and thus limits the employees that are included to managers. The ***DAVERAGE function*** returns the average salary for just the managers. The ***DMAX*** and ***DMIN functions*** display the maximum and minimum salaries for the managers. The ***DSUM function*** computes the total salary for all the managers. The ***DCOUNT function*** indicates the number of managers.

Criteria range is A17:E18 (filters list to Managers)

Summary statistics for Managers

	A	B	C	D	E
1	Name	Location	Title	Hire Date	Salary
2	Adams	Atlanta	Trainee	11/24/93	$19,500
3	Adamson	Chicago	Manager	3/16/92	$52,000
4	Brown	Atlanta	Trainee	11/24/93	$18,500
5	Charles	Boston	Account Rep	3/16/92	$40,000
6	Coulter	Atlanta	Manager	11/24/93	$100,000
7	Elofson	Miami	Account Rep	10/31/92	$47,500
8	Gillenson	Miami	Account Rep	10/31/93	$55,000
9	James	Chicago	Account Rep	10/31/89	$42,500
10	Johnson	Chicago	Account Rep	10/31/90	$47,500
11	Manin	Boston	Account Rep	3/16/92	$49,500
12	Marder	Chicago	Account Rep	10/31/91	$38,500
13	Milgrom	Boston	Manager	3/16/92	$57,500
14	Rubin	Boston	Account Rep	3/16/92	$45,000
15	Smith	Atlanta	Account Rep	11/24/93	$65,000
16					
17	Name	Location	Title	Hire Date	Salary
18			Manager		
19					
20					
21			Summary Statistics		
22	Average Salary:				$69,833
23	Maximum Salary:				$100,000
24	Minimum Salary:				$52,000
25	Total Salary:				$209,500
26	Number of Employees:				3

FIGURE 1.9 Database Functions and the Data Extract Command

Each database function has three arguments: the range for the list on which it is to operate, the field to be processed, and the criteria range. Consider, for example, the DAVERAGE function as shown below:

=DAVERAGE(list,"field",criteria)

- The criteria range can be entered as a cell range (such as A17:E18) or as a name assigned to a cell range (e.g., Criteria)
- The name of the field to be processed is enclosed in quotation marks
- The list can be entered as a cell range (such as A1:E15) or as a name assigned to a cell range (e.g., Database).

FORMAT THE DATABASE

Formatting has no effect on the success or failure of database commands, so you can format the entries in a list to any extent you like. Select currency format where appropriate, change fonts, use borders or shading, or any other formatting option. Be sure to format the row containing the column names differently from the rest of the list, so that it can be recognized as the header row in conjunction with the Ascending and Descending Sort buttons on the Standard toolbar.

The entries in the criteria range may be changed at any time, in which case the values of the database functions are automatically recalculated. The other database functions have arguments identical to those used in the DAVERAGE example.

Name Command

The ***Name command*** in the Insert menu equates a mnemonic name such as *employee_list* to a cell or cell range such as *A1:E15,* then enables you to use that name to reference the cell(s) in all subsequent commands. A name can be up to 255 characters in length, but must begin with a letter or an underscore. It can include upper- or lowercase letters, numbers, periods, and underscore characters.

Once defined, names adjust automatically for insertions and/or deletions within the range. If, in the previous example, you were to delete row 4, the definition of *employee_list* would change to A1:E14. And, in similar fashion, if you were to add a new column between columns B and C, the range would change to A1:F14.

A name can be used in any formula or function instead of a cell address; for example, =SALES−EXPENSES instead of =C1−C10, where Sales and Expenses have been defined as the names for cells C1 and C10, respectively. A name can also be entered into any dialog box where a cell range is required.

THE GO TO COMMAND

Names are frequently used in conjunction with the Go To command. Pull down the Edit menu and click Go To (or click the F5 key) to display a dialog box containing the names that have been defined within the workbook. Double click a name to move directly to the first cell in the associated range and simultaneously select the entire range.

HANDS-ON EXERCISE 2

Data versus Information

Objective: To sort a list on multiple keys; to demonstrate the AutoFilter and Advanced Filter commands; to define a named range; to use the DSUM, DAVERAGE, DMAX, DMIN, and DCOUNT functions. Use Figure 1.10 as a guide in the exercise.

STEP 1: Calculate the Years of Service

- Start Excel. Reset the TipWizard. Open the **Finished Employee List** workbook created in the previous exercise.
- Click the **column heading** in **column D.** Click the **right mouse button** to display a shortcut menu. Click **Insert.** The column of hire dates has been moved to column E.
- Click in **cell D1.** Type **Service** and press **enter.**

- Click in **cell D2** and enter the formula to compute the years of service **=(Today()-E2)/365** as shown in Figure 1.10a. Press **enter;** the years of service for the first employee are displayed in cell D2.
- Click in **cell D2,** then click the **Decrease Decimal button** on the Formatting toolbar several times to display the length of service with only one decimal place. Reduce the column width as appropriate.
- Drag the **fill handle** in cell D2 to the remaining cells in that column (**cells D3** through **D15**) to compute the service for the remaining employees.

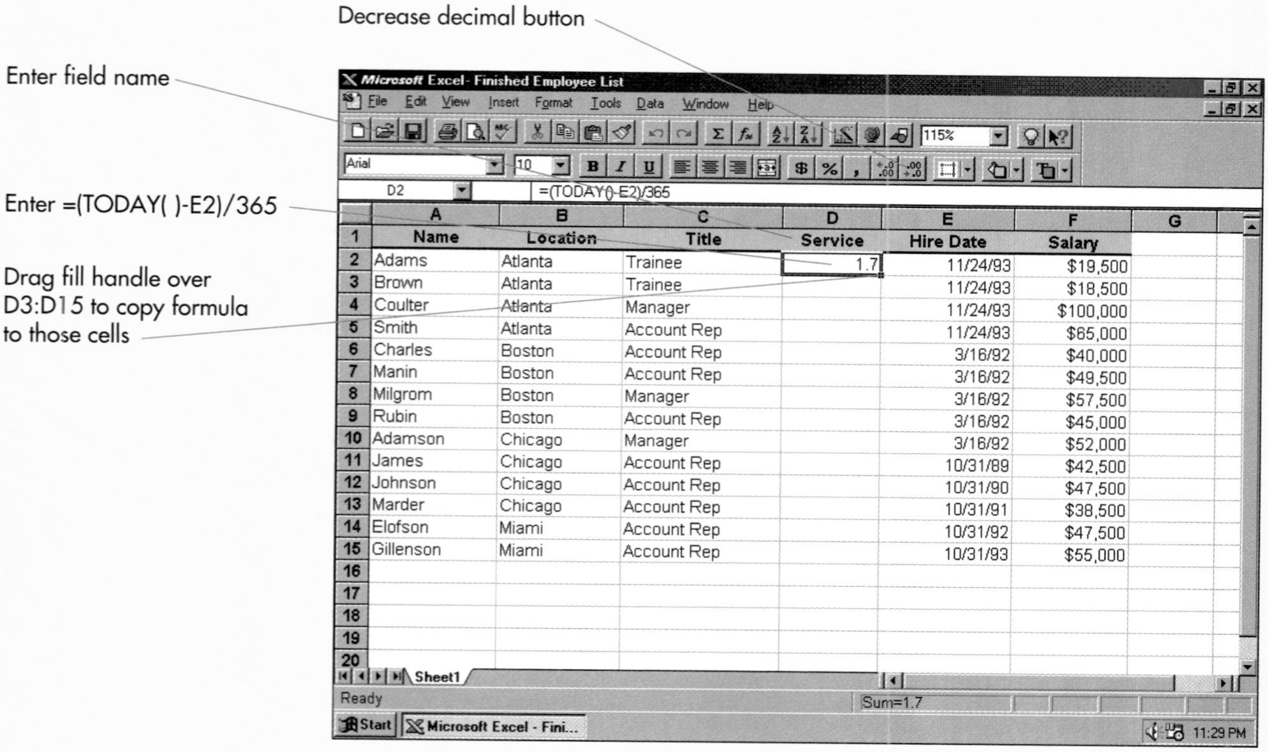

Decrease decimal button

Enter field name

Enter =(TODAY( )-E2)/365

Drag fill handle over D3:D15 to copy formula to those cells

Microsoft Excel - Finished Employee List

D2 =(TODAY()-E2)/365

	A	B	C	D	E	F	G
1	Name	Location	Title	Service	Hire Date	Salary	
2	Adams	Atlanta	Trainee	1.7	11/24/93	$19,500	
3	Brown	Atlanta	Trainee		11/24/93	$18,500	
4	Coulter	Atlanta	Manager		11/24/93	$100,000	
5	Smith	Atlanta	Account Rep		11/24/93	$65,000	
6	Charles	Boston	Account Rep		3/16/92	$40,000	
7	Manin	Boston	Account Rep		3/16/92	$49,500	
8	Milgrom	Boston	Manager		3/16/92	$57,500	
9	Rubin	Boston	Account Rep		3/16/92	$45,000	
10	Adamson	Chicago	Manager		3/16/92	$52,000	
11	James	Chicago	Account Rep		10/31/89	$42,500	
12	Johnson	Chicago	Account Rep		10/31/90	$47,500	
13	Marder	Chicago	Account Rep		10/31/91	$38,500	
14	Elofson	Miami	Account Rep		10/31/92	$47,500	
15	Gillenson	Miami	Account Rep		10/31/93	$55,000	

(a) Calculate the Years of Service (step 1)

FIGURE 1.10 Hands-on Exercise 2

THE COLUMN HIDE (UNHIDE) COMMAND

The Column Hide command does as its name implies and hides a column from view. Point to the column heading, then click the right mouse button to select the column and display a shortcut menu. Click the Hide command, and the column is no longer visible (although it remains in the worksheet). The column headings will reflect a hidden column in that the letter for the hidden column is not seen. To display (unhide) a hidden column, select (click) the column headings of the adjacent columns on either side, click the right mouse button to display a shortcut menu, then click the Unhide command.

STEP 2: The AutoFilter Command

- Click a single cell anywhere within the list. Pull down the **Data menu.** Click the **Filter** command.
- Click **AutoFilter** from the resulting cascade menu to display the down arrows to the right of each field name.
- Click the **down arrow** next to **Title** to display the list of titles in Figure 1.10b. Click **Account Rep.**
  - The display changes to show only those employees who meet the filter condition.
  - The worksheet is unchanged, but only those rows containing account reps are visible.
  - The row numbers for the visible records are blue.
  - The drop-down arrow for Title is also blue, indicating that it is part of the filter condition.
- Click the **down arrow** next to **Location.** Click **Boston** to display only the employees in this city. The combination of the two filter conditions shows only the account reps in Boston.
- Click the **down arrow** next to **Location** a second time. Scroll until you can click **All** to remove the filter condition on location. Only the account reps are displayed since the filter on Title is still in effect.
- Save the workbook.

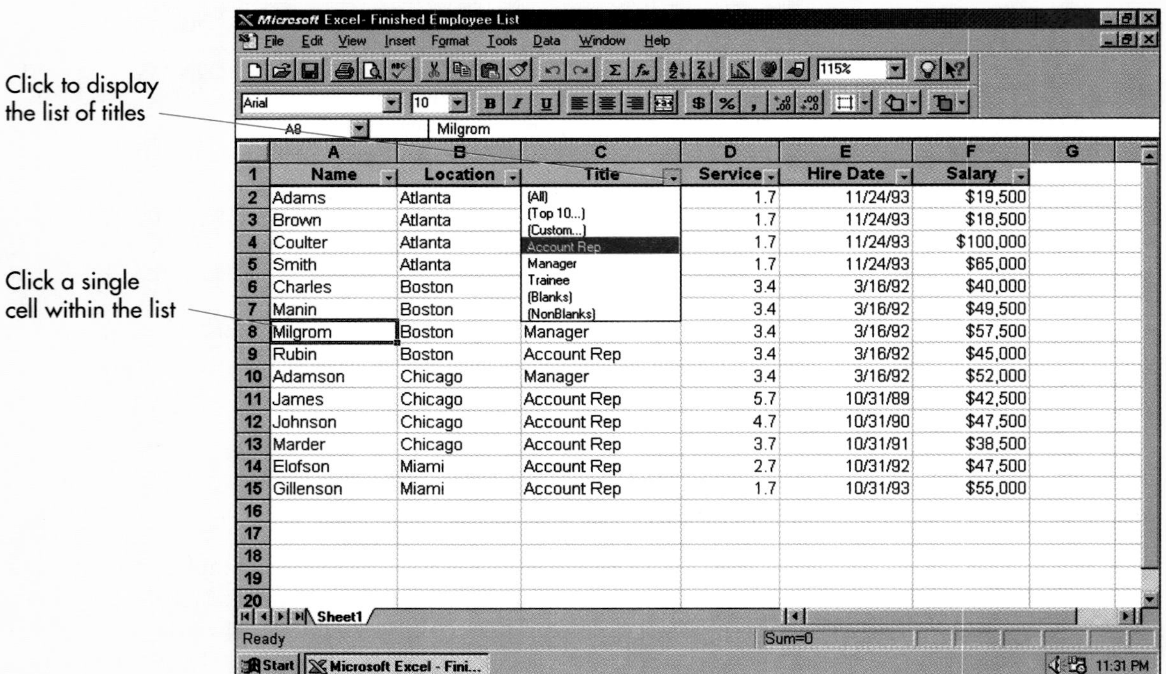

(b) The AutoFilter Command (step 2)

FIGURE 1.10 Hands-on Exercise 2 (continued)

THE TOP 10 AUTOFILTER

To see the records containing the top 10 values in a specific field, turn the AutoFilter condition on, then click the drop-down arrow next to the column heading. Click Top 10 from the list of AutoFilter options, then choose the options you want. You can see any number of the top (or bottom) records by entering the desired values in the Top 10 AutoFilter dialog box. You can also see a desired (top or bottom) percentage rather than a specified number of records. Click the Sort Ascending or Sort Descending button to display the selected records in order.

STEP 3: The Custom AutoFilter Command

- Click the **arrow** next to **Salary** to display the list of salaries. Click **Custom** to display the dialog box in Figure 1.10c.
- Click the **arrow** in the leftmost drop-down list box for **Salary.** Click the **greater than** sign.
- Click in the text box for the salary amount. Type **45000.** Click **OK.**
- The list changes to display only those employees whose title is account rep *and* who earn more than $45,000.

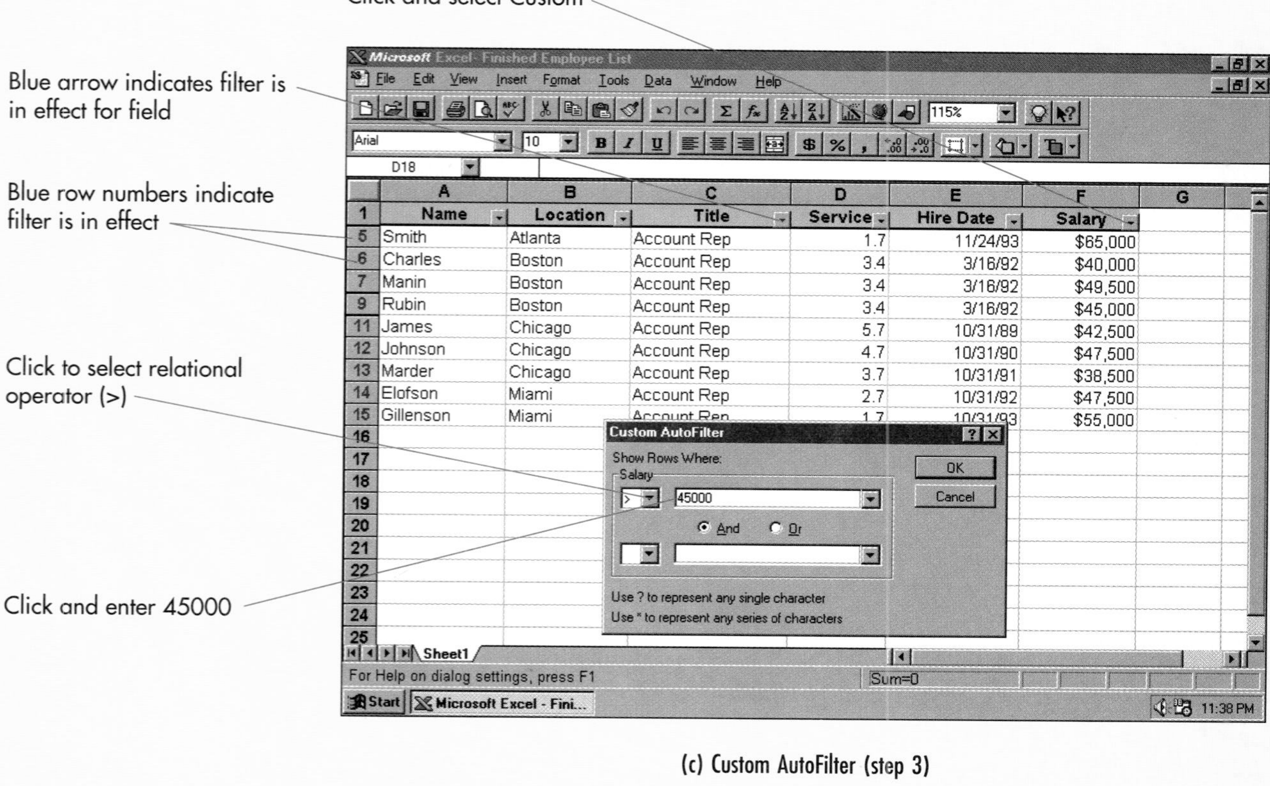

(c) Custom AutoFilter (step 3)

FIGURE 1.10 Hands-on Exercise 2 (continued)

- Pull down the **Data menu.** Click **Filter.** Click **AutoFilter** to toggle the AutoFilter command off, which removes the arrows next to the field names and cancels all filter conditions. All of the records in the list are visible.

> **WILD CARDS**
>
> Excel recognizes the question mark and asterisk as wild cards in the specification of criteria. A question mark stands for a single character in the exact position; for example, B?ll returns Ball, Bill, Bell, and Bull. An asterisk stands for any number of characters; e.g., *son will find Samson, Johnson, and Yohanson.

STEP 4: The Advanced Filter Command

- The field names in the criteria range must be spelled exactly the same way as in the associated list. The best way to ensure that the names are identical is to copy the entries from the list to the criteria range.
  - Click and drag to select **cells A1** through **F1.**
  - Click the **Copy button** on the Standard toolbar. A moving border appears around the selected cells.
  - Click in **cell A17.** Click the **Paste button** on the Standard toolbar to complete the copy operation. Press **Esc** to cancel the moving border.

> **DRAG AND DROP TO NONADJACENT RANGES**
>
> You can use the mouse to copy selected cells to a *nonadjacent* range provided the source and destination ranges are the same size and shape. Select the cells to be copied, point to any border of the selected cells (the mouse pointer changes to an arrow), then press and hold the Ctrl key (a plus sign appears) as you drag the selection to its destination. Release the mouse to complete the operation. Follow the same procedure, without pressing the Ctrl key, to move rather than copy the selected cells to a nonadjacent range.

- Click in **cell C18.** Enter **Manager.** (Be sure you spell it correctly.)
- Click a single cell anywhere within the employee list. Pull down the **Data menu.** Click **Filter.** Click **Advanced Filter** from the resulting cascade menu to display the dialog box in Figure 1.10d. (The range is already entered because you had selected a cell in the list prior to executing the command.)
- Click in the **Criteria Range** text box. Click in **cell A17** in the worksheet and drag the mouse to cell F18. Release the mouse. A moving border appears around these cells in the worksheet, and the corresponding cell reference is entered in the dialog box.
- Check that the **option button** to Filter the List, in-place is selected. Click **OK.** The display changes to show just the managers; that is, only rows 4, 8, and 10 are visible.

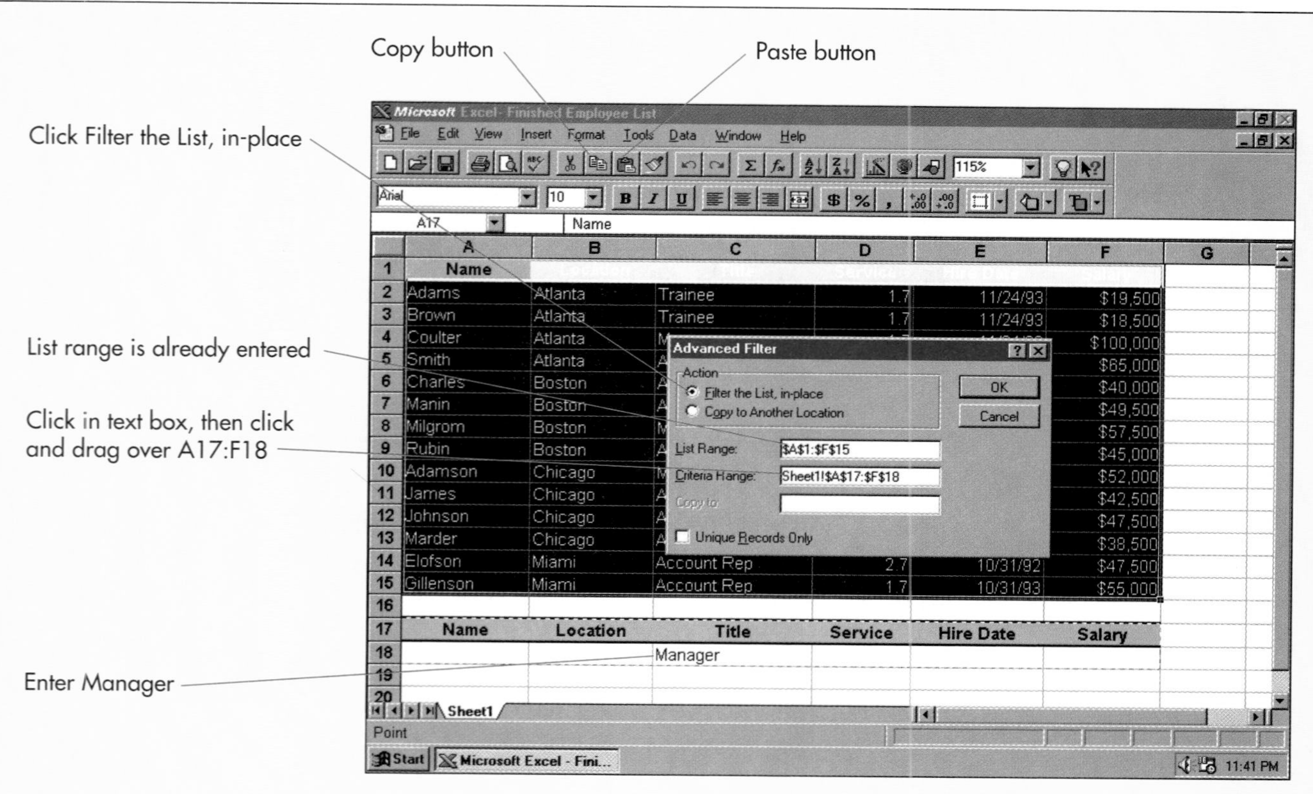

(d) Advanced Filter Command (step 4)

FIGURE 1.10 Hands-on Exercise 2 (continued)

- Click in **cell B18.** Type **Atlanta.** Press **enter.**
- Pull down the **Data menu.** Click **Filter.** Click **Advanced Filter.** The Advanced Filter dialog box already has the cell references for the List and Criteria ranges (which were the last entries made).
- Click **OK.** The display changes to show just the manager in Atlanta; that is, only row 4 is visible.
- Pull down the **Data menu.** Click **Filter.** Click **Show All** to remove the filter condition. The entire list is visible.

STEP 5: The Insert Name Command

- Click and drag to select **cells A1** through **F15** as shown in Figure 1.10e.
- Pull down the **Insert menu.** Click **Name.** Click **Define.** Type **Database** in the Define Name dialog box. Click **OK.**
- Pull down the **Edit menu** and click **Go To** (or press the **F5 key**) to display the Go To dialog box. There are two names in the box: Database, which you just defined, and Criteria, which was defined automatically when you specified the criteria range in step 4.
- Double click **Criteria** to select the criteria range (**cells A17** through **F18**). Click elsewhere in the worksheet to deselect the cells.
- Save the workbook.

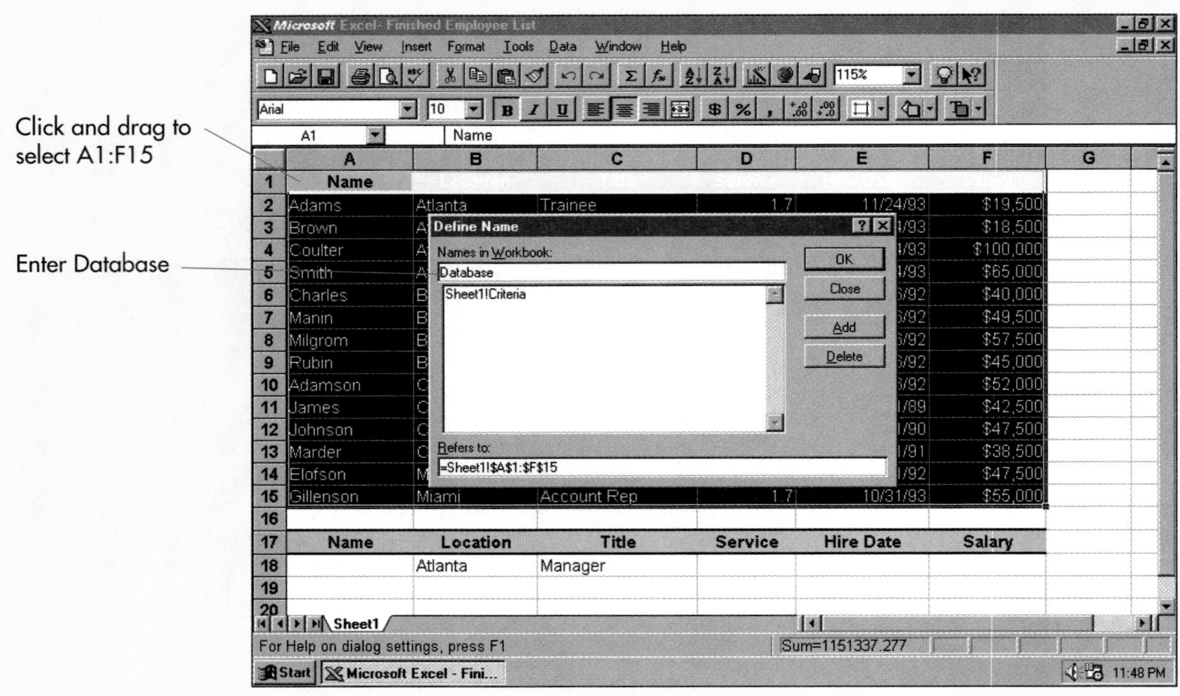

(e) Name Define Command (step 5)

FIGURE 1.10 Hands-on Exercise 2 (continued)

THE NAME BOX

Use the ***Name box*** on the formula bar to select a cell or named range by clicking in the box and then typing the appropriate cell reference or name. You can also click the down arrow next to the Name box to select a named range from a drop-down list. And, finally, you can use the Name box to define a named range, by first selecting the cell(s) in the worksheet to which the name is to apply, clicking in the Name box in order to enter the range name, and then pressing the enter key.

STEP 6: Database Functions (The Function Wizard)

- Click in **cell A21.** Type **Summary Statistics.** Select **cells A21** through **F21,** then click the **Center Across Columns** button on the Formatting toolbar to center the heading over the selected cells.
- Enter the labels for **cells A22** through **A26** as shown in Figure 1.10f.
- Click in **cell B18.** Press the **Del key.** The criteria range is now set to select only managers.
- Click in **cell F22.** Click the **Function Wizard button** on the Standard toolbar to display the dialog box in Figure 1.10f.
- Select **Database** in the Function Category list box. Select **DAVERAGE** as the function name, then click the **Next command button** to move to step 2 of the Function Wizard.

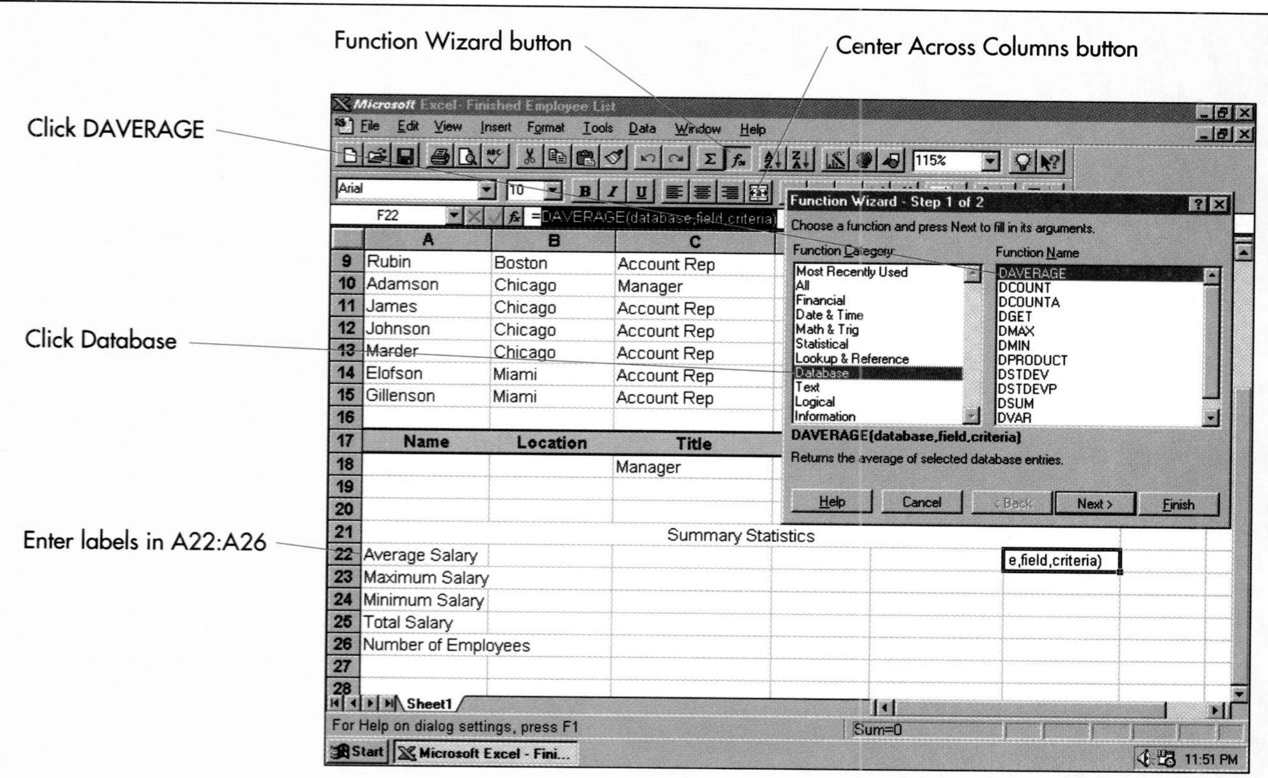

(f) Function Wizard (step 6)

FIGURE 1.10 Hands-on Exercise 2 (continued)

DATABASE FUNCTIONS

Database functions should always be placed above or below the list to which they refer, rather than to the left or right. This is done to ensure that (the rows containing) the database functions will always be visible, even when a filter condition is in effect.

STEP 7: The DAVERAGE Function

- Click the **database** text box in the Function Wizard dialog box of Figure 1.10g. Type **Database** (the range name defined in step 5), which references the employee list.
- Click the **field** text box. Type **Salary,** which is name of the field within the list that you want to average.
- Click the **criteria** text box. Type **Criteria** (the range name defined during the Advanced Filter operation). The Function Wizard displays the computed value of 69833.33333.
- Click the **Finish command button** to enter the DAVERAGE function into the worksheet.
- Save the workbook.

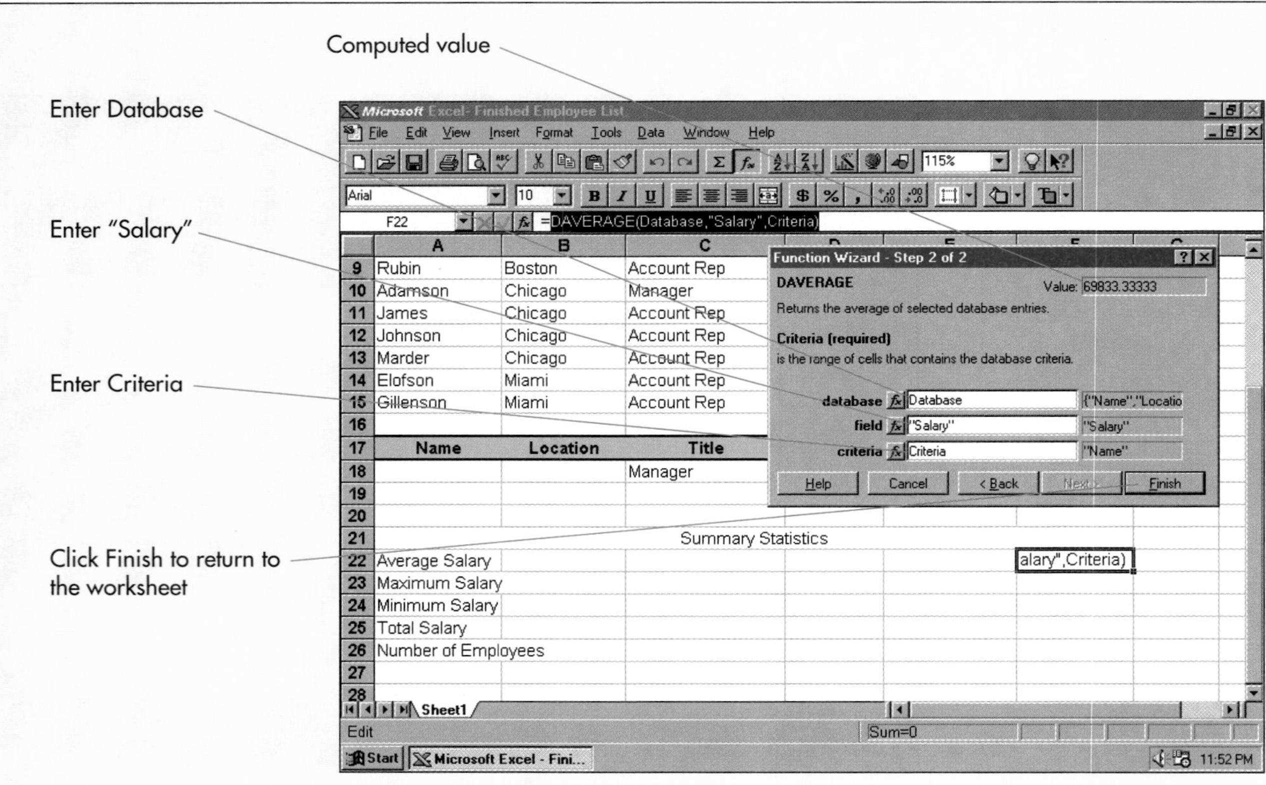

(g) DAVERAGE Function (step 7)

FIGURE 1.10 Hands-on Exercise 2 (continued)

STEP 8: The DMAX, DMIN, DSUM, and DCOUNT Functions

➤ Enter the DMAX, DMIN, DSUM, and DCOUNT functions in cells F23 through F26, respectively. You can use the Function Wizard to enter each function individually, *or* you can copy the DAVERAGE function and edit appropriately:

- Click in **cell F22.** Drag the **fill handle** to **cells F23** through **F26** to copy the DAVERAGE function to these cells.
- Double click in **cell F23** to edit the contents of this cell, then click within the displayed formula to substitute **DMAX** for DAVERAGE. Press **enter** when you have completed the change.
- **Double click** in the remaining cells and edit them appropriately. Figure 1.10h shows how double clicking a cell displays the cell contents, enabling you to edit within the cell itself rather than on the formula bar.

➤ The computed values (except for the DCOUNT function, which has a computed value of 3) are shown in Figure 1.10h.

➤ Select **cells F22** through **F25,** then format these cells to currency with no decimals. Widen the column if necessary.

➤ Save the workbook.

STEP 9: Change the Criteria

➤ Click in the **Name box.** Type **B18** and press **enter** to make cell B18 the active cell. Type **Chicago** to change the criteria to Chicago managers. Press **enter.**

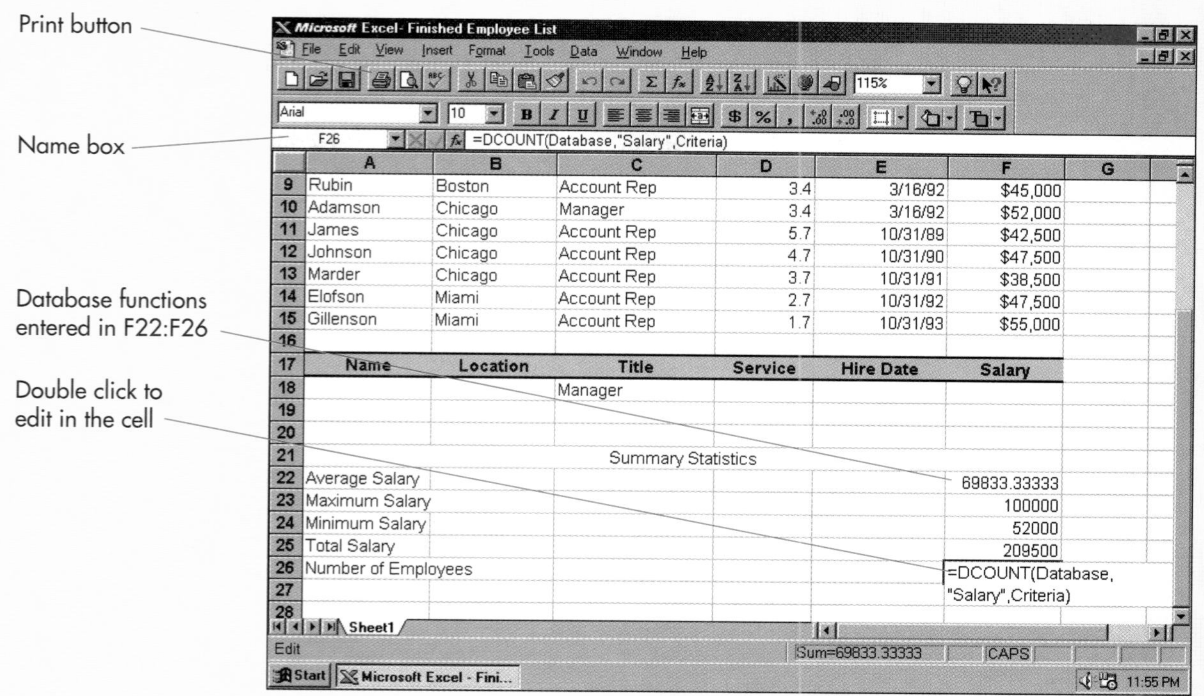

(h) DMAX, DMIN, DSUM, and DCOUNT Functions (step 8)

FIGURE 1.10 Hands-on Exercise 2 (continued)

- The values displayed by the DAVERAGE, DMIN, DMAX, and DSUM functions change to $52,000, reflecting the one employee (Adamson) who meets the current criteria (a manager in Chicago). The value displayed by the DCOUNT function changes to 1 to indicate one employee.
- Click in **cell C18.** Press the **Del key.**
- The average salary changes to $45,125, reflecting all employees in Chicago.
- Click in **cell B18.** Press the **Del key.**
- The criteria range is now empty. The DAVERAGE function displays $48,429, which is the average salary of all employees in the database.
- Click in **cell C18.** Type **Manager** and press the **enter key.** The average salary is $69,833, the average salary for all managers.

CLEAR THE CRITERIA RANGE

Clear the existing values within the criteria range before you enter new values, especially when the selection criteria are based on different fields. If, for example, you are changing from managers in any location (Title = Manager) to all employees in Chicago (Location = Chicago), you must clear the title field, or else you will get only employees who are managers and work in Chicago.

STEP 10: Print the Worksheet

- Save the worksheet. To print the entire worksheet, click the **Print button** on the Standard toolbar.
- To print only a portion of the worksheet (e.g., just the summary statistics), select the cells you wish to print, pull down the **File menu,** and click **Print.** Click the **Selection option button.** Click **OK** to print the selected cells.
- Close the workbook. Exit Excel if you do not want to continue with the next exercise at this time.

SUBTOTALS

The ***Subtotals command*** in the Data menu computes subtotals based on data groups in a selected field. It also computes a grand total. The totals may be displayed with or without the detail lines as shown in Figure 1.11. Figure 1.11a displays the employee list as well as the totals. Figure 1.11b displays only the totals.

Execution of the Subtotals command inserts a subtotal row into the list whenever the value of the selected field (Location in this example) changes from row to row. In Figure 1.11a the subtotal for the Atlanta employees is inserted into

	A	B	C	D	E	F
1	Name	Location	Title	Service	Hire Date	Salary
2	Adams	Atlanta	Trainee	1.7	11/24/93	$19,500
3	Brown	Atlanta	Trainee	1.7	11/24/93	$18,500
4	Coulter	Atlanta	Manager	1.7	11/24/93	$100,000
5	Smith	Atlanta	Account Rep	1.7	11/24/93	$65,000
6		Atlanta Total				$203,000
7	Charles	Boston	Account Rep	3.4	3/16/92	$40,000
8	Manin	Boston	Account Rep	3.4	3/16/92	$49,500
9	Milgrom	Boston	Manager	3.4	3/16/92	$57,500
10	Rubin	Boston	Account Rep	3.4	3/16/92	$45,000
11		Boston Total				$192,000
12	Adamson	Chicago	Manager	3.4	3/16/92	$52,000
13	James	Chicago	Account Rep	5.7	10/31/89	$42,500
14	Johnson	Chicago	Account Rep	4.7	10/31/90	$47,500
15	Marder	Chicago	Account Rep	3.7	10/31/91	$38,500
16		Chicago Total				$180,500
17	Elofson	Miami	Account Rep	2.7	10/31/92	$47,500
18	Gillenson	Miami	Account Rep	1.7	10/31/93	$55,000
19		Miami Total				$102,500
20		Grand Total				$678,000

(a) Detail Lines

	A	B	C	D	E	F
1	Name	Location	Title	Service	Hire Date	Salary
6		Atlanta Total				$203,000
11		Boston Total				$192,000
16		Chicago Total				$180,500
19		Miami Total				$102,500
20		Grand Total				$678,000

(b) Summary Lines (SUM function)

FIGURE 1.11 The Subtotals Command

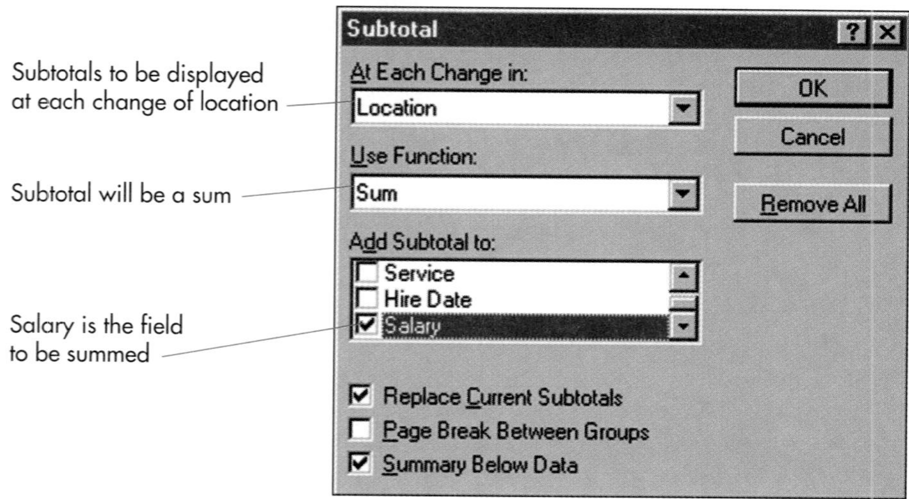

(c) Subtotals Dialog Box

FIGURE 1.11 The Subtotals Command (continued)

the list as we go from the last employee in Atlanta to the first employee in Boston. In similar fashion, the subtotal for Boston is inserted into the list as we go from the last employee in Boston to the first employee in Chicago. It is critical, therefore, that the list be in sequence according to the field on which the subtotals will be based, *prior* to executing the Subtotals command.

Figure 1.11c displays the Subtotal dialog box set to display the subtotals in Figure 1.11a. The various list boxes within the dialog box show the flexibility within the command. You can specify when the subtotals will be computed (in this example, at each change in the Location field). You can specify the function to use (sum in this example, but average, max, min, and count are also available). Finally, you can specify the field(s) for which the computation is to take place (Salary). Subtotals are removed from a worksheet by re-executing the Subtotals command and clicking the Remove All command button.

PIVOT TABLES

A ***pivot table*** extends the capability of individual database functions by presenting the data in summary form. It divides the records in a list into categories, then computes summary statistics for those categories. The pivot tables in Figure 1.12, for example, compute statistics based on salary and location.

The pivot table in Figure 1.12a displays the number of employees in each location according to job title. The column labels are the unique values within the list for the Location field. The row labels are the unique values within the list for the Title field. The values in the table show the number of employees in each

	A	B	C	D	E	F
1	Count of Name	Location				
2	Title	Atlanta	Boston	Chicago	Miami	Grand Total
3	Account Rep	1	3	3	2	9
4	Manager	1	1	1	0	3
5	Trainee	2	0	0	0	2
6	Grand Total	4	4	4	2	14

Number of Account Reps in Atlanta

(a) Number of Employees in Each Job Title at Each Location

FIGURE 1.12 Pivot Tables

Total salaries for Account Reps in Atlanta

	A	B	C	D	E	F
1	Sum of Salary	Location				
2	Title	Atlanta	Boston	Chicago	Miami	Grand Total
3	Account Rep	$65,000	$134,500	$128,500	$102,500	$430,500
4	Manager	$100,000	$57,500	$52,000	$0	$209,500
5	Trainee	$38,000	$0	$0	$0	$38,000
6	Grand Total	$203,000	$192,000	$180,500	$102,500	$678,000

(b Total Salaries for Each Job Title and at Each Location

FIGURE 1.12 Pivot Tables (continued)

Title–Location combination. Figure 1.12b uses the identical categories (Title and Location) but computes the total salaries instead of the number of employees. Both pivot tables are based on the employee list we have been using throughout the chapter.

A pivot table is created by using the ***PivotTable Wizard,*** which prompts you for the information to develop the pivot table. You indicate the field names for the row and column labels (Title and Location in Figures 1.12a and 1.12b). You also indicate the field on which the computation is to be based and the means of computation (a count of names in Figure 1.12a and a summation of Salary in Figure 1.12b). The PivotTable Wizard does the rest. It creates the pivot table in its own worksheet within the same workbook as the list on which it is based.

Pivot tables provide the utmost in flexibility, in that you can vary the row or column categories and/or the way the statistics are computed. Figure 1.13a illustrates a different pivot table, in which we analyze by gender rather than location. This table computes two statistics rather than one, and displays the number of employees as well as the average salary for each combination of title and gender.

The PivotTable dialog box in Figure 1.13b shows just how easy it is to create a pivot table. The field names within the associated list appear at the right of the dialog box. To create the pivot table, you simply drag a field name(s) to the row, column, or data areas of the table. Click the Next command button to supply the finishing touches to the pivot table, after which the pivot table will appear in its own worksheet.

Once a pivot table has been created, you can easily add or remove categories by dragging the field names on or off the table within the PivotTable Wizard. You can also switch the orientation (pivot the table) by dragging a field to or from the row or column area. And finally, you can modify the worksheet on which the pivot table is based (by adding, editing, or deleting employee records), then refresh the pivot table to reflect the changes made to the worksheet.

Two statistics computed (count and average salary)

	A	B	C	D	E
1			Gender		
2	Title	Data	F	M	Grand Total
3	Account Rep	Count of Name	5	4	9
4		Average of Salary	$45,600	$50,625	$47,833
5	Manager	Count of Name	1	2	3
6		Average of Salary	$52,000	$78,750	$69,833
7	Trainee	Count of Name	1	1	2
8		Average of Salary	$18,500	$19,500	$19,000
9	Total Count of Name		7	7	14
10	Total Average of Salary		$42,643	$54,214	$48,429

(a) The Pivot Table

FIGURE 1.13 The PivotTable Wizard

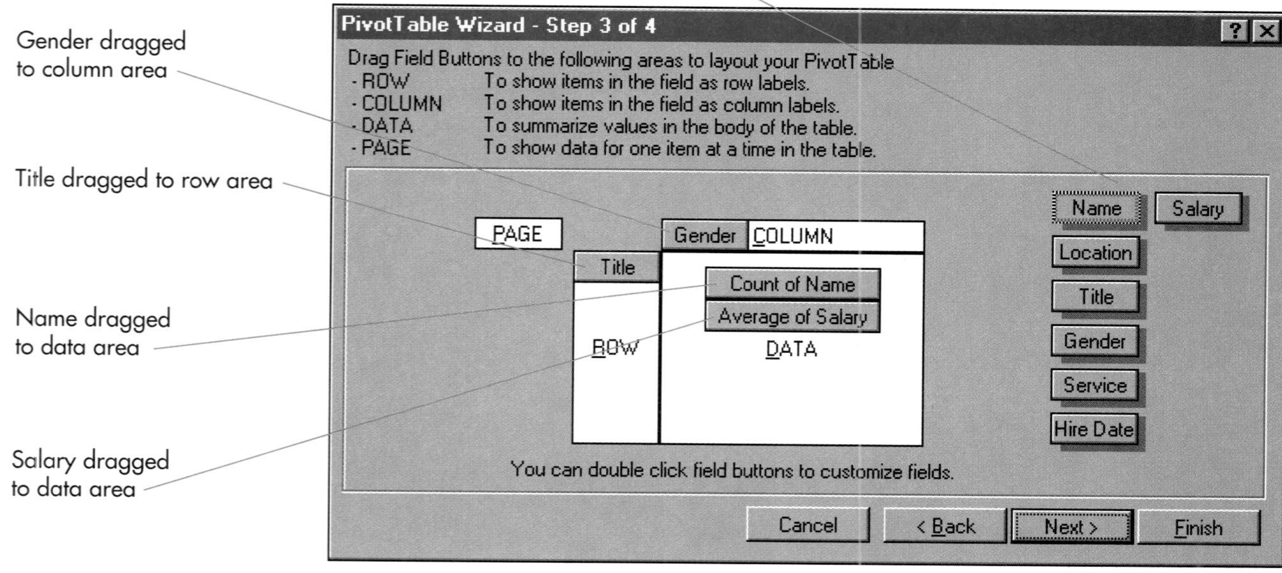

(b) The PivotTable Wizard

FIGURE 1.13 The PivotTable Wizard (continued)

HANDS-ON EXERCISE 3

Subtotals and Pivot Tables

Objective: To display and modify subtotals within a list; to use the PivotTable Wizard to create and modify a pivot table. Use Figure 1.14 as a guide in the exercise.

STEP 1: Open the Workbook

- Open the **Finished Employee List** workbook from the previous exercise. Clear the criteria range in row 18 so that the summary statistics pertain to all employees.
- Click any cell in **column C,** the column containing the employee titles. Click the **Sort Ascending button** on the Standard toolbar. The employees should be arranged according to title within the worksheet, as shown in Figure 1.14a. (This is the field on which the subtotals will be grouped.)
- Point to the **column heading** in **column D,** which presently contains the length of service. Press the **right mouse button** to display a shortcut menu. Click **Insert** to insert a new column.
- Click in **cell D1.** Type **Gender** (the field name). Press the **down arrow key** to move to **cell D2.** Type **M.**
- Add the remaining entries in column D to match those in Figure 1.14a.
- Drag the border between the column headings for columns D and E to the left to make column D narrower.

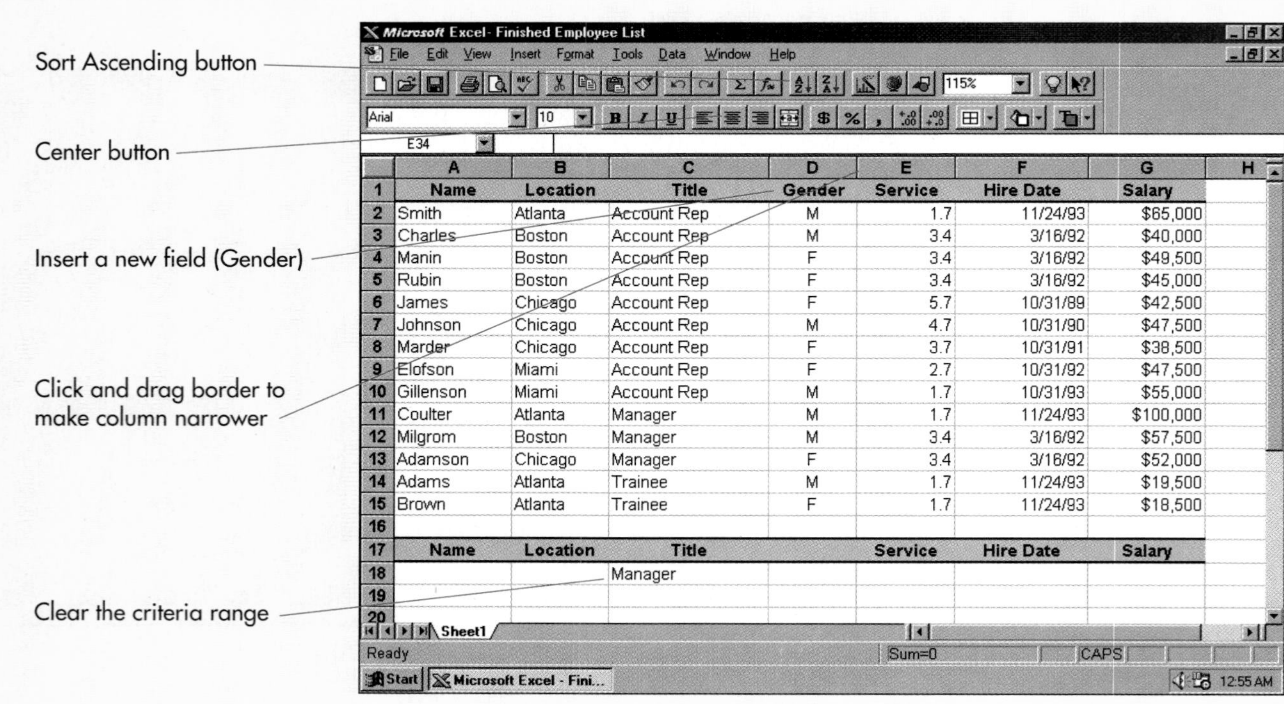

	A	B	C	D	E	F	G
1	Name	Location	Title	Gender	Service	Hire Date	Salary
2	Smith	Atlanta	Account Rep	M	1.7	11/24/93	$65,000
3	Charles	Boston	Account Rep	M	3.4	3/16/92	$40,000
4	Manin	Boston	Account Rep	F	3.4	3/16/92	$49,500
5	Rubin	Boston	Account Rep	F	3.4	3/16/92	$45,000
6	James	Chicago	Account Rep	F	5.7	10/31/89	$42,500
7	Johnson	Chicago	Account Rep	M	4.7	10/31/90	$47,500
8	Marder	Chicago	Account Rep	F	3.7	10/31/91	$38,500
9	Elofson	Miami	Account Rep	F	2.7	10/31/92	$47,500
10	Gillenson	Miami	Account Rep	M	1.7	10/31/93	$55,000
11	Coulter	Atlanta	Manager	M	1.7	11/24/93	$100,000
12	Milgrom	Boston	Manager	M	3.4	3/16/92	$57,500
13	Adamson	Chicago	Manager	F	3.4	3/16/92	$52,000
14	Adams	Atlanta	Trainee	M	1.7	11/24/93	$19,500
15	Brown	Atlanta	Trainee	F	1.7	11/24/93	$18,500
16							
17	Name	Location	Title		Service	Hire Date	Salary
18			Manager				
19							
20							

(a) Insert a Field (step 1)

FIGURE 1.14 Hands-on Exercise 3

- ➤ Click and drag to select **cells D2** through **D15.** Click the **Center button** on the Formatting toolbar.
- ➤ Click outside the selected cells to deselect the range. Save the workbook.

THE DOCUMENTS SUBMENU

One of the fastest ways to get to a recently used document, regardless of the application, is through the Windows 95 Start menu, which includes a Documents submenu containing the last 15 documents that were opened. Click the Start button, click (or point to) the Documents submenu, then click the document you wish to open (e.g., Finished Employee List), assuming that it appears on the submenu.

STEP 2: Create the Subtotals

- ➤ Click anywhere in the employee list. Pull down the **Data menu.** Click **Subtotals** to display the Subtotal dialog box in Figure 1.14b.
- ➤ Click the **arrow** in the At Each Change in list box. Click **Title** to create a subtotal whenever there is a change in title.
- ➤ Set the other options to match the dialog box in Figure 1.14b. Click **OK** to create the subtotals.

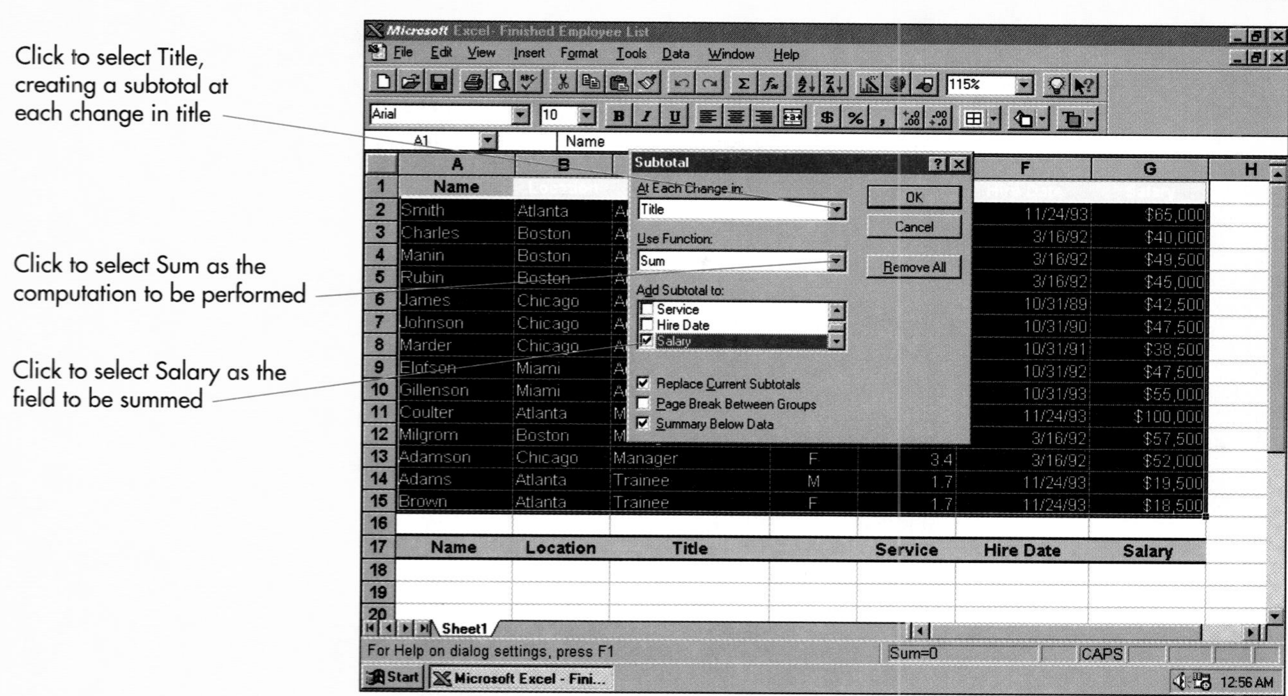
Click to select Title, creating a subtotal at each change in title
Click to select Sum as the computation to be performed
Click to select Salary as the field to be summed

(b) Create the Subtotals (step 2)

FIGURE 1.14 Hands-on Exercise 3 (continued)

STEP 3: Examine the Subtotals

- ➤ Your worksheet should display subtotals as shown in Figure 1.14c.
- ➤ Click in **cell G11,** the cell containing the Account Rep subtotal. The formula bar displays =SUBTOTAL(9,G2:G10), which computes the sum for cells G2 through G10. (The number 9 within the argument of the function indicates a sum.)
- ➤ Click in **cell G15,** the cell containing the Manager subtotal. The formula bar displays =SUBTOTAL(9,G12:G14), which computes the sum for cells G12 through G14.
- ➤ Click the **level 2 button** (under the Name box) to suppress the detail lines. The list collapses to display the subtotals and grand total.

THE SUBTOTAL FUNCTION

The ***SUBTOTAL function*** can be entered explicitly into a worksheet or implicitly (and more easily) through the Subtotal command in the Data menu. The function has two arguments: a function number to indicate the type of computation, and the associated cell range. A function number of 9 indicates a sum; thus, the entry =SUBTOTAL(9,E2:E10) computes the sum for cells E2 through E10. Pull down the Help menu and search on the SUBTOTAL function for additional information.

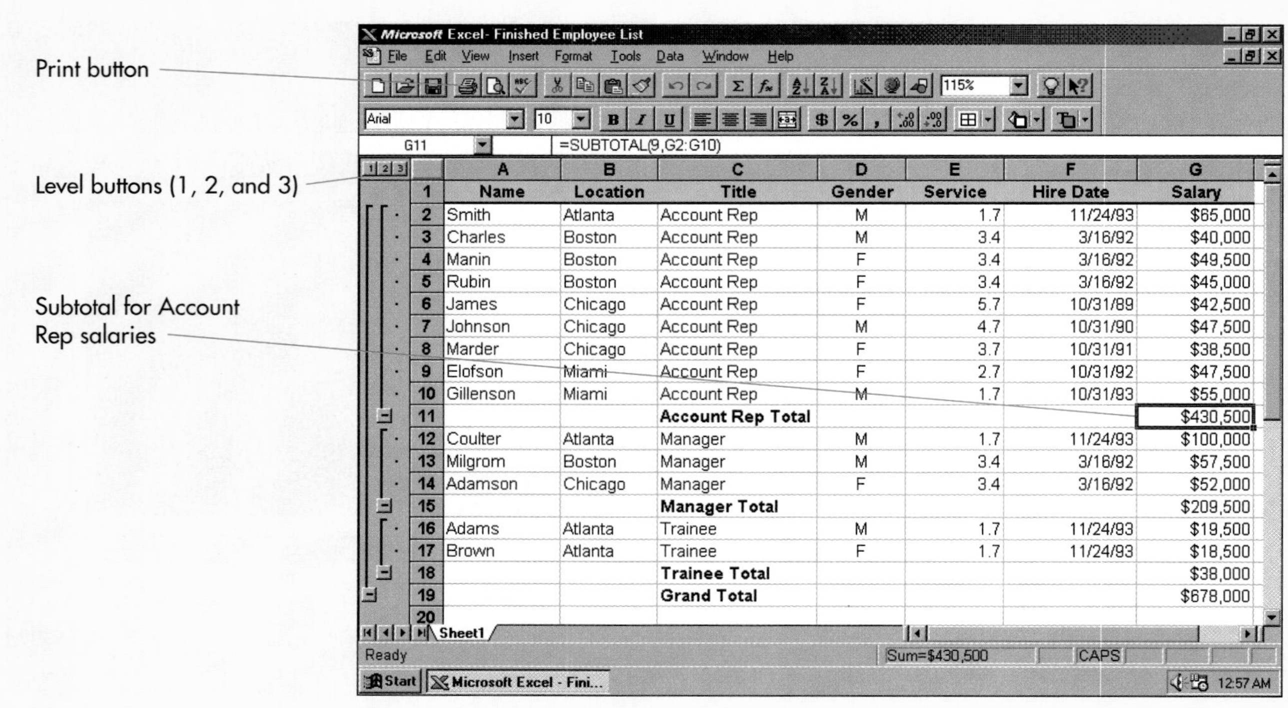

	A	B	C	D	E	F	G
1	Name	Location	Title	Gender	Service	Hire Date	Salary
2	Smith	Atlanta	Account Rep	M	1.7	11/24/93	$65,000
3	Charles	Boston	Account Rep	M	3.4	3/16/92	$40,000
4	Manin	Boston	Account Rep	F	3.4	3/16/92	$49,500
5	Rubin	Boston	Account Rep	F	3.4	3/16/92	$45,000
6	James	Chicago	Account Rep	F	5.7	10/31/89	$42,500
7	Johnson	Chicago	Account Rep	M	4.7	10/31/90	$47,500
8	Marder	Chicago	Account Rep	F	3.7	10/31/91	$38,500
9	Elofson	Miami	Account Rep	F	2.7	10/31/92	$47,500
10	Gillenson	Miami	Account Rep	M	1.7	10/31/93	$55,000
11			Account Rep Total				$430,500
12	Coulter	Atlanta	Manager	M	1.7	11/24/93	$100,000
13	Milgrom	Boston	Manager	M	3.4	3/16/92	$57,500
14	Adamson	Chicago	Manager	F	3.4	3/16/92	$52,000
15			Manager Total				$209,500
16	Adams	Atlanta	Trainee	M	1.7	11/24/93	$19,500
17	Brown	Atlanta	Trainee	F	1.7	11/24/93	$18,500
18			Trainee Total				$38,000
19			Grand Total				$678,000
20							

(c) Examine the Subtotals (step 3)

FIGURE 1.14 Hands-on Exercise 3 (continued)

- Click the **level 1 button** to suppress the subtotals. The list collapses further to display only the grand total.
- Click the **level 3 button** to restore the detail lines and subtotals. The list expands to display the employee records, subtotals, and grand total.
- Save the workbook. Click the **Print button** on the Standard toolbar if you wish to print the list with the subtotals.

STEP 4: The PivotTable Wizard

- The subtotals must be cleared in order to create a pivot table. Click anywhere within the employee list or subtotals. Pull down the **Data menu.** Click **Subtotals.** Click the **Remove All command button.**
- Pull down the **Data menu.** Click **PivotTable** to produce step 1 of the PivotTable Wizard. The option button indicates the pivot table will be created from data in a Microsoft Excel List or Database.
- Click the **Next command button** to move to step 2 of the PivotTable Wizard. You will see a dialog box where **Database** (the name assigned to the employee list in Hands-on Exercise 2) has already been entered in the Range text box.
- Click the **Next command button** to move to step 3 as shown in Figure 1.14d:
  - Click the **Title field button** and drag it to the row area.
  - Click the **Location field button** and drag it to the column area.
  - Click the **Salary field button** and drag it to the data area. (Sum is the default computation for a numeric field, such as Salary. Count is the default computation for a text field, such as Name.)

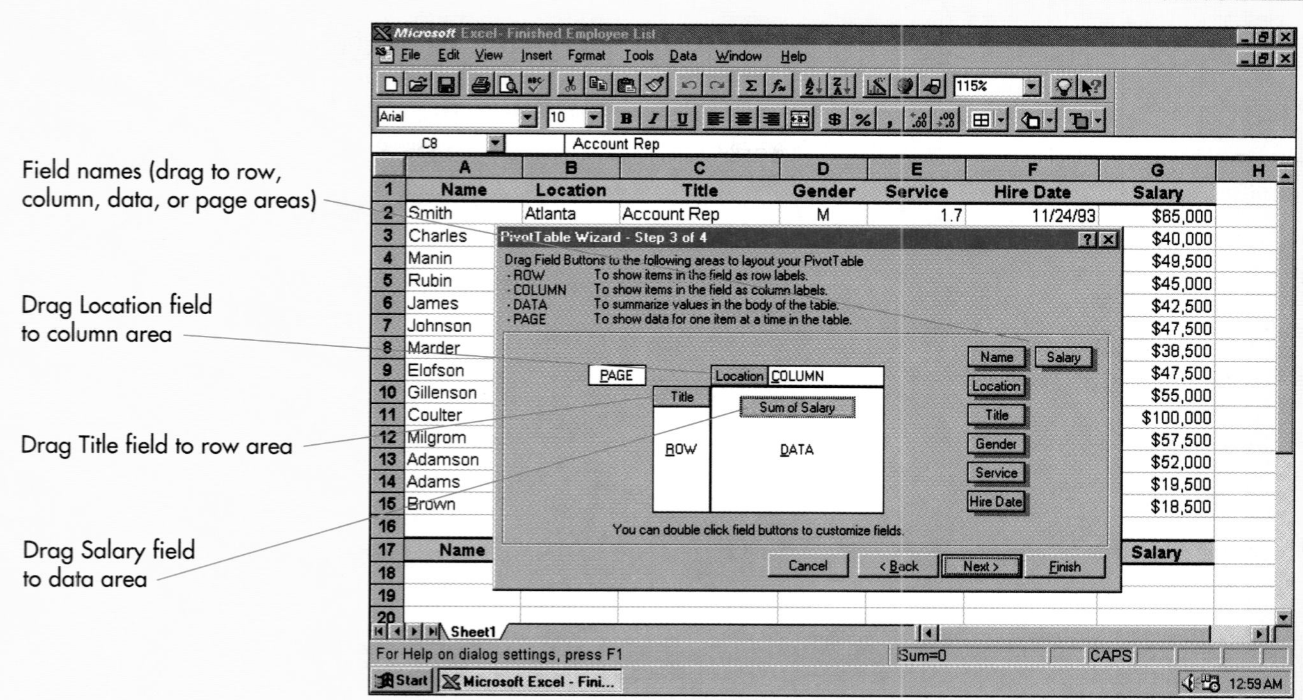

(d) The PivotTable Wizard (step 4)

FIGURE 1.14 Hands-on Exercise 3 (continued)

- Click the **Next command button** to move to step 4, the final step in the PivotTable Wizard:
  - The check boxes for all four options should be selected.
  - The text box for the PivotTable starting cell should be blank so that the pivot table is created in its own worksheet.
- Click the **Finish command button** to create the pivot table and exit the PivotTable Wizard. Save the workbook.

FIXED VERSUS FLOATING TOOLBARS

Any toolbar can be docked along the edge of the application window, or it can be displayed as a floating toolbar within the application window. To move a docked toolbar, drag the toolbar background. To move a floating toolbar, drag its title bar. To size a floating toolbar, drag any border in the direction you want to go. Double click the background of any toolbar to toggle between a floating toolbar and a docked (fixed) toolbar.

STEP 5: Modify the Pivot Table

- The pivot table is in its own worksheet, and the Query and Pivot toolbar is displayed automatically as shown in Figure 1.14e.

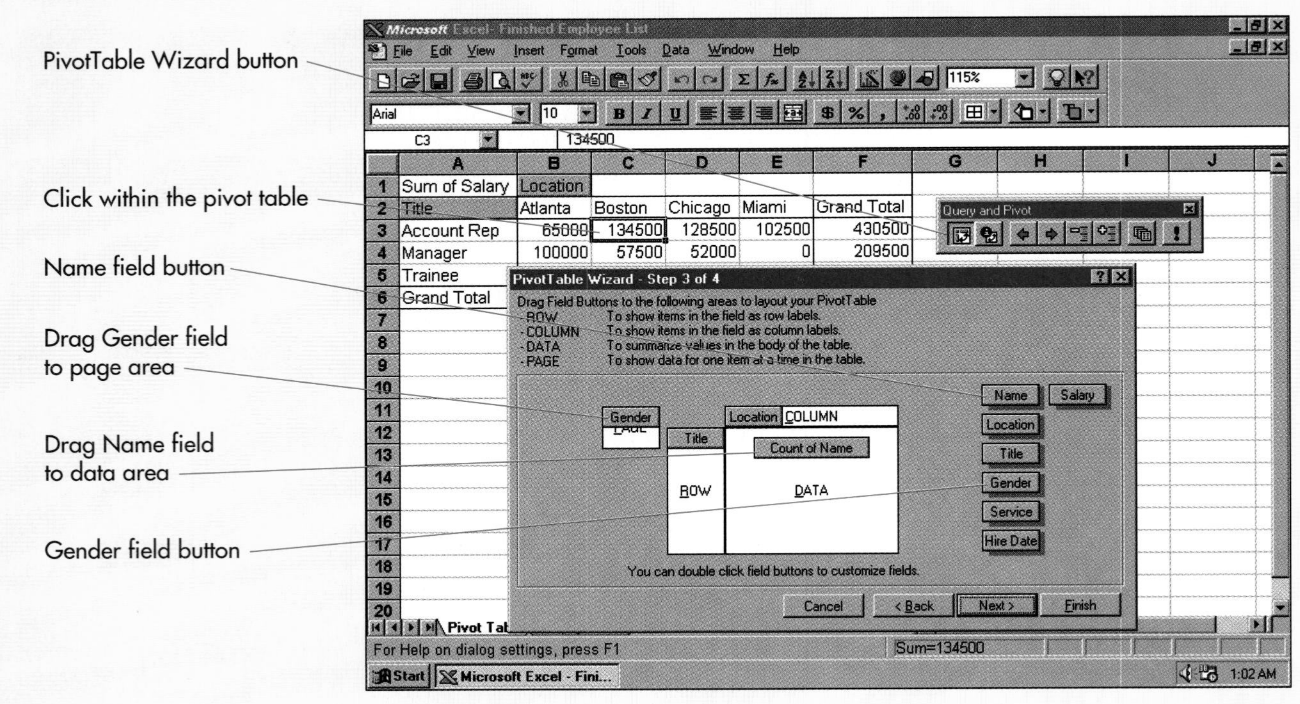

(e) Modify the Pivot Table (step 5)

FIGURE 1.14 Hands-on Exercise 3 (continued)

- Rename the worksheets within the workbook:
  - Point to the **Sheet2 tab** and click the **right mouse button** to display a shortcut menu. Click **Rename** to display the Rename sheet dialog box. Type **Pivot Table** as the new name of the tab. Click **OK.**
  - Point to the **Sheet1 tab** and click the **right mouse button** to display a shortcut menu. Click **Rename** to display the Rename Sheet dialog box. Type **Employee List** as the new name. Click **OK.**
- Click the **PivotTable tab** to return to this worksheet, then click anywhere within the pivot table.
- Click the **PivotTable Wizard button** on the Query and Pivot toolbar to reopen the PivotTable wizard as shown in Figure 1.14e. (If you are not on step 3 of the PivotTable Wizard, it is because you did not click in the pivot table prior to invoking the Wizard. Click Cancel, click in the pivot table, then click the PivotTable Wizard button.)
  - Click and drag the **Name field button** to the data area. The button displays "Count of Name" (the default function for a text field).
  - Click and drag the **Gender field** to the page area.
  - Click and drag the **Salary field button** out of the data area.
  - Click the **Next command button.** Click the **Finish command button.**
- The pivot table changes to display the number of employees for each location–title combination. Note that there are two account reps and no managers or trainees in Miami.

THE PAGE FIELD

A page field adds a third dimension to a pivot table. Unlike items in the row and column fields, however, the items in a page field are displayed one at a time. Creating a page field on gender, for example, enables you to view the data for each gender separately, by clicking the drop-down arrow on the page field list box, then clicking the appropriate value of gender. You can see the statistics for all male employees, for all female employees, or for all employees (both male and female).

STEP 6: Modify the Employee List

- Click the **Employee List tab** to return to the employee worksheet.
- Click in **cell C10.** Type **Manager.** Press **enter** to change Gillenson's title from account rep to manager. Note that Gillenson works in Miami.
- Click the **PivotTable tab** to return to the pivot table. There are still two account reps and no managers or trainees in Miami because Gillenson's change in title is not yet reflected in the pivot table.
- Click within the pivot table, then click the **Refresh Data button** on the Query and Pivot toolbar to update the pivot table.
- Miami now has one manager and one account rep, which reflects the change made to the employee list with respect to Gillenson's change of title. Save the workbook.

REFRESH THE PIVOT TABLE

The data in a pivot table is tied to an underlying list and cannot be edited directly. Thus, to change the data in a pivot table, you must edit the underlying list. Any changes in the list, however, are not reflected in the pivot table until the pivot table is refreshed. Click anywhere in the pivot table, then click the Refresh Data button on the Query and Pivot toolbar to update the pivot table.

STEP 7: Pivot the Table

- The pivot table on your monitor should match Figure 1.14f with Gender, Title, and Location as the page, row, and column fields, respectively.
- Click and drag the **Gender button** next to the Location button. The page field disappears, and there are now two column fields, Gender and Location.
- Click and drag the **Location button** to the previous location of the Gender field to make Location a page field. You have changed the orientation of the table and have a completely different analysis.

STEP 8: The Completed Pivot Table

- The pivot table has been modified as shown in Figure 1.14g. Location is now the page field and Gender is the column field. This arrangement of the table

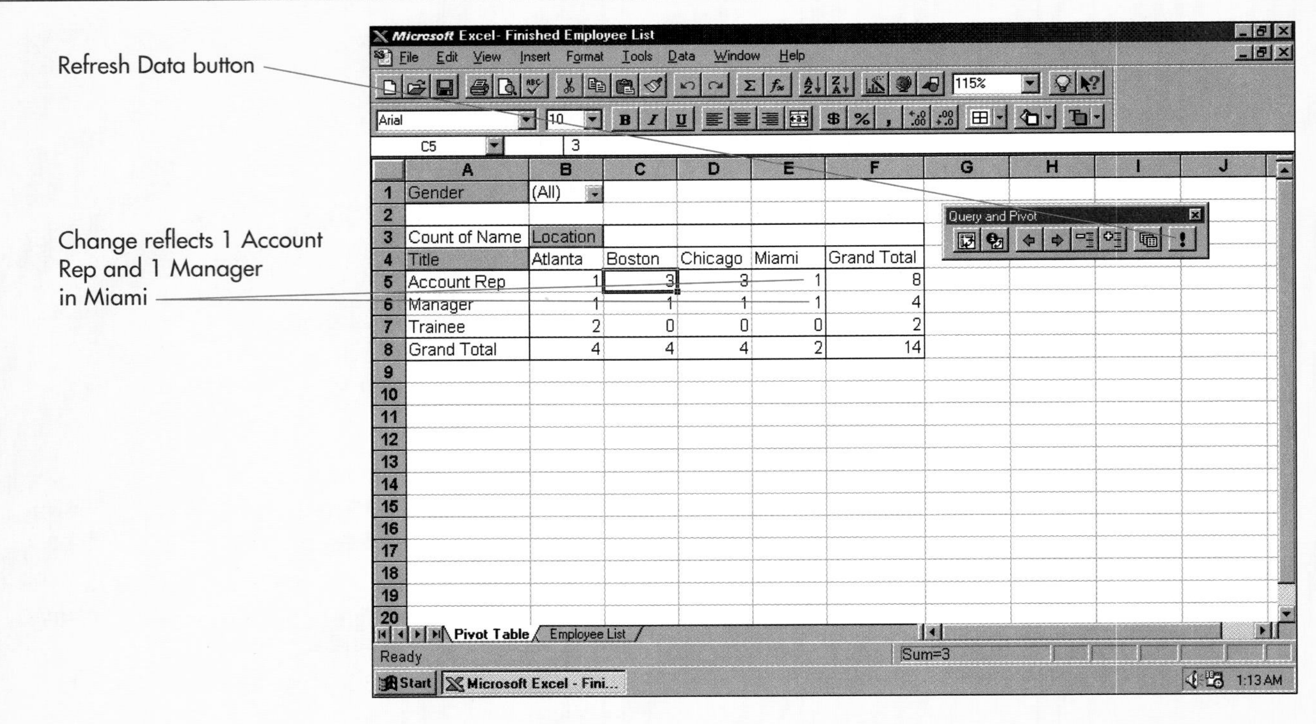

(f) Pivot the Table (step 7)

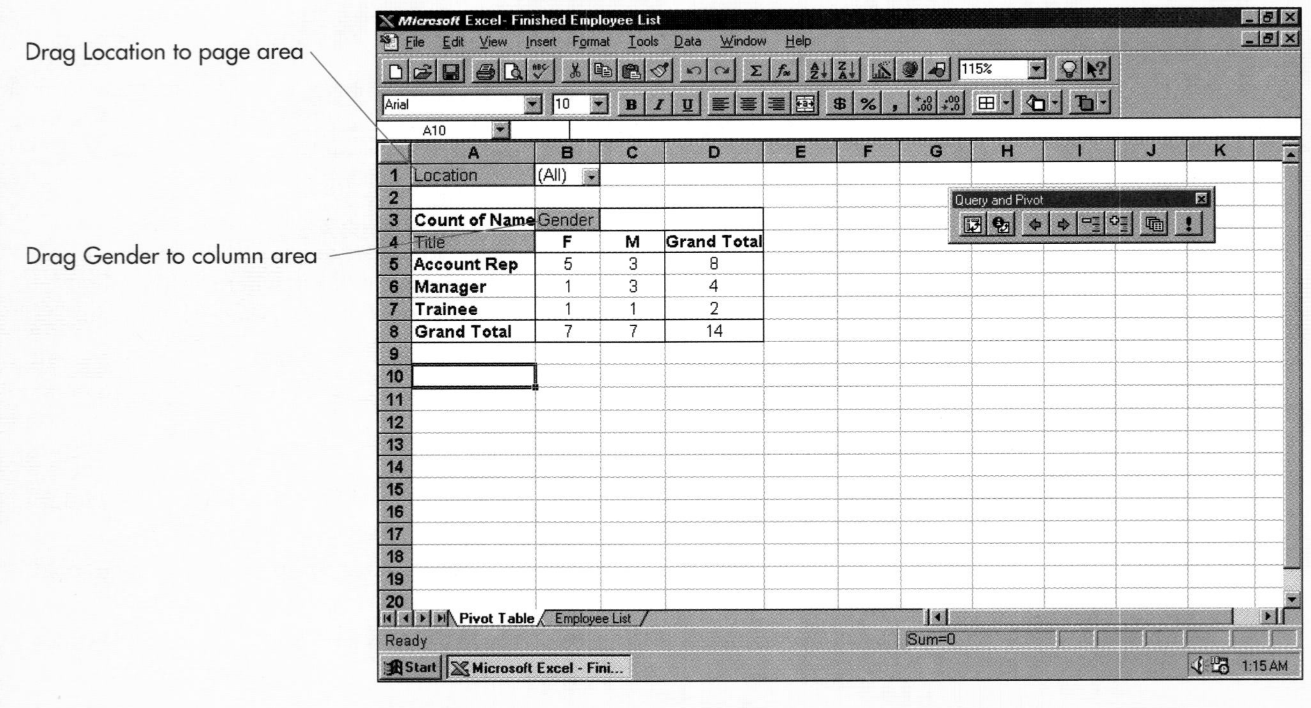

(g) The Completed Pivot Table (step 8)

FIGURE 1.14 Hands-on Exercise 3 (continued)

makes it easy to see the number of male and female employees in each job classification.

- Boldface the row and column labels of the pivot table in order to improve its appearance.
- Center the column labels. Center all of the values in the pivot table under their respective headings.
- Save the workbook. Print the completed workbook and submit it to your instructor. Exit Excel.

SUMMARY

A list is an area in a worksheet that contains rows of similar data. The first row contains the column labels (field names), and each additional row contains a record. A data form provides an easy way to add, edit, and delete records in a list.

Data and information are not synonymous. Data refers to a fact or facts about a specific record, such as an employee's name, title, or salary. Information is data that has been rearranged into a form perceived as useful by the recipient.

A date is stored internally as an integer number corresponding to the number of days in this century. (January 1, 1900 is stored as the number 1.) The number of elapsed days between two dates can be determined by simple subtraction. The TODAY function always returns the current date (the date on which a worksheet is created or retrieved).

A filtered list displays only those records that meet specific criteria. Filtering is implemented through AutoFilter or the Advanced Filter command.

The Sort command arranges a list according to the value of one or more keys. Each key may be in ascending or descending sequence.

The database functions (DSUM, DAVERAGE, DMAX, DMIN, and DCOUNT) have three arguments: the associated list, the field name, and the criteria range. The simplest criteria range consists of two rows and as many fields as there are in the list.

The Subtotals command inserts subtotals (based on a variety of functions) into a list. A list should be sorted prior to execution of the Subtotals command.

A pivot table extends the capability of individual database functions by presenting the data in summary form. It divides the records in a list into categories, then computes summary statistics for those categories. Pivot tables provide the utmost flexibility in that you can vary the row or column categories and/or the way that the statistics are computed.

KEY WORDS AND CONCEPTS

Advanced Filter command
Ascending sequence
AutoFilter command
Criteria range
Data
Data form
Database functions
DAVERAGE function
DCOUNT function
Delete command
Descending sequence
DMAX function
DMIN function
DSUM function
Field
Field name
File
Filtered list
Form command
Information

Insert Columns command
Insert Rows command
Key
List
Name box
Name command
Pivot table
PivotTable Wizard
Primary key
Record
Secondary key
Sort command
Subtotals command
SUBTOTAL function
Tertiary key
TODAY() function
Wild card

MULTIPLE CHOICE

1. Which of the following describes the implementation of data management in Excel?
   (a) The rows in a list correspond to records in a file
   (b) The columns in a list correspond to fields in a record
   (c) Both (a) and (b)
   (d) Neither (a) nor (b)
2. Which of the following is suggested for the placement of a list within a worksheet?
   (a) There should be at least one blank row between the list and the other entries in the worksheet
   (b) There should be at least one blank column between the list and the other entries in the worksheet
   (c) Both (a) and (b)
   (d) Neither (a) nor (b)
3. Which of the following is suggested for the placement of database functions within a worksheet?
   (a) Above or below the list with at least one blank row separating the database functions from the list to which they refer
   (b) To the left or right of the list with at least one blank column separating the database functions from the list to which they refer
   (c) Both (a) and (b)
   (d) Neither (a) nor (b)
4. Assume that cells A21:B22 have been defined as the criteria range, that cells A21 and B21 contain the field names City and Title, respectively, and that cells A22 and B22 contain New York and Manager. The selected records will consist of:
   (a) All employees in New York, regardless of title
   (b) All managers, regardless of the city
   (c) Only the managers in New York
   (d) All employees in New York (regardless of title) or all managers (regardless of city)
5. Assume that cells A21:B23 have been defined as the criteria range, that cells A21 and B21 contain the field names City and Title, respectively, and that cells A22 and B23 contain New York and Manager, respectively. The selected records will consist of:
   (a) All employees in New York regardless of title
   (b) All managers regardless of the city

(c) Only the managers in New York
(d) All employees in New York (regardless of title) or all managers (regardless of city)

6. If employees are to be listed so that all employees in the same city appear together in alphabetical order by the employee's last name:
(a) City and last name are both considered to be the primary key
(b) City and last name are both considered to be the secondary key
(c) City is the primary key and last name is the secondary key
(d) Last name is the primary key and city is the secondary key

7. Which of the following can be used to delete a record from a database?
(a) The Edit Delete command
(b) The Data Form command
(c) Both (a) and (b)
(d) Neither (a) nor (b)

8. Which of the following is true about the DAVERAGE function?
(a) It has a single argument
(b) It can be entered into a worksheet using the Function Wizard
(c) Both (a) and (b)
(d) Neither (a) nor (b)

9. The Name box can be used to:
(a) Define a range name
(b) Select the range
(c) Both (a) and (b)
(d) Neither (a) nor (b)

10. Which of the following is recommended to distinguish the first row in a list (the field names) from the remaining entries (the data)?
(a) Insert a blank row between the first row and the remaining rows
(b) Insert a row of dashes between the first row and the remaining rows
(c) Either (a) or (b)
(d) Neither (a) nor (b)

11. The AutoFilter command:
(a) Permanently deletes records from the associated list
(b) Requires the specification of a criteria range elsewhere in the worksheet
(c) Either (a) or (b)
(d) Neither (a) nor (b)

12. Which of the following is true of the Sort command?
(a) The primary key must be in ascending sequence
(b) The secondary key must be in descending sequence
(c) Both (a) and (b)
(d) Neither (a) nor (b)

13. What is the best way to enter January 21, 1996 into a worksheet, given that you create the worksheet on that date, and further, that you always want to display that specific date?
(a) =TODAY()
(b) 1/21/96

(c) Both (b) and (b) are equally acceptable
(d) Neither (a) nor (b)

14. Which of the following best describes the relationship between the Sort and Subtotals commands?
    (a) The Sort command should be executed before the Subtotals command
    (b) The Subtotals command should be executed before the Sort command
    (c) The commands can be executed in either sequence
    (d) There is no relationship because the commands have nothing to do with one another

15. Which of the following changes may be implemented in an existing pivot table?
    (a) A row field may be added or deleted
    (b) A column field may be added or deleted
    (c) Both (a) and (b)
    (d) Neither (a) nor (b)

ANSWERS

1. c	**6.** c	**11.** d
2. c	**7.** c	**12.** d
3. a	**8.** b	**13.** b
4. c	**9.** c	**14.** a
5. d	**10.** d	**15.** c

EXPLORING MICROSOFT EXCEL 7.0

1. Use Figure 1.15 to match each action with its result; a given action may be used more than once or not at all.

Action		**Result**
a. Click at 3, drag to 2, click at 7	_____	Create a pivot table
b. Click at 9	_____	Select a range name
c. Click at 13	_____	Add a record, using a data form
d. Click at 11	_____	Create salary subtotals for each location
e. Click at 4, click at 6	_____	Hide records not meeting the current criteria
f. Click at 5 and enter the new data	_____	Sort the list
g. Click at 10	_____	Rename the active worksheet
h. Click at 8	_____	Delete Adamson's record
i. Click at 12	_____	Enter a new city for Manin
j. Click at 1, then click the right mouse button	_____	Assign a name to the criteria range

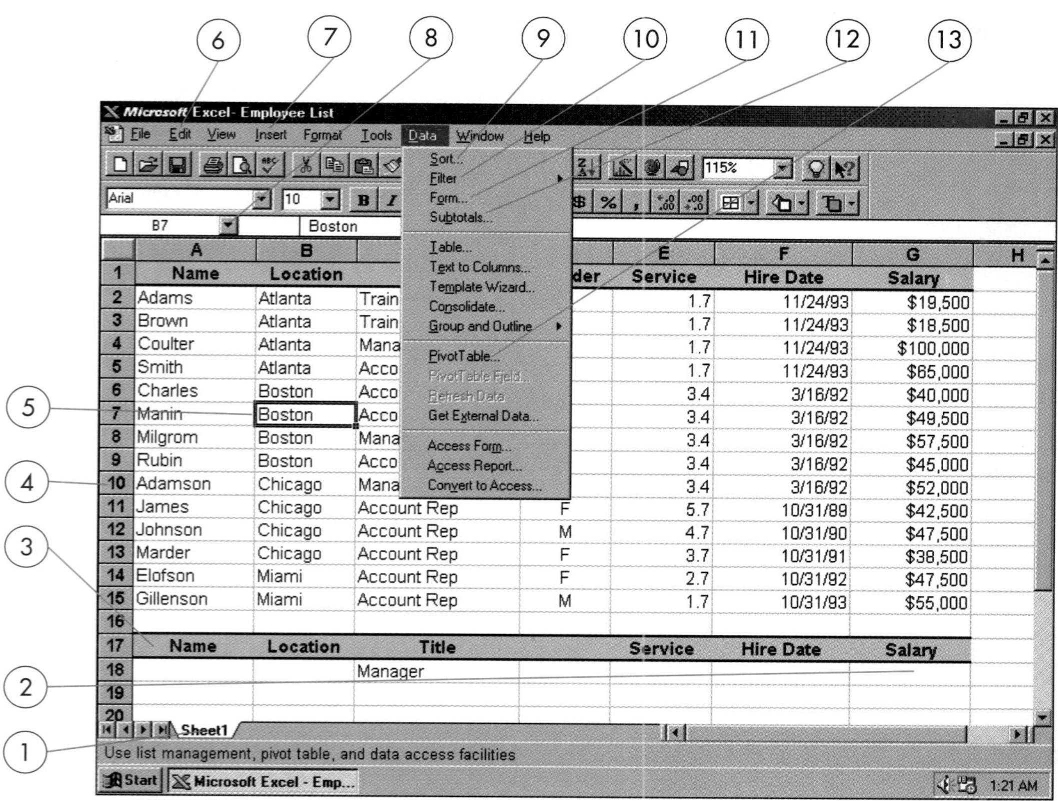

FIGURE 1.15 Screen for Problem 1

2. Careful attention must be given to designing a list, or else the resulting system will not perform as desired. Consider the following:
   a. An individual's age may be calculated from his or her birth date, which in turn can be stored as a field within a record. An alternate technique would be to store age directly in the record and thereby avoid the calculation. Which field—that is, age or birth date—would you use? Why?
   b. Social security number is typically chosen as a record key instead of a person's name. What attribute does the social security number possess that makes it the superior choice?
   c. Zip code is normally stored as a separate field to save money at the post office in connection with a mass mailing. Why?
   d. An individual's name is normally divided into two (or three) fields corresponding to the last name and first name (and middle initial). Why is this done; that is, what would be wrong with using a single field consisting of the first name, middle initial, and last name, in that order?

3. Troubleshooting: The informational messages in Figure 1.16 appeared (or could have appeared) in response to commands that were executed in the various hands-on exercises in the chapter. Indicate the command that was executed prior to each message and the appropriate response.

4. Answer the following with respect to the pivot table in Figure 1.17:
   a. What are the row field(s)? The column field(s)? The page field(s)?
   b. What are the data field(s)? What is the means of computation for each data field?

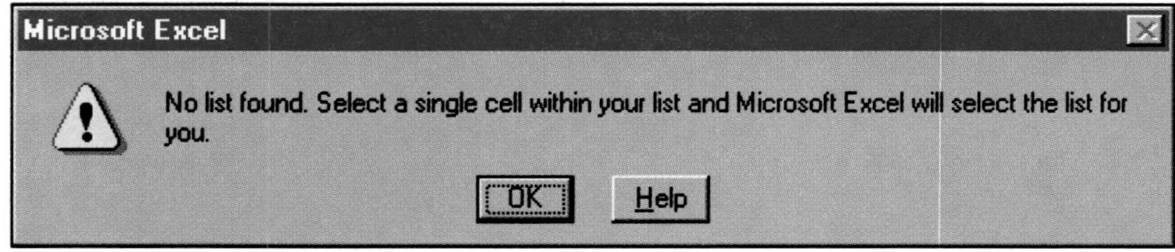

(a) Informational Message 1

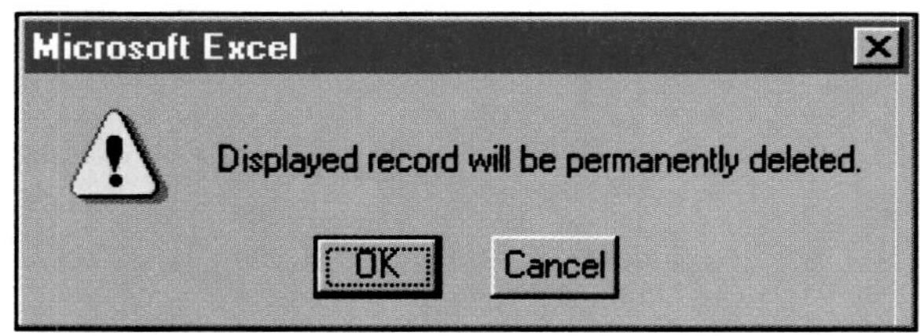

(b) Informational Message 2

(c) Informational Message 3

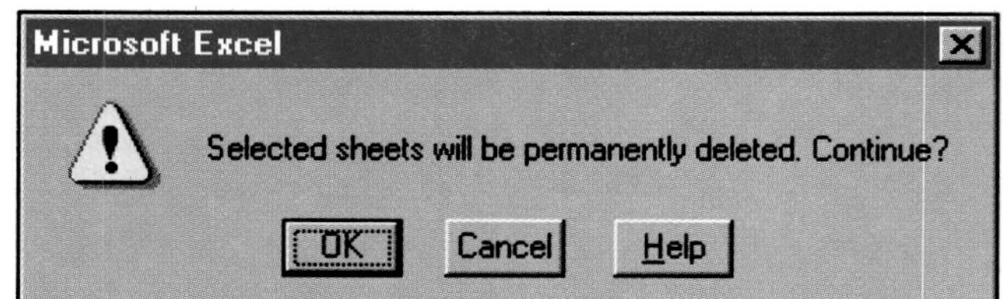

(d) Informational Message 4

FIGURE 1.16 **Informational Messages for Problem 3**

	A	B	C	D	E
1	Location	Boston			
2					
3			Gender		
4	Title	Data	F	M	Grand Total
5	Account Rep	Count of Name	2	1	3
6		Average of Salary	$47,250	$40,000	$44,833
7	Manager	Count of Name	0	1	1
8		Average of Salary	#DIV/0!	$57,500	$57,500
9	Total Count of Name		2	2	4
10	Total Average of Salary		$47,250	$48,750	$48,000

FIGURE 1.17 **Pivot Table for Problem 4**

c. Why does the pivot table display data for only four employees when the underlying worksheet contains 14 employees? Would refreshing the pivot table display the data for all 14 employees?

d. What is the significance of the #DIV/0! entry?

e. A second manager, Ms. Henderson, was hired to manage the Boston office at a salary of $62,250. What values will change in the pivot table as a result of the new employee?

PRACTICE WITH MICROSOFT EXCEL 7.0

1. Figure 1.18 displays the *Volume II Chapter 1 Practice 1* workbook as it exists on the data disk. Open the workbook, then implement the following changes:

   a. Delete the record for Julie Rubin, who has dropped out of school.

   b. Change the data in Rick Fegin's record to show 193 quality points.

   c. Use the Data Form command to add a transfer student, Jimmy Flynn, majoring in Engineering. Jimmy has completed 65 credits and has 200 quality points. Use the Tab key to move from one field to the next within the data form; be sure to enter the data in the appropriate text boxes. You cannot enter Jimmy's GPA as it will be computed automatically.

   d. Sort the list so that the students are listed in alphabetical order. Specify last name and first name as the primary and secondary keys, respectively.

   e. Create the Dean's List by using the Advanced Filter command to copy the qualified students (those with a GPA > 3.20) to cells A22 through A27. Use A19:F20 as the criteria range.

   f. Create the list of students on academic probation by using the Advanced Filter command to copy the selected students (those with a GPA < 2.00) to cells A33 through A40. Use A30:F31 as the criteria range for this Advanced Filter command.

   g. Add your name as the academic advisor in cell C1. Print the worksheet two ways, with displayed values and cell formulas, and submit both to your instructor.

2. The worksheet in Figure 1.19 is used to determine information about Certificates of Deposit purchased at First National Bank of Miami. A partially completed version of the worksheet can be found in the *Volume II Chapter 1 Practice 2* workbook on the data disk. Retrieve the workbook from the data disk, then develop the necessary formulas so that your workbook matches the completed version.

   Realize, however, that displayed values on your worksheet will be different from those displayed in the figure in that you are making the calculations on a different day. Thus, when you retrieve the workbook, the entry in cell B1 will reflect the current date, rather than the date in the figure. Other numbers, such as the days to maturity and the indication of whether a CD has matured, will change as well.

   Completion of the workbook reviews material from earlier chapters, specifically the use of relative and absolute addressing, and the IF function to determine the maturity status. The determination of whether or not the CD has matured can be made by comparing the Maturity date to the current date; that is, if the Maturity date is greater than the current date, the CD has not yet matured.

	A	B	C	D	E	F
1	Academic Advisor:					
2						
3	Last Name	First Name	Major	Quality Points	Credits	GPA
4	Moldof	Alan	Engineering	60	20	3.00
5	Stutz	Joel	Engineering	180	75	2.40
6	Rubin	Julie	Liberal Arts	140	65	2.15
7	Milgrom	Richard	Liberal Arts	400	117	3.42
8	Grauer	Jessica	Liberal Arts	96	28	3.43
9	Moldof	Adam	Business	160	84	1.90
10	Grauer	Benjamin	Business	190	61	3.11
11	Rudolph	Eleanor	Liberal Arts	185	95	1.95
12	Ford	Judd	Engineering	206	72	2.86
13	Fegin	Rick	Communications	190	64	2.97
14	Flynn	Sean	Business	90	47	1.91
15	Coulter	Maryann	Liberal Arts	135	54	2.50
16						
17						
18	The Dean's List					
19	Last Name	First Name	Major	Quality Points	Credits	GPA
20						
21						
22	Last Name	First Name	Major	Quality Points	Credits	GPA
23						
24						
25						
26						
27						
28						
29	Academic Probation					
30	Last Name	First Name	Major	Quality Points	Credits	GPA
31						
32						
33	Last Name	First Name	Major	Quality Points	Credits	GPA
34						
35						
36						
37						
38						
39						
40						

FIGURE 1.18 Spreadsheet for Practice Exercise 1

	A	B	C	D	E	F
1	Date:	7/30/95				
2						
3	Certificates of Deposit					
4	First National Bank of Miami					
5						
6	Customer	Amount of CD	Date Purchased	Duration	Maturity Date	# Days Remaining Til Mature
7	Harris	$500,000	4/15/95	180	10/12/95	74
8	Bodden	$50,000	1/5/95	180	7/4/95	Mature
9	Dorsey	$25,000	7/18/95	180	1/14/96	168
10	Rosell	$10,000	8/1/94	365	8/1/95	2
11	Klinger	$10,000	5/31/95	365	5/30/96	305

FIGURE 1.19 Spreadsheet for Practice Exercise 2

The workbook on the data disk is unformatted, so you will have to add formatting. Be sure to add your name to the worksheet as a bank officer. Print the worksheet two ways, with displayed values and cell formulas, and submit both to your instructor.

3. Figure 1.20 is a revised version of the employee list that was used throughout the chapter. A field has been added for an employee's previous salary as well as two additional fields for computations based on the previous salary. A partially completed version of this worksheet can be found on the data disk as *Volume II Chapter 1 Practice 3.*

	A	B	C	D	E	F	G	H	I	J
	Name	Location	Title	Gender	Service	Hire Date	Salary	Previous Salary	Increase	Percentage
1	Johnson	Chicago	Account Rep	M	4.7	10/31/90	$47,500	$40,000	$7,500	18.75%
2	Rubin	Boston	Account Rep	F	3.4	3/16/92	$45,000	$40,000	$5,000	12.50%
3	Coulter	Atlanta	Manager	M	1.7	11/24/93	$100,000	$90,000	$10,000	11.11%
4	Manin	Boston	Account Rep	F	3.4	3/16/92	$49,500	$45,000	$4,500	10.00%
5	Marder	Chicago	Account Rep	F	3.7	10/31/91	$38,500	$35,000	$3,500	10.00%
6	Elofson	Miami	Account Rep	F	2.7	10/31/92	$47,500	$45,000	$2,500	5.56%
7	Gillenson	Miami	Account Rep	M	1.7	10/31/93	$55,000	$52,500	$2,500	4.76%
8	Milgrom	Boston	Manager	M	3.4	3/16/92	$57,500	$55,000	$2,500	4.55%
9	James	Chicago	Account Rep	F	5.7	10/31/89	$42,500	$41,000	$1,500	3.66%
10	Adams	Atlanta	Trainee	M	1.7	11/24/93	$19,500			
11	Brown	Atlanta	Trainee	F	1.7	11/24/93	$18,500			
12	Smith	Atlanta	Account Rep	M	1.7	11/24/93	$65,000			
13	Charles	Boston	Account Rep	M	3.4	3/16/92	$40,000			
14	Adamson	Chicago	Manager	F	3.4	3/16/92	$52,000			
15										
16	Name	Location	Title	Gender	Service	Hire Date	Salary	Previous Salary	Increase	Percentage
17								>0		
18										
19										
20										
21					Evaluation of Salary Increase					
22					Average Increase			$4,389	8.99%	
23					Maximum Increase			$10,000	18.75%	
24					Minimum Increase			$1,500	3.66%	
25					Number of Employees			9	9	

FIGURE 1.20 Spreadsheet for Practice Exercise 3

The employees in the workbook on the data disk appear in a different sequence from the list in Figure 1.20. Hence, when you open the workbook, you must first determine the proper sequence in which to sort the employees. Note, too, that the recently hired employees do not have a previous salary, and thus the formulas to compute the amount of the salary increase and the associated percent salary increase must first determine if the employee actually had an increase. (You can suppress zero values in a spreadsheet through the View tab in the Options command of the Tools menu.) The summary statistics at the bottom of the worksheet reflect only those employees who actually had an increase.

Complete the workbook on the data disk so that it matches Figure 1.20. Add your name somewhere in the workbook as compensation analyst. Print the cell formulas as well as the displayed values and submit both to your instructor.

4. The compound document in Figure 1.21 consists of a memo created in Microsoft Word and a modified version of the pivot table created in the third hands-on exercise. The document was created in such a way that any change in the worksheet will be automatically reflected in the memo.

The methodology for linking an Excel worksheet to a Word document can be found in Appendix A in the section of the book on Microsoft Word.

Soleil Shoes

Italy, London, Madrid

Dear John,

Enclosed please find the salary analysis you requested last Friday. I have broken down the salaries by title and location.

Sum of Salary	Location				
Title	Atlanta	Boston	Chicago	Miami	Grand Total
Account Rep	$65,000	$134,500	$128,500	$47,500	$375,500
Manager	$100,000	$57,500	$52,000	$55,000	$264,500
Trainee	$38,000	$0	$0	$0	$38,000
Grand Total	$203,000	$192,000	$180,500	$102,500	$678,000

I noticed that the manager in Atlanta is paid disproportionately well compared to his counterparts in the other cities. Let me know if you need any other information.

Bob

FIGURE 1.21 Compound Document for Practice Exercise 4

Use the same technique to create the compound document in Figure 1.21. Sign your name so that your instructor will know the document came from you.

We want you to create the compound document and submit it to your instructor. You will have to return to the pivot table at the end of the third hands-on exercise in order to modify the table so that it matches Figure 1.21. (Don't forget to format the table.) Then you will have to open Microsoft Word in order to create the memo, and finally you will have to link the worksheet to the memo. *Print this version of the memo and submit it to your instructor.*

Prove to yourself that Object Linking and Embedding really works by returning to the Excel worksheet *after* you have created the document in Figure 1.21. Change Milgrom's salary in cell G12 to $75,000, then refresh (and reformat) the pivot table in the Excel workbook. Switch back to the Word memo, and the pivot table should reflect the adjusted salary (the total of all salaries should be $695,500). Add a postscript to the memo indicating that this reflects Milgrom's revised salary, then print the revised memo and submit it to your instructor with the earlier version.

CASE STUDIES

The United States of America

What is the total population of the United States? What is its area? Can you name the 13 original states or the last five states admitted to the Union? Do you know the 10 states with the highest population or the five largest states in terms of area? Which states have the highest population density (people per square mile)?

The answers to these and other questions are readily available provided you can analyze the data in the *United States* workbook that is available on the data disk. This assignment is completely open-ended and requires only that you print out the extracted data in a report on the United States database. Format the reports so that they are attractive and informative.

The Super Bowl

How many times has the National Football Conference (NFC) won the Super Bowl? When was the last time the American Football Conference (AFC) won? What was the largest margin of victory? What was the closest game? What is the most points scored by two teams in one game? How many times have the Miami Dolphins appeared? How many times did they win? Use the data in the *Super Bowl* workbook to prepare a trivia sheet on the Super Bowl, then incorporate your analysis into a letter addressed to NBC Sports. Convince them you are a super fan and that you merit two tickets to next year's game.

Personnel Management

You have been hired as the Personnel Director for a medium-sized firm (500 employees) and are expected to implement a system to track employee compensation. You want to be able to calculate the age of every employee as well as their length of service. You want to know each employee's most recent performance evaluation. You want to calculate the amount of the most recent salary increase, in dollars as well as a percentage of the previous salary. You also want to know how long the employee had to wait for that increase—that is, how much time elapsed between the present and previous salary.

Design a worksheet capable of providing this information. Enter test data for at least five employees to check the accuracy of your formulas. Format the worksheet so that it is attractive and easy to read.

Equal Employment Opportunity

Are you paying your employees fairly? Is there any difference between the salaries paid to men and women? between minorities and nonminorities? between minorities of one ethnic background versus those of another ethnic background? Use the *Equal Employment* workbook on the data disk to analyze the data for the current employees. Are there any other factors not included in the database that might reasonably be expected to influence an employee's compensation? Write up your findings in the form of a memo to the Vice President for Human Resources.

2

CONSOLIDATING DATA: 3-D WORKBOOKS AND FILE LINKING

OBJECTIVES

After reading this chapter you will be able to:

1. Distinguish between a cell reference, a worksheet reference, and a 3-D reference; use appropriate references to consolidate data from multiple worksheets within a workbook.
2. Select and group multiple worksheets in order to enter common formulas and/or formats.
3. Explain the advantage of using a function rather than a formula when consolidating data from multiple worksheets.
4. Explain the importance of properly organizing and documenting a workbook.
5. Use the Copy and Paste commands to copy selected data to a second workbook; copy an entire worksheet by dragging its tab from one workbook to another.
6. Distinguish between a source workbook and a dependent workbook; create external references to link workbooks to one another.

OVERVIEW

This chapter considers the problem of combining data from different sources into a summary report. Assume, for example, that you are the marketing manager for a national corporation with offices in several cities. Each branch manager reports to you on a quarterly basis, providing detailed information about each product sold in his or her office. Your job is to consolidate the data from the individual offices into a single report.

The situation is depicted graphically in Figure 2.1. Figures 2.1a, 2.1b, and 2.1c show reports for the Atlanta, Boston, and Chicago

Atlanta Office				
	Qtr 1	Qtr 2	Qtr 3	Qtr 4
Product 1	$10	$20	$30	$40
Product 2	$1,100	$1,200	$1,300	$1,400
Product 3	$200	$200	$300	$400

(a)

Boston Office				
	Qtr 1	Qtr 2	Qtr 3	Qtr 4
Product 1	$55	$25	$35	$45
Product 2	$150	$250	$350	$450
Product 3	$1,150	$1,250	$1,350	$1,400

(b)

Chicago Office				
	Qtr 1	Qtr 2	Qtr 3	Qtr 4
Product 1	$850	$950	$1,050	$1,150
Product 2	$100	$0	$300	$400
Product 3	$75	$150	$100	$200

(c)

Corporate Totals				
	Qtr 1	Qtr 2	Qtr 3	Qtr 4
Product 1	$915	$995	$1,115	$1,235
Product 2	$1,350	$1,450	$1,950	$2,250
Product 3	$1,425	$1,600	$1,750	$2,000

(d)

FIGURE 2.1 Consolidating Data

offices, respectively. Figure 2.1d shows the summary report for the corporation as a whole.

You should be able to reconcile the corporate totals with the detail amounts in each office. Consider, for example, the sales of Product 1 in the first quarter. The Atlanta office has sold $10, the Boston office $55, and the Chicago office $850; thus, the corporation as a whole has sold $915 ($10+$55+$850). In similar fashion, the Atlanta, Boston, and Chicago offices have sold $1100, $150, and $100, respectively, of Product 2 in the first quarter, for a corporate total of $1,350.

The chapter presents two different approaches to compute the corporate totals in Figure 2.1. One approach is to use the three-dimensional capability within Excel, in which one workbook contains multiple worksheets. The workbook contains a separate worksheet for each of the three branch offices, and a fourth worksheet to hold the corporate data. An alternate technique is to keep the data for each branch office in its own workbook, then create a summary workbook that uses file linking to reference cells in the other workbooks.

There are advantages and disadvantages to each technique, as will be discussed in the chapter. As always, the hands-on exercises are essential to mastering the conceptual material.

THE THREE-DIMENSIONAL WORKBOOK

An Excel workbook is the electronic equivalent of the three-ring binder. It contains one or more worksheets, each of which is identified by a tab at the bottom of the document window. The workbook in Figure 2.2, for example, contains four worksheets. The title bar displays the name of the workbook (Corporate Sales).

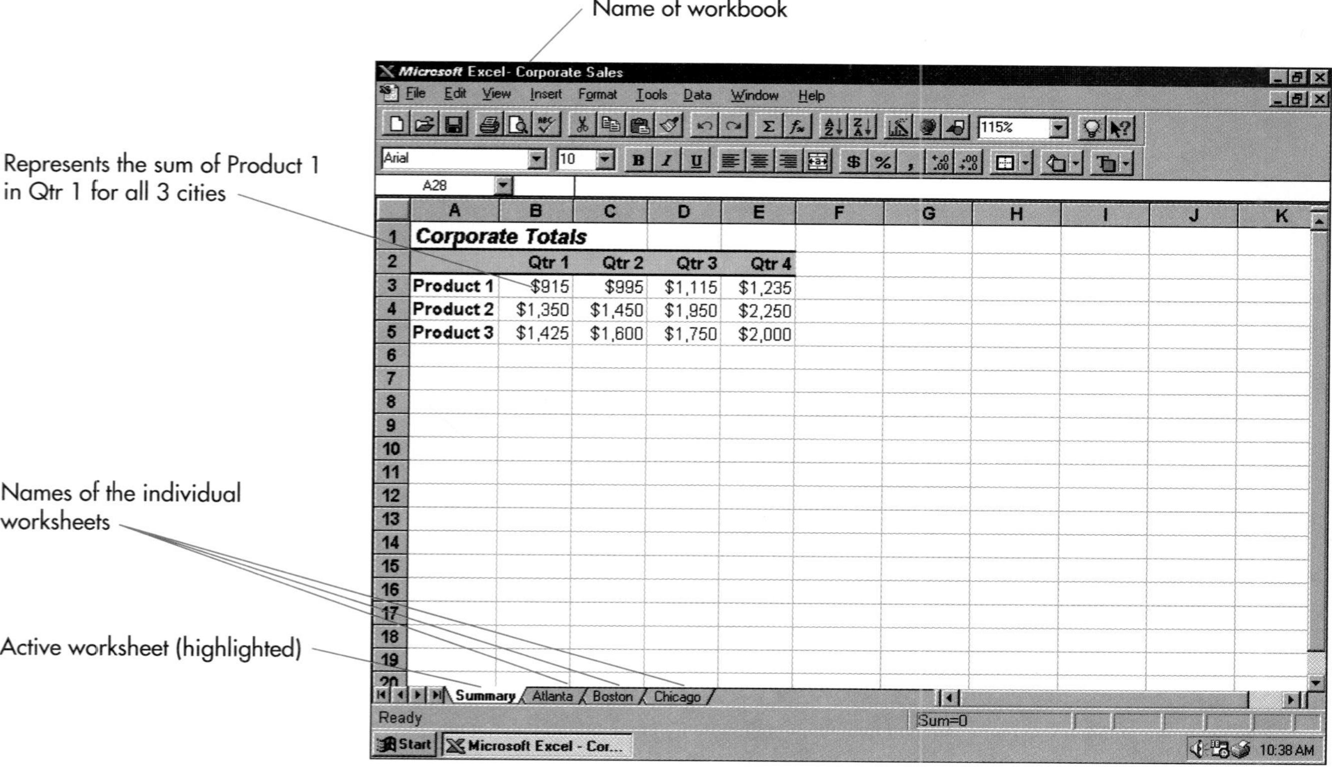

FIGURE 2.2 A Three-dimensional Workbook

The tabs at the bottom of the workbook window display the names of the individual worksheets (Summary, Atlanta, Boston, and Chicago). The highlighted tab indicates the name of the active worksheet (Summary). To display a different worksheet, click on a different tab; for example, click the Atlanta tab to display the Atlanta worksheet.

The Summary worksheet shows the total amount for each product in each quarter. The data in the worksheet reflects the amounts shown earlier in Figure 2.1; that is, each entry in the Summary worksheet represents the sum of the corresponding entries in the worksheets for the individual cities. The amounts in the individual cities, however, are not visible in Figure 2.2. It is convenient, therefore, to open multiple windows in order to view the individual city worksheets at the same time you view the summary sheet.

Figure 2.3 displays the four worksheets in the Corporate Sales workbook, with a different sheet displayed in each window. The individual windows are smaller than the single view in Figure 2.2, but you can see at a glance how the Summary worksheet consolidates the data from the individual worksheets. The ***New Window command*** (in the Window menu) is used to open each additional window. Once the windows have been opened, the ***Arrange command*** (in the Window menu) is used to tile or cascade the open windows.

Only one window can be active at a time, and all commands apply to just the active window. In Figure 2.3, for example, the window in the upper left is active, as can be seen by the highlighted title bar. (To activate a different window, just click in that window.)

Copying Worksheets

The workbook in Figure 2.3 summarizes the data in the individual worksheets, but how was the data placed in the workbook? You could, of course, manually type

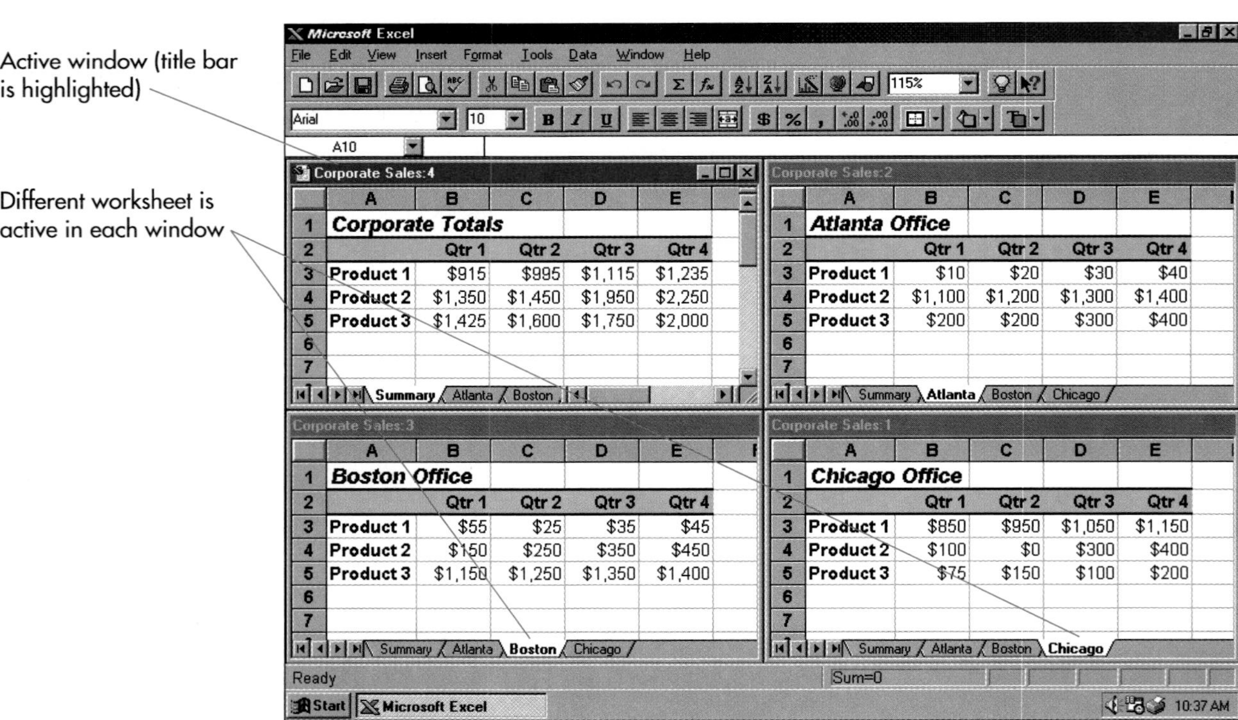

FIGURE 2.3 Multiple Worksheets

in the entries, but there is an easier way, given that each branch manager sends you a workbook with the data for his or her office. All you have to do is copy the data from the individual workbooks into the appropriate worksheets in a new corporate workbook. (The specifics for how this is done are explained in detail in a hands-on exercise.)

Consider now Figure 2.4, which at first glance appears almost identical to Figure 2.3. The two figures are very different, however. Figure 2.3 displayed four different worksheets from the same workbook. Figure 2.4, on the other hand, displays four different workbooks. There is one workbook for each city (Atlanta, Boston, and Chicago) and each of these workbooks contains only a single worksheet. The fourth workbook, Corporate Sales, contains four worksheets (Atlanta, Boston, Chicago, and Summary) and is the workbook displayed in Figure 2.3.

THE HORIZONTAL SCROLL BAR

The horizontal scroll bar contains four ***tab scrolling buttons*** to scroll through the worksheet tabs in a workbook. (The default workbook has 16 worksheets.) Click ◀ or ▶ to scroll one tab to the left or right. Click |◀ or ▶| to scroll to the first or last tab in the workbook. Once the desired tab is visible, click the tab to select it. The number of tabs that are visible simultaneously depends on the setting of the horizontal scroll bar; that is, you can drag the ***tab split box*** to change the number of tabs that can be seen at one time.

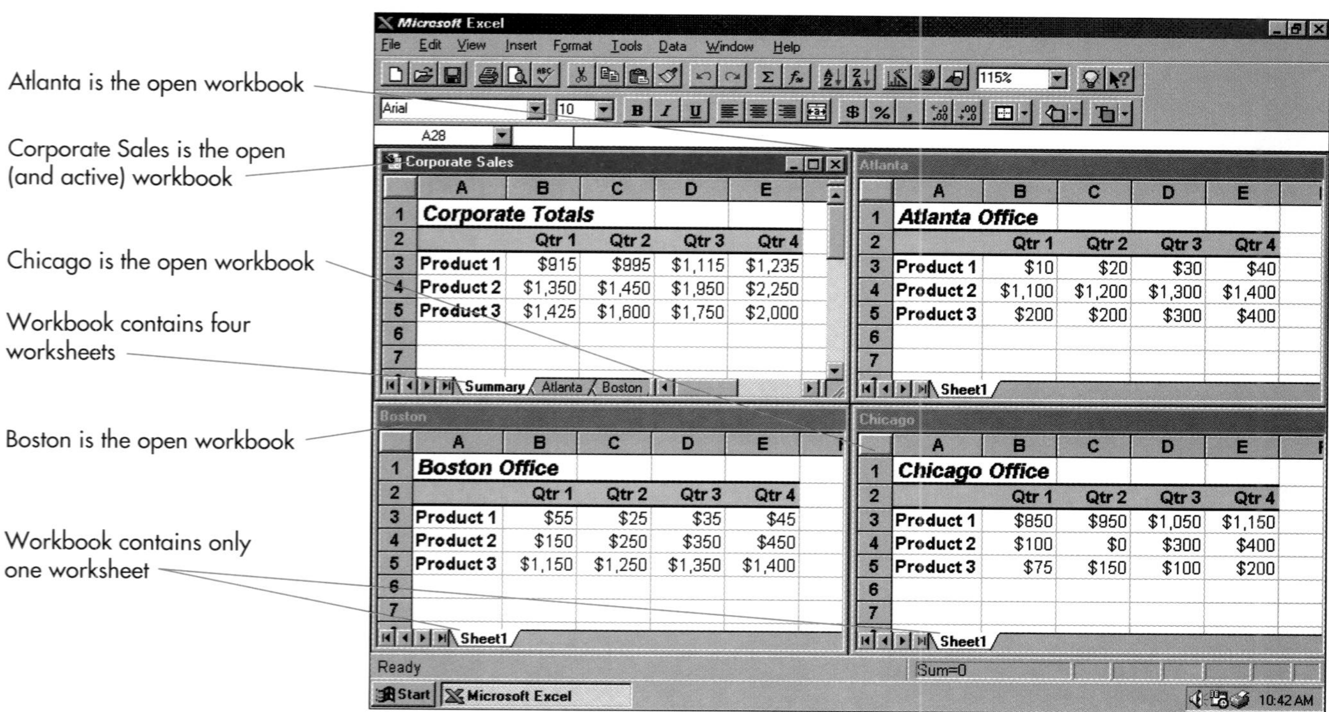

FIGURE 2.4 Multiple Workbooks

HANDS-ON EXERCISE 1

Copying Worksheets

Objective: Open multiple workbooks; use the Windows Arrange command to tile the open workbooks; copy a worksheet from one workbook to another. Use Figure 2.5 as a guide in the exercise.

STEP 1: Open a New Workbook

➤ Start Excel. If necessary, click the **New button** on the Standard toolbar to open a new workbook.

➤ Delete all worksheets except for Sheet1:

- Click the tab for **Sheet2.** Press the ▶| **key** to scroll to the last sheet in the workbook (Sheet16).
- Press the **Shift key** as you click the tab for Sheet 16. (Sheets 2 through 16 should be selected and their worksheet tabs appear in white.)
- Point to the tab for **Sheet16** and click the **right mouse button** to display a shortcut menu. Click **Delete.** Click **OK** in response to the warning that the selected sheets will be permanently deleted.

➤ The workbook should contain only Sheet1 as shown in Figure 2.5a. Save the workbook as **Corporate Sales** in the **Exploring Excel folder.**

THE DEFAULT WORKBOOK

A new workbook contains 16 worksheets, but you can change the default value to any number. Pull down the Tools menu, click Options, then click the General tab. Click the up (down) arrow in the Sheets in New Workbook text box to enter a new default value, then click OK to exit the Options dialog box and continue working. The next time you open a new workbook, it will contain the new number of worksheets.

STEP 2: Open the Individual Workbooks

➤ Pull down the **File menu.** Click **Open** to display the Open dialog box as shown in Figure 2.5a.

➤ Click the **Atlanta workbook,** then press and hold the **Ctrl key** as you click the **Boston** and **Chicago workbooks** to select all three workbooks at the same time.

➤ Click **Open** to open the selected workbooks. The workbooks will be opened one after another with a brief message appearing on the status bar as each workbook is opened.

➤ Pull down the **Window menu,** which should indicate the four open workbooks at the bottom of the menu. Only the Chicago workbook is visible at this time.

➤ Click **Arrange** to display the Arrange Windows dialog box. If necessary, select the Tile option, then click **OK.** You should see four open workbooks as shown in Figure 2.5b. (Do not be concerned if your workbooks are arranged differently from ours.)

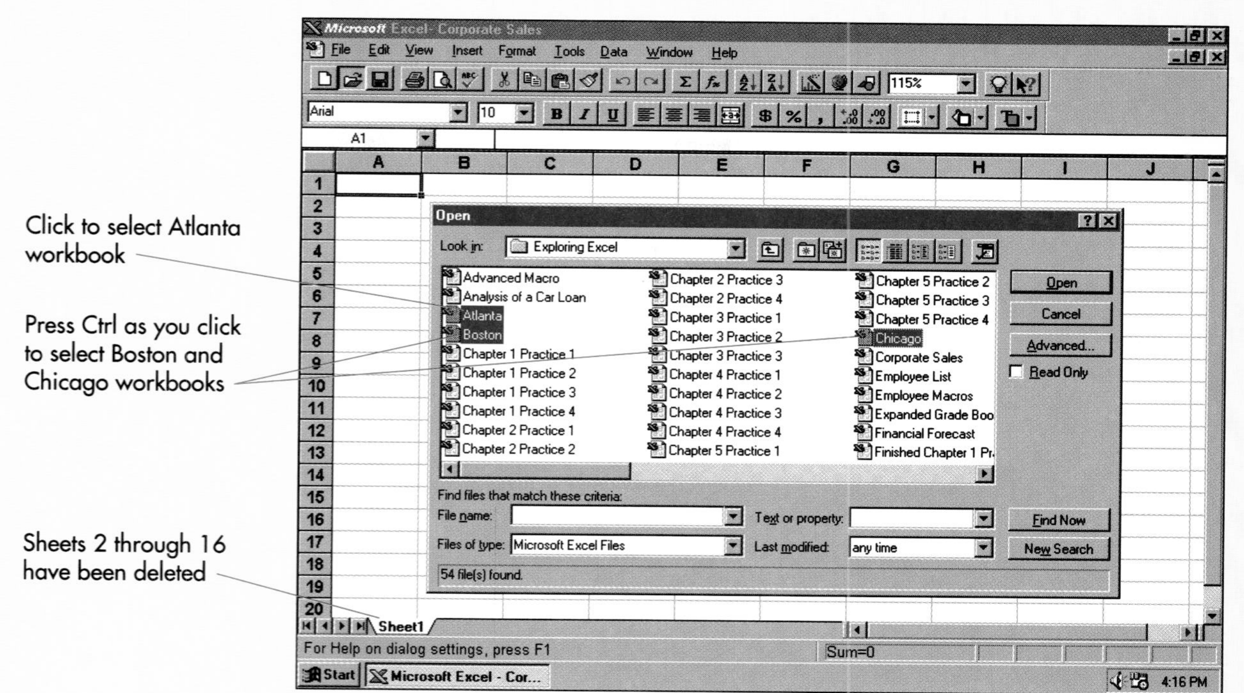

(a) Open Multiple Workbooks (steps 1 and 2)

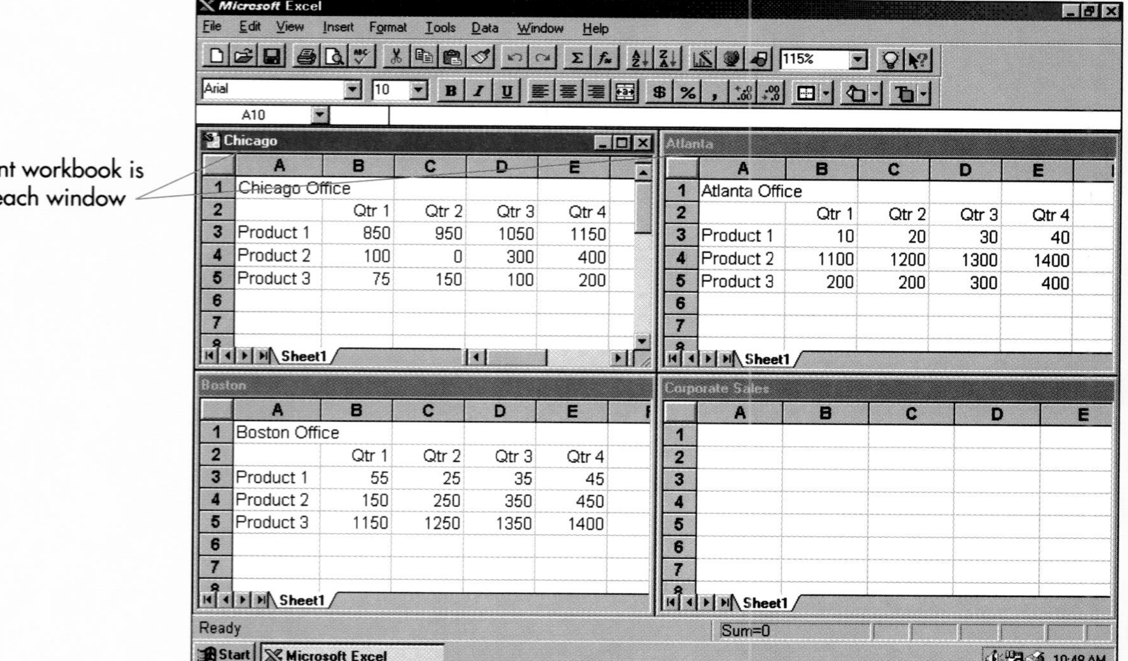

(b) Tile the Open Workbooks (step 2)

FIGURE 2.5 **Hands-on Exercise 1**

THE XLS EXTENSION—NOW YOU SEE IT, NOW YOU DON'T

Long-time DOS users will recognize a three-character extension at the end of a filename to indicate the file type. XLS, for example, indicates an Excel workbook. The extension is displayed or hidden in the application's title bar (and in the Open and Save dialog boxes) according to an option in the View menu of My Computer or the Windows Explorer. We suggest you hide the extension if it is currently visible. Open either My Computer or the Explorer, pull down the View menu, click the Options command, click the View tab, then check the box to hide MS-DOS file extensions. Click OK to accept the setting and exit the dialog box. The Excel title bar will display the name of the workbook, but not the XLS extension.

STEP 3: Copy the Atlanta Data

- Click in the **Atlanta workbook** to make it the active workbook. Reduce the column widths (if necessary) so that you can see the entire worksheet in the window.
- Click and drag to select **cells A1** through **E5** as shown in Figure 2.5c. Pull down the **Edit menu** and click **Copy** (or click the **Copy button** on the Standard toolbar).

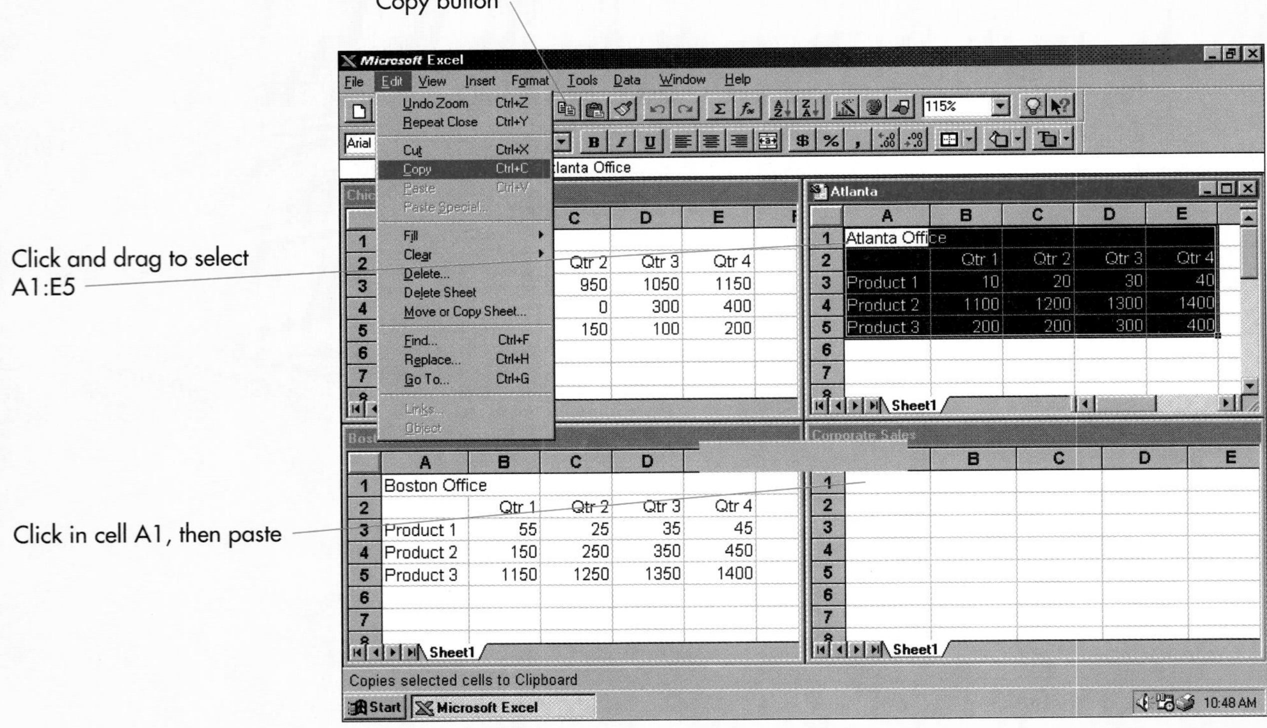

(c) Copy the Atlanta Data (step 3)

FIGURE 2.5 Hands-on Exercise 1 (continued)

➤ Click in **cell A1** of the **Corporate Sales workbook.** Click the **Paste button** on the Standard toolbar to copy the Atlanta data into this workbook.

➤ Point to the **Sheet1 tab** at the bottom of the Corporate Sales worksheet window, then click the **right mouse button** to produce a shortcut menu. Click **Rename.**

➤ Type **Atlanta** in the Rename Sheet dialog box and click **OK.** The worksheet tab has been changed from Sheet1 to Atlanta.

➤ Click the **Save button** to save the active workbook (Corporate Sales).

RENAMING A WORKSHEET

The fastest way to rename a worksheet is to double click the worksheet tab, which automatically displays the Rename Sheet dialog box. Type the new name for the worksheet, then press the enter key.

STEP 4: Copy the Boston and Chicago Data (a Shortcut)

➤ Click in the **Boston workbook** to make it the active workbook as shown in Figure 2.5d.

➤ Click the **Sheet1 tab,** then press and hold the **Ctrl key** as you drag the tab to the right of the Atlanta tab in the Corporate Sales workbook. You will see a tiny spreadsheet with a plus sign as you drag the tab. The plus sign indicates

Click in window to make Boston the active workbook

Click the Sheet1 tab, press Ctrl as you drag the tab to the right of the Atlanta tab in the Corporate Sales workbook

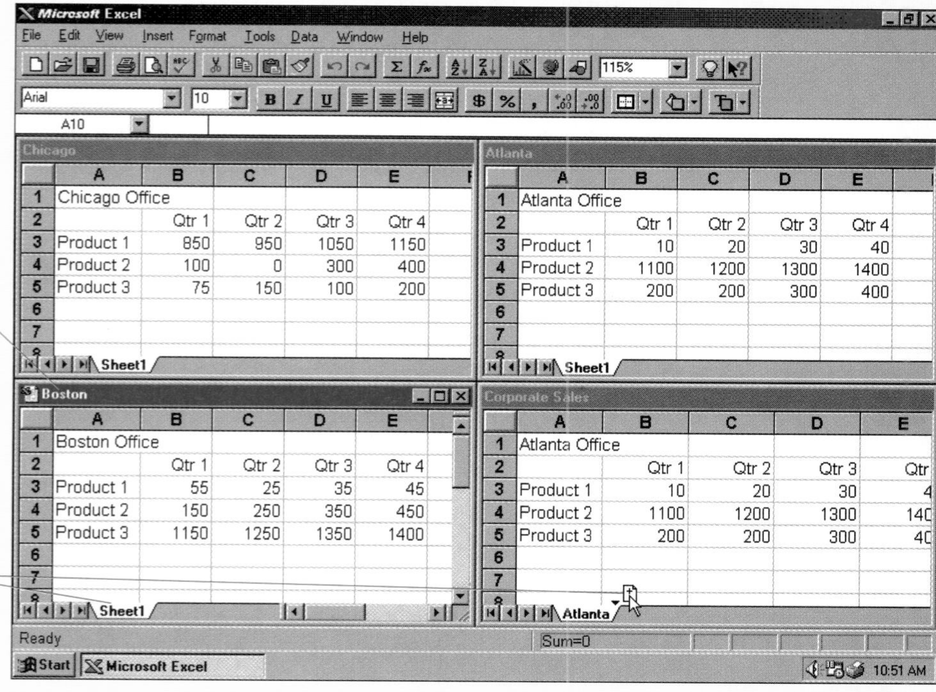

(d) A Shortcut (step 4)

FIGURE 2.5 Hands-on Exercise 1 (continued)

that the worksheet is being copied; the ▼ symbol indicates where the worksheet will be placed.

- Release the mouse, then release the Ctrl key. The worksheet from the Boston workbook should have been copied to the Corporate Sales workbook and appears as Sheet1 in that workbook.
- The Boston workbook should still be open; if it isn't, it means that you did not press the Ctrl key as you were dragging the tab to copy the worksheet. If this is the case, pull down the **File menu,** reopen the Boston workbook, and if necessary, tile the open windows.
- Double click the **Sheet1 tab** in the Corporate Sales workbook in order to rename the tab. Type **Boston** in the Rename Sheet text box and click **OK.**
- The Boston worksheet should appear to the right of the Atlanta worksheet; if the worksheet appears to the left of Atlanta, click and drag the tab to its desired position. (The ▼ symbol indicates where the worksheet will be placed.)
- Repeat the previous steps to copy the Chicago data to the Corporate Sales workbook, placing the new sheet to the right of the Boston sheet. Rename the copied worksheet **Chicago.** Remember, you must click in the window containing the Chicago workbook to activate the window before you can copy the worksheet.
- Save the Corporate Sales workbook. (The Summary worksheet will be built in the next exercise.)

MOVING AND COPYING WORKSHEETS

You can move or copy a worksheet within a workbook by dragging its tab. To move a worksheet, click its tab, then drag the tab to the new location (a black triangle shows where the new sheet will go). To copy a worksheet, click its tab, then press and hold the Ctrl key as you drag the tab to its new location. The copied worksheet will have the same name as the original worksheet, followed by a number in parentheses indicating the copy number.

STEP 5: The Corporate Sales Workbook

- Check that the Corporate Sales workbook is the active workbook. Click the **Maximize button** so that this workbook takes the entire screen.
- The Corporate Sales workbook contains three worksheets. Click the **Atlanta tab** to display the worksheet for Atlanta. Click the **Boston tab** to display the worksheet for Boston. Click the **Chicago tab** to display the worksheet for Chicago.
- Pull down the **File menu.** Click **Print.** Click the **Entire Workbook option button** as shown in Figure 2.5e. Click **OK** to print the workbook.
- Close the open workbooks, saving changes if requested to do so. Exit Excel if you do not want to continue with the next exercise at this time.

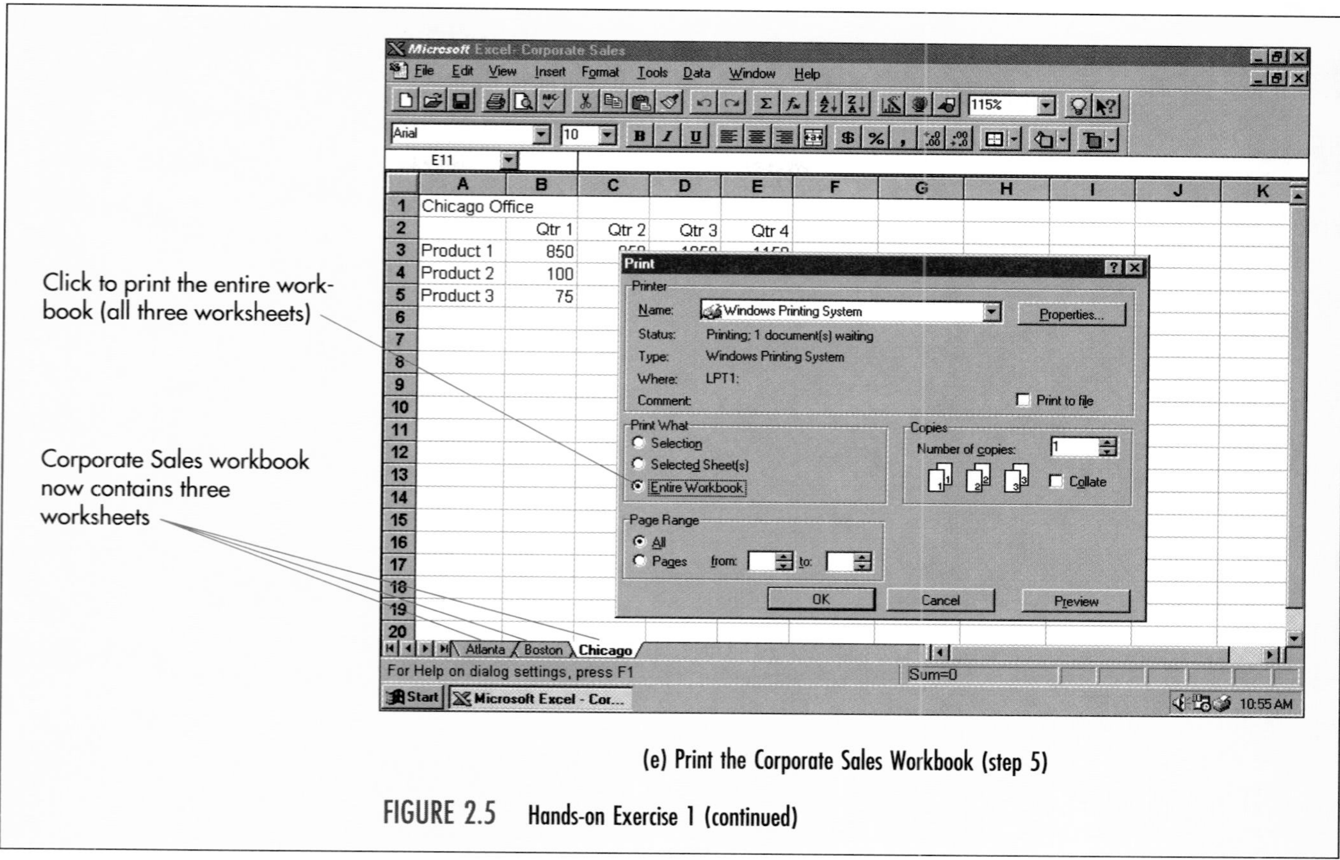

(e) Print the Corporate Sales Workbook (step 5)

FIGURE 2.5 Hands-on Exercise 1 (continued)

WORKSHEET REFERENCES

The presence of multiple worksheets in a workbook creates an additional requirement for cell references. You continue to use the same row and column convention when you reference a cell on the current worksheet; that is, cell A1 is still A1. What if, however, you want to reference a cell on another worksheet within the same workbook? It is no longer sufficient to refer to cell A1 because every worksheet has its own cell A1.

To reference a cell (or cell range) in a worksheet other than the current (active) worksheet, you need to preface the cell address with a ***worksheet reference;*** for example, Atlanta!A1 references cell A1 in the Atlanta worksheet. A worksheet reference may also be used in conjunction with a cell range—for example, Summary!B2:E5 to reference cells B2 through E5 on the Summary worksheet. Omission of the worksheet reference in either example defaults to the cell reference in the active worksheet.

An exclamation point separates the worksheet reference from the cell reference. The worksheet reference (e.g., Atlanta or Summary) is always an absolute reference. The cell reference can be either relative (e.g., Atlanta!A1 or Summary!B2:E5) or absolute (e.g., Atlanta!$A$1 or Summary!$B$2:$E$5).

Consider how worksheet references are used in the Summary worksheet in Figure 2.6. Each entry in the Summary worksheet computes the sum of the corresponding cells in the Atlanta, Boston, and Chicago worksheets. The cell formula in cell B3, for example, would be entered as follows:

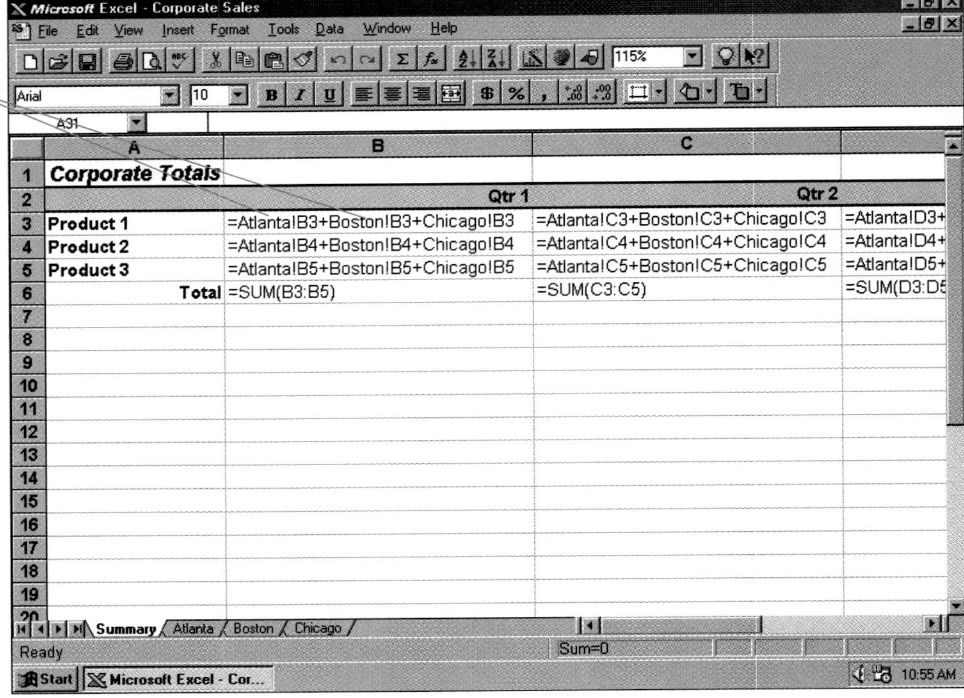

FIGURE 2.6 Worksheet References

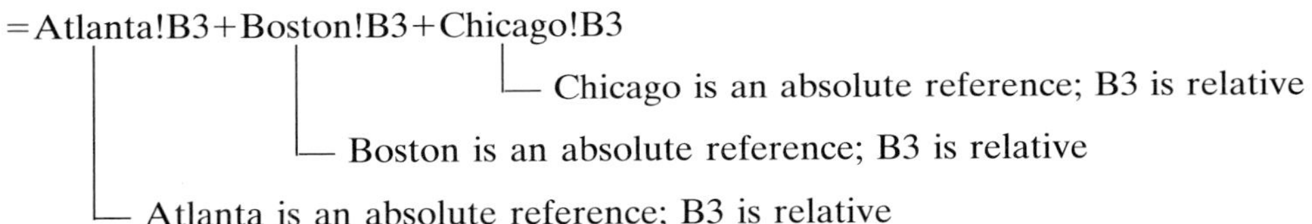

The combination of relative and absolute addresses enables you to enter the formula once (in cell B3), then copy it to the remaining cells in the worksheet. In other words, you enter the formula in cell B3 to compute the total sales for Product 1 in Quarter 1, then you copy that formula to the other cells in row three (C3 through E3) to obtain the totals for Product 1 in Quarters 2, 3, and 4. You then copy the entire row (B3 through E3) to rows four and five (cells B4 through E5) to obtain the totals for Products 2 and 3 in all four quarters.

The proper use of relative and absolute references in the original formula in cell B3 is what makes it possible to copy the cell formulas. Consider, for example, the formula in cell C3 (which was copied from cell B3):

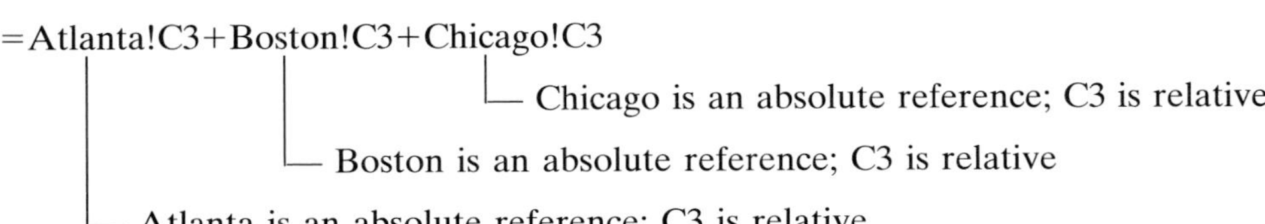

The worksheet references remain absolute (e.g., Atlanta!) while the cell references adjust for the new location of the formula (cell C3). Similar adjustments are made in all of the other copied formulas.

3-D Reference

A ***3-D reference*** is a range that spans two or more worksheets in a workbook; for example, =SUM(Atlanta:Chicago!B3) to sum cell B3 in the Atlanta, Boston, and Chicago worksheets. The sheet range is specified with a colon between the beginning and ending sheets. An exclamation point follows the ending sheet, followed by the cell reference. The worksheet references are absolute. The cell reference may be relative or absolute.

Three-dimensional references can be used in the Summary worksheet as an alternative way to compute the corporate total for each product–quarter combination. To compute the corporate sales for Product 1 in Quarter 1 (which appears in cell B3 of the Summary worksheet), you would use the function:

=SUM(Atlanta:Chicago!B3)

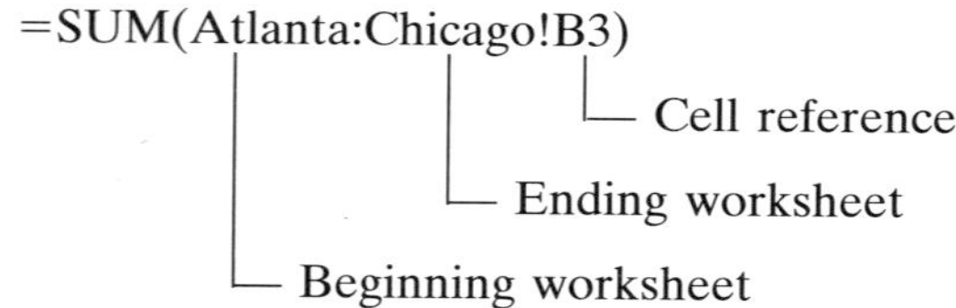

The 3-D reference includes all worksheets between the Atlanta and Chicago worksheets. (Only one additional worksheet, Boston, is present in the example, but the reference would adjust automatically for the insertion of any additional worksheets.) Note, too, that the cell reference is relative and thus the formula can be copied from cell B3 in the Summary worksheet to the remaining cells in row 3 (C3 through E3). Those formulas can then be copied to the appropriate cells in rows 4 and 5.

A 3-D reference can be typed directly into a cell formula, but it is easier to enter the reference by pointing. Click in the cell that is to contain the 3-D reference, then enter an equal sign to begin the formula. To reference a cell in another workbook, click in the window containing that workbook, click the tab for the worksheet you want to reference, then click the cell or cell range you want to include in the formula.

FORMULAS VERSUS FUNCTIONS

Many worksheet calculations, such as an average or a sum, can be performed in one of two ways. You can either enter a formula—for example, =Atlanta!B3+Boston!B3+Chicago!B3—or you can use the equivalent function, =SUM(Atlanta:Chicago!B3). Functions are preferable in that they will adjust automatically for the deletion of existing worksheets or the insertion of new worksheets (within the existing range).

Grouping Worksheets

The worksheets in a workbook are often similar to one another in terms of content and/or formatting. In Figure 2.3, for example, the formatting is identical in all four worksheets of the workbook. You can format the worksheets individually or more easily through grouping.

Excel provides the capability for ***grouping worksheets*** in order to enter or format data in multiple worksheets at the same time. Once the worksheets are grouped, anything you do in one of the worksheets is automatically done to the other sheets in the group. You could, for example, group all of the worksheets together when you enter row and column labels, when you format data, or when you enter formulas to compute row and column totals. You must, however, ungroup the worksheets when you enter data in a specific worksheet. Grouping and ungrouping is illustrated in the following hands-on exercise.

HANDS-ON EXERCISE 2

3-D References

Objective: Use 3-D references to summarize data from multiple worksheets within a workbook; group worksheets to enter common formatting and formulas; open multiple windows to view several worksheets at the same time. Use Figure 2.7 as a guide in the exercise.

STEP 1: Insert a Worksheet

- Start Excel. Open the **Corporate Sales workbook** created in the previous exercise. The workbook contains three worksheets: Atlanta, Boston, and Chicago.
- Click the **Atlanta tab** to select this worksheet. Pull down the **Insert menu,** and click the **Worksheet command.** You should see a new worksheet, Sheet1, which is displayed on the screen and whose tab is to the left of the Atlanta tab.
- Double click the **tab** of the newly inserted worksheet. Type **Summary** in the Rename Sheet dialog box and press **enter.** The name of the new worksheet has been changed to Summary.
- Save the workbook.

SHORTCUT MENUS

Shortcut menus provide an alternate (and generally faster) way to execute common commands. Point to a tab, then click the right mouse button to display a shortcut menu with commands to insert, delete, rename, move, or copy, or select all worksheets. Point to the desired command, then click the left mouse button to execute the command from the shortcut menu. Press the Esc key or click outside the menu to close the menu without executing the command.

STEP 2: The AutoFill Command

- Click in **cell A1** of the Summary worksheet. Type **Corporate Totals** as shown in Figure 2.7a.
- Click in **cell B2.** Enter **Qtr 1.** Click in **cell B2,** then point to the fill handle in the lower-right corner of cell B2. The mouse pointer changes to a thin crosshair.

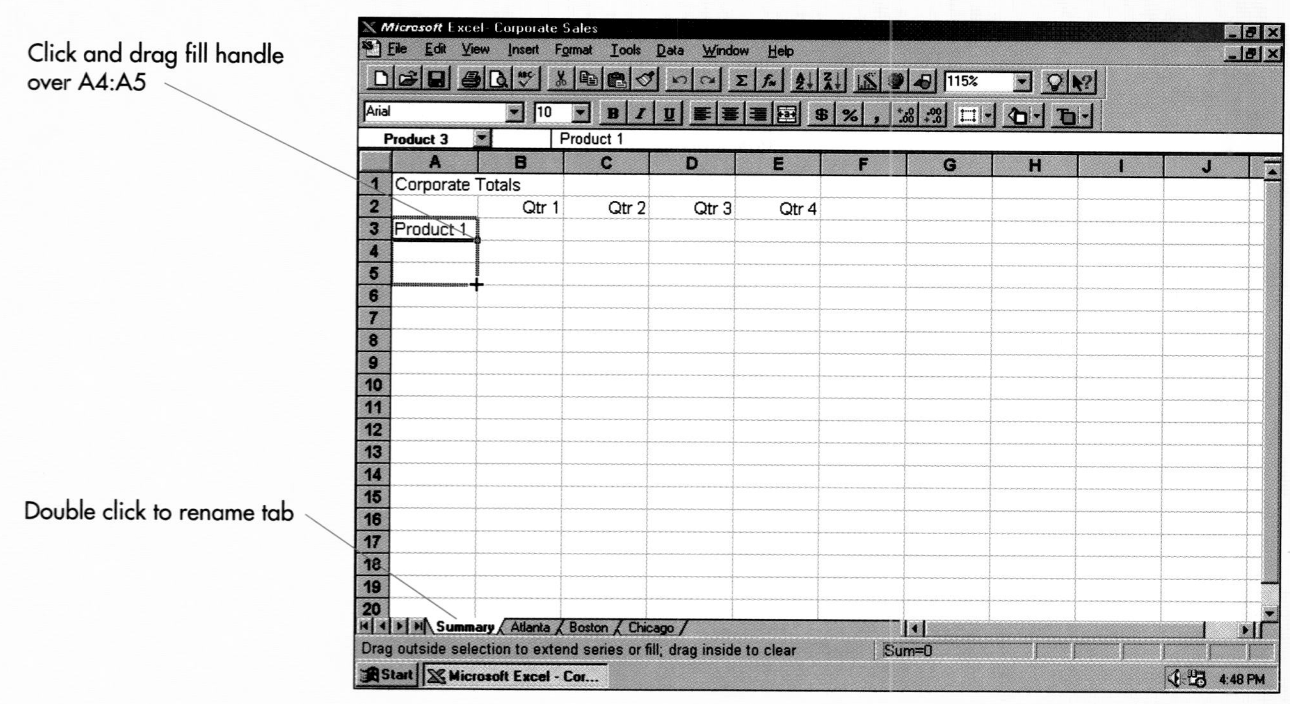

(a) The AutoFill Command (step 2)

FIGURE 2.7 Hands-on Exercise 2

- Drag the fill handle over **cells C2, D2,** and **E2.** A border appears to indicate the destination range. Release the mouse. Cells C2 through E2 contain the labels Qtr 2, Qtr 3, and Qtr 4, respectively. Right align the column labels.
- Click in **cell A3.** Enter **Product 1.** Use the AutoFill capability to enter the labels **Product 2** and **Product 3** in cells A4 and A5.

THE AUTOFILL COMMAND

The AutoFill command is the fastest way to enter any type of series in adjacent cells. If, for example, you needed the months of the year in 12 successive cells, you would enter January (or Jan) in the first cell, then drag the fill handle over the next 11 cells in the direction you want to fill. If you need the days of the week, enter Monday (or Mon) and drag over the appropriate number of cells. You can also create a numeric series by entering the first two numbers in that series; for example, to enter the years 1990 through 1999, enter 1990 and 1991 in the first two cells, then select both cells and drag the fill handle.

STEP 3: Sum the Worksheets

- Click in **cell B3** of the Summary worksheet as shown in Figure 2.7b. Enter **=SUM(Atlanta:Chicago!B3),** then press the **enter key.** You should see 915

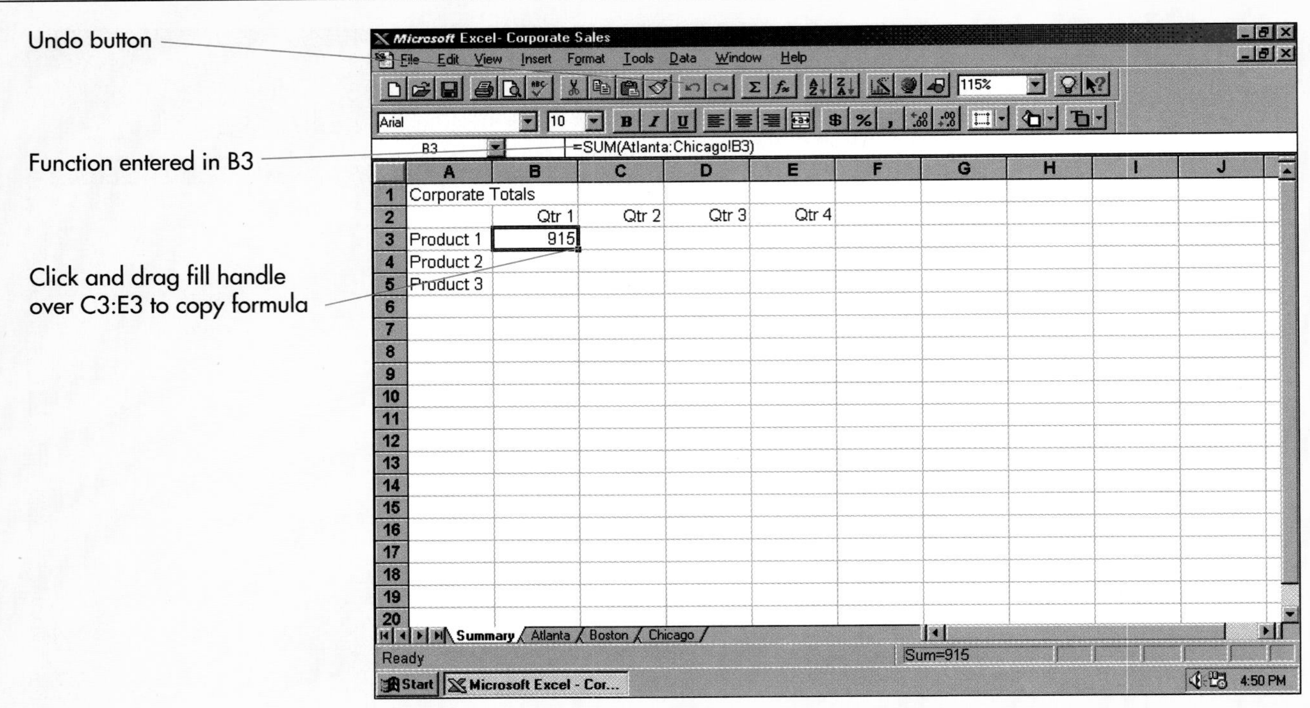

(b) Sum the Worksheets (step 3)

FIGURE 2.7 Hands-on Exercise 2 (continued)

as the sum of the sales for Product 1 in Quarter 1 for the three cities (Atlanta, Boston, and Chicago).

- Click the **Undo button** on the Standard toolbar to erase the function so that you can re-enter the function by using pointing:
- Check that you are in cell B3 of the Summary worksheet. Enter **=SUM(.**
  - Click the **Atlanta tab** to begin the pointing operation.
  - Press and hold the **Shift key,** click the **Chicago tab** (scrolling if necessary), then release the Shift key and click **cell B3.** The formula bar should now contain =SUM(Atlanta:Chicago!B3.
  - Press the **enter key** to complete the function (which automatically enters the closing right parenthesis) and return to the Summary worksheet.
- You should see once again the displayed value of 915 in cell B3 of the Summary worksheet.
- If necessary, click in **cell B3,** then drag the fill handle over cells **C3** through **E3** to copy this formula and obtain the total sales for Product 1 in quarters two, three, and four.
- Be sure that cells B3 through E3 are still selected, then drag the fill handle to **cell E5.** You should see the total sales for all products in all quarters as shown in Figure 2.7c.
- Click **cell E5** to examine the formula in this cell and note that the worksheet references are absolute (i.e., they remained the same), whereas the cell references are relative (they were adjusted). Click in other cells to review their formulas in similar fashion.
- Save the workbook.

POINTING TO CELLS IN OTHER WORKSHEETS

A worksheet reference can be typed directly into a cell formula, but it is easier to enter the reference by pointing. Click in the cell that is to contain the reference, then enter an equal sign to begin the formula. To reference a cell in another worksheet, click the tab for the worksheet you want to reference, then click the cell or cell range you want to include in the formula. Complete the formula as usual, continuing to first click the tab whenever you want to reference a cell in another worksheet.

STEP 4: The Arrange Windows Command

- Pull down the **Window menu.** The bottom of the menu displays the names of the open windows, with only one window open at this time. (If the list of open windows includes Book1, close that workbook.)
- Click **New Window** to open a second window. Note, however, that your display will not change at this time, because the windows are maximized and only one window is displayed at a time.
- Pull down the **Window menu** a second time. Click **New Window** to open a third window. Open a fourth window in similar fashion.
- Pull down the **Window menu** once again. You should see the names of the four open windows as shown in Figure 2.7c.
- Click **Arrange** to display the Arrange Windows dialog box. If necessary, select the **Tile** option, then click **OK.** You should see four tiled windows.

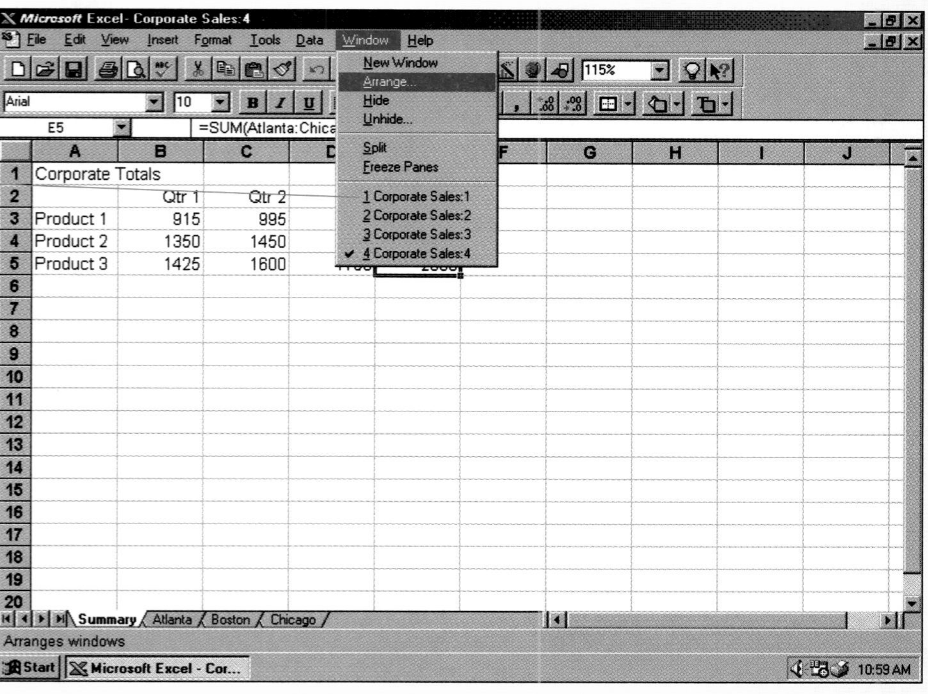

(c) Arrange Windows Command (step 4)

FIGURE 2.7 Hands-on Exercise 2 (continued)

STEP 5: Changing Data

- Click in the **upper-right window** in Figure 2.7d. Click the **Atlanta tab** to display the Atlanta worksheet in this window.
- Click the **lower-left window.** Click the **Boston tab** to display the Boston worksheet in this window.
- Click in the **lower-right window.** Click the **Tab scrolling button** until you can see the Chicago tab, then click the **Chicago tab** to display the Chicago worksheet.
- Note that cell B3 in the Summary worksheet displays the value 915, which reflects the total sales for Product 1 in Quarter 1 for Atlanta, Boston, and Chicago (10, 55, and 850, respectively).
- Click in **cell B3** of the Chicago worksheet. Enter **250.** Press **enter.** The value of cell B3 in the Summary worksheet changes to 315 to reflect the decreased sales in Chicago.
- Click the **Undo button** on the Standard toolbar. The sales for Chicago revert to 850 and the Corporate total is again 915.

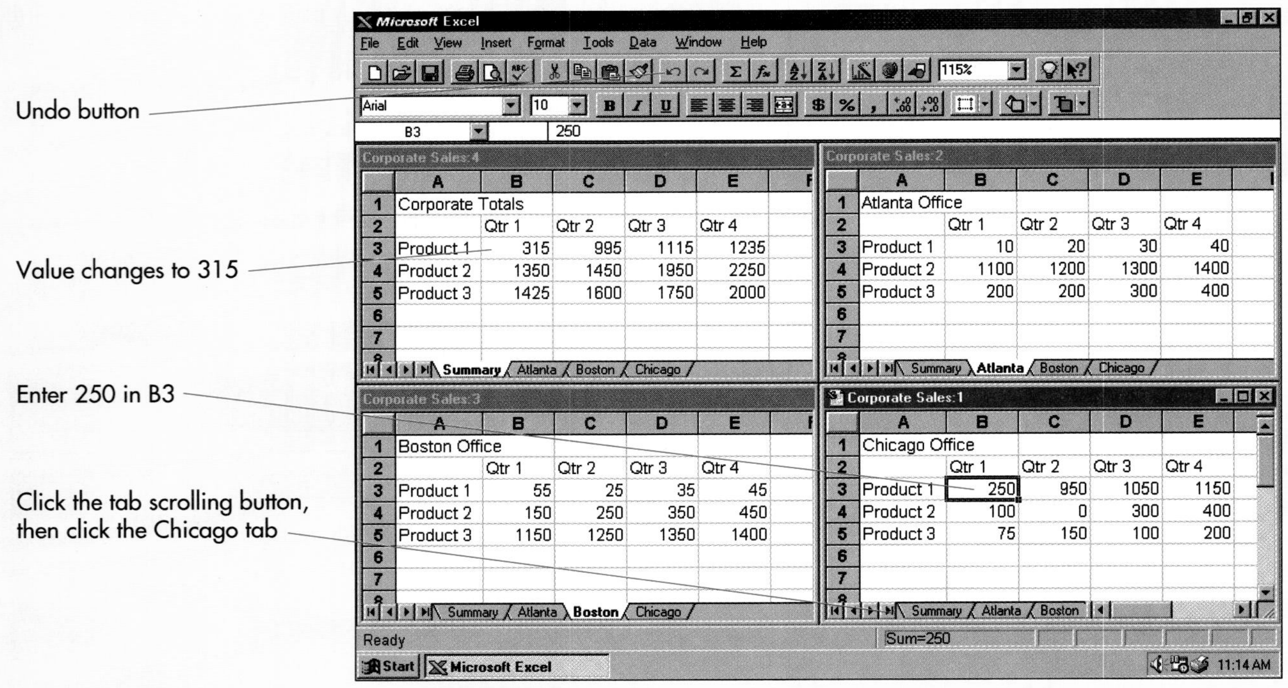

(d) Changing the Data (step 5)

FIGURE 2.7 Hands-on Exercise 2 (continued)

STEP 6: Group Editing

- Click in the **upper-left window,** which displays the Summary worksheet. Point to the split box separating the tab scrolling buttons from the horizontal scroll bar. (The pointer becomes a two-headed arrow.) Click and drag to the right until you can see all four tabs at the same time.
- If necessary, click the **Summary tab.** Press and hold the **Shift key** as you click the tab for the **Chicago worksheet.** All four tabs should be selected (and are displayed in white) as in Figure 2.7e, and you see [Group] in the title bar.

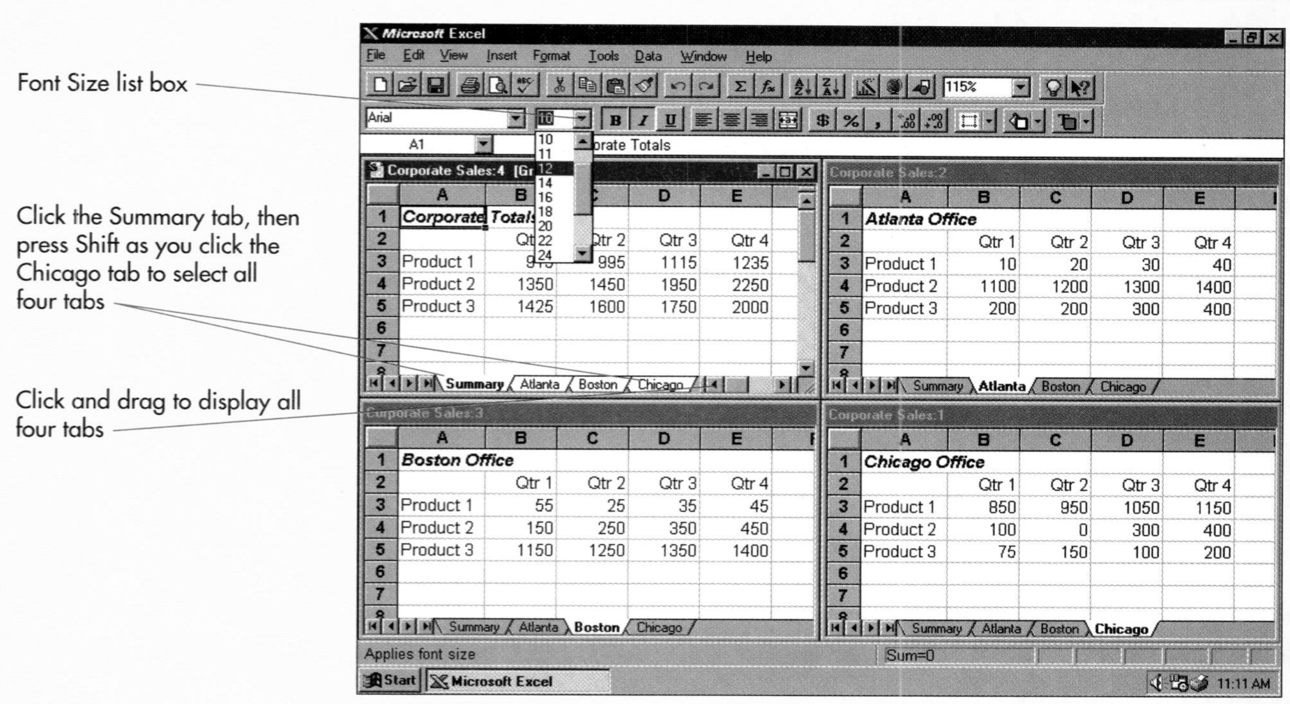
Font Size list box
Click the Summary tab, then press Shift as you click the Chicago tab to select all four tabs
Click and drag to display all four tabs

(e) Group Editing (step 6)

FIGURE 2.7 Hands-on Exercise 2 (continued)

- Click in **cell A1,** then click the **Bold** and **Italic buttons** to boldface and italicize the title of each worksheet. Click the **drop-down arrow** for the Font Size list box and change the font to 12.
- Boldface the quarterly and product labels. Note that all four sheets are being formatted simultaneously because of group editing.
- Click and drag to select **cells B3** through **E5,** the cells containing the numerical values. Format these cells in currency format with zero decimals. Add borders and color as desired.
- Save the workbook.

SELECTING MULTIPLE SHEETS

You can group (select) multiple worksheets simultaneously, then perform the same operation on the selected sheets. To select adjacent sheets, select (click) the first sheet in the range, then press and hold the Shift key as you click the last sheet in the group. If the worksheets are not adjacent to one another, click the first tab, then press and hold the Ctrl key as you click the tab of each additional sheet you want to include in the group. To select all of the sheets at one time, right click the active tab, then choose Select All from the shortcut menu. Once multiple sheets have been selected, Excel indicates that grouping is in effect by appending [Group] to the workbook name in the title bar. Click any tab within the selected group to deselect the group.

STEP 7: Sum the Rows and Columns

- Be sure that all four tabs are still selected so that group editing is still in effect.
- Scroll until you can click in **cell F3** in the Summary worksheet. Enter the function **=SUM(B3:E3).** Copy this formula to **cells F4** through **F6.**
- Click in **cell B6** as shown in Figure 2.7f. Enter the function **=SUM(B3:B5).** Copy this formula to **cells C6** through **E6.** Note that the formula is being entered in all four sheets simultaneously since group editing is still in effect.
- Enter **Total** in cell F2, then center and boldface the label in the cell. Enter **Total** in cell A6 and boldface it. Boldface the row and column totals.
- Save the workbook.

THE AUTOSUM BUTTON

The ***AutoSum*** button on the Standard toolbar invokes the Sum function over a suggested range of cells. To sum a single row or column, click in the blank cell at the end of the row or column, click the AutoSum button to see the suggested function, then click the button a second time to enter the function into the worksheet. To sum multiple rows or columns, select all of the cells that are to contain the Sum function prior to clicking the AutoSum button.

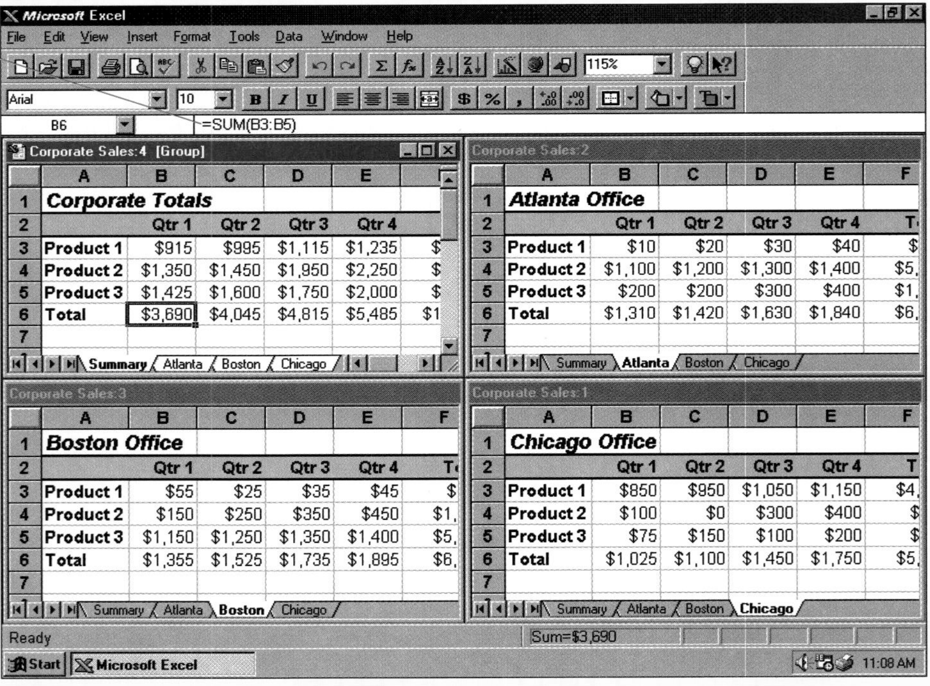

(f) Sum the Rows and Columns (step 7)

FIGURE 2.7 Hands-on Exercise 2 (continued)

STEP 8: Print the Workbook

- Pull down the **File menu** and click the **Page Setup command.**
- Click the **Margins tab,** then click the check box to center the worksheet horizontally.
- Click the **Sheet tab.** Check the boxes to include row and column headings and gridlines.
- Click **OK** to exit the Page Setup dialog box.
- Pull down the **File menu.** Click **Print** to display the Print dialog box. Click the option button to print the **Entire Workbook.**
- Click **OK** to print the workbook, which will print on four separate pages, one worksheet per page.

STEP 9: Exit Excel

- Close all four windows, clicking **Yes** to save the workbook as you close the last window.
- Exit Excel if you do not want to continue with the next exercise at this time.

THE DOCUMENTATION WORKSHEET

A well-designed worksheet should isolate the assumptions and initial conditions on which the worksheet is based. A workbook can contain up to 256 worksheets, and it, too, should be well designed so that the purpose of every worksheet is evident. Documenting a workbook, and the various worksheets within the workbook, is important because spreadsheets are frequently used by individuals other than the author. You are familiar with every aspect of your workbook because you created it. Your colleague down the hall (or across the country) is not, however, and that person needs to know at a glance the purpose of the workbook and its underlying structure. Even if you don't share your worksheet with others, you will appreciate the documentation six months from now, when you have forgotten some of the nuances you once knew so well.

One way of documenting a workbook is through the creation of a ***documentation worksheet*** that describes the contents of each worksheet within the workbook as shown in Figure 2.8. The worksheet in Figure 2.8 has been added to the Corporate Sales workbook that was created in the first two exercises. (The Insert menu contains the command to add a worksheet.)

The documentation worksheet shows the author and date the spreadsheet was last modified. It contains a description of the overall workbook, a list of each sheet within the workbook, and the contents of each worksheet. The information in the documentation worksheet may seem obvious to you, but it will be greatly appreciated by someone seeing the workbook for the first time.

The documentation worksheet is attractively formatted and takes advantage of the ability to wrap text within a cell. The description in cell B6, for example, wraps over several lines (just as in a word processor). The worksheet also takes advantage of color and larger fonts to call attention to the title of the worksheet. The grid lines have been suppressed through the View tab in the Options command of the Tools menu. The documentation worksheet is an important addition to any workbook.

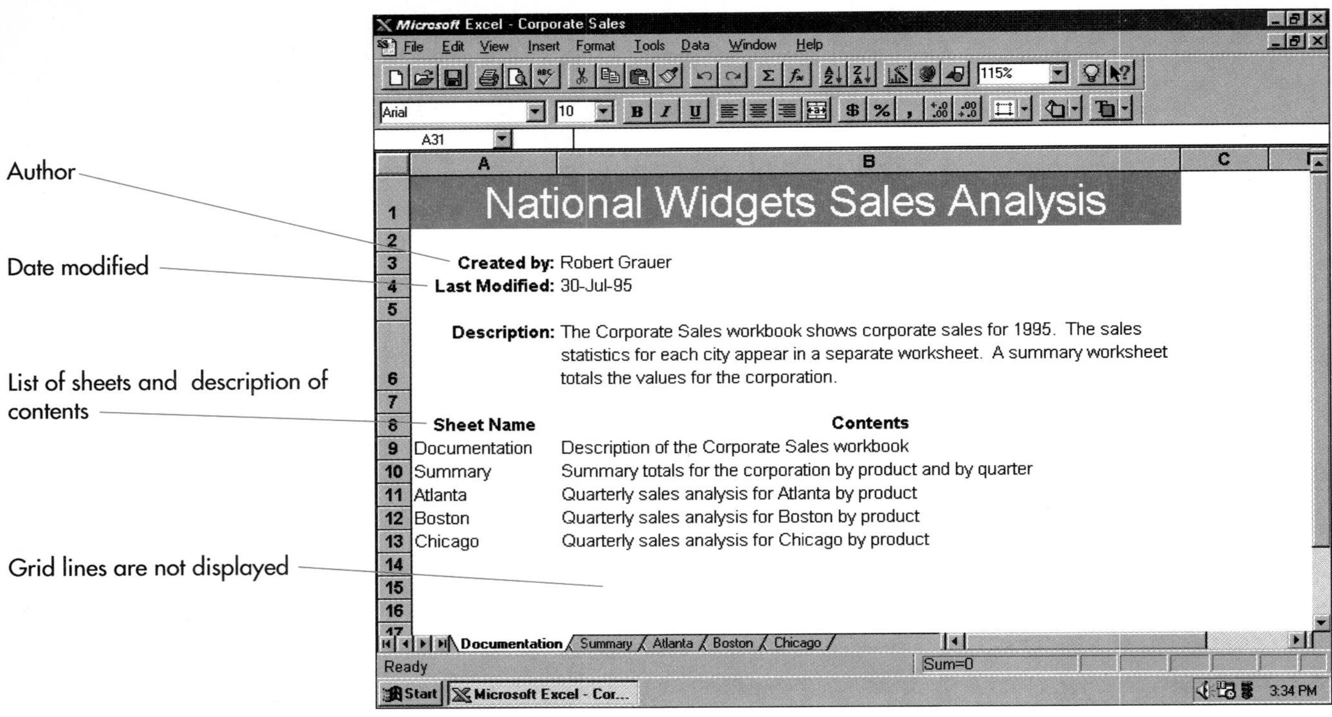

FIGURE 2.8 The Documentation Worksheet

HANDS-ON EXERCISE 3

The Documentation Worksheet

Objective: To improve the design of a workbook through the inclusion of a documentation worksheet. To illustrate sophisticated formatting. Use Figure 2.9 as a guide in the exercise.

STEP 1: Insert a Worksheet

- Start Excel. Open the **Corporate Sales workbook** created in the previous exercise. The workbook contains four worksheets: Summary, Atlanta, Boston, and Chicago, each in its own window. Close all but one of the windows, then maximize that window.
- Click the **Summary tab** to select this worksheet. Pull down the **Insert menu,** and click the **Worksheet command.** You should see a new worksheet, Sheet1, whose tab is to the left of the Summary worksheet. Do not be concerned if the worksheet is other than Sheet1.
- Double click the **tab** of the newly inserted worksheet. Enter **Documentation** in the Rename Sheet dialog box and press **enter.** The name of the new worksheet has been changed to Documentation as shown in Figure 2.9a.
- Save the workbook.

STEP 2: Enter the Documentation Information

- Enter the descriptive entries in cells A3, A4, and A6 as shown in Figure 2.9a.
- Click and drag to select **cells A3** through **A6** so that you can format these cells at the same time. Click the **Bold button.** Click the **Align Right button.**

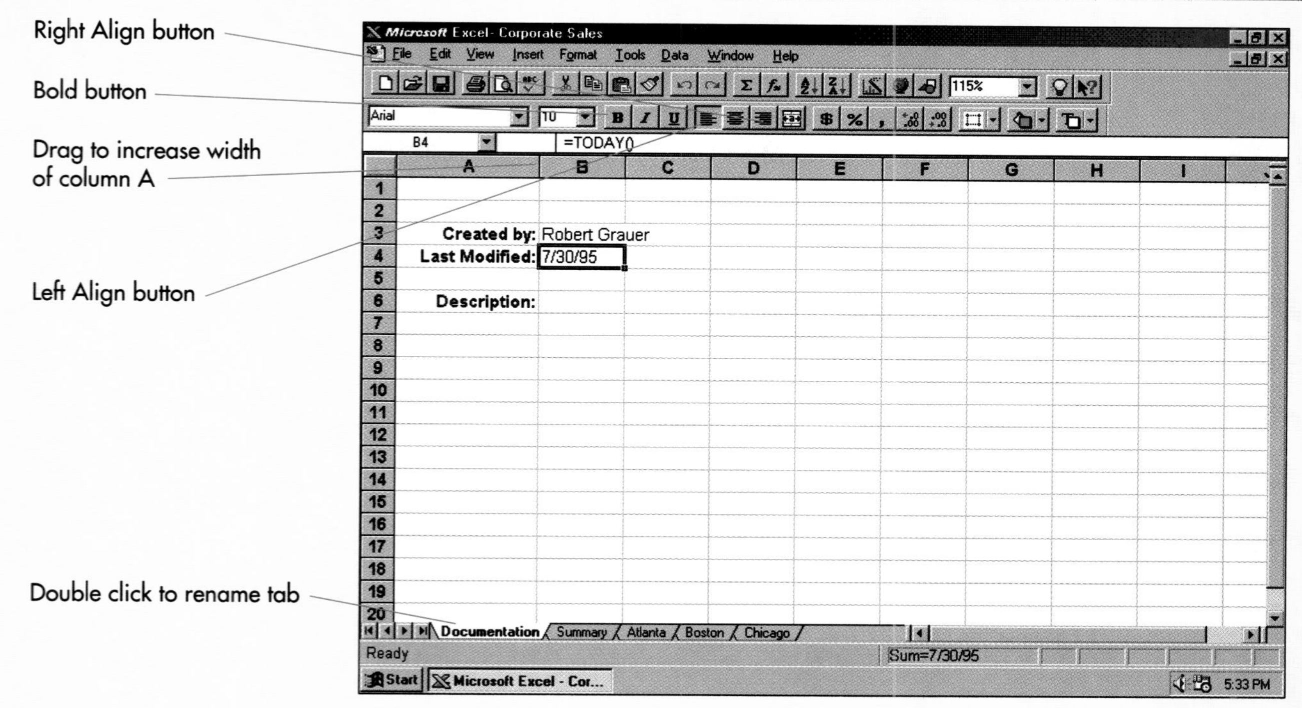

(a) Add the Documentation Worksheet (steps 1 and 2)

FIGURE 2.9 Hands-on Exercise 3

- Increase the width of column A so that the contents of column A are completely visible.
- Enter your name in cell B3. Enter **=Today()** in cell B4. Press **enter.** Click the **Left Align button** to align the date as shown in Figure 2.9a.

STEP 3: The Format Cells Command

- Increase the width of column B as shown in Figure 2.9b, then click in **cell B6** and enter the descriptive entry shown in the formula bar.
- Type the entire entry *without* pressing the enter key as you will be able to wrap the text within the cell. (You are limited to a maximum of 256 characters in the entry.) Do not be concerned if the text in cell B6 appears to spill into the other cells in row six.
- Press the **enter key** when you have completed the entry. Click in **cell B6,** then pull down the **Format menu** and click **Cells** (or right click **cell B6** and click **Format Cells**) to display the dialog box in Figure 2.9b.
- Click the **Alignment tab.** Click the box to **Wrap Text** as shown in the figure. Click **OK** to close the dialog box. The text in cell B6 wraps to the width of column B. (You can change the width of the column, and the text will wrap automatically.)
- Point to **cell A6,** then click the **right mouse button** to display a shortcut menu. Click **Format Cells** to display the Format Cells dialog box. If necessary, click the **Alignment tab,** then click the **Top option button** in the Vertical section of the dialog box.
- The entry in cell A6 (the word "Description") now aligns with the top of the description in cell B6.
- Save the workbook.

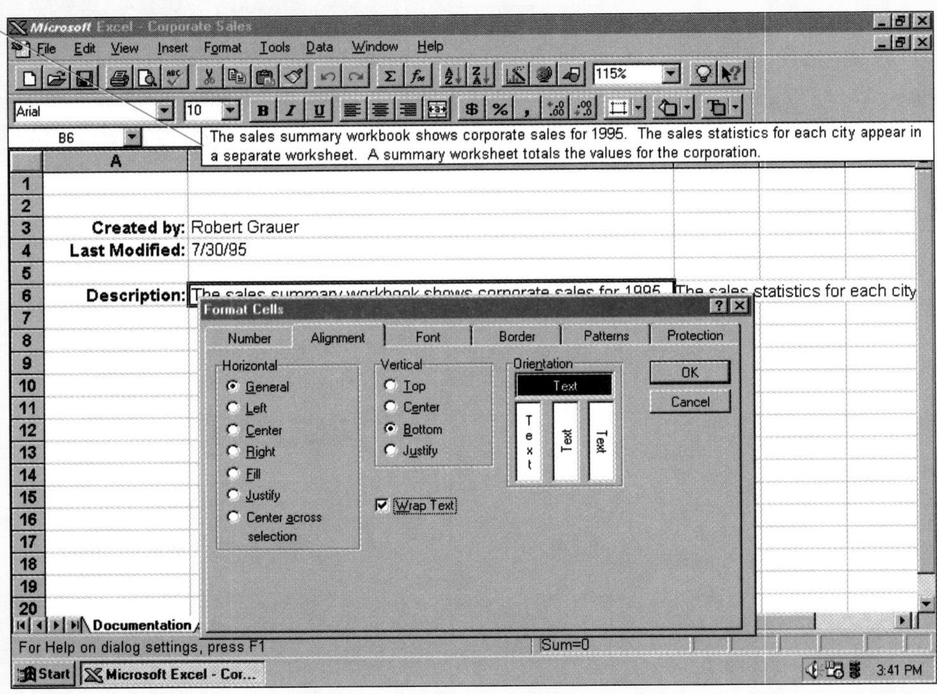

(b) Wrap Text Command (step 3)

FIGURE 2.9 Hands-on Exercise 3 (continued)

EDIT WITHIN A CELL

Double click within the cell whose contents you want to change, then make the changes directly in the cell itself rather than on the formula bar. Use the mouse or arrow keys to position the insertion point at the point of correction. Press the Ins key to toggle between the insertion and overtype modes and/or use the Del key to delete a character. Press the Home and End keys to move to the first and last characters, respectively.

STEP 4: Complete the Descriptive Entries

- Complete the text entries in cells A8 through B13 as shown in Figure 2.9c. Click and drag to select cells **A8** and **B8.** Click the **Bold** and **Center buttons** to match the formatting in the figure.
- Save the workbook.

STEP 5: Add the Worksheet Title

- Click in **cell A1.** Enter **National Widgets Sales Analysis.** Change the font size to **24.**
- Click and drag to select **cells A1** and **B1.** Click the **Center Across Columns button** to center the title across cells A1 and B1.
- Check that cells A1 and B1 are still selected. Pull down the **Format menu.** Click **Cells** to display the Format Cells dialog box as shown in Figure 2.9d.

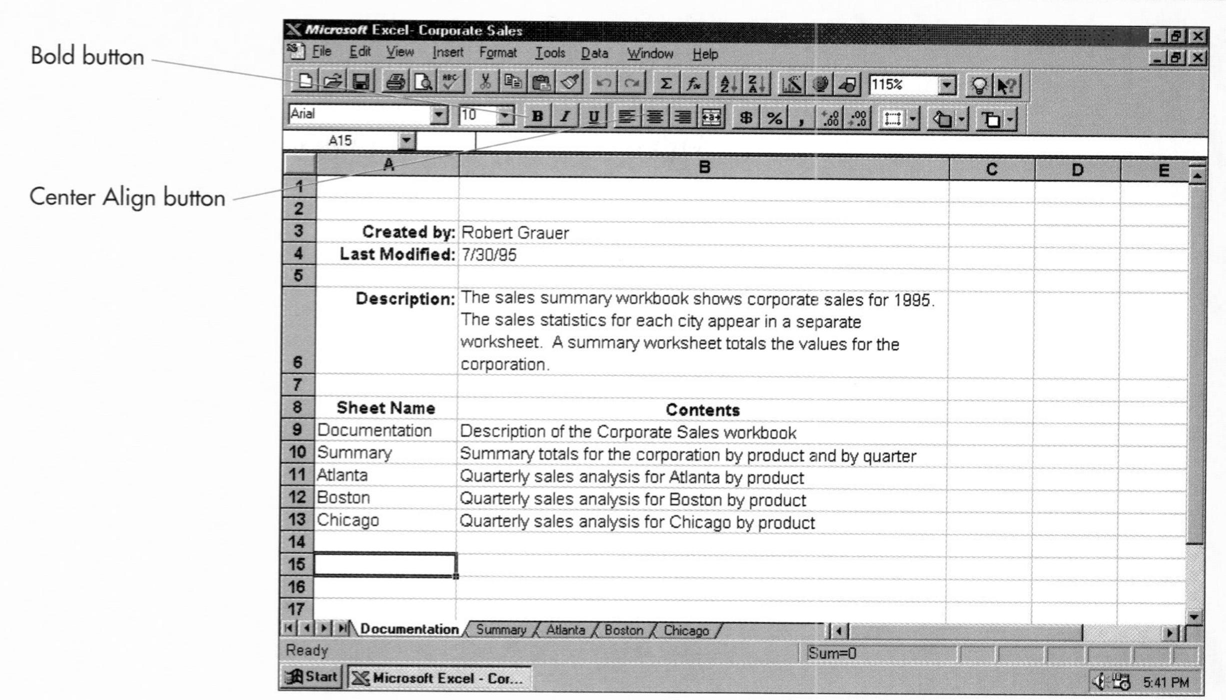

(c) Complete the Descriptive Entries (step 4)

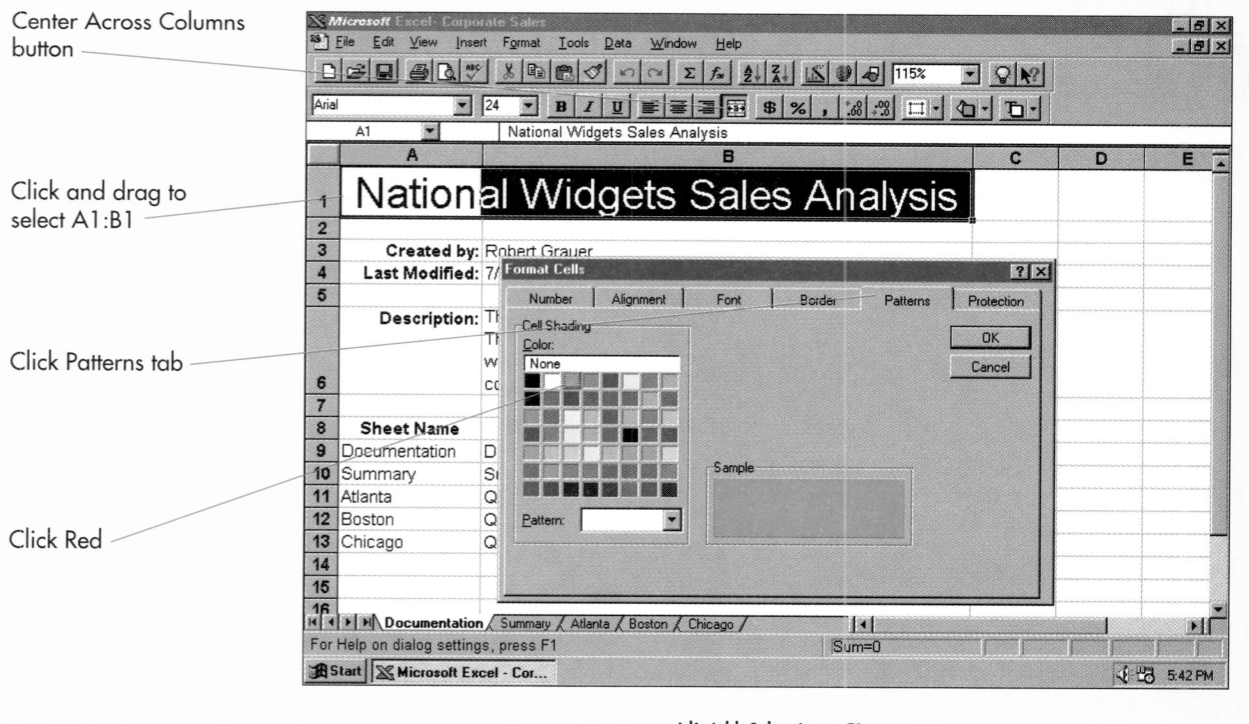

(d) Add Color (step 5)

FIGURE 2.9 Hands-on Exercise 3 (continued)

- Click the **Patterns tab.** Click the **Red** color to shade the selected cells.
- Click the **Font tab.** Click the **drop-down arrow** in the Color list box. Click the **White** color.
- Click **OK** to accept the settings and close the Format Cells dialog box.

➤ Click outside the selected cells to see the effects of the formatting change. You should see white letters on a red background.

➤ Remove the gridlines. Pull down the **Tools menu.** Click **Options.** Click the **View tab** and clear the check box for Gridlines in the Window options area.

➤ Save the workbook.

THE FORMATTING TOOLBAR

Use the Color and Font Color buttons on the Formatting toolbar to change the shading (pattern color) and font color, respectively. Select the cell(s) you wish to format, click the down arrow of the appropriate button to display the palette, then click the desired color.

STEP 6: Exit Excel

➤ Click the **Spelling button** on the Standard toolbar to initiate the spell check. Make corrections as necessary.

➤ You have completed the descriptive worksheet shown earlier in Figure 2.8. Exit Excel if you do not want to continue with the next exercise at this time.

THE SPELL CHECK

Anyone familiar with a word processor takes the spell check for granted, but did you know the same capability exists within Excel? Click the Spelling button on the Standard toolbar to initiate the spell check, then implement corrections just as you do in Microsoft Word. All of the applications in Microsoft Office share the same custom dictionary, so that any words you add to the custom dictionary in one application are automatically recognized in other applications.

LINKING WORKBOOKS

As indicated at the beginning of the chapter, there are in essence two different approaches to combining data from multiple sources. You can store all of the data on separate sheets in a single workbook, then create a summary worksheet within that workbook that references values in the other worksheets. Alternatively, you can retain the source data in separate workbooks, and create a summary workbook to reference those workbooks.

The two approaches are equally valid, and the choice depends on where you want to keep the source data. In general, it's easier to keep all of the data in a single workbook as has been done throughout the chapter. Occasionally, however, it may be impractical to keep all of the data in a single workbook, in which case it becomes necessary to link the individual workbooks to one another.

Linking is established through the creation of ***external references*** that specify a cell (or range of cells) in another workbook. The ***dependent workbook*** (the Corporate Links workbook in our example) contains the external references and thus reflects (is dependent on) data in the source workbook(s). The ***source workbooks*** (the Atlanta, Boston, and Chicago workbooks in our example) contain the data referenced by the dependent workbook.

Figure 2.10 illustrates the use of linking within the context of the example we have been using. The figure resembles figures that have appeared earlier in the chapter, but with subtle differences.

Four different workbooks are open, each with one worksheet. The Corporate Links workbook is the dependent workbook and contains external references to obtain the summary totals. The Atlanta, Boston, and Chicago workbooks are the source workbooks.

Cell B3 is the active cell, and its contents are displayed in the formula bar. The corporate sales for Product 1 in the first quarter are calculated by summing the corresponding values in the source workbooks. Note how the workbook names are enclosed in square brackets to indicate the external references to the Atlanta, Boston, and Chicago workbooks. The precise format of an external reference is as follows:

=[ATLANTA.XLS]Sheet1!B3

- The cell reference (can be relative or absolute)
- The sheet name is followed by an exclamation point
- The name of the source workbook is enclosed in square brackets

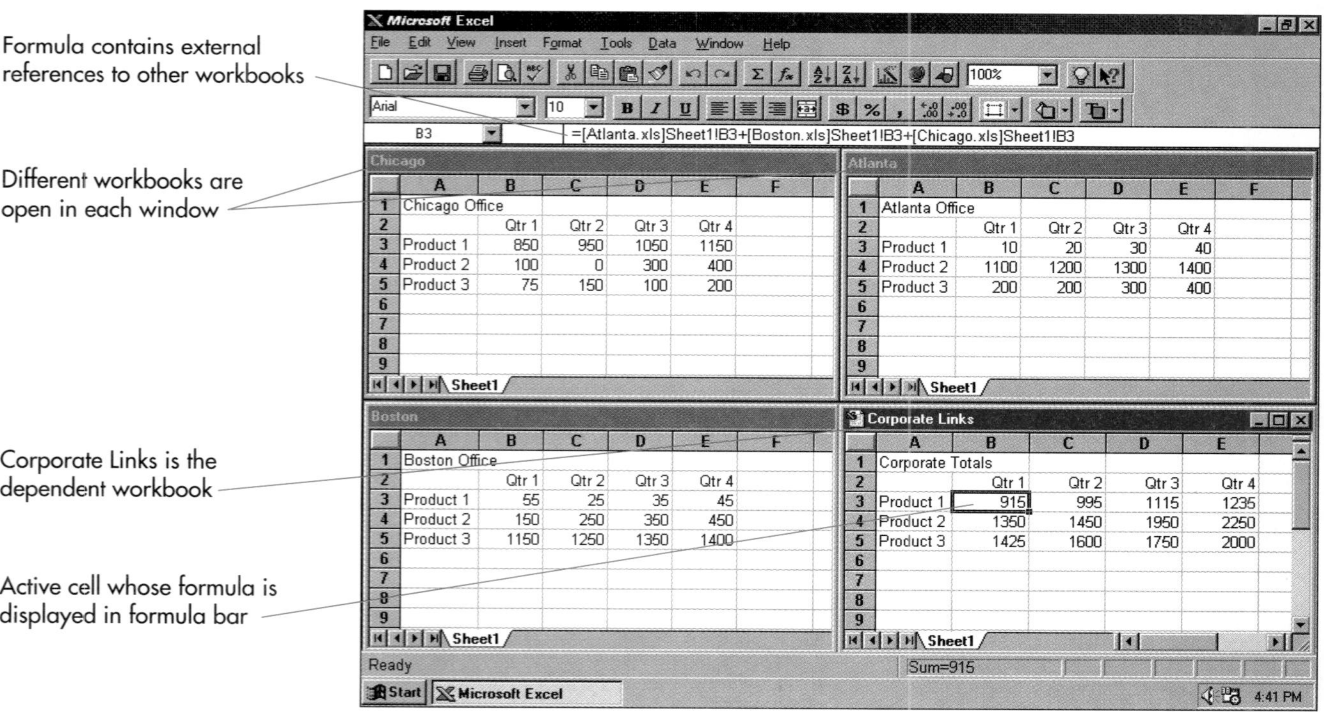

FIGURE 2.10 File Linking

The formulas to compute the corporate totals for Product 1 in the second, third, and fourth quarters contain external references similar to those shown in the formula bar of Figure 2.10. The ***workbook references*** and sheet references are always absolute, whereas the cell reference may be relative (as in this example) or absolute. Once the formula has been entered in cell B3, it may be copied to the remaining cells in this row to compute the totals for Product 1 in the remaining quarters. Cells B3 through E3 may then be copied to rows 4 and 5 to obtain the totals for the other products.

HANDS-ON EXERCISE 4

Linked Workbooks

Objective: Create a dependent workbook with external references to multiple source workbooks; use pointing to create the external reference rather than entering the formula explicitly. Use Figure 2.11 as a guide in the exercise.

STEP 1: Open the Workbooks

- Start Excel. If necessary, click the **New Workbook button** on the Standard toolbar to open a new workbook.
- Delete all worksheets except for Sheet1 as you did in step 1 of the first hands-on exercise. Save the workbook as **Corporate Links** in the **Exploring Excel folder.**
- Pull down the **File menu.** Click **Open** to display the Open dialog box. Click the **Atlanta workbook.** Press and hold the **Ctrl key** as you click the **Boston** and **Chicago workbooks** to select all three workbooks at the same time.
- Click **Open** to open the selected workbooks. The workbooks will be opened one after another with a brief message appearing on the status bar as each workbook is opened.
- Pull down the **Window menu,** which should indicate four open workbooks at the bottom of the menu. Click **Arrange** to display the Arrange Windows dialog box. If necessary, select the **Tile** option, then click **OK.**
- You should see four open workbooks as shown in Figure 2.11a, although the row and column labels have not yet been entered in the Corporate Links workbook. (Do not be concerned if your workbooks are arranged differently.)

STEP 2: The AutoFill Command

- Click in **cell A1** in the **Corporate Links workbook** to make this the active cell in the active workbook. Enter **Corporate Totals** as shown in Figure 2.11a.
- Click **cell B2.** Enter **Qtr 1.** Click in **cell B2,** then point to the fill handle in the lower-right corner. The mouse pointer changes to a thin crosshair.
- Drag the fill handle over **cells C2, D2,** and **E2.** A border appears, to indicate the destination range. Release the mouse. Cells C2 through E2 contain the labels Qtr 2, Qtr 3, and Qtr 4, respectively.
- Right-align the entries in **cells B2** through **E2,** then reduce the column widths so that you can see the entire worksheet in the window.
- Click **cell A3.** Enter **Product 1.** Use the AutoFill capability to enter the labels **Product 2** and **Product 3** in cells A4 and A5.

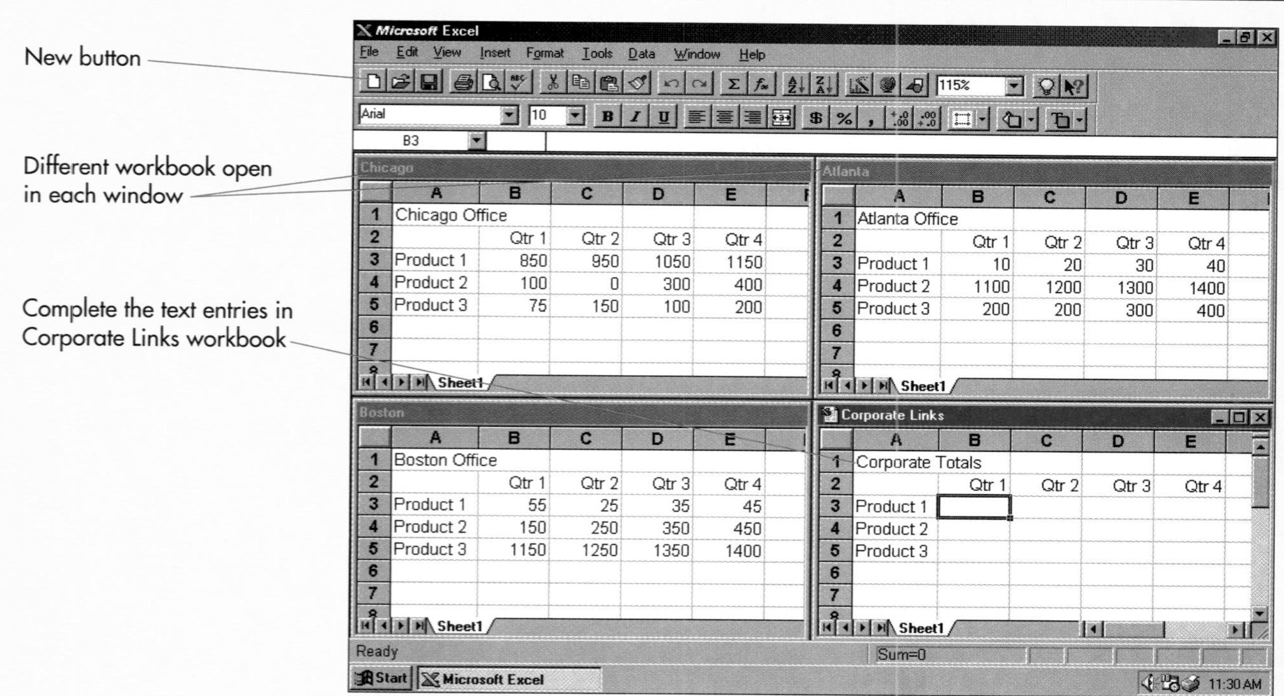

(a) Open the Workbooks (step 2)

FIGURE 2.11 Hands-on Exercise 4

STEP 3: File Linking

➤ Click **cell B3** of the **Corporate Links workbook.** Enter an **equal sign** so that you can create the formula by pointing:

- Click in the window for the **Atlanta workbook.** Click **cell B3.** The formula bar should display =[ATLANTA.XLS]Sheet1!$B$3. Press the **F4 key** continually until the cell reference changes to B3.
- Enter a **plus sign.** Click in the window for the **Boston workbook.** Click **cell B3.** The formula expands to include +[BOSTON.XLS]Sheet1!$B$3. Press the **F4 key** continually until the cell reference changes to B3.
- Enter a **plus sign.** Click in the window for the **Chicago workbook.** Click **cell B3.** The formula expands to include +[CHICAGO.XLS]Sheet1!$B$3. Press the **F4 key** continually until the cell reference changes to B3.

THE F4 KEY

The F4 key cycles through relative, absolute, and mixed addresses. Click on any reference within the formula bar; for example, click on A1 in the formula =A1+A2. Press the F4 key once, and it changes to an absolute reference, $A$1. Press the F4 key a second time, and it becomes a mixed reference, A$1; press it again, and it is a different mixed reference, $A1. Press the F4 key a fourth time, and it returns to the original relative address, A1.

- Press **enter.** The formula is complete, and you should see 915 in cell B3 of the Corporate Links workbook. Click in **cell B3.** The entry on the formula bar should match the entry in Figure 2.11b. Save the workbook.

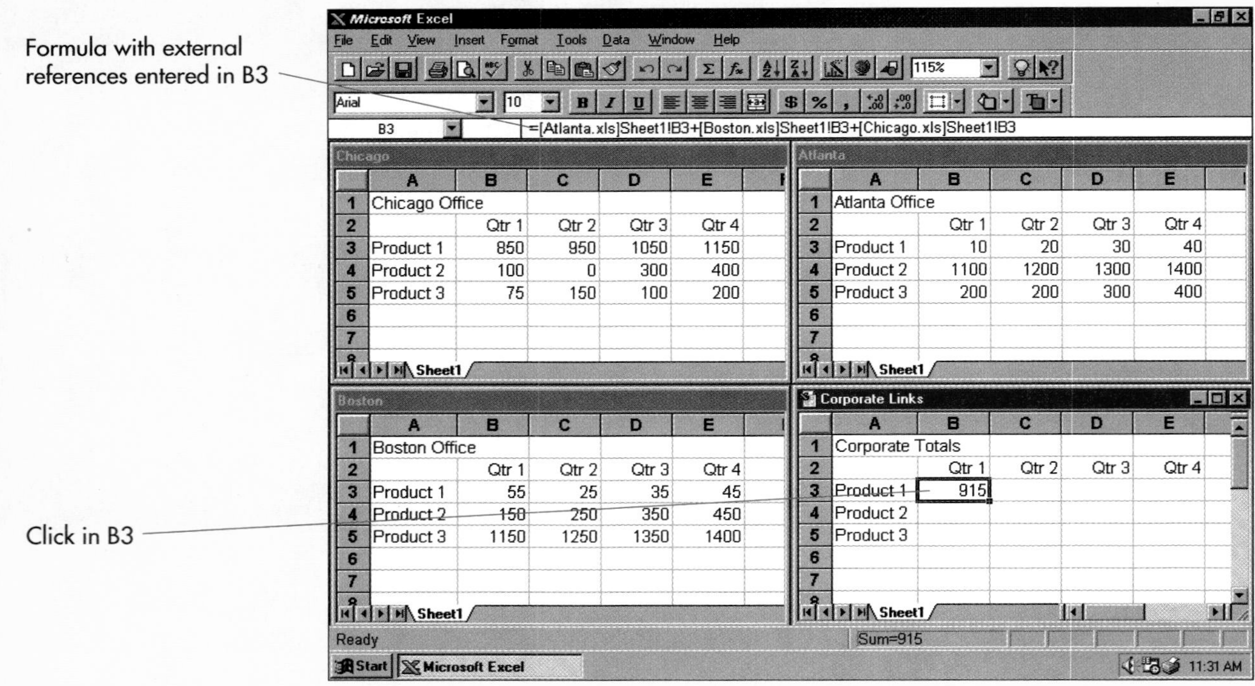

(b) File Linking (step 3)

FIGURE 2.11 Hands-on Exercise 4 (continued)

STEP 4: Copy the Formulas

- If necessary, click **cell B3** in the **Corporate Links workbook,** then drag the fill handle over **cells C3** through **E3** to copy this formula to the remaining cells in row 3.
- Be sure that cells B3 through E3 are still selected, then drag the fill handle to **cell E5.** You should see the total sales for all products in all quarters as shown in Figure 2.11c.
- Click **cell E5** to view the copied formula as shown in the figure. Note that the workbook and sheet references are absolute but that the cell references are relative. Save the workbook.

DRIVE AND FOLDER REFERENCE

An external reference is updated regardless of whether or not the source workbook is open. The reference is displayed differently, however, depending on whether or not the source workbook is open. The references include the path (the drive and folder) if the source workbook is closed; the path is not shown if the source workbook is open.

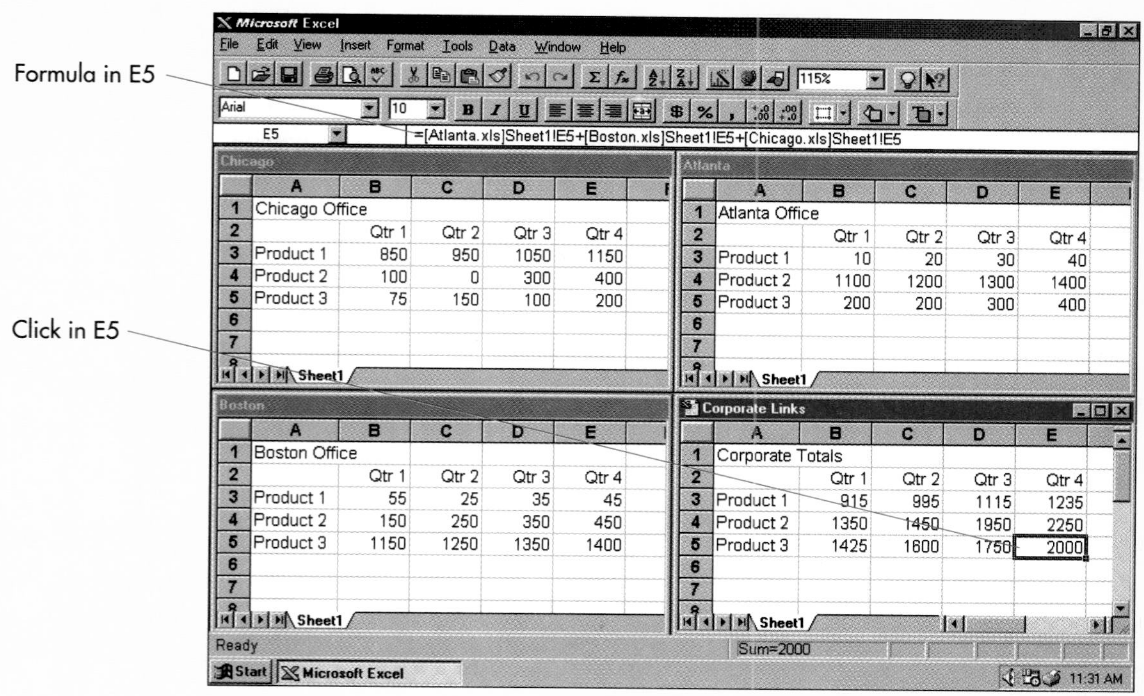

(c) Copy the Formulas (step 4)

FIGURE 2.11 Hands-on Exercise 4 (continued)

STEP 5: Change the Data

- Click **cell B3** to make it the active cell. Note that the value displayed in the cell is 915.
- Pull down the **File menu.** Click **Close.** Answer **Yes** if asked whether to save the changes.
- Click in the window containing the **Chicago workbook,** click **cell B3,** enter **250,** and press **enter.** Pull down the **File menu.** Click **Close.** Answer **Yes** if asked whether to save the changes. Only two workbooks, Atlanta and Boston, are now open.
- Pull down the **File menu** and open the **Corporate Links workbook.** You should see the dialog box in Figure 2.11d, asking whether to re-establish the links. (Note that cell B3 still displays 915). Click **Yes** to re-establish the links.
- The value in cell B3 of the Corporate Links workbook changes to 315 to reflect the change in the Chicago workbook, even though the latter is closed.
- If necessary, click in **cell B3.** The formula bar displays the contents of this cell, which include the drive and folder reference for the Chicago workbook, because the workbook is closed.

STEP 6: Close the Workbooks

- Close the Atlanta and Boston workbooks. Close the Corporate Links workbook. Saving the source workbook(s) before the dependent workbook

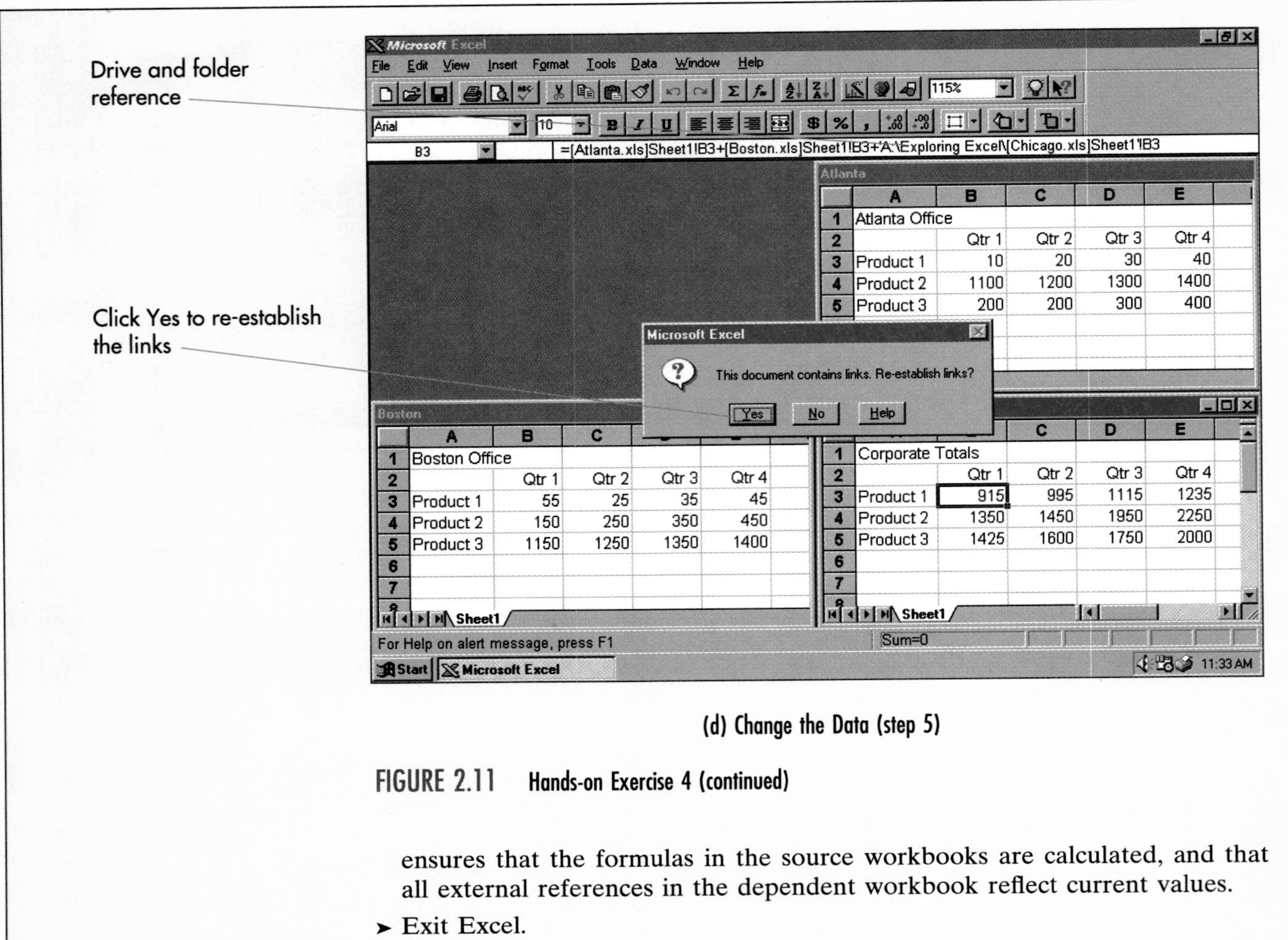

(d) Change the Data (step 5)

FIGURE 2.11 Hands-on Exercise 4 (continued)

ensures that the formulas in the source workbooks are calculated, and that all external references in the dependent workbook reflect current values.

➤ Exit Excel.

SUMMARY

The chapter showed how to combine data from different sources into a summary report. The example is quite common and applicable to any business scenario requiring both detail and summary reports. One approach is to store all of the data in separate sheets of a single workbook, then summarize the data in a summary worksheet within that workbook. Alternatively, the source data can be kept in separate workbooks and analyzed through linking to a summary workbook. Both approaches are valid, and the choice depends on where you want to keep the source data.

An Excel workbook may contain up to 256 worksheets, each of which is identified by a tab at the bottom of the window. Worksheets may be added, deleted, moved, copied, or renamed through a shortcut menu. The highlighted tab indicates the active worksheet.

A worksheet reference is required to indicate a cell in another worksheet of the same workbook. An exclamation point separates the worksheet reference from the cell reference. The worksheet reference is always absolute. The cell reference may be relative or absolute. A 3-D reference is a range that spans two or more worksheets in a workbook.

A workbook should be clearly organized so that the purpose of every worksheet is evident. One way of documenting a workbook is through the creation of a documentation worksheet that describes the purpose of each worksheet within the workbook.

Linking is used when it is impractical to keep all of the data in the same workbook. Linking is established through an external reference that specifies a cell (or range of cells) in a source workbook. The dependent workbook contains the external references and uses (is dependent on) the data in the source workbook(s).

KEY WORDS AND CONCEPTS

3-D reference
Arrange command
AutoSum
Dependent workbook
Documentation worksheet
External reference
Grouping worksheets
Linking
New Window command
Repeat command
Source workbook
Tab scrolling buttons
Tab split box
Workbook reference
Worksheet reference

MULTIPLE CHOICE

1. Which of the following is true regarding workbooks and worksheets?
   (a) A workbook contains one or more worksheets
   (b) Only one worksheet can be selected at a time within a workbook
   (c) Every workbook contains the same number of worksheets
   (d) All of the above
2. Assume that a workbook contains three worksheets. How many cells are included in the function =SUM(Sheet1:Sheet3!A1)?
   (a) Three
   (b) Four
   (c) Twelve
   (d) Twenty-four
3. Assume that a workbook contains three worksheets. How many cells are included in the function =SUM(Sheet1:Sheet3!A1:B4)?
   (a) Three
   (b) Four
   (c) Twelve
   (d) Twenty-four
4. Which of the following is the preferred way to sum the value of cell A1 from three different worksheets?
   (a) =Sheet1!A1+Sheet2!A1+Sheet3!A1
   (b) =SUM(Sheet1:Sheet3!A1)
   (c) Both (a) and (b) are equally good
   (d) Neither (a) nor (b)

5. The reference CIS120!$A$2:
   (a) Is an absolute reference to cell A2 in the CIS120 workbook
   (b) Is a relative reference to cell A2 in the CIS120 workbook
   (c) Is an absolute reference to cell A2 in the CIS120 worksheet
   (d) Is a relative reference to cell A2 in the CIS120 worksheet
6. Assume that Sheet1 is the active worksheet and that cells A2 through A4 are currently selected. What happens if you press and hold the Shift key as you click the tab for Sheet3, then press the Del key?
   (a) Only Sheet1 will be deleted from the workbook
   (b) Only Sheet3 will be deleted from the workbook
   (c) Sheet1, Sheet2, and Sheet3 will be deleted from the workbook
   (d) The contents of cells A2 through A4 will be erased from Sheet1, Sheet2, and Sheet3
7. Which of the following is true about the reference Sheet1:Sheet3!A1:B2?
   (a) The worksheet reference is relative, the cell reference is absolute
   (b) The worksheet reference is absolute, the cell reference is relative
   (c) The worksheet and cell references are both absolute
   (d) The worksheet and cell references are both relative
8. You are in the Ready mode and are positioned in cell B2 of Sheet1. You enter an equal sign, click the worksheet tab for Sheet2, click cell B1, and press enter.
   (a) The content of cell B2 in Sheet1 is =Sheet2!B1
   (b) The content of cell B1 in Sheet2 is = Sheet1!B2
   (c) Both (a) and (b)
   (d) Neither (a) nor (b)
9. You are in the Ready mode and are positioned in cell A10 of Sheet1. You enter an equal sign, click the worksheet tab for the worksheet called This Year, and click cell C10. You then enter a minus sign, click the worksheet tab for the worksheet called LastYear, click cell C10, and press enter. What are the contents of cell A10?
   (a) =ThisYear:LastYear!C10
   (b) =(ThisYear−LastYear)!C10
   (c) =ThisYear!C10-LastYear!C10
   (d) =ThisYear:C10-LastYear:C10
10. Which of the following can be accessed from a shortcut menu?
    (a) Inserting or deleting a worksheet
    (b) Moving or copying a worksheet
    (c) Renaming a worksheet
    (d) All of the above
11. The Arrange Windows command can display:
    (a) Multiple worksheets from one workbook
    (b) One worksheet from multiple workbooks
    (c) Both (a) and (b)
    (d) Neither (a) nor (b)
12. Pointing can be used to reference a cell in:
    (a) A different worksheet
    (b) A different workbook

(c) Both (a) and (b)
(d) Neither (a) nor (b)

13. The appearance of [Group] within the title bar indicates that:
(a) Multiple workbooks are open and are all active
(b) Multiple worksheets are selected within the same workbook
(c) Both (a) and (b)
(d) Neither (a) nor (b)

14. You are in the Ready mode and are positioned in cell A1 of Sheet1 of Book1. You enter an equal sign, click in the open window for Book2, click the tab for Sheet1, click cell A1, then press the F4 key continually until you have a relative cell reference. What reference appears in the formula bar?
(a) =[BOOK1.XLS]Sheet1!$A$1
(b) =[BOOK1.XLS]Sheet1!A1
(c) =[BOOK2.XLS]Sheet1!$A$1
(d) =[BOOK2.XLS]Sheet1!A1

15. Which of the following is true regarding the example on file linking that was developed in the chapter?
(a) The Atlanta, Boston, and Chicago workbooks were dependent workbooks
(b) The Linked workbook was a source workbook
(c) Both (a) and (b)
(d) Neither (a) nor (b)

ANSWERS

1. a	**6.** d	**11.** c
2. a	**7.** b	**12.** c
3. d	**8.** a	**13.** b
4. b	**9.** c	**14.** d
5. c	**10.** d	**15.** d

EXPLORING MICROSOFT EXCEL 7.0

1. Use Figure 2.12 to match each action with its result; a given action may be used more than once or not at all.

Action		Result
a. Click at 2; enter =; click at B3 in the Atlanta sheet; enter +; click at B3 in the Boston sheet; enter +; click at B3 in the Chicago sheet; press enter	_____	Display the Chicago sheet in the lower-right window
	_____	Select all four sheets in upper-left window
	_____	Close the upper-left window
	_____	Change the name of the Sheet1 tab to Corporate Summary
b. Click at 3	_____	Change the size of the selected text in the Summary sheet

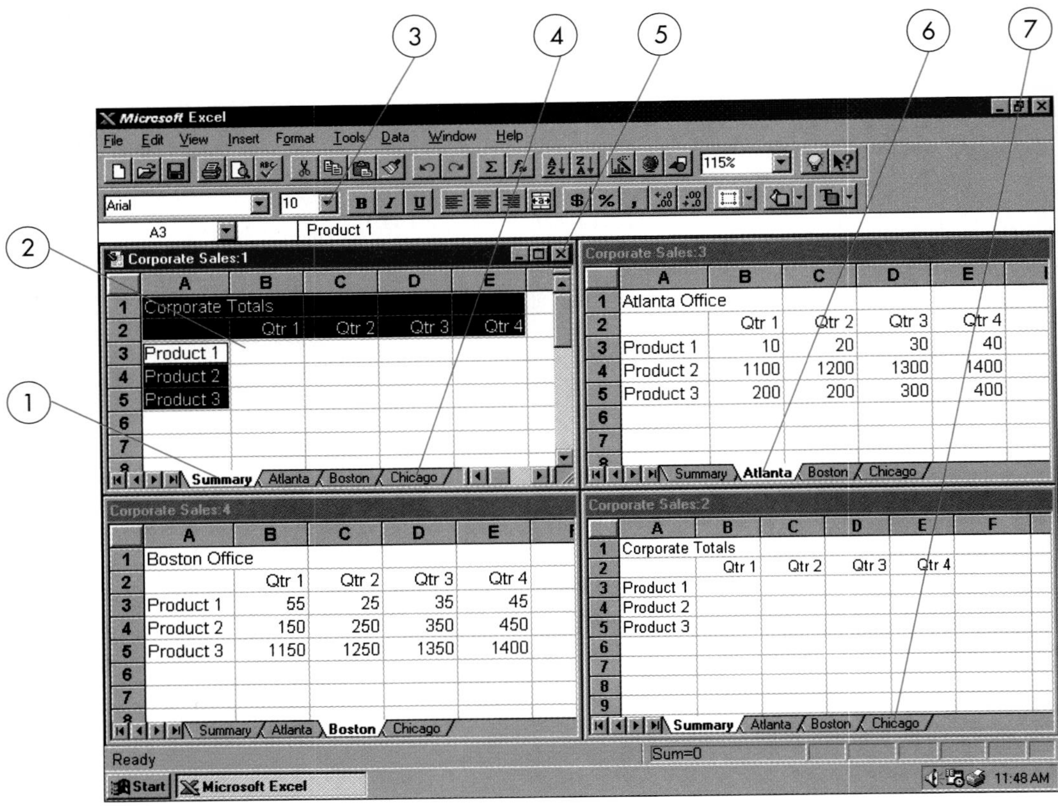

FIGURE 2.12 Screen for Problem 1

Action		Result
c. Click at 1, press the Shift key as you click at 4	_____	Change the size of the selected text in all four sheets
d. Click and drag at 6	_____	Move the Atlanta sheet to the right of the Boston sheet
e. Press the Ctrl key as you click and drag at 6	_____	Copy the Atlanta sheet so that it appears to the right of the Boston sheet
f. Click at 7	_____	Delete the Summary sheet
g. Double click at 1	_____	Enter the formula to determine the total sales for Product 1 in the first Quarter
h. Click at 5		
i. Click at 1, press the Shift key as you click at 4, then click at 3		
j. Point to 1, click the right mouse button, and click Delete		

2. Answer the following with respect to the formula:

   =Sheet1!C10+Sheet2!C10+Sheet3!C10

   versus the function:

   =SUM(Sheet1:Sheet3!C10)

   a. Which entry (the formula, function, or both) contains a relative cell reference? An absolute worksheet reference?

b. How many cells are included in the computation for the formula? In the computation for the function?

c. Assume that a new worksheet is inserted between Sheet1 and Sheet3. Will the computed value of the formula change? Will the computed value of the function change?

d. Assume that Sheet2 is deleted. Which entry (the formula, function, or both) will return an error?

3. Figure 2.13 displays a workbook containing worksheets for individual stores as well as a summary worksheet with totals for all stores.

a. What is the name of the workbook displayed in the figure? How many worksheets does it contain?

b. What was the gross profit for the Downtown store in the first quarter? For the Midtown store in the second quarter? For the Uptown store in the third quarter?

c. Assume that the sales in the first quarter for the Downtown store are changed to $109,500. Which other value(s) will change within the Downtown worksheet? Within the All Stores Worksheet?

d. Which worksheet is active? What is the active cell in that worksheet? What are its contents?

e. What formula (function) would you expect to find in cell B10 of the Uptown worksheet? of the Midtown worksheet?

f. What formula (function) would you expect to find in cell B3 in the All Stores worksheet? in cell B4 in the All Stores worksheet? in cell B5 in the All Stores worksheet?

g. Which formula (function) would you expect to find in cell B7 of the All Stores worksheet, given that the formula (function) references only cells within the All Stores worksheet?

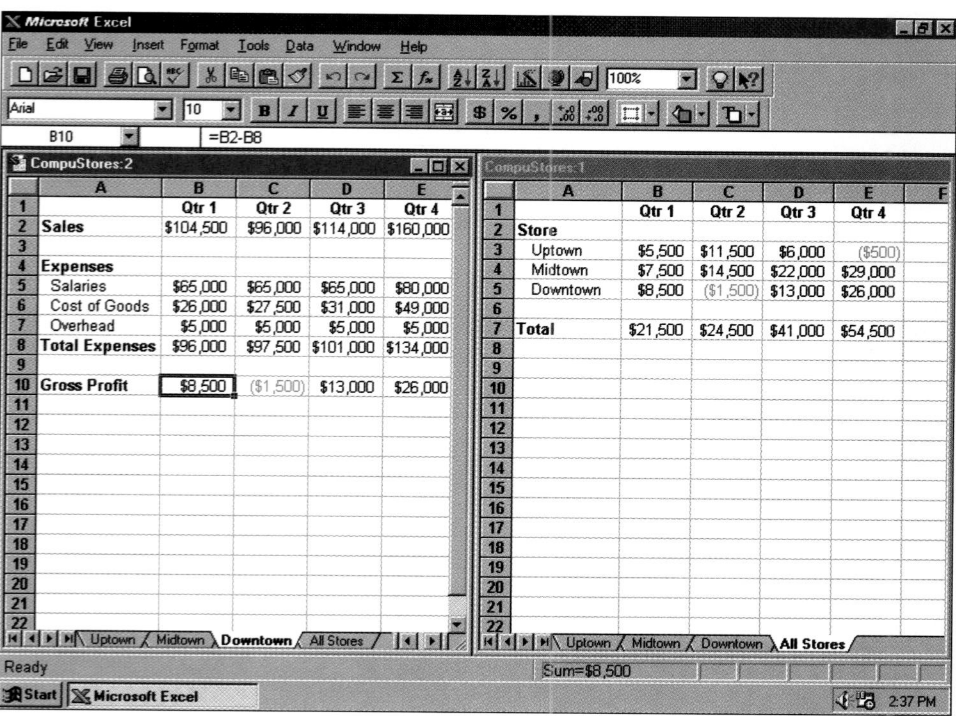

FIGURE 2.13 Screen for Problem 3

4. Answer the following with respect to the workbook(s) shown in Figure 2.14:
   a. How many workbooks are open in Figure 2.14?
   b. Which workbook is the source workbook? Which workbook is the dependent workbook?
   c. Which workbook contains an external reference?
   d. What is the active workbook? What is the active worksheet in this workbook? What is the active cell?
   e. What are the contents of the formula bar? Why are the drive and folder shown for the San Diego workbook, but not for the Miami workbook?

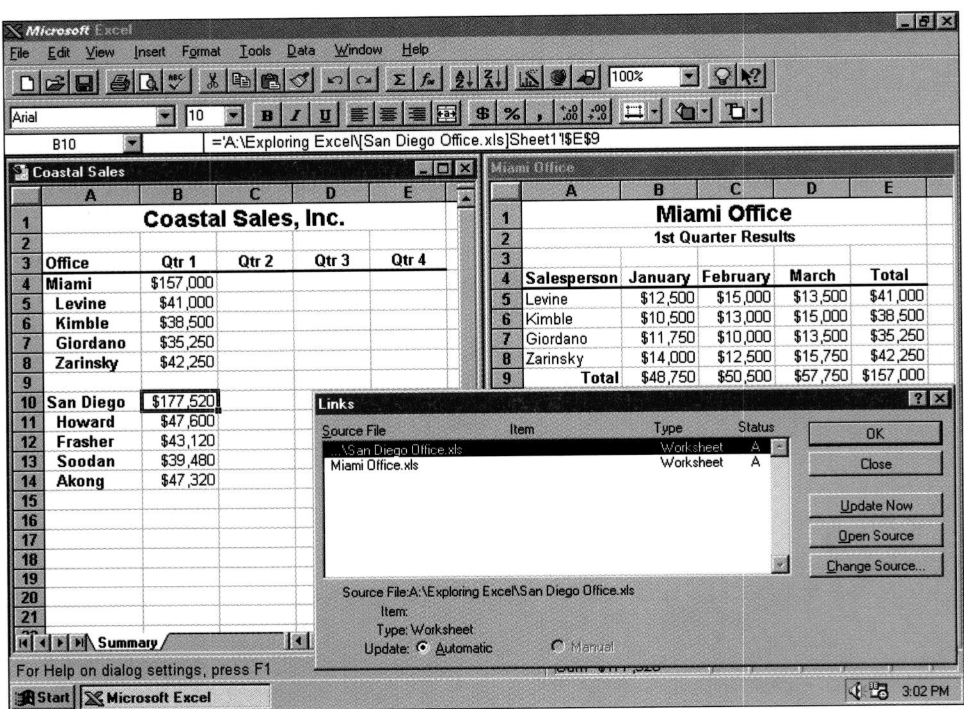

FIGURE 2.14 Screen for Problem 4

PRACTICE WITH MICROSOFT EXCEL 7.0

1. A partially completed version of the workbook in Figure 2.15 can be found on the data disk as *Volume II Chapter 2 Practice 1.* This workbook contains worksheets for the individual sections but does not contain the summary worksheet.
   a. Retrieve the *Volume II Chapter 2 Practice 1* workbook from the data disk, then open multiple windows so that the display on your monitor matches Figure 2.15.
   b. Complete the individual worksheets by adding the appropriate formulas (functions) to compute the class average on each test.
   c. Add a summary worksheet that includes the test averages from each of the sections as shown in the figure.

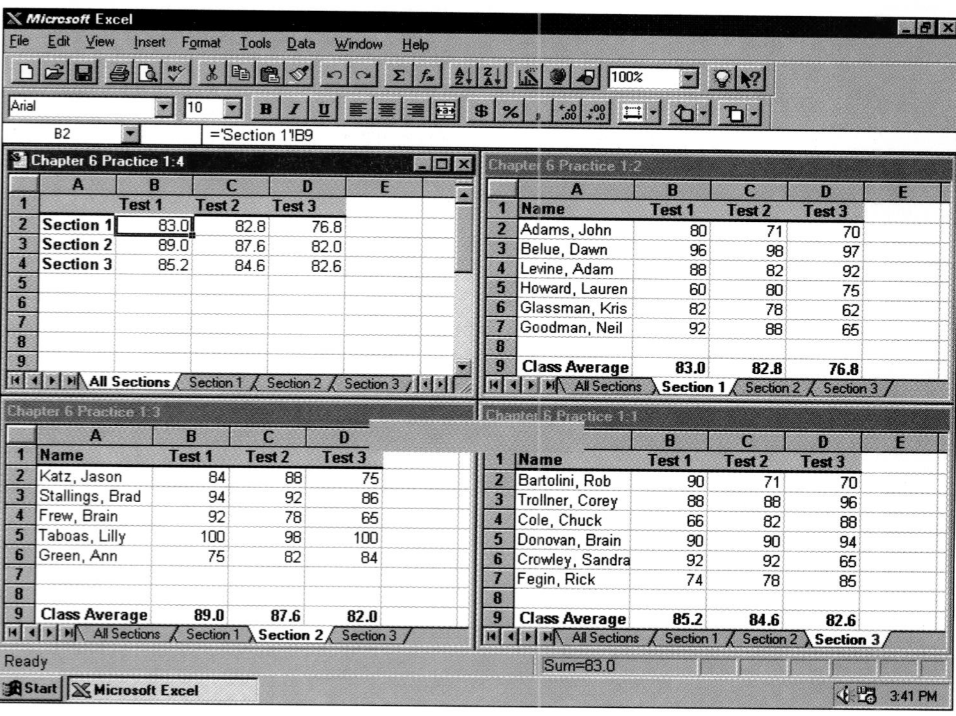

FIGURE 2.15 Screen for Practice Exercise 1

d. Add a documentation worksheet that includes your name as the grading assistant, the date of modification, and lists all of the worksheets in the workbook.

e. Print the entire workbook and submit it to your instructor.

2. A partially completed version of the workbook in Figure 2.16 can be found on the data disk as *Volume II Chapter 2 Practice 2.* The workbook contains a separate worksheet for each month of the year as well as a summary worksheet for the entire year. Thus far, only the months of January, February, and March are complete. Each monthly worksheet tallies the expenses for five departments in each of four categories to compute a monthly total for each department. The summary worksheet displays the total expense for each department.

a. Retrieve the *Volume II Chapter 2 Practice 2* workbook from the data disk, then open multiple windows so that the display on your monitor matches Figure 2.16.

b. Use the Group Editing feature to select the worksheets for January, February, and March simultaneously. Enter the formula to compute the monthly total for each department in each month.

c. Use the Group Editing feature to format the worksheets.

d. Enter the appropriate formulas in the summary worksheet to compute the year-to-date totals for each department.

e. Add an additional worksheet for the month of April. Assume that department 1 spends $100 in each category, department 2 spends $200 in each category, and so on. Update the summary worksheet to include the expenses for April.

f. Add a documentation worksheet that includes your name, the date of modification, plus a description of each worksheet within the workbook.

g. Print the entire workbook (all five worksheets), then print the cell formulas for the summary worksheet only.

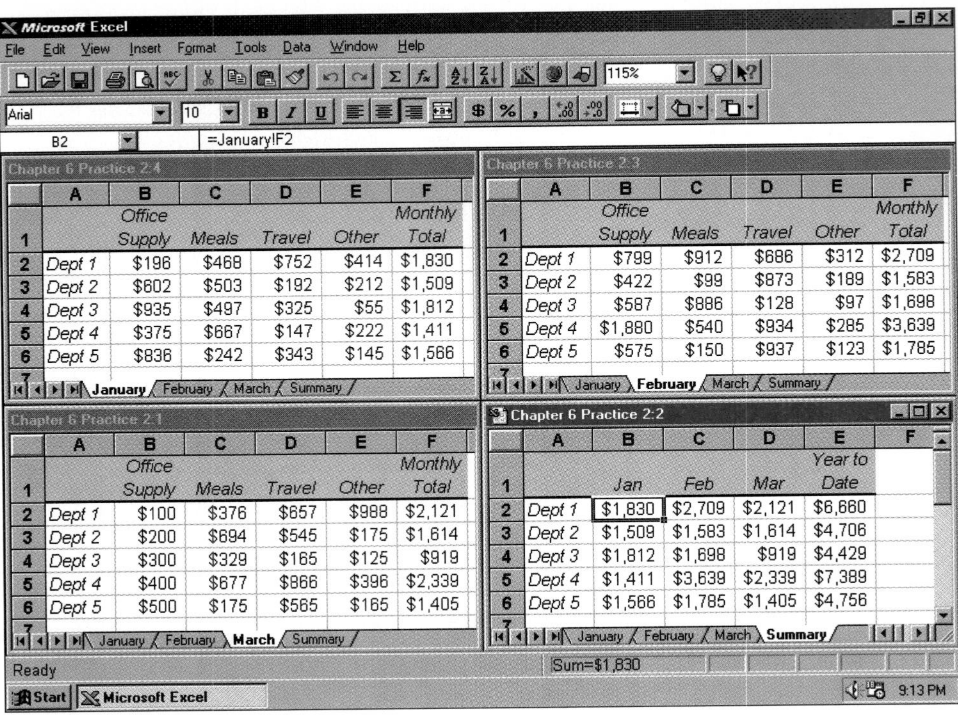

FIGURE 2.16 Screen for Practice Exercise 2

3. Object Linking and Embedding: Create the compound document in Figure 2.17, which consists of a memo, summary worksheet, and three-dimensional chart. The chart is to be created in its own chart sheet within the Corporate Sales workbook, then incorporated into the memo. Address the memo to your instructor, sign your name, then print the memo as it appears in Figure 2.17.

Prove to yourself that Object Linking and Embedding really works by returning to the Atlanta worksheet *after* you have created the document in Figure 2.17. Change the sales for Product 2 in Quarter 4 to $3,000. Switch back to the Word memo, and the chart should reflect the dramatic increase in the sales for Product 1. Add a postscript to the memo, indicating that the corrected chart reflects the last-minute sale of Product 1 in Atlanta. Print the revised memo and submit it to your instructor with the earlier version.

4. Figure 2.18 on page 96 contains a pivot table that was created from the Corporate Sales workbook used throughout the chapter. The pivot table was created *without* the benefit of a list (as was done in Chapter 1) by specifying multiple consolidation ranges. Do Hands-on Exercises 1, 2, and 3 as they appear in this chapter. Review the material on pivot tables from Chapter 1, then follow the steps below to create the pivot table in its own worksheet within the Corporate Sales workbook.
   a. Pull down the Data menu and click the Pivot Table command. Click the option button to select Multiple Consolidation Ranges in step 1 of the Pivot Table Wizard. Click Next.
   b. Click the option button to create a single-page field for me in step 2. Click Next.

National Widgets, Inc.

Atlanta • Boston • Chicago

To: John Graves, President
National Widgets, Inc.

From: Susan Powers
Vice President, Marketing

Subject: Sales Analysis Data

Our overall fourth quarter sales have improved considerably over those in the first quarter. Please note, however, that Product 1, despite a growth in sales, is still trailing the others, and discontinuing its production should be considered. I will await your reply on this matter.

Corporate Totals					
	Qtr 1	Qtr 2	Qtr 3	Qtr 4	Totals
Product 1	$915	$995	$1,115	$1,235	$4,260
Product 2	$1,350	$1,450	$1,950	$2,250	$7,000
Product 3	$1,425	$1,600	$1,750	$2,000	$6,775
Total	$3,690	$4,045	$4,815	$5,485	$18,035

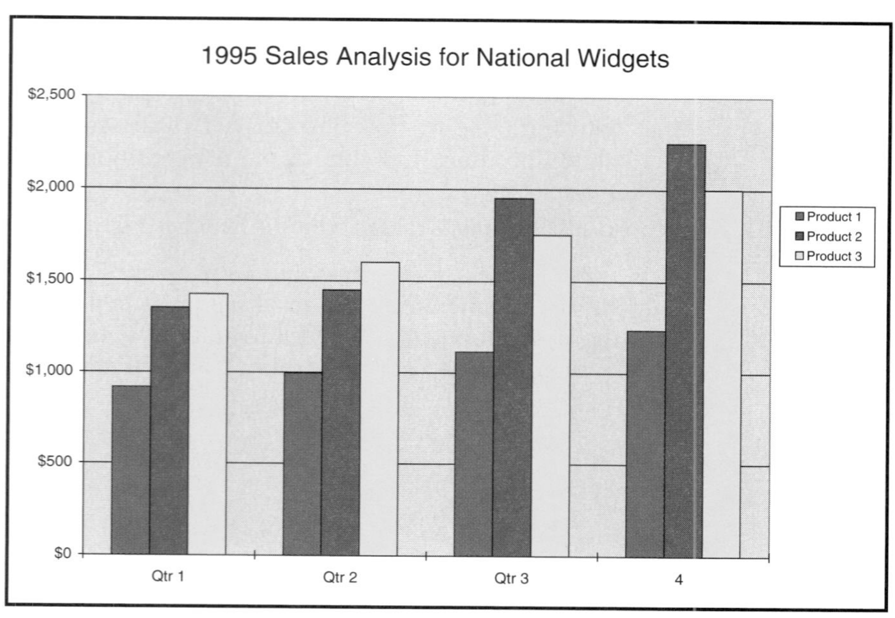

FIGURE 2.17 Memo for Practice Exercise 3

Sum of Amount		Product			
Quarter	City	Product 1	Product 2	Product 3	Grand Total
Qtr 1	Atlanta	$10	$1,100	$200	$1,310
	Boston	$55	$150	$1,150	$1,355
	Chicago	$850	$100	$75	$1,025
Qtr 1 Total		$915	$1,350	$1,425	$3,690
Qtr 2	Atlanta	$20	$1,200	$200	$1,420
	Boston	$25	$250	$1,250	$1,525
	Chicago	$950	$0	$150	$1,100
Qtr 2 Total		$995	$1,450	$1,600	$4,045
Qtr 3	Atlanta	$30	$1,300	$300	$1,630
	Boston	$35	$350	$1,350	$1,735
	Chicago	$1,050	$300	$100	$1,450
Qtr 3 Total		$1,115	$1,950	$1,750	$4,815
Qtr 4	Atlanta	$40	$1,400	$400	$1,840
	Boston	$45	$450	$1,400	$1,895
	Chicago	$1,150	$400	$200	$1,750
Qtr 4 Total		$1,235	$2,250	$2,000	$5,485
Grand Total		$4,260	$7,000	$6,775	$18,035

FIGURE 2.18 **Pivot Table for Practice Exercise 4**

c. Specify the range in step 3 of the PivotTable wizard through pointing. Click the Sheet tab for Atlanta, select cells A2 through E5, then click the Add command button. You should see Atlanta!$A$2:$E$5 in the Range box. Repeat this step for the other two cities. You should see the same range for Atlanta, Boston, and Chicago.
d. Click the Finish command button to create the pivot table.
e. Edit the pivot table so that it matches Figure 2.18. Click in cell B3 (the field name is Column), then click the formula bar and enter Quarter. Change the entry in cell A4 from Row to Product in similar fashion. Change the entry in cell A1 from Page to City.
f. Click in cell B1, click the drop-down arrow, select Item1, click the formula bar, and enter Atlanta. Click OK when asked to rename Item1 to Atlanta. Repeat these steps to replace Items 2 and 3 with Boston and Chicago, respectively.
g. Pivot the table by dragging Quarter to the row position, Product to the column position, and City to the row position below and to the right of Quarter.
h. Format the pivot table so that it matches Figure 2.18. Save the workbook.

The process seems long, but with practice, it's done rather easily, and the flexibility inherent in the resulting pivot table is worth the effort. Modify the description on the Documentation worksheet to include the pivot table, then print the entire workbook and submit it to your instructor.

Urban Sophisticates

The *Urban Sophisticates* workbook on the data disk is only partially complete as it contains worksheets for individual stores, but does not as yet have a summary worksheet. Your job is to retrieve the workbook and create a summary worksheet, then use the summary worksheet as the basis of a three-dimensional column chart reflecting the sales for the past year. Add a documentation worksheet containing your name as financial analyst, then print the entire workbook and submit it to your instructor.

External References

As marketing manager you are responsible for consolidating the sales information for all of the branch offices within the corporation. Each branch manager creates an identically formatted workbook with the sales information for his or her branch office. Your job is to consolidate the information into a single table, then graph the results appropriately. The branch data is to remain in the individual workbooks; that is, the formulas in your workbook are to contain external references to the *Eastern, Western,* and *Foreign workbooks* on the data disk. Your workbook is to be developed in such a way that any change in the individual workbooks should be automatically reflected in the consolidated workbook.

Pivot Tables

What advantages, if any, does a pivot table have over a conventional worksheet with respect to analyzing and consolidating data from multiple sources? What are the disadvantages? Does the underlying data have to be entered in the form of a list, or can it be taken directly from a worksheet? Use what you learn to extend the analysis of the Atlanta, Boston, and Chicago data that appeared throughout the chapter. (See practice exercise 4 for one example of a pivot table.)

The Spreadsheet Audit

Which tools are found on the Auditing toolbar? What is the difference between precedent and dependent cells? Can the Auditing toolbar detect precedent cells that are located in a different worksheet? In a different workbook? The answers to these and other questions can be found by studying Appendix A, then experimenting on your own. A spreadsheet audit is an important concept and one with which you should become familiar.

3

AUTOMATING REPETITIVE TASKS: MACROS AND VISUAL BASIC

OBJECTIVES

After reading this chapter you will be able to:

1. Define a macro; explain how macros facilitate the execution of repetitive tasks.
2. Record and run a macro; view and edit the statements in a simple macro.
3. Use the InputBox statement to obtain input for a macro as it is running.
4. Use a keyboard shortcut and/or a customized toolbar to run a macro; create a custom button to execute a macro.
5. Describe where macros are stored; explain the function of the Personal Macro workbook.
6. Use the Step mode to execute a macro one statement at a time.
7. Use the Copy and Paste commands to duplicate an existing macro; modify the copied macro to create an entirely new macro.
8. Use the Visual Basic If and Do statements to implement decision making and looping within an Excel macro.

OVERVIEW

Have you ever pulled down the same menus and clicked the same sequence of commands over and over? Easy as the commands may be to execute, it is still burdensome to have to continually repeat the same mouse clicks or keystrokes. If you can think of any task that you do repeatedly, whether in one workbook or in a series of workbooks, you are a perfect candidate to use macros.

A ***macro*** is a set of instructions that tells Excel which commands to execute. It is in essence a program, and its instructions are written in Visual Basic, a programming language. Fortunately, however, you don't have to be a programmer to write macros. Instead, you use the macro recorder within Excel to record your commands, and let Excel write the macros for you.

This chapter introduces you to the power of Excel macros. We begin by creating a simple macro to insert your name, class, and date into a worksheet. We show you how to modify the macro once it has been created and how to execute the macro one statement at a time. We also show you how to store the macro in the Personal Macro workbook, so that it will be available automatically whenever you start Excel.

The second half of the chapter describes how to create more powerful macros that automate commands associated with list management, as presented in Chapter 1. We show you how to copy and edit a macro, and how to create customized buttons with which to execute a macro. We also show you how the power of an Excel macro can be extended through the inclusion of additional Visual Basic statements that implement loops and decision making.

VISUAL BASIC

Visual Basic is a powerful programming language that can be used to develop all types of applications. It may appear intimidating at first, but it is quite easy to learn once you understand its overall structure. We believe the best introduction to Visual Basic is to use the macro recorder in Excel to create simple macros, which are in fact complete programs in Visual Basic. You get results that are immediately usable and can learn a good deal about Visual Basic through observation and intuition.

INTRODUCTION TO MACROS

The ***macro recorder*** stores Excel commands, in the form of Visual Basic instructions, on a ***macro sheet*** within a workbook. To use the recorder, you pull down the Tools menu and click the Record Macro command. From that point on (until you stop recording), every command you execute will be stored by the recorder. It doesn't matter whether you execute commands from pull-down menus via the mouse, or whether you use the toolbar or keyboard shortcuts. The macro recorder captures every action you take and stores the equivalent Visual Basic statements in a macro within the workbook.

Once the macro has been created, you can run (execute) the macro at a later time. Sure, you spend time creating the macro, but once this has been accomplished, you have the macro forever, and can run it whenever you need it. The more powerful the macro, the more time it will save you.

Figure 3.1 contains a simple macro to enter your name and class in cells A1 and A2 of the active worksheet. The macro is a ***Visual Basic*** program and consists of statements that were created through the macro recorder. We don't expect you to be able to write the Visual Basic program yourself, but you don't have to. You just invoke the recorder and let it capture the keystrokes for you. We think it important, however, for you to understand the macro, and so we proceed to explain its statements. As you read our discussion, do not be concerned with the precise syntax of every statement, but try to get an overall appreciation for what the statements do.

The first several statements begin with an apostrophe and are known as ***comments.*** (Comments appear in green on a color monitor, but it is the apostrophe that is significant rather than the color of the statement.) Comments provide documentation about a macro but do not affect its execution; that is, the results of

Comments begin with an apostrophe

Sub statement begins the executable part of the macro and contains its name

Last macro statement

```
'
' NameAndCourse Macro
' Macro recorded 8/6/95 by Darren Krein
'
' Keyboard Shortcut: Ctrl+n
'
Sub NameAndCourse()
    Range("A1").Select
    ActiveCell.FormulaR1C1 = "Darren Krein"
    Range("A2").Select
    ActiveCell.FormulaR1C1 = "CIS 622"
    Range("A1:A2").Select
    Selection.Font.Bold = True
    Selection.Font.Italic = True
    With Selection.Font
        .Name = "Arial"
        .Size = 12
    End With
    Range("A3").Select
End Sub
```

FIGURE 3.1 A Simple Macro

the macro are the same, whether or not the comments are included. Comments are inserted automatically by the recorder to document the macro name, its author, and shortcut key (if any). You can add additional comments (a comment line must begin with an apostrophe), or delete or modify existing comments, as you see fit.

The executable portion of a macro begins and ends with the Sub and End Sub statements, respectively. The ***Sub statement*** contains the name of the macro—for example, NameAndCourse in Figure 3.1. (Spaces are not allowed in a macro name.) The ***End Sub statement*** is physically the last statement and indicates the end of the macro. Sub and End Sub are Visual Basic key words and appear in blue.

Each instruction in a macro is a Visual Basic statement that corresponds to commands in Excel; for example, the statements

Range ("A1").Select
and ActiveCell.FormulaR1C1 = "Darren Krein"

select cell A1 as the active cell, then enter the text "Darren Krein" into the active cell. These statements are equivalent to clicking in cell A1 of a worksheet, typing the indicated entry into the active cell, then pressing the enter key (or an arrow key) to complete the entry. In similar fashion, the statements

Range ("A2").Select
and ActiveCell.FormulaR1C1 = "CIS622"

select cell A2 as the active cell, then enter the text entry "CIS622" into that cell. The concept of select-then-do applies equally well to statements within a macro. Thus, the statements

Range ("A1:A2").Select
Selection.Font.Bold = True
Selection.Font.Italic = True

select cells A1 through A2, then change the font for the selected cells to bold italic. The ***With statement*** enables you to perform multiple actions on the same object.

All commands between the With and corresponding ***End With statements*** are executed collectively; for example, the statements

```
With Selection.Font
    .Name = "Arial"
    .Size = 12
End With
```

change the formatting of the selected cells (A1:A2) to 12 point Arial. The statements are equivalent to selecting cells A1 and A2, selecting Arial as the typeface, then specifying 12 point type. The last statement in the macro, Range ("A3").Select, deselects all other cells, a practice we use throughout the chapter.

As we have already indicated, you are not expected to be able to write the Visual Basic statements from scratch, but you should be able to understand the statements once they have been recorded. Moreover, you can edit the macro (after it has been recorded) to change the selected cells and/or their values. You can also change the typeface, point size, or style, simply by changing the appropriate statement in the macro.

PLAN AHEAD

The macro recorder records everything you do, including entries that are made by mistake or commands that are executed incorrectly. Plan the macro in advance, before you begin recording. Write down what you intend to do, then try out the commands with the recorder off. Be sure you go all the way through the intended sequence of operations prior to turning the macro recorder on.

HANDS-ON EXERCISE 1

Introduction to Macros

Objective: Record, run, view, and edit a simple macro; establish a keyboard shortcut to run a macro. Use Figure 3.2 as a guide in the exercise.

STEP 1: Open a New Workbook

➤ Start Excel. Open a new workbook if one is not already open.

➤ Delete all worksheets except for Sheet1:

- Click the tab for **Sheet2.** Click the **►| scrolling button** to scroll to the last worksheet in the workbook (Sheet16 is the default).
- Press the **Shift key** as you click the tab for **Sheet16.** (Sheets 2 through 16 should be selected.)
- Point to the tab for **Sheet16** and click the **right mouse button** to display a shortcut menu. Click **Delete.** Click **OK** in response to the warning that the selected sheets will be permanently deleted.

➤ Your workbook should contain only Sheet1 as shown in Figure 3.2a. Save the workbook as **My Macros** in the **Exploring Excel folder.**

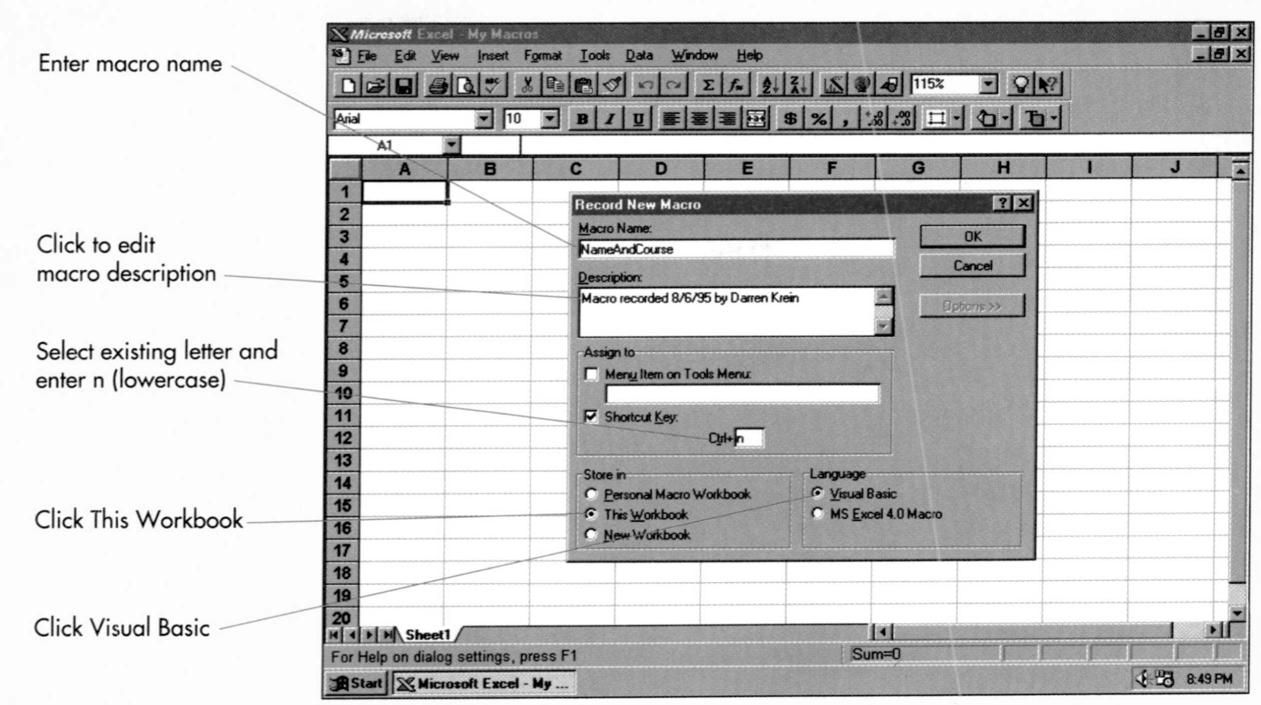

(a) Set the Macro Options (step 2)

FIGURE 3.2 Hands-on Exercise 1

STEP 2: Set the Macro Options

- Pull down the **Tools menu,** click (or point to) the **Record Macro command,** then click **Record New Macro.**
- You will see the Record New Macro dialog box in Figure 3.2a. Only the Macro Name and Description text boxes are visible at this time.
- Enter **NameAndCourse** as the name of the macro. Do not leave any spaces in the macro name.
- The description is entered automatically and contains today's date and the name of the person in whose name this copy of Excel is registered. If necessary, change the description to include your name.
- Click the **Options command button** to display additional options within the Record New Macro dialog box as shown in Figure 3.2a:
  - Check the **Shortcut Key check box,** click in the Shortcut key text box, then delete (or select) the existing shortcut (the letter e).
  - Enter a **lowercase n** as shown in Figure 3.2a. Ctrl+n should appear as the shortcut. (If you see Ctrl+Shift+N it means you typed an uppercase "N" rather than a lowercase letter; correct the entry to a lowercase n.)
  - Check that the options buttons for **This Workbook** and **Visual Basic** have been selected.
- Click **OK** to begin recording the macro. The Stop Macro button appears on the screen.
- Pull down the **Tools menu** a second time and click (or point to) the **Record Macro command:**

- If there is a check next to Use Relative References, click the command to toggle it off. (Relative references are explained on page 113.)
- If Use Relative References does not have a check, click outside the menu to close it.

> **THE PERSONAL MACRO WORKBOOK**
>
> Macros are stored in one of two places: either on a module sheet in the current workbook or in a Personal Macro workbook. The latter is intended for generic macros that you want to use with many workbooks and is discussed in detail, beginning on page 115.

STEP 3: Record the Macro

➤ You should be in Sheet1, ready to record, as shown in Figure 3.2b. A macro sheet (Module1) has been added to the workbook, and the status bar indicates that you are recording the macro:

- Click in **cell A1** even if it is already selected. Enter your name.
- Click in **cell A2.** Enter the course you are taking.
- Click and drag to select **cells A1** through **A2.** Click the **Bold button.** Click the **Italic button.**

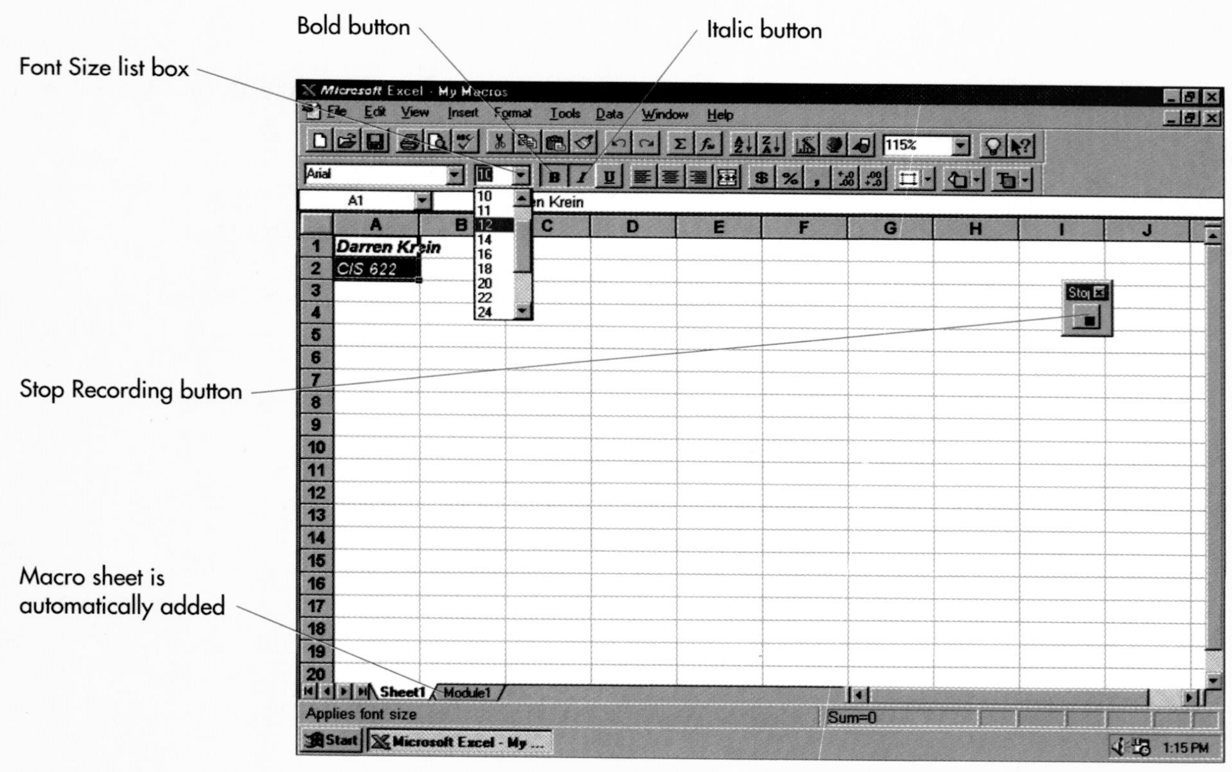

(b) Record the Macro (step 3)

FIGURE 3.2 Hands-on Exercise 1 (continued)

- Click the **arrow** on the **Font Size** list box. Click **12** to change the point size.
- Click in **cell A3** to deselect all other cells prior to ending the macro.

➤ Click the **Stop Recording button** to end the macro. The macro has been recorded on its own worksheet named Module1.

➤ Save the workbook.

THE END RESULT

The macro recorder records only the result of the selection process, with no indication of how the selection was arrived at. It doesn't matter how you get to a particular cell. You can click in the cell directly, use the Go To command in the Edit menu, or use the mouse or arrow keys. The end result is the same, and the macro indicates only the selected cell(s).

STEP 4: Run the Macro

➤ To run (test) the macro, you have to remove the contents and formatting from cells A1 and A2. Click and drag to select **cells A1** through **A2.**

➤ Pull down the **Edit menu.** Click **Clear.** Click **All** from the cascaded menu to erase both the contents and formatting from the selected cells. Cells A1 through A2 are empty as shown in Figure 3.2c.

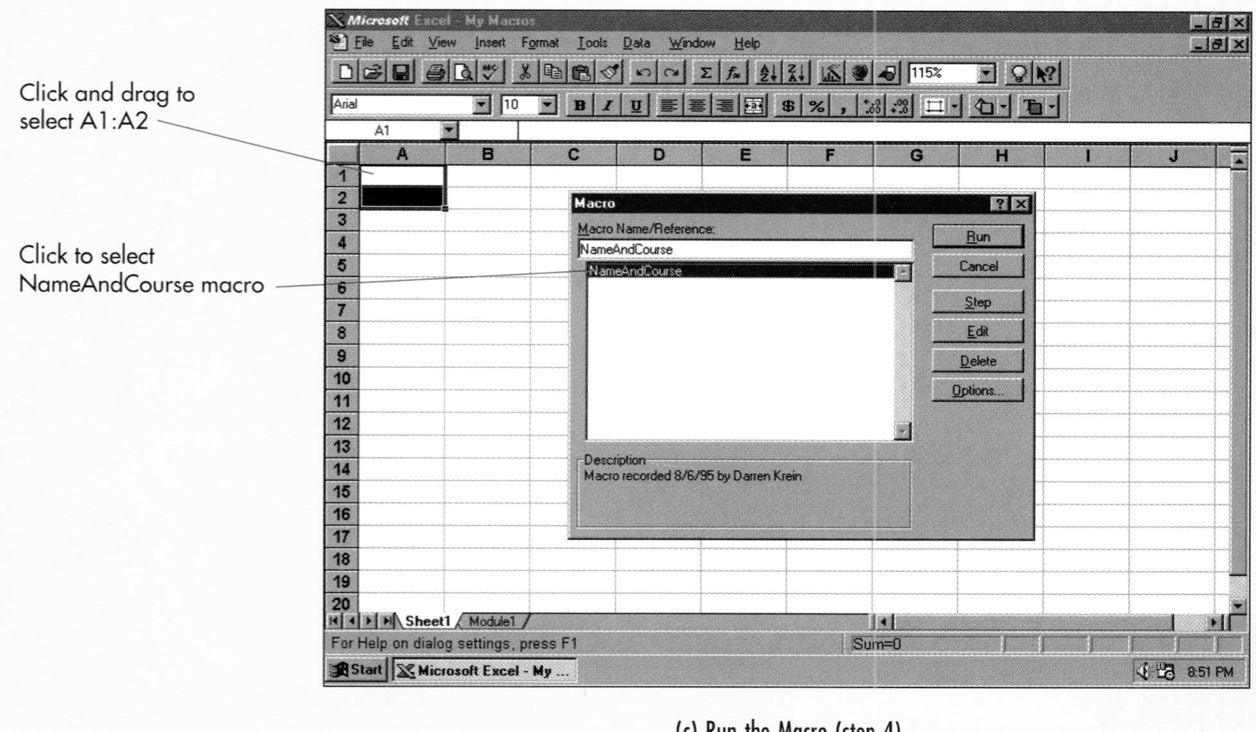

(c) Run the Macro (step 4)

FIGURE 3.2 Hands-on Exercise 1 (continued)

➤ Pull down the **Tools menu.** Click **Macro** to produce the dialog box shown in Figure 3.2c.

➤ Click **NameAndCourse,** which is the macro you just recorded. Click **Run.** Your name and class are entered in cells A1 and A2, then formatted according to the instructions in the macro.

> **MACRO NAMES**
>
> Macro names must begin with a letter and are not allowed to contain spaces or punctuation except for the underscore character. To create a macro name containing more than one word, capitalize the first letter of each word to make the words stand out and/or use the underscore character—for example, NameAndCourse or Name_And_Course.

STEP 5: Simplify the Macro

➤ Click the **Module1 tab** to view the macro you just created. Use the **down (up) arrows** on the vertical scroll bar to display the macro as shown in Figure 3.2d. The commands in your macro may vary slightly from ours if you did not follow the exact instructions in step 3.

➤ Click immediately after the number **12,** then click and drag to select the highlighted statements as shown in Figure 3.2d. Press the **Del key** to delete these

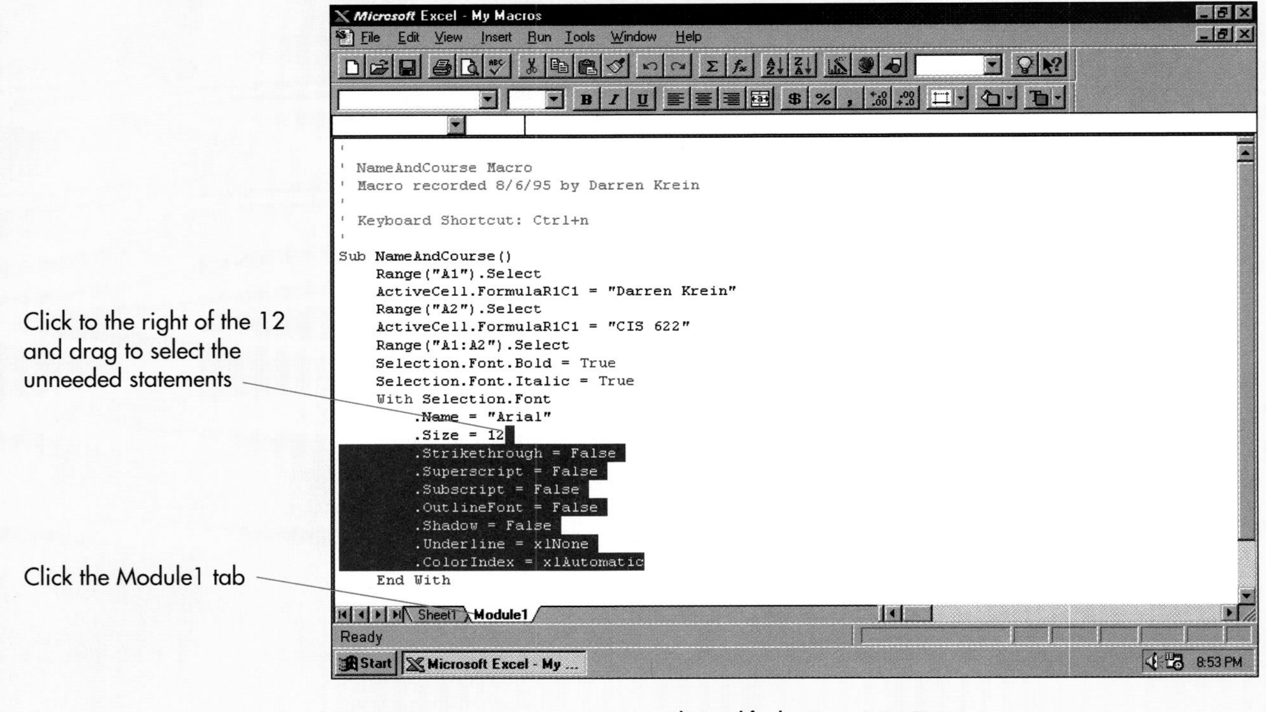

(d) Simplify the Macro (step 5)

FIGURE 3.2 Hands-on Exercise 1 (continued)

statements from the macro. (These statements contain default values and are unnecessary.)

- ➤ Click the tab for **Sheet1.** Clear the entries and formatting in cells A1 and A2 as you did in step 4, then rerun the **NameAndCourse** macro. Your name and class should once again be entered in cells A1 and A2. (If the macro does not execute correctly, click the Module1 tab and re-edit your macro so that it matches the one in Figure 3.2d.)
- ➤ Click the **Save button** to save the workbook with the revised macro.

SIMPLIFY THE MACRO

The macro recorder usually sets all possible options for an Excel command or dialog box even if you do not change those options explicitly. We suggest, therefore, that you make a macro easier to read by deleting the unnecessary statements.

STEP 6: Create the Erase Macro

- ➤ Pull down the **Tools menu.** Click (or point to) the **Record Macro command,** then click **Record New Macro** from the cascaded menu. You will see the Record New Macro dialog box as described earlier.
- ➤ Enter **EraseNameAndCourse** as the name of the macro. Do not leave any spaces in the macro name. If necessary, change the description to include your name.
- ➤ Click the **Options command button** to display additional options within the Record New Macro dialog box.
  - Check the **Shortcut Key check box,** then (if necessary) delete the current entry and enter a **lowercase e.**
  - Check that the options buttons for **This Workbook** and **Visual Basic** have been selected.
- ➤ Click **OK** to begin recording the macro. The Stop Macro button appears on the screen.
- ➤ Click and drag to select **cells A1** through **A2** as shown in Figure 3.2e, even if they are already selected.
- ➤ Pull down the **Edit menu.** Click **Clear.** Click **All** from the cascaded menu to erase both the contents and formatting from the selected cells. Cells A1 through A2 should now be empty.

TO SELECT OR NOT SELECT

If you start recording, then select a cell(s), you limit the macro to the cell(s) you selected from within the macro. If, however, you select the cell(s), then record, the macro is generic and will operate on the selected cells regardless of their location. Both techniques are valid, and the decision on which to choose depends on what you want the macro to do.

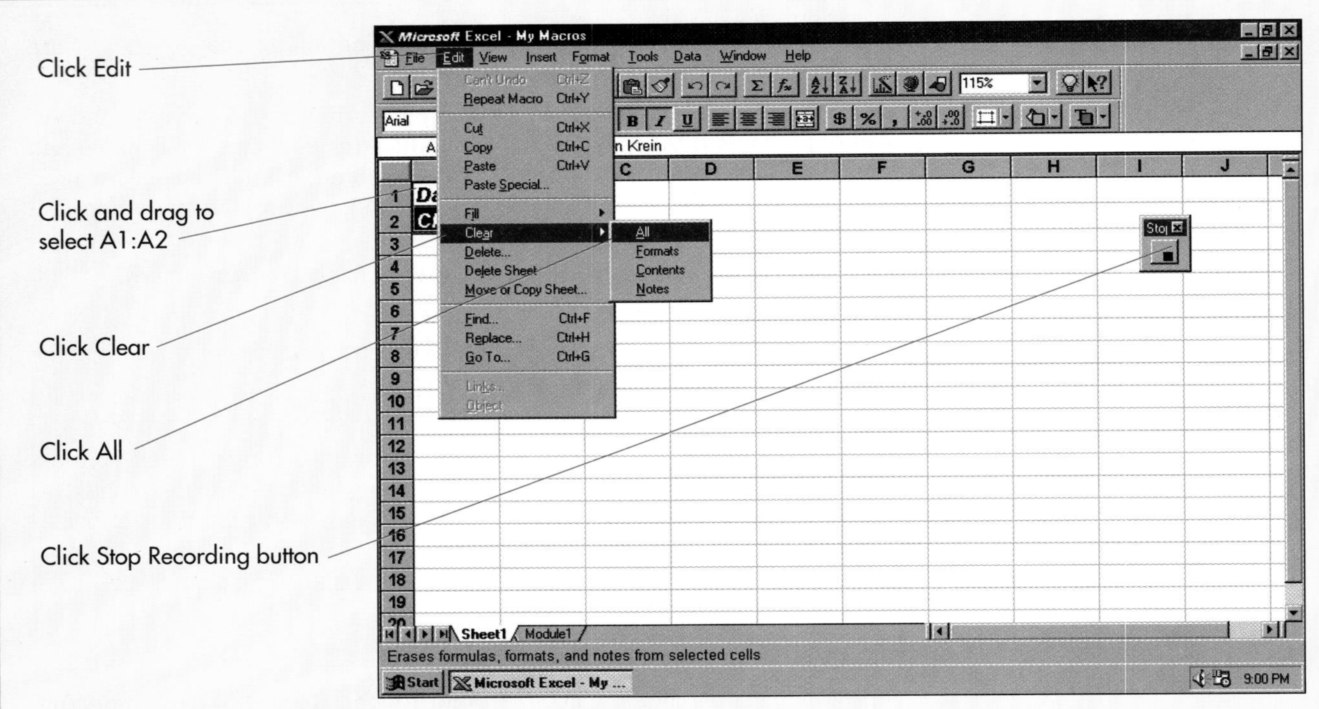

(e) Create the Erase Macro (step 6)

FIGURE 3.2 Hands-on Exercise 1 (continued)

- Click in **cell A3** to deselect all other cells prior to ending the macro.
- Click the **Stop Recording button** to end the macro. The macro is inserted in the Module1 worksheet below the NameAndCourse macro created earlier.

STEP 7: Shortcut Keys

- Press **Ctrl+n** to execute the NameAndCourse macro. (You need to reenter your name and course in order to test the newly created EraseNameAnd-Course macro.)
- Your name and course should again appear in cells A1 and A2.

TROUBLESHOOTING

If the shortcut keys do not work, it is probably because they were not defined properly. Pull down the Tools menu, select the Macro command, choose the desired macro in the Macro Name/Reference list box, then click the Options command button. Check the Shortcut Key check box, then click in the associated text box to enter the shortcut. Enter a *lowercase letter* to create a shortcut with just the Ctrl key; for example, a lowercase "n" establishes Ctrl+n as the shortcut. Enter an *uppercase letter* to create a shortcut with the Ctrl and Shift keys; e.g., typing an uppercase "N" establishes Ctrl+Shift+n as the shortcut.

➤ Press **Ctrl+e** to execute the EraseNameAndCourse macro. Cells A1 and A2 should again be empty.

➤ You can press Ctrl+n and Ctrl+e repeatedly, to enter, then erase your name and course. End this step after having erased the data.

STEP 8: Edit the Macro

➤ Click the **Module1 tab** to return to the macros. Click the **down (up) arrow** on the vertical scroll bar to view both macros as shown in Figure 3.2f.

➤ Edit the NameAndCourse macro as follows:

- Change the Font Name to **Times New Roman.**
- Delete the statement **Selection.Font.Bold = True.**

➤ Click the **Sheet1 tab** to test the macro. Press **Ctrl+n** to run the revised NameAndCourse macro. Your name and course should appear in 12 point Times New Roman Italic.

USE WHAT YOU KNOW

The ***Cut, Copy,*** and ***Paste commands*** are the mainstays of editing, regardless of the application. Select the statements to cut or copy to the clipboard, then paste them elsewhere in the macro, as necessary. If the results are different from what you expected or intended, click the Undo command immediately to reverse the effects of the previous command.

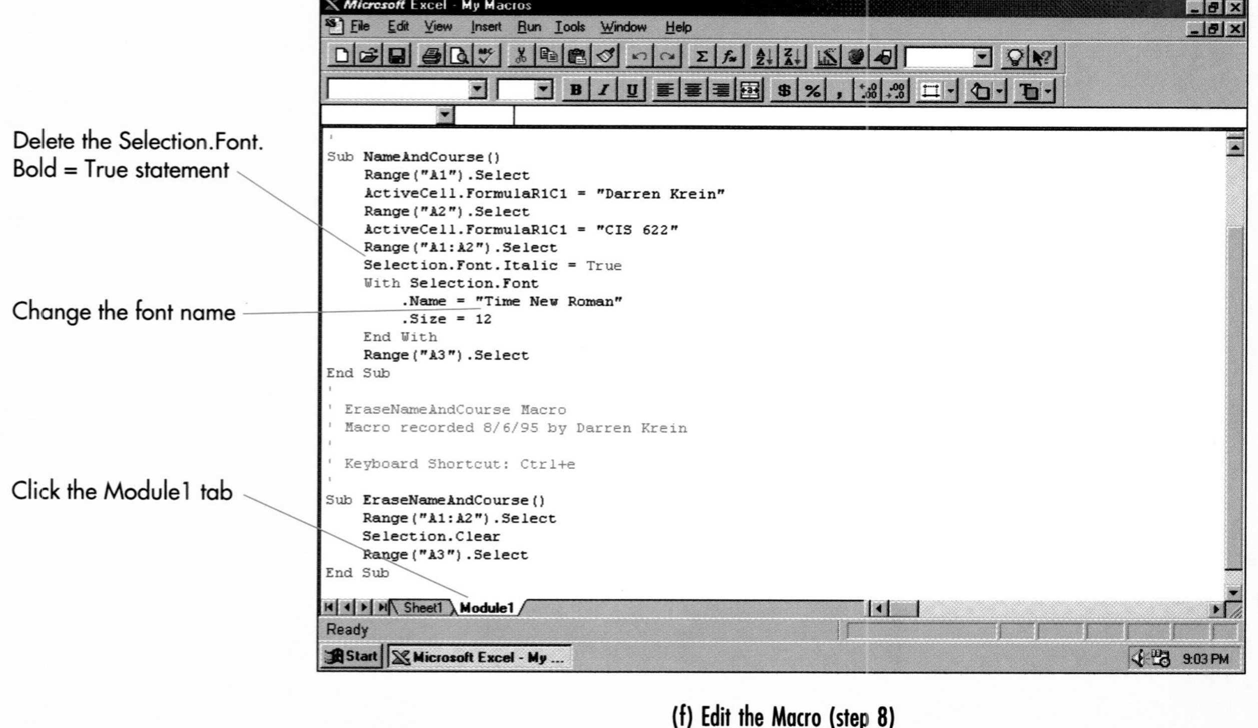

(f) Edit the Macro (step 8)

FIGURE 3.2 Hands-on Exercise 1 (continued)

STEP 9: Step through the Macro

- Press **Ctrl+e** to execute the Erase macro and clear the contents and formatting in cells A1 and A2.
- Point to any toolbar, then click the **right mouse button** to display a shortcut menu. Check **Visual Basic** to display the Visual Basic toolbar. Dock the toolbar below the Formatting toolbar.
- Click the **Run Macro button** on the Visual Basic toolbar. Click the **NameAndCourse macro** from the list of macros within the workbook, then click the **Step command button.**
- You should see a Debug window similar to Figure 3.2g. Drag the left border of the Debug window so that columns A and B of Sheet1 are visible as in Figure 3.2g. There is a rectangle around the Sub statement that begins the macro.
- Click and drag the line dividing the two halves of the Debug window to increase the size of the lower window. Click the **Step Into button** on the Visual Basic toolbar to step into the macro.
- The first Range statement is selected. Click the **Step Into button** to execute this statement (and select the next statement). Look at the worksheet. Cell A1 is selected as a result of executing the first macro statement.
- The ActiveCell statement to enter your name is selected. Click the **Step Into button** to execute this statement (and select the next statement). Look at the worksheet. Your name has been entered into cell A1.

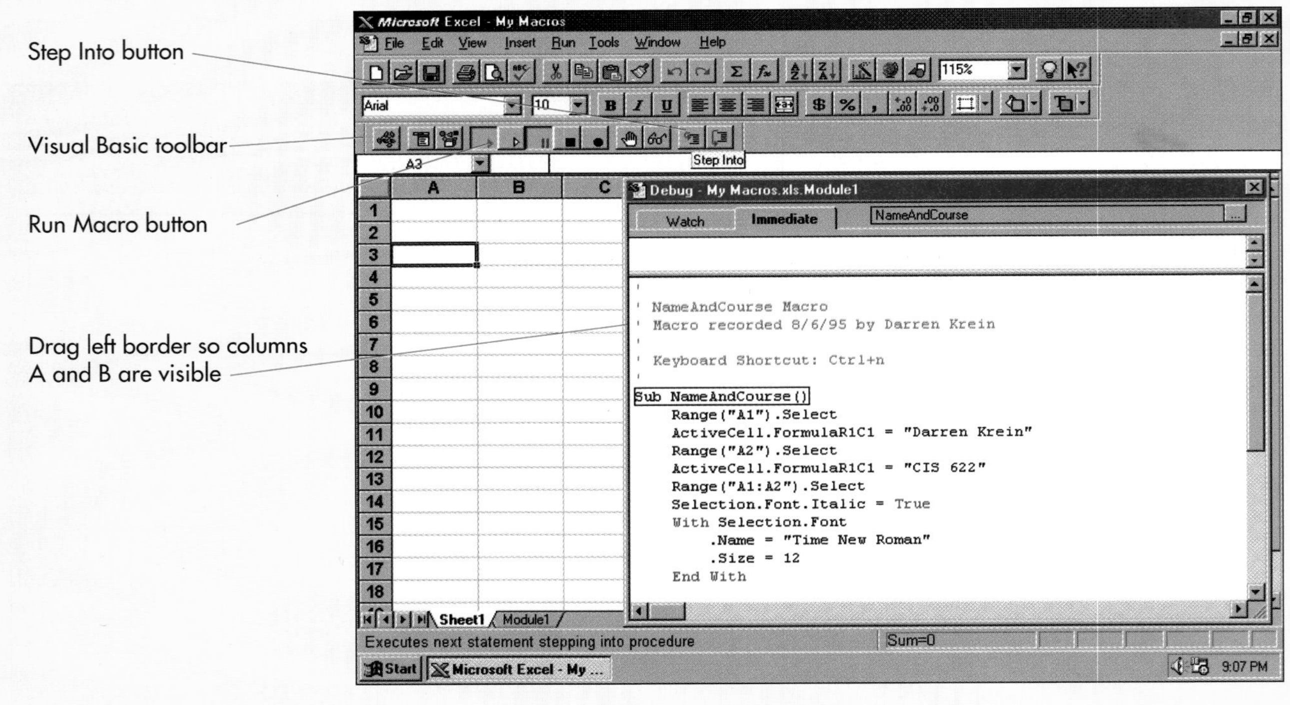

(g) Step through the Macro (step 9)

FIGURE 3.2 Hands-on Exercise 1 (continued)

➤ Continue to click the **Step Into button** until the macro has completed execution, and you again see your name and course in Sheet1, and the Debug window has closed.

> ### THE FIRST BUG
>
> A bug is a mistake in a computer program; hence debugging refers to the process of correcting program errors. According to legend, the first bug was an unlucky moth crushed to death on one of the relays of the electromechanical Mark II computer, bringing the machine's operation to a halt. The cause of the failure was discovered by Grace Hopper, who promptly taped the moth to her logbook, noting, *"First actual case of bug being found."*

STEP 10: Add to the Macro

➤ Click the **Module1 tab.** Click immediately to the left of the Range ("A1:A2").Select statement as shown in Figure 3.2h. This is the position in the macro where you want to insert additional statements.

➤ Pull down the **Tools menu.** Click the **Record Macro command.** Click **Mark Position for Recording** from the cascaded menu as shown in Figure 3.2h.

➤ Click the **Sheet1 tab** and pull down the **Tools menu.** Click the **Record Macro command,** then click **Record at Mark.**

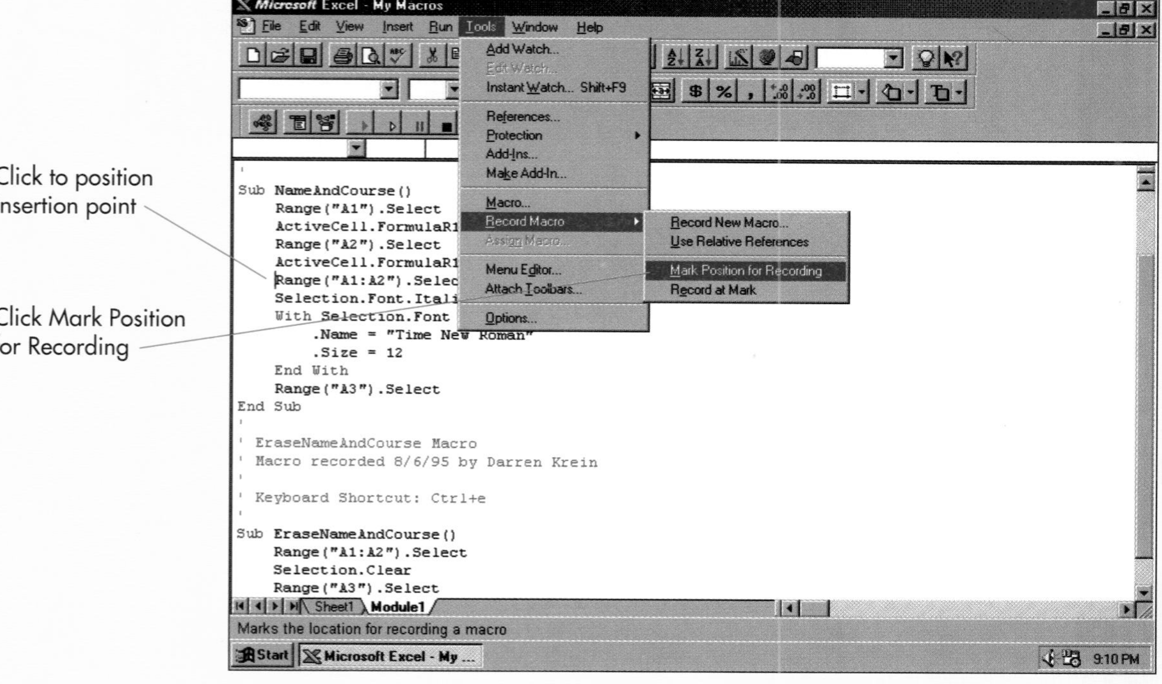

(h) Mark Position for Recording (step 10)

FIGURE 3.2 Hands-on Exercise 1 (continued)

- ➤ Click **cell A3** (even if it is currently selected), then enter **=TODAY().** Press **enter** to complete the entry in cell A3. Click the **Stop Recording Button** to cease recording.
- ➤ Click the **Save button** to save the workbook, which includes the revised macro.

> **MARK THE POSITION**
>
> Whenever you close and then reopen a workbook, the macro recorder will record new macros on a new module sheet. You can, however, record a new macro on an existing module sheet by marking the position prior to recording. Click the tab for the macro sheet in which you want the macro recorded, click where you want the new macro to go, pull down the Tools menu, click (or point to) the Record Macro command, then click Mark Position for Recording. Click the worksheet tab, pull down the Tools menu, click Record Macro, click Record New Macro, and proceed as usual.

STEP 11: The Completed Macro

- ➤ Click the **Module1 tab** to view the revised macro as shown in Figure 3.2i. Three additional statements have been inserted into the macro at the position previously marked for recording.

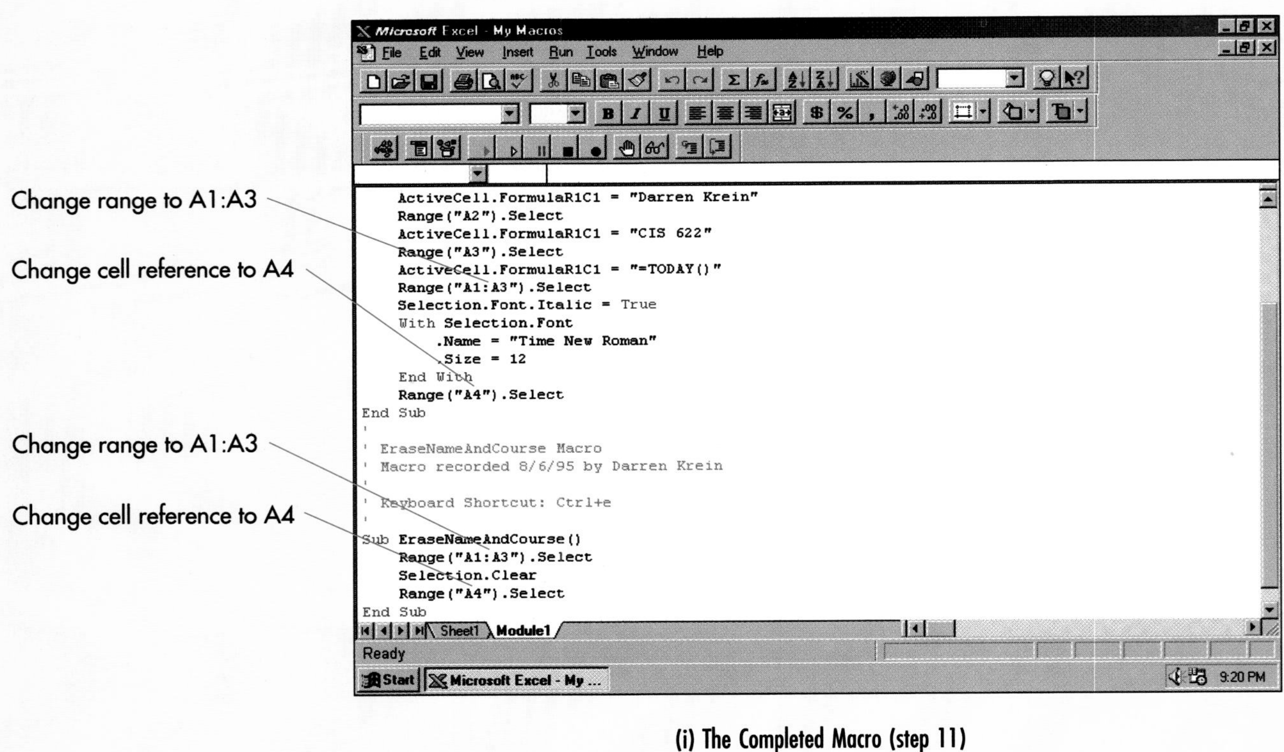

(i) The Completed Macro (step 11)

FIGURE 3.2 Hands-on Exercise 1 (continued)

- Change the Range ("A1:A2").Select statement to reference **cells A1:A3** so that cells A1 through A3 will be formatted.
- Delete the Range ("A4").Select statement, which is unnecessary and was entered because you pressed the enter key after entering the TODAY function in cell A3.
- Change the last statement in the macro to reference **cell A4** (rather than A3).

➤ Edit the Range ("A1:A2").Select statement in the EraseNameAndCourse macro so that it, too, reflects **cells A1** through **A3.** Be sure to change the last statement in this macro to reference **cell A4.**

➤ Click the **Sheet1 tab.** Press **Ctrl+e** to clear the contents of cells A1 through A3.

➤ Press **Ctrl+n** to run the revised NameAndCourse macro.

STEP 12: Print the Macro Sheet

➤ Click the **Module1 tab.**

➤ Pull down the **File menu** and select the **Print command.** If necessary, click the option button to print the **Selected Sheet(s).** Click **OK.**

➤ Save the workbook a final time. Close the workbook. Exit Excel if you do not want to continue with the next exercise at this time.

RELATIVE VERSUS ABSOLUTE REFERENCES

One of the most important options to specify when recording a macro is whether the references are to be relative or absolute. A reference is a cell address. An ***absolute reference*** is a constant address that always refers to the same cell. A ***relative reference*** is variable in that the reference will change from one execution of the macro to the next, depending on the location of the active cell when the macro is executed.

To appreciate the difference, consider Figure 3.3, which displays the NameAndCourse macro from the previous exercise with absolute and relative references. Figure 3.3a uses absolute references to place your name, course, and date in cells A1, A2, and A3. The data will always be entered in these cells regardless of which cell is selected when you execute the macro.

Figure 3.3b enters the same data, but with relative references, so that the cells in which the data is entered depend on where you are when the macro is executed. If you happen to be in cell A1, your name, course, and date will be entered in cells A1, A2, and A3. If, however, you are in cell E4 when you execute the macro, then your name, course, and date will be entered in cells E4, E5, and E6.

A relative reference is specified by an ***offset*** that indicates the number of rows and columns from the active cell. An offset of (1,0) indicates a cell one row below the active cell. An offset of (0,1) indicates a cell one column to the right of the active cell. In similar fashion, an offset of (1,1) indicates a cell one row below and one column to the right of the active cell. Negative offsets are used for cells above or to the left of the current selection.

Relative references may appear confusing at first, but they extend the power of a macro by making it more general. You will appreciate this capability as you learn more about macros. Let us begin by recognizing that the statement:

```
ActiveCell.Offset (1,0).Range ("A1").Select
```

Absolute reference to specified cell

```
'
' NameAndCourse Macro
' Macro recorded 8/6/95 by Darren Krein
'
' Keyboard Shortcut: Ctrl+n
'
Sub NameAndCourse()
    Range("A1").Select
    ActiveCell.FormulaR1C1 = "Darren Krein"
    Range("A2").Select
    ActiveCell.FormulaR1C1 = "CIS 622"
    Range("A3").Select
    ActiveCell.FormulaR1C1 = "=TODAY()"
    Range("A1:A3").Select
    Selection.Font.Italic = True
    With Selection.Font
        .Name = "Time New Roman"
        .Size = 12
    End With
    Range("A4").Select
End Sub
```

(a) Absolute References

Relative reference to the cell one row below the active cell

Indicates a column of three cells, not cells A1 to A3

```
'
' RelativeName Macro
' Macro recorded 8/6/95 by Darren Krein
'
' Keyboard Shortcut: Ctrl+n
'
Sub RelativeName()
    ActiveCell.Select
    ActiveCell.FormulaR1C1 = "Darren Krein"
    ActiveCell.Offset(1, 0).Range("A1").Select
    ActiveCell.FormulaR1C1 = "CIS 662"
    ActiveCell.Offset(1, 0).Range("A1").Select
    ActiveCell.FormulaR1C1 = "=TODAY()"
    ActiveCell.Offset(-2, 0).Range("A1:A3").Select
    Selection.Font.Italic = True
    With Selection.Font
        .Name = "Arial"
        .Size = 12
    End With
    ActiveCell.Offset(3, 0).Range("A1").Select
End Sub
```

(b) Relative References

FIGURE 3.3 Absolute versus Relative References

means select the cell one row below the active cell. It has nothing to do with cell A1, and you might wonder why the entry Range ("A1") is included. The answer is that the offset specifies the location of the new range (one row below the current cell), and the A1 indicates that the size of that range is a single cell (A1).

In similar fashion, the statement:

ActiveCell.Offset (-2,0).Range ("A1:A3").Select

selects a range, starting two rows above the current cell, that is one column by three rows in size. Again, it has nothing to do with cells A1 through A3. The offset specifies the location of a new range (two rows above the current cell) and the shape of that range (a column of three cells). If you are in cell D11 when the statement is executed, the selected range will be cells D9 through D11. The selection starts with the cell two rows above the active cell (cell D9), then it continues from that point to select a range consisting of one column by three rows (cells D9:D11).

THE PERSONAL MACRO WORKBOOK

The hands-on exercise at the beginning of the chapter created the NameAndCourse macro in the My Macros workbook, where it is available to that workbook (or to any other workbook that is in memory when the My Macros workbook is open). What if, however, you want the macro to be available at all times, not just when the My Macros workbook is open? This is easily accomplished by selecting the option button to store the macro in the Personal Macro workbook when it is first recorded.

The ***Personal Macro workbook*** is a special workbook that opens automatically whenever Excel is loaded. (The workbook is hidden by default until the ***Unhide command*** in the Window menu is executed.) The macros within the Personal Macro workbook are available to any workbook as long as the Personal Macro workbook is open. The following hands-on exercise modifies the NameAndCourse macro to include relative references, then stores that macro in the Personal Macro workbook.

NETWORK PRIVILEGES

If you are on a network, as opposed to a stand-alone machine, you will not be able to save the Personal Macro workbook in the startup folder, as only the network supervisor has rights to that folder. Ask your instructor or the network administrator how to establish your own Personal Macro workbook.

HANDS-ON EXERCISE 2

The Personal Macro Workbook

Objective: To create and store a macro in the Personal Macro workbook; to assign a toolbar button to a macro; to use the Visual Basic InputBox statement. Use Figure 3.4 as a guide in the exercise.

STEP 1: Record Relative References

- Start Excel and open a new workbook. Delete all worksheets except for Sheet1.
- Pull down the **Tools menu.** Click (or point to) the **Record Macro command,** then click **Record New Macro** from the cascaded menu to produce the Record New Macro dialog box.
- Enter **NameAndCourse** in the Macro Name text box, then click the **Options command button** to display additional options within the dialog box.

- Check the **Shortcut Key check box,** delete (or select) the existing letter, then enter a **lowercase n** in the appropriate text box. Ctrl+n should appear as the shortcut. (If you see Shift+Ctrl+n, it means you typed an uppercase "N" rather than a lowercase letter.)
- Check the option button for **Personal Macro workbook.** (This is a different option from the one used in the previous exercise.)
- Check the option button for **Visual Basic.**

➤ Click **OK** to begin recording the macro.

➤ Pull down the **Tools menu,** then click (or point to) the **Record Macro command.** If there is no check mark next to **Use Relative References,** click the command to toggle it on, as shown in Figure 3.4a. (The command functions as a toggle switch; click it once and a check appears and relative references are in effect; click the command a second time and the check disappears.)

RELATIVE VERSUS ABSOLUTE REFERENCES

Relative references appear confusing at first, but they extend the power of a macro by making it more general. Macro statements that have been recorded with relative references include an offset to indicate the number of rows and columns the selection is to be from the active cell. An offset of (1,0) indicates a cell one row below the active cell, whereas an offset of (0,1) indicates a cell one column to the right of the active cell. Negative offsets indicate cells above or to the left of the current selection.

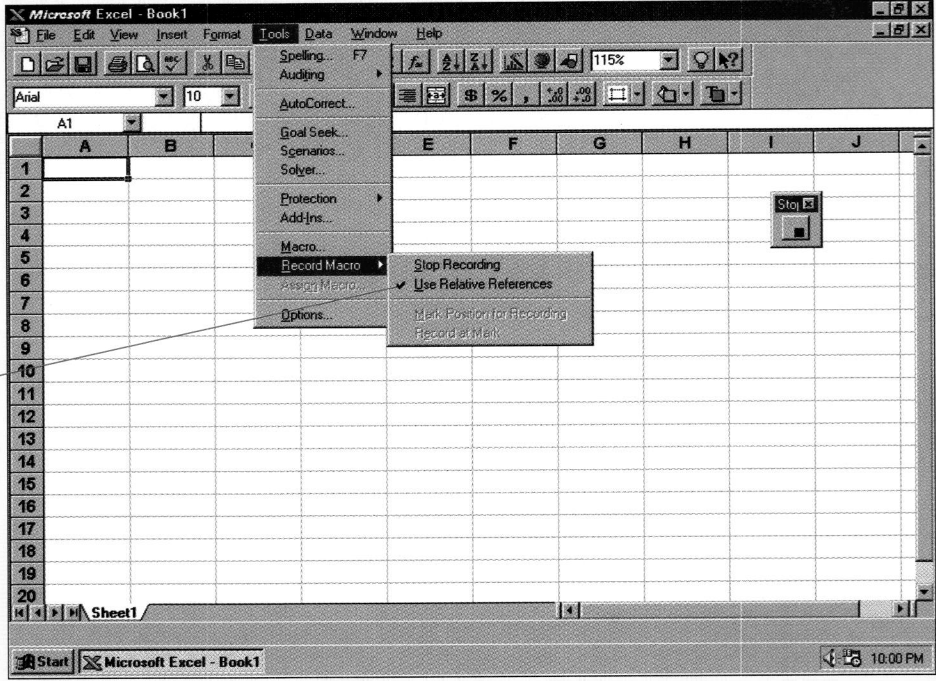

(a) Relative Reference (step 1)

FIGURE 3.4 Hands-on Exercise 2

STEP 2: Record the Macro

- You should be in Sheet1 with cell A1 selected. Enter your name in the active cell.
- Press the **down arrow key** to move to the cell immediately underneath the current cell. Enter the course you are taking.
- Press the **down arrow key** to move to the next cell. Enter **=TODAY()** to enter today's date.
- Click and drag to select the three cells containing the data values you just entered (**cells A1** through **A3** in Figure 3.4b).
  - Click the **Bold button.**
  - Click the **Italic button.**
  - Click the **arrow** on the **Font Size** list box. Click **12** to change the point size.
  - Drag the border between the column headings for Columns A and B to increase the width of column A if you see a series of number signs in cell A3. (The latter indicate the column is too narrow to display the date in its current format.)
  - Click in **cell A4** to deselect all other cells prior to ending the macro.
- Click the **Stop Recording button** to end the macro.

STEP 3: Unhide the Personal Macro workbook

- The macro has been recorded but is not yet visible; that is, unlike the previous exercise, there is no Module1 sheet in the current workbook.

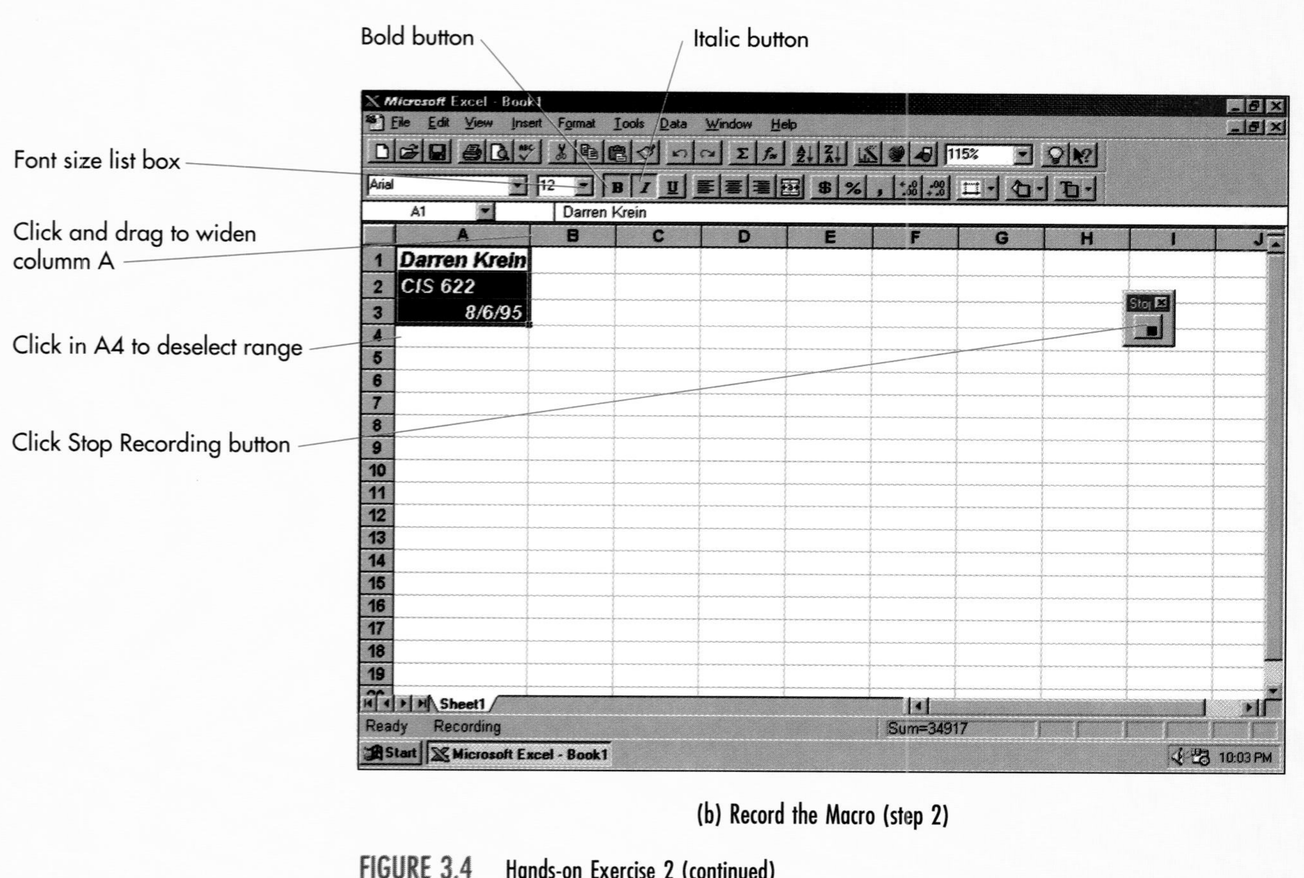

(b) Record the Macro (step 2)

FIGURE 3.4 Hands-on Exercise 2 (continued)

- ➤ Pull down the **Window menu.** Click **Unhide** to produce the Unhide dialog box. The Personal Macro workbook is already selected. Click **OK** (or press **enter**) to show (unhide) the workbook. If necessary, click the **Maximize button** so that you can edit the macro more easily.

STEP 4: Edit the Macro

- ➤ The commands in your macro may be slightly different from ours, but they must reflect relative rather than absolute addresses. (You will have to return to the beginning of the exercise and start over if your macro does not contain relative references. Close both workbooks without saving them, then start again, replacing the existing macro when prompted to do so.)
- ➤ Click immediately after the number **12,** then click and drag to select the highlighted statements in Figure 3.4c. Press the **Del key** to delete the highlighted statements from the macro.
- ➤ Delete the **Selection.Font.Bold = True** statement, which appears above the With statement.
- ➤ Change the third statement in the macro (which contains the name of the course) to **ActiveCell.FormulaR1C1 = InputBox("Enter the Course You Are Taking").** Be sure you enter this statement correctly with beginning and ending parentheses, and with beginning and ending quotation marks, as shown.
- ➤ Click the **Save button** to save the revised workbook.

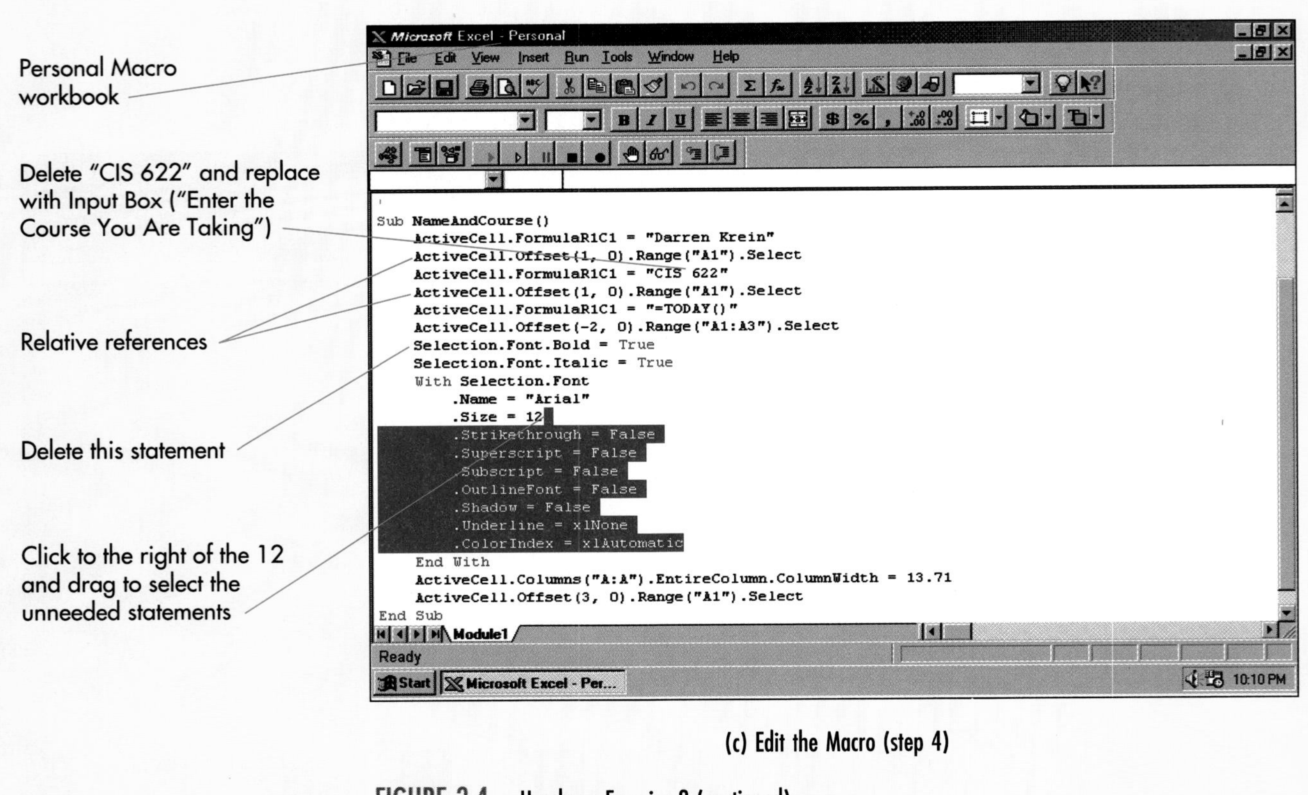

(c) Edit the Macro (step 4)

FIGURE 3.4 Hands-on Exercise 2 (continued)

WHAT DOES RANGE ("A1:A3") REALLY MEAN?

The statement ActiveCell.Offset(−2,0).Range ("A1:A3").Select has nothing to do with cells A1 through A3, so why is the entry Range ("A1:A3") included? The effect of the statement is to select three cells (one cell under the other), starting with the cell two rows above the current cell. The offset (−2,0) specifies the starting point of the selected range (two rows above the current cell). The range ("A1:A3") indicates the size and shape of the selected range (a vertical column of three cells) from the starting cell.

STEP 5: Test the Revised Macro

- Pull down the **Window menu.** Click **Book1** to select the window containing the workbook on which you are working. (The Book number is not important, and you may see a different number, depending on how many other workbooks you have opened in this session.)
- Click in any cell—for example, **cell C5** as shown in Figure 3.4d. Pull down the **Tools menu.** Click **Macro,** select **PERSONAL.XLS!NameAndCourse,** then click the **Run command button** to run the macro. (Alternatively, you can use the **Ctrl+n** shortcut.)
- The macro enters your name in cell C5 (the active cell), then displays the input dialog box in Figure 3.4d. Enter any appropriate course and press the **enter key.** You should see the course you entered followed by the date.

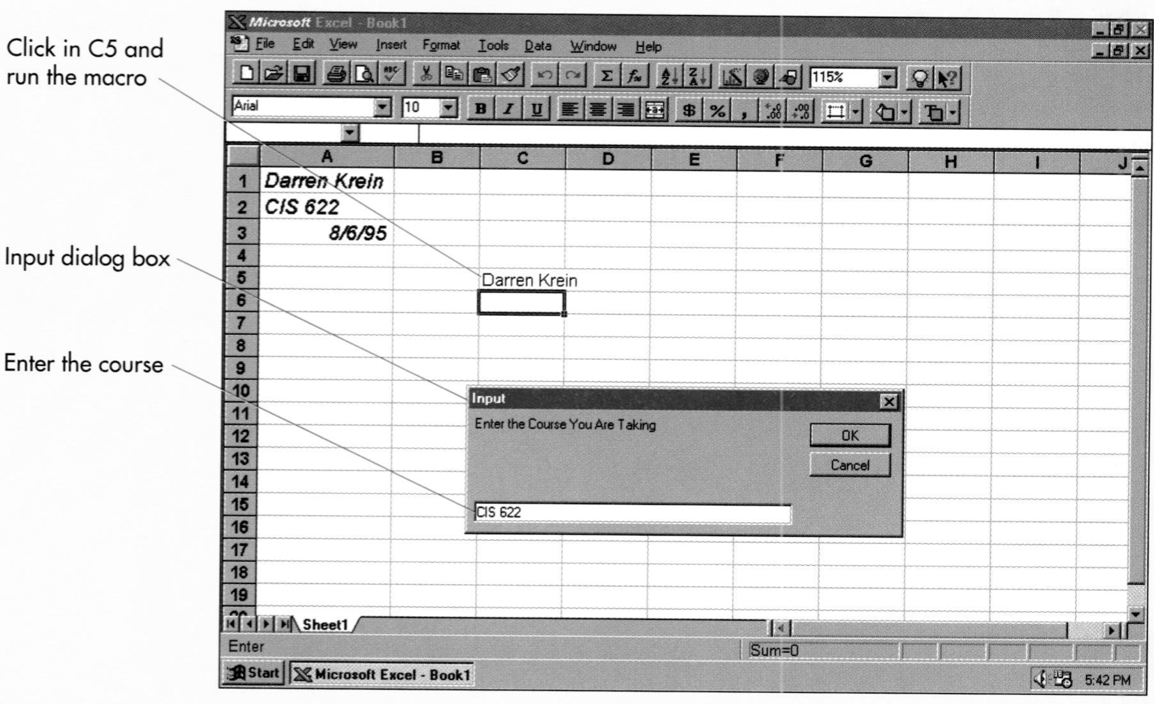

(d) Test the Revised Macro (step 5)

FIGURE 3.4 Hands-on Exercise 2 (continued)

- ➤ Click in a different cell (you can click in any cell because the macro uses relative references), then press **Ctrl+n** to rerun the macro. The macro will enter your name, the course you specify, and the date in the selected location.
- ➤ Be sure you are in Book1 (and not the Personal Macro workbook). Pull down the **File menu.** Click **Close.** Click **No** when prompted to save the changes in Book1, since this workbook is not significant and need not be saved.
- ➤ The Personal Macro workbook remains open, and its macros can be used in this (or any future) session.

STEP 6: Add a Custom Tool Button

- ➤ Point to any toolbar, then click the **right mouse button** to display a shortcut menu. Click **Customize** to display the Customize dialog box in Figure 3.4e.
- ➤ Click the **down arrow** to scroll through the Categories list box until you can select the Custom category.
- ➤ Click and drag the **Happy Face button** to an available space at the right of the Standard toolbar. Release the mouse. You will see the Assign Macro dialog box. Choose **NameAndCourse** from the open list box and click **OK.** Click **Close** to exit the Custom dialog box.

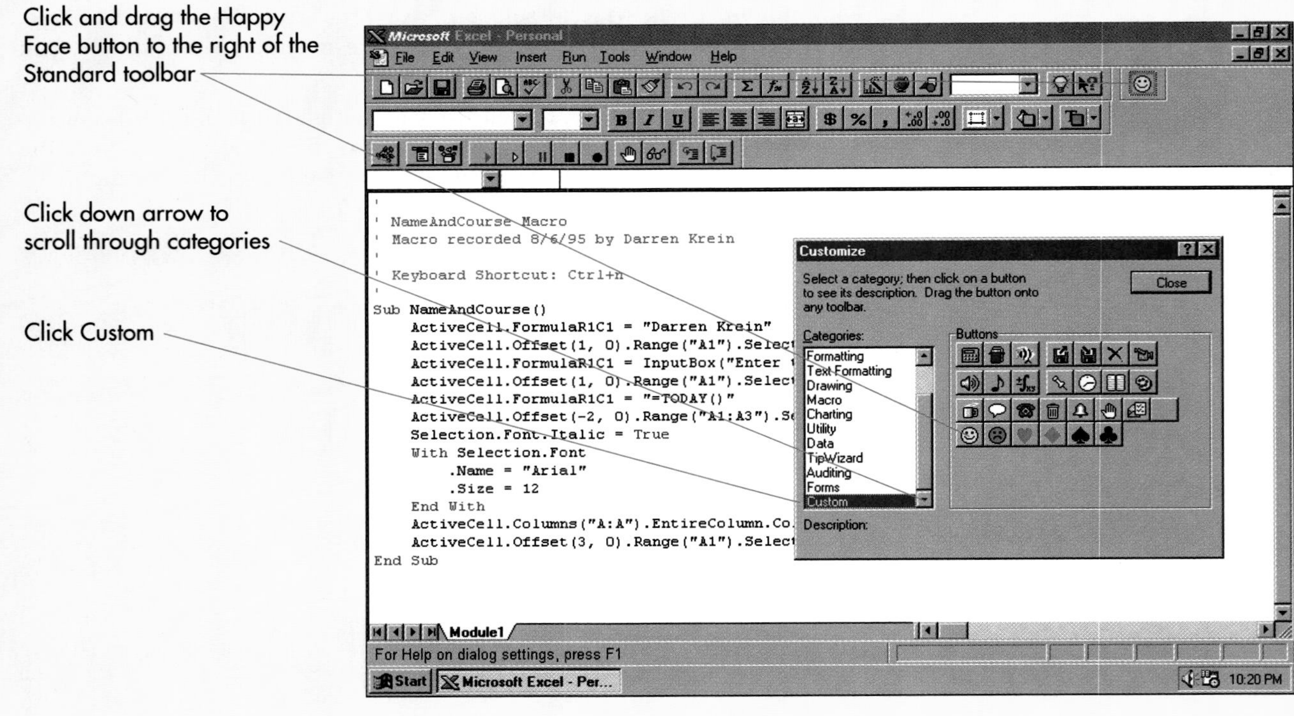

(e) Customize the Toolbar (step 6)

FIGURE 3.4 Hands-on Exercise 2 (continued)

STEP 7: Test the Custom Button

- ➤ Click the **New Workbook button** on the Standard toolbar to open a new workbook (Book2 in Figure 3.4f; the book number is not important). Click **cell B2** as the active cell from which to execute the macro.

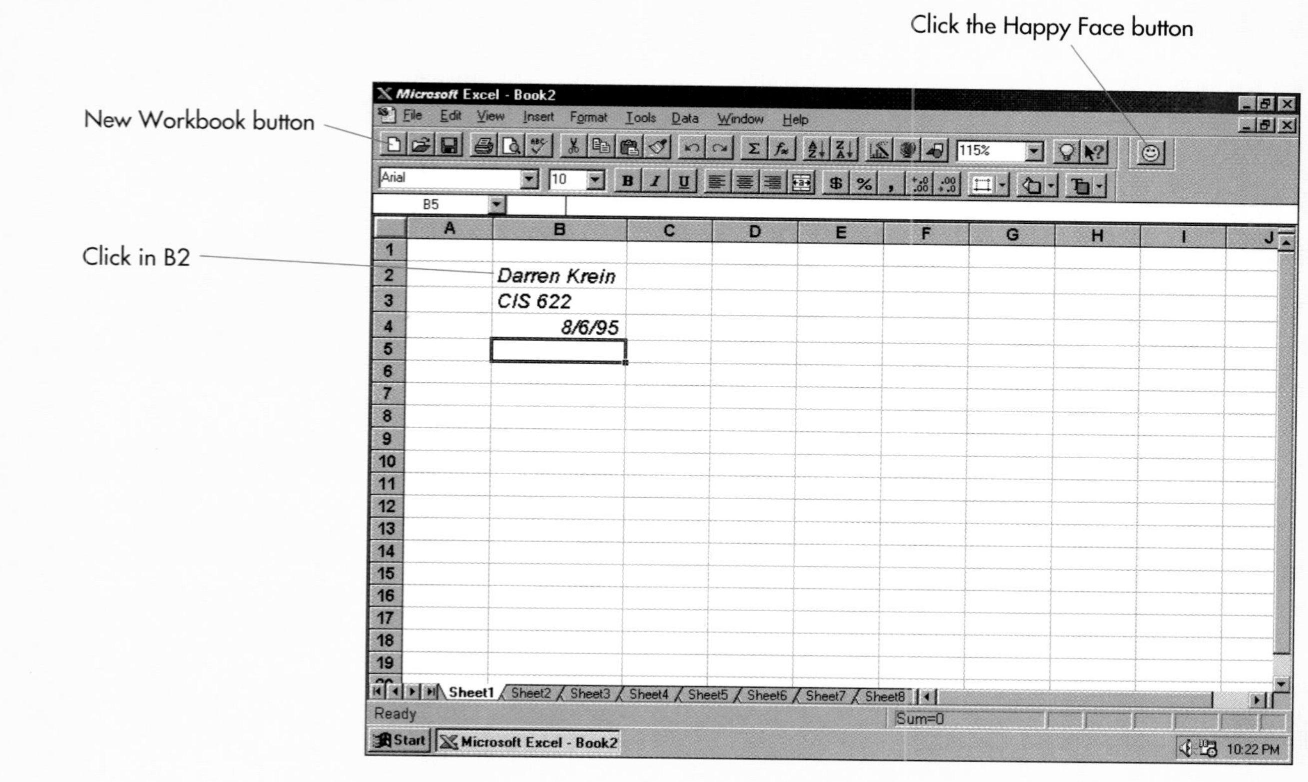

(f) Test the Macro (step 7)

FIGURE 3.4 Hands-on Exercise 2 (continued)

- Click the **Happy Face button** to execute the NameAndCourse macro. Enter the name of a course you are taking. The macro inserts your name, course, and today's date in cells B2 through B4 as shown in Figure 3.4f.

STEP 8: Hide the Personal Macro Workbook

- Pull down the **Window menu.** Click **Personal** to activate the Personal Macro workbook, then save the workbook if you have your own machine. (You will probably not be able to save the Personal Macro workbook if you are on a network.)
- Pull down the **Window menu** a second time. Click **Hide** to hide the Personal Macro workbook.
- Close, but don't save, Book2 (the workbook opened at the beginning of this exercise). Exit Excel if you do not wish to continue with the next exercise at this time.

DATA MANAGEMENT MACROS

Thus far we have covered the basics of macros in the context of entering your name, course, and today's date in a worksheet. As you might expect, macros are capable of much more and can be used to automate any repetitive task. The next several pages illustrate the use of macros in conjunction with the list (data) management examples that were presented in Chapter 1.

The worksheet in Figure 3.5a displays an employee list and the associated summary statistics. As you already know, a list is an area in a worksheet that contains rows of similar data. The first row in the list contains the column labels or field names. Each additional row contains a record. Every record contains the same fields in the same order. The list in Figure 3.5a has 14 records. Each record has seven fields: name, location, title, gender, service, hire date, and salary.

A criteria range has been established in cells A17 through G18 for use with the database functions in cells G22 through G26. Criteria values have not been entered in Figure 3.5a, and so the database functions reflect the values of the entire list (all 14 employees).

Field names — row 1
Data records — rows 2 and 3
Criteria range (A17:G18) — row 17
Database functions (G22:G26) compute summary statistics

	A	B	C	D	E	F	G
1	Name	Location	Title	Gender	Service	Hire Date	Salary
2	Adams	Atlanta	Trainee	M	1.8	11/24/93	$19,500
3	Adamson	Chicago	Manager	F	3.5	3/16/92	$52,000
4	Brown	Atlanta	Trainee	F	1.8	11/24/93	$18,500
5	Charles	Boston	Account Rep	M	3.5	3/16/92	$40,000
6	Coulter	Atlanta	Manager	M	1.8	11/24/93	$100,000
7	Elofson	Miami	Account Rep	F	2.9	10/31/92	$47,500
8	Gillenson	Miami	Manager	M	1.9	10/31/93	$55,000
9	James	Chicago	Account Rep	F	5.9	10/31/89	$42,500
10	Johnson	Chicago	Account Rep	M	4.9	10/31/90	$47,500
11	Manin	Boston	Account Rep	F	3.5	3/16/92	$49,500
12	Marder	Chicago	Account Rep	F	3.9	10/31/91	$38,500
13	Milgrom	Boston	Manager	M	3.5	3/16/92	$57,500
14	Rubin	Boston	Account Rep	F	3.5	3/16/92	$45,000
15	Smith	Atlanta	Account Rep	M	1.8	11/24/93	$65,000
16							
17	Name	Location	Title	Gender	Service	Hire Date	Salary
18							
19							
20							
21	Summary Statistics						
22	Average Salary						$48,429
23	Maximum Salary						$100,000
24	Minimum Salary						$18,500
25	Total Salary						$678,000
26	Number of Employees						14

(a) All Employees

List is filtered to employees who work in Chicago — row 3
Summary statistics reflect only the Chicago employees

	A	B	C	D	E	F	G
1	Name	Location	Title	Gender	Service	Hire Date	Salary
3	Adamson	Chicago	Manager	F	3.5	3/16/92	$52,000
9	James	Chicago	Account Rep	F	5.9	10/31/89	$42,500
10	Johnson	Chicago	Account Rep	M	4.9	10/31/90	$47,500
12	Marder	Chicago	Account Rep	F	3.9	10/31/91	$38,500
16							
17	Name	Location	Title	Gender	Service	Hire Date	Salary
18		Chicago					
19							
20							
21	Summary Statistics						
22	Average Salary						$45,125
23	Maximum Salary						$52,000
24	Minimum Salary						$38,500
25	Total Salary						$180,500
26	Number of Employees						4

(b) Chicago Employees

FIGURE 3.5 Data Management Macros

The worksheet in Figure 3.5b displays selected employees, those who work in Chicago. Look carefully at the worksheet and you will see that only rows 3, 9, 10, and 12 are visible. The other rows within the list have been hidden by the Advanced Filter command, which displays only those employees who satisfy the specified criteria. The summary statistics reflect only the Chicago employees; for example, the DCOUNT function in cell G26 shows four employees (as opposed to the 14 employees in Figure 3.5a).

You already know how to execute the list management commands to modify the existing criteria and filter a list accordingly. The process is not difficult, but it does require the execution of several commands. Consider, for example, the steps that would be necessary to modify the worksheet in Figure 3.5b if you wanted to display managers rather than Chicago employees.

You would have to clear the existing criterion (Chicago) in cell B18, then enter the new criterion (Manager) in cell C18. You would then execute the Advanced Filter command, which requires the specification of the list (cells A1 through G15), the location of the criteria range (cells A17 through G18), and the option to filter the list in place.

And what if you wanted to see the Chicago employees after you executed the commands to display the managers? You would have to repeat all of the previous commands to change the criterion back to what it was, then filter the list accordingly. Suffice it to say that the entire process can be simplified through creation of the appropriate macros.

The following exercise develops the macro to select the Chicago employees from the worksheet in Figure 3.5a. A subsequent exercise, beginning on page 132, develops two additional macros, one to select the managers and another to select the managers who work in Chicago.

NAMED RANGES

Use the Name command in the Insert menu to establish a mnemonic name (e.g., Database) for a cell range (e.g., A1:G15). Once defined, names adjust automatically for insertions and/or deletions within the range or a movement of the range within the worksheet. A name can be used in any command or function that requires a cell reference, and its use is highly recommended. This is especially true in macros, both to make the macro easier to read and to make it immune from changes to the worksheet.

HANDS-ON EXERCISE 3

Data Management Macros

Objective: To create a data management macro in conjunction with an employee list; to create a custom button to execute a macro. Use Figure 3.6 as a guide in the exercise.

STEP 1: The Management Functions

- Start Excel. Open the **Finished Employee List** workbook that you created in Chapter 1.

- ➤ Click any cell between A2 and A15, then click the **Ascending Sort button** on the Standard toolbar. The employees should be listed in alphabetical order as shown in Figure 3.6a.
- ➤ Click in **cell D17.** Type **Gender** to complete the field names in the criteria range. Clear all entries in the range **A18** through **G18.**
- ➤ Click in **cell G22,** which contains the DAVERAGE function, to compute the average salary of all employees who satisfy the specified criteria. No criteria have been entered, however, so the displayed value of $48,429 represents the average salary of all fourteen employees.
- ➤ Click **cell B18.** Enter **Chicago.** Press **enter.** The average salary changes to $45,125 to indicate the average salary of the four Chicago employees.
- ➤ Click **cell C18.** Enter **Manager.** Press **enter.** The average salary changes to $52,000 to indicate the average salary of the one Chicago manager.

PLAN AHEAD

Plan a macro ahead of time by testing its commands prior to turning on the macro recorder. Go through every command to make sure you produce the desired results. Determine the cells you will need to select so that you can assign names to these cells prior to recording the macro.

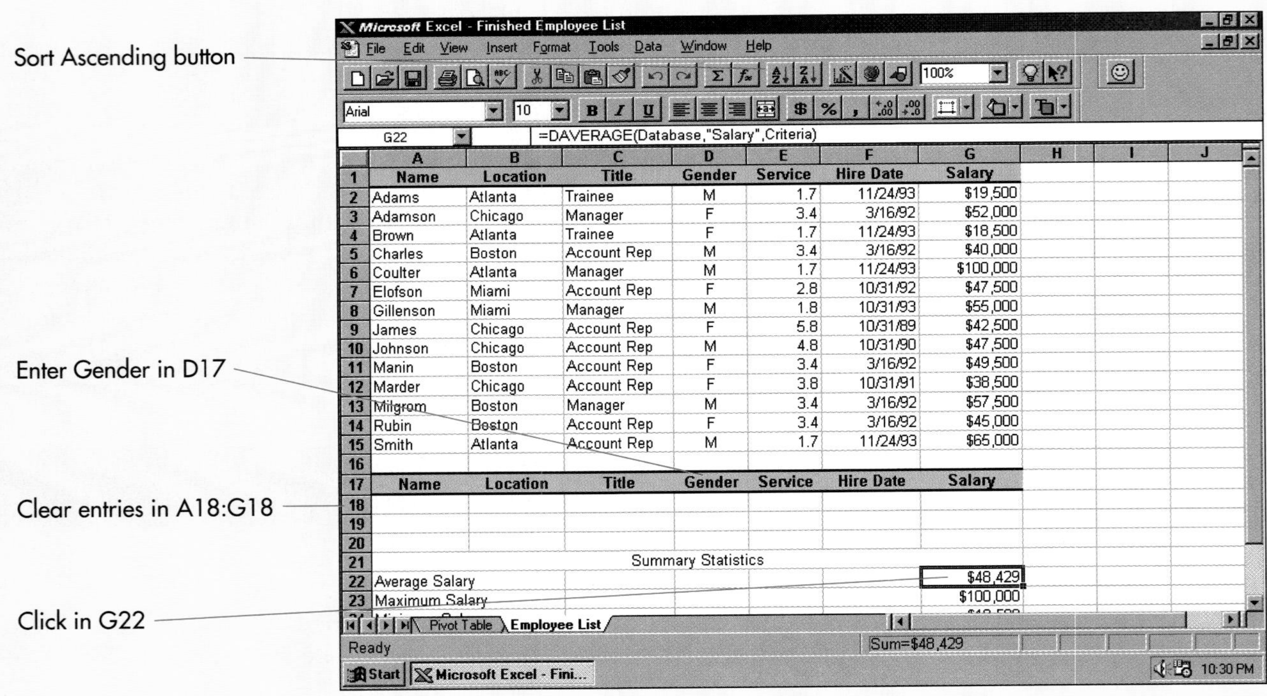

	A	B	C	D	E	F	G
1	Name	Location	Title	Gender	Service	Hire Date	Salary
2	Adams	Atlanta	Trainee	M	1.7	11/24/93	$19,500
3	Adamson	Chicago	Manager	F	3.4	3/16/92	$52,000
4	Brown	Atlanta	Trainee	F	1.7	11/24/93	$18,500
5	Charles	Boston	Account Rep	M	3.4	3/16/92	$40,000
6	Coulter	Atlanta	Manager	M	1.7	11/24/93	$100,000
7	Elofson	Miami	Account Rep	F	2.8	10/31/92	$47,500
8	Gillenson	Miami	Manager	M	1.8	10/31/93	$55,000
9	James	Chicago	Account Rep	F	5.8	10/31/89	$42,500
10	Johnson	Chicago	Account Rep	M	4.8	10/31/90	$47,500
11	Manin	Boston	Account Rep	F	3.4	3/16/92	$49,500
12	Marder	Chicago	Account Rep	F	3.8	10/31/91	$38,500
13	Milgrom	Boston	Manager	M	3.4	3/16/92	$57,500
14	Rubin	Boston	Account Rep	F	3.4	3/16/92	$45,000
15	Smith	Atlanta	Account Rep	M	1.7	11/24/93	$65,000
16							
17	Name	Location	Title	Gender	Service	Hire Date	Salary
18							
19							
20							
21				Summary Statistics			
22	Average Salary						$48,429
23	Maximum Salary						$100,000

(a) Data Management Functions (step 1)

FIGURE 3.6 Hands-on Exercise 3

STEP 2: The Create Name Command

- Click and drag to select **cells A17** through **G18** as shown in Figure 3.6b. Pull down the **Insert menu,** click **Name,** then click **Create** to display the Create Names dialog box.
- Check the box to **Create Names in Top Row.** Click **OK.** This command assigns the text in each cell in row 17 to the corresponding cell in row 18; for example, cells B18 and C18 will be assigned the names Location and Title, respectively.
- Click and drag to select only **cells A18** through **G18.** (You need to assign a name to these seven cells collectively as you will have to clear the criteria values in row 18 later in the chapter.)
- Pull down the **Insert menu.** Click **Name.** Click **Define.** Enter **CriteriaValues** in the Define Name dialog box. Click **OK.**

THE NAME BOX

Use the Name box to define a range by selecting the cell(s) in the worksheet to which the name is to apply, clicking the Name box, then entering the name. For example, to assign the name CriteriaValues to cells A18:G18, select the range, click the Name box, and type CriteriaValues. The Name box can also be used to select a previously defined range by clicking the drop-down arrow next to the box and choosing the desired name from the drop-down list.

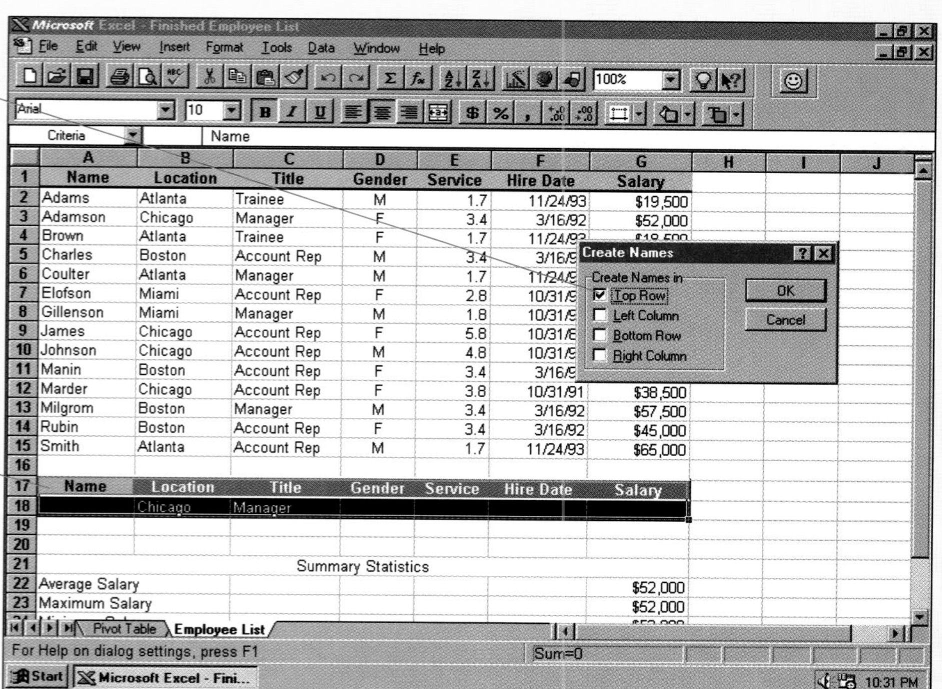

(b) The Create Name Command (step 2)

FIGURE 3.6 Hands-on Exercise 3 (continued)

The Go To Command

- Pull down the **Edit menu.** Click **Go To** to produce the Go To dialog box in Figure 3.6c. You should see the names you defined (CriteriaValues, Gender, Hire_Date, Location, Name, Salary, Service, and Title) as well as the two names defined previously by the authors (Criteria and Database).
- Click **Database.** Click **OK.** Cells A1 through G5 should be selected, corresponding to cells assigned to the name Database.
- Press the **F5 key** (a shortcut for the Edit Go To command), which again produces the Go To dialog box. Click **Criteria.** Click **OK.** Cells A17 through G18 should be selected.
- Click the **drop-down arrow** next to the Name box. Click **Location.** Cell B18 should be selected.
- You are now ready to record the macro.

Click to see a list of defined names

List of defined names produced with Edit Go To command or by pressing F5

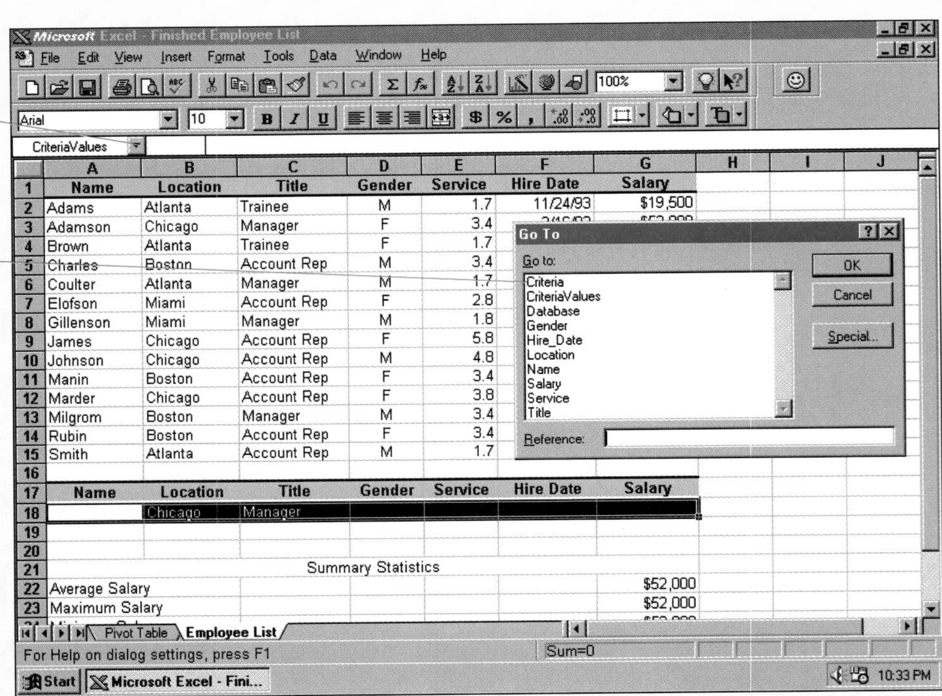

(c) The Go To Command (step 3)

FIGURE 3.6 Hands-on Exercise 3 (continued)

STEP 4: Set the Macro Options

- Pull down the **Tools menu** and click the **Record Macro command.** (Use absolute references; that is, Use Relative References should be toggled off.)
- Click **Record New Macro** from the cascaded menu to produce the Record New Macro dialog box. Enter **Chicago** in the Macro Name text box.
- Click the **Options command button** to display additional options within the dialog box. If necessary, clear the **Shortcut Key check box.** Check the option button for **This Workbook.** Check the option button for **Visual Basic.**
- Click **OK** to begin recording the macro.

STEP 5: Record the Macro (Edit Clear Command)

- Pull down the **Edit menu,** click **Go To,** select **CriteriaValues** from the Go To dialog box, and click **OK.** Cells A18 through G18 should be selected as shown in Figure 3.6d. (Alternatively, you can also use the **F5 key** or the Name box to select CriteriaValues.)
- Pull down the **Edit menu.** Click **Clear,** then click **All** from the cascaded menu as shown in Figure 3.6d. Cells A18 through G18 should be empty.

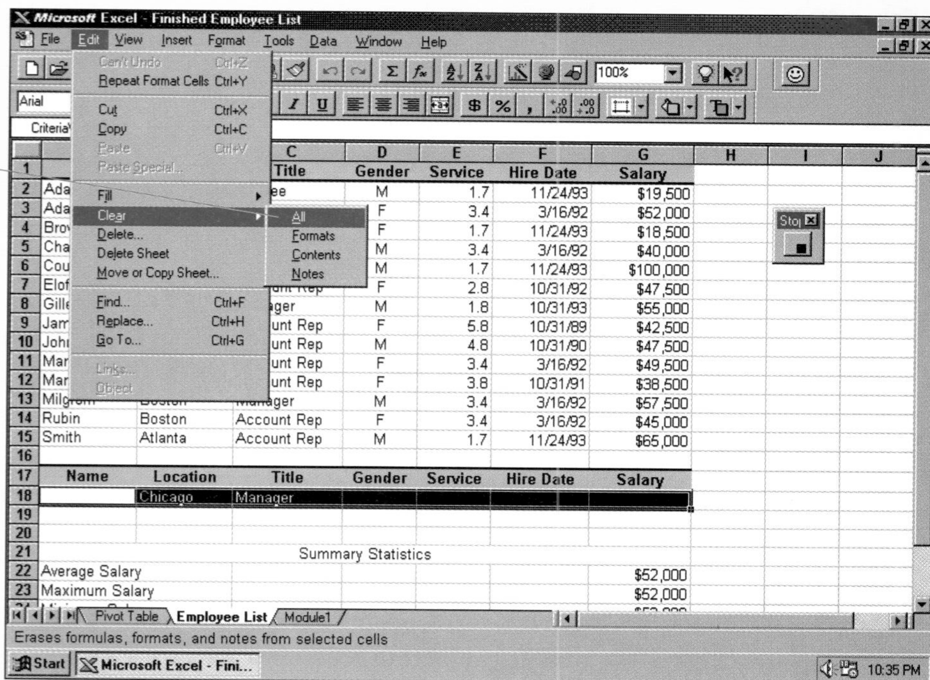

(d) The Edit Clear Command (step 5)

FIGURE 3.6 Hands-on Exercise 3 (continued)

STEP 6: Record the Macro (Advanced Filter Command)

- Pull down the **Edit menu,** click **Go To,** select **Location** from the Go To dialog box, and click **OK.**
- Cell B18 should be selected. Enter **Chicago** to establish the criterion for both the database functions and the Advanced Filter command.
- Click in **cell A2** to position the active cell within the employee list. Pull down the **Data menu.** Click **Filter,** then click **Advanced Filter** from the cascaded menu to display the dialog box in Figure 3.6e.
- Enter **Database** as the List Range. Press the **tab key.** Enter **Criteria** as the Criteria Range.
- Check that the option to **Filter the List in-place** is checked.
- Click **OK.** You should see only those employees who satisfy the current criteria (i.e., Adamson, James, Johnson, and Marder, who are the employees who work in Chicago).
- Click the **Stop Record button** to stop recording.
- Click the **Save button** to save the workbook with the macro.

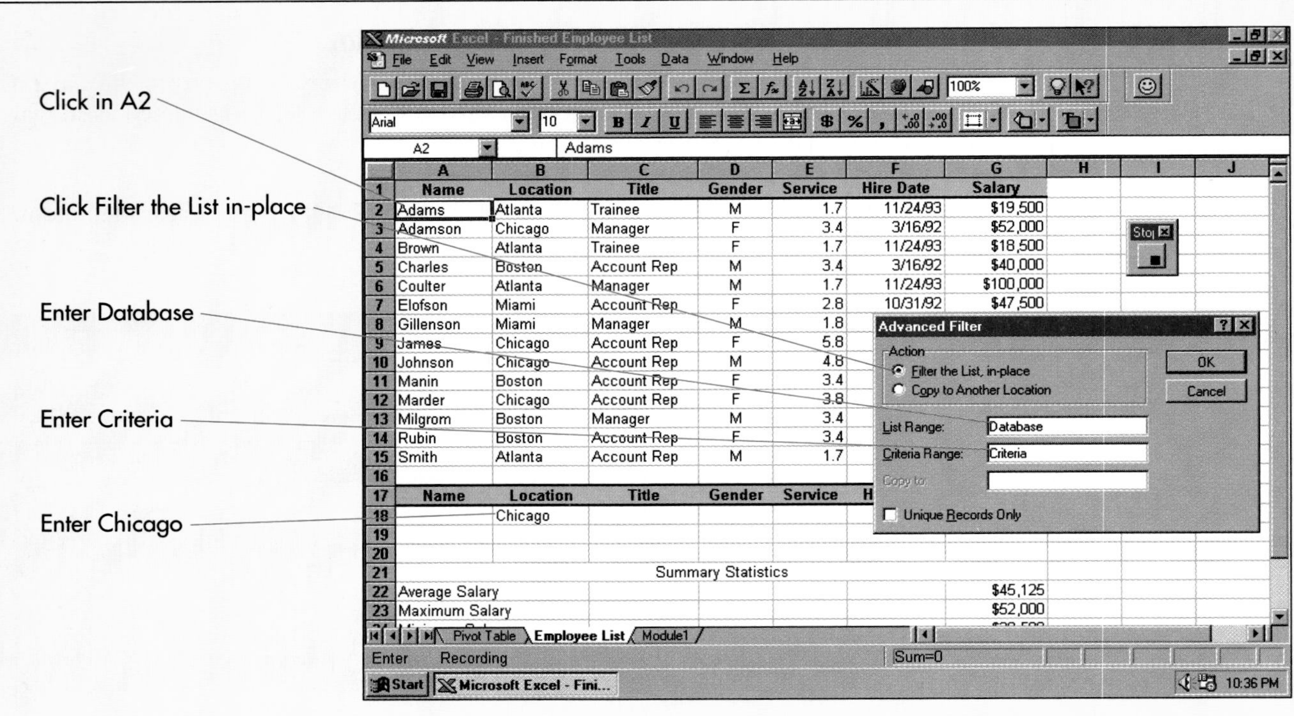

(e) Record the Macro (steps 4 and 5)

FIGURE 3.6 Hands-on Exercise 3 (continued)

STEP 7: View the Macro

- Click the **Module1 tab** to display the Chicago macro as shown in Figure 3.6f.
  - If you do not see a new tab, it means that the macro was recorded in the Personal Macro workbook because you chose the wrong option in step 4.
  - If your macro does not contain references to Database and Criteria within the Advanced Filter function, it means you specified cell ranges rather than defined names.
- Correct your macro so that it matches the macro in Figure 3.6f.
  - If the correction is minor, it is easiest to edit the macro directly.
  - If the changes are significant, delete the macro, then return to step 4 and rerecord the macro from the beginning. (To delete a macro, pull down the **Tools menu,** click **Macro,** select the macro you wish to delete, then click the **Delete button.**)
- Click the **Employee List tab** to continue working.

STEP 8: Customize the Toolbar

- Pull down the **View menu.** Click **Toolbars.** Click the **Customize command button** to display the Customize dialog box in Figure 3.6g.
- Click **Utility** from the Categories list box to display the buttons in the Utility category.
- Click the **Macro button** to see its description as shown in Figure 3.6g. Drag the Macro button onto any toolbar or to the gray area to the right of any docked toolbar.
- Click the **Close command button** to return to your worksheet.

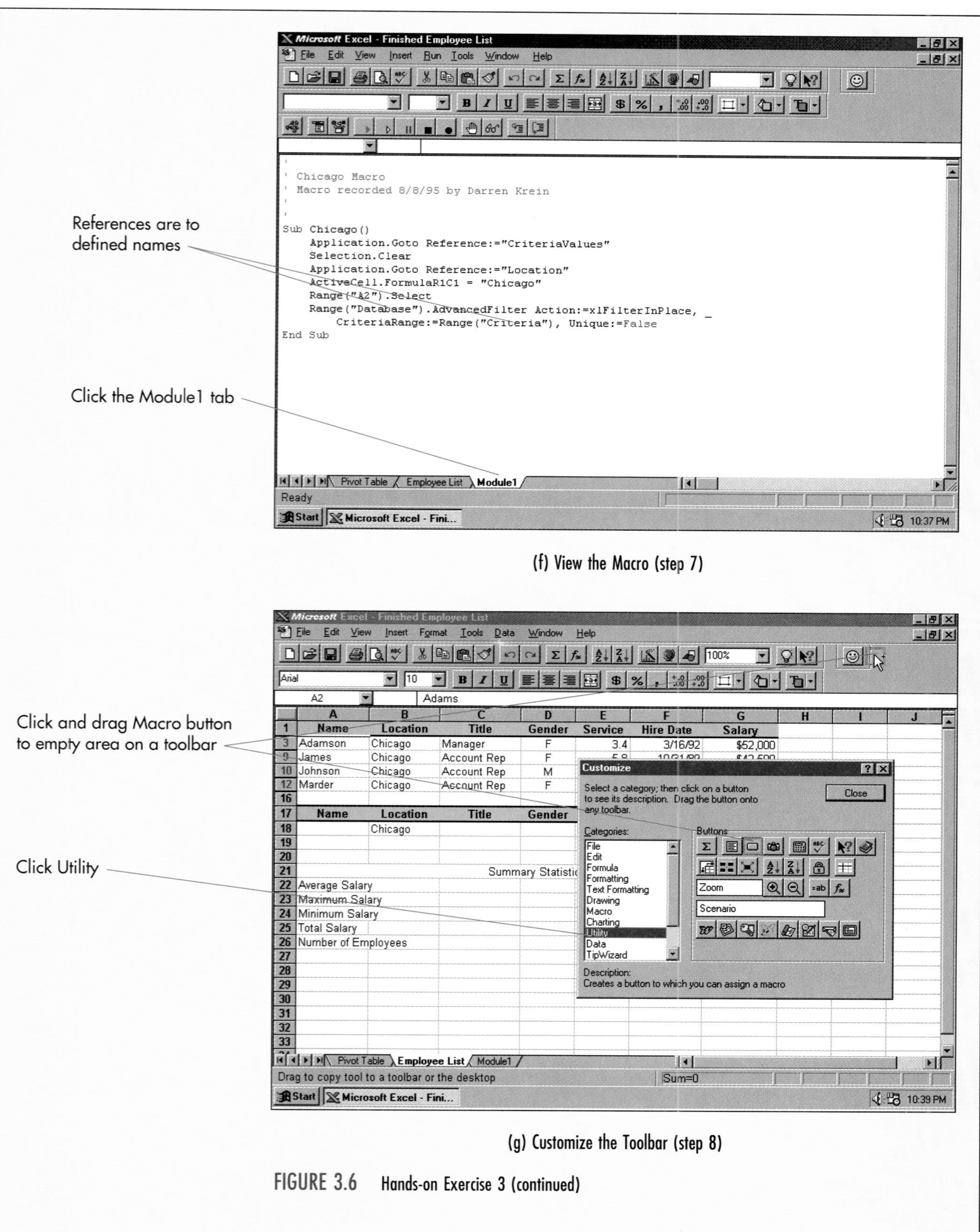

Microsoft Excel - Finished Employee List
References are to defined names
' Chicago Macro
' Macro recorded 8/8/95 by Darren Krein
Sub Chicago()
Application.Goto Reference:="CriteriaValues"
Selection.Clear
Application.Goto Reference:="Location"
ActiveCell.FormulaR1C1 = "Chicago"
Range("A2").Select
Range("Database").AdvancedFilter Action:=xlFilterInPlace, _
CriteriaRange:=Range("Criteria"), Unique:=False
End Sub
Click the Module1 tab
Pivot Table
Employee List
Module1
Ready

(f) View the Macro (step 7)

Click and drag Macro button to empty area on a toolbar
Click Utility
Customize
Select a category; then click on a button to see its description. Drag the button onto any toolbar.
Close
Categories:
Buttons
Description:
Creates a button to which you can assign a macro
Drag to copy tool to a toolbar or the desktop

(g) Customize the Toolbar (step 8)

FIGURE 3.6 Hands-on Exercise 3 (continued)

STEP 9: Assign the Macro

- Click the **Macro button** (the mouse pointer changes to a tiny crosshair). Click and drag in the worksheet as shown in Figure 3.6h to draw a button on the worksheet. Be sure to draw the button *below* the employee list, or the button may be hidden when a subsequent Data Filter command is executed.
- Release the mouse, and the Assign Macro dialog box will appear. Choose **Chicago** (the macro you just created) from the list of macro names. Click **OK** to close the Assign Macro dialog box.
- The button should still be selected. Click and drag to select the name of the button, **Button 1.**
- Type **Chicago** as the new name. Do *not* press the enter key.
- Click outside the button to deselect it. You should see a button named Chicago on your worksheet.

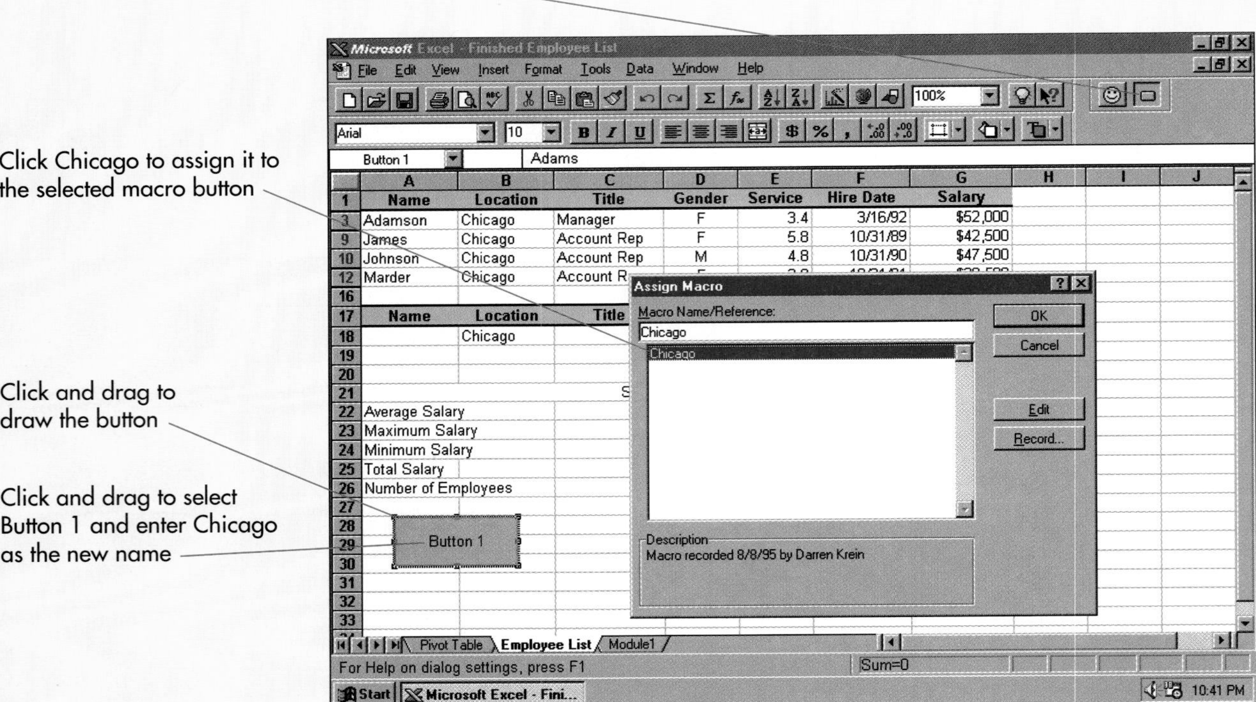

Macro button
Click Chicago to assign it to the selected macro button
Click and drag to draw the button
Click and drag to select Button 1 and enter Chicago as the new name
Assign Macro
Macro Name/Reference:
Chicago
OK
Cancel
Edit
Record...
Description
Macro recorded 8/8/95 by Darren Krein
Button 1

(h) Assign the Macro (step 9)

FIGURE 3.6 Hands-on Exercise 3 (continued)

STEP 10: Test the Macro

- Pull down the **Data menu,** click **Filter,** then click **Show All.**
- Click **cell B12.** Enter Miami to change the location for Marder. Press **enter.** The number of employees changes in the summary statistics area, as do the results of the other summary statistics.

- ➤ Click the **Chicago button** as shown in Figure 3.6i to execute the macro. Marder is *not* listed this time because she is no longer in Chicago.
- ➤ Pull down the **Data menu.** Click **Filter.** Click **Show All** to display the entire employee list.
- ➤ Click **cell B12.** Enter **Chicago** to change the location for this employee back to Chicago. Press **enter.** Click the **Chicago button** to execute the macro a second time. Marder is once again displayed with the Chicago employees.
- ➤ Pull down the **Data menu.** Click **Filter.** Click **Show All.**
- ➤ Save the workbook. Close the workbook. Exit Excel if you do not want to continue with the next exercise at this time.

SELECTING A BUTTON

The standard Windows convention to select an object is simply to click the object. You cannot, however, select a ***Macro button*** in this way, because if you click the button, you execute the associated macro. To select a Macro button, press and hold the Ctrl key as you click the left mouse button. (You can also select a button by clicking the right mouse button to produce a shortcut menu.) Once the button has been selected, you can edit its name, and/or move or size the button just as you can any other Windows object.

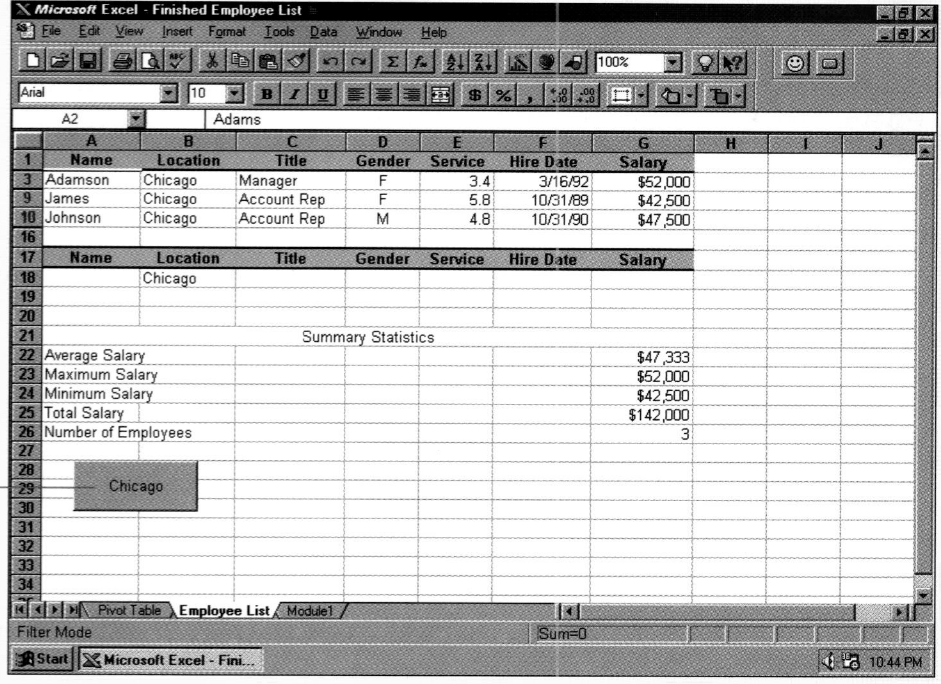

(i) Test the Macro (step 10)

FIGURE 3.6 Hands-on Exercise 3 (continued)

CREATING ADDITIONAL MACROS

The macro to filter the Chicago employees is only one of several macros that could be developed in conjunction with the employee list with which we have been working. It's reasonable to assume that you might want additional macros to select other groups of employees, such as employees in another city or employees with a particular job title.

You could develop the additional macros by recording them from scratch as you did the Chicago macro. Alternatively, you could copy the Chicago macro, give it a different name, then edit the copied macro so that it performs the desired function. This is the approach we follow in the next hands-on exercise.

Visual Basic statements are edited the same way text is edited in a word processing program. Thus, you toggle back and forth between the insertion or overtype modes to insert or type over text. You can also use the Cut, Copy, and Paste commands just as you would with a word processor. Text (Visual Basic commands) is cut or copied from one location to the clipboard, from where it can be pasted to another location.

THE FIND AND REPLACE COMMANDS

Anyone familiar with a word processor takes the Find and Replace commands for granted, but did you know the same capabilities exist in Excel? Pull down the Edit menu and choose either command. You have the same options as in the parallel command in Word, such as a case-sensitive (or insensitive) search or a limitation to a whole word search.

HANDS-ON EXERCISE 4

Creating Additional Macros

Objective: Use the Copy and Paste commands to duplicate an existing macro, then modify the copied macro to create an entirely new macro. Use Figure 3.7 as a guide in the exercise.

STEP 1: Copy the Chicago Macro

- Start Excel. Open the **Finished Employee List** workbook from the previous exercise.
- Click the **Module1 tab** to make it active. Click at the beginning of the **Chicago** macro, then click and drag to select the entire macro as shown in Figure 3.7a.
- Pull down the **Edit menu** and click **Copy** (or click the **Copy button** on the Standard toolbar).
- Click below the End Sub statement to deselect the macro and simultaneously establish the position of the insertion point. Press **enter** to insert a blank line below the End Sub statement.
- Pull down the **Edit menu** and click **Paste** (or click the **Paste button** on the Standard toolbar). The Chicago macro has been copied and now appears twice in Module1.

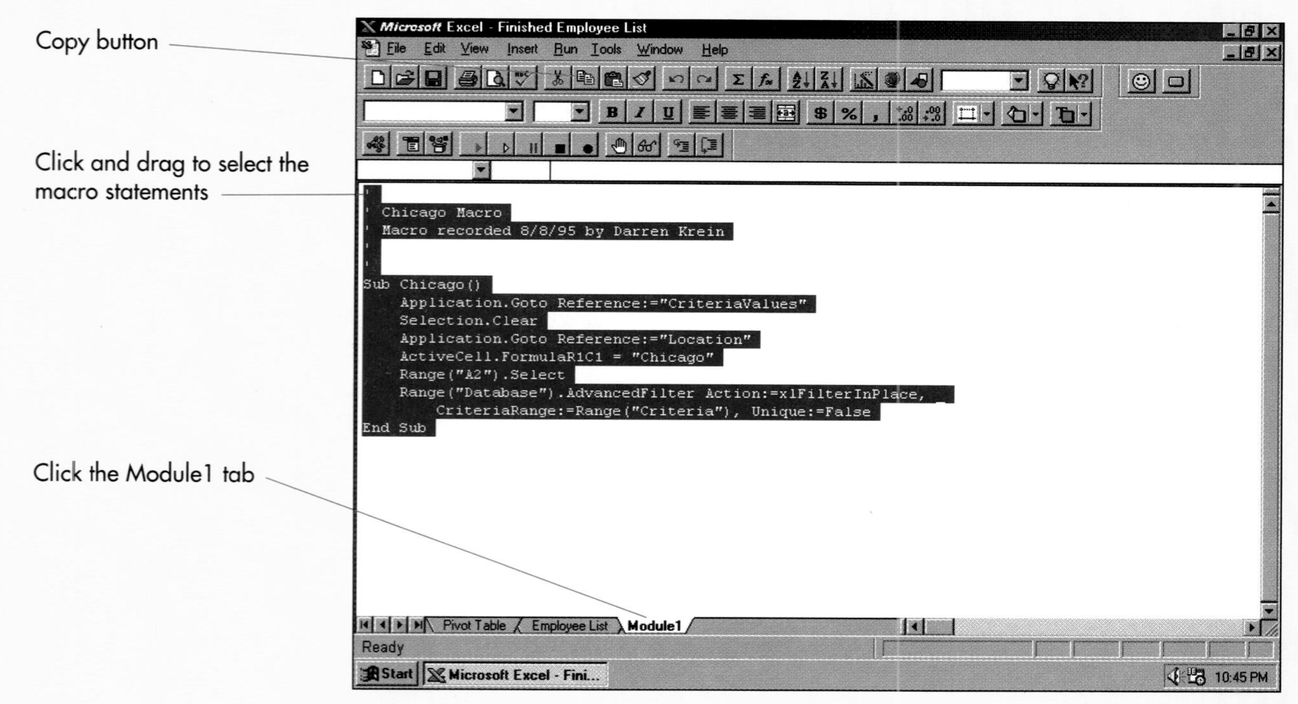

(a) Copy the Chicago Macro (step 1)

FIGURE 3.7 Hands-on Exercise 4

THE SHIFT KEY

You can select text for editing (or replacement) with the mouse, or alternatively, you can select by using the cursor keys on the keyboard. Set the insertion point where you want the selection to begin, then press and hold the Shift key as you use the cursor keys to move the insertion point to the end of the selection.

STEP 2: Create the Manager Macro

- Click in front of the second Chicago macro to set the insertion point. Pull down the **Edit menu.** Click **Replace** to display the Replace dialog box as shown in Figure 3.7b.
- Enter **Chicago** in the Find What text box. Press the **tab key.** Enter **Manager** in the Replace with text box. Click the **Find Next command button.**
- Excel searches for the first occurrence of Chicago, which should be in the comment statement of the copied macro. (If this is not the case, click the **Find Next command button** until your screen matches Figure 3.7b.)
- Click the **Replace command button.** Excel substitutes Manager for Chicago, then looks for the next occurrence of Chicago. Click **Replace.** Click **Replace** a third time to make another substitution. You are now positioned at the top of the sheet (at the beginning of the Chicago macro), where you *don't* want to make the substitution. Click the **Close command button.**

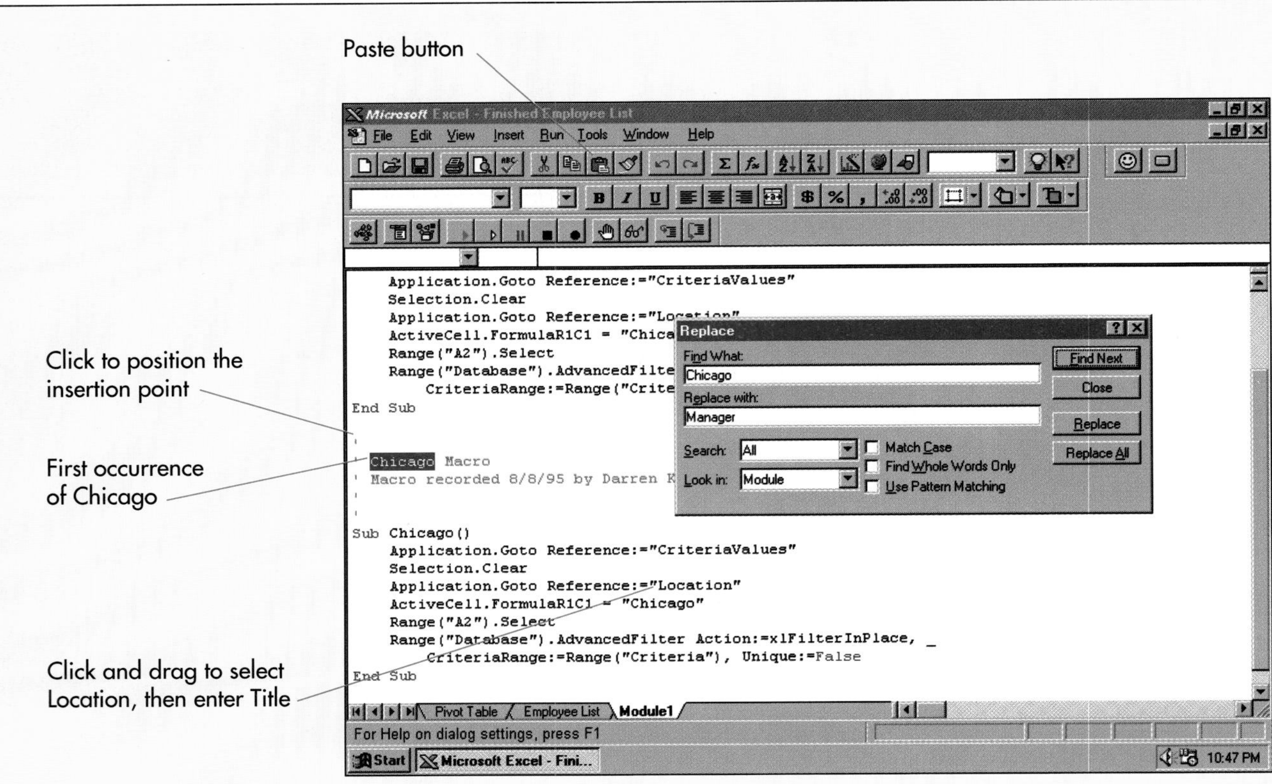
Paste button
Click to position the insertion point
First occurrence of Chicago
Click and drag to select Location, then enter Title
Microsoft Excel - Finished Employee List
File Edit View Insert Run Tools Window Help
Application.Goto Reference:="CriteriaValues"
Selection.Clear
ActiveCell.FormulaR1C1 = "Chica
Range("A2").Select
Range("Database").AdvancedFilte
CriteriaRange:=Range("Crite
End Sub
Chicago Macro
Macro recorded 8/8/95 by Darren K
Sub Chicago()
Application.Goto Reference:="CriteriaValues"
Selection.Clear
Application.Goto Reference:="Location"
ActiveCell.FormulaR1C1 = "Chicago"
Range("A2").Select
Range("Database").AdvancedFilter Action:=xlFilterInPlace, _
CriteriaRange:=Range("Criteria"), Unique:=False
End Sub
Replace
Find What:
Chicago
Replace with:
Manager
Search: All
Look in: Module
Match Case
Find Whole Words Only
Use Pattern Matching
Find Next
Close
Replace
Replace All
Pivot Table
Employee List
Module1
For Help on dialog settings, press F1
Start
Microsoft Excel - Fini...
10:47 PM

(b) The Replace Command (step 2)

FIGURE 3.7 Hands-on Exercise 4 (continued)

- Click and drag to select **Location** within the Application.Goto.Reference statement in the Manager macro. Enter **Title.** (The criteria within the macro have been changed from employees who work in Chicago to those whose title is Manager.)
- Save the workbook.

STEP 3: Run the Manager Macro

- Click the **Employee List tab** to return to the worksheet. Pull down the **Tools menu.** Click **Macro** to display the Macro dialog box as shown in Figure 3.7c.
- You should see two macros: Chicago, which was created in the previous exercise, and Manager, which you just created. (If the Manager macro does not appear, click the **Module1 tab** and correct the appropriate Sub statement to include Manager() as the name of the macro.)
- Select the **Manager macro,** then click **Run** to run the macro, after which you should see four employees (Adamson, Coulter, Gillenson, and Milgrom). If the macro does not execute correctly, click the **Module1 tab** to make the necessary corrections, then rerun the macro.

STEP 4: Assign a Button

- Click the **Macro button** on the toolbar (the mouse pointer changes to a tiny crosshair), then click and drag in the worksheet to draw a button on the worksheet. Release the mouse.
- Choose **Manager** (the macro you just created) from the list of macro names as shown in Figure 3.7d. Click **OK** to close the Assign Macro dialog box.

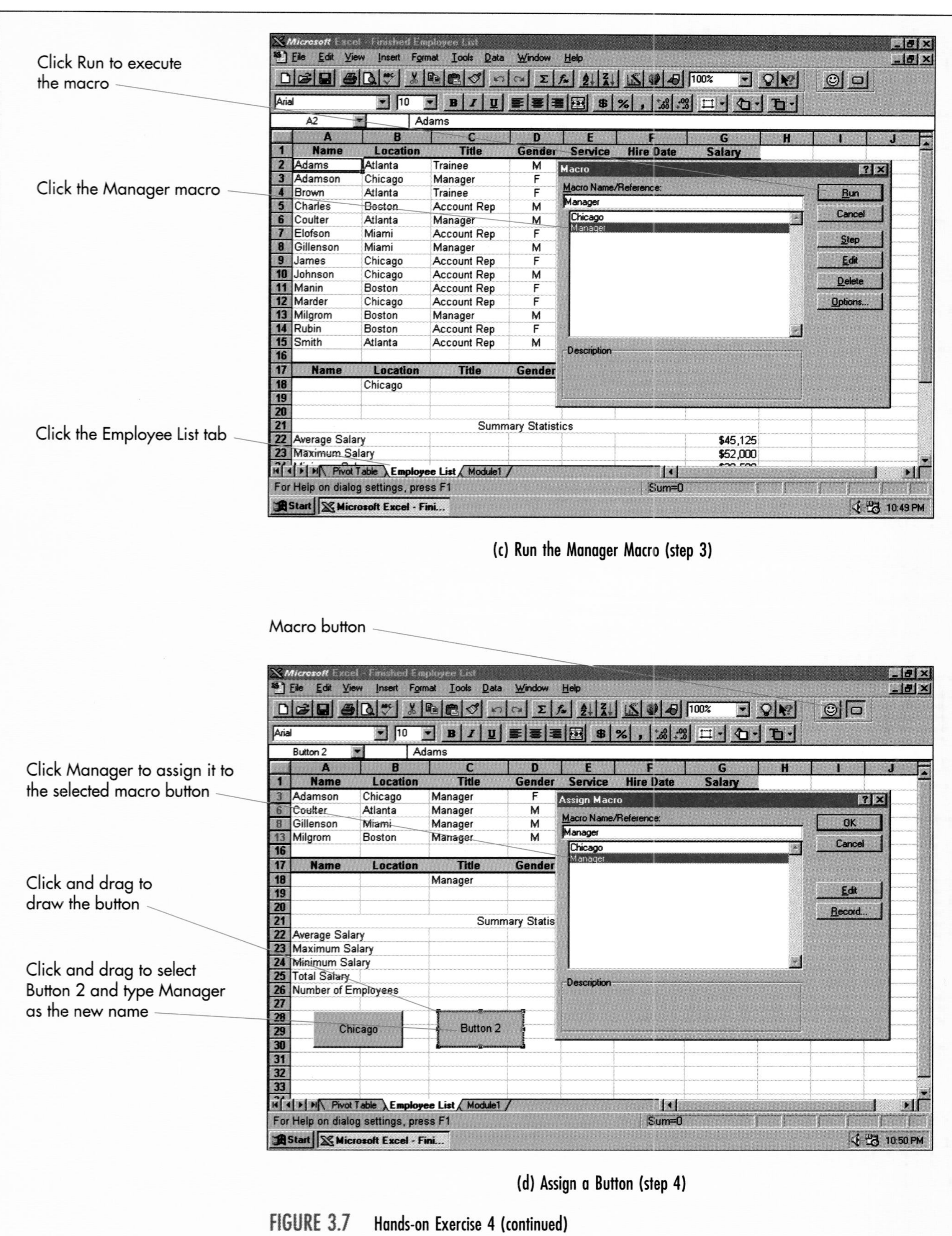

Click Run to execute the macro
Click the Manager macro
Click the Employee List tab
Macro button
Click Manager to assign it to the selected macro button
Click and drag to draw the button
Click and drag to select Button 2 and type Manager as the new name

(c) Run the Manager Macro (step 3)

(d) Assign a Button (step 4)

FIGURE 3.7 Hands-on Exercise 4 (continued)

- ➤ The button should still be selected. Click and drag to select the name of the button, **Button 2,** then type **Manager** as the new name. Do *not* press the enter key. Click outside the button to deselect it.
- ➤ There should be two buttons on your worksheet, one each for the Chicago and Manager macros.
- ➤ Click the **Chicago button** to execute the Chicago macro. You should see four employees with an average salary of $45,125.
- ➤ Click the **Manager button** to execute the Manager macro. You should see four employees with an average salary of $66,125.

THE STEP INTO COMMAND

The Step Into command helps to debug a macro, as it executes the statements one at a time. Pull down the Tools menu, click Macro, select the macro to debug, then click the Step command button. Move and/or size the Debug window so that you can see both the worksheet and the macro. Click the ***Step Into button*** on the Visual Basic toolbar to move into the macro, then click the Step Into button again to execute the first statement in the macro and view its results. Continue to click the Step Into button to execute the statements one at a time until the macro has completed execution.

STEP 5: Create the Chicago Manager Macro

- ➤ Click the **Module1 tab.** Press **Ctrl+Home** to move to the beginning of Module 1. Click and drag to select the entire Chicago macro. Be sure to include the End Sub statement in your selection.
- ➤ Click the **Copy button** on the Standard toolbar to copy the selected macro to the clipboard.
- ➤ Press **Ctrl+End** to move to the end of the module sheet. Click the **Paste button** on the Standard toolbar to complete the copy operation.
- ➤ Change **Chicago** to **ChicagoManager** in both the comment statement and the Sub statement as shown in Figure 3.7e.
- ➤ Click at the end of the line ActiveCell.FormulaR1C1 = "Chicago". Press **enter** to begin a new line, then enter the two statements to include managers as part of the criteria:
  - Click and drag to select the two statements in the **Manager macro** as shown in Figure 3.7e.
  - Click the **Copy button** to copy these statements to the clipboard.
  - Click in the **ChicagoManager macro** where you want the statements to go.
  - Click the **Paste button** to complete the copy operation.
  - Delete any unnecessary blank lines or spaces that may remain.
- ➤ Save the workbook.

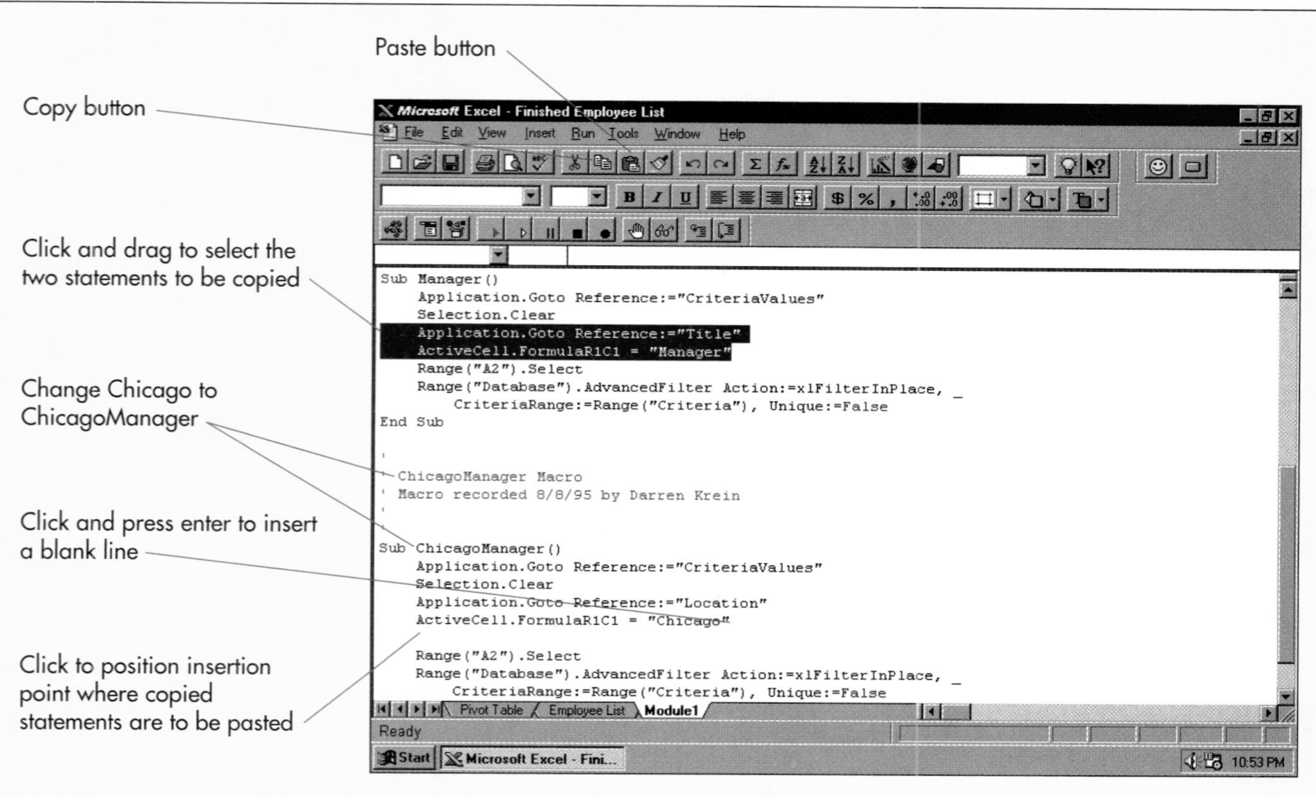

(e) Create the ChicagoManager Macro (step 5)

FIGURE 3.7 Hands-on Exercise 4 (continued)

> **THE INPUT BOX STATEMENT**
>
> The Visual Basic InputBox adds flexibility to a macro by obtaining input from the user when the macro is executed. You can generalize the ChicagoManager macro to select employees with any title from any location by using the InputBox statement instead of specifying the specific selection criteria. See practice exercise 1 at the end of the chapter.

STEP 6: Assign a Button

- Click the **Employee List tab.** Click the Macro button on the toolbar, then click and drag to draw a new button on the worksheet. Assign the **ChicagoManager macro** to this button. Click and drag to select the name of the Button, **Button 3.** Enter **Chicago Manager** as the new name. Do not press enter.
- Click outside the button to deselect it. Point to the **ChicagoManager button,** then press and hold the **Ctrl key** as you click the mouse to select the button. Drag a sizing handle to size it appropriately. Click outside the button to deselect it.
- Click the **ChicagoManager button** to execute the macro. You should see one employee, Adamson, who is the only Chicago manager.

- Click the **Chicago button** to execute the Chicago macro. You should see an average salary of $45,125.
- Click the **Manager button** to execute the Manager macro. You should see an average salary of $66,125.

CREATE UNIFORM BUTTONS

The easiest way to make all buttons the same size is to create the first button, then copy that button to create the others. To copy a button, press the Ctrl key as you select (click) the button, then click the Copy button on the Standard toolbar. Click in the worksheet where you want the new button to appear, then click the Paste button. Click and drag over the name of the button and enter a new name. Right click the new button, then click Assign Macro from the shortcut menu. Select the name of the new macro, then click OK.

STEP 7: Object Properties

- Point to the **ChicagoManager button,** then press and hold the **Ctrl key** to select this button.
- Press the **Ctrl key,** then press and hold the **Shift key** as you click the **Chicago button.** The ChicagoManager and Chicago buttons are both selected.
- Press and hold both the **Shift** and **Ctrl keys** as you click the **Manager button** to add it to the selection.
- All three buttons should be selected as shown in Figure 3.7f. Point to any of the buttons and click the **right mouse button** to display a shortcut menu. Click **Format Object.**
- Click the **Properties tab** in the Format Object dialog box:
  - Check the **Print Object box** so that the macro buttons are included on the printed output.
  - Click the **Move but Don't Size with Cells** option button.
  - Click **OK** to exit the dialog box and return to the worksheet.
- Click anywhere in the worksheet to deselect the buttons.
- Click the **Print button** on the Standard toolbar to print the worksheet.
- Click the **Module1 tab.** Click the **Print button** to print the macros.
- Save the workbook a final time. Close the workbook. Exit Excel if you don't want to continue with the next exercise at this time.

OBJECT PROPERTIES

The size and/or position of a macro button changes in accordance with the cell(s) on which it is positioned. To prevent this from happening, select the macro button, click the right mouse button to display a shortcut menu, then click the Format Object command. Click the Properties tab, choose the appropriate Object Positioning option button, then click OK to close the Format Object dialog box.

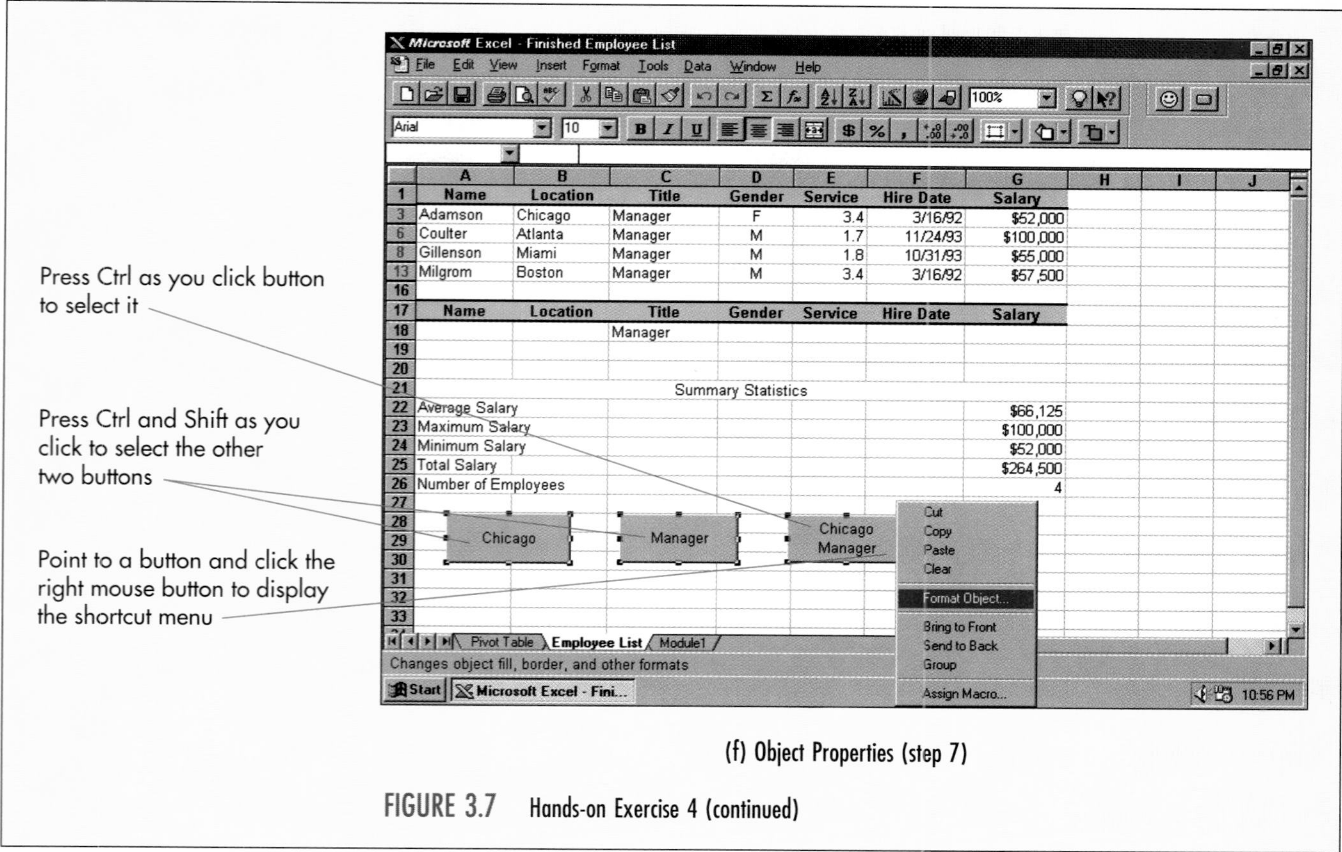

(f) Object Properties (step 7)

FIGURE 3.7 Hands-on Exercise 4 (continued)

LOOPS AND DECISION MAKING

Thus far, all of the macros in the chapter have consisted entirely of Excel commands that were captured by the macro recorder as they were executed. Excel macros can be made significantly more powerful by incorporating additional Visual Basic statements that enable true programming. These include the If statement for decision making, and the Do statement to implement a ***loop*** (one or more commands that are executed repeatedly until a condition is met).

Consider, for example, the worksheet and associated macro in Figure 3.8. The worksheet is similar to those used in the preceding exercises, except that the font color of the data for managers is red. Think for a minute how you would do this manually. You would look at the first employee in the list, examine the employee's title to determine if that employee is a manager, and if so, change the font color for that employee. You would then repeat these steps for all of the other employees on the list. It sounds tedious, but that is exactly what you would do if asked to change the font color for the managers.

Now ask yourself whether you could implement the entire process with the macro recorder. You could use the recorder to capture the commands to select a specific row within the list and change the font color. You could not, however, use the recorder to determine whether or not to select a particular row (i.e., whether the employee is a manager) because you make that decision by comparing the cell contents to a specific criterion. Nor is there a way to tell the recorder to repeat the process for every employee. In other words, you need to go beyond merely capturing Excel commands. You need to include additional Visual Basic statements to enable true programming.

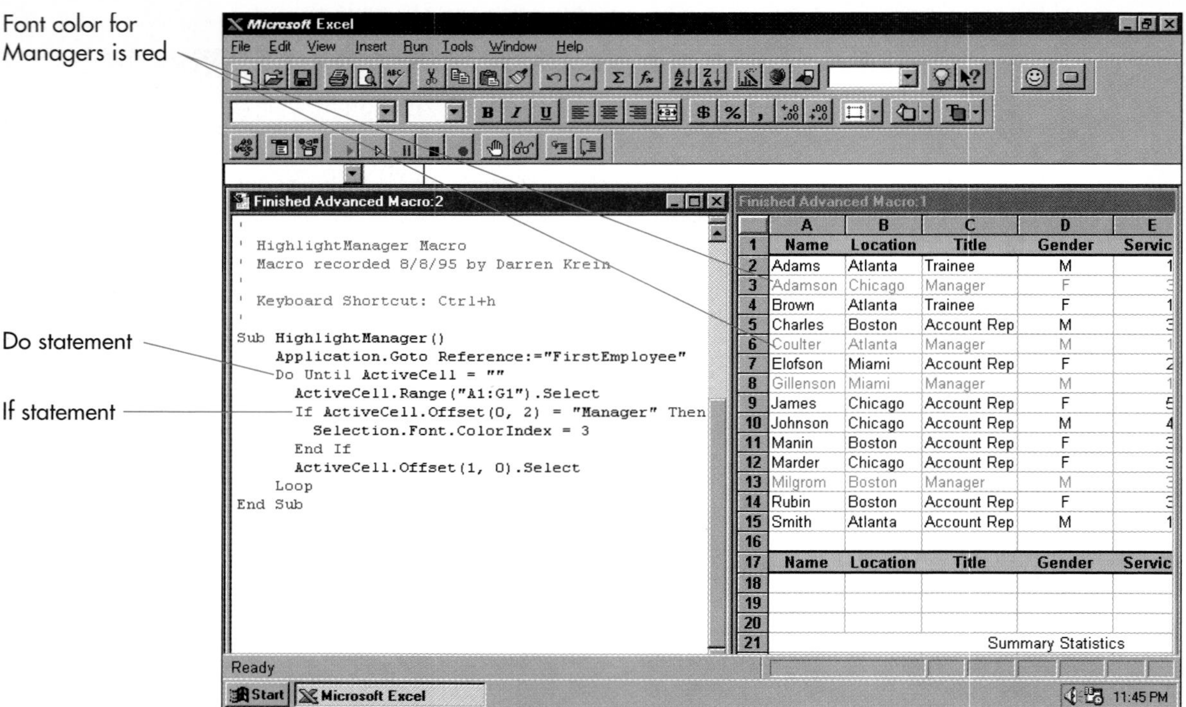

FIGURE 3.8 Loops and Decision Making

The HighlightManager macro in Figure 3.8 uses the If statement to implement a decision (to determine whether the selected employee is a manager) and the Do statement to implement a loop (to repeat the commands until all employees in the list have been processed). To understand how the macro works, you need to know the basic syntax of each statement.

If Statement

The ***If statement*** conditionally executes a statement (or group of statements), depending on the value of an expression (condition). The If statement determines whether an expression is true, and if so, executes the commands between the If and End If. For example:

```
If ActiveCell.Offset(0, 2) = "Manager" Then
    Selection.Font.ColorIndex = 3
End If
```

IF-THEN-ELSE

The If statement includes an optional Else clause whose statements are executed if the condition is false. Consider:

If condition Then statements [Else statements] End If

The condition is evaluated as either true or false. If the condition is true, the statements following Then are executed; otherwise the statements following Else are executed. Either way, execution continues with the statement following End If. Use the Help command for additional information and examples.

This If statement determines whether the cell two columns to the right of the active cell (the offset indicates a relative reference) contains the text "Manager", and if so, changes the font color of the (previously) selected text. The number three corresponds to the color red. No action is taken if the condition is false. Either way, execution continues with the command below the End If.

Do Statement

The ***Do statement*** repeats a block of statements until a condition becomes true. For example:

```
Do Until ActiveCell = ""
    ActiveCell.Range("A1:G1").Select
    If ActiveCell.Offset(0, 2) = "Manager" Then
        Selection.Font.ColorIndex = 3
    End If
    ActiveCell.Offset(1, 0).Select
Loop
```

The statements within the loop are executed repeatedly until the active cell is empty (i.e., ActiveCell = ""). The first statement in the loop selects the cells in columns A through G of the current row. (Relative references are used, and you may want to refer to the earlier discussion on page 113, which indicated that A1:G1 specifies the shape of a range rather than a specific cell address.) The If statement determines whether the current employee is a manager and, if so, changes the font color for the selected cells. The last statement selects the cell one row below the active cell to process the next employee. (Omission of this statement would process the same row indefinitely, creating what is known as an infinite loop.)

The macro in Figure 3.8 is a nontrivial macro that illustrates the potential of Visual Basic. Try to gain a conceptual understanding of how the macro works, but do not be concerned if you are confused initially. Do the hands-on exercise, and you'll be pleased at how much clearer it will be when you have created the macro yourself.

A SENSE OF FAMILIARITY

Visual Basic has the basic capabilities found in any other programming language. If you have programmed before, whether in Pascal, C, or even COBOL, you will find all of the logic structures you are used to. These include the Do While and Do Until statements, the If-Then-Else statement for decision making, nested If statements, a Case statement, and/or calls to subprograms.

HANDS-ON EXERCISE 5

Loops and Decision Making

Objective: To implement loops and decision making in a macro through the Do Until and If statements. Use Figure 3.9 as a guide in doing the exercise.

STEP 1: The ClearColor Macro

- Open the **Advanced Macro workbook** in the **Exploring Excel folder,** then save the workbook as **Finished Advanced Macro** workbook. The data for the employees in rows 3, 6, 8, and 13 appears in red to indicate these employees are managers.
- Pull down the **Tools menu.** Click the **Macro** command to produce the dialog box in Figure 3.9a.
- Select **ClearColor,** then click **Run** to execute this macro and clear the red color from the managerial employees. It is important to know that the ClearColor macro works, as you will use it throughout the exercise.

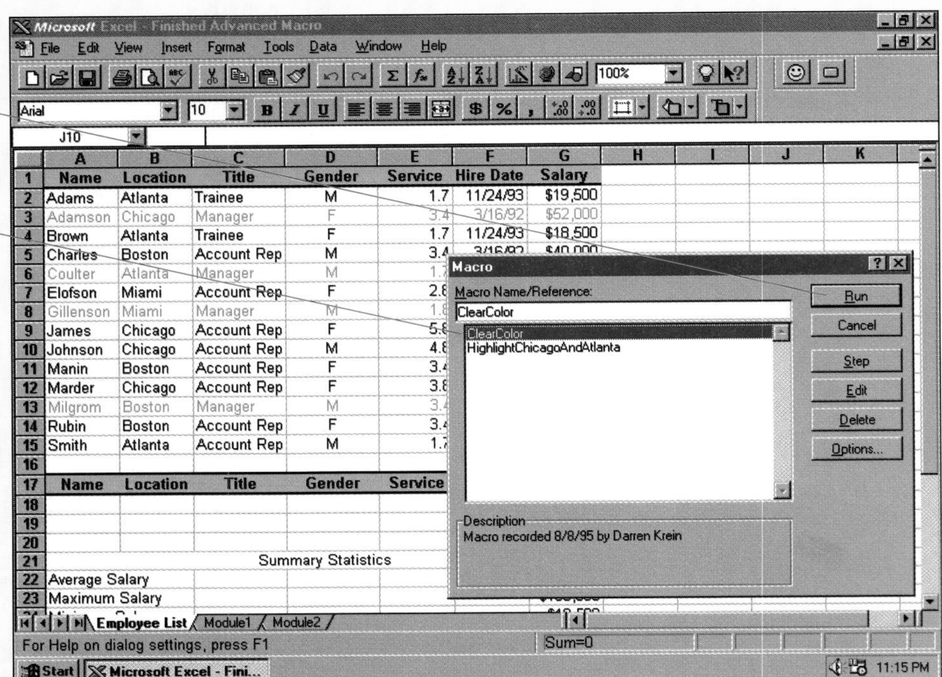

(a) The ClearColor Macro (step 1)

FIGURE 3.9 Hands-on Exercise 5

STEP 2: Mark the Position for Recording

- Click the tab for **Module1.** Press **Ctrl+End** to move the insertion point to the end of the ClearColor macro. Press **enter** to insert a blank line.
- Pull down the **Tools menu,** then click (or point to) the **Record Macro command.** Click **Mark Position for Recording** (so that the new macro will be inserted on the existing macro sheet instead of on a new sheet).
- Click the **Employee List tab** to return to the worksheet and begin recording the macro.

STEP 3: Record the Macro

- You must choose the active cell before recording the macro. Click **cell A3,** the cell containing the name of the first manager.
- Pull down the **Tools menu,** then click the **Record Macro** command.

- If **Use Relative References** is already checked, click **Record New Macro** from the cascaded menu to produce the Record New Macro dialog box.
- If **Use Relative References** is not checked, click the command on, then pull down the **Tools menu** and click (or point to) the **Record Macro command** a second time. Click **Record New Macro** from the cascaded menu to produce the Record New Macro dialog box.

➤ Enter **HighlightManager** in the Macro Name text box.

➤ Click the **Options command button** to display additional options within the dialog box. Check the **Shortcut Key check box,** delete the existing letter (e), and replace the existing shortcut with a **lowercase h.** (Ctrl+h should appear as the shortcut.)

➤ Check the option button for **This Workbook.** Check the option button for **Visual Basic.** Click **OK** to begin recording the macro.

➤ Click and drag to select **cells A3** through **G3** as shown in Figure 3.9b. Click the **drop-down arrow** in the **Font color** list box. Click **Red.** Click the **Stop Recording button.**

➤ Click anywhere in the worksheet to deselect cells A3 through G3 so you can see the effect of the macro; cells A3 through G3 should be displayed in red.

➤ Save the workbook.

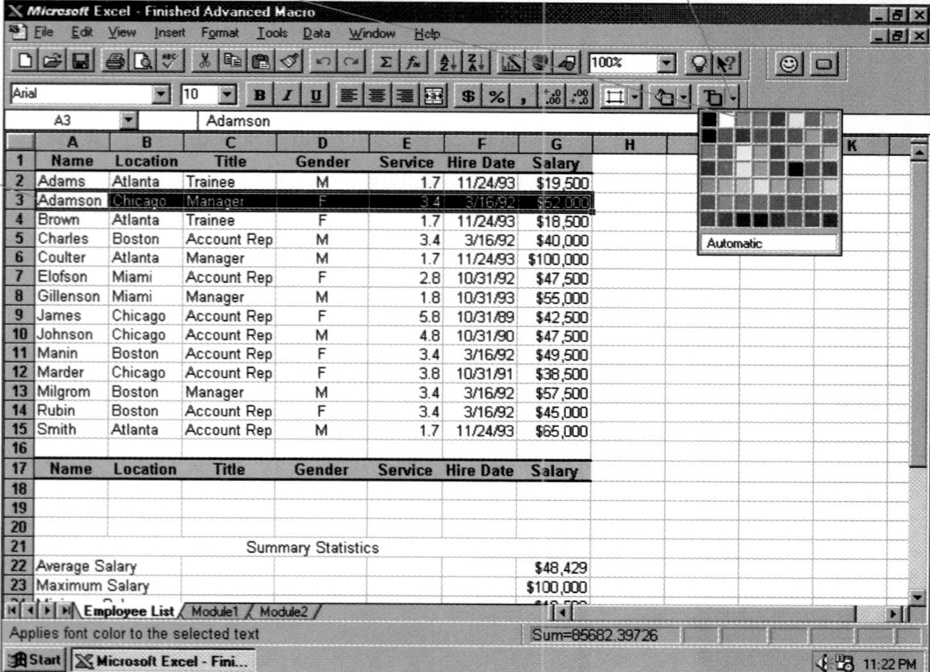

(b) Record the Macro (step 3)

FIGURE 3.9 Hands-on Exercise 5 (continued)

STEP 4: View and Test the Macro

➤ Pull down the **Window menu** (and close Book1 if it is open). Click **New Window** to open a second window as shown in Figure 3.9c.

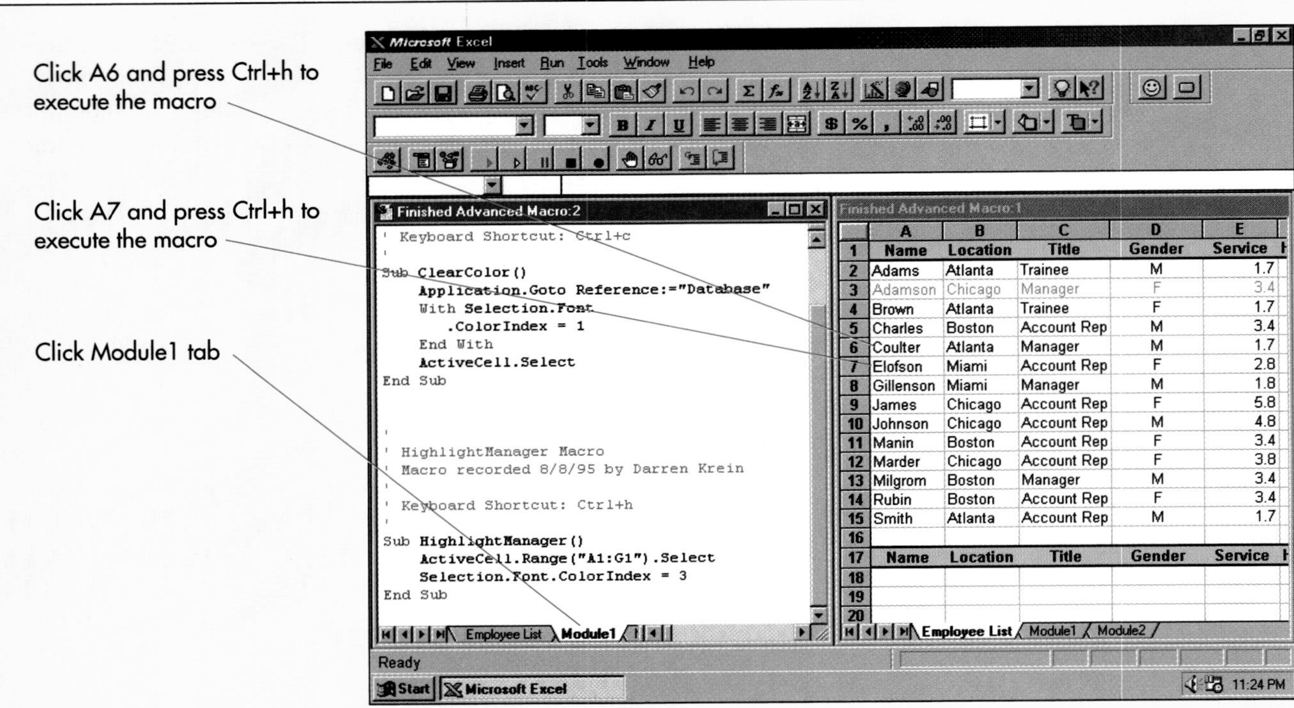

(c) View and Test the Macro (step 4)

FIGURE 3.9 Hands-on Exercise 5 (continued)

- Pull down the **Window menu** a second time. Click **Arrange.** Chose the **Tiled option button,** then click **OK** to display the open windows side by side.
- Click in the window on the left. Click the **Module1 tab** to view the newly created macro in this window. Your screen should match Figure 3.9c.
- Click in the window on the right. Click **cell A6** (the cell containing the name of the next manager). Press **Ctrl+h** to execute the HighlightManager macro. The font in cells A6 through G6 changes to red.
- Click **cell A7.** Press **Ctrl+h** to execute the HighlightManager macro. The font for this employee is also red, although the employee is *not* a manager.

STEP 5: Add the If Statement

- Press **Ctrl+c** to execute the ClearColor macro. The data for all employees is again displayed in black.
- Click in the window containing the **HighlightManager** macro. Add the **If** and **End If** statements exactly as they are shown in Figure 3.9d. Use the **Tab key** (or press the **space bar**) to indent the Selection statement within the If and End If statements.
- Click in the window containing the worksheet, then click **cell A3.** Press **Ctrl+h** to execute the modified HighlightManager macro. Cells A3 through G3 are highlighted since this employee is a manager.
- Click **cell A4.** Press **Ctrl+h.** The row is selected, but the color of the font remains unchanged. The If statement prevents these cells from being highlighted because the employee is not a manager. Press **Ctrl+c** to remove all highlighting.
- Save the workbook.

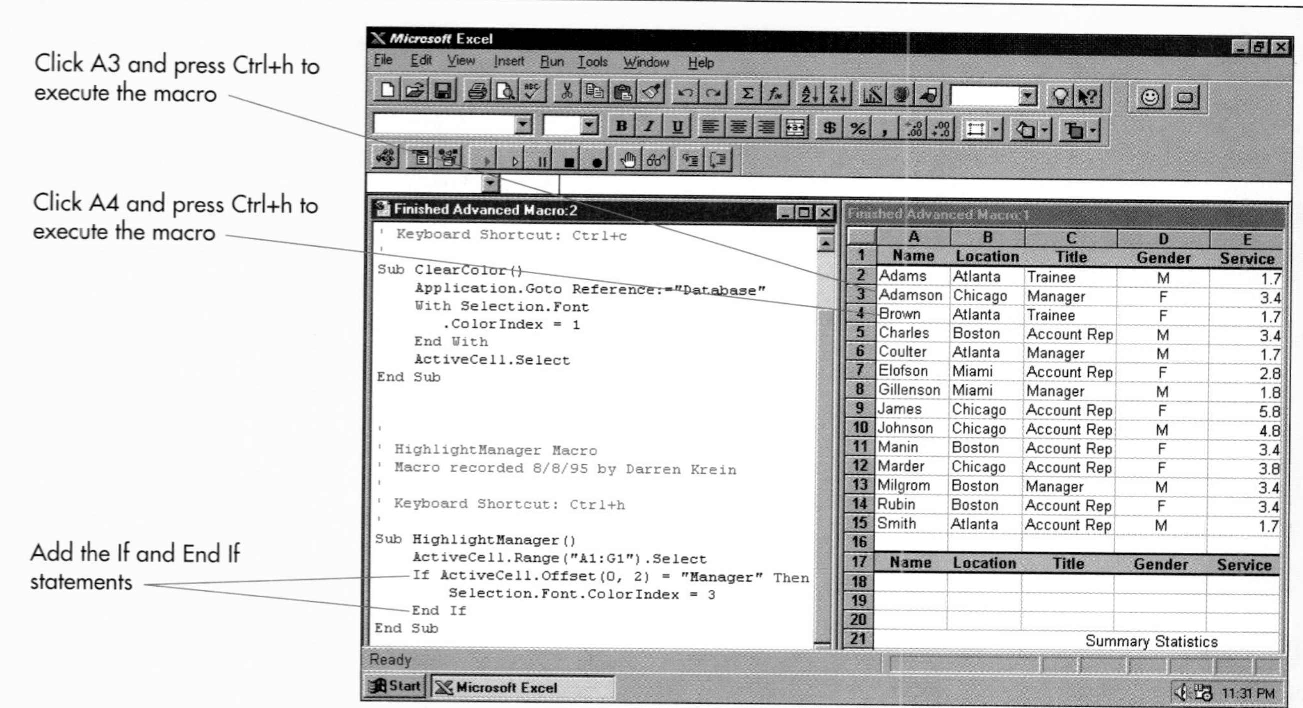

(d) Add the IF Statement (step 5)

FIGURE 3.9 Hands-on Exercise 5 (continued)

INDENT

Indentation does not affect the execution of a macro. It, does, however, make the macro easier to read, and we suggest you follow common conventions in developing your macros. Indent the conditional statements associated with an If statement by a consistent amount. Place the End If statement on a line by itself, directly under the associated If.

STEP 6: An Endless Loop

- Click in the window containing the **HighlightManager** macro. Add the **Do Until** and **Loop** statements exactly as they appear in Figure 3.9e. Indent the other statements as shown in the figure.
- Click **cell A3** of the worksheet. Press **Ctrl+h** to execute the macro. Cells A3 through G3 will be displayed in red, but the macro continues to execute indefinitely as it applies color to the same record over and over. The macro is in an infinite loop (as can be seen by the hourglass that remains on your monitor).
- Press **Ctrl+Break** to cease execution of the macro. You will see the dialog box in Figure 3.9e, indicating that an error has been encountered during the execution of the macro.
- Click the **Debug command button** to debug the macro, then continue as described in step 7.

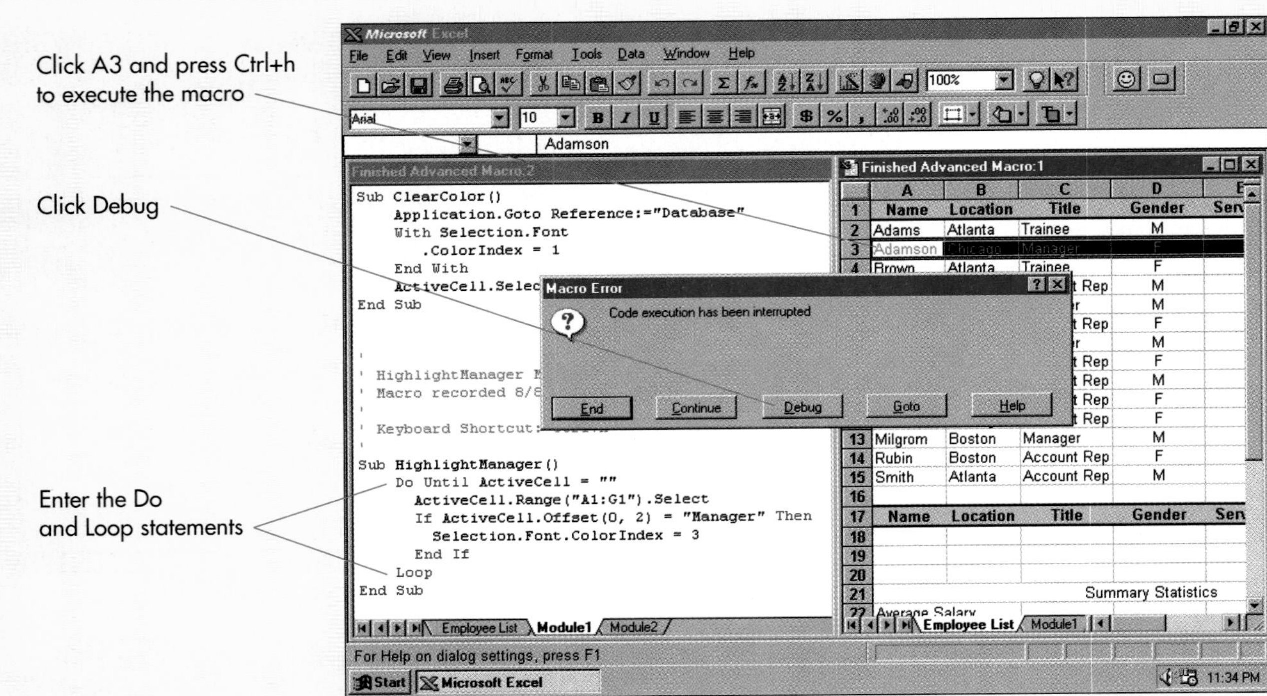

(e) An Endless Loop (step 6)

FIGURE 3.9 Hands-on Exercise 5 (continued)

AN ENDLESS LOOP

The glossary in the Programmer's Guide for a popular database contains the following definitions:

Endless loop—See loop, endless
Loop, endless—See endless loop

We don't know whether these entries were deliberate or not, but the point is made either way. Endless loops are a common and frustrating bug. Press Ctrl+Break to halt execution, then click the Debug command button to step through the macro and locate the source of the error.

STEP 7: Debug the Macro

- Click and drag the **Debug window** so that its position approximates that of Figure 3.9f.
- Click the **Step Into button** on the Visual Basic toolbar several times to view the execution of the next several steps in the macro. You will see that the macro is stuck in a loop as the If statement is executed indefinitely.
- Close the Debug window.

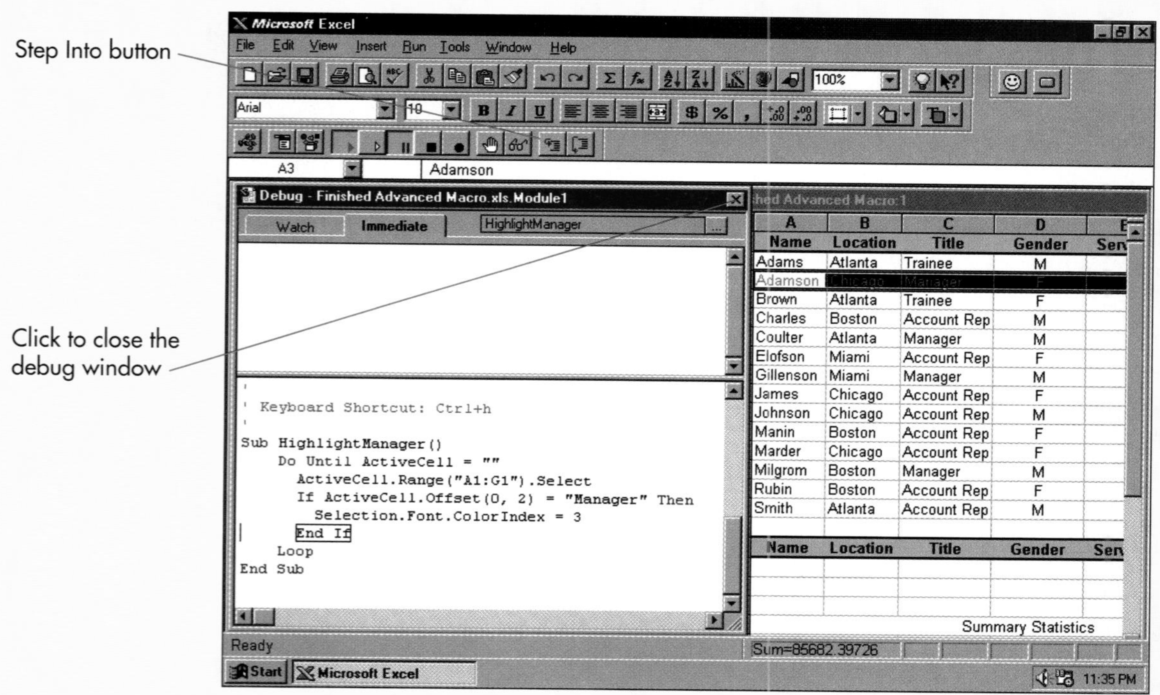

(f) Debug the Macro (step 7)

FIGURE 3.9 Hands-on Exercise 5 (continued)

RED, GREEN, AND BLUE

Visual Basic automatically assigns different colors to different types of statements (or a portion of those statements). Any statement containing a syntactical error appears in red. Comments appear in green. Key words such as Sub, End Sub, If, End If, Do Until, and Loop appear in blue.

STEP 8: Complete the Macro

- Click in **cell A2** of the worksheet. Click in the **Name Box.** Enter **FirstEmployee** to name this cell. Press **enter.**
- Click in the window containing the macro. Click at the end of the Sub statement and press **enter** to insert a blank line. Add the statement to select the cell named FirstEmployee as shown in Figure 3.9g. This ensures that the macro always begins in row two by selecting the cell named FirstEmployee.
- Click immediately after the End If statement. Press **enter.** Add the statement containing the offset (1,0) as shown in Figure 3.9g, which selects the cell one row below the current row.
- Click anywhere in the worksheet except cell A2. Press **Ctrl+c** to clear the color. Press **Ctrl+h** to execute the HighlightManager macro.
- The macro begins by selecting cell A2, then proceeds to highlight all managers in red. Save the workbook a final time. Exit Excel.

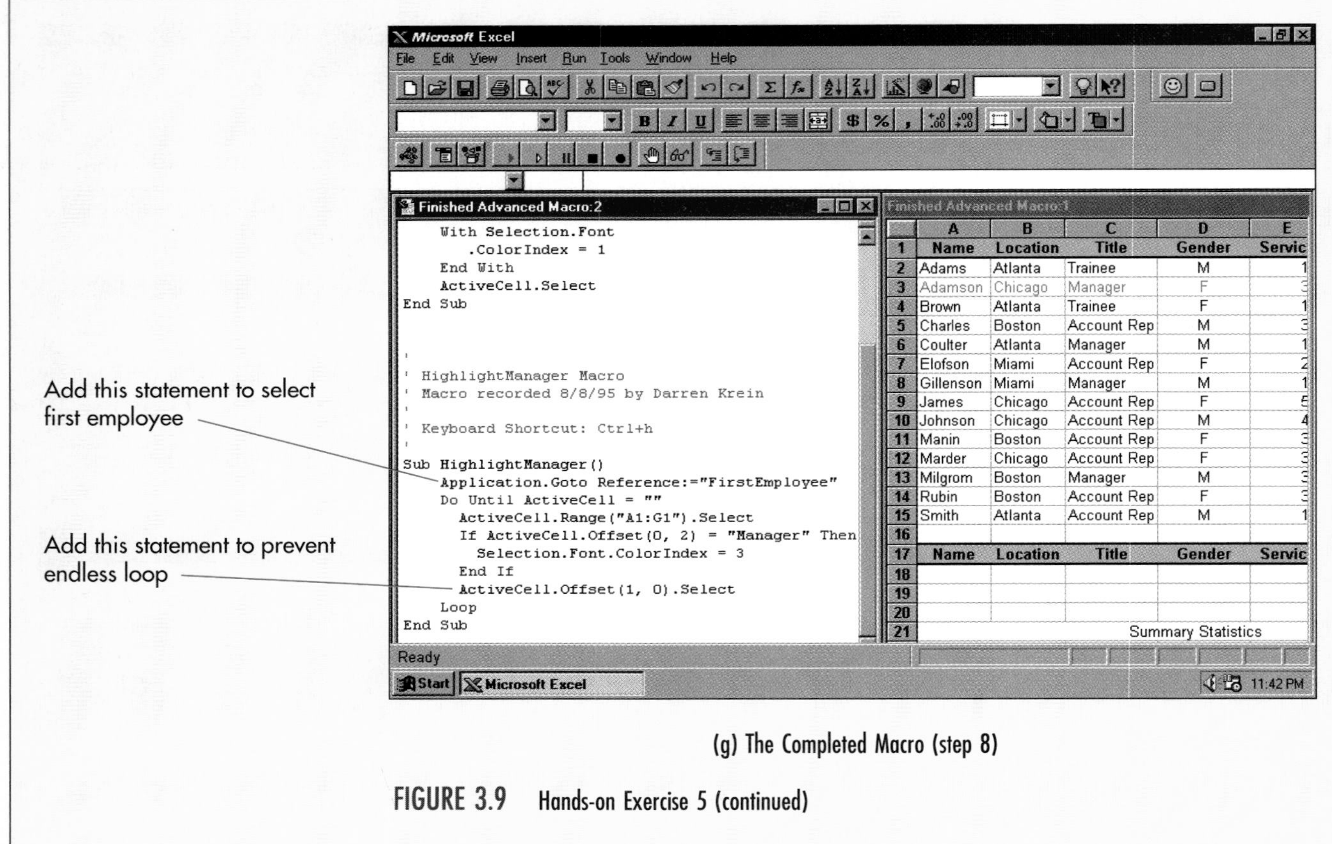

(g) The Completed Macro (step 8)

FIGURE 3.9 Hands-on Exercise 5 (continued)

HELP FOR VISUAL BASIC

Click within any Visual Basic key word, then press the F1 key for context-sensitive help. You will see a help screen containing a description of the statement, its syntax, key elements, and several examples. You can print the help screen by clicking the Options command button and selecting Print Topic. (If you do not see the help screens, ask your instructor to install Visual Basic Help.)

SUMMARY

A macro is a set of instructions that automates a repetitive task. It is, in essence, a program, and its instructions are written in Visual Basic, a programming language. The macro recorder in Excel records your commands and writes the macro for you. Once a macro has been created, it can be edited by manually inserting, deleting, or changing its statements.

Macros are stored in one of two places, either in the current workbook or in a Personal Macro workbook. Macros that are specific to a particular workbook should be stored in that workbook. Generic macros that can be used with any workbook should be stored in the Personal Macro workbook.

A macro is run (executed) by pulling down the Tools menu and selecting the Run Macro command. A macro can also be executed through a keyboard shortcut, by placing a button on the worksheet, or by customizing a toolbar to include an additional button to run the macro.

A comment is a nonexecutable statement that begins with an apostrophe. Comments are inserted automatically at the beginning of a macro by the macro recorder to remind you of what the macro does. Comments may be added, deleted, or modified, just as any other statement.

A macro begins and ends with the Sub and End Sub statements, respectively. The Sub statement contains the name of the macro.

The With statement enables you to perform multiple actions on the same object. All commands between the With and corresponding End With statements are executed collectively.

A macro records either absolute or relative references. An absolute reference is constant; that is, Excel keeps track of the exact cell address and selects that specific cell. A relative reference depends on the previously selected cell, and is entered as an offset, or number of rows and columns from the current cell.

An Excel macro can be made more powerful through inclusion of Visual Basic statements that enable true programming. These include the If statement to implement decision making and the Do statement to implement a loop.

KEY WORDS AND CONCEPTS

Absolute reference
Comment statement
Copy command
Cut command
Debugging
Do Statement
End If statement
End Sub statement
End With statement
Find command
If statement
Keyboard shortcut
Loop
Macro
Macro button
Macro recorder
Macro sheet
Mark Position for Recording
Name
Name box
Offset
Paste command
Personal Macro workbook
Relative reference
Replace command
Shortcut key
Step Into button
Sub statement
Unhide command
Visual Basic
With statement

MULTIPLE CHOICE

1. Which of the following best describes the recording and execution of a macro?
   (a) A macro is recorded once and executed once
   (b) A macro is recorded once and executed many times
   (c) A macro is recorded many times and executed once
   (d) A macro is recorded many times and executed many times
2. Which of the following can be used to execute a macro?
   (a) A keyboard shortcut
   (b) A customized toolbar button

(c) Both (a) and (b)
(d) Neither (a) nor (b)

3. A macro is stored in a:
   (a) Separate sheet within the current workbook
   (b) Personal Macro workbook
   (c) Both (a) and (b)
   (d) Neither (a) nor (b)

4. Which of the following is true regarding comments in Visual Basic?
   (a) A comment is executable; that is, its inclusion or omission affects the outcome of a macro
   (b) A comment begins with an apostrophe
   (c) Both (a) and (b)
   (d) Neither (a) nor (b)

5. Which statement must contain the name of the macro?
   (a) The Sub statement at the beginning of the macro
   (b) The first comment statement
   (c) Both (a) and (b)
   (d) Neither (a) nor (b)

6. Which commands(s) are necessary to record additional statements within an existing macro?
   (a) Mark the position for recording
   (b) Record at the marked position
   (c) Both (a) and (b)
   (d) Neither (a) nor (b)

7. The statement Selection.Offset (1,0).Range ("A1").Select will select the cell:
   (a) In the same column as the active cell but one row below
   (b) In the same row as the active cell but one column to the right
   (c) In the same column as the active cell but one row above
   (d) In the same row as the active cell but one column to the left

8. The statement Selection.Offset (1,1).Range ("A1").Select will select the cell:
   (a) One cell below and one cell to the left of the active cell
   (b) One cell below and one cell to the right of the active cell
   (c) One cell above and one cell to the right of the active cell
   (d) One cell above and one cell to the left of the active cell

9. The statement Selection.Offset (1,1).Range ("A1:A2").Select will select:
   (a) Cell A1
   (b) Cell A2
   (c) Both (a) and (b)
   (d) Neither (a) nor (b)

10. Which commands are used to duplicate an existing macro so that it can become the basis of a new macro?
    (a) Copy command
    (b) Paste command
    (c) Both (a) and (b)
    (d) Neither (a) nor (b)

11. Which of the following is used to protect a macro from the subsequent insertion or deletion of rows or columns in the associated worksheet?
   (a) Range names
   (b) Absolute references
   (c) Both (a) and (b)
   (d) Neither (a) nor (b)

12. Which of the following is true regarding a customized button that has been inserted as an object onto a worksheet and assigned to an Excel macro?
   (a) Point to the customized button, then click the left mouse button to execute the associated macro
   (b) Point to the customized button, then click the right mouse button to select the macro button and simultaneously display a shortcut menu
   (c) Point to the customized button, then press and hold the Ctrl key as you click the left mouse to select the button
   (d) All of the above

13. You want to create a macro to enter your name in a specific cell. The best way to do this is to:
   (a) Select the cell for your name, turn on the macro recorder with absolute references, then type your name
   (b) Turn on the macro recorder with absolute references, select the cell for your name, then type your name
   (c) Either (a) or (b)
   (d) Neither (a) nor (b)

14. You want to create a macro to enter your name in the active cell (which will vary whenever the macro is used) and the course you are taking in the cell immediately below. The best way to do this is to:
   (a) Select the cell for your name, turn on the macro recorder with absolute references, type your name, press the down arrow, and type the course
   (b) Turn on the macro recorder with absolute references, select the cell for your name, type your name, press the down arrow, and type the course
   (c) Select the cell for your name, turn on the macro recorder with relative references, type your name, press the down arrow, and type the course
   (d) Turn on the macro recorder with relative references, select the cell for your name, type your name, press the down arrow, and type the course

15. The InputBox statement:
   (a) Displays a message (prompt) requesting input from the user
   (b) Stores the user's response in a designated cell
   (c) Both (a) and (b)
   (d) Neither (a) nor (b)

ANSWERS

1. b	**6.** c	**11.** a
2. c	**7.** a	**12.** d
3. c	**8.** b	**13.** b
4. b	**9.** d	**14.** c
5. a	**10.** c	**15.** c

1. Use Figure 3.10 to match each action with its result; a given action may be used more than once or not at all.

Action		Result
a. Click at 13	_____	Step through the macro one statement at a time
b. Click at 11	_____	Unhide the Personal Macro workbook
c. Click at 14, then click at 5	_____	Record a new macro
d. Click at 10	_____	Run the Chicago macro
e. Click at 3, then click at 8 to mark the position for recording	_____	Create a button for the Manager macro
f. Click the right mouse button at 1	_____	Copy the Chicago macro
g. Click at 8	_____	Run the Manager macro
h. Click at 12	_____	Add additional steps within the Chicago macro

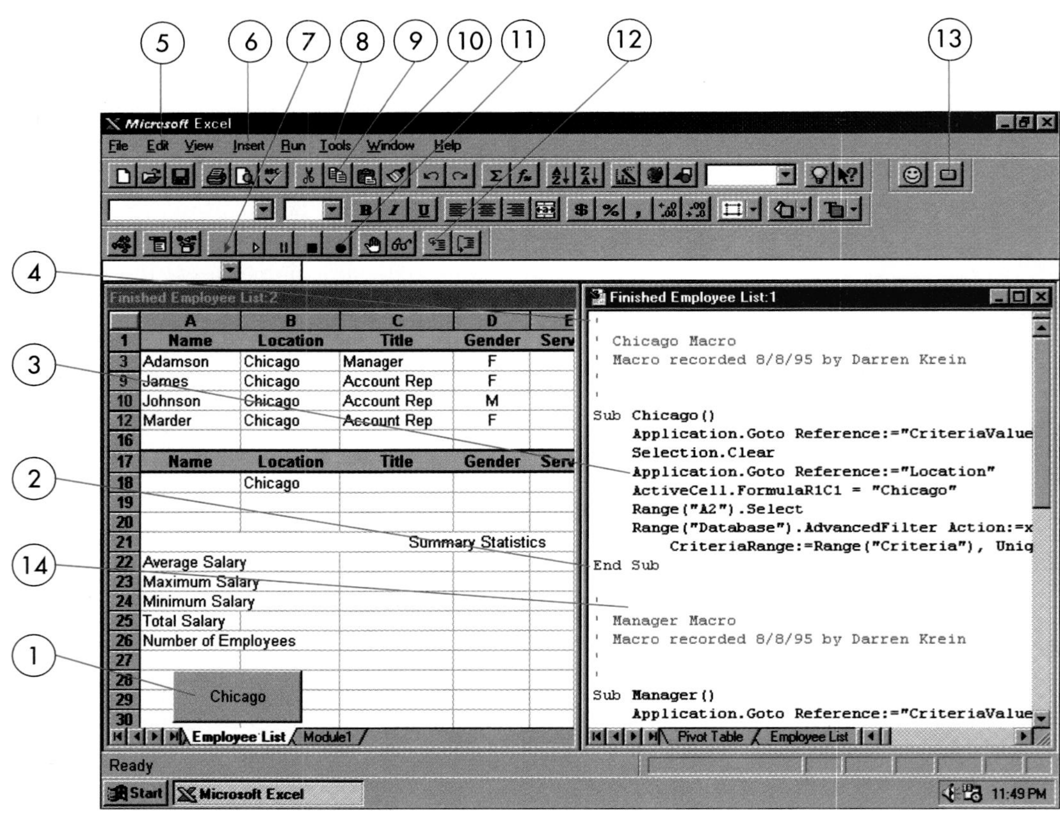

FIGURE 3.10 Screen for Problem 1

Action		Result
i. Click at 4 and drag to 2, then click at 9	_____	Change the Manager macro to an Account Rep macro by changing all occurrences of Manager to Account Rep
j. Click the left mouse button at 1	_____	Change the properties of the Chicago button so that it will print with the worksheet

2. Each of the messages in Figure 3.11 appeared (or could have appeared) in conjunction with the exercises in the chapter. Explain the meaning of each message and indicate what (if any) corrective action is required.

(a) Message 1

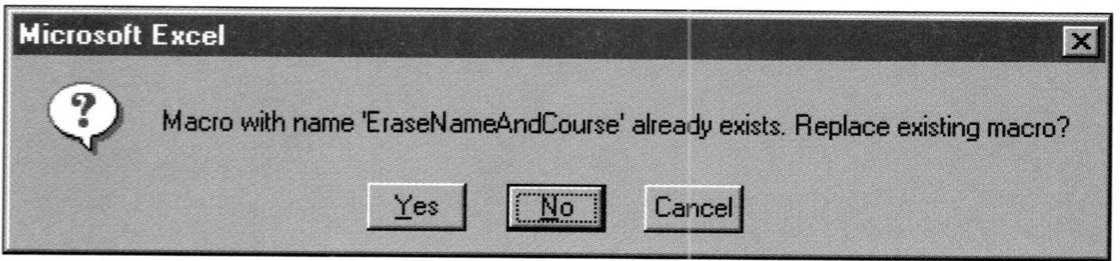

(b) Message 2

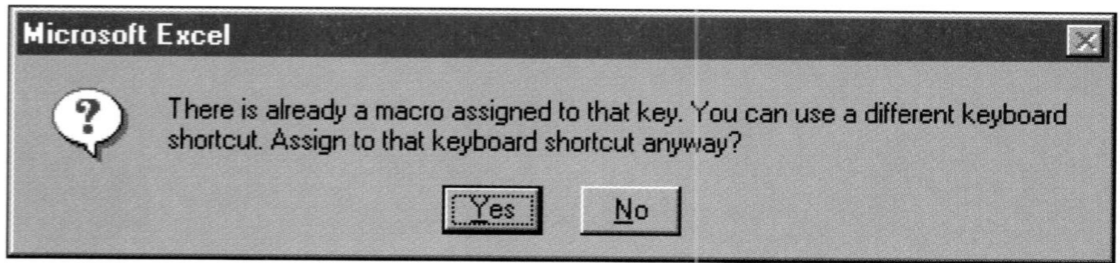

(c) Message 3

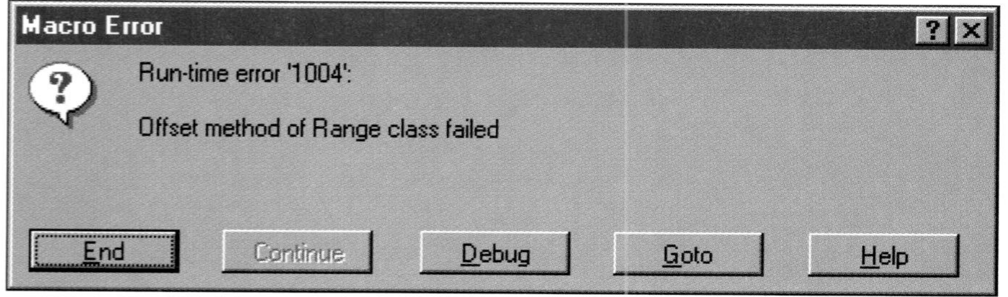

(d) Message 4

FIGURE 3.11 Messages for Problem 2

3. Answer the following with respect to the macros in Figure 3.12, both of which enter a student's name, class, and today's date in a worksheet:
   a. In which cells does Macro1 enter the data?
   b. In which cells does Macro2 enter the data?
   c. Which macro was recorded with absolute references? With relative references?
   d. Which macro was created by selecting the active cell, then turning on the macro recorder? Which macro was created by turning on the macro recorder, then selecting the active cell within the macro?
   e. Assume that the first statement of Macro1 is deleted. In which cells will the data appear after the macro has been modified?
   f. Assume that the first statement of (the original) Macro1 is entered as the first statement in Macro2. In which cells will the data appear after the statement is added to Macro2?
   g. Where should the macros be stored if they are to be accessible from any workbook?

```
' Macro1 Macro
'
' Keyboard Shortcut: Ctrl+e
'
Sub Macro1()
    Range("D5").Select
    ActiveCell.FormulaR1C1 = "John Smith"
    Range("D6").Select
    ActiveCell.FormulaR1C1 = "CIS 622"
    Range("D7").Select
    ActiveCell.FormulaR1C1 = "=TODAY()"
End Sub
'
' Macro2 Macro
'
' Keyboard Shortcut: Ctrl+f
'
Sub Macro2()
    ActiveCell.FormulaR1C1 = "John Smith"
    ActiveCell.Offset(1, 0).Range("A1").Select
    ActiveCell.FormulaR1C1 = "CIS 622"
    ActiveCell.Offset(1, 0).Range("A1").Select
    ActiveCell.FormulaR1C1 = "=TODAY()"
End Sub
```

FIGURE 3.12 Macros for Problem 3

4. Answer the following with respect to the screen displayed in Figure 3.13.
   a. How many workbooks are open in the figure? Which workbook is active?
   b. How many sheets are there in the active workbook? Which sheet is active?
   c. What is the name of the visible macro? What shortcut key (if any) has been established for that macro?
   d. Which macro statements are comments?
   e. Does the macro use relative or absolute references?
   f. What does the macro do?

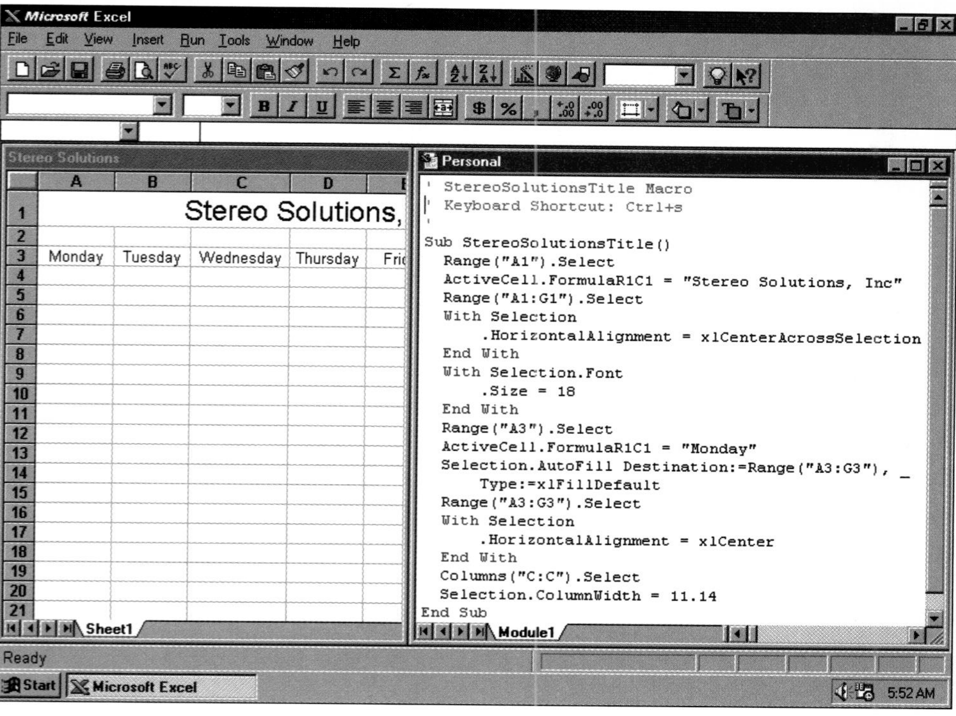

FIGURE 3.13 Screen for Problem 4

PRACTICE WITH MICROSOFT EXCEL 7.0

1. Figure 3.14 displays a modified version of the Finished Employee List workbook that was developed in Hands-on Exercises 3 and 4. The worksheet contains the three command buttons (Chicago, Manager, and Chicago/Manager) that correspond to the macros that were developed in the chapter. It also contains a fourth command button that is the focus of this problem.
   a. Do Hands-on Exercises 3 and 4 as they are described in the chapter in order to create the first three macros and associated command buttons.
   b. Create a fourth macro that prompts the user to enter a city, prompts the user a second time to enter a title, then displays all employees with that city–title combination.
   c. Create a command button corresponding to the macro in part b as shown in the figure.
   d. Add a documentation worksheet (see pages 75–80) that describes all of the macros in the workbook. Be sure your name and date are on this worksheet.
   e. Submit a disk containing the completed workbook to your instructor.
2. Figure 3.15 displays a partially completed macro that can be found on the Module2 sheet in the Finished Advanced Macro workbook described in the fifth hands-on exercise. The macro is intended to highlight the Chicago employees in red and the Atlanta employees in blue.
   a. Do Hands-on Exercise 5 as it is described in the chapter, which introduced loops and decision making within a macro.

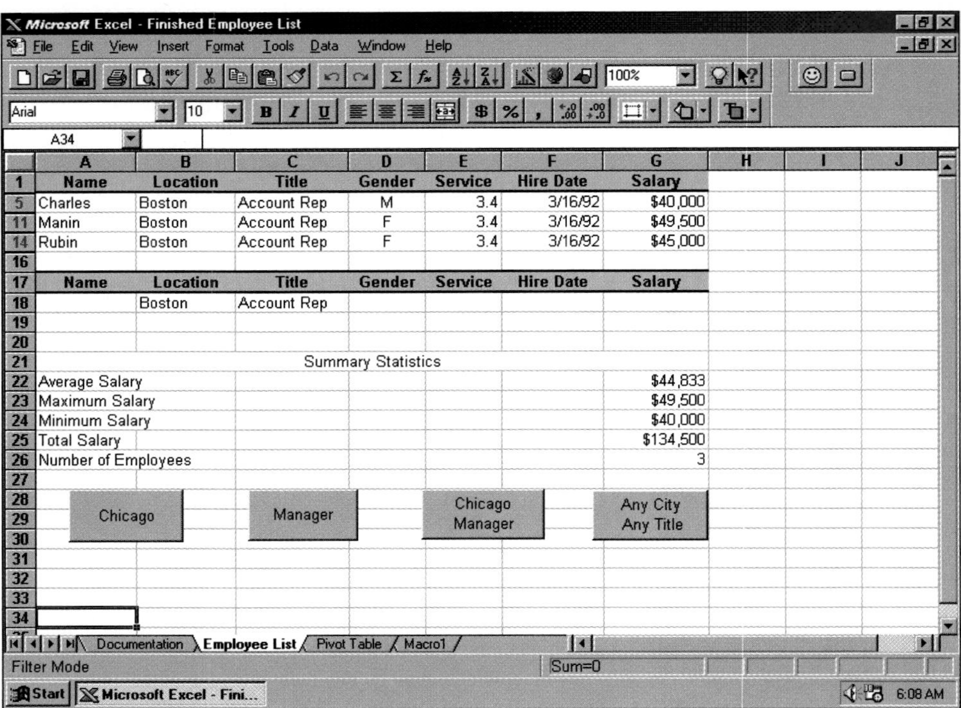

FIGURE 3.14 Data Management Macros for Practice Exercise 1

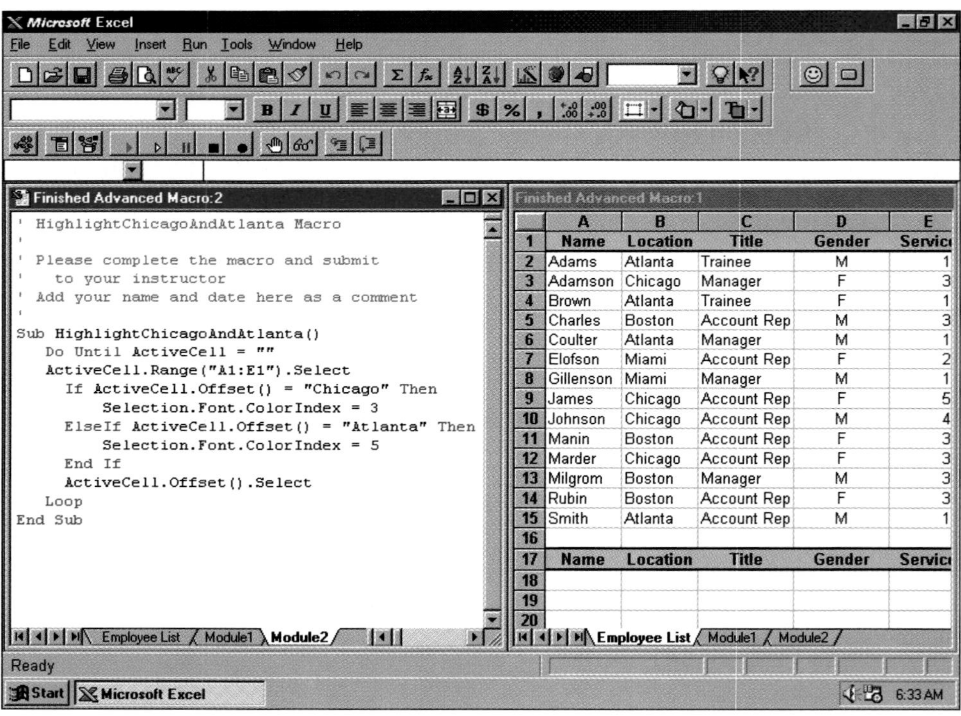

FIGURE 3.15 Advanced Macro for Practice Exercise 2

b. Complete the HighlightChicagoAndAtlanta macro by entering the appropriate offsets in three different statements within the macro. Completion of the macro also requires you to enter a statement at the beginning of the macro that positions you at the first employee within the list.

c. Test the completed macro to be sure that it works properly. You can use the existing ClearColor macro within the workbook (press Ctrl+c as a shortcut) to clear the color within the employee list.

d. Assign Ctrl+a as the shortcut for the macro. The workbook should now have three shortcuts. Ctrl+c and Ctrl+h to clear color and highlight the managers are shortcuts for the ClearColor and HighlightManager macros from the existing hands-on exercise.

e. Add a documentation worksheet that describes all of the macros in the workbook. Be sure your name and date are on this worksheet.

f. Submit a disk containing the completed workbook to your instructor.

3. The workbook in Figure 3.16 is based on the three-dimensional example from Chapter 2. Open the *Volume II Chapter 3 Practice 3* workbook as it exists on the data disk and save it as *Finished Volume II Chapter 3 Practice 3*. Do the following:

a. Run Macro1, Macro2, and Macro3 in succession. What does each of these macros do?

b. Run the StartOver macro. What does this macro do?

c. Run Macro4. What does it do? How many statements does the macro contain? Explain why the macro is so powerful even though it contains a limited number of statements.

d. A branch office has been opened in a fourth city, and its sales are found in the New York workbook. Determine which macro(s) have to be modified so that the sales of the New York office are included in the corporate totals, then modify those macros appropriately.

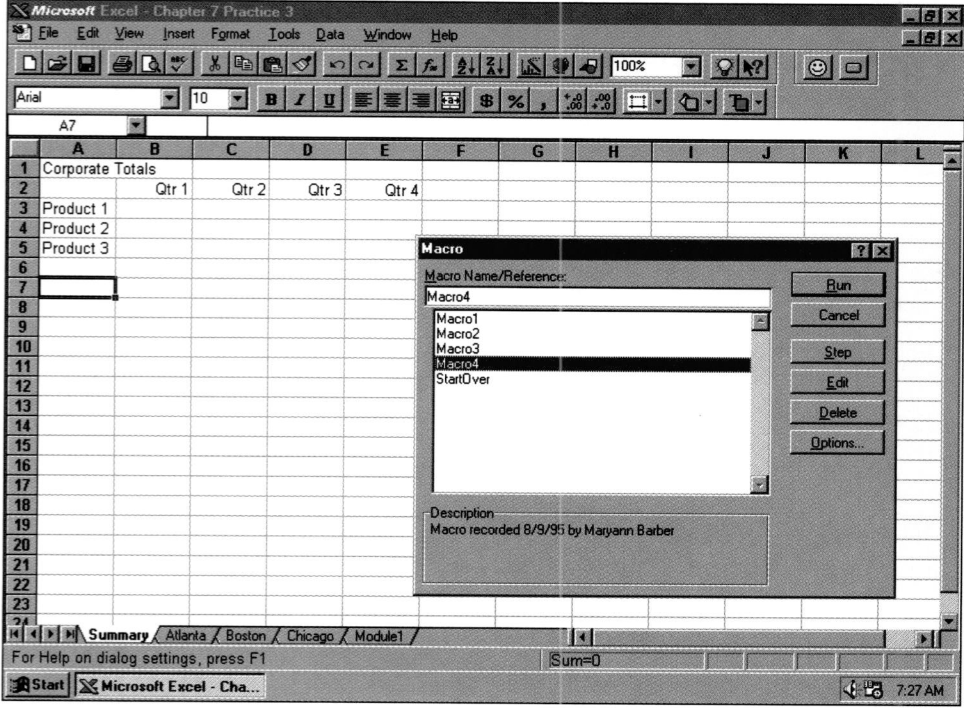

FIGURE 3.16 Screen for Practice Exercise 3

e. Modify Macro4 and the StartOver macro so that they can be run with the keyboard shortcuts Ctrl+a and Ctrl+b, respectively.

f. Submit a disk containing the finished workbook to your instructor. (The disk should also contain the Atlanta, Boston, Chicago, and New York workbooks.)

4. Microsoft Excel includes several templates to help run a business or plan your personal finances. A template is a partially completed workbook that contains formatting, text, formulas, and macros, and it is the macros that make the template so valuable. One of those templates, the Loan Manager, is the basis of the workbook in Figure 3.17. The workbook contains four worksheets and several macros, which Microsoft has chosen to hide. The macros execute automatically, however, as you enter data in the workbook and move from one worksheet to another.

To create the workbook in Figure 3.17, pull down the File menu, click New, click the Spreadsheet Solutions tab, open the Loan Manager template, then save it as *Volume II Chapter 3 Practice 4.* Click the Customize Your Loan Manager tab and enter your personal information. Enter the parameters for a real (or imaginary) loan, then explore the workbook by examining its worksheets. Enter a beginning date at least two years prior to today's date so that the workbook will record several loan payments. Print the Loan Data, Loan Amortization Table, and Summary worksheets, then submit all three pages as proof that you did the exercise.

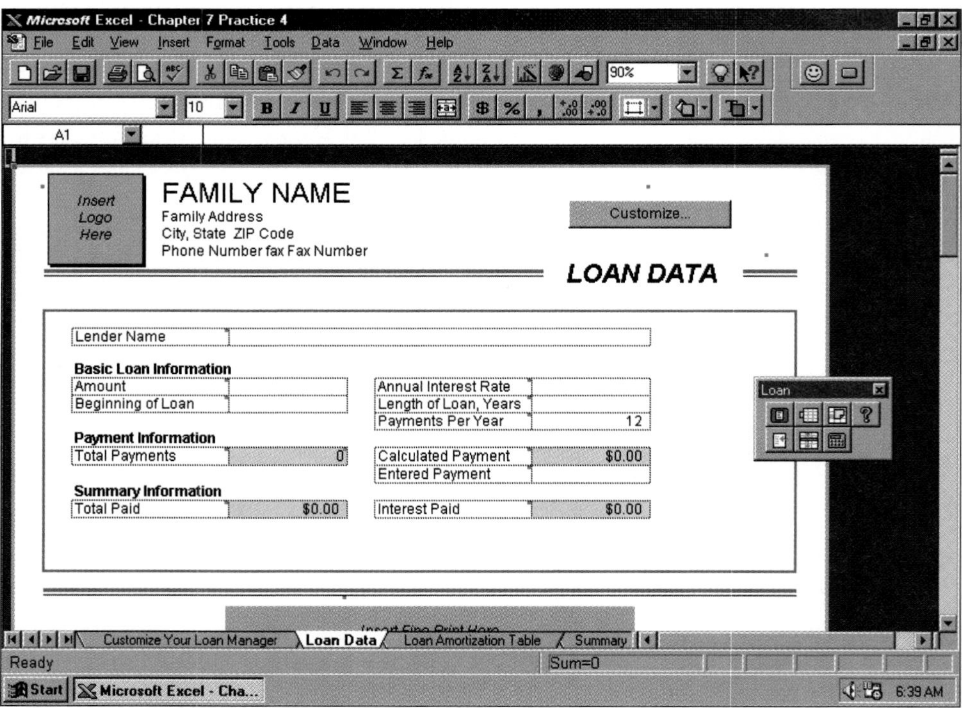

FIGURE 3.17 Screen for Practice Exercise 4

Spreadsheet Solutions

The Loan Manager is one of several templates that are supplied with Microsoft Excel. The other templates include a Sales Invoice, Purchase Order, Expense Statement, Business Planner, and Personal Budget. Choose any template that seems of interest to you, then enter real or hypothetical data. Print one or more worksheets from the workbook and submit the output to your instructor.

Microsoft Word

Do you use Microsoft Word on a regular basis? Are there certain tasks that you do repeatedly, whether in the same document or in a series of different documents? If so, you would do well to explore the macro capabilities within Microsoft Word. How are these capabilities similar to Excel's? How do they differ?

Starting Up

Your instructor is very impressed with the Excel workbook and associated macros that you have created. He would like you to take the automation process one step further and simplify the way in which Excel is started and the workbook is loaded. Use your knowledge of Windows 95 to implement your instructor's request. The problem is open ended, and there are many different approaches. You might, for example, create a shortcut on the desktop to open the workbook. You might also explore the use of the Startup folder.

Dade County Metro Zoo

The Dade County Metro Zoo workbook is similar in concept to the Employee List workbook that was used throughout the chapter. Open the workbook and run the three existing macros. Create two additional macros of your own that you think are appropriate, then submit a disk containing the completed workbook to your instructor.

A

APPENDIX A: THE SPREADSHEET AUDIT

OVERVIEW

In one of the most celebrated spreadsheet errors of all time, the comptroller of James A. Cummings, Inc, a Florida construction company, used a spreadsheet to develop a bid on a multi-million dollar office complex. At the last minute, he realized that he had forgotten to include $254,000 for overhead, and so he inserted this number at the top of a column of numbers. Unfortunately for both the comptroller and the company, the $254,000 was not included in the final total, and the contract was underbid by that amount. The company was awarded the contract and forced to make good on its unrealistically low estimate.

Seeking to recover its losses, the construction company brought suit against the spreadsheet vendor, claiming that a latent defect within the spreadsheet failed to add the entry in question. The vendor contended that the mistake was in fact a *user error* and the court agreed, citing the vendor's licensing agreement:

> *". . . Because software is inherently complex and may not be completely free of errors, you are advised to verify your work. In no event will the vendor be liable for direct, indirect, special, incidental, or consequential damages arising out of the use of or inability to use the software or documentation, even if advised of the possibility of such damages. In particular, said vendor is not responsible for any costs including, but not limited to, those incurred as a result of lost profits or revenue."*

The purpose of this appendix is to remind you that the spreadsheet is only a tool, and like all other tools it must be used properly, or there can be serious consequences. Think, for a moment, how business has become totally dependent on the spreadsheet, and how little validity checking is actually done. Ask yourself if any of your spreadsheets contained an error, and if so, what the consequences would have been if those spreadsheets represented real applications rather than academic exercises.

USE FUNCTIONS RATHER THAN FORMULAS

The entries =A1+A2+A3+A4 and =SUM(A1:A4) may appear equivalent, but the function is inherently superior and should be used whenever possible. A function adjusts automatically for the insertion (deletion) of rows within the designated range, whereas a formula does not. Including a blank row at the beginning and end of the function's range ensures that any value added to the top or bottom of a column of numbers will automatically be included in the sum. Had this technique been followed by the James A. Cummings company, the error would not have occurred.

A WORD OF CAUTION

The formatting capabilities within Excel make it all too easy to get caught up in the appearance of a worksheet without paying attention to its accuracy. Consider, for example, the grade book in Figure A.1, which is used by a hypothetical professor to assign final grades in a class. The grade book is nicely formatted, *but its calculations are wrong*, and no amount of fancy formatting can compensate for the erroneous results. Consider:

- Baker should have received an A rather than a B. He has an 87 average on his quizzes, he received an 87 on the final exam, and with two bonus points for each of his two homeworks, he should have had an overall final average of 91.
- Charles should have received a B rather than a C. True, he did not do any homework and he did do poorly on the final, but, with the semester quizzes and final exam counting equally, his semester average should have been 80.

	Name	HW 1	HW 2	HW 3	Quiz 1	Quiz 2	Quiz 3	Quiz Average	Final Exam	HW Bonus	Semester Average	Grade
2	Baker		OK	OK	77	89	95	87	87	2	89	B
3	Charles				84	76	86	82	78	0	79	C
4	Goodman	OK	OK			95	94	63	95	4	89	B
5	Johnson	OK	OK		90	86	70	82	90	4	92	A
6	Jones		OK	OK	75	85	71	77	86	2	85	B
7	Irving	OK		OK	65	85	75	75	78	2	79	C
8	Lang				84	88	83	85	94	0	91	A
9	London		OK		72	69	75	72	82	2	81	B
10	Milgrom	OK	OK		100	65	90	85	100	4	100	A
11	Mills	OK	OK		75	85	80	80	65	4	74	C
12	Nelson	OK	OK		65	60	61	62	60	4	65	D

Grading Criteria	
Bonus for each homework	2
Weight of semester quizzes	50%
Weight of final exam	50%

Grading Scale	
Average	Grade
0	F
60	D
70	C
80	B
90	A

Baker should have received an A

Charles should have received a B

Goodman should have received an A

FIGURE A.1 The Professor's Grade Book

- Goodman should have received an A rather than a B. She aced both quizzes (she was excused from the first quiz) as well as the final, and in addition, she received a four-point bonus for homework.

The errors in our example are contrived, but they could occur. Consider:

- At the class's urging, the professor decided at the last minute to assign a third homework but neglected to modify the formulas to include the additional column containing the extra homework.
- The professor changed the grading scheme at the last minute and decided to count the semester quizzes and final exam evenly. (The original weights were 30% and 70%, respectively.) Unfortunately, however, the formulas to compute each student's semester average specify constants (.30 and .70) rather than absolute references to the cells containing the exam weights. Hence the new grading scheme is not reflected in the student averages.
- The professor forgot that he had excused Goodman from the first quiz and hence did not adjust the formula to compute Goodman's average on the basis of two quizzes rather than three.

Our professor is only human, but he would have done well to print the cell formulas in order to audit the mechanics of the worksheet and double check its calculations. Suffice it to say that the accuracy of a worksheet is far more important than its appearance, and you are well advised to remember this thought as you create and/or use a spreadsheet.

THE SPREADSHEET AUDIT

The ***Auditing toolbar*** helps you understand the relationships between the various cells in a worksheet. It enables you to trace the ***precedents*** for a formula and identify the cells in the worksheet that are referenced by that formula. It also enables you to trace the ***dependents*** of a cell and identify the formulas in the worksheet that reference that cell.

The identification of precedent and/or dependent cells is done graphically by displaying tracers on the worksheet. You simply click in the cell for which you want the information, then you click the appropriate button on the Auditing toolbar. The blue arrows (tracers) appear on the worksheet, and will remain on the worksheet until you click the appropriate removal button. The tracers always point forward, from the precedent cells to the dependent formula.

To see how valuable the tracers can be, consider Figure A.2, which contrasts the professor's original worksheet (Figure A.2a) with the corrected worksheet (Figure A.2b). Consider first the precedents for cell J2, which contains the formula to compute Baker's homework bonus. The tracers (the blue lines) in the invalid worksheet identify homeworks 1 and 2 (note the box around cells B2 and C2) as precedents. The corrected worksheet, however, shows that all three homeworks (cells B2, C2, and D2) are used in the determination of the bonus. (Both worksheets show that cell G15, which contains the homework bonus, is also a precedent for cell J2.)

The analysis of dependent cells is equally telling. There are no dependent cells for cell G16 in the invalid spreadsheet because the formulas to compute the students' semester averages do not reference this cell. The valid worksheet, however, corrects the error, and hence each cell in column K is dependent on cell G16.

The Auditing toolbar is displayed through the View menu and is shown in both Figures A.2a and A.2b. You can point to any button on the Auditing toolbar to display a ToolTip to indicate the purpose of that button.

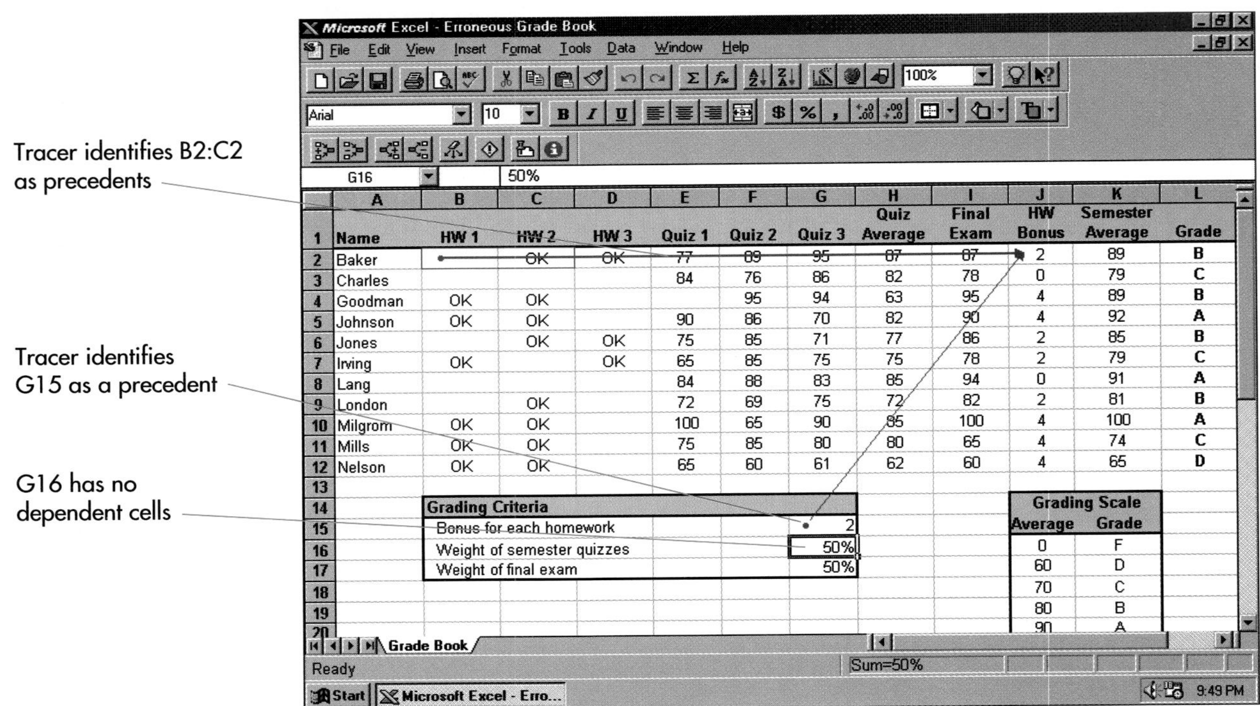

(a) The Invalid Worksheet

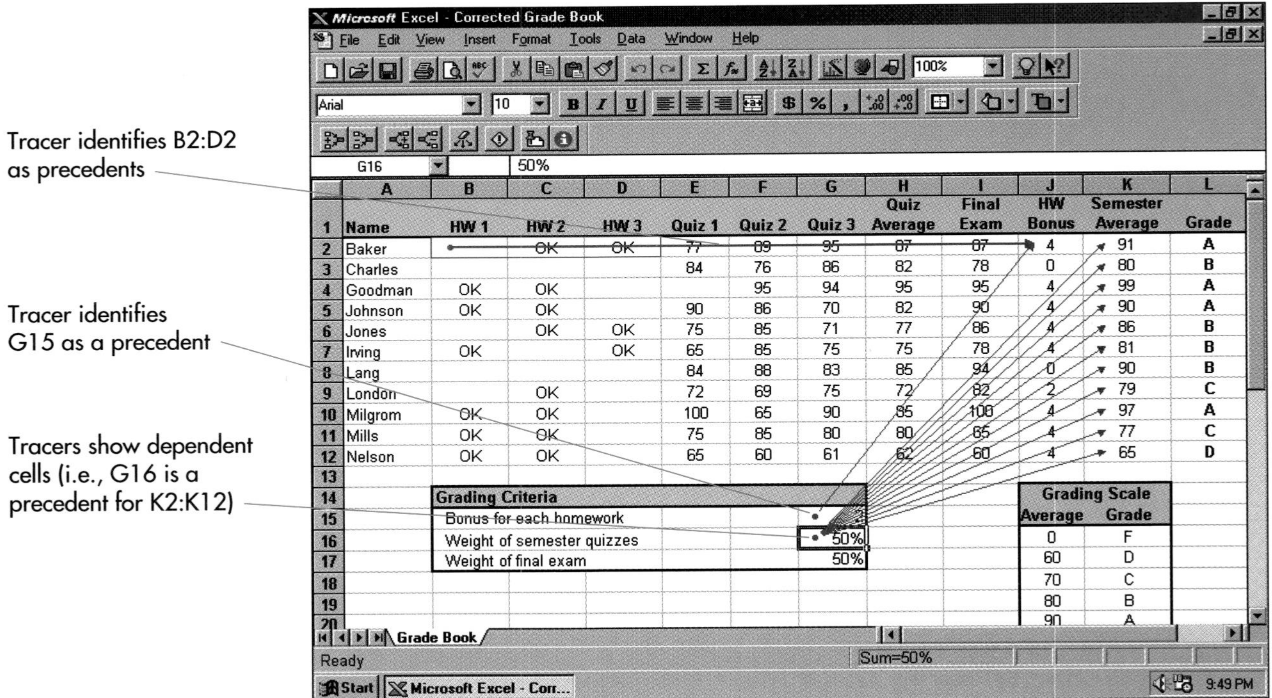

(b) The Corrected Worksheet

FIGURE A.2 The Spreadsheet Audit

ANNOTATE YOUR SPREADSHEETS

The Attach Note button on the Auditing Toolbar enables you to create the equivalent of your own ToolTip for any cell in a spreadsheet. It is an excellent way to annotate a spreadsheet and attach an explanation to any cell containing a complex formula. See step 5 in the hands-on exercise for details on attaching a note.

A SECOND EXAMPLE

Financial planning and budgeting is one of the most common business applications of spreadsheets. Figure A.3 contains an *erroneous* version of a financial forecast for Get Rich Quick Enterprises. As in the professor's grade book, the spreadsheet is nicely formatted, but its calculations are wrong, as will be explained shortly. Any decisions based on the spreadsheet will also be in error.

How do you know when a spreadsheet displays invalid results? One way is to "eyeball" the spreadsheet and try to approximate its results. Look for any calculations that are obviously incorrect. Look at the financial forecast, for example, and see whether all the values are growing at the projected rates of change. The number of units sold and the unit price increase every year as expected, but the cost of the production facility remains constant after 1997. This is an obvious error because the production facility is supposed to increase at eight percent annually, according to the assumptions at the bottom of the spreadsheet. The consequence of this error is that the production costs (after 1997) are too low and hence the projected earnings are too high. The error was easy to find, even without the use of a calculator.

Cost of the production facility is not increasing as expected after 1977

Earnings should be 0 ($225,000 – $225,000)

	A	B	C	D	E	F
1		Get Rich Quick - Financial Forecast				
2		1996	1997	1998	1999	2000
3	Income					
4	Units sold	100,000	110,000	121,000	133,100	146,410
5	Unit price	$2.25	$2.36	$2.48	$2.60	$2.73
6	Gross revenue	$225,000	$259,875	$300,156	$346,680	$400,415
7						
8	Fixed costs					
9	Production facility	$50,000	$54,000	$54,000	$54,000	$54,000
10	Administration	$25,000	$26,250	$27,563	$28,941	$30,388
11	Variable cost					
12	Unit mfg cost	$1.50	$1.65	$1.82	$2.00	$2.20
13	Variable mft cost	$150,000	$181,500	$219,615	$265,734	$321,538
14						
15	Earnings before taxes	$25,000	$24,375	$26,541	$26,946	$24,877
16						
17	Initial conditions			Annual increase		
18	First year sales	100,000		10%		
19	Selling price	$2.25		5%		
20	Unit mfg cost	$1.50		10%		
21	Production facility	$50,000		8%		
22	Administration	$25,000		5%		
23	First year of forecast	1996				

FIGURE A.3 The Erroneous Financial Forecast

A more subtle error occurs in the computation of the earnings before taxes. Look at the numbers for 1996. The gross revenue is $225,000. The total cost is also $225,000 ($50,000 for the production facility, $25,000 for administration, and $150,000 for the manufacturing cost). The projected earnings should be zero, but are shown incorrectly as $25,000, because the administration cost was not subtracted from the gross revenue in determining the profit.

The errors in the financial forecast are easy to discover if only you take the time to look. Unfortunately, however, too many people are prone to accept the results of a spreadsheet, simply because it is nicely formatted on a laser printer. We urge you, therefore, to "eyeball" every spreadsheet for obvious errors, and if a mistake is found, a spreadsheet audit is called for.

TEST WITH SIMPLE AND PREDICTABLE DATA

Test a spreadsheet initially with simple and predictable data that you create yourself so that you can manually verify the spreadsheet is performing as expected. Once you are confident the spreadsheet works with data you can control, test it again with real data to further check its validity. Adequate testing is time consuming, but it can save you from embarrassing, not to mention costly, mistakes.

HANDS-ON EXERCISE 1

The Auditing Toolbar

Objective: To illustrate the tools on the Auditing toolbar; to trace errors in spreadsheet formulas; to identify precedent and dependent cells; to attach a note to a cell. Use Figure A.4 as a guide in the exercise.

STEP 1: Display the Auditing Toolbar

- Load Excel. Open the **Erroneous Financial Forecast** workbook in the **Exploring Excel folder** as shown in Figure A.4a. Save the workbook as **Finished Erroneous Financial Forecast.**
- Point to any toolbar, click the **right mouse button** to display the shortcut menu in Figure A.4a, then click **Auditing** to display the Auditing toolbar.
- If necessary, click and drag the title bar of the Auditing toolbar to dock the toolbar under the Formatting toolbar.

FIXED VERSUS FLOATING TOOLBARS

Any toolbar can be docked along the edge of the application window, or it can be displayed as a floating toolbar within the application window. To move a docked toolbar, drag the toolbar background. To move a floating toolbar, drag its title bar. To size a floating toolbar, drag any border in the direction you want to go. Double click the background of any toolbar to toggle between a floating toolbar and a docked (fixed) toolbar.

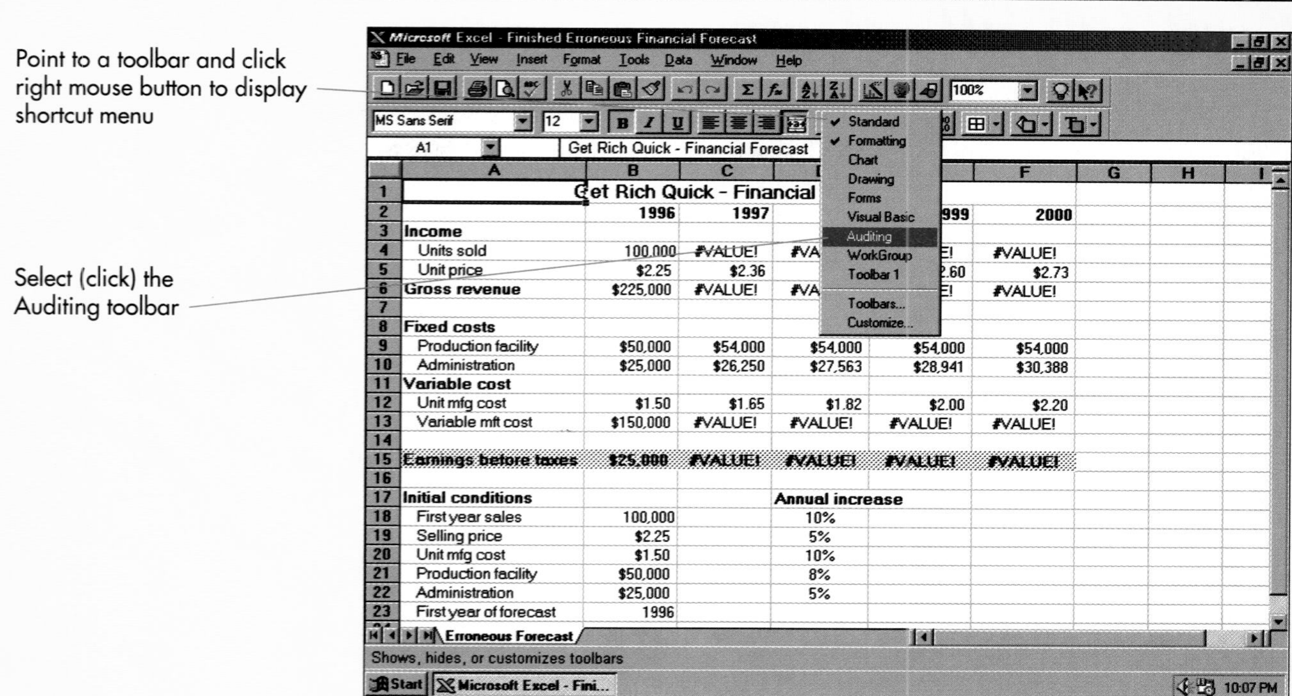

(a) Display the Auditing Toolbar (step 1)

FIGURE A.4 Hands-on Exercise 1

STEP 2: The Trace Error Command

- Click in **cell C4,** the first cell that displays the #VALUE error. Click the **Trace Error button** on the Auditing toolbar to display the tracers shown in Figure A.4b.
- The tracers identify the error in graphic fashion and show that cell C4 is dependent on cells A4 and D18 (i.e., cells A4 and D18 are precedents of cell C4). Cell A4 contains a text entry and is obviously incorrect.
- Click in the formula bar to edit the formula for cell C4 so that it references cell B4 rather than cell A4. (The correct formula is =B4+B4*$D$18). Press **enter** when you have corrected the formula.
- The tracer arrows disappear (they disappear automatically whenever you edit a formula to which they refer). The #VALUE errors are also gone because the formula has been corrected and all dependent formulas have been automatically recalculated.

THE #VALUE ERROR

The #VALUE error occurs when the wrong type of entry is used in a formula or as an argument in a function. It typically occurs when a formula references a text rather than a numeric entry. The easiest way to resolve the error is to display the Auditing toolbar, select the cell in question, then click the Trace Error button.

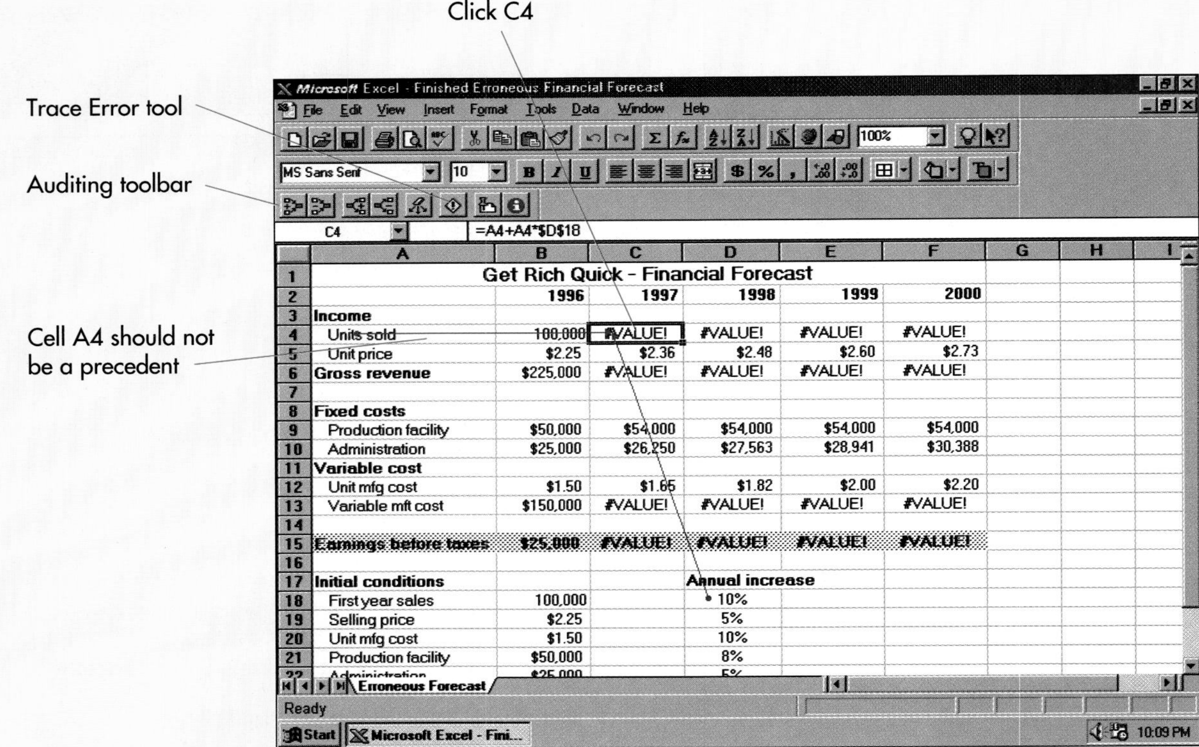

(b) The Trace Error Command (step 2)

FIGURE A.4 Hands-on Exercise 1 (continued)

STEP 3: Trace Dependents

- The worksheet is in error because the production costs do not increase after 1997. Click in **cell D21** (the cell containing the projected increase in the cost of the production facility).
- Click the **Trace Dependents button** to display the dependent cells as shown in Figure A.4c. Only one dependent cell (cell C9) is shown. This is clearly an error because cells D9 through F9 should also depend on cell D1.
- Click in **cell C9** to examine its formula (=B9+B9*D21). The production costs for the second year are based on the first-year costs (cell B9) and the rate of increase (cell D21). The latter, however, was entered as a relative rather than an absolute address.
- Change the formula in cell C9 to include an absolute reference to cell D21 (i.e., the correct formula is =B9+B9*$D$21). The tracer arrow disappears due to the correction.
- Drag the fill handle in **cell C9** to copy the corrected formula to **cells D9, E9,** and **F9.** (The displayed value for cell F9 should be $68,024.)
- Click in **cell D21.** Click the **Trace Dependents button,** and this time it points to the production costs for years 2 through 5 in the forecast. Click the **Remove Dependents button** to remove the arrows.

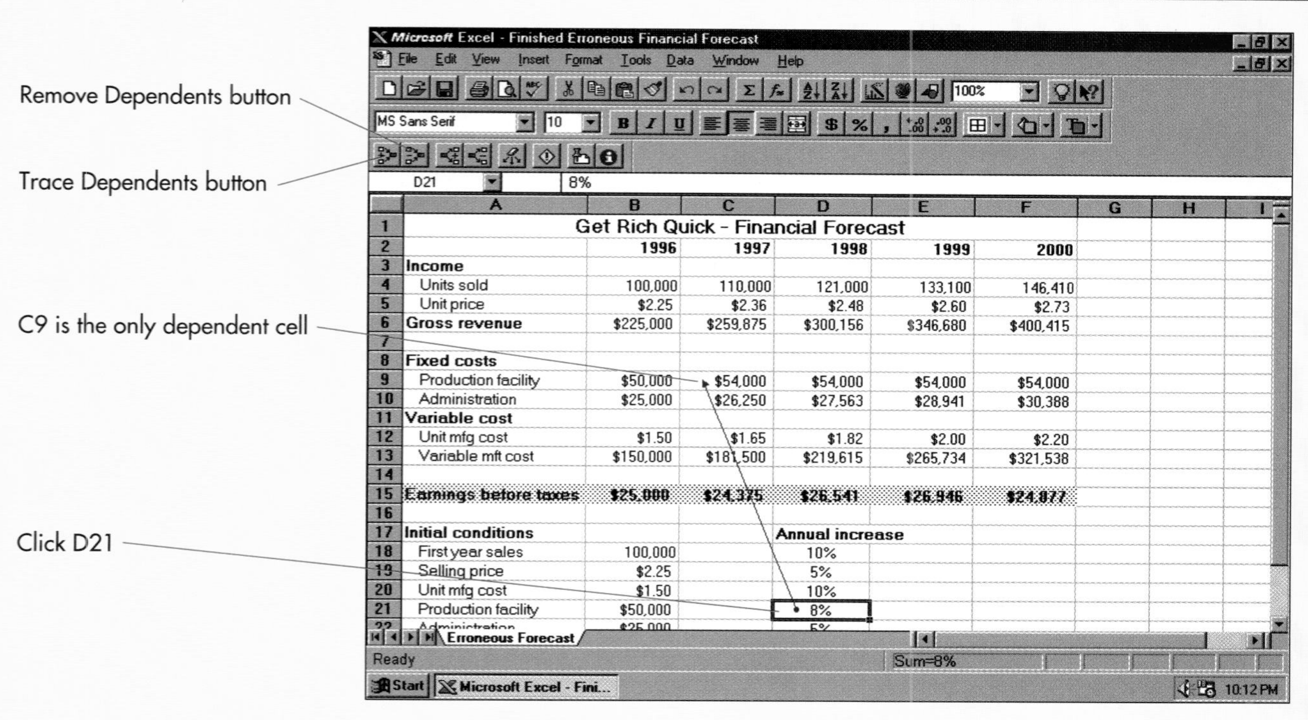

	A	B	C	D	E	F
1	Get Rich Quick - Financial Forecast					
2		1996	1997	1998	1999	2000
3	Income					
4	Units sold	100,000	110,000	121,000	133,100	146,410
5	Unit price	$2.25	$2.36	$2.48	$2.60	$2.73
6	Gross revenue	$225,000	$259,875	$300,156	$346,680	$400,415
7						
8	Fixed costs					
9	Production facility	$50,000	$54,000	$54,000	$54,000	$54,000
10	Administration	$25,000	$26,250	$27,563	$28,941	$30,388
11	Variable cost					
12	Unit mfg cost	$1.50	$1.65	$1.82	$2.00	$2.20
13	Variable mft cost	$150,000	$181,500	$219,615	$265,734	$321,538
14						
15	Earnings before taxes	$25,000	$24,375	$26,541	$26,946	$24,877
16						
17	Initial conditions			Annual increase		
18	First year sales	100,000		10%		
19	Selling price	$2.25		5%		
20	Unit mfg cost	$1.50		10%		
21	Production facility	$50,000		8%		
22	Administration	$25,000		5%		

(c) The Trace Dependents Command (step 3)

FIGURE A.4 Hands-on Exercise 1 (continued)

ISOLATE ASSUMPTIONS AND INITIAL CONDITIONS

A spreadsheet is first and foremost a tool for decision making, and as such, the subject of continual what-if speculation. It is critical, therefore, that the input and assumptions be isolated and clearly visible, and further that all formulas in the spreadsheet accurately reflect the cells containing these values.

STEP 4: Trace Precedents

- The earnings before taxes in cell B15 should be zero. (The gross revenue is $225,000, as are the total expenses, which consist of production, administration, and manufacturing costs of $50,000, $25,000, and $150,000, respectively.) Click in **cell B15.**
- Click the **Trace Precedents button** to display the precedent cells as shown in Figure A.4d. The projected earnings depend on the revenue (cell B6) and various expenses (cells B9 and B13). The problem is that the administration expense (cell B10) is omitted, and hence the earnings are too high.
- Change the formula in cell B15 to **=B6−(B9+B10+B13)** so that the administration expense is included in the expenses that are deducted from the gross revenue. The tracer arrow disappears.
- Drag the fill handle in **cell B15** to copy the corrected formula to **cells C15** through **F15.** (The displayed value in cell F15 is a *negative* $19,535.)

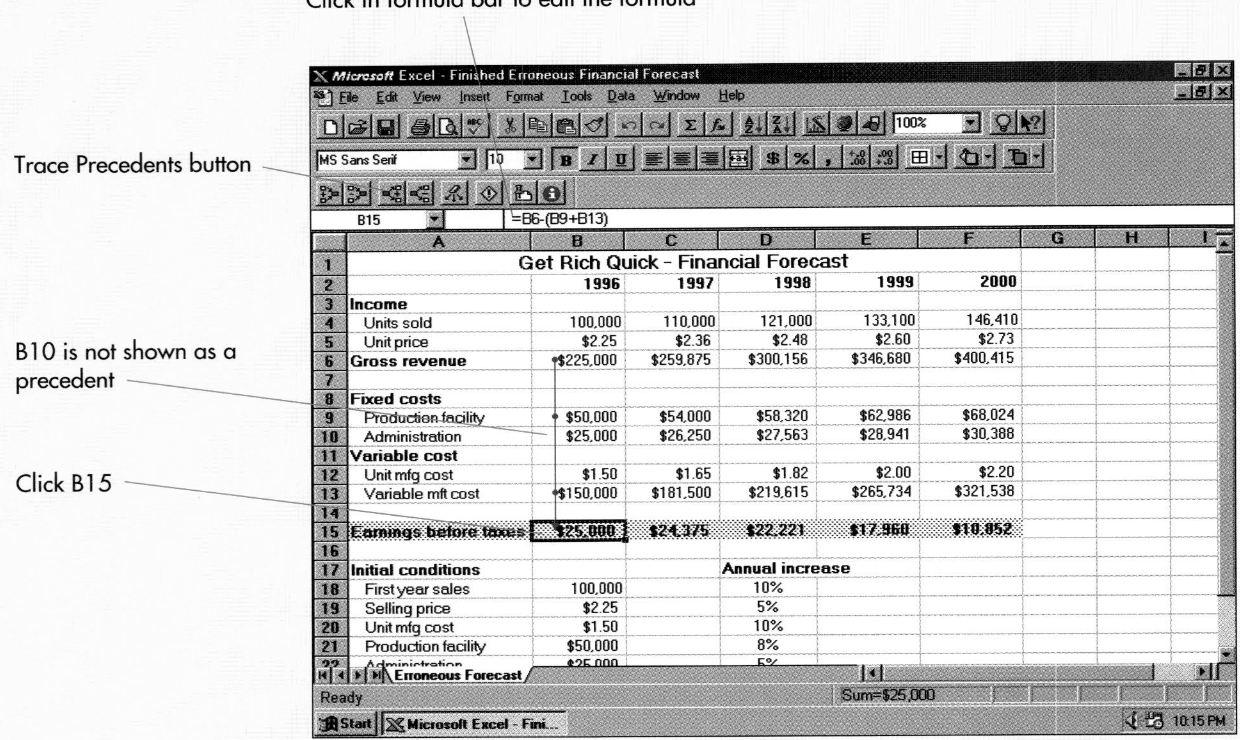

(d) The Trace Precedents Command (step 4)

FIGURE A.4 Hands-on Exercise 1 (continued)

STEP 5: Attach a Note

- Click in **cell B19** (the cell containing the selling price for the first year). Click the **Attach Note button** to display the Cell Note dialog box as shown in Figure A.4e.
- Type the text of the note you want attached to cell B19. Click **OK** to close the dialog box and return to the worksheet.
- Click outside cell B19 to deselect this cell. Look carefully at cell B19 in Figure A.4f. You should see a red dot in the upper-right corner of the cell, indicating that a note has been attached.
- Point to cell B19, and the text of the note you just created appears over the spreadsheet in the form of a ToolTip. Point to a different cell, and the note disappears from view.
- Save the workbook.

THE EDIT CLEAR COMMAND

The Clear command in the Edit menu erases the contents, format, and/or notes within a cell. Select the cell(s), pull down the Edit menu, click (or point to) the Clear command, then select the desired option (All, Format, Contents, or Notes) from the resulting submenu.

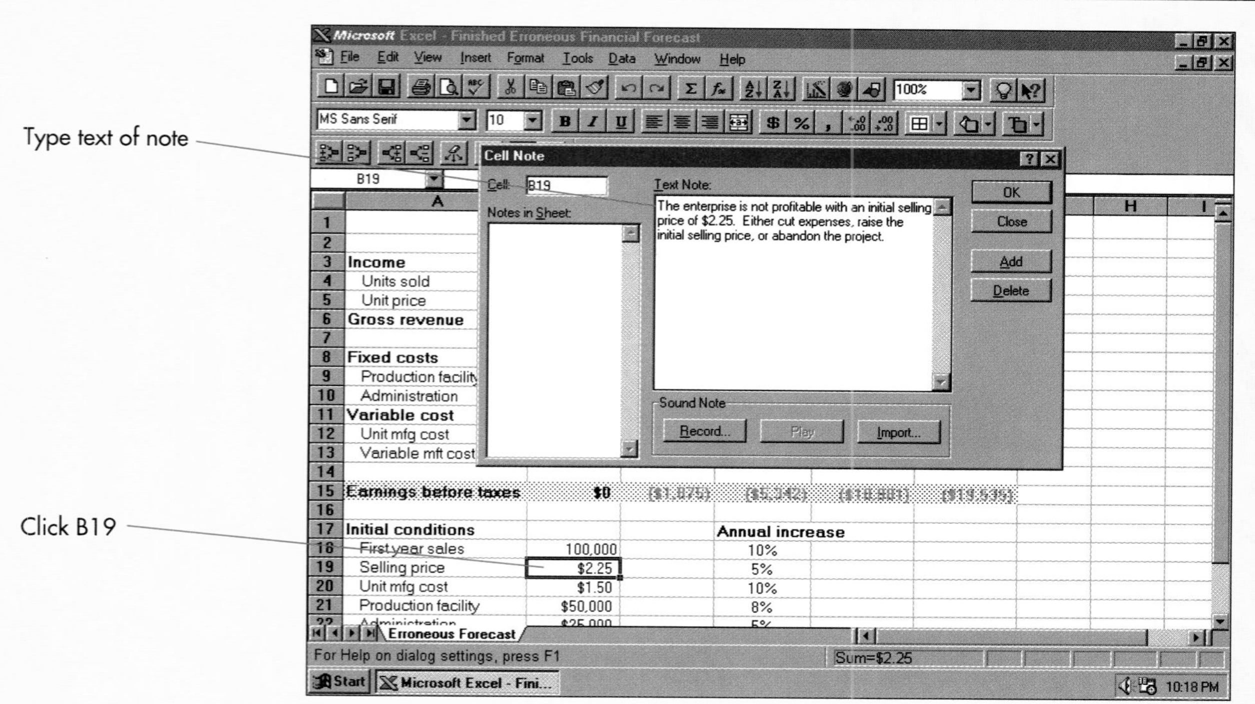

(e) Attach a Note (step 5)

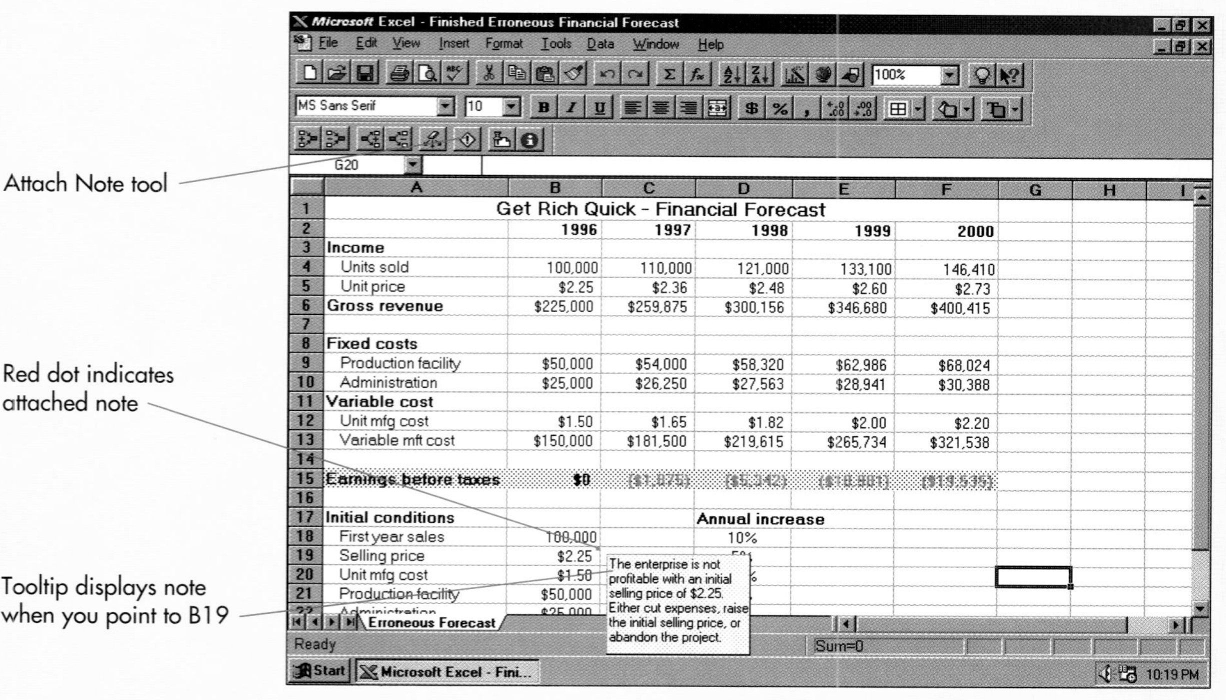

(f) The Completed Worksheet (step 6)

FIGURE A.4 Hands-on Exercise 1 (continued)

STEP 6: Conduct Your Own Audit

- The erroneous grade book is on the data disk so that you can continue to practice. Open the **Erroneous Gradebook** workbook in the **Exploring Excel folder.**
- You should see the professor's grade book that was described at the beginning of the appendix. Conduct your own audit of the grade book, using the techniques in the exercise.
- Exit Excel when you have completed the exercise.

SUMMARY

A spreadsheet is only a tool, and like all other tools, it must be used properly, or else there can be serious consequences. The essential point in the grade book and financial forecast examples is that the potential for spreadsheet error does exist, and that you cannot blindly accept the results of a spreadsheet. Every spreadsheet should be checked for obvious errors, and if any are found, a spreadsheet audit is called for.

The Auditing toolbar helps you understand the relationships between the various cells in a worksheet. It enables you to trace the precedents for a formula and identify the cells in the worksheet that are referenced by that formula. It also enables you to trace the dependents of a cell and identify the formulas in the worksheet that reference that cell.

KEY WORDS AND CONCEPTS

Audit
Attach Note command
Auditing toolbar
Dependents
Precedents
Trace Error command

B

APPENDIX B: SOLVER

OVERVIEW

The use of a spreadsheet in decision making has been emphasized throughout the text. We showed you how to design a spreadsheet based on a set of initial conditions and assumptions, then see at a glance the effect of changing one or more of those values. We introduced the Scenario Manager to store sets of assumptions so that they could be easily recalled and reevaluated. We discussed the Goal Seek command, which enables you to set the value of a target cell, then determine the input needed to arrive at that target value. The Goal Seek command, useful as it is, however, is limited to a *single* input variable. This appendix discusses ***Solver,*** a powerful add-in that is designed for problems involving *multiple* variables.

Solver is an optimization and resource allocation tool that helps you achieve a desired goal. You specify a goal, such as maximizing profit or minimizing cost. You indicate the constraints (conditions) that must be satisfied for the solution to be valid, and you specify the cells whose values can change in order to reach that goal. Solver will then determine the values for the changing cells (i.e., it will tell you how to allocate your resources) in order to reach the desired goal.

This appendix provides an introduction to Solver through two different examples. The first example shows how to maximize profit. The second example minimizes cost. Both examples are accompanied by a hands-on exercise.

EXAMPLE 1—MAXIMIZE PROFIT

Assume that you are the production manager for a company that manufactures computers. Your company divides its product line into two basic categories, desktop computers and laptops. Each product is sold under two different labels, a discount line and a premium line. As production manager you are to determine how many computers of each type, and of each product line, to make each week.

Your decision is subject to various constraints that must be satisfied during the production process. Each computer requires a specified number of hours for assembly. Discount and premium-brand desktops require two and three hours, respectively. Discount and premium-brand laptops use three and five hours, respectively. The factory is working at full capacity, and you have only 4,500 hours of labor to allocate among the different products.

Your production decision is also constrained by demand. The marketing department has determined that you cannot sell more than 800 desktop units, nor more than 900 laptops, per week. The total demand for the discount and premium lines is 700 and 1,000 computers, respectively, per week.

Your goal (objective) is to maximize the total profit, which is based on a different profit margin for each type of computer. A desktop and a laptop computer from the discount line have unit profits of $600 and $800, respectively. The premium desktop and laptop computers have unit profits of $1,000 and $1,300, respectively. How many computers of each type do you manufacture each week in order to maximize the total profit?

This is a complex problem, but one which can be easily solved provided you can design the spreadsheet to display all of the information. Figure B.1 illustrates one way to set up the problem. In essence, you need to determine the values of cells B2 through B5, which represent the quantity of each computer to produce. You might be able to solve the problem manually through trial and error, by substituting different values and seeing the impact on profit. That is exactly what Solver will do for you, only it will do it much more quickly. (Solver uses various optimization techniques that are beyond the scope of this discussion.)

Once Solver arrives at a solution, assuming that it can find a solution, it creates a report such as the one shown in Figure B.2. The solution shows the value of the target cell (the profit in this example), based on the values of the adjustable cells (the quantity of each type of computer). The solution that will maximize profit is to manufacture 700 discount laptops and 800 premium desktops for a profit of $1,270,000.

The report in Figure B.2 also examines each constraint and determines whether it is binding or not binding. A ***binding constraint*** is one in which the resource is fully utilized (i.e., the slack is zero). The number of available hours, for example, is a binding constraint because every available hour is used, and hence the value of the target cell (profit) is limited by the amount of this resource (the number of hours). Or stated another way, any increase in the number of available hours (above 4,500) will also increase the profit.

A ***nonbinding constraint*** is just the opposite. It has a nonzero slack (i.e., the resource is not fully utilized), and hence it does not limit the value of the target cell. The laptop demand, for example, is not binding because a total of only 700 laptops were produced, yet the allowable demand was 900 (the value in cell E13). In other words, there is a slack value of 200 for this constraint, and increasing the allowable demand will have no effect on the profit. (The demand could actually be decreased by up to 200 units with no effect on profit.)

SOLVER

The information required by Solver is entered through the ***Solver Parameters dialog box*** as shown in Figure B.3. The dialog box is divided into three sections: the target cell, the changing cells, and the constraints. The dialog box in Figure B.3 corresponds to the spreadsheet shown earlier in Figure B.1.

Need to determine the values of cells B2:B5

	A	B	C	D	E
1		Quantity	Hours	Unit Profit	
2	Discount desktop		2	$600	
3	Discount laptop		3	$800	
4	Premium desktop		3	$1,000	
5	Premium laptop		5	$1,300	
6					
7	Constraints				
8	Total number of hours used				
9	Labor hours available				4,500
10	Number of desktops produced				
11	Total demand for desktop computers				800
12	Number of laptops produced				
13	Total demand for laptop computers				900
14	Number of discount computers produced				
15	Total demand for discount computers				700
16	Number of premium computers produced				
17	Total demand for premium computers				1,000
18	Hourly cost of labor				$20
19	Profit				

FIGURE B.1 The Initial Worksheet

Value of target cell (profit)

Quantity of each type of computer to be produced

Indicates whether constraint is binding or nonbinding

Target Cell (Max)

Cell	Name	Original Value	Final Value
$E$19	Profit	$0	$1,270,000

Adjustable Cells

Cell	Name	Original Value	Final Value
$B$2	Discount desktop Quantity	0	0
$B$3	Discount laptop Quantity	0	700
$B$4	Premium desktop Quantity	0	800
$B$5	Premium laptop Quantity	0	0

Constraints

Cell	Name	Cell Value	Formula	Status	Slack
$E$8	Total number of hours used	4500	$E$8<=$E$9	Binding	0
$E$10	Number of desktops produced	800	$E$10<=$E$11	Binding	0
$E$12	Number of laptops produced	700	$E$12<=$E$13	Not Binding	200
$E$14	Number of discount computers produced	700	$E$14<=$E$15	Binding	0
$E$16	Number of premium computers produced	800	$E$16<=$E$17	Not Binding	200
$B$2	Discount desktop Quantity	0	$B$2>=0	Binding	0
$B$3	Discount laptop Quantity	700	$B$3>=0	Not Binding	700
$B$4	Premium desktop Quantity	800	$B$4>=0	Not Binding	800
$B$5	Premium laptop Quantity	0	$B$5>=0	Binding	0

FIGURE B.2 The Solution

The ***target cell*** identifies the goal (or objective function)—that is, the cell whose value you want to maximize, minimize, or set to a specific value. Our problem seeks to maximize profit, the formula for which is found in cell E19 (the target cell) of the underlying spreadsheet.

The ***changing cells*** (or decision variables) are the cells whose values are adjusted until the constraints are satisfied and the target cell reaches its optimum value. The changing cells in this example contain the quantity of each computer to be produced and are found in cells B2 through B5.

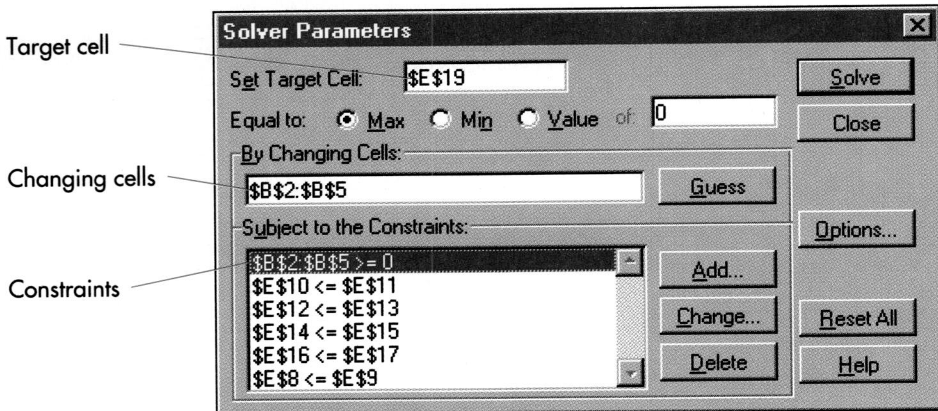

FIGURE B.3 Solver Parameters Dialog Box

The ***constraints*** specify the restrictions. Each constraint consists of a cell or cell range on the left, a relational operator, and a numeric value or cell reference on the right. (The constraints can be entered in any order, but they always appear in alphabetical order.) The first constraint references a cell range, cells B2 through B5, and indicates that each of these cells must be greater than or equal to zero. The remaining constraints reference a single cell rather than a cell range.

The functions of the various command buttons are apparent from their names. The Add, Change, and Delete buttons, are used to add, change, or delete a constraint. The Options button enables you to set various parameters that determine how Solver attempts to find a solution. The Reset All button clears all settings and resets all options to their defaults. The Solve button begins the search for a solution.

THE GREATER-THAN-ZERO CONSTRAINT

One constraint that is often overlooked is the requirement that the value of each changing cell be greater than or equal to zero. Physically, it makes no sense to produce a negative number of computers in any category. Mathematically, however, a negative value in a changing cell may produce a higher value for the target cell. Hence the nonnegativity (greater than or equal to zero) constraint should always be included for the changing cells.

HANDS-ON EXERCISE 1

Maximize Profit

Objective: Use Solver to maximize profit; create a report containing binding and nonbinding constraints. Use Figure B.4 as a guide in the exercise.

STEP 1: Enter the Cell Formulas

➤ Start Excel. Open the **Optimization** workbook in the **Exploring Excel folder.** Save the workbook as **Finished Optimization** so that you can return to the original workbook if necessary.

- If necessary, click the tab for the **Production Mix** worksheet, then click **cell E8** as shown in Figure B.4a. Enter the formula shown in Figure B.4a to compute the total number of hours used in production.
- Enter the remaining cell formulas as shown below:
  - Cell E10 (Number of desktops produced) **=B2+B4**
  - Cell E12 (Number of laptops produced) **=B3+B5**
  - Cell E14 (Number of discount computers produced) **=B2+B3**
  - Cell E16 (Number of premium computers produced) **=B4+B5**
  - Cell E19 (Profit) **=B2*D2+B3*D3+B4*D4+B5*D5–E18*E8**
- Save the workbook.

USE POINTING TO ENTER CELL FORMULAS

A cell reference can be typed directly into a formula, or it can be entered more easily through pointing. The latter is also more accurate as you use the mouse or arrow keys to reference cells directly. To use pointing, select (click) the cell to contain the formula, type an equal sign to begin entering the formula, then click (or move to) the cell containing the reference. Type any arithmetic operator to place the cell reference in the formula, then continue pointing to additional cells. Press the enter key (instead of typing an arithmetic operator) to complete the formula.

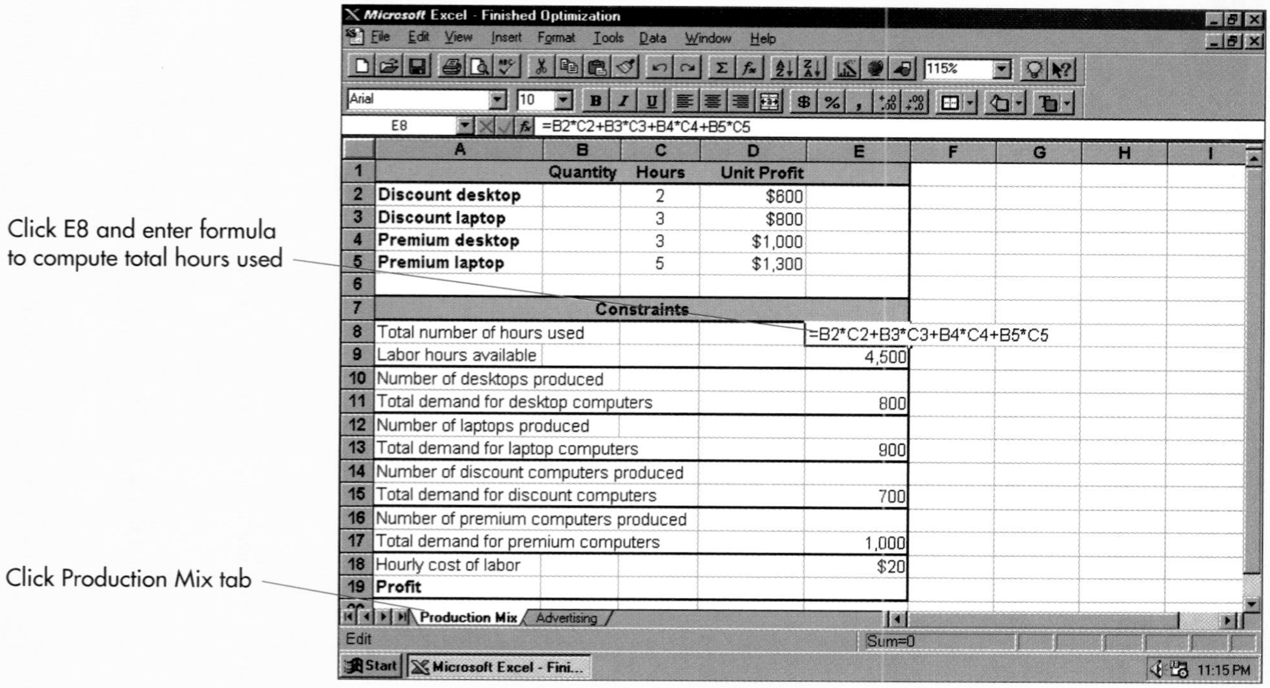

Microsoft Excel - Finished Optimization

E8 =B2*C2+B3*C3+B4*C4+B5*C5

	A	B	C	D	E
1		Quantity	Hours	Unit Profit	
2	**Discount desktop**		2	$800	
3	**Discount laptop**		3	$800	
4	**Premium desktop**		3	$1,000	
5	**Premium laptop**		5	$1,300	
6					
7			Constraints		
8	Total number of hours used				=B2*C2+B3*C3+B4*C4+B5*C5
9	Labor hours available				4,500
10	Number of desktops produced				
11	Total demand for desktop computers				800
12	Number of laptops produced				
13	Total demand for laptop computers				900
14	Number of discount computers produced				
15	Total demand for discount computers				700
16	Number of premium computers produced				
17	Total demand for premium computers				1,000
18	Hourly cost of labor				$20
19	**Profit**				

Production Mix / Advertising

Click E8 and enter formula to compute total hours used

Click Production Mix tab

(a) Enter the Cell Formulas (step 1)

FIGURE B.4 Hands-on Exercise 1

STEP 2: Set the Objective and Variable Cells

- Check that the formula in cell E19 is entered correctly as shown in Figure B.4b. Pull down the **Tools menu.** Click **Solver** to display the Solver Parameters dialog box shown in Figure B.4b.
- The target cell is already set to **cell E19** (since this was the active cell when you started Solver). The **Max option button** is selected by default.
- Click in the **By Changing Cells** text box. Click and drag **cells B2** through **B5** in the worksheet to select these cells.
- Click the **Add command button** to add the first constraint as described in step 3.

> **MISSING SOLVER**
>
> Solver is an optional component of Excel and hence may not be loaded or installed on your system. Pull down the Tools menu and click Add-ins, then check the box next to Solver to load it. If Solver does not appear, you need to install it. Click the Windows 95 Start button, click Settings, then click Control Panel. Double click the icon to Add/Remove programs, click the Install/Uninstall tab, click Microsoft Office application, then click the Add/Remove command button and follow the instructions.

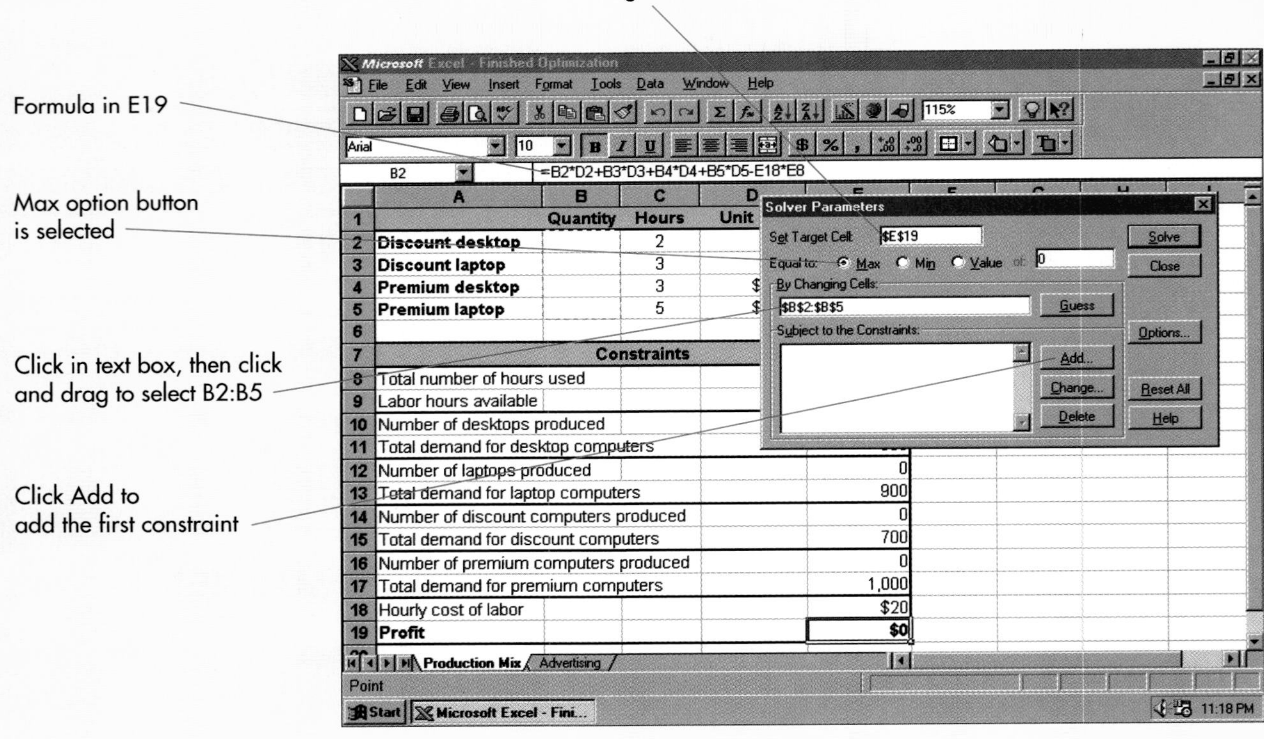

(b) Set the Objective and Variable Cells (step 2)

FIGURE B.4 Hands-on Exercise 1 (continued)

STEP 3: Add the Constraints

- You should see the Add Constraint dialog box in Figure B.4c with the insertion point (a flashing vertical line) in the Cell Reference text box.
  - Click in **cell E8** (the cell containing the formula to compute the total number of hours used).
  - The <= constraint is selected by default.
  - Click in the text box to contain the value of the constraint, then click **cell E9** in the worksheet to enter the cell reference.
  - Click **Add** to complete this constraint and add another.
- You will see a new (empty) Add Constraint dialog box, which enables you to enter additional constraints. Use pointing to enter each of the constraints shown below. (Solver automatically converts each reference to an absolute reference.):
  - Enter the constraint **E10<=E11.** Click **Add.**
  - Enter the constraint **E12<=E13.** Click **Add.**
  - Enter the constraint **E14<=E15.** Click **Add.**
  - Enter the constraint **E16<=E17.** Click **Add.**
- Add the last constraint. Click and drag to select **cells B2** through **B5.** Click the >= operator in the Add Constraint dialog box. Type **0** in the text box to indicate that the production quantities for all computers must be greater than zero. Click **OK** to return to the Solver Parameters dialog box.

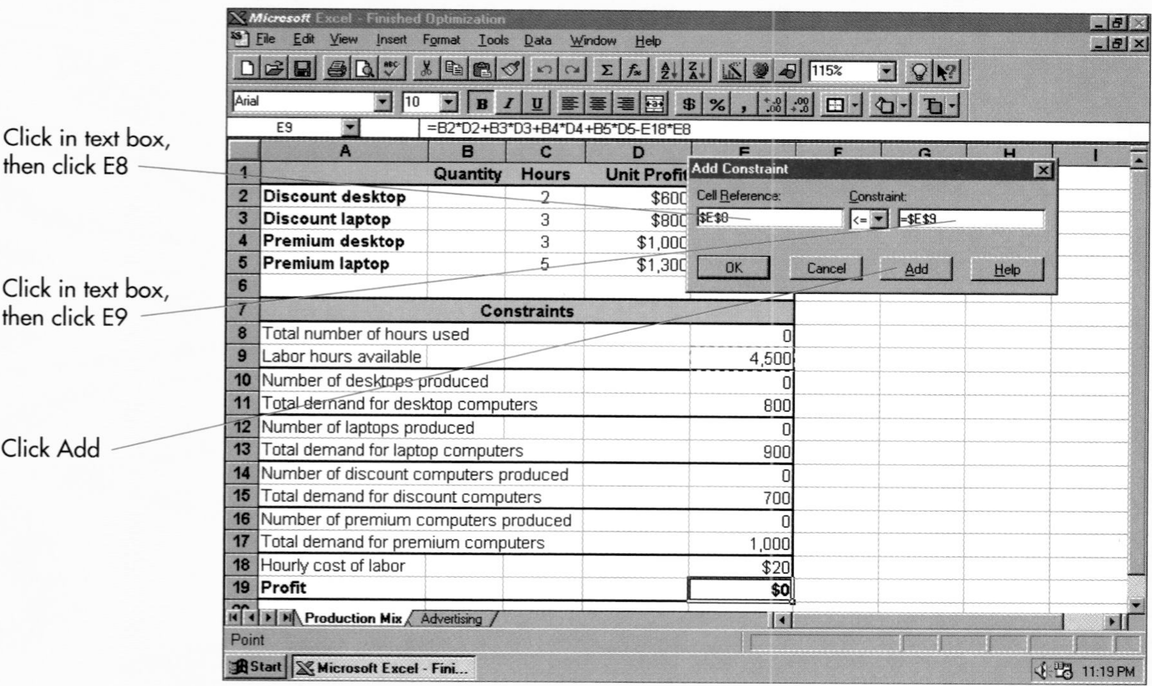

(c) Enter the Constraints (step 3)

FIGURE B.4 Hands-on Exercise 1 (continued)

ADD VERSUS OK

Click the Add button to complete the current constraint and display an empty dialog box in order to enter another constraint. Click OK only when you have completed the last constraint and want to return to the Solver Parameters dialog box in order to solve the problem.

STEP 4: Solve the Problem

- Check that the contents of the Solver Parameters dialog box match those of Figure B.4d. (The constraints appear in alphabetical order rather than the order in which they were entered.)
  - To change the Target cell, click the **Set Target Cell** text box, then click the appropriate target cell in the worksheet.
  - To change (edit) a constraint, select the constraint, then click the **Change button.**
  - To delete a constraint, select the constraint and click the **Delete button.**
- Click the **Solve button** to solve the problem.

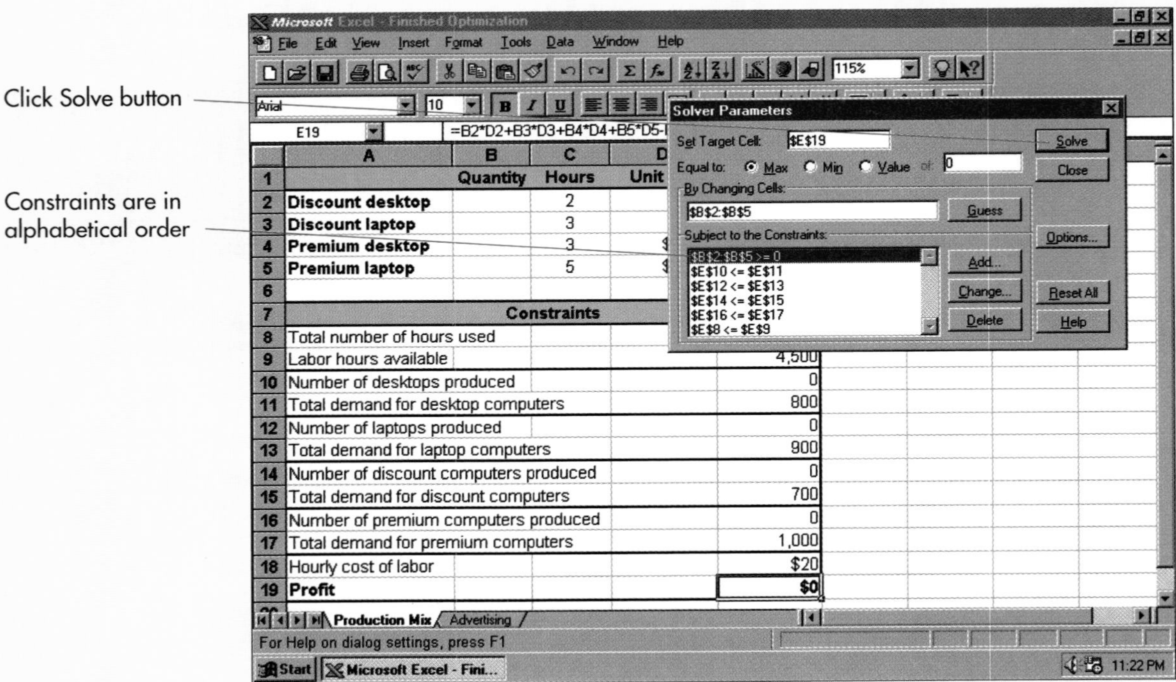

(d) Solve the Problem (step 4)

FIGURE B.4 Hands-on Exercise 1 (continued)

STEP 5: Create the Report

- You should see the Solver Results dialog box in Figure B.4e, indicating that Solver has found a solution. The option button to Keep Solver Solution is selected by default.

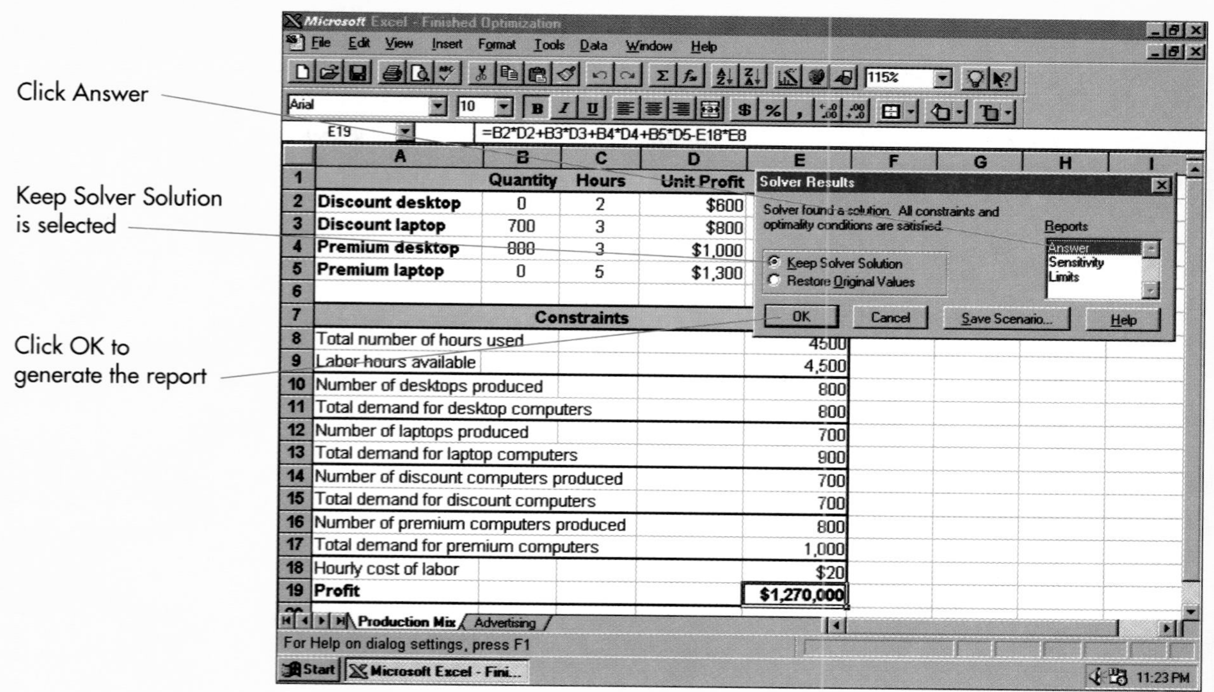

(e) Create the Report (step 5)

FIGURE B.4 Hands-on Exercise 1 (continued)

➤ Click **Answer** in the Reports list box, then click **OK** to generate the report. You will see the report being generated, after which the Solver Results dialog box closes automatically.

➤ Save the workbook.

STEP 6: View the Report

➤ Click the **Answer Report 1 worksheet tab** to view the report as shown in Figure B.4f. Click in **cell A4,** the cell immediately under the entry showing the date and time the report was created. (The gridlines and row and column headings are suppressed by default for this worksheet.)

➤ Enter your name in boldface as shown in the figure, then press **enter** to complete the entry. Print the answer sheet and submit it to your instructor as proof you did the exercise.

➤ Exit Excel if you do not wish to continue with the next exercise at this time.

VIEW OPTIONS

Any worksheet used to create a spreadsheet model will display gridlines and row and column headers by default. Worksheets containing reports, however, especially worksheets generated by Excel, often suppress these elements to make the reports easier and more appealing to read. To suppress (display) these elements, pull down the Tools menu, click Options, click the View tab, then clear (check) the appropriate check boxes under Window options.

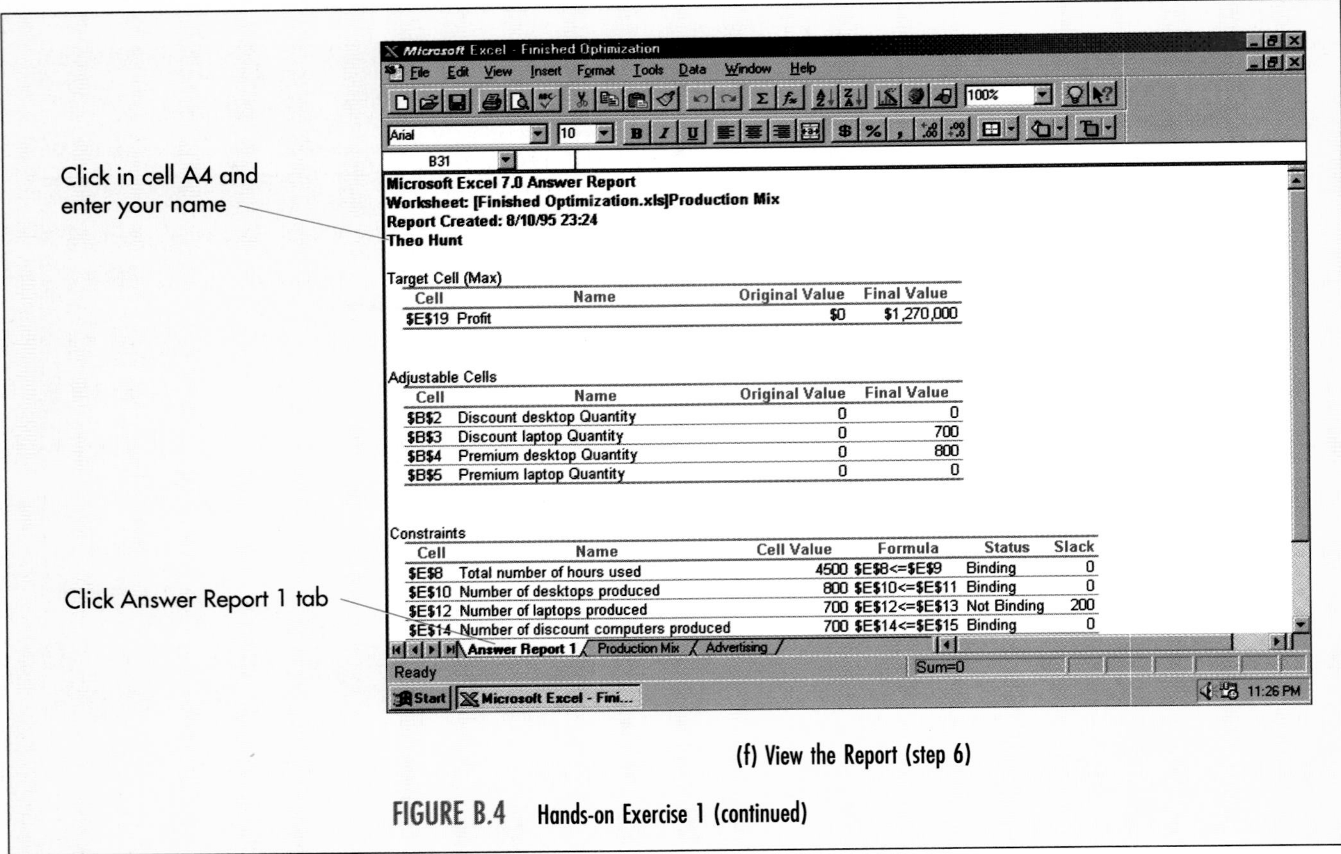

(f) View the Report (step 6)

FIGURE B.4 Hands-on Exercise 1 (continued)

EXAMPLE 2—MINIMIZE COST

The example just concluded introduced you to the basics of Solver. We continue now with a second hands-on exercise, to provide additional practice, and to discuss various subtleties that can occur. This time we present a minimization problem in which we seek to minimize cost subject to a series of constraints. The problem will focus on the advertising campaign that will be conducted to sell the computers that you have produced.

The director of marketing has allocated a total of $125,000 in his weekly advertising budget. He wants to establish a presence in both magazines and radio, and requires a minimum of four magazine ads and ten radio ads each week. Each magazine ad costs $10,000 and is seen by one million readers. Each radio commercial costs $5,000 and is heard by 250,000 listeners. How many ads of each type should be placed in order to reach at least 10 million customers at minimum cost?

All of the necessary information is contained within the previous paragraph. You must, however, display that information in a worksheet before you can ask Solver to find a solution. Accordingly, reread the previous paragraph, then try to set up a worksheet from which you can call Solver. (Our worksheet appears in step 1 of the following hands-on exercise. Try, however, to set up your own worksheet before you look at ours.)

FINER POINTS OF SOLVER

Figure B.5 displays the ***Solver Options dialog box*** that enables you to specify how Solver will approach the solution. The Max Time and Iterations entries determine

Settings determine how long Solver will work on finding a solution

Setting determines how close the computed value will come to the specified value

Solver Options		
Max Time:	100 seconds	OK
Iterations:	100	Cancel
Precision:	0.000001	
Tolerance:	5 %	Load Model...
☐ Assume Linear Model		Save Model...
☐ Show Iteration Results		
☐ Use Automatic Scaling		Help
Estimates	Derivatives	Search
⦿ Tangent	⦿ Forward	⦿ Newton
○ Quadratic	○ Central	○ Conjugate

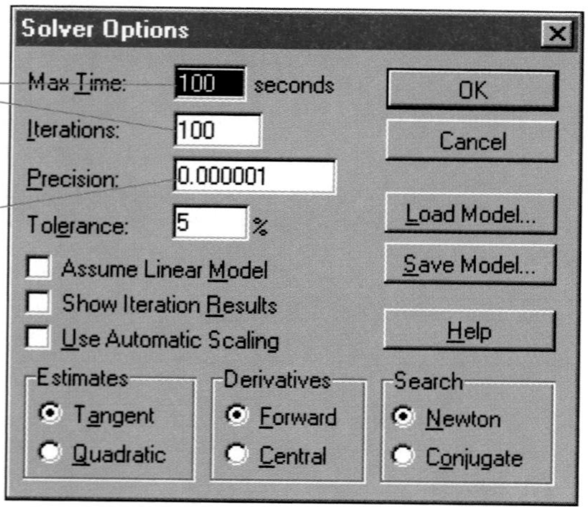

FIGURE B.5 Options Dialog Box

how long Solver will work on finding the solution. If either limit is reached before a solution is found, Solver will ask whether you want to continue. The default settings of 100 seconds and 100 iterations are sufficient for simpler problems, but may fall short for complex problems with multiple constraints.

The Precision setting determines how close the computed values in the constraint cells come to the specified value of the resource. The smaller the precision, the longer Solver will take in arriving at a solution. The default setting of .0000001 is adequate for most problems and should not be decreased. The remaining options are beyond the scope of our discussion.

HANDS-ON EXERCISE 2

Minimize Cost

Objective: Use Solver to minimize cost; impose an integer constraint and examine its effect on the optimal solution; relax a constraint in order to find a feasible solution. Use Figure B.6 as a guide in the exercise.

STEP 1: Enter the Cell Formulas

- Open the **Finished Optimization** workbook from the previous exercise.
- Click the tab for the **Advertising** worksheet, then click in **cell E6.** Enter the formula **=B2*C2+B3*C3** as shown in Figure B.6a.
- Click in **cell E10.** Enter the formula **=B2*D2+B3*D3** to compute the size of the audience. Save the workbook.

THE ANSWER WIZARD

The Answer Wizard lets you ask questions in your own words. Pull down the Help menu, click Answer Wizard, type the question "What is Solver?", then press the enter key. The Answer Wizard will return a list of available help topics pertaining to Solver.

Click E6 and enter the formula

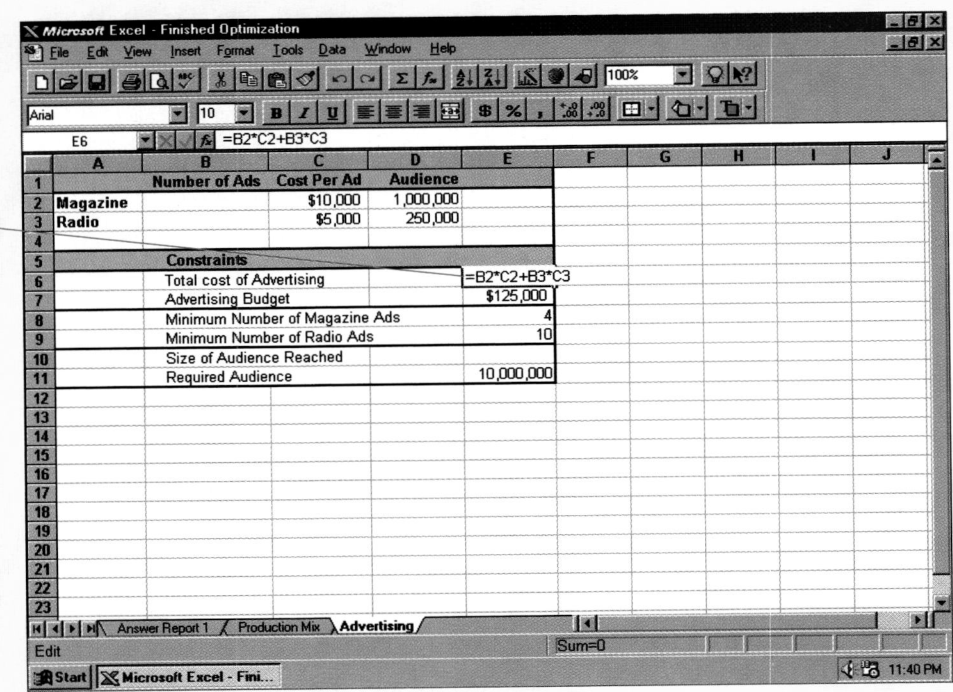

(a) Enter the Cell Formulas (step 1)

FIGURE B.6 Hands-on Exercise 2

STEP 2: Set the Objective and Variable Cells

- Pull down the **Tools menu.** Click **Solver** to display the Solver Parameters dialog box shown in Figure B.6b.
- Set the target cell to **cell E6.** Click the **Min (Minimize) option button.** Click in the **By Changing Cells** text box.
- Click and drag **cells B2** and **B3** in the worksheet to select these cells as shown in Figure B.6b.
- Click the **Add command button** to add the first constraint as described in step 3.

STEP 3: Add the Constraints

- You should see the Add Constraint dialog box in Figure B.6c with the insertion point (a flashing vertical line) in the Cell Reference text box.
  - Click in **cell E6** (the cell containing the formula to compute the total cost of advertising).
  - The <= constraint is selected by default.
  - Click in the text box to contain the value of the constraint, then click **cell E7** in the worksheet to enter the cell reference in the Add Constraint dialog box.
  - Click **Add** to complete this constraint and add another.

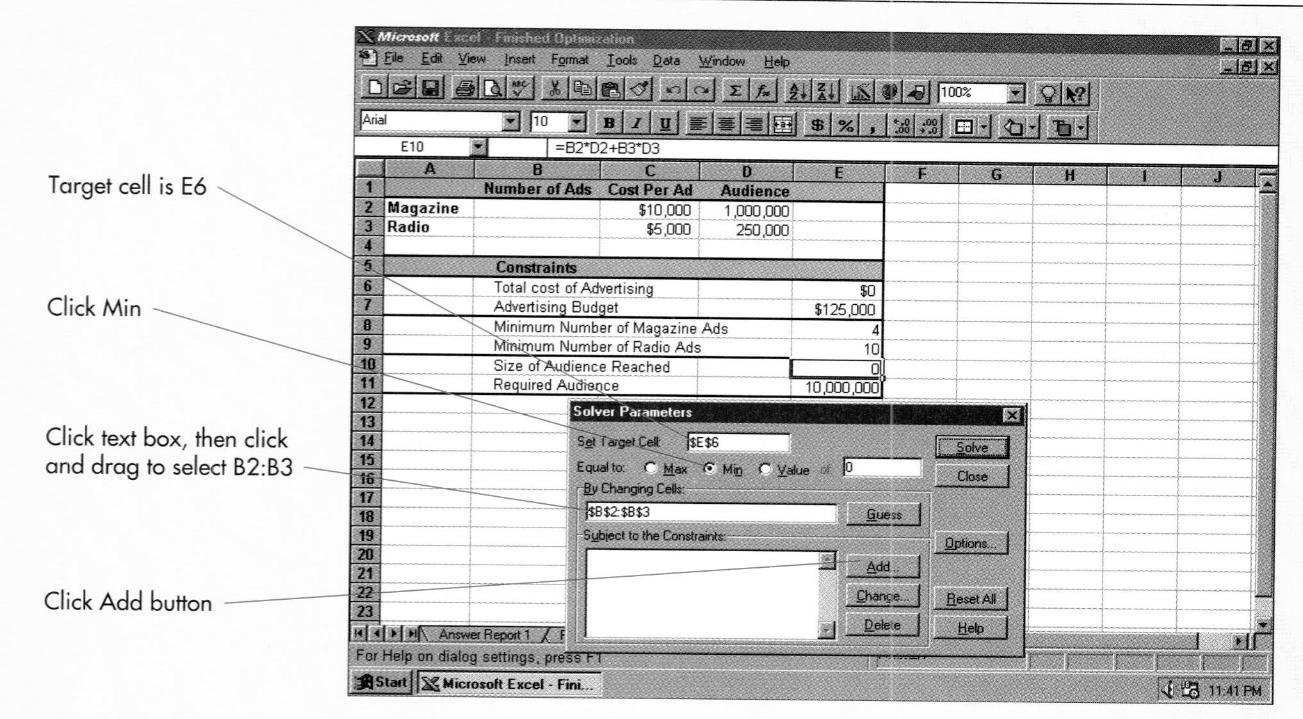

(b) Set the Objective and Variable Cells (step 2)

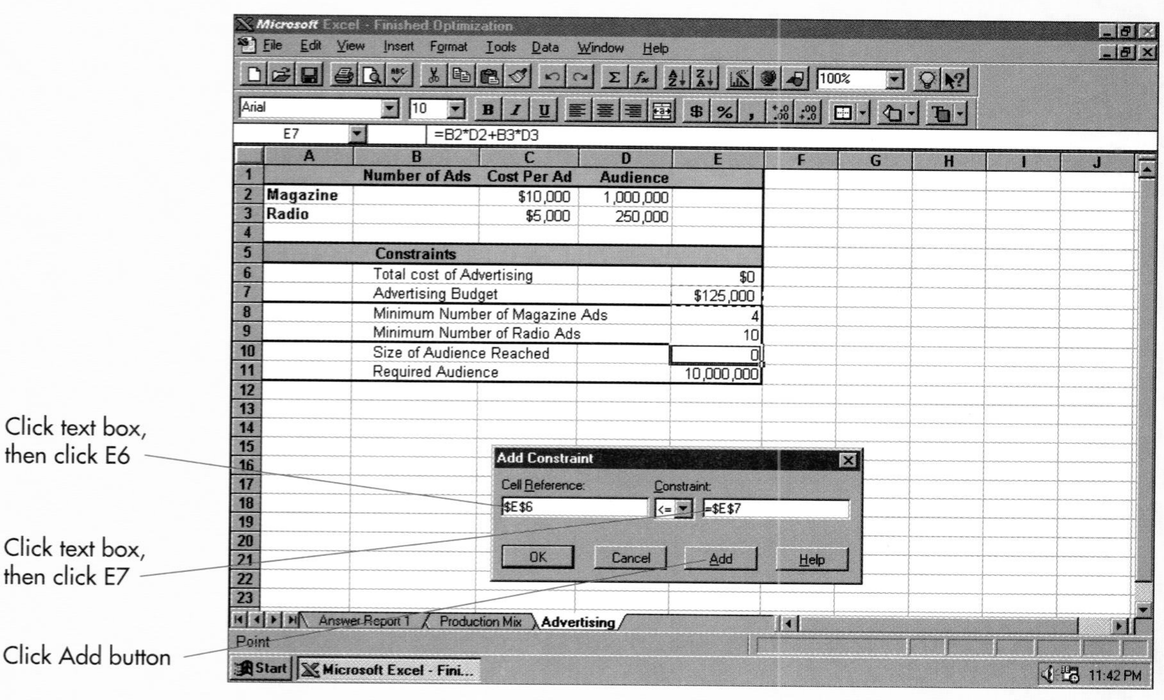

(c) Enter the Constraints (step 3)

FIGURE B.6 Hands-on Exercise 2 (continued)

- You will see a new (empty) Add Constraint dialog box, which enables you to enter additional constraints. Use pointing to enter each of the constraints shown below. (Solver automatically converts each reference to an absolute reference.)
  - Enter the constraint **E10>=E11.** Click **Add.**
  - Enter the constraint **B2>=E8.** Click **Add.**
  - Enter the constraint **B3>=E9.** Click **OK** since this is the last constraint.

SHOW ITERATION RESULTS

Solver uses an iterative (repetitive) approach in which each iteration (trial solution) is one step closer to the optimal solution. It may be interesting, therefore, to examine the intermediate solutions, especially if you have a knowledge of optimization techniques, such as linear programming. Click the Options command button in the Solver Parameters dialog box, check the Show Iterations Results box, click OK to close the Solver Options dialog box, then click the Solve command button in the usual fashion. A Show Trial Solutions dialog box will appear as each intermediate solution is displayed in the worksheet. Click Continue to move from one iteration to the next until the optimal solution is reached.

STEP 4: Solve the Problem

- Check that the contents of the Solver Parameters dialog box match those in Figure B.6d. (The constraints appear in alphabetical order rather than the order in which they were entered.)
- Click the **Solve button** to solve the problem. The Solver Results dialog box appears and indicates that Solver has arrived at a solution.
- The option button to Keep Solver Solution is selected by default. Click **OK** to close the Solver Results dialog box and display the solution.

STEP 5: Impose an Integer Constraint

- The number of magazine ads in the solution is 7.5 as shown in Figure B.6e. This is a noninteger number, which is reasonable in the context of Solver but not in the "real world" as one cannot place half an ad.
- Pull down the **Tools menu.** Click **Solver** to once again display the Solver Parameters dialog box. Click the **Add button** to display the Add Constraint dialog box in Figure B.6e.
- The insertion point is already positioned in the Cell Reference text box. Click and drag to select **cells B2** through **B3.** Click the **drop-down arrow** in the Constraint list box and click **int** (for integer).
- Click **OK** to accept the constraint and close the Add Constraint dialog box.
- The Solver Parameters dialog box appears on your monitor with the integer constraint added. Click **Solve** to solve the problem.

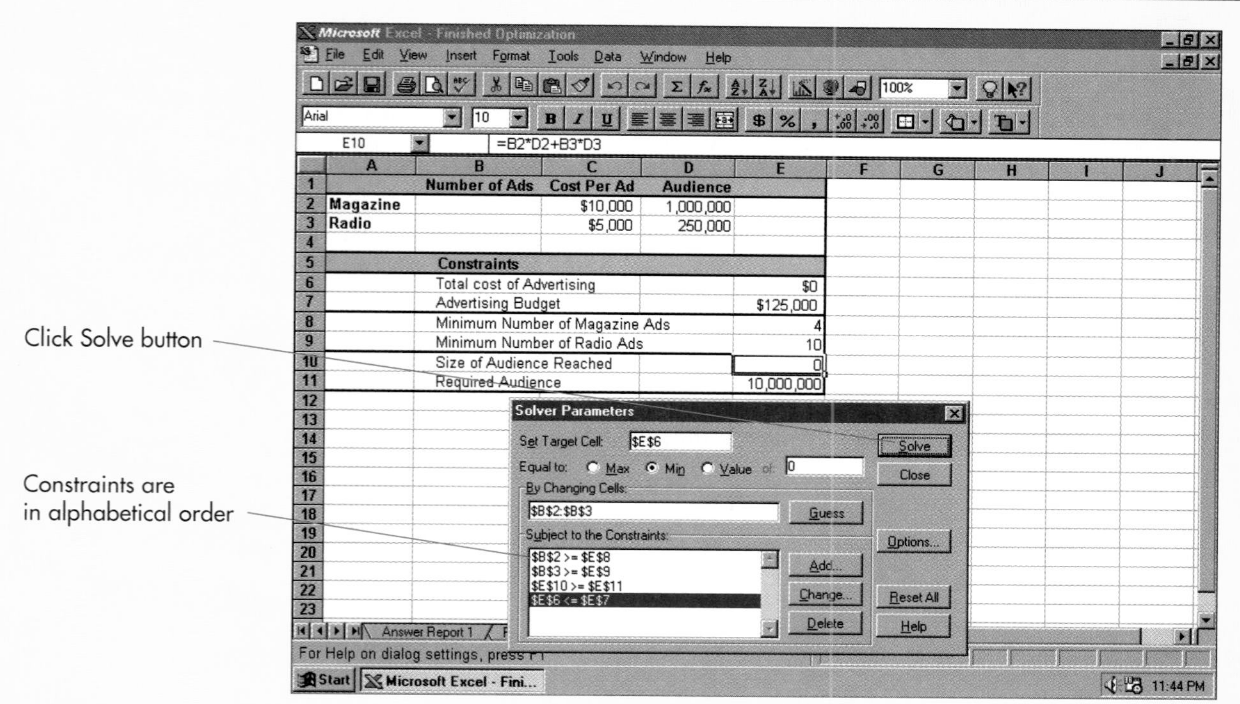

(d) Solve the Problem (step 4)

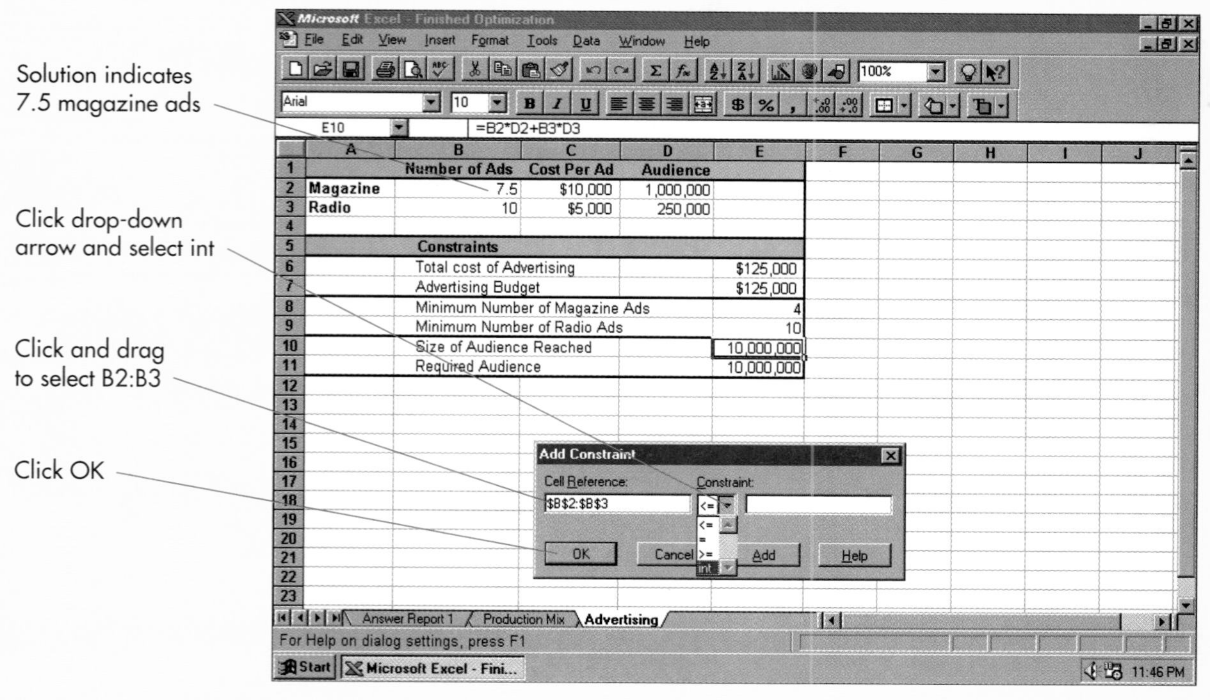

(e) Add the Integer Constraint (step 5)

FIGURE B.6 Hands-on Exercise 2 (continued)

DO YOU REALLY NEED AN INTEGER SOLUTION?

It seems like such a small change, but specifying an integer constraint can significantly increase the amount of time required for Solver to reach a solution. The examples in this chapter are relatively simple and did not take an inordinate amount of time to solve. Imposing an integer constraint on a more complex problem, however, especially on a slower microprocessor, may challenge your patience as Solver struggles to reach a solution.

STEP 6: The Infeasible Solution

- You should see the dialog box in Figure B.6f, indicating that Solver could *not* find a solution that satisfied the existing constraints. This is because the imposition of the integer constraint raised the number of magazine ads from 7.5 to 8, which increased the total cost of advertising to $130,000, which exceeded the budget of $125,000.
- The desired audience can still be reached but only by relaxing one of the binding constraints. You can, for example, retain the requisite number of magazine and radio ads by increasing the budget. Alternatively, the budget can be held at $125,000, while still reaching the audience by decreasing the required number of radio ads.
- Click **Cancel** to exit the dialog box and return to the worksheet.

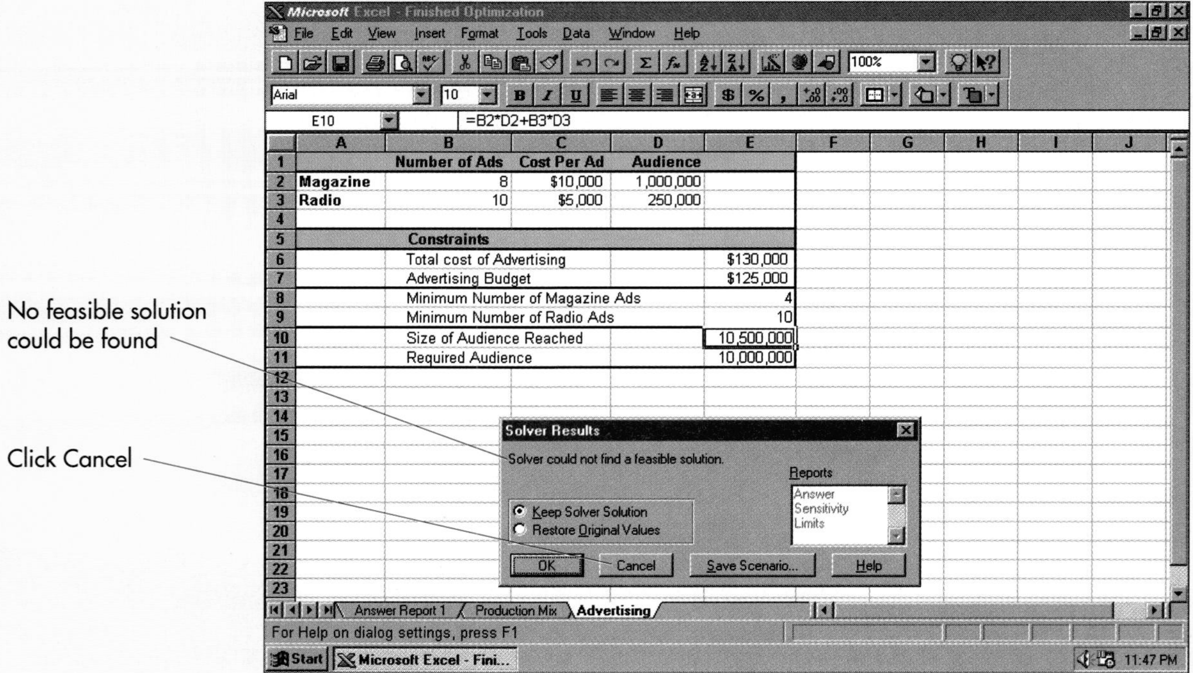

(f) The Infeasible Solution (step 6)

FIGURE B.6 Hands-on Exercise 2 (continued)

UNABLE TO FIND A SOLUTION

Solver is a powerful tool, but it cannot do the impossible. Some problems simply do not have a solution because the constraints may conflict with one another, and/or because the constraints exceed the available resources. Should this occur, and it will, check your constraints to make sure they were entered correctly. If Solver is still unable to reach a solution, it will be necessary to relax one or more constraints.

STEP 7: Relax a Constraint

- Click in **cell E9** (the cell containing the minimum number of radio ads). Enter **9** and press **enter.**
- Pull down the **Tools menu.** Click **Solver** to display the Solver Parameters dialog box. Click **Solve.** This time Solver finds a solution as shown in Figure B.6g.
- Click **Answer** in the Reports list box, then click **OK** to generate the report. You will see the report being generated, after which the Solver Results dialog box closes automatically.
- Click the **Answer Report 2 worksheet tab** to view the report. Add your name to the report, boldface your name, print the answer report, and submit it to your instructor.
- Save the workbook a final time. Exit Excel.

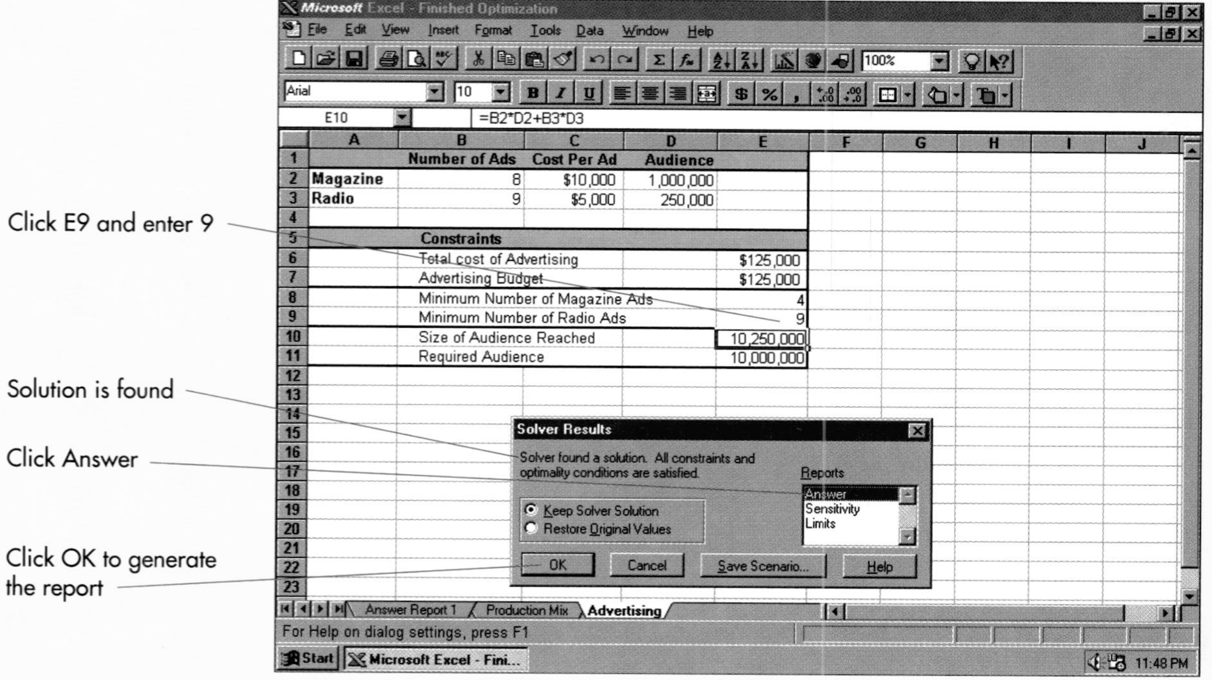

(g) Relax a Constraint (step 7)

FIGURE B.6 Hands-on Exercise 2 (continued)

SUMMARY

Solver is an optimization and resource allocation tool that helps you achieve a desired goal, such as maximizing profit or minimizing cost. The information required by Solver is entered through the Solver Parameters dialog box, which is divided into three sections: the target cell, the changing cells, and the constraints.

The target cell identifies the goal (or objective function), which is the cell whose value you want to maximize, minimize, or set to a specific value. The changing cells are the cells whose values are adjusted until the constraints are satisfied and the target cell reaches its optimum value. The constraints specify the restrictions. Each constraint consists of a comparison, containing a cell or cell range on the left, a relational operator, and a numeric value or cell reference on the right.

The Solver Options dialog box lets you specify how Solver will attempt to find a solution. The Max Time and Iterations entries determine how long Solver will work on finding a solution. If either limit is reached before a solution is found, Solver will ask whether you want to continue. The default settings of 100 seconds and 100 iterations are sufficient for simpler problems, but may fall short for complex problems with multiple constraints.

KEY WORDS AND CONCEPTS

Adjustable cells
Answer Report
Binding constraint
Changing cells
Constraint
Feasible solution
Integer constraint
Iteration
Nonbinding constraint
Nonnegativity constraint
Precision
Solver Options dialog box
Solver Parameters dialog box
Target cell

C

APPENDIX C: DATA MAPPING

OVERVIEW

"A picture is worth 1,000 words." It is a well-documented fact that a chart can convey information more effectively than the corresponding table of numbers. You are already familiar with the use of conventional charts (pie charts, column charts, line charts, and so on) as an effective way to represent the information in a worksheet. This appendix extends that discussion to the use of maps, a capability that is built into Microsoft Office.

Consider, for example, the worksheet and associated maps in Figure C.1, which display the results of the 1992 presidential election as well as a strategy for 1996. The worksheet in Figure C.1a contains the statistical data on which the maps are based. It lists the states in alphabetical order, and for each state, the number of electoral votes and the candidate who received those votes. The worksheet also shows the number of popular votes received by each candidate, although that information is not conveyed in either map. (The District of Columbia is not shown in the worksheet, but its three electoral votes are included in Mr. Clinton's total.)

The maps in Figures C.1b and C.1c display (some of the) information that is contained within the worksheet, but in a form that is more quickly grasped by the reader. Figure C.1b shows at a glance which candidate won which state by assigning different colors to each candidate. Figure C.1c groups the states according to the number of electoral votes in order to develop a strategy for the 1996 election.

This appendix shows you how to use the Data Mapping application in Microsoft Office to create the maps in Figure C.1. The appendix also introduces you to the Mapstats workbook that contains demographic information for the United States as well as several foreign countries, and enables you to create a variety of additional maps.

	State	Electoral Votes	Winner	Bush	Clinton	Perot
1	State	Electoral Votes	Winner	Bush	Clinton	Perot
2	Alabama	9	Bush	804,283	690,080	183,109
3	Alaska	3	Bush	102,000	78,294	73,481
4	Arizona	8	Bush	572,086	543,050	253,741
5	Arkansas	6	Clinton	337,324	505,823	99,132
6	California	54	Clinton	3,630,574	5,121,325	2,296,006
7	Colorado	8	Clinton	562,850	629,681	366,010
8	Connecticut	8	Clinton	578,313	682,318	348,771
9	Delaware	3	Clinton	102,313	126,055	59,213
10	Florida	25	Bush	2,173,310	2,072,798	1,053,067
11	Georgia	13	Clinton	995,252	1,008,966	309,657
12	Hawaii	4	Clinton	136,822	179,310	53,003
13	Idaho	4	Bush	202,645	137,013	130,395
14	Illinois	22	Clinton	1,734,096	2,453,350	840,515
15	Indiana	12	Bush	989,375	848,420	455,934
16	Iowa	7	Clinton	504,891	586,353	253,468
17	Kansas	6	Bush	449,951	390,434	312,358
18	Kentucky	8	Clinton	617,178	665,104	203,944
19	Louisiana	9	Clinton	733,386	815,971	211,478
20	Maine	4	Clinton	206,504	263,420	206,820
21	Maryland	10	Clinton	707,094	988,571	281,414
22	Massachusetts	12	Clinton	805,039	1,318,639	630,731
23	Michigan	18	Clinton	1,554,940	1,871,182	824,813
24	Minnesota	10	Clinton	747,841	1,020,997	562,506
25	Mississippi	7	Bush	487,793	400,258	85,626
26	Missouri	11	Clinton	811,159	1,053,873	518,741
27	Montana	3	Clinton	144,207	154,507	107,225
28	Nebraska	5	Bush	344,346	217,344	174,687
29	Nevada	4	Clinton	175,828	189,148	132,580
30	New Hampshire	4	Clinton	202,484	209,040	121,337
31	New Jersey	15	Clinton	1,356,865	1,436,206	521,829
32	New Mexico	5	Clinton	212,824	261,617	91,895
33	New York	33	Clinton	2,346,649	3,444,450	1,090,721
34	North Carolina	14	Bush	1,134,661	1,114,042	357,864
35	North Dakota	3	Bush	136,244	99,168	71,084
36	Ohio	21	Clinton	1,894,310	1,984,942	1,036,426
37	Oklahoma	8	Bush	592,929	473,066	319,878
38	Oregon	7	Clinton	475,757	621,314	354,091
39	Pennsylvania	23	Clinton	1,791,841	2,239,164	902,667
40	Rhode Island	4	Clinton	131,605	213,302	105,051
41	South Carolina	8	Bush	577,507	479,514	138,872
42	South Dakota	3	Bush	136,718	124,888	73,295
43	Tennessee	11	Clinton	841,300	933,521	199,968
44	Texas	32	Bush	2,496,071	2,281,815	1,354,781
45	Utah	5	Bush	322,632	183,429	203,400
46	Vermont	3	Clinton	88,122	133,592	65,991
47	Virginia	13	Bush	1,150,517	1,038,650	348,639
48	Washington	11	Clinton	731,235	993,039	541,801
49	West Virginia	5	Clinton	241,974	331,001	108,829
50	Wisconsin	11	Clinton	930,855	1,041,066	544,479
51	Wyoming	3	Bush	79,347	68,160	51,263
52						
53	Total	535		39,083,847	44,717,270	19,632,586
54						
55	Electoral Vote totals					
56	Clinton	370				
57	Bush	168				

(a) Worksheet Data

FIGURE C.1 Data Mapping

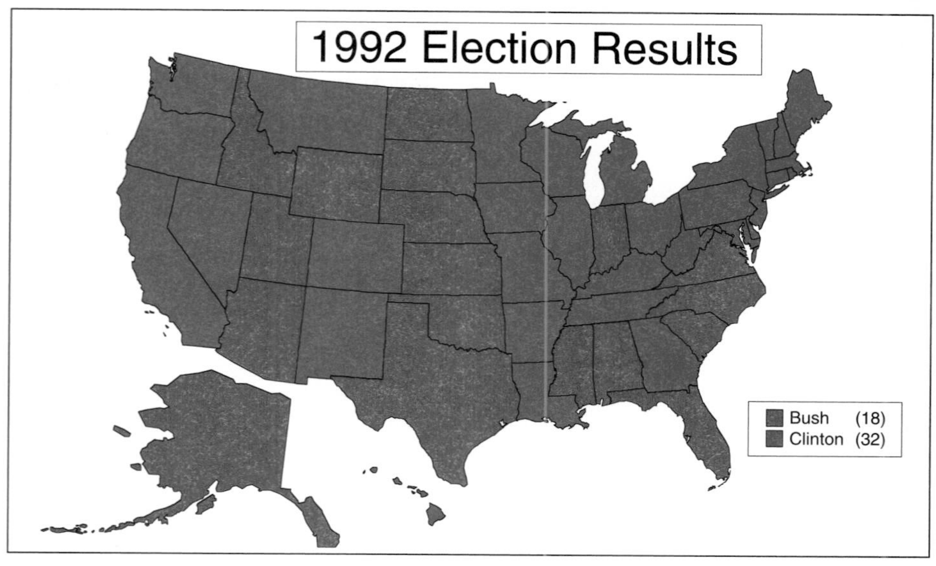

(b) 1992 Election Results

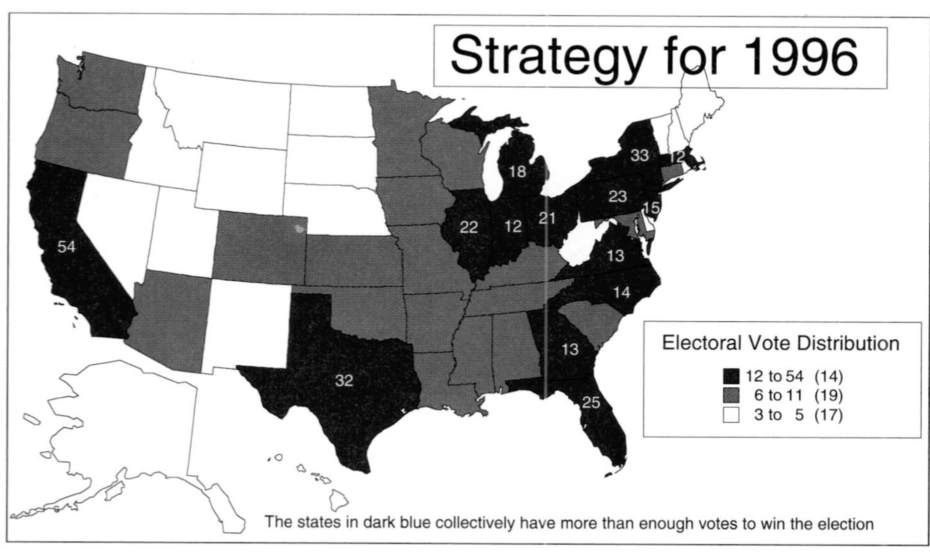

(c) Strategy for 1996

FIGURE C.1 Data Mapping (continued)

CREATING A MAP

The exercise that follows shortly illustrates the basic commands in the Data Mapping application and gives you an appreciation for its overall capability. Creating a map is easy provided you have a basic proficiency with Microsoft Excel. In essence, you do the following:

1. Select the cell range(s) containing the data for the map. (At least one column of the data must be recognizable as geographic names that are present in one of the available maps.)

2. Click the Map button on the Standard toolbar, then click and drag in the worksheet where you want the map to go.
3. Determine the type of map you want to create by selecting one of several formatting options. (The formatting options are specified in the Data Map Control dialog box, which is described in greater detail on page 201.)
4. Add the finishing touches by changing the title, legend, or other features.

Each step displays a dialog box in which you specify the options you want. The best way to learn is to create a map. Let's begin.

HANDS-ON EXERCISE 1

Introduction to Data Mapping

Objective: Illustrate basic features of the Data Mapping application to create a map showing the winning candidate in each state in the 1992 presidential election. Use Figure C.2 as a guide in the exercise.

STEP 1: Insert a Cell Note

- Start Excel. Open the **Presidential Election** workbook in the **Exploring Excel folder.** Save the workbook as **Finished Presidential Election** so that you can return to the original workbook if necessary.
- Press **Ctrl+End** to move to the end of the worksheet as shown in Figure C.2a. You can see the number of popular votes received by each candidate as well as the number of electoral votes.
- Click in **cell B56.** Pull down the **Insert menu.** Click **Note** to display the dialog box in Figure C.2a. Enter the cell note shown in the figure, then click **OK** to insert the note.
- There should be a tiny red dot in the upper-right corner of cell B56. Point to cell B56 and you will see a ToolTip that displays the note you just added. (To remove a note, select the cell, pull down the **Edit menu,** click **Clear,** then click **Notes.**)

RESOLVE UNKNOWN GEOGRAPHIC DATA

The Data Mapping application uses its own version of a spell check to ensure that the selected data matches predefined geographic data. The states must be spelled correctly, for example, or else mapping is not possible. Any unrecognized entry is flagged as unknown geographic data. You may be offered suggestions for a simple misspelling, in which case you can accept the suggestion. A more serious error, however, such as including an extraneous row (e.g., totals) in the data range, requires you to discard the entry.

STEP 2: Draw the Map

- Press **Ctrl+Home** to move to the beginning of the worksheet. Click in **cell A1,** then click and drag to select **cells A1** through **C51.** The AutoCalculate

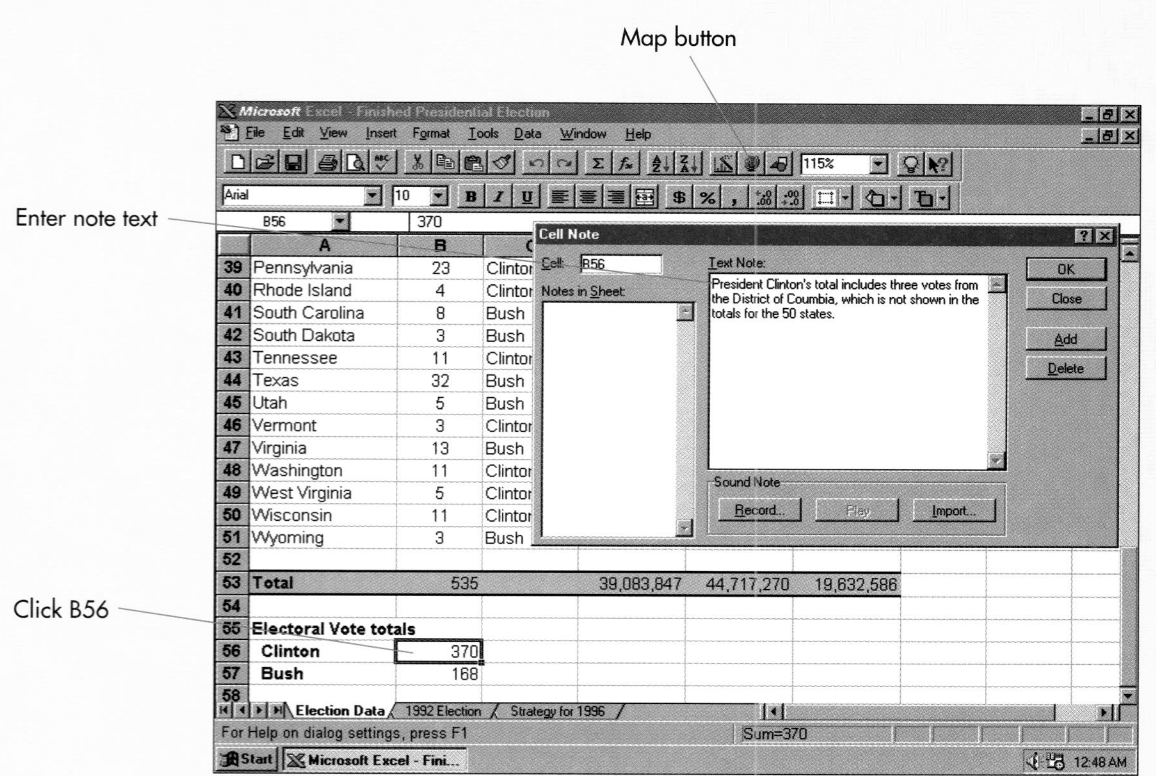

(a) Insert a Note (step 1)

FIGURE C.2 Hands-on Exercise 1

indicator on the status bar (see boxed tip) should display 535 as the total number of electoral votes in the selected range.

- Click the **Map button** on the Standard toolbar. Click the **down scroll arrow** until cell A59 comes into view. Click in **cell A59,** then click and drag as shown in Figure C.2b. (Excel requires that the map be created on the same sheet as the data. You can, however, move the map to a different sheet after it has been created to facilitate printing.) Release the mouse.
- A dialog box will appear on the screen with the message, "Retrieving current selection", followed by a second message, "Matching Data". You should then see the dialog box in Figure C.2b, indicating that multiple maps are available.

THE AUTOCALCULATE FEATURE

The AutoCalculate feature lets you check a total without having to use a calculator or enter a temporary formula in a worksheet. You can use the feature to check that you have selected all 50 states prior to drawing the map. Just select the range, and the status bar displays the result. You can change the AutoCalculate function (to display the count, average, maximum, or minimum value) by right clicking the AutoCalculate area of the status bar, then selecting the desired function.

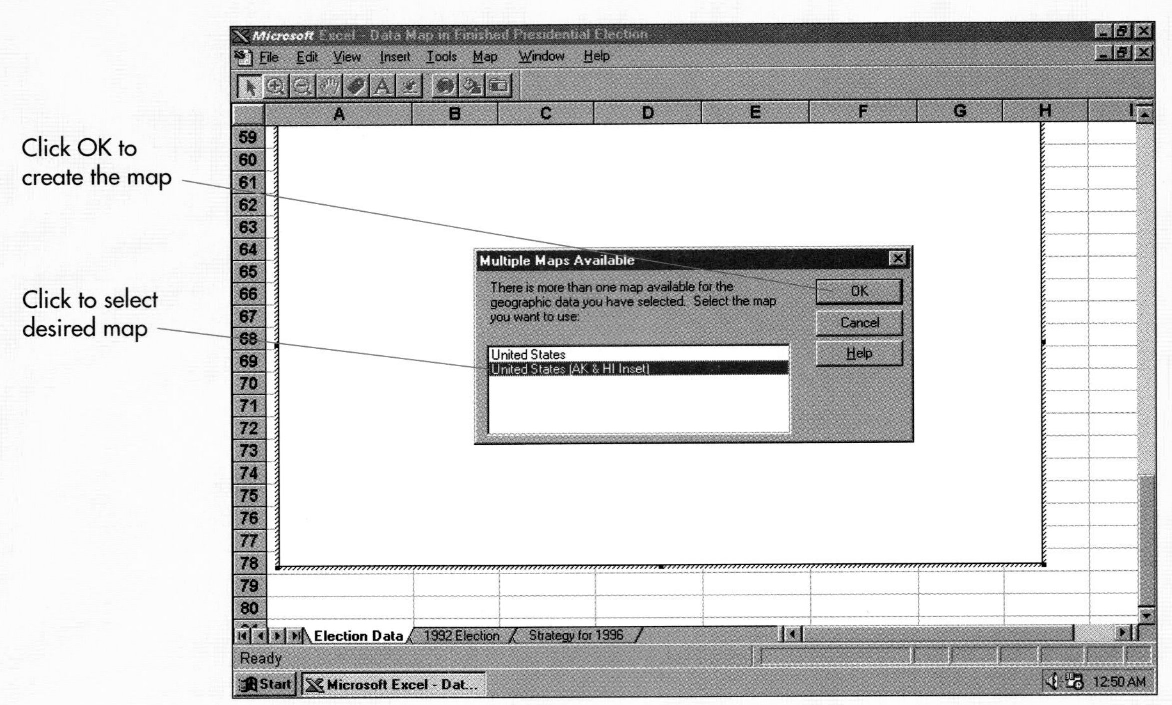

(b) Draw a Map (step 2)

FIGURE C.2 Hands-on Exercise 1 (continued)

- The program recognizes the state names in Column A and presents two options for U.S. maps. Click **United States (AK & HI Inset),** then click **OK** to create the map.

STEP 3: Data Map Control

- You should see the Data Map Control dialog box in Figure C.2c. Excel has (by default) plotted the number of electoral votes, rather than the candidate who won the votes.
- Click and drag the **Electoral Votes button** out of the Data Map Control dialog box work area until you see a recycle bin. Release the mouse. The data disappears from the map, and all of the states appear in light green.

CHANGE THE CATEGORY COLORS

You can change the category colors by double clicking the column heading button within the Data Map Control box. To change the color for President Clinton, for example, double click the Winner button within the work area of the Data Map Control box to display the Category Shading Options dialog box. Select the category (e.g., Clinton), then click the down arrow in the color list box to choose a different color. Click OK to accept the color change and close the Category Shading Options dialog box.

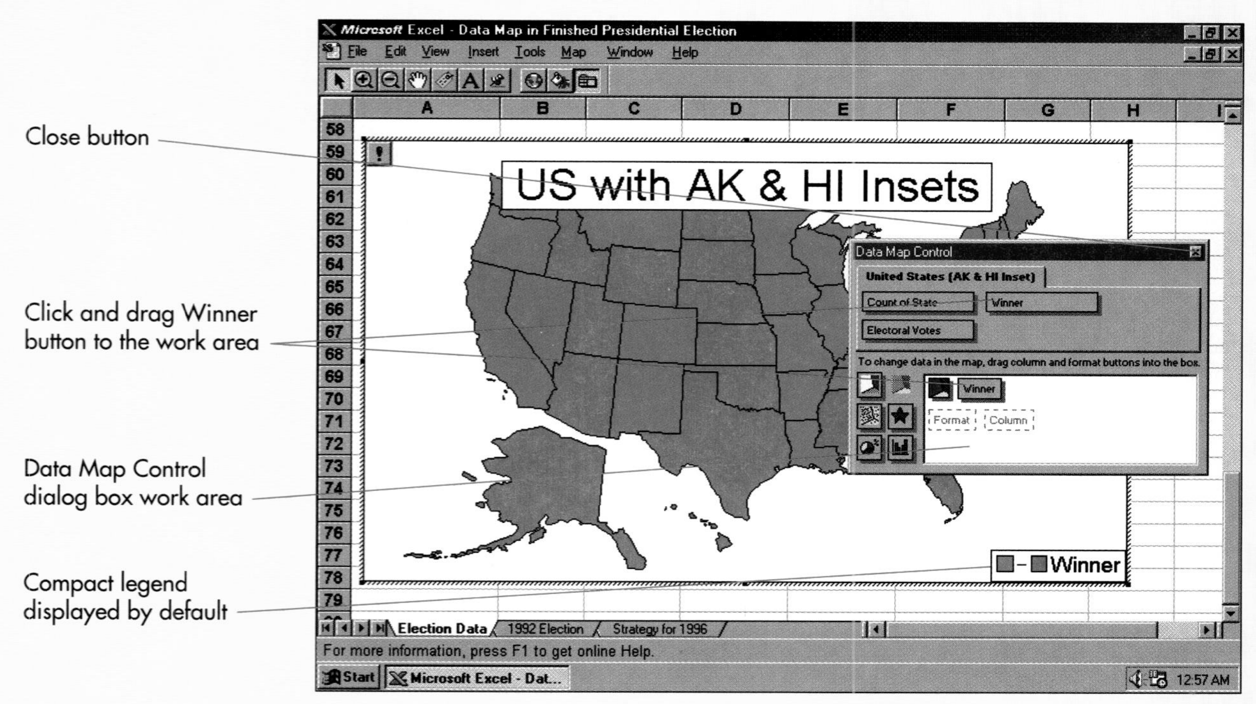

(c) Data Map Control Dialog Box (step 3)

FIGURE C.2 Hands-on Exercise 1 (continued)

- Click and drag the **Winner button** (the name of the button corresponds to the column heading in the worksheet) to the work area in the dialog box. Release the mouse.
- A map is created with the various states shaded in red or green according to the winning candidate in each state. The significance of the different colors is determined from the legend as explained in step 4.
- Click the **Close button** to close the Data Map Control dialog box.

STEP 4: Edit the Legend

- To determine the meaning of the shadings, you need to display the complete (not the compact) legend.
  - Pull down the **View menu.** Click **All Legends** if you do not see a legend.
  - Point to the legend (it may appear differently from the legend in Figure C.2d), then click the **right mouse button** to display a shortcut menu.
  - Click **Edit** to display the Edit Legend dialog box in Figure C.2d. If necessary, clear the Use Compact Legend check box.
- Click and drag to select the contents of the legend Title text box. Press the **Del key.** Clear the contents of the Subtitle text box in similar fashion.
- Click **OK** to accept the changes and close the dialog box. The legend should consist of two lines, Bush and Clinton, with the numbers 18 and 32, respectively, indicating the number of states each candidate carried.

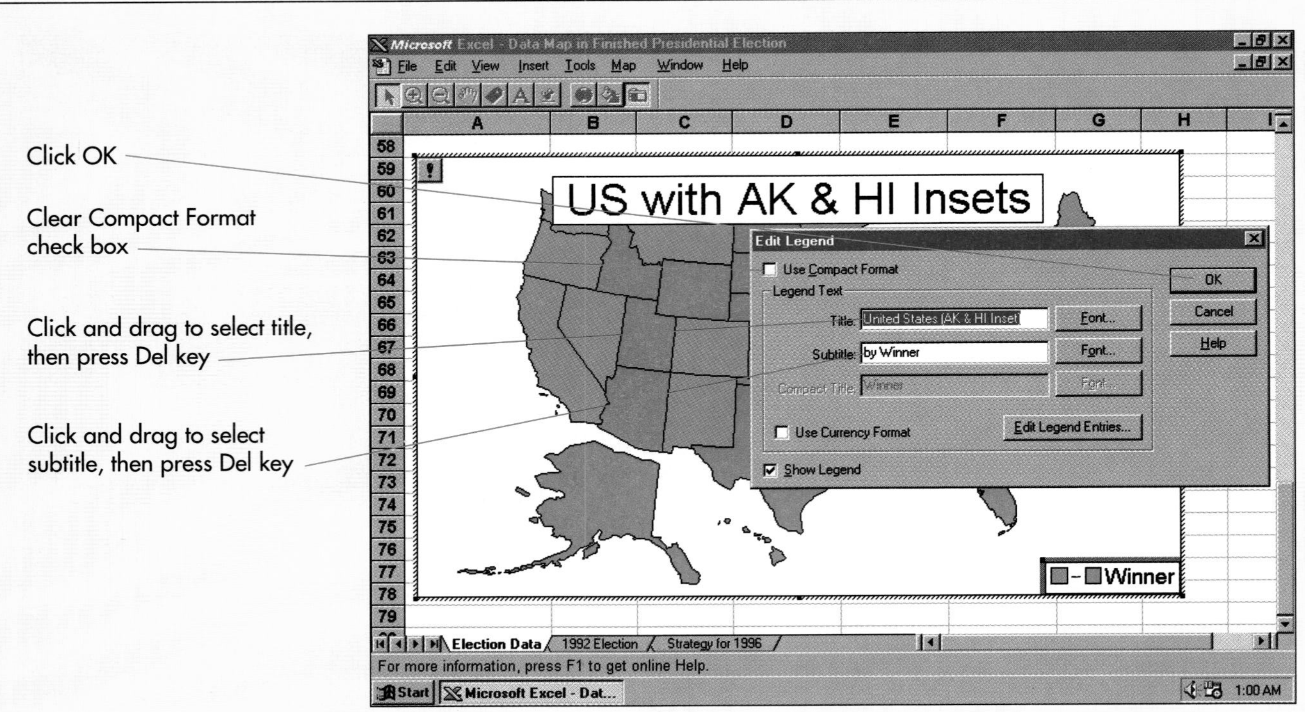

(d) Edit the Legend (step 4)

FIGURE C.2 Hands-on Exercise 1 (continued)

➤ Click inside the legend to select it. A shaded border appears around the legend. If necessary, click and drag the legend to position it within the map frame.

IN-PLACE EDITING

In-place editing enables you to edit an embedded object by using the toolbar and pull-down menus of the server application. Thus, when editing a map that has been embedded into an Excel worksheet, the title bar is that of the client application (Microsoft Excel), but the toolbars and pull-down menus reflect the server application (the Data Map application within Microsoft Office). There are, however, two exceptions; the File and Window menus are those of the client application (Excel). The File menu enables you to save the worksheet. The Window menu enables you to view (and edit) multiple workbooks in different windows.

STEP 5: The Finishing Touches

➤ Double click immediately in front of the "U" in "US with AK and HI Insets" in order to edit the title. A flashing vertical line (the insertion point) will appear at the place where you double clicked.

➤ Click and drag to select the entire title, then type **1992 Election Results** as the new title. Press **enter** to complete the title.

➤ Point to the title, then click the **right mouse button** to display the shortcut menu shown in Figure C.2e.

➤ Click **Format Font** to display the Format Font dialog box. Change the font size to **20 points.** Change the other parameters (e.g., font color) as you see fit, then close the Format Font dialog box.

➤ You can position the title, legend, and map independently within the frame:

- Click and drag the **title** to move the title anywhere within the frame.
- Click and drag the **legend** to move the legend anywhere within the frame.
- Click the **Grabber button** (a hand) on the Data Map toolbar to select it. Point to the map (the mouse pointer changes to a hand), then click and drag the **map** to move it within the frame.
- Pull down the **File menu.** Click **Save** to save the worksheet.

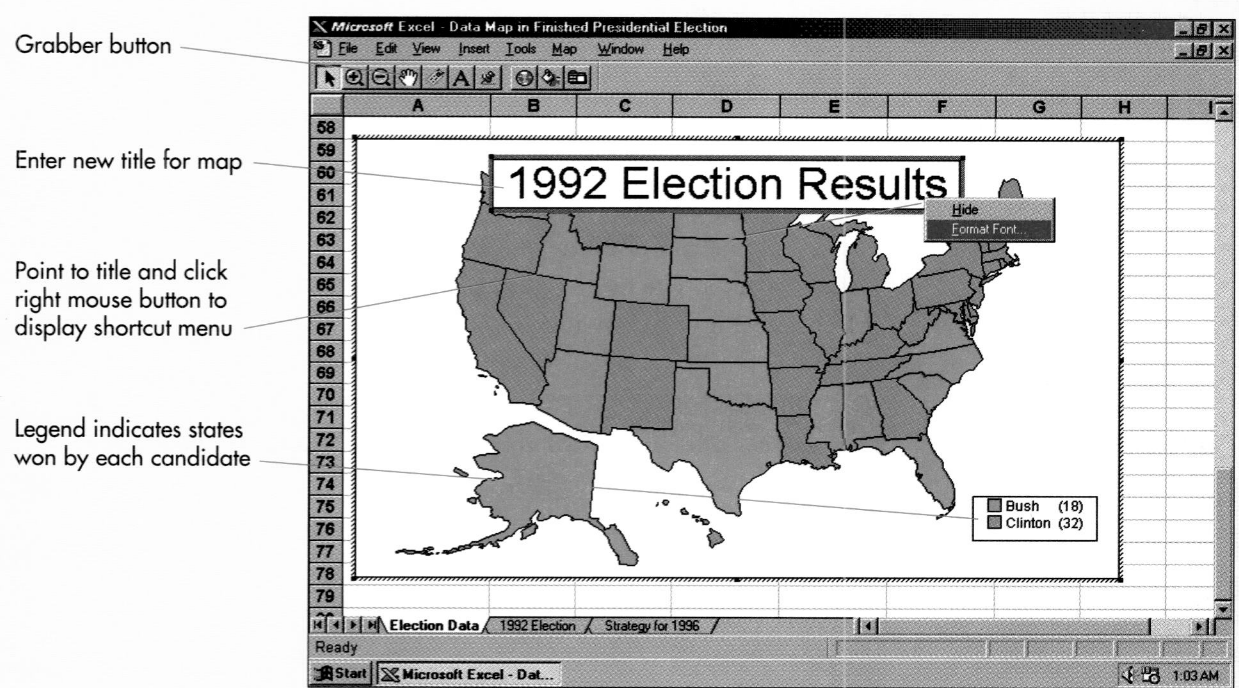

(e) The Finishing Touches (step 5)

FIGURE C.2 Hands-on Exercise 1 (continued)

TO CLICK OR DOUBLE CLICK

Clicking a map selects the map and displays the sizing handles that are used to move or size the frame containing the map. Double clicking the map loads the underlying Data Mapping application that created the map and enables you to edit the map.

STEP 6: Place the Map in Its Own Worksheet

➤ Click outside the map to exit the Data Mapping application, then click anywhere on the map to select the map as an Excel object.

➤ Click the **Cut button.** The map is placed in the clipboard and disappears from the worksheet.

➤ Click the **1992 Election tab.** Click in **cell A1.** Click the **Paste button** to paste the map onto this worksheet.

STEP 7: The Print Preview Command

➤ Pull down the **File menu.** Click **Page Setup** to display the Page Setup dialog box.

- Click the **Page tab.** Click the **Landscape orientation button.**
- Click the option button to adjust **Scaling to 120%** of size.
- Click the **Margins tab.** Check the box to center the worksheet **Horizontally.**
- Click the **Sheet tab.** Clear the boxes to include Row and Column Headings and Gridlines.

➤ Click the **Print Preview button** to preview the map before printing as shown in Figure C.2f.

- If you are satisfied with the appearance of the worksheet, click the **Print button** within the Preview window, then click **OK** to print the worksheet.
- If you are not satisfied with the appearance of the map, click the **Setup button** within the Preview window to make the necessary changes, after which you can print the worksheet.

➤ Pull down the **File menu.** Click **Close.** Click **Yes** if prompted to save changes.

➤ Exit Excel if you do not want to continue with the next exercise at this time.

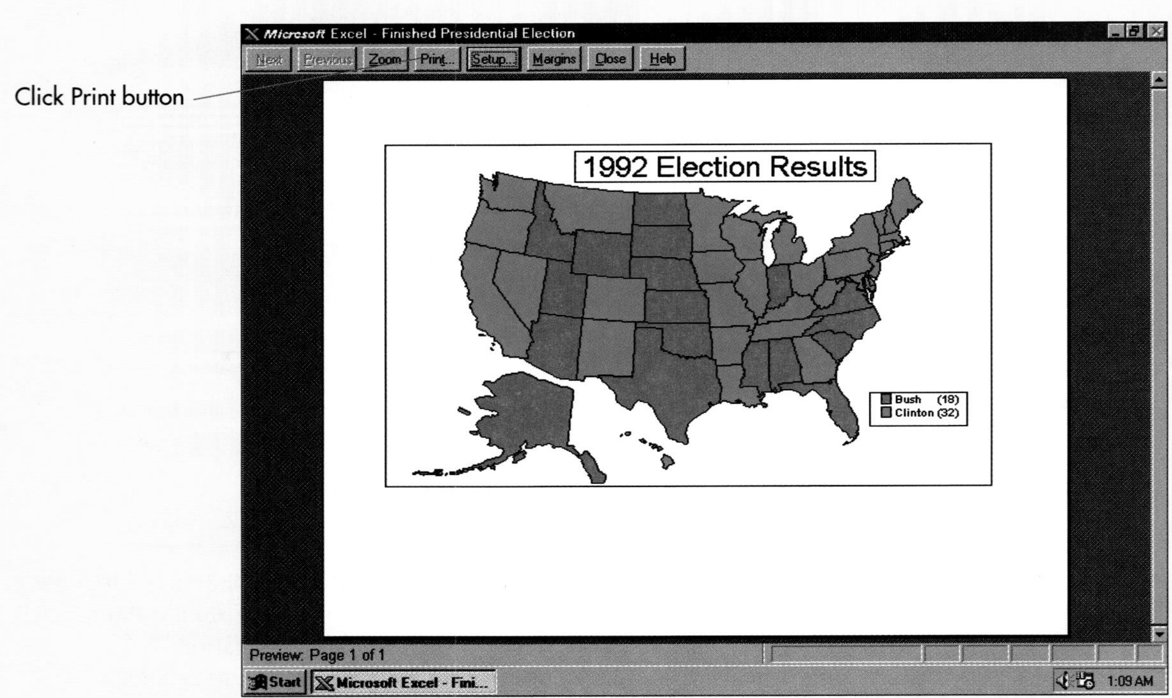

(f) Print Preview Command (step 7)

FIGURE C.2 Hands-on Exercise 1 (continued)

We trust you completed the hands-on exercise without difficulty. The exercise introduced you to the basic features in the Data Mapping application and enabled you to create a map showing the winning candidate in each state. The format of the map was chosen automatically according to the nature of the data. The exercise had you plot a qualitative variable, which had one of two values (Bush or Clinton). The mapping program automatically selected ***category shading*** and assigned a different color to each value of a category, green to Mr. Clinton and red to Mr. Bush.

The next exercise directs you to plot a quantitative variable (the number of electoral votes in each state), then has you experiment with different formats for the resulting map. The selection is made in the ***Data Map Control dialog box*** as shown in Figure C.3. Six different formats are available, but not every format is suitable for every type of data. Figure C.3 illustrates three types of formatting.

Figure C.3a displays the Data Map Control dialog box, which appears automatically as the map is created. The top half of the dialog box indicates the columns that have been selected from the associated worksheet. The bottom half of the dialog box (the work area) shows the data that is to be plotted and the type of formatting in effect.

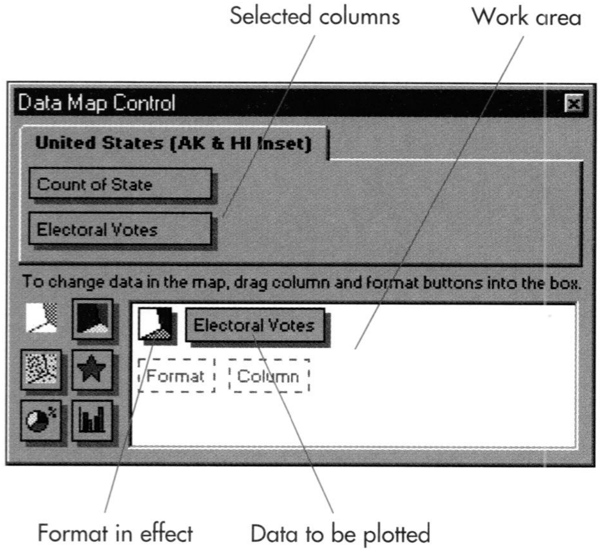

(a) Data Control Dialog Box

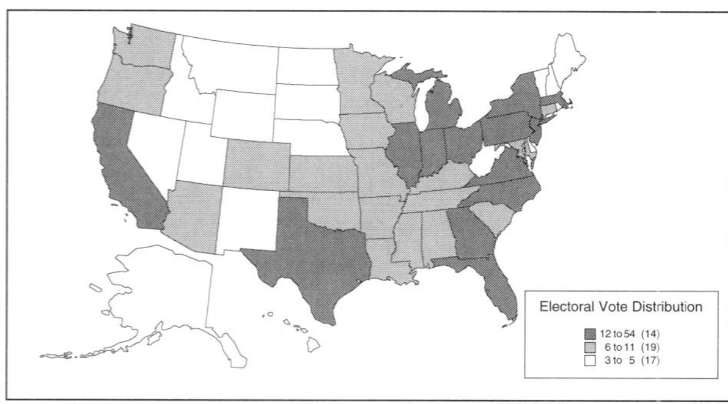

(b) Value Shading

FIGURE C.3 Data Map Control

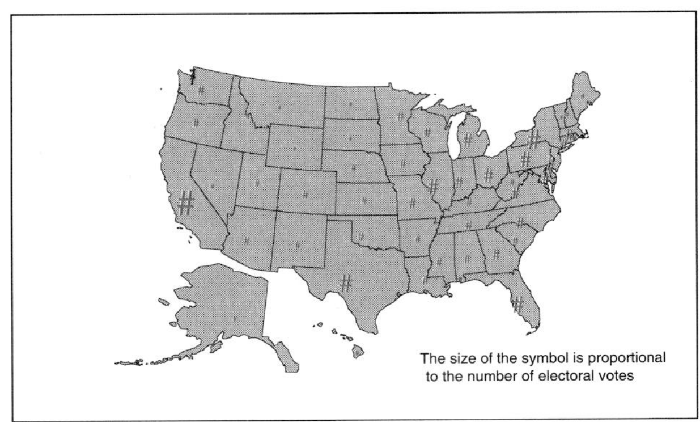

(c) Graduated Symbol

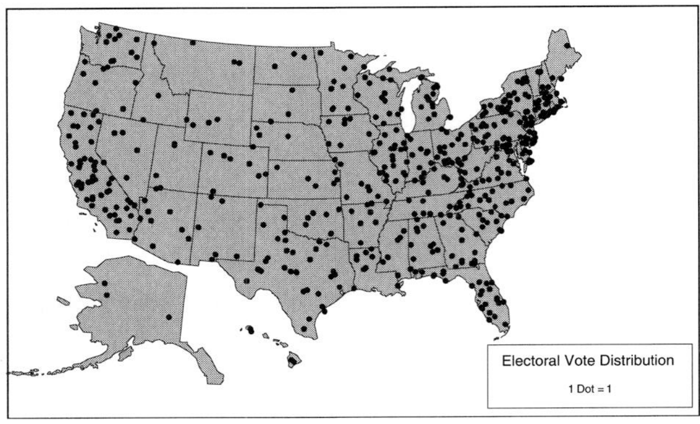

(d) Dot Density

FIGURE C.3 Data Map Control (continued)

The maps in Figure C.3 plot the identical data (the number of electoral votes in each state), but in three different formats. Figure C.3b uses ***value shading*** to divide the states into groups and assign a different shade to each group. Figure C.3c uses the ***graduated symbol*** format to convey the same information. (The size of the symbol corresponds to the number of electoral votes.) Figure C.3d uses the ***dot density*** format to enable the user to see the actual number of electoral votes in each state. (Each dot corresponds to one electoral vote.) The choice between these maps is one of personal preference as will be seen in the next exercise.

HANDS-ON EXERCISE 2

Data Map Control

Objective: To create a map showing the distribution of electoral votes in the United States; to experiment with different formatting options in the Data Map Control dialog box. Use Figure C.4 as a guide in the exercise.

STEP 1: Draw the Map

- Start Excel. Open the **Finished Presidential Election** workbook from the previous exercise. Click the **Election Data tab.**

- ➤ Click in **cell A1,** then click and drag to select **cells A1** through **B51.** (The AutoCalculate indicator on the status bar should display 535 as the total number of electoral votes in the selected range.)
- ➤ Click the **Map button** on the Standard toolbar. Click the **down scroll arrow** until cell A59 comes into view. Click in **cell A59,** then click and drag to draw the frame that will contain the map. Release the mouse.
- ➤ A dialog box will appear on the screen with the message, "Retrieving current selection", followed by a second message, "Matching Data".
- ➤ The program recognizes the state names in Column A and presents two options. Click **United States (AK & HI Inset),** then click **OK** to create the map as shown in Figure C.4a.
- ➤ Close the Data Map Control box. Pull down the **File menu.** Click **Save** to save the worksheet.

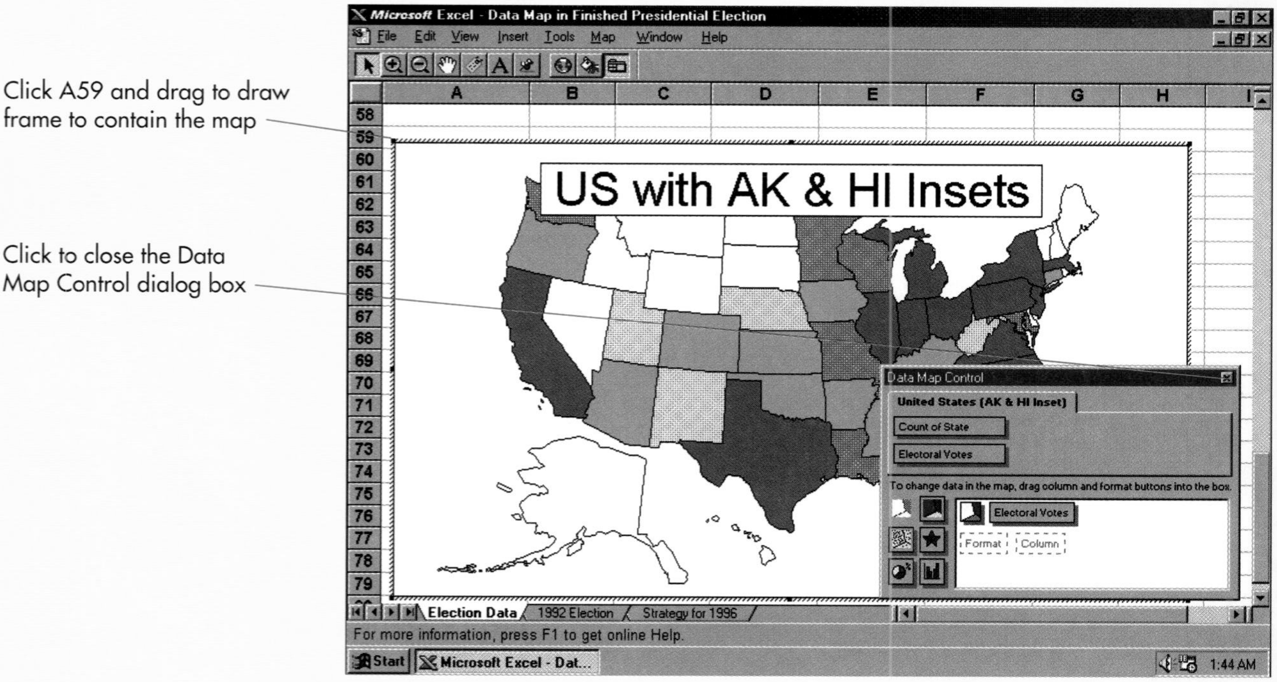

Click A59 and drag to draw frame to contain the map

Click to close the Data Map Control dialog box

(a) Create the Map (step 1)

FIGURE C.4 Hands-on Exercise 2

STEP 2: Edit the Legend

- ➤ The various states are shaded according to the number of electoral votes in each state. To determine the meaning of the shadings, you need to display the complete (not the compact) legend.
  - Pull down the **View menu** and click **All Legends** if you do not see a legend.
  - Point to the legend (it may appear differently from the legend in Figure C.4b), then click the **right mouse button** to display a shortcut menu.
  - Click **Edit** to display the Edit Legend dialog box. If necessary, clear the Use Compact Legend check box so that your legend will match the one in the figure.

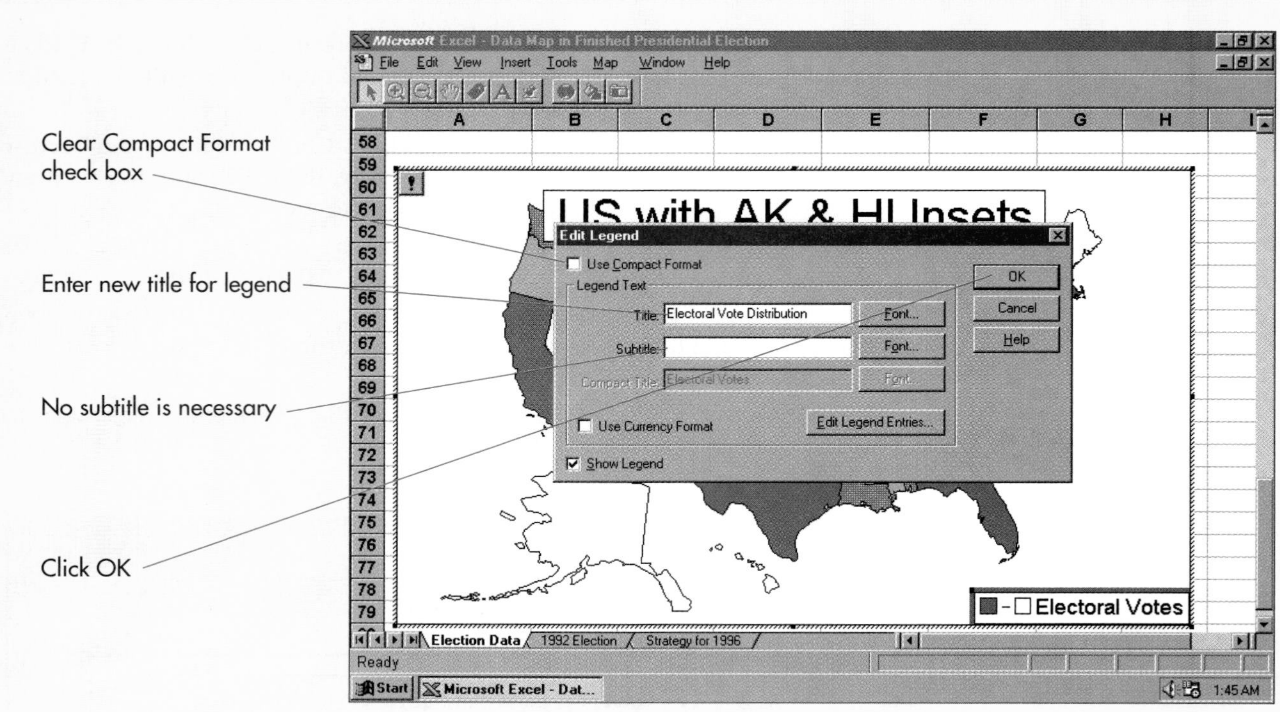

(b) Change the Legend (step 2)

FIGURE C.4 Hands-on Exercise 2 (continued)

- Click and drag to select the contents of the Title text box. Type **Electoral Vote Distribution** to replace the selected text. Clear the contents of the Subtitle text box as shown in Figure C.4b.
- Click **OK** to accept the changes and close the dialog box.
- Pull down the **File menu** and click the **Save command.**

STEP 3: Data Map Control

- Click the **Show/Hide Data Map Control button** to open the Data Map Control box as shown in Figure C.4c. Click **OK** if asked to refresh the map.
  - Click and drag the **Dot Density button** to a position next to the Electoral Votes button as shown in Figure C.4c. The shading on the map changes so that each state contains a number of dots proportional to its electoral votes.
  - Click and drag the **Graduated Symbol button** to a position next to the Electoral Votes button. The map changes to place a graduated symbol (the same symbol in different sizes) in each state according to its number of electoral votes.
  - Click and drag the **Category Shading button** to a position next to the Electoral Votes button. The states are displayed in a variety of colors, which is totally *inappropriate* for this map. (Category shading is used only when the number of distinct values is small; e.g., to indicate the winning candidate in each state as in the earlier map.)
  - Click and drag the **Value Shading button** to a position next to the Electoral Votes button.
- Close the Data Map Control box. Pull down the **File menu.** Click **Save** to save the worksheet.

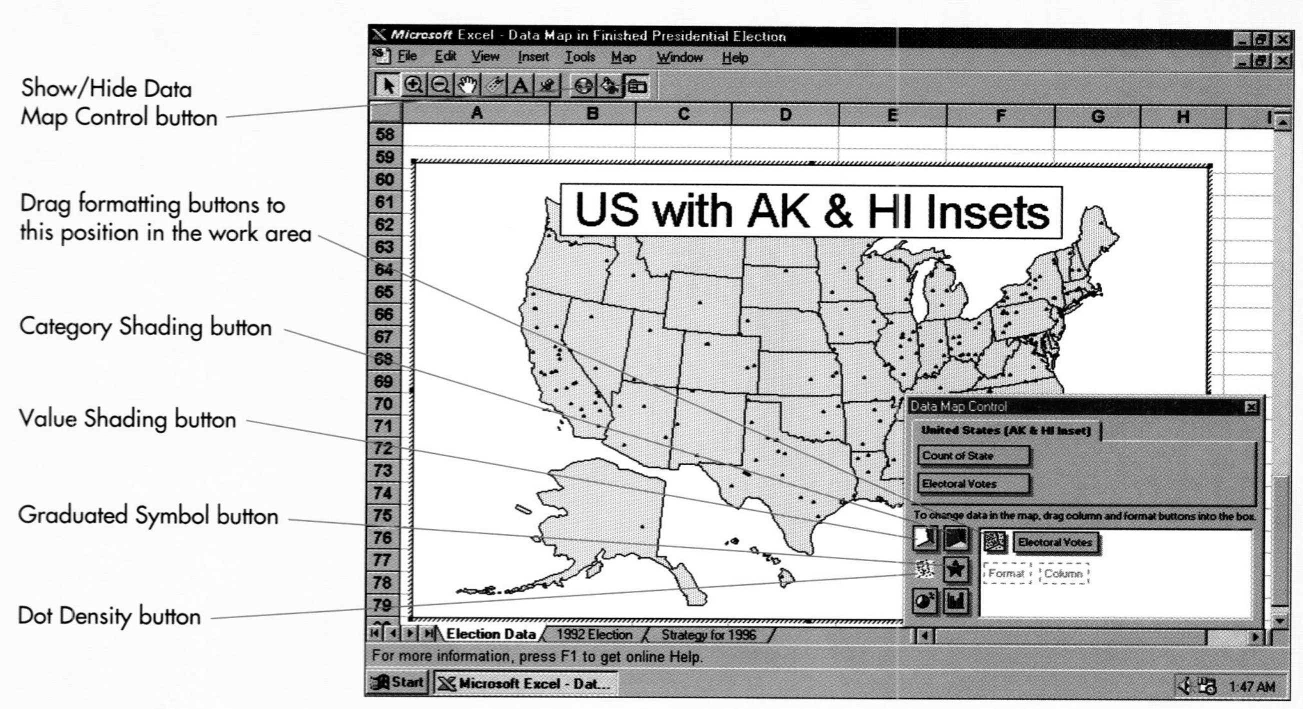

(c) Data Map Control (step 3)

FIGURE C.4 Hands-on Exercise 2 (continued)

CATEGORY SHADING VERSUS VALUE SHADING

Category shading is used with a nonquantitative variable (such as a candidate's name) and assigns a different color to each value of the category—for example, green to Mr. Clinton and red to Mr. Bush as was done in the map in exercise 1. Value shading is used with a quantitative variable (such as the number of electoral votes in each state) and is necessary when there are a large number of distinct values. Value shading divides the states into groups with a different shade assigned to each group.

STEP 4: Value Shading Options

- Pull down the **Map menu.** Click **Value Shading Options** to display the dialog box in Figure C.4d. (Click **OK** if asked to refresh the map.)
- Click the **drop-down arrow** to change the number of value ranges to **three.** Click the **drop-down arrow** in the **color** list box to change the color of the shading to **blue.**
- Click the option button for an equal number of items in each range of values. Click **OK** to close the Value Shading Options dialog box.
- The number of groups changes to three. The legend shows 14 states with 12 to 54 votes, 19 states with 6 to 12 votes, and 17 states with 3 to 6 votes. The legend uses *inclusive* ranges and needs to be modified.

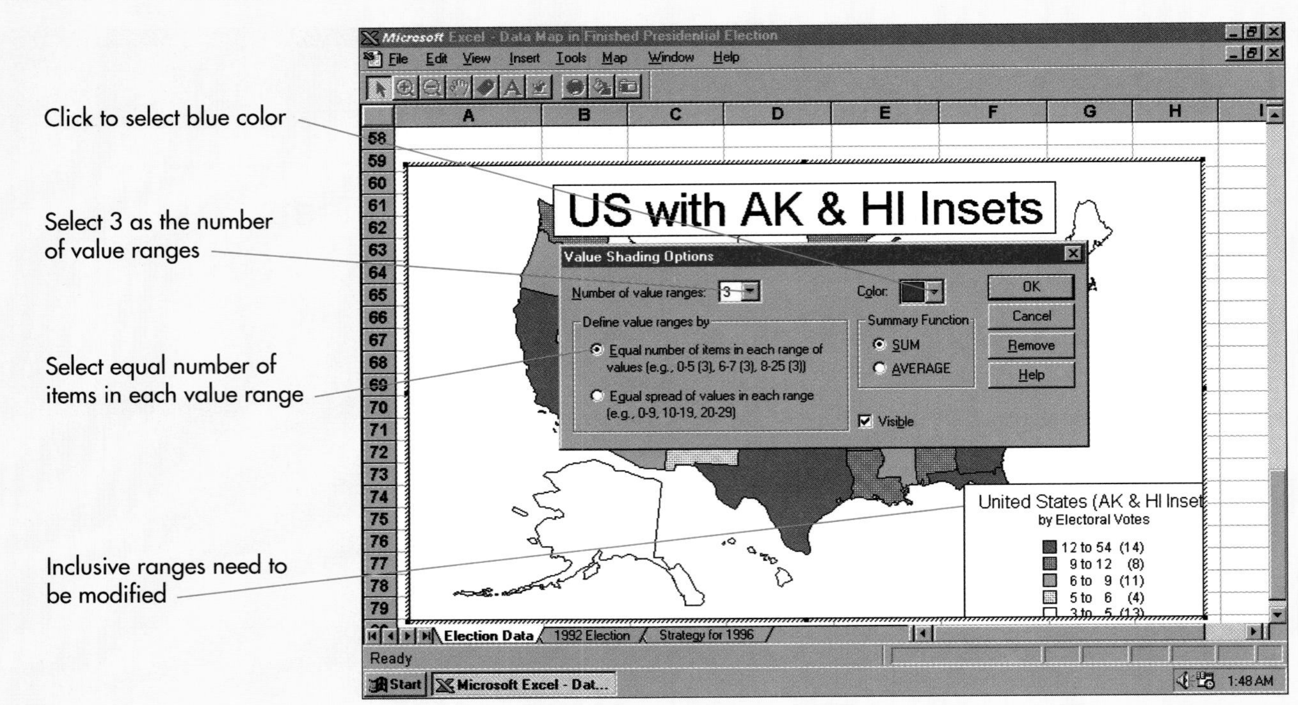

(d) Value Shading Options (step 4)

FIGURE C.4 Hands-on Exercise 2 (continued)

- ➤ Point to the legend, click the **right mouse button** to display a shortcut menu, then click **Edit** to display the Edit Legend dialog box.
- ➤ Click the command button to **Edit Legend Entries,** then change the text for the latter two groups to read **6 to 11** and **3 to 5.** Click **OK** to close the Edit Legend Entries dialog box. Click **OK** to close the Edit Legend dialog box.

MISLEADING LEGEND

The legend created by the data mapping program incorrectly uses inclusive values, which need to be adjusted manually if the legend is to make sense. In creating groups for the electoral vote distribution, the number 12 is used as a break point in that there is a group of states with 12 to 54 electoral votes and a second group with 6 to 12 electoral votes. In actuality, the latter group consists of states with 6 to 11 electoral votes (i.e., the upper bound is less than 12).

STEP 5: Map Labels

- ➤ Click the **Map Labels button** to display the Map Labels dialog box. Click the option button to **Create labels from Values from Electoral Votes** (the only option in the drop-down list). Click **OK** to close the Map Labels dialog box.
- ➤ Point to a state (the mouse pointer changes to a crosshair), and you see the corresponding number of electoral votes. Point to California, for example, and you see 54. Point to Texas and you see 32.
- ➤ Point to a state, such as California, then **click the mouse** to create a label

containing the number of electoral votes. The number 54 is entered on the map and surrounded in sizing handles to indicate that the label is currently selected.

- Click the **Select Objects button** (the arrow) on the Data Map toolbar to turn off the labeling feature so that we can change the color of the label and make it easier to read. Point to the number 54 and click the **right mouse button** to display a shortcut menu.
- Click **Format Font** to display the Font dialog box in Figure C.4e:
  - Click the **drop-down arrow** on the **Color** list box. Click **aqua** as the color of the text.
  - If necessary, change the type size to **8** points.
  - Click **OK** to accept the color change and close the Font dialog box.
- Click the **Map Labels button,** click **OK** to close the Map Labels dialog box, then label all of the other states in the category with the highest numbers of electoral votes. When you are finished, click the **Select Objects button** (the arrow) on the Data Map toolbar to turn off the labeling feature.
- Pull down the **File menu** and click the **Save command.**

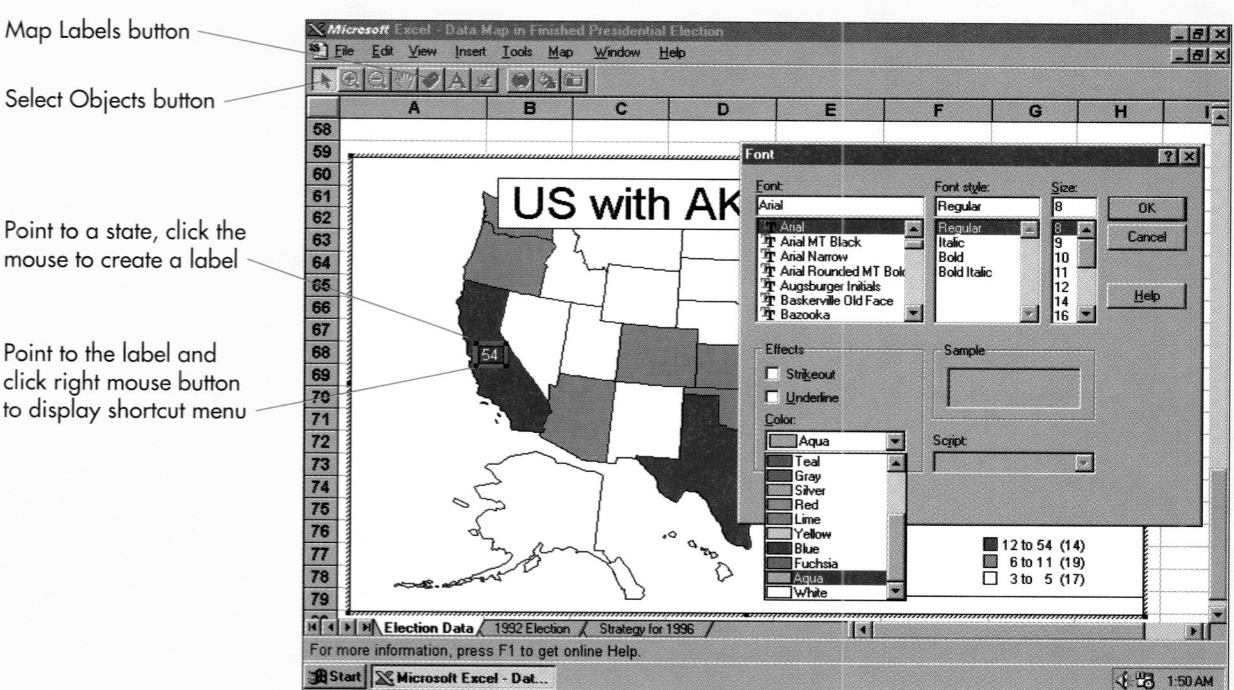

(e) Map Labels (step 5)

FIGURE C.4 Hands-on Exercise 2 (continued)

STEP 6: Complete the Map

- Click the **Text tool,** click at the bottom of the map as shown in Figure C.4f, then start to type the text shown in the figure. The text appears in aqua.
- Click the **right mouse button,** click **Format Font,** and change the color back to black. Click **OK** to close the Font dialog box, then finish entering the text.
- Click the title to select it. Click before the first character in the title, drag to select the entire title, then enter **Strategy for 1996** as shown in Figure C.4f.

➤ You can position the title, legend, and map independently within the frame:

- Click and drag the **title** to move the title anywhere within the frame.
- Click and drag the **legend** to move the legend anywhere within the frame.
- Click the **Grabber button** on the Data Map toolbar to select it, then click and drag the **map** (the mouse pointer changes to a hand) to move it within the frame.

➤ Pull down the **File menu** and click the **Save command.**

STEP 7: Place the Map in Its Own Worksheet

➤ Click outside the map to exit the Data Mapping application, then click anywhere on the map to select it as an Excel object.

➤ Click the **Cut button.** The map is placed in the clipboard and disappears from the worksheet.

➤ Click the **Strategy for 1996 tab.** Click in **cell A1.** Click the **Paste button** to paste the map onto this worksheet.

➤ Print the worksheet and map. Save the workbook a final time. Exit Excel.

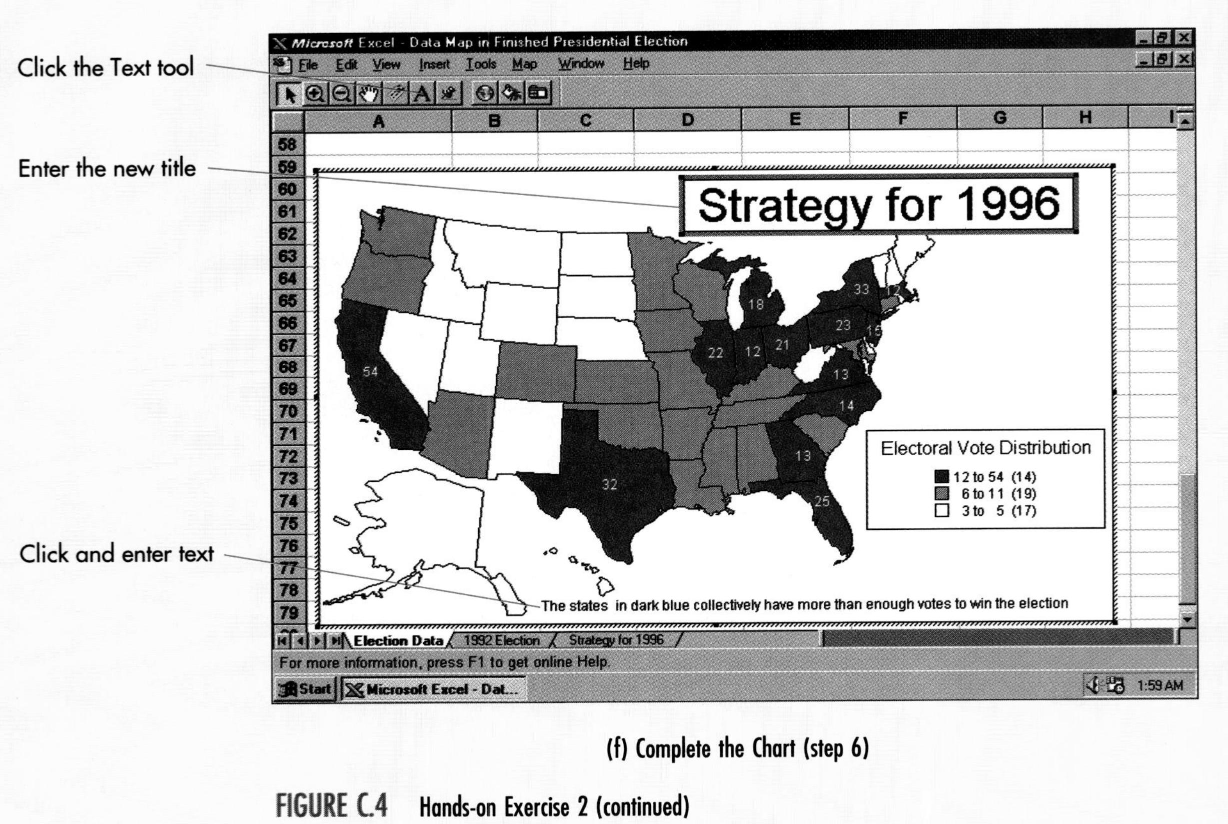

(f) Complete the Chart (step 6)

FIGURE C.4 Hands-on Exercise 2 (continued)

THE MAPSTATS WORKBOOK

Microsoft Excel comes with an assortment of maps, together with demographic data for each map. The demographic data is contained in the ***Mapstats workbook*** as shown in Figure C.5. The Table of Contents worksheet in Figure C.5a shows the countries for which a map and demographic data are supplied. Figure C.5b displays (some of) the demographic data for the United States.

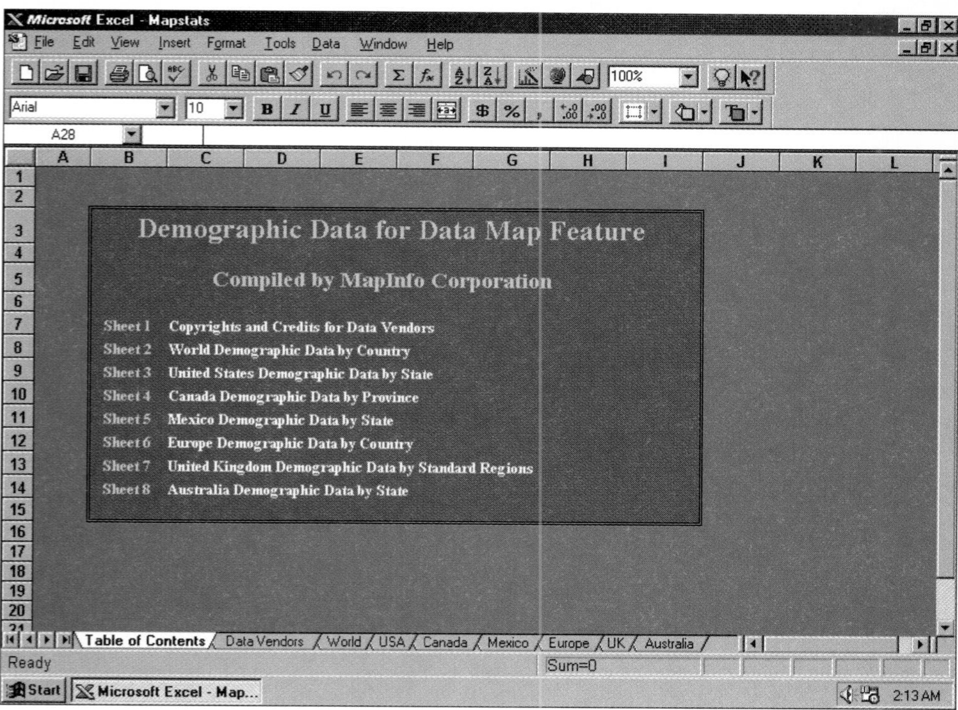

(a) Table of Contents Page

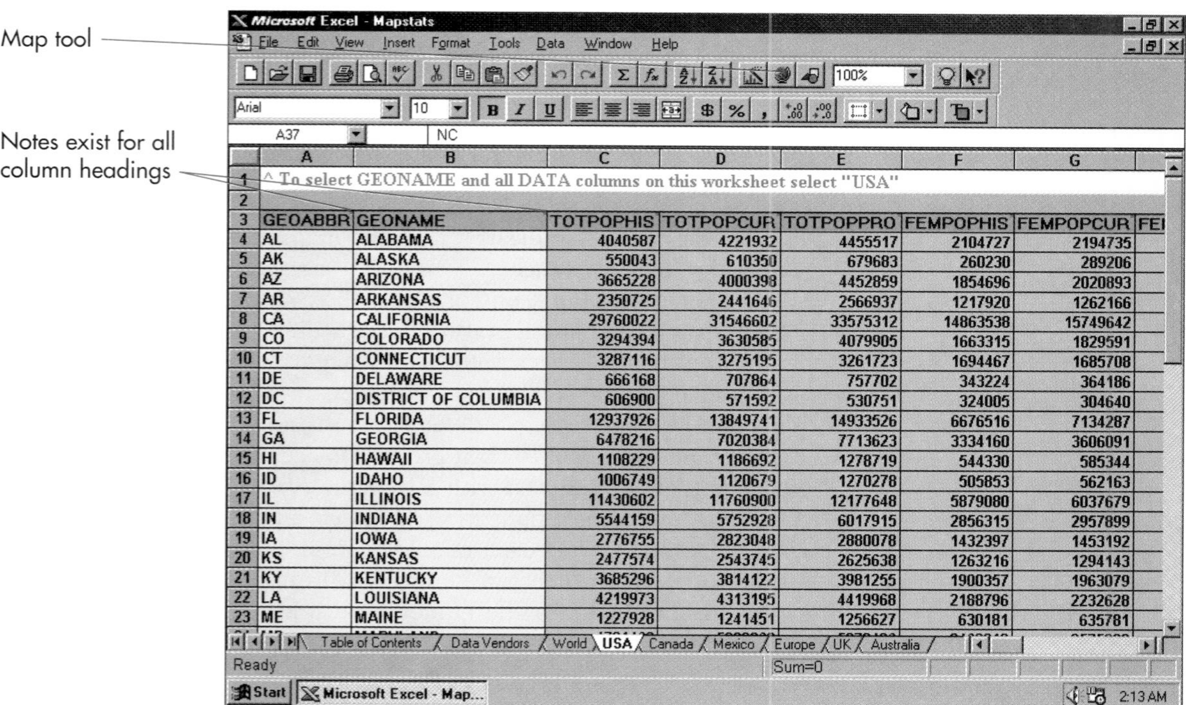

GEOABBR	GEONAME	TOTPOPHIS	TOTPOPCUR	TOTPOPPRO	FEMPOPHIS	FEMPOPCUR
AL	ALABAMA	4040587	4221932	4455517	2104727	2194735
AK	ALASKA	550043	610350	679683	260230	289206
AZ	ARIZONA	3665228	4000398	4452859	1854696	2020893
AR	ARKANSAS	2350725	2441646	2566937	1217920	1262166
CA	CALIFORNIA	29760022	31546602	33575312	14863538	15749642
CO	COLORADO	3294394	3630585	4079905	1663315	1829591
CT	CONNECTICUT	3287116	3275195	3261723	1694467	1685708
DE	DELAWARE	666168	707864	757702	343224	364186
DC	DISTRICT OF COLUMBIA	606900	571592	530751	324005	304640
FL	FLORIDA	12937926	13849741	14933526	6676516	7134287
GA	GEORGIA	6478216	7020384	7713623	3334160	3606091
HI	HAWAII	1108229	1186692	1278719	544330	585344
ID	IDAHO	1006749	1120679	1270278	505853	562163
IL	ILLINOIS	11430602	11760900	12177648	5879080	6037679
IN	INDIANA	5544159	5752928	6017915	2856315	2957899
IA	IOWA	2776755	2823048	2880078	1432397	1453192
KS	KANSAS	2477574	2543745	2625638	1263216	1294143
KY	KENTUCKY	3685296	3814122	3981255	1900357	1963079
LA	LOUISIANA	4219973	4313195	4419968	2188796	2232628
ME	MAINE	1227928	1241451	1256627	630181	635781

(b) USA Data Worksheet

FIGURE C.5 The Mapstats Workbook

The column headings in Figure C.5b are abbreviated, and hence the precise nature of the data is not immediately apparent. The cells containing the column headings are annotated, however (note the red dot in each cell), so that you can point to any heading and display the cell tip that fully describes the data. There are more than 30 categories of demographic data available for the United States. Similar, but not necessarily identical, data is available for the other countries in the workbook.

You can create a map based on any column of demographic data by following the steps in the hands-on exercise. Just select the data, click the Map button on the Standard toolbar, then click in the worksheet where you want the map to go. Choose the type of map you want, add the finishing touches as was done in the exercises, and you will be able to create a variety of useful and attractive maps. Cartography has never been so easy.

FINDING THE MAPSTATS WORKBOOK

The easiest way to open the Mapstats workbook is through the Windows 95 Find command. Click the Start button, click (or point to) the Find command, then click Files or Folders to display the Find dialog box. Enter Mapstats in the Named text box and My Computer in the Look In box. Click Find Now. Double click the icon next to the Mapstats workbook to start Excel and open the workbook. Save the workbook under a different name so that you can return to the original workbook should it become necessary.

SUMMARY

Computer mapping enables you to visualize quantitative data and is made possible through the Data Mapping application included with Microsoft Office 95. Creation of a map is straightforward and consists of four general steps. You select the data to be mapped, indicate where the map is to go, choose the type of map, then apply the finishing touches.

The Data Map Control dialog box determines the type of formatting in effect. Category shading is always used with a nonquantitative variable and assigns a different color to each value of a category. Value shading is one of several different formats that can be used with a quantitative variable and is used when many different outcomes are possible. The outcomes are divided into groups with a different shade assigned to each group. Dot density and graduated symbol are other formats that can be used with a quantitative variable.

The mapping application includes an assortment of maps together with demographic data for each map. The demographic data is contained in the Mapstats workbook (which can be located through the Windows 95 Find command). Maps are available for the United States, Mexico, Canada, Australia, the United Kingdom, and the world.

KEY WORDS AND CONCEPTS

AutoCalculate
Category shading
Data Map Control
Dot density
Graduated symbol
In-place editing
Label
Legend
Mapstats workbook
Value shading

D

APPENDIX D: TOOLBARS

OVERVIEW

Microsoft Excel has thirteen predefined toolbars to provide access to commonly used commands. The toolbars are displayed in Figure D.1 and are listed here for convenience. They are: the Auditing, Chart, Drawing, Formatting, Forms, Full Screen, Microsoft, Query and Pivot, Standard, Stop Recording, TipWizard, Visual Basic, and WorkGroup toolbars. The Standard and Formatting toolbars are displayed by default and appear immediately below the menu bar. The other toolbars can be displayed as needed or, in some cases, may appear automatically when you access their corresponding feature (e.g., the Chart toolbar and the Query and Pivot toolbar).

The buttons on the toolbars are intended to be indicative of their function. Clicking the Printer button (the fourth button from the left on the Standard toolbar), for example, executes the Print command. If you are unsure of the purpose of any toolbar button, point to it, and a ToolTip will appear that displays its name.

You can display multiple toolbars at one time, move them to new locations on the screen, customize their appearance, or suppress their display.

- To display or hide a toolbar, pull down the View menu and click the Toolbars command. Select (deselect) the toolbar(s) that you want to display (hide). The selected toolbar(s) will be displayed in the same position as when last displayed. You may also point to any toolbar and click with the right mouse button to bring up a shortcut menu, after which you can select the toolbar to be displayed (hidden).
- To change the size of the buttons, display them in monochrome rather than color, or suppress the display of the ToolTips, pull down the View menu, click Toolbars, and then select (deselect) the appropriate check box. Alternatively, you can click on any

toolbar with the right mouse button, select Toolbars, and then select (deselect) the appropriate check box.

- Toolbars may be either docked (along the edge of the window) or left floating (in their own window). A toolbar moved to the edge of the window will dock along that edge. A toolbar moved anywhere else in the window will float in its own window. Docked toolbars are one tool wide (high), whereas floating toolbars can be resized by clicking and dragging a border or corner as you would with any window.
  - To move a docked toolbar, click anywhere in the gray background area and drag the toolbar to its new location.
  - To move a floating toolbar, drag its title bar to its new location.
- To customize one or more toolbars, display the toolbar(s) on the screen, pull down the View menu, click Toolbars, and then click the Customize command button. Alternatively, you can click on any toolbar with the right mouse button and select Customize from the shortcut menu.
  - To move a button, drag the button to its new location on that toolbar or any other displayed toolbar.
  - To copy a button, press the Ctrl key as you drag the button to its new location on that toolbar or any other displayed toolbar.
  - To delete a button, drag the button off the toolbar and release the mouse button.
  - To add a button, select the category from the Categories list box and then drag the button to the desired location on the toolbar. (To see a description of a tool's function prior to adding it to a toolbar, click the tool in the Customize dialog box and read the displayed description.)
  - To restore a predefined toolbar to its default appearance, pull down the View menu, click Toolbars, select (highlight) the desired toolbar, and click the Reset command button.
- The Borders, Color, and Font Color buttons on the Formatting toolbar, the Chart Type button on the Chart toolbar, and the Pattern button on the Drawing toolbar also function as movable tear-off palettes. Display the desired palette by clicking the associated down arrow, then drag the palette onto the worksheet in order to make it more accessible as you work. Click the Close button to close the palette.
- To create your own toolbar, pull down the View menu and click Toolbars. Alternatively, you can click on any toolbar with the right mouse button and select Toolbars from the shortcut menu.
  - Enter a name for the toolbar in the Toolbar Name text box. The name can be any length and can contain spaces.
  - Click the New command button.
  - The new toolbar will appear at the top left of the screen. Initially, it will be big enough to hold only one button. Add, move, and delete buttons following the same procedures as outlined above. The toolbar will automatically size itself as new buttons are added and deleted.
- To delete a custom toolbar, pull down the View menu, click Toolbars, and make sure that the custom toolbar to be deleted is the only one selected (highlighted). Click the Delete command button. Click OK to confirm the deletion. (Note that a predefined toolbar cannot be deleted.)

MICROSOFT EXCEL 7.0 TOOLBARS

Auditing Toolbar

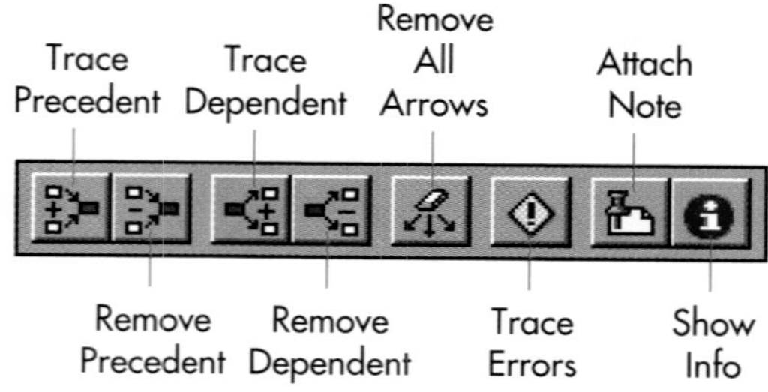

Chart Toolbar

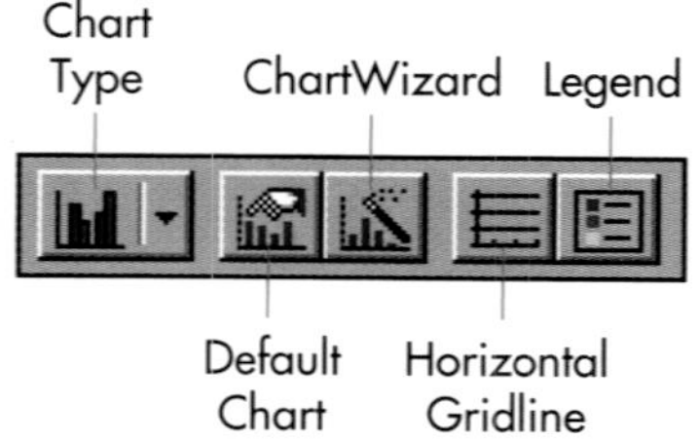

Drawing Toolbar

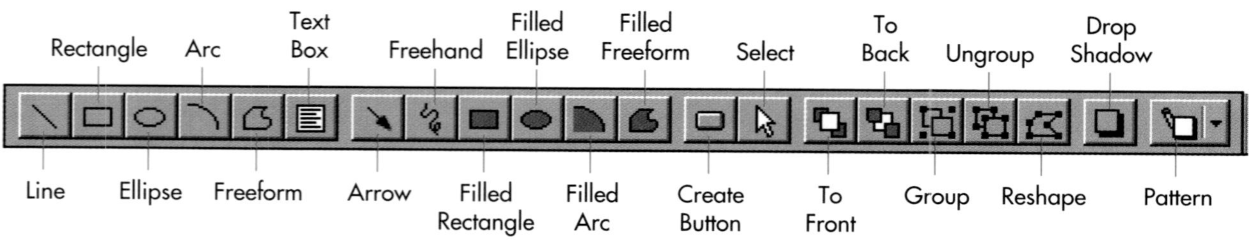

Formatting Toolbar

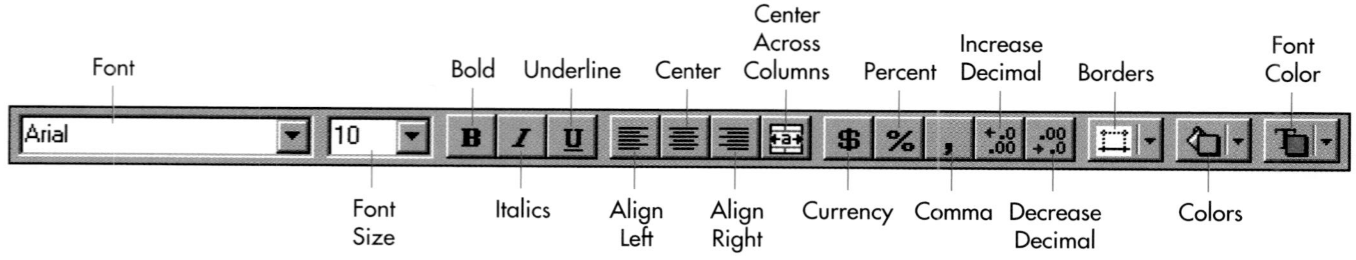

FIGURE D.1 Toolbars

Forms Toolbar

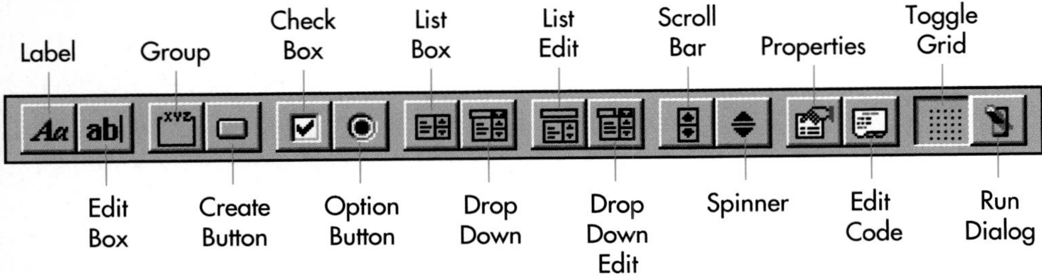

Full Screen Toolbar

Microsoft Toolbar

Query and Pivot Toolbar

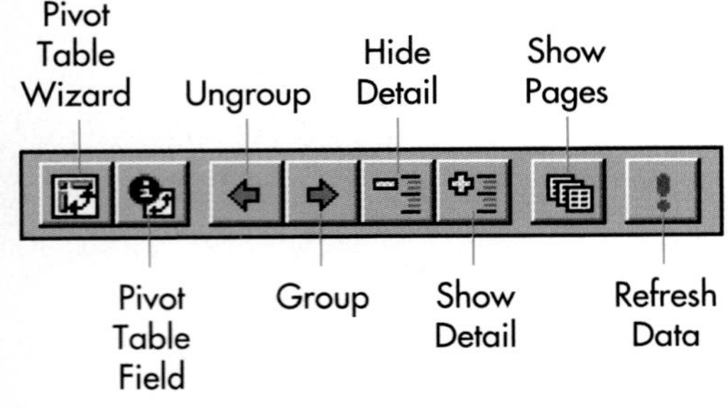

Standard Toolbar

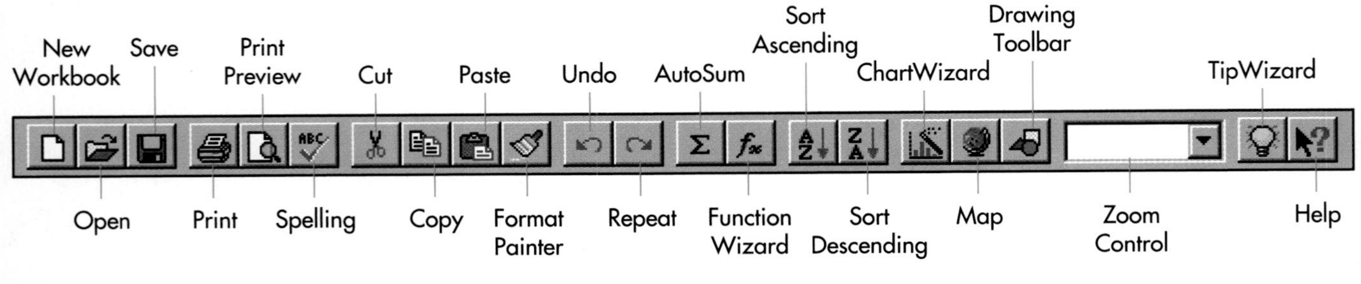

FIGURE D.1 Toolbars (continued)

Stop Recording Toolbar

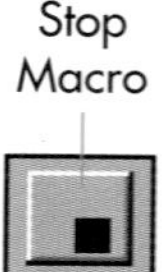

TipWizard Toolbar

TipWizard Box

1) You can double-click a workbook icon in the File Manager to start Microsoft Excel and open the workbook at the same time.

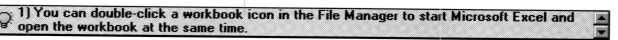

Visual Basic Toolbar

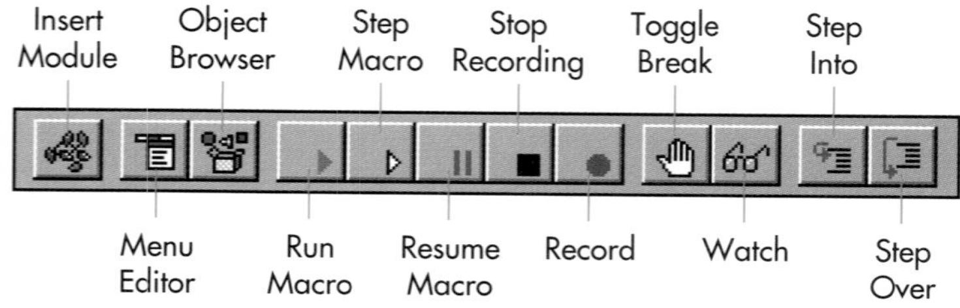

WorkGroup Toolbar

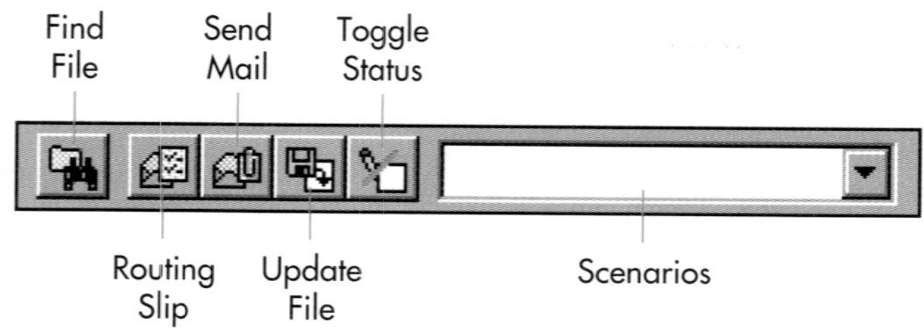

FIGURE D.1 Toolbars (continued)

7

ONE-TO-MANY RELATIONSHIPS: SUBFORMS AND MULTIPLE TABLE QUERIES

OBJECTIVES

After reading this chapter you will be able to:

1. Explain how a one-to-many relationship is essential in the design of a database; differentiate between a primary key and a foreign key.
2. Use the Relationships window to implement a one-to-many relationship within an Access database.
3. Define referential integrity; explain how the enforcement of referential integrity maintains consistency within a database.
4. Distinguish between a main form and a subform; explain how a subform is used in conjunction with a one-to-many relationship.
5. Create a query based on multiple tables, then create a report based on that query.
6. Create a main form containing two subforms linked to one another

OVERVIEW

We assume you are familiar with the different types of objects in an Access database: tables, forms, queries, and reports. The databases you have studied, however, were simple databases because they contained only one table. The real power of Access stems from its use as a relational database, which contains multiple tables.

This chapter presents a new case study that focuses on a relational database. The case is that of a consumer loan system within a bank. The database contains two tables, one for customers and one for loans. There is a one-to-many relationship between the tables, in that one customer can have many loans, but a loan is tied to only one customer.

The case solution includes a discussion of database concepts. It reviews the definition of a primary key and explains how the primary key of one table exists as a foreign key in a related table. It also introduces the concept of referential integrity, which ensures that the tables within the database are consistent with one another. And most important, it shows how to implement these concepts in an Access database.

The chapter builds on what you already know by expanding the earlier material on forms, queries, and reports. It describes how to create a main form and a corresponding subform that contains data from a related table. It develops a query that contains data from multiple tables, then creates a report based on that query.

Suffice it to say that this is a critically important chapter because it is built around a relational database, as opposed to a single table. Thus, when you complete the chapter, you will have a much better appreciation of what can be accomplished within Access. As always, the hands-on exercises are essential to your understanding of the material.

CASE STUDY: CONSUMER LOANS

Let us assume that you are in the Information Systems department of a commercial bank and are assigned the task of implementing a system for consumer loans. The bank needs complete data about every loan (the amount, interest rate, term, and so on). It also needs data about the customers holding those loans (name, address, telephone, etc.)

The problem is how to structure the data so that the bank will be able to obtain all of the information it needs from its database. The system must be able to supply the name and address of the person associated with a loan. The system must also be able to retrieve all of the loans for a specific individual.

The solution calls for a database with two tables, one for loans and one for customers. To appreciate the elegance of this approach, consider first a single table containing a combination of loan and customer data as shown in Figure 1.1. At first glance this solution appears to be satisfactory. You can, for example, search for a specific loan (e.g., L022) and determine that Lori Sangastiano is the customer associated with that loan. You can also search for a particular customer (e.g., Michelle Zacco) and find all of her loans (L028, L030, and L060).

There is a problem, however, in that the table duplicates customer data throughout the database. Thus, when one customer has multiple loans, the customer's name, address, and other data are stored multiple times. Maintaining the data in this form is a time-consuming and error-prone procedure, because any change to the customer's data has to be made in many places.

A second problem arises when you enter data for a new customer that occurs before a loan has been approved. The bank receives the customer's application data prior to granting a loan, and it wants to retain the customer data even if a loan is turned down. Adding a customer to the database in Figure 1.1 is awkward, however, because it requires the creation of a "dummy" loan record to hold the customer data.

The deletion (payoff) of a loan creates a third type of problem. What happens, for example, when Ted Myerson pays off loan L020? The loan record would be deleted, but so too would Ted's data as he has no other outstanding loans. The bank might want to contact Mr. Myerson about another loan in the future, but it would lose his data with the deletion of the existing loan.

The database in Figure 1.2 represents a much better design because it eliminates all three problems. It uses two different tables, a Loans table and a Customers table. Each record in the Loans table has data about a specific loan (LoanID, Date, Amount, Interest Rate, Term, Type, and CustomerID). Each record in the Customers table has data about a specific customer (CustomerID, First Name, Last Name, Address, City, State, Zip Code, and Phone Number). Each record in the Loans table is associated with a matching record in the Cus-

LoanID	Loan Data (Date, Amount, Interest Rate...)	Customer Data (First Name, Last Name, Address...)
L001	Loan Data for Loan L001	Customer data for Wendy Solomon
L004	Loan Data for Loan L004	Customer data for Wendy Solomon
L010	Loan Data for Loan L010	Customer data for Alex Rey
L014	Loan Data for Loan L014	Customer data for Wendy Solomon
L020	Loan Data for Loan L020	Customer data for Ted Myerson
L022	Loan Data for Loan L022	Customer data for Lori Sangastiano
L026	Loan Data for Loan L026	Customer data for Matt Hirsch
L028	Loan Data for Loan L028	Customer data for Michelle Zacco
L030	Loan Data for Loan L030	Customer data for Michelle Zacco
L031	Loan Data for Loan L031	Customer data for Eileen Faulkner
L032	Loan Data for Loan L032	Customer data for Scott Wit
L033	Loan Data for Loan L033	Customer data for Alex Rey
L039	Loan Data for Loan L039	Customer data for David Powell
L040	Loan Data for Loan L040	Customer data for Matt Hirsch
L047	Loan Data for Loan L047	Customer data for Benjamin Grauer
L049	Loan Data for Loan L049	Customer data for Eileen Faulkner
L052	Loan Data for Loan L052	Customer data for Eileen Faulkner
L053	Loan Data for Loan L053	Customer data for Benjamin Grauer
L054	Loan Data for Loan L054	Customer data for Scott Wit
L057	Loan Data for Loan L057	Customer data for Benjamin Grauer
L060	Loan Data for Loan L060	Customer data for Michelle Zacco
L062	Loan Data for Loan L062	Customer data for Matt Hirsch
L100	Loan Data for Loan L100	Customer data for Benjamin Grauer
L109	Loan Data for Loan L109	Customer data for Wendy Solomon
L120	Loan Data for Loan L120	Customer data for Lori Sangastiano

FIGURE 1.1 Single Table Solution

tomers table through the CustomerID field common to both tables. This solution may seem complicated, but it is really quite simple and elegant.

Consider, for example, how easy it is to change a customer's address. If Michelle Zacco were to move, you would go into the Customers table, find her record (Customer C08), and make the necessary change. You would not have to change any of the records in the Loans table, because they do not contain customer data, but only a CustomerID that indicates who the customer is. In other words, you would change Michelle's address in only one place, and the change would be automatically reflected for every associated loan.

The addition of a new customer is done directly in the Customer table. This is much easier than the approach of Figure 1.1, which required an existing loan in order to add a new customer. And finally, the deletion of an existing loan is also easier than with the single table organization. A loan can be deleted from the Loans table without losing the corresponding customer data.

The database in Figure 1.2 is composed of two tables in which there is a ***one-to-many relationship*** between customers and loans. One customer (Michelle Zacco) can have many loans (Loan numbers L028, L030, and L060), but a specific loan (L028) is associated with only one customer (Michelle Zacco). The tables are related to one another by a common field (CustomerID) that is present in both the Customer and the Loans table.

Access enables you to create the one-to-many relationship between the tables, then uses that relationship to answer questions about the database. It can retrieve information about a specific loan, such as the name and address of the customer holding that loan. It can also find all of the loans for a particular customer as illustrated in the queries that follow.

LoanID	Date	Amount	Interest Rate	Term	Type	CustomerID
L001	1/15/96	$475,000	6.90%	15	M	**C04**
L004	1/23/96	$35,000	7.20%	5	C	**C04**
L010	1/25/96	$10,000	5.50%	3	C	**C05**
L014	1/31/96	$12,000	9.50%	10	O	**C04**
L020	2/8/96	$525,000	6.50%	30	M	**C06**
L022	2/12/96	$10,500	7.50%	5	O	**C07**
L026	2/15/96	$35,000	6.50%	5	O	**C10**
L028	2/20/96	$250,000	8.80%	30	M	**C08**
L030	2/21/96	$5,000	10.00%	3	O	**C08**
L031	2/28/96	$200,000	7.00%	15	M	**C01**
L032	3/1/96	$25,000	10.00%	3	C	**C02**
L033	3/1/96	$20,000	9.50%	5	O	**C05**
L039	3/3/96	$56,000	7.50%	5	C	**C09**
L040	3/10/96	$129,000	8.50%	15	M	**C10**
L047	3/11/96	$200,000	7.25%	15	M	**C03**
L049	3/21/96	$150,000	7.50%	15	M	**C01**
L052	3/22/96	$100,000	7.00%	30	M	**C01**
L053	3/31/96	$15,000	6.50%	3	O	**C03**
L054	4/1/96	$10,000	8.00%	5	C	**C02**
L057	4/15/96	$25,000	8.50%	4	C	**C03**
L060	4/18/96	$41,000	9.90%	4	C	**C08**
L062	4/22/96	$350,000	7.50%	15	M	**C10**
L100	5/1/96	$150,000	6.00%	15	M	**C03**
L109	5/3/96	$350,000	8.20%	30	M	**C04**
L120	5/8/96	$275,000	9.20%	15	M	**C07**

(a) Loans Table

CustomerID	First Name	Last Name	Address	City	State	Zip Code	Phone Number
C01	Eileen	Faulkner	7245 NW 8 Street	Minneapolis	MN	55346	(612) 894-1511
C02	Scott	Wit	5660 NW 175 Terrace	Baltimore	MD	21224	(410) 753-0345
C03	Benjamin	Grauer	10000 Sample Road	Coral Springs	FL	33073	(305) 444-5555
C04	Wendy	Solomon	7500 Reno Road	Houston	TX	77090	(713) 427-3104
C05	Alex	Rey	3456 Main Highway	Denver	CO	80228	(303) 555-6666
C06	Ted	Myerson	6545 Stone Street	Chapel Hill	NC	27515	(919) 942-7654
C07	Lori	Sangastiano	4533 Aero Drive	Santa Rosa	CA	95403	(707) 542-3411
C08	Michelle	Zacco	488 Gold Street	Gainesville	FL	32601	(904) 374-5660
C09	David	Powell	5070 Battle Road	Decatur	GA	30034	(301) 345-6556
C10	Matt	Hirsch	777 NW 67 Avenue	Fort Lee	NJ	07624	(201) 664-3211

(b) Customers Table

FIGURE 1.2 Multiple Table Solution

Query: What are the name, address, and phone number of the customer associated with loan number L010?

Answer: Alex Rey, at 3456 Main Highway is the customer associated with loan L010. His phone number is (303) 555-6666.

To determine the answer, Access searches the Loans table for loan L010 to obtain the CustomerID (C05 in this example). It then searches the Customers table for the customer with the matching CustomerID and retrieves the name, address, and phone number. Consider a second example:

Query: What loans are associated with Wendy Solomon?
Answer: Wendy Solomon has four loans: loan L001 for $475,000, loan L004 for $35,000, loan L014 for $12,000, and loan L109 for $350,000.

This time Access begins in the Customers table and searches for Wendy Solomon to determine the CustomerID (C04). It then searches the Loans table for all records with a matching CustomerID.

PEDAGOGY VERSUS REALITY

Our design requires that the CustomerID and LoanID begin with the letters C and L, respectively, to emphasize the tables in which these fields are found and to facilitate data entry in the hands-on exercises. This convention places artificial limits on the number of customers and loans at 100 and 1000, respectively. (CustomerID goes from C00 to C99, and LoanID goes from L000 to L999.)

Implementation in Access

An Access database contains multiple tables. Each table stores data about a specific subject, such as customers or loans. Each table has a ***primary key,*** which is a field (or combination of fields) that uniquely identifies each record. CustomerID is the primary key in the Customers table. LoanID is the primary key in the Loans table.

A one-to-many relationship uses the primary key of the "one" table as a ***foreign key*** in the "many" table, and it is through the foreign key that the relationship is established. (A foreign key is simply the primary key of another table.) The CustomerID appears in both the Customers table and the Loans table. It is the primary key in the Customers table, where its values are unique; it is a foreign key in the Loans table, where its values are not unique. Thus, multiple records in the Loans table can have the same CustomerID to implement the one-to-many relationship between customers and loans.

To create a one-to-many relationship, you open the ***Relationships window*** in Figure 1.3 and add the necessary tables. You then drag the field on which the relationship is built, from the field list of the "one" table (Customers) to the matching field in the ***related table*** (Loans). Once the relationship has been established, you will see a ***join line*** connecting the tables, which indicates the "one" and "many" sides of the relationship. The line extends from the primary key in the "one" table to the foreign key in the "many" table and uses the symbols 1 and ∞, respectively.

RELATED FIELDS AND DATA TYPES

The related fields must have the same data type—both text or both number. In addition, number fields must also have the same field size. The exception is an AutoNumber (counter) field in the primary table, which is matched against a Long Integer field in the related table. AutoNumber fields are discussed in Chapter 2.

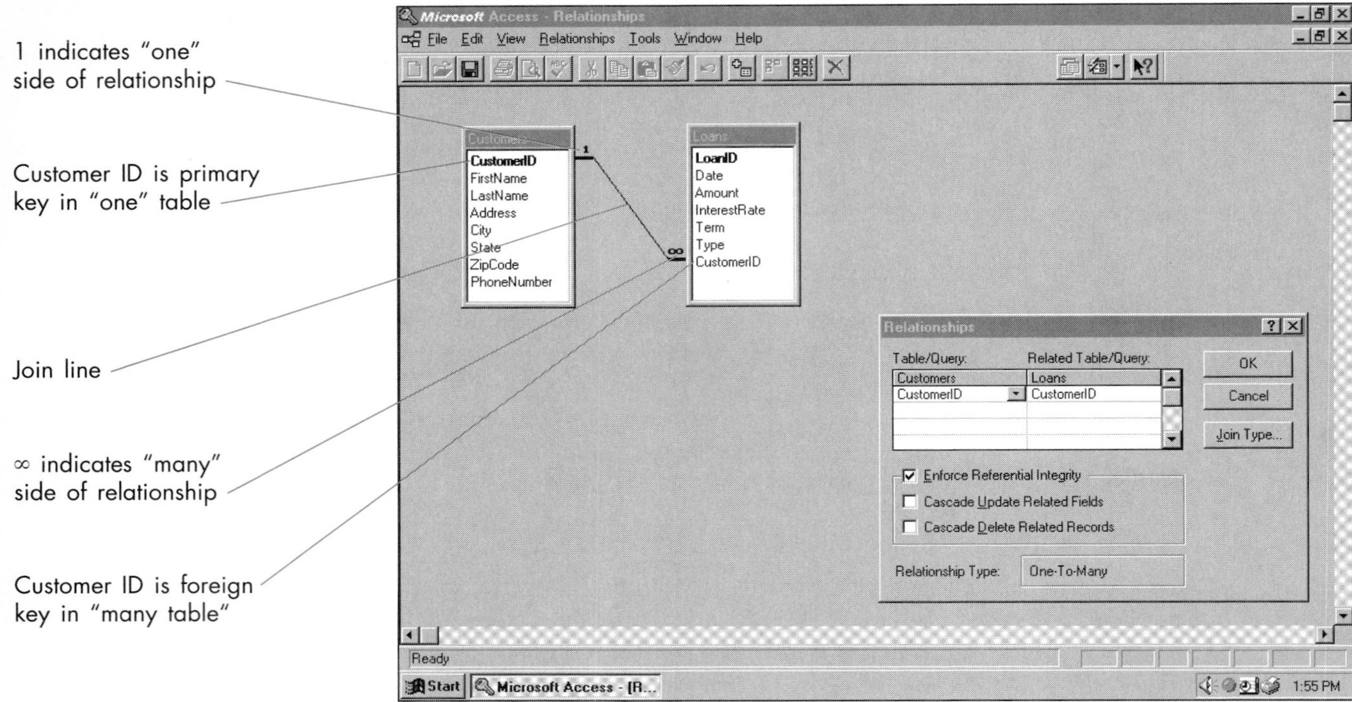

FIGURE 1.3 The Relationships Window

Referential Integrity

Referential integrity ensures that the records in related tables are consistent with one another. When enforcement of referential integrity is in effect, Access will prevent you from adding records to a related table when there is no associated record in the primary table. In other words, you cannot add a record to the Loans table unless there is a corresponding Customer record, because every loan must be associated with an existing customer. Or stated another way, you must add a Customer record before assigning a loan to that customer.

Enforcement of referential integrity will also prevent you from deleting a record in the primary (Customers) table if there is a corresponding record in the related (Loans) table. (Thus, to delete a customer, you would first have to delete all loans for that customer.) In similar fashion, you cannot change the primary key of a Customer record when there are matching Loan records. (These restrictions are relaxed if you check the Cascade Delete Related Records or Cascade Update Fields option in the Relationships dialog box. These options are discussed further in Chapter 2.)

HANDS-ON EXERCISE 1

One-to-Many Relationships

Objective: To create a one-to-many relationship between existing tables in a database; to demonstrate referential integrity between the tables in a one-to-many relationship. Use Figure 1.4 as a guide in the exercise.

STEP 1: Open the National Bank Database

- Start Access. Open the **National Bank database** in the **Exploring Access folder.** The database contains three tables: for Customers, Loans, and Payments. (The Payments table will be used later in the chapter.)
- Pull down the **Tools menu** and click **Relationships** to open the Relationships window as shown in Figure 1.4a. (The Customers and Loans tables are not yet visible.) If you do not see the Show Table dialog box, pull down the **Relationships menu** and click the **Show Table command.**
- The **Tables tab** is selected within the Show Table dialog box. Click (select) the **Customers table,** then click the **Add Command button** to add the table to the Relationships window.
- Click the **Loans table,** then click the **Add Command button** (or simply double click the **Loans table**) to add this table to the Relationships window.
- Do *not* add the Payments table at this time. Click the **Close button** to close the Show Table dialog box.

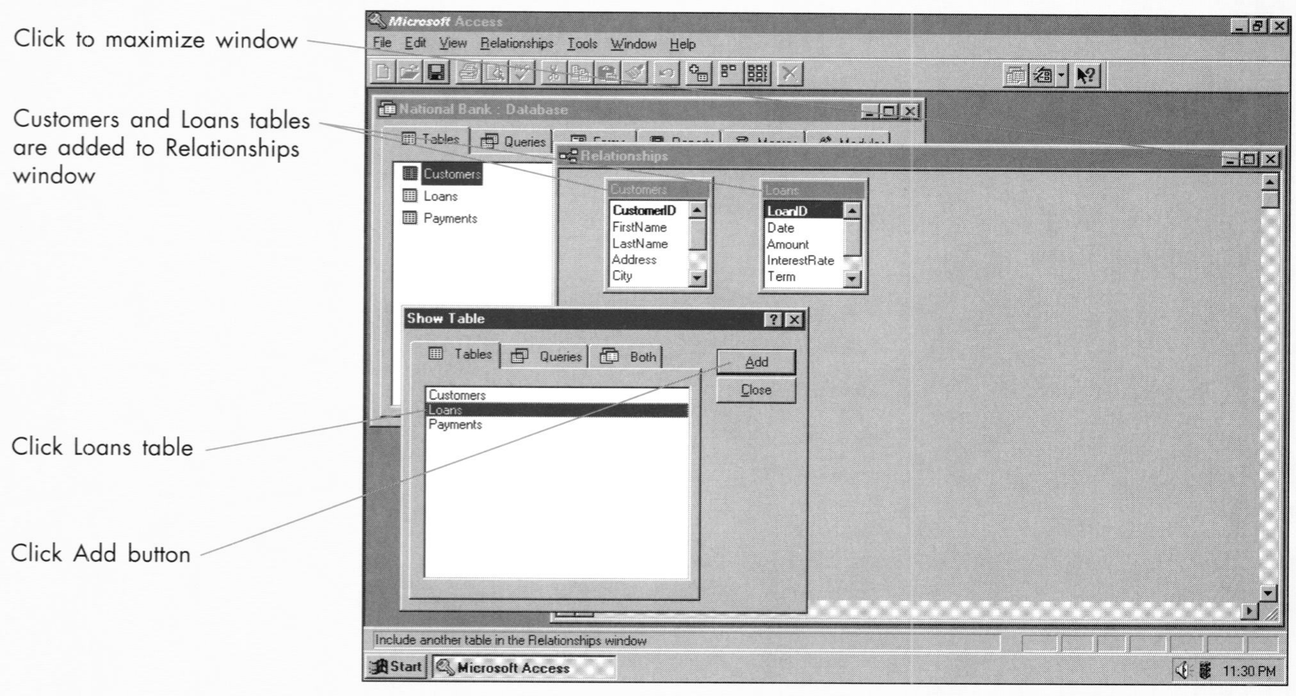

(a) The Relationships Window (step 1)

FIGURE 1.4 Hands-on Exercise 1

STEP 2: Create the Relationships

- Maximize the Relationships window so that you have more room in which to work. Point to the bottom border of the **Customers field list** (the mouse pointer changes to a double arrow), then click and drag the border until all of the fields are visible.
- Click and drag the bottom border of the **Loans field list** until all of the fields are visible.

- Click and drag the title bar of the **Loans field list** so that it is approximately one inch away from the Customers field list.
- Click and drag the **CustomerID field** in the Customers field list to the **CustomerID field** in the Loans field list. You will see the Relationships dialog box in Figure 1.4b.
- Check the **Enforce Referential Integrity** check box. (If necessary, clear the check boxes to Cascade Update Related Fields and Delete Related Records.)
- Click the **Create Command button** to establish the relationship and close the Relationships dialog box. You should see a line indicating a one-to-many relationship between the Customers and Loans tables.

THE RELATIONSHIPS ARE VISUAL

Access displays a relationship (join) line between related tables to indicate the relationship between those tables. It uses the number 1 and the infinity symbol (∞) to indicate a one-to-many relationship in which referential integrity is enforced. The 1 appears at the end of the join line near the primary (one) table. The infinity symbol appears at the end nearest the related (many) table. Access shows the primary keys in each table in bold.

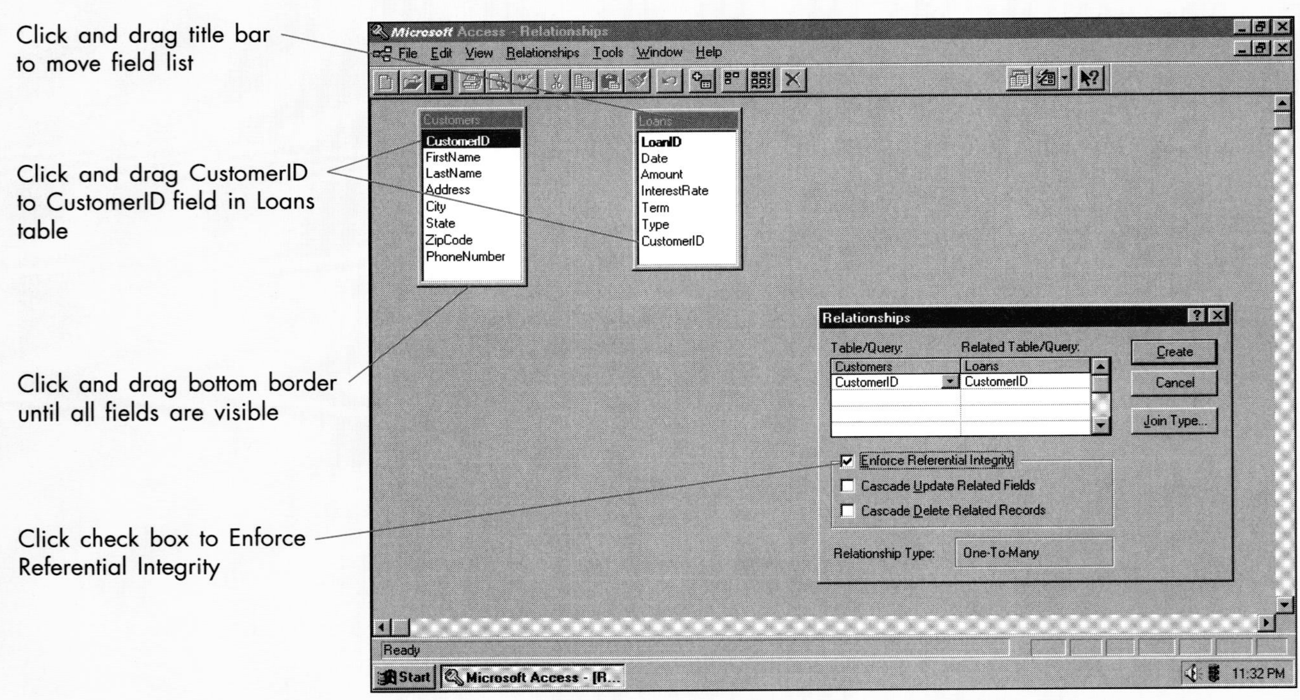

(b) Create the Relationship (step 2)

FIGURE 1.4 Hands-on Exercise 1 (continued)

STEP 3: Deleting a Relationship

- Point to the line indicating the relationship between the tables, then click the **right mouse button** to select the relationship and display a shortcut menu.
- Click the **Delete Relationship command.** You will see the dialog box in Figure 1.4c, asking whether you want to delete the relationship. Click **No** since you do *not* want to delete the relationship.
- Close the Relationships window. Click **Yes** when asked whether to save the layout changes.

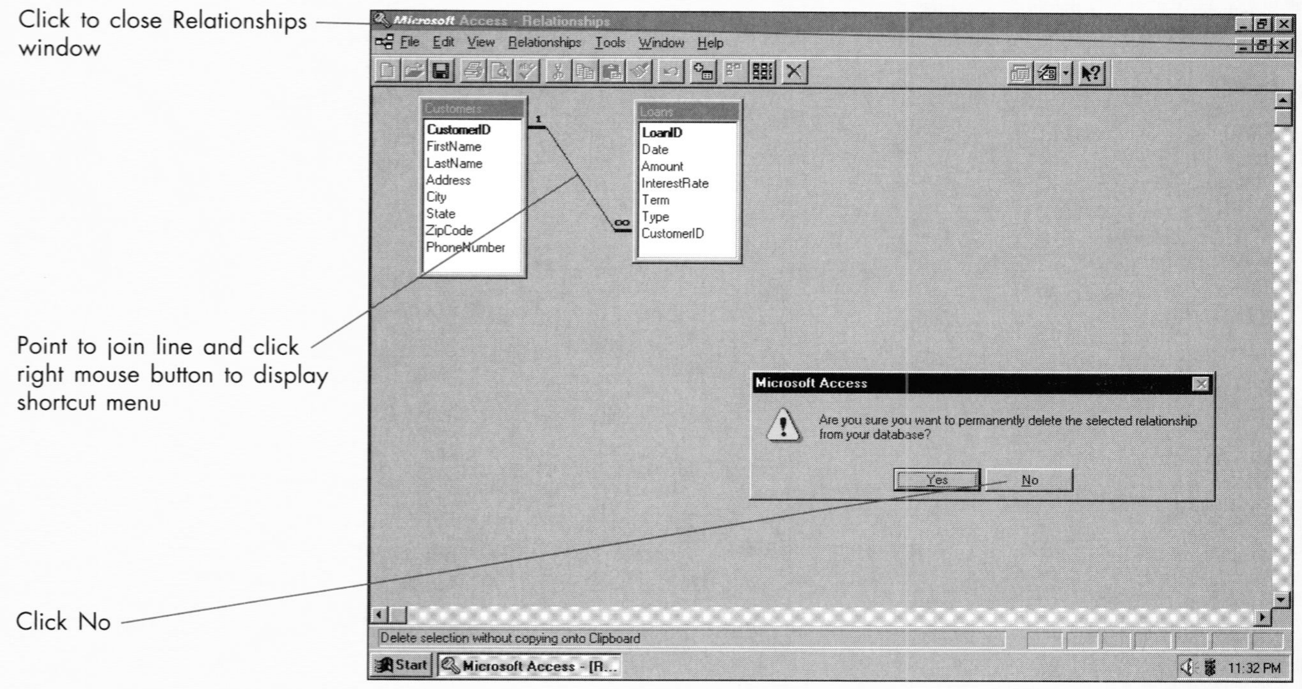

(c) Deleting a Relationship (step 3)

FIGURE 1.4 Hands-on Exercise 1 (continued)

STEP 4: Add a Customer Record

- The Database window is again visible with the Tables tab selected. Open the **Customers table.** If necessary, click the **Maximize button** to give yourself additional room when adding a record. Widen the fields as necessary to see the data.
- Click the **New Record button** on the toolbar. The record selector moves to the last record (record 11).
- Enter **C11** as the CustomerID as shown in Figure 1.4d. The record selector changes to a pencil as soon as you enter the first character.
- Enter data for yourself as the new customer. Data validation has been built into the Customers table, so you must enter the data correctly, or it will not be accepted.
  - The message, *Customer ID must begin with the letter C followed by a two-digit number,* indicates that the CustomerID field is invalid.

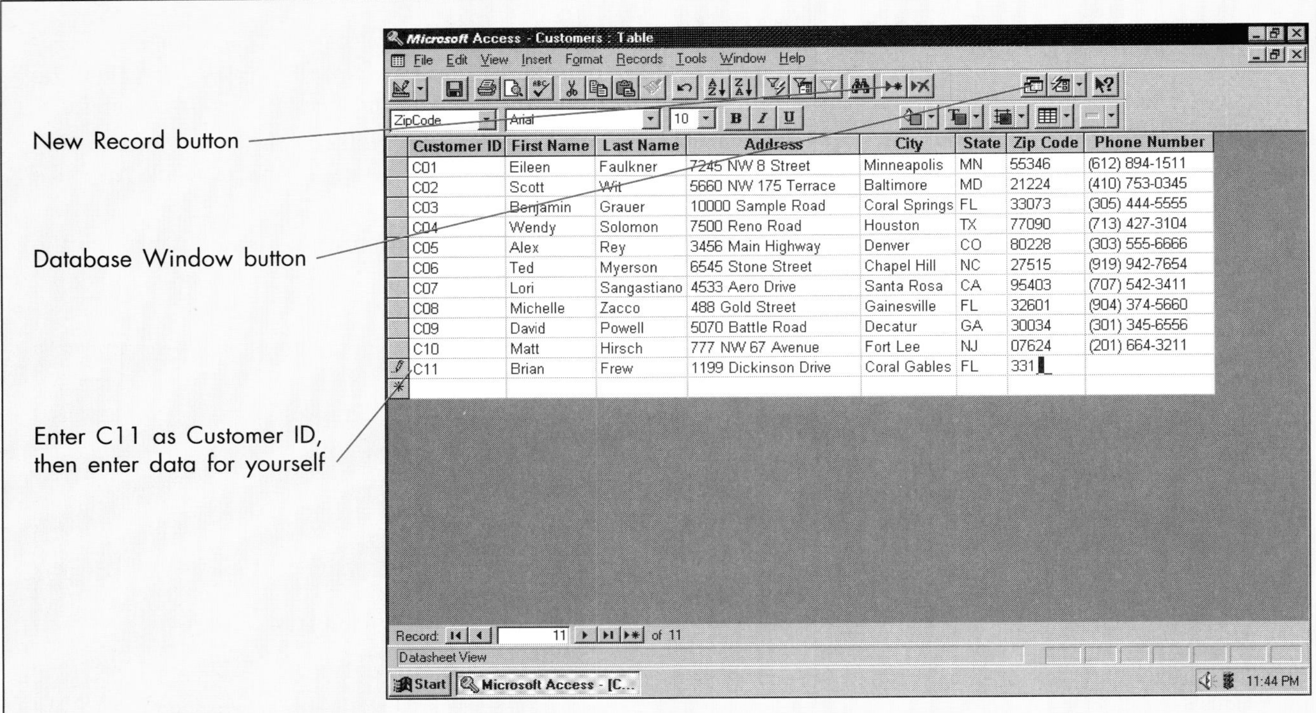

(d) Add a Customer Record (step 4)

FIGURE 1.4 Hands-on Exercise 1 (continued)

- The message, *Field 'Customer'sLastName' can't contain a null value,* indicates that you must enter a last name.
- A beep in either the ZipCode or PhoneNumber field indicates that you are entering a nonnumeric character.
- If you encounter a data validation error, press **Esc** (or Click **OK**), then reenter the data.

➤ Press **enter** when you have completed your record. Remember your CustomerID (C11) because you will need to enter it in the corresponding loan records.

THE RECORD SELECTOR

The record selector symbol indicates the status of the record. A triangle means the data in the current record has not changed. A pencil indicates you are in the process of entering (or changing) the data. An asterisk appears next to the blank record at the end of every table.

STEP 5: Add a Loan Record

➤ Click the **Database Window button** on the toolbar, then open the **Loans table.** Maximize the window containing the Loans table to give yourself additional room when adding a record.

➤ Click the **New Record button** on the toolbar. The record selector moves to the blank record at the end of the table. Add a new loan record as shown in Figure 1.4e.

- Use **L121** for the LoanID and enter the terms of the loan as you see fit.
- Data validation has been built into the Loans table so you will have to enter data correctly for it to be accepted. The term of the loan, for example, cannot exceed 30 years. The interest rate must be entered as a decimal. The type of the loan must be C, M, or O for Car, Mortgage, or Other. Enter **C** for a car loan.
- Be sure to enter **C11** as the CustomerID field. (This is your CustomerID from step 4.).

➤ Press **enter** when you have completed the loan record.

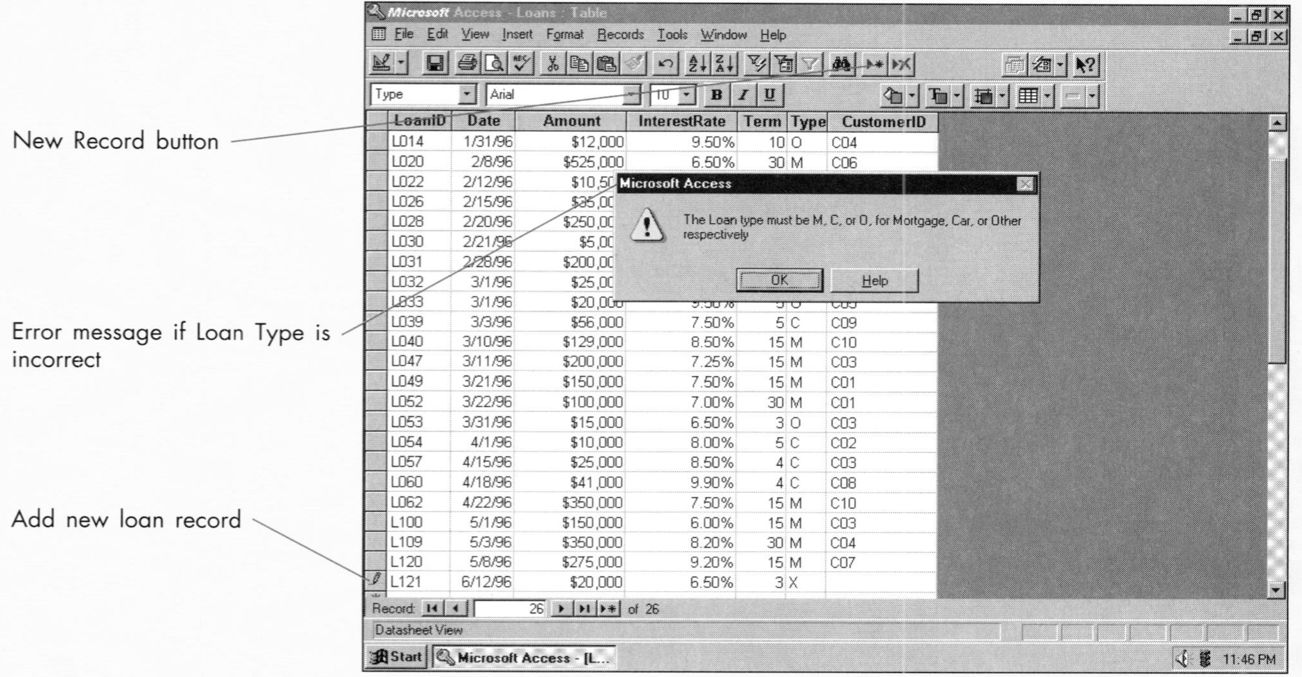

(e) Add a Loan Record (step 5)

FIGURE 1.4 Hands-on Exercise 1 (continued)

GARBAGE IN, GARBAGE OUT

The information produced by a system depends entirely on the quality of the data. It is important, therefore, that you validate data as it is being entered to ensure that the data is as accurate as possible. A well-designed system will anticipate errors that a user may make during data entry and will include data validation checks that will prevent invalid data from being accepted into the system.

STEP 6: Referential Integrity

- Pull down the **Window menu.** Click **Cascade** to cascade the open windows (the Database window, the Customers table, and the Loans table.)
- Click the **Database window,** then click the **Minimize button** to minimize this window. Move and size the Customers and Loans windows so that your desktop matches ours in Figure 1.4f.
- Click in the **Loans window.** Click the **CustomerID field** of your loan record and (attempt to) replace the CustomerID (C11) with **C88.** Press **enter.** You will see the dialog box in Figure 1.4f, indicating that referential integrity has been violated because there is no corresponding Customer record.
- Click **OK.** Reenter **C11** as the valid CustomerID. Press **enter.**
- Click the window for the **Customers table.** Click the **row selector** to select the first record (Customer C01). Press the **Del key** (in an attempt) to delete this record.
- Access indicates that you cannot delete this record because related records exist and referential integrity rules would be violated. Click **OK.**

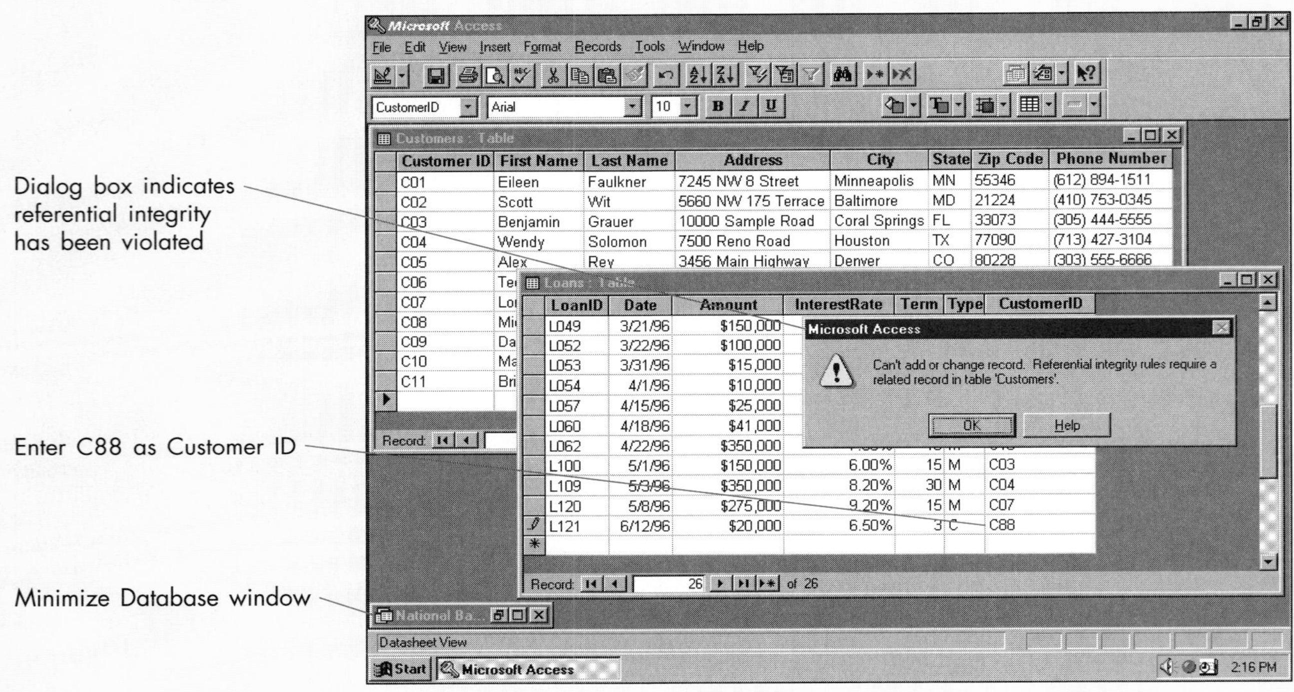
Dialog box indicates referential integrity has been violated
Enter C88 as Customer ID
Minimize Database window
Microsoft Access
Can't add or change record. Referential integrity rules require a related record in table 'Customers'.
OK
Help

(f) Referential Integrity (step 6)

FIGURE 1.4 Hands-on Exercise 1 (continued)

ARRANGING THE DESKTOP

An Access database contains several objects that can be open at the same time. Pull down the Window menu, then click the Cascade or Tile command to arrange the open windows on the desktop. If you cascade the windows, you will most likely size and/or move them afterwards. To size a window, point to any border or corner and drag in the desired direction. To move a window, point to the title bar and drag the window to its new position.

STEP 7: Close the Database

- Close the Customers table. Close the Loans table.
- Close the Database window if you do not want to continue with the next hands-on exercise at this time.

SUBFORMS

A ***subform*** is a form within a form. It appears inside a main form to display records from a related table. A main form and its associated subform, to display the loans for one customer, are shown in Figure 1.5. The ***main form*** (also known as the primary form) is based on the ***primary table*** (the Customers table). The subform is based on the related table (the Loans table).

The main form and the subform are linked to one another so that the subform displays only the records related to the record currently displayed in the main form. The main form shows the "one" side of the relationship (the customer). The subform shows the "many" side of the relationship (the loans). The main form displays the customer data for one record (Eileen Faulkner with CustomerID C01). The subform shows the loans for that customer. The main form is displayed in the ***Form view,*** whereas the subform is displayed in the ***Datasheet view.*** (A subform can also be displayed in the Form view, in which case it would show one loan at a time.)

Each form in Figure 1.5a has its own status bar and associated navigation buttons. The status bar for the main form indicates that the active record is record 1 of 11 records in the Customers table. The status bar for the subform indicates record 1 of 3 records. (The latter shows the number of loans for this customer rather than the number of loans in the Loans table.) Click the navigation button to move to the next customer record, and you will automatically see the loans associated with that customer. If, for example, you were to move to the last customer record (C11, which contains the data you entered in the first hands-on exercise), you would see your loan information.

The Loans form also contains a calculated control, the payment due, which is based on the loan parameters. Loan L031, for example (a $200,000 mortgage with a 15-year term), has a monthly payment of $1,797.66. The amount of the payment is calculated using a predefined function, as will be described in the next hands-on exercise.

Figure 1.5b displays the Design view of the Customers form in Figure 1.5a. The Loans subform control is an object on the Customers form and can be moved and sized (or deleted) just like any other object. It should also be noted that the Loans subform is a form in and of itself, and can be opened in either the Datasheet

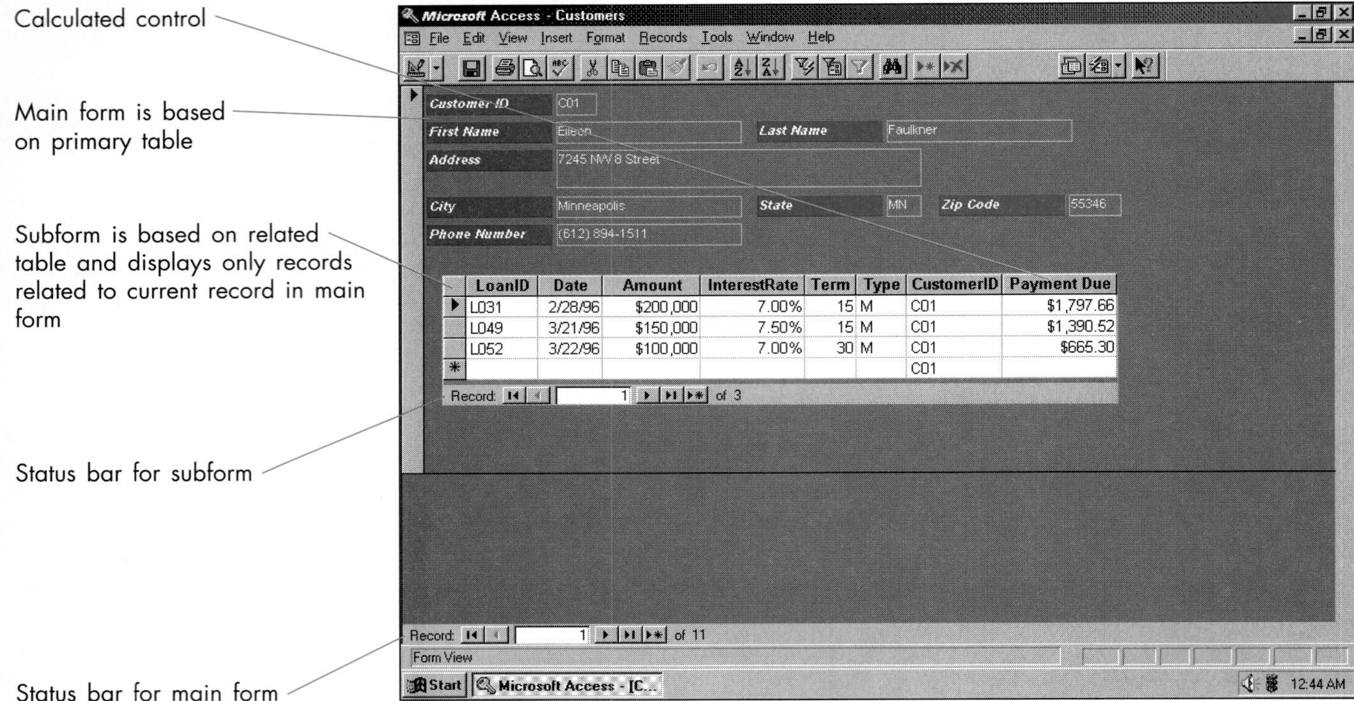

(a) Form View

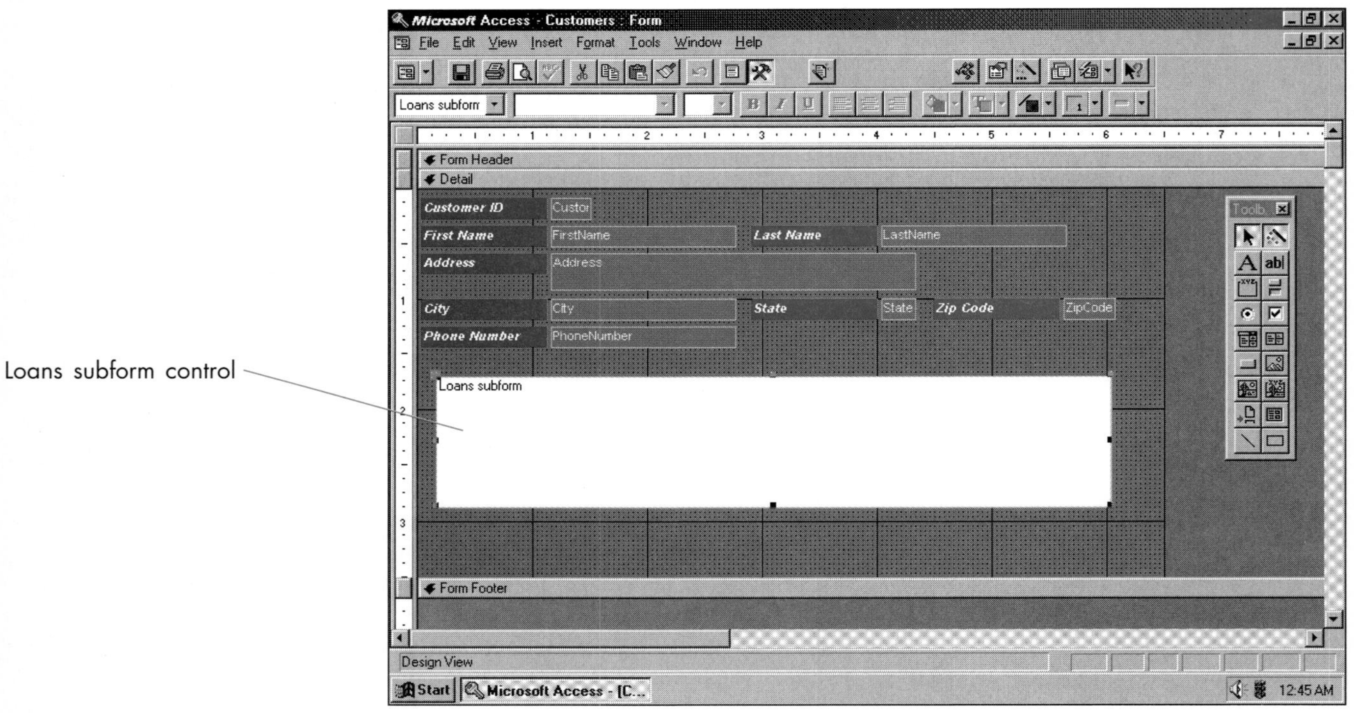

(b) Design View

FIGURE 1.5 A Main Form and a Subform

view or the Form view. It can also be opened in the Design view (to modify its appearance) as will be done in the next hands-on exercise.

> **THE PMT FUNCTION**
>
> The Pmt function is one of several predefined ***functions*** built into Access. It calculates the payment due on a loan based on the principal, interest rate, and term and is similar to the PMT function in Excel. The Pmt function is reached most easily through the Expression Builder and can be entered onto any form, query, or report. (See step 7 in the hands-on exercise.)

The Subform Wizard

A subform can be created as a separate form, then dragged onto the main form. It can also be created directly on the main form by selecting the Subform/Subreport button, then clicking and dragging on the main form to size and position the subform. This in turn opens the ***Subform Wizard*** as shown in Figure 1.6. You specify whether to build the subform from an existing form or from a table or query

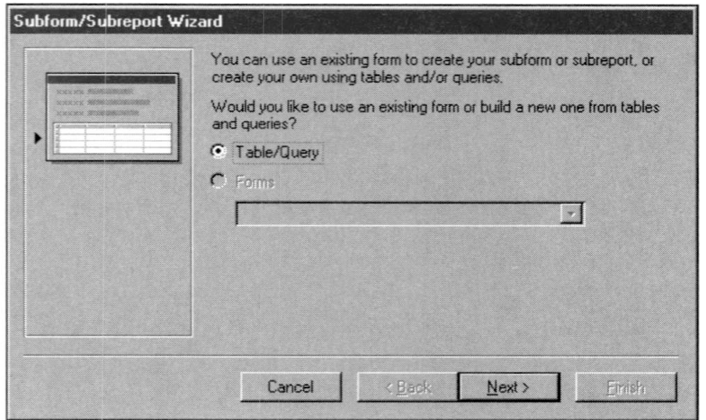

(a) Use an Existing Table/Query

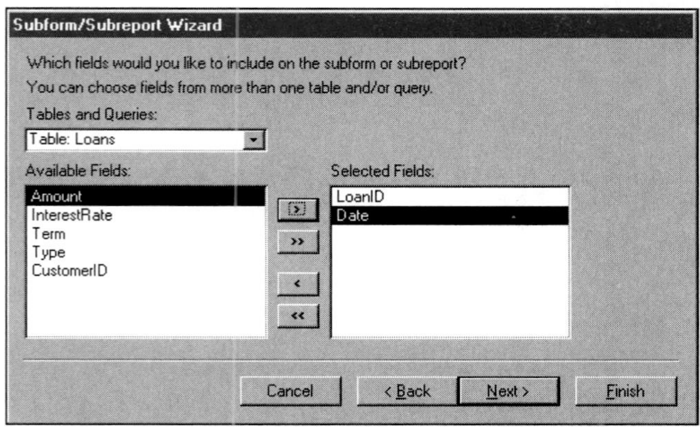

(b) Select the Fields

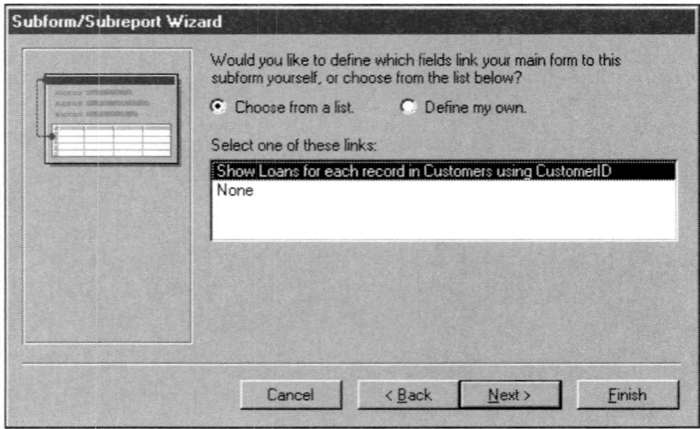

(c) Create the Link

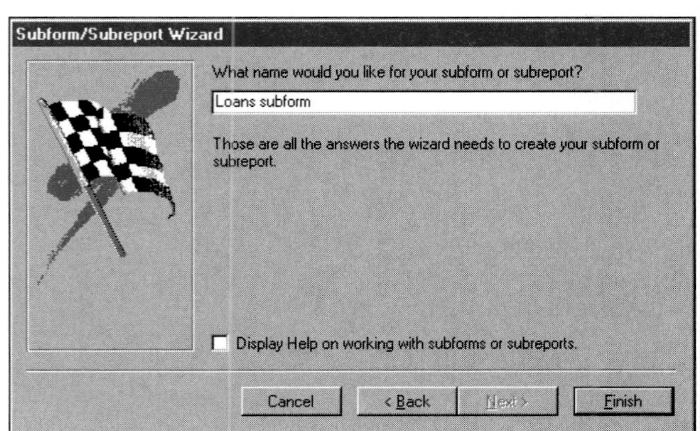

(d) Save the Subform

FIGURE 1.6 The Subform Wizard

as shown in Figure 1.6a, then you select the desired fields in Figure 1.6b. Next, you specify the relationship between the main form and the subform as shown in Figure 1.6c. The subform in this example will show all of the loans for a particular customer. And finally, you specify the name for the subform as in Figure 1.6d to save the subform as an object within the database.

The Subform Wizard provides an excellent starting point, but as with the Form Wizard and a regular form, you usually need to customize the subform so that it meets your requirements. This is done using the identical techniques for a regular form to move and size the controls and/or to modify their properties.

THE POWER OF SUBFORMS

A subform exists as a separate object within the database and can be opened or modified just like any other form. A main form can have any number of subforms, and a subform in turn can have its own subform. (See Hands-on Exercise 4 at the end of the chapter.)

HANDS-ON EXERCISE 2

Creating a Subform

Objective: To create a subform that displays the many records in a one-to-many relationship; to move and size controls in an existing form; to enter data in a subform. Use Figure 1.7 as a guide in doing the exercise.

STEP 1: Create the Customers Form

- Open the **National Bank database** from the previous exercise. Click the **Forms tab** in the Database window. Click **New** to display the New Form dialog box as shown in Figure 1.7a. Click **Form Wizard** in the list box.
- Click the **drop-down arrow** to display the available tables and queries in the database on which the form can be based. Click **Customers** to select the Customers table, then click **OK** to start the Form Wizard.

STEP 2: The Form Wizard

- You should see the dialog box in Figure 1.7b, which displays all of the fields in the Customers table. Click the **>> button** to enter all of the fields in the table on the form. Click **Next.**
- The **Columnar layout** is already selected. Click **Next.**
- Click **Colorful 1** as the style for your form. Click **Next.**
- The Form Wizard suggests **Customers** as the title of the form. (Keep this entry.) Click the option button to **Modify the form's design,** then click the **Finish Command button** to create the form and exit the Form Wizard.

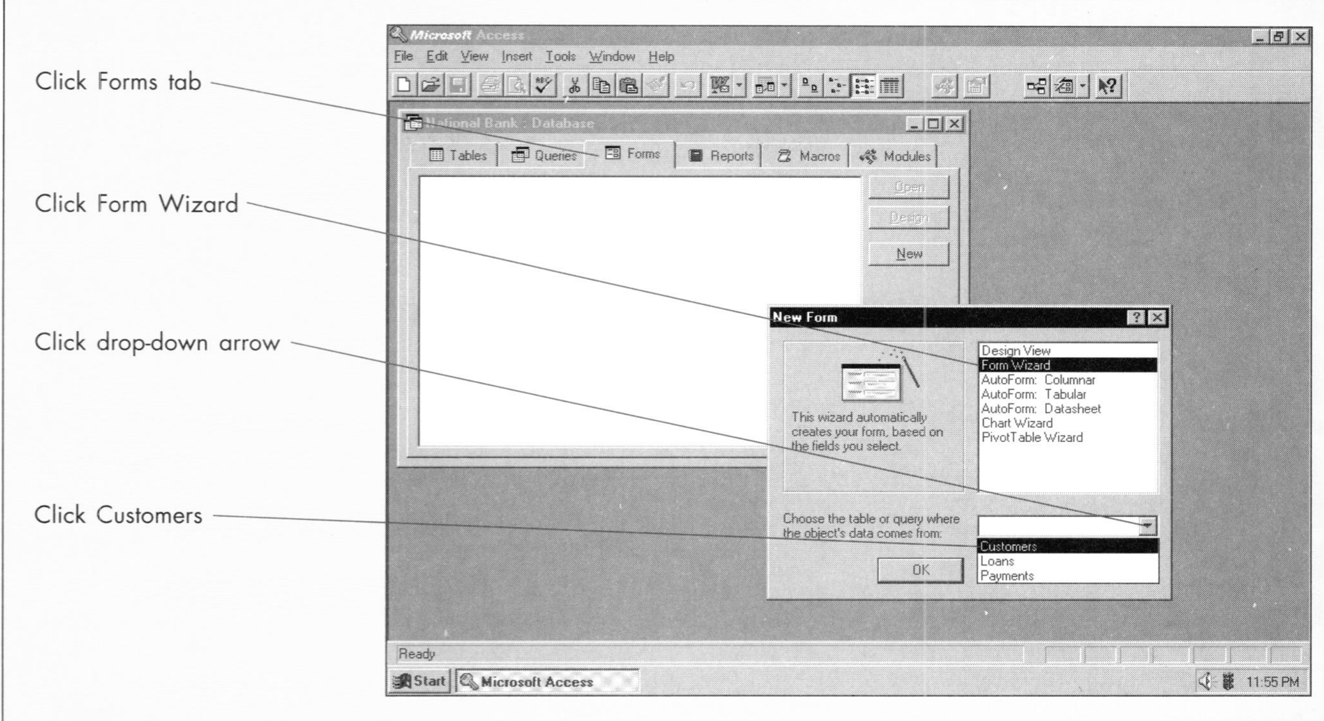

(a) The Form Wizard (step 1)

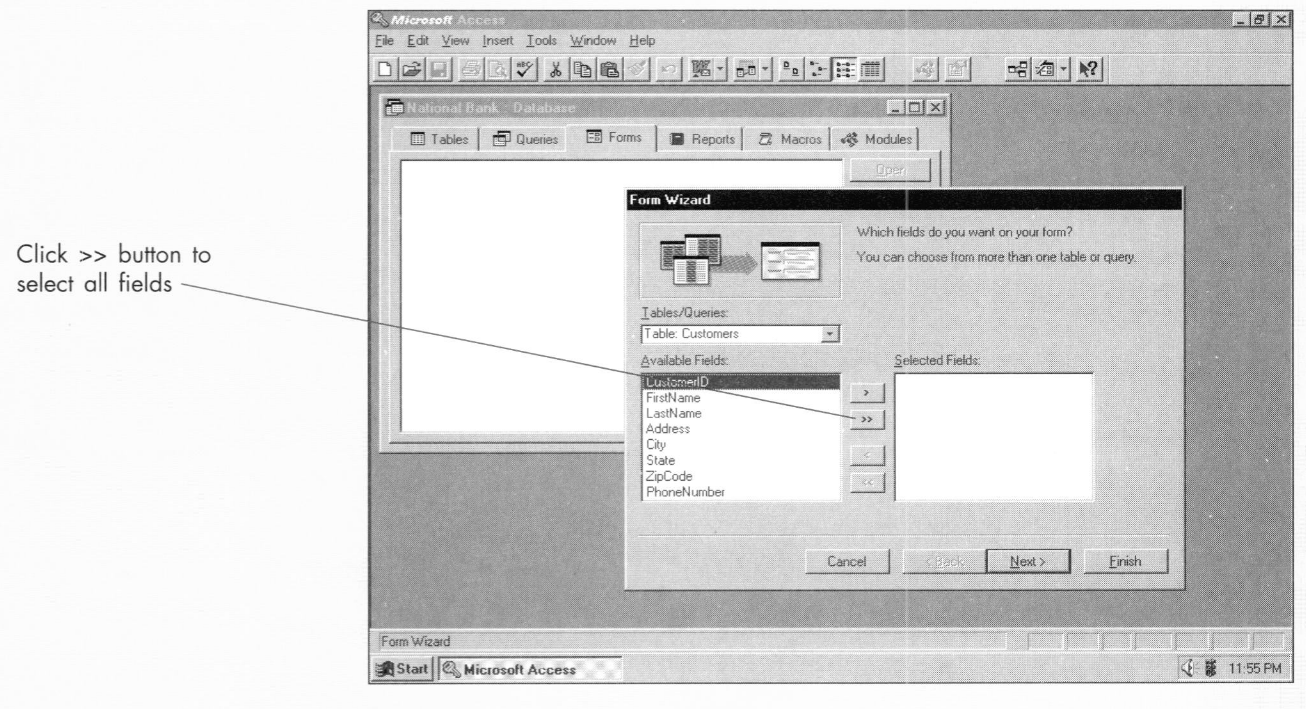

(b) The Form Wizard (continued)

FIGURE 1.7 Hands-on Exercise 2

THE NAME'S THE SAME

The Form Wizard automatically assigns the name of the underlying table (or query) to each form (subform) it creates. The Report Wizard works in similar fashion. The intent of the similar naming convention is to help you select the proper object from the Database window when you want to subsequently open the object. This becomes increasingly important in databases that contain a large number of objects.

STEP 3: Modify the Customers Form

- You should see the Customers form in Figure 1.7c. Maximize the window. Click and drag the right edge of the form to widen the form to **6½ inches.**
- Click the control for **LastName** to select the control and display the sizing handles, then drag the **LastName control** so that it is next to the FirstName control.
- Click and drag the other controls to complete the form:
  - Click and drag the **Address control** under the control for FirstName.
  - Place the controls for **City, State,** and **ZipCode** on the same line, then move these controls under the Address control.
  - Move the control for **PhoneNumber** under the control for City.
- Click the **Save button** to save the form.

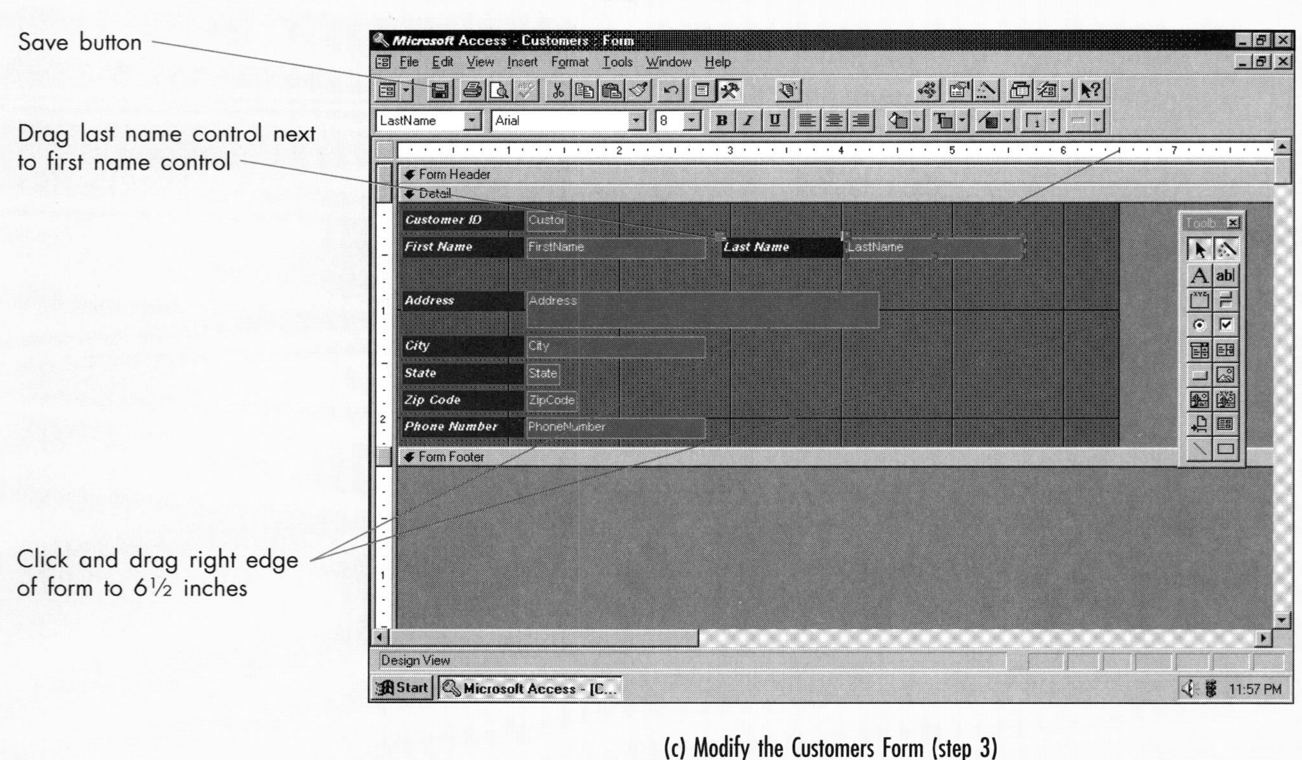

(c) Modify the Customers Form (step 3)

FIGURE 1.7 Hands-on Exercise 2 (continued)

ALIGN THE CONTROLS

To align the controls in a straight line (horizontally or vertically), press and hold the Shift key as you click the labels of the controls to be aligned. Pull down the Format menu and select the edge to align (Left, Right, Top, or Bottom). Click the Undo button if you are not satisfied with the result.

STEP 4: Create the Loans Subform

- Click and drag the bottom edge of the **Detail section** so that you have approximately 2 inches of blank space in the Detail section as shown in Figure 1.7d. (This is where the subform will go.)
- Click the **Subform/Subreport button** on the Toolbox toolbar, then click and drag in the Customers form where you want the subform to go. Release the mouse to start the Subform/Subreport Wizard.
- The **Table/Query Option button** is selected, indicating that we will build the subform from a table or query. Click **Next.**
- You should see the Subform/Subreport Wizard dialog box in Figure 1.7d. Click the **down arrow** on the Tables and Queries list box to select the **Loans table.** Click the **>> button** to enter all of the fields in the Loans table onto the subform. Click **Next.**

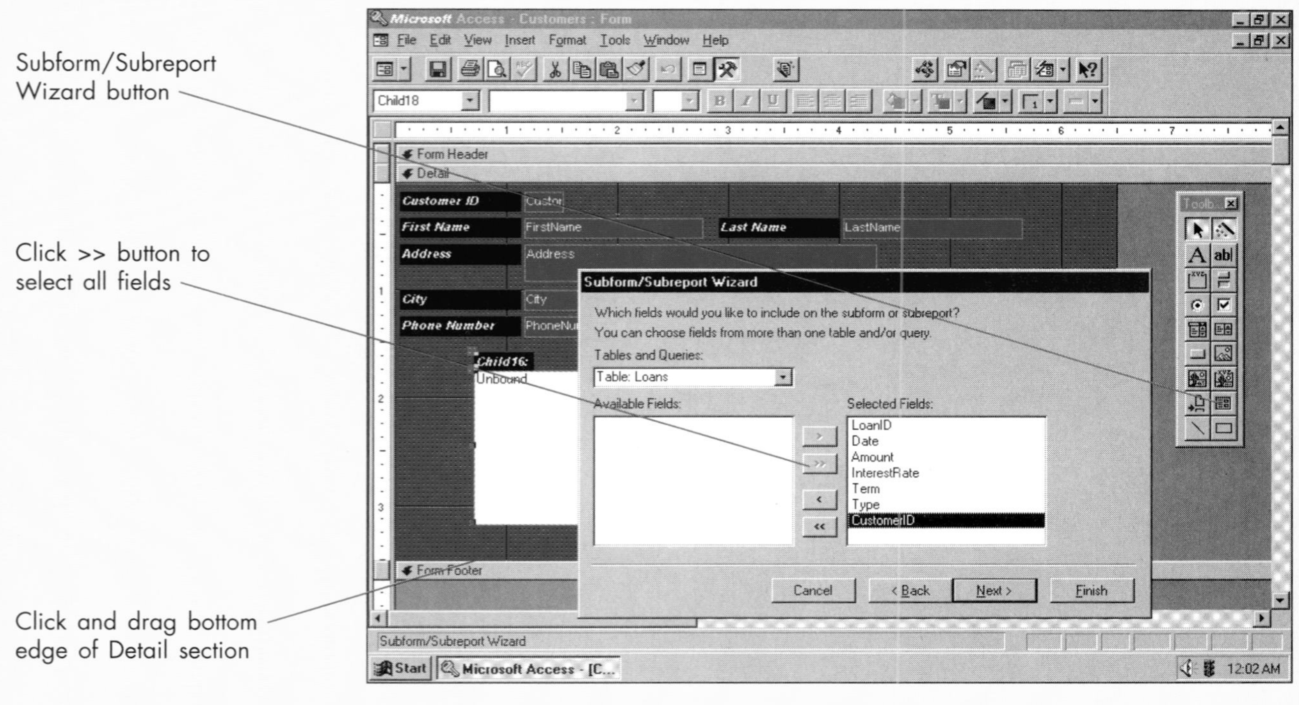

(d) Create the Subform (step 4)

FIGURE 1.7 Hands-on Exercise 2 (continued)

- ➤ The next step asks you to define the fields that link the main form to the subform. The option button to **Choose from a list** is selected. The selected link will **Show Loans for each record in Customers using CustomerID.** Click **Next.**
- ➤ The Wizard suggests **Loans subform** as the name of the subform. Click **Finish** to exit the Subform/Subreport wizard.

STEP 5: The Loans Subform (Datasheet view)

- ➤ You should be in the Design view for the Customers form, which contains a white rectangular area indicating the position of the Loans subform control. Maximize the window.
- ➤ Click the label attached to the subform control and press the **Del key.** Be sure you delete only the label and not the control for the subform.
- ➤ You need to open the Loans subform to check the column width of its fields. This is done in one of two ways:
    - Deselect the Loans subform (by clicking anywhere in the main form), then double click the **Loans subform** to open it. Change to the **Datasheet view,** *or*
    - Pull down the **Window menu** to change to the **Database window,** click the **Forms tab,** and open the **Loans subform.**
- ➤ You should see the Datasheet view of the Loans subform as shown in Figure 1.7e. Click and drag the various column headings to the approximate sizes shown in the figure so that you can see the complete field names.
- ➤ Save the Loans subform. Close the Loans subform.

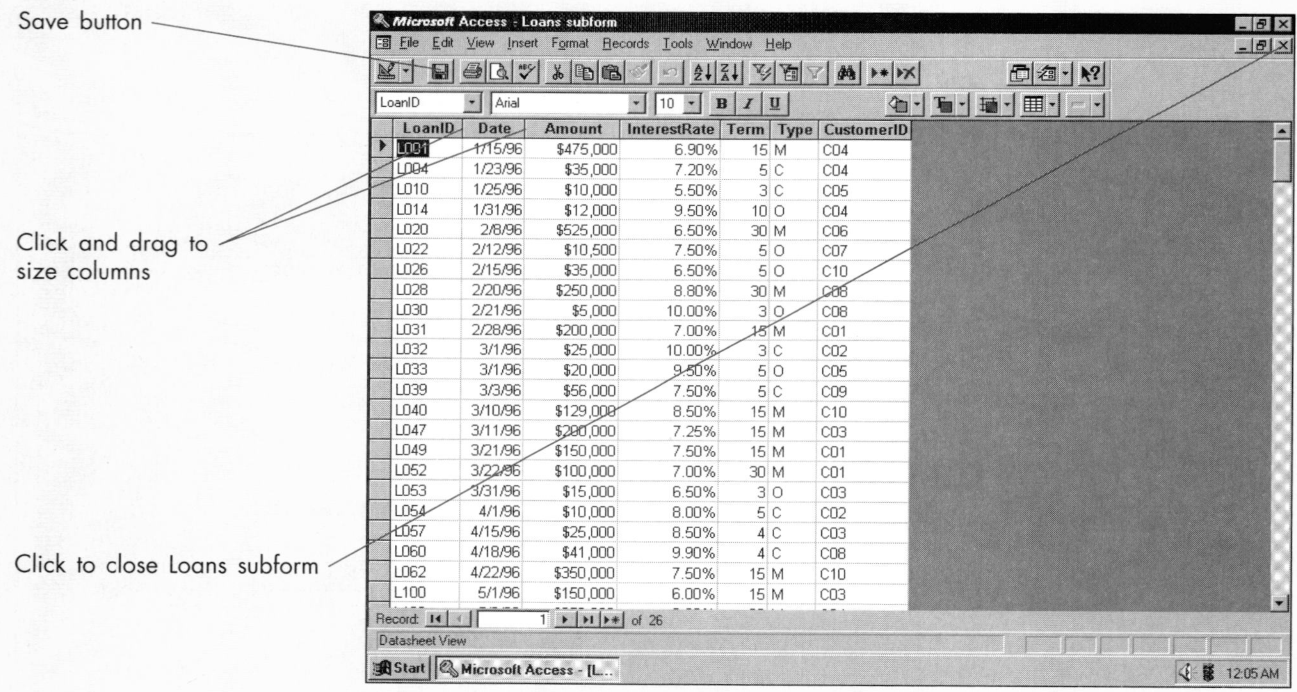

LoanID	Date	Amount	InterestRate	Term	Type	CustomerID
L001	1/15/96	$475,000	6.90%	15	M	C04
L004	1/23/96	$35,000	7.20%	5	C	C04
L010	1/25/96	$10,000	5.50%	3	C	C05
L014	1/31/96	$12,000	9.50%	10	O	C04
L020	2/8/96	$525,000	6.50%	30	M	C06
L022	2/12/96	$10,500	7.50%	5	O	C07
L026	2/15/96	$35,000	6.50%	5	O	C10
L028	2/20/96	$250,000	8.80%	30	M	C08
L030	2/21/96	$5,000	10.00%	3	O	C08
L031	2/28/96	$200,000	7.00%	15	M	C01
L032	3/1/96	$25,000	10.00%	3	C	C02
L033	3/1/96	$20,000	9.50%	5	O	C05
L039	3/3/96	$56,000	7.50%	5	C	C09
L040	3/10/96	$129,000	8.50%	15	M	C10
L047	3/11/96	$200,000	7.25%	15	M	C03
L049	3/21/96	$150,000	7.50%	15	M	C01
L052	3/22/96	$100,000	7.00%	30	M	C01
L053	3/31/96	$15,000	6.50%	3	O	C03
L054	4/1/96	$10,000	8.00%	5	C	C02
L057	4/15/96	$25,000	8.50%	4	C	C03
L060	4/18/96	$41,000	9.90%	4	C	C08
L062	4/22/96	$350,000	7.50%	15	M	C10
L100	5/1/96	$150,000	6.00%	15	M	C03

(e) The Loans Subform in Datasheet View (step 5)

FIGURE 1.7 Hands-on Exercise 2 (continued)

CHANGE THE VIEW

A subform can be displayed in either the Datasheet view or the Form view. To change the default view, open the subform in Design view, point to the Form Selection box in the upper-left corner, click the right mouse button to display a shortcut menu, and click Properties. Click the Default View box, click the drop-drop arrow, select the desired view, and close the Properties dialog box.

STEP 6: View the Customers Form

➤ You are either in the Database window or the Customers form, depending on how you opened the Loans subform. Use the **Window menu** to change to the Customers form (if necessary), then click the **Maximize button** so that the form takes the entire window.

➤ Change to the **Form view** as shown in Figure 1.7f. You may have to return to the Design view of the Customers form to increase the space allotted for the Loans subform. Size and/or move the subform control as necessary, then save the form. You may also have to reopen the Loans subform in the Datasheet view to adjust the column widths.

➤ Note the following:

- The customer information for the first customer (C01) is displayed in the main portion of the form. The loans for that customer are displayed in the subform.

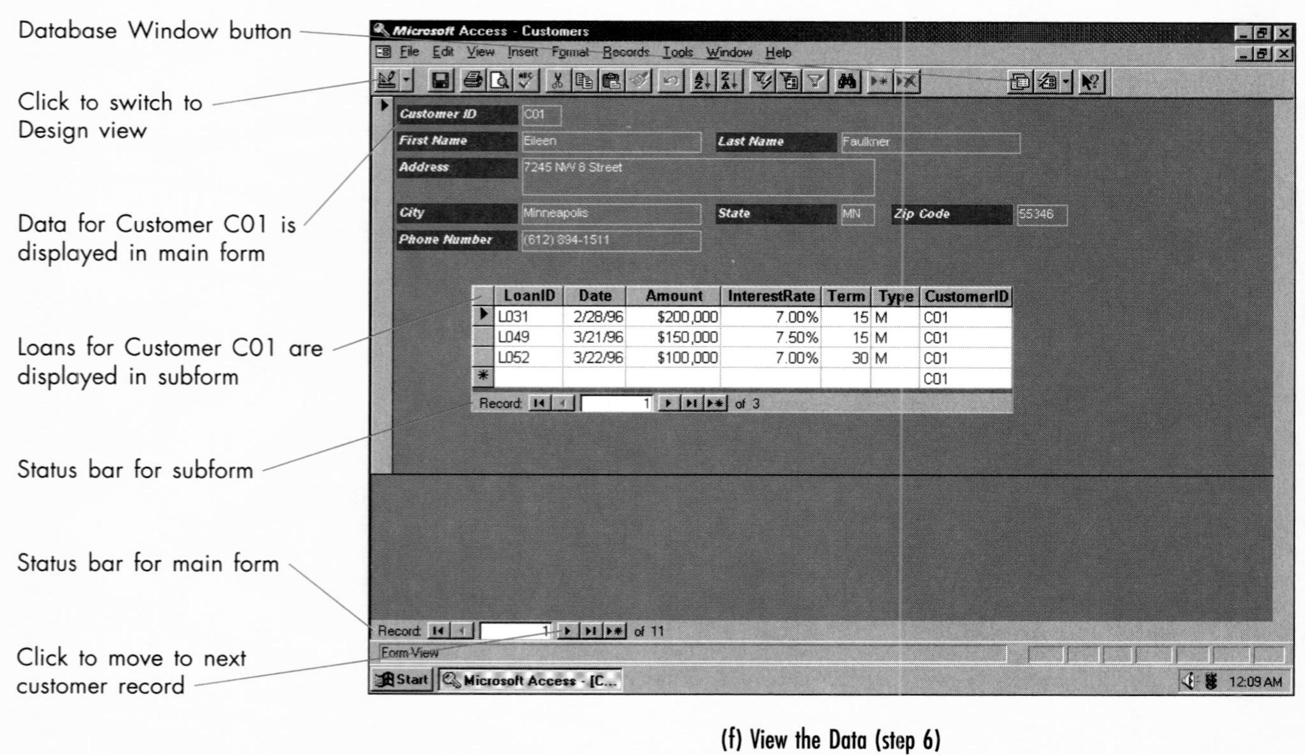

(f) View the Data (step 6)

FIGURE 1.7 Hands-on Exercise 2 (continued)

- The status bar at the bottom of the window (corresponding to the main form) displays record 1 of 11 records (you are looking at the first record in the Customers table).
- The status bar for the subform displays record 1 of 3 records (you are on the first of three loan records for this customer).

➤ Click the ▶ **button** on the status bar for the main form to move to the next customer record. The subform is updated automatically to display the two loans belonging to this customer.

➤ Press the **PgDn key** to move through the customer records until you come to the last record in the Customers table.

WHY IT WORKS

The main form (Customers) and subform (Loans) work in conjunction with one another so that you always see all of the loans for a given customer. The link between the forms is established through a common field as described at the beginning of the chapter. To see how the link is actually implemented, change to the Design view of the Customers form and point anywhere inside the Loans subform. Click the right mouse button to display a shortcut menu, click Properties to display the Subform/Subreport properties dialog box, and if necessary, click the All tab within the dialog box. You should see CustomerID next to two properties (Link Child Fields and Link Master Fields), which define how the main and subforms are linked to one another.

STEP 7: Add the Payment Amount

➤ Click the **Database Window button,** click the **Forms tab,** select the **Loans subform,** then click the **Design button.** The Loans subform is open in the Design view as shown in Figure 1.7g. (The dialog boxes are not yet visible.)

➤ If necessary, maximize the window. Click and drag the right edge of the form to **6½ inches** to make room for a new control and its associated label.

➤ Click the **Label button,** then click and drag in the **Form Header** to create an unbound control. Enter **Payment Due** as the text for the label as shown in Figure 1.7g.

➤ Click the **Textbox button** on the Toolbox toolbar, then click and drag in the **Detail section** to create an unbound control that will contain the amount of the monthly payment. Click the label for the control (e.g., Text 15), then press the **Del key** to delete the label.

➤ Point to the unbound control, click the **right mouse button** to display a shortcut menu, then click **Properties** to open the properties dialog box. Click the **All tab** to view all existing properties.

➤ Click the **Name property.** Enter **Payment Due** in place of the existing label (e.g., Text 15).

➤ Click the **Control Source property,** then click the **Build (...) button** to display the Expression Builder dialog box.

- Double click **Functions** (if there is a plus sign in its button), then click **Built-In Functions.** Click **Financial** in the second column, then double click **Pmt** to enter the Pmt function in the Expression Builder.

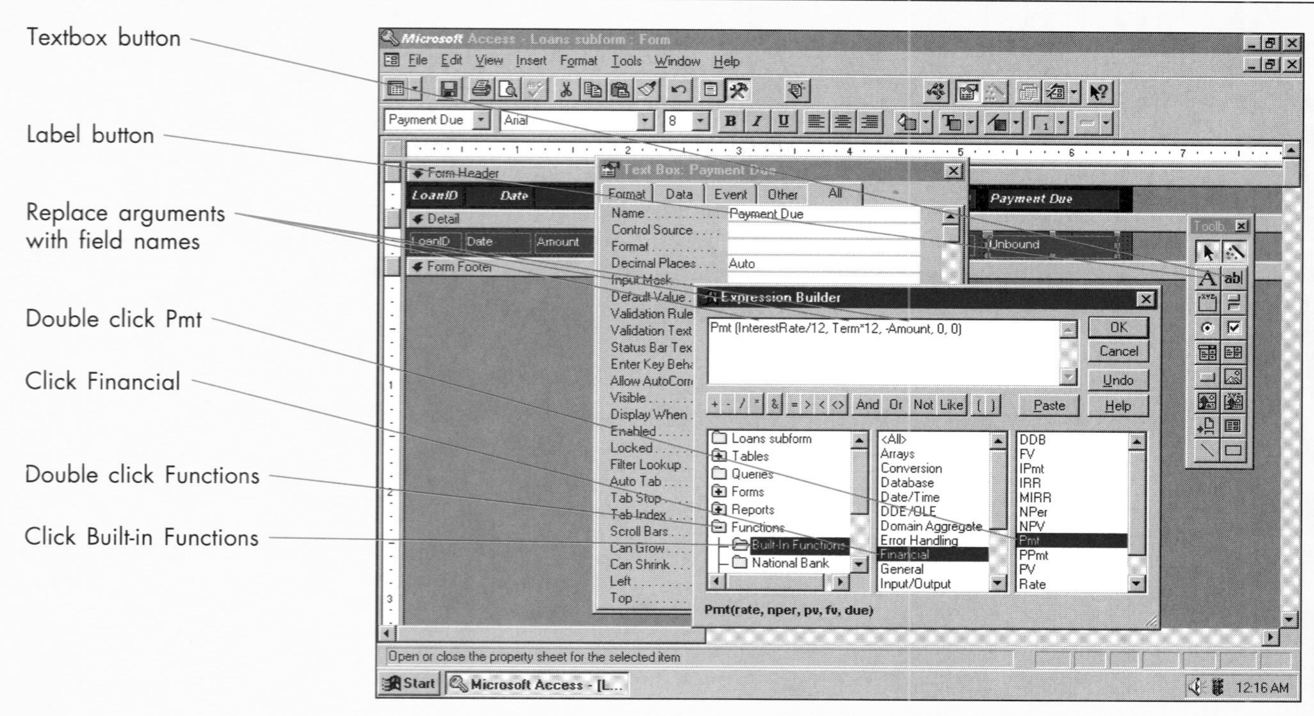

(g) Add the Payment Function (step 7)

FIGURE 1.7 Hands-on Exercise 2 (continued)

- You need to replace each of the arguments in the Pmt function with the appropriate field names from the Loans table. Select the arguments one at a time and enter the replacement for that argument exactly as shown in Figure 1.7g. Click **OK** when finished.

➤ Click the **Format property,** click the **down arrow,** and specify **Currency** (scrolling if necessary). Click the **Decimal Places property,** click the **down arrow,** and select **2.**

➤ Close the Properties dialog box. Change to the Datasheet view and check the column widths, making adjustments as necessary. Close the Loans subform. Click **Yes** to save the changes.

THE ZOOM WINDOW

Trying to enter or edit a long expression directly in the Control Source properties box can be confusing in that you may not be able to see the entire expression. Access anticipates the situation and provides a Zoom window to increase the space in which you can work. Press Shift+F2 to open the Zoom window, enter or edit the expression as necessary, then click OK to accept the changes and close the Zoom window.

STEP 8: Enter a New Loan

- Open the **Customers form** in the Form view as shown in Figure 1.7h. (You may have to return to the Design view of the Customers form to increase the space allotted for the Loans subform. You may also have to reopen the Loans subform to adjust the column widths.)
- Click the ►| on the status bar of the main form to move to the last record (customer C11), which is the record you entered in the previous exercise. (Click the **PgUp key** if you are on a blank record.)
- Click the **LoanID field** next to the asterisk in the subform. The record selector changes to a triangle. Enter data for the new loan as shown in Figure 1.7h:
  - The record selector changes to a pencil as soon as you begin to enter data.
  - The payment due will be computed automatically as soon as you complete the Term field.
  - You do *not* have to enter the CustomerID since it appears automatically due to the relationship between the Customers and Loans tables.
- Press the **down arrow** when you have entered the last field (Type), which saves the data in the current record. (The record selector symbol changes from a pencil to a triangle.)

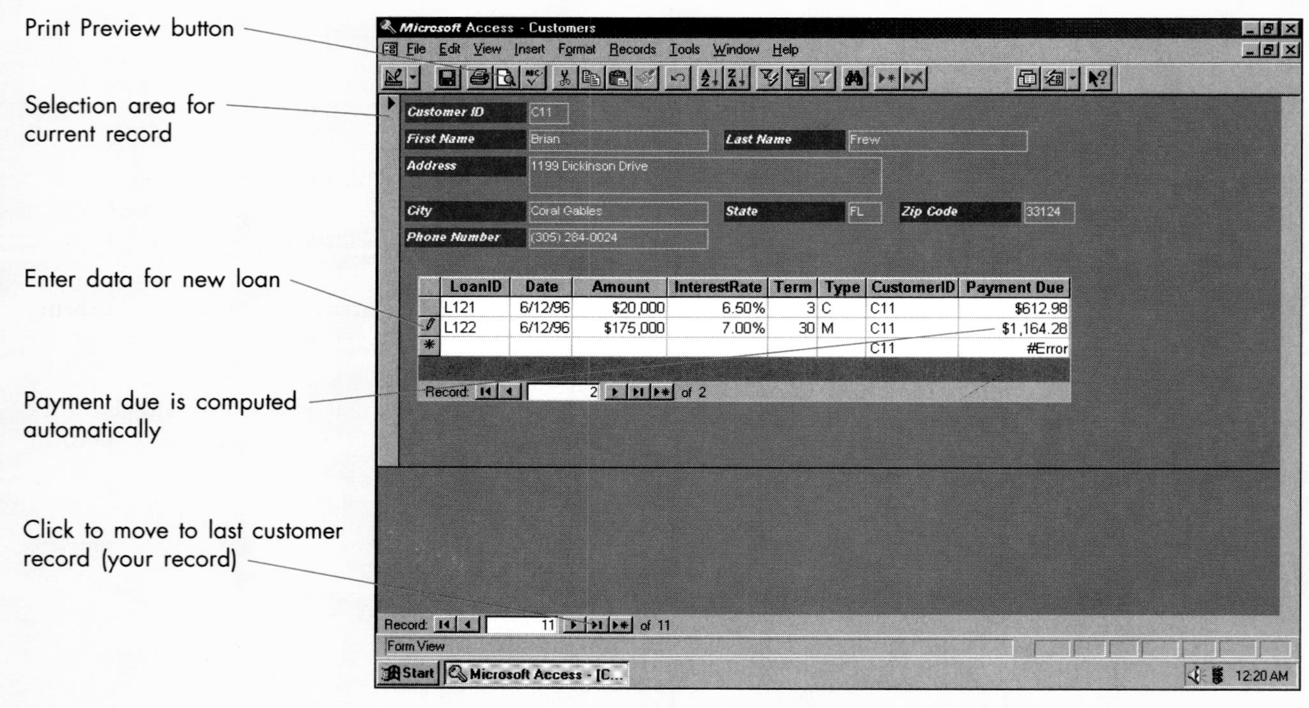

(h) Enter a New Loan (step 8)

FIGURE 1.7 Hands-on Exercise 2 (continued)

#ERROR AND HOW TO AVOID IT

A #Error message will be displayed if the Pmt function is unable to compute a periodic payment—for example, in a new record prior to entering the term of the loan. You can, however, suppress the display of the message by using the IIf (Immediate If) function to test for a null argument. In other words, if the term of the loan has not been entered, do not display anything, otherwise compute the payment in the usual way. This is accomplished by using the IIf function =IIf([Term] Is Null,"",Pmt([InterestRate]/12,[Term]*12,-[Amount],)) as the control source for the payment amount. Use Help for additional information.

STEP 9: Print the Form

- Click the **Print Preview button** to view the form prior to printing to be sure that the form fits on one page. (See boxed tip on the Page Setup command if the form does not fit.) Click the **Close button** to return to the Form view.
- Check that you are still on the record for customer 11 (the record containing your data), then click the **selection area** at the left of the form to select this record.
- Pull down the **File menu** and click **Print** (or click the **Print button**) to display the Print dialog box. Click the **Selected Record(s) option button.** Click **OK** to print the selected form.
- Close the Customers form. Click **Yes** if asked to save the changes to the form.
- Close the National Bank database and exit Access if you do not want to continue with the next hands-on exercise at this time.

THE PAGE SETUP COMMAND

The Page Setup command controls the appearance of the printed page in Access just as it does in other applications. Pull down the File menu and click Page Setup. You can change the orientation from Landscape to Portrait. You can also change the top, bottom, left, and right margins to fit more or less on a page.

MULTIPLE TABLE QUERIES

A relational database consists of multiple tables, each dealing with a specific subject. The related data can be displayed in a main form/subform combination as was done in the preceding exercise. It can also be displayed in a select query that is developed from multiple tables.

The real power of a select query is its ability to include fields from several tables. If, for example, you wanted the name and address of all customers holding a certain type of loan, you would need data from both the Customers table and the Loans table. You would create the select query using the QBE grid in which you display fields from both tables. You would select the customer's name and address fields from the Customers table, and the various loan parameters from the Loans table.

Figure 1.8a shows the Design view of a query to select the 15-year mortgages (the term is 15 and the loan type is "M") issued after April 1, 1996. Figure 1.8b displays the resulting dynaset. You should recognize the QBE grid and the Field, Sort, Show, and Criteria rows from our earlier discussion. The ***Table row*** is new and displays the name of the table containing the field.

In Figure 1.8a the LastName and the FirstName fields are taken from the Customers table. All of the other fields are from the Loans table. The one-to-many relationship between the Customers table and the Loans table is shown graphically within the Query window. The tables are related through the CustomerID field, which is the primary key in the Customers table and a foreign key in the Loans table. The line between the two field lists is called a join line and tells Access how to relate the data in the tables.

Return for a moment to the discussion at the beginning of the chapter, where we asked the name and address of the customer holding loan L010 (Alex Rey at

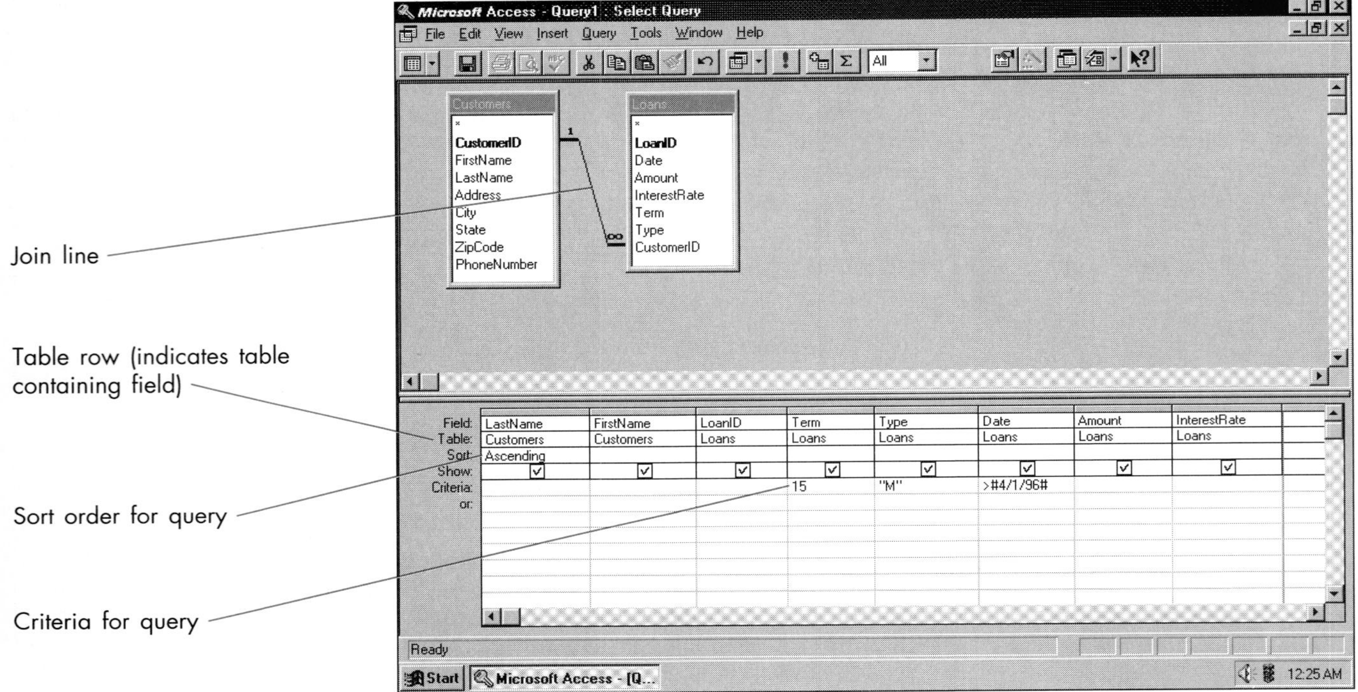

(a) Query Window

Query1 : Select Query

	Last Name	First Name	LoanID	Term	Type	Date	Amount	InterestRate
▶	Grauer	Benjamin	L100	15	M	5/1/96	$150,000	6.00%
	Hirsch	Matt	L062	15	M	4/22/96	$350,000	7.50%
	Sangastiano	Lori	L120	15	M	5/8/96	$275,000	9.20%
*								

Record: 1 of 3

(b) Dynaset

FIGURE 1.8 A Multitable Query

3456 Main Highway). Look at the data in Figure 1.2 at the beginning of the chapter and see how you have to consult both tables to answer the query. You do it intuitively; Access does it using a query containing fields from both tables.

Forms and reports become more interesting and contain more useful information when they are based on multiple table queries. The following exercise has you create a query similar to the one in Figure 1.8, then create a report based on that query.

THE JOIN LINE

Access joins the tables in a query automatically if a relationship exists between the tables. Access will also join the tables (even if no relationship exists) if both tables have a field with the same name and data type, and if one of the fields is a primary key. You can also create the join yourself by dragging a field from one table to the other, but this type of join applies only to the query in which it was created.

HANDS-ON EXERCISE 3

Queries and Reports

Objective: Create a query that relates two tables to one another, then create a report based on that query. Use Figure 1.9 as a guide in the exercise.

STEP 1: Create a Select Query

- Open the **National Bank database** from the previous exercise.
- Click the **Queries tab** in the Database window. Click the **New Command button** to display the New Query dialog box. **Design View** is already selected as the means of creating a query. Click **OK** to begin creating the query.
- The Show Table dialog box appears as shown in Figure 1.9a, with the Tables tab already selected. Click the **Customers table,** then click the **Add button** (or double click the **Customers table**) to add the Customers table to the query (the field list should appear within the Query window).
- Double click the **Loans table** to add the Loans table to the query.
- Click **Close** to close the Show Table dialog box.

ADDING AND DELETING TABLES

To add a table to an existing query, pull down the Query menu, click Show Table, then double click the name of the table from the Table/Query list. To delete a table, click anywhere in its field list and press the Del key, or pull down the Query menu and click Remove Table.

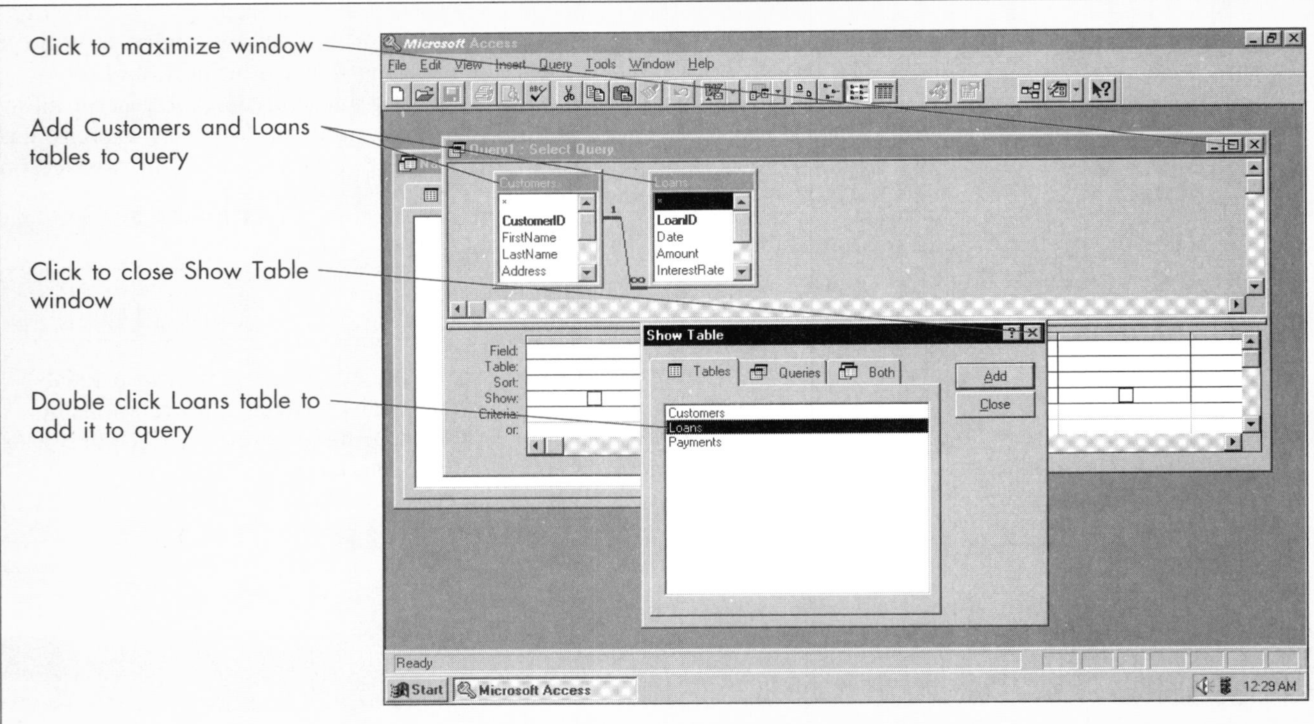

(a) Add the Tables (step 1)

FIGURE 1.9 Hands-on Exercise 3

STEP 2: Move and Size the Field Lists

- Click the **Maximize button** so that the Query Design window takes the entire desktop.
- Point to the line separating the field lists from the QBE grid (the mouse pointer changes to a cross), then click and drag in a downward direction. This gives you more space to display the field lists for the tables in the query as shown in Figure 1.9b.
- Click and drag the bottom of the **Customers table field list** until you can see all of the fields in the Customers table. Click and drag the bottom of the **Loans table field list** until you can see all of the fields in the Loans table.
- Click and drag the title bar of the **Loans table** to the right until you are satisfied with the appearance of the line connecting the tables.

CONVERSION TO STANDARD FORMAT

Access is flexible in accepting text and date expressions in the Criteria row of a select query. A text entry can be entered with or without quotation marks (e.g., M or "M"). A date entry can be entered with or without pound signs (you can enter 1/1/96 or #1/1/96#). Access does, however, convert your entries to standard format as soon you move to the next cell in the QBE grid. Thus, text entries are always displayed in quotation marks, and dates are always enclosed in pound signs.

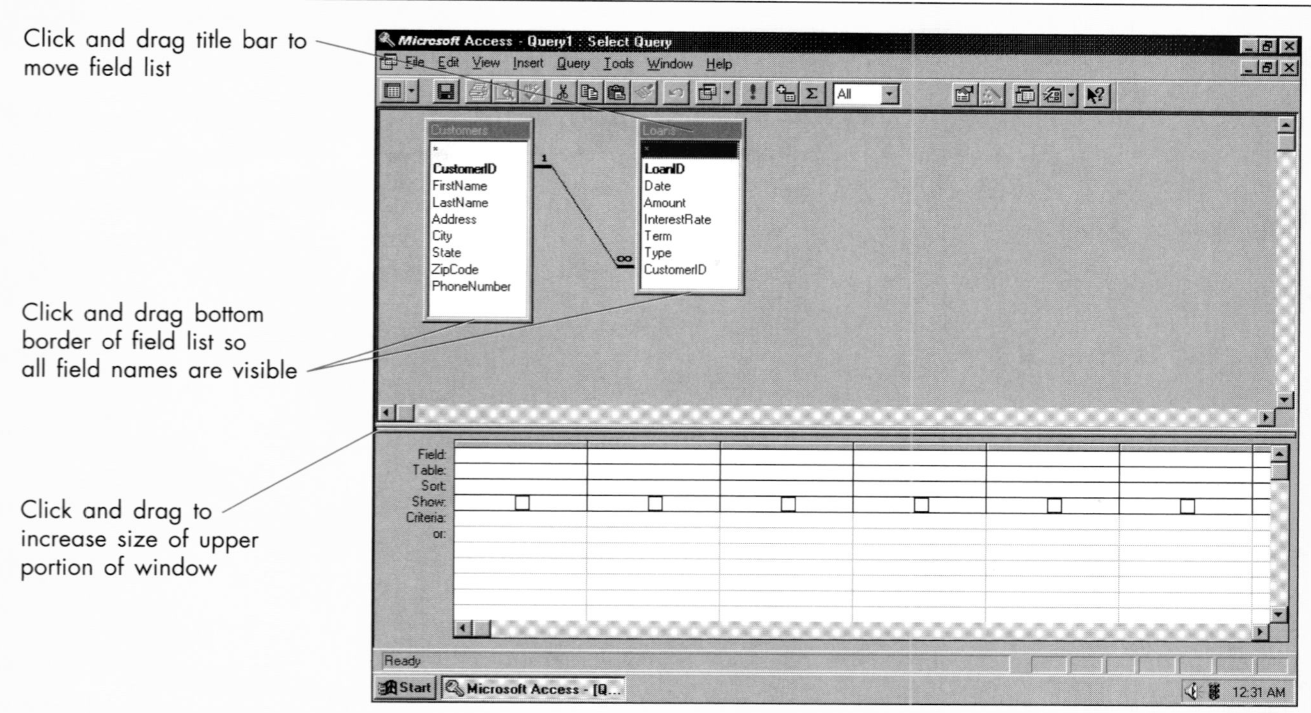

(b) Move and Size the Field Lists (step 2)

FIGURE 1.9 Hands-on Exercise 3 (continued)

STEP 3: Create the Query

- The Table row should be visible within the QBE grid. If not, pull down the **View menu** and click **Table Names** to display the Table row in the QBE grid as shown in Figure 1.9c.
- Double click the **LastName** and **FirstName fields,** in that order, from the Customers table to add these fields to the QBE grid. Double click the **title bar** of the Loans table to select all of the fields, then drag the selected group of fields to the QBE grid.
- Enter the selection criteria (scrolling if necessary) as follows:
  - Click the **Criteria row** under the **Date field.** Type **Between 1/1/96 and 3/31/96.** (You do not have to type the pound signs.)
  - Click the **Criteria row** for the **Amount field.** Type **>200000.**
  - Type **M** in the Criteria row for the **Type field.** (You do not have to type the quotation marks.)
- Select all of the columns in the QBE grid by clicking the column selector in the first column, then pressing and holding the **Shift key** as you scroll to the last column and click its column selector. Double click the right edge of any column selector to adjust the column width of all the columns simultaneously.
- Click the **Sort row** under the LastName field, then click the **down arrow** to open the drop-down list box. Click **Ascending.**
- Click the **Save button** on the Query Design toolbar. Save the query as **First Quarter 1996 Jumbo Loans.**

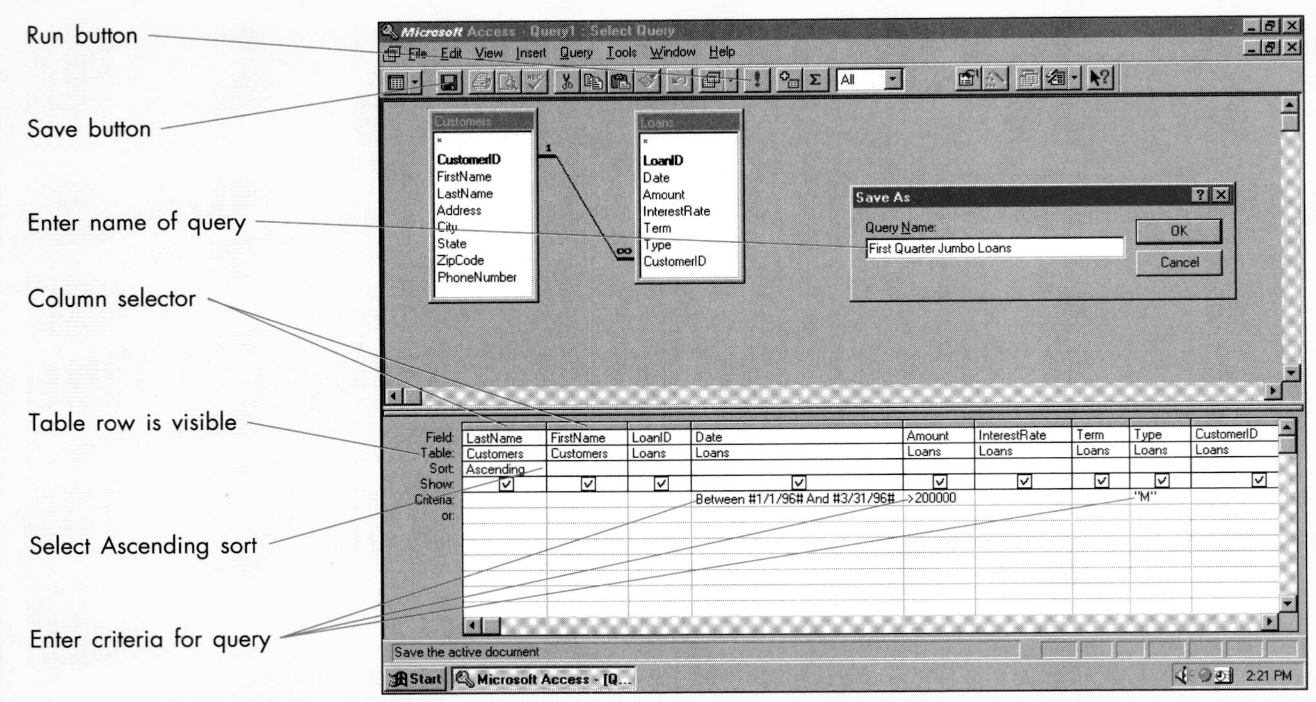

(c) Create the Query (step 3)

FIGURE 1.9 Hands-on Exercise 3 (continued)

SORTING ON MULTIPLE FIELDS

A query can be sorted on more than one field, but you must be certain that the fields are in the proper order within the QBE grid. Access sorts from left to right (the leftmost field is the primary key), so the fields must be arranged in the desired sort sequence. To move a field within the QBE grid, click the column selector above the field name to select the column, then drag the column to its new position.

STEP 4: Run the Query

- Click the **Run button** (the exclamation point) to run the query and create the dynaset in Figure 1.9d. Three jumbo loans are listed.
- Click the **Amount field** for loan L028. Enter **100000** as the corrected amount and press **enter.** (This will reduce the number of jumbo loans in subsequent reports to two.)
- Click the **Close button** to close the query. Click **Yes** if asked whether to save the changes to the query.

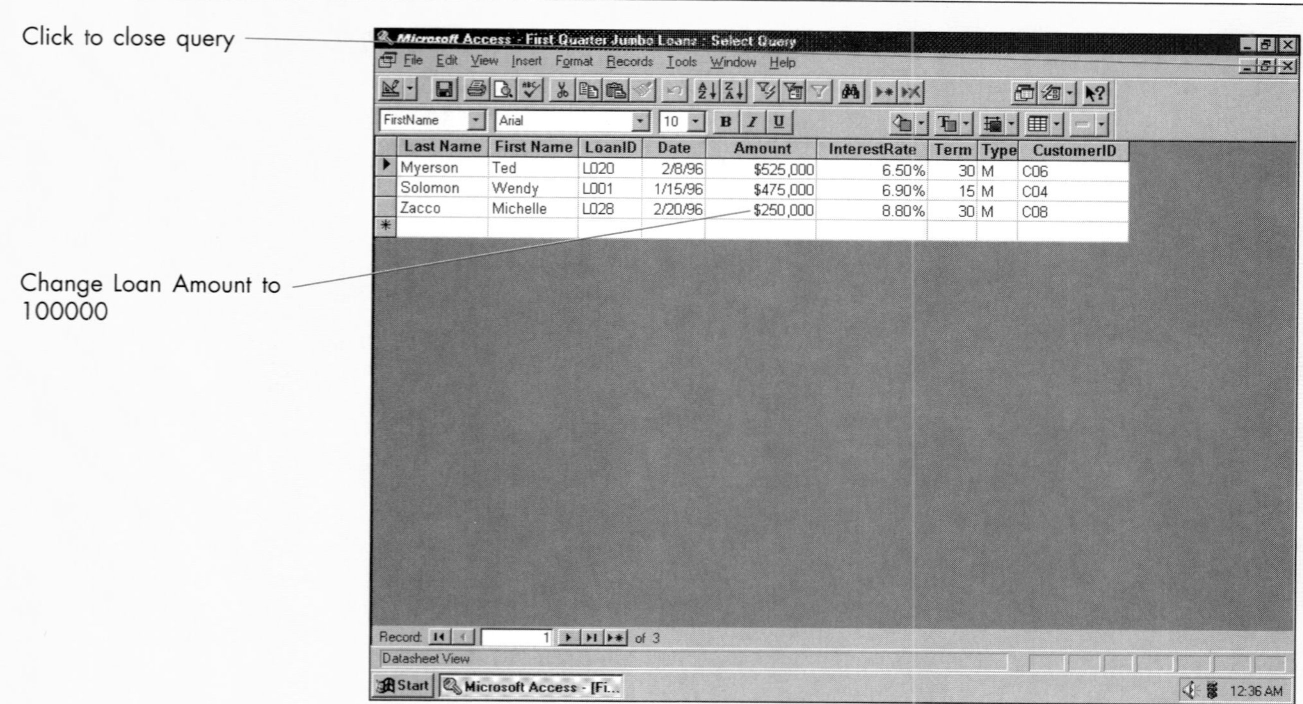

(d) The Dynaset (step 4)

FIGURE 1.9 Hands-on Exercise 3 (continued)

TYPE MISMATCH

The data type determines the way in which criteria appear in the QBE grid. A text field is enclosed in quotation marks. Number, currency, and counter fields are shown as digits with or without a decimal point. Dates are enclosed in pound signs. A Yes/No field is entered as Yes or No without quotation marks. Entering criteria in the wrong form produces a Type Mismatch error when attempting to run the query.

STEP 5: Create a Report

- The National Bank database should be open (although the size of your window may be different from the one in the figure).
- Click the **Reports tab** in the Database window, then click the **New command button** to display the New Report dialog box as shown in Figure 1.9e. Select the **Report Wizard** as the means of creating the report.
- Click the **drop-down arrow** to display the tables and queries in the database in order to select the one on which the report will be based. Select **First Quarter 1996 Jumbo Loans** (the query you just created) as the basis of your report. Click **OK** to start the Report Wizard.

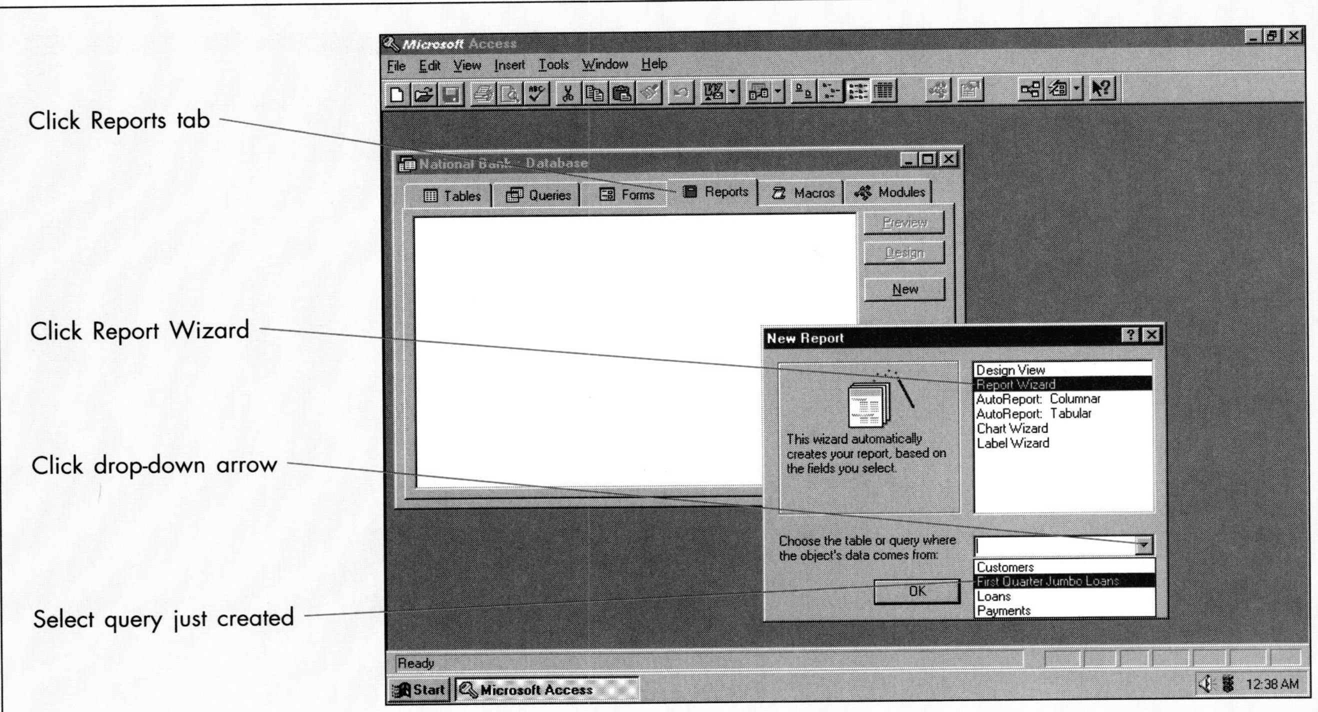

(e) Create a Report (step 5)

FIGURE 1.9 Hands-on Exercise 3 (continued)

REPORTS WITHOUT QUERIES

You can create a report containing fields from multiple tables or queries without having to first create the underlying query. Use the Report Wizard as the basis for your design, and select fields from the first table or query in normal fashion. Click the down arrow in the Table/Query list box, select the next table or query, and enter the appropriate fields. Click the down arrow to select additional tables or queries as necessary, and continue in this fashion until you have selected all of the necessary fields.

STEP 6: The Report Wizard

- Double click **LoanID** from the Available Fields list box to add this field to the report. Add the **LastName, FirstName, Date,** and **Amount** fields as shown in Figure 1.9f. Click **Next.**
- The **by Loans option** is selected as the means of viewing your report. (This means that the report will display the loans in sequence by the LoanID field.) Click **Next.**
- There is no need to group the records. Click **Next.**
- There is no need to sort within a group. Click **Next.**

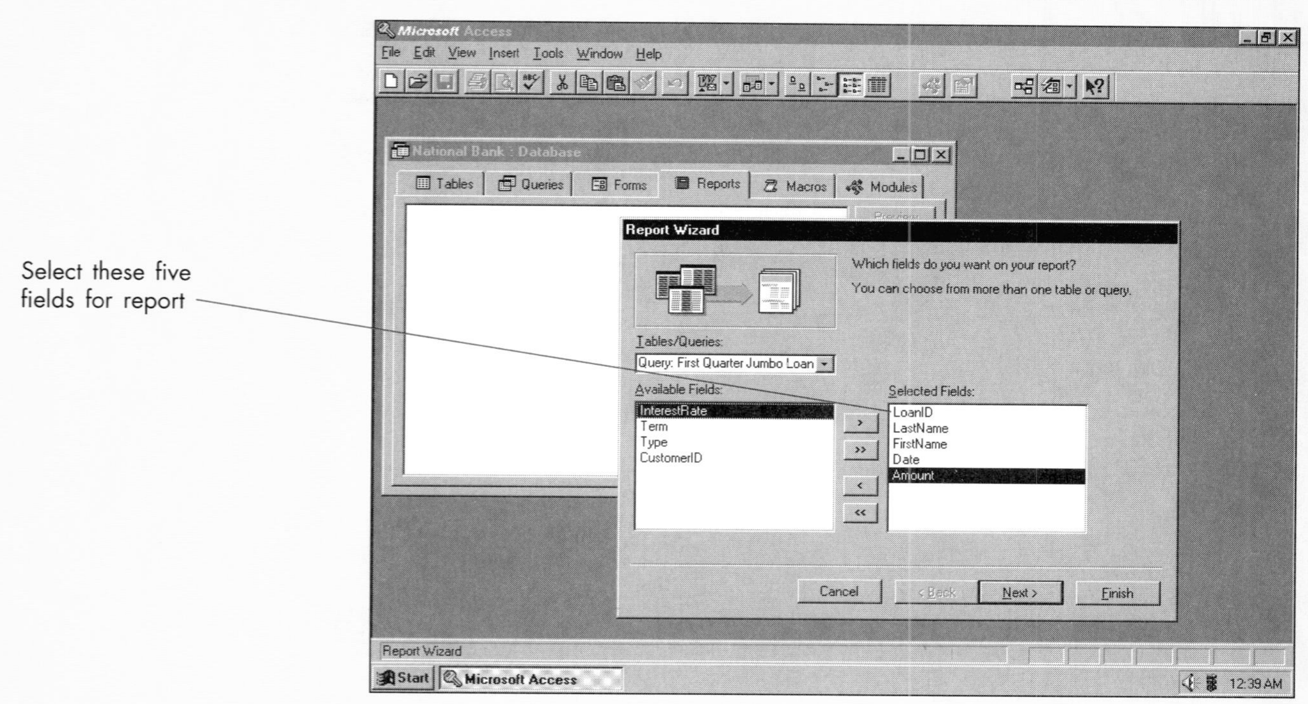

(f) The Report Wizard (step 6)

FIGURE 1.9 Hands-on Exercise 3 (continued)

- The **Tabular layout** is selected, as is **Portrait orientation.** Be sure the box is checked to **Adjust field width so all fields fit on a page.** Click **Next.**
- Choose **Soft Gray** as the style. Click **Next.**
- Enter **First Quarter 1996 Jumbo Loans** as the title for your report. The option button to **Preview the Report** is already selected.
- Click the **Finish Command button** to exit the Report Wizard and preview the report.

STEP 7: Print the Completed Report

- Click the **Maximize button.** If necessary, click the **Zoom button** in the Print Preview window so that you can see the whole report as in Figure 1.9g.
- The report is based on the query created earlier. Michelle Zacco is *not* in the report because the amount of her loan was updated in the query's dynaset in step 4.
- Click the **Print button** to print the report. Close the Preview window, then close the Report window. Click **Yes** if asked to save the changes.
- Close the National Bank database and exit Access if you do not want to continue with the next exercise at this time.

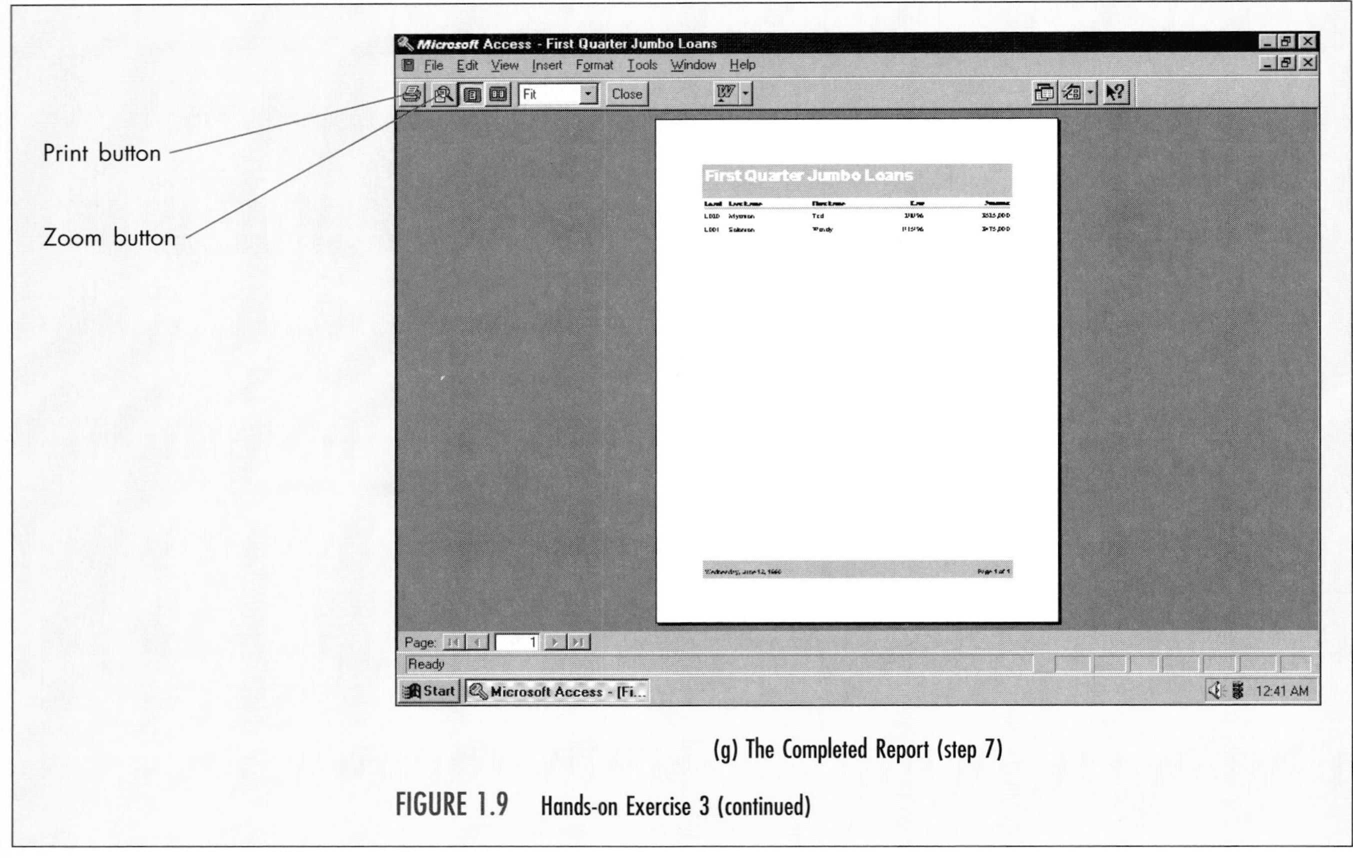

(g) The Completed Report (step 7)

FIGURE 1.9 Hands-on Exercise 3 (continued)

EXPANDING THE DATABASE

One of the advantages of a relational database is that it can be easily expanded to include additional data without disturbing the existing tables. The database used throughout the chapter consisted of two tables: a Customers table and a Loans table. Figure 1.10 extends the database to include a partial listing of the Payments table containing the payments received by the bank. Each record in the Payments table has four fields: LoanID, PaymentNumber, Date (the date the payment was received), and PaymentReceived (the amount sent in).

The original database had a one-to-many relationship between customers and loans. One customer may have many loans, but a given loan is associated with only one customer. The expanded database contains a second one-to-many relationship between loans and payments. One loan has many payments, but a specific payment is associated with only one loan. Thus, the primary key of the Loans table (LoanID) appears as a foreign key in the Payments table.

Look carefully at the Payments table and note that it contains multiple records with the same payment number (e.g., every loan has a payment number 1). In similar fashion, there are multiple records with the same LoanID. Loan L001, for example, has five payments. The combination of LoanID and PaymentNumber is unique, however (there is only one payment 1 for loan L001), and thus the combination of the two fields serves as the primary key in the Payments table.

We began the chapter by showing you hypothetical records in the database and asking you to answer queries based on that data. We end the chapter the same way, by asking you to reference one or more tables in Figure 1.10. As you consider each query, think of how it would appear in the QBE grid.

CustomerID	First Name	Last Name	Address	City	State	Zip Code	Phone Number
C01	Eileen	Faulkner	7245 NW 8 Street	Minneapolis	MN	55346	(612) 894-1511
C02	Scott	Wit	5660 NW 175 Terrace	Baltimore	MD	21224	(410) 753-0345
C03	Benjamin	Grauer	10000 Sample Road	Coral Springs	FL	33073	(305) 444-5555
C04	Wendy	Solomon	7500 Reno Road	Houston	TX	77090	(713) 427-3104
C05	Alex	Rey	3456 Main Highway	Denver	CO	80228	(303) 555-6666
C06	Ted	Myerson	6545 Stone Street	Chapel Hill	NC	27515	(919) 942-7654
C07	Lori	Sangastiano	4533 Aero Drive	Santa Rosa	CA	95403	(707) 542-3411
C08	Michelle	Zacco	488 Gold Street	Gainesville	FL	32601	(904) 374-5660
C09	David	Powell	5070 Battle Road	Decatur	GA	30034	(301) 345-6556
C10	Matt	Hirsch	777 NW 67 Avenue	Fort Lee	NJ	07624	(201) 664-3211

(a) Customers Table

LoanID	Date	Amount	Interest Rate	Term	Type	CustomerID
L001	1/15/96	$475,000	6.90%	15	M	C04
L004	1/23/96	$35,000	7.20%	5	C	C04
L010	1/25/96	$10,000	5.50%	3	C	C05
L014	1/31/96	$12,000	9.50%	10	O	C04
L020	2/8/96	$525,000	6.50%	30	M	C06
L022	2/12/96	$10,500	7.50%	5	O	C07
L026	2/15/96	$35,000	6.50%	5	O	C10
L028	2/20/96	$250,000	8.80%	30	M	C08
L030	2/21/96	$5,000	10.00%	3	O	C08
L031	2/28/96	$200,000	7.00%	15	M	C01
L032	3/1/96	$25,000	10.00%	3	C	C02
L033	3/1/96	$20,000	9.50%	5	O	C05
L039	3/3/96	$56,000	7.50%	5	C	C09
L040	3/10/96	$129,000	8.50%	15	M	C10
L047	3/11/96	$200,000	7.25%	15	M	C03
L049	3/21/96	$150,000	7.50%	15	M	C01
L052	3/22/96	$100,000	7.00%	30	M	C01
L053	3/31/96	$15,000	6.50%	3	O	C03
L054	4/1/96	$10,000	8.00%	5	C	C02
L057	4/15/96	$25,000	8.50%	4	C	C03
L060	4/18/96	$41,000	9.90%	4	C	C08
L062	4/22/96	$350,000	7.50%	15	M	C10
L100	5/1/96	$150,000	6.00%	15	M	C03
L109	5/3/96	$350,000	8.20%	30	M	C04
L120	5/8/96	$275,000	9.20%	15	M	C07

(b) Loans Table

LoanID	Payment Number	Date	Payment Received
L001	1	2/15/96	$4,242.92
L001	2	3/15/96	$4,242.92
L001	3	4/15/96	$4,242.92
L001	4	5/15/96	$4,242.92
L001	5	6/15/96	$4,242.92
L004	1	2/23/96	$696.35
L004	2	3/23/96	$696.35
L004	3	4/23/96	$696.35
L004	4	5/23/96	$696.35
L004	5	6/23/96	$696.35
L010	1	2/25/96	$301.96
L010	2	3/25/96	$301.96
L010	3	4/25/96	$301.96
L010	4	5/25/96	$301.96
L010	5	6/25/96	$301.96
L014	1	2/28/96	$155.28
L014	2	3/31/96	$155.28
L014	3	4/30/96	$155.28
L014	4	5/30/96	$155.28
L014	5	6/30/96	$155.28
L020	1	3/8/96	$3,318.36
L020	2	4/8/96	$3,318.36
L020	3	5/8/96	$3,318.36
L020	4	6/8/96	$3,318.36
L022	1	3/12/96	$210.40
L022	2	4/12/96	$210.40
L022	3	5/12/96	$210.40
L022	4	6/12/96	$210.40
L026	1	3/15/96	$684.82
L026	2	4/15/96	$684.82
L026	3	5/15/96	$684.82
L026	4	6/15/96	$684.82
L028	1	3/20/96	$1,975.69
L028	2	4/20/96	$1,975.69
L028	3	5/20/96	$1,975.69
L028	4	6/20/96	$1,975.69
L030	1	3/21/96	$161.34
L030	2	4/21/96	$161.34
L030	3	5/21/96	$161.34
L030	4	6/21/96	$161.34

(c) Payments Table (partial list)

FIGURE 1.10 Expanding the Database

Query: How many payments have been received for loan L022? What was the date of the most recent payment?
Answer: Four payments have been received for loan L022. The most recent payment was received on 6/12/96.

The query can be answered with reference to just the Payments table by finding all payments for loan L022. To determine the most recent payment, you would retrieve the records in descending order by Date and retrieve the first record.

Query: How many payments have been received from Michelle Zacco since May 1, 1996?
Answer: Four payments have been received. Two of the payments were for loan L028 on May 20th and June 20th. Two were for loan L030 on May 21st and June 21st.

To answer this query, you would look in the Customers table to determine the CustomerID for Ms. Zacco, search the Loans table for all loans for this customer, then retrieve the corresponding payments (those made after May 1) from the Payments table. (Michelle is also associated with loan L060. The Payments table, however, is truncated in Figure 1.10, and hence the payments for this loan are not visible.) The exercises at the end of the chapter ask you to create queries such as these, then use those queries as the basis of a form or a report.

Multiple Subforms

Subforms were introduced earlier in the chapter as a means of displaying data from related tables. Figure 1.11 continues the discussion by showing a main form with two levels of subforms. The main (Customers) form has a one-to-many relationship with the first (Loans) subform. The Loans subform in turn has a one-to-many relationship with the second (Payments) subform. The Customers form and the Loans subform are the forms you created in the second hands-on exercise. (The Loans subform is opened in the Form view as opposed to the Data sheet view.) The Payments subform is new and will be developed in our next exercise.

The records displayed in the three forms are linked to one another according to the relationships within the database. There is a one-to-many relationship between customers and loans so that the first subform displays all of the loans for one customer. There is also a one-to-many relationship between loans and payments so that the second subform (Payments) displays all of the payments for the selected loan. Click on a different loan (for the same customer), and the Payments subform is updated automatically to show all of the payments for that loan.

The status bar for the main form indicates record 5 of 11, meaning that you are viewing the fifth of 11 Customer records. The status bar for the Loans subform indicates record 2 of 2, corresponding to the second of two loan records for the fifth customer. The status bar for the Payments subform indicates record 1 of 3, corresponding to the first of three Payment records for this loan and customer.

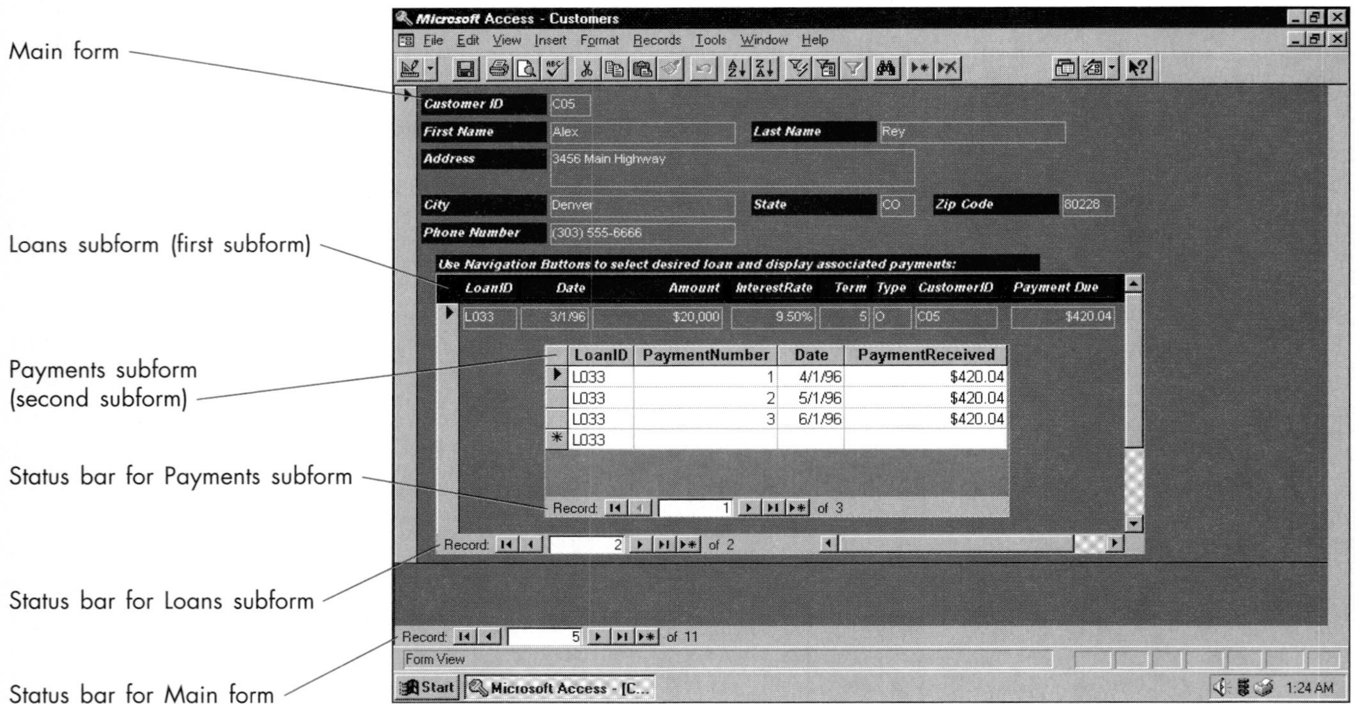

FIGURE 1.11 Multiple Subforms

The three sets of navigation buttons enable you to advance to the next record(s) in any of the forms. The records move in conjunction with one another. Thus, if you advance to the next record in the Customers form you will automatically display a different set of records in the Loans subform, as well as a different set of Payment records in the Payments subform.

HANDS-ON EXERCISE 4

Linked Subforms

Objective: To create a main form with two levels of subforms; to display a subform in Form view or Datasheet view. Use Figure 1.12 as a guide.

STEP 1: Add a Relationship

- Open the **National Bank database.** Pull down the **Tools menu.** Click **Relationships** to open the Relationships window as shown in Figure 1.12a. Maximize the Relationships window.
- Pull down the **Relationships menu.** Click **Show Table** to display the Show Table dialog box.

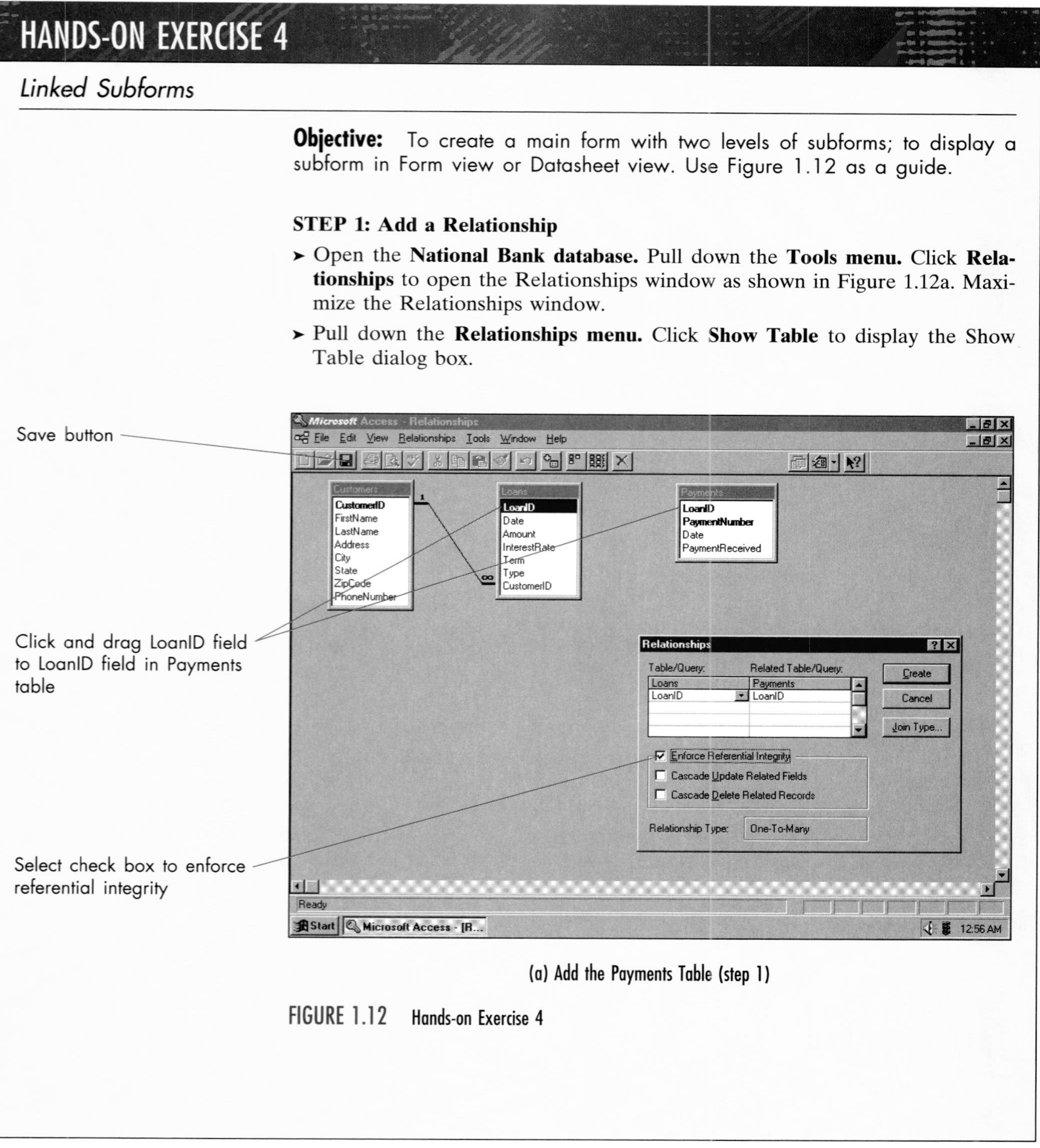

(a) Add the Payments Table (step 1)

FIGURE 1.12 Hands-on Exercise 4

- The **Tables tab** is selected within the Show Table dialog box. Double click the **Payments table** to add the table to the Relationships window. Close the Show Table dialog box.
- Click and drag the title bar of the **Payments Field list** so that it is positioned approximately one inch from the Loans table.
- Click and drag the **LoanID field** in the Loans field list to the **LoanID field** in the Payments field list. You will see the Relationships dialog box.
- Check the **Enforce Referential Integrity** check box. (If necessary, clear the check boxes to Cascade Update Related Fields and Delete Related Records.)
- Click the **Create Command button** to establish the relationship. You should see a line indicating a one-to-many relationship between the Loans and Payments tables.
- Click the **Save button** to save the Relationships window, then close the Relationships window.

A CONCATENATED PRIMARY KEY

The primary key is defined as the field, or combination of fields, that is unique for every record in a table. The Payments table contains multiple records with the same payment number (i.e., every loan has a payment number 1, 2, 3, and so on) as well as multiple payments for the same LoanID. The combination of LoanID and PaymentNumber is unique, however, and serves as the primary key for the Payments table.

STEP 2: Create the Payments Subform

- You should be back in the Database window. Click the **Forms tab,** then open the **Loans subform** (from the second exercise) in Design view as shown in Figure 1.12b. If necessary, maximize the Form Design window.
- Click and drag the bottom edge of the **Details section** so that you have approximately 2 to 2½ inches of blank space in the Detail section. (This is where the Payments subform will go.)
- Click the **Subform/Subreport button** on the Toolbox toolbar, then click and drag in the Loans form to create the Payments subform. Release the mouse to begin the Subform/Subreport Wizard.
- The **Table/Query Option button** is selected, indicating that we will build the subform from a table or query. Click **Next.** You should see the Subform/Subreport dialog box in Figure 1.12b.
- Click the **drop-down arrow** on the Tables and Queries list box to select the **Payments table.** Click the **>> button** to add all of the fields in the Payments table to the subform. Click **Next.**
- The Subform Wizard asks you to define the fields that link the main form to the subform. The option button to **Choose from a list** is selected, as is **Show Payments for each record in <SQL Statement> using LoanID.** Click **Next.**
- The Wizard suggests **Payments Subform** as the name of the subform. Click **Finish** to exit the Subform/Subreport wizard.

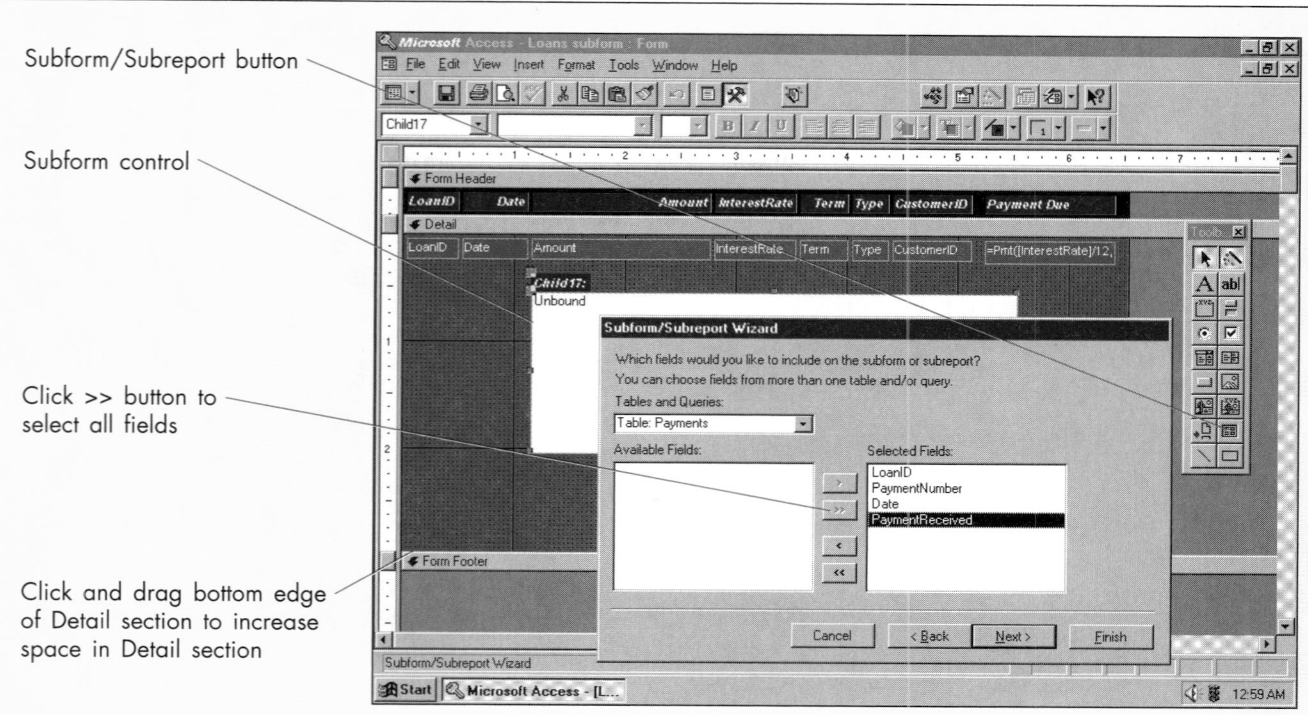

(b) Create the Payments Subform (step 2)

FIGURE 1.12 Hands-on Exercise 4 (continued)

LINKING FIELDS, FORMS, AND SUBFORMS

Linking fields do not have to appear in the main form and subform but must be included in the underlying table or query. The LoanID, for example, is used to link the Loans form and the Payments form and need not appear in either form. We have, however, chosen to display the LoanID in both forms to emphasize the relationship between the corresponding tables.

STEP 3: Change the Default View

- Maximize the window. Point to the **Form Selector box** in the upper-left corner of the Design window, click the **right mouse button** to display a shortcut menu, and click **Properties** to display the Form Properties dialog box in Figure 1.12c.
- Click in the **Default View box,** click the **drop-down arrow** to display the views, then click **Single Form.** Close the Properties dialog box.
- Select the label for the Payments subform control, then press the **Del key** to delete the label. Save the form.

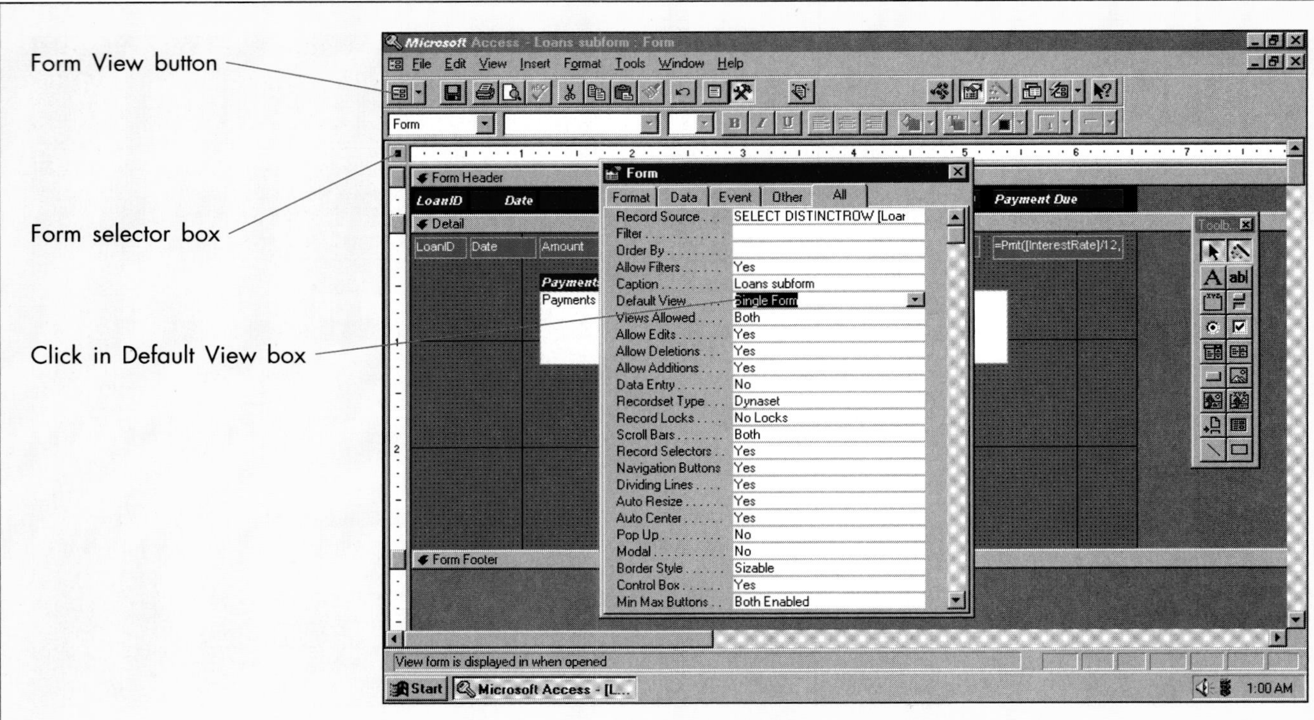

(c) Change the Loans Subform View (step 3)

FIGURE 1.12 Hands-on Exercise 4 (continued)

STEP 4: The Loans Subform in Form View

- Click the **Form View button** to switch to the Form view for the Loans subform as shown in Figure 1.12d.
- Do not be concerned if the size and/or position of your form is different from ours as you can return to the Design view in order to make the necessary changes.
  - The status bar of the Loans form indicates record 1 of 27, meaning that you are positioned on the first of 27 records in the Loans table.
  - The status bar for the Payments subform indicates record 1 of 5, corresponding to the first of five payment records for this loan.
- Change to the **Design view** to adjust the column widths within the Payments subform. This is accomplished by opening the subform in the Datasheet view (see boxed tip on page 41 on modifying a subform) and adjusting the column headings.
- You will most likely have to size and/or move the Payments subform control within the Loans subform. Click and drag the subform control as necessary.
- Save, then close, the Loans subform.

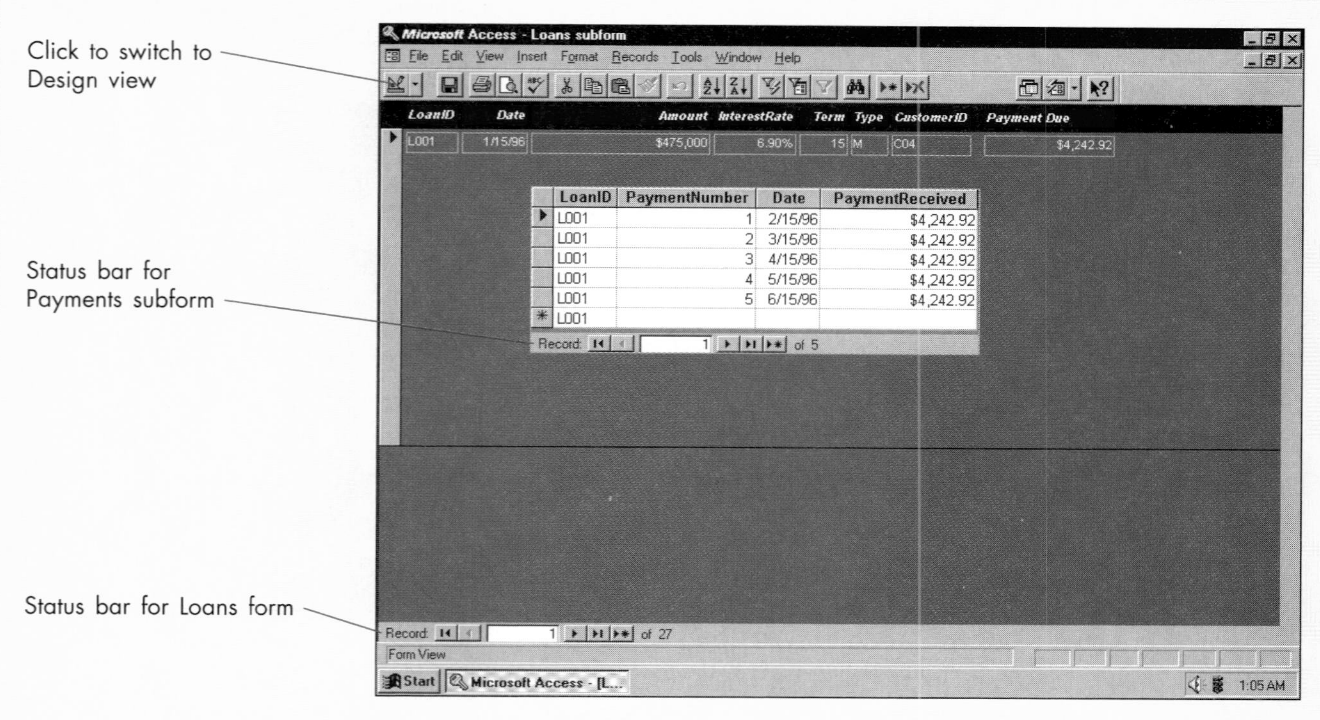

(d) The Form View (step 4)

FIGURE 1.12 Hands-on Exercise 4 (continued)

STEP 5: The Customers Form

- You should be back in the Database window. Click the **Forms tab** (if necessary), then open the **Customers form** as shown in Figure 1.12e. Do not be concerned if the size of the Loans or Payments subforms are different from ours as you can return to the Design view to make the necessary changes.
  - The status bar of the Customers form indicates record 1 of 11, meaning that you are positioned on the first of 11 records in the Customers table.
  - The status bar for the Loans subform indicates record 1 of 3, corresponding to the first of three records for this customer.
  - The status bar for the Payments subform indicates record 1 of 4, corresponding to the first of four payments for this loan.
- Change to the **Design view** to move and/or size the control for the Loans subform. You may also need to open the subform in the Datasheet view to adjust the column widths.

MODIFYING A SUBFORM

The Payment subform appears as an object in the Design view of the Loans form, but it can be opened and modified as an independent form. To open a subform, click outside the subform to deselect it, then double click the subform to open it.

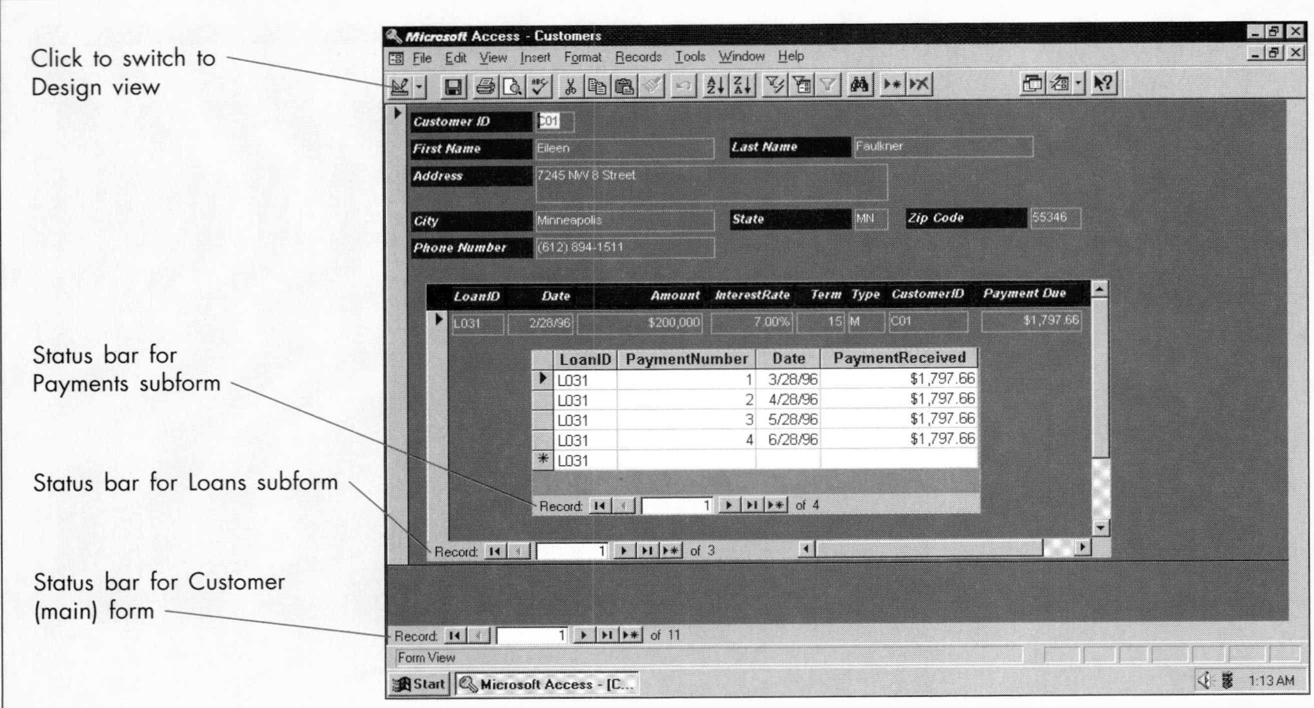

(e) The Customers Form (step 5)

FIGURE 1.12 Hands-on Exercise 4 (continued)

STEP 6: The Finishing Touches

- Point to the **Label tool,** then click and drag in the **Customers form** to create an unbound control as shown in Figure 1.12f.
- Release the mouse, then enter **Use navigation buttons to select desired loan and display associated payments.** Click outside the control when you have completed the text.
- Click the **Save button** to save the Customers form, which contains the two subforms.

USER-FRIENDLY FORMS

The phrase "user friendly" appears so frequently that we tend to take it for granted. The intention is clear, however, and you should strive to make your forms as clear as possible so that the user is provided with all the information he or she may need. It may be obvious to the designer that one has to click the Navigation buttons to move to a new loan, but a user unfamiliar with Access may not know that. Adding a descriptive label to the form goes a long way toward making the system successful.

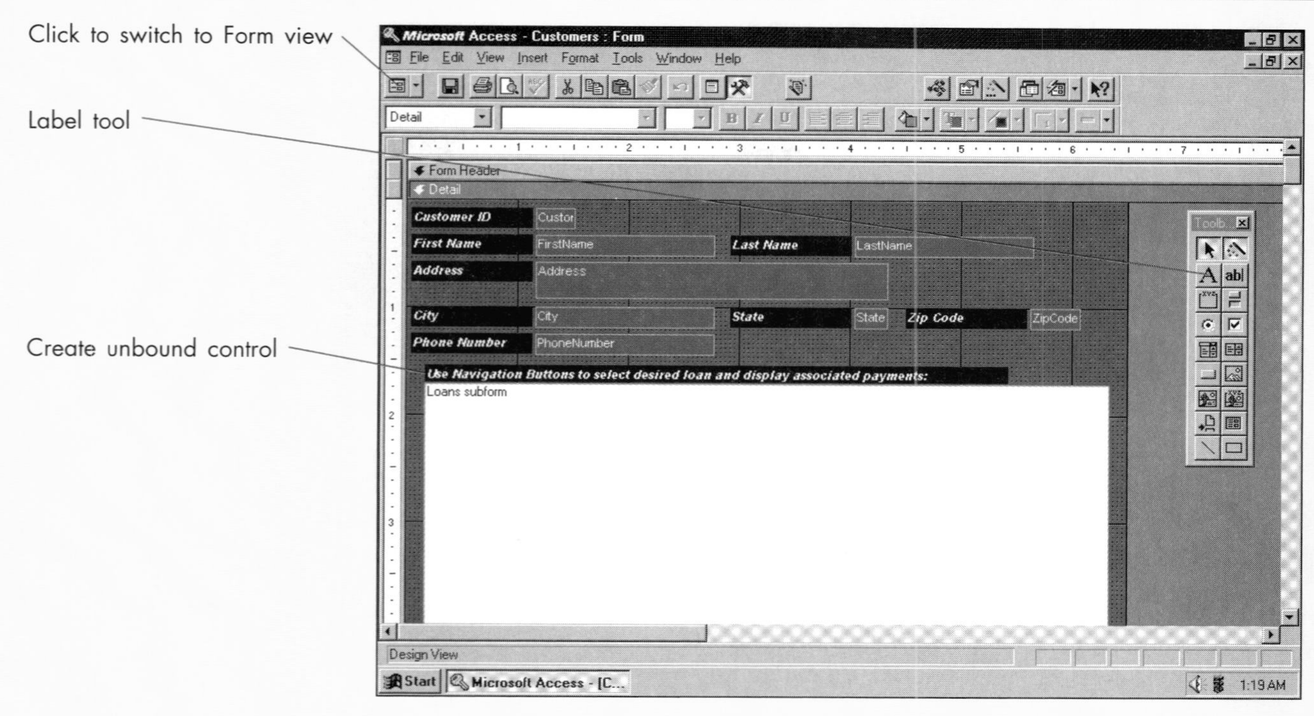

(f) The Finishing Touches (step 6)

FIGURE 1.12 Hands-on Exercise 4 (continued)

STEP 7: Make Your Payments

- Change to the **Form view.** Click the ▶| on the status bar for the Customers form to move to the last record as shown in Figure 1.12g. This should be Customer C11 (your record) that you entered in the earlier exercises in this chapter. You currently have two loans, L121 and L122, the first of which is displayed.
- Click in the **Payments subform.** Enter the payment number, press **Tab,** enter the date of your first payment, press **Tab,** then enter the amount paid. Press **enter** to move to the next payment record and enter this payment as well. Press **enter** and enter a third payment.
- Click the **selection area** at the left of the form to select this record. Pull down the **File menu** and click **Print** (or click the **Print button**) to display the Print dialog box. Click the **Selected Records Option button.** Click **OK** to print the selected form.
- Close the Customers form. Click **Yes** if asked to save the changes to the form.
- Close the National Bank database and exit Access.

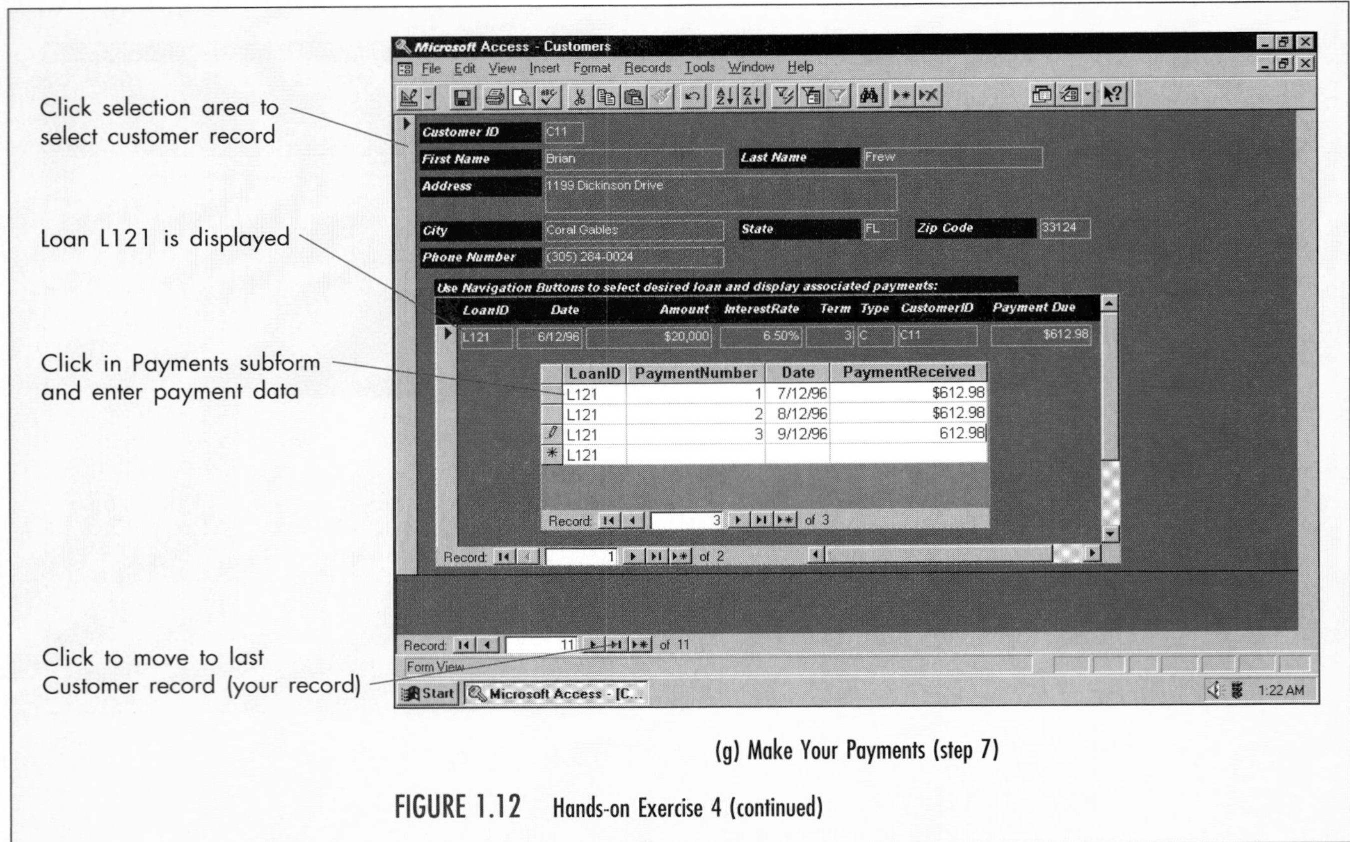

(g) Make Your Payments (step 7)

FIGURE 1.12 Hands-on Exercise 4 (continued)

SUMMARY

An Access database may contain multiple tables. Each table stores data about a specific subject. Each table has a primary key, which is a field (or combination of fields) that uniquely identifies each record.

A one-to-many relationship uses the primary key of the "one" table as a foreign key in the "many" table. (A foreign key is simply the primary key of another table.) The Relationships window enables you to graphically create a one-to-many relationship by dragging the join field from one table to the other.

Referential integrity ensures that the tables in a database are consistent with one another. When referential integrity is enforced, Access prevents you from adding records to a related table when there is no associated record in the primary table. It also prevents you from deleting a record in the primary table if there is a corresponding record in the related table.

A subform is a form within a form and is used to display data from a related table. It is created most easily with the Form Wizard, then modified in the Form Design view just as any other form. A main form can have any number of subforms. Subforms can extend to two levels, enabling a subform to be created within a subform.

The power of a select query lies in its ability to include fields from several tables. The query shows the relationships that exist between the tables by drawing a join line that indicates how to relate the data. The Tables row displays the name of the table containing the corresponding field. Once created, a multiple table query can be the basis for a form or report.

Tables can be added to a relational database without disturbing the data in existing tables. A database can have several one-to-many relationships.

KEY WORDS AND CONCEPTS

Build button
Control Source property
Datasheet view
Foreign key
Form view
Function
Join line
Main form
One-to-many relationship
Primary key
Primary table
Referential integrity
Related table
Relationships window
Subform
Subform Wizard
Table row

MULTIPLE CHOICE

1. Which of the following will cause a problem of referential integrity when there is a one-to-many relationship between customers and loans?
   (a) The deletion of a customer record that has corresponding loan records
   (b) The deletion of a customer record that has no corresponding loan records
   (c) The deletion of a loan record with a corresponding customer record
   (d) All of the above

2. Which of the following will cause a problem of referential integrity when there is a one-to-many relationship between customers and loans?
   (a) The addition of a new customer prior to entering loans for that customer
   (b) The addition of a new loan without a corresponding customer record
   (c) Both (a) and (b)
   (d) Neither (a) nor (b)

3. Which of the following is true about a database that monitors players and the teams to which those players are assigned?
   (a) The PlayerID will be defined as a primary key within the Teams table
   (b) The TeamID will be defined as a primary key within the Players table
   (c) The PlayerID will appear as a foreign key within the Teams table
   (d) The TeamID will appear as a foreign key within the Players table

4. Which of the following best expresses the relationships within the expanded National Bank database as it appeared at the end of the chapter?
   (a) There is a one-to-many relationship between customers and loans
   (b) There is a one-to-many relationship between loans and payments
   (c) Both (a) and (b)
   (d) Neither (a) nor (b)

5. A database has a one-to-many relationship between branches and employees (one branch can have many employees). Which of the following is true?
   (a) The EmployeeID will be defined as a primary key within the Branches table
   (b) The BranchID will be defined as a primary key within the Employees table
   (c) The EmployeeID will appear as a foreign key within the Branches table
   (d) The BranchID will appear as a foreign key within the Employees table

6. Every table in an Access database:
   (a) Must be related to every other table
   (b) Must have one or more foreign keys
   (c) Both (a) and (b)
   (d) Neither (a) nor (b)

7. Which of the following is true of a main form and subform that are created in conjunction with the one-to-many relationship between customers and loans?
   (a) The main form should be based on the Customers table
   (b) The subform should be based on the Loans table
   (c) Both (a) and (b)
   (d) Neither (a) nor (b)

8. Which of the following is true regarding the navigation buttons for a main form and its associated subform?
   (a) The navigation buttons pertain to just the main form
   (b) The navigation buttons pertain to just the subform
   (c) There are separate navigation buttons for each form
   (d) There are no navigation buttons at all

9. How do you open a subform?
   (a) Go to the Design view of the associated main form, click anywhere in the main form to deselect the subform, then double click the subform
   (b) Go to the Database window, select the subform, then click the Open or Design buttons, depending on the desired view
   (c) Both (a) and (b)
   (d) Neither (a) nor (b)

10. Which of the following is true?
    (a) A main form may contain multiple subforms
    (b) A subform may contain another subform
    (c) Both (a) and (b)
    (d) Neither (a) nor (b)

11. Which command displays the open tables in an Access database in equal-sized windows one on top of another?
    (a) The Tile command in the Window menu
    (b) The Cascade command in the Window menu
    (c) The Tile command in the Relationships menu
    (d) The Cascade command in the Relationships menu

12. Which of the following describes how to move and size a field list within the Relationships window?
    (a) Click and drag the title bar to size the field list
    (b) Click and drag a border or corner to move the field list
    (c) Both (a) and (b)
    (d) Neither (a) nor (b)

13. Which of the following is true regarding entries in a Criteria row of a select query?
    (a) A text field may be entered with or without quotation marks
    (b) A date field may be entered with or without surrounding number (pound) signs
    (c) Both (a) and (b)
    (d) Neither (a) nor (b)

14. Which of the following is true about a select query?
    (a) It may reference fields in one or more tables
    (b) It may have one or more criteria rows
    (c) It may sort on one or more fields
    (d) All of the above

15. A report may be based on:
    (a) A table
    (b) A query
    (c) Both (a) and (b)
    (d) Neither (a) nor (b)

ANSWERS

1. a	**6.** d	**11.** b
2. b	**7.** c	**12.** d
3. d	**8.** c	**13.** c
4. c	**9.** c	**14.** d
5. d	**10.** c	**15.** c

EXPLORING MICROSOFT ACCESS 7.0

1. Use Figure 1.13 to match each action with its result. A given action may be used more than once or not at all.

Action		Result
a. Click and drag at 1	____	Modify the form properties
b. Click and drag at 2	____	Change the column widths for the subform
c. Double click at 3	____	Create a second subform on the main form
d. Click and drag at 4	____	Create an unbound control (label) with instructions on how to use the subform
e. Click at 5	____	Change the size of the subform control
f. Right click at 6	____	Change the width of the main form to 7 inches
g. Click at 7	____	Display the form in Form view
h. Click and drag at 8	____	Return to the Database window
i. Click at 9	____	Move the subform control
j. Click at 10	____	Change the height of the detail section

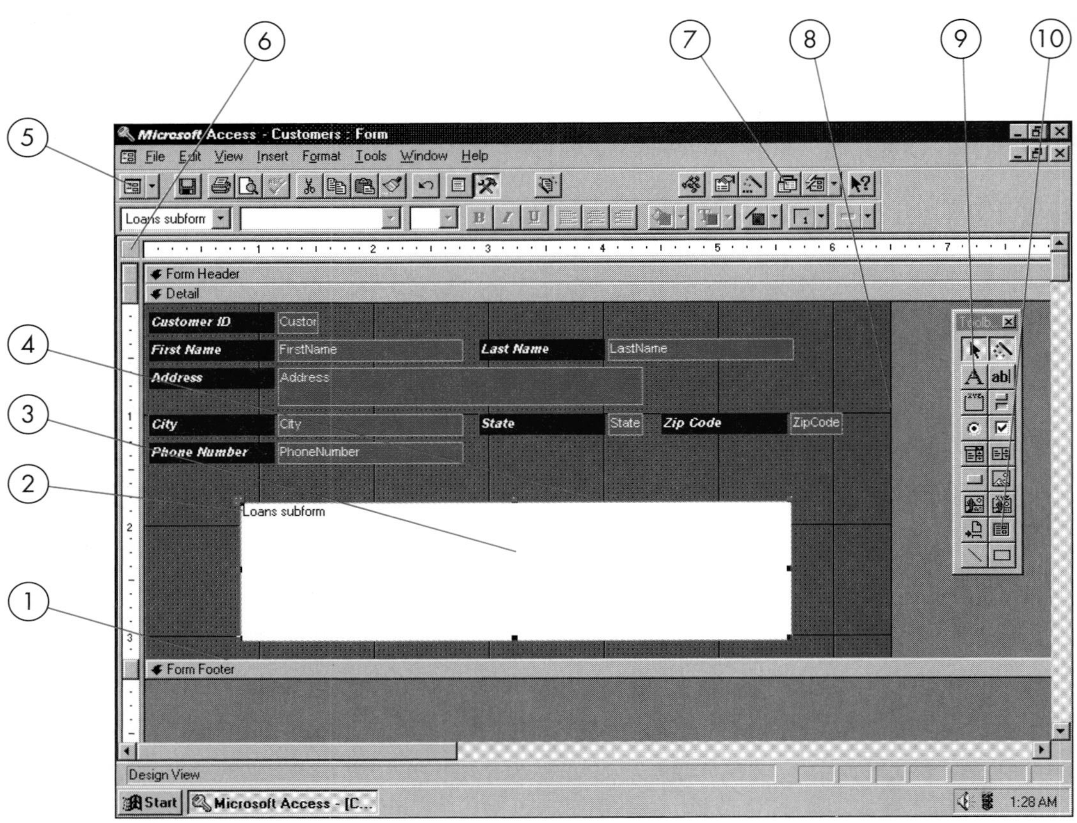

FIGURE 1.13 Screen for Problem 1

2. Answer the following with respect to the Relationships window in Figure 1.14:
   a. What are the relationships in Figure 1.14?
   b. What is the primary key of each table? How is this indicated in the Relationships window?
   c. What foreign keys (if any) are in the Teams table? in the Players table? in the Coaches table?
   d. What is the main table in the Team-Coach relationship? What is the related table?
   e. Can you delete a Team record if there is a matching Player record? Can you delete a Player record if there is a matching Team record?
   f. Can you change the value of the TeamID field in the Teams table if there is a matching Player record?

3. Answer the following with respect to the Relationships window in Figure 1.15:
   a. What are the relationships in Figure 1.15?
   b. What is the primary key of each table? How is this indicated in the Relationships window?
   c. What foreign keys (if any) are in the Offices table? In the Brokers table? In the Clients table?
   d. Can you delete a Broker record if there is a matching Client record? Can you delete a Client record if there is a matching Broker record?
   e. Can you change the value of the OfficeID field in the Offices table if there is a matching Broker record?

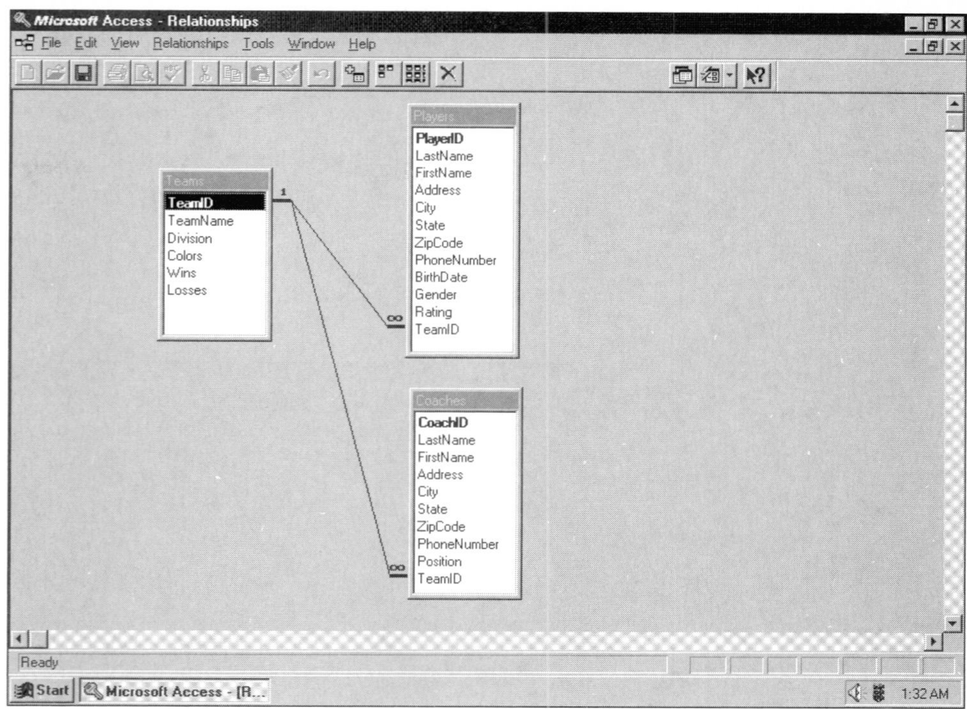

FIGURE 1.14 Screen for Problem 2

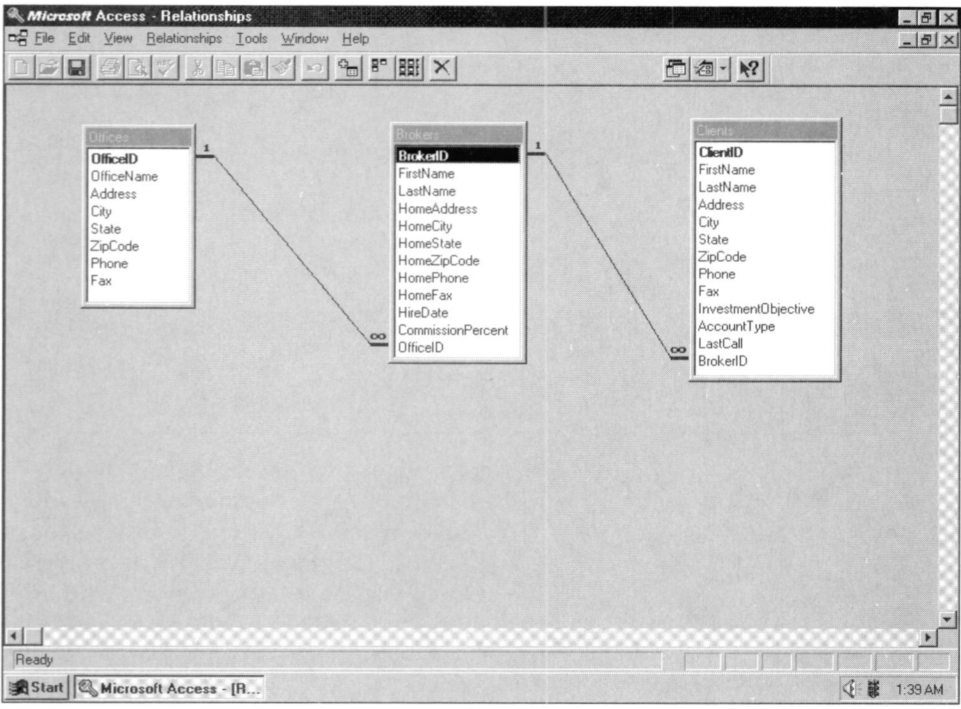

FIGURE 1.15 Screen for Problem 3

4. Answer the following with respect to the query in Figure 1.16:
   a. How many tables are represented in the query? How many fields are taken from the Customers table? From the Loans table? From the Payments table?
   b. Will all of the fields in the query be visible when the query is run?
   c. What criteria are in effect? In which order will the selected records appear?
   d. What is the name of the query as it is stored in the database? Is this an apt description of what the query accomplishes?

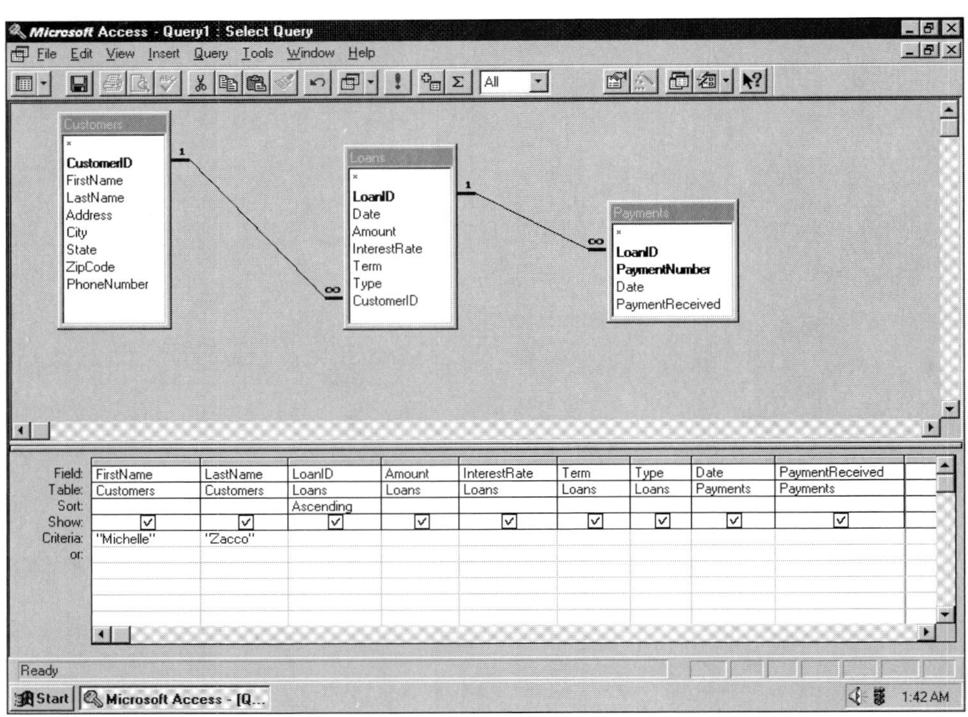

FIGURE 1.16 Screen for Problem 4

PRACTICE WITH MICROSOFT ACCESS 7.0

1. Figure 1.17 contains a modified version of the Customers form and its associated subforms. Complete the hands-on exercises in the chapter, then modify the completed Customers form so that it matches Figure 1.17. (The easiest way to add the label at the top of the form is to create a form header.) Follow the steps below to add the clip art image. (The faster your machine, the more you will enjoy the exercise.)
   a. Open the Customers form in the Design view. Double click the Loans subform control to open the Loans subform in the Design view. Move the control for the Payments subform to the left to allow room for the OLE object.

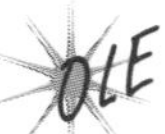

   b. Click the Unbound Object Frame tool on the toolbox. (If you are unsure as to which tool to click, just point to the tool to display the name of the tool.)

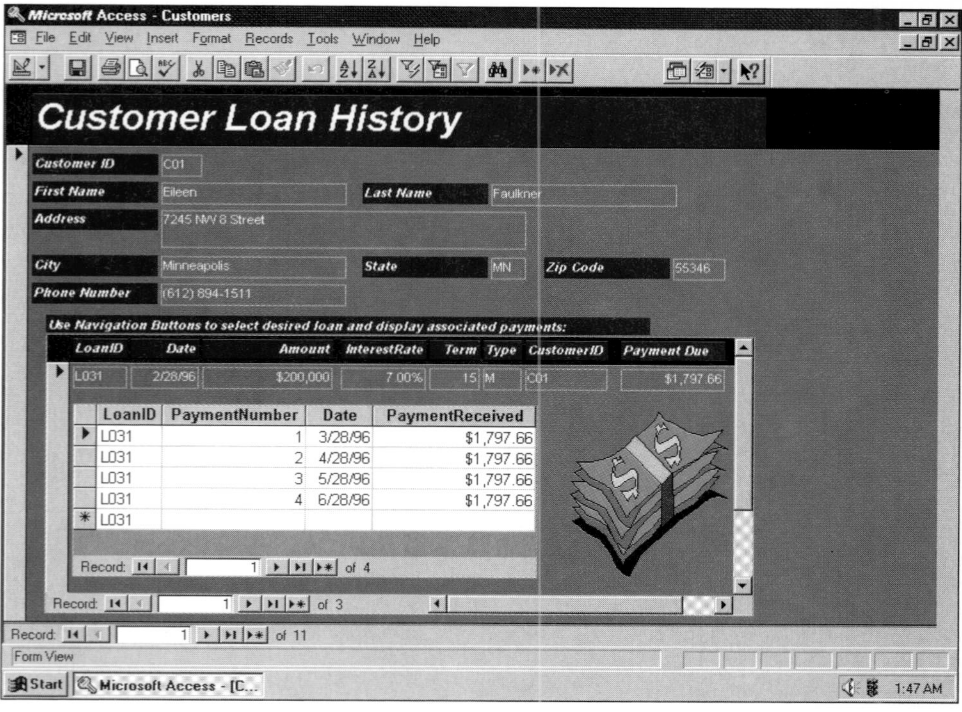

FIGURE 1.17 Screen for Practice Exercise 1

c. Click and drag in the Loans subform to size the frame, then release the mouse to display an Insert Object dialog box.

d. Click the Create New Option button. Select the Microsoft ClipArt Gallery as the object type. Click OK.

e. Choose the category and picture you want from within the ClipArt Gallery. Click the Insert button to insert the picture into the Access form and simultaneously close the ClipArt Gallery dialog box. Do *not* be concerned if only a portion of the picture appears on the form.

f. Right click the newly inserted object to display a shortcut menu, then click Properties to display the Properties dialog box. Click the Format tab, then select (click) the Size Mode property and select Stretch from the associated list. Change the Back Style property to Transparent, the Special Effect property to Flat, and the Border Style property to Transparent. Close the Properties dialog box.

g. You should see the entire clip art image, although it may be distorted because the size and shape of the frame you inserted in steps (a) and (b) does not match the image you selected. Click and drag the sizing handles on the frame to size the object so that its proportions are correct. Click anywhere in the middle of the frame (the mouse pointer changes to a hand) to move the frame elsewhere in the form.

h. If you want to display a different object, double click the clip art image to return to the ClipArt Gallery in order to select another object. View the completed form, then make any final changes.

i. Print the completed form with your customer information. Remember to click the selection area prior to printing. (You are still customer C11.)

2. Interest rates have come down and National Bank has decided to run a promotion on car loans. The loan officer would like to contact all existing customers with a car loan to inform them of their new rates. Create a report similar to the one in Figure 1.18 in response to the request from the loan officer.

The report may be based on a query that contains fields from both the Customers and the Loans tables, or it may be created directly in the Report Wizard. Note, too, the clip art image, which is required in the Report heading and which can be added using the techniques described in the previous problem. Be sure to add your name to the heading so that your instructor will know the report came from you.

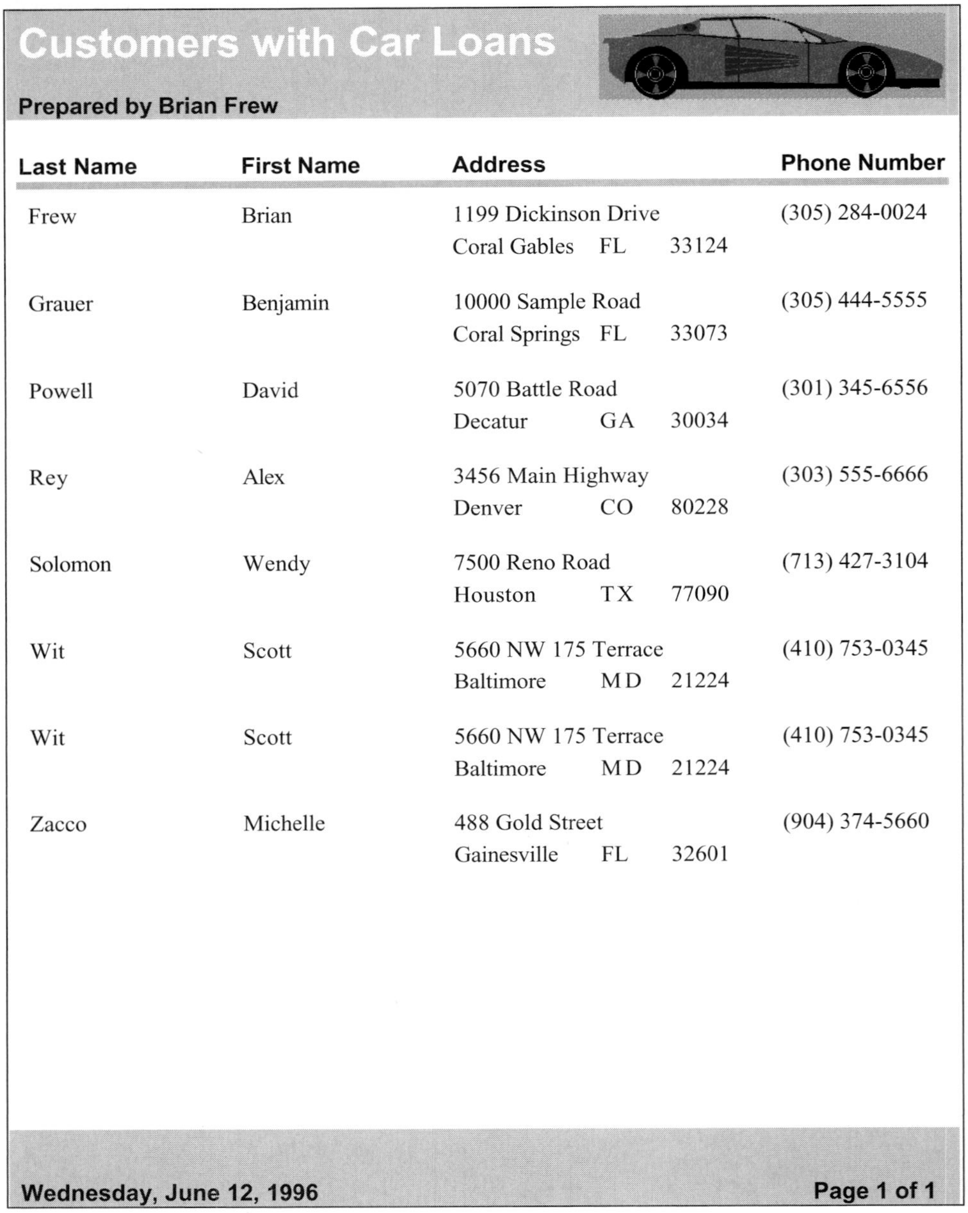

Customers with Car Loans

Prepared by Brian Frew

Last Name	First Name	Address	Phone Number
Frew	Brian	1199 Dickinson Drive Coral Gables FL 33124	(305) 284-0024
Grauer	Benjamin	10000 Sample Road Coral Springs FL 33073	(305) 444-5555
Powell	David	5070 Battle Road Decatur GA 30034	(301) 345-6556
Rey	Alex	3456 Main Highway Denver CO 80228	(303) 555-6666
Solomon	Wendy	7500 Reno Road Houston TX 77090	(713) 427-3104
Wit	Scott	5660 NW 175 Terrace Baltimore MD 21224	(410) 753-0345
Wit	Scott	5660 NW 175 Terrace Baltimore MD 21224	(410) 753-0345
Zacco	Michelle	488 Gold Street Gainesville FL 32601	(904) 374-5660

Wednesday, June 12, 1996 **Page 1 of 1**

FIGURE 1.18 Report for Practice Exercise 2

3. Use the Employee database in the Exploring Access folder on the data disk to create the main form and subform combination shown in Figure 1.19. There is a one-to-many relationship between locations and employees (one location contains many employees), and you need to define this relationship prior to creating the form.

   You also need to modify the underlying Employee table to use a Location code rather than the Location name. (The change in design was requested by the end-user after the initial database was completed. This is not a trivial task, and you will see how important it is to arrive at a satisfactory design as early as possible in a project.)

   In creating the form we used the Colorful 2 style, but you are free to use any style you like. You can create the forms using the techniques in the second hands-on exercise. Alternatively, you can access the Subform/Subreport Wizard directly from the Form Wizard by following the steps below.

   a. Click the Forms tab in the Database window, click New to display the New Form dialog box, then click Form Wizard as the means of creating the form. Select Locations as the table on which to base the main form, and click OK to start the Form Wizard.
   b. Click the >> button to select all of the fields in the Locations table for the form. Do *not,* however, click Next at this time as you will select additional fields from the Employees table for inclusion on the form.
   c. Click the drop-down arrow on the Tables/Queries list box, select the Employees table, then click the >> button to select all of the fields in the Employees table. Click Next.
   d. View your data by Locations and be sure the Form with subform(s) option button is selected. Click Next.

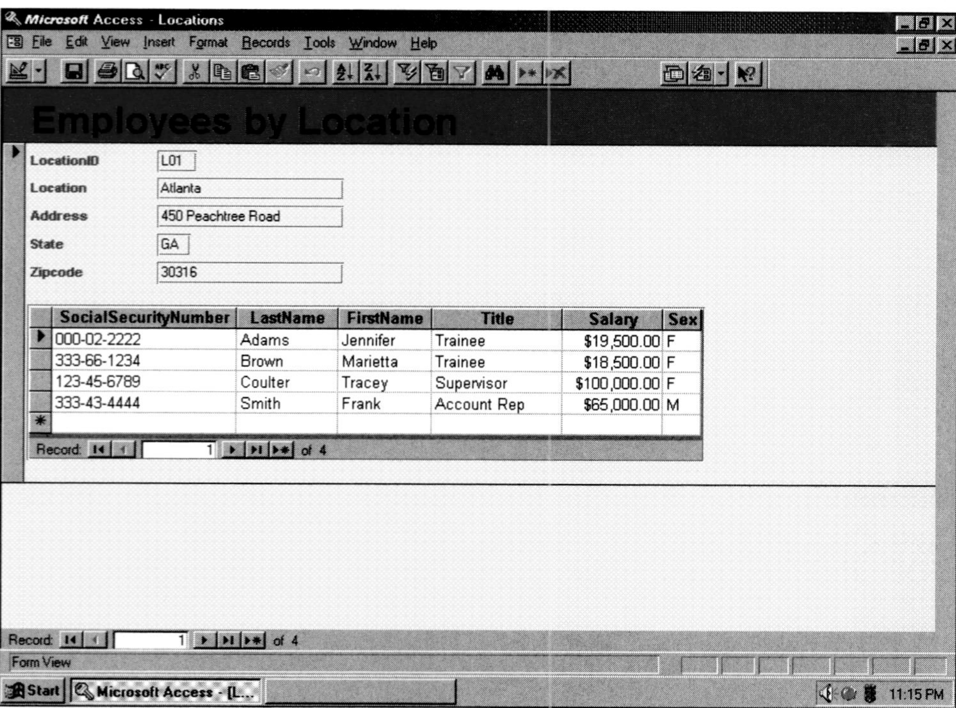

FIGURE 1.19 Screen for Practice Exercise 3

e. Choose the Datasheet layout for your subform, then answer the remaining questions to complete the forms.

f. Add your name as an Account Rep in Miami at a salary of $50,000. Print the location form for the Miami location only, and submit it to your instructor as proof you did this exercise.

4. The Titles form in Figure 1.20 is based on the Employees database referenced in problem 3. Open the Employee database and add the one-to-many relationship between titles and employees, then create the form in Figure 1.20. (The Titles table contains a memo field for the job description.)

Use the technique described in problem 1 to add a clip art logo of your choice to the form. (As in the previous exercise, you will need to change the Employees table to accommodate a Title code rather than a Title description.)

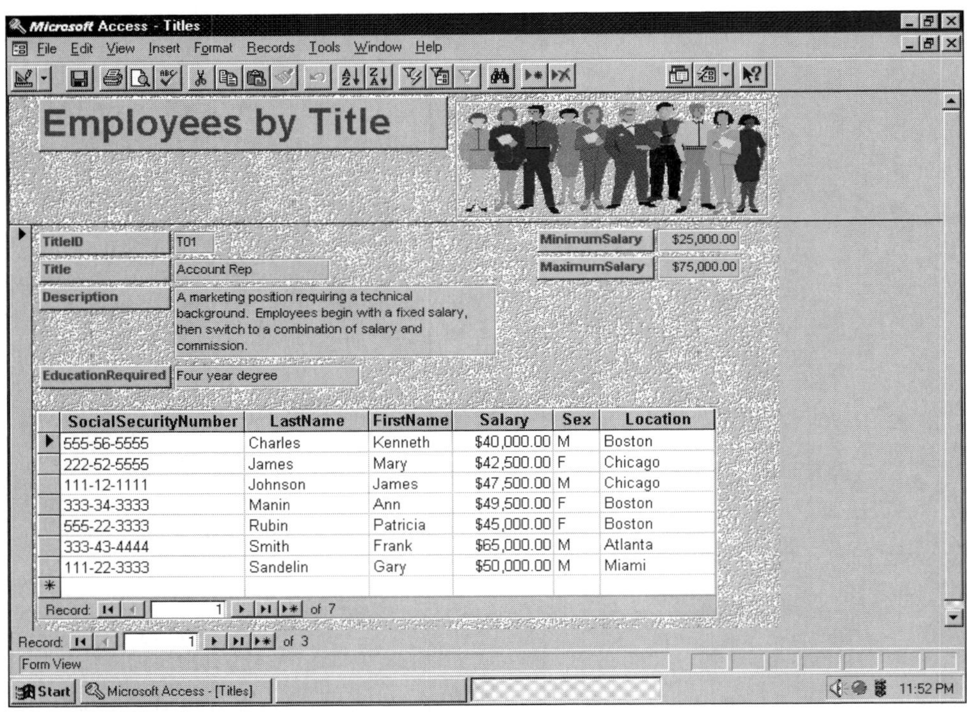

FIGURE 1.20 Report for Practice Exercise 4

CASE STUDIES

Recreational Sports League

Design a database for a recreational sports league that will monitor players, coaches, and sponsors. There may be any number of teams in the league, with each team having any number of players. A player is associated with only one team.

Each team has at least one coach. The league also imposes the rule that a person may not coach more than one team. Each team has a sponsor such as a local business. One sponsor can be associated with multiple teams.

Your solution should make the system as realistic as possible. The player table, for example, requires not only the identifying information for each player (name, address, phone, and so on) but additional fields such as birth date (to implement age limits on various teams), ability ratings, and so on. Your system should be capable of producing reports that will display all information about a specific team, such as its players, coach, and sponsor. The league administrators would also like master lists of all teams, players, coaches, and sponsors.

Show the required tables in the database, being sure to indicate the primary key and foreign keys in each table. Indicate one or two other fields in each table (you need not list them all).

The Personnel Director

You have been hired as a personnel director for a medium-sized company with offices in several cities. You require the usual personal data for each employee (birth date, hire date, home address, and so on.) You also need to reach an employee at work, and must be able to retrieve the office address, office phone number, and office fax number for each employee. Each employee is assigned to only one branch office.

Your duties also include the administration of various health plans offered by the company. Each employee is given his or her choice of several health plans. Each plan has a monthly premium and deductible amount. Once the deductible is reached, each plan pays a designated percentage of all subsequent expenses.

Design a database that will include the necessary data to provide all of the information you need. Show the required tables in the database, being sure to indicate the primary key and foreign keys in each table. Indicate one or two other fields in each table (you need not list them all).

The Franchise

The management of a national restaurant chain is automating its procedure for monitoring its restaurants, restaurant owners (franchisees), and the contracts that govern the two. Each restaurant has one owner (franchisee). There is no limit on the number of restaurants an individual may own, and franchisees are encouraged to apply for multiple restaurants.

The payment from the franchisee to the company varies according to the contract in effect for the particular restaurant. The company offers a choice of contracts, which vary according to the length of the contract, the franchise fee, and the percentage of the restaurant's sales paid to the company for marketing and royalty fees. Each restaurant has one contract, but a given contract may pertain to many restaurants.

The company needs a database capable of retrieving all data for a given restaurant, such as its annual sales, location, phone number, owner, and type of contract in effect. It would also like to know all restaurants owned by one person as well as all restaurants governed by a specific contract type.

Widgets of America

Widgets of America gives its sales staff exclusive rights to specific customers. Each sales person has many customers, but a specific customer always deals with the same sales representative. The company needs to know all of the orders placed by a specific customer as well as the total business generated by each sales representative. The data for each order includes the date the order was placed and the amount of the order. Design a database capable of producing the information required by the company.

Show the required tables in the database, being sure to indicate the primary key and foreign keys in each table. Indicate one or two other fields in each table (you need not list them all).

2

MANY-TO-MANY RELATIONSHIPS: A MORE COMPLEX SYSTEM

OBJECTIVES

After reading this chapter you will be able to:

1. Define a many-to-many relationship and explain how it is implemented in Access.
2. Use the Cascade Update and Cascade Delete options in the Relationships window to relax enforcement of referential integrity.
3. Explain how the AutoNumber field type simplifies the entry of new records.
4. Create a main and subform based on a query; discuss the advantage of using queries rather than tables as the basis for a form or report.
5. Create a parameter query; explain how a parameter query can be made to accept multiple parameters.
6. Use aggregate functions in a select query to perform calculations on groups of records.
7. Use the Get External Data command to add external tables to an existing database.

OVERVIEW

This chapter introduces a new case study to give you additional practice in database design. The system extends the concept of a relational database that was introduced in the previous chapter to include both a one-to-many and a many-to-many relationship. The case solution reviews earlier material on establishing relationships in Access and the importance of referential integrity. Another point of particular interest is the use of an AutoNumber (counter) field to facilitate the addition of new records.

The chapter extends what you already know about subforms and queries, and uses both to present information from related tables. The forms created in this chapter are based on multiple table queries rather than tables. The queries themselves are of a more advanced nature. We show you how to create a parameter query, where you enter the criteria at the time you run the query. We also show you how to create queries that use the aggregate functions built into Access to perform calculations on groups of records.

The chapter contains four hands-on exercises to implement the case study. We think you will be pleased with what you have accomplished by the end of the chapter, working with a sophisticated system that is typical of real-world applications.

CASE STUDY: THE COMPUTER SUPER STORE

The case study in this chapter is set within the context of a computer store that requires a database for its customers, products, and orders. The store maintains the usual customer data (name, address, phone, etc.). It also keeps data about the products it sells, storing for each product a product ID, description, quantity on hand, quantity on order, and unit price. And finally, the store has to track its orders. It needs to know the date an order was received, the customer who placed it, the products that were ordered, and the quantity of each product.

Think, for a moment, about the tables that are necessary and the relationships between those tables, then compare your thoughts to our solution in Figure 2.1. You probably have no trouble recognizing the need for the Customers, Products, and Orders tables. Initially, you may be puzzled by the Order Details table, but you will soon appreciate why it is there and how powerful it is.

You can use the Customers, Products, and Orders tables individually to obtain information about a specific customer, product, or order, respectively. For example:

Query: What is Jeffrey Muddell's phone number?
Answer: Jeffrey Muddell's phone is (305) 253-3909.

Query: What is the price of a Pentium 133 system? How many are in stock?
Answer: A Pentium 133 sells for $2,599. Fifteen systems are in stock.

Query: When was Order O0003 placed?
Answer: Order O0003 was placed on April 18, 1996.

Other queries require you to relate the tables to one another. There is, for example, a ***one-to-many relationship*** between customers and orders. One customer can place many orders, but a specific order can be associated with only one customer. The tables are related through the CustomerID, which appears as the ***primary key*** in the Customers table and as a ***foreign key*** in the Orders table. Consider:

Query: What is the name of the customer who placed order number O0003?
Answer: Order O0003 was placed by Jeffrey Muddell.

Query: How many orders were placed by Jeffrey Muddell?
Answer: Jeffrey Muddell placed five orders: O0003, O0014, O0016, O0024, and O0025.

These queries require you to use two tables. To answer the first query, you would search the Orders table to find order O0003 and obtain the CustomerID (C0006 in this example). You would then search the Customers table for the

Customer ID	First Name	Last Name	Address	City	State	Zip Code	Phone Number
C0001	Benjamin	Lee	1000 Call Street	Tallahassee	FL	33340	(904) 327-4124
C0002	Eleanor	Milgrom	7245 NW 8 Street	Margate	FL	33065	(305) 974-1234
C0003	Neil	Goodman	4215 South 81 Street	Margate	FL	33065	(305) 444-5555
C0004	Nicholas	Colon	9020 N.W. 75 Street	Coral Springs	FL	33065	(305) 753-9887
C0005	Michael	Ware	276 Brickell Avenue	Miami	FL	33131	(305) 444-3980
C0006	Jeffrey	Muddell	9522 S.W. 142 Street	Miami	FL	33176	(305) 253-3909
C0007	Ashley	Geoghegan	7500 Center Lane	Coral Springs	FL	33070	(305) 753-7830
C0008	Serena	Sherard	5000 Jefferson Lane	Gainesville	FL	32601	(904) 375-6442
C0009	Luis	Couto	455 Bargello Avenue	Coral Gables	FL	33146	(305) 666-4801
C0010	Derek	Anderson	6000 Tigertail Avenue	Coconut Grove	FL	33120	(305) 446-8900
C0011	Lauren	Center	12380 S.W. 137 Avenue	Miami	FL	33186	(305) 385-4432
C0012	Robert	Slane	4508 N.W. 7 Street	Miami	FL	33131	(305) 635-3454

(a) Customers Table

Product ID	Product Name	Units In Stock	Units On Order	Unit Price
P0001	Pentium/75 System	50	0	$1,899.00
P0002	Pentium/90 System	25	5	$1,999.00
P0003	Pentium/100 System	125	15	$2,099.00
P0004	Pentium/120 System	25	50	$2,299.00
P0005	Pentium/133 System	15	25	$2,599.00
P0006	15" SVGA Monitor	50	0	$499.00
P0007	17" SVGA Monitor	25	10	$899.00
P0008	19" Multisync Monitor	50	20	$1,599.00
P0009	500 MB Hard Drive	15	20	$399.00
P0010	1 GB Hard Drive	25	15	$799.00
P0011	2 GB Hard Drive	10	0	$1,245.00
P0012	CD-ROM: 4X	40	0	$249.00
P0013	CD-ROM: 6X	50	15	$449.95
P0014	HD Floppy Disks	500	200	$9.99
P0015	HD Data Cartridges	100	50	$14.79
P0016	250 MB Tape Backup	15	3	$179.95
P0017	Serial Mouse	150	50	$69.95
P0018	Trackball	55	0	$59.95
P0019	Joystick	250	100	$39.95
P0020	Fax/Modem 28.8 Kbps	35	10	$189.95
P0021	Fax/Modem 14.4Kbps	20	0	$65.95
P0022	Laser Printer	100	15	$1,395.00
P0023	24Pin Dot Matrix	50	50	$249.95
P0024	Color Printer	125	25	$569.95
P0025	Windows 95	400	200	$95.95
P0026	Windows 95 Plus	150	50	$45.95
P0027	Norton Utilities 7.0	150	50	$115.95
P0028	Microsoft Scenes Screen Saver	75	25	$29.95
P0029	Microsoft Bookshelf	250	100	$129.95
P0030	Microsoft Cinemania	25	10	$59.95
P0031	Professional Photos on CD-ROM	15	0	$45.95

(b) Products Table

Order ID	Customer ID	Order Date
O0001	C0004	4/15/96
O0002	C0003	4/18/96
O0003	C0006	4/18/96
O0004	C0007	4/18/96
O0005	C0001	4/20/96
O0006	C0001	4/21/96
O0007	C0002	4/21/96
O0008	C0002	4/22/96
O0009	C0001	4/22/96
O0010	C0002	4/22/96
O0011	C0001	4/24/96
O0012	C0007	4/24/96
O0013	C0004	4/24/96
O0014	C0006	4/25/96
O0015	C0009	4/25/96
O0016	C0006	4/26/96
O0017	C0011	4/26/96
O0018	C0011	4/26/96
O0019	C0012	4/27/96
O0020	C0012	4/28/96
O0021	C0010	4/29/96
O0022	C0010	4/29/96
O0023	C0008	4/30/96
O0024	C0006	5/ 1/96
O0025	C0006	5/ 1/96

(c) Orders Table

Order ID	Product ID	Quantity
O0001	P0013	1
O0001	P0014	4
O0001	P0027	1
O0002	P0001	1
O0002	P0006	1
O0002	P0020	1
O0002	P0022	1
O0003	P0005	1
O0003	P0020	1
O0003	P0022	1
O0004	P0003	1
O0004	P0010	1
O0004	P0022	2
O0005	P0003	2
O0005	P0012	2
O0005	P0016	2
O0006	P0007	1
O0006	P0014	10
O0007	P0028	1
O0007	P0030	3
O0008	P0001	1
O0008	P0004	3
O0008	P0008	4
O0008	P0011	2
O0008	P0012	1
O0009	P0006	1
O0010	P0002	2
O0010	P0022	1
O0010	P0023	1
O0011	P0016	2
O0011	P0020	2
O0012	P0021	10
O0012	P0029	10
O0012	P0030	10
O0013	P0009	4
O0013	P0016	10
O0013	P0024	2
O0014	P0019	2
O0014	P0028	1
O0015	P0018	1
O0015	P0020	1
O0016	P0029	2
O0017	P0019	2
O0018	P0009	1
O0018	P0025	2
O0018	P0026	2
O0019	P0014	25
O0020	P0024	1
O0021	P0004	1
O0022	P0027	1
O0023	P0021	1
O0023	P0028	1
O0023	P0029	1
O0024	P0007	1
O0024	P0013	5
O0024	P0014	3
O0024	P0016	1
O0025	P0012	2
O0025	P0029	2

(d) Order Details Table

FIGURE 2.1 Super Store Database

customer with this CustomerID and retrieve the customer's name. To answer the second query, you would begin in the Customers table and search for Jeffrey Muddell to determine the CustomerID (C0006), then search the Orders table for all records with this CustomerID.

The system is more complicated than earlier examples in that there is a ***many-to-many relationship*** between orders and products. One order can include many products, and at the same time a specific product can appear in many orders. The implementation of a many-to-many relationship requires an additional table, the Order Details table, containing (at a minimum) the primary keys of the individual tables.

The Order Details table will contain many records with the same OrderID, because there is a separate record for each product in a given order. It will also contain many records with the same ProductID, because there is a separate record for every order pertaining to that product. However, the *combination* of OrderID and ProductID is unique, and this ***combined key*** becomes the primary key in the Order Details table. The Order Details table also contains an additional field (Quantity) whose value depends on the primary key (the *combination* of OrderID and ProductID). Thus:

Query: How many units of product P0014 were included in order O0001?
Answer: Order O0001 included four units of product P0014. (The order also included one unit of Product P0013 and one unit of P0027.)

The Order Details table has four records with a ProductID of P0014. It also has three records with an OrderID of O0001. There is, however, only one record with a ProductID P0014 *and* an OrderID O0001, which is for four units.

The Order Details table makes it possible to determine all products in one order or all orders for one product. You can also use the Products table in conjunction with the Order Details table to determine the names of those products. Consider:

Query: Which orders include a Pentium 75 system?
Answer: A Pentium 75 is found in orders O0002 and O0008.

Query: Which products were included in Order O0003?
Answer: Order O0003 consisted of products P0005 (a Pentium/133 system), P0020 (a 28.8Kbps fax/modem), and P0022 (a laser printer).

To answer the first query, you would begin in the Products table to find the ProductID for a Pentium 75 system (P0001). You would then search the Order Details table for records containing a ProductID of P0001, which in turn identifies orders O0002 and O0008. The second query is processed in similar fashion except that you would search the Order Details table for an OrderID of O0003. This time you would find three records with ProductIDs P0005, P0020, and P0022, respectively. You would then go to the Products table to look up the ProductIDs to return the name of each product.

We've emphasized that the power of a relational database comes from the inclusion of multiple tables and the relationships between those tables. As you already know, you can use data from several tables to compute the answer to more complex queries. For example:

Query: What is the total cost of order O0006?
Answer: Order O0006 costs $998.90.

To determine the cost of an order, you must first identify all of the products associated with that order, the quantity of each product, and the price of each product. The previous queries have shown how you would find the products in an order and the associated quantities. The price of a specific product is obtained from the Products table, which enables you to compute the invoice by multiplying the price of each product by the quantity. Thus, the total cost of order O0006 is $998.90. (One unit of P0007 at $899.00 and ten units of product P0014 at $9.99.)

PRACTICE WITH DATABASE DESIGN

An Access database consists of multiple tables, each of which stores data about a specific subject. To use Access effectively, you must be able to relate the tables to one another, which in turn requires a knowledge of database design. Appendix B provides additional examples that enable you to master the principles of a relational database.

The AutoNumber Field Type

Look carefully at the Customer, Order, and Product numbers in their respective tables and note that each set of numbers is consecutive. This is accomplished by specifying the ***AutoNumber field*** type for each of these fields in the design of the individual tables. The AutoNumber specification automatically assigns the next sequential number to the primary key of a new record. If, for example, you were to add a new customer to the existing Customers table, that customer would be assigned the number 13. In similar fashion, the next order will be order number 26, and the next product will be product number 32. (Deleting a record does not, however, renumber the remaining records in the table; that is, once a value is assigned to a primary key, the primary key will always retain that value.)

The C, O, and P that appear as the initial character of each field, as well as the high-order zeros, are *not* part of the fields themselves, but are displayed through the ***Format property*** associated with each field. In other words, the internal value of the first CustomerID is the number 1 (not C0001). The letters function as a prefix and identify the table to which the field belongs; for example, C0001, O0001, and P0001 correspond to the first record in the Customers, Orders, and Products tables, respectively. The zeros provide a uniform appearance for that field throughout the table.

SIMPLIFIED DATA ENTRY

The AutoNumber field type is often assigned to the primary key of a table to ensure a unique value (the next consecutive number) in each new record. This simplifies data entry in situations where the user has no knowledge of what the primary key should be, as in the case of a customer number other than a social security number. The Format property can be used in conjunction with an AutoNumber field to improve its appearance through the addition of a letter prefix and/or high-order zeros.

The Relationships Window

The Relationships window in Figure 2.2 shows the Computer Store database as it will be implemented in Access. The database contains the Customers, Orders,

Many-to-many relationship implemented by a pair of one-to-many relationships

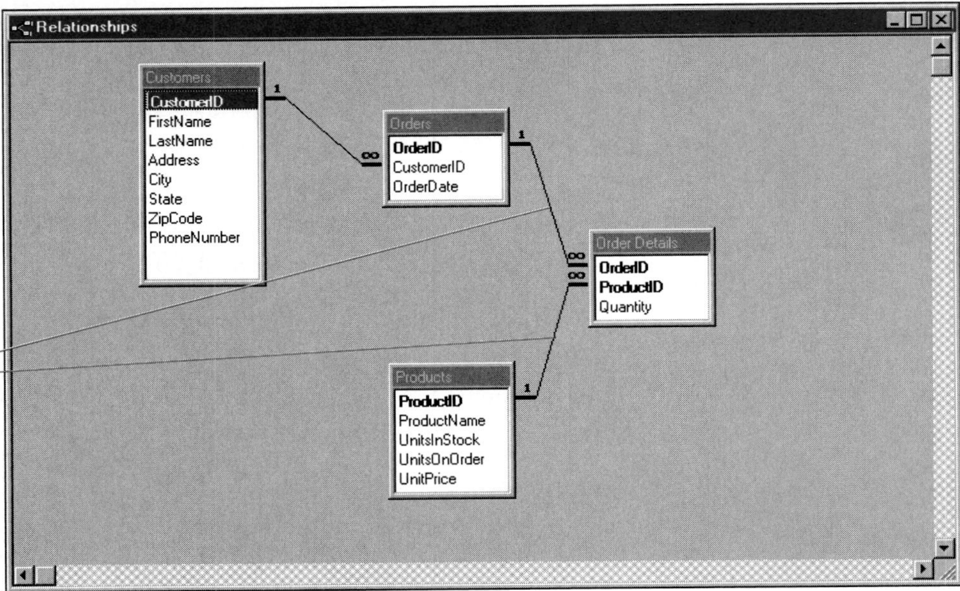

FIGURE 2.2 The Relationships Window

Products, and Order Details tables as per the previous discussion. The field lists display the fields within each table, with the primary key shown in bold. The OrderID and ProductID are both shown in bold in the Order Details table, to indicate that the primary key consists of the combination of these fields.

The many-to-many relationship between Orders and Products is implemented by a *pair* of one-to-many relationships. There is a one-to-many relationship between the Orders table and the Order Details table. There is a second one-to-many relationship between the Products table and the Order Details table. In other words, the Orders and Products tables are not related to each other directly, but indirectly through the pair of one-to-many relationships with the Order Details table.

The ***join lines*** show the relationships between the tables. The number 1 appears next to the Orders table on the join line connecting the Orders table and the Order Details table. The infinity symbol appears at the end of the line next to the Order Details table. The one-to-many relationship between these tables means that each record in the Orders table can be associated with many records in the Order Details table. Each record in the Order Details table, however, can be associated with only one record in the Orders table.

In similar fashion, there is also a one-to-many relationship between the Products table and the Order Details table. The number 1 appears on the join line next to the Products table. The infinity symbol appears at the end of the join line next to the Order Details table. Each record in the Products table can be associated with many records in the Order Details table, but each record in the Order Details table is associated with only one product.

Referential Integrity

The concept of ***referential integrity,*** which was introduced in the previous chapter, ensures that the records in related tables are consistent with one another. Enforcement of referential integrity prevents you from adding a record to the related table when there is no associated record in the primary table. It means, for example, that you cannot add a record to the Orders table unless there is a corresponding Customer record. Or stated another way, a Customer record must exist before you can assign an order to that customer. Enforcement of referential integrity will also prevent you from deleting a record in the primary (Customers) table when there are corresponding records in the related (Orders) table. Nor will it let you change the primary key of the primary (Customers) table if there are matching records in the related (Orders) table.

Consider, for example, the application of referential integrity to the one-to-many relationship between the Orders table and the Order Details table. Referential integrity prevents the addition of a record to the related (Order Details) table unless there is a corresponding record in the primary (Orders) table. It prevents the deletion of a record in the Orders table when there are corresponding records in the Order Details table. And finally, it prevents the modification of the OrderID in any record in the Orders table when there are matching records in the Order Details table.

There may be times, however, when you want to delete an order and simultaneously delete the corresponding records in the Order Details table. This is accomplished by enabling the ***cascaded deletion*** of related records, so that when you delete a record in the Orders table, Access automatically deletes the associated records in the Order Details table.

You might also want to enable the ***cascaded updating*** of related fields to correct the value of an OrderID. Enforcement of referential integrity would ordinarily prevent you from changing the value of the OrderID field in the Orders table when there are corresponding records in the Order Details table. You could, however, specify the cascaded updating of related fields so that if you were to change the OrderID in the Orders table, the corresponding fields in the Order Details table would also change. In either case, however, you will still be prevented from adding a record to the Order Details table unless there is a corresponding record in the Orders table.

USE WITH CAUTION

The cascaded deletion of related records relaxes referential integrity and eliminates errors that would otherwise occur during data entry. That does not mean, however, that the option should always be selected, and in fact, most of the time it is disabled. What would happen, for example, in an employee database with a one-to-many relationship between branch offices and employees, if cascade deleted records was in effect and a branch office was eliminated?

HANDS-ON EXERCISE 1

Relationships and Referential Integrity

Objective: To create relationships between existing tables in order to demonstrate referential integrity; to edit an existing relationship to allow the cascaded deletion of related records. Use Figure 2.3 as a guide in the exercise.

STEP 1: Add a Customer (the AutoNumber field type)

- Start Access. Open the **Computer Store database** in the **Exploring Access folder.**

- The **Tables tab** is already selected in the Database window. Open the **Customers table,** then click the **Maximize button** (if necessary) so that the table takes the entire screen as shown in Figure 2.3a.
- Click the **New Record button,** then click in the **First Name field.** Enter the first letter of your first name (e.g., "J" as shown in the figure:
  - The record selector changes to a pencil to indicate that you are in the process of entering a record.
  - The CustomerID is assigned automatically as soon as you begin to enter data. *Remember your customer number as you will use it throughout the chapter.* (Your CustomerID is 13, not C0013. The prefix and high-order zeros are displayed through the Format property. See boxed tip.)

THE AUTONUMBER FIELD TYPE AND FORMAT PROPERTY

The Format property can enhance the appearance of an AutoNumber field by displaying a prefix and/or high-order zeros. To view (or assign) the Format property of a field, open the table in Design view, select (click) the field name in the upper part of the window, then click the Format property and enter the desired format. Our Customers table, for example, uses the format \C0000, which displays a C in front of the field and pads it with high-order zeros. The Format property determines how a value is displayed, but does not affect how it is stored in the table. The CustomerID of the first customer, for example, is stored as the number 1, rather than C0001.

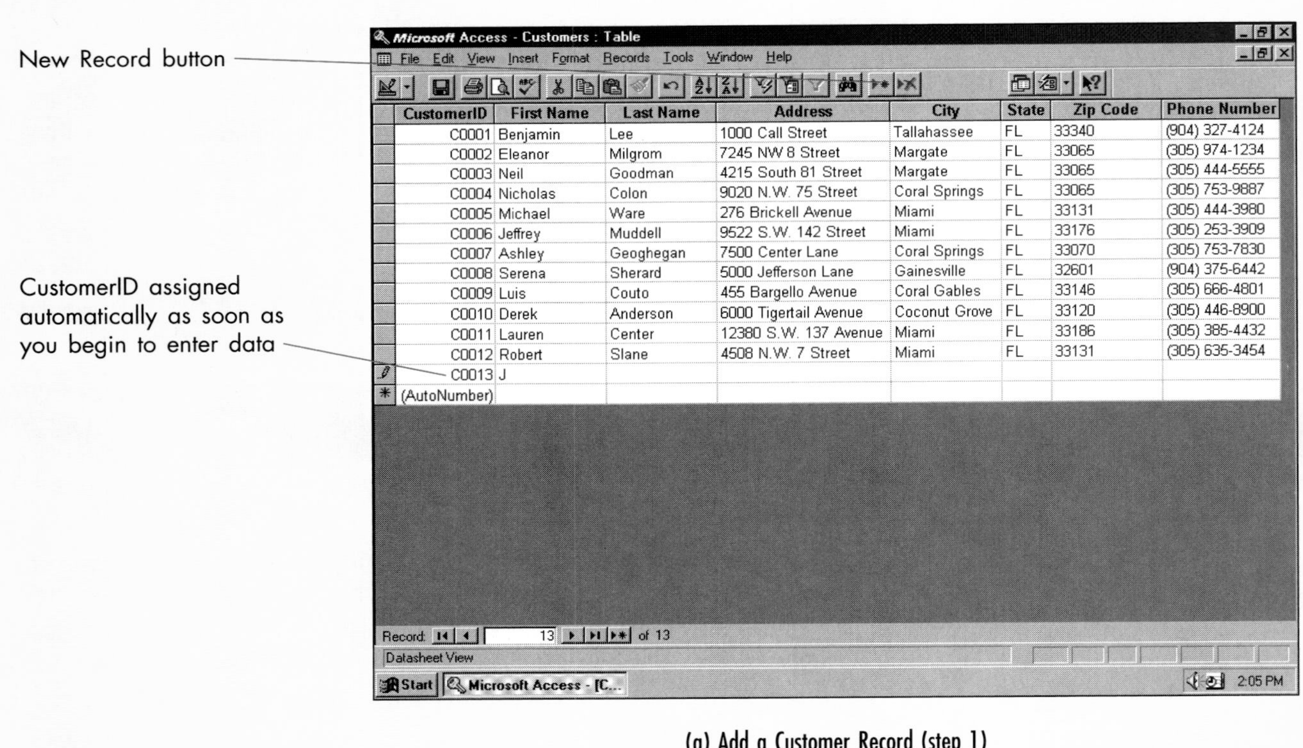

CustomerID	First Name	Last Name	Address	City	State	Zip Code	Phone Number
C0001	Benjamin	Lee	1000 Call Street	Tallahassee	FL	33340	(904) 327-4124
C0002	Eleanor	Milgrom	7245 NW 8 Street	Margate	FL	33065	(305) 974-1234
C0003	Neil	Goodman	4215 South 81 Street	Margate	FL	33065	(305) 444-5555
C0004	Nicholas	Colon	9020 N.W. 75 Street	Coral Springs	FL	33065	(305) 753-9887
C0005	Michael	Ware	276 Brickell Avenue	Miami	FL	33131	(305) 444-3980
C0006	Jeffrey	Muddell	9522 S.W. 142 Street	Miami	FL	33176	(305) 253-3909
C0007	Ashley	Geoghegan	7500 Center Lane	Coral Springs	FL	33070	(305) 753-7830
C0008	Serena	Sherard	5000 Jefferson Lane	Gainesville	FL	32601	(904) 375-6442
C0009	Luis	Couto	455 Bargello Avenue	Coral Gables	FL	33146	(305) 666-4801
C0010	Derek	Anderson	6000 Tigertail Avenue	Coconut Grove	FL	33120	(305) 446-8900
C0011	Lauren	Center	12380 S.W. 137 Avenue	Miami	FL	33186	(305) 385-4432
C0012	Robert	Slane	4508 N.W. 7 Street	Miami	FL	33131	(305) 635-3454
C0013	J						
(AutoNumber)							

(a) Add a Customer Record (step 1)

FIGURE 2.3 Hands-on Exercise 1

- Complete your customer record, pressing the **Tab key** to move from one field to the next. Press **Tab** after you have entered the last field (phone number) to complete the record.
- Close the Customers table.

STEP 2: The Relationships Window

- Pull down the **Tools menu** and click **Relationships** to open the Relationships window as shown in Figure 2.3b. (The tables are not yet visible.) Maximize the Relationships window so that you have more room in which to work.
- Pull down the **Relationships menu** and click **Show Table** (or click the **Show Table button** on the Relationships toolbar) to display the Show Table dialog box.
- The **Tables tab** is selected within the Show Table dialog box, and the **Customers table** is selected. Click the **Add Command button** (or double click the **table name**) to add the Customers table to the Relationships window.
- Add the **Order Details, Orders,** and **Products** tables in similar fashion. Close the Show Table dialog box.
- Point to the bottom border of the **Customers field list** (the mouse pointer changes to a double arrow), then click and drag the border until all of the fields are visible. (The vertical scroll bar will disappear.)
- If necessary, click and drag the bottom border of the other tables until all of their fields are visible.
- Click and drag the title bars to move the field lists so that they are positioned as in Figure 2.3b.

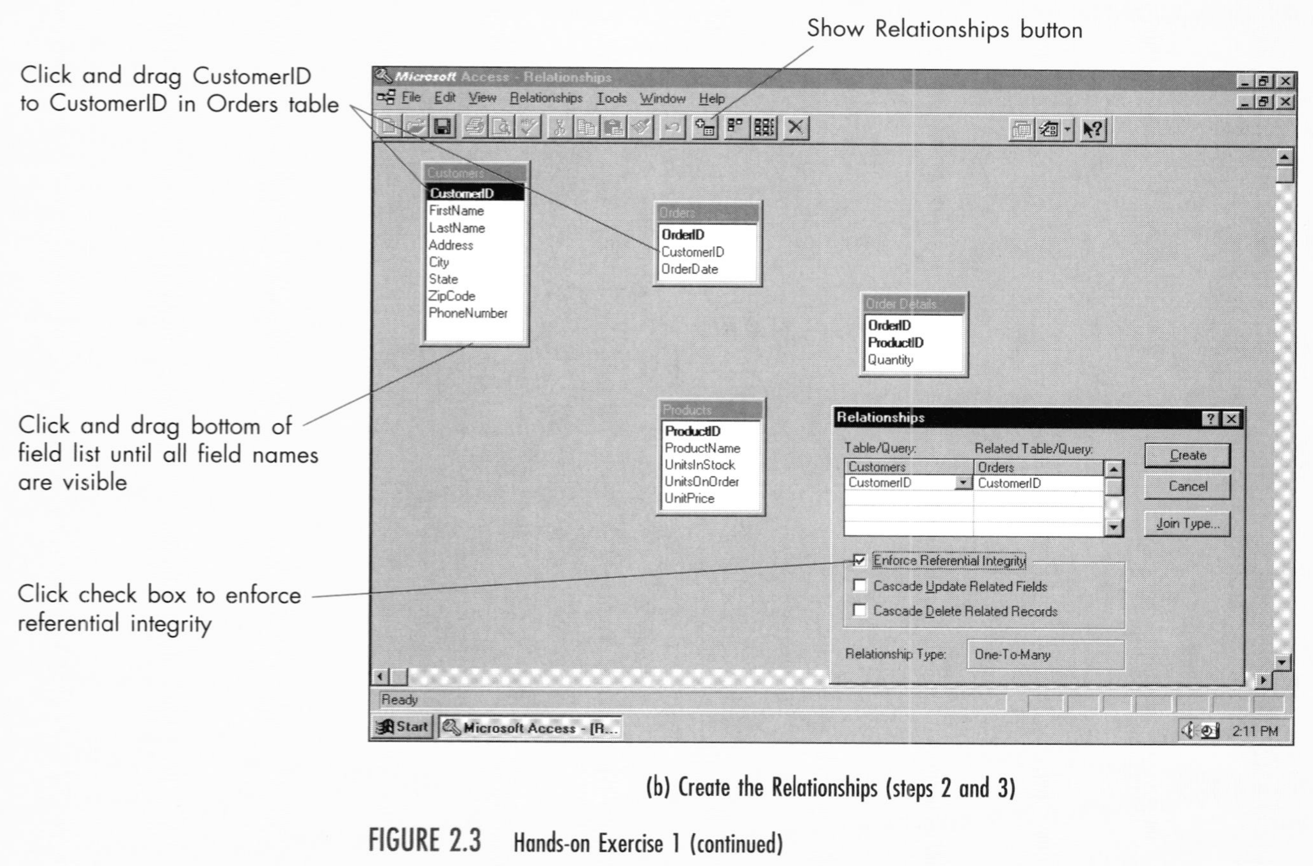

(b) Create the Relationships (steps 2 and 3)

FIGURE 2.3 Hands-on Exercise 1 (continued)

STEP 3: Create the Relationships

- Click and drag the **CustomerID field** in the Customers field list to the **CustomerID field** in the Orders field list. You will see the Relationships dialog box in Figure 2.3b when you release the mouse.
- Click the **Enforce Referential Integrity** check box. Click the **Create Command button** to establish the relationship and close the Relationships dialog box. You should see a line indicating a one-to-many relationship between the Customers and Orders tables.
- Click and drag the **OrderID field** in the Orders field list to the **OrderID field** in the Order Details field list. Click the **Enforce Referential Integrity** check box, then click the **Create Command button.**
- Click and drag the **ProductID field** in the Products field list to the **ProductID field** in the Order Details field list. Click the **Enforce Referential Integrity** check box, then click the **Create Command button.**
- Click the **Save button** to save the relationships, then close the Relationships window.

JOIN FIELDS

The join fields on both sides of a relationship must be the same data type—for example, both number fields or both text fields. (Number fields must also have the same field size setting.) You cannot, however, specify an AutoNumber field on both sides of a relationship. Accordingly, if the join field in the primary table is an AutoNumber field, the join field in the related table must be specified as a number field, with the Field Size property set to Long Integer.

STEP 4: Open the Orders and Order Details Tables

- You should be in the Database window. Click the **Restore button** to return the window to its previous size, then click the **Tables tab** (if necessary) and open the **Orders table.**
- Return to the Database window:
  - Click in the **Database window** (if it is visible), *or*
  - Click the **Database Window button** on the toolbar, *or*
  - Pull down the **Window menu** and click **Computer Store: Database.**
- Open the **Order Details table.** Your desktop should resemble Figure 2.3c although the precise arrangement of the open windows will be different.
- Return to the Database window, then click the **Minimize button** to lessen the clutter on the desktop.

STEP 5: Delete an Order Details Record

- Pull down the **Window menu.** Click **Tile Vertically** to display the Orders table and the Order Details table side by side as in Figure 2.3d. (It doesn't matter whether the Orders table appears on the left or right.)
- Click the **Order Details window.** Click the row selector column for the last Order Details record for order O0005. You should have selected the record for product **P0016** in order **O0005.**

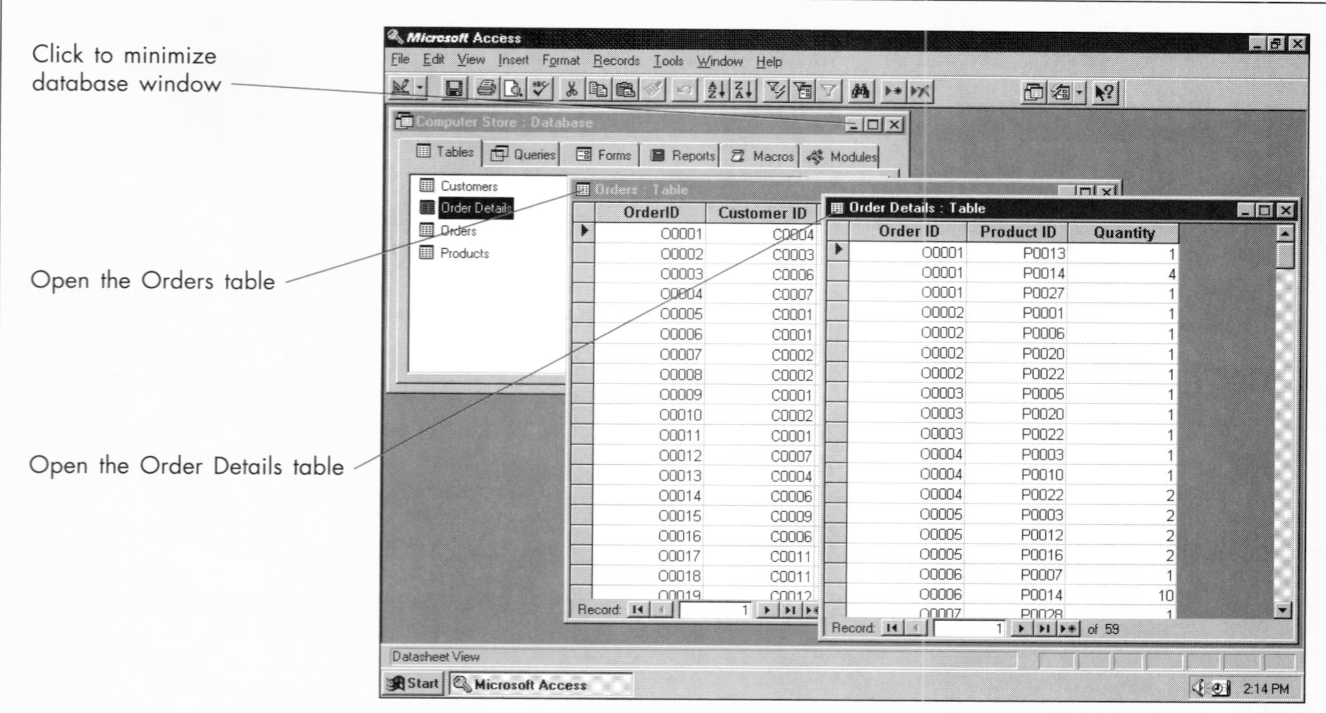

(c) Arranging the Desktop (step 4)

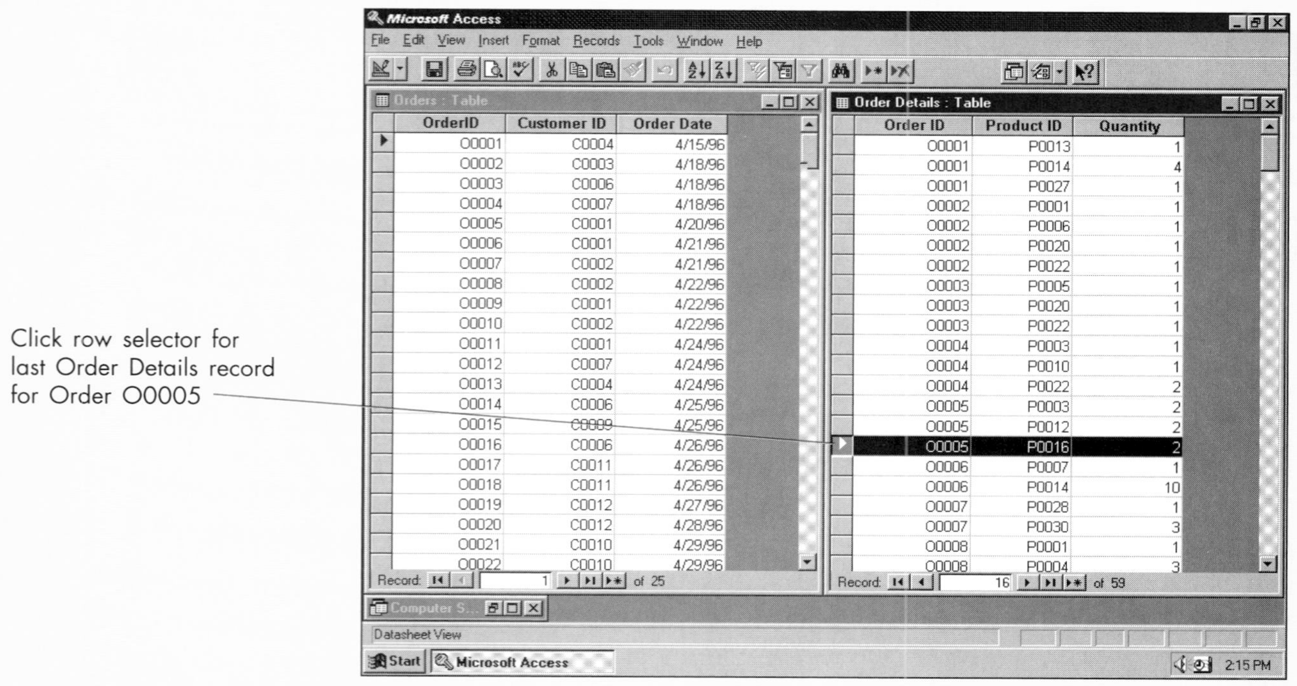

(d) Delete an Order Details Record (step 5)

FIGURE 2.3 Hands-on Exercise 1 (continued)

- Press the **Del key.** You will see a message indicating that you have just deleted one record. Click **Yes** to delete the record. The Delete command works because you are deleting a "many record" in a one-to-many relationship.

STEP 6: Referential Integrity

- Click the **Orders window.** Click the row selector column for **Order O0005** as shown in Figure 2.3e. Press the **Del key** to (attempt to) delete the record.
- You will see the message in Figure 2.3e, indicating that you cannot delete the record. The Delete command does not work because you are attempting to delete the "one record" in a one-to-many relationship. Click **OK.**

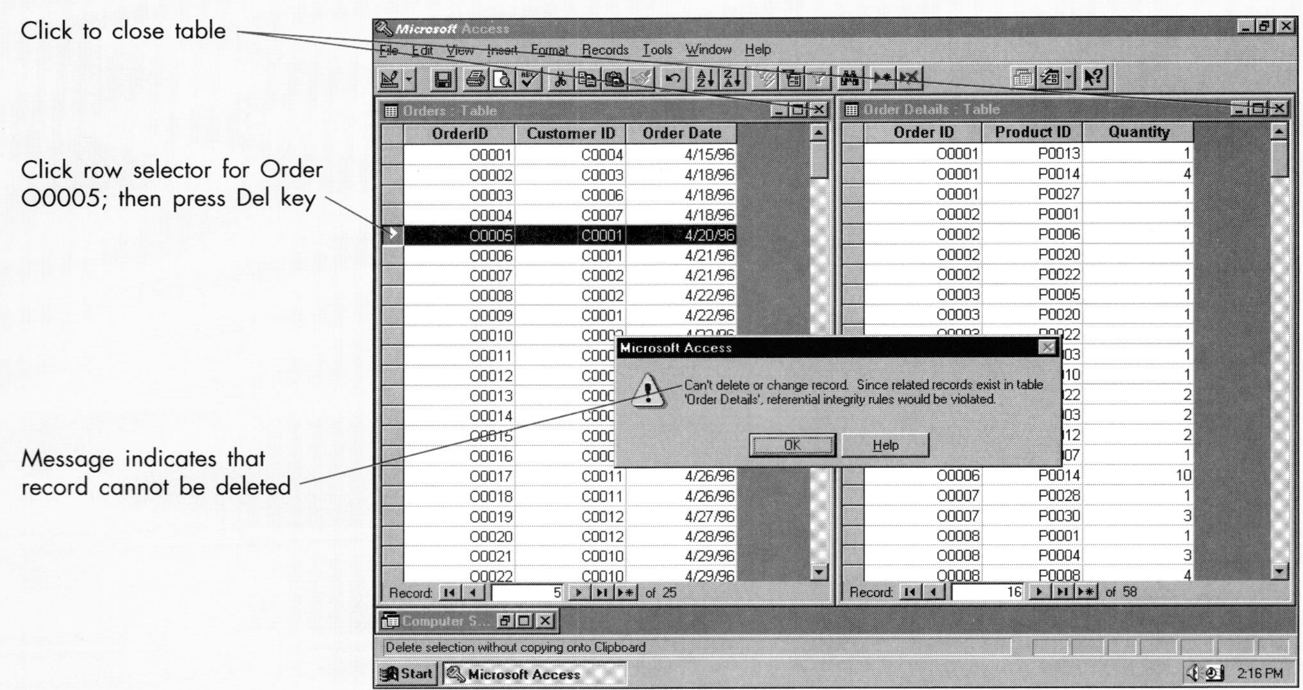

(e) Referential Integrity (step 6)

FIGURE 2.3 Hands-on Exercise 1 (continued)

STEP 7: Edit a Relationship

- Close the Orders table. Close the Order Details table. (The tables in a relationship must be closed before the relationship can be edited.)
- Pull down the **Tools menu** and click **Relationships** to reopen the Relationships window (or click the **Relationships button** on the toolbar). Maximize the window.
- Point to the line connecting the Orders and Order Details tables, then click the **right mouse button** to display a shortcut menu. Click **Edit Relationship** to display the Relationships dialog box in Figure 2.3f.
- Check the box to **Cascade Delete Related Records,** then click **OK** to accept the change and close the dialog box.
- Click the **Save button** to save the edited relationship. Close the Relationships window.

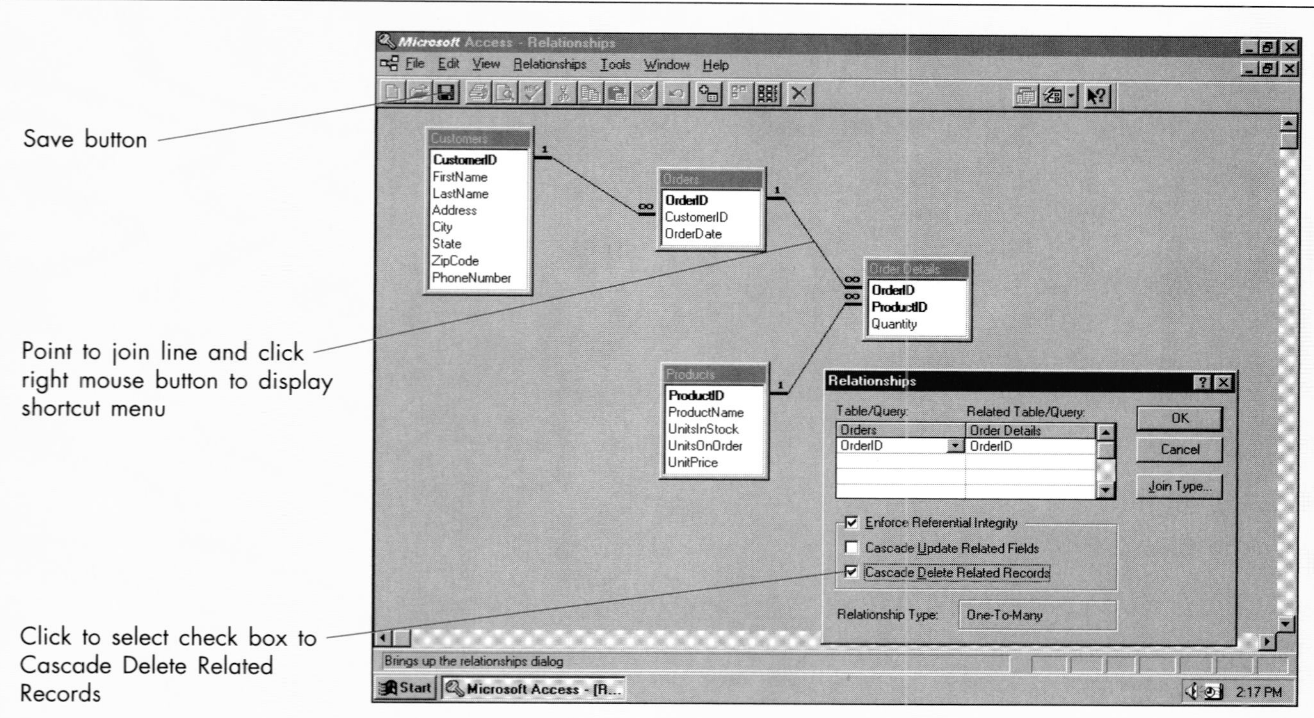

(f) Edit a Relationship (step 7)

FIGURE 2.3 Hands-on Exercise 1 (continued)

TO CLICK OR DOUBLE CLICK

Click the join line connecting two tables to select the relationship, then press the Del key to delete the relationship. Double click the join line to select the relationship and bring up the Relationships window to edit the relationship.

STEP 8: Delete the Related Records

- If necessary, restore the Database window, then open the **Orders table** and the **Order Details table.** Minimize the Database window, then tile the open windows vertically as shown in Figure 2.3g.
- Click the **Orders window** and select the record for **Order O0005.** Press the **Del key** to delete the record.
- You will see a message about cascaded deletes, indicating that records in the Orders table as well as related tables are about to be deleted. Click **Yes.** Order O0005 is gone from the Orders table.
- The related records in the Order Details table have also been deleted but are displayed with the #Deleted indicator as shown in Figure 2.3g. (The records will be gone the next time the Order Details table is opened.)

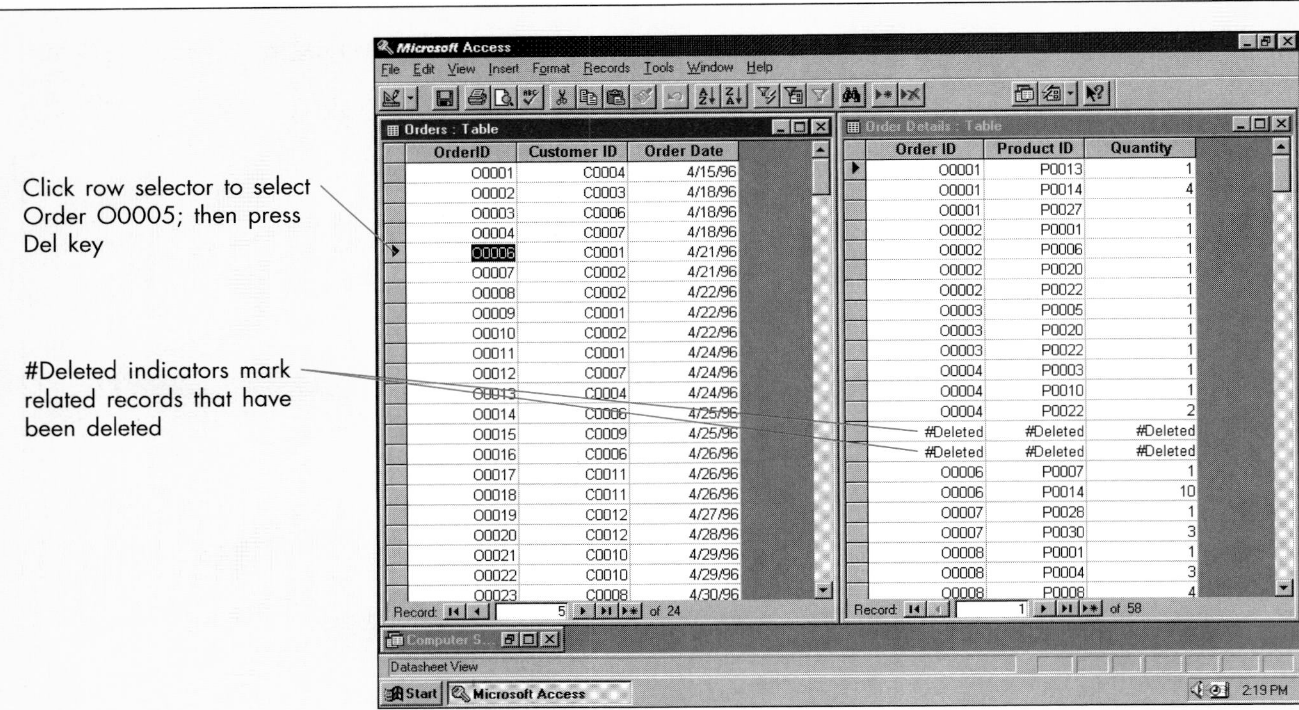
Click row selector to select Order O0005; then press Del key
#Deleted indicators mark related records that have been deleted

(g) Delete Related Records (step 8)

FIGURE 2.3 Hands-on Exercise 1 (continued)

- The Delete command works this time (unlike the previous attempt in step 5) because the relationship was changed to permit the deletion of related records.

STEP 9: Document the Relationships

- Pull down the **Tools menu,** click (or point to) **Analyze,** then click **Documentor** to display the Database Documentor dialog box.
- Click the **drop-down arrow** in the Object Type list box, choose **Current database** as the object type, check the box for **Relationships,** then click **OK.**
- Be patient as it takes a little while for Access to check the relationships within the database and to display the Object Definition window in Figure 2.3h. Maximize the window.
- Scroll through the report to note the relationship between the Orders and Order Details tables (one-to-many; enforced, cascade deletes), which is consistent with the edited relationship.
- Click the **Print button** to print the definition. Close the Object Definition window to continue.
- Close the Orders table. Close the Order Details table. Close the database. Click **Yes** if prompted to save the tables or relationships.
- Exit Access if you do not want to continue with the next exercise at this time.

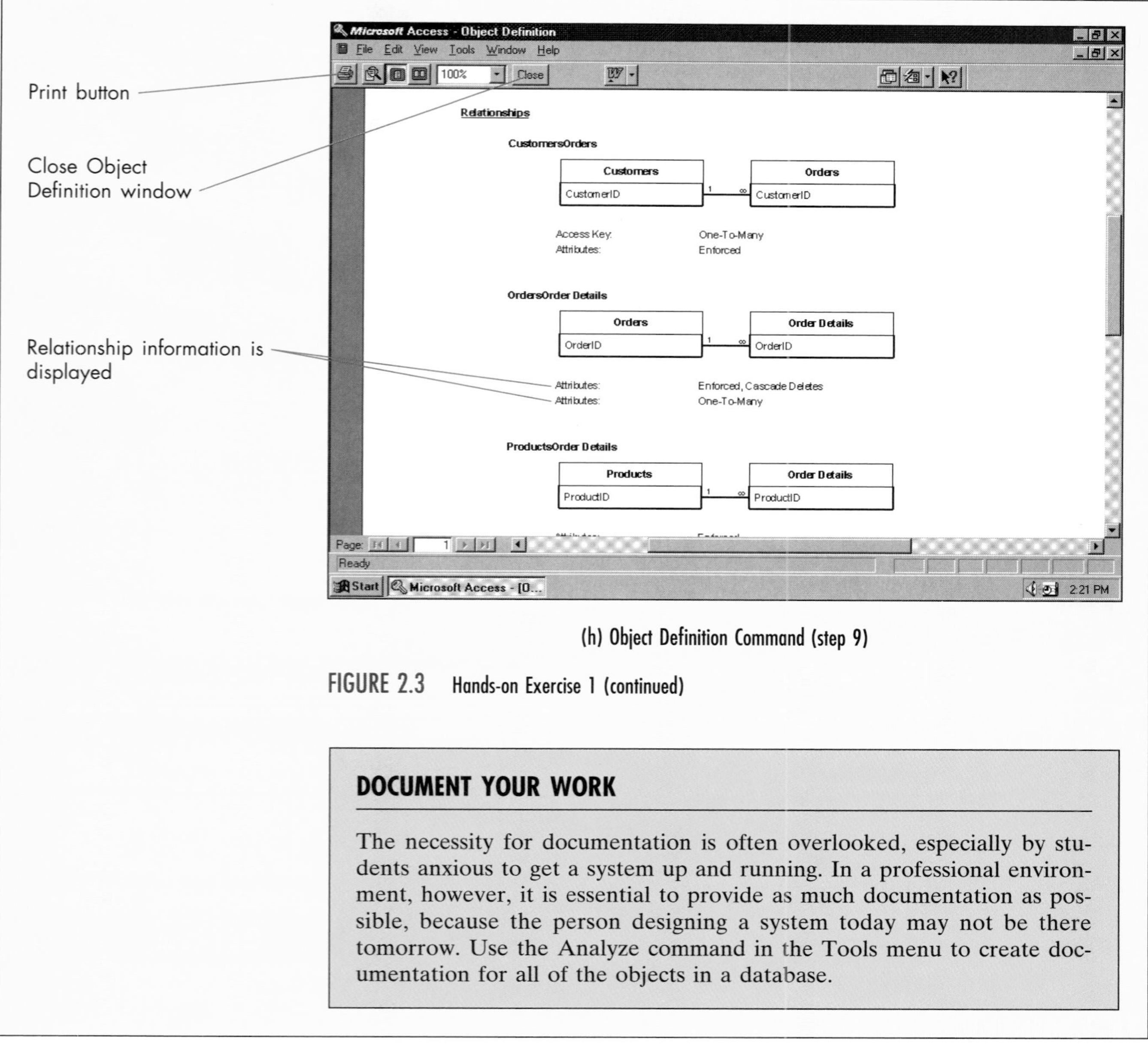

(h) Object Definition Command (step 9)

FIGURE 2.3 Hands-on Exercise 1 (continued)

DOCUMENT YOUR WORK

The necessity for documentation is often overlooked, especially by students anxious to get a system up and running. In a professional environment, however, it is essential to provide as much documentation as possible, because the person designing a system today may not be there tomorrow. Use the Analyze command in the Tools menu to create documentation for all of the objects in a database.

SUBFORMS, QUERIES, AND AUTOLOOKUP

The main and subform combination in Figure 2.4 is used by the store to enter a new order for an existing customer. The forms are based on queries (rather than tables) for several reasons. A query enables you to display data from multiple tables, to display a calculated field, and to take advantage of AutoLookup, a feature that is explained shortly.

The main form contains fields from both the Orders table and the Customers table. The OrderID, OrderDate, and CustomerID (the join field) are taken from the Orders table. The other fields are taken from the Customers table. The query is designed so that you do not have to enter any customer information other than the CustomerID; that is, you enter the CustomerID, and Access will automatically look up (***AutoLookup***) the corresponding customer data.

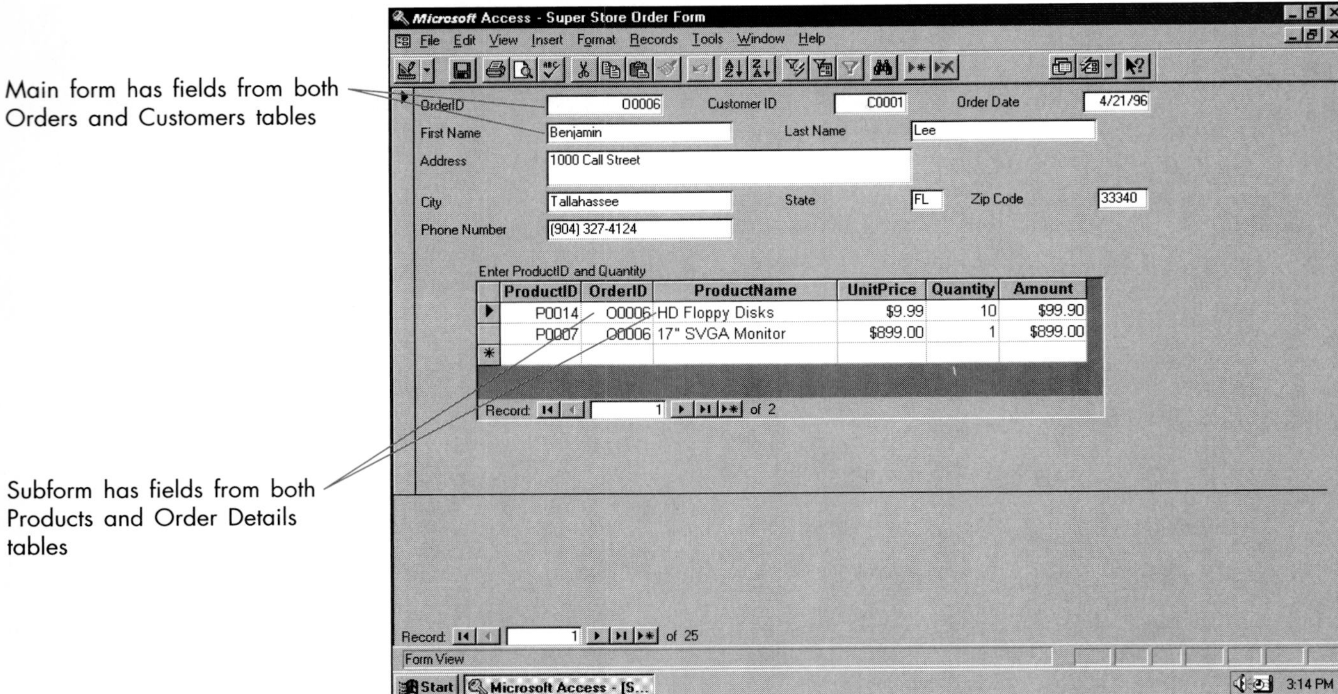

FIGURE 2.4 The Super Store Order Form

The subform is based on a second query containing fields from the Order Details table and the Products table. The OrderID, Quantity, and ProductID (the join field) are taken from the Order Details table. The ProductName and UnitPrice fields are from the Products table. AutoLookup works here as well so that when you enter the ProductID, Access automatically displays the Product Name and Unit Price. You then enter the quantity, and the amount (a calculated field) is determined automatically.

The queries for the main form and subform are shown in Figures 2.5a and 2.5b, respectively. The upper half of the Query window displays the field list for each table and the relationship between the tables. The lower half of the Query window contains the QBE grid. Any query intended to take advantage of AutoLookup must adhere to the following:

1. The tables in the query must have a one-to-many relationship, such as customers to orders in Figure 2.5a or products to order details in Figure 2.5b.
2. The join field on the "one" side of the relationship must have a unique value in the primary table. The CustomerID in Figure 2.5a and the ProductID in Figure 2.5b are primary keys in their respective tables and therefore unique.
3. The join field in the query must be taken from the "many" side of the relationship. Thus, CustomerID is from the Orders table in Figure 2.5a rather than from the Customers table. In similar fashion, ProductID is taken from the Order Details table in Figure 2.5b, not from the Products table.

The following exercise has you create the main and subform in Figure 2.4. We supply the query for the main form (Figure 2.5a), but we ask you to create the query for the subform (Figure 2.5b).

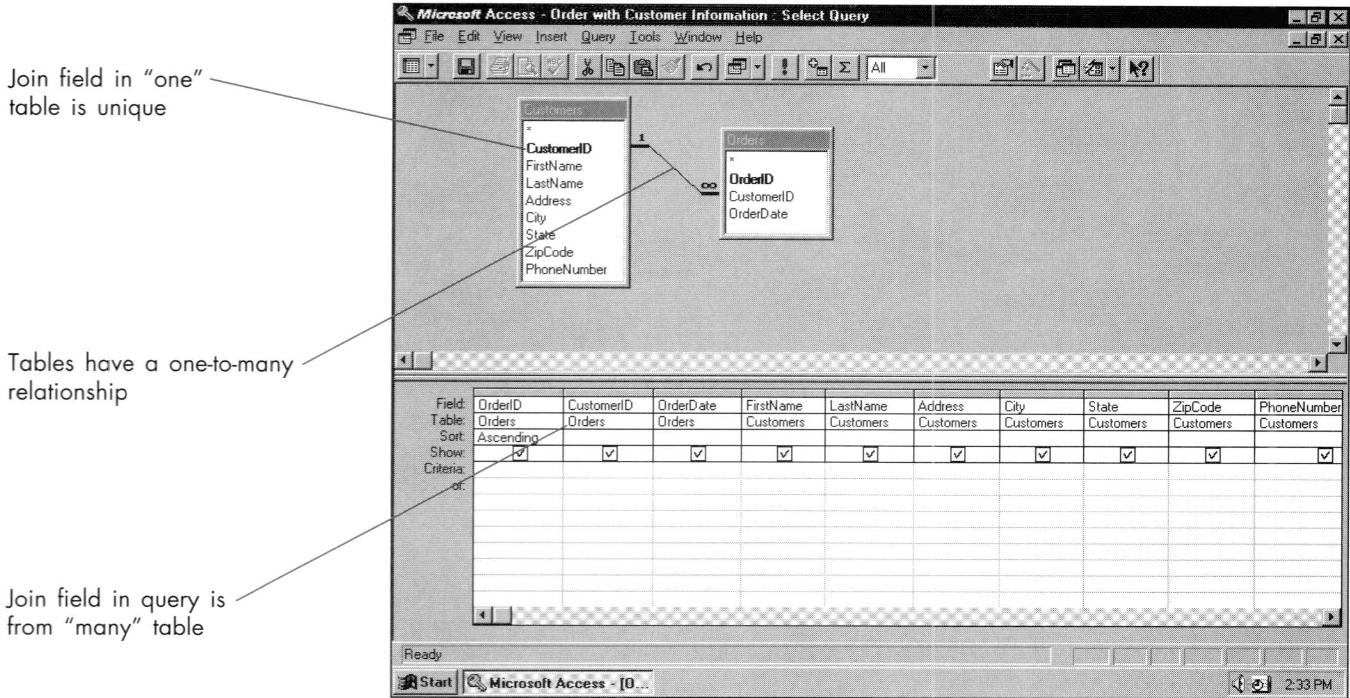

(a) Order with Customer Information Query (used for the main form)

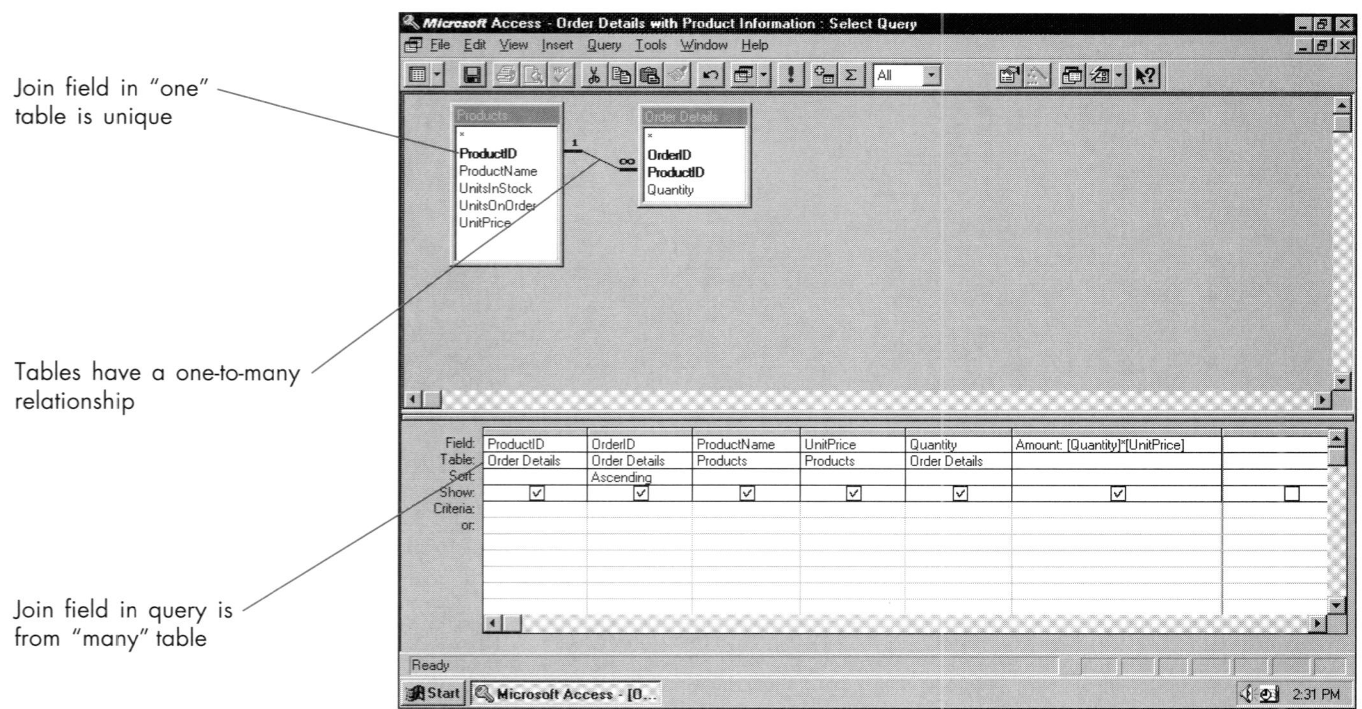

(b) Order Details with Product Information Query (used for the subform)

FIGURE 2.5 Multiple Table Queries

HANDS-ON EXERCISE 2

Subforms and Multiple Table Queries

Objective: To use multiple table queries as the basis for a main form and its associated subform; to create the link between a main form and subform manually. Use Figure 2.6 as a guide in the exercise.

STEP 1: Create the Subform Query

- Open the **Computer Store database** from the previous exercise. Click the **Queries tab** in the Database window, click **New** to display the New Query dialog box, select **Design View** as the means of creating the query, then click **OK.**
- The Show Table dialog box appears in Figure 2.6a with the Tables tab already selected.
- Double click the **Products table** to add this table to the query. Double click the **Order Details table** to add this table to the query. A join line showing the one-to-many relationship between the Products and Order Details table appears automatically.
- Click **Close** to close the Show Table dialog box. If necessary, click the **Maximize button.**

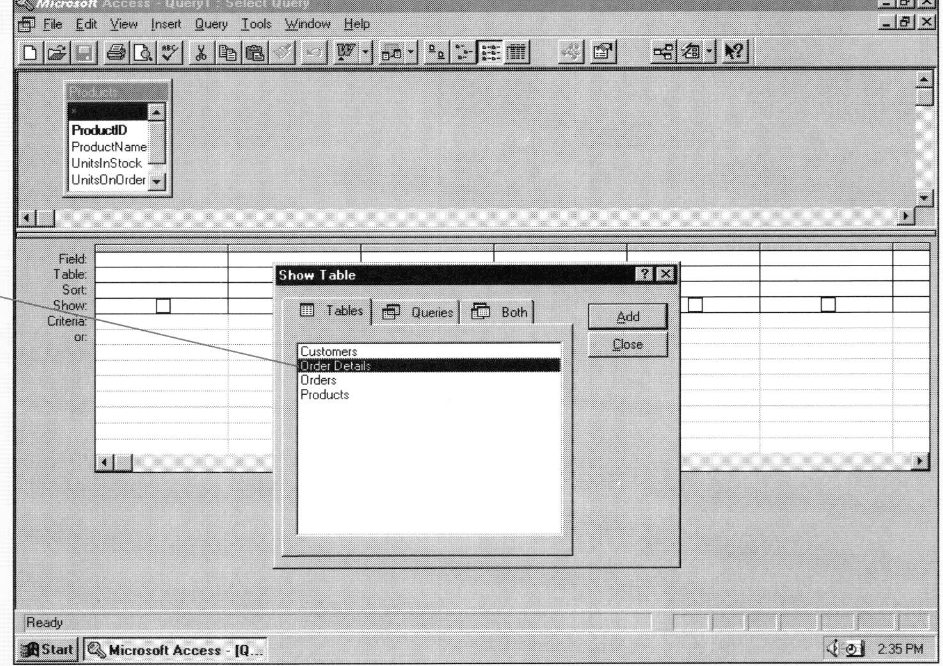

(a) Add the Tables (step 1)

FIGURE 2.6 Hands-on Exercise 2

CUSTOMIZE THE QUERY WINDOW

The Query window displays the field list and QBE grid in its upper and lower halves, respectively. To increase (decrease) the size of either portion of the window, drag the line dividing the upper and lower sections. Drag the title bar to move a field list. You can also size a field list by dragging a border just as you can size any other window.

STEP 2: Create the Subform Query (continued)

➤ Add the fields to the query as follows:

- Double click the **ProductID** and **OrderID fields** in that order from the Order Details table.
- Double click the **ProductName** and **UnitPrice fields** in that order from the Products table.
- Double click the **Quantity field** from the Order Details table.

➤ Click the **Sort row** under the **OrderID field.** Click the **drop-down arrow,** then specify an **ascending** sequence.

➤ Click the first available cell in the Field row. Type **=[Quantity]*[UnitPrice].** Do not be concerned if you cannot see the entire expression, but be sure you put square brackets around each field name.

➤ Press **enter.** Access has substituted Expr1: for the equal sign you typed. Drag the column boundary so that the entire expression is visible as in Figure 2.6b. (You may need to make the other columns narrower in order to see all of the fields in the QBE grid.)

➤ Click and drag to select **Expr1.** (Do not select the colon.) Type **Amount** to substitute a more meaningful field name.

➤ Point to the expression and click the **right mouse button** to display a shortcut menu. Click **Properties** to display the Field Properties dialog box in Figure 2.6b.

➤ Click the box for the **Format property.** Click the **drop-down arrow,** then click **Currency.** Close the Properties dialog box.

➤ Save the query as **Order Details with Product Information.** Click the **Run button** to test the query so that you know the query works prior to using it as the basis of a form.

THE ZOOM BOX

Creating a long expression can be confusing in that you cannot see the entire expression as it is entered. Access anticipates the situation and provides a Zoom box to increase the space in which you can work. Press Shift+F2 as you enter the expression (or select Zoom from the shortcut menu) to display the Zoom box. Click OK to close the Zoom box and continue working in the QBE grid.

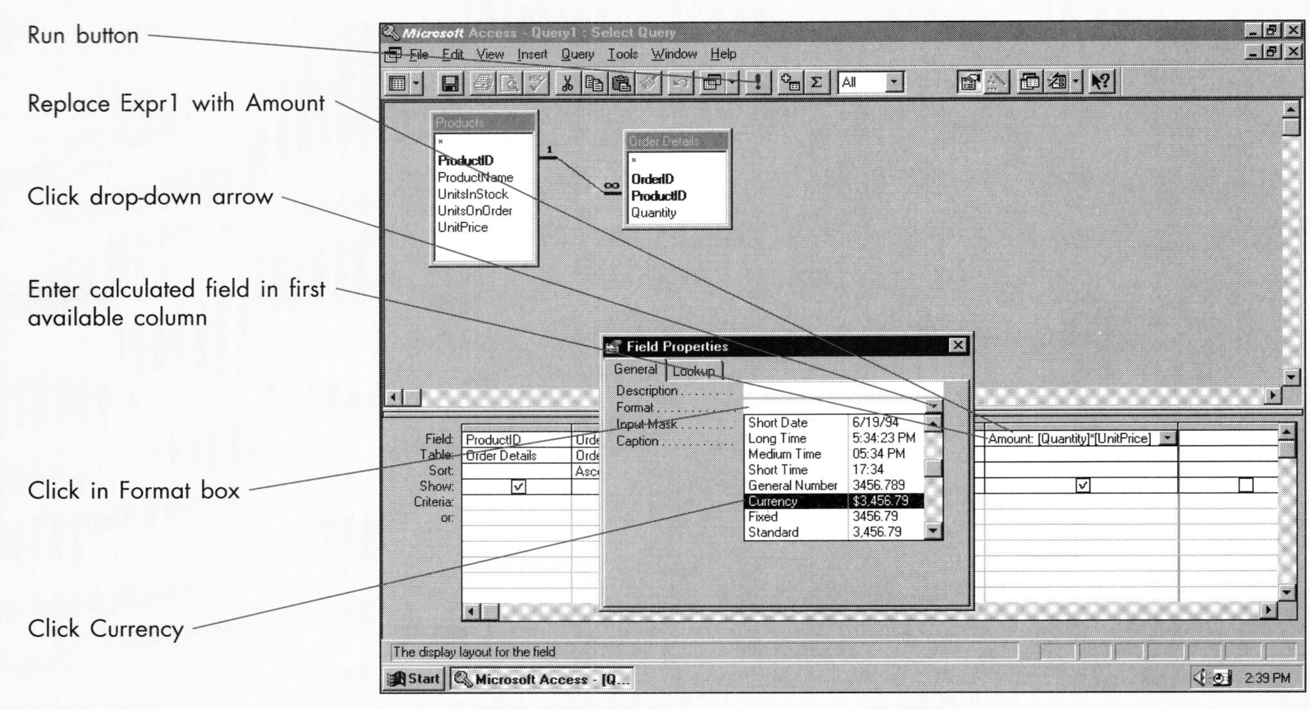

(b) Create the Subform Query (step 2)

FIGURE 2.6 Hands-on Exercise 2 (continued)

STEP 3: Test the Query

- You should see the dynaset shown in Figure 2.6c. (See the boxed tip below if the dynaset does not appear.)
- Enter **1** (not P0001) to change the ProductID to 1 (from 14) in the very first record. (The Format property automatically displays the letter P and the high-order zeros.)
- Press **enter.** The Product Name changes to a Pentium/75 system as you hit the enter key. The unit price also changes, as does the computed amount.
- Click the **Undo button** to cancel the change. The ProductID returns to P0014, and the Product Name changes back to HD Floppy Disks. The unit price also changes, as does the computed amount.
- Close the query.

A PUZZLING ERROR

If you are unable to run a query, it is most likely because you misspelled a field name in the QBE grid. Access interprets the misspelling as a parameter query (see page 83) and asks you to enter a parameter value (the erroneous field name is displayed in the dialog box). Press the Esc key to exit the query and return to the Design view. Click the field row for the problem field and make the necessary correction.

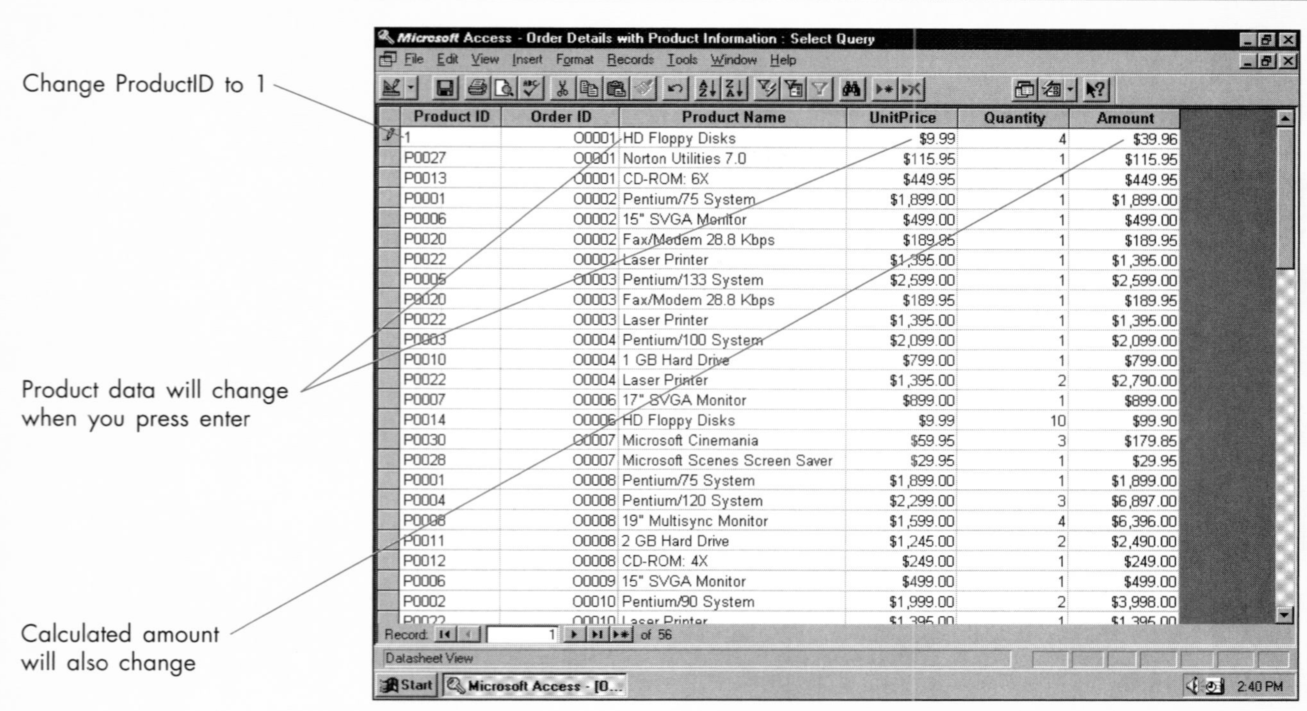

Product ID	Order ID	Product Name	UnitPrice	Quantity	Amount
1	O0001	HD Floppy Disks	$9.99	4	$39.96
P0027	O0001	Norton Utilities 7.0	$115.95	1	$115.95
P0013	O0001	CD-ROM: 6X	$449.95	1	$449.95
P0001	O0002	Pentium/75 System	$1,899.00	1	$1,899.00
P0006	O0002	15" SVGA Monitor	$499.00	1	$499.00
P0020	O0002	Fax/Modem 28.8 Kbps	$189.95	1	$189.95
P0022	O0002	Laser Printer	$1,395.00	1	$1,395.00
P0005	O0003	Pentium/133 System	$2,599.00	1	$2,599.00
P0020	O0003	Fax/Modem 28.8 Kbps	$189.95	1	$189.95
P0022	O0003	Laser Printer	$1,395.00	1	$1,395.00
P0003	O0004	Pentium/100 System	$2,099.00	1	$2,099.00
P0010	O0004	1 GB Hard Drive	$799.00	1	$799.00
P0022	O0004	Laser Printer	$1,395.00	2	$2,790.00
P0007	O0006	17" SVGA Monitor	$899.00	1	$899.00
P0014	O0006	HD Floppy Disks	$9.99	10	$99.90
P0030	O0007	Microsoft Cinemania	$59.95	3	$179.85
P0028	O0007	Microsoft Scenes Screen Saver	$29.95	1	$29.95
P0001	O0008	Pentium/75 System	$1,899.00	1	$1,899.00
P0004	O0008	Pentium/120 System	$2,299.00	3	$6,897.00
P0008	O0008	19" Multisync Monitor	$1,599.00	4	$6,396.00
P0011	O0008	2 GB Hard Drive	$1,245.00	2	$2,490.00
P0012	O0008	CD-ROM: 4X	$249.00	1	$249.00
P0006	O0009	15" SVGA Monitor	$499.00	1	$499.00
P0002	O0010	Pentium/90 System	$1,999.00	2	$3,998.00
P0022	O0010	Laser Printer	$1,395.00	1	$1,395.00

(c) Test the Query (step 3)

FIGURE 2.6 Hands-on Exercise 2 (continued)

STEP 4: Create the Orders Form

- ➤ You should be back in the Database window. Click the **Forms tab.** Click the **New Command button** to display the New Form dialog box, click **Form Wizard** in the list box, then click the **drop-down arrow** to display the available tables and queries.
- ➤ Select the **Order with Customer Information query** (the query we provided) as the basis for the form, then click **OK** to start the Form Wizard.
- ➤ You should see the Form Wizard dialog box, which displays all of the fields in the selected query. Click the **>> button** to enter all of the fields onto the form. Click **Next.**
- ➤ **By Orders** is selected as the means of viewing your data. Click **Next.** The **Columnar layout** is already selected. Click **Next.** Click **Standard** as the style for your form. Click **Next.**
- ➤ Save the form as **Super Store Order Form.** Click the option button to **Modify the form's design,** then click the **Finish Command button** to create the form and exit the Form Wizard.

STEP 5: Modify the Orders Form

- ➤ You should see the Super Store Order Form in Figure 2.6d. Click the **CustomerID control** to select the control and display the sizing handles, then drag the **CustomerID control** so that it is next to the OrderID.
- ➤ Click and drag the **OrderDate control** so that it is next to the CustomerID. (The width of the form will change automatically, but you will need to extend the width a little further when you release the mouse.)

Save button

Click CustomerID control, then drag it next to OrderID control

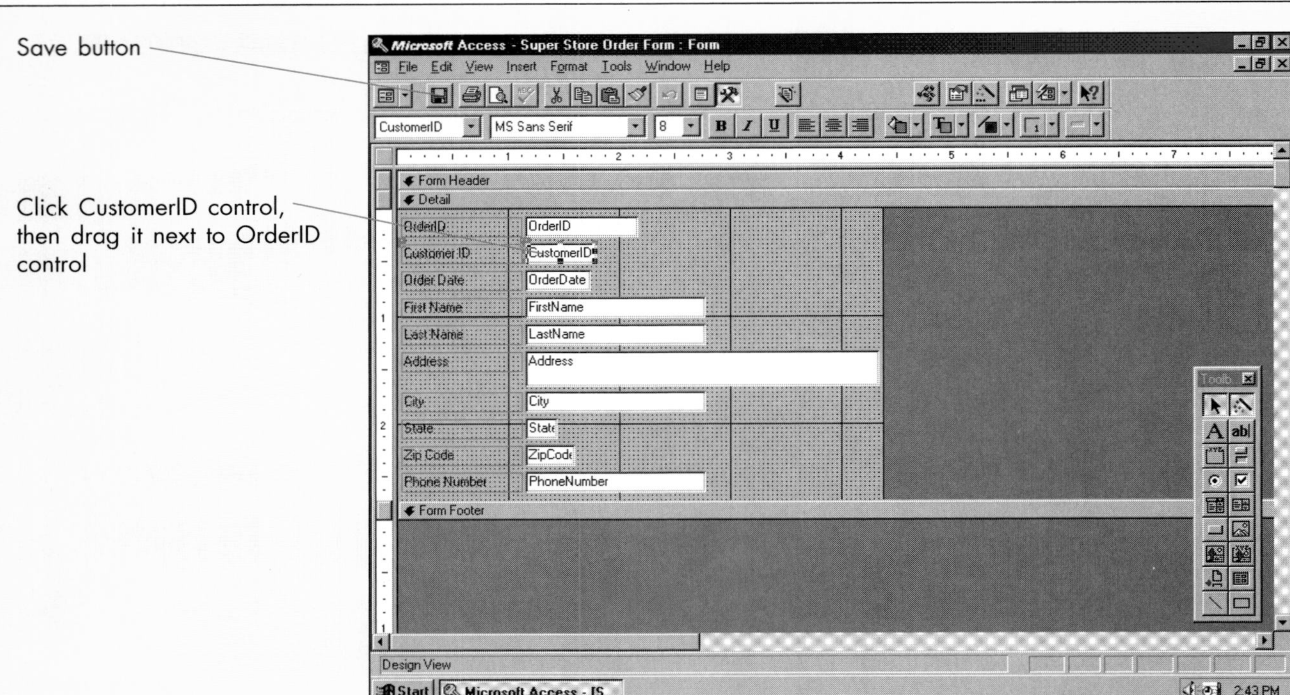

(d) Create the Super Store Order Form (steps 4 and 5)

FIGURE 2.6 Hands-on Exercise 2 (continued)

➤ Click and drag the other controls to complete the form:
- Click and drag the **LastName control** so that it is next to the FirstName control.
- Click and drag the **Address control** under the control for FirstName.
- Place the controls for **City, State,** and **ZipCode** on the same line and move them under the Address control.
- Move the control for **PhoneNumber** under the control for City.
- Move all of the controls under the OrderID control.

➤ Click the **Save button** to save the form.

SIZING OR MOVING A CONTROL AND ITS LABEL

A bound control is created with an attached label. Select (click) the control, and the control has sizing handles and a move handle, but the label has only a move handle. Select the label (instead of the control) and the opposite occurs: The control has only a move handle, but the label will have both sizing handles and a move handle. To move a control and its label, click and drag the border of either object. To move either the control or its label, click and drag the move handle (a tiny square in the upper-left corner) of the appropriate object.

STEP 6: Create the Order Details Subform

- Click and drag the bottom edge of the **Detail section** so that you have approximately 2 inches of blank space as shown in Figure 2.6e. (This is where the subform will go.)
- Click the **Subform/Subreport button** on the Toolbox toolbar, then click and drag in the **Orders form** where you want the subform to go. Release the mouse to begin the Subform/Subreport Wizard.
- The **Table/Query option button** is selected, indicating that we will build the subform from a table or query. Click **Next.**
- You should see the Subform/Subreport dialog box. Click the **drop-down arrow** on the Tables and Queries list box to select the **Order Details with Product Information query** as shown in Figure 2.6e. (This is the query you created in steps 1 and 2.)
- Click the **>> button** to enter all of the fields in the query onto the subform. Click **Next.**
- The next step asks you to define the fields that link the main form to the subform: The option button to **Choose from a list** is selected. The selected link will **Show Order Details with Product Information.** Click **Next.**
- The Wizard suggests **Order Details with Product Information subform** as the name of the subform. Click **Finish** to exit the Subform/Subreport wizard.

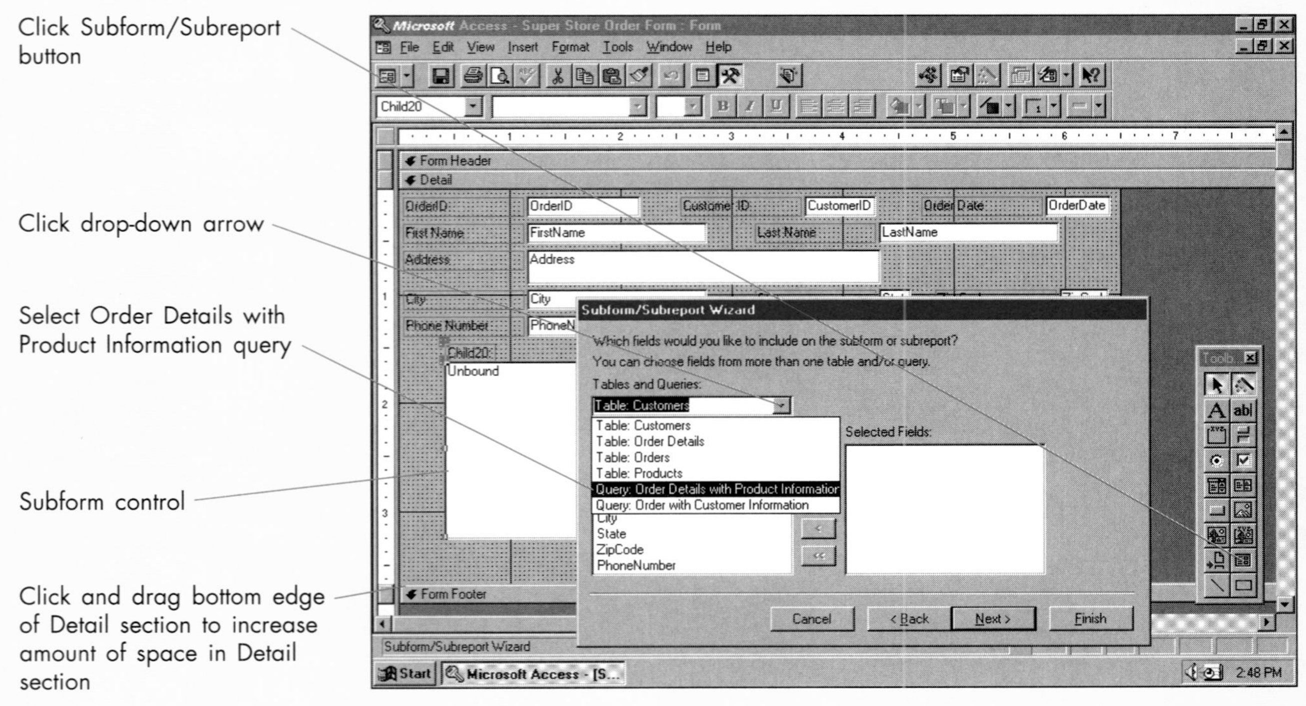

(e) Create the Subform (step 6)

FIGURE 2.6 Hands-on Exercise 2 (continued)

STEP 7: The Order Details Subform (Datasheet view)

- You should be in the Design view for the Super Store Order Form. The white rectangular control indicates the position of the Order Details subform within the main form. Maximize the window.
- You need to open the **Order Details subform** to check the column width of its columns. Accordingly:
  - Deselect the Order Details subform (by clicking anywhere in the main form), then double click the **Order Details subform** to open it. Change to the Datasheet view, *or*
  - Change to the **Database window,** click the **Forms tab,** and open the **Order Details subform.**
- You should see the Datasheet view of the Order Details with Product Information subform as shown in Figure 2.6f. Click and drag the various column headings until you can read all of the information.
- Click the **Save button** to save the new layout, then close the subform. This returns you to the Design view of the Orders form. (Alternatively, you may be back in the Database window, in which case you need to pull down the Window menu to return to the Super Store Order Form.)
- Select (click) the label of the **subform control,** then click and drag the existing text (Order Details with Product Information subform). Type **Enter Product ID and Quantity** (to provide descriptive help to the user).
- Save the completed form.

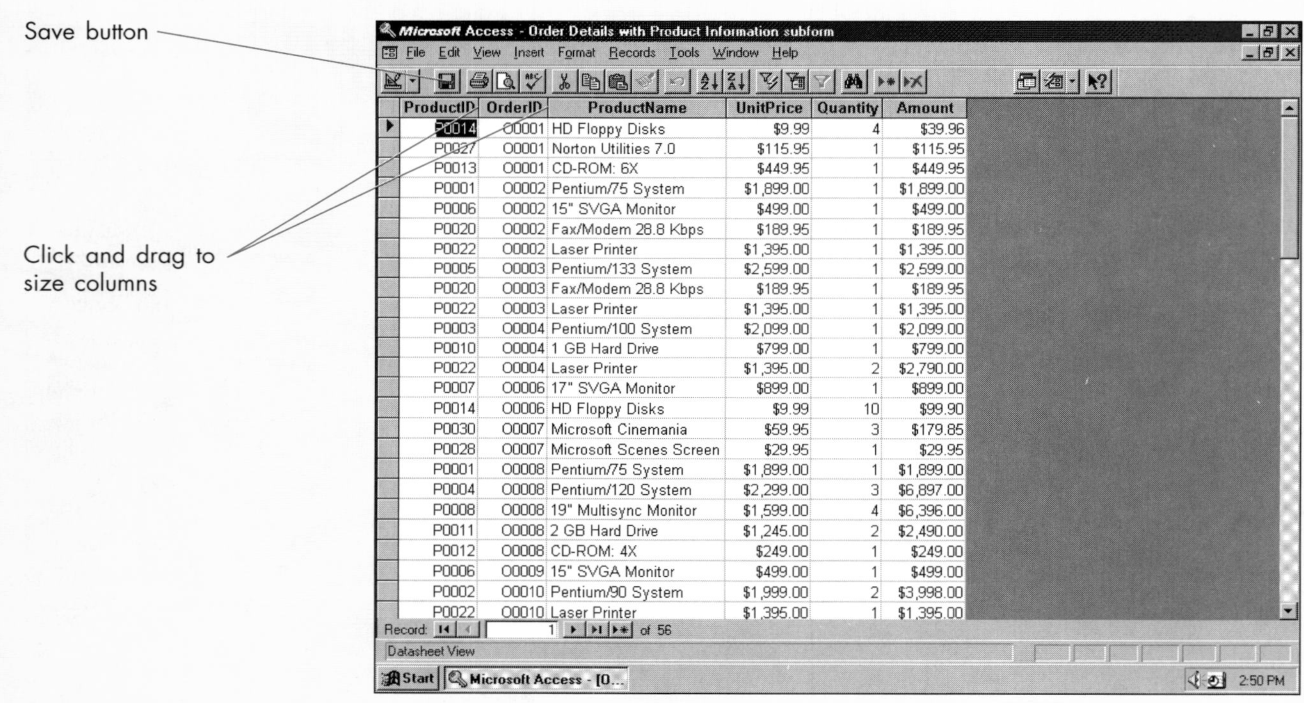

ProductID	OrderID	ProductName	UnitPrice	Quantity	Amount
P0014	O0001	HD Floppy Disks	$9.99	4	$39.96
P0027	O0001	Norton Utilities 7.0	$115.95	1	$115.95
P0013	O0001	CD-ROM: 6X	$449.95	1	$449.95
P0001	O0002	Pentium/75 System	$1,899.00	1	$1,899.00
P0006	O0002	15" SVGA Monitor	$499.00	1	$499.00
P0020	O0002	Fax/Modem 28.8 Kbps	$189.95	1	$189.95
P0022	O0002	Laser Printer	$1,395.00	1	$1,395.00
P0005	O0003	Pentium/133 System	$2,599.00	1	$2,599.00
P0020	O0003	Fax/Modem 28.8 Kbps	$189.95	1	$189.95
P0022	O0003	Laser Printer	$1,395.00	1	$1,395.00
P0003	O0004	Pentium/100 System	$2,099.00	1	$2,099.00
P0010	O0004	1 GB Hard Drive	$799.00	1	$799.00
P0022	O0004	Laser Printer	$1,395.00	2	$2,790.00
P0007	O0006	17" SVGA Monitor	$899.00	1	$899.00
P0014	O0006	HD Floppy Disks	$9.99	10	$99.90
P0030	O0007	Microsoft Cinemania	$59.95	3	$179.85
P0028	O0007	Microsoft Scenes Screen	$29.95	1	$29.95
P0001	O0008	Pentium/75 System	$1,899.00	1	$1,899.00
P0004	O0008	Pentium/120 System	$2,299.00	3	$6,897.00
P0008	O0008	19" Multisync Monitor	$1,599.00	4	$6,396.00
P0011	O0008	2 GB Hard Drive	$1,245.00	2	$2,490.00
P0012	O0008	CD-ROM: 4X	$249.00	1	$249.00
P0006	O0009	15" SVGA Monitor	$499.00	1	$499.00
P0002	O0010	Pentium/90 System	$1,999.00	2	$3,998.00
P0022	O0010	Laser Printer	$1,395.00	1	$1,395.00

(f) Datasheet View of Subform (step 7)

FIGURE 2.6 Hands-on Exercise 2 (continued)

STEP 8: Enter a New Order

- Change to the **Form view** of the Orders form as shown in Figure 2.6g. (You will probably need to return to the Design view to move and/or size the subform control.)
- Click the **New Record button** to display a blank form so that you can place an order.
- Click in the **Customer ID text box.** Enter **13** (your customer number from the first exercise), then press the **Tab** or **enter key** to move to the next field.
  - The OrderID is entered automatically as it is an AutoNumber field and assigned the next sequential number.
  - All of your customer information (your name, address, and phone number) is entered automatically because of the AutoLookup feature that is built into the underlying query.
  - Today's date is entered automatically because of the default value (=Date()) that is built into the Orders table.
- Click the **ProductID text box** in the subform. Enter **1** (not P0001) and press the **enter key** to move to the next field. The OrderID (O0026) is entered automatically, as is the Product Name and Unit Price.
- Press the **Tab key** three times to move to the Quantity field, enter **1,** and press the **Tab key** twice more to move to the ProductID field for the next item. (The amount is calculated automatically.)
- Complete your order as shown in Figure 2.6g. (If necessary, re-open the subform in the Datasheet view as described in step 7 to adjust the column widths.)

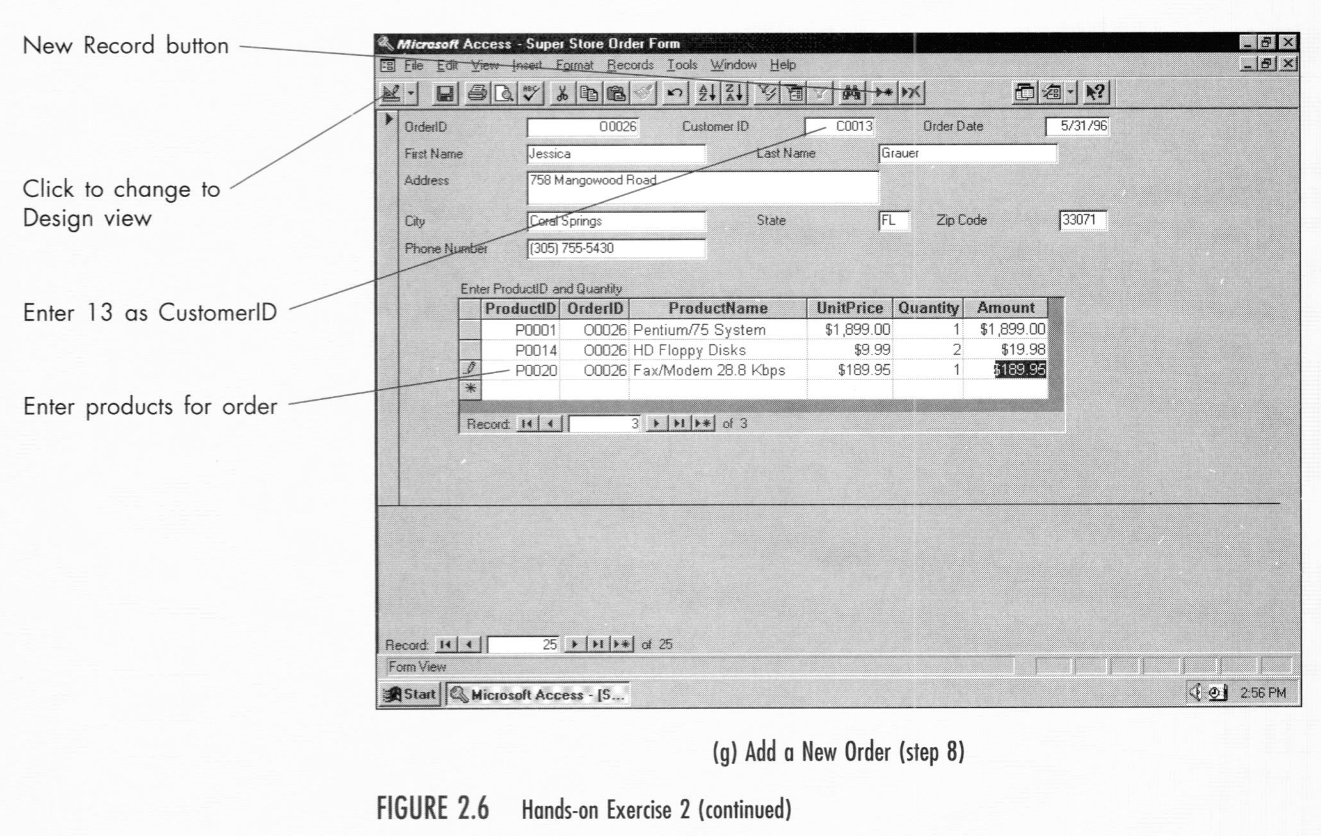

(g) Add a New Order (step 8)

FIGURE 2.6 Hands-on Exercise 2 (continued)

AUTOLOOKUP—WHY IT WORKS

The main form is based on a query containing a one-to-many relationship between Customers and Orders, in which CustomerID is the join field and appears in both tables. The CustomerID is the primary key in the Customers table and is unique in that table. The query, however, must contain the CustomerID field from the Orders table for the AutoLookup feature to take effect. AutoLookup is implemented in similar fashion in the subform, which is based on a query containing a one-to-many relationship between the Products and Order Details tables. The ProductID field is common to both tables and must be taken from the Order Details table (the "many" table) in order for AutoLookup to work.

STEP 9: Print the Completed Order

- Click the **Selection Area** to select the current record (the order you just completed). This is done to print only the current record.
- Pull down the **File menu.** Click **Page Setup** to display the Page Setup dialog box as shown in Figure 2.6h. Click the **Page tab,** then click the **Landscape option button** so that your form will fit on the page. (Alternatively, you could click the **Margins tab** and decrease the left and right margins.) Click **OK** to close the Print Setup dialog box.

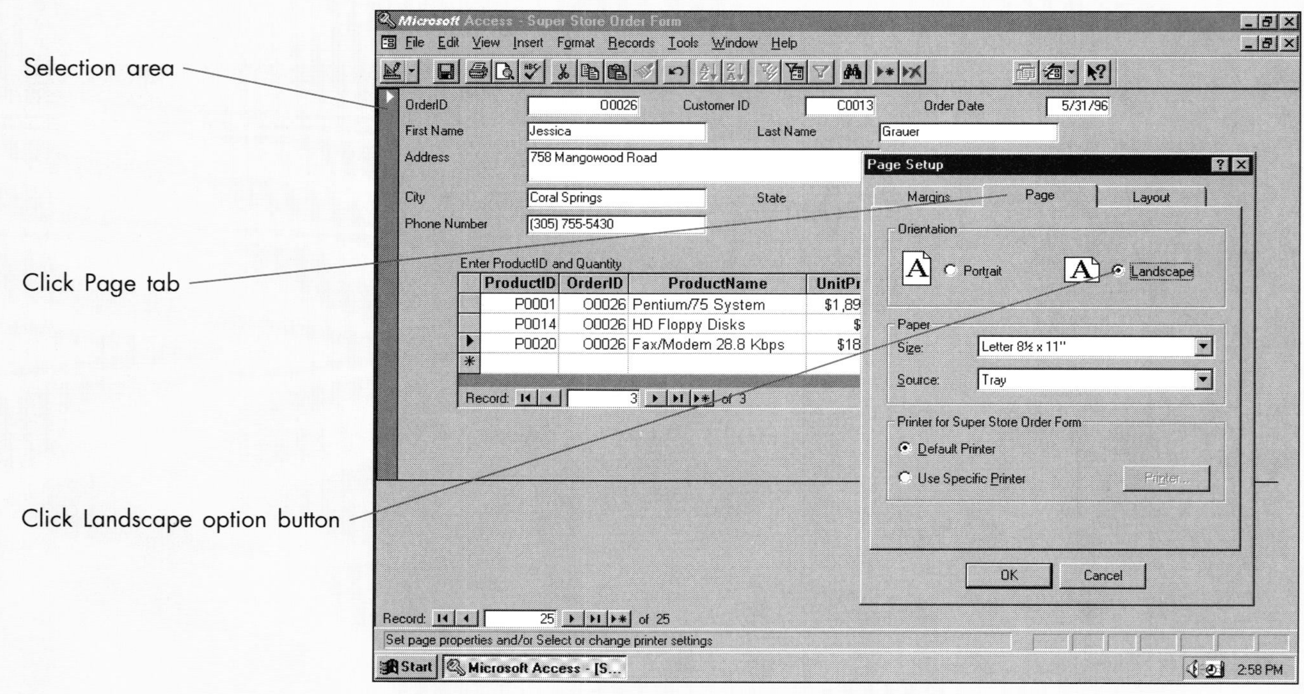

(h) Print Your Order (step 9)

FIGURE 2.6 Hands-on Exercise 2 (continued)

- ➤ Pull down the **File menu,** click **Print** to display the Print dialog box, then click the option button to specify **Selected Record(s)** as the print range. (You cannot click the Print button on the toolbar as that will print every record.)
- ➤ Click **OK** to print the form and submit it to your instructor as proof that you did this exercise. Close the form, then close the database. Answer **Yes** if asked to save the changes.
- ➤ Exit Access if you do not want to continue with the next exercise at this time.

ADDING CUSTOMERS

The form that you just created enables you to add an order for an existing customer, provided you know the CustomerID. It does not, however, let you add an order for a new customer because the underlying query does not contain the primary key from the Customers table. See practice exercises 3 and 4 at the end of the chapter for instructions on how to overcome these limitations.

ADVANCED QUERIES

A select query, powerful as it is, has its limitations. It requires you to enter the criteria directly in the query, which means you have to change the query every time you vary the criteria. What if you wanted to use a different set of criteria (e.g., a different customer's name) every time you ran the "same" query?

A second limitation of select queries is that they do not produce summary information about groups of records. How many orders have we received this month? What was the largest order? What was the smallest order? This section introduces two additional types of queries to overcome both limitations.

Parameter Queries

A ***parameter query*** prompts you for the criteria each time you execute the query. It is created in similar fashion to a select query and is illustrated in Figure 2.7. The difference between a parameter query and an ordinary select query is the way in which the criteria are specified. A select query contains the actual criteria. A parameter query, however, contains a ***prompt*** (message) that will request the criteria when the query is executed.

The QBE grid in Figure 2.7a creates a parameter query that will display the orders for a particular customer. The query does not contain the customer's name, but a prompt for that name. The prompt is enclosed in square brackets and is displayed in a dialog box in which the user enters the requested data when the query is executed. Thus, the user supplies the customer's name in Figure 2.7b, and the query displays the resulting dynaset in Figure 2.7c. This enables you to run the same query with different criteria; that is, you can enter a different customer name every time you execute the query.

A parameter query may prompt for any number of variables (parameters), which are entered in successive dialog boxes. The parameters are requested in order from left to right, according to the way in which they appear in the QBE grid.

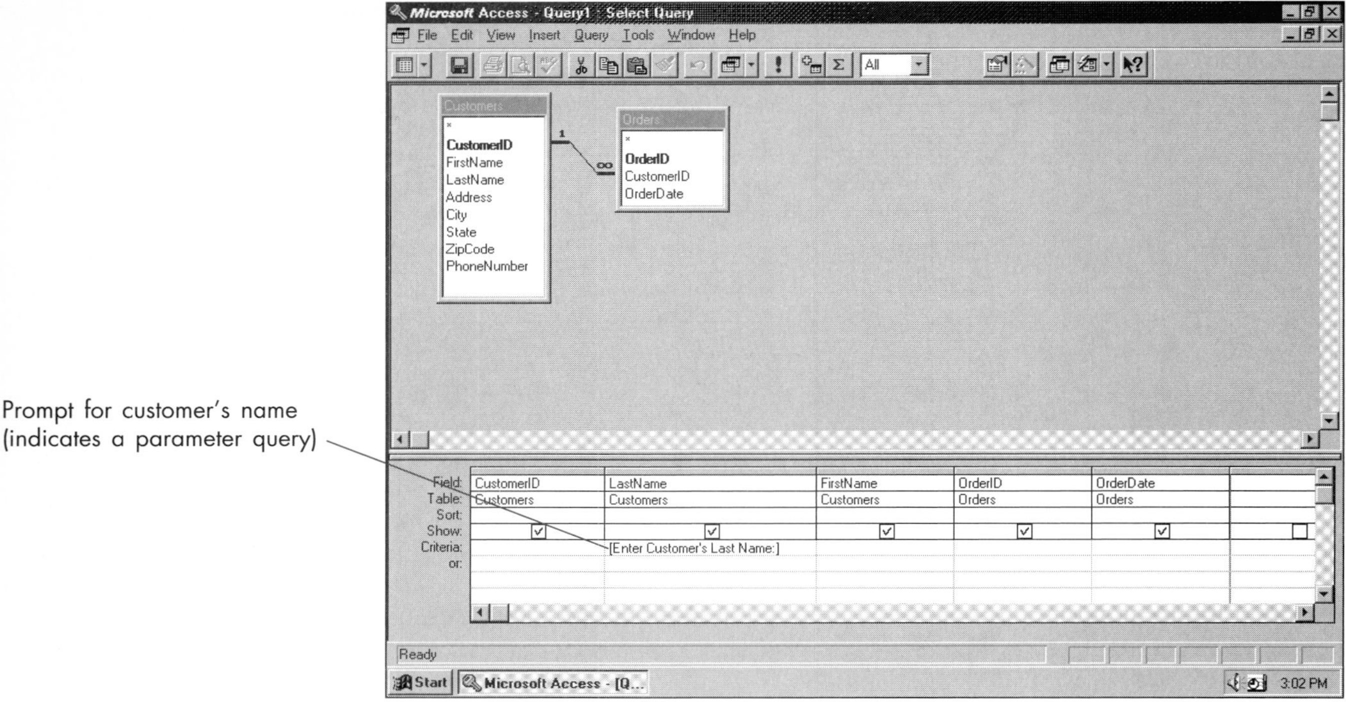

(a) QBE Grid

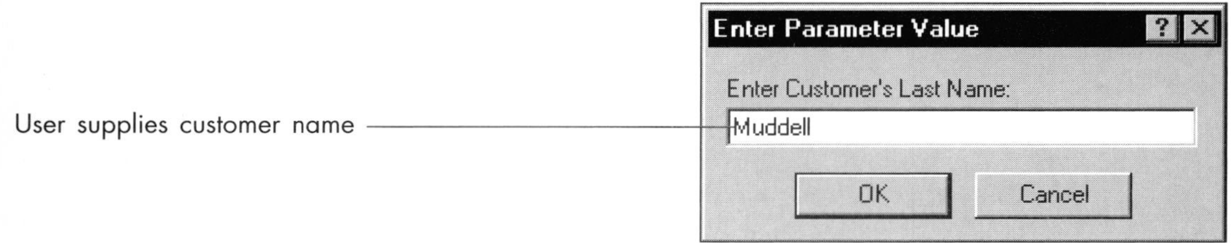

(b) Dialog Box

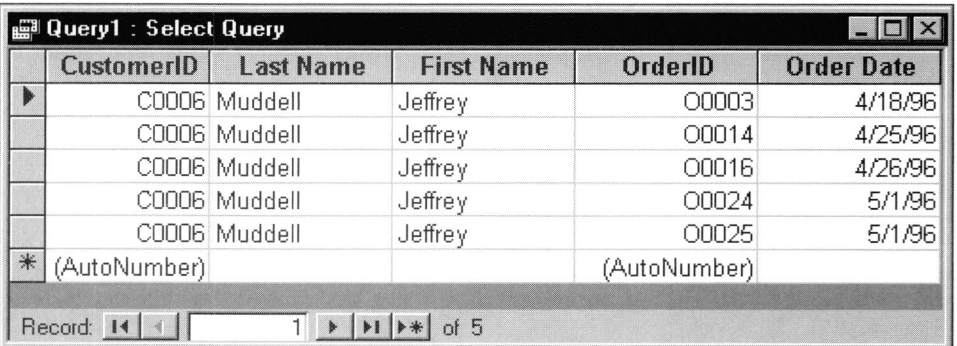
Query1 : Select Query

CustomerID	Last Name	First Name	OrderID	Order Date
C0006	Muddell	Jeffrey	O0003	4/18/96
C0006	Muddell	Jeffrey	O0014	4/25/96
C0006	Muddell	Jeffrey	O0016	4/26/96
C0006	Muddell	Jeffrey	O0024	5/1/96
C0006	Muddell	Jeffrey	O0025	5/1/96
(AutoNumber)			(AutoNumber)	

Record: 1 of 5

(c) Dynaset

FIGURE 2.7 Parameter Query

PARAMETER QUERIES, FORMS, AND REPORTS

A parameter query can be used as the basis for a form or report. Create the form or report in the normal way (with or without a wizard), but specify the parameter query when asked which table or query to use. Then, when you open the form or report, Access will display a dialog box with the prompt(s) contained within the parameter query. Supply the requested information, and the form or report is created based on the criteria you entered.

Total Queries

A ***total query*** performs calculations on a *group* of records using one of several summary (aggregate) functions available within Access. These include the Sum, Count, Avg, Max, and Min functions to determine the total, number, average, maximum, and minimum values, respectively. Figure 2.8 illustrates the use of a total query to compute the total amount for each order.

Figure 2.8a displays the dynaset from a select query with fields from both the Products and Order Details tables. (The dynaset contains one record for each product in each order and enables us to verify the results of the total query in Figure 2.8c.) Each record in Figure 2.8a contains the price of the product, the quantity ordered, and the amount for that product. There are, for example, three products in order O0001. The first product costs $449.95, the second product costs $39.96 (four units at $9.99 each), and the third product costs $115.95). The total for the order comes to $602.86, which is obtained by (manually) adding the amount field in each of the records for this order.

Figure 2.8b shows the Design view of the total query to calculate the cost of each order. The query contains only two fields, OrderID and Amount. The QBE grid also displays a ***Total row*** in which each field in the query has either a Group By or aggregate entry. The ***Group By*** entry under OrderID indicates that the records in the dynaset are to be grouped (aggregated) according to the like values of OrderID; that is, there will be one record in the total query for each distinct value of OrderID. The ***Sum function*** specifies the arithmetic operation to be performed on each group of records.

The dynaset in Figure 2.8c displays the result of the total query and contains *aggregate* records, as opposed to *individual* records. There are, for example, three records for order O0001 in Figure 2.8a, but only one record in Figure 2.8c. This is because each record in a total query contains a calculated result for a group of records.

THE UNMATCHED QUERY WIZARD

The Unmatched Query Wizard identifies records in one table that do not have matching records in another table. It can, for example, tell you whether there are products in inventory that have never been ordered; that is, it will find the records in the Products table that do not appear in the Order Details table. Such information is extremely useful and can be used to reduce the cost of inventory. The Unmatched Query Wizard is explored in problem 2 at the end of the chapter.

Contains multiple records for order O0001

Orders with Products : Select Query

Order ID	Product ID	Product Name	Quantity	UnitPrice	Amount
O0001	P0013	CD-ROM: 6X	1	$449.95	$449.95
O0001	P0014	HD Floppy Disks	4	$9.99	$39.96
O0001	P0027	Norton Utilities 7.0	1	$115.95	$115.95
O0002	P0001	Pentium/75 System	1	$1,899.00	$1,899.00
O0002	P0006	15" SVGA Monitor	1	$499.00	$499.00
O0002	P0020	Fax/Modem 28.8 Kbps	1	$189.95	$189.95
O0002	P0022	Laser Printer	1	$1,395.00	$1,395.00
O0003	P0005	Pentium/133 System	1	$2,599.00	$2,599.00
O0003	P0020	Fax/Modem 28.8 Kbps	1	$189.95	$189.95
O0003	P0022	Laser Printer	1	$1,395.00	$1,395.00
O0004	P0003	Pentium/100 System	1	$2,099.00	$2,099.00
O0004	P0010	1 GB Hard Drive	1	$799.00	$799.00
O0004	P0022	Laser Printer	2	$1,395.00	$2,790.00
O0006	P0007	17" SVGA Monitor	1	$899.00	$899.00
O0006	P0014	HD Floppy Disks	10	$9.99	$99.90
O0007	P0028	Microsoft Scenes Screen Saver	1	$29.95	$29.95
O0007	P0030	Microsoft Cinemania	3	$59.95	$179.85
O0008	P0001	Pentium/75 System	1	$1,899.00	$1,899.00
O0008	P0004	Pentium/120 System	3	$2,299.00	$6,897.00
O0008	P0008	19" Multisync Monitor	4	$1,599.00	$6,396.00
O0008	P0011	2 GB Hard Drive	2	$1,245.00	$2,490.00
O0008	P0012	CD-ROM: 4X	1	$249.00	$249.00

Record: 1 of 59

(a) Order Details with Product Information Dynaset

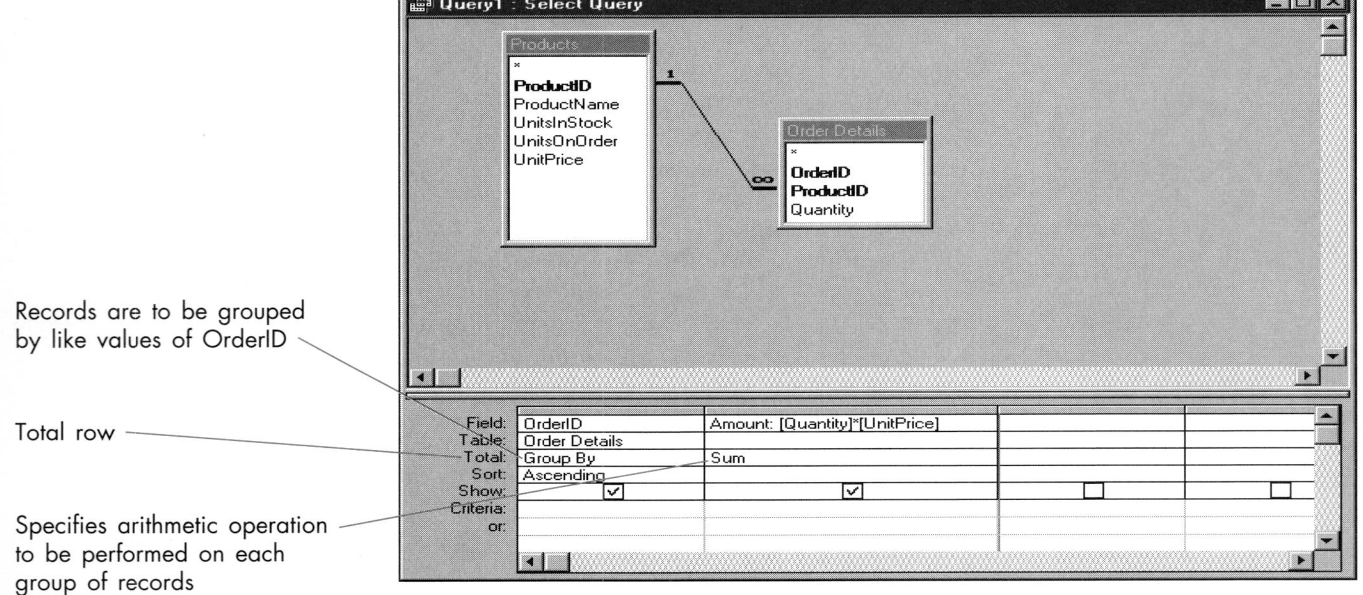

(b) QBE Grid

Order ID	Amount
O0001	$605.86
O0002	$3,982.95
O0003	$4,183.95
O0004	$5,688.00
O0006	$998.90
O0007	$209.80
O0008	$17,931.00

Record: 1 of

(c) Dynaset

FIGURE 2.8 Total Query

The exercise that follows begins by having you create the report in Figure 2.9. The report is a detailed analysis of all orders, listing every product in every order. The report is based on a query containing fields from the Orders, Customers, Products, and Order Details tables. The exercise also provides practice in creating parameter queries and total queries.

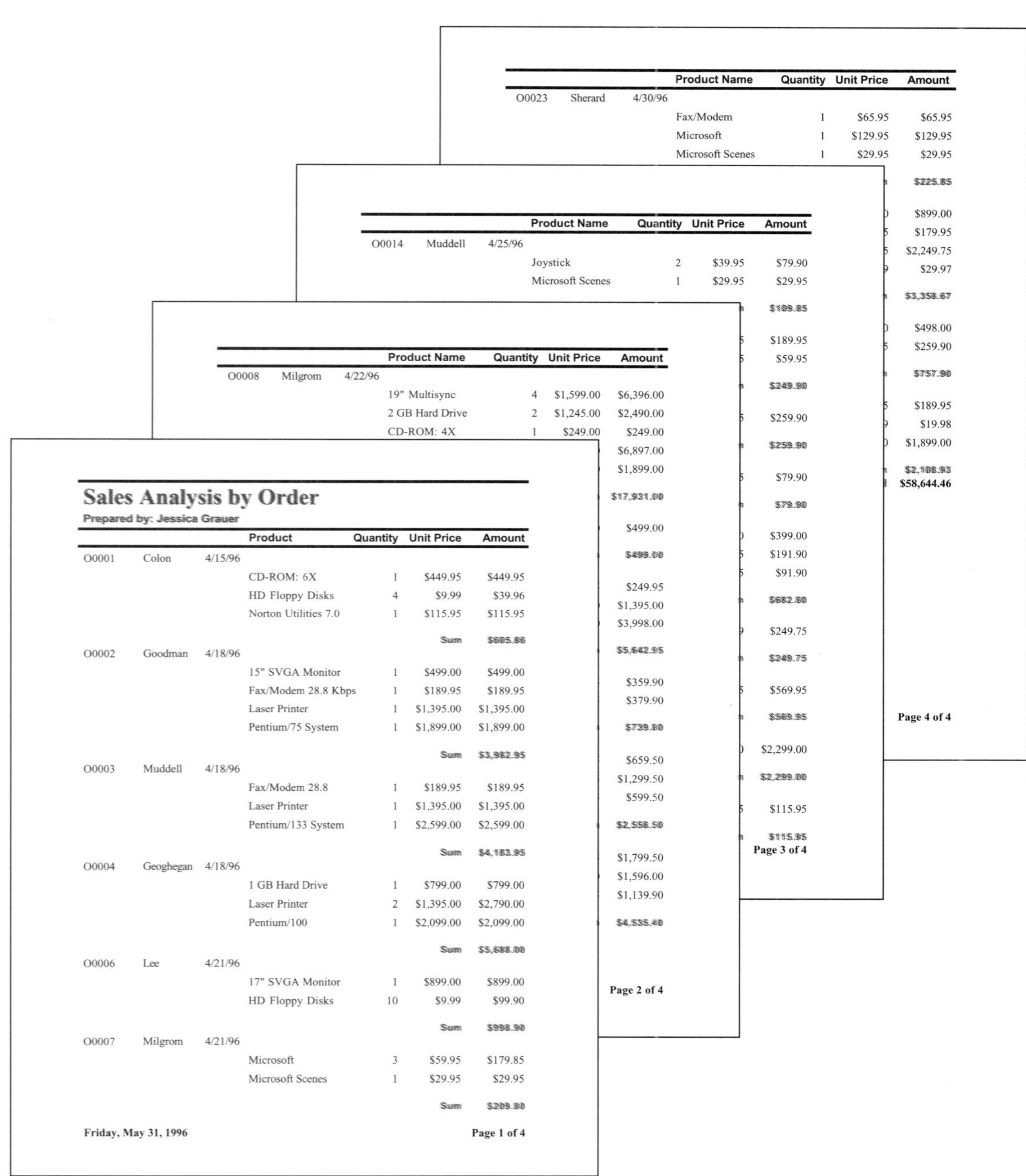

Sales Analysis by Order

Prepared by: Jessica Grauer

			Product	Quantity	Unit Price	Amount
O0001	Colon	4/15/96				
			CD-ROM: 6X	1	$449.95	$449.95
			HD Floppy Disks	4	$9.99	$39.96
			Norton Utilities 7.0	1	$115.95	$115.95
					Sum	$605.86
O0002	Goodman	4/18/96				
			15" SVGA Monitor	1	$499.00	$499.00
			Fax/Modem 28.8 Kbps	1	$189.95	$189.95
			Laser Printer	1	$1,395.00	$1,395.00
			Pentium/75 System	1	$1,899.00	$1,899.00
					Sum	$3,982.95
O0003	Muddell	4/18/96				
			Fax/Modem 28.8	1	$189.95	$189.95
			Laser Printer	1	$1,395.00	$1,395.00
			Pentium/133 System	1	$2,599.00	$2,599.00
					Sum	$4,183.95
O0004	Geoghegan	4/18/96				
			1 GB Hard Drive	1	$799.00	$799.00
			Laser Printer	2	$1,395.00	$2,790.00
			Pentium/100	1	$2,099.00	$2,099.00
					Sum	$5,688.00
O0006	Lee	4/21/96				
			17" SVGA Monitor	1	$899.00	$899.00
			HD Floppy Disks	10	$9.99	$99.90
					Sum	$998.90
O0007	Milgrom	4/21/96				
			Microsoft	3	$59.95	$179.85
			Microsoft Scenes	1	$29.95	$29.95
					Sum	$209.80

Friday, May 31, 1996 — Page 1 of 4

			Product Name	Quantity	Unit Price	Amount
O0008	Milgrom	4/22/96				
			19" Multisync	4	$1,599.00	$6,396.00
			2 GB Hard Drive	2	$1,245.00	$2,490.00
			CD-ROM: 4X	1	$249.00	$249.00

$6,897.00 $1,899.00 $17,931.00 $499.00 $499.00 $249.95 $1,395.00 $3,998.00 $5,642.95 $359.90 $379.90 $739.80 $659.50 $1,299.50 $599.50 $2,558.50 $1,799.50 $1,596.00 $1,139.90 $4,535.40

Page 2 of 4

			Product Name	Quantity	Unit Price	Amount
O0014	Muddell	4/25/96				
			Joystick	2	$39.95	$79.90
			Microsoft Scenes	1	$29.95	$29.95

$109.85 $189.95 $59.95 $249.90 $259.90 $259.90 $79.90 $79.90 $399.00 $191.90 $91.90 $682.80 $249.75 $249.75 $569.95 $569.95 $2,299.00 $2,299.00 $115.95 $115.95

Page 3 of 4

			Product Name	Quantity	Unit Price	Amount
O0023	Sherard	4/30/96				
			Fax/Modem	1	$65.95	$65.95
			Microsoft	1	$129.95	$129.95
			Microsoft Scenes	1	$29.95	$29.95

$225.85 $899.00 $179.95 $2,249.75 $29.97 $3,358.67 $498.00 $259.90 $757.90 $189.95 $19.98 $1,899.00 $2,108.93 $58,644.46

Page 4 of 4

FIGURE 2.9 Sales Analysis by Order

HANDS-ON EXERCISE 3

Advanced Queries

Objective: To copy an existing query; to create a parameter query; to create a total query using the aggregate Sum function. Use Figure 2.10 as a guide.

STEP 1: Create the Query

- Open the **Computer Store database** from the previous exercise. Click the **Queries tab** in the Database window, click **New** to display the New Query dialog box, select **Design View,** then click **OK.**
- By now you have had sufficient practice creating a query, so we will just outline the steps:
  - Add the **Customers, Orders, Products,** and **Order Details** tables. Move and size the field lists within the Query window to match Figure 2.10a. Maximize the window.
  - Add the indicated fields to the QBE grid. Be sure to take each field from the appropriate table.
  - Add the calculated field to compute the amount by multiplying the quantity by the unit price. Point to the expression, click the **right mouse button** to display a shortcut menu, then change the Format property to **Currency.**
  - Check that your query matches Figure 2.10a. Save the query as **Sales Analysis by Order.**
- Click the **Run button** (the exclamation point) to run the query. The dynaset contains one record for every item in every order. Close the query.

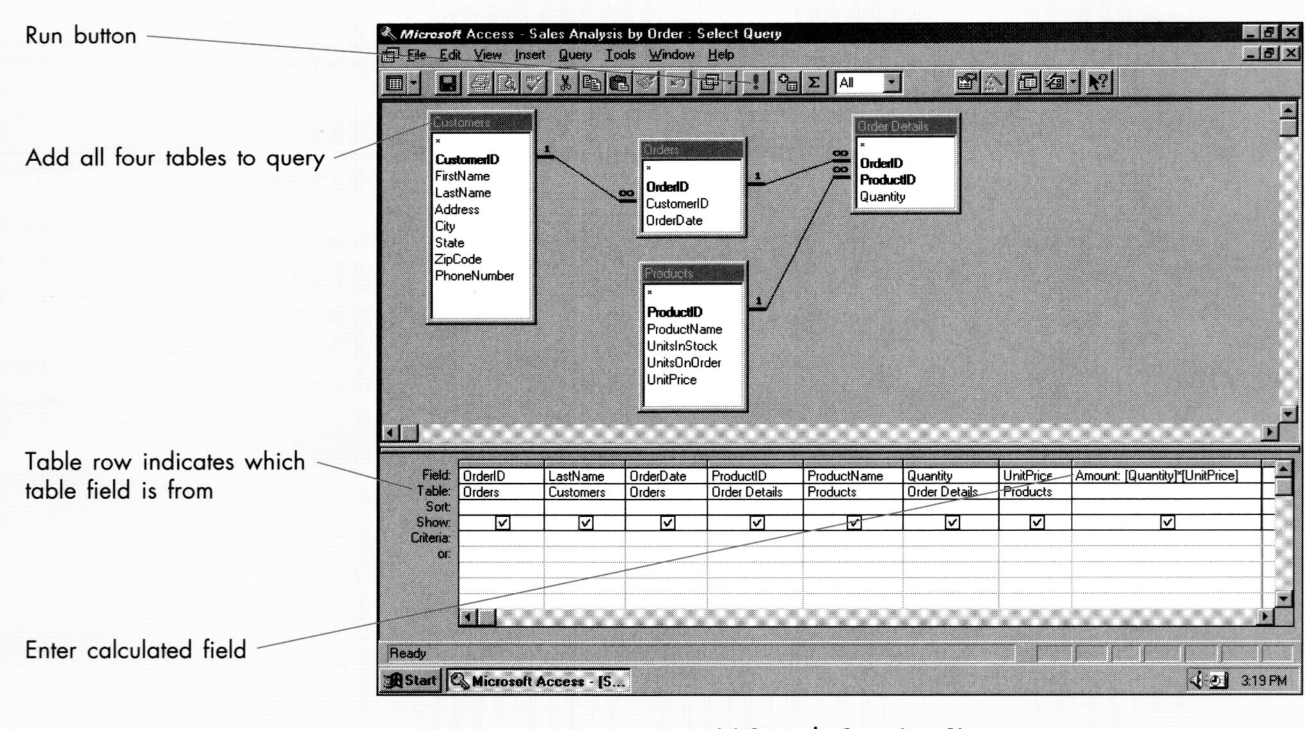

(a) Create the Query (step 1)

FIGURE 2.10 Hands-on Exercise 3

STEP 2: The Report Wizard

- Click the **Reports tab** in the Database window, then click the **New Command button** to display the New Report dialog box. Select the **Report Wizard.**
- Click the **drop-down arrow** to display the tables and queries in the database, then select **Sales Analysis by Order** (the query you just created). Click **OK.**
- By now you have had sufficient practice using the Report Wizard, so we will just outline the steps:
  - Select all of the fields in the query *except* the ProductID. Click the **>> button** to move every field in the Available Fields list box to the Selected field list, then select the **ProductID field** within the Selected field list and click the **< button** to remove this field. Click **Next.**
  - Group the report by **OrderID.** Click **Next.**
  - Sort the report by **ProductName.** Click the **Summary Options button** to display the Summary Options dialog box in Figure 2.10b. Check **Sum** under the Amount field. The option button to **Show Detail and Summary** is selected. Click **OK** to close the Summary Options dialog box. Click **Next.**
  - The **Stepped Layout** is selected, as is **Portrait orientation.** Be sure the box is checked to **Adjust field width so all fields fit on a page.** Click **Next.**
  - Choose **Bold** as the style. Click **Next.**
  - **Sales Analysis by Order** is entered as the title of the report. The option button to **Preview the Report** is selected. Click **Finish.**
- The report you see approximates the finished report, but requires several modifications to improve the formatting. The OrderDate and LastName, for example, are repeated for every product in an order, when they should appear only once in the group (OrderID) header.

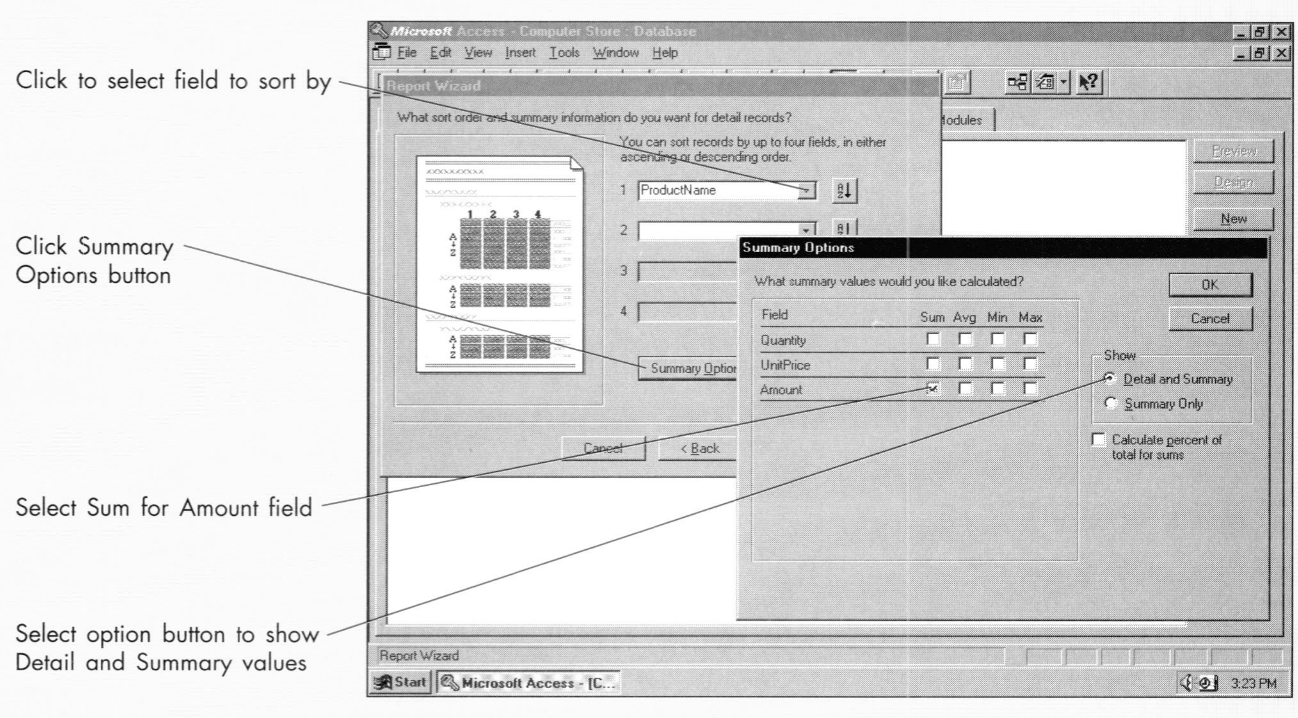

(b) The Report Wizard (step 2)

FIGURE 2.10 Hands-on Exercise 3 (continued)

STEP 3: Modify the Report

- Click the **Close button** to change to the Design view to modify the report as shown in Figure 2.10c.
- Press and hold the **Shift key** as you click the **OrderDate** and **LastName** controls to select both controls, then drag the controls to the group header next to the OrderID.
- Click anywhere in the report to deselect the controls after they have been moved. Press and hold the **Shift key** to select the **OrderID, OrderDate,** and **LastName** labels in the Page Header. Press the **Del key** to delete the labels.
- Size the **Quantity, UnitPrice,** and **Amount controls** (and their **labels**). Move the **ProductName control** and its **label** closer to the other controls.
- Click the **OrderID control** in the group header. Click the **right mouse button,** click **Properties,** and change the Border Style to **Transparent.** Close the Properties dialog box.
- Click and drag the **Label tool** to create an unbound control under the title of the report. Type **Prepared by:** followed by your name as shown in Figure 2.10c.
- Select (click) the first control in the OrderID footer (which begins with the literal "Summary for). Press the **Del key.** Click and drag the unbound control containing the word **Sum** to the right of the group footer so that the label is next to the computed total for each order. Do the same for the Group Total label in the Report footer.
- Click the **Save button** to save the report, then click the **Report View button** to preview the report.

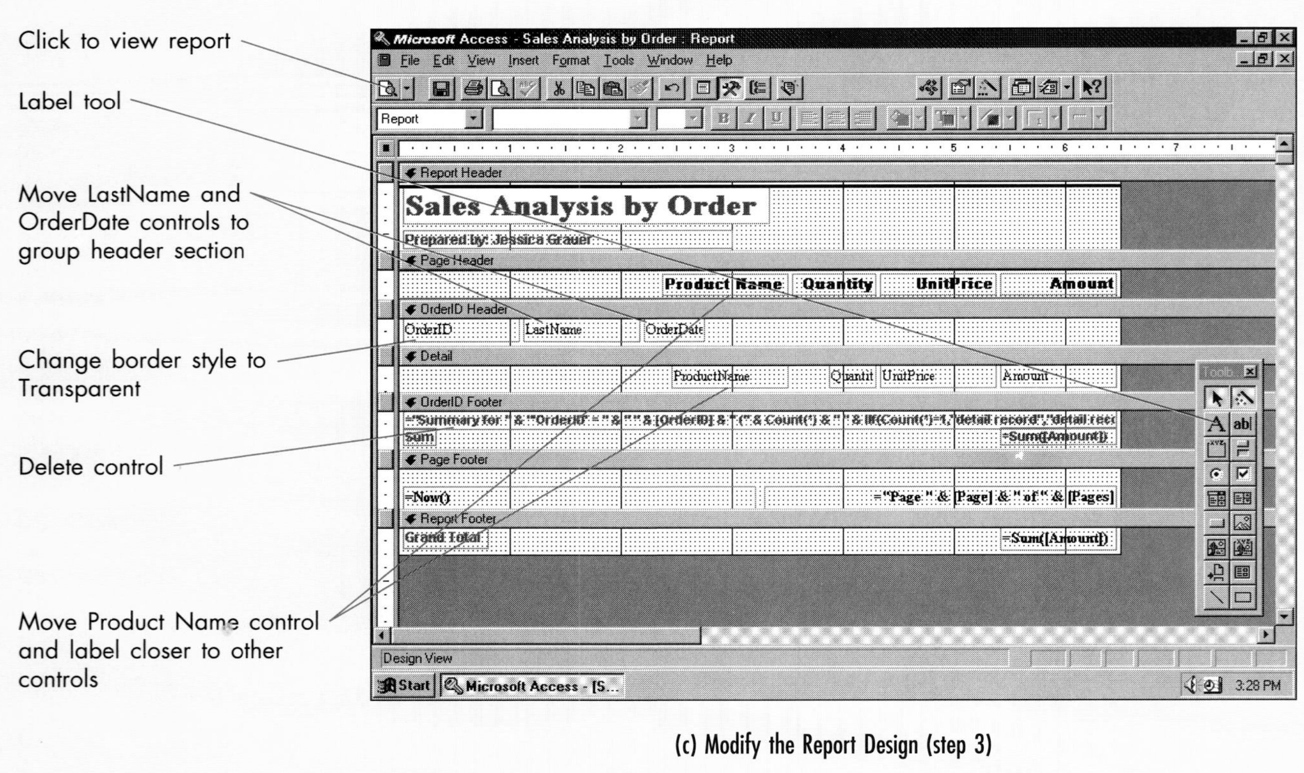

(c) Modify the Report Design (step 3)

FIGURE 2.10 Hands-on Exercise 3 (continued)

SELECTING MULTIPLE CONTROLS

Select (click) a column heading in the page header, then press and hold the Shift key as you select the corresponding control in the Detail section. This selects both the column heading and the bound control and enables you to move and size the objects in conjunction with one another. Continue to work with both objects selected as you apply formatting through various buttons on the Formatting toolbar, or change properties through the property sheet. Click anywhere on the report to deselect the objects when you are finished.

STEP 4: Print the Report

- You should see the report in Figure 2.10d, which groups the reports by Order ID. The products are in alphabetical order within each order.
- Click the **Zoom button** to see the entire page. Click the **Zoom button** a second time to return to the higher magnification.
- Click the **Printer button** if you are satisfied with the appearance of the report, or return to the Design view to make any needed changes.
- Pull down the **File menu** and click **Close** to close the report. Click **Yes** if asked whether to save the changes.

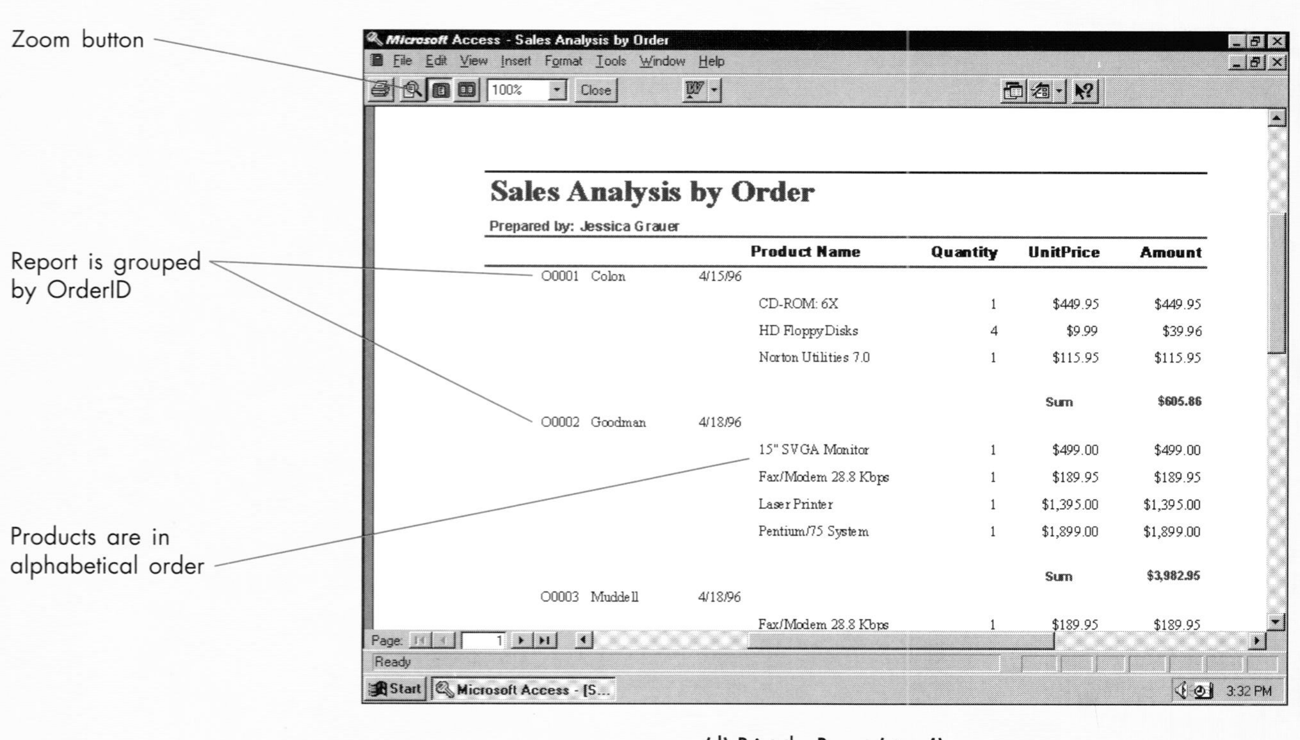

(d) Print the Report (step 4)

FIGURE 2.10 Hands-on Exercise 3 (continued)

STEP 5: Copy a Query

- ➤ If necessary, return to the Database window, then click the **Queries tab** in the Database window.
- ➤ Click the **Sales Analysis by Order query** to select the query as shown in Figure 2.10e.
- ➤ Pull down the **Edit menu.** Click **Copy** to copy the query to the clipboard.
- ➤ Pull down the **Edit menu.** Click **Paste** to produce the Paste As dialog box in Figure 2.10e. Type **Sales Totals.** Click **OK.** The Database window contains the original query (Sales Analysis by Order) as well as the copied version (Sales Totals) you just created.

COPY, DELETE, OR RENAME A REPORT

The Database window enables you to copy, delete, or rename any object (a table, form, query, or report) in an Access database. To copy an object, select the object, pull down the Edit menu, and click Copy. Pull down the Edit menu a second time, click Paste, then enter the name of the copied object. To delete or rename an object, point to the object, then click the right mouse button to display a shortcut menu, and select the desired operation.

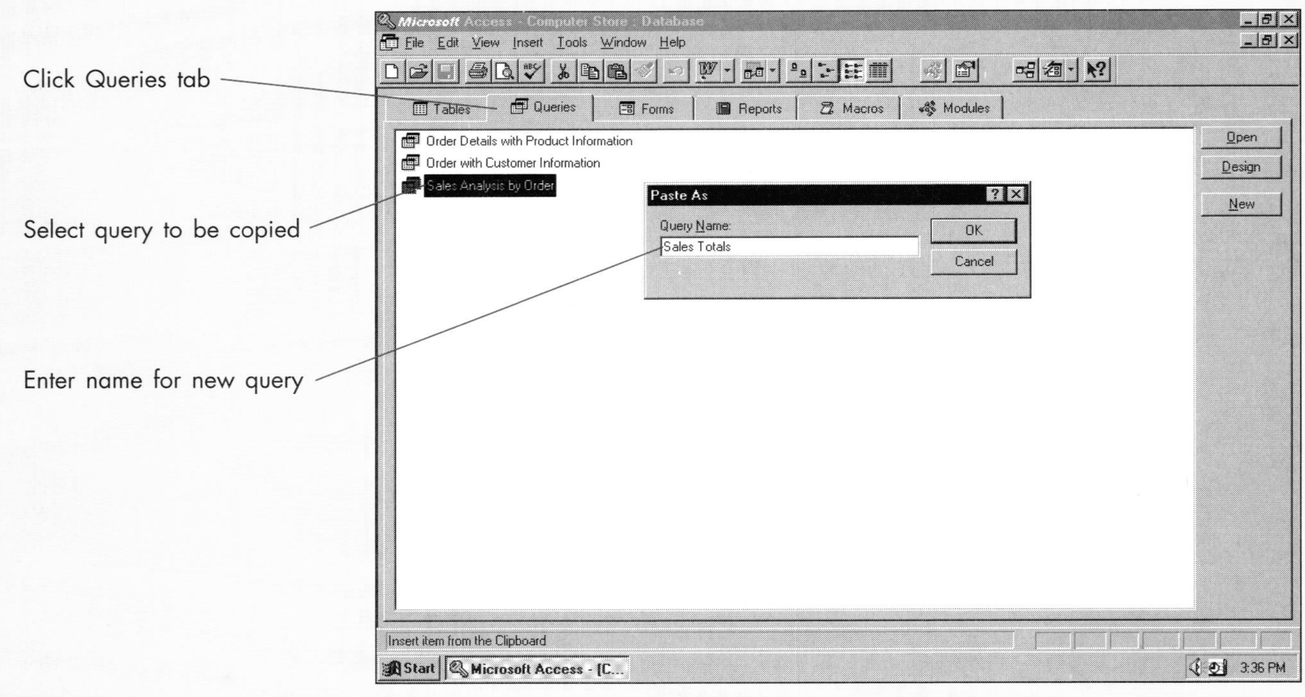

(e) Copy an Existing Query (step 5)

FIGURE 2.10 Hands-on Exercise 3 (continued)

STEP 6: Create a Total Query

- Select the newly created **Sales Totals query.** Click the **Design button** to open the Query Design window in Figure 2.10f.
- Click the **column selector** for the **OrderDate field** to select the column. Press the **Del key** to delete the field from the query. Delete the **ProductID, ProductName, Quantity,** and **UnitPrice fields** in similar fashion.
- Pull down the **View menu** and click **Totals** to display the Total row (or click the **Totals button** on the toolbar).
- Click the **Total row** under the Amount field, then click the **drop-down arrow** to display the summary functions. Click **Sum** as shown in the figure.
- Save the query.

THE DESCRIPTION PROPERTY

A working database will contain many different objects of the same type, making it all too easy to forget the purpose of the individual objects. The Description property helps you to remember. Point to any object within the Database window, click the right mouse button to display a shortcut menu, click Properties to display the Properties dialog box, enter an appropriate description, then click OK to close the Properties sheet. Once a description has been created, you can right click any object in the Database window, then click the Properties command from the shortcut menu to display the information.

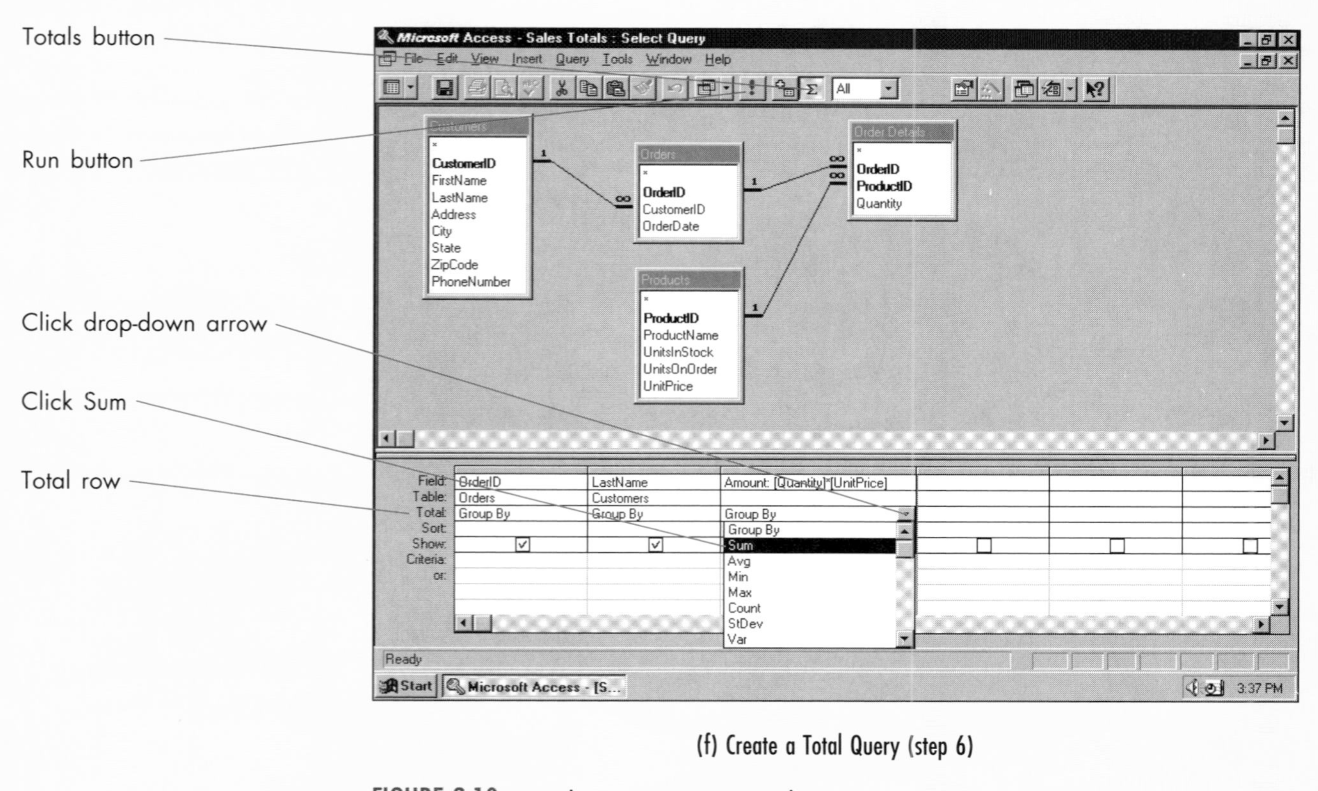

(f) Create a Total Query (step 6)

FIGURE 2.10 Hands-on Exercise 3 (continued)

STEP 7: Run the Query

- Pull down the **Query menu** and click **Run** (or click the **Run button**) to run the query. You should see the datasheet in Figure 2.10g, which contains one record for each order with the total amount of that order.
- Click any field and attempt to change its value. You will be unable to do so as indicated by the beep and the message in the status bar, indicating that the recordset is not updatable.
- Click the **Design View button** to return to the Query Design view.

> **UPDATING THE QUERY**
>
> The changes made to a query's dynaset are automatically made in the underlying table(s). Not every field in a query is updatable, however, and the easiest way to determine if you can change a value is to run the query, view the dynaset, and attempt to edit the field. Access will prevent you from updating a calculated field, a field based on an aggregate function (such as Sum or Count), or the join field on the "one side" of a one-to-many relationship. If you attempt to update a field you cannot change, the status bar will display a message indicating why the change is not allowed.

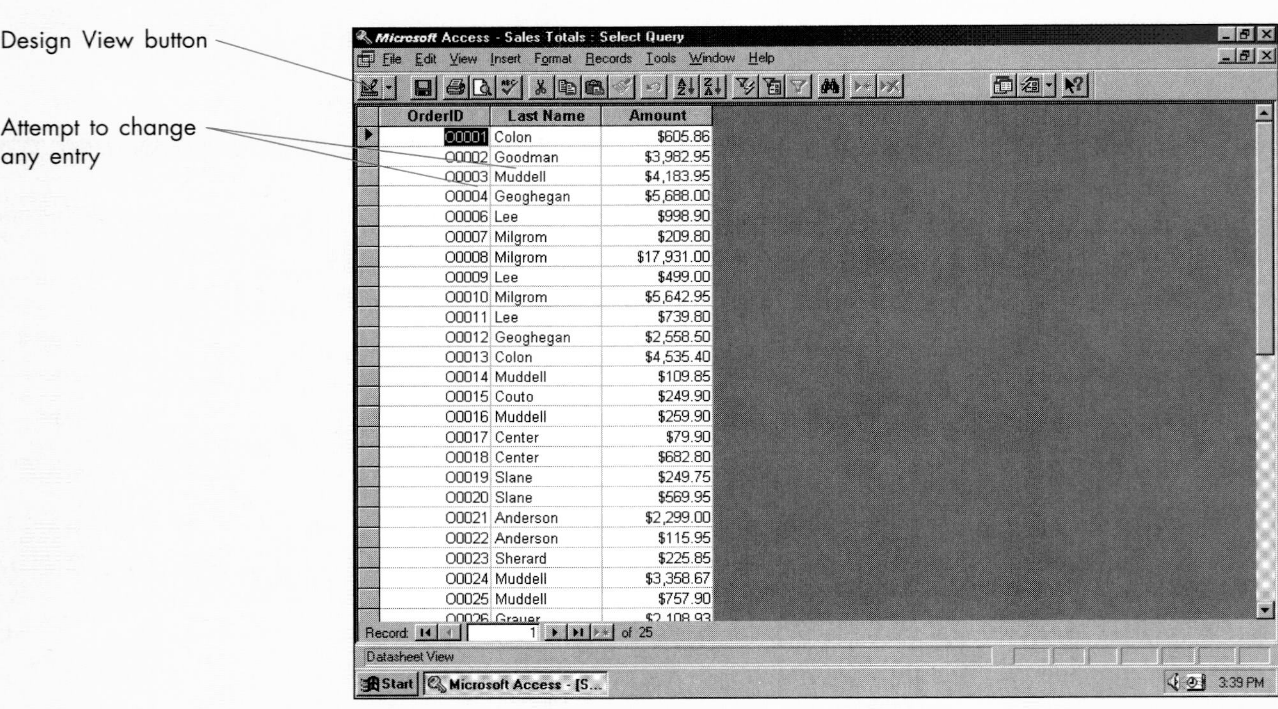

(g) The Total Query (step 7)

FIGURE 2.10 Hands-on Exercise 3 (continued)

STEP 8: Create a Parameter Query

- Click the **Criteria row** under **LastName.** Type **[Enter Customer's Last Name].** Be sure to enclose the entry in square brackets.
- Pull down the **File menu.** Click **Save As/Export.** Save the query as **Customer Parameter Query.**
- Run the query. Access will display the dialog box in Figure 2.10h, asking for the Customer's last name. Type **your name** and press **enter.** Access displays your last name, OrderID(s), and the date and amount of your order(s).
- Save the query. Close the query.

> **THE TOPVALUES PROPERTY**
>
> The TopValues property returns a designated number of records rather than the entire dynaset. Open the query in Design view, then click the right mouse button *outside* the QBE grid to display a shortcut menu. Click Properties, click the box for TopValues, and enter the desired value as either a number or a percent; for example, 5 to list the top five records, or 5% to display the records that make up the top five percent. The dynaset must be in sequence according to the desired field in order for the TopValues property to work properly. Hence you will need to clear the Sort row for all other fields, then click the Sort row in the desired field, and select a descending or ascending sequence to display the top or bottom values, respectively.

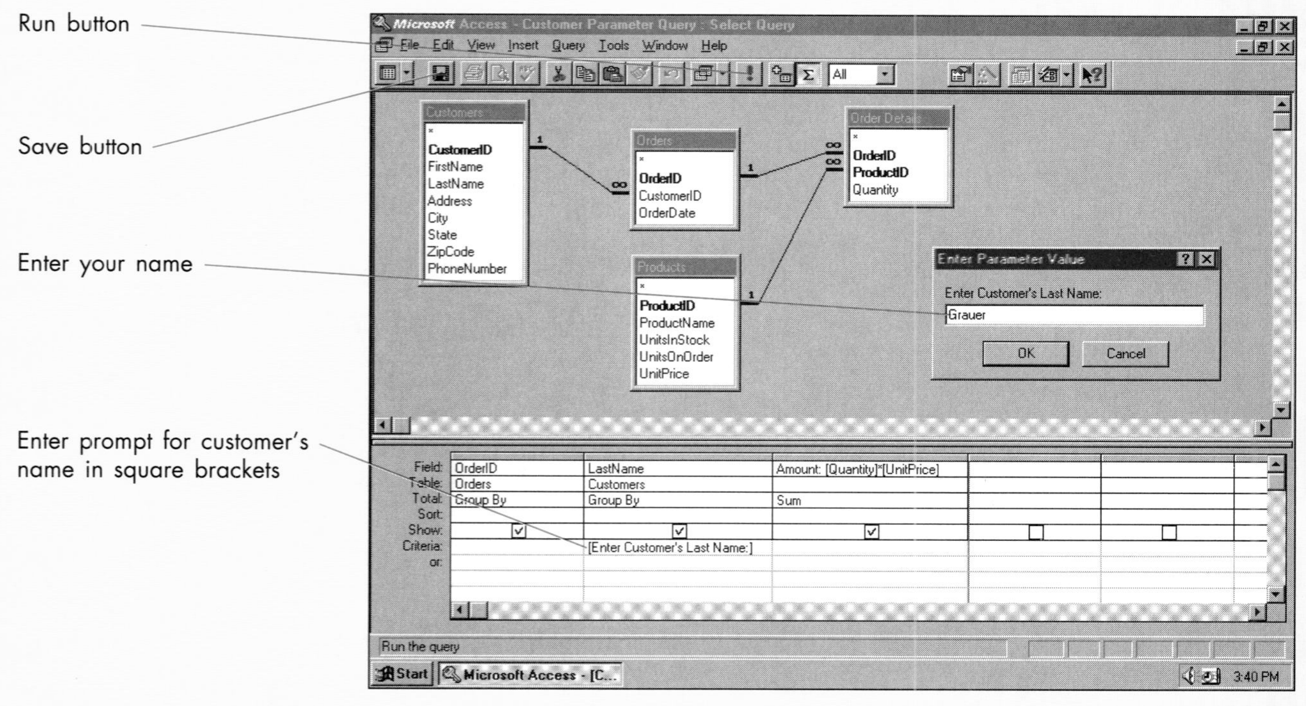

(h) Create a Parameter Query (step 8)

FIGURE 2.10 Hands-on Exercise 3 (continued)

STEP 9: Exit Access

➤ Close the Computer Store database. Exit Access if you do not want to continue with the next exercise at this time. (Do not be concerned by the message indicating that Access will empty the clipboard.)

EXPANDING THE DATABASE

One of the advantages of an Access database is that it can be easily expanded to include additional data without disturbing the existing tables. The database used throughout the chapter consisted of four tables: a Customers table, a Products table, an Orders table, and an Order Details table. Figure 2.11 extends the database to include a Sales Persons table with data about each member of the sales staff.

The salesperson helps the customer as he or she comes into the store, then receives a commission based on the order. There is a one-to-many relationship between the salesperson and orders. One salesperson can generate many orders, but an order can have only one salesperson. The Sales Persons and Orders tables are joined by the SalesPersonID field, which is common to both tables.

Figure 2.11 is similar to Figure 2.1 at the beginning of the chapter except that the Sales Persons table has been added and the Orders table has been expanded to include a SalesPersonID. This enables management to monitor the performance of the sales staff. Consider:

Query: How many orders has Cori Rice taken?
Answer: Cori has taken five orders.

The query is straightforward and easily answered. You would search the Sales Persons table for Cori Rice to determine her SalesPersonID (S03). You would then search the Orders table and count the records containing S03 in the SalesPersonID field.

The Sales Persons table is also used to generate a report listing the commissions due to each salesperson. The store pays a 5% commission on every sale. Consider:

Query: Which salesperson is associated with Order O0003? How much is the commission on that order?
Answer: Cori Rice is the salesperson for order O0003. Her commission for this order is $209.20.

The determination of the salesperson is straightforward, as all you have to do is search the Orders table to locate the order and obtain the SalesPersonID (S03). You then search the Sales Persons table for this value (S03) and find the corresponding name (Cori Rice).

The calculation of the commission is more complicated and requires a fair amount of arithmetic. First, you need to compute the total amount of the order. Thus, you would begin in the Order Details table, find each product in order O0003, and multiply the quantity of that product by its unit price. The total cost of order O0003 is $4,183.95, based on one unit of product P0005 at $2,599, one unit of product P0020 at $189.95, and one unit of product P0022 at $1,395. (You can also refer to the sales report in Figure 2.9 that was developed in the previous exercise to check these calculations.) Next, you compute the commission, which is 5% of the total order, or $209.20 (.05 x $4,183.95).

CustomerID	First Name	Last Name	Address	City	State	Zip Code	Phone Number
C0001	Benjamin	Lee	1000 Call Street	Tallahassee	FL	33340	(904) 327-4124
C0002	Eleanor	Milgrom	7245 NW 8 Street	Margate	FL	33065	(305) 974-1234
C0003	Neil	Goodman	4215 South 81 Street	Margate	FL	33065	(305) 444-5555
C0004	Nicholas	Colon	9020 N.W. 75 Street	Coral Springs	FL	33065	(305) 753-9887
C0005	Michael	Ware	276 Brickell Avenue	Miami	FL	33131	(305) 444-3980
C0006	Jeffrey	Muddell	9522 S.W. 142 Street	Miami	FL	33176	(305) 253-3909
C0007	Ashley	Geoghegan	7500 Center Lane	Coral Springs	FL	33070	(305) 753-7830
C0008	Serena	Sherard	5000 Jefferson Lane	Gainesville	FL	32601	(904) 375-6442
C0009	Luis	Couto	455 Bargello Avenue	Coral Gables	FL	33146	(305) 666-4801
C0010	Derek	Anderson	6000 Tigertail Avenue	Coconut Grove	FL	33120	(305) 446-8900
C0011	Lauren	Center	12380 S.W. 137 Avenue	Miami	FL	33186	(305) 385-4432
C0012	Robert	Slane	4508 N.W. 7 Street	Miami	FL	33131	(305) 635-3454
C0013	Jessica	Grauer	758 Mangowood Road	Coral Springs	FL	33071	(305) 755-5430

(a) Customers Table

ProductID	Product Name	Units In Stock	Units On Order	Unit Price
P0001	Pentium/75 System	50	0	$1,899.00
P0002	Pentium/90 System	25	5	$1,999.00
P0003	Pentium/100 System	125	15	$2,099.00
P0004	Pentium/120 System	25	50	$2,299.00
P0005	Pentium/133 System	15	25	$2,599.00
P0006	15" SVGA Monitor	50	0	$499.00
P0007	17" SVGA Monitor	25	10	$899.00
P0008	19" Multisync Monitor	50	20	$1,599.00
P0009	500 MB Hard Drive	15	20	$399.00
P0010	1 GB Hard Drive	25	15	$799.00
P0011	2 GB Hard Drive	10	0	$1,245.00
P0012	CD-ROM: 4X	40	0	$249.00
P0013	CD-ROM: 6X	50	15	$449.95
P0014	HD Floppy Disks	500	200	$9.99
P0015	HD Data Cartridges	100	50	$14.79
P0016	250 MB Tape Backup	15	3	$179.95
P0017	Serial Mouse	150	50	$69.95
P0018	Trackball	55	0	$59.95
P0019	Joystick	250	100	$39.95
P0020	Fax/Modem 28.8 Kbps	35	10	$189.95
P0021	Fax/Modem 14.4Kbps	20	0	$65.95
P0022	Laser Printer	100	15	$1,395.00
P0023	24Pin Dot Matrix	50	50	$249.95
P0024	Color Printer	125	25	$569.95
P0025	Windows 95	400	200	$95.95
P0026	Windows 95 Plus	150	50	$45.95
P0027	Norton Utilities 7.0	150	50	$115.95
P0028	Microsoft Scenes Screen Saver	75	25	$29.95
P0029	Microsoft Bookshelf	250	100	$129.95
P0030	Microsoft Cinemania	25	10	$59.95
P0031	Professional Photos (CD-ROM)	15	0	$45.95

(b) Products Table

OrderID	Customer ID	Order Date	SalesPersonID
O0001	C0004	4/15/96	S01
O0002	C0003	4/18/96	S02
O0003	C0006	4/18/96	S03
O0004	C0007	4/18/96	S04
O0006	C0001	4/21/96	S05
O0007	C0002	4/21/96	S01
O0008	C0002	4/22/96	S02
O0009	C0001	4/22/96	S03
O0010	C0002	4/22/96	S04
O0011	C0001	4/24/96	S05
O0012	C0007	4/24/96	S01
O0013	C0004	4/24/96	S02
O0014	C0006	4/25/96	S03
O0015	C0009	4/25/96	S04
O0016	C0006	4/26/96	S05
O0017	C0011	4/26/96	S01
O0018	C0011	4/26/96	S02
O0019	C0012	4/27/96	S03
O0020	C0012	4/28/96	S04
O0021	C0010	4/29/96	S05
O0022	C0010	4/29/96	S01
O0023	C0008	4/30/96	S02
O0024	C0006	5/ 1/96	S03
O0025	C0006	5/ 1/96	S04
O0026	C0013	5/31/96	S05

(c) Orders Table

Order ID	Product ID	Quantity
O0001	P0013	1
O0001	P0014	4
O0001	P0027	1
O0002	P0001	1
O0002	P0006	1
O0002	P0020	1
O0002	P0022	1
O0003	P0005	1
O0003	P0020	1
O0003	P0022	1
O0004	P0003	1
O0004	P0010	1
O0004	P0022	2
O0006	P0007	1
O0006	P0014	10
O0007	P0028	1
O0007	P0030	3
O0008	P0001	1
O0008	P0004	3
O0008	P0008	4
O0008	P0011	2
O0008	P0012	1
O0009	P0006	1
O0010	P0002	2
O0010	P0022	1
O0010	P0023	1
O0011	P0016	2
O0011	P0020	2
O0012	P0021	10
O0012	P0029	10
O0012	P0030	10
O0013	P0009	4
O0013	P0016	10
O0013	P0024	2
O0014	P0019	2
O0014	P0028	1
O0015	P0018	1
O0015	P0020	1
O0016	P0029	2
O0017	P0019	2
O0018	P0009	1
O0018	P0025	2
O0018	P0026	2
O0019	P0014	25
O0020	P0024	1
O0021	P0004	1
O0022	P0027	1
O0023	P0021	1
O0023	P0028	1
O0023	P0029	1
O0024	P0007	1
O0024	P0013	5
O0024	P0014	3
O0024	P0016	1
O0025	P0012	2
O0025	P0029	2
O0026	P0014	2
O0026	P0020	1

(d) Order Details Table

SalesPersonID	FirstName	LastName	WorkPhone	HireDate
S01	Linda	Black	(305) 284-6105	2/3/93
S02	Michael	Vaughn	(305) 284-3993	2/10/93
S03	Cori	Rice	(305) 284-2557	3/15/93
S04	Karen	Ruenheck	(305) 284-4641	1/31/94
S05	Richard	Linger	(305) 284-4662	1/31/94

(e) Sales Persons Table

FIGURE 2.11 Super Store Database

The Sales Commission Query

We think it important that you understand how the tables in a database are related to one another and that you can answer conceptual questions such as obtaining the commission for a specific order. Practically speaking, however, you would not do the calculations yourself, but would create the necessary queries to let Access do the work for you.

Consider, for example, Figure 2.12a, which contains a parameter query to calculate the commissions that are due to a specific salesperson. (This query provides the sales information for Cori Rice, which you computed manually in the previous discussion.) Enter the name of the sales associate, Cori Rice, and the query returns the dynaset in Figure 2.12b, showing all of her commissions. Note, too, that the commission returned for order O0003 is $209.20, which corresponds to the amount we arrived at earlier.

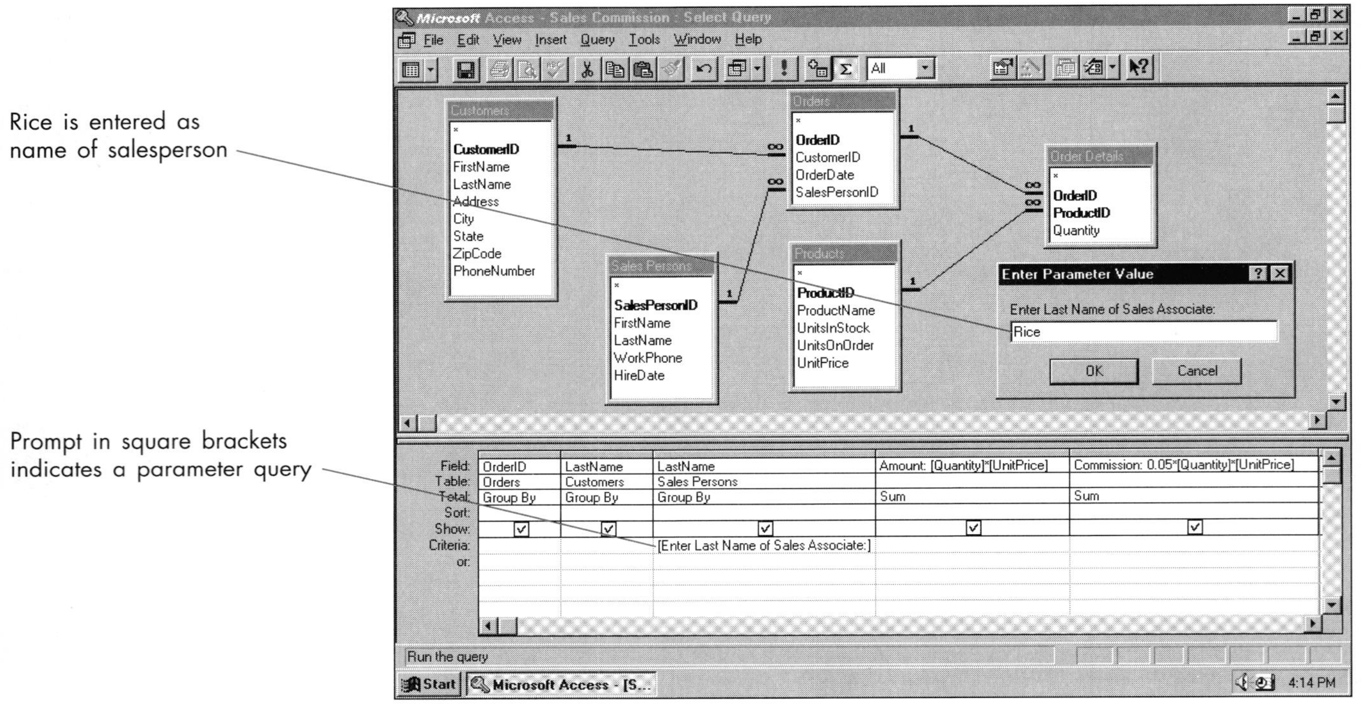

(a) Sales Commission Query

Commission earned on Order O0003

Sales Commission : Select Query

OrderID	Last Name	Sales Persons.LastName	Amount	Commission
O0003	Muddell	Rice	$4,183.95	$209.20
O0009	Lee	Rice	$499.00	$24.95
O0014	Muddell	Rice	$109.85	$5.49
O0019	Slane	Rice	$249.75	$12.49
O0024	Muddell	Rice	$3,358.67	$167.93

Record: 1 of 5

(b) Dynaset

FIGURE 2.12 Sales Commissions

The query in Figure 2.12a includes fields from all five tables in the database. The relationships are shown graphically in the top half of the query window and reflect the earlier discussion—for example, the one-to-many relationship between salespersons and orders. The tables are joined through the SalesPersonID field, which is the primary key in the Sales Persons table but a foreign key in the Orders table. (The Orders table has been modified to include this field.) Each field in the Total row contains either a Group By entry or an aggregate function, as explained in the previous discussion on total queries.

The Get External Data Command

The Computer Store database that you have been using in the hands-on exercises does not include the Sales Persons table. You could, of course, create the table manually, just as you would enter any other table. Alternatively, you could import the table from an external database, if it (the Sales Persons table) had been created independently. This is accomplished through the ***Get External Data command,*** which imports an object (a table, query, form, or report) from another database.

One benefit of this approach is that you can take advantage of any work that was previously done. The Sales Persons table, for example, may be part of an employee database in a completely different application. The Get External Data command also enables you to divide a large project (perhaps a class project) among many individuals.

The following exercise has you import the Sales Persons table from another Access database. It then directs you to modify the existing Orders table to include a SalesPersonID, which references the records in the Sales Persons table, and to modify the Super Store Order Form to include the salesperson data.

HANDS-ON EXERCISE 4

Expanding the Database

Objective: To import a table from another database; to modify the design of an existing table; to create a combined parameter/totals query. Use Figure 2.13 as a guide in the exercise.

STEP 1: Import the Sales Persons Table

- Open the **Computer Store database.** Click the **Tables tab.**
- Pull down the **File menu.** Click **Get External Data** to display a cascaded menu, then click **Import** to display the Import dialog box.
- Click (select) the **Sales Persons database** from the **Exploring Access folder,** then click **Import** to display the Import Objects dialog box in Figure 2.13a.
- If necessary, click the **Tables tab,** click **Sales Persons** (the only table in this database), then click **OK.** A dialog box will appear briefly on your screen as the Sales Persons table is imported into the Computer Store database.

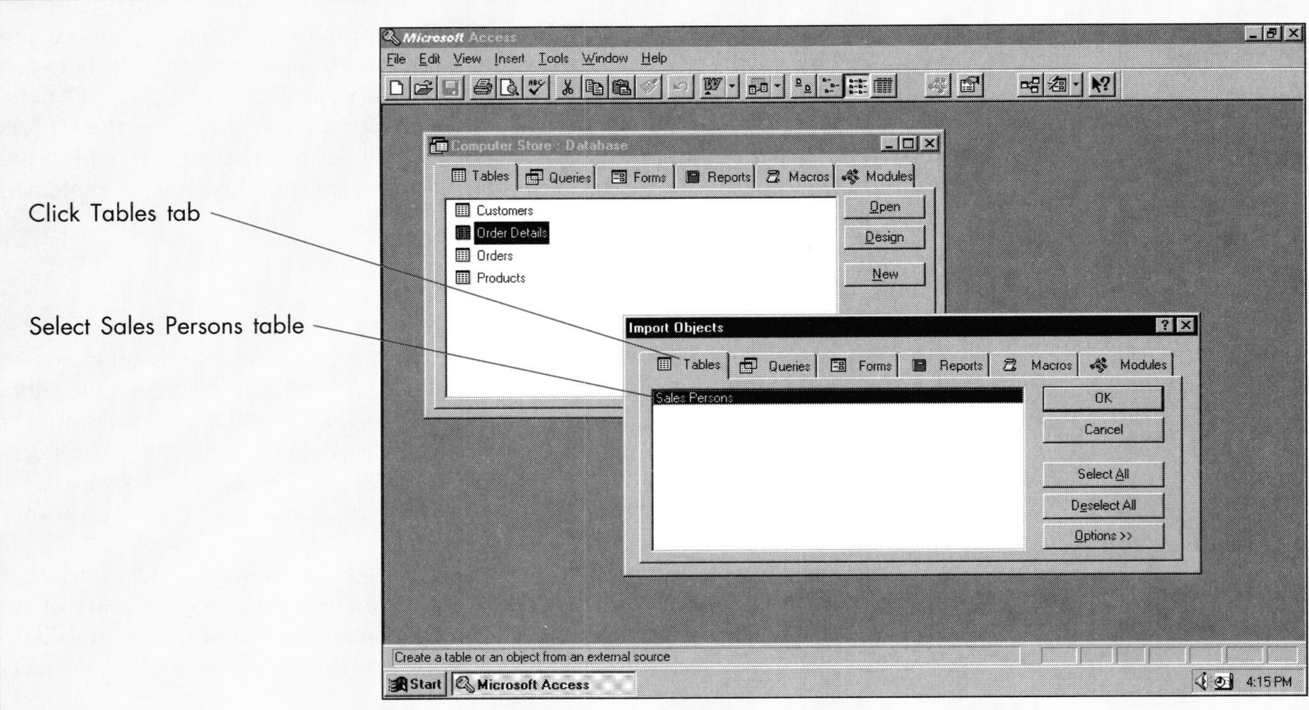

(a) Import the Sales Persons Table (step 1)

FIGURE 2.13 Hands-on Exercise 4

THE DOCUMENTS SUBMENU

One of the fastest ways to get to a recently used document, regardless of the application, is through the Windows 95 Start menu, which includes a Documents submenu containing the last 15 documents that were opened. Click the Start button, click (or point to) the Documents submenu, then click the document you wish to open (e.g., Computer Store), assuming that it appears on the submenu. Windows will start the application, then open the indicated document.

STEP 2: Modify the Orders Table Design

- Select the **Orders table** from the Database window as shown in Figure 2.13b. Click the **Design button.**
- Click in the first available row in the **Field Name** column. Enter **SalesPersonID** as shown in Figure 2.13b. Choose **Number** as the data type. The Field Size property changes to Long Integer by default.
  - Click the **Format** property. Enter **\S00.**
  - Click the **Default Value** property and delete the **0.**
- Click the **Save button** to save the modified design of the Orders table.

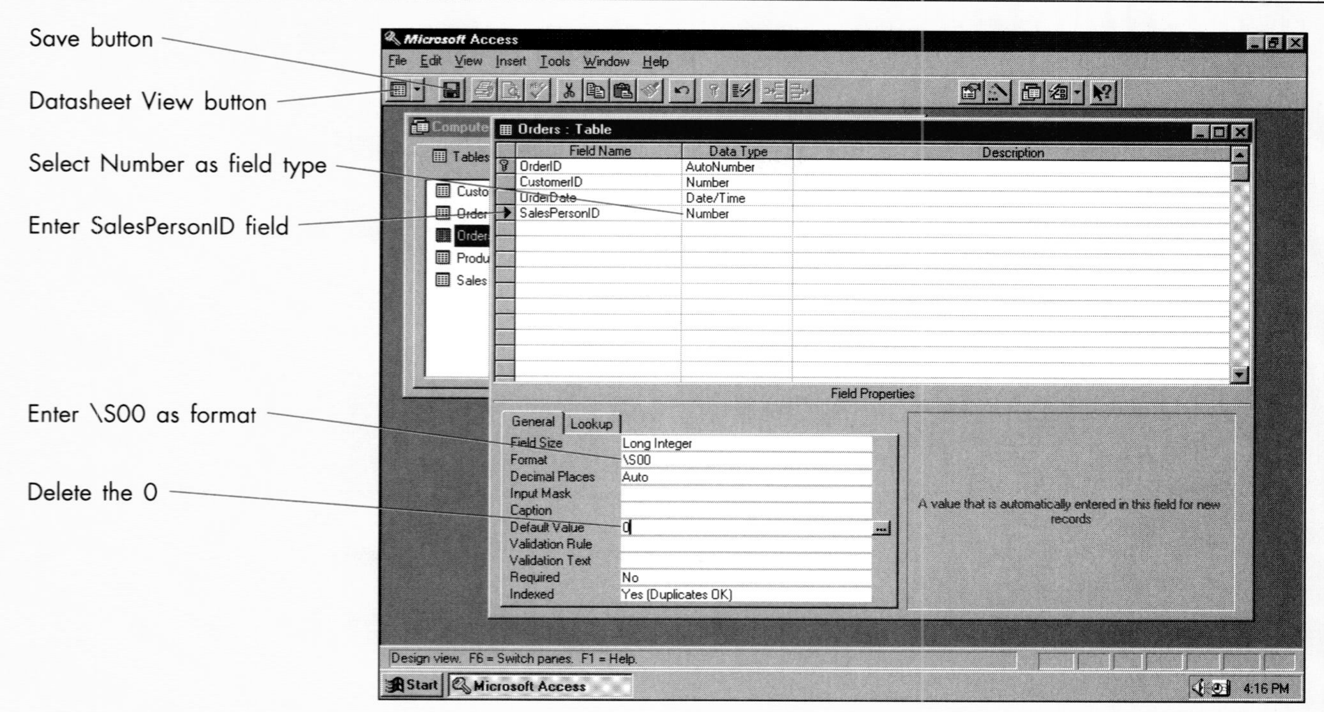

(b) Modify the Orders Table (step 2)

FIGURE 2.13 Hands-on Exercise 4 (continued)

RELATIONSHIPS AND THE AUTONUMBER FIELD TYPE

The join fields on both sides of a relationship must be the same data type—for example, both number fields or both text fields. The AutoNumber field type, however, cannot be specified on both sides of a relationship. Thus, if the join field (SalesPersonID) in the primary table (Sales Persons) is an AutoNumber field, the join field in the related table (Orders) must be specified as a Number field, with the Field Size property set to Long Integer.

STEP 3: Add the Sales Person to Existing Orders

- Click the **Datasheet View button** to change to the Datasheet view as shown in Figure 2.13c. Maximize the window.
- Enter the **SalesPersonID** for each existing order as shown in Figure 2.13c. Enter only the number (e.g., 1, rather than S01) as the S and leading 0 are displayed automatically through the Format property. (Orders O0001 and O0002 have salespersons 1 and 2 respectively, and are not visible in the figure.)
- Close the Orders table.

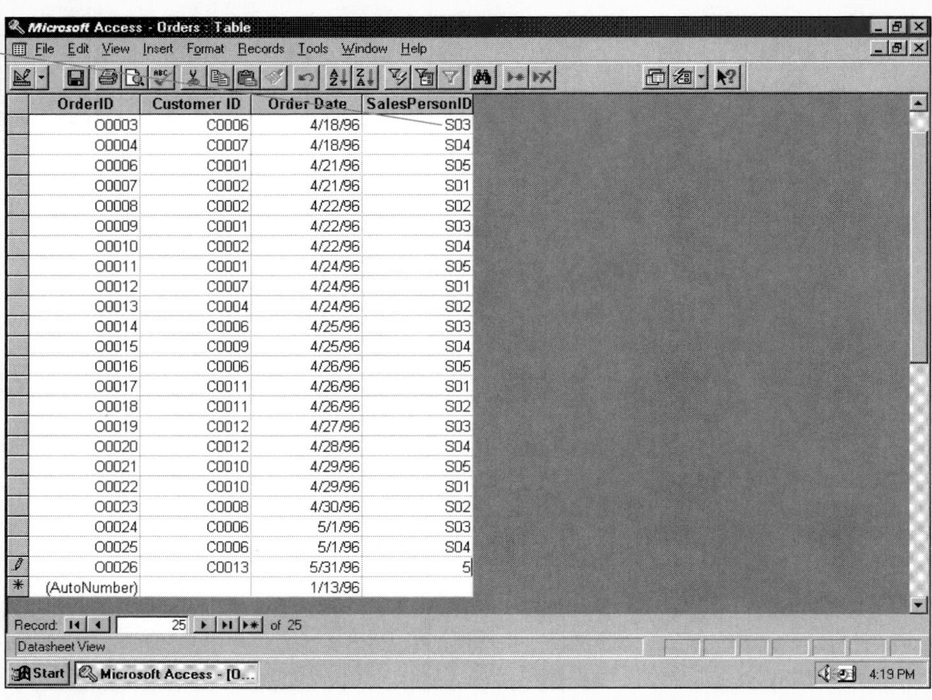

OrderID	Customer ID	Order Date	SalesPersonID
O0003	C0006	4/18/96	S03
O0004	C0007	4/18/96	S04
O0006	C0001	4/21/96	S05
O0007	C0002	4/21/96	S01
O0008	C0002	4/22/96	S02
O0009	C0001	4/22/96	S03
O0010	C0002	4/22/96	S04
O0011	C0001	4/24/96	S05
O0012	C0007	4/24/96	S01
O0013	C0004	4/24/96	S02
O0014	C0006	4/25/96	S03
O0015	C0009	4/25/96	S04
O0016	C0006	4/26/96	S05
O0017	C0011	4/26/96	S01
O0018	C0011	4/26/96	S02
O0019	C0012	4/27/96	S03
O0020	C0012	4/28/96	S04
O0021	C0010	4/29/96	S05
O0022	C0010	4/29/96	S01
O0023	C0008	4/30/96	S02
O0024	C0006	5/1/96	S03
O0025	C0006	5/1/96	S04
O0026	C0013	5/31/96	5
(AutoNumber)		1/13/96	

(c) Add the Sales Person (step 3)

FIGURE 2.13 Hands-on Exercise 4 (continued)

HIDE THE WINDOWS 95 TASKBAR

The Windows 95 taskbar is great for novices because it makes task switching as easy as changing channels on a TV. It also takes up valuable real estate on the desktop, and hence you may want to hide the taskbar when you don't need it. Point to an empty area on the taskbar, click the right mouse button to display a shortcut menu, and click Properties to display the Taskbar Properties dialog box. Click the Taskbar Options tab (if necessary), check the box to Auto hide the taskbar, and click OK. The taskbar should disappear. Now point to the bottom of the screen (or the edge where the taskbar was last displayed), and it will reappear.

STEP 4: Add a Relationship

- Pull down the **Tools menu.** Click **Relationships** to open the Relationships window as shown in Figure 2.13d. (The Sales Persons table is not yet visible.) Click the **Maximize button.**
- If necessary, drag the bottom border of the **Orders table** until you see the SalesPersonID (the field you added in step 2).
- Pull down the **Relationships menu.** Click **Show Table.** Click the **Tables tab** if necessary, select the **Sales Persons table,** then click the **Add button** to add the Sales Persons table to the Relationships window. Close the Show Table dialog box.

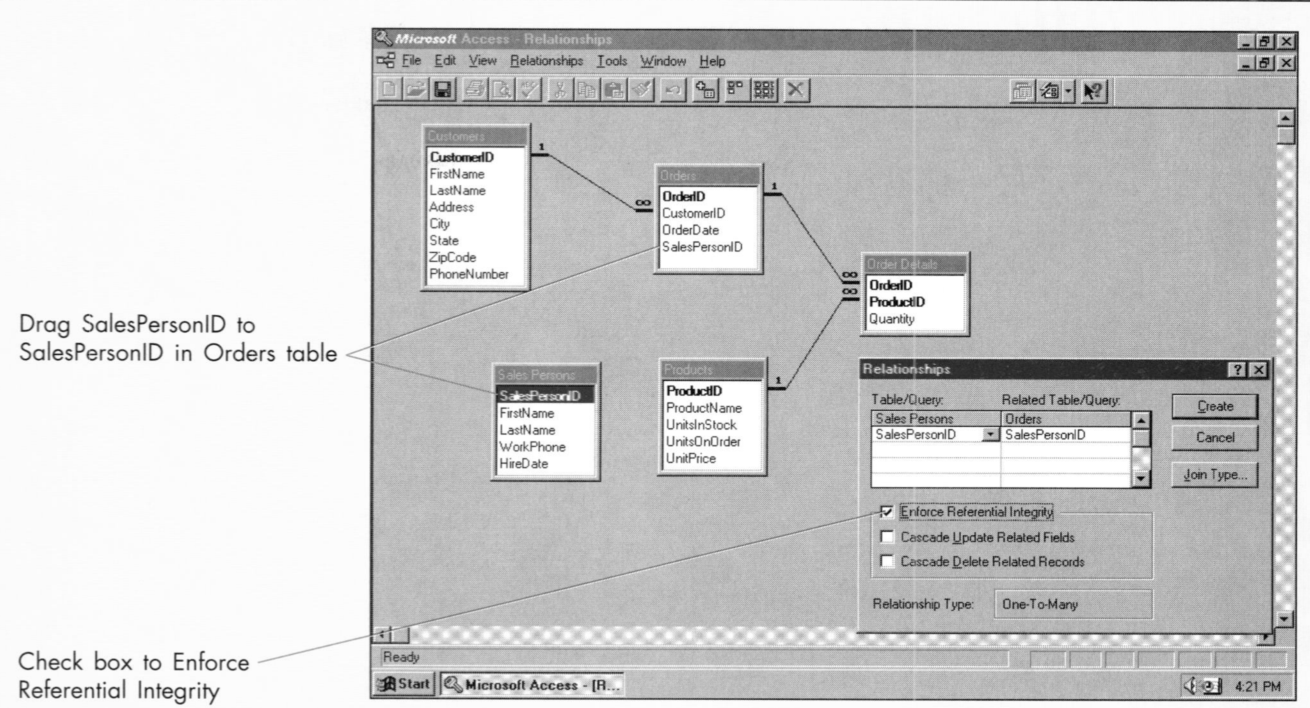

(d) Create the Relationship (step 4)

FIGURE 2.13 Hands-on Exercise 4 (continued)

- Drag the title bar of the **Sales Persons table** to position the table as shown in Figure 2.13d. Drag the **SalesPersonID field** from the Sales Persons table to the SalesPersonID in the Orders table. You will see the Relationships dialog box.
- Check the box to **Enforce Referential Integrity.** Click the **Create Command button** to create the relationship.
- Click the **Save button** to save the Relationships window. Close the Relationships window.

STEP 5: Modify the Order with Customer Information Query

- You should be back in the Database window. Click the **Queries tab,** select the **Order with Customer Information query,** then click the **Design button** to open the query in the Design view as shown in Figure 2.13e.
- If necessary, click and drag the border of the **Orders table** so that the newly added SalesPersonID field is displayed. Click the **horizontal scroll arrow** until a blank column in the QBE grid is visible.
- Click and drag the **SalesPersonID** from the Orders table to the last column in the QBE grid.
- Save the query. Close the query.

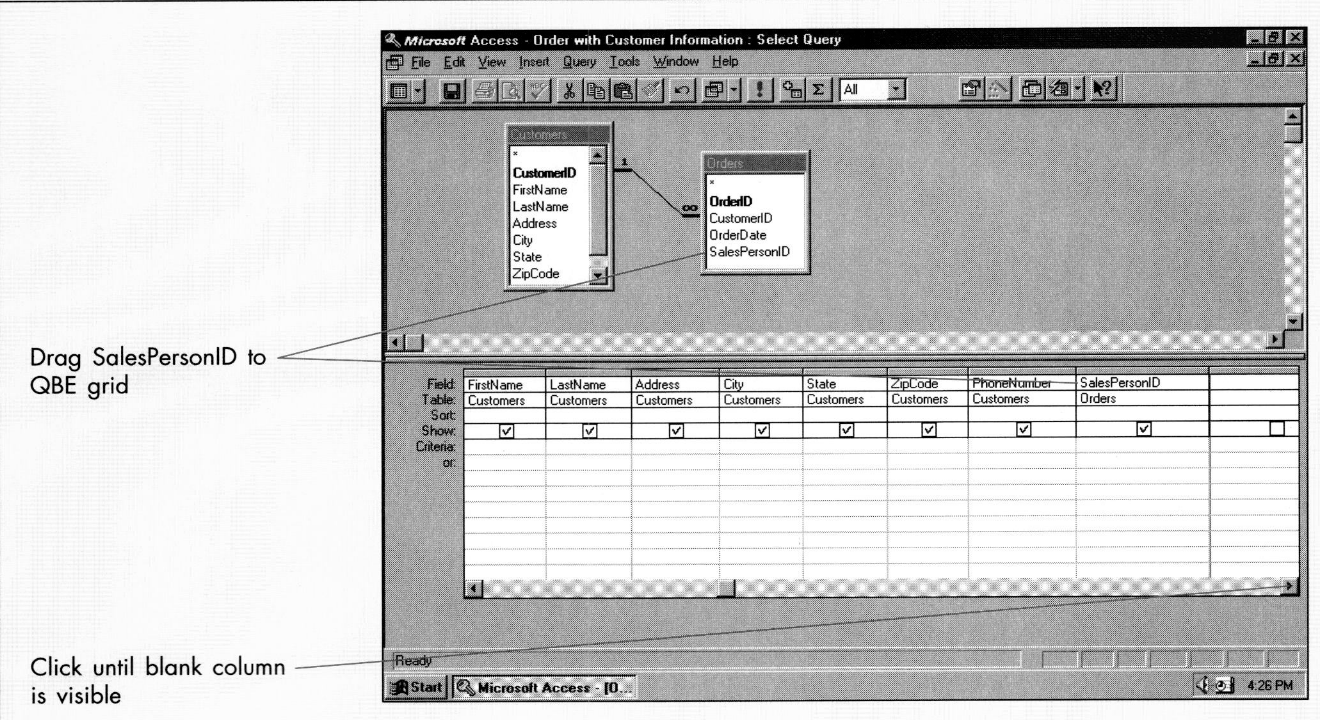

(e) Modify the Order with Customer Information Query (step 5)

FIGURE 2.13 Hands-on Exercise 4 (continued)

STEP 6: Modify the Order Form

- You should be back in the Database window. Click the **Forms tab,** select the **Super Store Order Form,** then click the **Design** button to open the form in the Design view.
- Right click the **form selector** and click **Properties** to display the Form Properties box. Click the **Data tab,** click the **Record Source property,** click the **drop-down arrow,** then select **Order with Customer Information.** This updates the form so that it looks for information from the modified (rather than the original) query. Close the Properties box.
- Move and size the controls so that there is room to add a control for the salesperson as shown in Figure 2.13f.
- Click the **Combo Box tool** on the Toolbox toolbar. Click and drag in the form where you want the combo box to go. Release the mouse. You will see the first step in the Combo Box Wizard.
  - Check the option button that indicates you want the combo box to look up values in a table or query. Click **Next.**
  - Choose the **Sales Persons table** in the next screen. Click **Next.**
  - Select the **SalesPersonID** and **LastName** from the Available Fields list box for inclusion in the Combo box columns list. Click **Next.**
  - Adjust the column widths if necessary. Be sure the box to hide the key column is checked. Click **Next.**
  - Click the option button to store the value in the field. Click the **drop-down arrow** to display the fields in the query and select the **SalesPersonID** field. Click **Next.**
  - Enter **Salesperson:** as the label for the combo box. Click **Finish.**

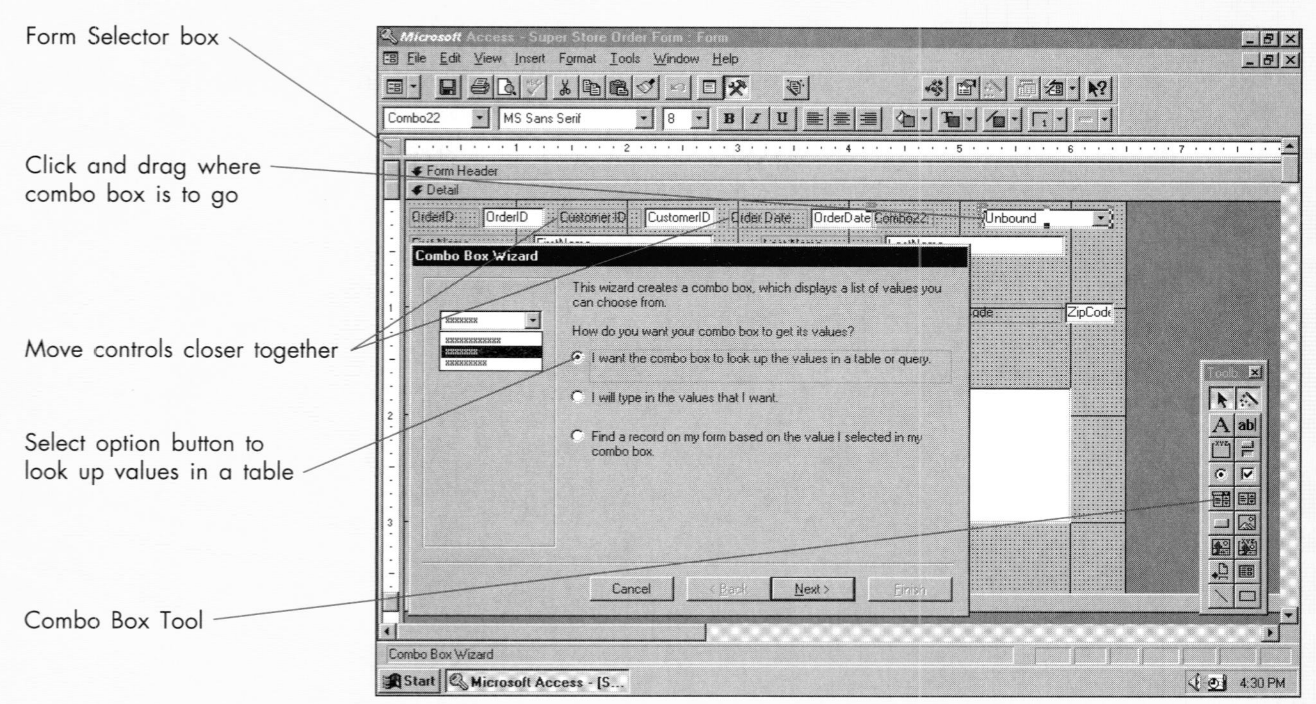

(f) Modify the Super Store Order Form (step 6)

FIGURE 2.13 Hands-on Exercise 4 (continued)

- Move and/or size the combo box and its label so that it is spaced attractively on the form.
- Point to the combo box, click the **right mouse button** to display a shortcut menu, and click **Properties.**
- Click the **Other tab.** Change the name of the box to **Sales Person.** Close the dialog box.
- Pull down the **View menu** and click **Tab Order.** Click the **AutoOrder button** to change the tab order so that the combo box is accessed in sequence. Click **OK.**
- Save the form. Change to the Form view.

STRUCTURED QUERY LANGUAGE

Structured Query Language (SQL) was developed by IBM during the 1970s and has since become the standard language for accessing a relational database. Access shields you from the subtleties of the SQL syntax through the QBE grid, which creates the equivalent SQL statement for you. An SQL statement may appear, however, as the record source property within the form and can be confusing if you are not familiar with SQL. Click the Record Source property, click the drop-down arrow to display the list of queries within the database, then click the desired query to replace the SQL statement.

STEP 7: The Completed Order Form

- You should see the completed form as shown in Figure 2.13g. Click the **New Record button** to display a blank form so that you can place an order.
- Click in the **Customer ID text box.** Enter **13** (your customer number from the first exercise), then press the **Tab key** to move to the next field.
  - The OrderID is entered automatically as it is an AutoNumber field and assigned the next sequential number.
  - All of your customer information (your name, address, and phone number) is entered automatically because of the AutoLookup feature that is built into the underlying query.
  - Today's date is entered automatically because of the default value (=Date()) that is built into the Orders table.
- Click the **drop-down arrow** on the Sales Person combo box. Select **Black** (or click in the box and type **B**), and the complete name is entered automatically.
- Click the **ProductID text box** in the subform. Enter **2** (not P0002) and press the **enter key** to move to the next field. The OrderID (O0027) is entered automatically, as is the Product Name and Unit Price.
- Press the **Tab key** three times to move to the Quantity field, enter **1,** and press the **Tab key** twice more to move to the ProductID field for the next item.
- Close the Order form.

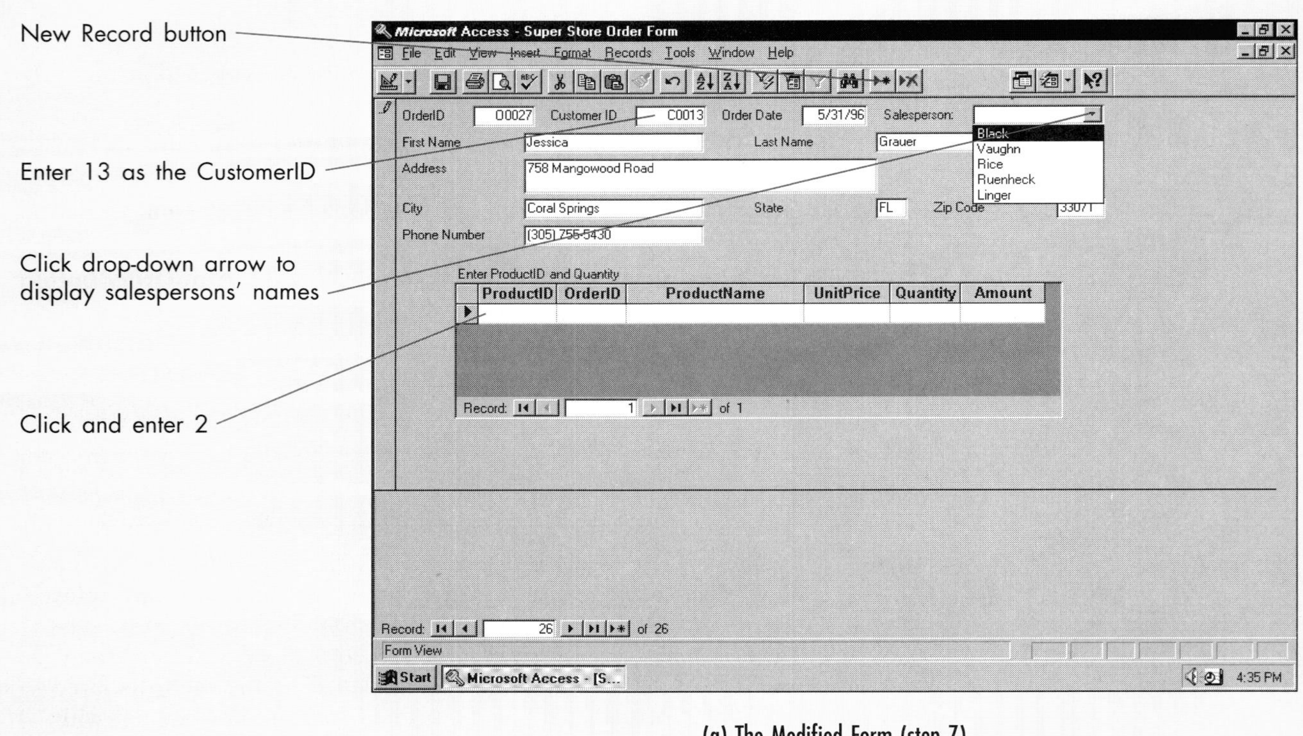

(g) The Modified Form (step 7)

FIGURE 2.13 Hands-on Exercise 4 (continued)

THE STARTUP PROPERTY

The Startup property determines how a database will appear when it is opened. One very common option is to open a form automatically so that the user is presented with the form without having to navigate through the Database window. Pull down the Tools menu, click Startup to display the Startup dialog box, then click the drop-down arrow in the Display Form list box. Select the desired form (e.g., the Orders with Customer Information form developed in this exercise), then click OK. The next time you open the database the designated form will be opened automatically.

STEP 8: Database Properties

➤ You should be back in the Database window. Pull down the **File menu** and click **Database Properties** to display the dialog box in Figure 2.13h.

➤ Click the **Contents tab** to display the contents of the Computer Store database on which you have been working:

- There are five tables (Customers, Order Details, Orders, Products, and Sales Persons).
- There are five queries, which include the Total and Parameter queries you created in exercise 3.

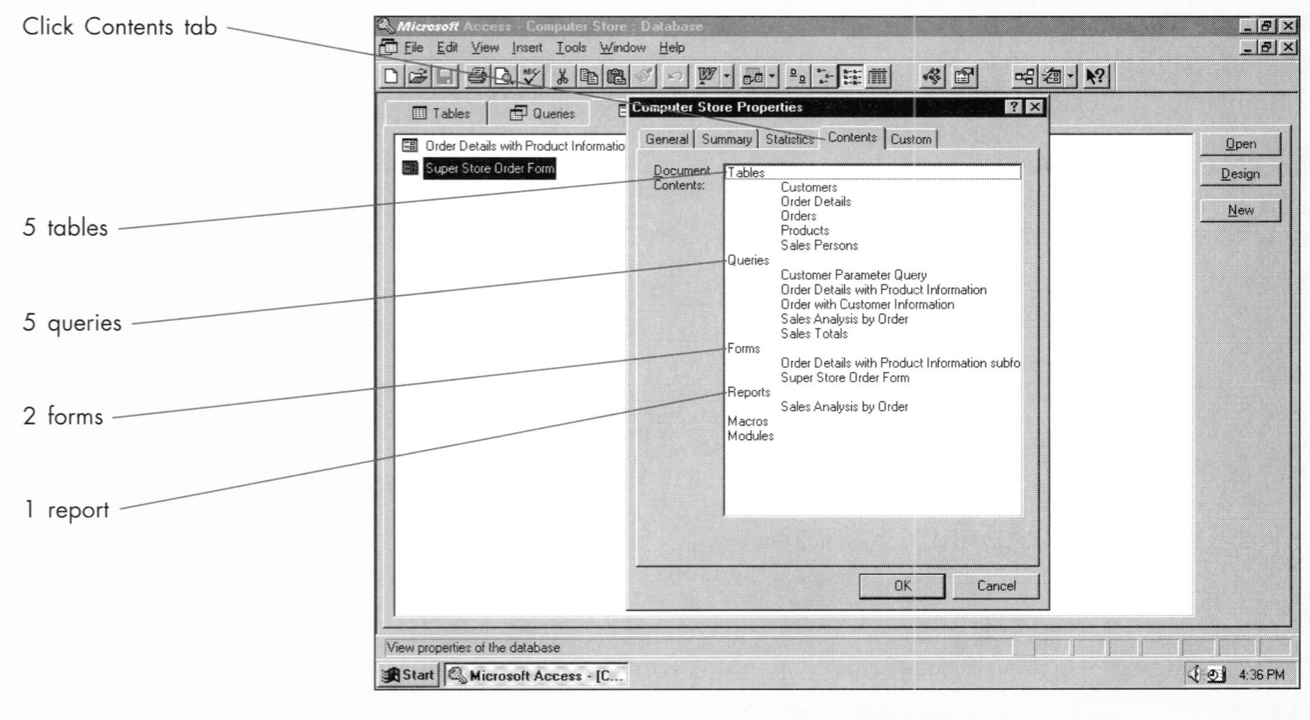

(h) Database Properties (step 8)

FIGURE 2.13 Hands-on Exercise 4 (continued)

- There are two forms—the main form, which you have completed in this exercise, and the associated subform.
- There is one report, the report you created in exercise 3.

➤ Congratulations on a job well done.

COMPACTING A DATABASE

The size of an Access database with multiple objects is quite large even if the database contains only a limited number of records. It is important, therefore, to compact the database periodically so that it is stored as efficiently as possible. Close the open database, but remain in Access. Pull down the Tools menu, click Database utilities, then click Compact Database to display a dialog box similar to the Open box. Select (click) the database you wish to compact, then enter a *different file name* for the compacted base. (This ensures that you still have the original database if there is a problem.) Click the Save button to compact the database and close the dialog box. Check that the compacted database is OK, delete the original database, then rename the compacted database to the original name. See online Help for additional information.

STEP 9: Exit Access

➤ Click OK to close the dialog box. Close the Computer Store database. Exit Access.

SUMMARY

The implementation of a many-to-many relationship requires an additional table whose primary key consists of (at least) the primary keys of the individual tables. The many-to-many table may also contain additional fields whose values are dependent on the combined key. All relationships are created in the Relationships window by dragging the join field from the primary table to the related table. A many-to-many relationship is implemented by a pair of one-to-many relationships.

Enforcement of referential integrity prevents you from adding a record to the related table without a corresponding record in the primary table. It also prevents the deletion and/or updating of records on the "one" side of a one-to-many relationship when there are matching records in the related table. The deletion (updating) can take place, however, if the relationship is modified to allow the cascaded deletion (updating) of related records (fields).

There are several reasons to base a form (or subform) on a query rather than a table. A query can contain a calculated field; a table cannot. A query can contain fields from more than one table and take advantage of AutoLookup. A query can also contain selected records from a table and/or display those records in a different sequence from that of the table on which it is based.

A parameter query prompts you for the criteria each time you execute the query. The prompt is enclosed in square brackets and is entered in the Criteria row within the Query Design view. Multiple parameters may be specified within the same query.

Aggregate functions (Avg, Min, Max, Sum, and Count) perform arithmetic on groups of records. Execution of the query displays an aggregate record for each group, and individual records do not appear. Updating of individual records is not possible in this type of query.

Tables may be added to an Access database without disturbing the data in existing tables. The Get External Data command enables you to import an object(s) from another database.

KEY WORDS AND CONCEPTS

AutoLookup
AutoNumber field
Cascaded deletion
Cascaded updating
Combined key
Description property
Foreign key
Format property
Get External Data command
Group By
Join field
Join line
Main form
Many-to-many relationship
One-to-many relationship
Parameter query
Primary key
Prompt
Referential integrity
Startup property
Sum function
Table row
TopValues property
Total query
Total row
Unmatched Query Wizard
Zoom box

MULTIPLE CHOICE

1. Which tables are necessary to implement a many-to-many relationship between students and the courses they take?
  (a) A Students table
  (b) A Courses table
  (c) A Students-Courses table
  (d) All of the above

2. Which of the following would be suitable as the primary key in a Students-Courses table, where there is a many-to-many relationship between Students and Courses, and further, when a student is allowed to repeat a course?
  (a) The combination of StudentID and CourseID
  (b) The combination of StudentID, CourseID, and semester
  (c) The combination of StudentID, CourseID, semester, and grade
  (d) All of the above are equally appropriate

3. Which of the following is necessary to add a record to the "one" side in a one-to-many relationship in which referential integrity is enforced?
  (a) A unique primary key for the new record
  (b) One or more matching records in the many table
  (c) Both (a) and (b)
  (d) Neither (a) nor (b)

4. Which of the following is necessary to add a record to the "many" side in a one-to-many relationship in which referential integrity is enforced?
   (a) A unique primary key for the new record
   (b) A matching record in the primary table
   (c) Both (a) and (b)
   (d) Neither (a) nor (b)
5. Under which circumstances can you delete a "many" record in a one-to-many relationship?
   (a) Under all circumstances
   (b) Under no circumstances
   (c) By enforcing referential integrity
   (d) By enforcing referential integrity with the cascaded deletion of related records
6. Under which circumstances can you delete the "one" record in a one-to-many relationship?
   (a) Under all circumstances
   (b) Under no circumstances
   (c) By enforcing referential integrity
   (d) By enforcing referential integrity with the cascaded deletion of related records
7. Which of the following would be suitable as the primary key in a Patients-Doctors table, where there is a many-to-many relationship between patients and doctors, and where the same patient can see the same doctor on different visits?
   (a) The combination of PatientID and DoctorID
   (b) The combination of PatientID, DoctorID, and the date of the visit
   (c) Either (a) or (b)
   (d) Neither (a) nor (b)
8. How do you implement the many-to-many relationship between patients and doctors described in the previous question?
   (a) Through a one-to-many relationship between the Patients table and the Patients-Doctors table
   (b) Through a one-to-many relationship between the Doctors table and the Patients-Doctors table
   (c) Both (a) and (b)
   (d) Neither (a) nor (b)
9. A database has a one-to-many relationship between teams and players, which is implemented through a common PlayerID field. Which data type and field size should be assigned to the PlayerID field in the Teams table, if PlayerID is defined as an AutoNumber field in the Players table?
   (a) AutoNumber and Long Integer
   (b) Number and Long Integer
   (c) Text and Long Integer
   (d) Lookup Wizard and Long Integer
10. Which of the following is true about a main form and an associated subform?
   (a) The main form can be based on a query
   (b) The subform can be based on a query
   (c) Both (a) and (b)
   (d) Neither (a) nor (b)

11. A parameter query:
    (a) Displays a prompt within brackets in the Criteria row of the query
    (b) Is limited to a single parameter
    (c) Both (a) and (b)
    (d) Neither (a) nor (b)

12. Which of the following is available as an aggregate function within a select query?
    (a) Sum and Avg
    (b) Min and Max
    (c) Both (a) and (b)
    (d) Neither (a) nor (b)

13. A query designed to take advantage of AutoLookup requires:
    (a) A unique value for the join field in the "one" side of a one-to-many relationship
    (b) The join field to be taken from the "many" side of a one-to-many relationship
    (c) Both (a) and (b)
    (d) Neither (a) nor (b)

14. Which of the following can be imported from another Access database?
    (a) Tables and forms
    (b) Queries and reports
    (c) Both (a) and (b)
    (d) Neither (a) nor (b)

15. Which of the following is true of the TopValues query property?
    (a) It can be used to display the top 10 records in a dynaset
    (b) It can be used to display the top 10 percent of the records in a dynaset
    (c) Both (a) and (b)
    (d) Neither (a) nor (b)

ANSWERS

1. d	**6.** d	**11.** a
2. b	**7.** b	**12.** c
3. a	**8.** c	**13.** c
4. c	**9.** b	**14.** c
5. a	**10.** c	**15.** c

EXPLORING MICROSOFT ACCESS 7.0

1. Use Figure 2.14 to match each action with its result. A given action may be used more than once or not at all.

Action		Result
a. Click at 1 and enter [Enter Order ID]	____	Display the Show Tables dialog box to add Sales Persons table to query

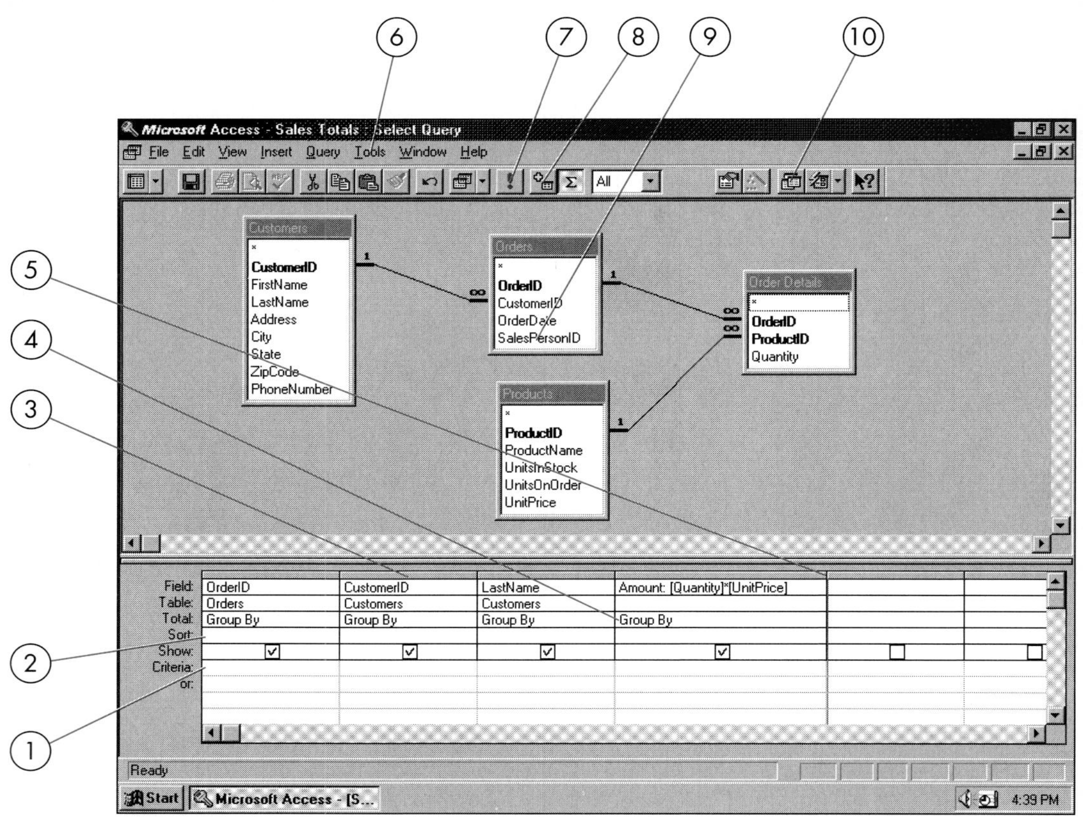

FIGURE 2.14 Screen for Problem 1

b. Click at 2
c. Click at 3, press Del key
d. Click at 4
e. Click and drag at 5
f. Click at 6
g. Click at 7
h. Click at 8
i. Double click at 9
j. Click at 10

____ Modify the query to get a total amount for each order
____ Add the SalesPersonID to the QBE grid
____ Sort the query in ascending order by OrderID
____ Run the query
____ Create a parameter query to reference a specific order
____ Switch to the Database window
____ Increase the width of the amount column
____ Open the Relationships window to edit an existing relationship
____ Delete the CustomerID from the QBE grid

2. Answer the following with respect to the Relationships window shown in Figure 2.15:

a. What relationships are shown in Figure 2.15?
b. What is the primary key in the Students table? in the Courses table? How is this indicated in the diagram?
c. What is the primary key in the Student Course table? Does this key permit a student to repeat a course?

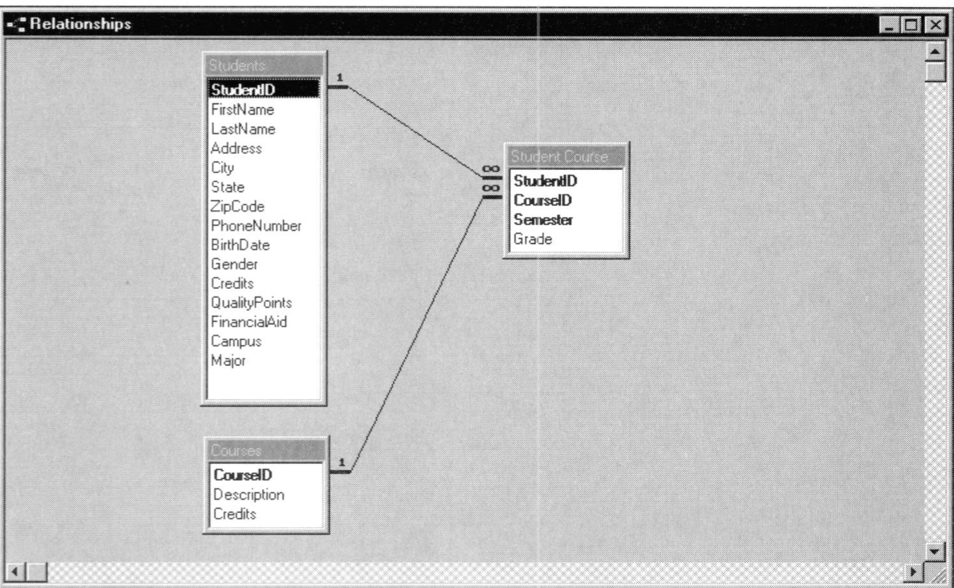

FIGURE 2.15 Screen for Problem 2

d. What foreign keys (if any) are present in the Students table? in the Courses table? in the Student Course table?

e. Can you add to the Students table a student who hasn't taken any courses?

f. Can you add a course to the Courses table prior to students enrolling in that course?

g. Under what circumstances can you delete a student from the Students table and simultaneously delete the courses taken by that student from the Student Course table?

3. The database in Figure 2.16 is intended to monitor information about doctors and patients in an HMO.

a. What is the primary key in the Patients table? in the Doctors table? in the Visits table?

b. Which table(s) have a foreign key?

c. Assume that referential integrity is enforced without cascading of any kind. Can you delete a record in the Patients table? in the Doctors table? in the Visits table?

PatientID	First Name	Last Name	Address	City	State	ZipCode	Phone Number	BirthDate	Sex
P001	Karen	Kinzer	5600 West 29 Court	Ft. Lauderdale	FL	33305	(305) 561-5347	7/ 2/65	F
P002	Brett	Gibson	9200 S.W. 142 Street	Miami	FL	33176	(305) 235-0506	5/ 1/90	M
P003	Matthew	Karlaftis	425 Segovia Street	Coral Gables	FL	33124	(305) 443-8976	2/ 3/47	M
P004	Daniel	Passacantilli	1200 Brickell	Miami	FL	33021	(305) 595-0090	6/15/88	M
P005	Heather	Warren	7890 N.E. 71 Street	Miami	FL	33075	(305) 271-8008	9/30/55	F
P006	Rocio	Diaz	875 West 7 Street	Hialeah	FL	33390	(305) 874-6676	10/ 5/93	F
P007	Sandra	Anon	6220 Miracle Mile	Coral Gables	FL	33124	(305) 284-6629	12/22/68	F
P008	William	Blaney	4777 S.W. 88 Street	Miami	FL	33152	(305) 385-6656	4/18/25	M
P009	Rozelle	Marder	922 Queen Avenue	Hialeah	FL	33395	(305) 874-3309	5/31/87	F
P010	Florence	Hecht	1120 Main Highway	Coconut Grove	FL	33130	(305) 854-6789	8/22/41	F
P011	Frank	Costa	1210 Brickell	Miami	FL	33021	(305) 595-2202	3/15/94	M
P012	Pat	Conroy	5090 South Island	Miami	FL	33021	(305) 595-7878	11/11/52	M
P013	Michell	Lopez	8888 Kendall Drive	Miami	FL	33156	(305) 274-5665	12/ 2/72	F

(a) Patients Table

FIGURE 2.16 Tables for Problem 3

DoctorID	First Name	Last Name	Address	City	State	ZipCode	Phone	Fax	Specialty
D001	Kenneth	Flicker	8700 S.W. 144 Street	Miami	FL	33156	(305) 253-5585	(305) 235-5590	Pediatrics
D002	Grace	Wolfe	2445 N.W. 12 Avenue	Miami	FL	33120	(305) 444-8990	(305) 444-9000	Cardiology
D003	Daniel	McLeod	9225 S.W. 88 Street	Miami	FL	33165	(305) 274-5500	(305) 274-5600	Obstetrics
D004	Phillip	Paul	8700 S.W. 144 Street	Miami	FL	33156	(305) 253-5585	(305) 235-5590	Pediatrics
D005	Victor	Dembrow	1415 N.W. 12 Avenue	Miami	FL	33120	(305) 446-6200	(305) 446-6205	General

(b) Doctors Table

PatientID	DoctorID	VisitDate	Complaint	Diagnosis	LabWork	Amount	Paid
P001	**D003**	3/ 5/96	Pregnancy	Pregnancy	1	$95.00	Yes
P001	**D003**	5/ 5/96	Pregnancy	Pregnancy	1	$95.00	Yes
P001	**D003**	6/ 5/96	Pregnancy	Pregnancy	1	$95.00	Yes
P001	**D005**	4/ 5/96	Sore Throat	Mild Flu	1	$95.00	Yes
P002	**D001**	1/12/96	Annual Checkup	Annual Checkup	2	$145.00	No
P002	**D004**	3/15/96	Fever	Flu	1	$95.00	Yes
P002	**D004**	3/21/96	Fever Follow-up	No follow up	0	$0.00	No
P003	**D002**	5/ 1/96	Palpitations	Cardiac Disease	3	$195.00	No
P003	**D002**	5/15/96	Palpitations	Cardiac Disease	0	$45.00	Yes
P004	**D004**	2/ 3/96	Annual Check-up	Annual Checkup	2	$145.00	Yes
P005	**D002**	4/ 1/96	Chest Pains	Anxiety	3	$195.00	No
P005	**D005**	5/ 1/96	Fever	Flu	0	$45.00	Yes
P007	**D003**	4/18/96	Nausea	Flu	1	$95.00	Yes
P008	**D005**	2/12/96	Sore Throat	Strep Throat	1	$95.00	Yes
P008	**D005**	2/19/96	Sore Throat	Strep Throat	0	$45.00	No
P009	**D004**	5/ 1/96	Annual Check-up	Annual Check-up	2	$145.00	No
P010	**D002**	3/ 1/96	Chest Pains	Irregular Heart	1	$95.00	Yes
P010	**D005**	6/12/96	Annual Check-up	Annual Check-up	3	$195.00	Yes
P011	**D001**	5/31/96	Well Baby Check-up	Well Baby Check-up	0	$45.00	No
P012	**D005**	2/ 1/96	Fever/Aches	Flu	1	$95.00	No
P012	**D005**	3/15/96	Twisted Ankle	Broken Ankle	0	$45.00	Yes
P013	**D003**	1/12/96	Sore Throat	Pregnancy	3	$195.00	Yes
P013	**D003**	3/12/96	Pregnancy	Pregnancy	3	$195.00	Yes
P013	**D003**	5/12/96	Pregnancy	Pregnancy	3	$195.00	Yes

(c) Visits Table

FIGURE 2.16 Tables for Problem 3 (continued)

d. Use the data in the figure to answer the following questions:

   i. List all visits for Heather Warren, showing the doctor's name, complaint, and amount charged for each visit.

   ii. When was Heather Warren's last visit?

   iii. How much has Heather Warren paid to the HMO in 1996?

   iv. Which doctors has Heather seen?

4. Figure 2.17 displays a (partially completed) Relationships window for the database used by a college bookstore. There is a one-to-many relationship between publishers and books. (One publisher can have many books, but a book has only one publisher.) There is also a many-to-many relationship between books and orders. (One order can specify several books, and at the same time, one book can appear in many orders.)

a. What is the primary key in each table? Which tables have a foreign key?

b. Why is the quantity field included in the Order Details table, rather than the Orders table or the Books table?

c. How would you implement the many-to-many relationship that exists between books and orders?

d. What field type should be assigned to the OrderID in the Orders table so that the order numbers are generated automatically when a new order is added? What field type should be specified for the OrderID field in the Order Details table?

e. What other fields (in other tables) could be generated automatically in conjunction with the addition of a new record?

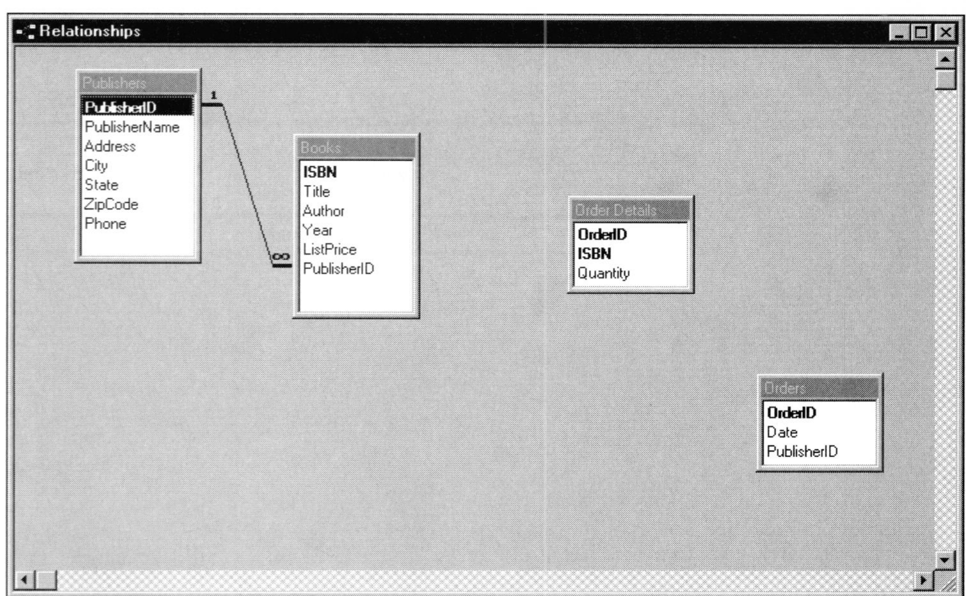

FIGURE 2.17 Screen for Problem 4

Practice with Microsoft Access 7.0

1. The Sales Commission report in Figure 2.18 is based on a query similar to the parameter query used to determine the commissions due a particular salesperson. Create the necessary query, then use the Report Wizard to create the report in Figure 2.18. This exercise illustrates the power of Access as both the report and underlying query are based on five different tables.

2. The query in Figure 2.19 identifies products that have never been ordered. The query was created through the Unmatched Query Wizard according to the instructions below.
   a. Click the Queries tab in the Database window. Click New, select the Find Unmatched Query Wizard, then click OK.
   b. Choose Products as the table whose records you want to see in the query results. Click Next.
   c. Choose Order Details as the table that contains the related records. Click Next.
   d. ProductID is automatically selected as the matching field. Click Next.
   e. Select every field from the Available Fields list. Click Next.
   f. Products without Matching Order Details is entered as the name of the query. Click the Finish Command button to exit the Wizard and see the results of the query.
   g. What advice will you give to management regarding unnecessary inventory?
   h. What advantage (if any) is there in using the Unmatched Query Wizard to create the query, as opposed to creating the query by entering the information directly in the Query Design view?

Sales Commissions Report

	OrderID	Order Date	Last Name	Amount	Commission
Black					
	O0001	4/15/96	Colon	$605.86	$30.29
	O0007	4/21/96	Milgrom	$209.80	10.49
	O0012	4/24/96	Geoghegan	$2,558.50	127.92
	O0017	4/26/96	Center	$79.90	4.00
	O0022	4/29/96	Anderson	$115.95	5.80
	O0027	5/31/96	Grauer	$1,999.00	99.95
			Sum	**$5,569.01**	**$278.45**
Linger					
	O0006	4/21/96	Lee	$998.90	49.95
	O0011	4/24/96	Lee	$739.80	36.99
	O0016	4/26/96	Muddell	$259.90	13.00
	O0021	4/29/96	Anderson	$2,299.00	114.95
	O0026	5/31/96	Grauer	$2,108.93	105.45
			Sum	**$6,406.53**	**$320.34**
Rice					
	O0003	4/18/96	Muddell	$4,183.95	209.20
	O0009	4/22/96	Lee	$499.00	24.95
	O0014	4/25/96	Muddell	$109.85	5.49
	O0019	4/27/96	Slane	$249.75	12.49
	O0024	5/1/96	Muddell	$3,358.67	167.93
			Sum	**$8,401.22**	**$420.06**
Ruenheck					
	O0004	4/18/96	Geoghegan	$5,688.00	284.40
	O0010	4/22/96	Milgrom	$5,642.95	282.15
	O0015	4/25/96	Couto	$249.90	12.50
	O0020	4/28/96	Slane	$569.95	28.50
	O0025	5/1/96	Muddell	$757.90	37.90
			Sum	**$12,908.70**	**$645.45**

Friday, May 31, 1996 **Page 1 of 2**

FIGURE 2.18 Report for Practice Exercise 1

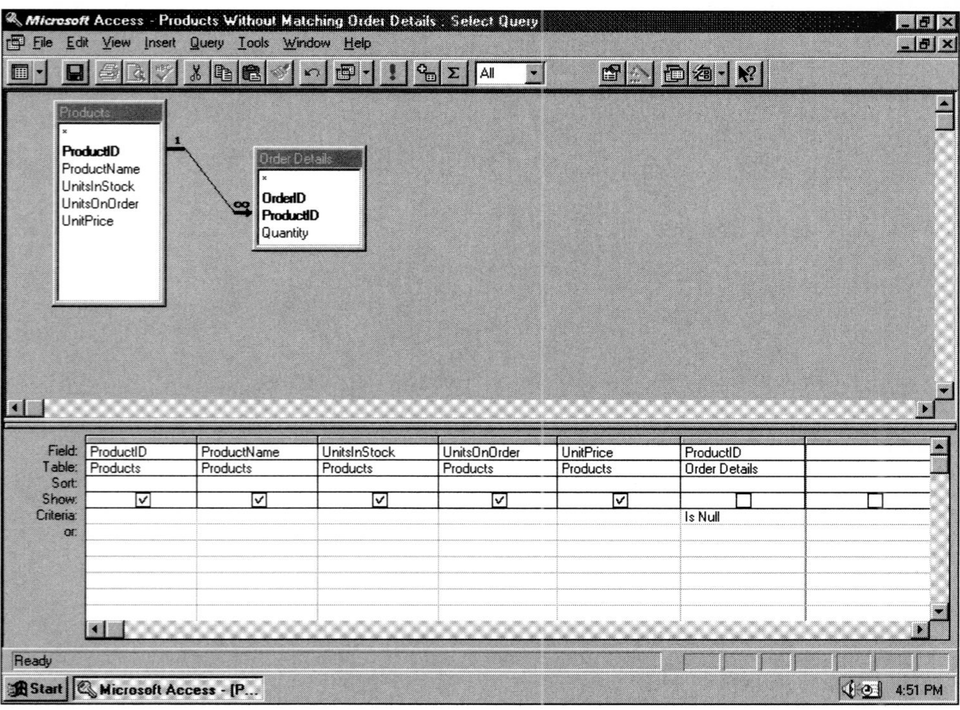

FIGURE 2.19 Screen for Practice Exercise 2

3. Create the form in Figure 2.20, which displays either the information for an existing customer or a blank form to add a new customer. This is accomplished by basing the form on a parameter query rather than the Customers table. Execution of the query displays a blank form when the customer's

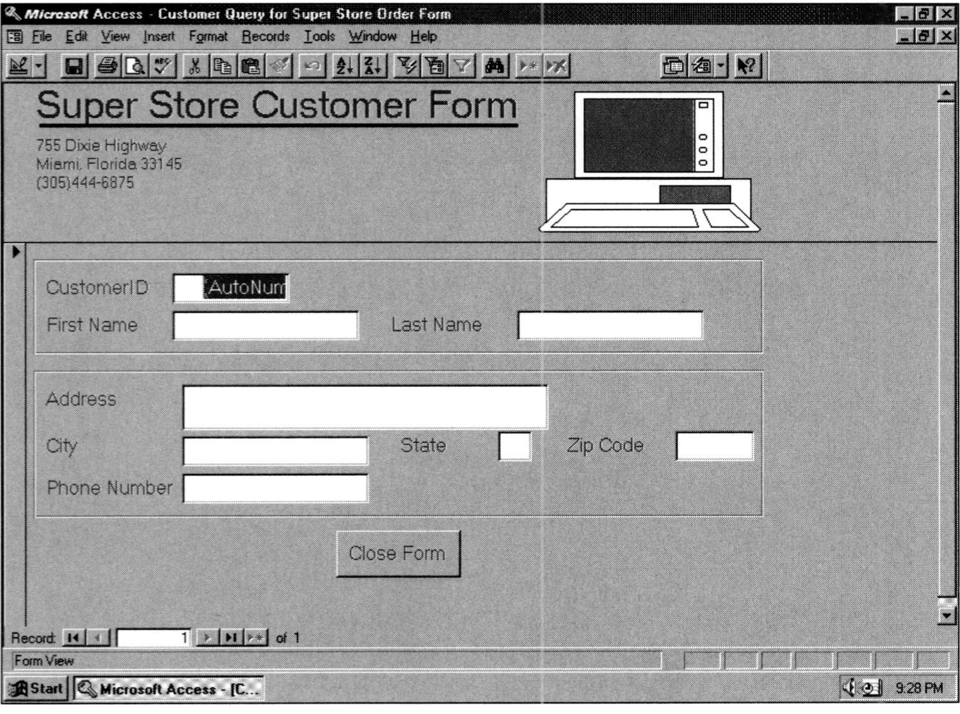

FIGURE 2.20 Screen for Practice Exercise 3

name is not in the database (as in Figure 2.20), or it will display a completed form when it finds the name.

a. Create the necessary parameter query that requests the customer's last name followed by the customer's first name.
b. Create the form based on the parameter query. You are free to improve upon our design.

4. The best way to open the Customer form that was created in the previous exercise is by adding a command button to the Super Store Order Form as shown in Figure 2.21. The user would click the Find/Add Command button to display the Parameter Value dialog box, then he or she would enter the customer's last name as indicated. The system would return a completed Customer form for an existing customer (from which to obtain the CustomerID) or a blank form to add a new customer. Closing the customer form, in either case, would return you to the Order form where you can enter the new order.

a. Open the Super Store Order form that was created in the chapter (and completed in Hands-on Exercise 4), then use the Command Button Wizard to add the buttons in Figure 2.21. The Find/Add a Customer button should open the form from the previous problem. The Add Order button should add a new order, and the Close Form button should close the Order form.
b. You can improve the form further by modifying the subform to display a combo box for the product name. This way, the user clicks on the combo box within an order, and selects the products by name rather than having to enter a ProductID. Open the subform in Design view, delete the existing ProductID and ProductName controls, then follow the procedure that was used to add a combo box for the salesperson (see step 6 on page 104).
c. Add a new order for yourself consisting of a Pentium 133, 17-inch monitor, laser printer, and 28.8 bps modem. Print this order (be sure to print only a single order) and submit it to your instructor.

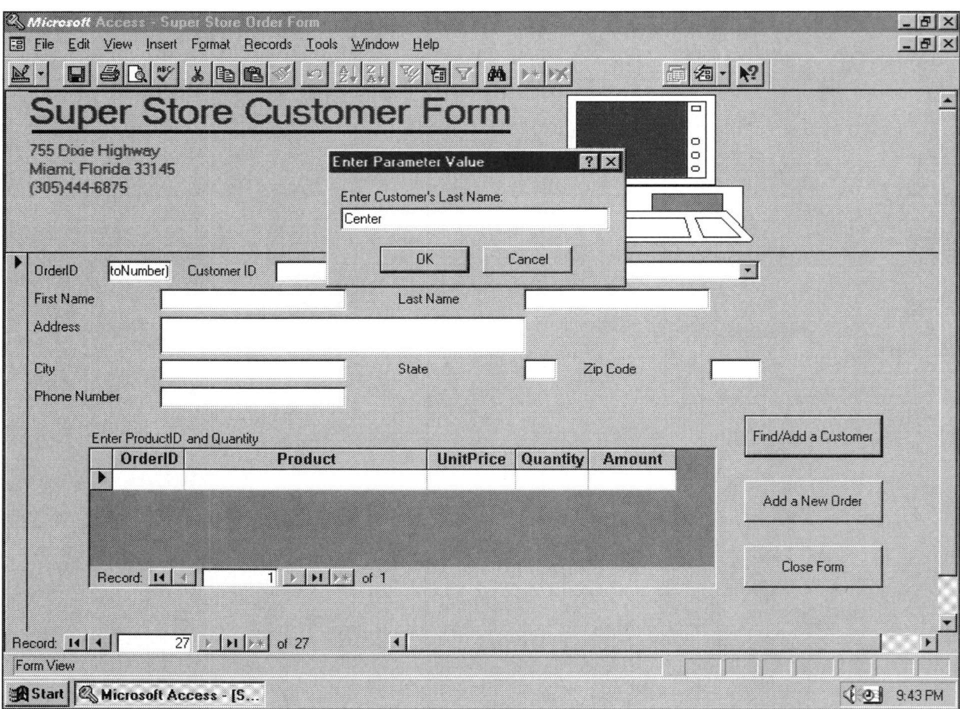

FIGURE 2.21 Screen for Practice Exercise 4

Medical Research

Design a database for a medical research project that will track specific volunteers and/or specific studies. A study will require several subjects, but a specific person may participate in only one study. The system should also be able to track physicians. Many physicians can work on the same study. A given physician may also work on multiple studies.

The system should be able to display all facts about a particular volunteer (subject) such as name, birth date, sex, height, weight, blood pressure, and cholesterol level. It should be able to display all characteristics associated with a particular study—for example, the title, beginning date, ending date, as well as the names of all physicians who work on that study. It should also show whether the physician is a primary or secondary investigator in each study.

Show the required tables in the database, being sure to indicate the primary key and foreign keys in each table. Indicate one or two other fields in each table as appropriate. (You need not list them all.)

The Stock Broker

You have been hired as a consultant to a securities firm that wants to track its clients and the stocks they own. The firm prides itself on its research and maintains a detailed file for the stocks it follows. Among the data for each stock are its symbol (ideal for the primary key), the industry it is in, its earnings, dividend, etc.

The firm requires the usual client data (name, address, phone number, social security number, etc.). One client can hold many different stocks, and the same stock can be held by different clients. The firm needs to know the date the client purchased the stock, the number of shares that were purchased, and the purchase price.

Show the required tables in the database, being sure to indicate the primary key and foreign keys in each table. Indicate one or two other fields in each table (you need not list them all).

The Video Store

You have been hired as a database consultant to the local video store, which rents and/or sells tapes to customers. The store maintains the usual information about every customer (name, address, phone number, and so on). It also has detailed information about every movie, such as its duration, rating, rental price, and purchase price. One customer can rent several tapes, and the same tape will (over time) be rented to many customers.

The owner of the store needs a detailed record of every rental that identifies the movie, the customer, the date the rental was made, and the number of days the customer may keep the movie without penalty.

Class Scheduling

Class scheduling represents a major undertaking at any university. It entails the coordination of course offerings as published in a registration schedule together with faculty assignments. All courses have a formal title but are more commonly known by a six-position course-id. Microcomputer Applications, for example, is better known as CIS120. The first three characters in the course-id denote the department (e.g., CIS stands for Computer Information Systems). The last three indicate the particular course.

The university may offer multiple sections of any given course at different times. CIS120, for example, is offered at four different times: at 9:00, 10:00, 11:00, and 12:00, with all sections meeting three days a week (Mondays, Wednesdays, and Fridays). The information about when a class meets is summarized in the one-letter section designation; for example, section A meets from 9:00 to 9:50 on Mondays, Wednesdays, and Fridays.

The published schedule should list every section of every course together with the days, times, and room assignments. It should also display the complete course title, number of credits, and the name of the faculty member assigned to that section. It should be able to list all classes taught by a particular faculty member or all sections of a particular course. Design a relational database to satisfy these requirements.

3

BUILDING APPLICATIONS: INTRODUCTION TO MACROS AND PROTOTYPING

OBJECTIVES

After reading this chapter you will be able to:

1. Explain how forms are used to develop an automated user interface; create a form with multiple command buttons to serve as a menu.
2. Use the Link Tables command to associate tables in one database with objects in a different database.
3. Describe how macros are used to automate an application; explain the special role of the AutoExec macro.
4. Describe the components of the Macro window; distinguish between a macro action and an argument.
5. Use the On Click property to change the action associated with a command button.
6. Use the Unmatched Query Wizard to identify records in one table that do not have a corresponding record in another table.
7. Explain how prototyping facilitates the development of an application; use the MsgBox action as the basis of a prototype macro.
8. Create a macro group; explain how macro groups simplify the organization of macros within a database.

OVERVIEW

You have completed several chapters in our text and have developed some impressive databases. You have created systems with multiple tables that contained both one-to-many and many-to-many relationships. You have created sophisticated forms and queries that relate data from several tables to one another. In short, you have become proficient in Microsoft Access and have learned how to create the objects (tables, forms, queries, and reports) that comprise a database.

You have not, however, developed a user interface that ties the objects together so that the database is easy to use. In other words, you have created a database, but have not yet created an application. An application contains the same objects as a database. The difference between the two is subtle and has to do with how the objects are presented to the user. An application has an intuitive user interface that does not require a knowledge of Microsoft Access on the part of the user.

This chapter has you develop an application for the Coral Springs Soccer Association. The discussion starts with an existing database that is expanded to include a user interface that enables a nontechnical person to use the application. The application includes macros that automate common command sequences and further simplify the system for the end user. And finally, the application includes the concept of prototyping, which enables you to demonstrate its "look and feel" to potential users, even before the application is complete.

Four hands-on exercises are included that progressively build the application. The end result is a system that is fully functional and one that can be used by any youth-oriented sports league.

THE CORAL SPRINGS SOCCER ASSOCIATION

The Coral Springs Soccer Association (CSSA) has approximately three thousand players organized into teams in various age groups. The Association registers the players and coaches, then holds a draft (among the coaches) to divide the players into teams. The Association has designed a database with three tables (Teams, Players, and Coaches) and has implemented the following relationships:

- A one-to-many relationship between teams and players (one team has many players, but a player is assigned to only one team).
- A one-to-many relationship between teams and coaches (one team has many coaches, but a coach is assigned to only one team).

The Access database developed by the CSSA contains multiple forms, queries, and reports based on these tables. There is a Players form through which you add a new player, or edit or delete the record of an existing player. A similar form exists for the Coaches table. There is also a sophisticated main and subform combination for the Teams table that displays the players and coaches on each team, and through which data for any table (Team, Player, or Coach) can be added, edited, or deleted.

The CSSA database contains a variety of reports, including a master list of players in alphabetical order, mailing labels for all coaches and players, a list of players according to their ability rating, and printed team rosters. The CSSA database also contains queries to find a specific player or coach, and to locate all players and/or coaches who have not been assigned to a team.

It would not be difficult for a person knowledgeable in Access to open the database and then select the various objects from the Database window as the need arose. The Soccer database, however, is used by nontechnical volunteers during registration, at which time hundreds of players (accompanied by their parents) sign up for the coming season. It is essential, therefore, that the database be easy to use, and that a nontechnical person be able to register the players and produce the queries and reports. This, in turn, gives rise to the menu-driven system in Figure 3.1.

The ***user interface*** (the screens the user sees) is the most important part of any system, at least from the viewpoint of the end-user. A system that is intuitive and easy to use will be successful. Conversely, a system that is difficult to use or

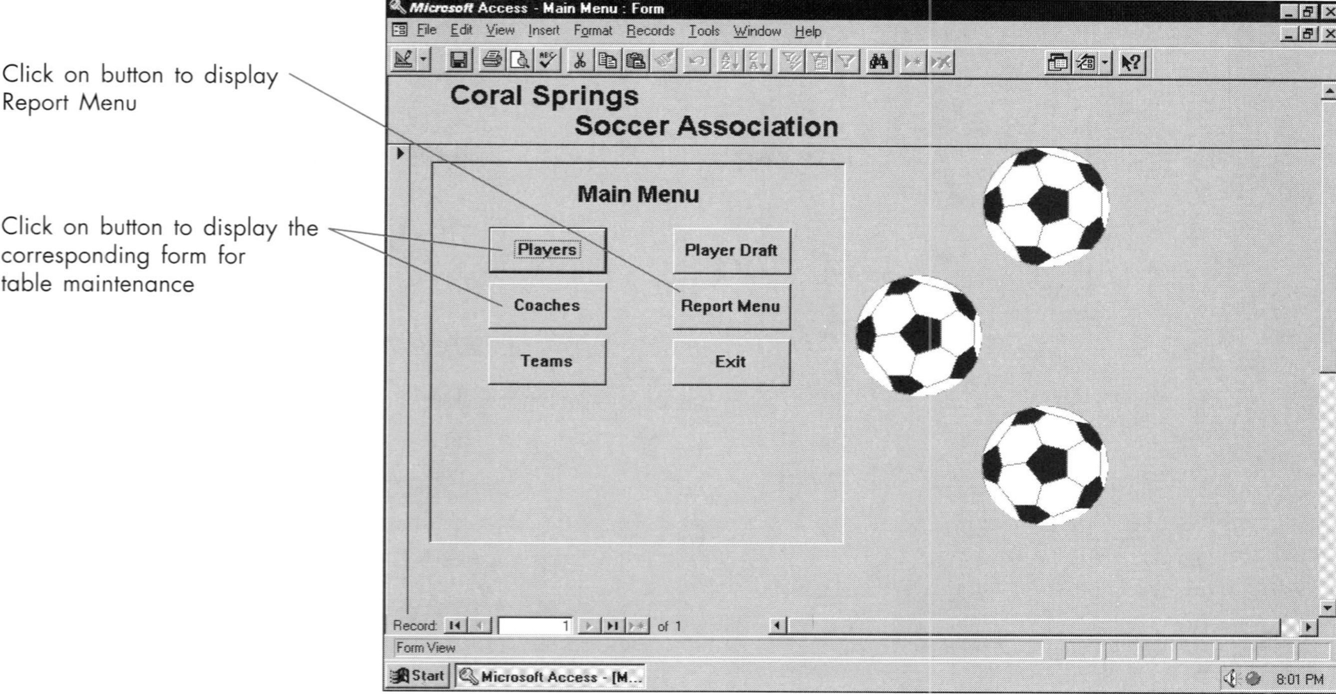

FIGURE 3.1 A User Interface

visually unappealing is sure to fail. You don't have to know anything about soccer or the workings of our system to use the menu in Figure 3.1.

You would, for example, click the Players, Coaches, or Teams command buttons and expect a screen that would enable you to maintain records in the corresponding table. In similar fashion, you would click the Report Menu button to display a menu listing the various reports, each of which could be produced by clicking the corresponding button. You would click the Player Draft button to assign players to teams after registration has taken place.

The menu in Figure 3.1 is a form similar to those that you have developed in other chapters. Each of the command buttons was created through the Command Button Wizard. The form is created in such a way that when a user clicks a button, Access interprets that action as an ***event*** and responds with an action that has been assigned to that event. Clicking the Teams button, for example, causes Access to open the Teams form. Clicking the Players button is a different event and causes Access to open the Players form.

To develop a menu, you create a form, then add command buttons through the Command Button Wizard. The Wizard prompts you for the action you want to take in response to the event (e.g., clicking the button), then creates an ***event procedure*** for you. The event procedure is an Access Basic program that executes automatically each time the event occurs. Eventually, you may want to learn Access Basic so that you can develop more advanced applications and create your own procedures. Access Basic is, however, beyond the scope of this text.

THE LINK TABLES COMMAND

All applications consist of tables *and* objects (forms, queries, reports, macros, and modules) based on those tables. The tables and objects may be stored in the same database (as was done throughout the book), or they may be stored in separate databases, as shown in Figure 3.2. In this example the tables are stored in one

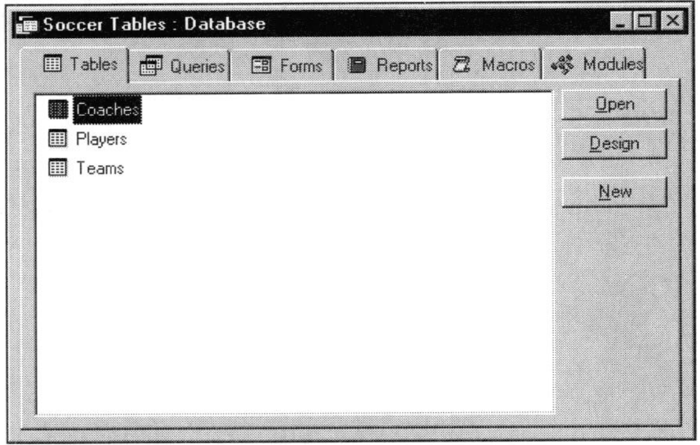

(a) Soccer Tables Database (contains only the tables)

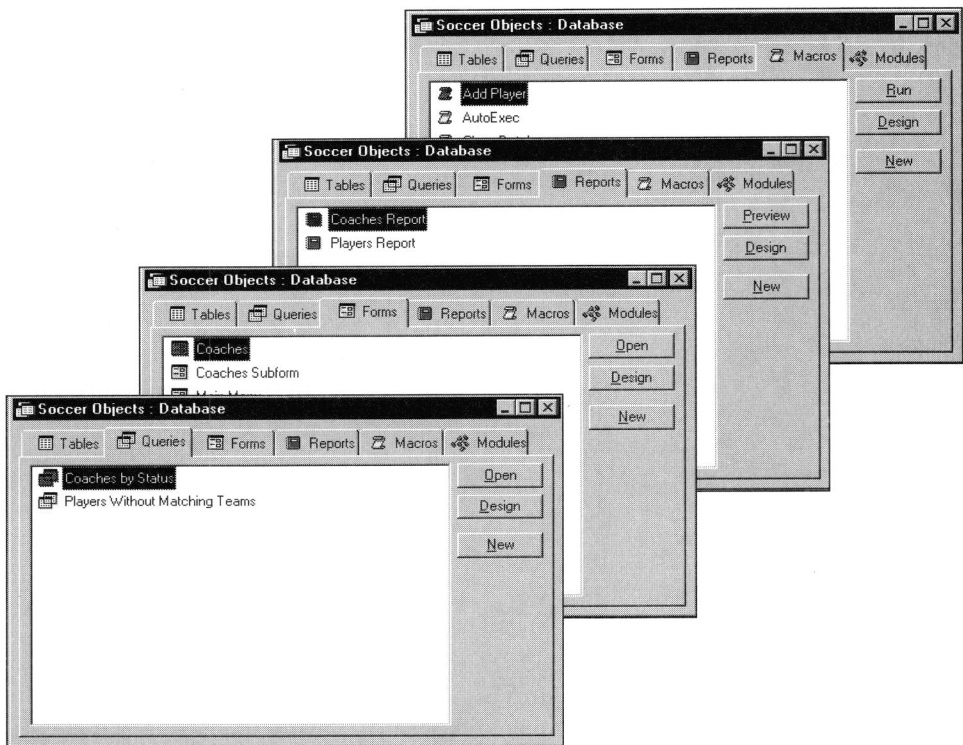

(b) Soccer Objects Database (contains the Queries, Forms, Reports, and Macros)

FIGURE 3.2 Separating the Tables and Objects

database (the Soccer Tables database), while the objects are stored in a different database (the Soccer Objects database).

The advantage to this approach is that you can create new versions of an application *without* disturbing the data. In other words, you can develop an upgraded release of the application (Soccer Objects Two) and distribute it to the users without affecting the various tables. The new version contains additional and/or improved features (e.g., new reports and queries) but attaches to the original data, and thus retains all of the transactions that have been processed.

You can also create other databases with different sets of objects for different users according to their needs and/or privileges. The Director, for example, may be given access to all tables within the database where he or she can perform any type of operation. Other users, however, may be given only restricted access, such as being able to add players or coaches, but prevented from making team assignments.

The tables and objects are tied to one another through the ***Link Tables command,*** which is executed from within the Soccer Objects database. The command associates the tables in one database (Soccer Tables) with the objects in another database (Soccer Objects). Once the Link Tables command has been executed, it is as though the tables were in the Soccer Objects database with respect to maintaining the data. You can add, edit, and delete a record in any (linked) table; you cannot, however, change the design of a linked table from within the Soccer Objects database.

The following exercise has you link the tables from one database to the objects in a different database, then develop the Main Menu (shown earlier in Figure 3.1) for the Coral Springs Soccer Association.

HANDS-ON EXERCISE 1

Creating a User Interface

Objective: Use the Link Tables command to associate tables in one database with the objects in a different database. Create a form with multiple command buttons to provide the user with a menu. Use Figure 3.3 as a guide in the exercise.

STEP 1: Open the Soccer Objects Database

- Start Access. Change to the **Exploring Access folder** as you have been doing throughout the text.
- Open the **Soccer Objects database** as shown in Figure 3.3a, then click the various tabs in the Database window to view the contents of this database. This database contains the various objects (forms, queries, and reports) in the soccer application, but not the tables.
  - Click the **Tables tab.** There are currently no tables in the database.
  - Click the **Forms tab.** There are six forms in the database.
  - Click the **Queries tab.** There is one query in the database.
  - Click the **Reports tab.** There are currently no reports in the database.
- Pull down the **File menu,** click **Database Properties,** then click the **Contents tab** to see the contents of the database as shown in Figure 3.3a. Click **OK** to close the dialog box.

DATABASE PROPERTIES

The tabs within the Database window display the objects within a database, but show only one type of object at a time. You can, for example, see all of the reports or all of the queries, but you cannot see the reports and queries at the same time. There is another way. Pull down the File menu, click Database Properties, then click the Contents tab to display the contents (objects) in the database. You cannot, however, use the Database Properties dialog box to open those objects.

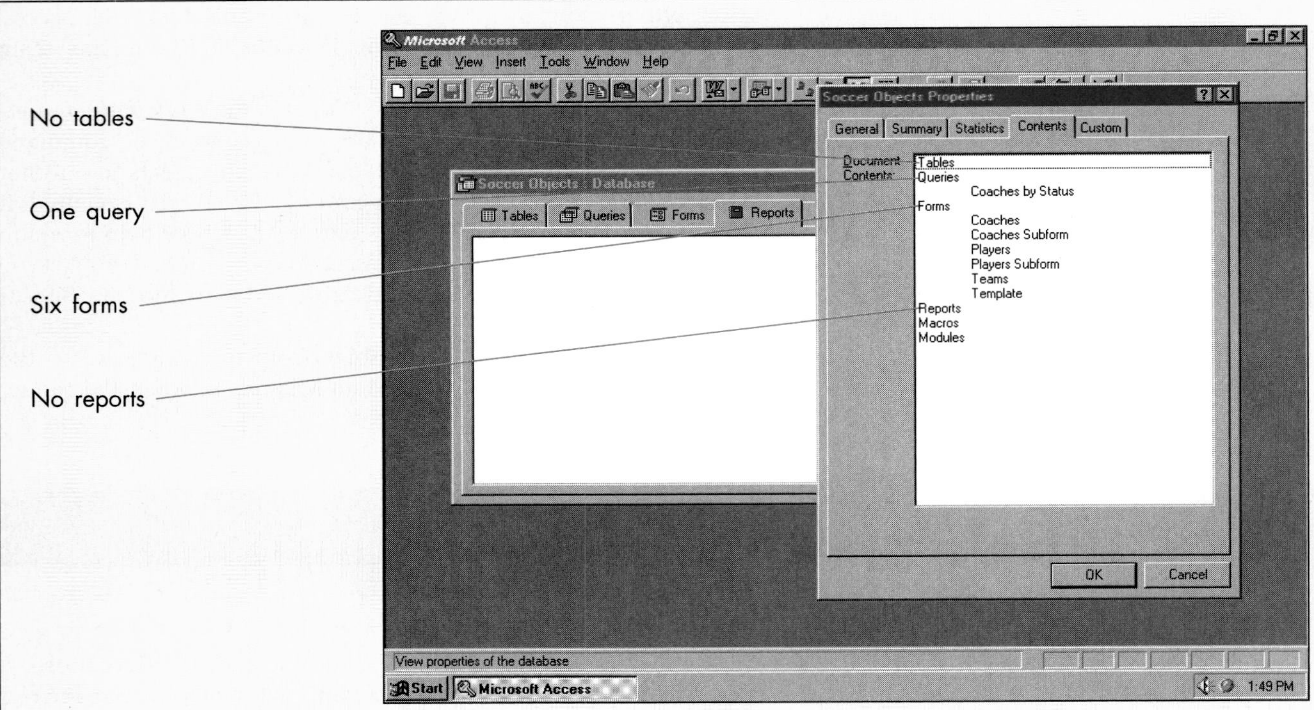

(a) The Soccer Objects Database (step 1)

FIGURE 3.3 Hands-on Exercise 1

STEP 2: The Link Tables Command

- Pull down the **File menu.** Click **Get External Data,** then click **Link Tables** from the cascaded menu. You should see the Link dialog box.
- Select the **Exploring Access folder.** Scroll (if necessary) until you can select the **Soccer Tables database,** then click the **Link Command button.**
- You should see the Link Tables dialog box in Figure 3.3b. Click the **Select All Command button** to select all three tables, then click **OK.**
- The system (briefly) displays a message indicating that it is linking the tables, after which the tables should appear in the Database window. (If necessary, click the **Tables tab** in the Database window.) The arrow next to each table indicates that the table physically resides in another database.

IMPORTING VERSUS LINKING

The Get External Data command displays a cascaded menu to import or link an object from another database. (Any type of object can be imported. A table is the only type of object that can be linked.) Importing an object brings a copy of the object into the current database and does not maintain a tie to the original object. Thus, any changes to the object in the current database are not reflected in the original object. Linking, on the other hand, does not bring the table into the database but only a pointer to the table. Any changes to the linked table are reflected in the original table as well as any other databases that are linked to that table.

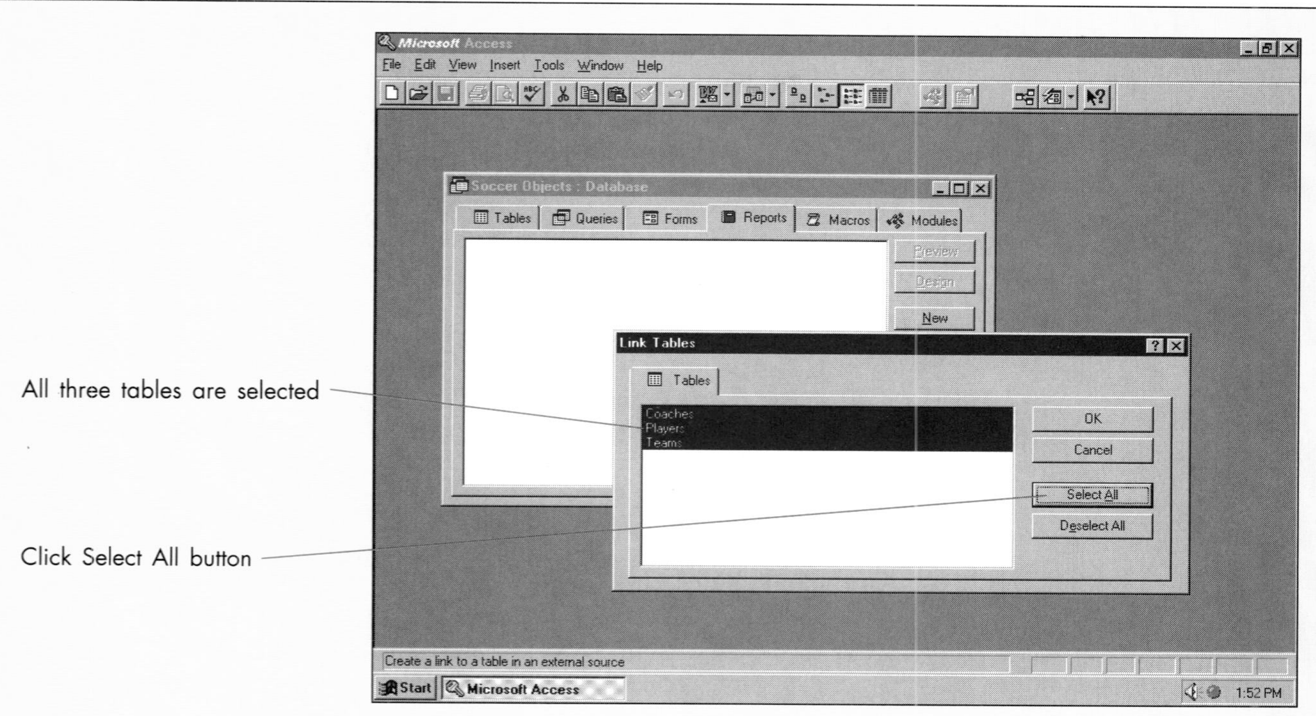

(b) Link Tables Command (step 2)

FIGURE 3.3 Hands-on Exercise 1 (continued)

STEP 3: Add a New Player

- Click the **Forms tab** to display the available forms, then double click the **Players form** to open the form. Click the **Maximize button** so that the form takes the entire window as shown in Figure 3.3c.
- Click the **Add Player Command button** on the bottom of the form. Click the **text box** to enter your first name. (The PlayerID is an AutoNumber field that is updated automatically.) Enter your name, then press the **Tab key** to move to the next field.
- Continue to enter the appropriate data for yourself, but please assign yourself to the **Comets team.** Note, too, that various defaults and data validation have been built into the system:
  - As soon as you begin to enter data, a unique PlayerID is assigned automatically since PlayerID is an AutoNumber field.
  - The phone number must be numeric and must contain both the area code and phone number.
  - Coral Springs and FL are entered as default values for city and state, respectively, but can be changed by entering new values.
  - The team is entered via a drop-down list. Type **C** (the first letter in Comets) and Comets is entered automatically from the drop-down list for teams.
  - The player rating is a required field (all players are evaluated for ability in order to balance the teams) and must be A, B, C, or D.
- Click the **Close Form Command button** to complete the data entry and return to the Database window.

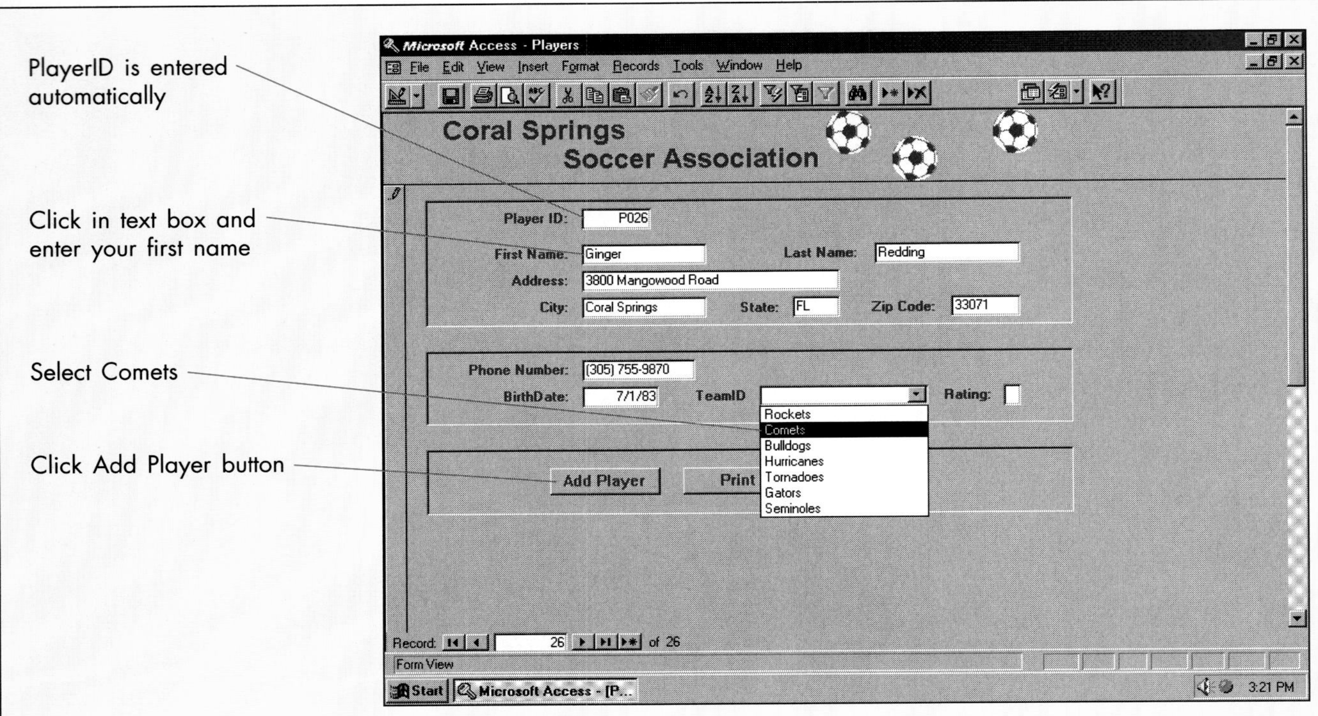

(c) Add a Player (step 3)

FIGURE 3.3 Hands-on Exercise 1 (continued)

A LOOK AHEAD

The Add Record button in the Players form was created through the Command Button Wizard. The Wizard creates an *event procedure* that creates a blank record at the end of the underlying table and enables you to add a new player. The procedure does not, however, position you at a specific control within the Players form; that is, you still have to click in the First Name text box to start entering the data. You can, however, create a macro that displays a blank record *and* automatically moves to the First Name control. See steps 6 and 7 in the next hands-on exercise.

STEP 4: View the Team Form

- Double click the **Teams form** to open this form. You will see the players and coaches for Team T01 (Rockets).
- Click the ▶| on the Team status bar (or press the **PgDn key**) to move to the next team, which is team T02 (Comets) as shown in Figure 3.3d.
- Your name has been added as the last player on this team because of the team assignment you made in the previous step. Don't be concerned that your team doesn't have a coach, as we will take care of that in step 9.
- Click the **Close Form Command button** to return to the Database window.

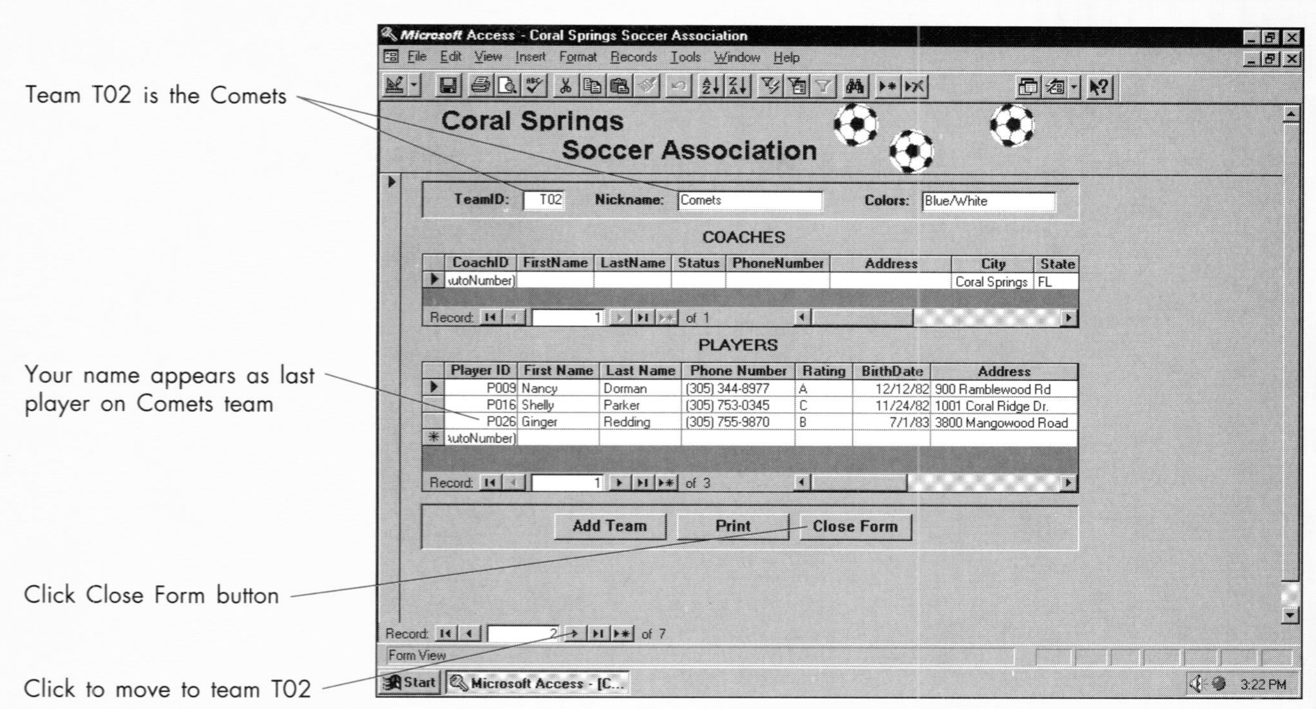

(d) View a Team Roster (step 4)

FIGURE 3.3 Hands-on Exercise 1 (continued)

STEP 5: Create the Main Menu Form

- Select (click) the **Template form,** but do *not* open the form. Pull down the **Edit menu** and click **Copy** (or click the **Copy button** on the Database toolbar). The form has been copied to the clipboard, although there is no visible indication that this has been accomplished.
- Pull down the **Edit menu** and click **Paste** (or click the **Paste button** on the Database toolbar). You will see the Paste As dialog box in Figure 3.3e.
- Type **Main Menu** as the name of the form. Press **enter** or click **OK.** The Database window should now contain the Main Menu form you just created.

USE A TEMPLATE

Avoid the routine and repetitive work of creating a new form by basing all forms for a given application on the same template. A template is a partially completed form that contains graphic elements and other formatting specifications. A template does not, however, have an underlying table or query. We suggest that you create a template for your application and store it within the database, then use that template whenever you need to create a new form. (All you do is copy the template.) It saves you time and trouble. It also promotes a consistent look that is critical to the application's overall success.

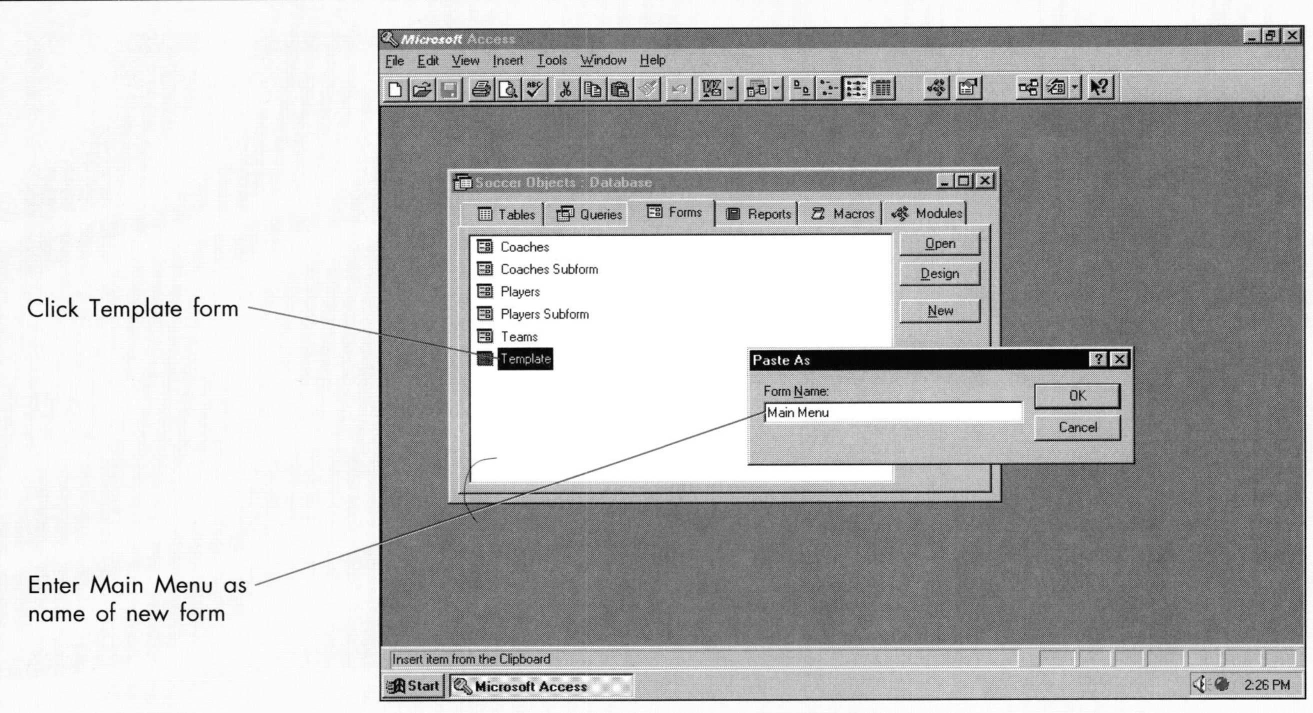

(e) Copy the Template Form (step 5)

FIGURE 3.3 Hands-on Exercise 1 (continued)

STEP 6: Add the Player Command Button

- Click the newly created **Main Menu form.** Click the **Design button** to open the form in Design view, then maximize the window.
- Click the text box containing the label, **Enter menu name here,** then click and drag to select the text. Enter **Main Menu** to replace the selected text as shown in Figure 3.3f.
- Check that the Form Design, Formatting (Form/Report Design), and Toolbox toolbars are all visible. (See boxed tip to display a missing toolbar.)
- Click the **Command button tool.** (The mouse pointer changes to a tiny crosshair attached to a command button when you point anywhere in the form.)
- Click and drag in the form where you want the button to go, then release the mouse. This draws a button and simultaneously opens the Command Button Wizard as shown in Figure 3.3f. (The number on your button may be different from ours.)
  - Click **Form Operations** in the Categories list box. Select **Open Form** from the list of actions. Click **Next.**
  - Select **Players** from the list of available forms. Click **Next.**
  - Click the option button to **Open the form and show all the records.** Click **Next.**

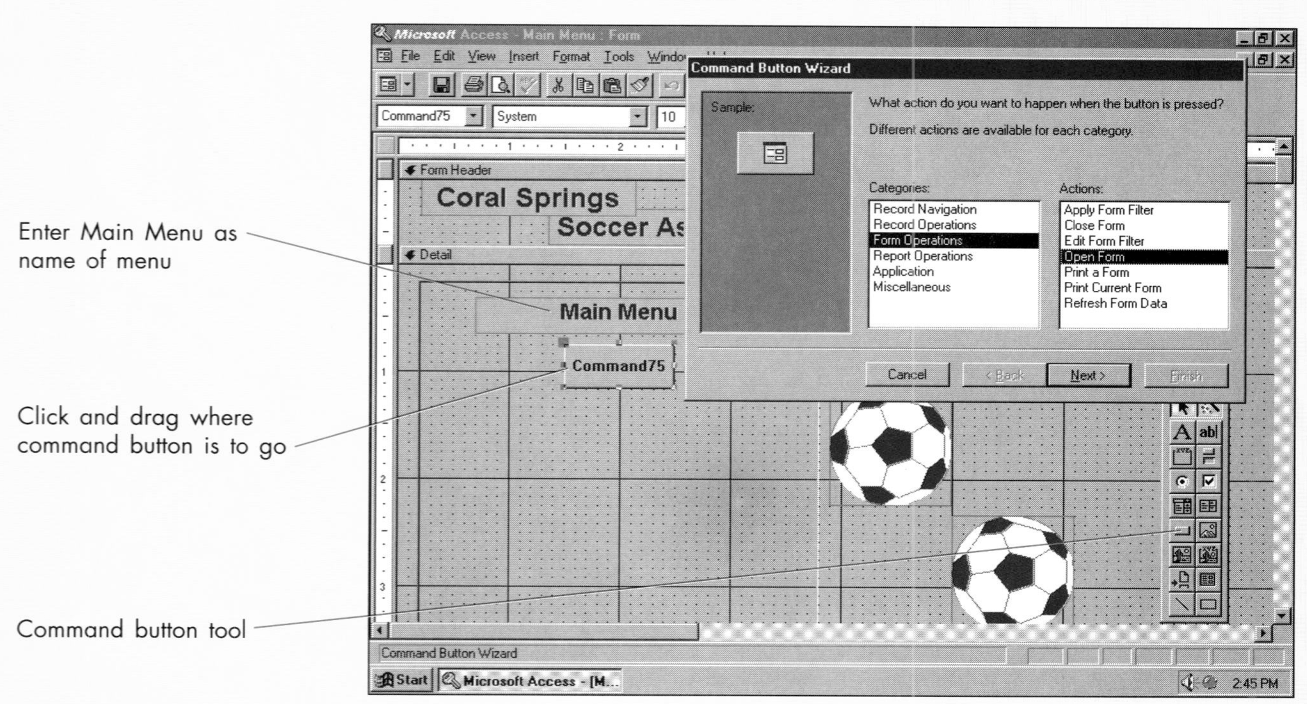

(f) Add the Command Button (step 6)

FIGURE 3.3 Hands-on Exercise 1 (continued)

- Click the **Text option button,** then click and drag to select the default text (Open Form). Type **Players** in the text box next to the option button. Click **Next.**
- Enter **Players** (in place of the button number) as the name of the button, then click the **Finish Command button.**

➤ The completed command button should appear on your form. This button will open the Players form when clicked.

FIXED VERSUS FLOATING TOOLBARS

A toolbar can be docked (fixed) along the edge of a window, or it can be displayed as a floating toolbar within the window. To move a docked toolbar, drag the toolbar background. To move a floating toolbar, drag its title bar. If a desired toolbar is not visible, point to any visible toolbar and click the right mouse button to display a shortcut menu from which you can display other toolbars.

STEP 7: Add the Remaining Command Buttons

➤ Add a command button to open the **Coaches form** following the procedure in the previous step. Click the **Command button tool,** click and drag in the form where you want the button to go, then release the mouse. Choose **Form Operations** in the Categories list box, select **Open Form,** and click **Next.**

- Choose **Coaches** from the list of available forms and click **Next.** Click the option button to **Open the form and show all the records.** Click **Next.**
- Click the **Text Option button,** enter **Coaches** in the text box, and click **Next.** Enter **Coaches** as the name of the button and click the **Finish Command button.**
- Add a **Teams button** in similar fashion.
- Add a fourth (and final) command button to close the Main Menu form. Choose **Form Operations,** then select **Close Form** as the action when the button is pressed.
- Enter **Exit** as the text to display on the button, and use **Exit** as the name of the button. Save the completed form.

THE FORMAT PAINTER

The Format Painter (common to all Office applications) copies the formatting of the selected object, such as a command button, to another object. Select (click) the object whose formatting you want to copy, then click or double click the Format Painter button. (Clicking the Format Painter will paint only one object. Double clicking will paint continuously until the feature is disabled by clicking the Format Painter button a second time.) Either way, the mouse pointer changes to a paintbrush to indicate that you can paint other objects with the current formatting. Just click the target object, which will assume the identical formatting characteristics as the original object.

STEP 8: Size and Align the Buttons

- Your form should contain four command buttons as shown in Figure 3.3g. Size one of the buttons to the height and width you want, then select all four command buttons by pressing and holding the **Shift key** as you click each button.
- Pull down the **Format menu.** Click **Size** to display the cascade menu shown in Figure 3.3g. Click **To Widest** to set a uniform width for the selected buttons.
- Pull down the **Format menu** a second time, click **Size** to display the cascade menu, and click **To Tallest** to set a uniform height for the selected buttons.
- Pull down the **Format menu** once again, click **Vertical Spacing,** then click **Make Equal.**
- Pull down the **Format menu** a final time, click **Align,** then click **Left** to complete the alignment.
- Click the **drop-down arrow** on the **Fore Color button** on the Formatting toolbar to display the available colors, then click **Blue** to change the text color of all four buttons.
- Save the form.

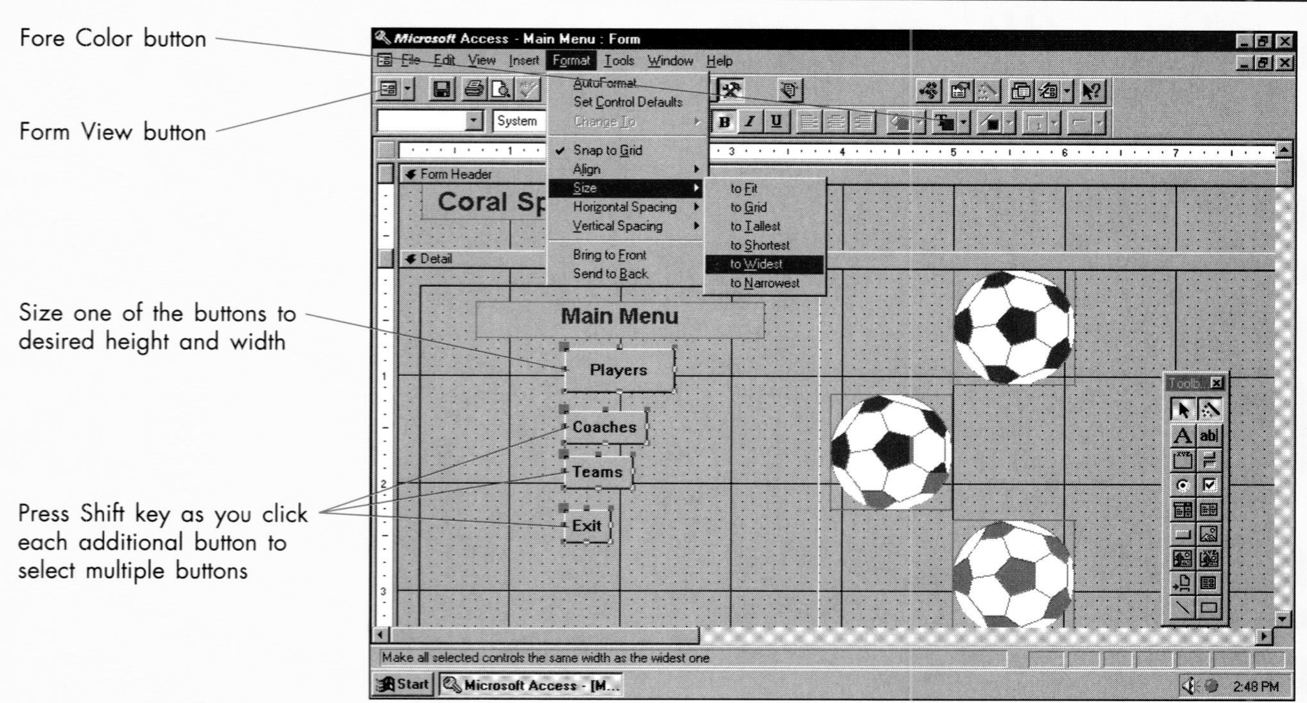

(g) Size and Align the Buttons (step 8)

FIGURE 3.3 Hands-on Exercise 1 (continued)

AVOID CLUTTER

Don't clutter a screen by displaying too much information or too many command buttons. (Seven or eight is the maximum that most people can handle comfortably.) Develop subservient (lower-level) menus if you find yourself with too many buttons on one screen. Don't crowd the command buttons. Make the buttons large enough (and of a uniform size) so that the text within a button is easy to read. Use sufficient blank space around the buttons so that they stand out from the rest of the screen.

STEP 9: Test the Menu

- Click the **Form View button** on the Form Design toolbar to switch to the Form view and view the completed menu in Figure 3.3h.
- Click the **Coaches Command button** to open this form. You should see a Coaches form similar to the Players and Teams forms.
- Click the **Add Coach Command button** at the bottom of the form. Click the text box to enter the coach's first name. (The CoachID is entered automatically as an AutoNumber field.)
- Enter data for your instructor as the coach. Click the appropriate **Option button** to make your instructor a **Head Coach.** Assign your instructor to the Comets (Team T02), which is the same team you joined in step 3.
- Click the **Close Form Command button** to complete data entry.

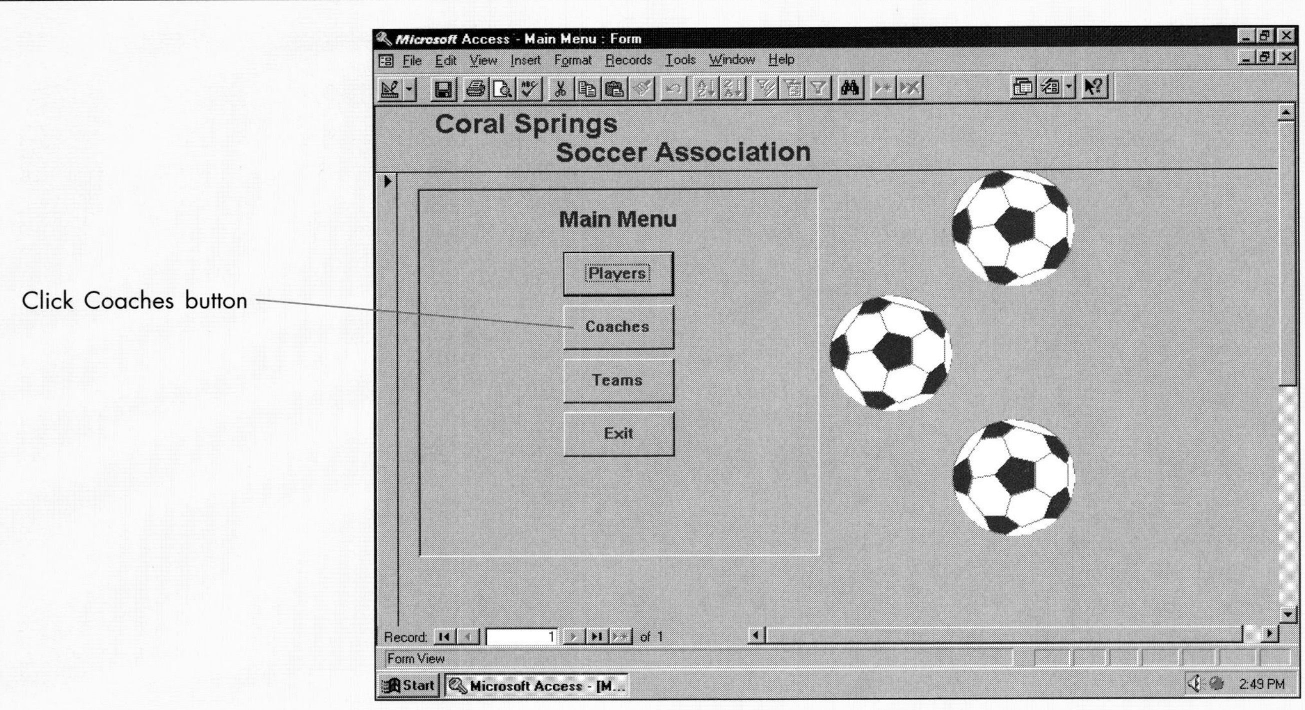

(h) The Completed Form (step 9)

FIGURE 3.3 Hands-on Exercise 1 (continued)

- Click the **Teams Command button** to open the Teams form, then click the ▶| (next record) or |◀ (previous record) button on the Team status bar to move to Team T02 (the Comets). You should see your instructor as the head coach and yourself as a player.
- Pull down the **Edit menu,** click **Select Record** to select the record for your team, then click the **Print button** on the form to print the roster and prove to your instructor that you have completed the exercise. Click the **Close Form button** to close the Teams form and return to the Main Menu.

OPTION GROUPS

An option group requires you to choose from one of several mutually exclusive choices and is an ideal way to guide the user during data entry. It is created most easily through the Option Group Wizard. Change to the Form Design view, click the Option Group button, click and drag in the form where you want the group to go, then let the Wizard do the rest.

STEP 10: Exit Access

- Click the **Exit button** to close the Main Menu form. (The next hands-on exercise will expand the action of this button to close the database in addition to closing the Main Menu.)
- Exit Access if you do not want to continue with the next exercise at this time.

The exercise just completed created a user interface to enable a nontechnical user to maintain the tables in the Soccer application. It did not, however, automate the system completely in that the user still has to open the form containing the Main Menu to get started, and further, has to close the same form at the end of a session to exit Access. You can make the application even easier to use by including macros that perform these tasks automatically.

A ***macro*** automates a command sequence. Thus, instead of using the mouse or keyboard to execute a series of commands, you store the commands (actions) in a macro and execute the macro. You can create a macro to open a table, query, form, or report. You can create a macro to display an informational message, then beep to call attention to that message. You can create a macro to move or size a window, or to minimize, maximize, or restore a window. In short, you can create a macro to execute any command in any Access menu and thus make an application easy to use.

The Macro Window

A macro is created in the ***Macro window*** as shown in Figure 3.4. The Macro window has two sections. You enter the ***actions*** (commands) that make up the macro and any optional comments in the upper section. You supply the additional information (***arguments***) for those actions in the lower section.

The macro in Figure 3.4 consists of a single action (MsgBox), which has four arguments (Message, Beep, Type, and Title). The ***MsgBox action*** displays a dialog box with the message you define. It's an ideal way to display an informational message to a user and is illustrated later in the chapter. The help area at the bottom right of the Macro window displays help information; the specific help information depends on where you are in the Macro window.

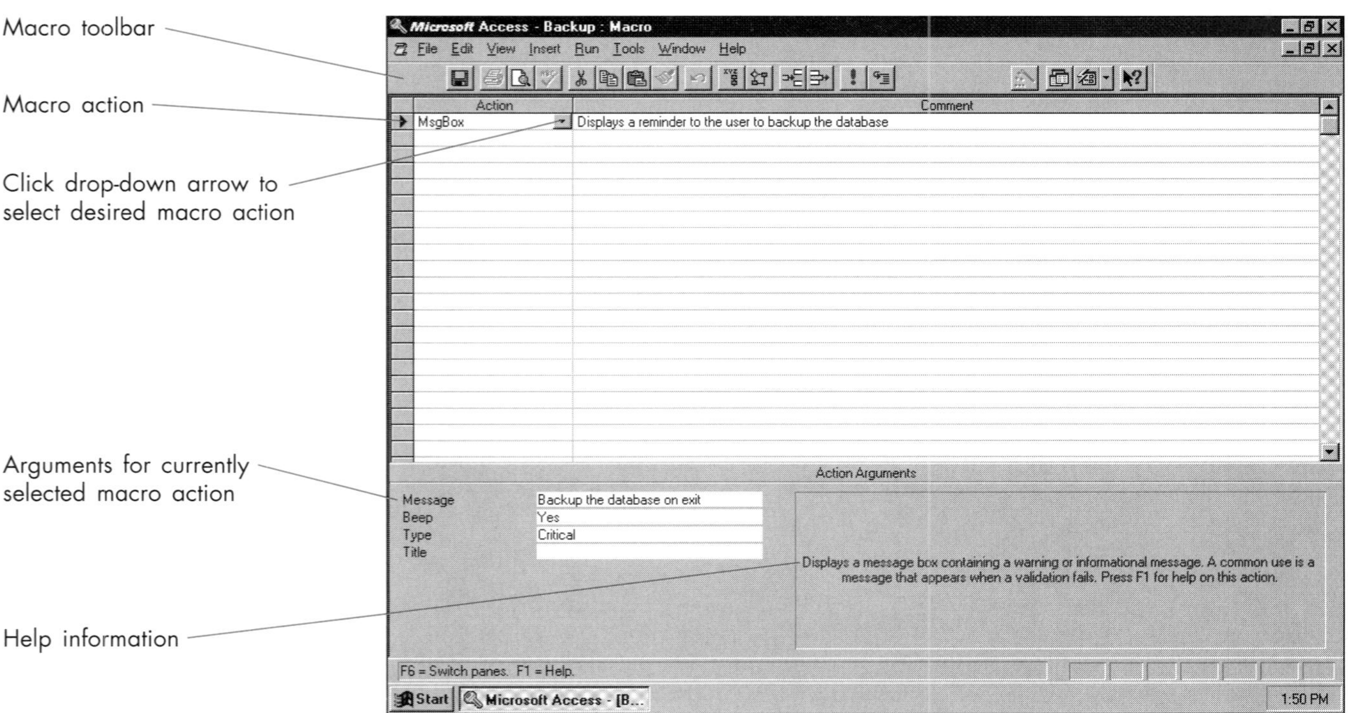

FIGURE 3.4 The Macro Window

A macro is created from the Database window by selecting the Macros tab and clicking the New button. It is stored as an object in the database in the same fashion as a form or report. Actions are added to a macro by choosing the action from a drop-down list or by typing the name of the action. The arguments for an action are entered in similar fashion; that is, by choosing from a drop-down list (when available) or by typing the argument directly. After a macro has been saved, it can be run from the Macro window or the Database window or assigned as a response to an event (e.g., clicking a command button) in a form or report.

The ***macro toolbar*** is displayed at the top of the Macro window and contains buttons that help create and test a macro. Many of the buttons (e.g., the Database Window, Save, and Help buttons) are common to other toolbars you have used in conjunction with other objects. Other buttons are specific to the Macro window and are referenced in the hands-on exercises as necessary. As with other toolbars, you can point to a button to display its ToolTip and determine its purpose.

ACCESS MACROS ARE DIFFERENT

Access lacks the macro recorder that is common to Word and Excel. This means that you have to explicitly enter the actions in the Macro window rather than have the recorder do it for you. Nevertheless, you can still create an Access macro to do virtually anything you would do via the keyboard or mouse.

The AutoExec Macro

After a macro is created, it is saved so that it can be run (executed) at a later time. A macro name can contain up to 64 characters (letters and numbers) and may include spaces. The name of the macro appears in the title bar of the Macro window (e.g., Backup in Figure 3.4). You can use any name at all for a macro, as long as you adhere to these simple rules.

One macro name, however, ***AutoExec,*** is reserved, and this macro has a unique function. The ***AutoExec macro*** (if it exists) is executed automatically whenever the database in which it is stored is opened. In other words, whenever you open a database, Access looks to see if the database contains an AutoExec macro, and if so, Access runs the macro for you.

The AutoExec macro is essential to automating a system for the end-user. It typically contains an OpenForm action to load the form containing the main (start-up) menu. The AutoExec macro may also perform other housekeeping chores to get the database ready to use, such as maximizing the current window.

Every database can have its own AutoExec macro, but there is no requirement for the AutoExec macro to be present. We recommend, however, that you include an AutoExec macro in every application to help the user get started quickly.

Debugging

Writing a macro is similar to writing a program in that mistakes are virtually certain to be made, and you need a way to correct those mistakes. Should Access encounter an error during the execution of a macro, it displays as much information as it can to help you determine the reason for the error—to assist you in ***debugging*** your program.

Figure 3.5a contains an erroneous version of the AutoExec macro that will be developed in the exercise that follows shortly. The macro contains two actions, Maximize and OpenForm. The Maximize action maximizes the Database window and affects all subsequent screens that will be displayed in the application. The OpenForm macro opens the form containing the menu developed in the previous exercise. The name of the form is deliberately misspelled to produce the error in Figure 3.5b.

When the AutoExec macro is executed, Access attempts to open the Main Menus form but is unable to do so. It displays the informational message in Figure 3.5b, followed by the Action Failed dialog box in Figure 3.5c. The latter is displayed whenever a macro is unable to execute successfully. Your only course of action is to click the Halt Command button, then attempt to correct the error using the displayed information.

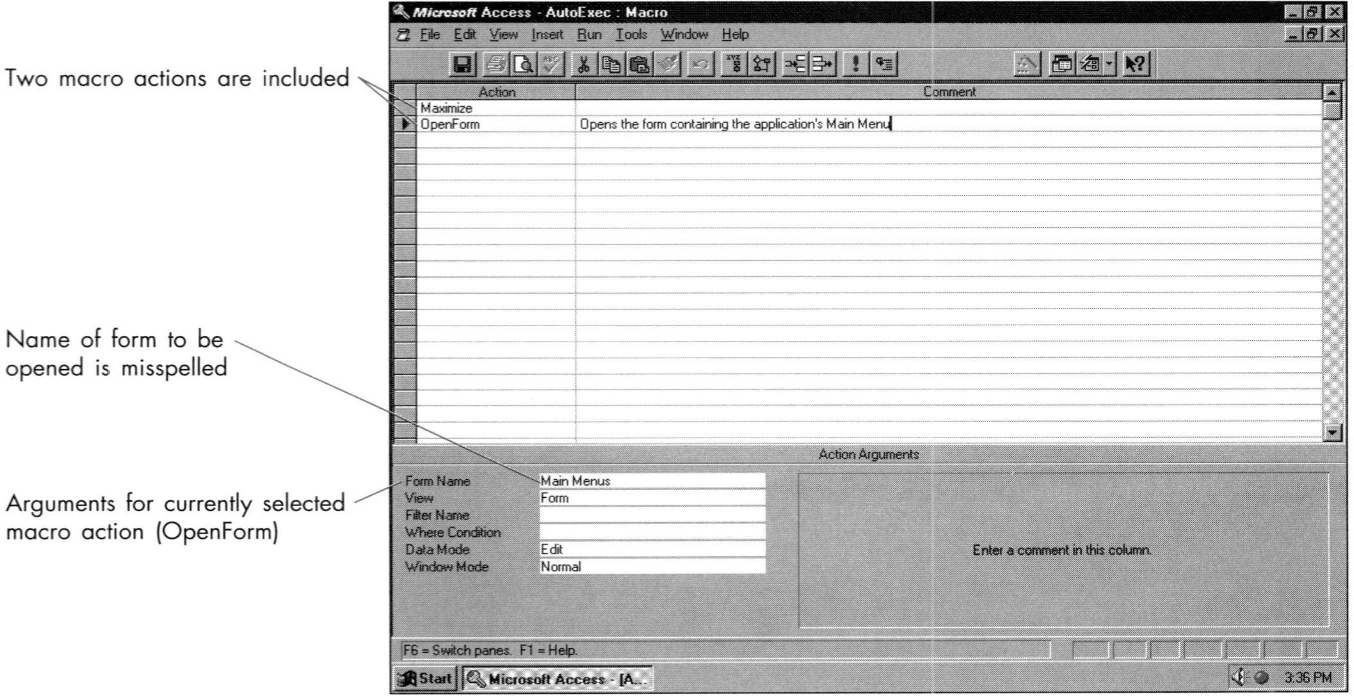

(a) AutoExec Macro

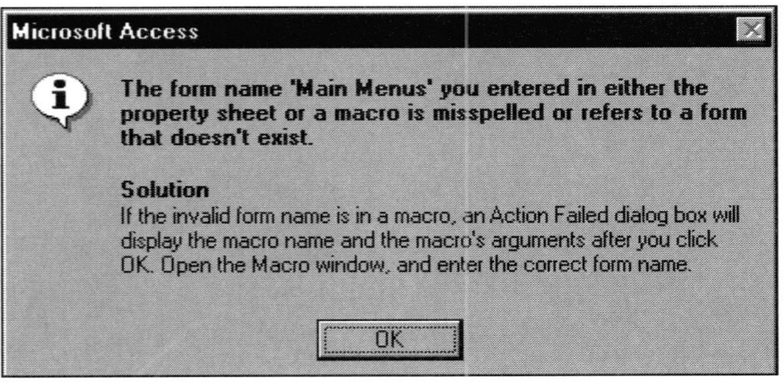

(b) Informational Message

FIGURE 3.5 Debugging

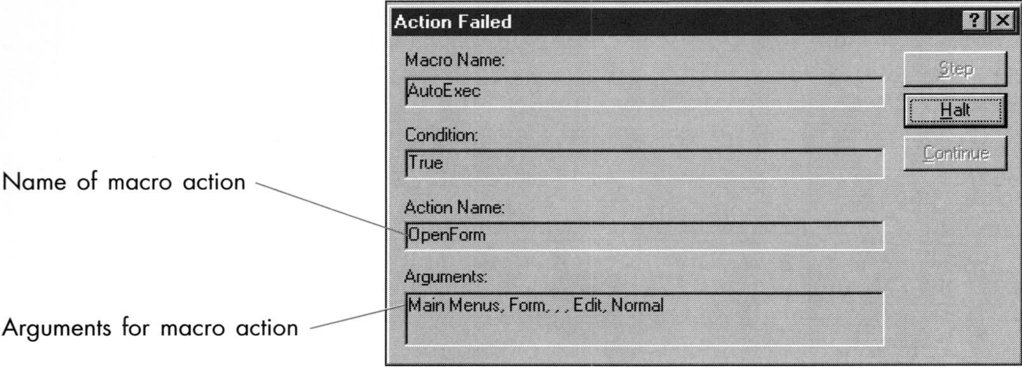

(c) Action Failed Dialog Box

FIGURE 3.5 Debugging (continued)

The Action Failed dialog box indicates the name of the failed macro (AutoExec). The Action Name indicates the failed action (OpenForm) within the macro, and the Arguments box shows the corresponding values. In this example the error is easy to find. The name of the form should have been Main Menu rather than Main Menus.

THE FIRST BUG

A bug is a mistake in a computer program; hence debugging refers to the process of correcting program errors. According to legend, the first bug was an unlucky moth crushed to death on one of the relays of the electromechanical Mark II computer, bringing the machine's operation to a halt. The cause of the failure was discovered by Grace Hopper, who promptly taped the moth to her logbook, noting, *"First actual case of bug being found."*

HANDS-ON EXERCISE 2

Introduction to Macros

Objective: Create an AutoExec macro to open a form automatically; create a Close Database macro to close the database and exit from the system. Use the On Click property to change the action associated with a command button. Use Figure 3.6 as a guide in the exercise.

STEP 1: Create the AutoExec Macro

- Start Access. Open the **Soccer Objects database** from the previous exercise.
- Click the **Macros tab** in the Database window (there are currently no macros in the database). Click the **New button** to create a new macro. If necessary, click the **Maximize button** so that the Macro window takes the entire screen as in Figure 3.6a.

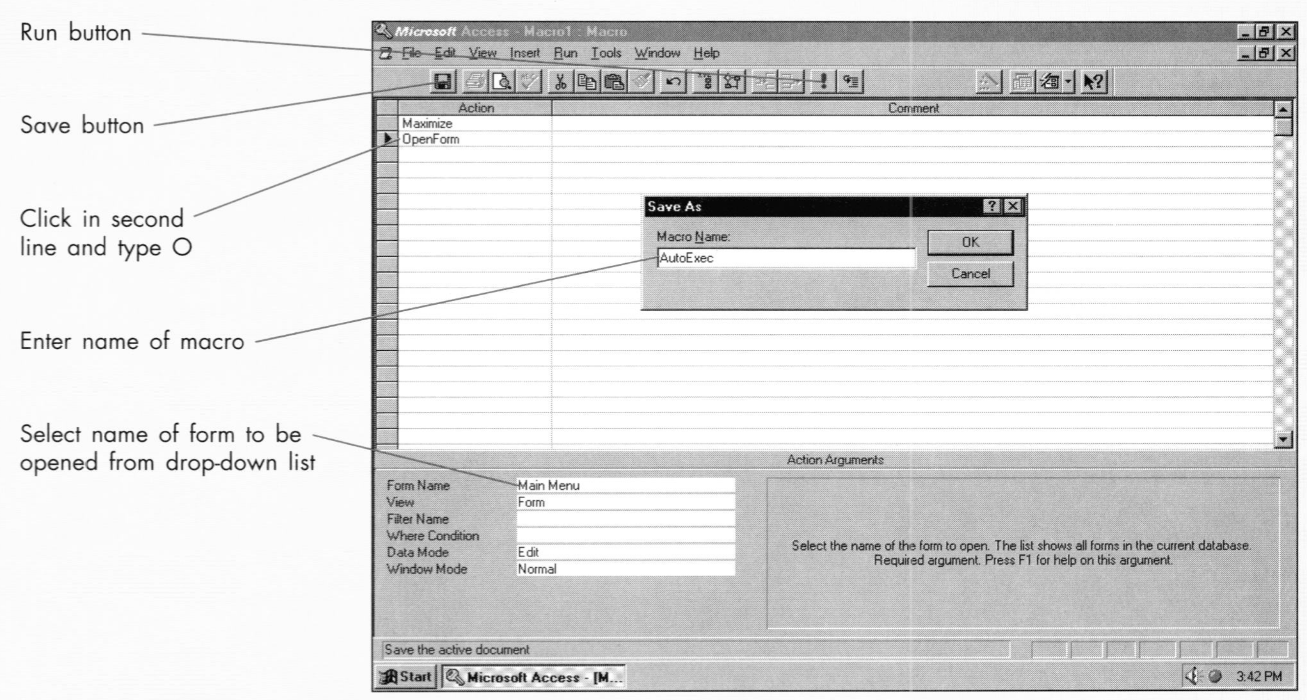

(a) Create the AutoExec Macro (step 1)

FIGURE 3.6 Hands-on Exercise 2

- Click the **drop-down arrow** to display the available macro actions. Scroll through the list until you can select **Maximize.**
- Click the **Action box** on the second line. Type the letter **O,** and the OpenForm action appears automatically. Press **enter** to accept this action, then click the text box for the **Form Name** argument in the lower section of the Macro window.
- Click the **drop-down arrow** to display the list of existing forms and select **Main Menu** (the form you created in the previous exercise).
- Click the **Save button** to display the Save As dialog box in Figure 3.6a. Type **AutoExec** as the macro name and click **OK.**
- Click the **Run button** to run the macro, which displays the Main Menu from the previous exercise. (The window is maximized on the screen.) Click the **Exit button** on the Main Menu to close the menu and return to the macro.
- Pull down the **File menu.** Click **Close** to close the AutoExec macro.

TYPE ONLY THE FIRST LETTER(S)

Click the Action box, then type the first letter of a macro action to move immediately to the first macro action beginning with that letter. Type an M, for example, and Access automatically enters the Maximize action. If necessary, type the second letter of the desired action; for example, type the letter I (after typing an M), and Access selects the Minimize action, which begins with the letters M and I.

STEP 2: The MsgBox Action

- You should be back in the Database window, which should display the name of the AutoExec macro. Click the **New button** to create a second macro, which automatically positions you at the first action.
- Type **MS** (the first two letters in the MsgBox action), then press **enter** to accept this action.
- Click the text box for the **Type** argument in the lower section of the Macro window. Click the **drop-down arrow** to display the list of message types. Select **Critical.**
- Click the text box for the **Message** argument. Press **Shift+F2** to display the zoom box so that you can see the contents of your entire message, then enter the message in Figure 3.6b. Click **OK.**

> **BACK UP YOUR DATABASE**
>
> It's not a question of if it will happen, but when. Hard disks die, files are lost, and viruses infect a system. Take our word for it, there are few things more unpleasant than searching for a file that isn't there or discovering that the file you do retrieve is missing most of its data. Adequate backup is the only insurance you can obtain against data loss. Backing up a system is easy, but you must remember to do it, and you must do it faithfully, without fail.

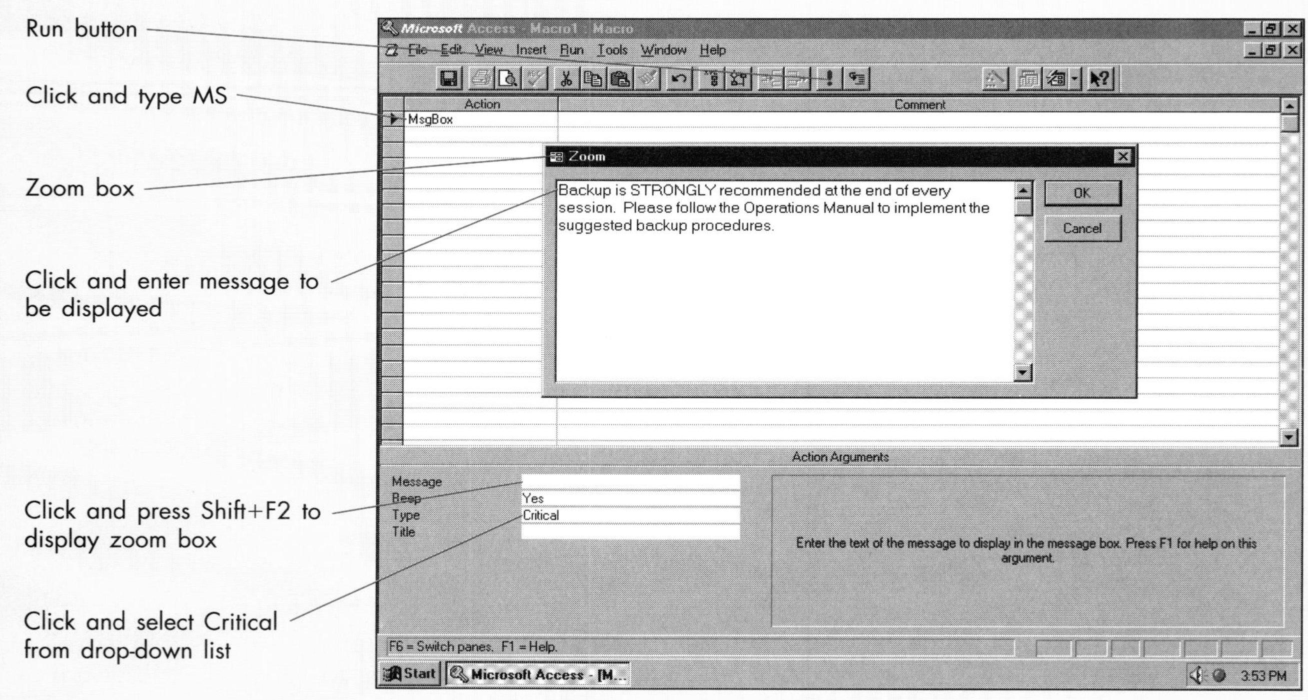

(b) The MsgBox Action (step 2)

FIGURE 3.6 Hands-on Exercise 2 (continued)

- Click the **Run button** to test the macro. You will see a message indicating that you have to save the macro. Click **Yes** to save the macro, type **Close Database** as the name of the macro, and click **OK.**
- You will see a dialog box containing the text of the message you just created. Click **OK** after you have read the message so that you can continue working on the macro.

STEP 3: Complete the Close Database Macro

- Click the **Action box** on the second line. Type **Cl** (the first two letters in **Close**) and press **enter.**
- Click the text box for the **Object Type** argument. Click the **drop-down arrow.** Choose **Form** as the Object type. Click the **Object Name** argument, click the **drop-down arrow,** and choose **Main Menu** as the Object (form) name.
- Click the **comment line** for this action. Type **Close the Main Menu form** as shown in Figure 3.6c.
- Click the **Action box** on the third line. Type **Do** (the first two letters in **DoMenuItem**) and press **enter.**
- Press the **F6 key** to move to the lower section of the Macro window. Choose **Database** for the Menu Bar, **File** for the Menu Name, and **Close** for the command. (This will execute the File Close command from the displayed menu bar when the Database window is active.)
- Click the **comments line** for this macro action and enter the comment shown in the figure.

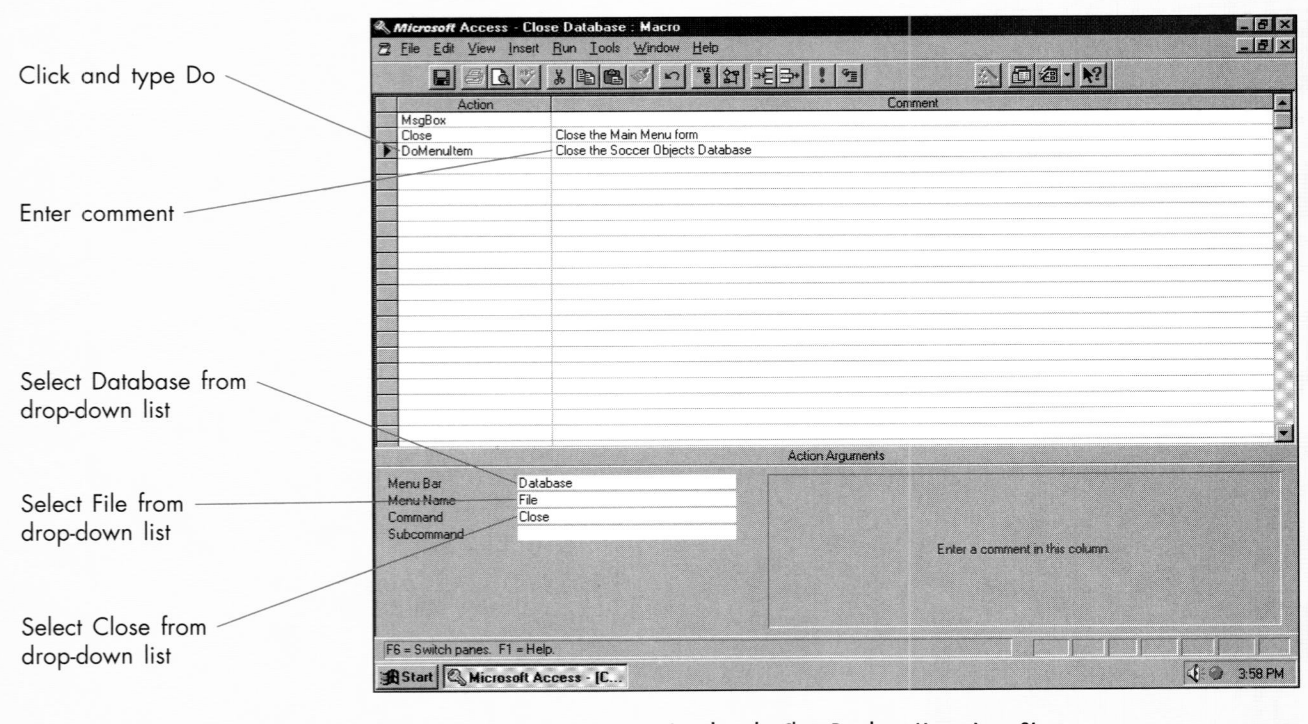

(c) Complete the Close Database Macro (step 3)

FIGURE 3.6 Hands-on Exercise 2 (continued)

➤ Pull down the **File menu** and click **Close** to close the macro. Click **Yes** when prompted whether to save the changes to the Close Database macro.

➤ If necessary, press the **F11 key** to switch to the Database window. You should see the names of both macros (AutoExec and Close Database).

> **THE F6 KEY**
>
> Press the F6 key to move back and forth between the top and bottom halves of the Macro window. You can also use the F6 key to move between the top and bottom portions of the Table and Query windows when they are open in Design view.

STEP 4: The On Click Property

➤ Click the **Forms tab,** select the **Main Menu form,** then click the **Design button** to open the form in Design view. If necessary, maximize the window.

➤ Point to the **Exit command button** (that was created in the first exercise) and click the **right mouse button** to display a shortcut menu. Click **Properties** to display the Properties dialog box in Figure 3.6d.

➤ Click the **down arrow** on the vertical scroll bar until you can see the On Click property, which is currently set to [Event Procedure]. This was set automatically when you used the Command Button Wizard to create the button in step 7 of the previous exercise.

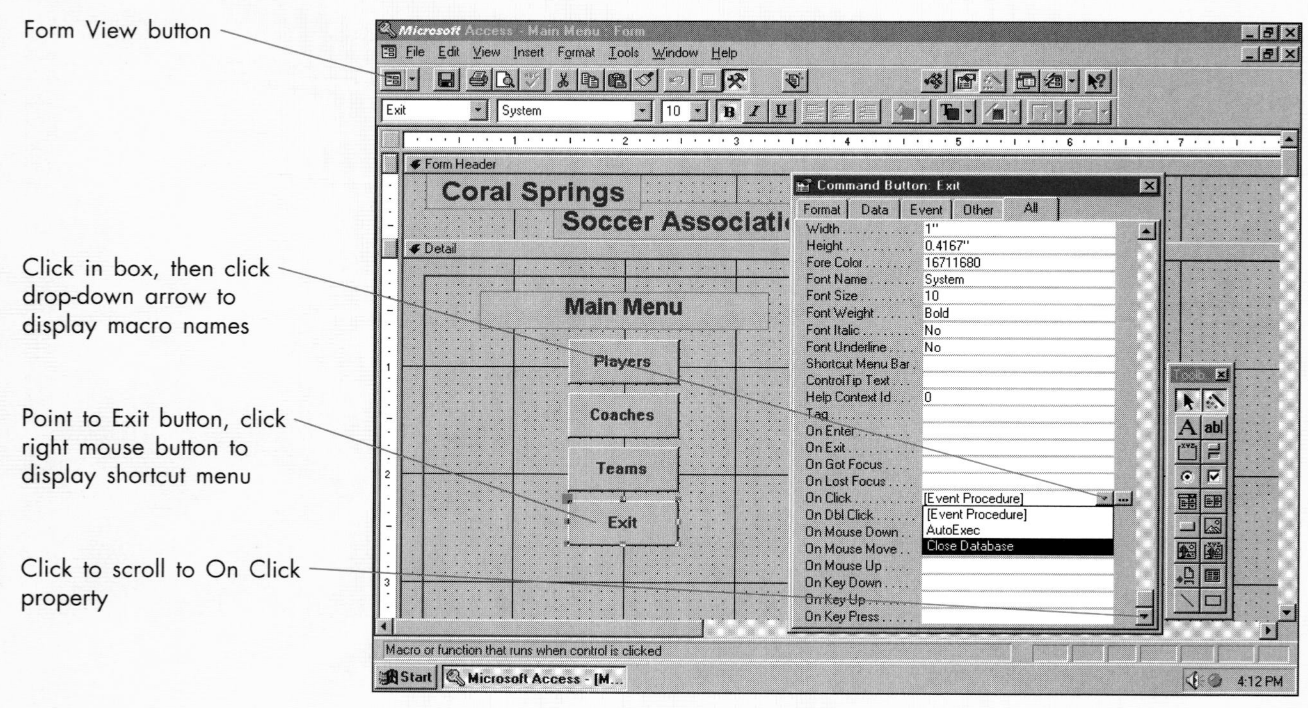

(d) The On Click Property (step 4)

FIGURE 3.6 Hands-on Exercise 2 (continued)

➤ Click the **On Click box,** then click the **drop-down arrow** to display the existing macros. Click **Close Database** (the macro you just created). Close the Properties dialog box.

➤ Save the form. Click the **Form View button** to switch to Form view so that you can test the macros you just created.

> **CREATE A HELP BUTTON**
>
> One of the nicest features you can provide your users is a means of obtaining technical support either by telephone or via e-mail. Use the MsgBox action to create a simple macro that displays your phone number and e-mail address, then assign that macro to a Help button on your Main Menu. See practice exercise 1 at the end of the chapter.

STEP 5: Test the AutoExec and Close Database Macros

➤ You should see the Main Menu form displayed in Figure 3.6e. Click the **Exit Command button,** which executes the Close Database macro you assigned to the button.

- You should see the informational message shown in the figure. (The message is displayed by the MsgBox action in the Close Database macro.)
- Click **OK** to accept the message. The Close Database macro then closes the database.

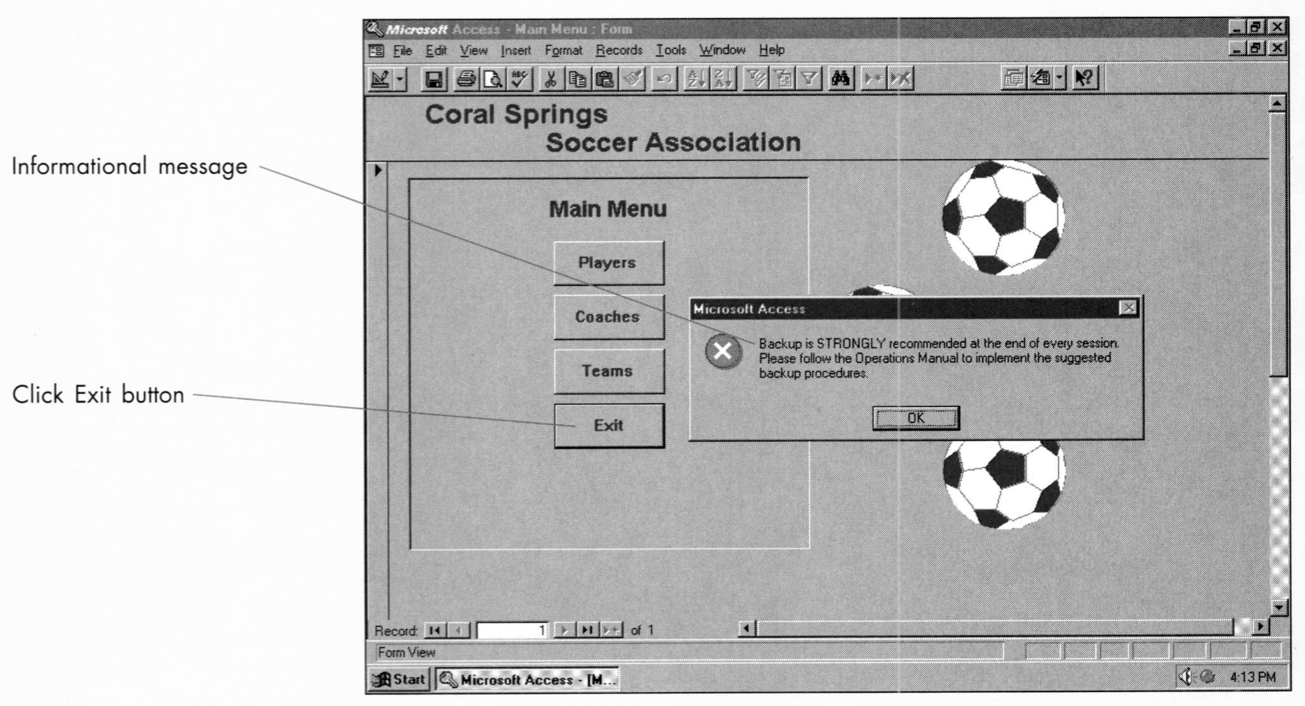

(e) Test the Macro (step 5)

FIGURE 3.6 Hands-on Exercise 2 (continued)

STEP 6: Reopen the Database

- Pull down the **File menu,** then click **Soccer Objects** from the list of recently opened databases. The AutoExec macro executes automatically, maximizes the current window, and displays the Main Menu.
- Pull down the **File menu** and click **Close** to close the form and continue working on this database. (You cannot click the Exit command button as that would close the database.) You should be back in the Database window.

STEP 7: Create the Add Player Macro

- Click the **Forms tab** in the Database window. Double click the **Players form** to open this form.
- Click the **Add Player button** on the Players form and note that in order to add a player, you must first click the First Name text box. We will correct this by creating an Add Player macro that will automatically move to the First Name text box. Click the **Close Form button** to exit the Players form.
- Click the **Macros tab** in the Database window. Click **New** to create a new macro, then create the Add Player macro as shown in Figure 3.6f:
  - Use the **F6 key** to switch between the top and bottom halves of the Macro window.
  - The first action, **DoMenuItem,** has three arguments: **Form, Insert,** and **Record,** corresponding to the name of the menu bar (Form), the specific menu (Insert), and the command (Record). The macro action and corresponding arguments are equivalent to moving to the end of the Player table in order to add a new record.

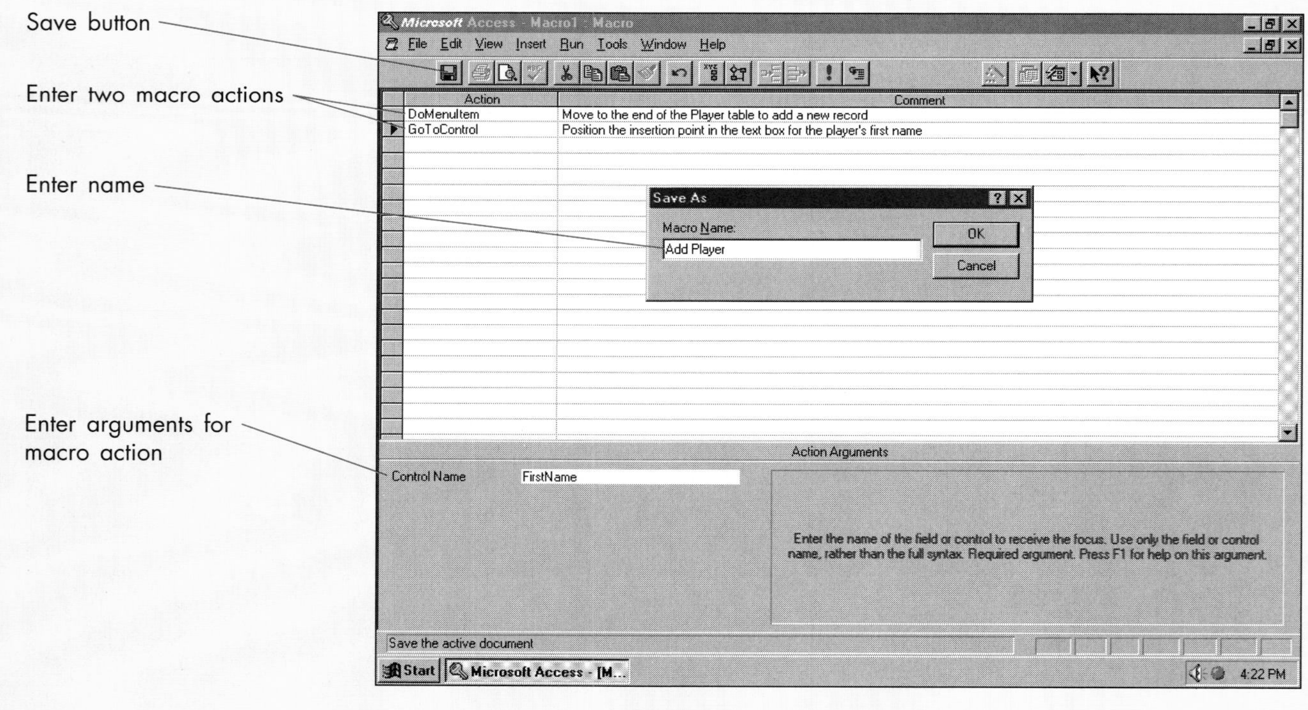

(f) The Add Player Macro (step 7)

FIGURE 3.6 Hands-on Exercise 2 (continued)

- The **GoToControl** action has a single argument, which is the name of the control on the Players form. Type **FirstName** (there is no space in the control name).

➤ Save the macro as **Add Player.** Do *not* attempt to run the macro at this time.

➤ Pull down the **File menu** and click **Close** to exit the macro and return to the Database window.

THE DISPLAY WHEN PROPERTY

The Add, Print, and Close Form Command buttons appear on the various forms (Team, Player, or Coach) when the forms are displayed on the screen, but not when the forms are printed. This was accomplished by setting the Display When property of the individual command buttons when the forms were created. Open a form in Design view, point to an existing command button, then click the right mouse button to display a shortcut menu. Click on the line for the Display When property and set the property accordingly.

STEP 8: The On Click Property

➤ Click the **Forms tab** in the Database window and select the **Players form.** Click the **Design button** to open the form in Design view as shown in Figure 3.6g.

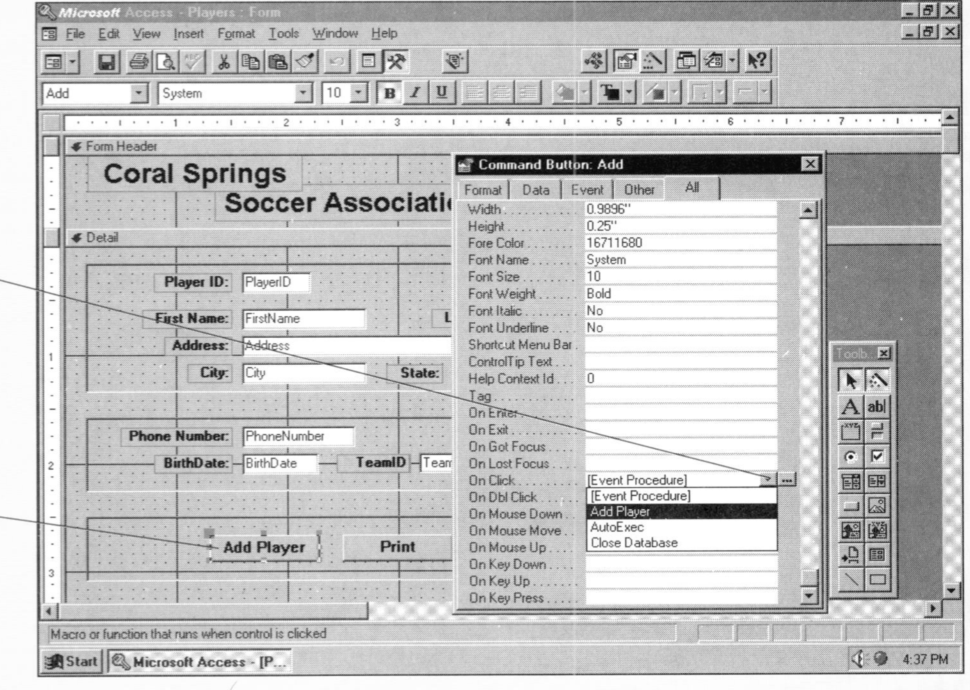

(g) The On Click Property (step 8)

FIGURE 3.6 Hands-on Exercise 2 (continued)

- Point to the **Add Player command button,** then click the **right mouse button** to display a shortcut menu. Click **Properties** to display the Properties dialog box.
- Click the **down arrow** on the vertical scroll bar until you can see the On Click property, which is currently set to [Event Procedure]. Click the **On Click property box,** then click the **drop-down arrow** to display the existing macros.
- Click **Add Player** (the macro you just created). Close the Properties dialog box.
- Click the **Form View button** to switch to Form view and test the Add Player macro.
  - Click the **Add Player command button.** You are automatically positioned in the First Name box (because of the Add Player macro) and can start typing immediately.
  - Enter data for a friend of yours. Assign your friend to the **Comets** (your team).
- Click the **Close Form command button** when you have completed the record. Click **Yes** if prompted to save the changes to the Players form.

THE CONTROLTIP TEXT PROPERTY

Point to any button on any Office toolbar and you see a ToolTip that describes the purpose of that button. Access enables you to create your own ToolTips through the ControlTip Text property. Open a form in Design view, right click the control for which you want to create a tip, then click the Properties command to open the Properties dialog box. Click the Other (or All) tab, click the ControlTip text box to enter the desired text, then close the dialog box. Change to Form view and point to the control. You will see the ToolTip you just created.

STEP 9: Close the Database

- You can close the database in one of two ways:
  - You should be back in the Database window. Pull down the **File menu** and click **Close** to close the Soccer Objects database, *or*
  - Click the **Forms tab,** double click the **Main Menu form** to open this form, click the **Exit button** on the form, then click **OK** in response to the message reminding you to back up the system.
- Pull down the **File menu.** Click **Exit** if you do not want to continue with the next exercise at this time.

THE PLAYER DRAFT

The implementation of a player draft is essential to the Soccer Association. Players sign up for the coming season at registration, after which the coaches meet to select players for their teams. All players are rated as to ability, and the CSSA strives to maintain a competitive balance between teams.

The coaches take turns selecting players from the pool of unassigned players as displayed in the form shown in Figure 3.7. The form is based on a query that identifies the players who have not yet been drafted. To aid in the selection process, the unassigned players are listed by ability and alphabetically within ability. Note, too, the use of a ***combo box*** to simplify data entry in conjunction with the team assignment. The user is able to click the drop-down arrow to display a list of team nicknames (or enter the nickname directly) rather than having to remember the associated team number.

In addition to displaying the list of unassigned players, the form in Figure 3.7 also contains three command buttons that are used during the player draft. The Find Player button moves directly to a specific player, and enables a coach to see whether a specific player has been assigned to a team, and if so, to which team. The Update List button refreshes the underlying query on which the list of unassigned players is based. It is used periodically during the draft as players are assigned to teams, to remove those players from the list of unassigned players. The End Draft button closes the form and returns to the Main Menu.

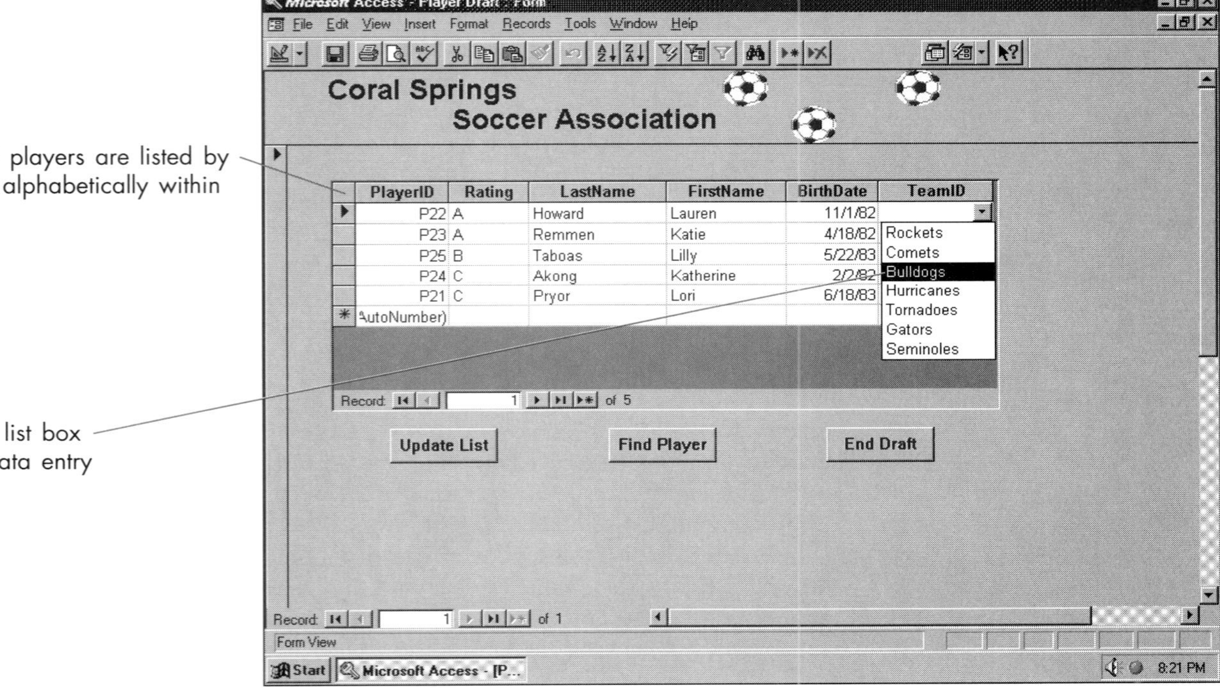

FIGURE 3.7 The Player Draft

SIMPLIFY DATA ENTRY

A drop-down list box simplifies data entry as it lets you select a value from a list, such as a team nickname, rather than having to remember the corresponding team number. A combo box combines the properties of a text box and a list box; that is, you can enter a new value directly in the box, or you can click the drop-down arrow to display a list of values from which to choose.

The Unmatched Query Wizard

Think, for a moment, how Access is able to display the list of unassigned players. You need to remember the one-to-many relationship between teams and players (one team has many players, but a player has only one team). Remember, too, that this relationship is implemented through the common TeamID field, which appears in both tables. The TeamID is the primary key in the Teams table and it is a foreign key in the Players table. A player is assigned to a team by entering the team number into the TeamID field in the Players table. Conversely, any player without a value in his or her TeamID field is an unassigned player.

To display a list of unassigned players, you need to create a query, based on the Players table, which selects records without an entry for TeamID. This can be done by creating the query explicitly (and specifying the Null criterion for TeamID) or more easily through the Unmatched Query Wizard, which creates the query for you. The Wizard asks the questions in Figure 3.8, then generates the query.

The ***Unmatched Query Wizard*** identifies the records in one table (e.g., the Players table) that do not have matching records in another table (e.g., the Teams table). The wizard begins by asking for the table that contains the unmatched records (Figure 3.8a) and for the related table (Figure 3.8b). It identifies the join field (TeamID in Figure 3.8c), then gives you the opportunity to select the fields you want to see in the query results (Figure 3.8d). The Wizard even suggests a name for the query (Players Without Matching Teams in Figure 3.8e), then displays the dynaset in Figure 3.8f.

The Unmatched Query Wizard has multiple applications within the CSSA database. It can identify players without teams (as in Figure 3.8), or conversely, teams without players. It can also identify coaches who have not been assigned to a team, and, conversely, teams without coaches.

Macro Groups

Implementation of the player draft requires three macros, one for each command button. Although you could create a separate macro for each button, it is convenient to create a ***macro group*** that contains the individual macros. The macro group has a name, as does each macro in the group. Only the name of the macro group appears in the Database window.

Figure 3.9 displays a Player Draft macro group containing three individual macros (Update List, Find Player, and End Draft), which run independently of one another. The name of each macro appears in the Macro Name column (which is displayed by clicking the Show/Hide Macro Names button on the Macro toolbar). The actions and comments for each macro are shown in the corresponding columns to the right of the macro name.

The advantage of storing related macros in a macro group, as opposed to storing them individually, is purely organizational. Large systems often contain many macros, which can overwhelm the developer as he or she tries to locate a specific macro. Storing related macros in macro groups limits the entries in the Database window, since only the (name of the) macro group is displayed. Thus, the Database window would contain a single entry (Player Draft, which is the name of the macro group), as opposed to three individual entries (Update List, Find Player, and End Draft, which correspond to the macros in the group).

Access must still be able to identify the individual macros so that each macro can be executed at the appropriate time. If, for example, a macro is to be executed when the user clicks a command button, the ***On Click property*** of that command button must specify both the individual macro and the macro group to which it belongs. The two names are separated by a period—for example, Player Draft.Update List—to indicate the Update List macro in the Player Draft group.

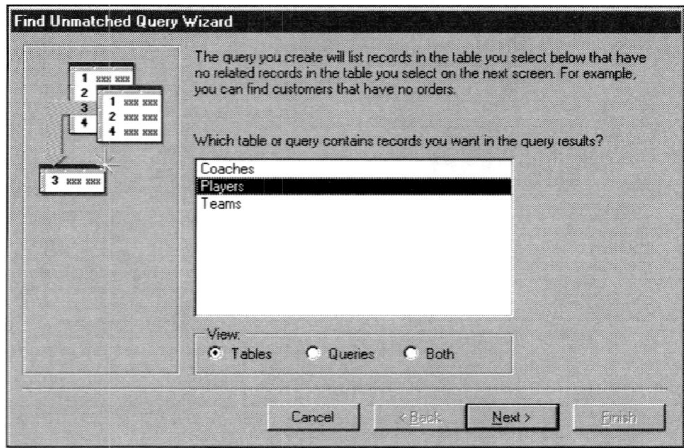

(a) Table Containing the Unmatched Records

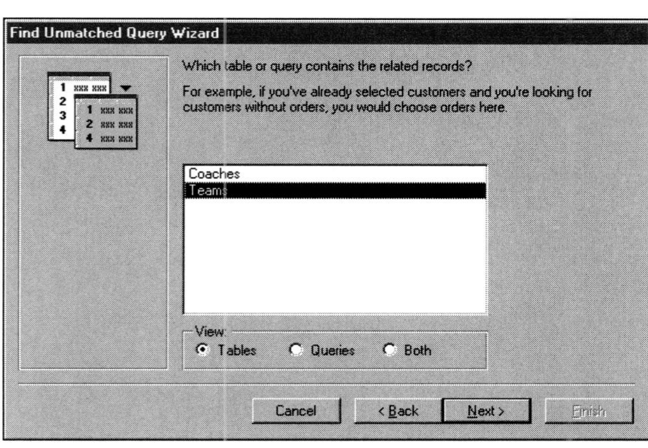

(b) The Related Table

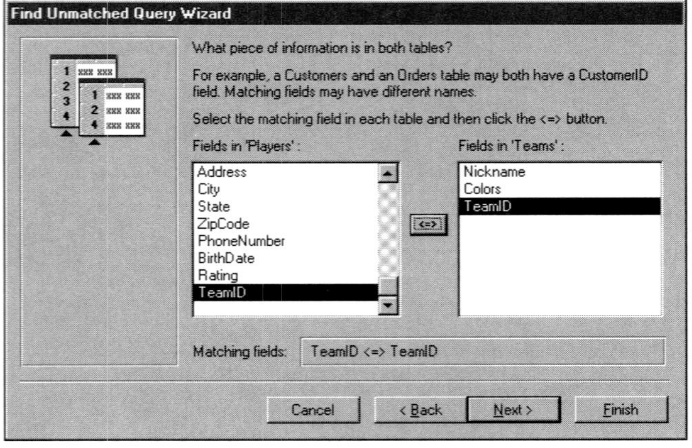

(c) Join Field

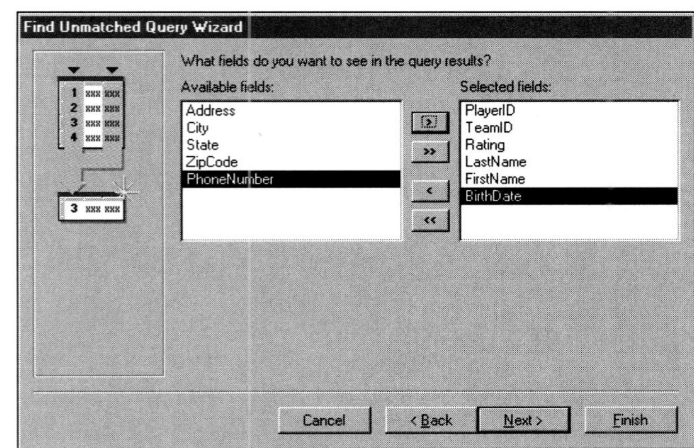

(d) Fields for Dynaset

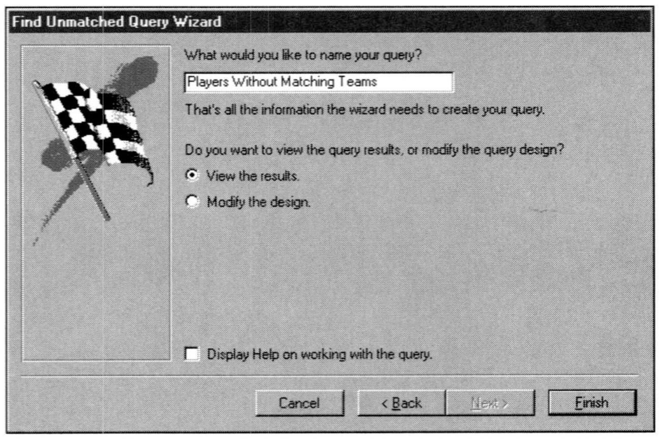

(e) Suggested Name

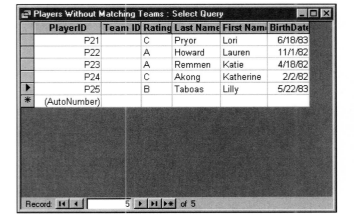

Players Without Matching Teams : Select Query

PlayerID	Team ID	Rating	Last Name	First Name	BirthDate
P21		C	Pryor	Lori	6/18/83
P22		A	Howard	Lauren	11/1/82
P23		A	Remmen	Katie	4/18/82
P24		C	Akong	Katherine	2/2/82
P25		B	Taboas	Lilly	5/22/83
(AutoNumber)					

Record: 5 of 5

(f) Dynaset

FIGURE 3.8 The Unmatched Query Wizard

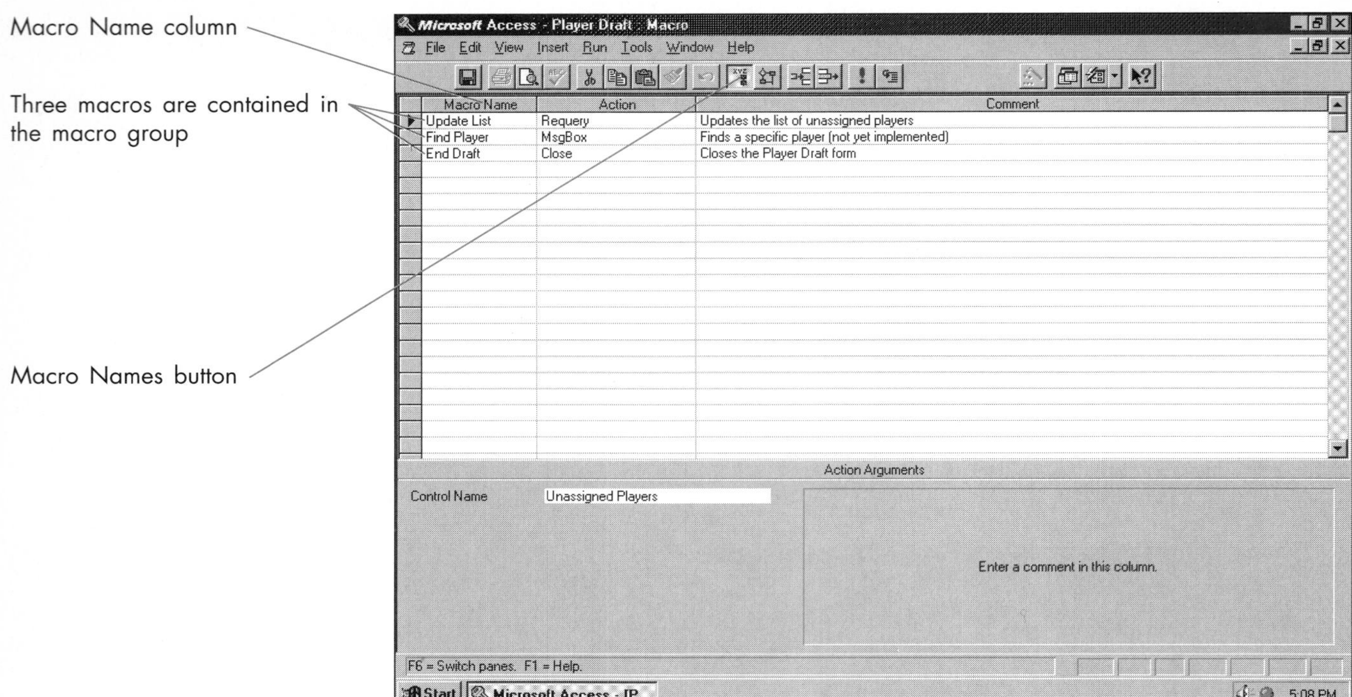

FIGURE 3.9 Macro Groups

As indicated, each macro in Figure 3.9 corresponds to a command button in the Player Draft form of Figure 3.7. The macros are created in the following hands-on exercise, which implements the player draft.

THE MACRO TOOLBAR

The Macro Name and Condition buttons on the Macro toolbar toggle the corresponding columns on and off. Click either button to display (hide) the indicated column. See practice exercise 3 at the end of the chapter for additional information on the Condition column.

HANDS-ON EXERCISE 3

The Player Draft

Objective: Create a macro group containing three macros to implement a player draft. Use Figure 3.10 as a guide in the exercise.

STEP 1: The Unmatched Query Wizard

- Start Access and open the **Soccer Objects database.** Pull down the **File menu** and click **Close** (or click the **Close button**) to close the Main Menu form but leave the database open. (You *cannot* click the Exit command button as that would close the database.)

➤ Click the **Queries tab** in the Database window. Click **New,** select the **Find Unmatched Query Wizard,** then click **OK** to start the Wizard:

- Select **Players** as the table whose records you want to see in the query results. Click **Next.**
- Select **Teams** as the table that contains the related records. Click **Next.**
- **TeamID** is automatically selected as the matching field. Click **Next.**
- Select the following fields from the Available Fields list: **PlayerID, Rating, LastName, FirstName, BirthDate,** and **TeamID.** Click **Next.**
- **Players Without Matching Teams** is entered as the name of the query. Check that the option button to **View the results** is selected, then click **Finish** to exit the Wizard and see the results of the query.

➤ You should see a dynaset containing five players (Pryor, Howard, Remmen, Akong, and Taboas) as shown in Figure 3.10a. The TeamID field for each of these players is blank, indicating these players are not on a team.

THE MOST RECENTLY OPENED FILE LIST

An easy way to open a recently used database is to select it from the Microsoft Access dialog box that appears when Access is first started. Check to see if your database appears on the list of the four most recently opened databases, and if so, simply double click the database to open it.

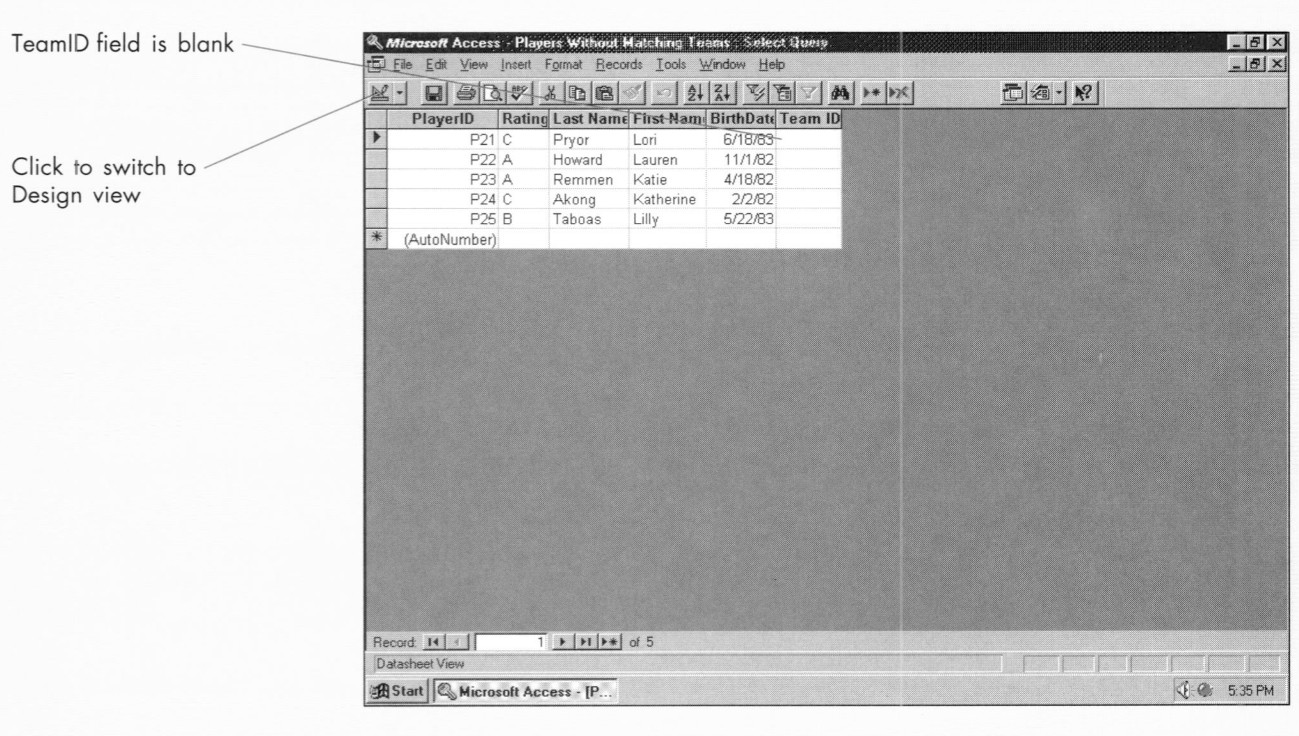

(a) The Unmatched Query Wizard (step 1)

FIGURE 3.10 Hands-on Exercise 3

STEP 2: Modify the Unmatched Query

- ➤ Change to Design view to see the underlying query as displayed in Figure 3.10b.
- ➤ Click and drag the line separating the upper and lower portions of the window. If necessary, click and drag the field lists to match the figure.
- ➤ Click in the **Sort row** for **Rating,** then click **Ascending** from the drop-down list. Click in the **Sort row** for **LastName,** then click **Ascending** from the drop-down list.
- ➤ Click the **Run button** to view the revised query, which lists players according to their player rating and alphabetically within rating.
- ➤ Close the query. Click **Yes** if asked whether to save the changes to the Players Without Matching Teams query.

THE IS NULL CRITERION

The Is Null criterion selects those records that do not have a value in the designated field. It is the essence of the Unmatched Query Wizard, which uses the criterion to identify the records in one table that do not have a matching record in another table. The NOT operator can be combined with the Is Null criterion to produce the opposite effect; that is, the criterion Is Not Null will select records with any type of entry (including spaces) in the specified field.

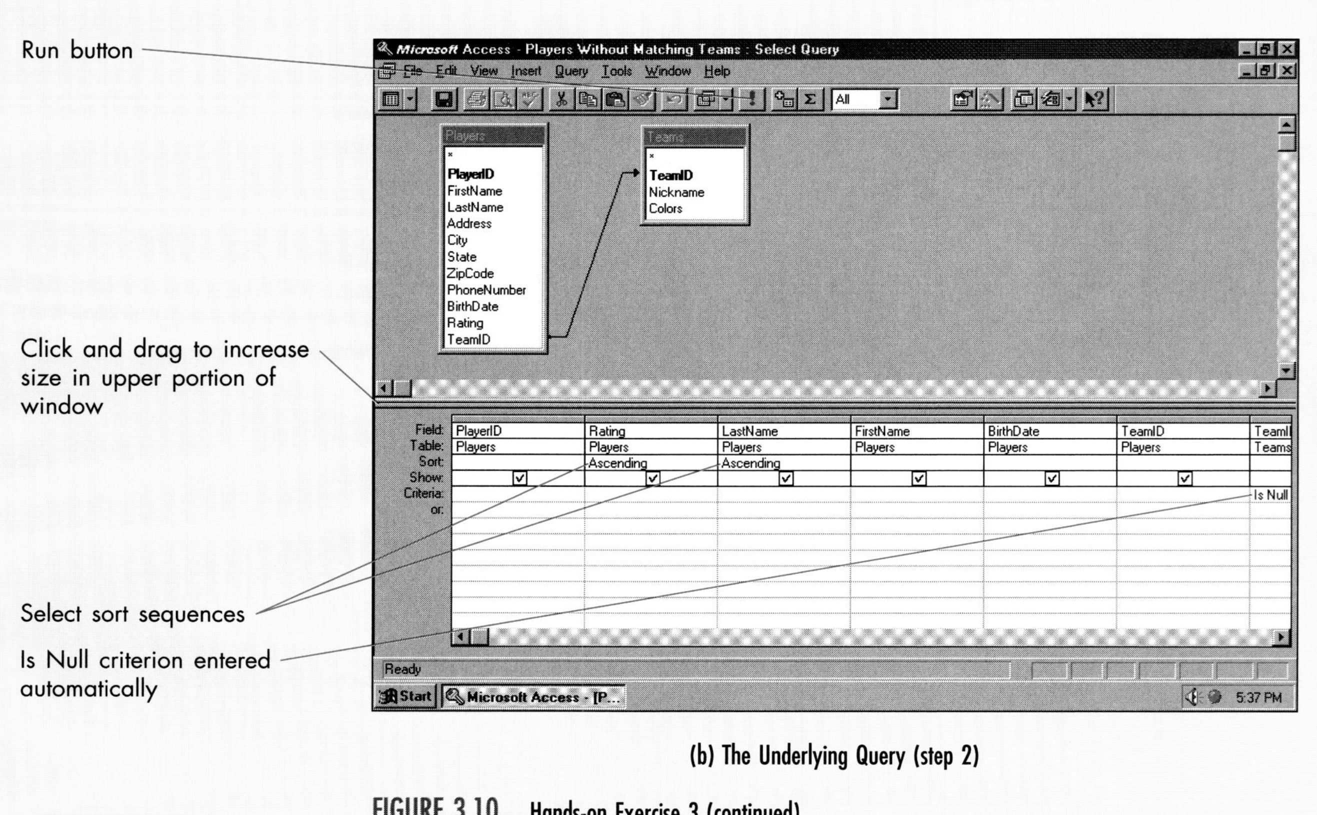

(b) The Underlying Query (step 2)

FIGURE 3.10 Hands-on Exercise 3 (continued)

STEP 3: Create the Unmatched Players Form

- Click the **Forms tab** in the Database window, click **New** to display the New Form dialog box, and select **AutoForm:Datasheet.**
- Click the **drop-down arrow** to choose a table or query. Select the **Players Without Matching Teams** (the query created in step 2). Click **OK.**
- Wait a few seconds as Access creates a form that lists the players who are not currently assigned to a team. The form is displayed in the Datasheet view and resembles the dynaset shown earlier.
- Maximize the form if necessary, then change to the Design view as shown in Figure 3.10c. Select the **TeamID control** in the Detail section, then press the **Del key** to delete the TeamID (which will be replaced with a combo box).
- Click the **Combo Box tool** on the Toolbox toolbar. Click and drag in the form where you want the combo box to go. Release the mouse. You will see the first step in the Combo Box Wizard:
  - Check the **Option button** that indicates you want the combo box to **look up values in a table or query.** Click **Next.**
  - Choose the **Teams table** in the next screen. Click **Next.**
  - Select the **TeamID** and **Nickname** from the Available Fields list box for inclusion in the combo box columns list. Click **Next.**
  - Adjust the column widths if necessary. Be sure the box to **Hide the key column** is checked. Click **Next.**
  - Click the **Option button** to store the value in the field. Click the **drop-down arrow** to display the fields in the query and select the **TeamID field.** Click **Next.**
  - Enter **TeamID** as the label for the combo box. Click **Finish.**
- Click (select) the label next to the control you just created. Press the **Del key** to delete the label.
- Point to the combo box, click the **right mouse button** to display a shortcut menu, and click **Properties.** Change the name of the control to **TeamID.** Close the Properties box.
- Click the **Save button** to display the Save As dialog box in Figure 3.10c. (Players Without Matching Teams is already entered as the default name.)
- Click **OK** to save the form, then close the form.

LIST BOXES VERSUS COMBO BOXES

The choice between a list box and a combo box depends on how you want the control to appear in the form. The advantage of a list box is that it is always visible, and further, that the user is restricted to entering a value from the list. The advantage of a combo box is that it takes less space because its values are not displayed until you open it. A combo box also enables you to control whether the user can enter just the values in the list or whether additional values are permitted. (The Limit to List property is set to Yes and No, respectively.) And finally, a combo box permits you to enter the first few characters in a value to move directly to that value. A list box, however, accepts only the first letter.

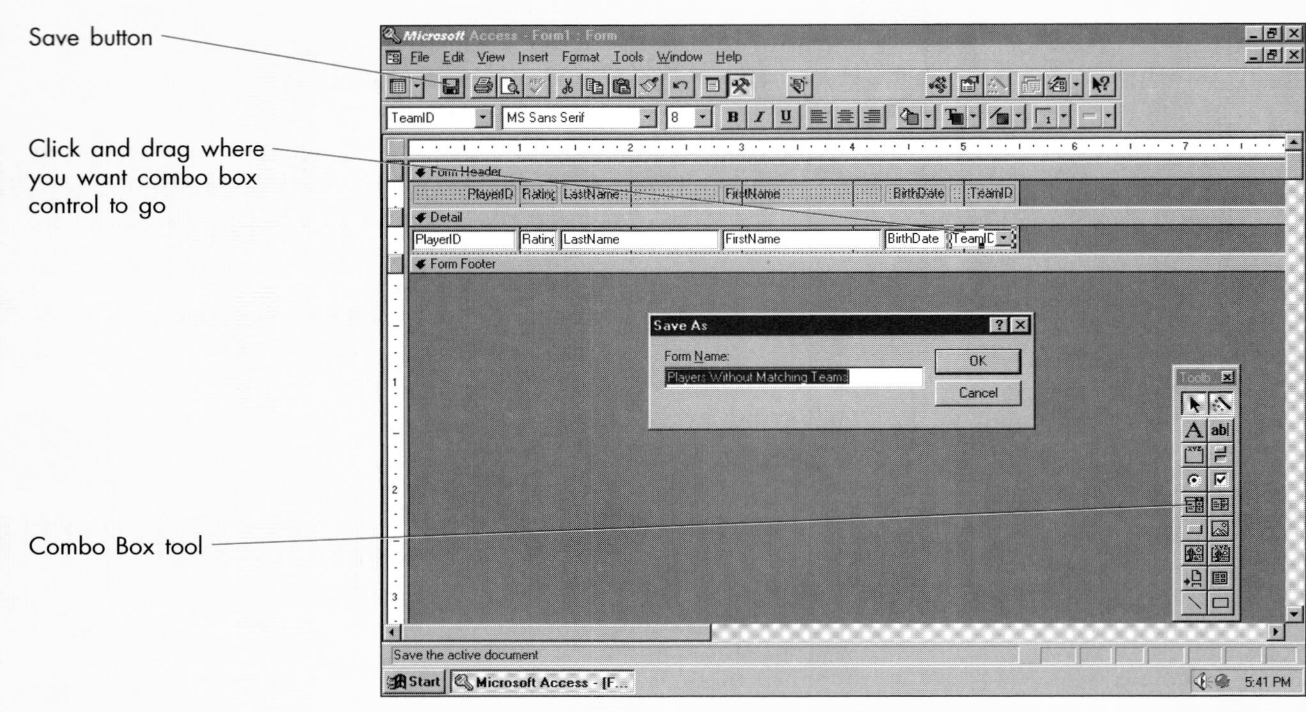

(c) Create the Unmatched Players Form (step 3)

FIGURE 3.10 Hands-on Exercise 3 (continued)

STEP 4: Create the Player Draft Macro Group

- Click the **Macros tab** in the Database window. Click **New** to create a new macro, and if necessary, click the **Maximize button** to maximize the Macro window.
- If you do not see the Macro Names column, pull down the **View menu** and click **Macro Names** to display the column. (Alternatively, you can click the **Macro Names button** on the Macro toolbar.)
- Enter the macro names, actions, and comments as shown in Figure 3.10d. Supply the arguments for each action as indicated below:
  - The Requery action (in the Update List macro) has a single argument in which you specify the control name (the name of the query).
  - Type **Players Without Matching Teams,** which is the query you created earlier in step 1.
  - The Find Player macro will be implemented as an assignment (see practice exercise 4), but in the interim, it will display a message and contain only the MsgBox action.
  - Enter **Not Yet Implemented** as the text of the message. Select **Information** as the type of message.
  - The arguments for the End Draft macro are visible in Figure 3.10d. The Player Draft form is created in the next step.
- Save the Macro group as **Player Draft** as shown in Figure 3.10d. Close the Macro window.

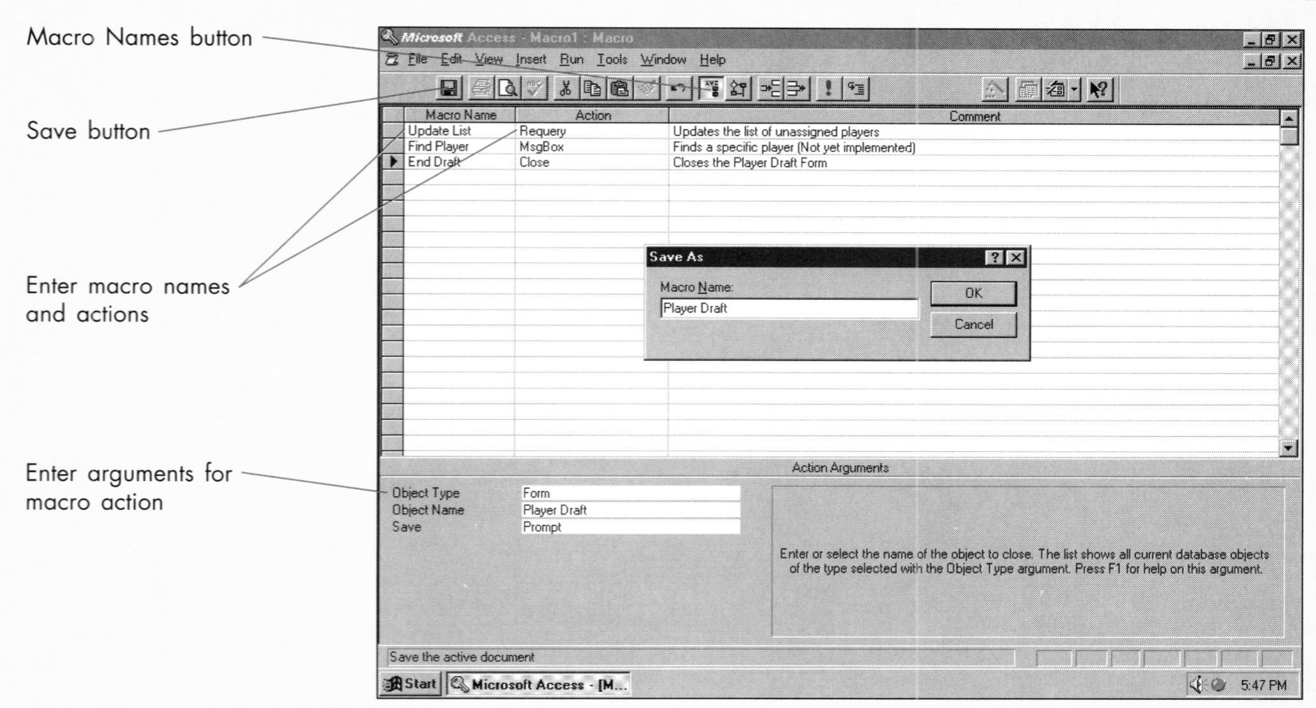

(d) Create the Player Draft Macro Group (step 4)

FIGURE 3.10 Hands-on Exercise 3 (continued)

REQUERY COMMAND NOT AVAILABLE

Most macros are designed to run at specified times and will fail if tested in isolation. The macros in the Player Draft group, for example, are designed to run only when the Player Draft form is open. Do not be concerned, therefore, if you attempt to test the macros at this time and the Action Failed dialog box appears. The macros will work correctly at the end of the exercise, when the entire player draft is in place. See problem 2 at the end of the chapter.

STEP 5: Create the Player Draft Form

- Click the **Forms tab** in the Database window. Select the **Template form,** click the **Copy button** to copy the form to the clipboard, then click the **Paste button** to complete the copy operation. Type **Player Draft** as the name of the copied form. Click **OK.**
- Open the **Player Draft form** in Design view. Delete the label and the rectangle from the Details section. Size the soccer balls, then move them to the Form Header section as shown in Figure 3.10e.
- Click the **Restore button,** then move and size the windows as shown in Figure 3.10e.
- Click the **Database window.** Click and drag the **Players Without Matching Teams form** onto the Player Draft form as shown in Figure 3.10e. Maximize the window.

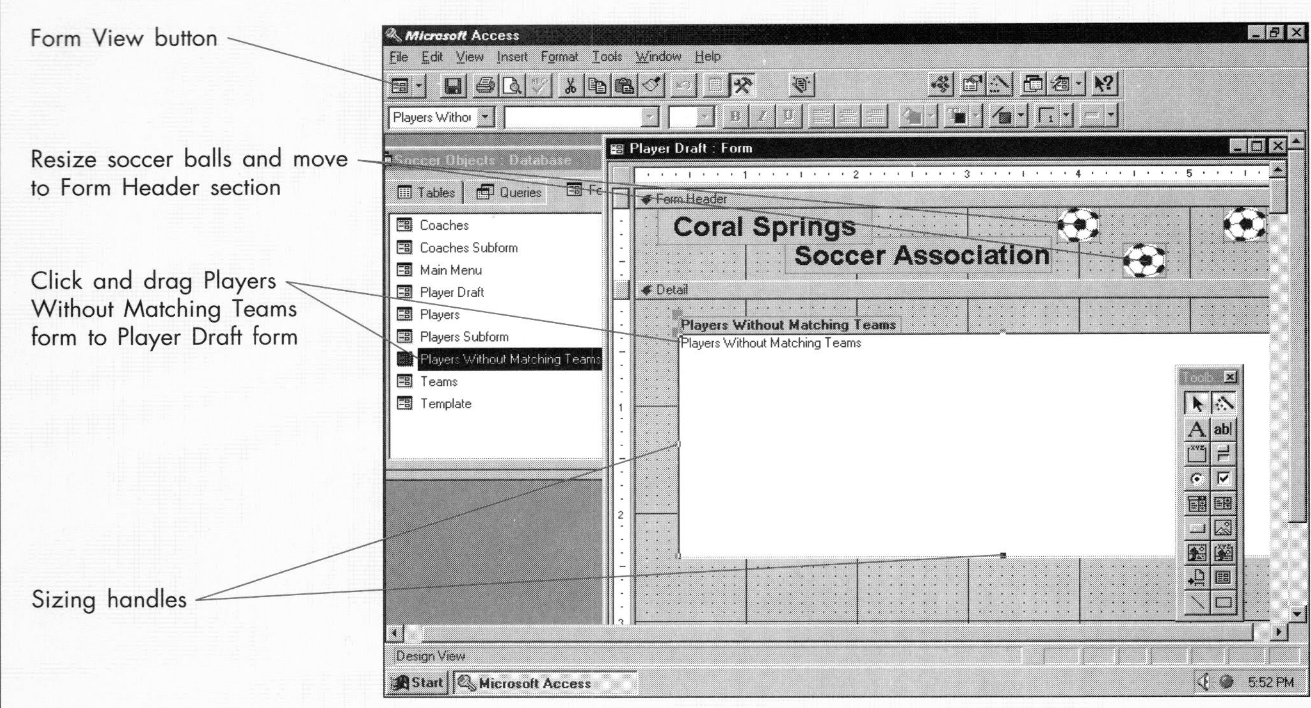

(e) Create the Player Draft Form (step 5)

FIGURE 3.10 Hands-on Exercise 3 (continued)

- Click and drag the **sizing handles** in the Players Without Matching Team form so that its size approximates the form in Figure 3.10e.
- Click the **Form View button** to view your progress. You should see the Datasheet view of the subform, which displays the players who have not yet been assigned to a team.
- Click the **Form Design button** to continue working on the form. If necessary, click off the subform control, then double click the subform control to open the subform in Design view. Switch to the Datasheet view to change the width of the columns within the query.
- Continue to switch back and forth between the Form view and the Design view until you are satisfied with the appearance of the subform. Close the form. Click **Yes** when asked whether to save the changes.
- Select (click) the **label** of the subform (Players Without Matching Teams), then press the **Del key** to delete the label. Be sure you delete the label and not the subform. (Click the **Undo button** if you make a mistake.) Save the form.

MODIFYING A SUBFORM

To modify the subform, click outside the subform to deselect it, then double click the subform to open it. Once the subform is open, you can change to the Design, Datasheet, or Form view by clicking the drop-down arrow on the Form View button on the Form Design toolbar.

STEP 6: Create the Command Buttons

- ➤ Click and drag the **Command Button tool** to create a command button, as shown in Figure 3.10f.
- ➤ Click **Miscellaneous** in the Categories list box. Select **Run Macro** from the list of actions. Click the **Next Command button.**
- ➤ Select **Player Draft.Update List** from the list of existing macros. Click the **Next Command button.**
- ➤ Click the **Text Option button.** Click and drag to select the default text (Run Macro), then type **Update List** as the text to display on the button. Click the **Next Command button.**
- ➤ Enter **Update List** (in place of the button number) and click the **Finish Command button.**
- ➤ Repeat these steps to create the additional command buttons shown in Figure 3.10f. Assign the Find Player and End Draft macros from the Player Draft group to the additional command buttons.
- ➤ Size, align, space, and color the command buttons as in the previous exercise. Save the completed form.
- ➤ Close the form.

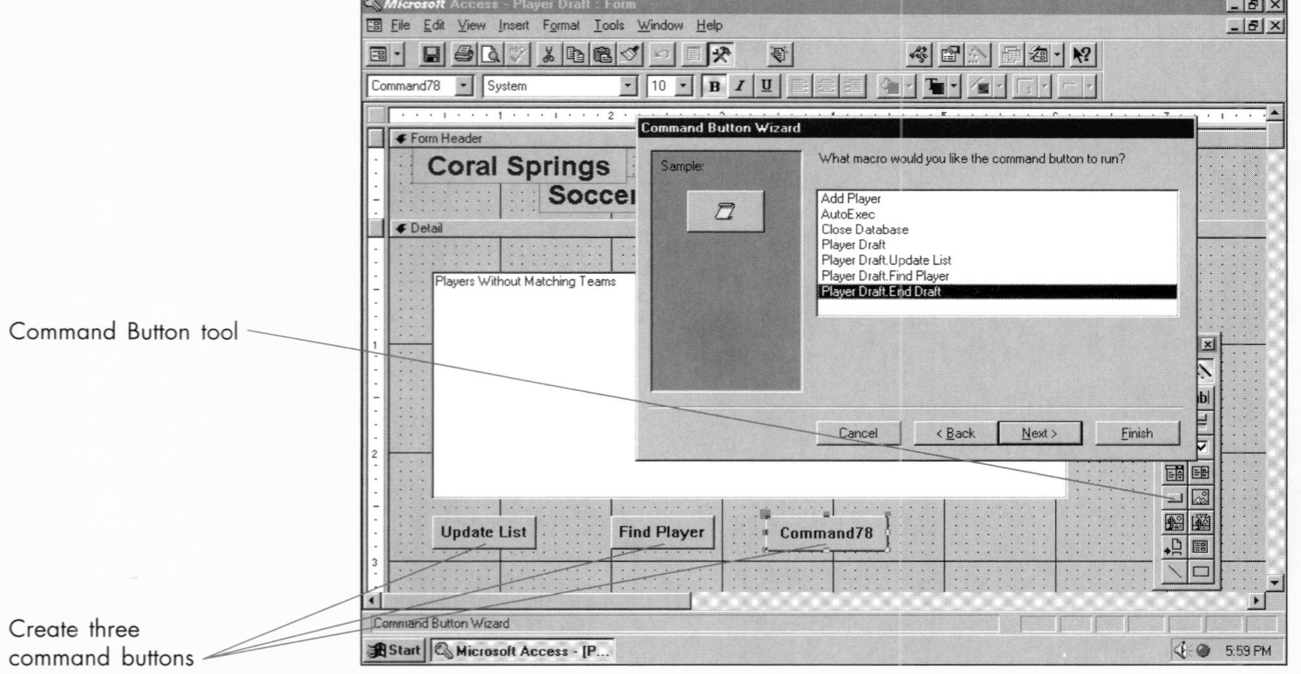

(f) Create the Command Buttons (step 6)

FIGURE 3.10 Hands-on Exercise 3 (continued)

UNIFORM COMMAND BUTTONS

Press and hold the Shift key to select multiple command buttons so that they can be formatted, sized, and aligned in a single command. After the buttons are selected, click the appropriate button on the Formatting toolbar to change the color, font, or point size, or to specify boldface or italics. Check that buttons are still selected, then pull down the Format menu to execute the Size and Alignment commands to arrange the buttons attractively on the form.

STEP 7: Modify the Main Menu

- You're almost finished. Open the **Main Menu form** in Design view. Move the four existing buttons to the left.
- Click and drag the **Command Button tool** to create the fifth command button as shown in Figure 3.10g. (Your button will display a different number.)
- Supply the necessary information to the Command Button Wizard so that the new button opens the Player Draft form just created. The text on the button should read **Player Draft.**
- Size, align, space, and color the command buttons as in the previous exercise. (Press and hold the **Shift key** to select multiple command buttons.)
- Save the completed form. Close the form, which returns you to the Database window.

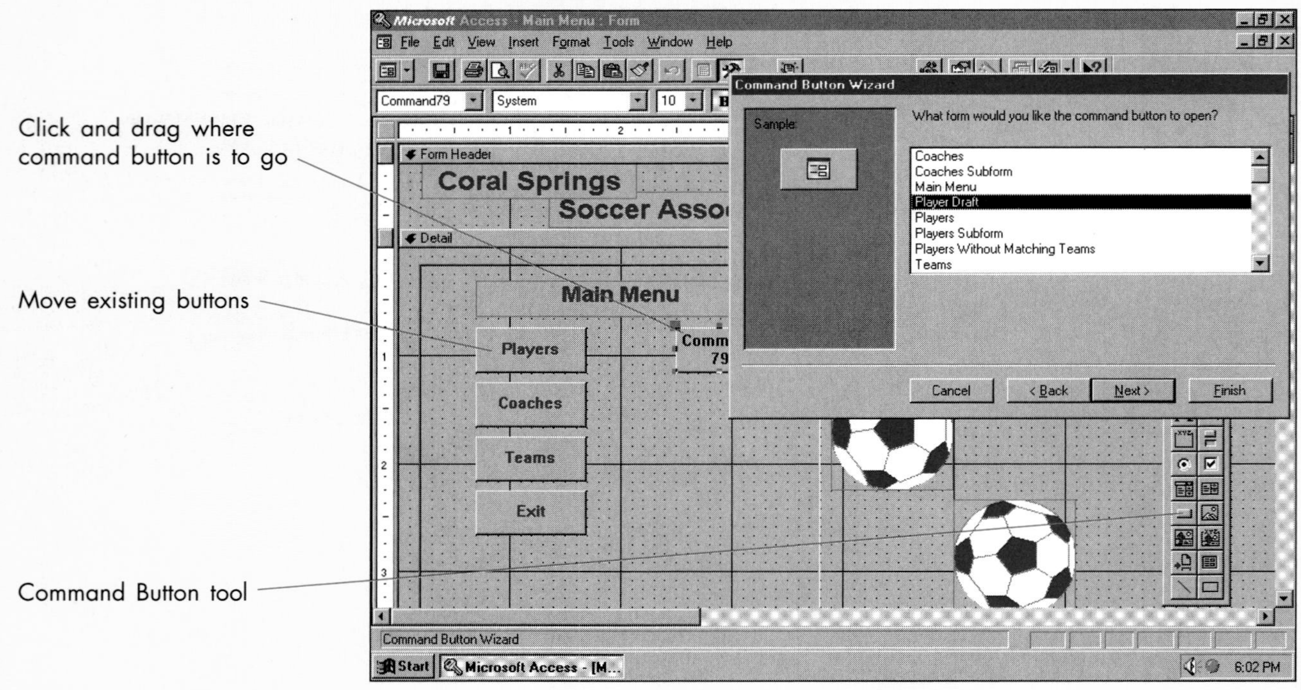

(g) Modify the Main Menu (step 7)

FIGURE 3.10 Hands-on Exercise 3 (continued)

THE F11 KEY

It's easy to lose the Database window, especially when you are maximizing objects within a database. Press the F11 key at any time to make the Database window the active window and place it in front of all the other open objects.

STEP 8: Test the Completed System

- Click the **Macros tab** in the Database window. Double click the **AutoExec macro** to execute this macro, as though you just opened the Soccer Objects database.
- Click the **Player Draft button** in the Main Menu to display the form you just created, as shown in Figure 3.10h. The Players are listed according to their ratings.
- Click the **TeamID field** for Katie Remmen. Type **R** (the first letter in Rockets) and Katie is assigned automatically to this team.
- Click the **Update List Command button.** Katie disappears from the list of unassigned players as she has just been drafted by the Rockets.
- Click the **End Draft button** to (temporarily) end the draft and return to the Main Menu.

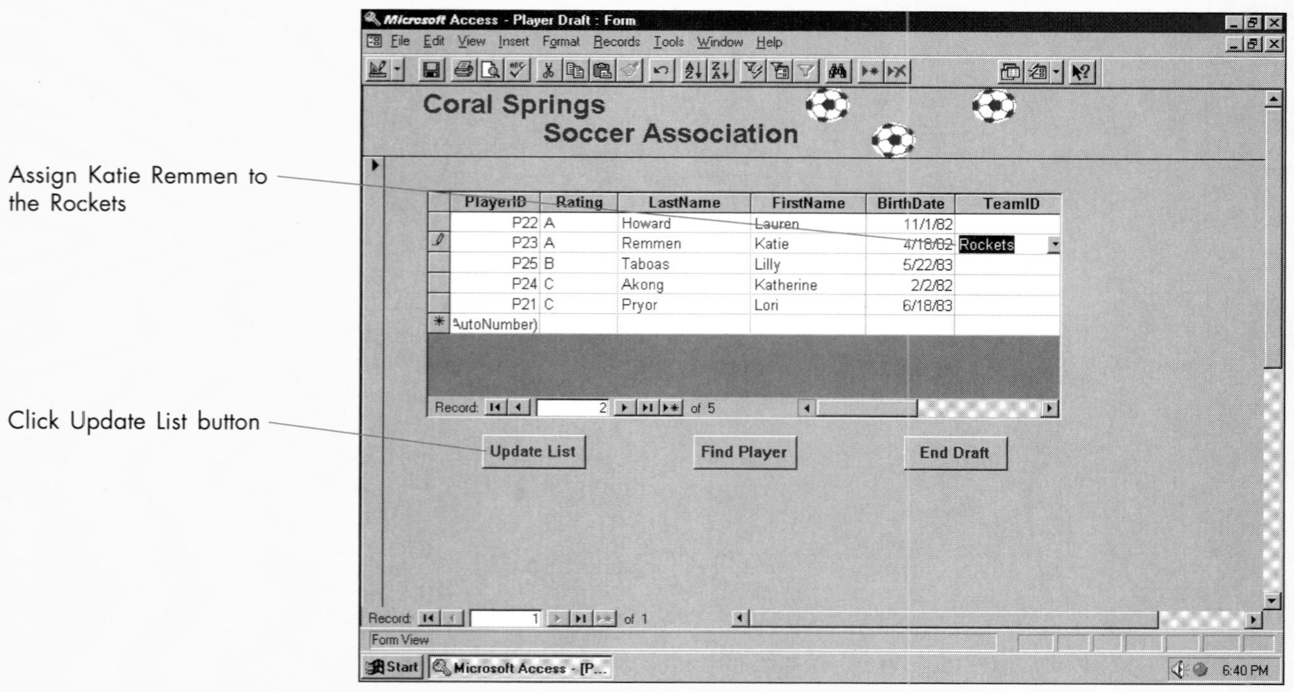

(h) The Completed Form (step 8)

FIGURE 3.10 Hands-on Exercise 3 (continued)

- ➤ Click the **Teams Command button** to view the team rosters. Team T01 (Rockets) is the first team you see, and Katie Remmen is on the roster. Click the **Close Form button** to return to the Main Menu.
- ➤ Click the **Exit Command button** to leave the system. Click **OK** in response to the message reminding you to back up the system.

A SIMPLE STRATEGY FOR BACKUP

We cannot overemphasize the importance of adequate backup. Backup procedures are personal and vary from individual to individual as well as installation to installation. Our suggested strategy is very simple, namely, that you back up whatever you cannot afford to lose and that you do so at the end of every session. Be sure to store the backup at a different location from the original file.

PROTOTYPING

Today's competitive environment demands that you develop applications quickly. This is especially true if you are creating an application for a client, where it is important for that person to see a working system as soon as possible. Prototyping enables you to do precisely that. Not only will the client appreciate your sense of urgency, but the sooner the client sees the initial version, the easier it is for you to make the necessary corrections.

A ***prototype*** is a partially completed version of an application that demonstrates the "look and feel" of the finished system. Consider, for example, Figure 3.11, which applies prototyping to the soccer application. The Main Menu in Figure 3.11a now includes a command button to display the Report Menu in Figure 3.11b. The Report Menu then enables a user to select any of the available reports.

The reports, however, have not yet been created; that is, clicking any of the command buttons in Figure 3.11b displays a message indicating that the report is not available. Nevertheless, the user has a better appreciation for how the eventual system will work and can provide immediate feedback on the portion of the system that has been completed. He or she may request changes in the user interface, the addition or deletion of reports, and so on. And, as indicated, the sooner the user communicates the requested changes to you, the easier it is for you to make those corrections. Once the prototype has been approved, the individual reports can be implemented one at a time, until the system is complete.

TOP-DOWN IMPLEMENTATION

An application should be developed in stages, beginning at the top (the form containing the Main Menu) and working toward the bottom (subsidiary forms, reports, and queries). Testing should go on continually, even before all of the objects are completed. This is accomplished through prototyping, which always presents a working application to the user, in which lower-level objects need not be completed. Development continues in top-down fashion, with each new version of the application containing additional objects until the system is finished.

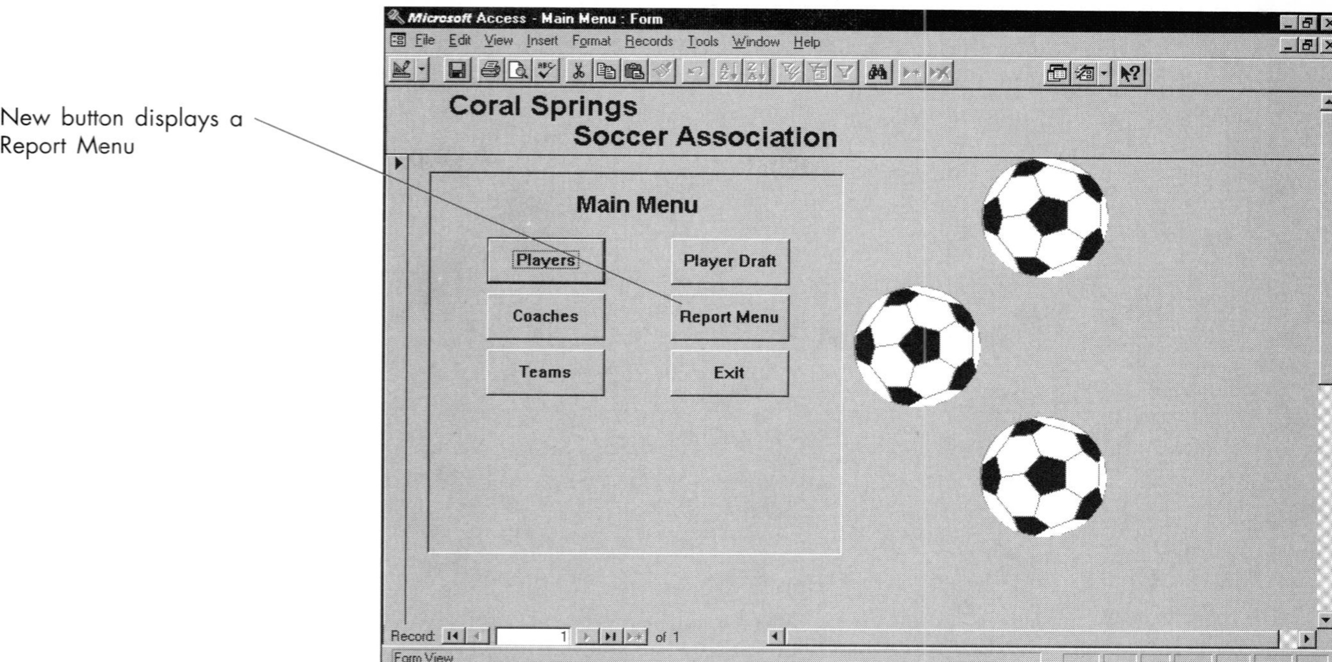

(a) Main Menu

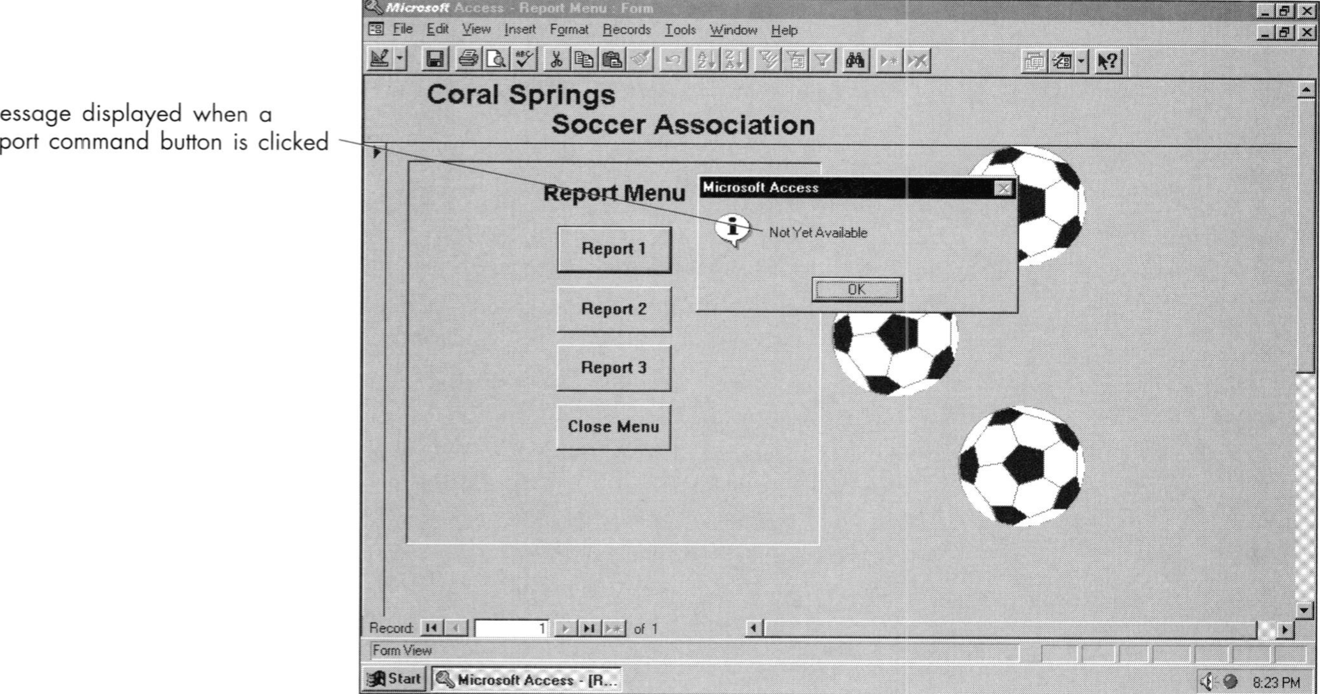

(b) Report Menu

FIGURE 3.11 Prototyping

Realize, too, how easy it is to produce the prototype shown in Figure 3.11. You need to create a macro (containing the MsgBox action) that will display the appropriate message when a report is not available. You also need to create a form that displays the Report Menu, and that form is easily created using the same template you used to create the Main Menu. And finally, you need to add a command button to the Main Menu to display the Report Menu. All of these steps are detailed in the following hands-on exercise.

HANDS-ON EXERCISE 4

Prototyping

Objective: Create a subsidiary Report Menu that is not fully implemented; use the MsgBox action as the basis of a prototyping macro. Use Figure 3.12 as a guide in the exercise.

STEP 1: Create the Prototype Macro

- Start Access and open the **Soccer Objects database.** Pull down the **File menu** and click **Close** (or click the **Close button**) to close the Main Menu form but leave the database open. (You *cannot* click the Exit command button as that would close the database.)
- Click the **Macros tab** in the Database window, which contains the four macros from the previous exercise. Click the **New button,** which opens the Macro window and automatically positions you at the first action. If necessary, click the **Maximize button** so that the Macro window takes the entire screen.
- Type **MS** (the first two letters in the MsgBox action), then press **enter** to accept this action. Press the **F6 key** or click the **box for the Message argument.** Type **Not Yet Available** as shown in Figure 3.12a.
- Press the **down arrow key** twice to move to the box for the **Type argument.** Click the **drop-down arrow** to display the list of message types and select **Information.**
- Click the **Save button.** Save the macro as **Prototype.**
- Click the **Run button** to test the macro, which displays the informational message in Figure 3.12a. Click **OK** to accept the message. Close the Macro window.

STEP 2: Create the Report Menu Form

- Click the **Forms tab** in the Database window. Click the **Template form** (on which all other forms are based), pull down the **Edit menu,** and click **Copy** (or press **Ctrl+C,** a universal Windows shortcut).
- Pull down the **Edit menu** a second time and click **Paste** (or click **Ctrl+V,** a universal Windows shortcut). Enter **Report Menu** as the name of the new form. Click **OK.**
- Select the newly created **Report Menu form.** Click the **Design button** to open the form in Design view as shown in Figure 3.12b.
- Click the **Restore button,** then size and/or move the Database and Form windows so that your desktop matches the arrangement in Figure 3.12b.
- Click the **label** in the Detail section, then click and drag to select the text **Enter Menu Name Here.** Enter **Report Menu** to replace the selected text. Save the form.

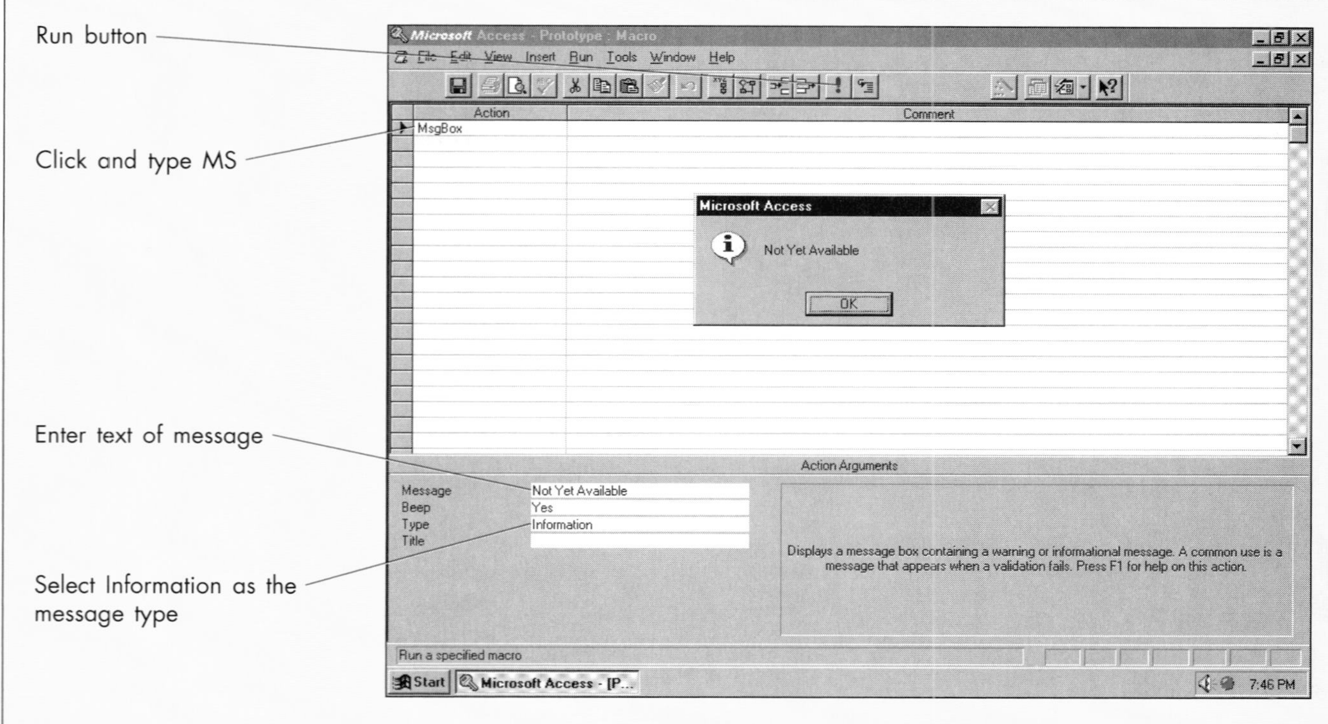

(a) The Prototype Macro (step 1)

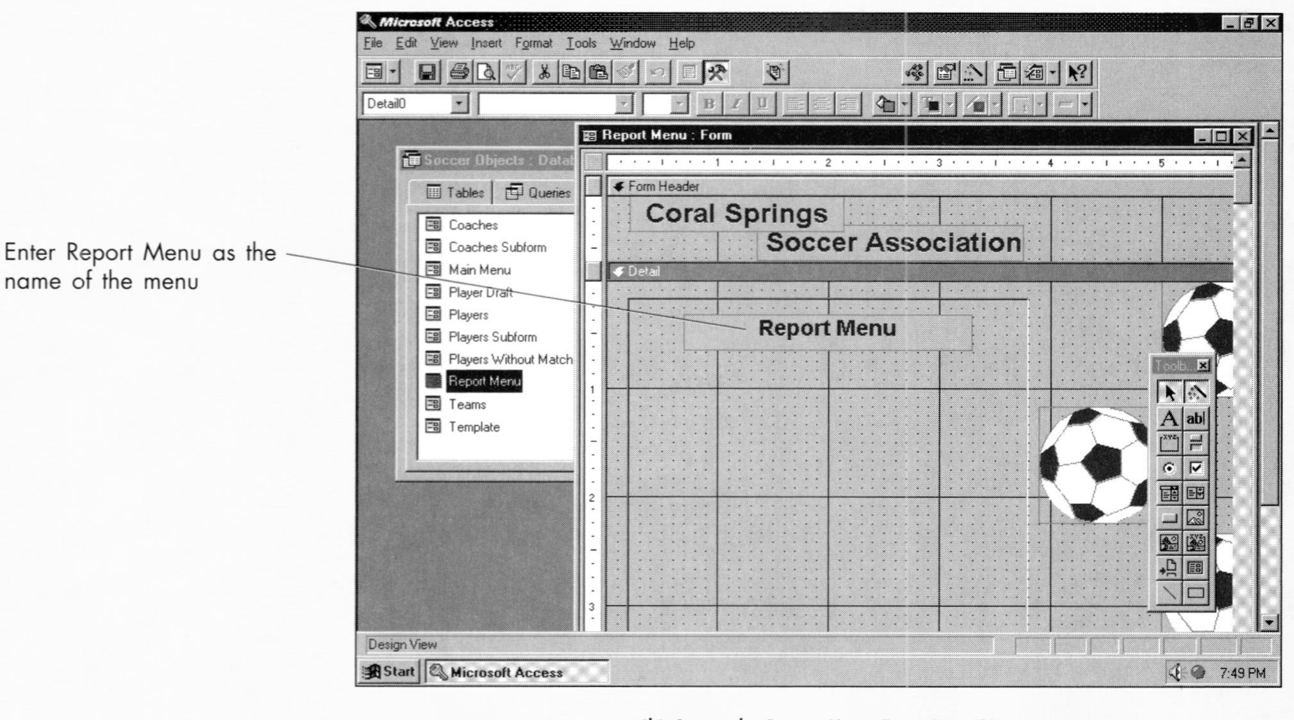

(b) Create the Report Menu Form (step 2)

FIGURE 3.12 Hands-on Exercise 4

ARRANGE THE DESKTOP

To size a window, point to any border (the mouse pointer changes to a double arrow), then drag the border in the direction you want to go: inward to shrink the window or outward to enlarge it. Alternatively, you can drag a corner to change both dimensions at the same time. To move a window while retaining its size, point to its title bar, then drag the window to its new position. Remember, too, that you cannot size a maximized window; that is, you must restore a maximized window if you want to change its size.

STEP 3: Add the Command Buttons

- Click the **Macros tab** in the Database window. Click and drag the **Prototype macro** to the Report Menu form as shown in Figure 3.12c. Release the mouse, and a command button is created to execute the Prototype macro.
- Click and drag to select the name of the button (Prototype), which corresponds to the name of the macro. Type **Report 1** as the new name. (Clicking this button in Form view will still execute the Prototype macro as you have changed only the text of the button, not the underlying macro.)
- Repeat these steps to create two additional buttons, **Report 2** and **Report 3,** as shown in Figure 3.12c. Do not worry about the size or position of the buttons at this time.

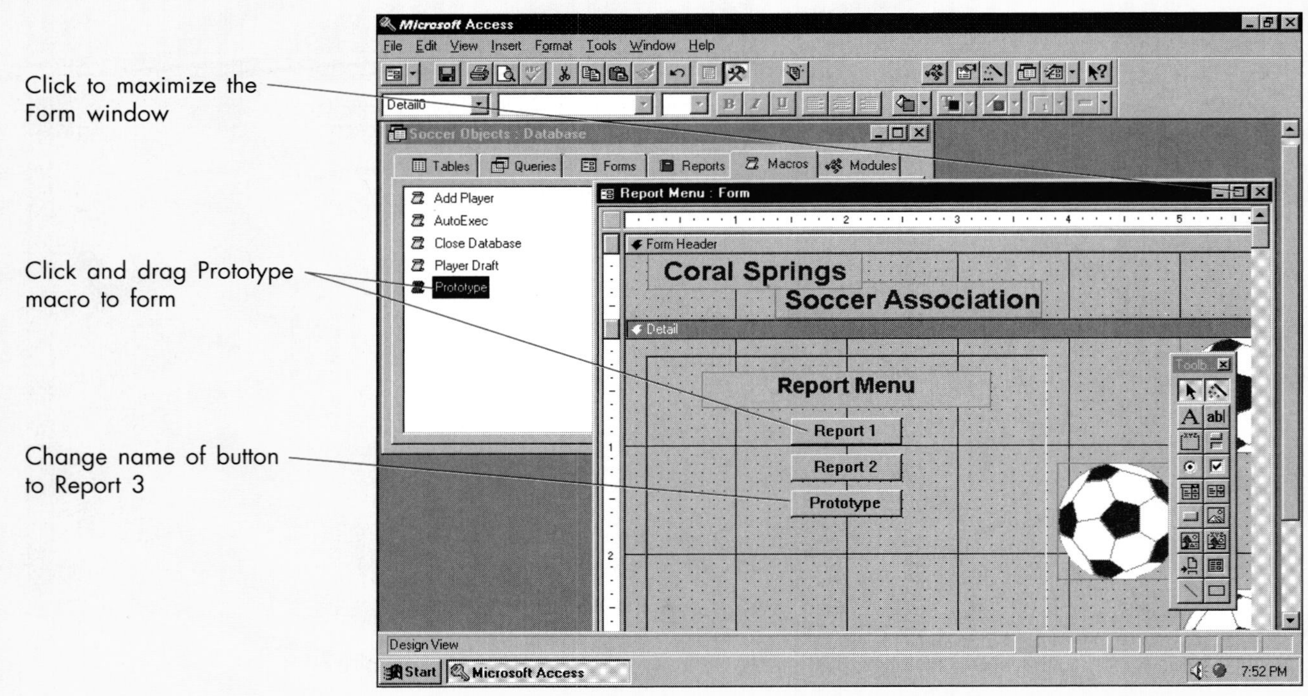

(c) Add the Command Buttons (step 3)

FIGURE 3.12 Hands-on Exercise 4 (continued)

STEP 4: Complete the Report Menu

- Maximize the Form window.
- Click the **Command Button tool** on the Forms Design toolbar, then click and drag in the form to create the command button shown in Figure 3.12d. (The number of your button will be different from ours.)
- The Command Button Wizard prompts you for the next several responses. Choose **Form operations** from the Categories list. Select **Close Form** as shown in Figure 3.12d. Click **Next.**
- Click the **Text option,** type **Close Menu** in the text box, and click **Next.** Type **Close Menu** as the name of the button. Click **Finish.**
- Size, align, color, and/or move the command buttons as you have done throughout the chapter.
- Click the **Form View button** to test the menu. Click the **Report 1 button,** which displays a message indicating that the report is not yet available. Click **OK** in response to the message.
- Click the buttons for **Report 2** and **Report 3,** then click **OK** as you see each informational message.
- Click the **Close Menu Command button** to close the Report Menu. Click **Yes** when asked whether to save the form.

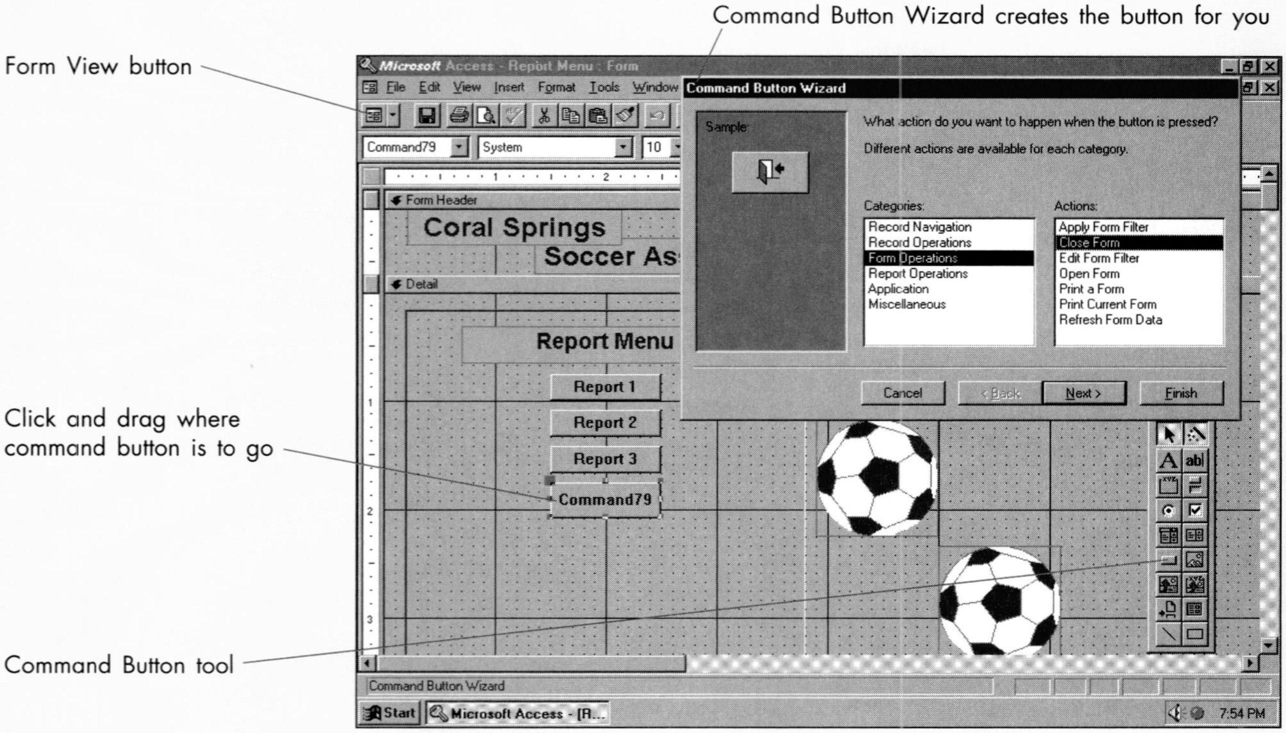

(d) Complete the Report Menu (step 4)

FIGURE 3.12 Hands-on Exercise 4 (continued)

GIVE YOUR USERS WHAT THEY WANT

Talk to the people who will eventually use your application to determine what they expect from the system. Ask for copies of the (paper) forms they currently have and aim for a similar look in your application. Try to obtain copies of the reports they currently prepare to be sure that your system produces the information expected from it.

STEP 5: Modify the Main Menu

- If necessary, click the **Forms tab** in the Database window. Select the **Main Menu form,** then click the **Design button** to open the form in Design view as shown in Figure 3.12e.
- Click the **Command Button tool** on the Forms Design toolbar, then click and drag in the form to create the command button shown in Figure 3.12e. (The number of your button will be different from ours.)
- The Command Button Wizard prompts you for several responses. Choose **Form operations** from the Categories list. Select **Open Form.** Click **Next.**
- Choose **Report Menu** as the name of the form. Click **Next.**
- Click the **Text option,** type **Report Menu** in the text box, and click **Next.** Type **Report Menu** as the name of the button. Click **Finish.**
- Size and align the command button within the Main Menu. (Press and hold the **Shift key** to select multiple buttons, then use the Size and Align commands on the Format menu.)
- Save the completed form.

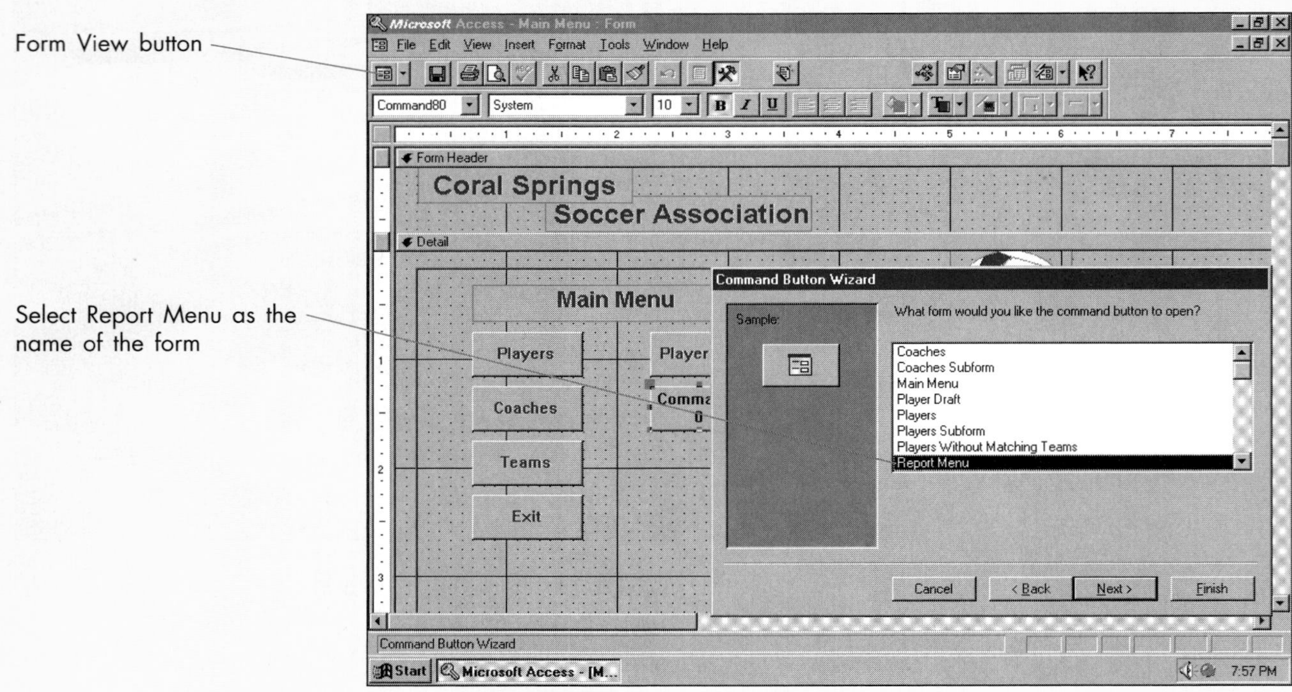

(e) Modify the Main Menu (step 5)

FIGURE 3.12 Hands-on Exercise 4 (continued)

BE CONSISTENT

Consistency within an application is essential to its success. Similar functions should be done in similar ways to facilitate learning and to build confidence in the application. The soccer application, for example, has similar screens for the Players, Coaches, and Teams forms, each of which contains the identical command buttons to add or print a record and close the form. The interface and means of navigation are consistent from one screen to the next.

STEP 6: Test the Completed System

- Click the **Form View button** to switch to the Form view and test the system. Click the **Report Menu button** on the Main Menu to display the Report Menu in Figure 3.12f.
- Click the command buttons for any of the reports, then click **OK** in response to the informational message.
- Click the **Close Menu Command button** to exit the Report Menu and return to the Main Menu.
- Click the **Exit Command button** to close the database. Click **Yes** if prompted to save any of the objects created in this exercise.
- Exit Access. Congratulations on a job well done.

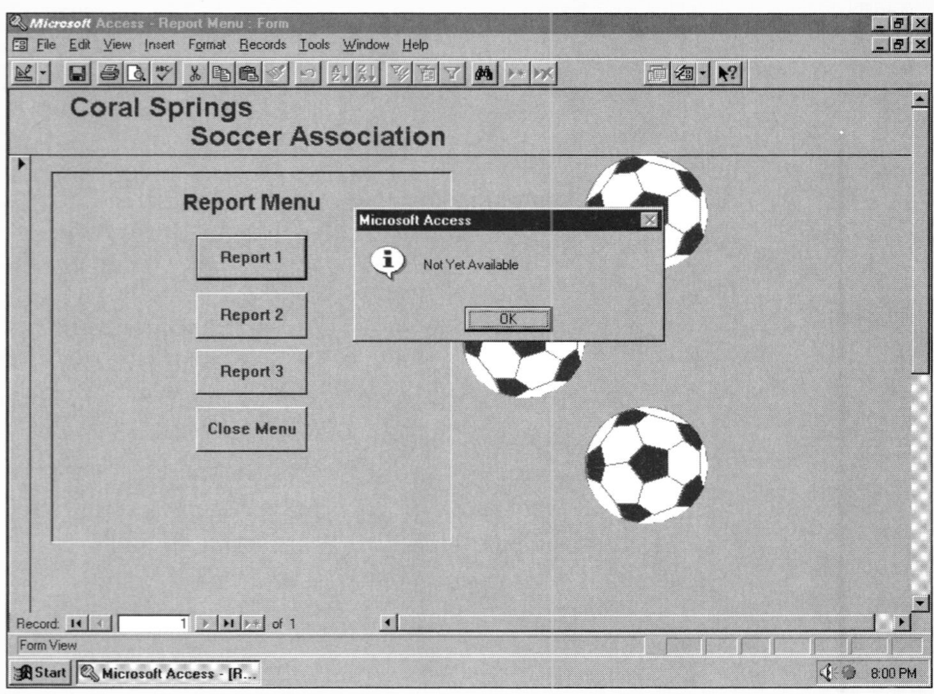

(f) Test the System (step 6)

FIGURE 3.12 Hands-on Exercise 4 (continued)

SUMMARY

An application contains the same objects as a database. The difference is in how the objects are presented to the user. An application has an intuitive user interface that does not require a knowledge of Microsoft Access on the part of the user.

The tables in a database can be separated from the other objects to enable the distribution of updated versions of the application without disturbing the data. The tables are stored in one database and the objects in another. The Link Tables command associates the tables with the objects.

A form is the basis of a user interface. The form contains text or list boxes in which to enter or edit data, and command buttons to move from one screen to the next. Clicking a command button causes Access to execute the underlying macro or event procedure.

A macro automates a command sequence and consists of one or more actions. An action is a command that performs a specific operation, such as opening a form or running a select query. A macro action has one or more arguments that supply information about how the command is to be executed.

The Macro window has two sections. The upper section contains the name (if any) of the macro, the condition (if any) under which it is executed, and most important, the actions (commands) that make up the macro. The lower section specifies the arguments for the various actions. A macro group consists of multiple macros and is used for organizational purposes.

The AutoExec macro is executed automatically whenever the database in which it is stored is opened. Each database can have its own AutoExec macro, but there is no requirement for an AutoExec macro to be present.

The Unmatched Query Wizard identifies the records in one table (e.g., the Players table) that do not have matching records in another table (e.g., the Teams table).

A prototype is a model (mockup) of a completed application that demonstrates the "look and feel" of the application. Prototypes can be developed quickly and easily through the use of simple macros containing the MsgBox action.

KEY WORDS AND CONCEPTS

Action
Application
Argument
AutoExec macro
Combo box
Command button
Database properties
Debugging
Display When property
Event
Event procedure
Is Null criterion
Link Tables command
List box
Macro
Macro group
Macro toolbar
Macro window
MsgBox action
On Click property
Prototype
Requery command
Template
Top-down implementation
Unmatched Query Wizard
User interface
Zoom box

Multiple Choice

1. The user interface of an application is based on a:
   (a) Table
   (b) Form
   (c) Query
   (d) Report
2. Which of the following describes the storage of the tables and objects for the application developed in the chapter?
   (a) Each table is stored in its own database
   (b) Each object is stored in its own database
   (c) The tables are stored in one database and the objects in a different database
   (d) The tables and objects are stored in the same database
3. Which of the following is true regarding the Link Tables command as it was used in the chapter?
   (a) It was executed from the Soccer Objects database
   (b) It was executed from the Soccer Tables database
   (c) Both (a) and (b)
   (d) Neither (a) nor (b)
4. What happens when an Access database is initially opened?
   (a) Access executes the AutoExec macro if the macro exists
   (b) Access opens the AutoExec form if the form exists
   (c) Both (a) and (b)
   (d) Neither (a) nor (b)
5. Which statement is true regarding the AutoExec macro?
   (a) Every database must have an AutoExec macro
   (b) A database may have more than one AutoExec macro
   (c) Both (a) and (b)
   (d) Neither (a) nor (b)
6. Which of the following are examples of arguments?
   (a) MsgBox and OpenForm
   (b) Message type (e.g., critical) and Form name
   (c) Both (a) and (b)
   (d) Neither (a) nor (b)
7. What happens if you drag a macro from the Database window onto a form?
   (a) A command button is created that opens the form
   (b) A command button is created that runs the macro
   (c) Both (a) and (b)
   (d) Neither (a) nor (b)

8. How do you change the properties of a command button on an existing form?
   (a) Open the form in Form view, then click the left mouse button to display a shortcut menu
   (b) Open the form in Form view, then click the right mouse button to display a shortcut menu
   (c) Open the form in Form Design view, then click the left mouse button to display a shortcut menu
   (d) Open the form in Form Design view, then click the right mouse button to display a shortcut menu

9. Which of the following is true regarding the Unmatched Query Wizard with respect to the CSSA database?
   (a) It can be used to identify teams without players
   (b) It can be used to identify players without teams
   (c) Both (a) and (b)
   (d) Neither (a) nor (b)

10. Which of the following can be associated with the On Click property of a command button?
    (a) An event procedure created by the Command Button Wizard
    (b) A macro created by the user
    (c) Either (a) or (b)
    (d) Neither (a) nor (b)

11. Which of the following was suggested as essential to a backup strategy?
    (a) Backing up files at the end of every session
    (b) Storing the backup file(s) at another location
    (c) Both (a) and (b)
    (d) Neither (a) nor (b)

12. The On Click property of a command button contains the entry, *Player Draft.Update List.* Which of the following is true?
    (a) Update List is an event procedure
    (b) Player Draft is an event procedure
    (c) Player Draft is a macro in the Update List macro group
    (d) Update List is a macro in the Player Draft macro group

13. Which columns are always visible in the Macro window?
    (a) Action and Comments
    (b) Macro Name and Conditions
    (c) Both (a) and (b)
    (d) Neither (a) nor (b)

14. The F6 and F11 function keys were introduced as shortcuts. Which of the following is true about these keys?
    (a) The F6 key switches between the top and bottom sections of the Macro window
    (b) The F11 key makes the Database window the active window
    (c) Both (a) and (b)
    (d) Neither (a) nor (b)

15. Which of the following was suggested as a way to organize macros and thus limit the number of macros that are displayed in the Database window?
    (a) Avoid macro actions that have only a single argument
    (b) Avoid macros that contain only a single action
    (c) Create a macro group
    (d) All of the above

ANSWERS

1. b	**6.** b	**11.** c
2. c	**7.** b	**12.** d
3. a	**8.** d	**13.** a
4. a	**9.** c	**14.** c
5. d	**10.** c	**15.** c

EXPLORING MICROSOFT ACCESS 7.0

1. Use Figure 3.13 to match each action with its result; a given action may be used more than once or not at all.

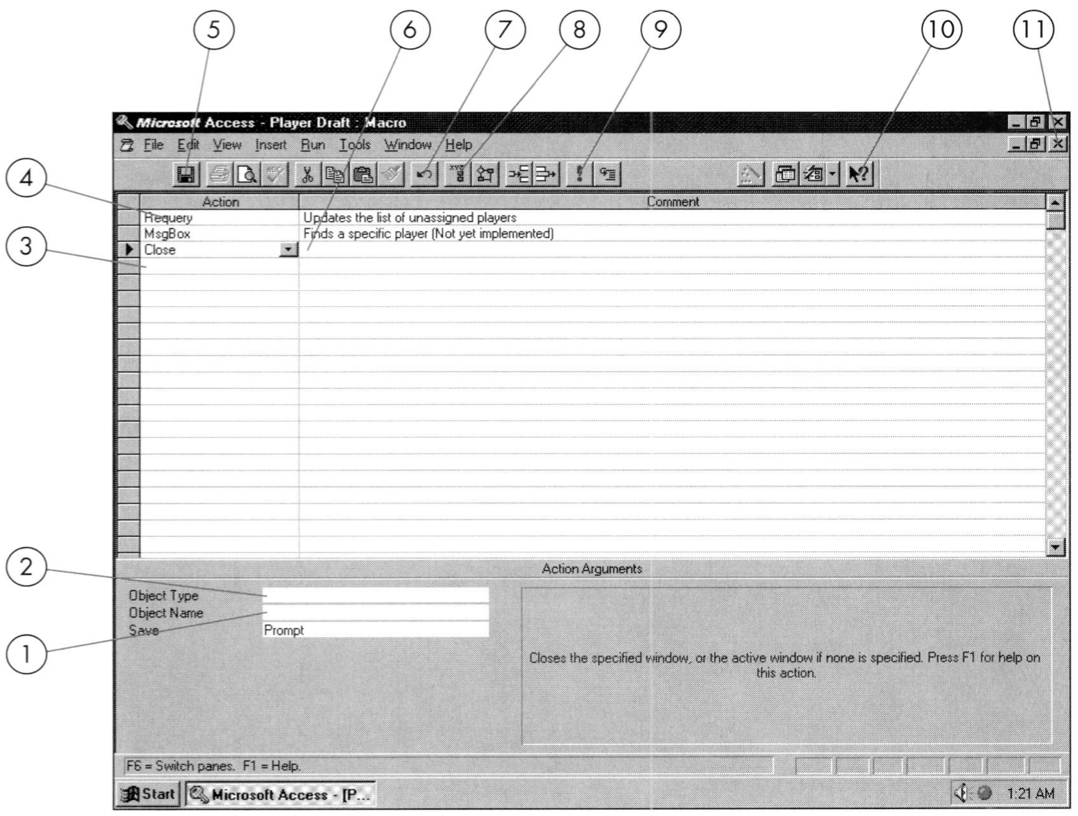

FIGURE 3.13 Screen for Problem 1

Action		Result
a. Click at 1	____	Enter a new macro action
b. Click at 2	____	Display the macro names
c. Click at 3	____	Enter the type of object to be closed
d. Click at 5	____	Enter the name of the object to be closed
e. Click at 6	____	Enter a description for the current macro action
f. Click at 7	____	Run the macro
g. Click at 8	____	Save the macro
h. Click at 9	____	Undo the most recent command
i. Click at 10, click at 4	____	Close the macro window
j. Click at 11	____	Get Help on the Requery action

2. The messages in Figure 3.14 appeared or could have appeared in conjunction with the hands-on exercises in the chapter. Indicate the probable reason why each message appeared and what (if any) corrective action is required.

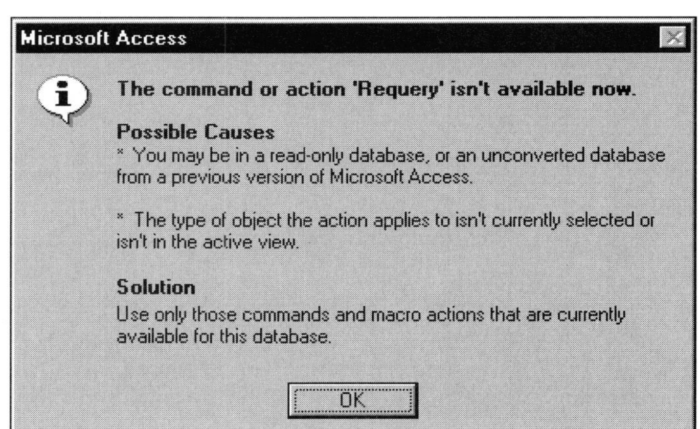

(a) Informational Message 1

Action Failed
Macro Name:
Player Draft
Condition:
True
Action Name:
Requery
Arguments:
Players Without Matching Teams
Step
Halt
Continue

(b) Informational Message 2

FIGURE 3.14 Screens for Problem 2

3. Answer the following with respect to the form in Figure 3.15:
   a. How do you display the property sheet in Figure 3.15?
   b. Which control(s) is selected? Which macro is associated with that control?
   c. What happens if you change to the Form view, then click the Update List Command button? If you double click the Update List Command button?
   d. What advantage (if any) is there to assigning different macros to different events for the same control?
   e. What is the difference between the On Enter and On Exit events?

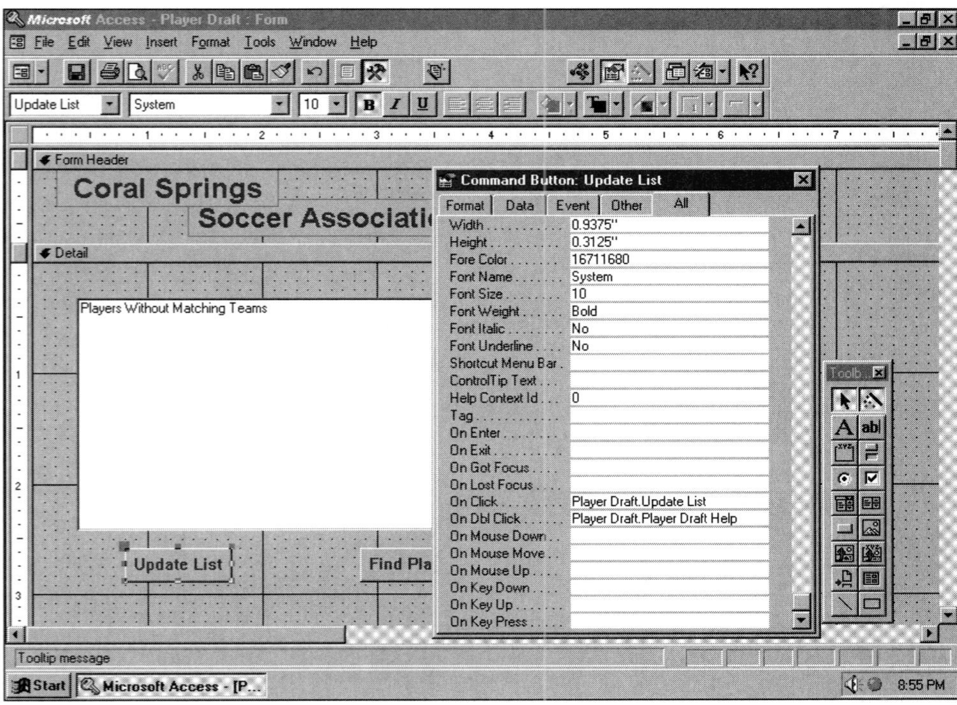

FIGURE 3.15 Screen for Problem 3

4. The Relationships window in Figure 3.16 contains a partial design for the database of a national corporation that franchises fast food restaurants. The database is to track the restaurants, the managers of those restaurants, and the companies that supply the restaurants. There is a one-to-many relationship between managers and restaurants and a many-to-many relationship between restaurants and suppliers.

   The system should be able to track all orders placed by a specific restaurant as well as all orders received by a given supplier. It should also be able to identify all restaurants for a specific manager. Complete the design of the system by:
   a. Adding new table(s), if any, that are necessary to satisfy the objectives of the system. Show all required fields in the new table(s).
   b. Adding additional field(s), if any, in the existing tables to establish the relationships that exist within the database.
   c. What is the primary key in each table?
   d. What is the foreign key (if any) in each table?

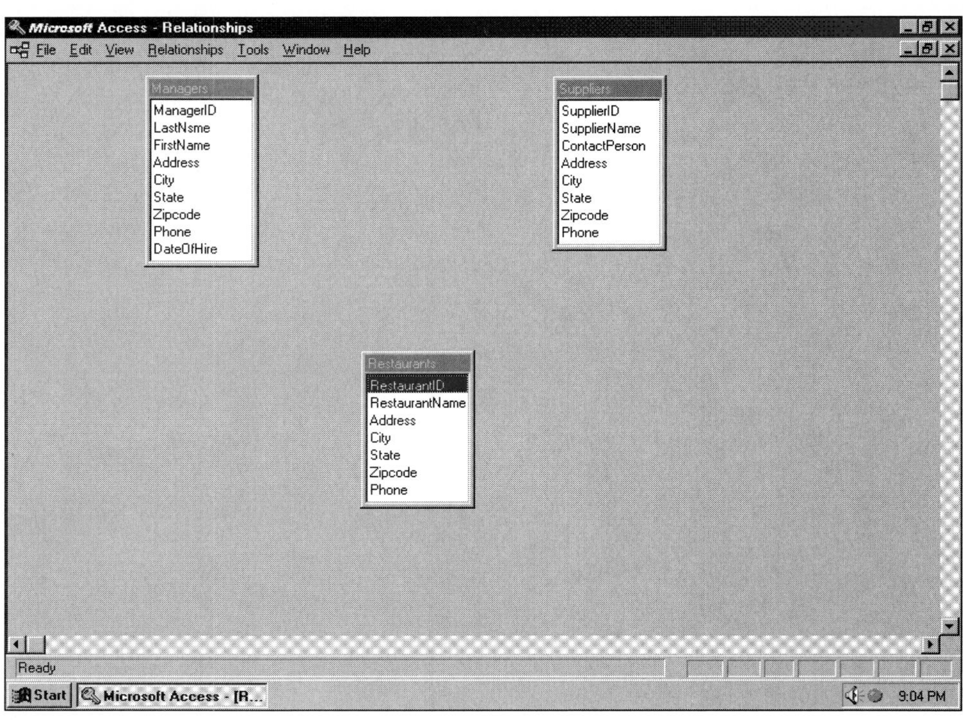

FIGURE 3.16 Screen for Problem 4

PRACTICE WITH MICROSOFT ACCESS 7.0

1. Prototyping was demonstrated in the fourth hands-on exercise to create the "look and feel" of the soccer application. It remains, however, to create the three reports in the Report Menu, to create a macro to open each of these reports, and finally to assign each macro to the appropriate command button. Create the following reports:

a. Report 1 is a master list of all players in alphabetical order. Include the player's first and last names, date of birth, rating, phone, and address in that order. Create the report in landscape rather than portrait orientation.

b. Report 2 is a master list of all coaches in alphabetical order. Include the coach's first and last names, phone, and address in that order. Create the report in landscape rather than portrait orientation.

c. Report 3 is to print the team rosters in sequence by TeamID. Each roster is to begin on a new page. The header line should contain the TeamID, nickname, and team colors as well as the name and phone number of the head coach. A detail line—containing the player's first and last names, telephone number, and date of birth—is to appear for each player. Players are to be listed alphabetically.

d. Create a macro group called Report Menu with three macros, one macro to open each report. Change the On Click property of each command button in the Report Menu (which is currently set to the Prototype macro) to the appropriate macro in the macro group.

e. Submit a disk with the CSSA database to your instructor.

2. Figure 3.17 displays a modified version of the Main Menu for the CSSA database, which has been enhanced through the addition of a Help button. The user clicks the Help button to execute a macro, which in turn displays the dialog box shown in the figure.
   a. Complete all of the hands-on exercises in the chapter, then add a Help macro containing your telephone and e-mail address. (The macro consists of a single MsgBox action.)
   b. Modify the existing Main Menu to include the Help button shown in Figure 3.17, which runs the macro you just created.
   c. Submit a disk with the CSSA database to your instructor.

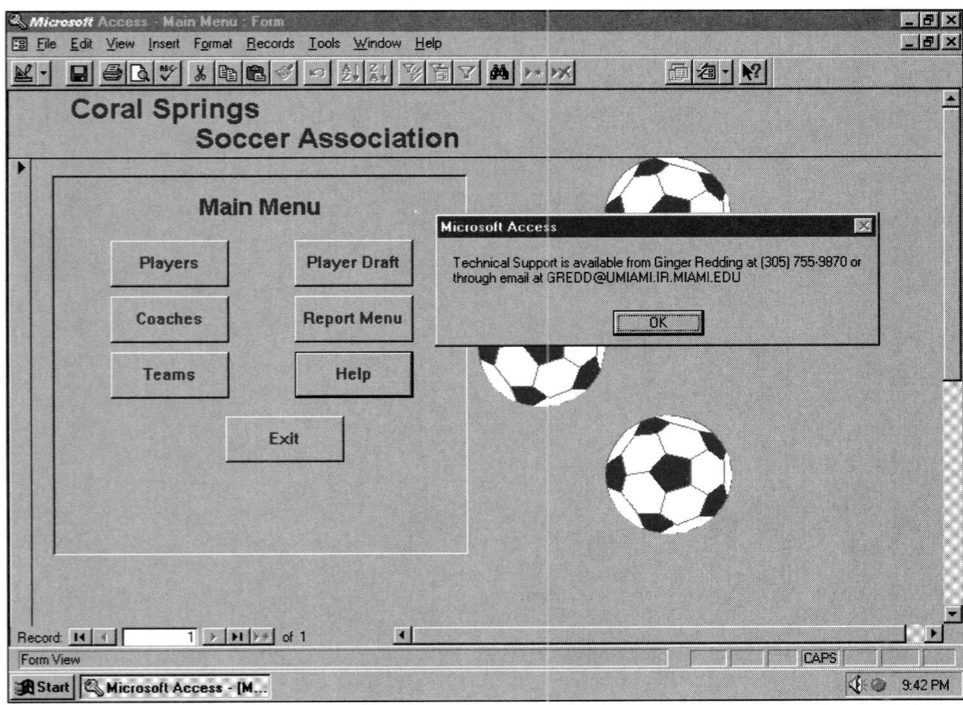

FIGURE 3.17 Screen for Practice Exercise 2

3. Figure 3.18 illustrates the use of the Condition column in the Macro window. The intent of the macro in Figure 3.18 is to display a message to "A"-rated players inviting them to try out for an All-City competitive team that plays against teams from other cities.
   a. Create the macro shown in Figure 3.18. (Click the Conditions button on the Macro toolbar to display the Conditions column in the Macro window.)
   b. Open the Players form in Design view. Right click the Rating control to display its Property sheet, then assign the macro you just created to the On Exit property.
   c. Prove to yourself that the macro works. Change to Form view, then move to the record containing the information you entered for yourself in step 3 of the first hands-on exercise. Click the text box containing the player rating, enter "A", then press the Tab key to move to the next control. You should see a message inviting you to try for the competitive team. Change your rating to a "B" and press the Tab key a second time. This time there is no message.
   d. Submit a disk with the CSSA database to your instructor.

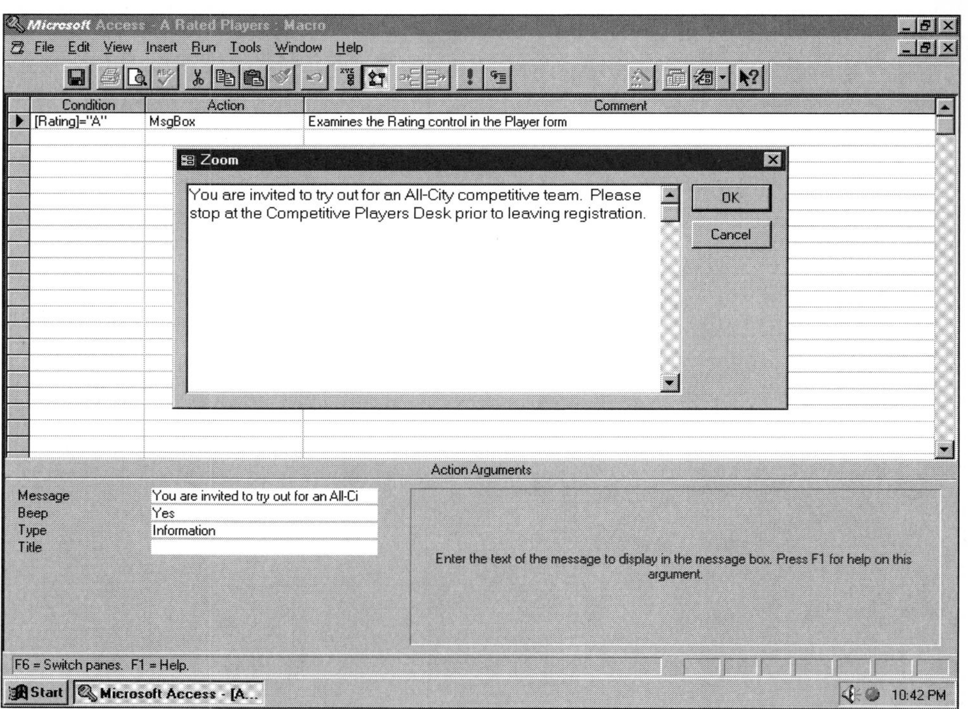

FIGURE 3.18 Screen for Practice Exercise 3

4. The player draft was only partially completed in the fourth hands-on exercise and still requires the completion of the Find Player function. After this has been accomplished, you will be able to click the Find Player button in Figure 3.19 to display the Find Parameter Value dialog box to enter a player's name, and then view the information for that player. Accordingly:

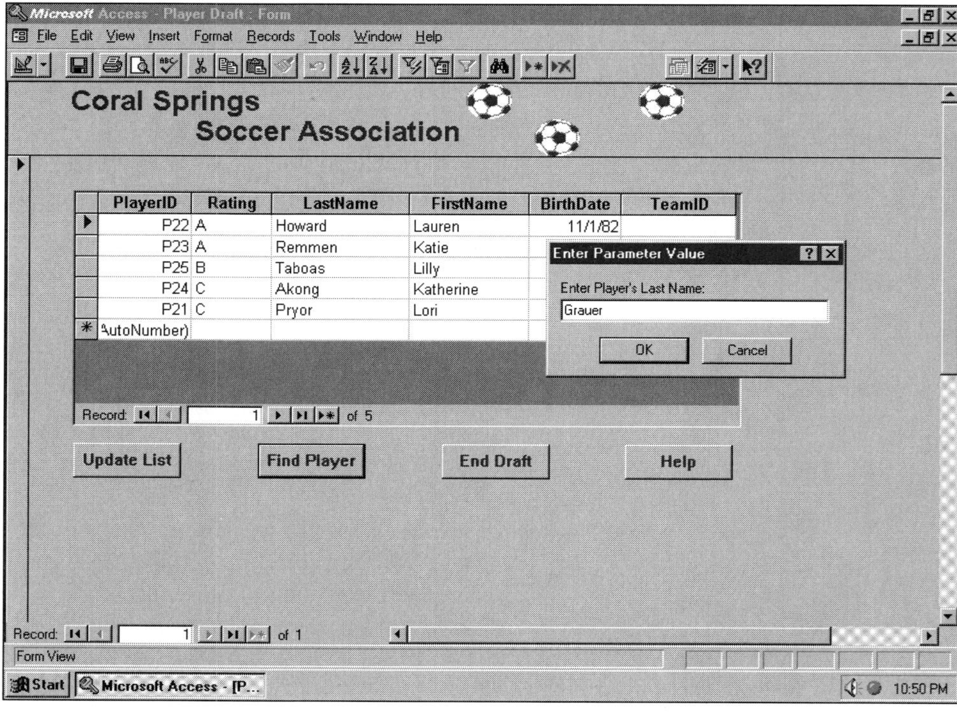

FIGURE 3.19 Screen for Practice Exercise 4

a. Create a parameter query that requests the last name of a player, then returns *all* fields for that player.
b. Copy the existing Players Form to a new form called Find Player. Change the Record Source property of the Find Player form to the parameter query you created in part a.
c. Change the Find Player macro in the Player Draft group so that it opens the Find Player form you just created.
d. Add the Help button to the Player Draft menu as described in practice exercise 1.
e. Submit the completed disk to your instructor.

CASE STUDIES

Client/Server Applications

The application for the Coral Springs Soccer Association was developed to run on a single PC; in practice, however, it would most likely be implemented on a network. Investigate the additional steps needed to load the Soccer Tables database on a server and enable multiple users (clients) to access the database simultaneously. How does Access prevent two users from modifying the same record simultaneously? What security features are available? How would backup be implemented? Where would the Soccer Objects database be stored?

A Project for the Semester

Choose any of the eight cases at the end of Chapter 1 or 2 (with the exception of the Recreational Sports League in Chapter 1) and develop a complete system. Design the tables and relationships and provide a representative series of forms to enter and edit the data. Create a representative set of queries and reports. And finally, tie the system together via a system of menus similar to those that were developed in this chapter.

The Database Wizard

The Database Wizard provides an easy way to create a database as it creates the database for you. The advantage of the Wizard is that it creates the tables, forms, and reports, together with a Main Menu (called a switchboard) in one operation. The disadvantage is that the Wizard is inflexible compared to creating the database yourself. Use the online Help facility to learn about the Database Wizard, then use the Wizard to create a simple database for your music collection. Is the Wizard a useful shortcut, or is it easier to create the database yourself?

Compacting versus Compressing

The importance of adequate backup has been stressed throughout the text. As a student, however, your backup may be limited to what you can fit on a single floppy disk, which in turn creates a problem if the size of your database grows beyond 1.4Mb. Two potential solutions involve compacting and/or compressing the database. Compacting is done from within Access, whereas compressing requires additional software. Investigate both of these techniques with respect to the CSSA database created in the chapter. Be sure to indicate to your instructor the reduction in file size that you were able to achieve.

A

APPENDIX A: TOOLBARS

OVERVIEW

Microsoft Access has nineteen predefined toolbars, which provide access to commonly used commands. Twelve of the toolbars are tied to a specific view and are displayed automatically when you work in that view. Eleven of these toolbars are shown in Figure A.1 and are listed here for convenience: the Database, Relationships, Table Design, Table Datasheet, Query Design, Query Datasheet, Form Design, Form View, Report Design, Print Preview, and Macro toolbars. The twelfth, the Visual Basic toolbar, is not shown as it is beyond the scope of this book.

Four of the remaining seven toolbars are shown in Figure A.2. The Toolbox and Formatting (Form/Report Design) toolbars are displayed by default in both the Form Design and Report Design views. The Formatting (Datasheet) toolbar is displayed by default in both the Table Datasheet and Query Datasheet views. The Microsoft toolbar can be displayed as needed, and is used to quickly access the other Microsoft applications. The Utility1 and Utility2 toolbars are not displayed in the figure as they are used to create custom toolbars that can be used with any database, and are initially blank. The Filter/Sort toolbar is also not displayed as it is beyond the scope of this book.

The buttons on the toolbars are intended to be indicative of their function. Clicking the Print button, for example (the fourth button from the left on the Database toolbar), executes the Print command. If you are unsure of the purpose of any toolbar button, point to it, and a ToolTip will appear that displays its name.

You can display multiple toolbars, move them to new locations on the screen, customize their appearance, or suppress their display.

- To display or hide a toolbar, pull down the View menu and click the Toolbars command. Select (deselect) the toolbar(s) that you want to display (hide). The selected toolbar(s) will be displayed in the same position as when last displayed. You may also point to any toolbar and click with the right mouse button to bring up a shortcut menu. The toolbars that are appropriate to that view are listed at the top of the menu and can be toggled on (off) by clicking the appropriate name. Other toolbars, not displayed by default in that view, can be displayed by clicking the Toolbars command from the shortcut menu. Note that when you explicitly elect to show a predefined toolbar in a view other than its default view, it will be displayed in every view. In similar fashion, when you explicitly hide a predefined toolbar, it will remain hidden in every view, including its default view.

- To change the size of the buttons, display them in monochrome rather than color, or suppress the display of the ToolTips, pull down the View menu, click Toolbars, and then select (deselect) the appropriate check box. Alternatively, you can click on any toolbar with the right mouse button, select Toolbars, and then select (deselect) the appropriate check box.
- Toolbars may be either docked (along the edge of the window) or left floating (in their own window). A toolbar moved to the edge of the window will dock along that edge. A toolbar moved anywhere else in the window will float in its own window. Docked toolbars are one tool wide (high), whereas floating toolbars can be resized by clicking and dragging a border or corner as you would with any other window.
  - To move a docked toolbar, click anywhere in the gray background area and drag the toolbar to its new location.
  - To move a floating toolbar, drag its title bar to its new location.
- To customize one or more toolbars, display the toolbar(s) on the screen, pull down the View menu, click Toolbars, and click the Customize command button. Alternatively, you can click on any toolbar with the right mouse button, and then select Customize from the shortcut menu.
  - To move a button, drag the button to its new location on that toolbar or any other displayed toolbar.
  - To delete a button, drag the button off the toolbar and release the mouse button.
  - To add a button, select the category from the Categories list box and then drag the button to the desired location on the toolbar. (To see a description of a tool's function prior to adding it to a toolbar, click the tool in the Customize dialog box and read the displayed description.)
  - To restore a predefined toolbar to its default appearance, pull down the View menu, click Toolbars, select (highlight) the desired toolbar, and click the Reset command button.
- To create a new toolbar that can be displayed for any database, pull down the View menu and click Toolbars, then select either the Utility1 or Utility2 toolbar, which is initially one tool wide and empty. (Alternatively, you can click any toolbar with the right mouse button and select Toolbars from the shortcut menu.) Add, move, and delete tools following the same procedure as outlined above. The toolbar will automatically resize itself as new tools are added and deleted.
- To create a toolbar that can be displayed only in the database in which it was created, pull down the View menu, click Toolbar, and click the New command button. Alternatively, you can click on any toolbar with the right mouse button, select Toolbars from the shortcut menu, and then click the New command button.
  - Enter a name for the toolbar in the dialog box that follows. The name can be any length and can contain spaces.
  - The new toolbar will appear at the top left of the screen. Initially it will be big enough to hold only one button. Add, move, and delete buttons fol-

lowing the same procedures as outlined above. The toolbar will automatically size itself as new buttons are added and deleted.

- To delete a custom toolbar, pull down the View menu, click Toolbars, and make sure that the custom toolbar to be deleted is the only one selected (highlighted). Click the Delete command button and respond Yes to confirm the deletion. (Note that a predefined toolbar cannot be deleted.)
- You may also quickly create a custom toolbar by dragging a button from the Customize window to any location on the screen other than a toolbar. The new toolbar will initially be one tool wide, and it will contain only the one tool. It will be named Toolbar, where *x* is the next sequential number available.

SOME TOOLS ARE DIM

We don't know why, but Microsoft chose to include several buttons on various toolbars that are rarely accessible. These buttons are dimmed initially. We reproduced the toolbars in this fashion so that our figures will match what you see on your monitor. We did, however, omit the captions from the dimmed buttons since they are rarely (if ever) used.

Database Toolbar

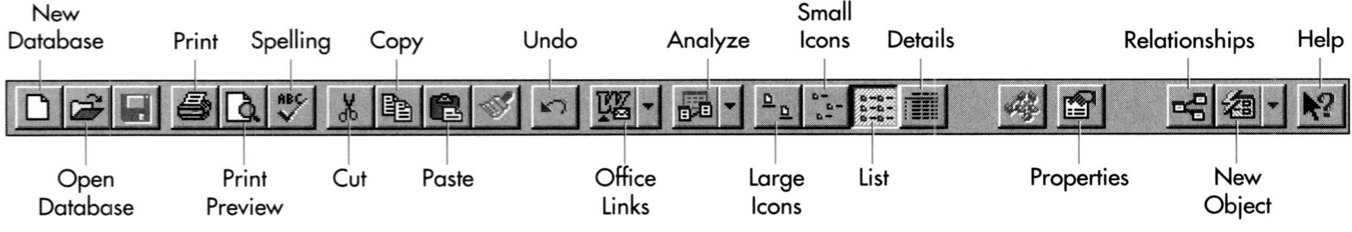

Relationships Toolbar

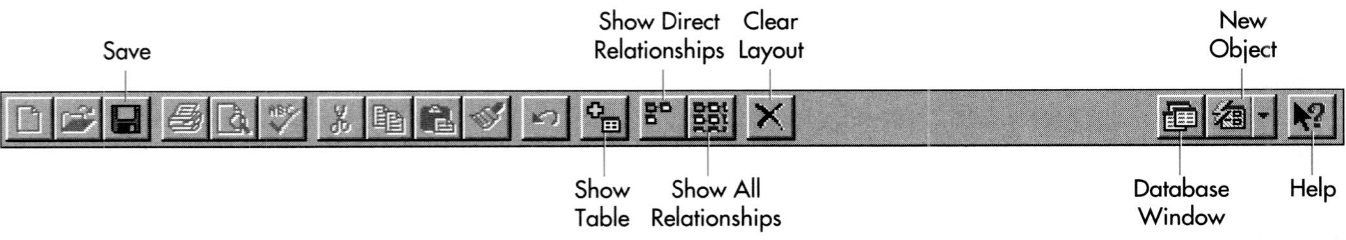

Table Design Toolbar

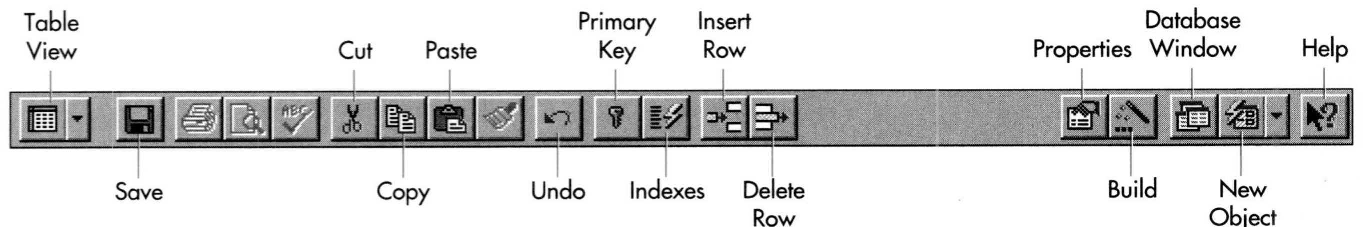

FIGURE A.1 Access Toolbars Tied to Specific Views

Table Datasheet Toolbar

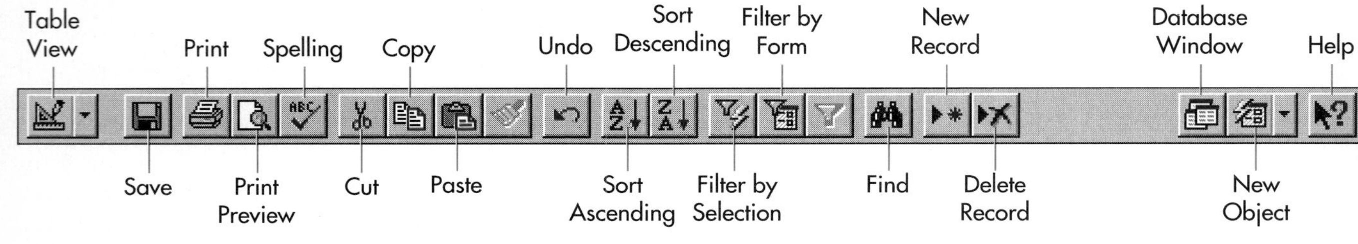

Query Design Toolbar

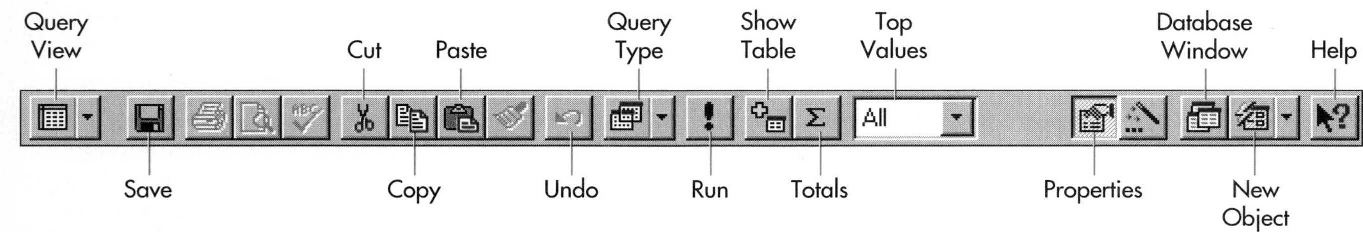

Query Datasheet Toolbar

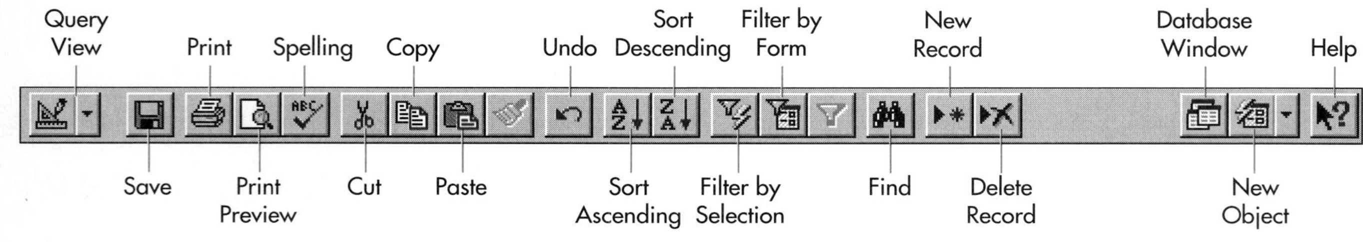

Form Design Toolbar

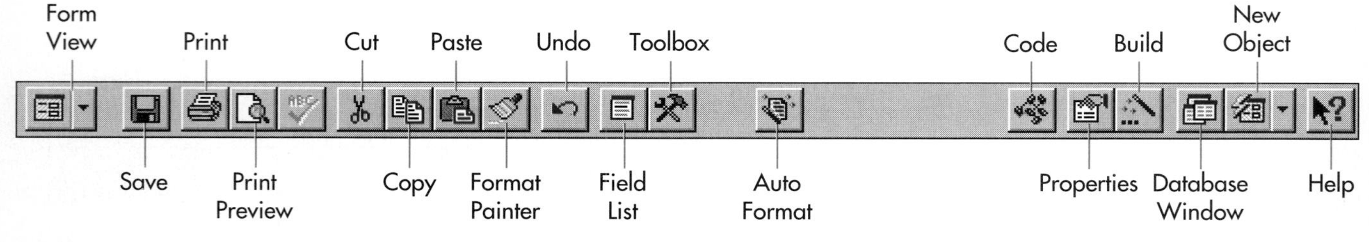

Form View Toolbar

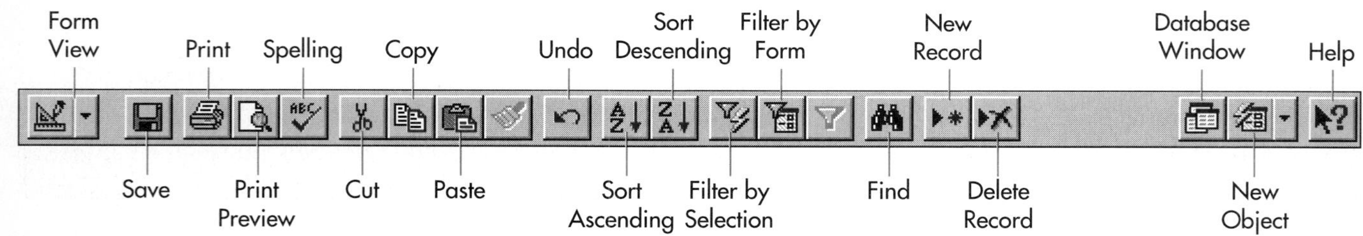

FIGURE A.1 Access Toolbars Tied to Specific Views (continued)

Report Design Toolbar

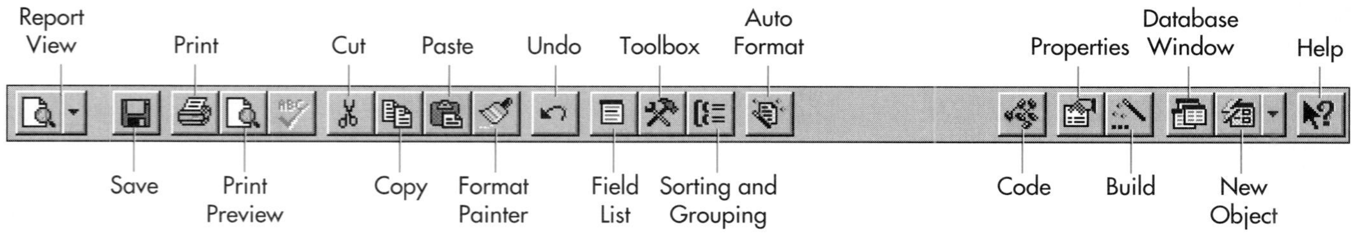

Print Preview Toolbar

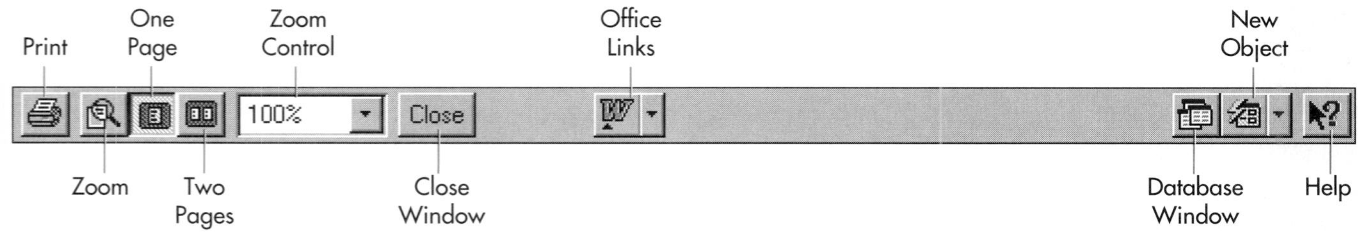

Macro Toolbar

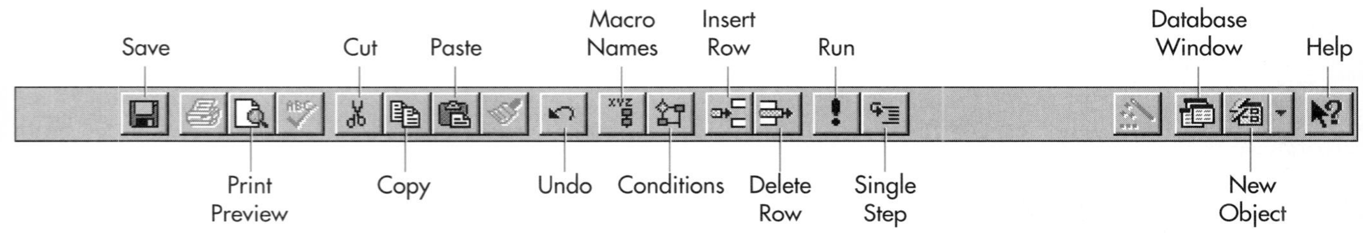

FIGURE A.1 Access Toolbars Tied to Specific Views (continued)

Toolbox Toolbar

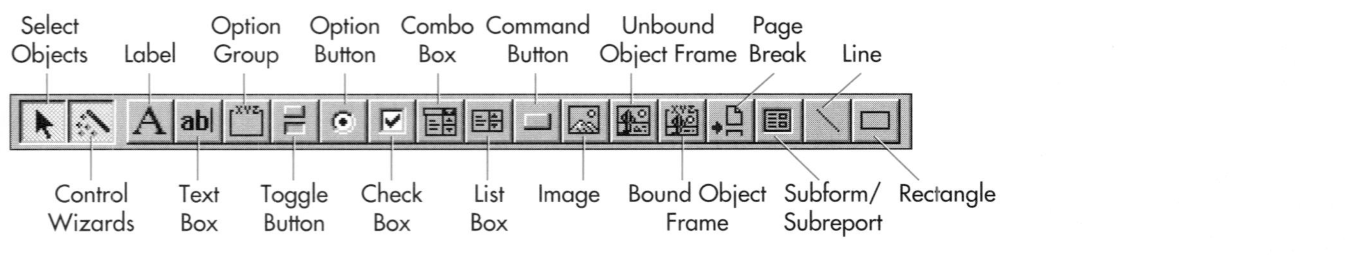

Formatting (Form/Report Design) Toolbar

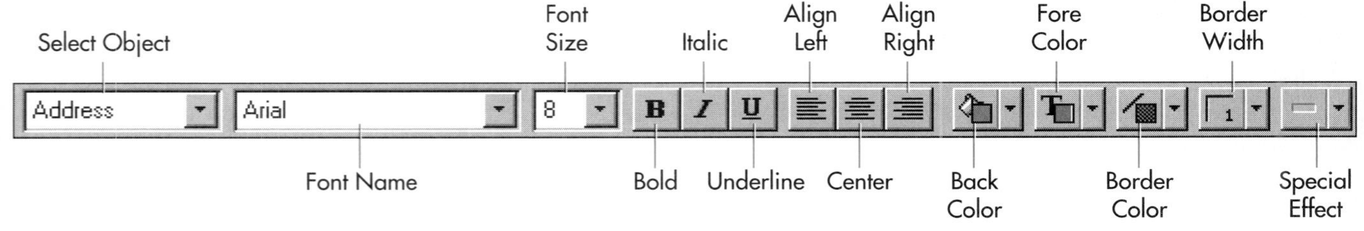

FIGURE A.2 Other Access Toolbars

Formatting (Datasheet) Toolbar

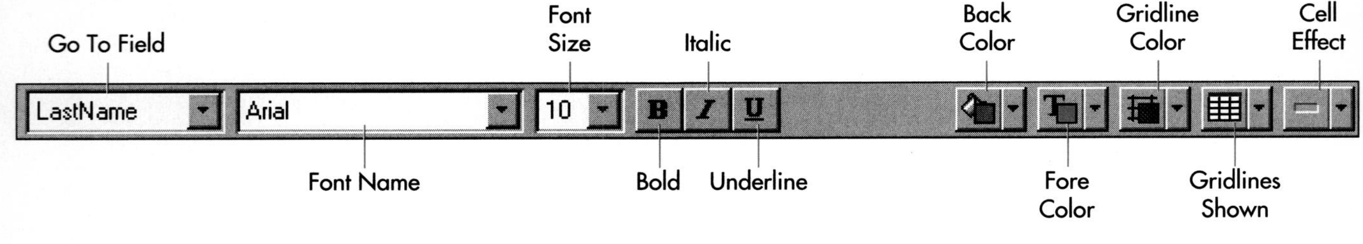

Microsoft Toolbar

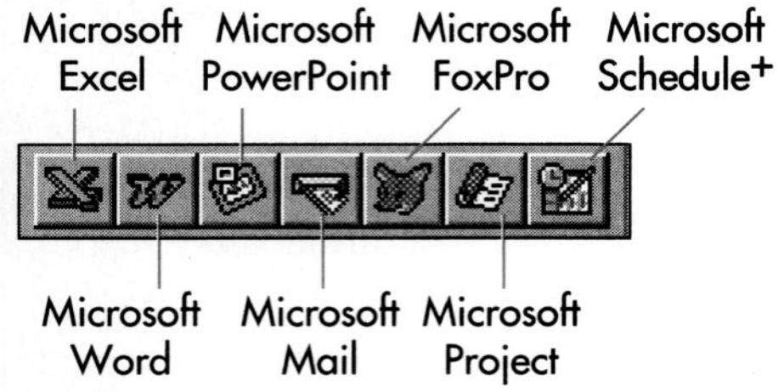

FIGURE A.2 Other Access Toolbars (continued)

B

APPENDIX B: DATABASE DESIGN—GETTING THE MOST FROM MICROSOFT ACCESS

OVERVIEW

An Access database consists of multiple tables, each of which stores data about a specific subject. To use Access effectively, you must relate the tables to one another. This in turn requires a knowledge of database design and an understanding of the principles of a relational database under which Access operates.

Our approach to teaching database design is to present two case studies, each of which covers a common application. (Additional case studies are presented in Chapters 1 and 2.) The first case centers on franchises for fast food restaurants and incorporates the concept of a one-to-many relationship. One person can own many restaurants, but a given restaurant is owned by only one person. The second case is based on a system for student transcripts and incorporates a many-to-many relationship. One student takes many courses, and one course is taken by many students. The intent in both cases is to design a database capable of producing the desired information.

CASE STUDY: FAST FOOD FRANCHISES

The case you are about to read is set within the context of a national corporation offering franchises for fast food restaurants. The concept of a franchise operation is a familiar one and exists within many industries. The parent organization develops a model operation, then franchises that concept to qualified individuals (franchisees) seeking to operate their own businesses. The national company teaches the franchisee to run the business, aids the person in site selection and staffing, coordinates national advertising, and so on. The franchisee pays an initial fee to open the business followed by subsequent royalties and marketing fees to the parent corporation.

The essence of the case is how to relate the data for the various entities (the restaurants, franchisees, and contracts) to one another. One approach is to develop a single restaurant table, with each restaurant record containing data about the owner and contract arrangement. As we shall see, that design leads to problems of redundancy whenever the same person owns more than one restaurant or when several restaurants are governed by the same contract type. A better approach is to develop separate tables, one for each of the objects (restaurants, franchisees, and contracts).

The entities in the case have a definite relationship to one another, which must be reflected in the database design. The corporation encourages individuals to own multiple restaurants, creating a ***one-to-many relationship*** between franchisees and restaurants. One person can own many restaurants, but a given restaurant is owned by only one person. There is also a one-to-many relationship between contracts and restaurants because the corporation offers a choice of contracts to each restaurant.

The company wants a database that can retrieve all data for a given restaurant, such as the annual sales, type of contract in effect (contract types are described below), and/or detailed information about the restaurant owner. The company also needs reports that reflect the location of each restaurant, all restaurants in a given state, and all restaurants managed by a particular contract type. The various contract arrangements are described below:

Contract 1: 99-year term, requiring a one-time fee of $250,000 payable at the time the franchise is awarded. In addition, the franchisee must pay a royalty of 2 percent of the restaurant's gross sales to the parent corporation, and contribute an additional 2 percent of sales to the parent corporation for advertising.

Contract 2: 5-year term (renewable at franchisee's option), requiring an initial payment of $50,000. In addition, the franchisee must pay a royalty of 4 percent of the restaurant's gross sales to the parent corporation, and contribute an additional 3 percent of sales to the parent corporation for advertising.

Contract 3: 10-year term (renewable at franchisee's option), requiring an initial payment of $75,000. In addition, the franchisee must pay a royalty of 3 percent of the restaurant's gross sales to the parent corporation, and contribute an additional 3 percent of sales to the parent corporation for advertising.

Other contract types may be offered in the future. The company currently has 500 restaurants, of which 200 are company owned. Expansion plans call for opening an additional 200 restaurants each year for the next three years, all of which are to be franchised. There is no limit on the number of restaurants an individual may own, and franchisees are encouraged to apply for multiple restaurants.

Single Table Solution

The initial concern in this, or any other, system is how best to structure the data so that the solution satisfies the information requirements of the client. We present two solutions. The first is based on a single restaurant table and will be shown to have several limitations. The second introduces the concept of a relational database and consists of three tables (for the restaurants, franchisee, and contracts).

The single table solution is shown in Figure B.1a. Each record within the table contains data about a particular restaurant, its franchisees (owner), and contract type. There are five restaurants in our example, each with a *unique* restaurant number. At first glance, Figure B.1a appears satisfactory; yet there are three specific types of problems associated with this solution. These are:

1. Difficulties in the modification of data for an existing franchisee or contract type, in that the same change may be made in multiple places.

Restaurant Number	Restaurant Data (Address, annual sales . . .)	Franchisee Data (Name, telephone, address . . .)	Contract Data (Type, term, initial fee . . .)
R1	Restaurant data for Miami . . .	Franchisee data (Grauer . . .)	Contract data (Type 1 . . .)
R2	Restaurant data for Coral Gables . . .	Franchisee data (Moldof . . .)	Contract data (Type 1 . . .)
R3	Restaurant data for Fort Lauderdale. . .	Franchisee data (Grauer . . .)	Contract data (Type 2 . . .)
R4	Restaurant data for New York . . .	Franchisee data (Glassman . . .)	Contract data (Type 1 . . .)
R5	Restaurant data for Coral Springs . . .	Franchisee data (Coulter . . .)	Contract data (Type 3 . . .)

(a) Single Table Solution

Restaurant Number	Restaurant Data	Franchisee Number	Contract Type
R1	Restaurant data for Miami . . .	F1	C1
R2	Restaurant data for Coral Gables . . .	F2	C1
R3	Restaurant data for Fort Lauderdale. . .	F1	C2
R4	Restaurant data for New York . . .	F3	C1
R5	Restaurant data for Coral Springs . . .	F4	C3

Contract Type	Contract Data
C1	Contract data. . .
C2	Contract data. . .
C3	Contract data. . .

Franchisee Number	Franchisee Data (Name, telephone, address, . . .)
F1	Grauer. . .
F2	Moldof. . .
F3	Glassman. . .
F4	Coulter. . .

(b) Multiple Table Solution

FIGURE B.1 Single versus Multiple Table Solution

2. Difficulties in the addition of a new franchisee or contract type, in that these entities must first be associated with a particular restaurant.
3. Difficulties in the deletion of a restaurant, in that data for a particular franchisee or contract type may be deleted as well.

The first problem, modification of data about an existing franchisee or contract type, stems from ***redundancy,*** which in turn requires that any change to duplicated data be made in several places. In other words, any modification to a duplicated entry, such as a change in data for a franchisee with multiple restaurants (e.g., Grauer, who owns restaurants in Miami and Fort Lauderdale), requires a search through the entire table to find all instances of that data so that the identical modification can be made to each of the records. A similar procedure would have to be followed should data change about a duplicated contract (e.g., a change in the royalty percentage for contract Type 1, which applies to restaurants R1, R2, and R4). This is, to say the least, a time-consuming and error-prone procedure.

The addition of a new franchisee or contract type poses a different type of problem. It is quite logical, for example, that potential franchisees must apply to the corporation and qualify for ownership before having a restaurant assigned to them. It is also likely that the corporation would develop a new contract type prior to offering that contract to an existing restaurant. Neither of these events is easily accommodated in the table structure of Figure B.1a, which would require the creation of a dummy restaurant record to accommodate the new franchisee or contract type.

The deletion of a restaurant creates yet another type of difficulty. What happens, for example, if the company decides to close restaurant R5 because of insufficient sales? The record for this restaurant would disappear as expected, but so too would the data for the franchisee (Coulter) and the contract type (C3), which is not intended. The corporation might want to award Coulter another restaurant in the future and/or offer this contract type to other restaurants. Neither situation would be possible as the relevant data has been lost with the deletion of the restaurant record.

Multiple Table Solution

A much better solution appears in Figure B.1b, which uses a different table for each of the entities (restaurants, franchisees, and contracts) that exist in the system. Every record in the restaurant table is assigned a unique restaurant number (e.g., R1 or R2), just as every record in the franchisee table is given a unique franchisee number (e.g., F1 or F2), and every contract record a unique contract number (e.g., C1 or C2).

The tables are linked to one another through the franchisee and/or contract numbers, which also appear in the restaurant table. Every record in the restaurant table is associated with its appropriate record in the franchisee table through the franchisee number common to both tables. In similar fashion, every restaurant is tied to its appropriate contract through the contract number, which appears in the restaurant record. This solution may seem complicated, but it is really quite simple and elegant.

Assume, for example, that we want the name of the franchisee for restaurant R5, and further, that we need the details of the contract type for this restaurant. We retrieve the appropriate restaurant record, which contains franchisee and contract numbers of F4 and C3, respectively. We then search through the franchisee table for franchisee F4 (obtaining all necessary information about Coulter) and search again through the contract table for contract C3 (obtaining the data for this contract type). The process is depicted graphically in Figure B.1b.

The multiple table solution may require slightly more effort to retrieve information, but this is more than offset by the advantages of table maintenance. Consider, for example, a change in data for contract C1, which currently governs restaurants R1, R2, and R4. All that is necessary is to go into the contract table, find record C1, and make the changes. The records in the restaurant table are *not* affected because the restaurant records do not contain contract data per se, only the number of the corresponding contract record. In other words, the change in data for contract C1 is made in one place (the contract table), yet that change would be reflected for all affected restaurants. This is in contrast to the single table solution of Figure B.1a, which would require the identical modification in three places.

The addition of new records for franchisees or contracts is done immediately in the appropriate tables of Figure B.1b. The corporation simply adds a franchisee or contract record as these events occur, without the necessity of a corresponding restaurant record. This is much easier than the approach of Figure B.1a, which required an existing restaurant in order to add one of the other entities.

The deletion of a restaurant is also easier than with the single table organization. You could, for example, delete restaurant R5 without losing the associated franchisee and contract data as these records exist in different tables.

Queries to the Database

By now you should be convinced of the need for multiple tables within a database and that this type of design facilitates all types of table maintenance. However, the ultimate objective of any system is to produce information, and it is in this area that the design excels. Consider now Figure B.2, which expands upon the multiple table solution to include additional data for the respective tables.

To be absolutely sure you understand the multiple table solution of Figure B.2, use it to answer the questions at the top of the next page. Check your answers with those provided.

Restaurant Number	Street Address	City	State	Zip Code	Annual Sales	Franchisee Number	Contract Type
R1	1001 Ponce de Leon Blvd	Miami	FL	33361	$600,000	F1	C1
R2	31 West Rivo Alto Road	Coral Gables	FL	33139	$450,000	F2	C1
R3	333 Las Olas Blvd	Fort Lauderdale	FL	33033	$250,000	F1	C2
R4	1700 Broadway	New York	NY	10293	$1,750,000	F3	C1
R5	1300 Sample Road	Coral Springs	FL	33071	$50,000	F4	C3

(a) Restaurant Table

Franchisee Number	Franchisee Name	Telephone	Street Address	City	State	Zip Code
F1	Grauer	(305) 755-1000	2133 NW 102 Terrace	Coral Springs	FL	33071
F2	Moldof	(305) 753-4614	1400 Lejeune Blvd	Miami	FL	33365
F3	Glassman	(212) 458-5054	555 Fifth Avenue	New York	NY	10024
F4	Coulter	(305) 755-0910	1000 Federal Highway	Fort Lauderdale	FL	33033

(b) Franchisee Table

Contract Type	Term (years)	Initial Fee	Royalty Pct	Advertising Pct
C1	99	$250,000	2%	2%
C2	5	$50,000	4%	3%
C3	10	$75,000	3%	3%

(c) Contract Table

FIGURE B.2 Fast Food Franchises

Questions

1. Who owns restaurant R2? What contract type is in effect for this restaurant?
2. What is the address of restaurant R4?
3. Which restaurant(s) are owned by Mr. Grauer?
4. List all restaurants with a contract type of C1.
5. Which restaurants in Florida have gross sales over $300,000?
6. List all contract types.
7. Which contract type has the lowest initial fee? How much is the initial fee? Which restaurant(s) are governed by this contract?
8. How many franchisees are there? What are their names?
9. What are the royalty and advertising percentages for restaurant R3?

Answers

1. Restaurant R2 is owned by Moldof and governed by contract C1.
2. Restaurant R4 is located at 1700 Broadway, New York, NY 10293.
3. Mr. Grauer owns restaurants R1 and R3.
4. R1, R2, and R4 are governed by contract C1.
5. The restaurants in Florida with gross sales over $300,000 are R1 ($600,000) and R2 ($450,000).
6. The existing contract types are C1, C2, and C3.
7. Contract C2 has the lowest initial fee ($50,000); restaurant R3 is governed by this contract type.
8. There are four franchisees: Grauer, Moldof, Glassman, and Coulter.
9. Restaurant R3 is governed by contract C2 with royalty and advertising percentages of four and three percent, respectively.

THE RELATIONAL MODEL

The restaurant case study illustrates a ***relational database,*** which requires a separate table for every entity in the physical system (restaurants, franchisees, and contracts). Each occurrence of an entity (a specific restaurant, franchisee, or contract type) appears as a ***row*** within a table. The properties of an entity (a restaurant's address, owner, or sales) appear as ***columns*** within a table.

Every row in every table of a relational database must be distinct. This is accomplished by including a column (or combination of columns) to uniquely identify the row. The unique identifier is known as the ***primary key.*** The restaurant number, for example, is different for every restaurant in the restaurant table. The franchisee number is unique in the franchisee table. The contract type is unique in the contract table.

The same column can, however, appear in multiple tables. The franchisee number, for example, appears in both the franchisee table, where its values are unique, and in the restaurant table, where they are not. The franchisee number is the primary key in the franchisee table, but it is a ***foreign key*** in the restaurant table. (A foreign key is simply the primary key of a related table.)

The inclusion of a foreign key in the restaurant table enables us to implement the one-to-many relationship between franchisees and restaurants. We enter the franchisee number (the primary key in the franchisee table) as a column in the restaurant table, where it (the franchisee number) is a foreign key. In similar fashion, contract type (the primary key in the contract table) appears as a foreign key in the restaurant table to implement the one-to-many relationship between contracts and restaurants.

It is helpful perhaps to restate these observations about a relational database in general terms:

1. Every entity in a physical system requires its own table in a database.
2. Each row in a table is different from every other row because of a unique column (or combination of columns) known as a primary key.
3. The primary key of one table can appear as a foreign key in another table.
4. The order of rows in a table is immaterial.
5. The order of columns in a table is immaterial, although the primary key is generally listed first.
6. The number of columns is the same in every row of the table.

THE KEY, THE WHOLE KEY, AND NOTHING BUT THE KEY

The theory of a relational database was developed by Dr. Edgar Codd, giving rise to the phrase, "*The key, the whole key, and nothing but the key . . . so help me Codd.*" The sentence effectively summarizes the concepts behind a relational database and helps to ensure the validity of a design. Simply stated, the value of every column other than the primary key depends on the key in that row, on the entire key, and on nothing but that key.

Referential Integrity

The concept of ***referential integrity*** requires that the tables in a database be consistent with one another. Consider once again the first row in the restaurant table of Figure B.2a, which indicates that the restaurant is owned by franchisee F1 and governed by contract Type C1. Recall also how these values are used to obtain additional information about the franchisee or contract type from the appropriate tables in Figures B.2b and B.2c, respectively.

What if, however, the restaurant table referred to franchisee number F1000 or contract C9, neither of which exists in the database of Figure B.2? There would be a problem because the tables would be inconsistent with one another; that is, the restaurant table would refer to rows in the franchisee and contract tables that do not exist. It is important, therefore, that referential integrity be strictly enforced and that such inconsistencies be prevented from occurring. Suffice it to say that data validation is critical when establishing or maintaining a database, and that no system, relational or otherwise, can compensate for inaccurate or incomplete data.

CASE STUDY: STUDENT TRANSCRIPTS

Our second case is set within the context of student transcripts and expands the concept of a relational database to implement a ***many-to-many relationship.*** The system is intended to track students and the courses they take. The many-to-many relationship occurs because one student takes many courses, while at the same time, one course is taken by many students. The objective of this case is to relate the student and course tables to one another to produce the desired information.

The system should be able to display information about a particular student as well as information about a particular course. It should also display information about a student-course combination, such as when a student took the course and the grade he or she received.

Solution

The (intuitive and incorrect) solution of Figure B.3 consists of two tables, one for courses and one for students, corresponding to the two entities in the physical system. The student table contains the student's name, address, major, date of entry into the school, cumulative credits, and cumulative quality points. The course table contains the unique six-character course identifier, the course title, and the number of credits.

There are no problems of redundancy. The data for a particular course (its description and number of credits) appears only once in the course table, just as the data for a particular student appears only once in the student table. New courses will be added directly to the course table, just as new students will be added to the student table.

The design of the student table makes it easy to list all courses for one student. It is more difficult, however, to list all students in one course. Even if this were not the case, the solution is complicated by the irregular shape of the student table. The rows in the table are of variable length, according to the number of courses taken by each student. Not only is this design awkward, but how do we know in advance how much space to allocate for each student?

Course Number	Course Description	Credits
ACC101	Introduction to Accounting	3
CHM100	Survey of Chemistry	3
CHM101	Chemistry Lab	1
CIS120	Microcomputer Applications	3
ENG100	Freshman English	3
MTH100	Calculus with Analytic Geometry	4
MUS110	Music Appreciation	2
SPN100	Spanish I	3

(a) Course Table

Student Number	Student Data	Courses Taken with Grade and Semester											
S1	Student data (Adams. . .)	ACC101	SP95	A	CIS120	FA94	A	MU100	SP94	B			
S2	Student data (Fox. . .)	ENG100	SP95	B	MTH100	SP95	B	SPN100	SP95	B	CIS120	FA94	A
S3	Student data (Baker. . .)	ACC101	SP95	C	ENG100	SP95	B	MTH100	FA94	C	CIS120	FA94	B
S4	Student data (Jones. . .)	ENG100	SP95	A	MTH100	SP95	A						
S5	Student data (Smith. . .)	CIS120	SP95	C	ENG100	SP95	B	CIS120	FA94	F			

(b) Student Table

FIGURE B.3 Student Transcripts (repeating groups)

The problems inherent in Figure B.3 stem from the many-to-many relationship that exists between students and courses. The solution is to eliminate the ***repeating groups*** (course number, semester, and grade), which occur in each row of the student table in Figure B.3, in favor of the additional table shown in Figure B.4. Each row in the new table is unique because the *combination* of student number, course number, and semester is unique. Semester must be included since students are allowed to repeat a course. Smith (student number S5), for example, took CIS120 a second time after failing it initially.

The implementation of a many-to-many relationship requires an additional table, with a ***combined key*** consisting of (at least) the keys of the individual entities. The many-to-many table may also contain additional columns, which exist as a result of the combination (intersection) of the individual keys. The combination of student S5, course CIS120, and semester SP95 is unique and results in a grade of C.

Note, too, how the design in Figure B.4 facilitates table maintenance as discussed in the previous case. A change in student data is made in only one place (the student table) regardless of how many courses the student has taken. A new student may be added to the student table prior to taking any courses. In similar fashion, a new course can be added to the course table before any students have taken the course.

Review once more the properties of a relational database, then verify that the solution in Figure B.4 adheres to these requirements. To be absolutely sure

Course Number	Course Description	Credits
ACC101	Introduction to Accounting	3
CHM100	Survey of Chemistry	3
CHM101	Chemistry Lab	1
CIS120	Microcomputer Applications	3
ENG100	Freshman English	3
MTH100	Calculus with Analytic Geometry	4
MUS110	Music Appreciation	2
SPN100	Spanish I	3

(a) Course Table

Student Number	Student Data
S1	Student data (Adams. . .)
S2	Student data (Fox. . .)
S3	Student data (Baker. . .)
S4	Student data (Jones. . .)
S5	Student data (Smith. . .)

(b) Student Table

Student Number	Course Number	Semester	Grade
S1	ACC101	SP95	A
S1	CIS120	FA94	A
S1	MU100	SP94	B
S2	ENG100	SP95	B
S2	MTH100	SP95	B
S2	SPN100	SP95	B
S2	CIS120	FA94	A
S3	ACC101	SP95	C
S3	ENG100	SP95	B
S3	MTH100	FA94	C
S3	CIS120	FA94	B
S4	ENG100	SP95	A
S4	MTH100	SP95	A
S5	CIS120	SP95	C
S5	ENG100	SP95	B
S5	CIS120	FA94	F

(c) Student-Course Table

FIGURE B.4 Student Transcripts (improved design)

that you understand the solution, and to illustrate once again the power of the relational model, use Figure B.4 to answer the following questions about the student database.

Questions

1. How many courses are currently offered?
2. List all three-credit courses.
3. Which courses has Smith taken during his stay at the university?
4. Which students have taken MTH100?
5. Which courses did Adams take during the Fall 1994 semester?
6. Which students took Microcomputer Applications in the Fall 1994 semester?
7. Which students received an A in Freshman English during the Spring 1995 semester?

Answers

1. Eight courses are offered.
2. The three-credit courses are ACC101, CHM100, CIS120, ENG100, and SPN100.
3. Smith has taken CIS120 (twice) and ENG100.
4. Fox, Baker, and Jones have taken MTH100.
5. Adams took CIS120 during the Fall 1994 semester.
6. Adams, Fox, Baker, and Smith took Microcomputer Applications in the Fall 1994 semester.
7. Jones was the only student to receive an A in Freshman English during the Spring 1995 semester.

SUMMARY

A relational database consists of multiple two-dimensional tables. Each entity in a physical system requires its own table in the database. Every row in a table is unique due to the existence of a primary key. The order of the rows and columns in a table is immaterial. Every row in a table contains the same columns in the same order as every other row.

A one-to-many relationship is implemented by including the primary key of one table as a foreign key in the other table. Implementation of a many-to-many relationship requires an additional table whose primary key combines (at a minimum) the primary keys of the individual tables. Referential integrity ensures that the information in a database is internally consistent.

KEY WORDS AND CONCEPTS

Column
Combined key
Entity
Foreign key
Many-to-many relationship
One-to-many relationship
Primary key
Query
Redundancy
Referential integrity
Relational database
Repeating group
Row
Table

C

APPENDIX C: COMBINING AN ACCESS DATABASE WITH A WORD FORM LETTER

OVERVIEW

One of the greatest benefits of using the Microsoft Office suite is the ability to combine data from one application with another. An excellent example is a ***mail merge,*** in which data from an Access ***table*** or ***query*** are input into a Word document to produce a set of individualized form letters. You create the ***form letter*** using Microsoft Word, then you merge the letter with the ***records*** in the Access table or query. The merge process creates the individual letters, changing the name, address, and other information as appropriate from letter to letter. The concept is illustrated in Figure C.1, in which John Smith uses a mail merge to seek a job upon graduation. John writes the letter describing his qualifications, then merges that letter with a set of names and addresses to produce the individual letters.

The mail merge process uses two input files (a main document and a data source) and produces a third file as output (the set of form letters). The ***main document*** (e.g., the cover letter in Figure C.1a) contains standardized text together with one or more ***merge fields*** that indicate where the variable information is to be inserted in the individual letters. The ***data source*** (the set of names and addresses in Figure C.1b) contains the data that varies from letter to letter and is a table (or query) within an Access database. (The data source may also be taken from an Excel list, or alternatively it can be created as a table in Microsoft Word. See Appendix B in the section on Microsoft Word, pages 113–126.)

The main document and the data source work in conjunction with one another, with the merge fields in the main document referencing the corresponding fields in the data source. The first line in the address of Figure C.1a, for example, contains three merge fields, each of which is enclosed in angle brackets, *<<Title>>* *<<FirstName>>* *<<LastName>>*. (These entries are not typed explicitly but are entered through special commands as described in the hands-on exercise that follows shortly.) The merge process examines each record in the data

John H. Smith

426 Jenny Lake Drive • Coral Gables, FL 33146 • (305) 666-4801

March 31, 1996

<<Title>> <<FirstName>> <<LastName>>
<<JobTitle>>
<<Company>>
<<Address1>>
<<City>>, <<State>> <<PostalCode>>

Dear <<Title>> <<LastName>>:

I am writing to inquire about a position with <<Company>> as an entry-level computer programmer. I have just graduated from the University of Miami with a bachelor's degree in Computer Information Systems (May 1995), and I am very interested in working for you. I have a background in both microcomputer applications (Windows 95, Word, Excel, PowerPoint, and Access) as well as extensive experience with programming languages (Visual Basic, C++, and COBOL). I feel that I am well qualified to join your staff as over the past two years I have had a great deal of experience designing and implementing computer programs, both as a part of my educational program and during my internship with Personalized Computer Designs, Inc.

I am eager to put my skills to work and would like to talk with you at your earliest convenience. I have enclosed a copy of my résumé and will be happy to furnish the names and addresses of my references, if you so desire. You may reach me at the above address and phone number. I look forward to hearing from you.

Sincerely,

John H. Smith

(a) The Form Letter (a Word document)

FIGURE C.1 The Mail Merge

source and substitutes the appropriate field values for the corresponding merge fields as it creates the individual form letters. For example, the first three fields in the first record will produce *Mr. Jason Frasher;* the same fields in the second record will produce, *Ms. Lauren Howard,* and so on.

In similar fashion, the second line in the address contains the *<<JobTitle>>* field. The third line contains the *<<Company>>* field. The fourth line references the *<<Address1>>* field, and the last line contains the *<<City>>, <<State>,* and *<<Postalcode>>* fields. The salutation repeats the *<<Title>>* and *<<LastName>>* fields. The first sentence in the letter uses the *<<Company>>* field a second time. The mail merge prepares the letters one at a time, with one letter created for every record in the data source until the file of names and addresses is exhausted. The individual form letters are shown in Figure C.1c. Each letter begins automatically on a new page.

	Title	First Name	Last Name	JobTitle	Company	Address1	City	State	Postal Code
▶	Mr	Jason	Frasher	President	Frasher Systems	100 S. Miami Avenue	Miami	FL	33103-
	Ms.	Lauren	Howard	Director of Human Resources	Unique Systems	475 LeJeune Road	Coral Gables	FL	33146-
	Ms.	Elizabeth	Scherry	Director of Personnel	Custom Computing	8180 Kendall Drive	Miami	FL	33156-
*									

Contacts : Table — Record: 1 of 3

(b) The Data Source (an Access Table or Query)

John H. Smith

426 Jenny Lake Drive • Coral Gables, FL 33146 • (305) 666-4801

March 31, 1996

Ms. Elizabeth Scherry
Director of Personnel
Custom Computing
8180 Kendall Drive
Miami, FL 33156

Dear Ms. Scherry:

I am writing to inquire about a position with Custom Computing as an entry-level computer programmer. I have just graduated from the U
Computer Information Systems (May 1995), a
background in both microcomputer applicatio
Access) as well as extensive experience with p
COBOL). I feel that I am well qualified to jo
great deal of experience designing and implem
educational program and during my internship

I am eager to put my skills to work and woul
have enclosed a copy of my résumé and will b
references, if you so desire. You may reach m
forward to hearing from you.

Sincerely,

John H. Smith

John H. Smith

426 Jenny Lake Drive • Coral Gables, FL 33146 • (305) 666-4801

March 31, 1996

Ms. Lauren Howard
Director of Human Resources
Unique Systems
475 LeJeune Road
Coral Gables, FL 33146

Dear Ms. Howard:

I am writing to inquire about a position with Unique Systems as an entry-level computer programmer. I have just graduated from th
Computer Information Systems (May 1995
background in both microcomputer applica
Access) as well as extensive experience wi
COBOL). I feel that I am well qualified to
great deal of experience designing and imp
educational program and during my intern

I am eager to put my skills to work and w
have enclosed a copy of my résumé and w
references, if you so desire. You may reac
forward to hearing from you.

Sincerely,

John H Smith

John H. Smith

426 Jenny Lake Drive • Coral Gables, FL 33146 • (305) 666-4801

March 31, 1996

Mr. Jason Frasher
President
Frasher Systems
100 S. Miami Avenue
Miami, FL 33103

Dear Mr. Frasher:

I am writing to inquire about a position with Frasher Systems as an entry-level computer programmer. I have just graduated from the University of Miami with a bachelor's degree in Computer Information Systems (May 1995), and I am very interested in working for you. I have a background in both microcomputer applications (Windows 95, Word, Excel, PowerPoint, and Access) as well as extensive experience with programming languages (Visual Basic, C++, and COBOL). I feel that I am well qualified to join your staff as over the past two years I have had a great deal of experience designing and implementing computer programs, both as a part of my educational program and during my internship with Personalized Computer Designs, Inc.

I am eager to put my skills to work and would like to talk with you at your earliest convenience. I have enclosed a copy of my résumé and will be happy to furnish the names and addresses of my references, if you so desire. You may reach me at the above address and phone number. I look forward to hearing from you.

Sincerely,

John H. Smith

(c) The Printed Letters

FIGURE C.1 The Mail Merge (continued)

Mail Merge Helper

A mail merge can be started from either ***Microsoft Word*** or ***Microsoft Access.*** Either way two input files are required—the form letter (main document) and the data source. The order in which these files are created depends on how the merge is initiated. When starting in Microsoft Word, you begin with the form letter, then create the data source. The process is reversed in Access—you start with a table or query, then exit to Word to create the form letter. The merge itself, however, is always performed from within Microsoft Word through the ***Mail Merge Helper*** as indicated in the next hands-on exercise.

The Mail Merge Helper guides you through the process. It enables you to create (or edit) the main document, to create or edit the data source, and finally, it enables you to merge the two.

> **PAPER MAKES A DIFFERENCE**
>
> Most of us take paper for granted, but the right paper can make a significant difference in the effectiveness of the document. Reports and formal correspondence are usually printed on white paper, but you would be surprised how many different shades of white there are. Other types of documents lend themselves to colored paper for additional impact. In short, the paper you use is far from an automatic decision. Our favorite source for paper is a company called Paper Direct (1-800-APAPERS). Ask for a catalog, then consider the use of a specialty paper the next time you have an important project, such as the cover letter for your résumé.

HANDS-ON EXERCISE 1

Mail Merge

Objective: To combine an Access table and a Word form letter to implement a mail merge and produce a set of form letters. Use Figure C.2 as a guide in the exercise.

STEP 1: Open the Names and Addresses Database

- Start Access. Open the **Names and Addresses** database in the **Exploring Access folder.** The **Tables tab** is selected. The **Contacts table** is the only table within the database.
- Pull down the **Tools menu,** click **Office Links** to display a cascaded menu in Figure C.2a, then click **Merge It** to begin the mail merge.
- The dialog box for the Microsoft Word Mail Merge Wizard appears after a few seconds.
- The option button to link your data to an existing Microsoft Word document is already selected. (We have created the form letter for you on the data disk.) Click **OK.**

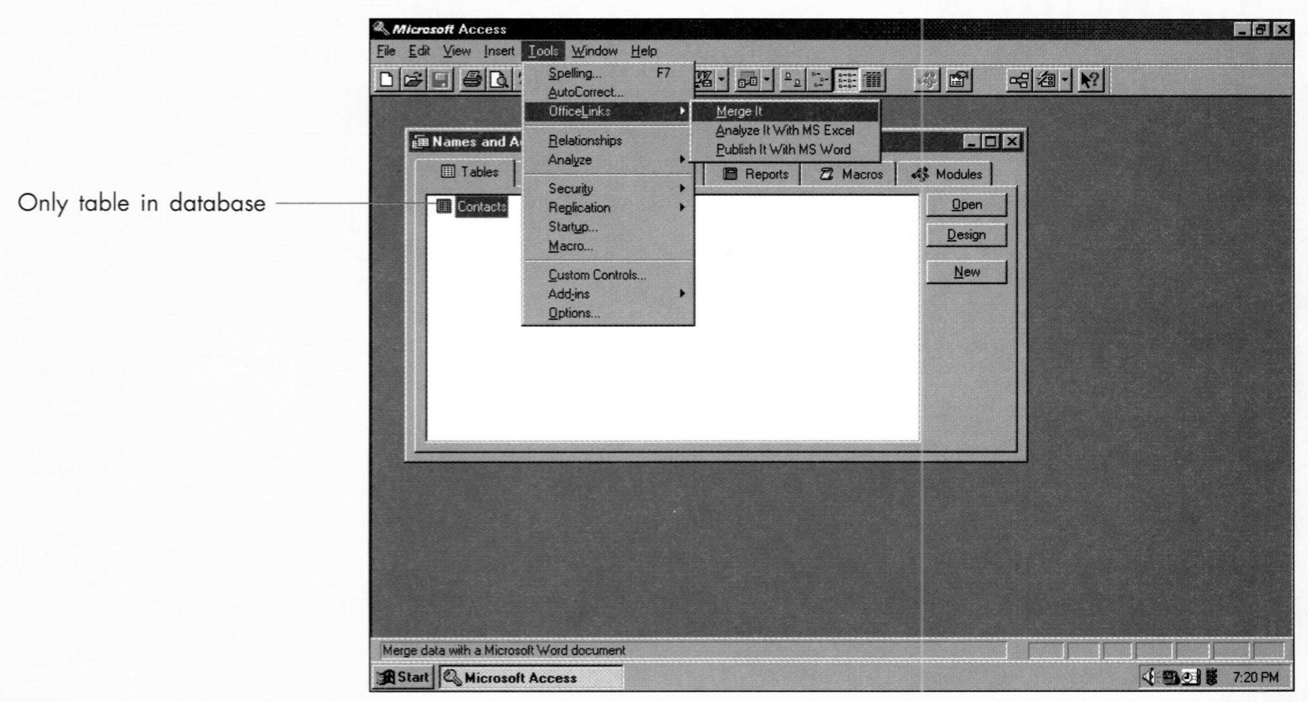

(a) Open the Database (step 1)

FIGURE C.2 Hands-on Exercise 1

STEP 2: Open the Form Letter

- ➤ You should see the dialog box to select the form letter as shown in Figure C.2b. If necessary, change to the **Exploring Access folder,** then select the **Form Letter document.** Click **Open.**
- ➤ Maximize the window containing the Word document (form letter). Pull down the **File menu,** click the **Save As** command to display the Save As dialog box, enter **Completed Form Letter** as the name of the document, then click the **Save command button.**
- ➤ There are now two identical copies of the file on disk: "Form Letter," which we supplied, and "Completed Form Letter," which you just created. The title bar references the latter, which is the document in memory. (You can always return to the original document if you modify this one beyond repair.)

THE MAIL MERGE TOOLBAR

The Microsoft Word Mail Merge toolbar is displayed automatically as soon as a merge is initiated. The toolbar contains various buttons that are used in conjunction with a mail merge and is referenced explicitly in step 5 of this exercise. Remember, too, that you can right click any toolbar in any Office application to display a shortcut menu, which enables you to explicitly display or hide the toolbars in that application.

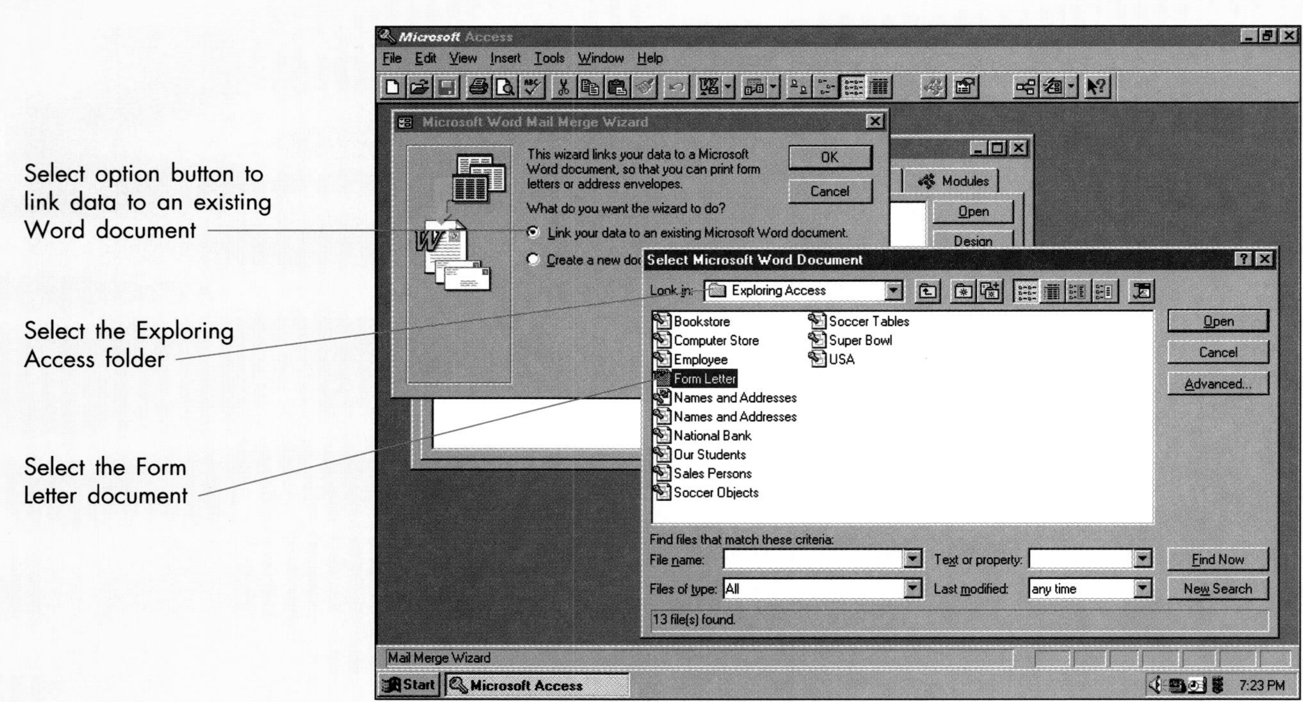

(b) Open the Form Letter (step 2)

FIGURE C.2 Hands-on Exercise 1 (continued)

STEP 3: Insert Today's Date

- The form letter should be visible on your monitor as shown in Figure C.2c.
  - If necessary, pull down the **View menu** and click **Page Layout** (or click the Page Layout button above the status bar).
  - If necessary, click the **Zoom control arrow** on the Standard toolbar to change to **Page Width.**
- Click to the left of the "D" in Dear Sir, then press **enter** twice to insert two lines. Press the **up arrow** two times to return to the first line you inserted.
- Pull down the **Insert menu** and click the **Date and Time** command to display the dialog box in Figure C.2c.
- Select (click) the date format you prefer and, if necessary, check the box to insert the date as a field. Click **OK** to close the dialog box

FIELD CODES VERSUS FIELD RESULTS

All fields in Microsoft Word are displayed in a document in one of two formats, as a ***field code*** or as a ***field result.*** A field code appears in braces and indicates instructions to insert variable data when the document is printed; a field result displays the information as it will appear in the printed document. You can toggle the display between the field code and field result by pressing Shift+F9 during editing.

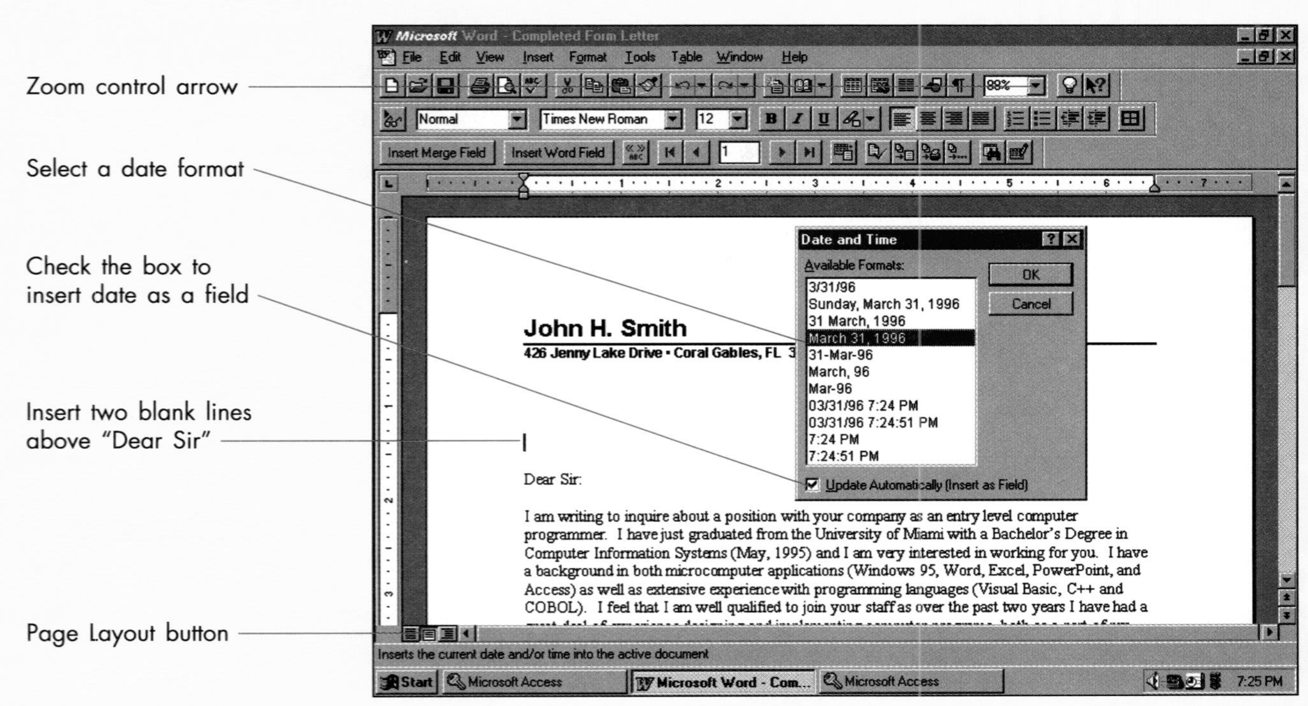

(c) Insert the Date (step 3)

FIGURE C.2 Hands-on Exercise 1 (continued)

STEP 4: Insert the Merge Fields

- Click in the document immediately below the date. Press **enter** to leave a blank line between the date and the first line of the address.
- Click the **Insert Merge Field** button on the Mail Merge toolbar to display the fields within the data source, then select (click) **Title** from the list of fields. The title field is inserted into the main document and enclosed in angle brackets as shown in Figure C.2d.
- Press the **space bar** to add a space between the words. Click the **Insert Merge Field** button a second time. Click **FirstName.** Press the **space bar.**
- Click the **Insert Merge Field** button again. Click **LastName.**
- Press **enter** to move to the next line. Enter the remaining fields in the address as shown in Figure C.2d. Be sure to add a comma as well as a space after the **City field.**
- Delete the word "Sir" in the salutation and replace it with the **Title** and **Last Name fields** separated by spaces. Delete the words "your company" in the first sentence and replace them with the **Company field.**
- Save the document.

STEP 5: The Mail Merge Toolbar

- The Mail Merge toolbar enables you to preview the form letters before they are created. Click the **<<abc>> button** on the Mail Merge toolbar to display field values rather than field codes.
- You will see, for example, Mr. Jason Frasher (instead of <<Title>> <<FirstName>> <<LastName>>) as shown in Figure C.2e

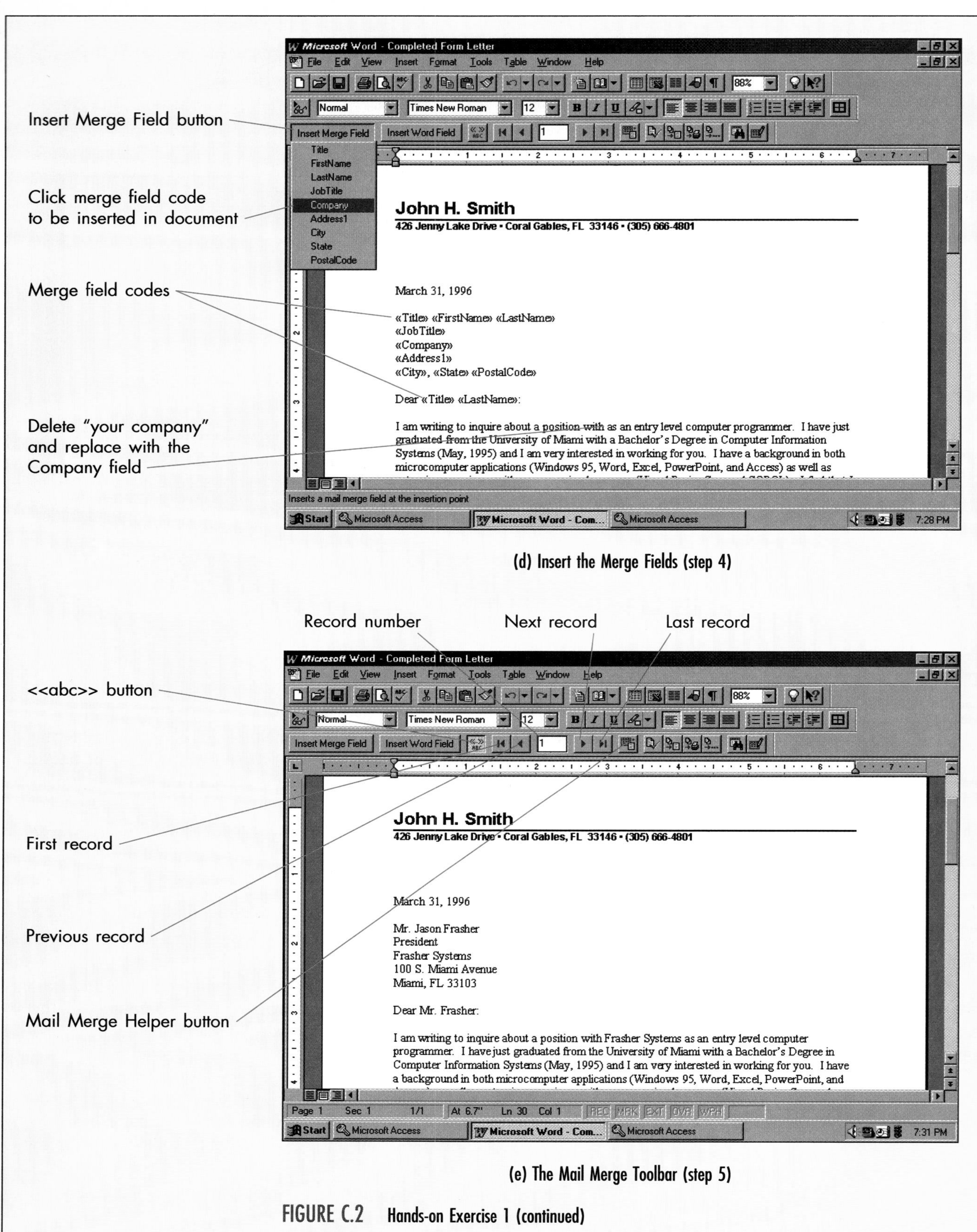

(d) Insert the Merge Fields (step 4)

(e) The Mail Merge Toolbar (step 5)

FIGURE C.2 Hands-on Exercise 1 (continued)

- The **<<abc>> button** functions as a toggle switch. Click it once and you switch from field codes to field values; click it a second time and you go from field values back to field codes. End with the field values displayed.
- Look at the text box on the Mail Merge toolbar, which displays the number 1 to indicate that the first record is displayed. Click the **► button** to display the form letter for the next record (Ms. Lauren Howard, in our example).
- Click the **► button** again to display the form letter for the next record (Ms. Elizabeth Scherry). The toolbar indicates you are on the third record. Click the **◄ button** to return to the previous (second) record.
- Click the **|◄ button** to move directly to the first record (Jason Frasher). Click the **►| button** to display the form letter for the last record (Elizabeth Scherry).
- Toggle the **<<abc>> button** to display the field codes.

STEP 6: The Mail Merge Helper

- Click the **Mail Merge Helper button** on the Merge toolbar to display the dialog box in Figure C.2f.
- The Mail Merge Helper shows your progress thus far:
  - The main document has been created and saved as Completed Form Letter on drive C.
  - The data source is the Contacts table within the Names and Addresses database.
- Click the **Merge command button** to display the Merge dialog box in Figure C.2f. The selected options should already be set, but if necessary, change your options to match those in the figure.

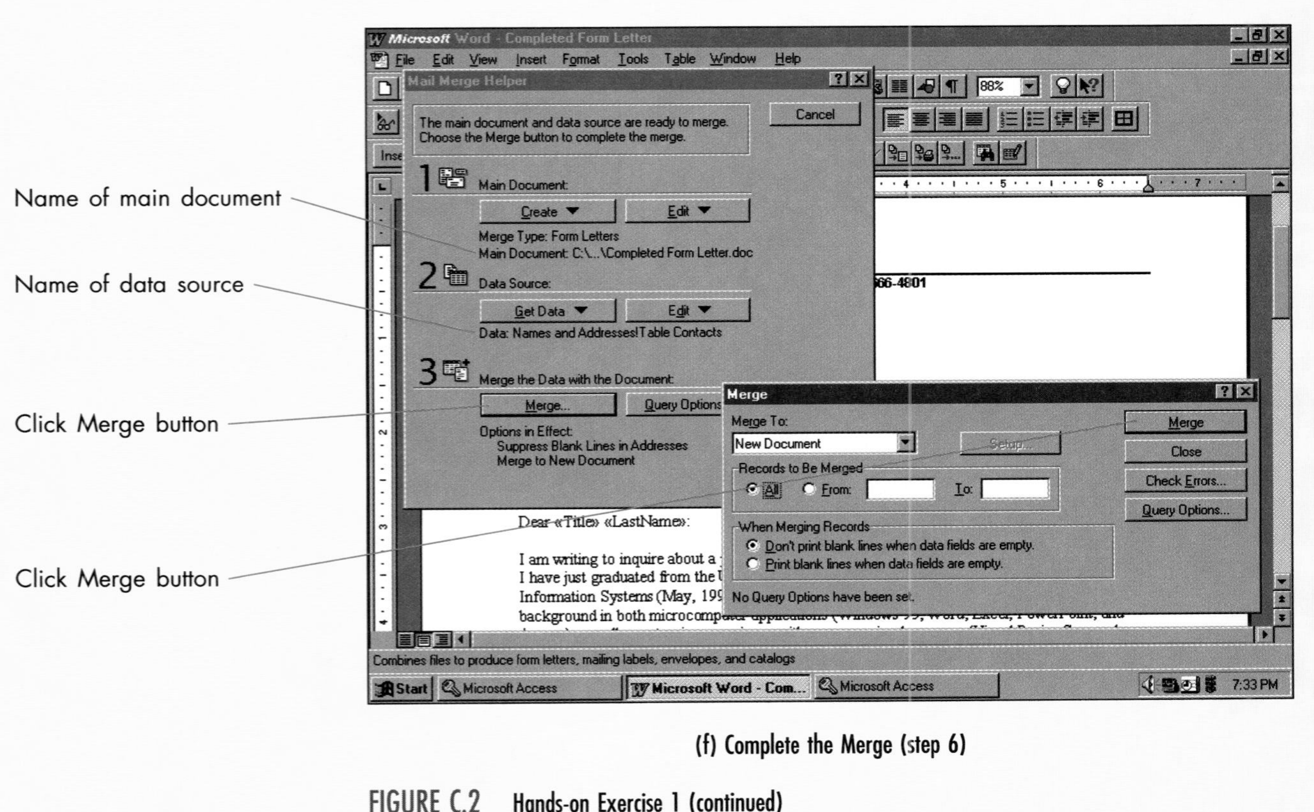

(f) Complete the Merge (step 6)

FIGURE C.2 Hands-on Exercise 1 (continued)

➤ Click the **Merge command button.** Word pauses momentarily, then generates the three form letters in a new document, which becomes the active document and is displayed on the monitor. The title bar of the active window changes to Form Letters1.

STEP 7: The Form Letters

➤ Scroll through the individual letters in the FormLetters1 document to review the letters one at a time.

➤ Pull down the **View menu.** Click **Zoom.** Click **Many Pages.** Click the **monitor icon,** then click and drag the icon within the resulting dialog box to display three pages side by side. Click **OK.** You should see the three form letters as shown in Figure C.2g.

➤ Print the letters to prove to your instructor that you did this exercise.

➤ Pull down the **File menu** and click **Exit** to exit Word. Pay close attention to the informational messages that ask whether to save the modified file(s):

- There is no need to save the merged document (Form Letters1) because you can always re-create the merged letters, provided you have saved the main document and data source.
- Save the Completed Form Letter if you are asked to do so.

➤ Exit Access. Congratulations on a job well done. We wish you good luck in your job hunting!

Title bar shows a new document

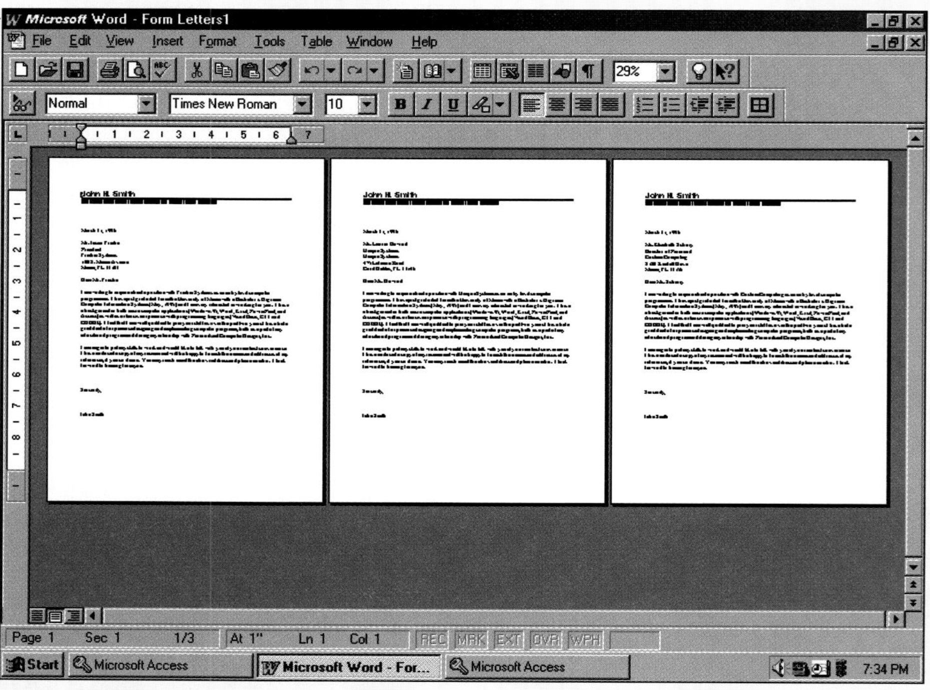

(g) The Individual Form Letters (step 7)

FIGURE C.2 Hands-on Exercise 1 (continued)

SUMMARY

A mail merge creates the same letter many times, changing only the variable data, such as the addressee's name and address, from letter to letter. The mail merge process uses two files as input, a main document and a data source. A set of form letters is created as output.

The main document contains standardized text together with one or more merge fields that indicate where variable information is to be inserted in the individual letters. The data source (e.g., a set of names and addresses) contains the information that varies from letter to letter and is a table or query within an Access database. (The data source can also be created as an Excel list or a Word table.)

The main document and the data source work in conjunction with one another, with the merge fields in the main document referencing the corresponding fields in the data source. The merge process examines each record in the data source and substitutes the appropriate field values for the corresponding merge fields as it creates the individual form letters.

KEY WORDS AND CONCEPTS

Data source
Field code
Field result
Form letter
Mail merge
Mail Merge Helper
Main document
Merge field
Microsoft Access
Microsoft Word
Query
Record
Table

7

ADDING IMPACT: OBJECT LINKING AND EMBEDDING

OBJECTIVES

After reading this chapter you will be able to:

1. Use Microsoft Graph to create and edit a graph within a presentation.
2. Use the Drawing and Drawing+ toolbars to modify existing clip art; describe the function of at least four different drawing tools.
3. Use Microsoft Organization Chart to embed an organization chart into a presentation.
4. Use Microsoft WordArt to embed a WordArt object into a presentation.
5. Link an Excel worksheet to a PowerPoint presentation.
6. Distinguish between linking and embedding; explain how in-place editing is used to modify an embedded object.
7. Embed a sound file into a PowerPoint presentation.
8. Use the Interactive Settings command to introduce branching into a presentation.

OVERVIEW

PowerPoint enables you to include a variety of visual elements that add impact to your presentation. You can add clip art from within PowerPoint through the ClipArt Gallery, or you can include clip art from other sources. You can use the supplementary applications that are included with Microsoft Office to add graphs, organization charts, and WordArt. You can also insert objects created in other applications, such as a worksheet from Microsoft Excel or a table from Microsoft Word.

We begin by introducing Microsoft Graph, an application that creates (and modifies) a graph based on data in an associated datasheet.

We show you how to use the Drawing and Drawing+ toolbars to modify existing clip art and/or develop original images, even if you are not artistic by nature. We describe how to create special text effects through WordArt and how to create organization charts. We show you how to embed a sound file, and we discuss Object Linking and Embedding, which incorporates objects from other applications. We also show you how to use the Interactive Settings command to allow branching in the presentation, so that you can view the slides in any order.

We think you will enjoy this chapter and be impressed with what you can do. As always, the hands-on exercises are essential to our learn-by-doing philosophy.

MICROSOFT GRAPH

The Microsoft Office suite includes a supplementary application called ***Microsoft Graph,*** which enables you to insert a graph into a presentation in support of numeric data. The program is called from within PowerPoint by choosing an Auto-Layout containing a graph placeholder, then double clicking the placeholder to start Microsoft Graph. You create the graph using commands within Microsoft Graph, then you exit Microsoft Graph and return to your presentation.

Figure 1.1 illustrates the basics of the Microsoft Graph program as it will be used in a hands-on exercise later in the chapter. The program has many of the same commands and capabilities as the charting component of Microsoft Excel. (See Grauer and Barber, *Exploring Microsoft Excel for Windows 95 Version 7.0,* pages 139–185, Prentice Hall, 1996, for additional information on graphs and charting.)

The ***datasheet*** in Figure 1.1a displays the quarterly sales for each of three salesmen: Tom, Dick, and Harry. The datasheet contains 12 ***data points*** (four quarterly values for each of three salesmen). The data points are grouped into ***data series,*** which appear as rows or columns in the datasheet.

The graph in Figure 1.1b plots the data by row so that you can see the relative performance of each salesman in each quarter. There are three data series (Sales for Tom, Sales for Dick, and Sales for Harry), each with four data points (1st Qtr, 2nd Qtr, 3rd Qtr, and 4th Qtr). The text entries in the first row of the datasheet appear on the X axis as the category names. The text entries in the first column of the datasheet appear as a legend to indicate the name associated with each series.

Figure 1.1c, on the other hand, plots the data by column, making it easy to see the progress of each salesman over the course of the year. This time there are four data series (Sales for 1st Qtr, Sales for 2nd Qtr, Sales for 3rd Qtr, and Sales for 4th Qtr), each with three data points (one each for Tom, Dick, and Harry). The text entries in the first column of the datasheet appear on the X axis as the category names. The text entries in the first row of the datasheet appear in the legend to indicate the name associated with each series.

Figure 1.1d also displays the data series in columns, but uses a different graph type, a stacked column rather than side-by-side columns as in Figure 1.1c. The choice between the two types of graphs depends on your message. If, for example, you want your audience to see each individual's sales in each quarter, the side-by-side graph is more appropriate. If, on the other hand, you want to emphasize the total sales for each salesperson, the stacked column graph is preferable. Note, too, the different scale on the Y axis in the two graphs. The side-by-side graph in Figure 1.1c shows the sales in each quarter and so the Y axis goes only to $90,000. The stacked bars in Figure 1.1d, however, reflect the total sales for each salesperson and thus the scale goes to $250,000.

All three graphs contain the same number of data points (12 in all) but plot them differently to emphasize different information. All three graphs are equally correct, and the choice depends on the message you want to convey.

EMPHASIZE YOUR MESSAGE

A graph exists to deliver a message, and you want that message to be as clear as possible. One way to help put your point across is to choose a title that leads the audience. A neutral title such as *Revenue by Quarter* does nothing and requires the audience to reach its own conclusion. A better title might be *Tom Is the Leading Sales Associate* if the objective were to emphasize Tom's contribution. A well-chosen title emphasizes your message.

My Chart - Datasheet

		A	B	C	D	E
		1st Qtr	2nd Qtr	3rd Qtr	4th Qtr	
1	Tom	20.4	50	90	75	
2	Dick	30.6	38.6	34.6	31.6	
3	Harry	45.9	46.9	45	12	
4						

(a) The Datasheet (sales in thousands)

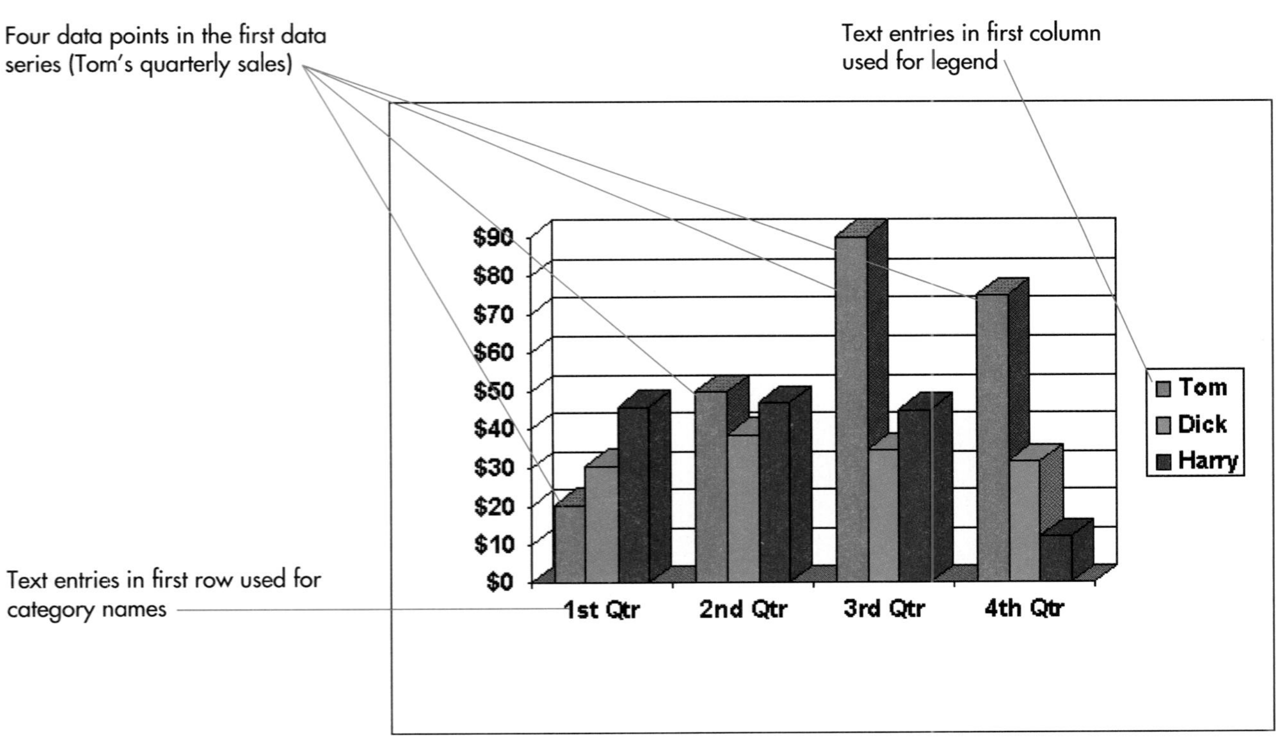

(b) Data Series in Rows (sales in thousands)

FIGURE 1.1 Microsoft Graph

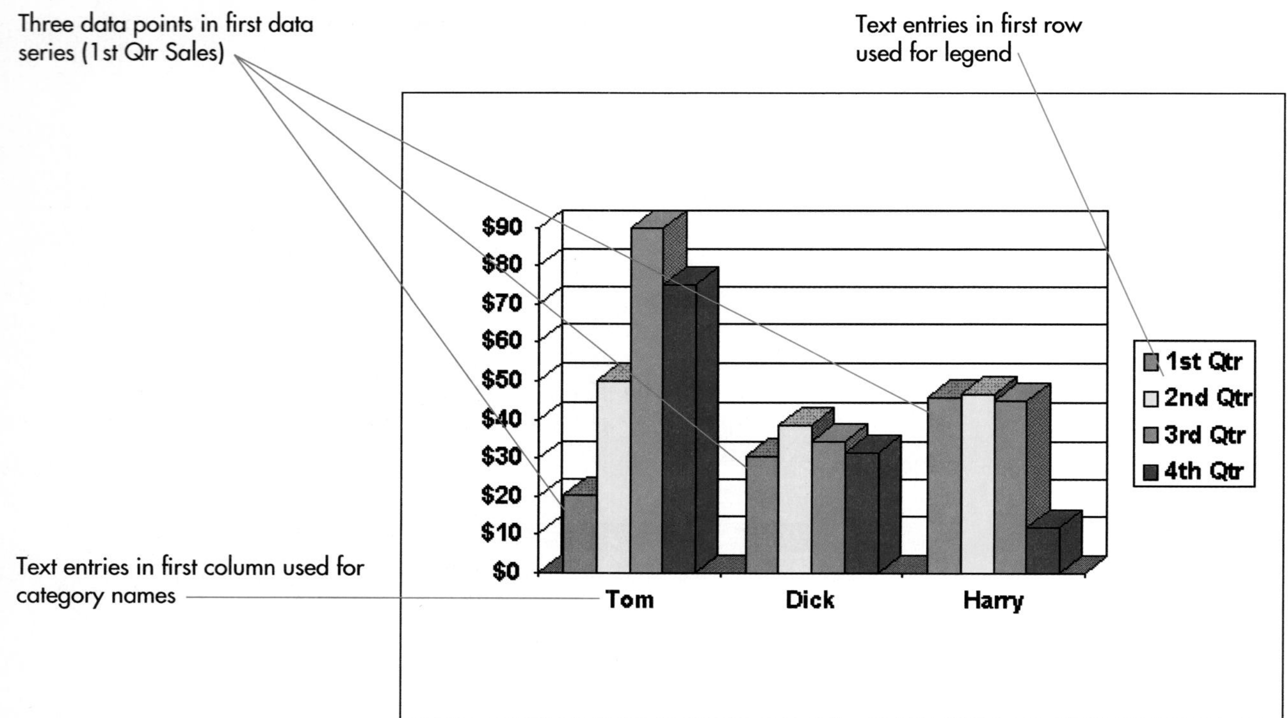

(c) Data Series in Columns (sales in thousands)

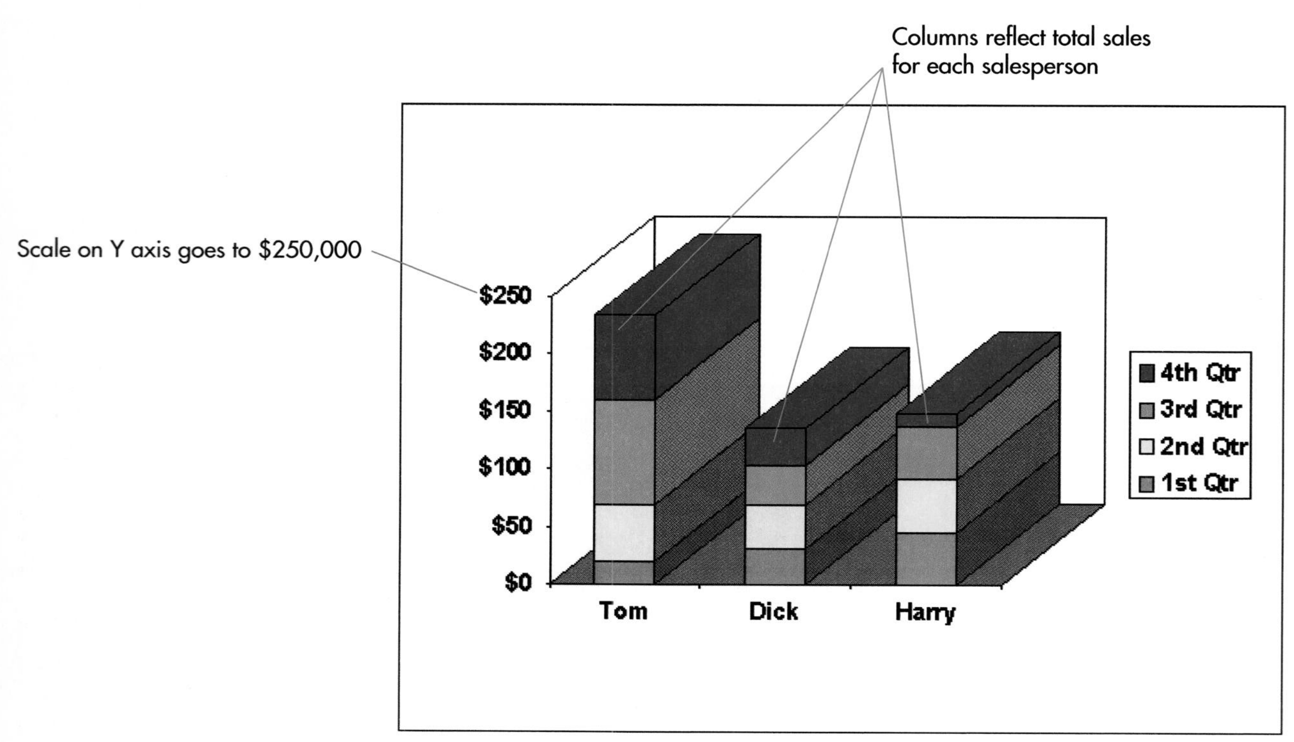

(d) Stacked Column Chart (sales in thousands)

FIGURE 1.1 Microsoft Graph (continued)

HANDS-ON EXERCISE 1

Microsoft Graph

Objective: Use Microsoft Graph to insert a graph into a presentation; modify the graph to display the data in rows or columns; change the graph format and underlying data. Use Figure 1.2 as a guide in the exercise.

STEP 1: Start Microsoft Graph

- Start PowerPoint. Click the option button to create a new presentation using a **Blank Presentation.** Click **OK.** You should see the New Slide dialog box.
- Select (click) the AutoLayout for a graph (it is the AutoLayout at the end of the second row), then click **OK** to add the slide as shown in Figure 1.2a. If necessary, maximize the document window.

INSERTING A GRAPH

There are several different ways to insert a graph into a presentation. You can choose one of three AutoLayouts containing a placeholder for a graph. You can also pull down the Insert menu and select Microsoft Graph, or you can click the Insert Graph button on the Standard toolbar. You can also insert a graph created in another application by executing the Insert Object command and selecting the appropriate object, such as a Microsoft Excel chart.

Double click placeholder to start Microsoft Graph

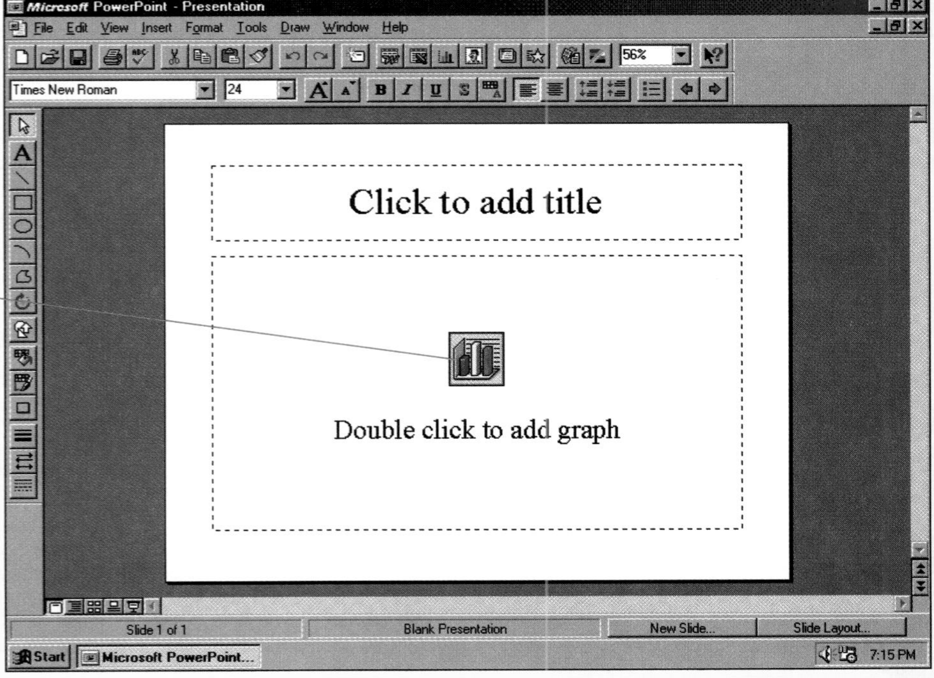

(a) Start Microsoft Graph (step 1)

FIGURE 1.2 Hands-on Exercise 1

➤ Double click the placeholder to add a graph, which starts the Microsoft Graph application.

STEP 2: The Default Graph

➤ The default datasheet and graph should be displayed on your monitor, as shown in Figure 1.2b. The menus and toolbar have changed to reflect the Microsoft Graph application.

➤ Do not be concerned if the numbers in your datasheet are different from those in the figure. (You can create your own graph simply by editing the text and numeric values, as will be described in the next step.)

➤ Click and drag the **title bar** of the datasheet so that you can see more of the graph, as in the figure.

IN-PLACE EDITING

Microsoft Graph enables in-place editing as you create and/or modify a graph; that is, you remain in PowerPoint, but the toolbar and pull-down menus are those of Microsoft Graph. The File and Window menus are exceptions, however, and contain PowerPoint commands (so that you can save the presentation and/or view multiple presentations). In-place editing requires that both applications support the Microsoft specification for Object Linking and Embedding 2.0.

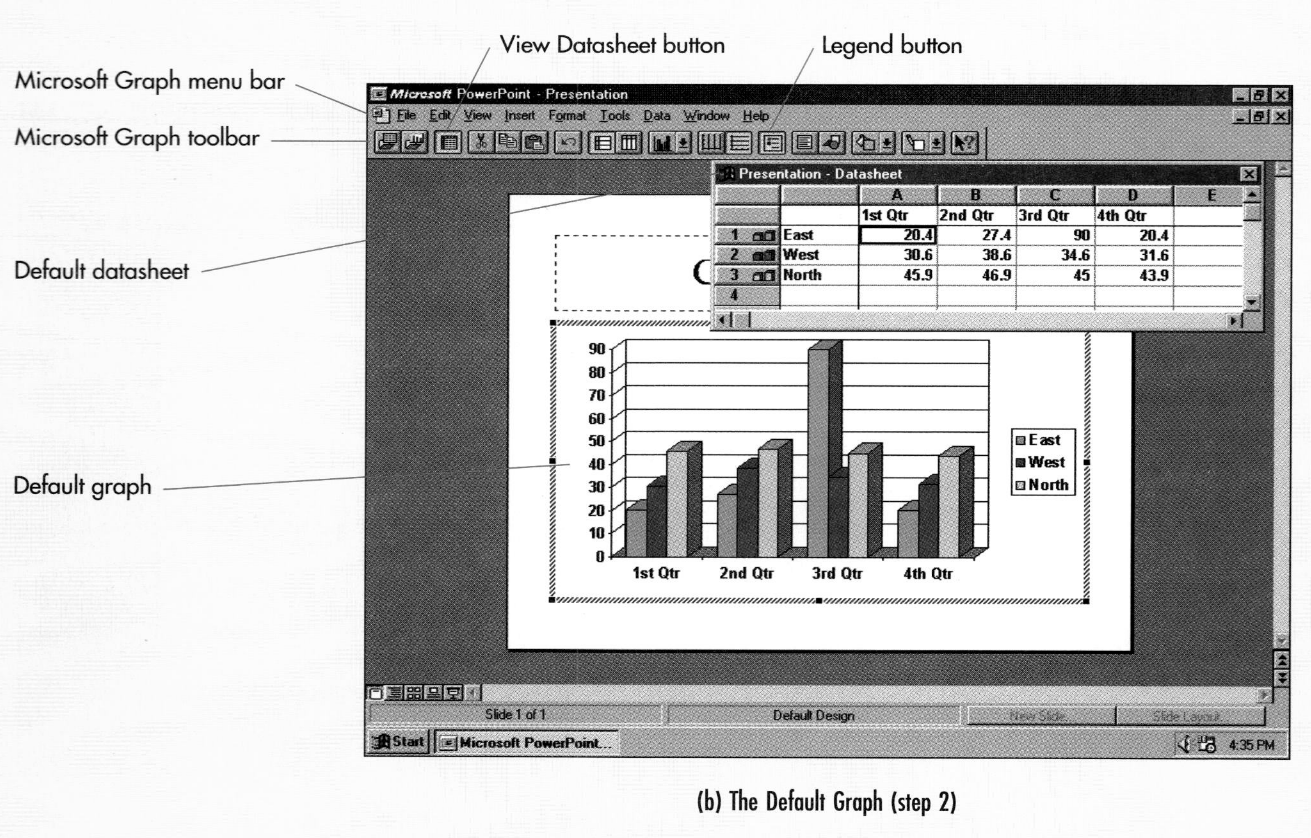

(b) The Default Graph (step 2)

FIGURE 1.2 Hands-on Exercise 1 (continued)

- Click the **View Datasheet button** on the (Microsoft Graph) Standard toolbar to close the datasheet. Click the **View Datasheet button** a second time to open the datasheet.
- Click the **Legend button** on the Standard toolbar to suppress the legend on the graph. Click the **Legend button** a second time to display the legend.

STEP 3: Change the Data

- Click in **cell B1** of the datasheet (the value for East in the 2nd Quarter). Type **50** and press **enter.** The graph changes automatically to reflect the new data.
- Change the values of the following cells as follows:
  - Click in **cell D1.** Type **75.**
  - Click in **cell D3.** Type **12.**
  - Click in the cell containing **East.** Type **Tom.**
  - Press the **down arrow key** to move to the cell containing **West.** Type **Dick.**
  - Press the **down arrow key** to move to the cell containing **North.** Type **Harry.**
- Check that all of the values in your datasheet match those in Figure 1.2c. Click the **Close button** to close the datasheet.

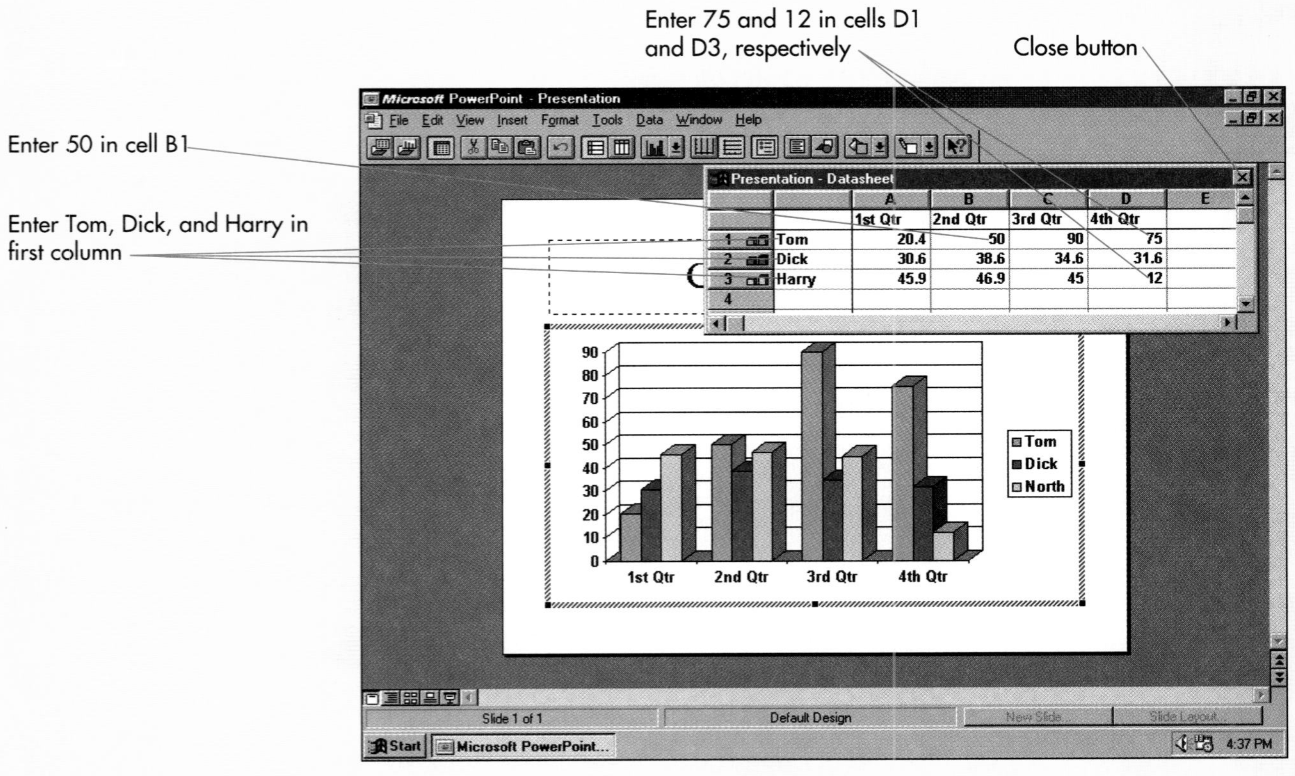

(c) Change the Data (step 3)

FIGURE 1.2 Hands-on Exercise 1 (continued)

IMPORT THE DATA

Microsoft Graph enables you to import data from another application (e.g., Microsoft Excel) and use that data as the basis for the graph. Click in the upper-left cell (the cell above row 1 and to the left of column A) to select the entire datasheet. Click the Import Data button on the Microsoft Graph toolbar to produce an Import Data dialog box. Select the appropriate drive and directory containing the file you want to import, select the file, then click the OK command button.

STEP 4: Change the Orientation and Graph Type

- Click the **By Column button** on the Standard toolbar to change the data series from rows to columns as shown in Figure 1.2d. The X axis changes to display the names of the salespersons, and the legend indicates the quarter.
- Click the **By Row button** on the Standard toolbar to change the data series back to rows.
- Click the **By Column button** a second time to match the orientation in Figure 1.2d.
- Pull down the **Format menu.** Click **AutoFormat** to produce the AutoFormat dialog box shown in Figure 1.2d.

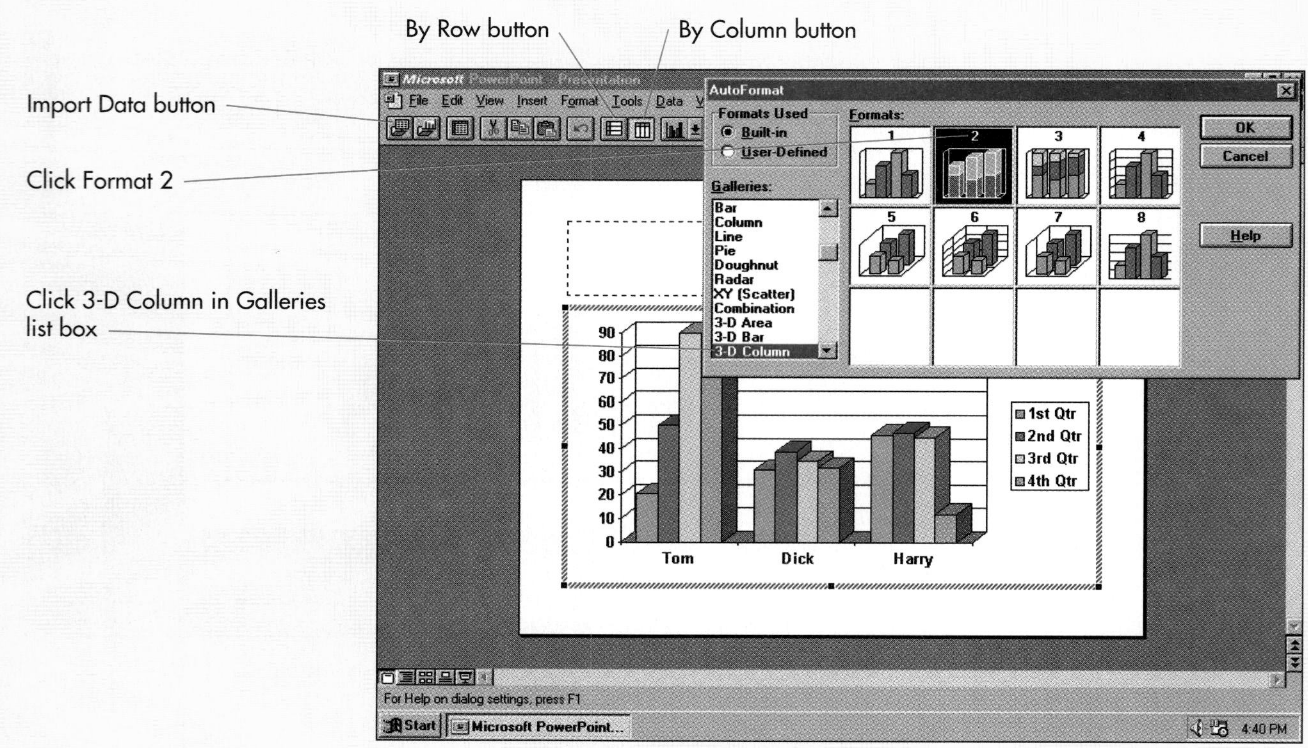

(d) Change the Orientation and Format (step 4)

FIGURE 1.2 Hands-on Exercise 1 (continued)

➤ If necessary, click **3-D Column** in the Galleries list box. Click **Format 2,** then click **OK** to create a stacked bar graph.

> **DON'T FORGET HELP**
>
> Microsoft Graph includes its own Help system, which functions identically to the Help in any other application. Pull down the Help menu and search on any topic for which you want additional information. Remember, too, that you can print the contents of a Help screen by pulling down the File menu and selecting the Print Topic command.

STEP 5: Return to PowerPoint

➤ Click outside the chart (and datasheet) to exit Microsoft Graph and return to PowerPoint. You should see the stacked column graph in Figure 1.2e.

➤ Click outside the graph to deselect it. The sizing handles disappear.

➤ Click inside the graph, and the sizing handles reappear to indicate the graph is selected. Click and drag a corner sizing handle to increase (decrease) the size of the graph within the slide.

➤ Click the **title placeholder,** which deselects the graph and positions the insertion point to enter the title. Type **Tom is the Top Sales Associate.**

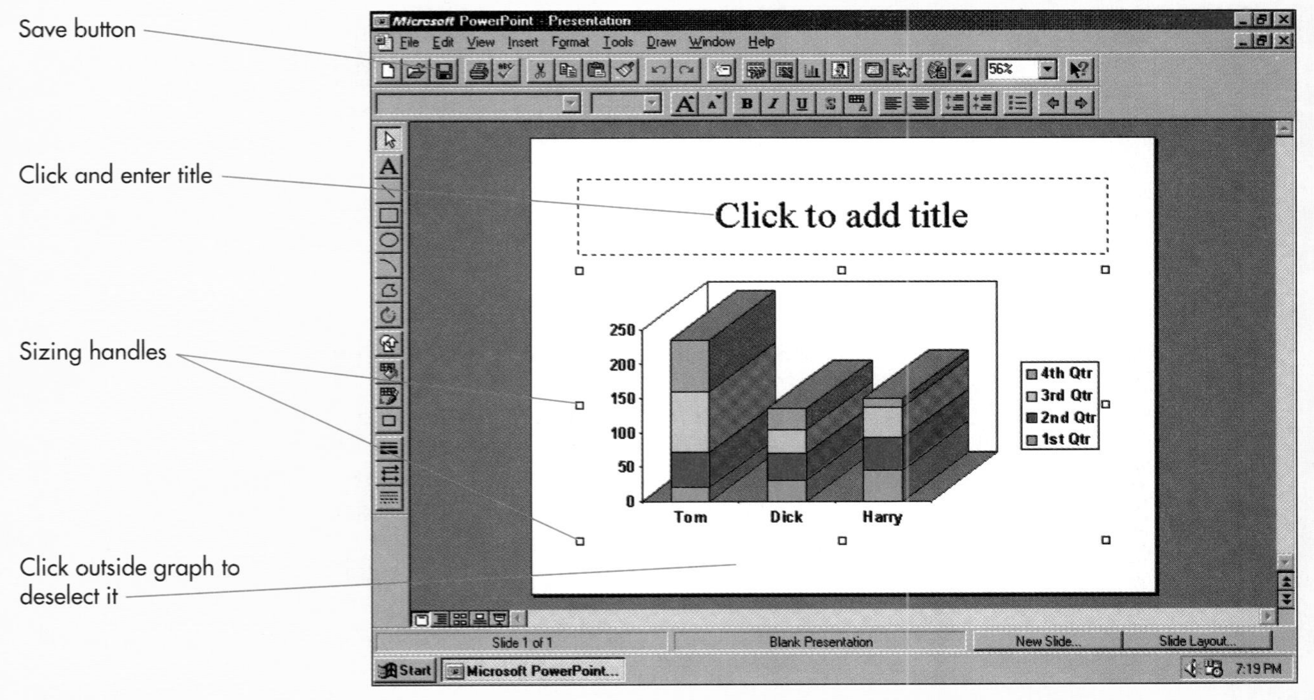

(e) Return to PowerPoint (step 5)

FIGURE 1.2 Hands-on Exercise 1 (continued)

➤ Pull down the **File menu** and click **Save** (or click the **Save button** on the Standard toolbar). Save the presentation as **My Chart** in the **Exploring PowerPoint folder.**

TO CLICK OR DOUBLE CLICK

Once you create a graph and return to your presentation, the graph becomes an embedded object, which retains its connection to Microsoft Graph for easy editing. You can click the graph to select it, then move or size the graph just as you would any other Windows object. You can also double click the graph to restart Microsoft Graph (the application that created the graph) and then edit it using the tools of the original application.

STEP 6: Add a Data Series

➤ Point to the graph and click the **right mouse button** to display a shortcut menu, then click **Edit Chart Object.** (You can also double click the graph as described in the previous tip.) Once again you are in Microsoft Graph, and the menus and toolbar have changed to reflect this application.

➤ Click the **View Datasheet button** to reopen the datasheet. If necessary, click and drag the title bar of the datasheet so you can see more of the graph.

➤ Add an additional data series as follows:

- Click in the cell under Harry. Type **George,** then press the **right arrow key** to move to cell A4. George appears as a category name on the X axis.
- Enter **10, 15, 20,** and **25** in cells A4, B4, C4, and D4, respectively. Notice that as you complete each entry, the graph adjusts automatically to reflect the value you just entered.

➤ The data for George is plotted automatically as shown in Figure 1.2f. Close the datasheet.

REMOVING A DATA SERIES

To delete a data series, open the datasheet, then click the row number or column header of the data series you want to delete, and press the Del key. The data series will disappear from both the datasheet and the associated graph. Alternatively, you can leave the data series in the datasheet but exclude it from the graph. (This enables you to subsequently include the data in the graph without having to reenter it.) Click the row number or column header to select the data series, pull down the Data menu, and select the Exclude Row/Column command. To restore the data series in the graph, select the series, pull down the Data menu, and select the Include Row/Column command.

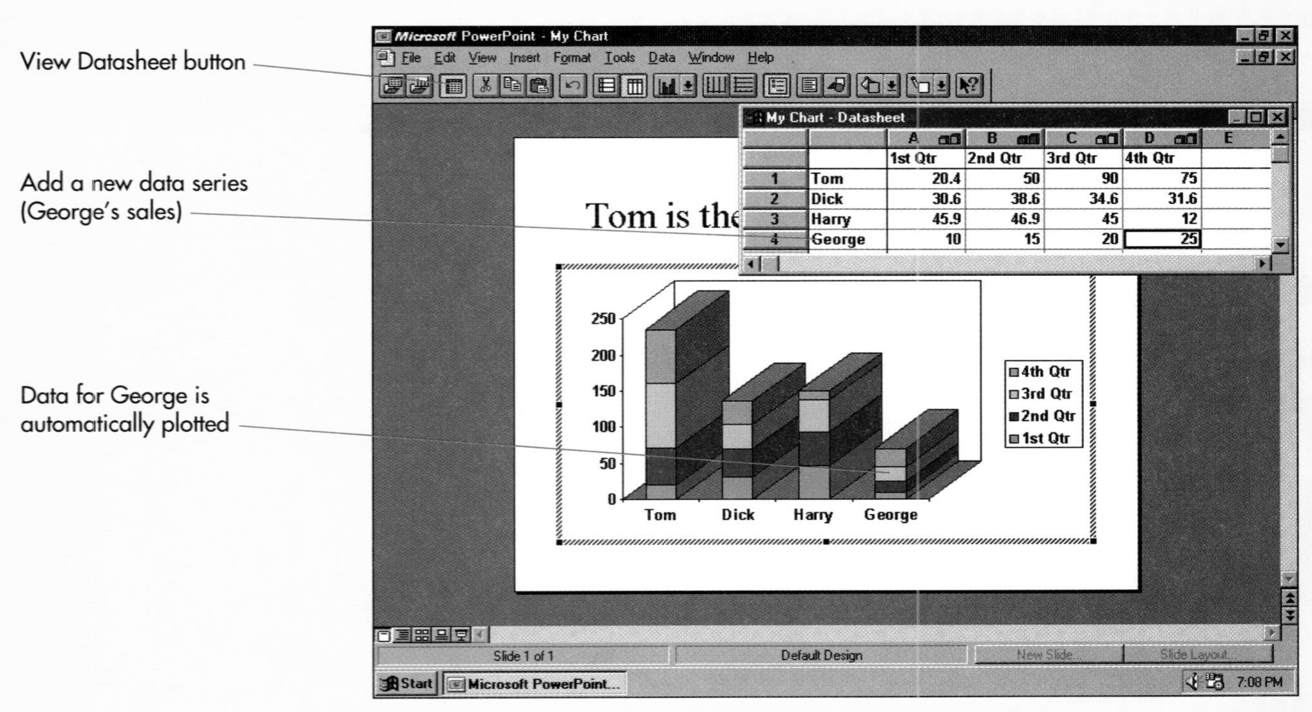

(f) Add a Data Series (step 6)

FIGURE 1.2 Hands-on Exercise 1 (continued)

STEP 7: The Finishing Touches

- You can customize every object within a chart (the legend, axis, plot area, and so on) by pointing to the object and clicking the right mouse button to display a shortcut menu.
- Close the datasheet. Point to the gray section (4th Qtr Sales) of any column and click the **right mouse button** to display a shortcut menu. Click **Format Data Series.**
- Click the **Patterns tab** (if necessary) in the Format Data Series dialog box and click **red** as the new color. Click **OK** to close the dialog box. The data series for the fourth quarter has been changed to red as shown in Figure 1.2g.
- Point to any value on the vertical axis, then click the **right mouse button** to display the shortcut menu in Figure 1.2g. Click **Format Axis.**
- Click the **Number tab** in the Format Number dialog box, then scroll within the Category list box until you can select the **Currency format.** Click **OK.** The format of the axis has been changed to include the dollar sign.

STEP 8: Save the Presentation

- Click outside the chart to exit Microsoft Graph and return to PowerPoint. Save the presentation.
- Pull down the **File menu** and click **Print** (or click the **Print button**). Click **OK** to print the slide.
- Exit PowerPoint if you do not want to continue with the next exercise at this time. Click **Yes** if prompted to save the changes to the presentation.

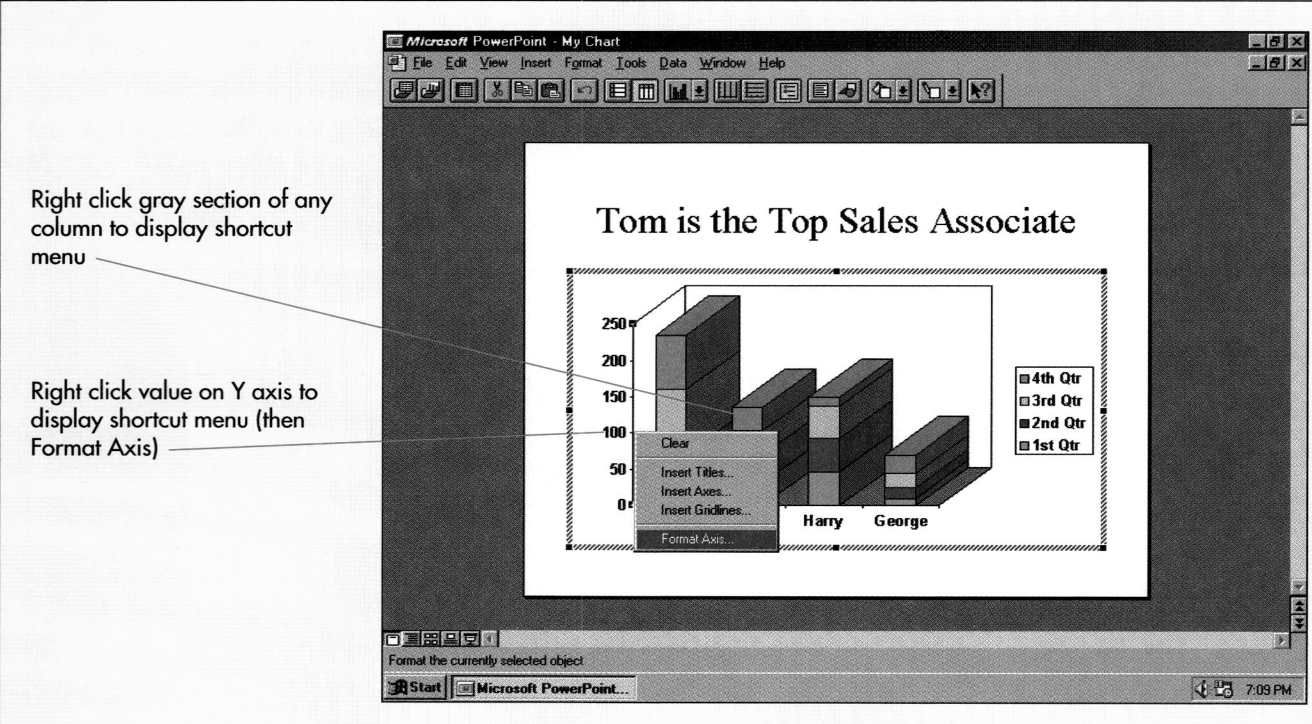

(g) The Finishing Touches (step 7)

FIGURE 1.2 Hands-on Exercise 1 (continued)

THE 3-D VIEW COMMAND

The 3-D View command enables you to fine-tune the appearance of a graph by controlling the rotation, elevation, and other parameters found within its dialog box. The rotation controls the rotation around the vertical axis and determines how much of the stacked bars you see. The elevation controls the height at which you view the graph. Pull down the Format menu, select the 3-D View command, then set these parameters as you see fit.

DRAWING IN POWERPOINT

PowerPoint provides a set of drawing tools to develop virtually any type of illustration. Even if you are not an artist, you can use these tools to modify existing clip art and thus create new and very different illustrations. Consider, for example, Figure 1.3, which contains an original piece of clip art and five variations. (The clip art was taken from the Cartoons category of the Microsoft ClipArt Gallery.)

We are not artistic by nature, and there is no way that we could have created the original duck. We did, however, create all of the variations, and you will too, in the hands-on exercise that follows. All it took was a little imagination and a sense of what can be done. The modifications were done with tools on the Drawing and Drawing+ toolbars.

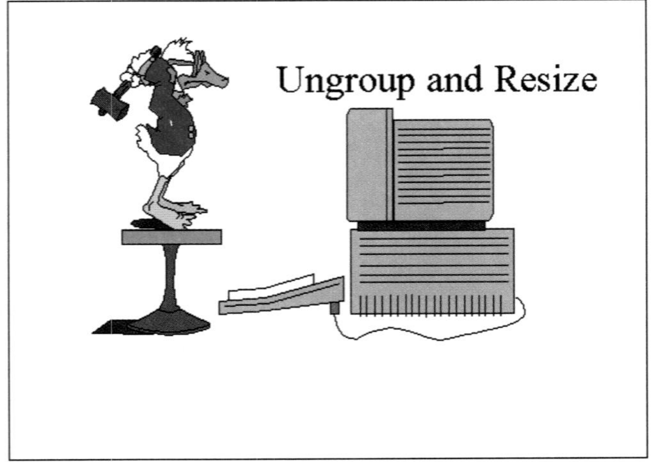

FIGURE 1.3 What You Can Do with Clip Art

The Drawing and Drawing+ Toolbars

The Drawing and Drawing+ toolbars are displayed in Figures 1.4a and 1.4b, respectively. The ***Drawing toolbar*** is displayed by default in the Slide view. The ***Drawing+ toolbar*** is displayed through the View menu or by pointing to any visible toolbar and clicking the right mouse button to display a shortcut menu.

As with the other toolbars, there is no need to memorize what the individual buttons do. You can, however, gain a better appreciation for their function by viewing the tools in groups as is done in Figure 1.4. And, as with all toolbars, you can point to any tool and PowerPoint will display the name of the tool. Finally, you can access the online help facility for detailed information on a specific tool.

An ***object*** is anything you put on a slide. The Drawing and Drawing+ toolbars are used to create objects such as a line, a shape, or text. Select a tool—for example, the Line tool on the Drawing toolbar—then click and drag in the slide to create the object. Objects are the building blocks of a drawing, in that any draw-

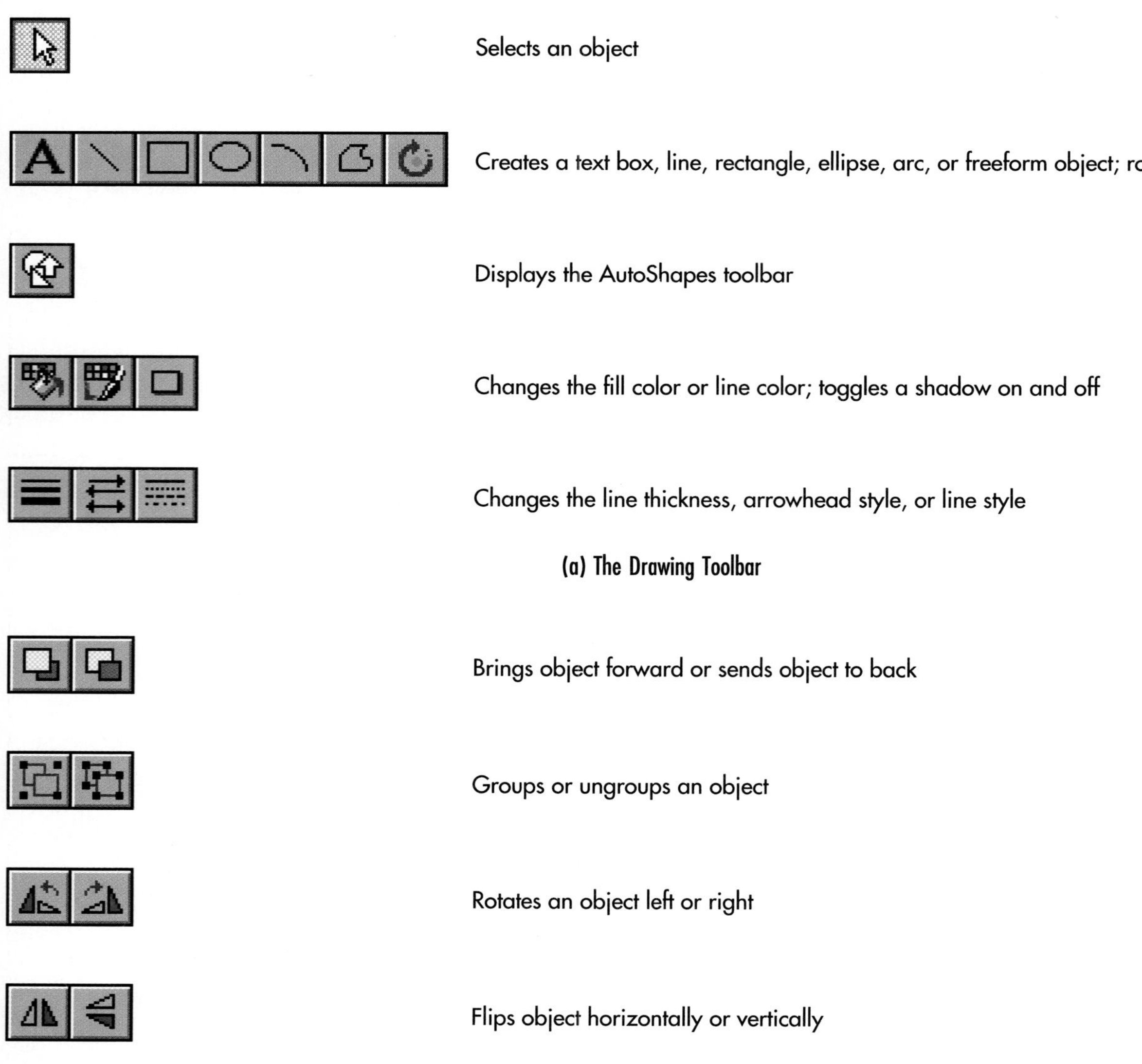
Selects an object
Creates a text box, line, rectangle, ellipse, arc, or freeform object; rotates an object
Displays the AutoShapes toolbar
Changes the fill color or line color; toggles a shadow on and off
Changes the line thickness, arrowhead style, or line style
(a) The Drawing Toolbar
Brings object forward or sends object to back
Groups or ungroups an object
Rotates an object left or right
Flips object horizontally or vertically
(b) The Drawing+ Toolbar

FIGURE 1.4 The Drawing Toolbars

ing can be broken down into a series of lines and shapes, each of which is considered an object.

As you create a drawing, you often work with many objects at the same time in order to apply the same command to those objects. The ***Group command*** combines individual objects so that you can work with them at the same time. The ***Ungroup (Disassemble Picture) command*** does the opposite, and breaks up an object into smaller objects so you can work with each object on an individual basis.

The exercise that follows has you insert a insert a clip art image into a presentation, then modify that image using various tools on the Drawing and Drawing+ toolbars. Be flexible and willing to experiment. Try, and try again, and don't be discouraged if you don't succeed initially. Just keep trying, and you will amaze yourself at what you will be able to do.

HANDS-ON EXERCISE 2

You Don't Have to Be an Artist

Objective: Insert clip art into a presentation, then use various tools on the Drawing and Drawing+ toolbars to modify the clip art. Use Figure 1.5 as a guide in the exercise.

STEP 1: Create the Title Slide

- Create a new presentation:
  - If necessary, start PowerPoint. Click the option button to create a **Blank Presentation** as you have been doing throughout the text. Click **OK.** If necessary, click the **Maximize button** so that PowerPoint takes the entire desktop.
  - If PowerPoint is already started, pull down the **File menu** and click **New** (or click the **New button** on the Standard toolbar). If necessary, double click the **Blank Presentation icon** to display the New Presentation dialog box.
- You should see the New slide dialog box with the **AutoLayout** for the title slide already selected. Click **OK** to create the title slide. Click the placeholder for the title. Type **What You Can Do With Clip Art** as shown in Figure 1.5a.
- Click the placeholder for the subtitle. Enter your name.
- Click the **Save button** on the Standard toolbar. Save the presentation as **You Don't Have to Be an Artist** in the **Exploring PowerPoint folder.**

STEP 2: The Drawing+ Toolbar

- Click the **New Slide command button** at the right of the status bar to display the New Slide dialog box.
- Select (click) the **Title Only AutoLayout.** (This is AutoLayout number 11 and is the third layout in the third row.) Click **OK** to create the slide shown in Figure 1.5b.
- Point to the **Drawing toolbar** (or any other toolbar), then click the **right mouse button** to display the shortcut menu shown in Figure 1.5b. Click **Drawing+** to display this toolbar.

STEP 3: Add the Clip Art

- If necessary, click and drag the title bar of the Drawing+ toolbar to anchor it at the left side of the window.

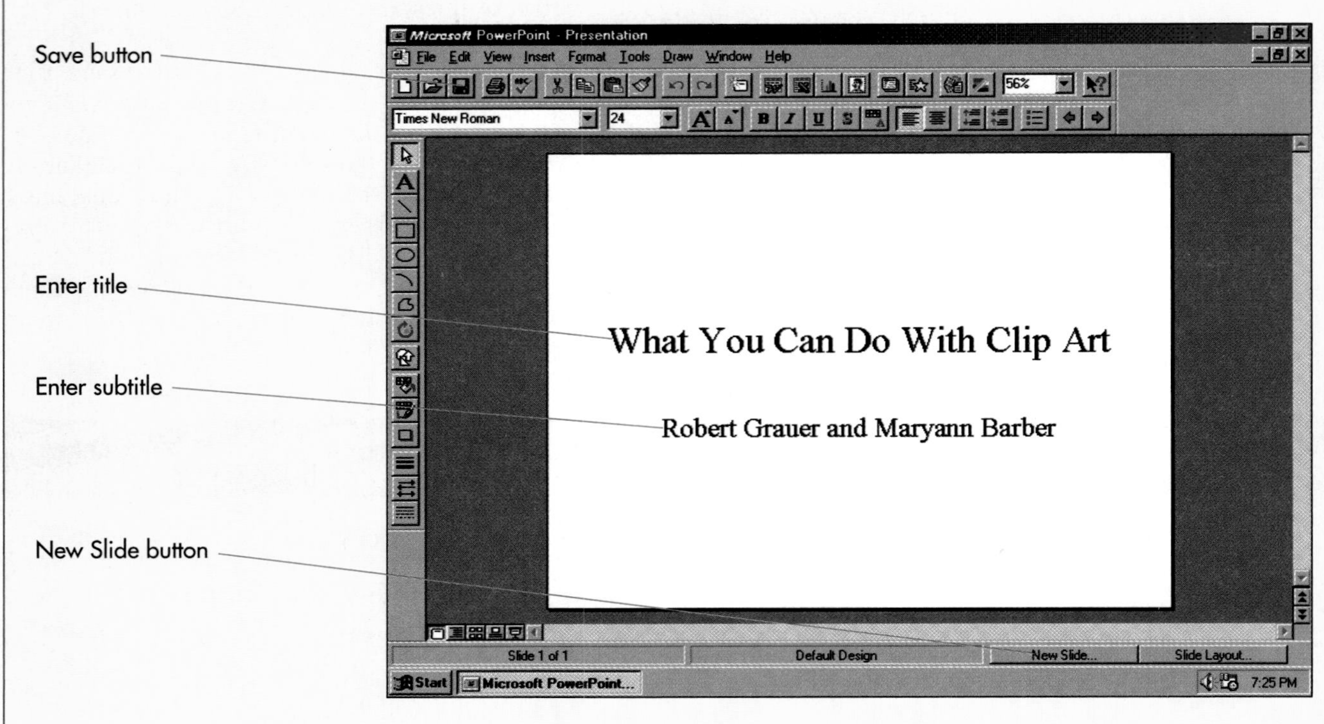

(a) Create the Title Slide (step 1)

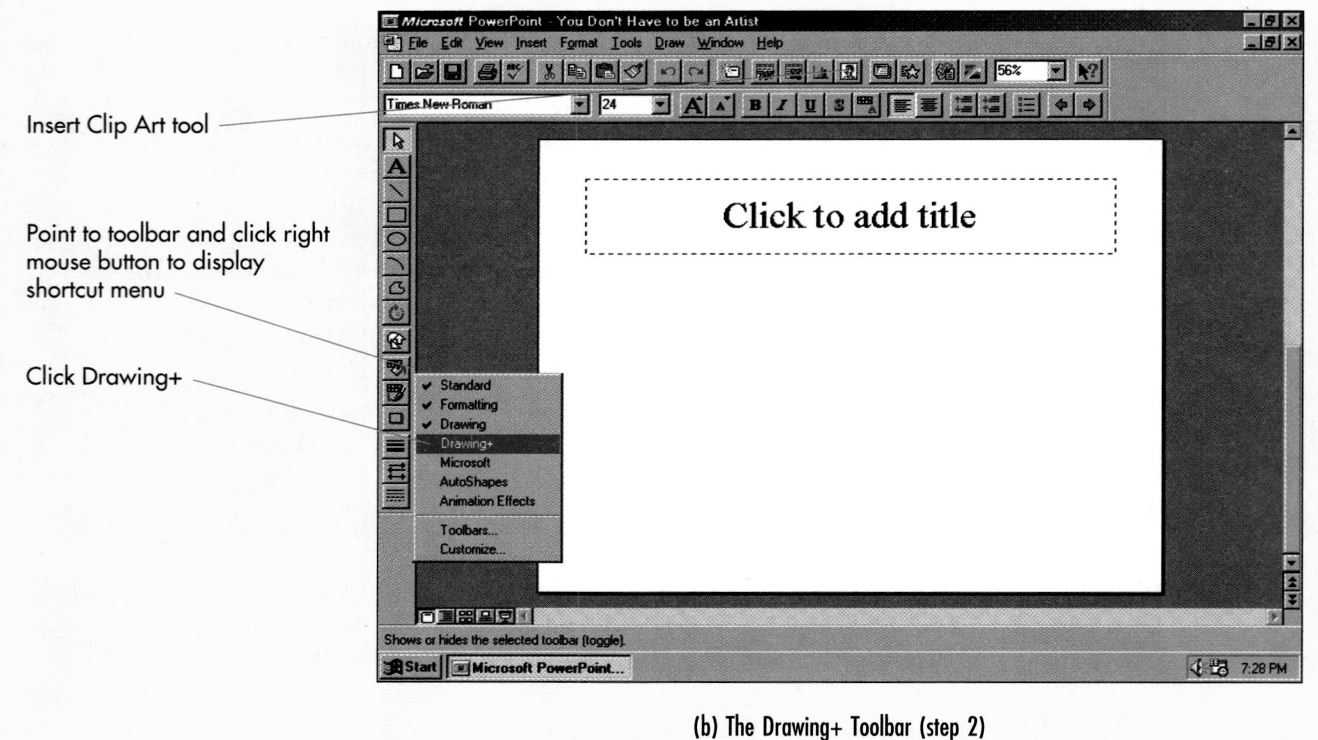

(b) The Drawing+ Toolbar (step 2)

FIGURE 1.5 Hands-on Exercise 2

➤ Click the **Insert Clip Art button** on the Standard toolbar to display the dialog box in Figure 1.5c. Select the **Cartoons category** (scrolling through the categories if required).

➤ Click the **down arrow** to scroll through the available cartoons until you can select the cartoon of the duck smashing the PC. Click **Insert** to insert the clip art onto the slide.

➤ Click the **placeholder** for the title. Type **The Original Clip Art** as the title of the slide. Save the presentation.

THE RECOLOR COMMAND

The Recolor command modifies an embedded object by substituting one color for another. Point to the embedded object, click the right mouse button to display a shortcut menu, then click the Recolor command to display the Recolor dialog box. Choose an existing (original) color, then click the associated down arrow to choose a new color. Change as many colors as you like, then click the OK command button to exit the command and return to the presentation. (The Recolor command is not available after an object has been ungrouped.)

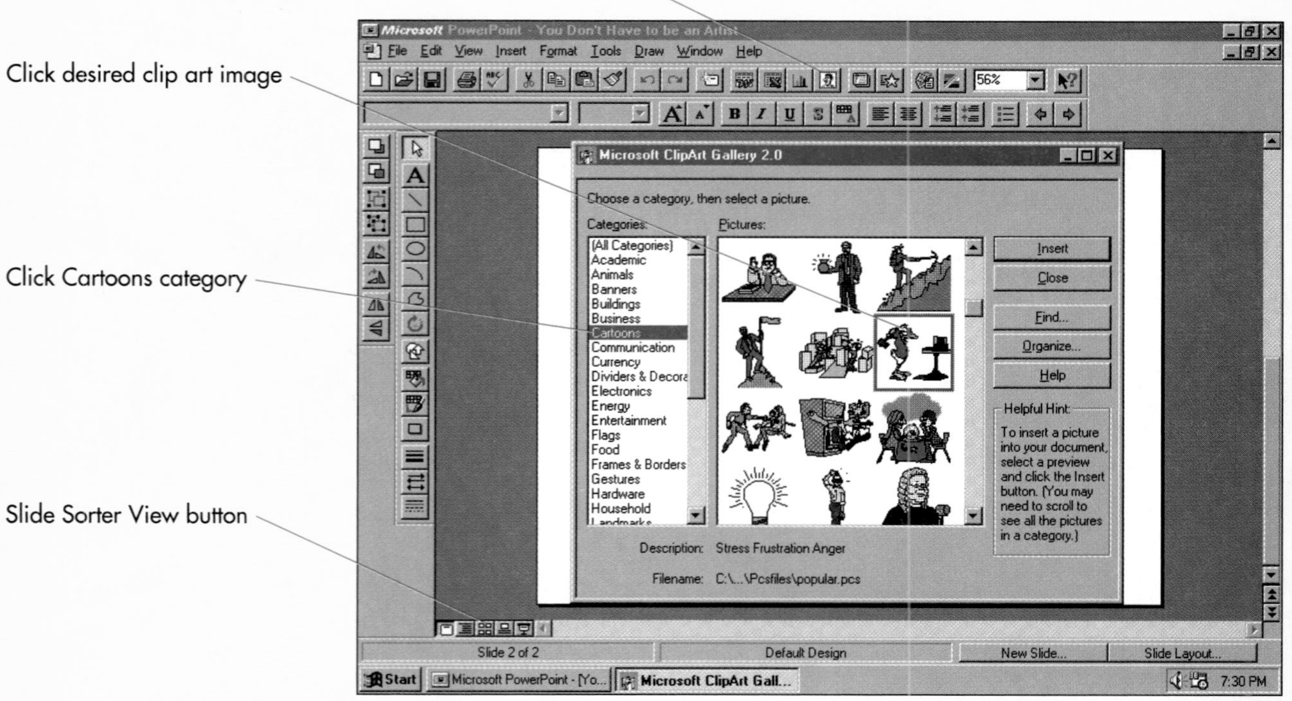

(c) Add the Clip Art (step 3)

FIGURE 1.5 Hands-on Exercise 2 (continued)

STEP 4: Copy the Slide

- Click the **Slide Sorter View button** on the status bar to change to the view in Figure 1.5d. Slide 2, the slide with the duck is selected.
- Click the **Copy button** on the Standard toolbar to copy the slide to the clipboard.
- Click the **Paste button** on the Standard toolbar to paste the contents of the clipboard into the presentation, which creates a new slide (slide 3) identical to slide 2.
- Click the **Paste button** four additional times so that you wind up with seven slides in all, as shown in Figure 1.5d.
- Save the presentation.

> **TOOL TIPS**
>
> Point to any button on any toolbar, and PowerPoint displays the name of the toolbar button, which is also indicative of its function. If pointing to a button has no effect, pull down the View menu, click Toolbars, and check the box to Show Tool Tips.

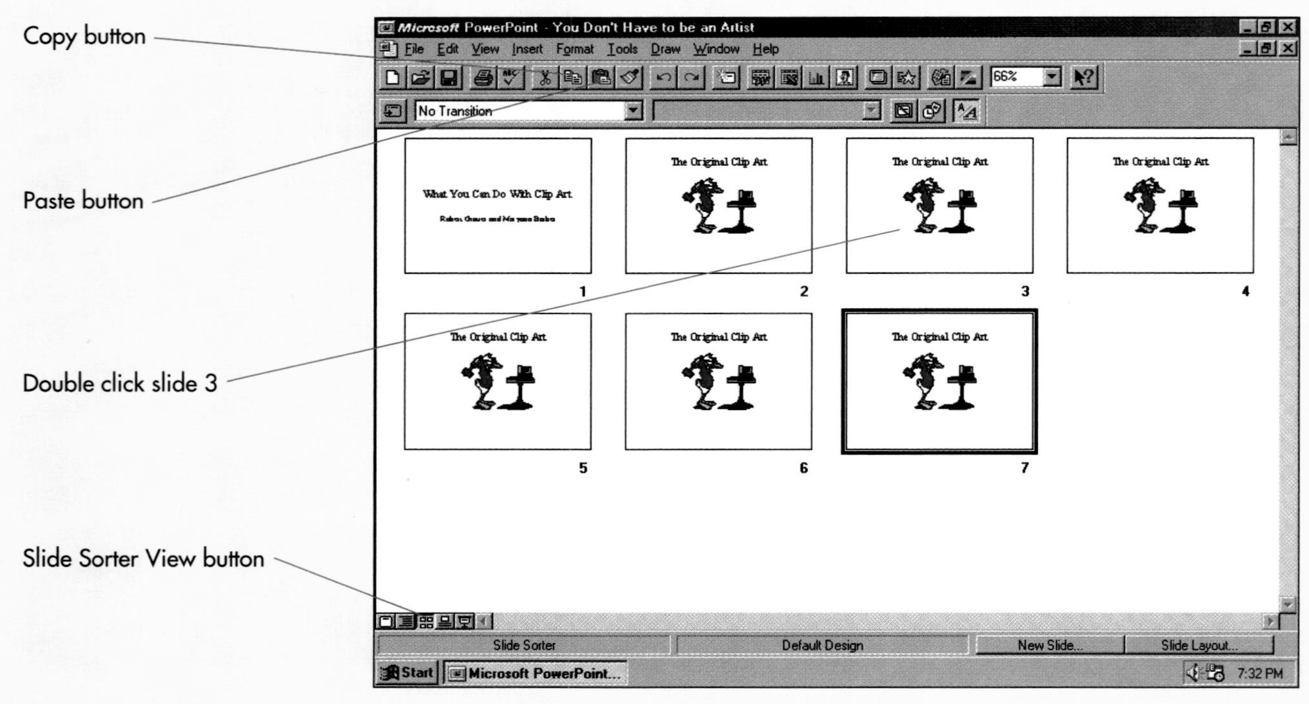

(d) Copy the Slide (step 4)

FIGURE 1.5 Hands-on Exercise 2 (continued)

STEP 5: Flip Vertically

- Double click **slide 3** to simultaneously select the slide and change to the Slide view, as shown in Figure 1.5e. The status bar should indicate that slide 3 is the current slide.
- Click and drag to select the text of the slide title, then type **Flip Vertically** as the new title.
- Click anywhere on the clip art to select the entire image. You should see eight sizing handles around the image as shown in the figure.
- Pull down the **Draw menu** and click **Ungroup,** or click the **Disassemble Picture (Ungroup) button** on the Drawing+ toolbar.
- You will see the dialog box in Figure 1.5e. Click **OK** to convert the object to a PowerPoint image, allowing you to use the PowerPoint tools to edit the image.
- You should see two sets of sizing handles: one set surrounding the duck, and the other set around the computer and the table.
- Click outside the selected area, then click anywhere on the duck to select just the duck.
- Click the **Flip Vertical button** on the Drawing+ toolbar. The duck is now upside down.
- Save the presentation.

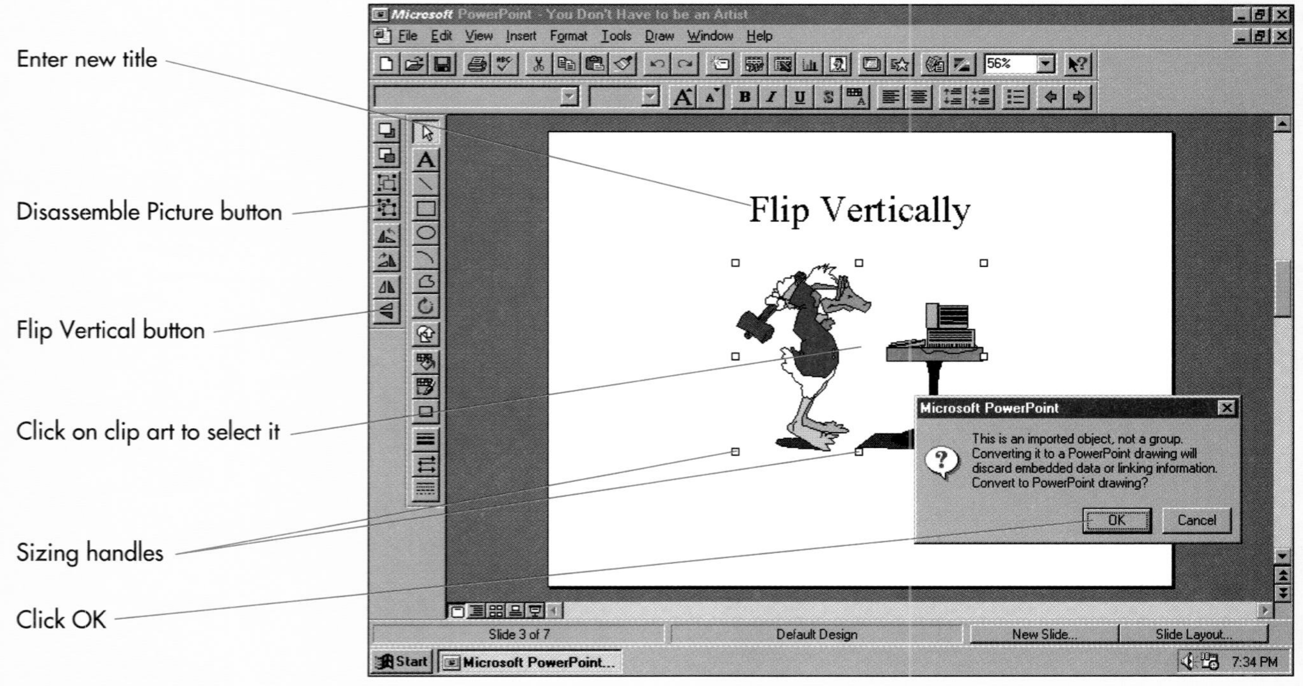

(e) The Ungroup Command (step 5)

FIGURE 1.5 Hands-on Exercise 2 (continued)

FLIP AND ROTATE

You can rotate an object 90 degrees to the left or right, or you can flip an object on its vertical or horizontal axis. If you are unable to use these tools, it is because the object is not a PowerPoint object. Just select the object, ungroup it, then regroup it. The object is transformed into a PowerPoint object, which can then be rotated or flipped.

STEP 6: Copy and Flip Horizontally

- Press the **PgDn key** (or click the **Next Slide button** at the bottom of the scroll bar) to move to slide 4. (You can also drag the scroll box (slide elevator) on the vertical scroll bar to move to slide 4.)
- Click and drag to select the slide title, then type **Copy and Flip Horizontally** as the new title as shown in Figure 1.5f.
- Click the clip art to select it, then drag the clip art to the left edge of the slide. Ungroup the duck and the computer as in step 5.
- Click outside the selected objects. Select just the duck. Click the **Copy button** on the Standard toolbar (which copies the duck to the clipboard).
- Click the **Paste button** on the Standard toolbar. You should see a second duck on top of the first duck.

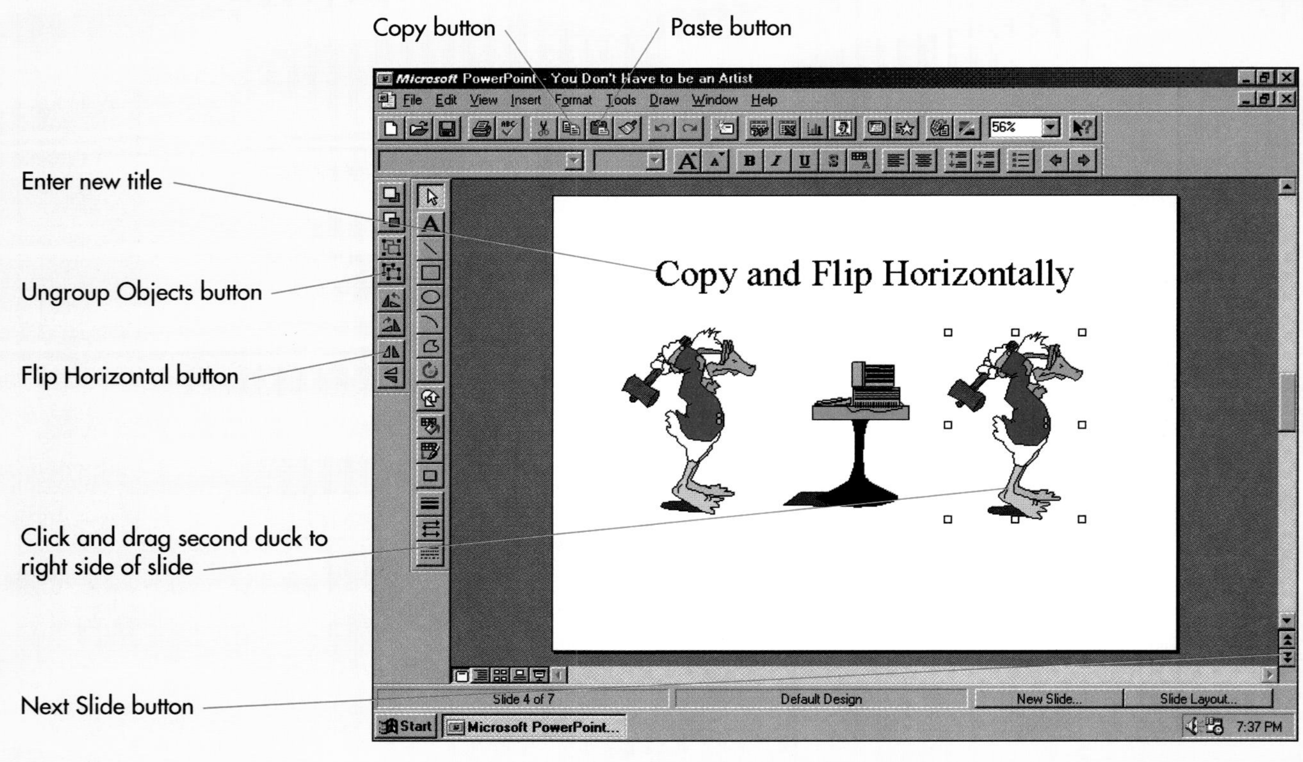

(f) Copy and Flip Horizontally (step 6)

FIGURE 1.5 Hands-on Exercise 2 (continued)

- Click and drag the second duck past the computer all the way to the right of the slide as shown in Figure 1.5f. Click the **Flip Horizontal button** to turn the duck around. Move the table and/or the ducks to adjust the spacing as desired.
- Save the presentation.

> **ALIGNING OBJECTS**
>
> You can improve the appearance of any slide by precisely aligning the objects it contains. Press and hold the Shift key to select the objects you want to align. Pull down the Draw menu, click Align, then choose the alignment you want (lefts, centers, rights, tops, middles, or bottoms) from the cascade menu.

STEP 7: Change Colors

- Press the **PgDn key** to move to slide 5. Click and drag to select the text of the slide title, then type **Change Colors** as the new title as shown in Figure 1.5g.
- Repeat the actions from the previous step to copy the duck and flip him horizontally:
  - Click and drag the clip art to the left side of the slide, then **ungroup** the duck and the computer.

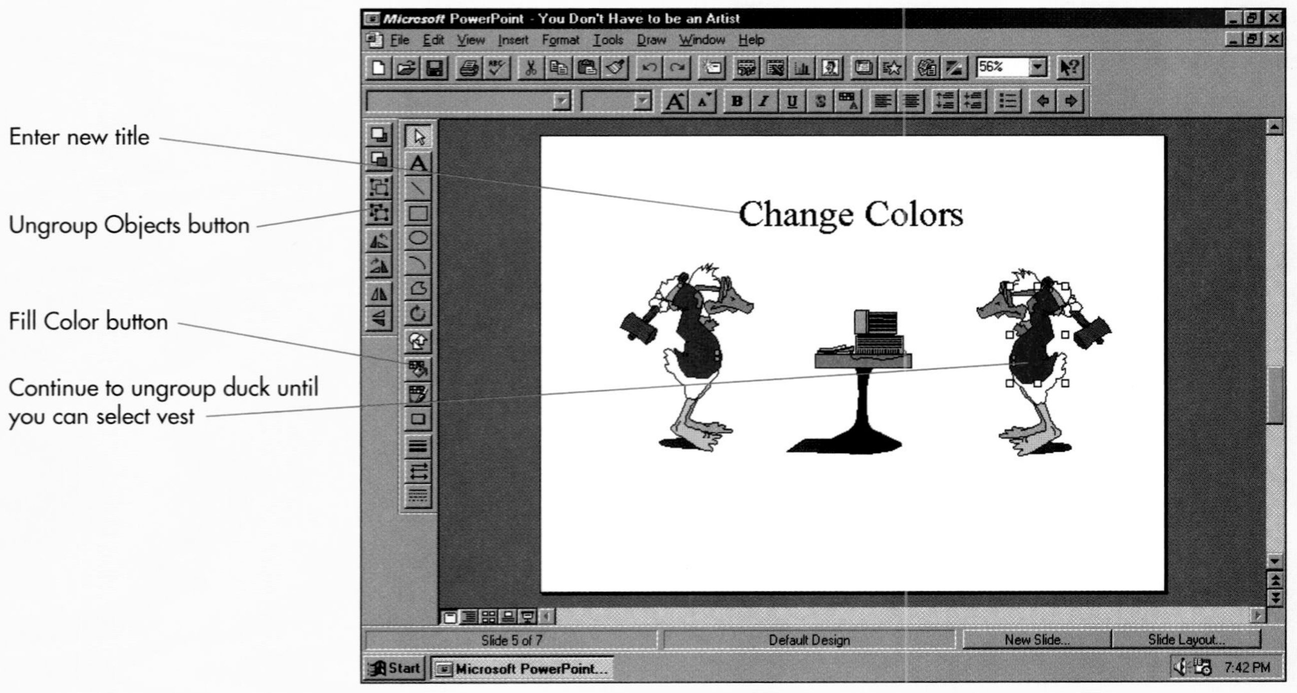

(g) Change Colors (step 7)

FIGURE 1.5 Hands-on Exercise 2 (continued)

- Click outside the selected area to deselect both objects. Select the duck, click the **Copy button,** click the **Paste button,** then drag the second duck to the right of the computer.
- Click the **Flip Horizontal** button to turn the duck around.

➤ Check that the duck on the right is still selected, then click the **Ungroup Objects button** to ungroup the objects that make up this duck and his hammer. The duck is now a separate object; the hammer and shadow are a second object.

➤ Click outside the selected objects, then click the duck. Click the **Ungroup Objects button** to ungroup the objects that make up the duck.

➤ Continue to ungroup the duck until you have separated his vest from his tie. Click outside the selected objects, then click the **duck's vest** to select just the vest as shown in Figure 1.5g.

➤ Click the **Fill Color button** to produce the available fill colors. Click **Green** to change the vest to green. Repeat these steps to change the costume of the other duck to a black vest with a blue tie.

➤ Save the presentation.

FILL, LINE, AND SHADOW

All drawn objects have attributes (characteristics) that determine the appearance of the object. To change an attribute, select the object, then click the appropriate tool on the Drawing+ toolbar. You can apply a shadow. You can change the style of the exterior line and/or the color of the line. You can also change the interior (fill) color of the object and/or the fill pattern.

STEP 8: Ungroup and Resize

➤ Press the **PgDn key** to move to slide 6. Click and drag to select the text of the slide title, then type **Ungroup and Resize** as the new title as shown in Figure 1.5h.

➤ Check that the title is still selected. Pull down the **Format menu.** Click **Alignment.** Click **Right** to move the slide title to the right as shown in Figure 1.5h.

➤ Ungroup the duck and computer as you have been doing throughout the exercise. Click outside the selected areas, then select the duck. Click and drag the duck to the upper left part of the slide.

➤ Click the computer and table. Click the **Ungroup Objects button** to separate these items.

➤ Click outside the selected items, then click and drag the table under the duck.

➤ Click the computer. Drag a **corner handle** to increase the size of the computer, then click and drag to position the computer closer to the duck.

➤ Save the presentation.

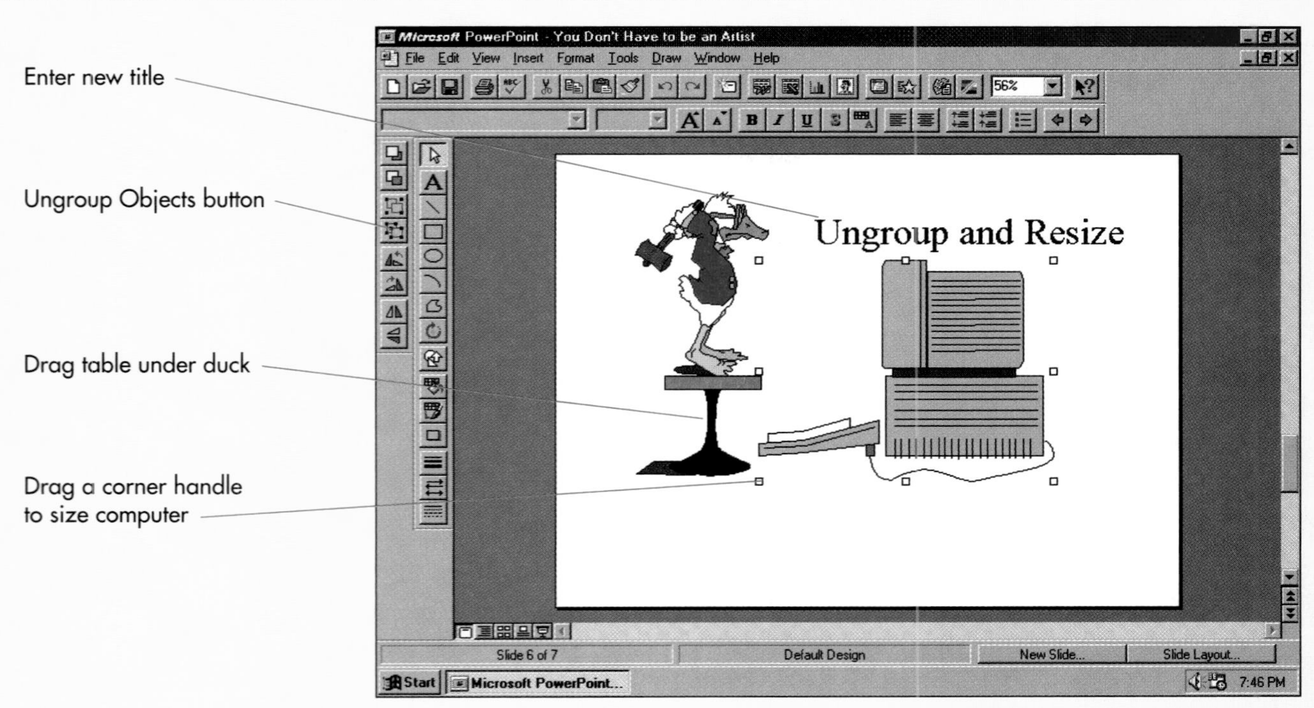

(h) Ungroup and Resize (step 8)

FIGURE 1.5 Hands-on Exercise 2 (continued)

PICK UP THE MOUSE

You always seem to run out of room on your real desk, just when you need to move the mouse a little further. The solution is to pick up the mouse and move it closer to you—the pointer will stay in its present position on the screen, but when you put the mouse down, you will have more room on your desk in which to work.

STEP 9: The Duplicate Command

- Press the **PgDn key** to move to slide 7. Click and drag to select the slide title, then type **Get Your Ducks in a Row** as the new title as shown in Figure 1.5i.
- Click and drag the clip art to the left side of the slide, then **ungroup** the duck and the computer. Click outside the selection to deselect both items, then click and drag the computer and table to the right of the slide.
- Select the duck. Pull down the **Edit menu** and click **Duplicate** (a combination of the Copy and Paste commands). You will see a second duck to the right of the first. Drag the second duck to the right until the ducks are separated as shown in Figure 1.5i.
- Pull down the **Edit menu** a second time and click **Duplicate Again.** A third duck will appear. (The distance between the second and third ducks is equal to the distance between the first and second ducks.)

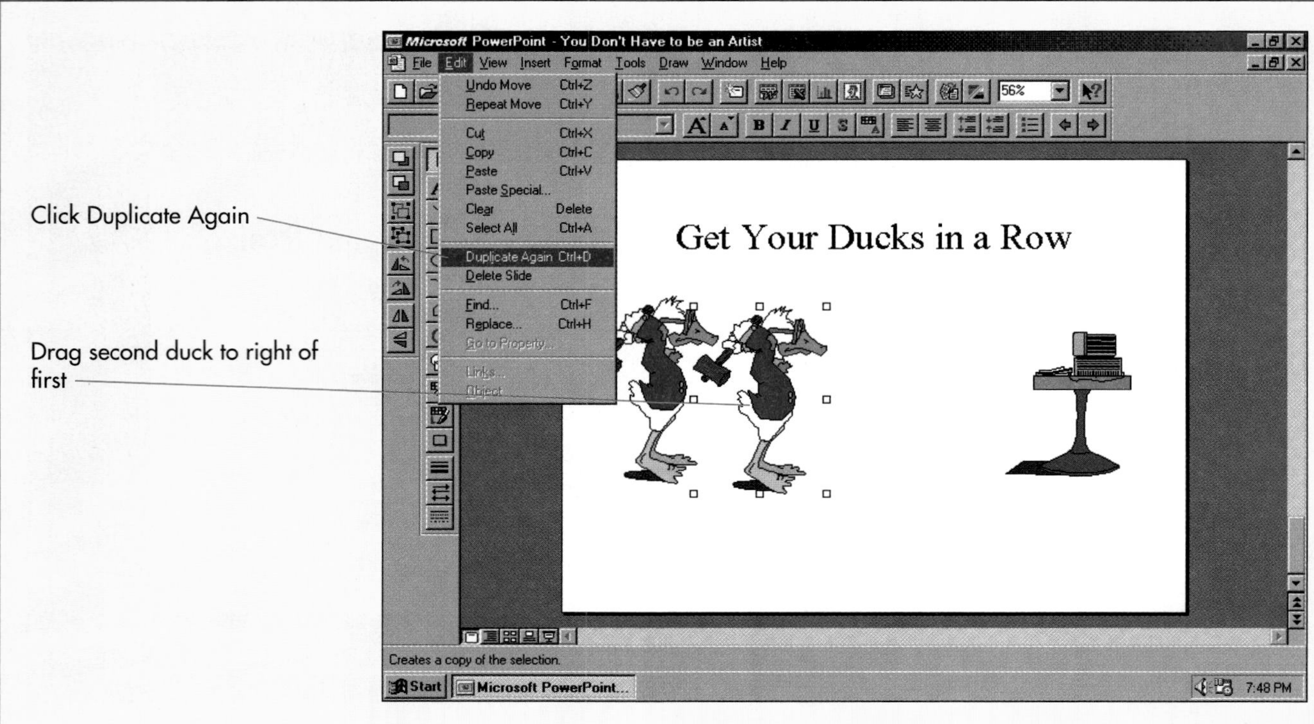

(i) The Duplicate Command (step 9)

FIGURE 1.5 Hands-on Exercise 2 (continued)

- ➤ Execute the **Duplicate Again** command a second time to create the fourth and final duck. Change the vest colors as you see fit.
- ➤ Save the presentation.

STEP 10: Print the Audience Handouts

- ➤ Pull down the **File menu.** Click **Slide Setup.** If necessary, click the **Portrait option button** to change the orientation for the Notes, Handouts, and Outline. Click **OK.**
- ➤ Pull down the **File menu.** Click **Print** to produce the Print dialog box. Click the **arrow** in the Print What drop-down list box. Click **Handouts (2 slides per page).**
- ➤ Check that the **All option button** is selected. Check the box to **Frame Slides.** Click **OK** to print the handouts.
- ➤ Save the presentation. Exit PowerPoint if you do not want to continue with the next exercise at this time.

OBJECT LINKING AND EMBEDDING

One of the primary advantages of the Windows environment is the ability to create a ***compound document*** containing data from multiple applications. This is accomplished through ***Object Linking and Embedding*** (OLE, pronounced "oh-lay") and it enables you to insert data (objects) from other applications into a PowerPoint presentation. You have, in fact, used OLE every time you inserted a clip art object into a presentation. You used it again at the beginning of this chapter to insert a graph created with the Microsoft Graph application. The next several pages describe other types of objects you can use to enhance a presentation.

In actuality, linking and embedding are two different techniques. The essential difference between the two is that embedding places the object into the presentation, whereas linking does not. In other words, an ***embedded object*** is stored within the presentation, and the presentation, in turn, becomes the only user (container) of that object. A ***linked object,*** on the other hand, is stored in its own file, and the presentation is one of many potential containers of that object. The presentation does not contain the object per se, but only a representation of the object as well as a pointer (link) to the file containing the object (the source document). The advantage of linking is that the presentation is updated automatically if the object is changed in the source document.

The choice between linking and embedding depends on how the object will be used. Linking is preferable if the object is likely to change and your presentation requires the latest version. Linking should also be used when the same object is placed in many documents, so that any change to the object has to be made in only one place (the source document). Embedding should be used if you need to take the presentation with you—for example, if you intend to show the presentation on a different computer.

The easiest way to link or embed an object is through the appropriate AutoLayout as shown in Figure 1.6. Choose the AutoLayout for an Object slide as shown in Figure 1.6a, then double click the object placeholder to produce the Insert Object dialog box in Figure 1.6b. The object types displayed within the dialog box depend on the applications that are installed on your system.

The option buttons to create a new object or to create the object from a file are mutually exclusive in that you choose one or the other. If you embed an object, you can choose either option. If you link, however, you must choose the Create from File option because a linked object has to exist in its own file. This in turn produces the dialog box in Figure 1.6c, in which you must enter the source file name as well as check the box to create a link. The example links the Excel workbook, Grade Book in the Exploring Excel folder, to the PowerPoint presentation and is illustrated in the next hands-on exercise.

WordArt

Microsoft WordArt is a separate application included with Microsoft Office that enables you to add special effects to text, then embed the text as an object into a presentation. WordArt is called from within PowerPoint by choosing the AutoLayout for an object slide, double clicking the object placeholder, and selecting WordArt object.

WordArt is intuitive and easy to use. In essence, you enter the text in the dialog box of Figure 1.7a, then choose a shape for the text from among the selections shown in Figure 1.7b. You can create special effects by choosing one of several different shadows as shown in Figure 1.7c. You can use any TrueType font installed on your system, and you can change the color and/or patterns of the WordArt object. Figure 1.7d shows the completed WordArt object.

Organization Charts

Microsoft Organization Chart is yet another application included with Microsoft Office; it enables you to create an organization chart and embed it into a presentation. You start the application by choosing the AutoLayout containing an organization chart or by creating an object slide and choosing Microsoft Organization Chart as the object.

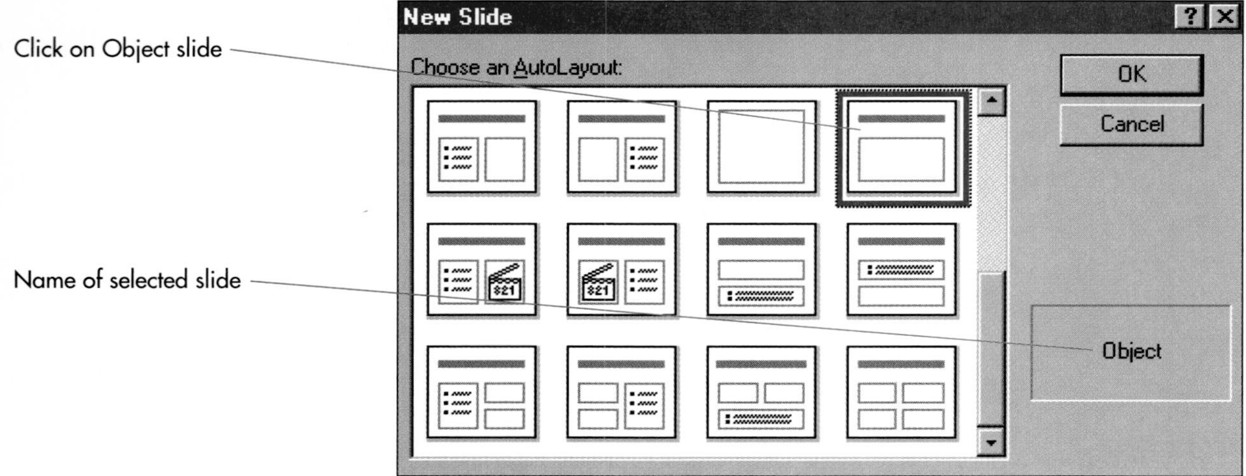

(a) The AutoLayout

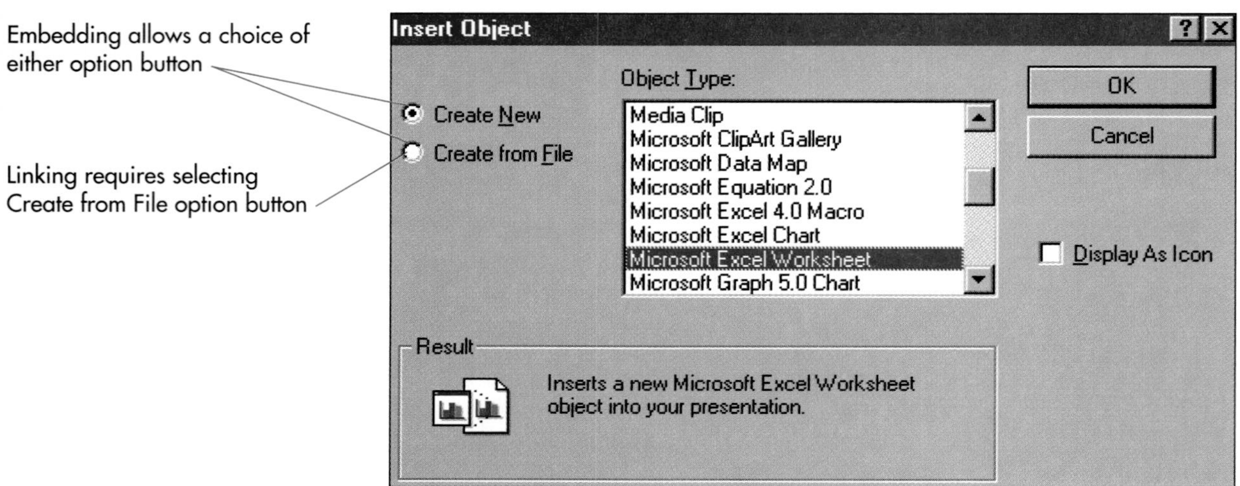

(b) Insert Object Dialog Box

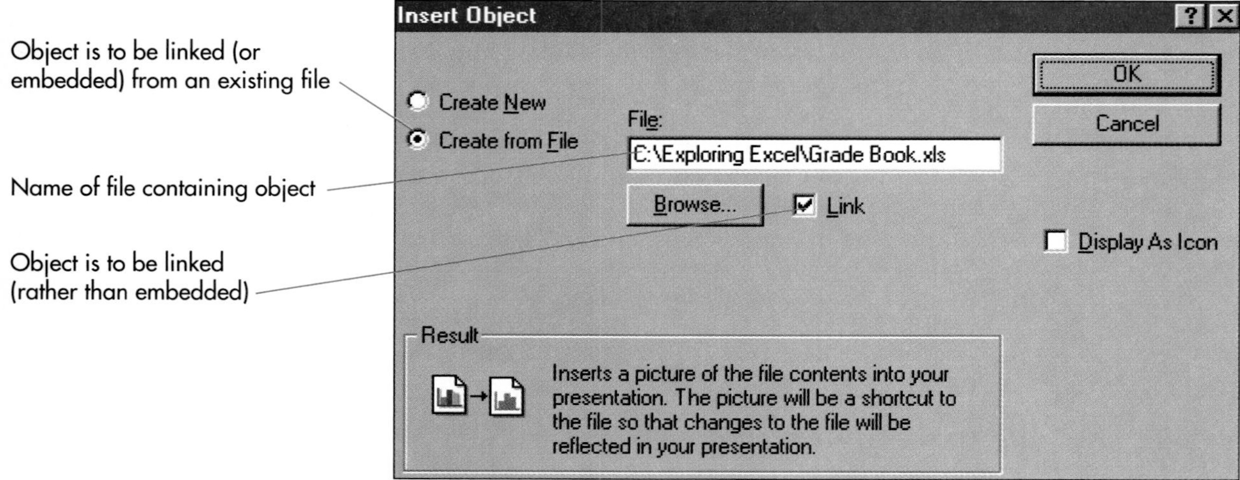

(c) Create the Link

FIGURE 1.6 Object Linking and Embedding

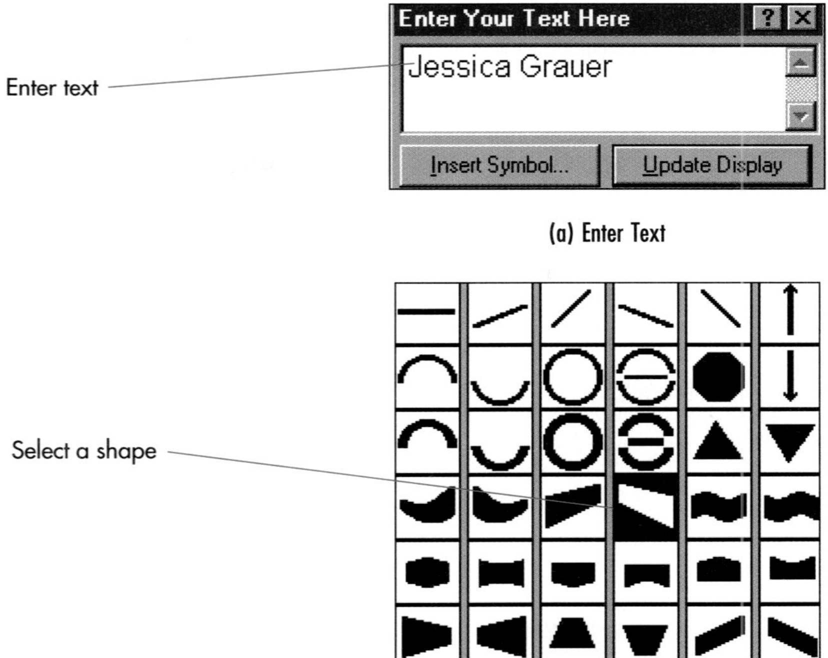

(a) Enter Text

(b) Text Shapes

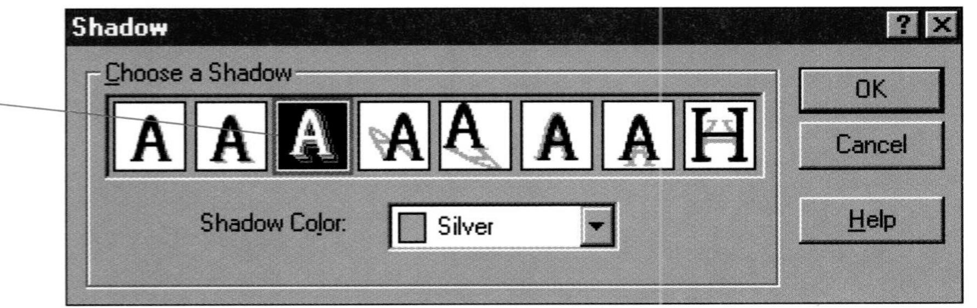

(c) Shadows

(d) Completed Text

FIGURE 1.7 WordArt

A partially completed organization chart is shown in Figure 1.8. To add additional boxes, you just click the appropriate command button at the top of the window. The coworker buttons create a box on the same level to the left or right of the current box. The subordinate command button creates a box under the current box, while the manager button creates a box above the current box. To delete a box, select the box, then press the Del key.

You can change the design of the connecting lines and/or the boxes in the chart, as well as their color. You can also change the font and/or alignment of the text within the individual boxes. Microsoft Organization Chart is illustrated in the hands-on exercise that follows shortly.

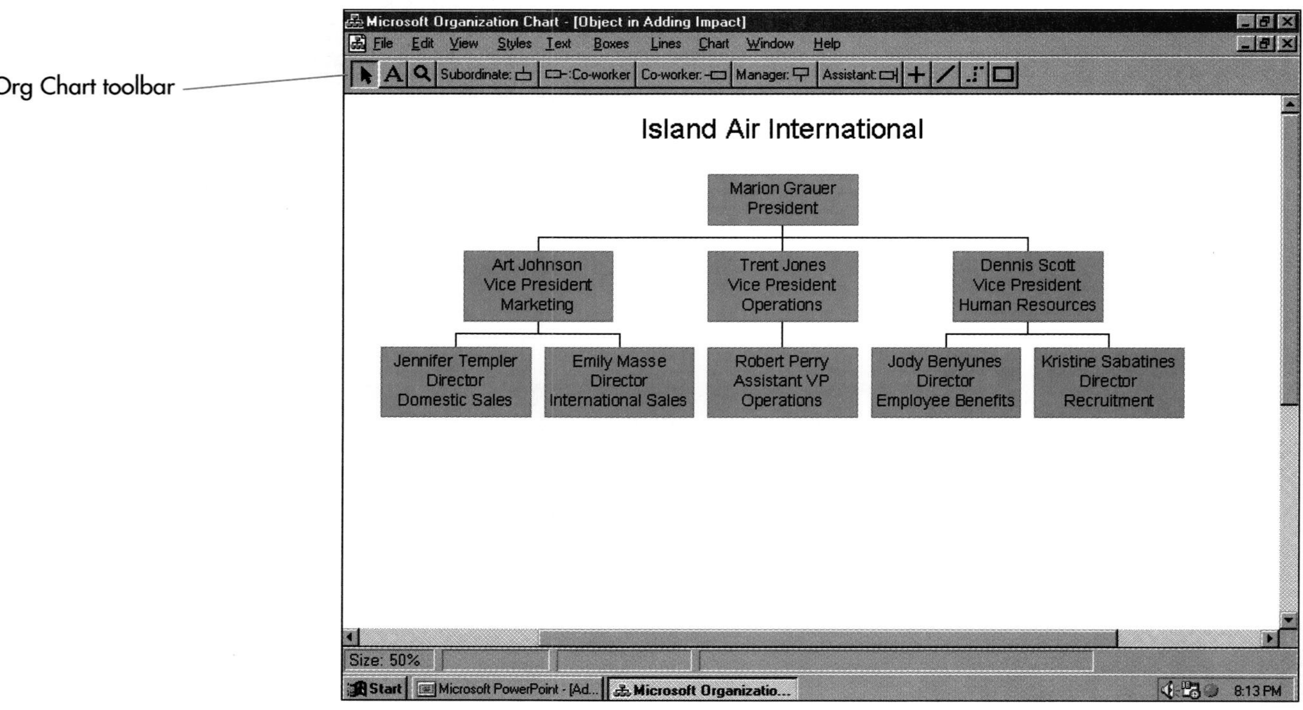

FIGURE 1.8 Organization Chart

Sound

Sound can be linked or embedded into a presentation just like any other object. Realize, however, that sound requires additional hardware, namely a sound card and speakers, and we urge you to include these options on any machine you buy. (Sound may not be available in a laboratory setting for obvious reasons.)

Sounds exist as separate files that are inserted into a presentation through the Insert Object command as illustrated in the following hands-on exercise. Additional information about the different types of sound files is found in Appendix B, Introduction to Multimedia.

HANDS-ON EXERCISE 3

Adding Impact through Object Linking and Embedding

Objective: To link an Excel worksheet to a PowerPoint presentation; to embed an organization chart, a WordArt object, and a sound file into a PowerPoint presentation. Use Figure 1.9 as a guide in doing the exercise. Completion of the exercise requires that Microsoft Excel be installed on your system.

STEP 1: Create the Title Slide

➤ Create a new presentation:

- If necessary, start PowerPoint. Click the option button to create a **Blank Presentation,** then click **OK.** If necessary, click the **Maximize button** so that PowerPoint takes the entire desktop.
- If PowerPoint is already started, pull down the **File menu** and click **New** (or click the **New button** on the Standard toolbar). If necessary, double click the **Blank Presentation icon** to display the New Presentation dialog box.

➤ You should see the New slide dialog box with the AutoLayout for the title slide already selected. Click **OK** to create the title slide. Click the placeholder for the title and enter **Adding Impact** as the title of the presentation. Click the placeholder for the subtitle. Enter your name.

➤ Click the **Save button** on the Standard toolbar. Save the presentation as **Adding Impact** in the **Exploring PowerPoint folder.**

STEP 2: Add an Object Slide

➤ Click the **New Slide button** on the status bar to add a second slide. You should see the New Slide dialog box. Click the **down arrow** and scroll through the available slide layouts until you can select the **Object slide** (AutoLayout number 16). Click **OK.**

➤ You should see the slide in Figure 1.9a.

THE AUTOLAYOUTS ARE NUMBERED

Each of the 24 AutoLayouts has an assigned number, corresponding to its position within the New Slide dialog box. (The layouts are numbered consecutively from left to right and top to bottom.) The number can be used as a shortcut to select the AutoLayout in lieu of clicking; type 2, for example, to select a bulleted list (the second slide in row 1). Other frequently used AutoLayouts include a title slide (number 1), a graph and title (number 8), an organization chart and title (number 7), an object and title (number 16), and a blank slide (number 12).

STEP 3: Insert the Excel Worksheet

➤ Double click the **placeholder** to add an object, producing the Insert Object dialog box. Scroll through the **Object Type** list box until you can select **Microsoft Excel Worksheet.** Then:

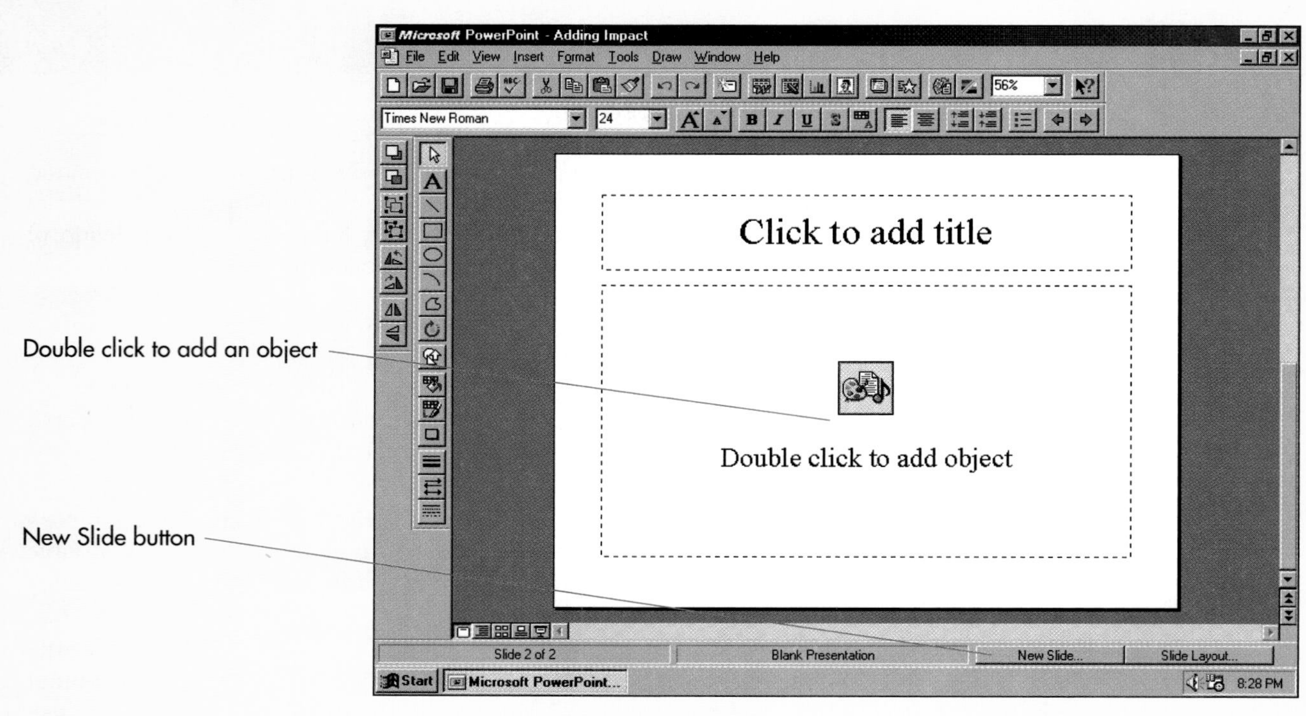

(a) Add an Object Slide (step 2)

FIGURE 1.9 Hands-on Exercise 3

- Click the option button for **Create from File** to produce the dialog box in Figure 1.9b.
- Click the **Browse button** to display the Browse dialog box. Click the **down arrow** on the Look In list box and select the **Exploring PowerPoint folder** (which contains the Excel workbook you are looking for).
- Select the **Grade Book workbook** from within the Exploring PowerPoint folder. Click **OK** to close the Browse dialog box.

LINKING VERSUS EMBEDDING

Linking is very different from embedding as it provides a dynamic connection between the source and container (destination) documents. A linked object (e.g., an Excel worksheet) is tied to the container document (e.g., a PowerPoint presentation) in such a way that any changes to the source file are automatically reflected in the container document. Linking is especially useful when the same object is inserted in multiple documents, as changes to the object are made in only one place (in the source file). A linked object must be saved as a separate file. An embedded object, on the other hand, is inserted directly into a source document and need not exist in its own file.

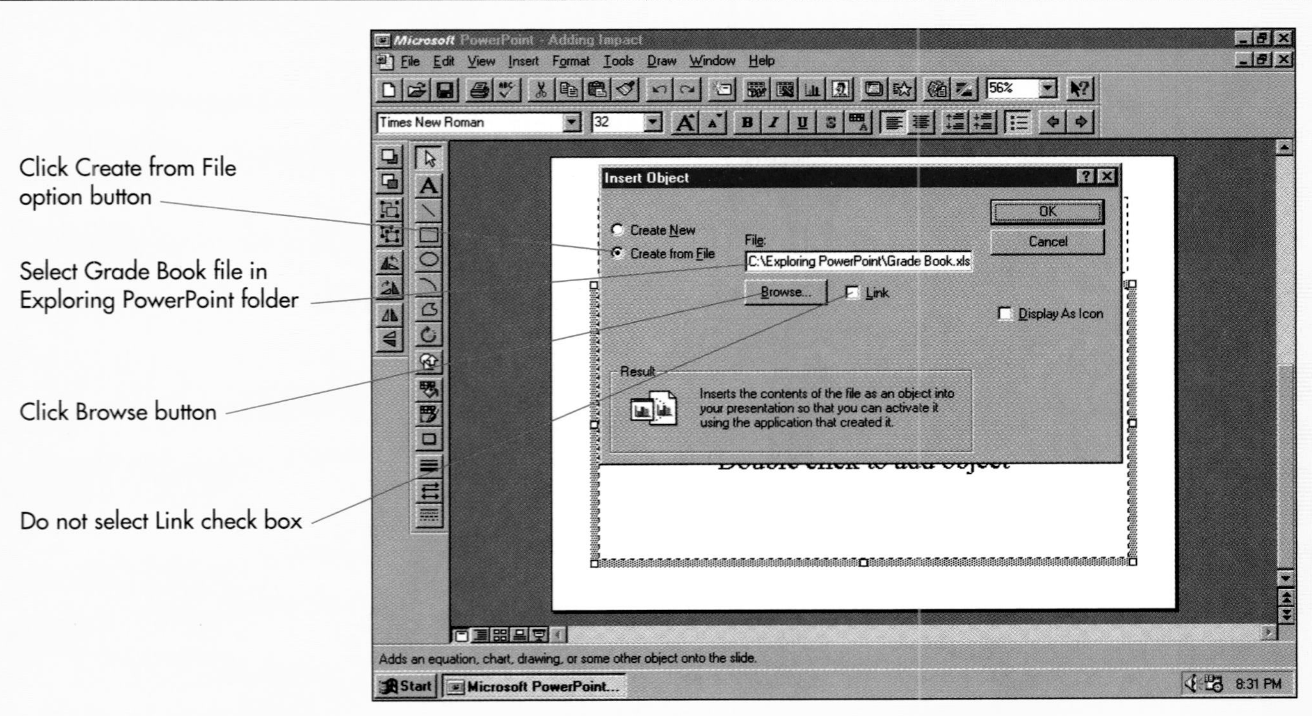

(b) Select the Object (step 3)

FIGURE 1.9 Hands-on Exercise 3 (continued)

- If necessary, clear the Link check box as we want to embed (rather than link) the worksheet into the presentation. Click **OK** to insert the worksheet into the presentation. (This may take a moment, depending on the speed of your system.)

➤ Save the presentation.

STEP 4: Move and Size the Worksheet

➤ You should see the worksheet in Figure 1.9c. The sizing handles indicate that the worksheet is currently selected and can be moved and sized like any other Windows object.

➤ Click anywhere outside the worksheet to deselect it. The sizing handles disappear.

➤ Click the **title placeholder** and type **CIS120 Grade Book** as the title of the slide.

➤ Save the presentation.

IN-PLACE EDITING

In-place editing enables you to double click an Excel worksheet in order to edit the object. You remain in PowerPoint, but the toolbar and pull-down menus are those of Excel. The File and Window menus are exceptions, however, and contain PowerPoint commands to save the presentation and/or view multiple presentations.

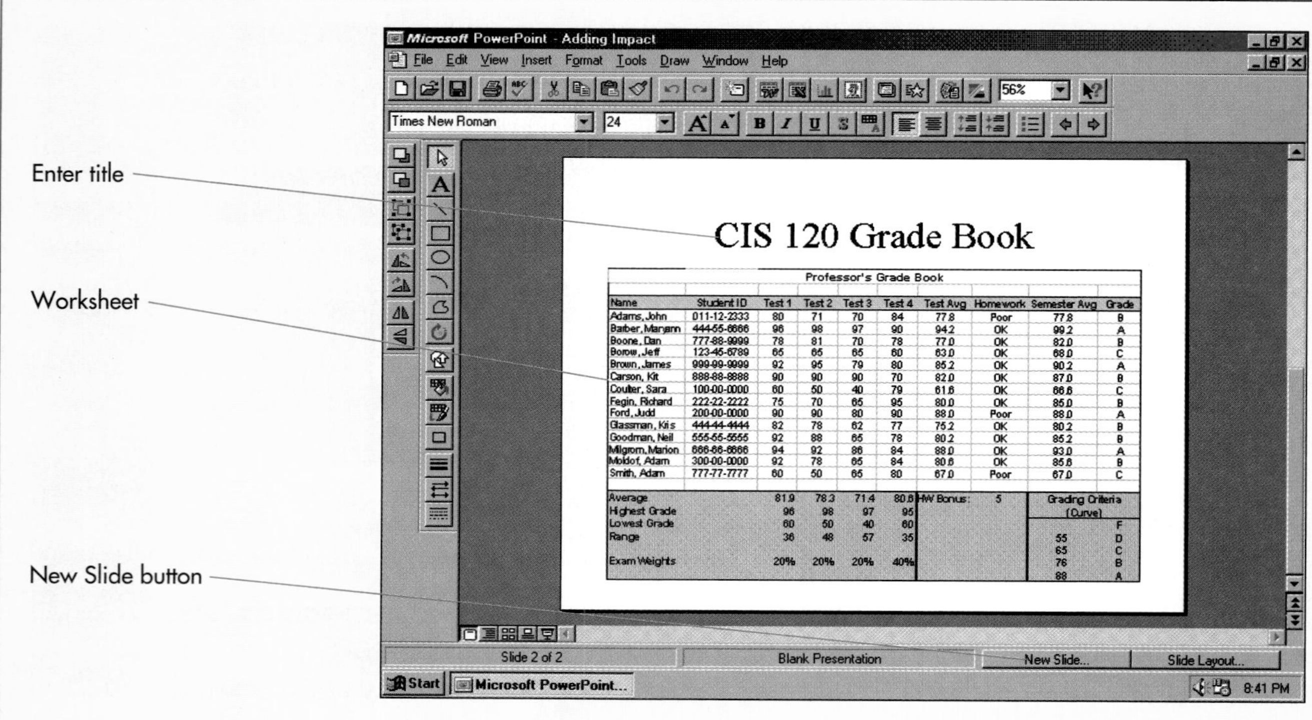

(c) Complete the Slide (step 4)

FIGURE 1.9 Hands-on Exercise 3 (continued)

STEP 5: Add the Organization Chart

- Click the **New Slide button** on the status bar. Click the AutoLayout for an **Organization chart** (or just type the number **7,** which is the number of the desired layout). Click **OK** to add the slide, then double click the placeholder to add the organization chart.
- You should see a window titled **Microsoft Organization Chart** open within the PowerPoint window, as shown in Figure 1.9d. Click the **Maximize button** of the Microsoft Organization Chart window.
- The text in the first box is already selected. Type your name and press **enter** to move to the second line. Type **President** for your title.
- Click in the first box in the second row. Enter the name of a friend as Vice President of Marketing. (Press **enter** to move to a second line.) Add two additional friends as Vice Presidents of Operations and Human Resources.

STEP 6: Complete the Organization Chart

- You can add detail to the chart by entering additional boxes for subordinates or coworkers. Enter the subordinates as shown in Figure 1.9e:
  - To add a subordinate, click the subordinate button on the Organization Chart toolbar, then click the box under which the subordinate is to appear.
  - To add a coworker, manager, or assistant, follow the same procedure as for a subordinate.
  - To enter a person's name and title in an existing box, click in the box, then enter the text. Press the **enter key** to go from line to line.
  - To delete a box, click in the box to select it, then press the **Del key.**

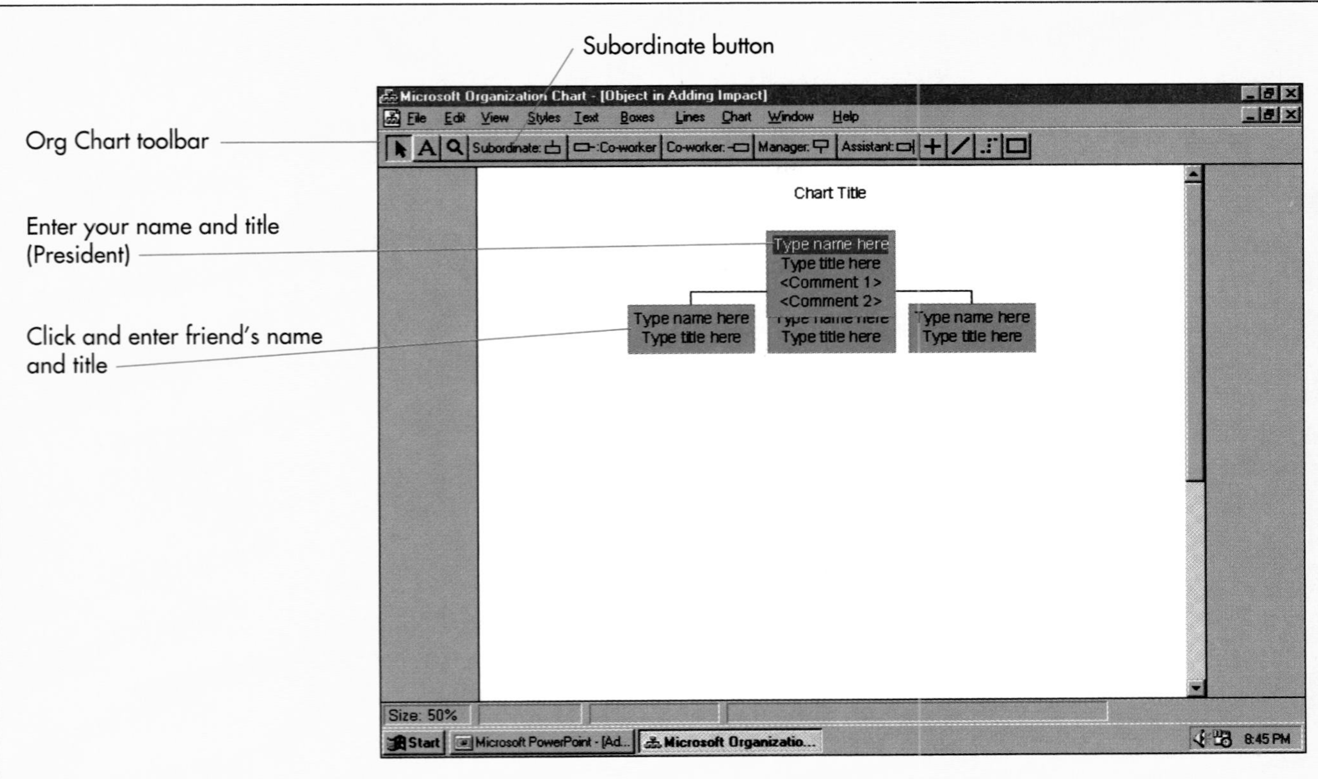

(d) Create the Organization Chart (step 5)

FIGURE 1.9 Hands-on Exercise 3 (continued)

- Pull down the **File menu.** Click **Exit and Return to Adding Impact** (the name of the presentation). Click **Yes** when asked whether to update the object. You should see an organization chart similar to the one in Figure 1.9e.
- Click the placeholder for the slide title and enter the title of your organization.
- Save the presentation.

SELECT, THEN DO

You can change the appearance of the various boxes within an organization chart by selecting the box, then executing the appropriate formatting command. It's generally best, however, to retain a uniform appearance for the chart as a whole by formatting the entire chart at one time. Thus, to select multiple boxes, press and hold the Shift key as you click each box in succession, or press Ctrl+A to select all of the boxes at the same time. Pull down the Boxes menu, then select the command to change the border style, border color, or border line style. To change the line color, style, or thickness, select all of the lines (pull down the Edit menu, click Select, and click Connecting lines), then choose the desired commands from the Lines menu.

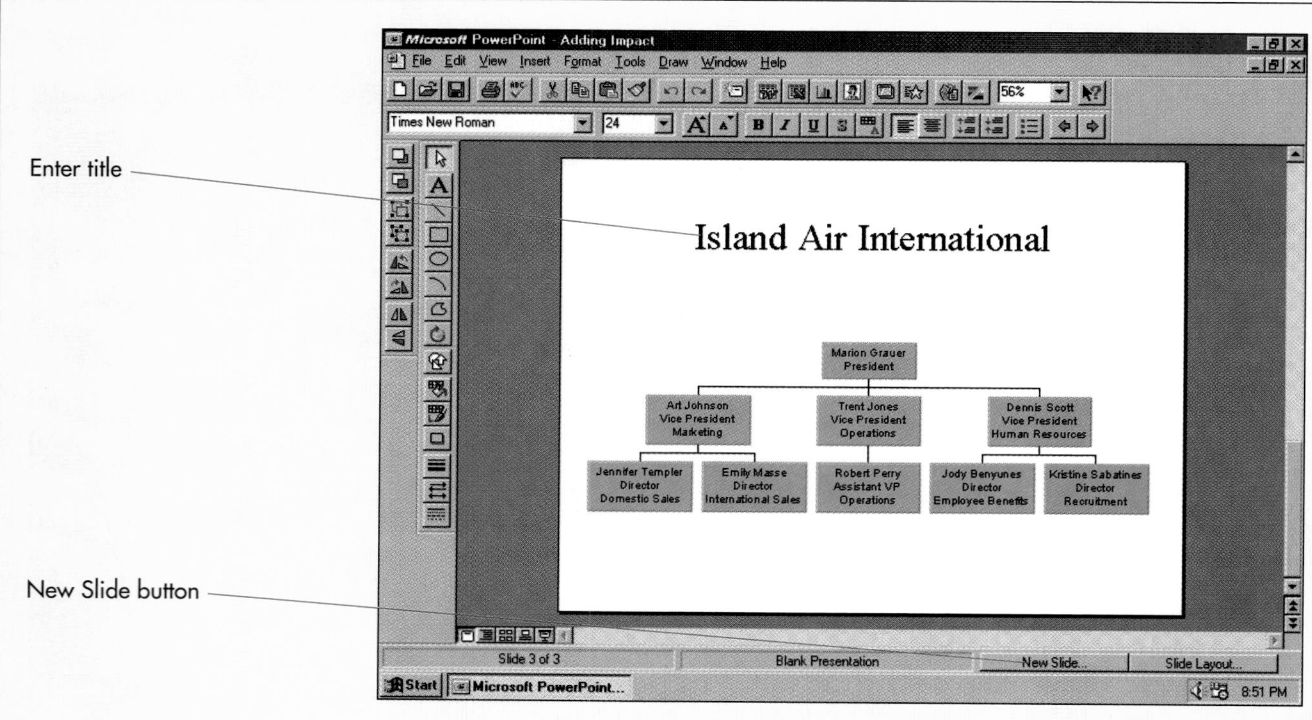

(e) The Completed Organization Chart (step 6)

FIGURE 1.9 Hands-on Exercise 3 (continued)

STEP 7: Clip Art and AutoShapes

➤ Click the **New Slide button** on the status bar, then do one of the following:

- Click **AutoLayout Number 11** (Title only), click **OK** to add the slide to the presentation, then click the **Insert Clip Art button** on the Standard toolbar to display the ClipArt Gallery dialog box, *or*
- Click **AutoLayout Number 16** (Object), click **OK** to add the slide to the presentation, then double click the placeholder to add the object. Choose **Microsoft ClipArt Gallery** from the list of available objects to display the ClipArt Gallery dialog box.

➤ Choose an appropriate clip art image. Click **Insert,** then move and size the clip art so that it is positioned as shown in Figure 1.9f. Click in the title placeholder, then enter **Clip Art and AutoShapes** as the title for this slide.

➤ Click the **AutoShapes button** on the Drawing toolbar to display the AutoShapes toolbar. Select (click) the **Balloon tool,** then click and drag on the slide where you want the balloon to go. Release the mouse.

➤ The balloon should be selected automatically with the sizing handles displayed:

- Type **I can do this!** as the caption. (You must enter the text when the balloon is selected.)
- If necessary, click and drag the balloon to adjust its size or position.
- To change the Fill color or Line color, click the appropriate tool on the Drawing toolbar, then select one of the displayed colors.

➤ Click outside the balloon to deselect it.

➤ Save the presentation. Close the AutoShapes toolbar.

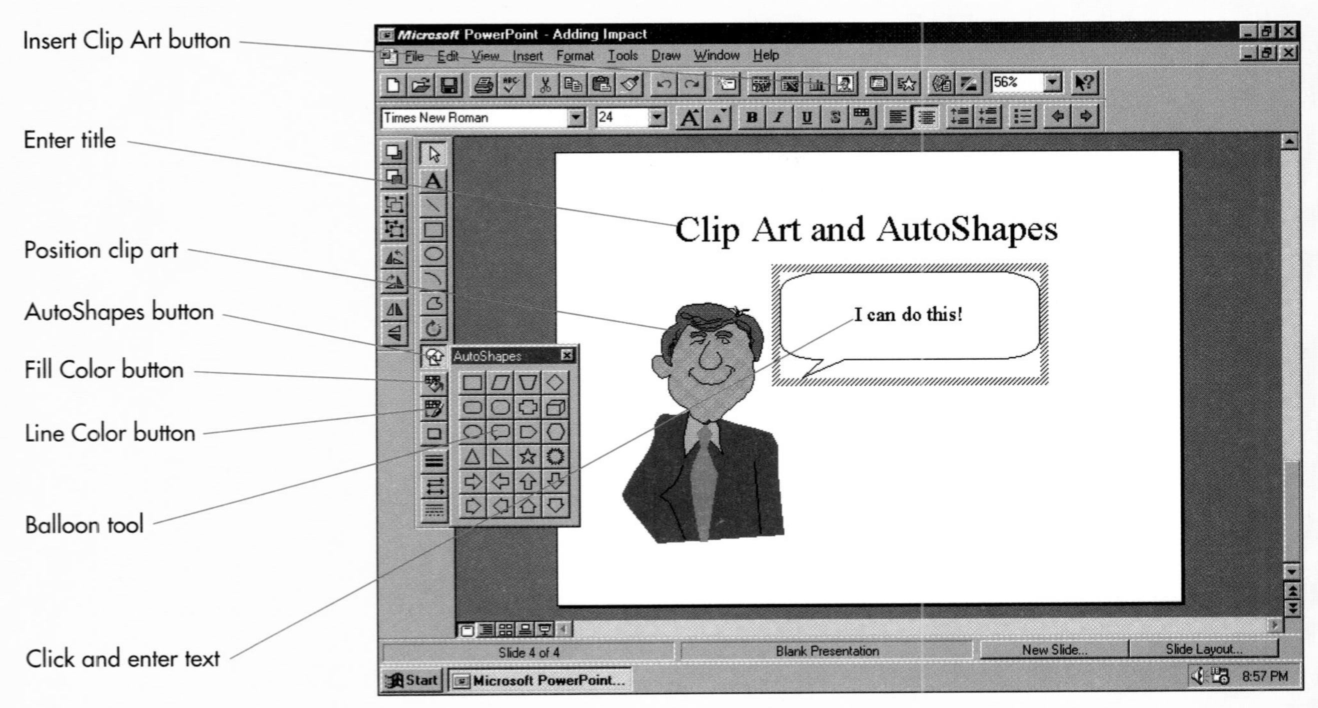

(f) Clip Art and AutoShapes (step 7)

FIGURE 1.9 Hands-on Exercise 3 (continued)

AUTOSHAPES

An AutoShape is a predefined shape that is drawn automatically when you select its icon from the AutoShapes toolbar, then click and drag in the slide. (To display the AutoShapes toolbar, click the AutoShape tool on the Drawing toolbar.) To place text inside an AutoShape, select the shape and start typing. You can also change the fill color or line thickness by selecting the shape, then clicking the appropriate button on the Drawing toolbar. See practice exercise 3 at the end of the chapter for additional information.

STEP 8: Insert a Slide

- Click the **Slide Sorter View button** above the status bar to change to the Slide Sorter view. Click the last slide (the one with the clip art that you just created) to position yourself at the point within the presentation where you want to add a slide. (The new slide will be inserted after the selected slide.)
- Pull down the **Insert menu** and click **Slides from File** to display the Insert File dialog box shown in Figure 1.9g.
- Select (click) the **My Chart presentation** (that you created in the first hands-on exercise), then click the **Insert button** to insert the slide(s) from that presentation into the current presentation. The graph from the first exercise has been inserted as the fifth slide in this presentation.

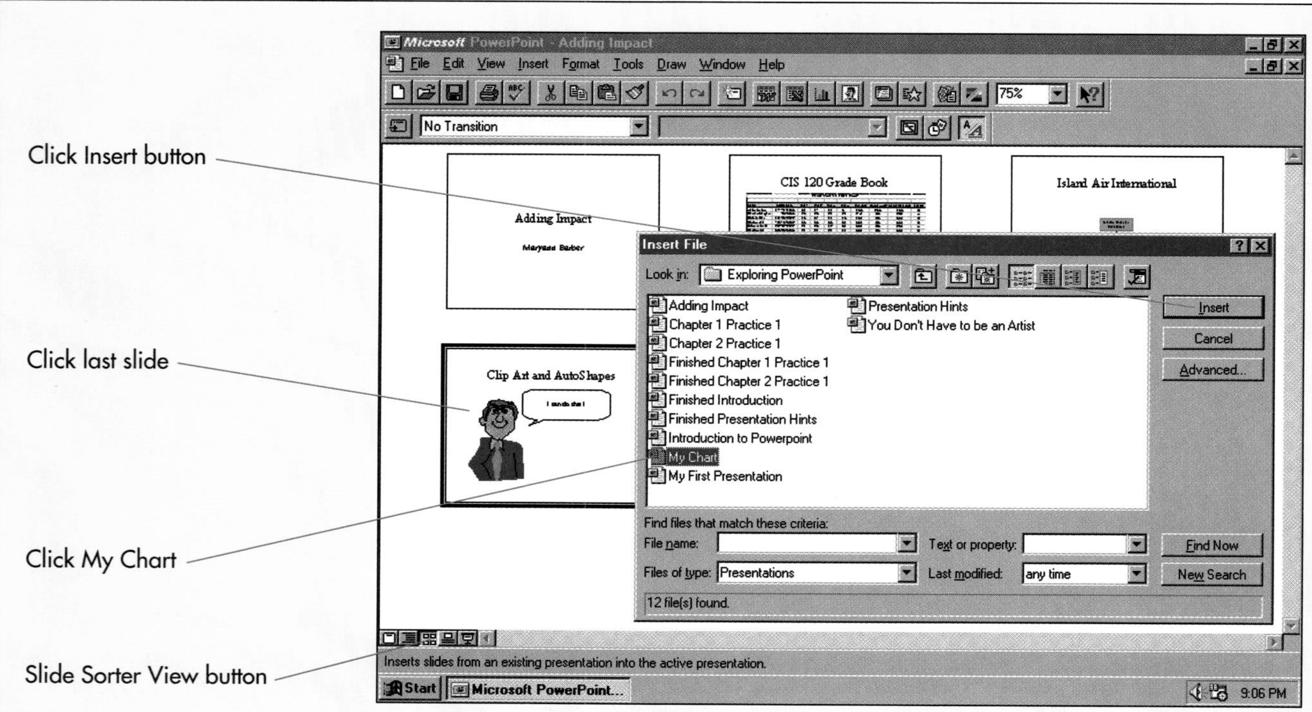

(g) Insert a Slide (step 8)

FIGURE 1.9 Hands-on Exercise 3 (continued)

USE WHAT YOU HAVE

You work hard to develop individual slides and thus you may find it useful to reuse a slide from one presentation to the next. Change to the Slide Sorter view in the current presentation, then click on the slide after which you want to insert a slide(s) from another presentation. Pull down the Insert menu, click the Slides from File command, then specify the presentation containing the slide(s) you want. The command is limited, however, in that it inserts every slide, and hence you may have to delete unwanted slides after they have been inserted. Press and hold the Shift key to select any slides you do not want, then press the Del key to delete those slides.

STEP 9: WordArt

- Click the slide containing the chart, then click the **New Slide button** on the status bar. Click the AutoLayout for a **blank slide** (or type **12** as the number of the desired layout). Click **OK** to add the slide.
- Change to the **Slide view.** Pull down the **Insert menu** and click **Object** to produce the Insert Object dialog box. Scroll until you can select **Microsoft WordArt 2.0** from the Object Type list box.
- Click the **Create New option button,** then click **OK.** You should see a screen similar to Figure 1.9h. Type **The End** in the Enter Your Text dialog box. Click the **Update Display command button.**

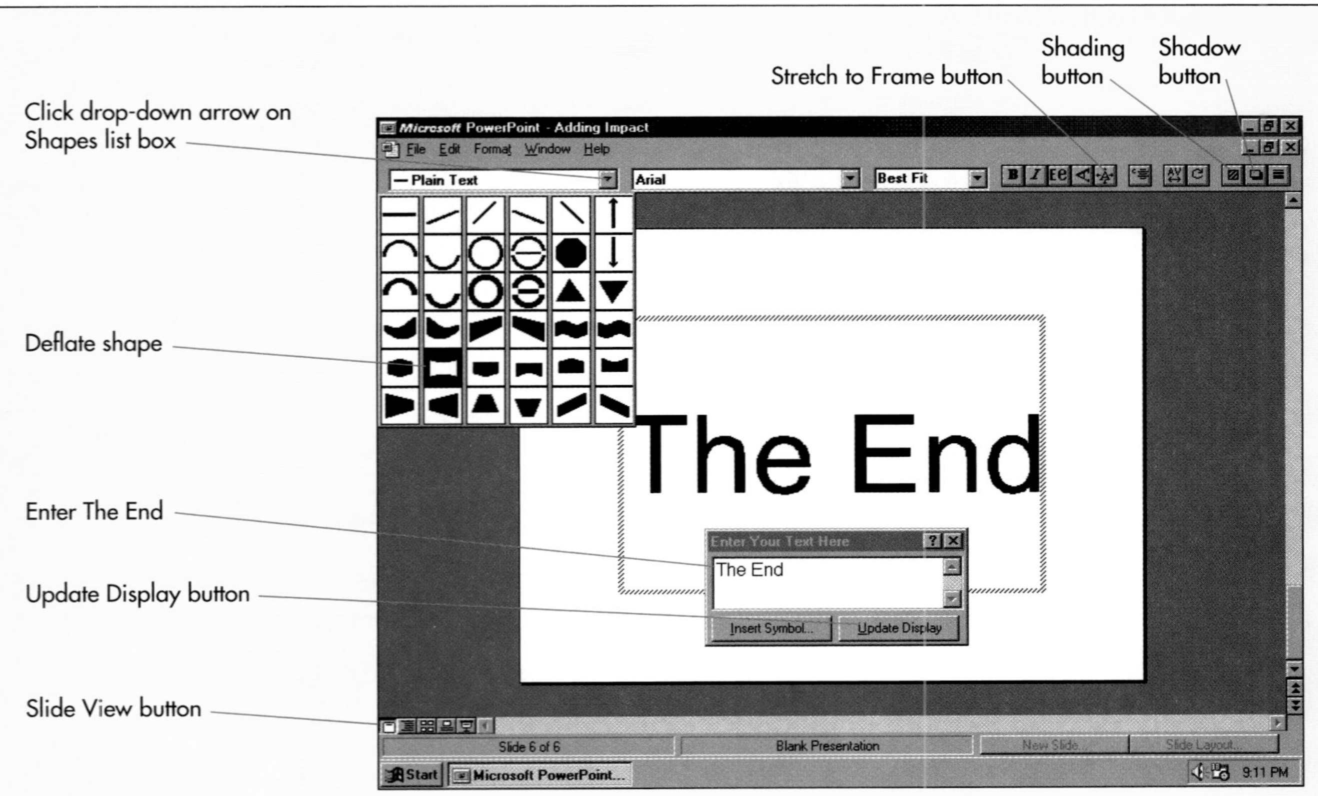

(h) WordArt (step 8)

FIGURE 1.9 Hands-on Exercise 3 (continued)

- Click the **drop-down arrow** on the Shapes list box and click **Deflate shape.** The shape of the text changes to match the shape chosen. Click the **Stretch to Frame button** on the WordArt toolbar so that the text will always fill the frame, regardless of the size of the frame.
- You can experiment with other effects to enhance the WordArt image. Click the **Shadow button** to add a shadow to the text and/or change the color of the shadow. Click the **Shading button** and change the **Foreground color** to **red.**
- Click outside the WordArt to deselect it and return to the PowerPoint presentation. The WordArt object should be selected with the sizing handles displayed. Click and drag a corner to enlarge the WordArt object so that it fills almost the entire slide.
- Save the presentation.

STEP 9: Sound (requires a sound card)

- Pull down the **Insert Menu.** Click **Sound** to display the Insert Sound dialog box in Figure 1.9i. If necessary, change to the **Exploring PowerPoint folder,** then double click the **Applause sound file** to insert the sound object into the presentation.
- A tiny microphone appears in the middle of the slide to indicate that the sound file has been embedded on the slide. Point to the microphone and click the **right mouse button** to display a shortcut menu, then click **Play Wave Sound Object** to play the sound and hear the applause.
- Save the presentation.

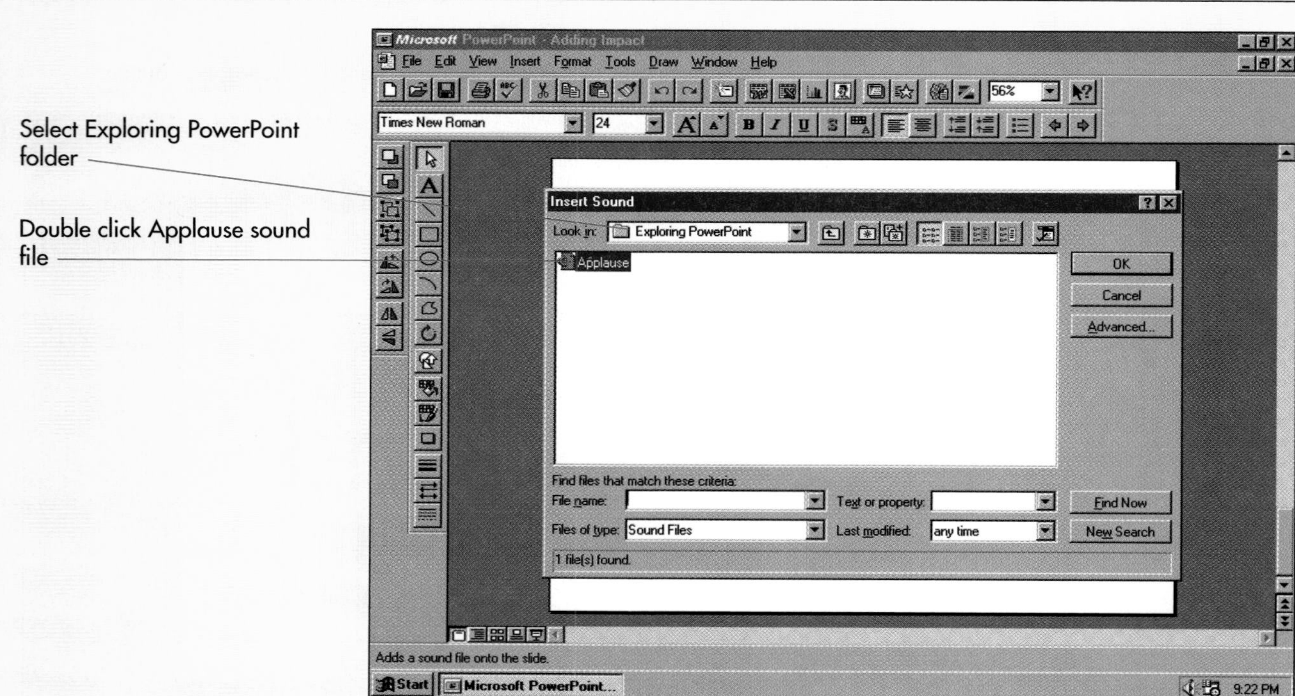

(i) Insert a Sound (step 9)

FIGURE 1.9 Hands-on Exercise 3 (continued)

THE WINDOWS 95 FIND COMMAND

We supplied the sound of applause, but you are likely to have many other sound files on your system, any one of which can be embedded into a presentation. The easiest way to locate these files is through the Windows 95 Find command. Click the Start button, click (or point to) the Find command, then click Files or Folders to display the Find dialog box. Enter *.wav (the "wav" indicates a sound file) in the Named text box and My Computer in the Look In box. Click Find Now. Use the right mouse button to click and drag a file from the Find Files window onto your presentation, release the mouse, then click the Copy Here command to embed the sound onto the slide.

STEP 10: Animation Settings

- Click and drag the sound icon to the upper right portion of the slide as shown in Figure 1.9j.
- Point to the icon, click the **right mouse button** to display a shortcut menu, then click **Animation Settings** to display the Animation Settings dialog box in Figure 1.9j.
- Click the **drop-down arrow** on the Play Options list box and click **Play.** Click the **More command button** to display the More Play Options dialog box.

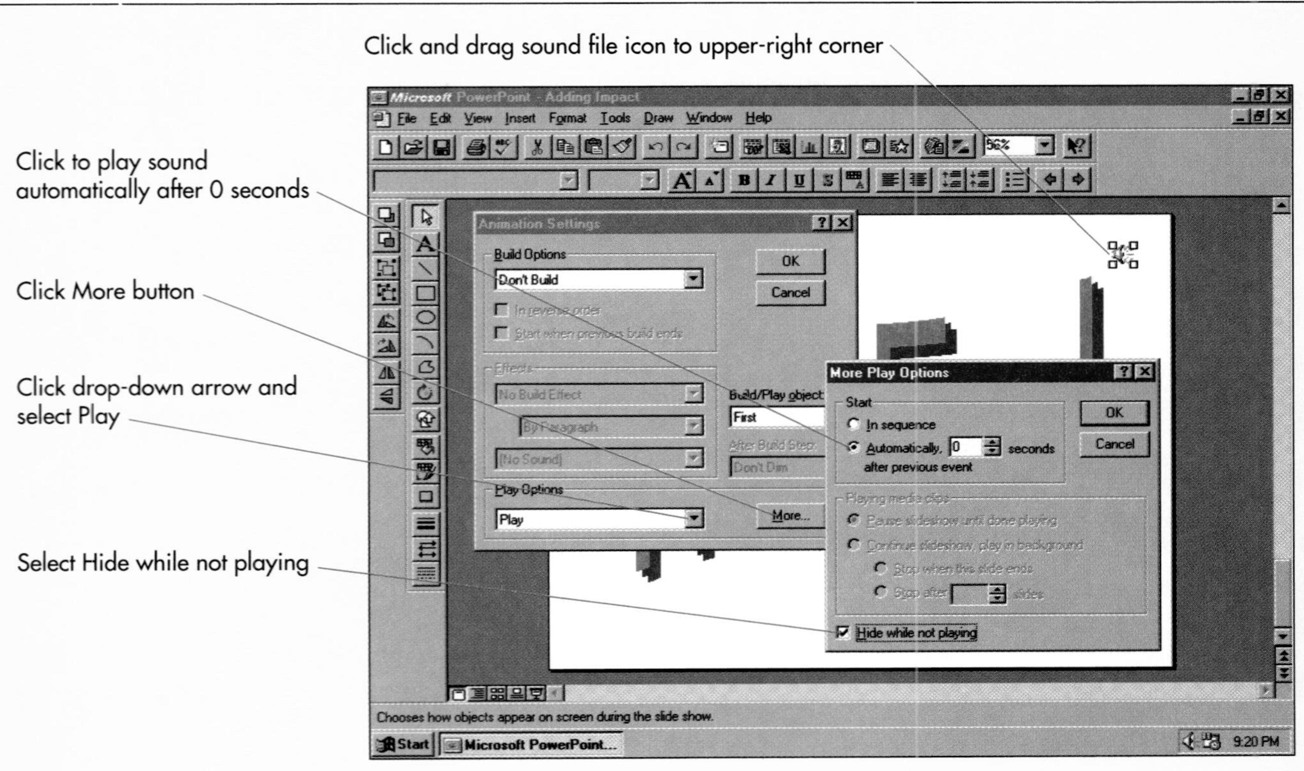

(j) Animation Settings (step 10)

FIGURE 1.9 Hands-on Exercise 3 (continued)

- Click the option button to play the sound automatically (after 0 seconds). Check the box to **Hide** the icon while not playing. Click **OK** to close the More Play Options dialog box. Click **OK** to close the Animation Settings dialog box.
- Save the presentation.

STEP 11: Applause, Applause

- Press **Ctrl+Home** to move to the first slide in the presentation, then click the **Slide Show button** to view the presentation.
- Click the **left mouse button** (or press the **PgDn key**) to move from slide to slide until you come to the end of the presentation. The applause you hear on the last slide is for your efforts in this exercise.
- Click the mouse a final time to return to the Slide view. Exit PowerPoint if you do not want to continue with the next exercise at this time.

BRANCHING WITHIN A PRESENTATION

The most effective public speakers are sensitive to their audiences and are able to adapt their presentations to specific situations. Thus far all of the presentations in our text have been designed to be viewed sequentially, starting with the first slide and ending with the last slide. Figure 1.10 introduces ***branching*** into a presenta-

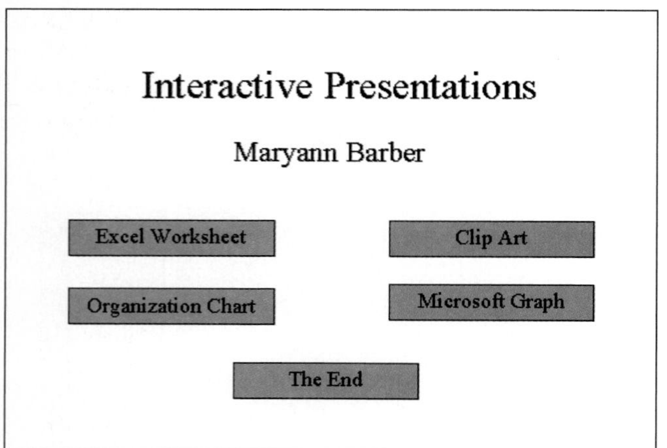

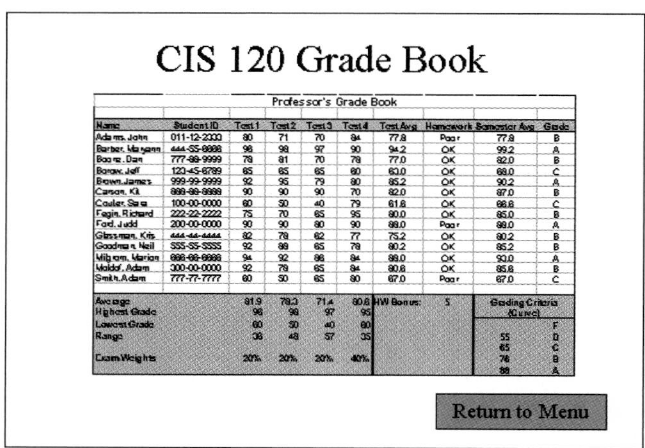

Professor's Grade Book

Name	Student ID	Test1	Test2	Test3	Test4	Test Avg	Homework	Semester Avg	Grade
Adams, John	011-12-2000	80	71	70	84	77.8	Poor	77.8	B
Barber, Maryann	444-55-8888	98	98	97	90	94.2	OK	99.2	A
Boone, Dan	777-88-9999	78	81	70	78	77.0	OK	82.0	B
Borow, Jeff	123-45-6789	65	65	65	80	63.0	OK	68.0	C
Brown, James	999-99-9999	92	95	79	80	85.2	OK	90.2	A
Carson, Kit	888-88-8888	90	90	90	70	82.0	OK	87.0	B
Coulter, Sara	100-00-0000	60	50	40	79	61.6	OK	66.6	C
Fegin, Richard	222-22-2222	75	70	65	95	80.0	OK	85.0	B
Ford, Judd	200-00-0000	90	90	80	90	88.0	Poor	88.0	A
Glassman, Kris	444-44-4444	82	78	62	77	75.2	OK	80.2	B
Goodman, Neil	555-55-5555	92	88	65	78	80.2	OK	85.2	B
Milgrom, Marion	888-88-8888	94	92	86	84	88.0	OK	90.0	A
Moldof, Adam	300-00-0000	92	78	65	84	80.8	OK	85.8	B
Smith, Adam	777-77-7777	80	50	65	80	67.0	Poor	67.0	C
Average		81.9	78.3	71.4	80.8	HW Bonus:	5	Grading Criteria (Curve)	
Highest Grade		98	98	97	95				F
Lowest Grade		60	50	40	60			55	D
Range		38	48	57	35			65	C
Exam Weights		20%	20%	20%	40%			76	B
								88	A

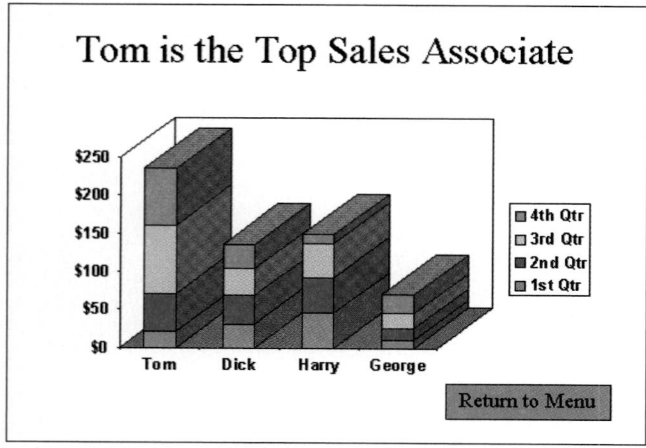

FIGURE 1.10 Branching within a Presentation

tion by placing buttons onto a slide that enable you to move nonsequentially through a presentation.

Figure 1.10 shows a slightly modified version of the presentation created in the previous hands-on exercise. The title slide has been modified to include five command buttons, each of which branches to a specific slide in the presentation. Click any of these buttons during the slide show, and you are transferred immediately to that slide. Click the "Return to Menu" button on any of the remaining slides, and you go back to the first slide in the presentation.

You are under no obligation to use the command buttons and can still move through the presentation sequentially by clicking the left mouse button (or pressing the PgDn key) to move to the next sequential slide. The command buttons are created through the ***Interactive Settings command*** in the Tools menu as demonstrated in the next hands-on exercise.

THE SLIDE NAVIGATOR

The Slide Navigator provides an alternate way to branch to various slides during a presentation. It is always accessible to the presenter regardless of whether or not branching has been built in. The disadvantage is that the Navigator is not intuitive to the novice, it lists every slide in a presentation (there may be many), and further, it requires additional mouse clicks when compared to predefined command buttons. See online Help for additional information.

HANDS-ON EXERCISE 4

Branching within a Presentation

Objective: To use the Interactive Settings command to enable branching within a presentation. Use Figure 1.11 as a guide in doing the exercise.

STEP 1: Create the Title Slide

- Open the **Adding Impact presentation** from the previous exercise.
- Click and drag to select the title of the presentation, then change the title to **Interactive Presentations.**
- Click the border of the title placeholder, then click and drag the border to move it the top of the slide as shown in Figure 1.11a.
- Click the **placeholder** containing your name, then click and drag that placeholder toward the top of the slide so that it is under the title.
- Pull down the **File menu,** click the **Save As command,** then save the presentation as **Interactive Presentations.**

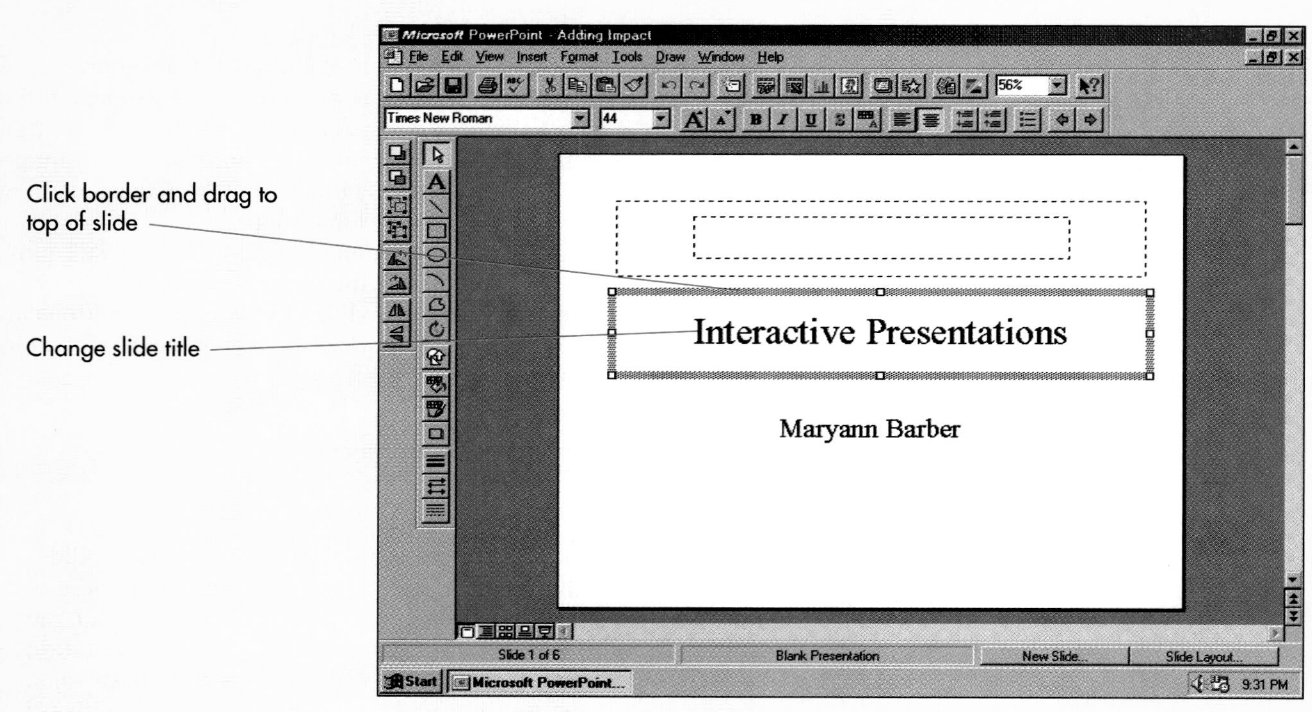

(a) Create the Title (step 1)

FIGURE 1.11 Hands-on Exercise 4

THE SAVE AS COMMAND

The Save As command saves a presentation under a different name, and is useful when you want to retain a copy of the original presentation prior to making any changes. The original (unmodified) presentation is kept on disk under its original name. A second copy of the presentation is saved under a new name and remains in memory. All subsequent editing is done on the new presentation.

STEP 2: Create the First Button (menu option)

- Click the **Text tool** on the Drawing toolbar, then click and drag in the slide where you want the first button to go. Release the mouse to create the button.
- Enter **Excel Worksheet** as the name of the first menu option as shown in Figure 1.11b.
- Click the **Center Alignment button** on the Formatting toolbar to center the text within the button.
- Click the **Line Style button** on the Drawing toolbar to display the available line styles as shown in Figure 1.11b. Click the second style to display a border around the button.
- Click the **Fill Color button** on the Drawing toolbar. Click **Green** as the color of the button.
- Save the presentation.

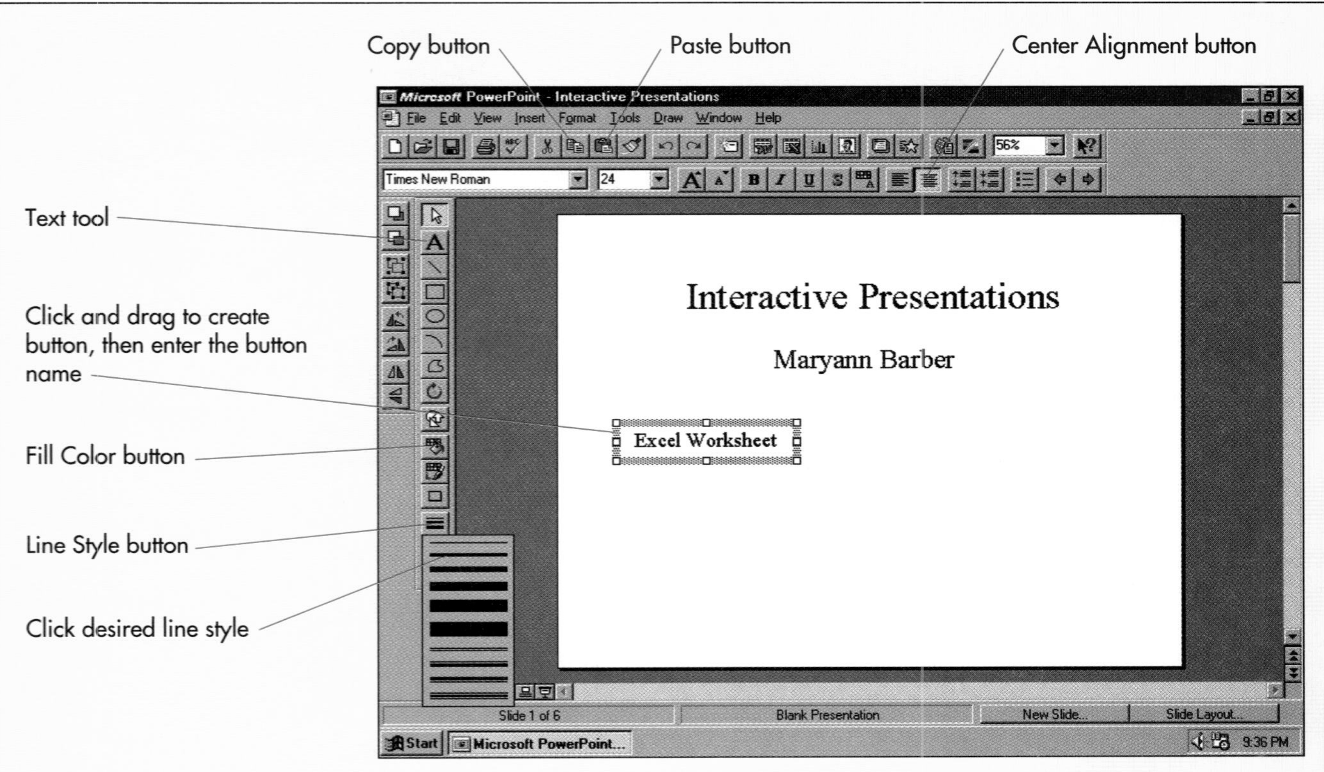

(b) Create the First Menu Option (step 2)

FIGURE 1.11 Hands-on Exercise 4 (continued)

STEP 3: Create the Other Buttons

- Select (click) the button you just created, then click the **Copy button** on the Standard toolbar to copy the button to the clipboard.
- Click the **Paste button,** then click and drag the copied button to the right of the original button. (Do not worry about the alignment or position of the two buttons.) You now have two Excel Worksheet buttons.
- Click in the second (copied) button, then change the text to **Clip Art.**
- Copy the button three more times, then move the buttons and change the names as shown in Figure 1.11c.
- Click the **Excel Worksheet button.** Press and hold the **Shift key** as you click the **Organization Chart button** to select both buttons.
- Pull down the **Draw menu.** Click the **Align command,** then click **Lefts** from the cascaded menu as shown in Figure 1.11c. The selected buttons should be aligned on their left side.
- Align the **Microsoft Graph** and **Clip Art buttons** by selecting the buttons two at a time and aligning them on their right side.
- Save the presentation.

STEP 4: Create the Branch

- Click outside all five buttons, then click the **Excel Worksheet button** to select just this button.

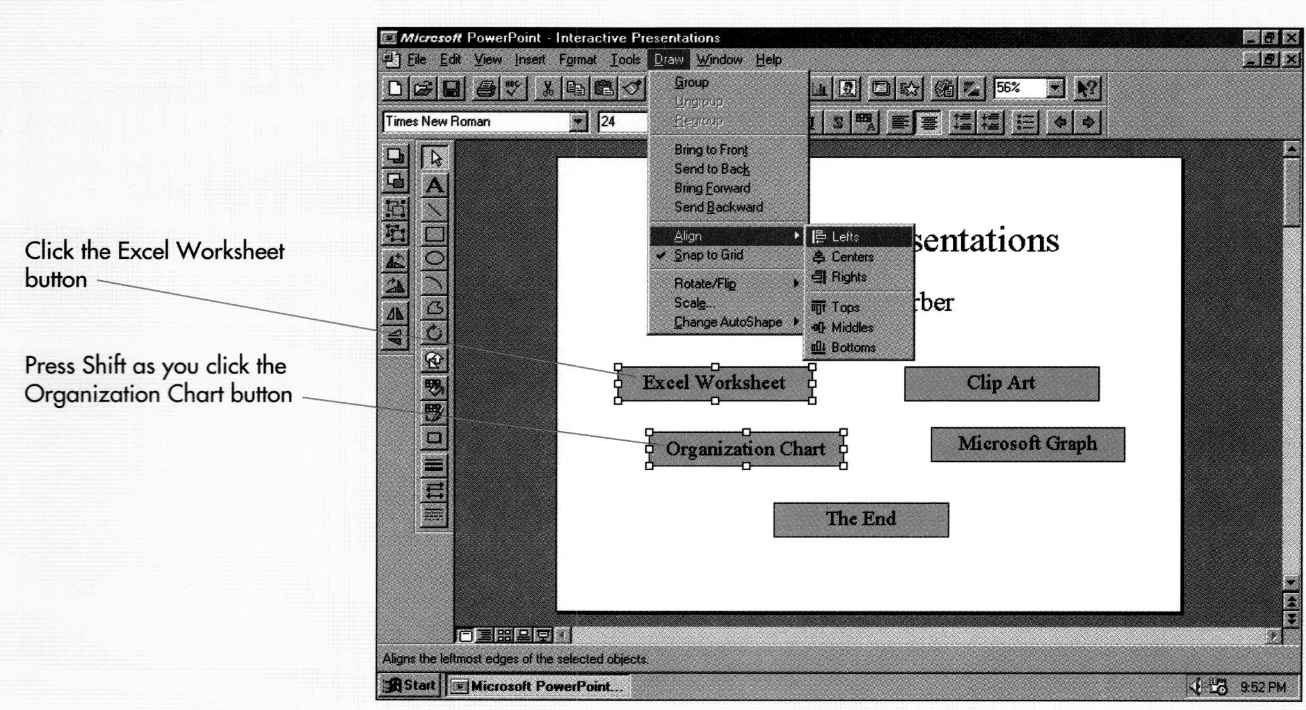

(c) Create the Other Buttons (step 3)

FIGURE 1.11 Hands-on Exercise 4 (continued)

- Pull down the **Tools menu.** Click **Interactive Settings** to display the Interactive Settings dialog box, then click the **Go to option button** as shown in Figure 1.11d.
- Click the **drop-down arrow** in the Slides list box, click **Slide . . .** from the displayed list of available slides to display the Go To Slide dialog box shown in the figure. Select slide 2 (CIS120 Grade Book) as shown in Figure 1.11d. Click **OK.** Click **OK** a second time.

STEP 5: Create the Return Branch

- Press the **PgDn key** to move to slide number 2 (the slide containing the Excel worksheet).
- Create a **Return to Menu** button in the lower-right corner of this slide, as shown in Figure 1.11e. (You may need to size and/or move the worksheet before creating the button.)
  - Click the **Text tool** on the Drawing toolbar, then click and drag in the slide where you want the button to go. Release the mouse and enter **Return to Menu** as the name of the button.
  - Click the **Center Alignment button** on the Formatting toolbar to center the text within the button. Click the **Line Style** and **Fill Color buttons** on the Drawing toolbar to format the button as we did in step 2. (Choose any line style and fill color.)
- Pull down the **Tools menu,** click **Interactive Settings** to display the Interactive Settings dialog box, then click the **Go to option button.** Click the **drop-down arrow** in the Slides list box, click **Slide . . .** from the displayed list, select

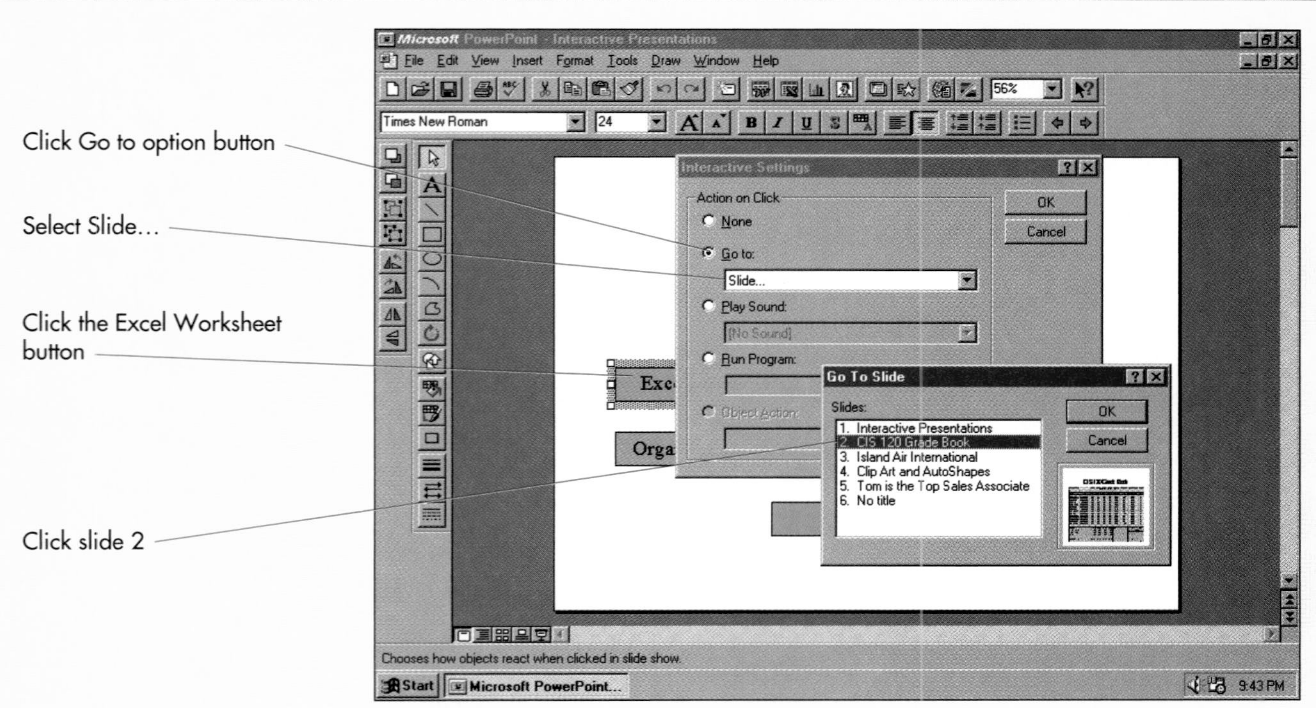

(d) Create the Branch (step 4)

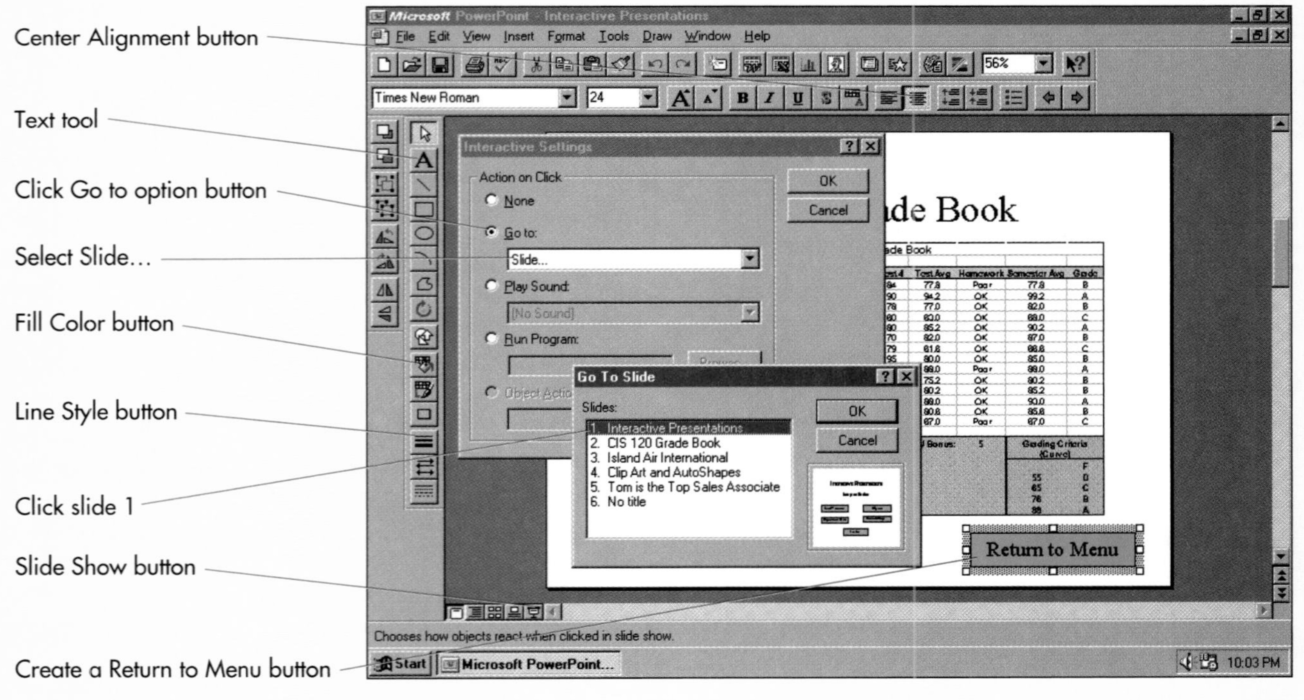

(e) Create the Return Branch (step 5)

FIGURE 1.11 Hands-on Exercise 4 (continued)

the title slide (**Interactive Presentations**) from the list of available slides, then click **OK.** Click **OK** to close the Interactive Settings dialog box.

➤ Save the presentation.

> **THE SLIDE ELEVATOR**
>
> PowerPoint uses the scroll box (common to all Windows applications) in the vertical scroll bar as an elevator to move up and down within the presentation. Click and drag the elevator to go to a specific slide; as you drag, you will see a Scroll Tip indicating the slide you are about to display. Release the mouse when you see the number (title) of the slide you want.

STEP 6: Test the Branching

➤ Press **Ctrl+Home** to return to the first slide in the presentation. Click the **Slide Show button** above the status bar to view the presentation and display the title slide.

➤ Click the **Excel Worksheet button** to branch to this slide. Click the **Return to Menu button** to return to the title slide. Click the **Excel Worksheet button** a second time to return to this slide.

➤ Press **Esc** to end the slide show and return to the Slide view.

STEP 7: Create Branches for the Remaining Buttons

➤ Press **Ctrl+Home** to return to the title slide in the presentation, then select (click) the **Organization Chart button.**

➤ Pull down the **Tools menu,** click **Interactive Settings,** then click the **Go to option button.** Click the **down arrow** in the Slides list box, and select slide 3 (**Island Air International**) to create the branch. Click **OK.** Click **OK** a second time.

➤ Create the branches for the remaining buttons in similar fashion.

STEP 8: Create the Remaining Return Buttons

➤ Press the **PgDn key** to move to the slide containing the Excel worksheet. Click the border of the **Return to Menu button** to select the button and display the sizing handles, then click the **Copy button** on the Standard toolbar to copy the button (including the branching) to the clipboard.

➤ Press the **PgDn key** to move to the next slide. Click the **Paste button** on the Standard toolbar to paste the contents of the clipboard (the Return to Menu button) onto this slide.

➤ Press the **PgDn key** to move to the next slide, then click the **Paste button** to paste the button onto this slide as well. Paste the **Return to Menu** button on each of the remaining slides in the presentation.

➤ Click the **Slide Sorter button** to change to the slide view to see the entire presentation as shown in Figure 1.11f.

- The title slide contains five buttons, one for each slide in the presentation.
- Each of the remaining slides contains a return button that branches back to the title slide.

➤ Save the presentation.

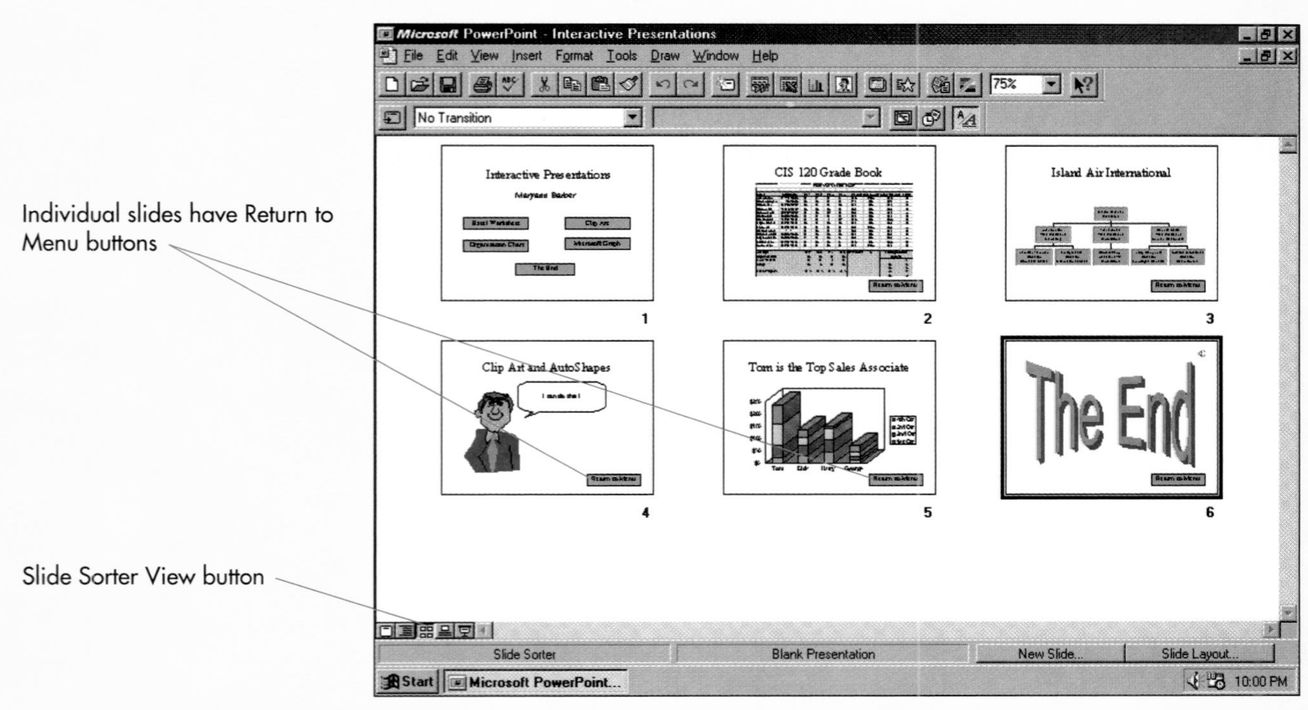

(f) Create the Remaining Buttons (step 8)

FIGURE 1.11 Hands-on Exercise 4 (continued)

CUT, COPY, AND PASTE

Ctrl+X, Ctrl+C, and **Ctrl+V** are shortcuts to cut, copy, and paste, respectively, and apply to all applications in the Office suite as well as to Windows applications in general. (The shortcuts are easier to remember when you realize that the operative letters—X, C, and V—are next to each other at the bottom left side of the keyboard.) You can also use the Cut, Copy, and Paste buttons on the Standard toolbar.

STEP 9: Show Time

- Press **Ctrl+Home** to move to the beginning of the presentation, then click the **Slide Show button** to view the presentation. The title slide is displayed on your monitor as shown in Figure 1.11g.
- You can branch to any slide in the presentation by clicking the appropriate command button on the title slide. You can return to the title slide at any time by clicking the **Return to Menu button** that is present on every slide except the title slide.
- You can also view the presentation in sequence by clicking the **left mouse button** (or by pressing the **PgDn key**) to move from one slide to the next.
- Go through the presentation (in any sequence) to review the material from the chapter. Click the **left mouse button** at the end of the presentation or press the **Esc key** to return to the Slide view.

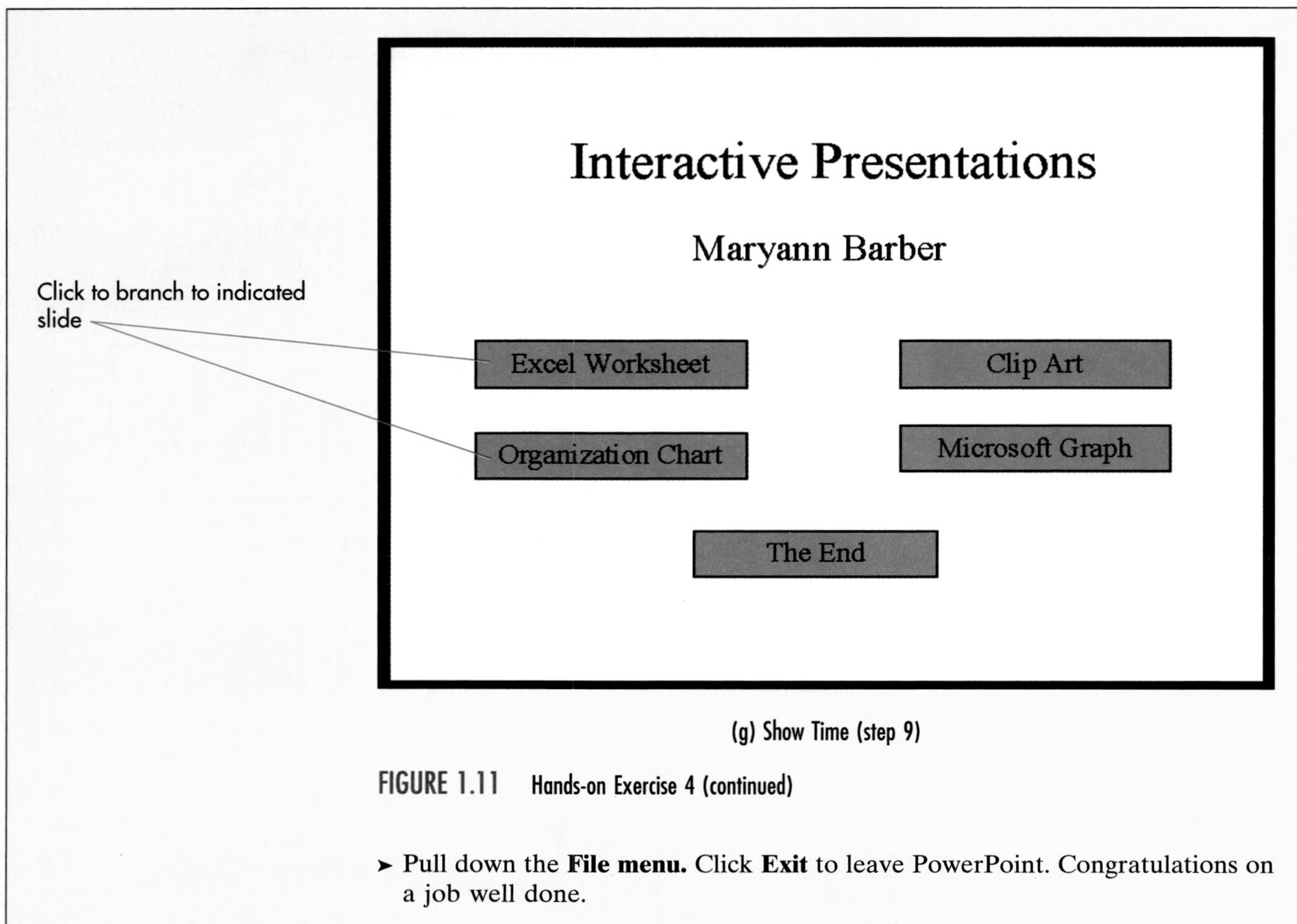

(g) Show Time (step 9)

FIGURE 1.11 Hands-on Exercise 4 (continued)

➤ Pull down the **File menu.** Click **Exit** to leave PowerPoint. Congratulations on a job well done.

SUMMARY

Microsoft Graph has many of the same commands and capabilities as the charting component of Microsoft Excel. After a graph has been inserted into a presentation, it becomes an embedded object that retains its connection to Microsoft Graph. Thus, you can double click the graph to restart Microsoft Graph and edit the graph. You can also click the graph to select it as an object on a PowerPoint slide, then move or size the graph just as you would any other Windows object.

A clip art image consists of a series of lines and shapes, each of which is considered an object in and of itself. The Group command combines individual objects so that you can work with them at the same time. The Ungroup command does the opposite and breaks up an object into smaller objects so you can work with the smaller objects individually.

Object Linking and Embedding (OLE) enables you to link or embed information (objects) created in other applications. The choice between linking and embedding depends on how the object will be used. Linking is preferable if the object is likely to change and your presentation requires the latest version, or when the same object is shared among many users. Embedding should be used if you plan to show the presentation on a different computer from the one used to create the presentation.

Microsoft WordArt enables you to add special effects to text, then embed the text object into a presentation. WordArt is called from within PowerPoint by choosing the AutoLayout for an Object slide, double clicking the object placeholder, and selecting a WordArt object.

Microsoft Organization Chart enables you to create an organization chart and embed it into a presentation. The application is called from within PowerPoint by choosing the AutoLayout containing an organization chart or by creating an object slide and choosing Microsoft Organization Chart as the object type.

PowerPoint enables you to embed a sound file or a video clip (a movie) as an object into a presentation. Movies do not require additional hardware. Sound requires a sound board and speakers.

The Interactive Settings command introduces branching into a presentation by placing command buttons onto a slide that let you to move directly to a specific slide.

KEY WORDS AND CONCEPTS

AutoShape
AutoShapes toolbar
Branching
Category names
Compound document
Data points
Data series
Datasheet
Drawing toolbar
Drawing+ toolbar
Embedded object
Group command
Interactive Settings command
In-place editing
Linked object
Microsoft Graph
Microsoft Organization Chart
Microsoft WordArt
Object
Object Linking and Embedding
Recolor command
Sound
Ungroup command

MULTIPLE CHOICE

1. What happens if you click the Datasheet button on the Microsoft Graph toolbar twice in a row?
   (a) The datasheet is closed (hidden)
   (b) The datasheet is opened (displayed)
   (c) The datasheet is in the same status (either opened or closed) as it was before it was clicked
   (d) Impossible to determine
2. Which of the following is true of data series that are plotted in rows?
   (a) The first row in the datasheet contains the category names for the X axis
   (b) The first column in the datasheet contains the legend
   (c) Both (a) and (b)
   (d) Neither (a) nor (b)

3. Which of the following is true of data series that are plotted in columns?
   (a) The first column in the datasheet contains the category names for the X axis
   (b) The first row in the datasheet contains the legend
   (c) Both (a) and (b)
   (d) Neither (a) nor (b)

4. What happens if you select a slide in the Slide Sorter view, click the Copy button, then click the Paste button twice in a row?
   (a) You have made one additional copy of the slide
   (b) You have made two additional copies of the slide
   (c) You have made three additional copies of the slide
   (d) The situation is impossible because you cannot execute the Paste command twice in a row

5. How do you size an object so that it maintains the original proportion between height and width?
   (a) Drag a sizing handle on the left or right side of the object to change its width, then drag a sizing handle on the top or bottom edge to change the height
   (b) Drag a sizing handle on any of the corners
   (c) Both (a) and (b)
   (d) Neither (a) nor (b)

6. What happens if you select an object, then click the Flip Vertical button twice in a row?
   (a) The object has been rotated 90 degrees
   (b) The object has been rotated 180 degrees (turned upside down)
   (c) The object has been rotated 270 degrees
   (d) The object has been rotated 360 degrees and is in the same position as when you started

7. What is the difference between clicking and double clicking an embedded object?
   (a) Clicking selects the object; double clicking starts the application that created the object
   (b) Double clicking selects the object; clicking starts the application that create the object
   (c) Clicking changes to the Slide Sorter view; double clicking changes to the Outline view
   (d) Double clicking changes to the Slide Sorter view; clicking changes to the Outline view

8. Under which circumstances would you choose linking over embedding?
   (a) When the same object is referenced in many different documents
   (b) When an object is constantly changing and you need the latest version
   (c) Both (a) and (b)
   (d) Neither (a) nor (b)

9. Under which circumstances would you choose embedding over linking?
   (a) When you need to show a presentation on a different computer
   (b) When the same object is referenced in many different documents
   (c) Both (a) and (b)
   (d) Neither (a) nor (b)

10. Which of the following can be created as an embedded object?
    (a) A graph created by Microsoft Graph
    (b) Text created by Microsoft WordArt
    (c) Clip art or WordArt
    (d) All of the above

11. Which of the following is true regarding the sequence of slides in a slide show?
    (a) The slides in a presentation must be viewed sequentially, starting with the first slide and ending with the last slide
    (b) The next slide in a presentation is displayed by clicking the left mouse button or by pressing the PgDn key
    (c) Both (a) and (b)
    (d) Neither (a) nor (b)

12. How do you insert clip art onto an existing slide?
    (a) Pull down the Insert menu, click Object, then choose Microsoft ClipArt Gallery from the list of available objects
    (b) Click the Insert Clip Art button on the Standard toolbar
    (c) Pull down the Insert menu and click the Clip Art command
    (d) All of the above

13. How do you create a new slide containing a graph?
    (a) Create a blank slide, then pull down the Insert menu and click the Microsoft Graph command
    (b) Create a blank slide, then click the Insert Graph button on the Standard toolbar
    (c) Click the New Slide button, select an AutoLayout containing a graph, then double click the placeholder for the graph in the Slide view
    (d) All of the above

14. What happens if you select an object, click the Copy command, move to a new slide, and click the Paste command?
    (a) Nothing because you cannot copy and paste an object on two different slides
    (b) The selected object has been moved from the first slide to the second slide
    (c) The selected object has been copied from the first slide to the second slide
    (d) The selected object has been copied from the first slide to the second slide, and in addition, remains on the clipboard from where it can be pasted onto another slide

15. What happens if you select an object, click the Cut command, move to a new slide, and click the Paste command?
    (a) Nothing because you cannot copy and paste an object on two different slides
    (b) The selected object has been moved from the first slide to the second slide
    (c) The selected object has been copied from the first slide to the second slide
    (d) The selected object has been copied from the first slide to the second slide, and in addition, remains on the clipboard from where it can be pasted onto another slide

ANSWERS

1. c	**6.** d	**11.** b
2. c	**7.** a	**12.** d
3. c	**8.** c	**13.** d
4. b	**9.** a	**14.** d
5. b	**10.** d	**15.** b

EXPLORING MICROSOFT POWERPOINT 7.0

1. Use Figure 1.12 to match each action with its result. A given action may be used more than once or not at all.

Action		**Result**
a. Click at 1	____	Suppress the display of the datasheet
b. Click at 2	____	Change the data series to columns
c. Click at 3	____	Change the format of the chart to stacked column
d. Click at 4	____	Return to PowerPoint
e. Click at 5	____	Suppress the display of the legend
f. Click at 6		
g. Click at 7 and enter the new city		

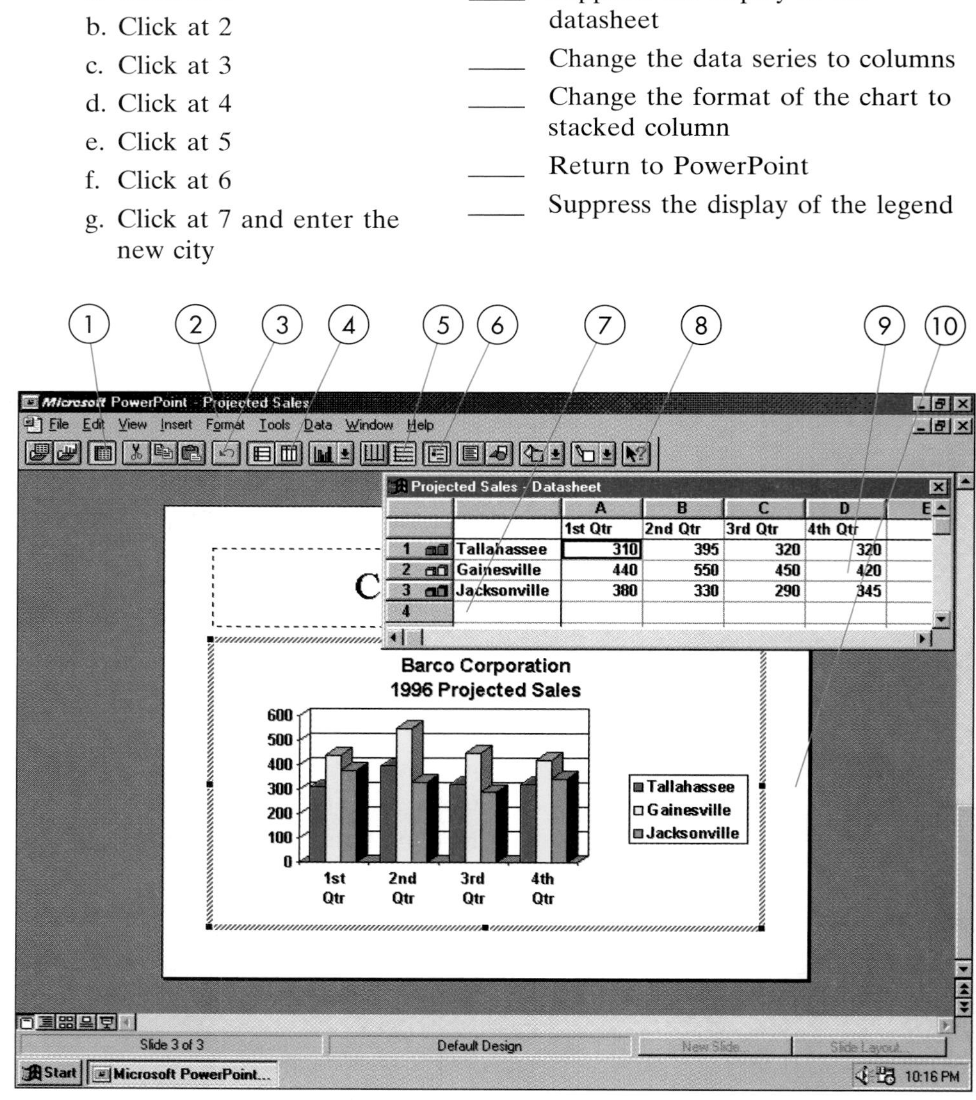

FIGURE 1.12 Screen for Problem 1

h. Click at 8
i. Click at 9 and enter the new data
j. Click at 10

____ Change Gainesville's 4th Quarter sales
____ Undo the last action taken
____ Add a new series for Orlando
____ Toggle the horizontal gridlines off
____ Access online Help

2. Answer the following with respect to Figure 1.13:

a. What is the name of the presentation containing the slide in Figure 1.13?
b. Which toolbars are currently displayed?
c. How many objects are displayed on the slide? How many different types of objects? Which object (if any) is currently selected?
d. What would happen if you pointed to the selected object and clicked the right mouse button? If you pressed the Delete key?
e. What is the difference between clicking and double clicking the WordArt object? How would you change the text on the slide to "CIS120"?

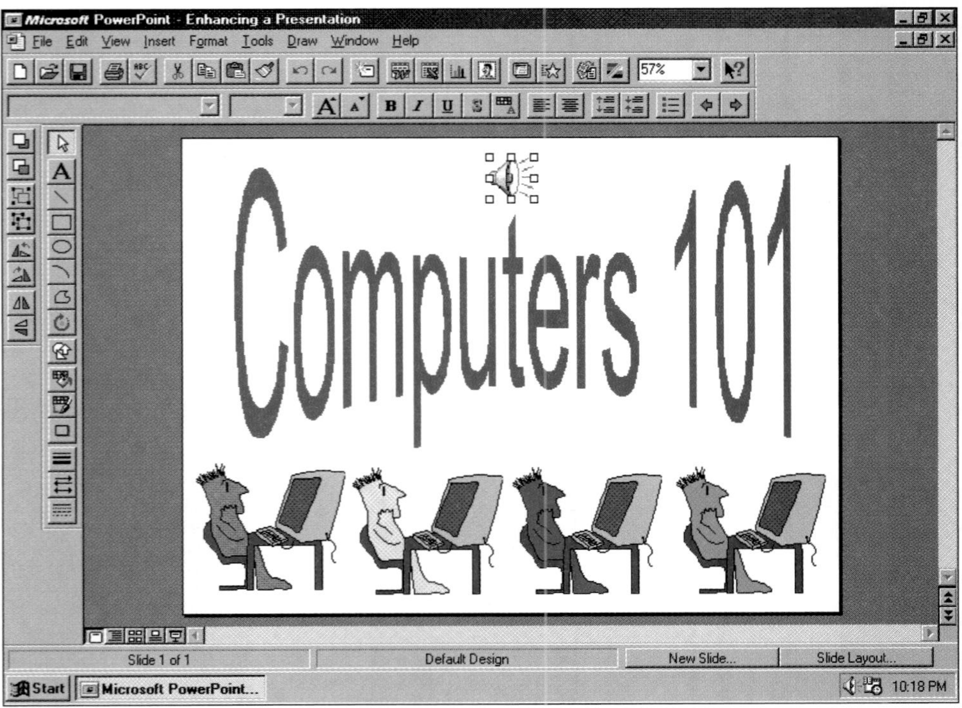

FIGURE 1.13 Screen for Problem 2

3. Answer the following with respect to Figure 1.14.

a. What is the name of the folder that is displayed in the figure?
b. Which view is used to display the files within the folder? What other views are available? How do you change the view?
c. How many objects are in the folder? What is the total amount of space taken by all of the objects?
d. How could you determine the file size of Beethoven's 5th Symphony? How could you play the file?
e. Why are there two different types of icons within the folder? (Hint: see Appendix B, Introduction to Multimedia.)

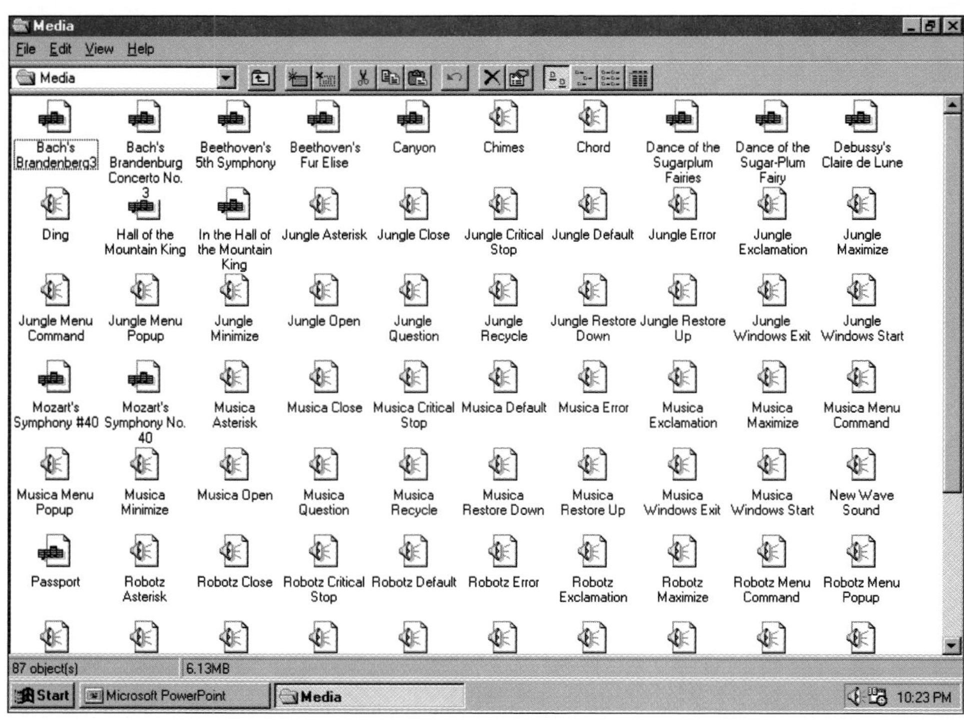

FIGURE 1.14 Screen for Problem 3

4. Answer the following with respect to Figure 1.15. (The presentation in Figure 1.15 is found in the Valupack\Audio\Cambium folder on the CD version of Microsoft Office.)
   a. What is the name of the presentation displayed in Figure 1.15? What is the significance of the words "Read Only" in the title bar?

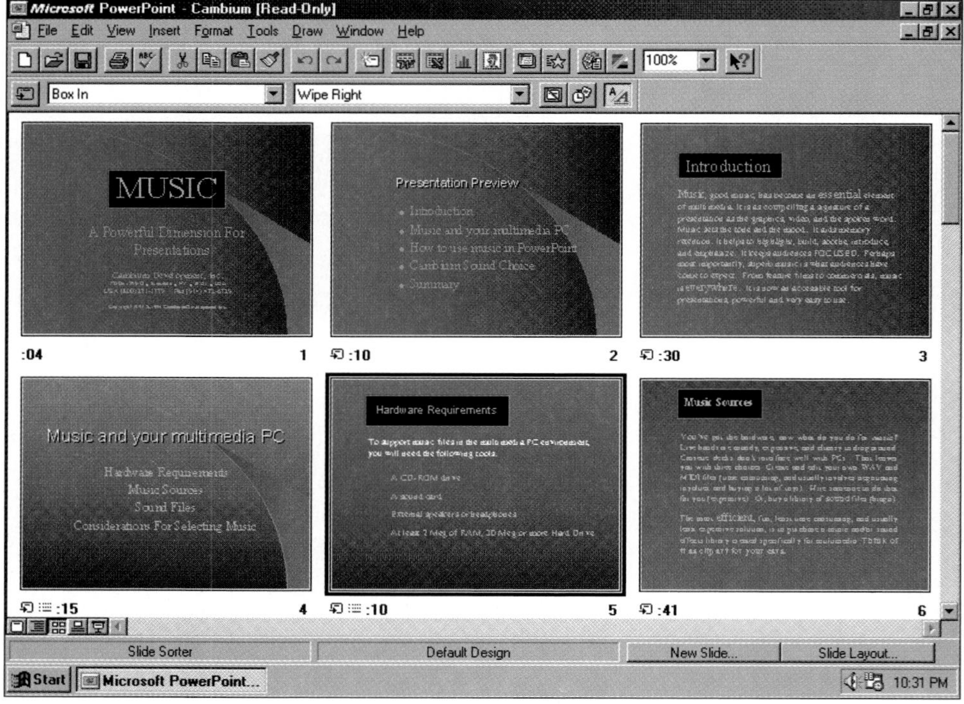

FIGURE 1.15 Screen for Problem 4

b. Which slide is currently selected? What transition effect (if any) is operative for this slide? What build effect (if any) is operative for this slide?

c. What happens if you click the selected slide? What happens if you double click the selected slide?

d. What happens if you click slide 2, then click the tiny slide icon below the slide?

e. What is the significance of the numbers that appear under each of the slides?

PRACTICE WITH MICROSOFT POWERPOINT 7.0

1. Microsoft WordArt is an ideal tool to create the title slide of a presentation, as can be seen from Figure 1.16. Open the Adding Impact presentation created in the third hands-on exercise and do the following:
   a. Switch to the Slide Sorter view. Select the Title Slide, then press the Del key to delete the slide.
   b. Click the New Slide button on the status bar to insert a new slide. Choose AutoLayout 12 for a blank slide. Click OK.
   c. Double click the new slide to change to the Slide view. Pull down the Insert menu and click Object to produce the Insert Object dialog box.
   d. Scroll until you can select Microsoft WordArt 2.0. Click the Create New option button, then click OK.
   e. You're on your own. Duplicate our slide or, better yet, create your own. Let's see how creative you can be and how much impact you can add.

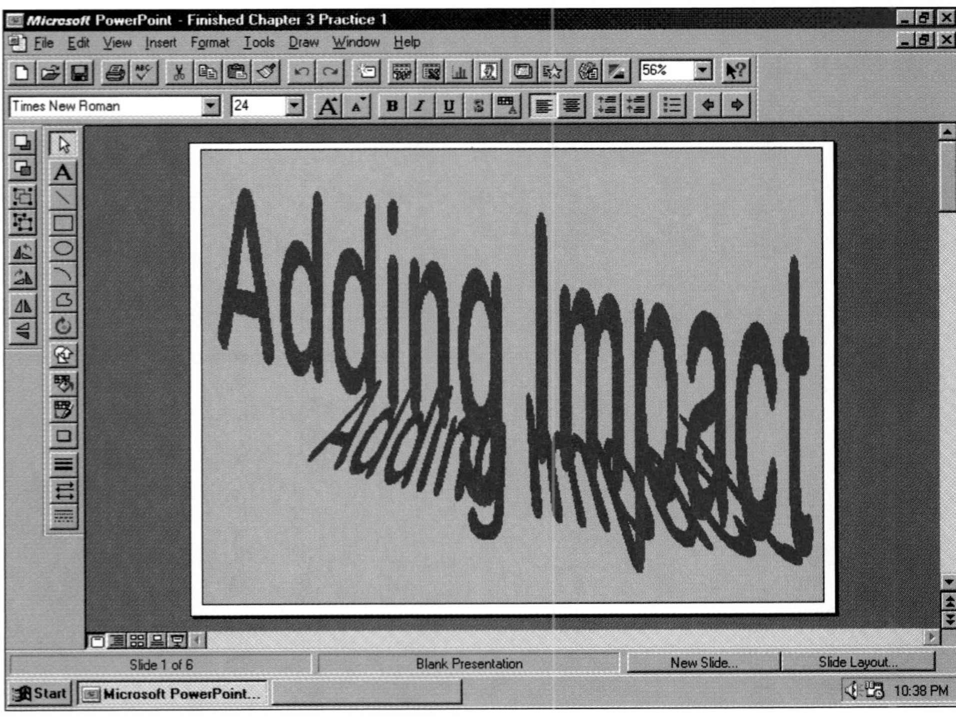

FIGURE 1.16 Screen for Practice Exercise 1

2. Microsoft Organization Chart offers considerable flexibility in the appearance of an organization chart as shown by the chart in Figure 1.17. You can change the line thickness, style, or color for the boxes or connecting lines. You can change the shape of a border and/or add a shadow effect. You can change the font and/or color of text within a box.

   All of these changes are done within the context of *select-then-do;* that is, you select the box (or boxes) for which the change is to apply, then you execute the appropriate command. (To select multiple boxes, press and hold the Shift key as you click additional boxes. You can also use the Select commands in the Edit menu.) Open the Adding Impact presentation created in the third hands-on exercise and do the following:

   a. Switch to the Slide Sorter view. Select the slide with the organization chart.
   b. Double click the slide to change to the Slide view. Double click the Organization Chart to edit the chart so that it matches Figure 1.17.
   c. Change the box and/or line style as you see fit.
   d. Print a full-page version of the revised slide and submit it to your instructor as proof you did the exercise.

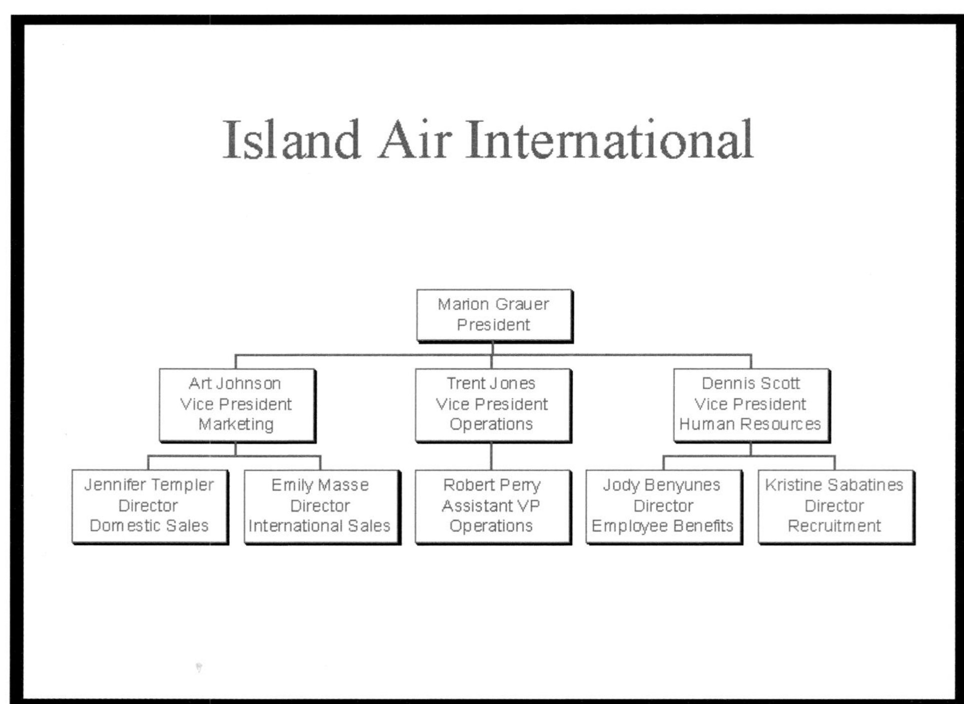

FIGURE 1.17 Screen for Practice Exercise 2

3. Exploring AutoShapes: Figure 1.18 displays a single slide containing a variety of AutoShapes. Open the presentation created in the third hands-on exercise and do the following:

   a. Add a blank slide immediately before the last slide.
   b. Click the AutoShapes tool on the Drawing toolbar to display the AutoShapes toolbar.

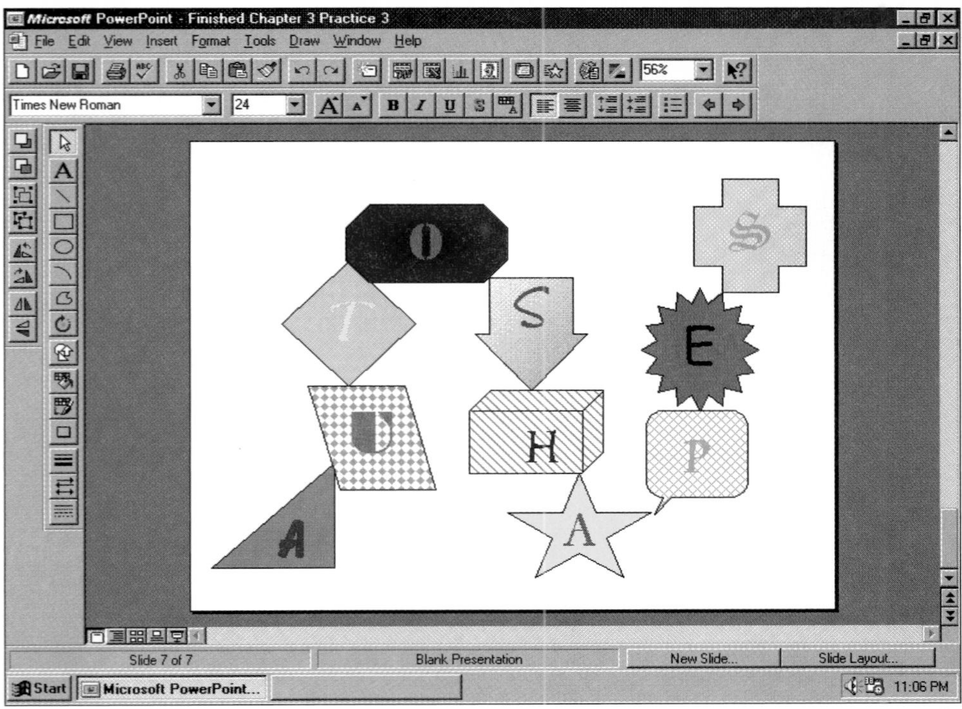

FIGURE 1.18 Screen for Practice Exercise 3

c. Point to an AutoShape, then click and drag in the slide to create the shape on the slide. (You can press and hold the Shift key as you drag for special effects; for example, press and hold the Shift key as you drag the ellipse or rectangle tool to draw a circle or square, respectively. You can also use the Shift key in conjunction with the Line tool to draw a perfect horizontal or vertical line, or a line at a 45-degree angle.)

d. To place text inside a shape, select the shape and start typing.

e. To change the fill color or line thickness, select the shape, then click the appropriate button on the Drawing toolbar.

f. Use these techniques to duplicate Figure 1.18, or better yet, create your own design. Add your name to the completed slide and submit it to your instructor.

4. Figure 1.19 shows two additional examples of what you can do with clip art. The smaller slide on the edge of the page contains the original clip art image. The full-size slide shows the modified slide and is the objective of the exercise. To create Figure 1.19a:

a. Create a blank slide in any presentation. Click the Insert Clip Art button on the Standard toolbar to open the ClipArt Gallery. Add the Worried image from the Cartoons category.

b. Select the clip art image and move it to the right side of the slide. Click the Copy and Paste buttons on the Standard toolbar to copy the image, then drag the copied image to the left side of the slide.

c. Point to the image on the left (it has not yet been flipped), click the right mouse button to display a shortcut menu, then click the Recolor command to produce the Recolor Picture dialog box. Click the check box for an original color (e.g., blue), then click the down arrow next to the corresponding new color to choose a different color (e.g., green). Click OK to

(a) Clip Art 1

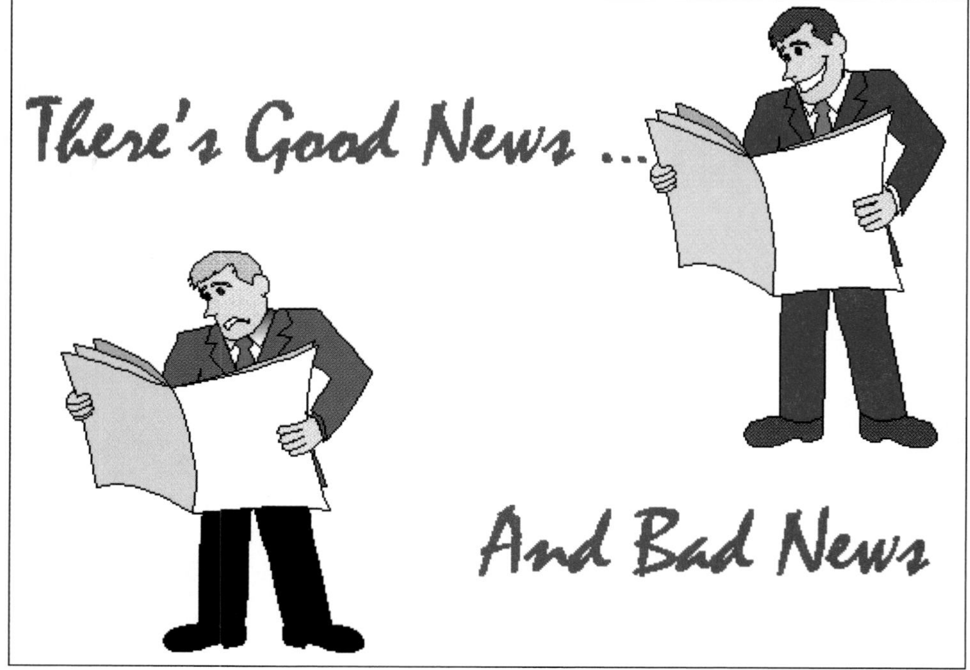

(b) Clip Art 2

FIGURE 1.19 Screen for Practice Exercise 4

implement the recoloring. Repeat these steps to change the hair coloring of the gentleman on the right. (You need not follow our color scheme exactly.)

d. Select the image on the left, recolor the image, then ungroup and regroup the clip art to convert it to a PowerPoint object. Click the Flip Horizontal button to reverse the image.

e. Click and drag the Rectangle tool to draw a rectangle under our puzzled friends. Do not be concerned if the rectangle is on top of the men and you cannot see their elbows. Check that the rectangle is still selected, then click the Fill Color button on the Drawing+ toolbar to change the color of the rectangle to brown. You can also change the texture (fill color).

f. Click outside the rectangle to deselect it. Press and hold the Shift key to select both of the men, then click the Bring Forward button on the Drawing+ toolbar.

g. Add the AutoShape with the indicated text. Add your name to the slide.

To create Figure 1.19b:

h. Create a blank slide in any presentation. Click the Insert Clip Art button on the Standard toolbar to open the ClipArt Gallery. Add the Information Newspaper image from the Cartoons category.

i. Click and drag the image to size and position it as shown in Figure 1.19b.

j. Copy the clip art image, then click and drag the copied image so that the figures are separated from one another.

k. Ungroup all of the elements in the copied image. Select just the smile, then flip and resize the smile to change it to a frown. (This takes a little practice.)

l. Use the Fill Color tool on the Drawing toolbar to recolor the clothing.

m. Click and drag the Text tool on the Drawing toolbar to create the first text box, then type *There's Good News* in the text box. Be sure the text is still selected, then change the font, size, and color as you see fit.

n. Repeat the previous steps to create the second text box. Print both slides and submit them to your instructor.

CASE STUDIES

The Federal Budget

The federal government spends billions more than it takes in. In fiscal year 1993, for example, government expenditures totaled $1,408 billion versus income of only $1,154 billion leaving a deficit of $254 billion. Thirty-one percent of the income came from Social Security and Medicare taxes, 36% from personal income taxes, 8% from corporate income taxes, and 7% from excise, estate, and other miscellaneous taxes. The remaining 18% was borrowed.

Social Security and Medicare accounted for 35% of the expenditures and the defense budget another 24%. Social programs including Medicaid and aid to dependent children totaled 17%. Community development (consisting of agricultural, educational, environmental, economic, and space programs) totaled 8% of the budget. Interest on the national debt amounted to 14%. The cost of law enforcement and government itself accounted for the final 2%.

Use the information contained within this problem to create a presentation that shows the distribution of income and expenditures. Do some independent research and obtain data on the budget, the deficit, and the national debt for the years 1945, 1967, and 1980. The numbers may surprise you; for example, how does the interest expense for the current year compare to the total budget in 1967 (at the height of the Viet Nam War)? to the total budget in 1945 (at the end of World War II)? Create additional graphs to reflect your findings, then write your representative in Congress. We are in trouble!

Before and After

As you already know, PowerPoint provides a set of drawing tools to develop virtually any type of illustration. Even if you are not artistic, you can use these tools to modify existing clip art and thus create new and very different illustrations. All it takes is a little imagination and a sense of what can be done. Choose any clip art image(s), then modify that image(s) to create an entirely different effect. Present your results in a three-slide presentation consisting of a title slide, a "before slide" showing the original image(s), and an "after slide" showing the modifications. Print the audience handouts for your presentation, three slides per page, and be sure to check the box to frame the slides. Ask your instructor to hold a class contest in which the class votes to determine the most creative application.

Photographs versus Clip Art

The right clip art can enhance a presentation, but there are times when clip art just won't do. It may be too juvenile or simply inappropriate. Photographs offer an alternative and are inserted into a presentation through the Insert Picture command. Once inserted into a presentation, photographs can be moved or sized just like any other Windows object. The CD-ROM version of Microsoft Office contains a Valuepack with a series of photographs from two different vendors. We invite you to explore these photographs, then report back to the class on their quality and cost.

Our Last Case

Once again we refer you to the Valuepack on the CD-ROM version of Microsoft Office to view a 45-slide presentation that introduces (and reviews) the major features in PowerPoint. The presentation is called "QuikPrev" (for quick preview) and is found in the PPQPREV folder within the Valuepack folder on the CD-ROM. It is a multimedia presentation that incorporates music, video, as well as the various other objects discussed in this chapter. Sit back, relax, and enjoy the show.

A

APPENDIX A: TOOLBARS

OVERVIEW

PowerPoint has nine predefined toolbars, which provide access to commonly used commands. The toolbars are displayed in Figure A.1 and are listed here for convenience. They are the Animation Effects, AutoShapes, Drawing, Drawing+, Formatting, Microsoft, Outlining, Slide Sorter, and Standard toolbars. When you first start PowerPoint, the Standard and Formatting toolbars are displayed immediately below the menu bar, and the Drawing toolbar is displayed along the left edge of the window. The Outlining and Slide Sorter toolbars are displayed automatically when you switch to the Outline and Slide Sorter views, respectively. The Animation Effects, AutoShape, Drawing+, and Microsoft toolbars are available for use as needed.

In addition to the PowerPoint predefined toolbars, Microsoft Graph, Microsoft WordArt, and Microsoft Organization Chart display application-specific toolbars when the applications are open. These toolbars are shown in Figure A.2.

The buttons on the toolbars are intended to be indicative of their functions. Clicking the Print button, for example (the fourth button from the left on the Standard toolbar), executes the Print command. If you are unsure of the purpose of any toolbar button, point to it, and a ToolTip will appear that displays its name.

You can display multiple toolbars at one time, move them to new locations on the screen, customize their appearance, or suppress their display.

- To display or hide a toolbar, pull down the View menu and click the Toolbars command. Select (deselect) the toolbar(s) that you want to display (hide). The selected toolbar(s) will be displayed in the same position as when last displayed. You may also point to any toolbar and click with the right mouse button to bring up a shortcut menu, after which you can select the toolbar to be displayed (hidden).

- To change the size of the buttons, display them in monochrome rather than color, or suppress the display of the ToolTips, pull down the View menu, click Toolbars, and then select (deselect) the appropriate check box. Alternatively, you can click on any toolbar with the right mouse button, select Toolbars, and then select (deselect) the appropriate check box.
- Toolbars may be either docked (along the edge of the window) or left floating (in their own window). A toolbar moved to the edge of the window will dock along that edge. A toolbar moved anywhere else in the window will float in its own window. Docked toolbars are one tool wide (high), whereas floating toolbars can be resized by clicking and dragging a border or corner as you would with any other window.
  - To move a docked toolbar, click anywhere in the gray background area and drag the toolbar to its new location.
  - To move a floating toolbar, drag its title bar to its new location.
- To customize one or more toolbars, display the toolbar(s) on the screen. Then pull down the View menu, click Toolbars, and click the Customize command button. Alternatively, you can click on any toolbar with the right mouse button, and then select Customize from the shortcut menu.
  - To move a button, drag the button to its new location on that toolbar or any other displayed toolbar.
  - To copy a button, press the Ctrl key as you drag the button to its new location on that toolbar or any other displayed toolbar.
  - To delete a button, drag the button off the toolbar and release the mouse button.
  - To add a button, select the category from the Categories list box and then drag the button to the desired location on the toolbar. (To see a description of a tool's function prior to adding it to a toolbar, click the tool in the Customize dialog box and read the displayed description.)
  - To restore a predefined toolbar to its default appearance, pull down the View menu, click Toolbars, select (highlight) the desired toolbar, and click the Reset command button.
- Buttons can also be moved, copied, or deleted without displaying the Customize dialog box.
  - To move a button, press the Alt key as you drag the button to the new location.
  - To copy a button, press the Alt and Ctrl keys as you drag the button to the new location.
  - To delete a button, press the Alt key as you drag the button off the toolbar.
- To create your own toolbar, pull down the View menu, click Toolbar, and click the New command button. Alternatively, you can click on any toolbar with the right mouse button, select Toolbars from the shortcut menu, and then click the New command button.
  - Enter a name for the toolbar in the dialog box that follows. The name can be any length and can contain spaces.
  - The new toolbar will appear at the top left of the screen. Initially it will be big enough to hold only one button. Add, move, and delete buttons following the same procedures as outlined above. The toolbar will automatically size itself as new buttons are added and deleted.
  - To delete a custom toolbar, pull down the View menu, click Toolbars, and make sure that the custom toolbar to be deleted is the only one selected

(highlighted). Click the Delete command button. Prior to closing the dialog box, you can undelete the toolbar by clicking the Undelete button. Once you have exited the dialog box, however, the custom toolbar cannot be undeleted. (Note that a predefined toolbar cannot be deleted.)

Animation Effects Toolbar

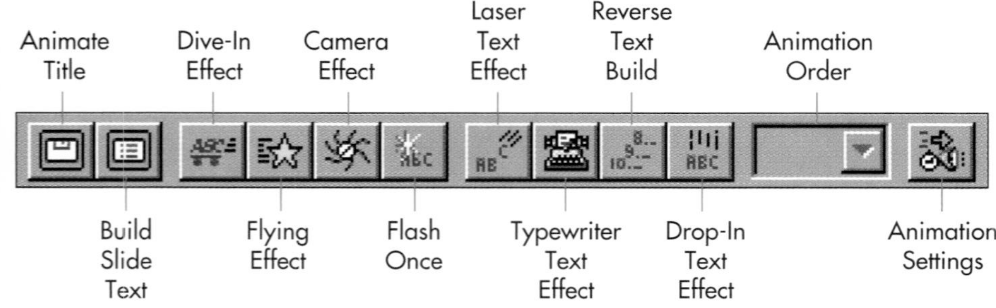

AutoShapes Toolbar

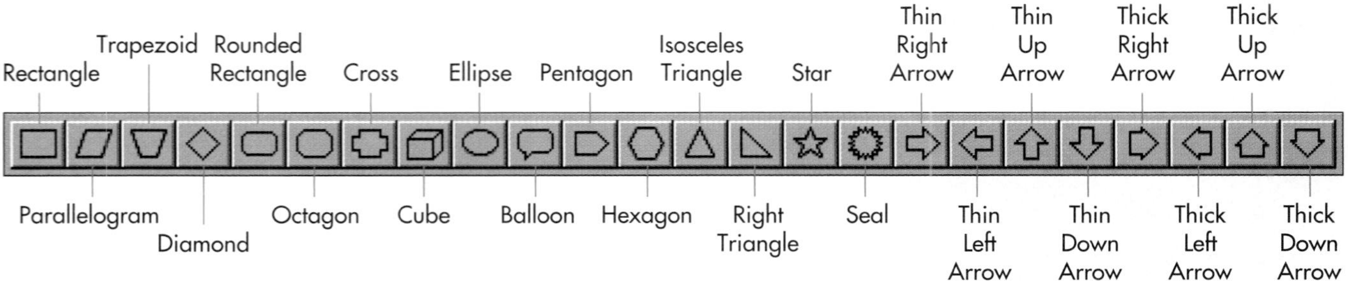

Drawing Toolbar

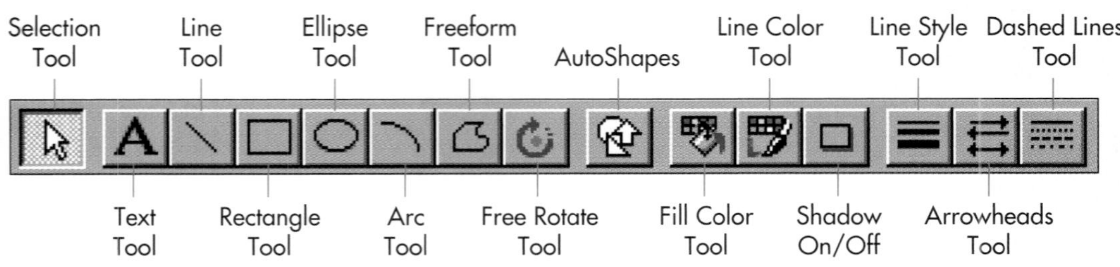

Drawing+ Toolbar

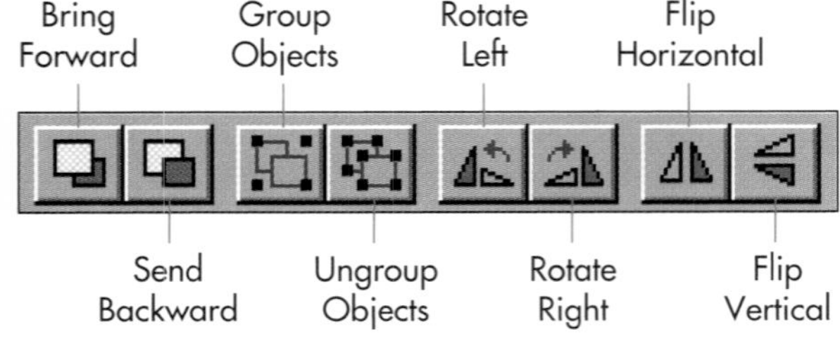

FIGURE A.1 PowerPoint Toolbars

Formatting Toolbar

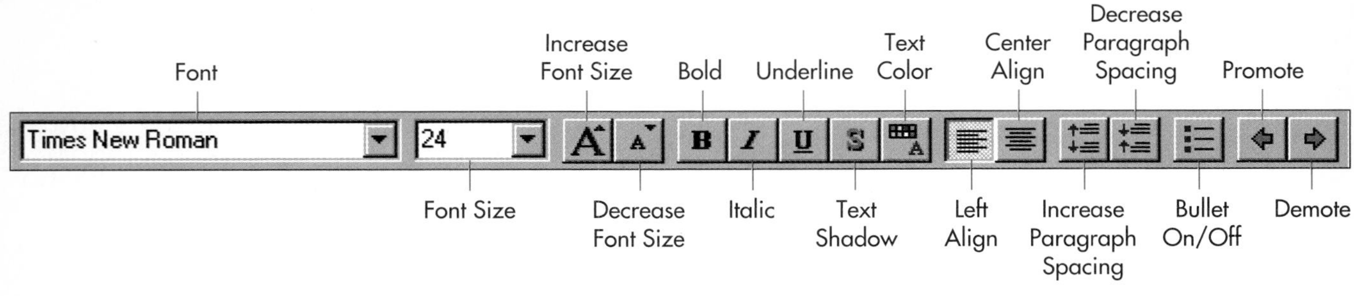

Microsoft Toolbar

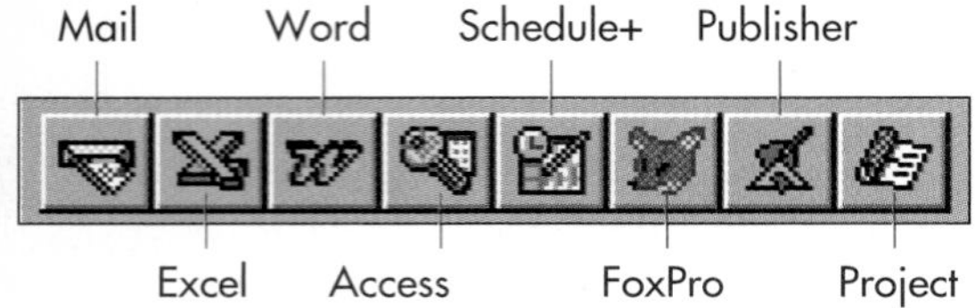

Outlining Toolbar

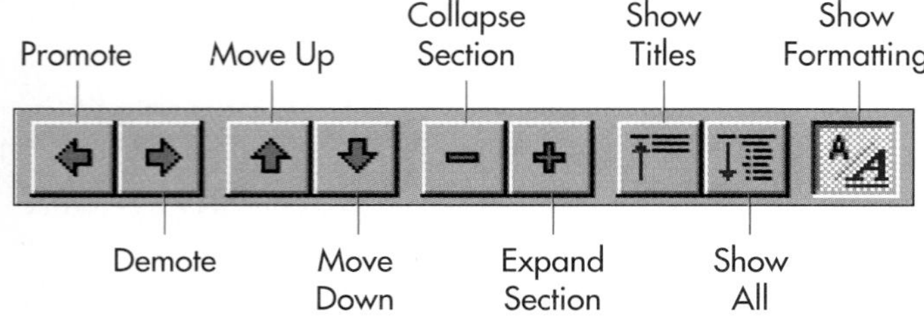

Slide Sorter Toolbar

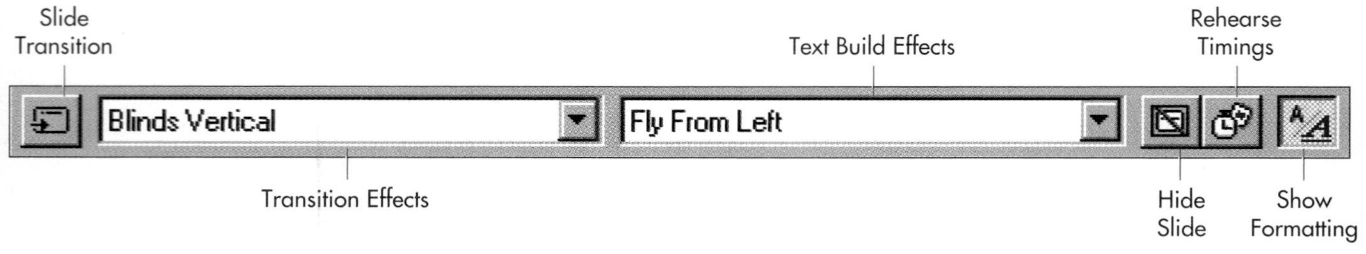

Standard Toolbar

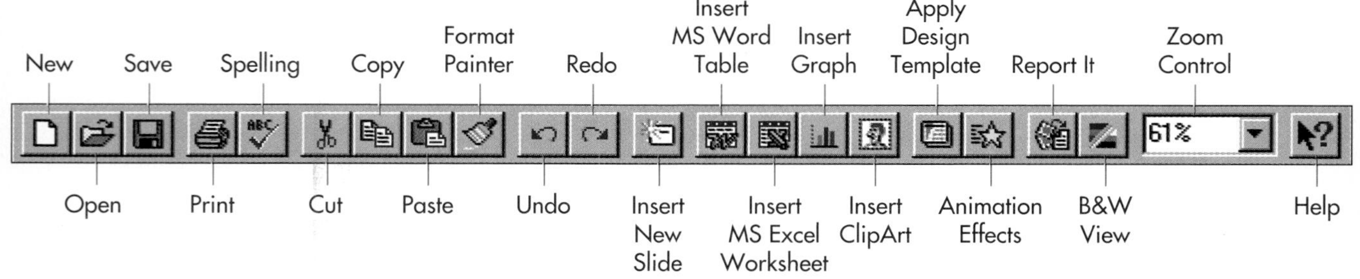

FIGURE A.1 PowerPoint Toolbars (continued)

Microsoft Graph

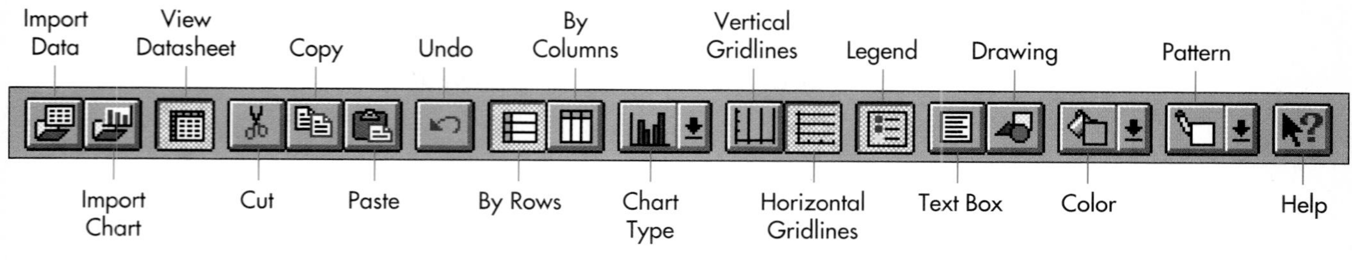

Microsoft Organization Chart

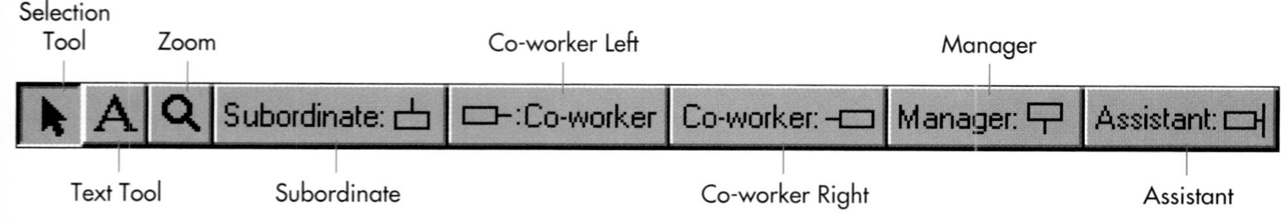

Microsoft WordArt

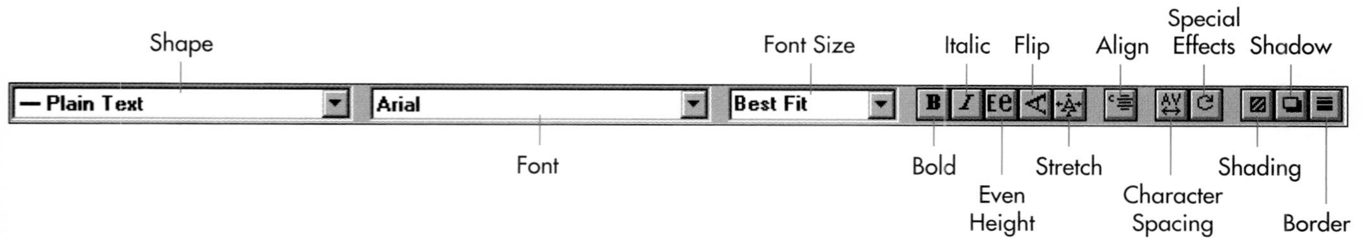

FIGURE A.2 Toolbars from Supplementary Applications

B

APPENDIX B: INTRODUCTION TO MULTIMEDIA

OVERVIEW

Multimedia combines the text and graphics capability of the PC with high-quality sound and video. The combination of different media, under the control of the PC, has opened up a new world of education and entertainment. This appendix introduces you to the basics of multimedia and shows you how to incorporate sound and video into a PowerPoint presentation.

We begin with a brief discussion of the hardware requirements needed to run multimedia applications. We explain the different file types that are associated with multimedia and discuss the support that is built into Windows 95. We also describe the royalty-free multimedia files that are available on the PowerPoint (or Office Professional) CD-ROM.

The appendix also contains two hands-on exercises that let you apply the conceptual material. The first exercise is independent of PowerPoint and has you experiment with various sound and video files to better acquaint you with the capabilities of multimedia. The second exercise shows you how to create your own multimedia presentation.

THE MULTIMEDIA COMPUTER

Multimedia is possible only because of recent advances in technology that include faster microprocessors, CD-ROM, and sophisticated sound and video boards. But how fast a microprocessor do you really need? What type of CD-ROM and sound card should you consider? The answers are critical to both the consumer and the developer. The consumer wants a system that is capable of running "typical" multimedia applications. The developer, on the other hand, wants to appeal to the widest possible audience and must write an application so that it runs on the "typical" configuration.

To guide developers, and to let the public know the specific hardware needed, the ***Multimedia PC Marketing Council (MPC)*** was established to determine the suggested minimum specification for a multimedia computer. Three standards have been published to date—***MPC-1, MPC-2,*** and ***MPC-3,*** in 1991, 1993, and 1995, respectively, as shown in Figure B.1. Implicit within each standard is the requirement that the system retail for less than $2,000. If your budget can afford it, you may want to go beyond the MPC-3 configuration (to a faster microprocessor, more memory, and a larger hard drive), but you should not consider a system with less capability. And don't forget to include speakers to amplify the sound, a microphone if you want to record your own sounds, and a joystick for games.

THE MULTIMEDIA UPGRADE

Computer magazines are filled with advertisements for multimedia upgrades—kits that contain a sound card and CD-ROM; but are they worth the investment? If your existing system meets our other minimum requirements—a 486/66 processor, 8MB of RAM, and a 350MB disk—by all means upgrade. If, on the other hand, you re lacking one or more of these components, you are better off waiting until you are ready to replace the entire system. And one final piece of advice if you do decide to upgrade. Installing a CD-ROM and sound card on an existing system is not easy! Purchase the hardware at a local store and have a professional install it for you.

	MPC-1 (1991)	**MPC-2 (1993)**	**MPC-3 (1995)**
CPU	80386 16MHz	80486SX 25MHz	75MHz Pentium
RAM	2MB	4MB	8MB
Disk capacity	30MB	160MB	540MB
Sound card	8 bit	8 bit	16 bit with multivoice internal synthesizer
CD-ROM	Single speed	Double speed	Quadruple speed
Video system	VGA (640 × 480)	SVGA (800 × 600)	30 frames/second at 320 × 240 pixels

FIGURE B.1 The Multimedia PC

THE BASICS OF MULTIMEDIA

A few years ago multimedia was an extra. Today it is a virtual standard, and everyone has a favorite multimedia application. But did you ever stop to think of how the application was created? Or of the large number of individual files that are needed for the sound and visual effects that are at the heart of the application? In this section we look at the individual components, the sound and video files, that comprise a multimedia application.

Sound

The sound you hear from your PC is the result of a sound file (stored on disk or a CD-ROM) being played through the sound card in your system. There are, however, two very different types of sound files: a WAV file and a MIDI file. Each is discussed in turn.

A ***WAV file*** is a digitized recording of an actual sound (a voice, music, or special effects). It is created by a chip in the sound card that converts a recorded sound (e.g., your voice by way of a microphone) into a file on disk. The sound card divides the sound wave into tiny segments (known as samples) and stores each sample as a binary number. The quality of the sound is determined by two factors—the sampling rate and the resolution of each sample. The higher each of these values, the better the quality, and the larger the corresponding file.

The ***sampling rate*** (or frequency) is the number of samples per second and is expressed in KHz (thousands of samples per second). The higher the sampling rate, the more accurately the sound will be represented in the wave file. Common sampling rates are 11KHz, 22KHz, and 44KHz. The ***resolution*** is the number of bits (binary digits) used to store each sample. The more bits, the better. The first sound cards provided for only eight bits and are obsolete. Sixteen bits are standard in today's environment.

WAV files, even those that last only a few seconds, grow large very quickly. Eight-bit sound, for example, at a sampling rate of 11KHz (11,000 samples a second), requires approximately 11KB of disk space per second. Thirty seconds of sound at this sampling rate will take some 330KB. If you improve the quality by using a 16-bit sound card, and by doubling the sampling rate to 22KHz, the same 30 seconds of sound will consume 1.3MB, or almost an entire high-density floppy disk!

A ***MIDI file*** (Musical Instrument Digital Interface) is very different from a WAV file and is used only to create music. It does not store an actual sound (as does a WAV file), but rather the instructions to create that sound. In other words, a MIDI file is the electronic equivalent of sheet music. The advantage of a MIDI file is that it is much more compact than a WAV file because it stores instructions to create the sound rather than the actual sound.

Video

An ***AVI*** (Audio-Video Interleaved) ***file*** is the Microsoft standard for a digital video (i.e., a multimedia) file. It takes approximately 4.5MB to store one second of *uncompressed* color video in the AVI format. That may sound unbelievable, but you can verify the number with a little arithmetic.

A single VGA screen contains approximately 300,000 (640 × 480) pixels, each of which requires (at least) one byte of storage to store the color associated with that pixel. Allocating one byte (or 8 bits) per pixel yields only 256 (or 2^8) different colors. It is more common, therefore, to define color palettes based on two or even three bytes per pixel, which yield 65,536 (2^{16}) and 16,777,216 (2^{24}) colors, respectively. The more colors you have, the better the picture, but the larger the file.

In addition, to fool the eye and create the effect of motion, the screen must display at least 15 screens (frames) a second. If we multiply 300,000 bytes per frame, times 15 frames per second, we arrive at the earlier number of 4.5MB of data for each second of video. Storage requirements of this magnitude are clearly prohibitive in that an entire 640MB CD would hold less than three minutes of video. And even if storage capacity were not a problem, it's simply not possible for a CD-ROM to deliver almost 5MB of data per second to the PC. Clearly, something has to be done.

Full-motion video is made possible in two ways: by reducing the size of the window in which the video clip is displayed, and through ***file compression.*** Think, for a moment, of the video clips you have seen (or consider the SIDEWALK.AVI file in Figure B.2) and realize that they are displayed in a window that is 320 × 240, or one quarter of a VGA screen. The smaller window immediately reduces the storage by a factor of four.

Video clip

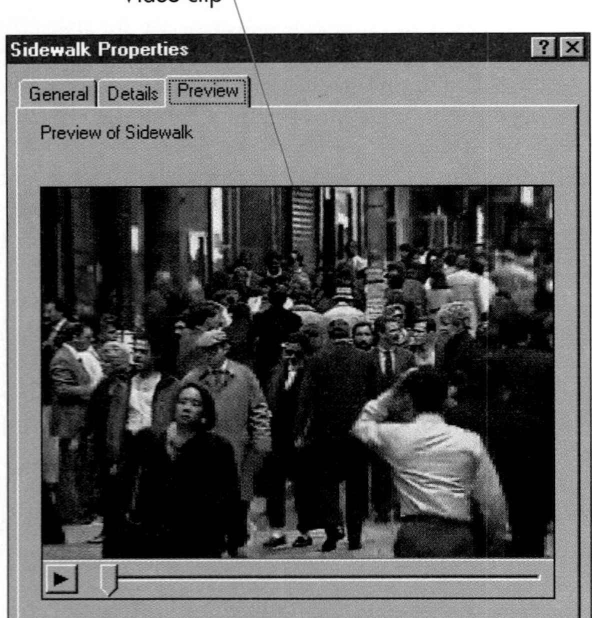

(a) Preview

Video is displayed at 320 x 240 (one quarter of VGA screen)

Duration of video clip

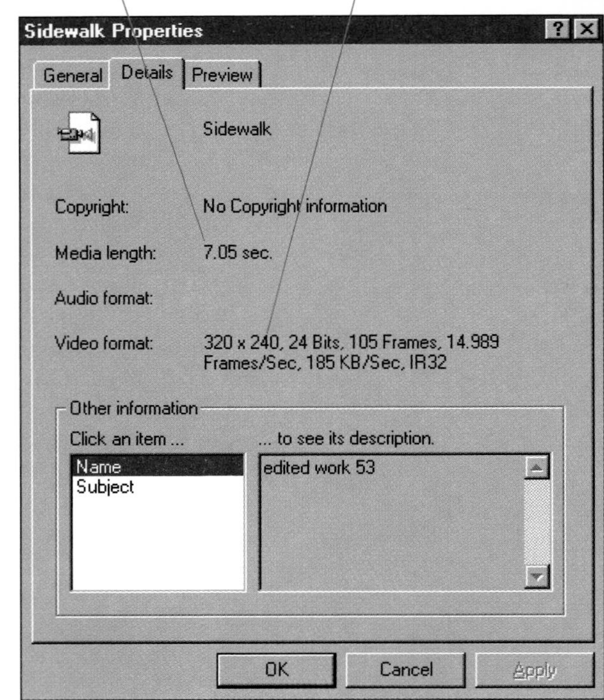

(b) Details

FIGURE B.2 A Video Clip

Even more significant than a reduced window is the availability of sophisticated compression-decompression algorithms, which dramatically reduce the storage requirements. In essence, these algorithms do not store every pixel in every frame, but only information about how pixels change from frame to frame. The details of file compression are not important at this time. What is important is that you appreciate the enormous amount of data that is required for multimedia applications.

Realize, too, that even with the smaller window and file compression, AVI files are still inordinately large. The seven-second movie clip in Figure B.2, for example, requires 1.3MB, or almost an entire high-density floppy disk. Nevertheless, compare this requirement to our earlier calculations, which showed that an uncompressed video running on a VGA screen would take approximately 4.5MB per second!

THE AVI (AUDIO-VIDEO INTERLEAVED) STANDARD

The AVI format was introduced in 1992 and specified a standard video clip of 160 × 120 pixels, or one sixteenth of a VGA screen. The tiny screen was not overly impressive to the public at large, but it represented a significant technical achievement. Improved technology such as the local bus, quad speed CD-ROM, better compression algorithms, and faster microprocessors have resulted in today's standard clip of 320 × 240, or one quarter of a VGA screen.

Windows 95 Support

Windows 95 includes the necessary software (in the form of accessories) to play various types of multimedia files. The tools can be accessed from the Start button or through shortcuts in the Multimedia folder shown in Figure B.3a. The appropriate accessory is also opened automatically when you double click the corresponding media file type.

The ***CD Player*** enables you to play audio CDs in a CD-ROM drive while you work on your PC. The controls on the Windows CD player look just like those on a regular CD player. It also has many of the same features, such as random play, and a programmable playback order.

The ***Media Player*** lets you play audio, video, or animation files. ***Volume Control*** enables you to control the volume and/or balance of your sound card.

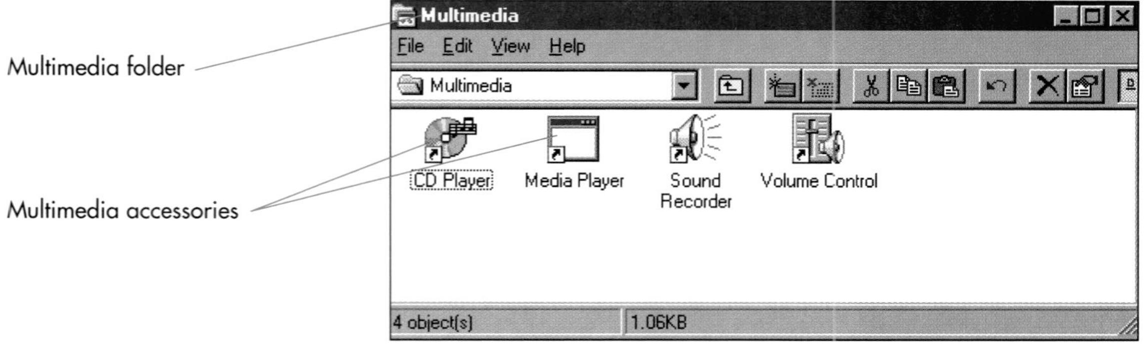

(a) Multimedia Tools

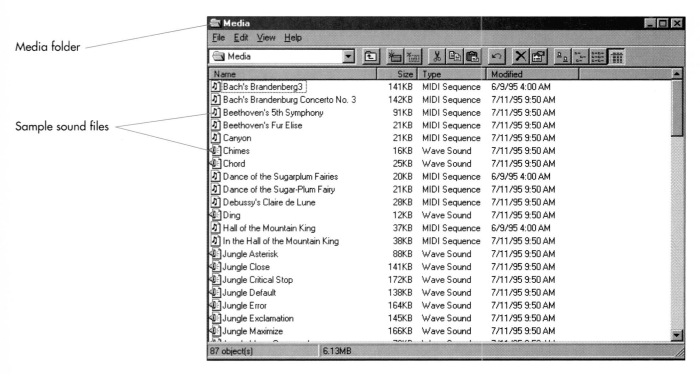

Media folder

Sample sound files

Media

File Edit View Help

Media

Name	Size	Type	Modified
Bach's Brandenberg3	141KB	MIDI Sequence	6/9/95 4:00 AM
Bach's Brandenburg Concerto No. 3	142KB	MIDI Sequence	7/11/95 9:50 AM
Beethoven's 5th Symphony	91KB	MIDI Sequence	7/11/95 9:50 AM
Beethoven's Fur Elise	21KB	MIDI Sequence	7/11/95 9:50 AM
Canyon	21KB	MIDI Sequence	7/11/95 9:50 AM
Chimes	16KB	Wave Sound	7/11/95 9:50 AM
Chord	25KB	Wave Sound	7/11/95 9:50 AM
Dance of the Sugarplum Fairies	20KB	MIDI Sequence	6/9/95 4:00 AM
Dance of the Sugar-Plum Fairy	21KB	MIDI Sequence	7/11/95 9:50 AM
Debussy's Claire de Lune	28KB	MIDI Sequence	7/11/95 9:50 AM
Ding	12KB	Wave Sound	7/11/95 9:50 AM
Hall of the Mountain King	37KB	MIDI Sequence	6/9/95 4:00 AM
In the Hall of the Mountain King	38KB	MIDI Sequence	7/11/95 9:50 AM
Jungle Asterisk	88KB	Wave Sound	7/11/95 9:50 AM
Jungle Close	141KB	Wave Sound	7/11/95 9:50 AM
Jungle Critical Stop	172KB	Wave Sound	7/11/95 9:50 AM
Jungle Default	138KB	Wave Sound	7/11/95 9:50 AM
Jungle Error	164KB	Wave Sound	7/11/95 9:50 AM
Jungle Exclamation	145KB	Wave Sound	7/11/95 9:50 AM
Jungle Maximize	166KB	Wave Sound	7/11/95 9:50 AM

87 object(s) 6.13MB

(b) Media Files

FIGURE B.3 Multimedia Support

The ***Sound Recorder*** is used to record and play back a WAV file. Options within the Sound Recorder enable you to record at different qualities (e.g., CD or radio). You can also add special effects to a recorded sound, such as an echo, or you can speed up or slow down the recording. You can even play it backwards.

In addition to the multimedia accessories, Windows also provides sample files on which you can experiment. The files are stored in the ***Media folder,*** as shown in Figure B.3b. The exercise that follows has you locate the Media folder on your system, then use the Windows accessories to play various files in the folder.

HANDS-ON EXERCISE 1

Introduction to Multimedia

Objective: Use the Windows 95 Find command to locate and demonstrate WAV, MIDI, and AVI files. The exercise requires a sound card but can be done without a CD-ROM. Use Figure B.4 as a guide in the exercise.

STEP 1: The Find Command

- Click the **Start Button** on the Windows 95 taskbar. Click (or point to) the **Find command,** then click **Files or Folders** to display the dialog box in Figure B.4a. (No files will be listed since the search has not yet taken place, and the Media folder will not be displayed.) The size and/or position of the dialog box may be different from the one in the figure.
- Type **Media** (the folder you are searching for) in the Named text box. Click the **drop-down arrow** in the Look in list box. Click **My Computer** to search all of the drives on your system. Be sure the **Include subfolders** box is checked as shown in Figure B.4a.
- Click the **Find Now button** to begin the search, then watch the status bar as Windows searches for the specified files and folders.
- The results of the search are displayed within the Find Files dialog box and should contain a Media folder as shown in Figure B.4a. (Your view may be different from ours.) If you do not see the folder, check the search parameters:
  - Be sure that you spelled **Media** correctly and that you are looking in **My Computer.**
  - Click the **Date Modified tab.** Click the **All Files option button.**
  - Click the **Advanced tab.** Be sure that **All Files and Folders** is specified in the Of Type list box and that the Containing text box is clear.

ORDINARY FILES

A multimedia file is just like any other file with respect to ordinary file operations. Point to the file (in My Computer or the Windows Explorer), then click the right mouse button to display a menu to cut or copy the file, rename or delete the file, or display its properties. You can also use the right mouse button to click and drag the file to a different drive or folder or create a shortcut on the desktop.

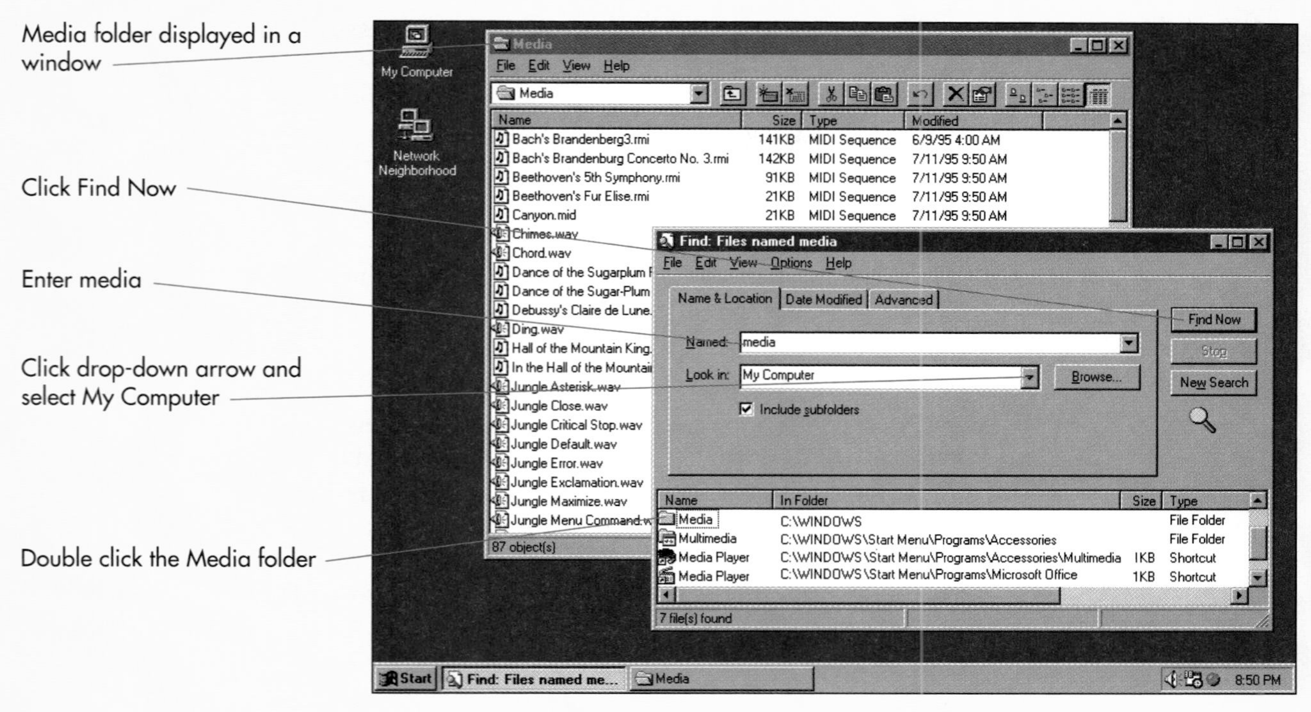

(a) Find the Media Folder (steps 1 & 2)

FIGURE B.4 Hands-on Exercise 1

- Pull down the **Options menu** and verify that the Case Sensitive option is off (i.e., that the option does not have a check).
- Click the **Find Now button** to repeat the search with these parameters.

➤ If you still do not see a Media folder, ask your instructor about reinstalling the multimedia component in Windows 95.

STEP 2: The Media Folder

➤ Double click the **Media folder** to open a window for this folder as shown in Figure B.4a. The size and position of your window may be different from ours.

FILE EXTENSIONS

Long-time DOS users will recognize the three-character extension at the end of a file name, which indicates the file type. The extensions are displayed or hidden according to an option set in the View menu in My Computer or the Windows Explorer. Windows 95 maintains the file extension for compatibility, and in addition, displays an icon next to the file name to indicate the file type. The icons are more easily recognized in the Large Icons view, as opposed to the Details view. Extensions of WAV and MID denote a wave form and MIDI file, respectively. An AVI (Audio-Video Interleaved) file is the Microsoft standard for a multimedia file with video and sound.

➤ To display the Details view and the file extensions within that view:

- Pull down the **View menu.** Click **Details.**
- Pull down the **View menu** a second time. Click **Options,** then click the **View tab** in the Options dialog box. Clear the box (if necessary) to **Hide MS-DOS file extensions.** Click **OK.**

➤ The view in your Media window should match Figure B.4a. You may, however, see a different number of objects.

➤ Click anywhere in the **Find window** (or click its button on the Taskbar). Click the **Close button** in this window so that only the Media folder remains open on the desktop.

STEP 3: WAV Files

➤ Point to the **Chord.wav** file, then click the **right mouse button** to display a menu with commands pertaining to the selected file.

➤ Click **Properties** to display the property sheet for the file. Click the **Details tab** as shown in Figure B.4b. Note that the duration of the sound (the media length) is just a little over one second, yet the file requires 25KB of storage.

➤ Close the Properties dialog box.

➤ Play the sound:

- Double click the icon next to the file name, or
- Right click the file, then click the **Play command.** The Sound Recorder will appear on the screen as the sound is played.
- If necessary, close the Sound Recorder after the sound has finished playing.

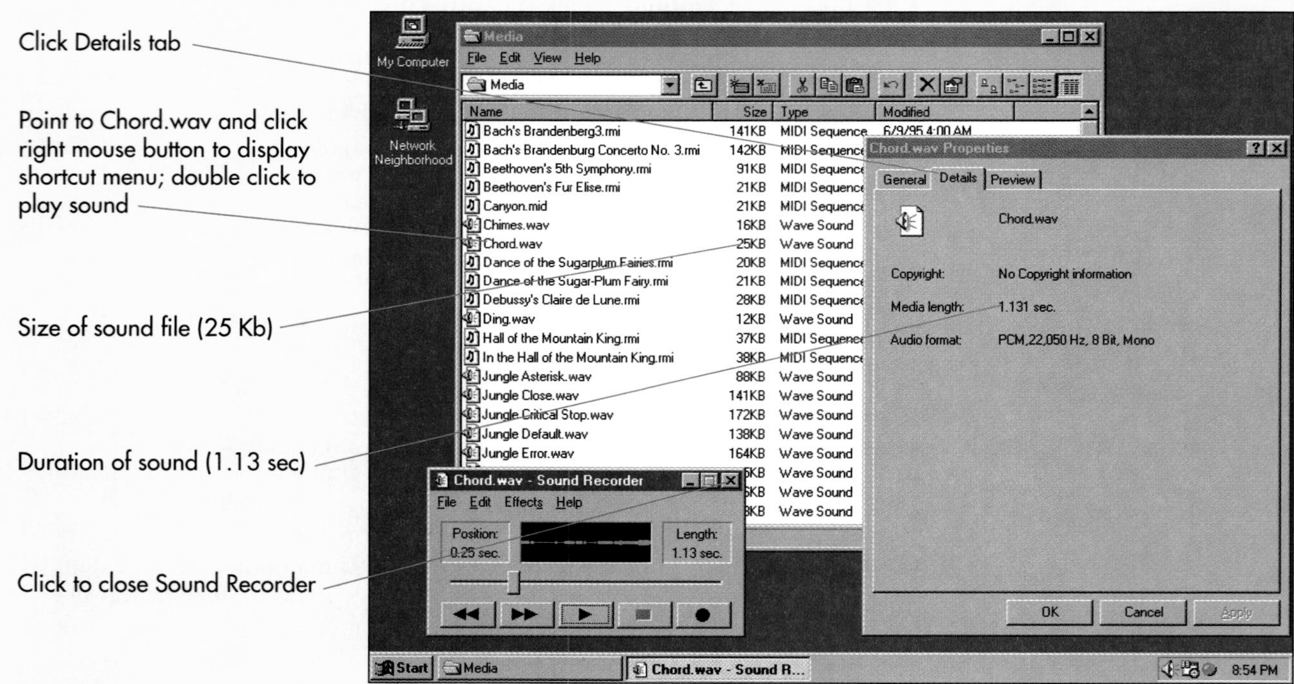

(b) WAV Files (step 3)

FIGURE B.4 Hands-on Exercise 1 (continued)

➤ Double click the other WAV files to play the other sound files. If necessary, close the Sound Recorder after playing each sound.

RECORD YOUR OWN WAV FILES

You can record your own WAV files (then link or embed those files in a PowerPoint presentation), provided you have a microphone. To create a new sound (WAV) file, right click in the folder that is to contain the file, click New, then click Wave Sound to specify the type of object you want to create. Change the default file name, then double click the file to open the Sound Recorder. Click the Record button to start recording and the Stop button when you have finished. Click the Play button to hear the recorded sound. Close the Sound Recorder, then use the Insert Sound command in PowerPoint to insert your new sound into a presentation.

STEP 4: MIDI Files

➤ Play either the **Canyon.mid** or the **Passport.mid** file:

- Double click the icon next to the file name, or
- Right click the file to select the file and display a menu. Click **Play.**

➤ The Media Player will appear on the screen as shown in Figure B.4c. Unlike the WAV files, which last but a second, the MIDI files are musical compositions that last two minutes each.

➤ Experiment with the controls on the Media Player:

- Click the **Pause button** to suspend playing.
- Click the **Play button** (which appears after you click the Pause button) to resume playing.
- Click the **Stop button** to stop playing.
- Click the **Rewind button** to return to the beginning of the recording.

➤ Close the Media Player when you are finished listening. Close the Media window.

WAV FILES VERSUS MIDI FILES

A WAV file stores an actual sound, whereas a MIDI file stores the instructions to create the sound. Because a WAV file stores a recorded sound, it can represent any type of sound—a voice, music, or special effects. A MIDI file can store only music. WAV files, even those that last only a few seconds, are very large because the sound is sampled thousands of times a second to create the file. MIDI files, however, are much more compact because they store the instructions to create the sound rather than the sound itself.

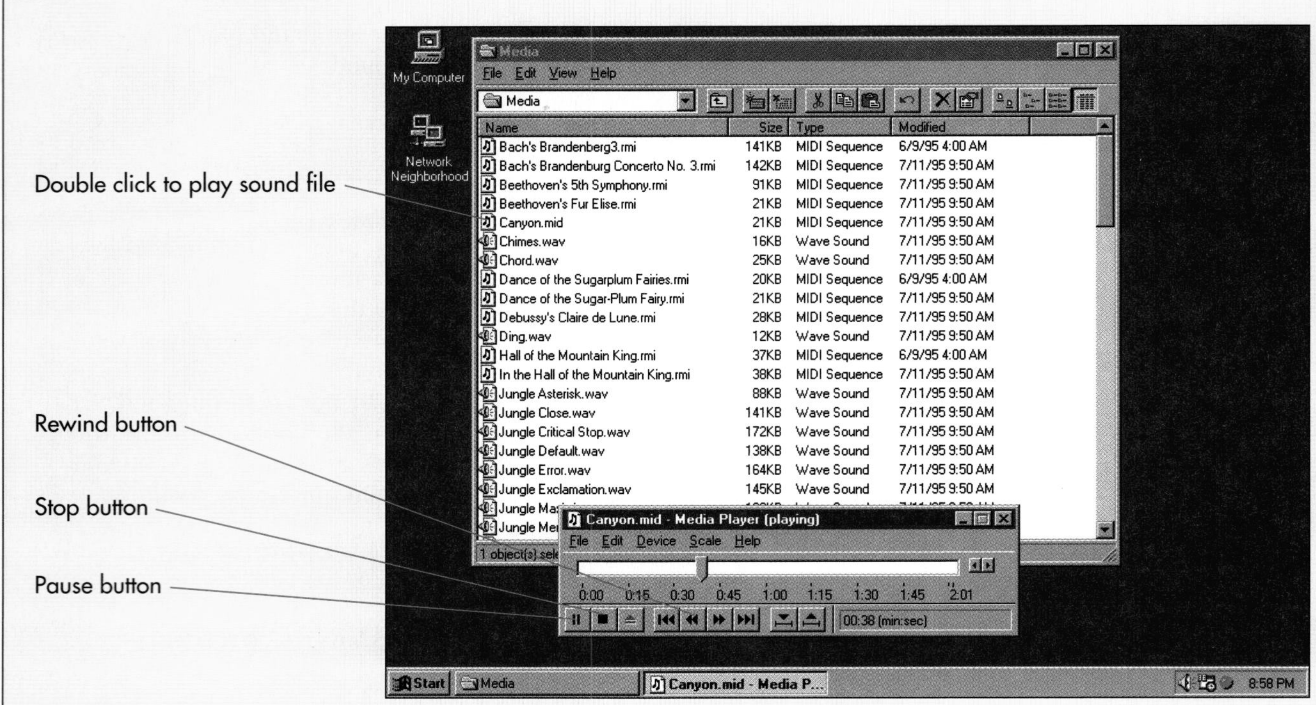

(c) MIDI Files (step 4)

FIGURE B.4 Hands-on Exercise 1 (continued)

STEP 5: Video Clips

- Click the **Start button** on the Windows 95 taskbar. Click (or point to) the **Find command,** then click **Files or Folders** to display the dialog box in Figure B.4d.
  - Place the PowerPoint or Office Professional CD in the CD-ROM drive, as the best AVI files, for purposes of demonstration, are found on this CD. (You can still do the exercise if you don't have the CD.)
  - Enter ***.avi** (the type of file you are searching for) in the Named text box. Click the **drop-down arrow** in the Look in list box and select **My Computer** (to search drive C and the CD-ROM).
  - Be sure the **include subfolders** box is checked.
  - Click the **Find Now button** to begin the search, then watch the status bar as Windows searches for the specified files and folders.
- The results of the search are displayed within the Find Files dialog box and should contain multiple AVI files. If you do not see any files at all, check the search parameters, then repeat the search.
- Select (click) a video clip (e.g., Sidewalk.avi in Figure B.4d), click the **right mouse button** to display a shortcut menu, then click **Play** to view the video clip (or double click the file name).
- View as many video clips as you like, then close the Find Files dialog box when you are finished.
- Exit Windows if you do not want to continue with the next exercise at this time.

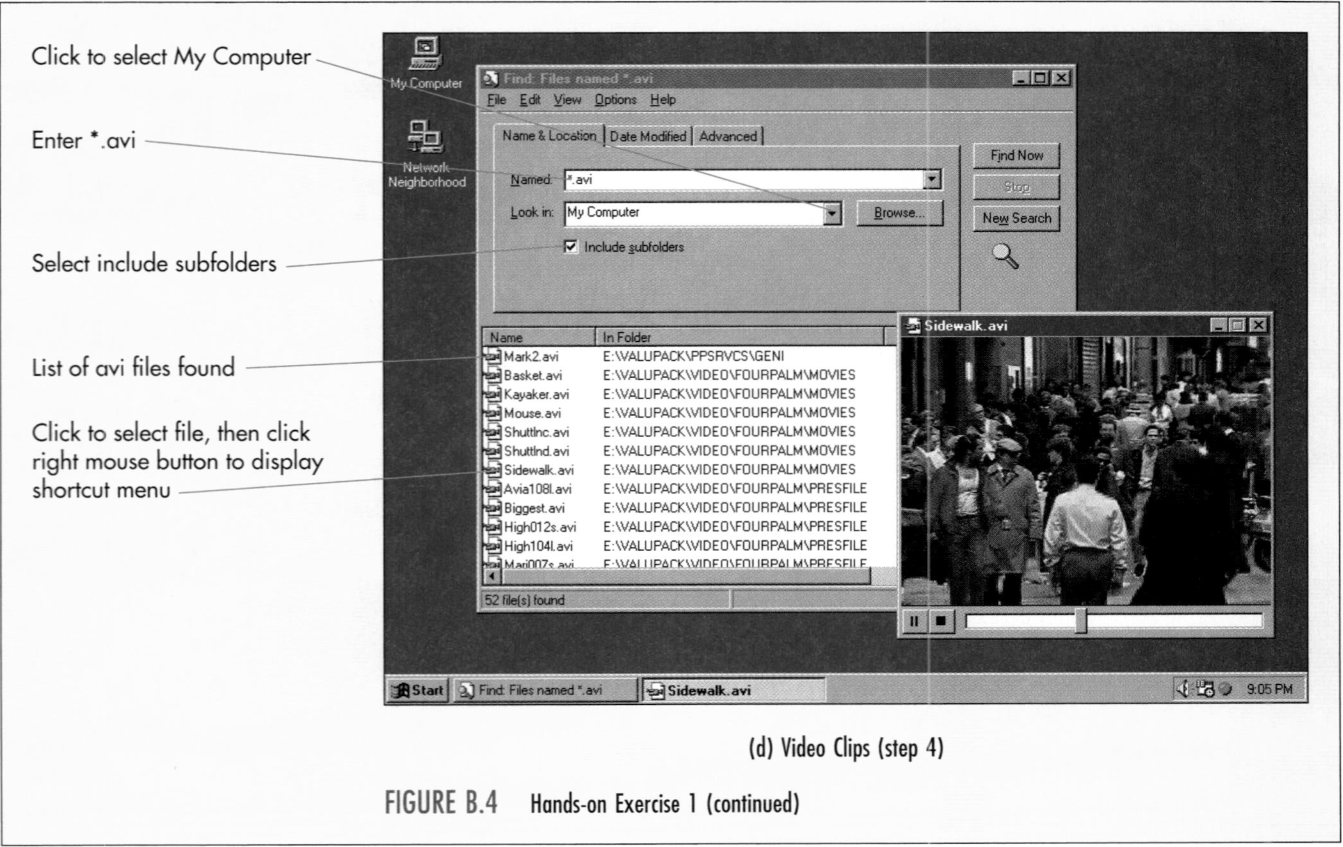

(d) Video Clips (step 4)

FIGURE B.4 Hands-on Exercise 1 (continued)

MULTIMEDIA PRESENTATIONS

The exercise just completed had you explore the elements of multimedia and experiment with individual files. You learned about the different types of sound files and saw the impact of a video clip. The effectiveness of multimedia, however, depends on integrating the various elements into a cohesive unit.

Perhaps the best way to explore the potential of multimedia is to view professional presentations such as those in Figure B.5. These presentations in Figures B.5a, B.5b, and B.5c can be found on the ***PowerPoint Multimedia CD*** and are interesting for two reasons. First, they show what can be done in PowerPoint by an individual knowledgeable in the basics of multimedia. Second, they acquaint you with some of the resources on the CD and tell you how to acquire royalty-free multimedia for inclusion in your own presentation.

THE VALUE PACK

Both the PowerPoint Multimedia and the Office Professional CDs contain a variety of professionally created multimedia presentations. Use the Windows 95 Find command to search for all PowerPoint presentations (files with a PPT extension), then view the presentations that are of interest to you. You will find information from companies offering audio and video files. You will also find additional resources on the CD (e.g., clip art and additional templates) that you can use in your presentations.

(a) 4PALMS (7.3 Mb)

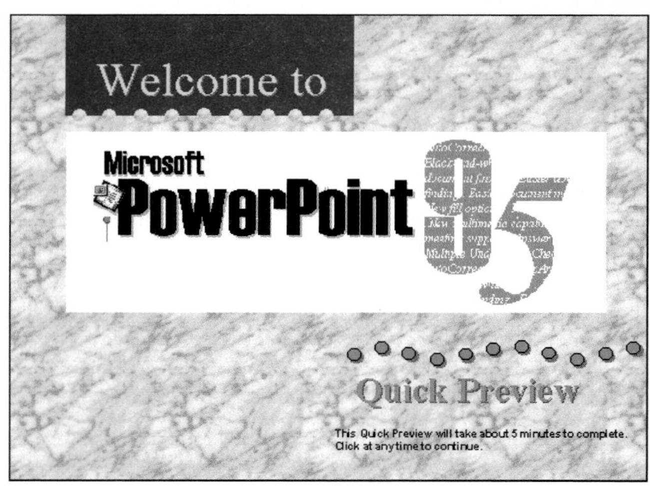

(b) QuikPrev (4.9 Mb)

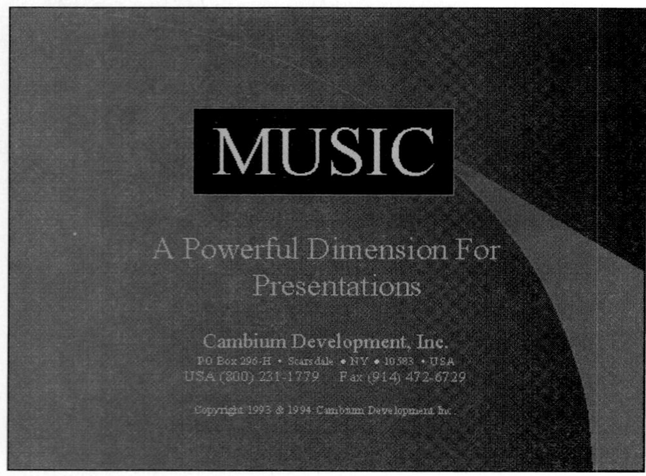

(c) Cambium (5.9 Mb)

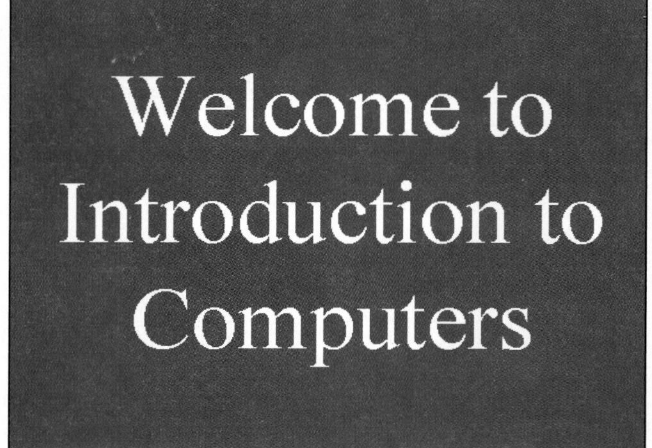

(d) Multimedia (278 Kb)

FIGURE B.5 Multimedia Presentations

A partially completed version of the presentation in Figure B.5d is found on the data disk and will be the basis of the next hands-on exercise in which you create your own multimedia presentation.

Implementation in PowerPoint

A multimedia presentation is a show, and like any show, it requires careful planning if it is to be successful. The actors in a show, or the objects on a PowerPoint slide, must be thoroughly scripted so that the performance is as effective as possible. Consider now Figure B.6, which contains one of the slides in the presentation you will create.

Figure B.6a contains the actual slide, whereas Figures B.6b and B.6c show the dialog boxes associated with two of the objects on the slide. The slide contains a total of nine objects (a single text box and eight students). Each of these objects is an "actor" in the presentation and requires instructions as to when to appear on stage and how to make that entrance.

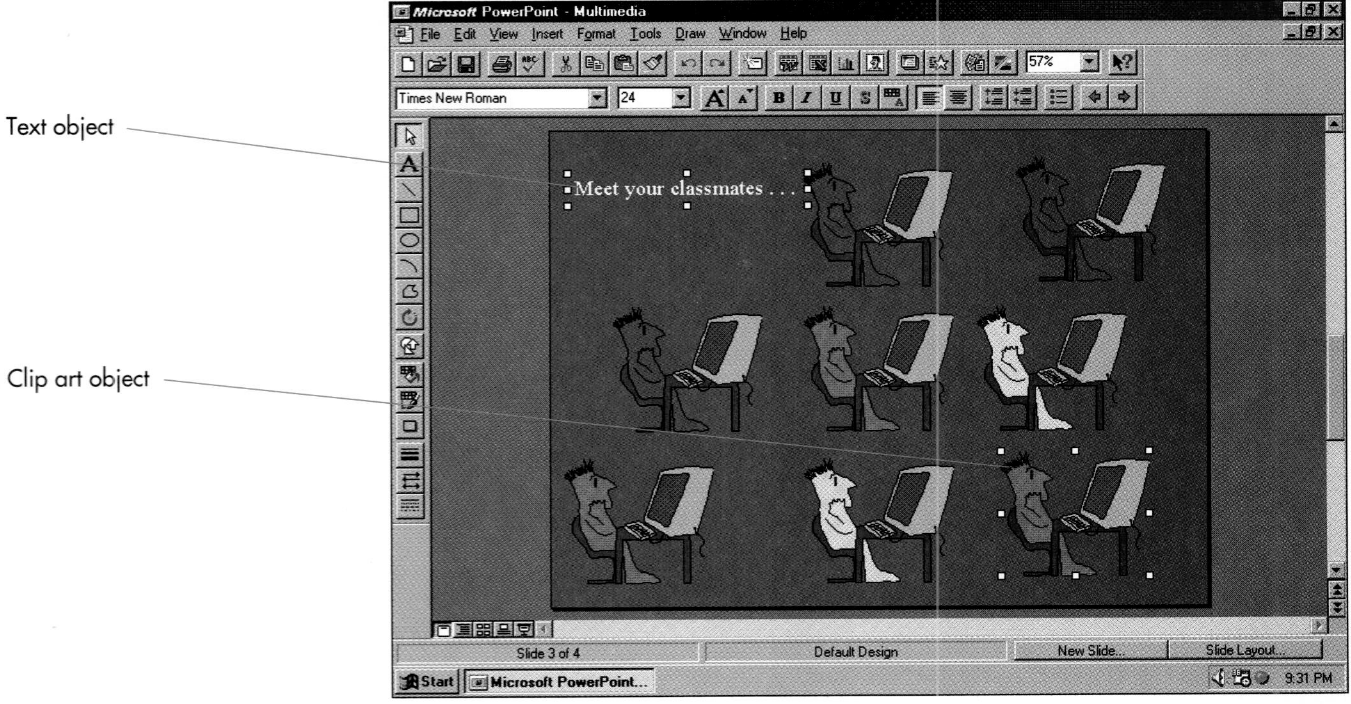

(a) The Slide

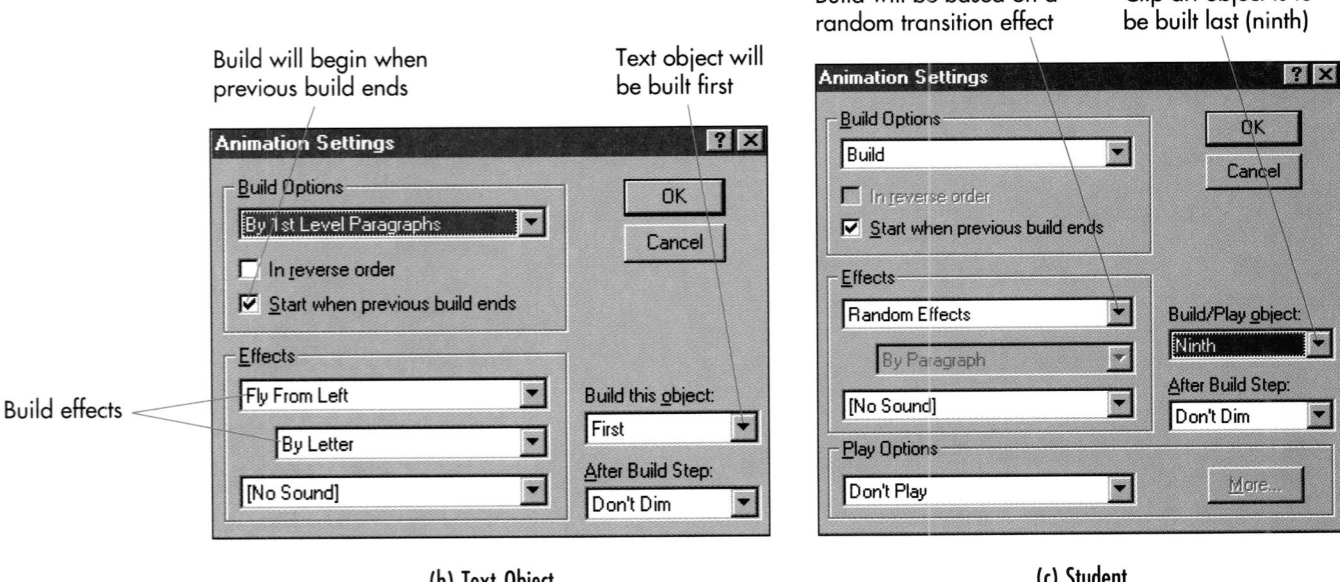

(b) Text Object

(c) Student

FIGURE B.6 Animation Settings

You, as director, have decided that the text box will fly in from the left of the slide and that this action will take place before any of the students appear. Once the text is displayed on screen, the students are to fly in from various directions, one student at a time, until all eight students are onstage. The ***Animation Settings command*** (in the Tools menu) is the means by which you convey these instructions to the object.

Figure B.6b displays the Animation Settings dialog box for the text. The text is to be built first, and the build is to begin as soon as the previous build ends (i.e., as soon as the slide appears and without the need to click the mouse.) The special effects call for the text to fly in from the left, letter by letter. Figure B.6c displays the instructions for the student in the lower-right corner of the slide, who is to appear last (the ninth object), and whose entrance will be based on a random transition effect. These instructions may sound complicated, but they work beautifully, as you will see in the next hands-on exercise.

HANDS-ON EXERCISE 2

Creating a Multimedia Presentation

Objective: Add music (a MIDI file) to the first slide of a presentation so that it plays continually throughout the presentation; use the Animation Settings command to control the appearance of objects on a slide. The exercise requires a sound card but can be done without a CD-ROM. Use Figure B.7 as a guide in the exercise.

STEP 1: Choose the Music

- Open the **Multimedia presentation** in the **Exploring PowerPoint folder** as shown in Figure B.7a.
- Click the **Start button** on the Windows 95 taskbar. Click (or point to) the **Find command,** then click **Files or Folders** to display the Find Files dialog

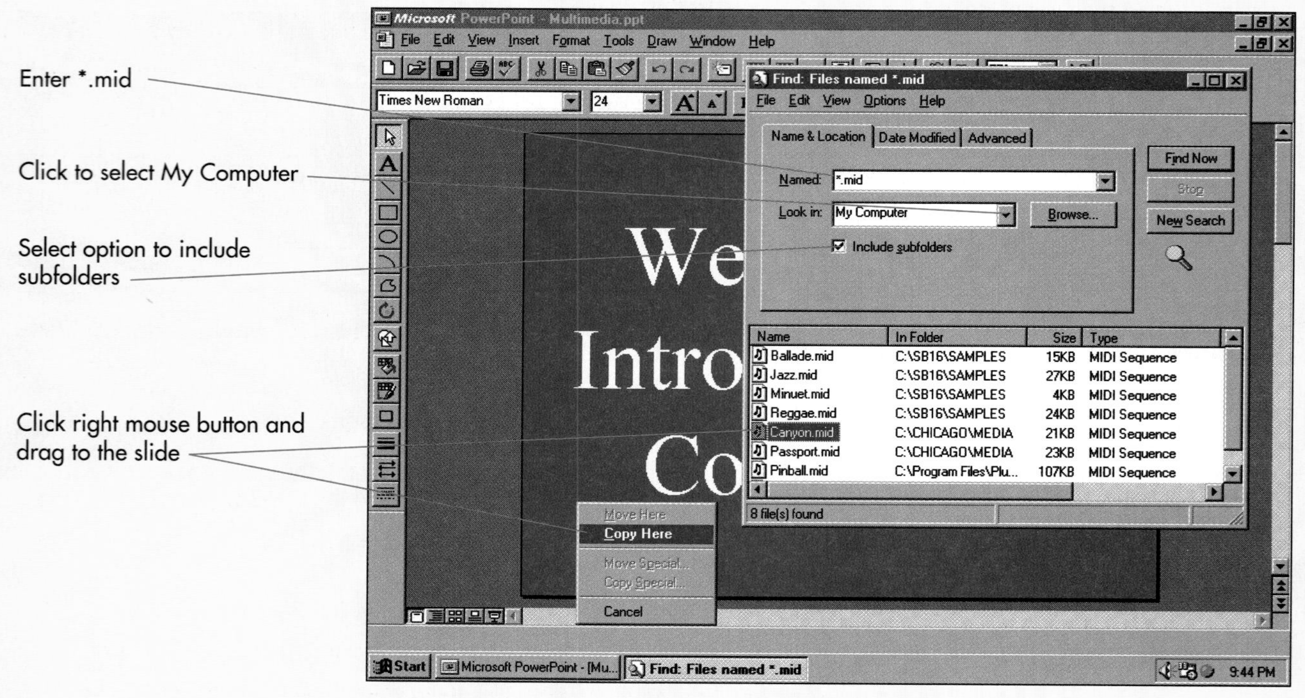

(a) Add the Music (step 1)

FIGURE B.7 Hands-on Exercise 2

box. The size and/or position of the dialog box may be different from the one in the figure:

- Enter ***.MID** (the type of file you are searching for) in the Named text box. Click the **drop-down arrow** in the Look in list box to select **My Computer** (to search all drives on your system).
- Be sure the **include subfolders** box is checked.
- Click the **Find Now button** to begin the search, then watch the status bar as Windows searches for the specified files and folders.

➤ The results of the search are displayed within the Find Files dialog box and should contain multiple files with the MID extension. If you do not see any files at all, check the search parameters, then repeat the search.

➤ Select (click) any file (e.g., Canyon.mid in Figure B.7a, click the **right mouse button** to display a shortcut menu, then click **Play** to hear the music. Close the Media Player when you are finished listening. (You can click the **Stop button** to stop playing.)

➤ Listen to as many files as you like, then choose the music you want to include. Point to the file you want, then click and drag the file icon with the **right mouse button** to the PowerPoint slide.

➤ Release the mouse to display the shortcut menu and click **Copy Here** to copy the sound object onto the PowerPoint slide. Close the Find Files dialog box.

ADDITIONAL TEMPLATES

The PowerPoint Multimedia (or Office Professional) CD contains 58 additional templates from which to choose. Pull down the Format menu and click the Apply Design Template command (or double click the Design Template portion of the status bar) to display the Apply Design Template dialog box. Click the drop-down arrow on the Look In list box, select the drive containing the CD-ROM, open the Valuepack folder, then open the Pptmpl folder to display the available templates.

STEP 2: Play Options

➤ The sound file should be selected. Pull down the **Tools menu** and click **Animation Settings** to display the Animation Settings dialog box as shown in Figure B.7b:

- Click the **drop-down arrow** on the Build Options list box and click **Build.**
- Check the box to **Start when previous build ends.**
- Click the **drop-down arrow** on the Play Options list box and click **Play.**

➤ Click the **More command button** to display the More Play Options dialog box.

- Click the option button to play **Automatically** (after 0 seconds).
- Click the option button to **Continue slide show, play in background.**
- Click the option button to **Stop after 4 slides** (click the **up arrow** to select 4 slides, the number of slides in the presentation).

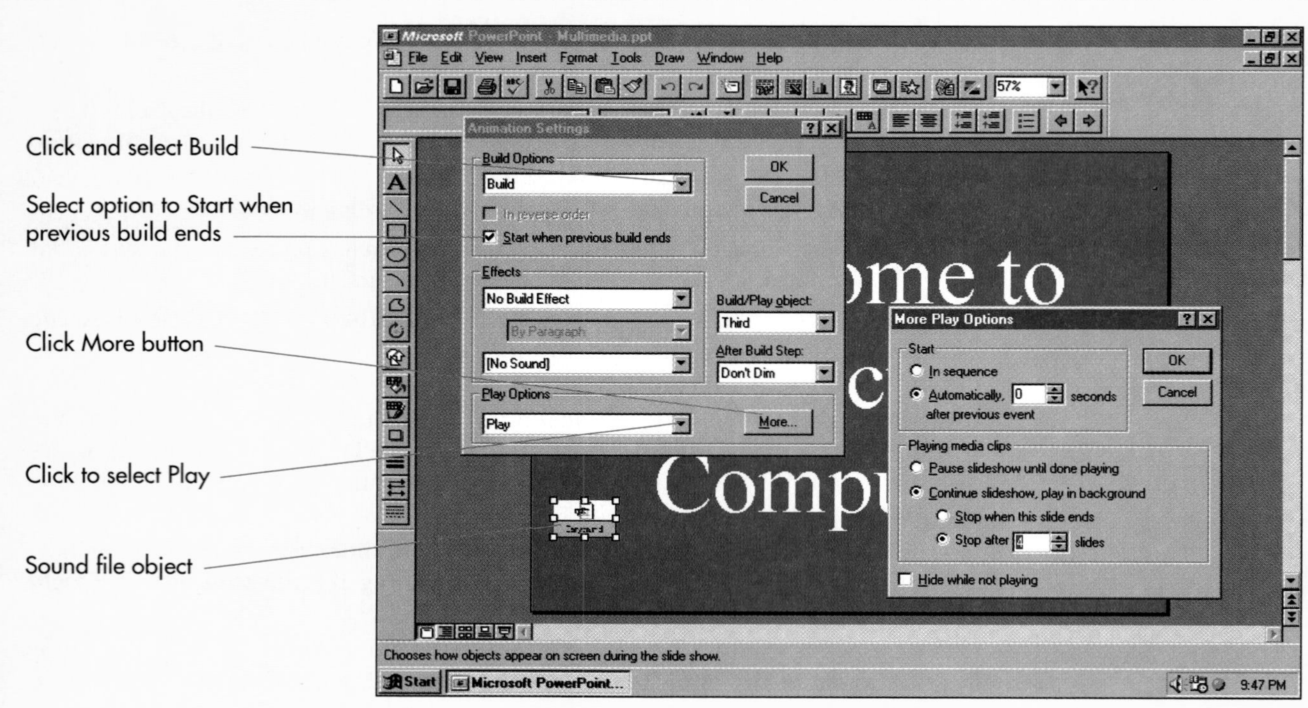

(b) Set the Music (step 2)

FIGURE B.7 Hands-on Exercise 2 (continued)

➤ Verify that your settings match those in Figure B.7b. Click **OK** to close the More Play Options dialog box. Click **OK** to close the Animation Settings dialog box.

➤ Click the **Slide Show button** above the status bar. You should see the title slide and hear the music. Click the **Stop button** on the Media Player when it appears, then press **Esc** to stop the show in order to return to the Slide view and continue working.

➤ Click and drag a corner sizing handle to shrink the icon on the slide so that the Media Player will not be visible during the actual show.

➤ Save the presentation.

THE VOICE OVER

Use the Sound Recorder to create a voice-over narration that you can play during a self-running presentation. Music and/or narration are especially effective in stand-alone presentations such as those found in a kiosk or demonstration booth.

(c) Complete the First Slide (step 3)

FIGURE B.7 Hands-on Exercise 2 (continued)

STEP 3: Animation Settings (the title slide)

➤ Click on the slide to select the title as shown in Figure B.7c. Pull down the **Tools menu** and click **Animation Settings** to display the Animation Settings dialog box:

- Click the **drop-down arrow** on the Build Options list box and select **By 1st Level Paragraphs.**
- Click the check box to **Start when previous build ends.**
- Click the **drop-down arrow** on the Effects list boxes and select **Fly From Left** and **By Letter.**
- Click the **drop-down arrow** on the Build this object list box and click **Second** (the letters are to appear after the music starts).
- Verify that your settings match those in Figure B.7c, then click **OK** to close the Animation Settings dialog box.

➤ Click the **Slide Show button** above the status bar. This time you will not only hear the music, but you will also see the letters fly in from the left. Press the **Esc key,** after you see the title, to stop the music (the Media Player is hidden), then press the **Esc key** a second time to return to the Slide view and continue working.

➤ Save the presentation.

YOU'RE THE DIRECTOR

No one ever said that multimedia was quick or easy. Creating an effective presentation takes time, much more time than you might expect initially, as each slide has to be choreographed in detail. Think of yourself as the director who must tell the actors (the objects on a slide) when to come on stage and how to make their entrance. It takes patience and practice.

STEP 4: Animation Settings (the students)

- Use the **Slide Elevator** (or press the **PgDn key** twice) to select the third slide as shown in Figure B.7d.
- Click the **Slide Show button** to view this slide as it will appear in the slide show. There are no animation effects on the slide as it currently exists, and all of the students appear at the same time. Press **Esc** to return to the Slide view.
- Press and hold the **Shift key** as you click each of the eight students to select all of the students at one time as shown in Figure B.7d.
- Point to any selected student and click the **right mouse button** to display a shortcut menu, then click **Animation Settings** to display the Animation Settings dialog box. (The settings will be applied to all the selected objects.)

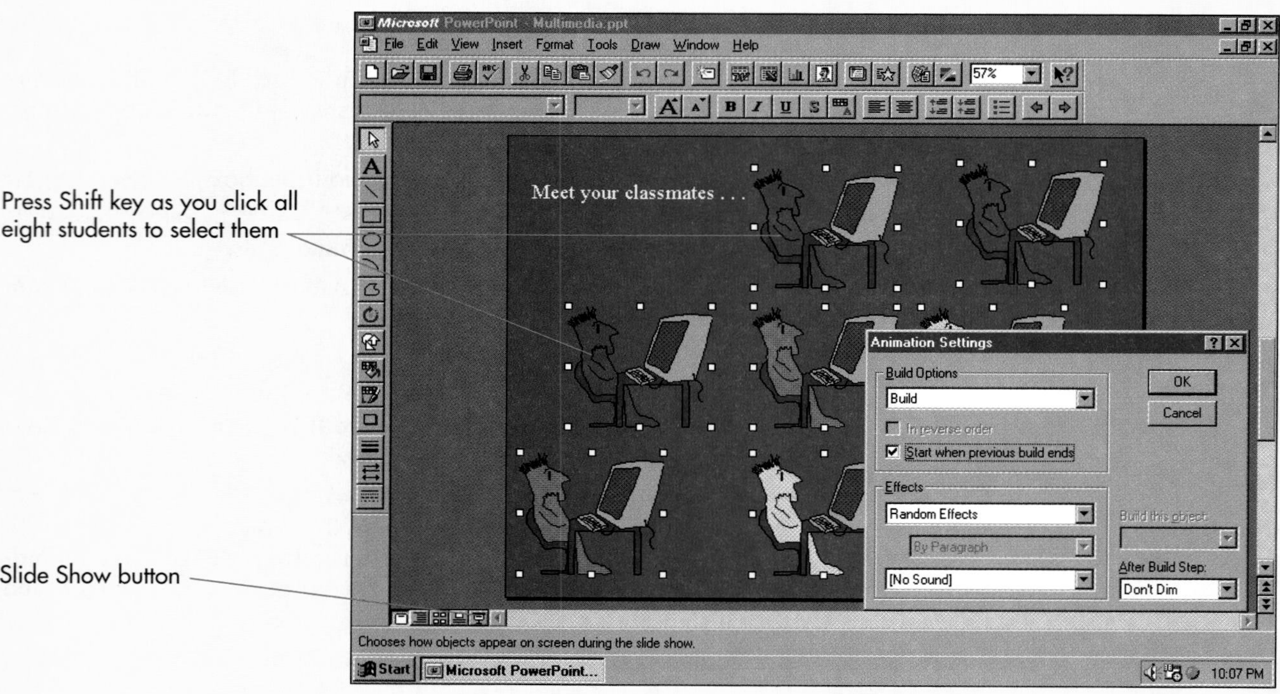

(d) Animation Settings (step 4)

FIGURE B.7 Hands-on Exercise 2 (continued)

- Click the **drop-down arrow** on the Build Effects list box and click **Build.**
- Click the check box to **Start when previous build ends.**
- If necessary, click the **drop-down arrow** in the Effects list box and choose **Random Effects.**
- Click **OK** to accept the settings and close the Animation Settings dialog box.

➤ Point to the placeholder for Meet Your Classmates, click the **right mouse button** to display a shortcut menu, then click **Animation Settings:**

- Click the **drop-down arrow** on the Build Options list box and select **By 1st Level Paragraphs.**
- Click the check box to **Start when previous build ends.**
- Click the **drop-down arrow** on the Effects list boxes and select **Fly From Left** and **By Letter.**
- Click the **drop-down arrow** on the Build this object list box and click **First** (the letters are to appear before the students).
- Click **OK** to close the Animation Settings dialog box.

➤ Click the **Slide Show button** to view this slide with the animation effects you added. (The students appear by default in the order they were added to the slide when the slide was created initially.) Press **Esc** to return to the Slide view.

➤ Save the presentation.

THE ANIMATION EFFECTS TOOLBAR

The Animation Effects toolbar is the easiest way to change the order in which objects are built on a slide. Point to any visible toolbar, click the right mouse button, then click Animation Effects to display (hide) the toolbar. Select the object on the slide, click the drop-down arrow on the Animation Order list box, then choose the appropriate number (e.g., 1, if the object is to appear first).

STEP 5: Rehearse the Timings

➤ Press **Ctrl+Home** to return to the first slide. Pull down the **View menu** and click **Slide Show** to display the Slide Show dialog box. Click the option button to **Rehearse New Timings,** then click the **Show button.**

➤ The first slide appears in the Slide Show view, and the Rehearsal dialog box is displayed in the lower-right corner of the screen. Click the mouse to register the elapsed time and move to the next slide.

➤ The second slide in the presentation should appear as shown in Figure B.7e with the animation effects built in. The cumulative time appears on the left (00:01:10 seconds). The time for this specific slide (00:00:17 seconds) is shown at the right.

- Click the **Repeat button** to redo the timing for the slide. (You won't see the new timing until the slide concludes.)
- Click the **Pause button** to (temporarily) stop the clock. Click the Pause button a second time to resume the clock. (The music continues to play.)

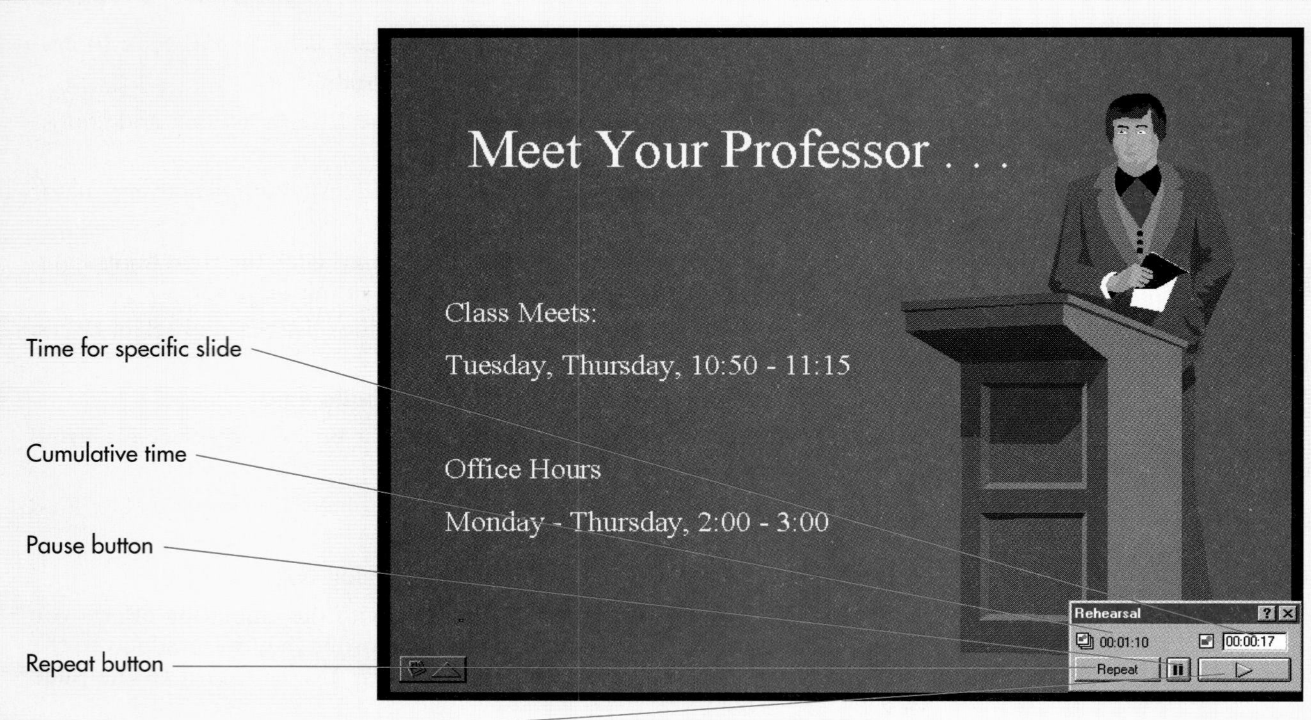

(e) Rehearse Timings (step 5)

FIGURE B.7 Hands-on Exercise 2 (continued)

- Click the **Next slide button** to record the timing and move to the next slide.
- Continue rehearsing the show until you reach the last slide (containing the PC and other equipment), then click on this last slide to end the presentation. Be sure to click the mouse to record the timing for the last slide.

➤ You should see a dialog box at the end of the presentation that indicates the total time of the slide show. Click **Yes** when asked whether you want to record the new timings.

➤ Save the presentation.

STEP 6: Slide Show Options

➤ You should be back in the Slide Sorter view as shown in Figure B.7f, with the timings recorded under each slide. Pull down the **View menu** and click **Slide Show** to display the Slide Show dialog box.

➤ Click the **All option button** under Slides, click the **Use Slide Timings option button** under Advance, and check the box to **Loop Continuously under Esc.**

➤ Click the **Show button,** then sit back and enjoy the show, which will cycle continually until you press the **Esc key.**

➤ End the show by clicking at the appropriate place in the last slide or by pressing the **Esc key.**

➤ Save the presentation. Exit PowerPoint. Welcome to Multimedia!!

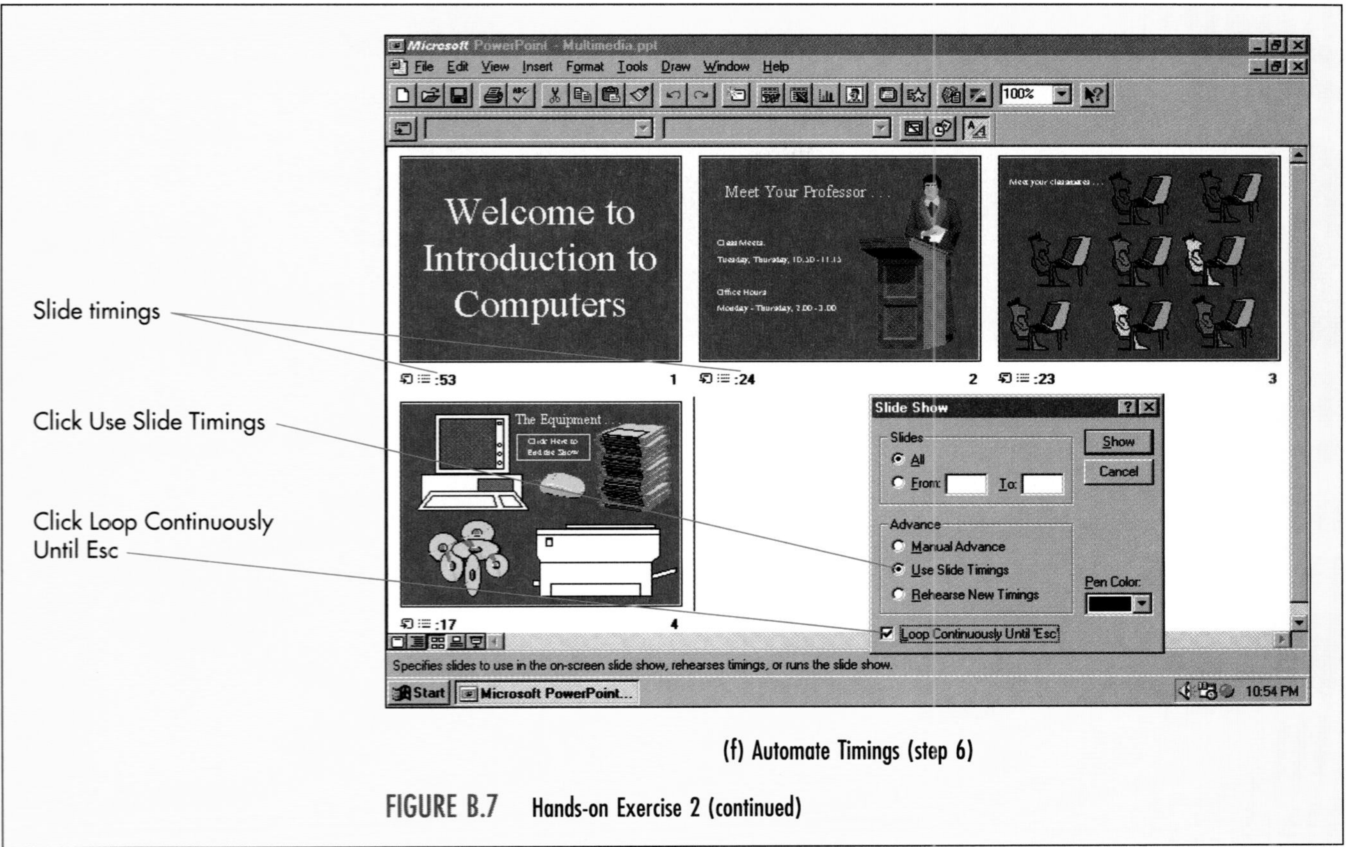

(f) Automate Timings (step 6)

FIGURE B.7 Hands-on Exercise 2 (continued)

SUMMARY

The Multimedia PC Marketing Council has established a minimum specification for a multimedia computer, which is intended to guide both the consumer and the developer. Three standards—MPC-1, MPC-2, and MPC-3—have been published to date.

There are two different types of sound files: WAV files and MIDI files. A WAV file records an actual sound and requires large amounts of disk space because the sound is sampled several thousand times a second to create the file. A MIDI file is much more compact than a WAV file because it stores the instructions to create the sound rather than the actual sound. A WAV file can represent any type of sound (a voice, music, or special effects) because it is a recorded sound. A MIDI file is the electronic equivalent of sheet music and can store only music.

An AVI (Audio-Video Interleaved) file is the Microsoft standard for a digital video (multimedia) file. AVI files are optimized to play at a resolution of 320 × 240 (one quarter of a VGA screen) to reduce the storage requirements.

Windows 95 provides the software tools necessary to play the different types of multimedia files. The accessories can be accessed through the Start button or through shortcuts in the Multimedia folder.

The slides in a multimedia production must be carefully scripted with respect to when and how each object is to appear. The Animation Settings command is the means by which the information is specified.

KEY WORDS AND CONCEPTS

Animation Settings command
AVI file
CD player
File compression
Media folder
Media Player
MIDI file
MPC-1
MPC-2
MPC-3
Multimedia PC Marketing Council
PowerPoint Multimedia CD
Resolution
Sampling rate
Sound Recorder
Volume control
WAV file

INDEX

A = Access E = Excel P = PowerPoint W = Word

I

J

K

L

U

V

W

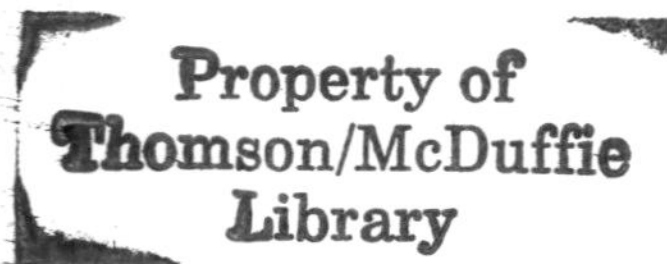
Property of Thomson/McDuffie Library

X

Z